Rabbi Meir Kahane

His Life and Thought

VOLUME ONE
1932–1975

by Libby Kahane

INSTITUTE FOR THE PUBLICATION
OF THE WRITINGS OF
RABBI MEIR KAHANE

JERUSALEM
5768 / 2008

INSTITUTE FOR PUBLICATION
OF THE WRITINGS OF
RABBI MEIR KAHANE

P. O. Box 39020
Jerusalem 91390
Israel

1412 Avenue M
Box 2387
Brooklyn, New York 11230

Distributed by
Urim Publications
P.O.B. 52287
Jerusalem 91521 Israel
www.UrimPublications.com

Computer composition: Moshe Kaplan

ISBN 13: 978-965-524-008-5
ISBN 10: 965-524-008-8

Printed in Israel

Dedicated to the Memory of

Fremette Fox

A True Supporter of Rabbi Meir Kahane
whose generous bequest made this book possible.
Fremette and her husband Morris (Mike), of blessed memory,
were among the founders of the Jewish Defense League in Miami
and supported the Kach movement from its inception

―――――――――――――

―――――――――

Rabbi Meir Kahane
August 1, 1932 (28 Tamuz 5692) – November 6, 1990 (18 Cheshvan 5751)

Contents

Acknowledgments

Countless people supplied the information that went into writing this book. Many of them had never been Meir's supporters, but they went out of their way to find the material I was seeking. Prof. Wendell B. Pols, reference librarian at Roger Williams University in Bristol, Rhode Island, sent me helpful information about a now-defunct school for speech therapy in Bristol. Stephen Barto sent me photocopies of material showing that Meir had been invited to the gala dinner Mayor Lindsay held for Golda Meir in 1969. Rabbi Hayim Schwartz perused the old records of the Rochdale Village Traditional Synagogue and sent me photocopies of those documents concerning Meir. They were but three of the many who kindly answered my requests for information, people I've never met, but who were willing to extend themselves. Their cooperation has unquestionably enriched this book.

My sincere thanks to them and –

To those who read my manuscript and made valuable suggestions: Shabtai Alboher, Elizabeth Berney, Khana Feiler, Becky Mark, Dr. Mordechai Nisan, Baruch Kahane, Tzipporah Kaplan, Jay Shapiro. Thanks to Judy Lee for editing the first 22 chapters and to Dvora Kiel for editing chapters 1-48.

To those who gave me original documents: Charley Cohen for his collection of JDL newspapers and documents; Samuel Shoshan for a far-ranging collection of clippings and letters; Dave Braverman, Jerry Blume, and Steve Smason for sending me the contents of the Kach-Los Angeles public storage bin; Nat Rosenwasser for his collection of clippings and letters. Their personal recollections were also invaluable.

To Abe Levine for audio tapes; to David Fein for video tapes; to Barbara Kanegis for a video tape of the film she shot in 1973.

To those who gave me photocopies of documents in their possession and shared their memories: Hilton Goldman, Shimon Rachamim, Murray Schneider, Bennett Levine, Janice Stern.

For their recollections of Meir as a child and young teenager: Dr. Jerry L. Shapiro, Rabbi Irwin E. (Yitzchak) Witty, and Rabbi Ephraim Zuroff.

For their recollections about Meir's attendance at the Mirrer Yeshiva: Rabbi Marcel Blitz, Rabbi Baruch Gelfand, Rabbi Avi Lieberman, Rabbi Moshe Bunim Pirutinsky, and Rabbi Chaim Plato. To Dinah Shira Foster, for sending me a photograph of Meir at a study session there and for her research assistance.

To the Betar members who generously shared their memories of Meir in Betar: Yitzhak Elitzur Friedman, Yitzhak Heimowitz, Arthur Heller, Lester Hering, Israel Herman, David Krakow, Shmuel Kraushar, Allan Mallenbaum, Yisrael Medad, Jenny Marden, Dov Troyansky.

To Dan Alter, who e-mailed me the entire text of his master's thesis, *Playing Utopia: Habonim Summer Camps in America* (Berkeley, Calif.: Graduate Theological Union, 1997) in answer to my query to the Jewish Music Internet list about the value of songs in Zionist youth groups.

To my friends from Bnei Akiva who shared their recollections of those early years: Miriam Brovender, Elsie Dudowitz, Yitzchak Fuchs, Avraham Greenhouse, Naomi Mauer, and Becky Mark. Thanks to Dov Gilor for photos of Meir from that period.

For their recollections about the late 1950s: Rabbi Chaim Druckman, Shoshana Silbert, Chaim and Rachel Spring, Shaul Kahan and Rabbi Eliezer Waldman. To Sarah Hamel, archivist of Kibbutz Saad, for photocopies of documents relating to Meir's bid to be rabbi at the kibbutz.

Stanley Bernstein, chairman of the Board Emeritus, Howard Beach Jewish Center, received my first query addressed to the HBJC and sent me the addresses of other members. Among them was Robert Falk, who supplied important information. Thanks also to Rabbi Benjamin Kamenetsky, Rabbi Abraham Levin, Belle Kirschenbaum and Alan Kirschenbaum for their recollections about the Howard Beach period.

Larry Dub, Esq., and Sharon Hirshmann supplied the sale prices of our homes in Laurelton and Howard Beach from the Deed Book of the City of New York.

For their recollections about Laurelton, I am indebted to Irwin Benjamin, Naomi Brody, Toby Fink, Helen Gluckman, Elliott Horowitz, Fred and Edith Horowitz, Malka Parnes, Robert Perlman, Gloria Podzeba, and Avraham (Jochnowitz) Ben Yochanan.

Ralph Weinstein sent me his recollections of the Traditional Synagogue of Rochdale Village; Arieh Lebowitz and Peter Eisenstadt supplied information about Rochdale Village.

Arnold Fine, Rabbi Avraham Goldreich, and Ralph Weinstein recalled the pre-JDL period. Rabbi Yehoshua Neeman and Rabbi O. Asher Reichel sent me documents pertaining to this period.

Glenn Richter and Jacob Birnbaum, leaders of the Student Struggle for Soviet Jewry, provided extensive input about Meir's early support for SSSJ and information about their struggle.

Michael Ravnitzky guided me to a treasure of information in the files of the FBI.

To all those who

– replied to my endless e-mail queries: Jerry Blume, David Fisch, Isaac Jaroslawicz, Meir Jolovitz, Charlotte Levine, Samson Levine, Glenn Richter, Fern Sidman, Dave Sommer, Yossi Templeman;

– shared their recollections in person and by mail: Joseph and Marilyn Alster, Barbara and Howie Ginsberg, Shifra and Ralph Hoffman, Mal and Yetta Lebowitz, Abe and Rita Levine, Murray Schneider;

– granted me interviews: Hy Beiber, Rabbi Zvi Block, Geula Cohen, Rabbi Kenny Cohen, Izzy Danziger, Bob Duchanov, Sammy Hirshmann, Rabbi Herzel Kranz, Garth Kravat, Sharon Katz Mittman, Barbara Oberman, Sherri Okin, Sy Polsky, Alan Rocoff, Neil Rothenberg, and attorney Barry Slotnick;

– took the time to reply to my letters: Tuvia Becker, Marilyn Betman, Renee Brown, Ari Calderon, Sonja Cohen Illouz, Russel Kelner, Charley Levine, Marty Lewinter, Richard Macales, and Alan Mandel.

To Yoel Lerner, for his readiness to share his phenomenal memory.

To my brother Phil Blum, for his recollections and research assistance.

To Avery Gross, Esq., for his readiness to answer my queries about legal issues and for giving me access to documents at the Kach office in Jerusalem.

To Naomi Mauer, who made the early bound issues of the *Jewish Press* available to me at the printing plant and kindly examined later issues that were not available at the National Library in Jerusalem.

To those of blessed memory: Rabbi Solomon Kahane, for family history; Dr. William Perl, who sent me his recollections; Rabbi Aryeh Julius, who told me about the early period in Israel, Avraham Hershkowitz, whose recollections spanned many years.

For research assistance: Keith Dickter, who searched the Rambam Yeshiva archives; David Fein and Barbara Benjamin, who examined the newspaper microfilms at the New York Public Library; Stefanie Pearson, who searched microfilmed newspapers at the National Library; my grandchildren, who looked for information in the microfilms of Hebrew newspapers during school vacations.

To those who generously gave me photographs for this book: Meir and Batsheva Indor, Isaac Jaroslawicz, the Jerusalem Post Photo Archives, Heshel Kupchin, and Nachum Bar Berel.

To Michael Harroch for his skillful graphic layout of the photo section and to Deanna Sperka for her expert advice on the photos.

To Moshe Kaplan for his patient dedication to this project and the excellence of his typesetting, layout, and preparation for printing.

Authors

My sincere thanks to the authors who generously granted me permission to quote from their articles. (Full citations are given in footnotes.)

Prof. Arnold Ages, Larry Ankewicz, Mark R. Arnold, Craig Aronoff, Kenneth Braiterman, Fern Marja Eckman, Jan Geliebter, Mati Golan, Larry Gordon, Yitta Halberstam, J. William Joynes, Dave Kahn, Dr. Michael Lerner for Max Lerner,

Stanley Marlin, Robert J. Milch, Fritz Plous Jr., Dick Polman, Don Pride, Allan Rabinowitz, Glenn Richter, Mrs. Irving J. Rosenbaum for Rabbi Rosenbaum, Marvin Schick, David Welcher, Donald L. Wolberg.

Newspaper Editors and Publishers

(Full citations are given in footnotes.)

The *Jewish Press*, for permission to quote Meir's articles.

The following newspapers, for freely granting permission to use excerpts:

The Anglo-Jewish press: *American Jewish World* (Mordecai Spektor, pub.), *American Jewish Year Book* (Larry Grossman, ed.), *B'nai B'rith Messenger* (Joe Bobker, pub.), *Jewish Exponent* (Jonathan Tobin, ed.), *Jewish Post and Opinion* (Jennie Cohen, ed.), *Jewish Spectator* (Robert Bleiweis, pub.), *Jewish Telegraphic Agency News Bulletin, Jewish Week* (Debra Rubin, ed.).

The general press: *Baltimore Sun, Chicago Sun-Times, Choice, Kirkus Reviews, The Miami Herald, Newark Star Ledger, Philadelphia Inquirer & Daily News, The Record* (Bergen County, N.J.), *Washington Post*.

The Israeli press: *Ha'aretz, Ma'ariv, Yedioth Ahronoth*.

College newspapers: *Daily Bruin* (University of California, Los Angeles), *Diamondback* (University of Maryland), *KEN* and *Kingsman* (Brooklyn College), *Hunter Envoy* (Hunter College), *Newsbeat* and *Phoenix* (Queens College).

Librarians and Archivists

My heartfelt appreciation to the many librarians and archivists who graciously responded to my requests for information:

Dr. Silvia Shenkolewski-Kroll, director, and Naomi Herman, Oren Mauer, and Rinat Klein, assistants, Archives for the Research of Religious Zionism, Bar Ilan University, Ramat Gan, Israel.

Shulamith Z. Berger, curator of Special Collections, Yeshiva University, New York.

Amira Stern, archivist, Jabotinsky Institute of Israel.

Roberta Saltzman, Dorot Jewish Division, New York Public Library, who searched issues of Anglo-Jewish newspapers unavailable in Jerusalem.

Prof. Bella Weinberg for her expert advice.

Denise Millman (of blessed memory), coordinator of reference, Long Island University Library, for searching library resources.

Mr. Reuven Schlenker, Gelman Library, George Washington University, sent me photocopies from the William Perl Collection.

Mira Levine, Institute of Contemporary Jewry, Hebrew University; Debby Steinmetz, Jewish Film Archive, Hebrew University; Edith Lubetski, Stern College for Women; Pearl Berger, Yeshiva University; Elliot Gertel, Curator of Judaica, University of Michigan.

Librarians at the National Library in Jerusalem:

General Reading Room: Kochevet Ben Shachar, Shelly Benvenisti, Brenda Coren, Ora Kravitz, Nili Zentler.

Reference Department: Nira Ilsar, Rachel Steiner (with appreciation for documents on the Yavneh organization), Chana Schwartz, Rachel Greenfield, Sarai Tsafrir, and Naomi Wahrman.

Archives and Manuscript Department: Raphael Weiser, Rivka Plesser.

National Sound Archives: Gila Flam, Ruth Freed, Avigdor Herzog, Yaakov Mazor, and Avi Nahamias.

Thanks are also due to many who helped in small but significant ways. Here is an example.

When I started to write about the Torah Dedication at Allenwood Prison in January 1976 in chapter 47, I thought it would be helpful to interview the prison's Jewish chaplain, Rabbi Abraham Yeret. I began my search for Rabbi Yeret on the Internet. There was only one "hit" for Abraham Yeret, a 1995 newspaper report that said he was rabbi of a synagogue in Ceara, Brazil. Now, ten years later, I wasn't sure he was still there. With the help of Rachel Steiner, head of the National Library's Reference Department, I found the address and phone number of the synagogue, But my letter went unanswered and the phone number was not in service.

Then, Rabbi Moshe (Marcel) Blitz of Baltimore, who had taken part in the Torah Dedication, replied to my e-mail query. He recalled Rabbi Yeret and his capable conduct of the Torah dedication ceremony. Rabbi Blitz searched the directory of the Rabbinical Council of America and sent me the e-mail address of Rabbi Moshe Yeres of Toronto, who might be a relative. Rabbi Yeres replied that he was not related to Rabbi Yeret, but he knew that he had been the rabbi of a congregation in Wilkes-Barre, Pennsylvania, and sent me the e-mail address of Congregation Ohav Zedek there. I felt I was on the right track now. It made sense for a part-time prison chaplain to be a local rabbi.

My June 22, 2005, e-mail query to Ohav Zedek was forwarded to Mr. Alvin Schwartz because it was known there that he had been in Betar with Meir. Schwartz sent my query to Mrs. Sarah Rosenblum, Rabbi Yeret's former wife. Within twelve hours, Mrs. Rosenblum sent me an e-mail with information about the chaplaincy position, and what is more, she gave me the phone number of her daughter in Israel, Avigail Witt. It turned out that Rabbi Yeret was arriving in Israel for his first visit in three years – that week! Mrs. Witt was sure he would be happy to phone me. He did, and he was able to give me the information I needed.

The chain of people who kindly helped me – Rabbi Blitz, Rabbi Yeres, Mr. Schwartz, Mrs. Rosenblum, Mrs. Witt – are just an example of the many people who answered my queries and helped me write this book. I thank them all.

Sources

1. Archival source material

Archives and Manuscript Department, National Library, Jerusalem. Of special interest are party platforms, pre-election advertisements, and a collection of Israeli press clippings on the JDL in the early 1970s.

Archives of the Jabotinsky Institute in Israel, Tel-Aviv. This was an invaluable source for research on Meir's years as a member of the Betar Zionist youth movement. Newspaper clippings and Betar publications such as the *Tel-Hai* newsletter were especially useful. Documents which I and others donated to the Jabotinsky Archives are in the Meir Kahane Collection.

Israel Broadcasting Authority, Television News Archive and Radio News Archive, Jerusalem. The subject files on Meir indicate the dates when he was given media exposure, while audio and video recordings show how he looked and sounded at various periods. I have described some of these.

Jerusalem Post Archives, Jerusalem. Articles prior to October 1988 were pasted into folders by subject. I consulted the "Meir Kahane" and "Jewish Defense League" folders. The archives were computerized in October 1988.

Jewish Defense League Collection, Yeshiva University Archives, New York. Bertram Zweibon, co-founder of JDL, donated papers covering the years 1969-1976. This was augmented by documents donated by Abe Levine, JDL archivist. I consulted this archive on a visit to the United States and subsequently by correspondence with the archivist.

National Sound Archives, National Library, Jerusalem. In researching Meir's teen years, I found that group singing and music were an important part of his life. Researchers at the Sound Archives helped me to identify songs he had taught and to analyze the musical background of the JDL Anthem he composed.

NBC News Archives, an Internet site (www.nbcnewsarchives.com). Its synopses of news programs were an important source of information. The site is also an indication of Meir's media coverage per year. For example, in 1970 Meir's name appeared three times; in 1971, twenty-four times; and in 1972 not at all.

Rabbi Meir Kahane Collection, Archives for the Research of Religious Zionism, Bar Ilan University, Ramat Gan, Israel. This holds Meir's extensive files on subjects ranging from Jewish education and intermarriage to social problems in Israel and international relations, which he drew on in his writing. He also saved every flyer, poster, and newspaper report related to his activities, as well as every letter he received. In his study at home there were floor-to-ceiling filing cabinets covering three walls. There are two types of files, topical and chronological. The first includes clippings, articles, and documents on the topics that interested him. The chronological files contain letters, clippings, flyers, press releases, legal documents, and itineraries. Additional material found here: JDL flyers and newspaper clippings, 1972-1978, from the collection of Abe Levine, JDL archivist, and audio and video recordings of Meir's public addresses, supplied by Abe Levine and David Fein.

Rabbi Meir Kahane Collection, Archives for the Research of Religious Zionism – Appendix. In the course of my research, I received letters and documents from many people as well as official documents from the Federal Bureau of Investigation and the U.S. State Department. Photocopies of the documents cited in the book are in this Appendix.

U.S. Federal Bureau of Investigation. I received hundreds of memos and reports written by FBI agents who were investigating Meir and the JDL. Files from the FBI offices in Los Angeles, New York and Washington, sent to me under the Freedom of Information Act, supplied information on Meir's speaking engagements and other activities not found in any other source.

U.S. State Department. Documents sent to me by the State Department under the Freedom of Information Act include memos and telegrams from the U.S. delegation at the United Nations and from the U.S. Consulate in Tel-Aviv. These provided significant information.

Zionist Archives, Jerusalem. I found important documentation here about Meir's years in the Bnei Akiva Zionist youth group.

2. Newspapers

I consulted newspaper indexes, both hard-copy and on-line, and read reports in such newspapers as the *New York Times*, the *Washington Post,* the *Jerusalem Post*, the *Jewish Press*, and *Yedioth Ahronoth.* At the New York Public Library, I read reports about the Jewish Defense League in local newspapers.

Because of their accessibility on the Internet, the majority of newspaper and TV reports cited in my book are from the *New York Times* and the NBC News Archive. As a rule, other newspapers and broadcasting stations carried the same story on the same day.

I found many newspaper reports in the various archives where I did research; their locations are cited in the footnotes. Most of the newspapers are readily available in major research and university libraries throughout the world, including the National Library in Israel.

3. Meir's Writings

On passport applications and similar forms, Meir gave his occupation as "writer." He wrote for the *Jewish Press* from 1960 up to his death on November 5, 1990. I was able to examine most of the issues in hard copy or microfilm at the National Library in Jerusalem. I saw the very early issues, not available on microfilm, at the *Jewish Press* printing plant in Brooklyn. Among the libraries that have the *Jewish Press* on microfilm are the New York Public Library, the Hebrew Union College Library in Cincinnati, and the University of California at Los Angeles Library.

Meir wrote several books. Seven were published by well-known American publishers and made Meir's ideas available to a wide public. Some of these were translated into Hebrew and published in Israel by JDL or Kach. Several other books and booklets in English were published under JDL or Kach auspices in the United States. A bibliography is appended.

Meir's writings are an important key to understanding his ideas. This book has many excerpts from his writings because they clearly explain the rationale behind his activities.

4. Interviews

When quoting from interviews, I was aware, as the reader should be too, that people's memories are not always reliable. With the passage of time the facts tend to blur. Without meaning to, people embellish and invent, and they alter details to suit their personal interpretations. Memory and imagination are close neighbors.

Nevertheless, interviews supplied important information. In addition to JDLers who live in Israel (as I do), I interviewed people who live in the United States – some during my visits there and some during their visits to Israel. Personal recollections in letters and e-mail messages also contributed significantly to this book.

Usage

The name Kahane: This is the spelling adopted by Meir's father when he arrived in the United States (pronounced Ka HAH nee). The spelling "Kahana" (Ka HAH nah) indicates a translation from a Hebrew text.

Dates: Although Hebrew dates were always used in JDL publications and in Meir's letters, for the sake of convenience, I have used only secular dates.

Transliteration: The Hebrew letter *chet* is denoted by *ch*; the letter *khaf* by *kh*. Where required for clarity, an apostrophe indicates an *aleph* or an *ayin*. A *shva* is expressed by the letter *e*, as in yeshiva, sefira, zemirot. *Kamatz-heh* is represented by *ah* or *a*, according to the accepted spelling (Torah, yeshiva). Sephardic pronunciation is followed.

The spelling of personal names, place names and journal titles does not follow this rule. For personal names, the spelling used by the individual is given (e.g. Chaim, Haim, Chayim, Hayyim.) Israeli place names are spelled according to Israel government usage, and the names of Hebrew newspapers and public bodies are spelled according to each one's own usage.

G-d; L-rd: In keeping with Jewish custom, the Deity's name is not written in full.

Ellipses: Three dots after an incomplete sentence indicate that part of a quote has been omitted. Four dots are used between two complete sentences to indicate an omission, and at the end of a quote to indicate additional text in the original.

Introduction

RABBI MEIR KAHANE'S life was one of intense activism on behalf of the Jewish people, marked by unconventional methods and unpopular views. Through it all, his steadfast commitment to the ideals of Judaism permeated and inspired all he did.

His influence on modern Jewish history was far-reaching; a comprehensive survey of his ideology and political strategy is crucial to understanding the history of American Jewry and of Israel during the past 35 years.

This book aims to be an authoritative study of his life and work, beginning with his childhood, with an emphasis on the shaping of his ideological outlook and political career. It is based on printed material, interviews, personal letters in the family's possession, and my own firsthand knowledge of events.

People who gave me interviews or replied to my letters referred to him respectfully as the Rabbi, the *Rav* (Hebrew for Rabbi), or the *Reb* (a term of endearment for Rabbi), but I will call him Meir in this book because that is how I knew him.

I have arranged the book chronologically, to show the development of Meir's ideas and actions. Using his own words from his writings, I have endeavored to provide the background against which his public activities took place and explain his motivation. During the period covered by this volume, Meir's writings expressed most of the ideas he promoted throughout his life. Thus, in addition to presenting an accurate historical record of his undertakings, this volume provides important insight into his philosophy.

As briefly as possible, I have presented the contemporary context – the situation of Jews in America and current issues in Israel – in which Meir acted.

Two books[1] were written about Meir during his lifetime, but they are seriously flawed by bias and inaccuracies. I have cited examples of those inaccuracies in the notes section. Unfortunately, even "unbiased" newspaper reports quoted from these books or from defamatory articles.

While no author can be completely objective about his subject, I believe that my twenty-seven years as a reference librarian at the National Library in Jerusalem gave me expertise and experience in the methods of careful research and proper documentation that make this book an accurate, authoritative study. Throughout the book, all statements are supported by documentation. I have not reported anything for which I have no personal knowledge or reliable source. In addition, thirty-four years of marriage to Meir gave me an advantage in locating his friends and associates, deciphering documents, and clarifying events.

This book is not a memoir about the wonderful people who supported JDL and Kach in America and in Israel. It is about Meir and about what he said and did. In this, I have followed Meir's lead in his book, *The Story of the Jewish Defense League*, where he named only a few individuals. I have described the activities of JDL or Kach only when Meir was directly involved in them. *The Story of the Jewish Defense League* relates the history of the JDL through 1972; I have written about that period from another perspective, based on archival sources and interviews, and I have covered later years as well.

Meir always dealt simultaneously with a number of topics. During different periods, his emphasis differed, but new topics were never "new." The seeds were always present earlier. His emphasis on Soviet Jewry in 1970 was preceded by articles he wrote as early as 1964. His emphasis on aliya in 1972 was preceded by earlier articles and speeches. His activities in Israel from 1972 on, such as his campaign against ceding the territories liberated during the Six Day War, flowed naturally from his perception of the Jewish character of the Land of Israel.

A Request

I hope that this book, the product of painstaking research, will be useful to future historians. Anyone who discovers an error or has additional information is requested to inform me. Corrections will be inserted in future editions.

Postscript

People often ask me what gave Meir the strength to act on his ideals in the face of the intense opposition of the Establishment. This book has many expressions of his unwavering belief in the truth of his ideals, especially during periods of crisis.

Meir himself supplied an interesting insight about the course of his life. It was one evening sometime in 1978, as Meir and I were eating supper in our tiny kitchen in Jerusalem. He said something profound and poetic, the kind of thing that would not appear in any of his own writing, so I noted it in my diary: "I have lines in my soul that serve as directional signals to tell me where I'm going and how far I've come."

Chapter 1

Roots

T O TRULY UNDERSTAND the profound love for the Jewish people and the Land of Israel that motivated Meir's every action, it is not enough to know the man – it is necessary to know his unique background. What made Meir form the Jewish Defense League and what drove his lifelong one-man struggle to promote the Torah way of life? His upbringing and schooling, and especially his remarkable roots, made his life a logical link in a multigenerational chain of devotion to the Torah, the Jews, and their land.

His father's support for the Irgun's* struggle against the British in Palestine showed him that Jews must not only love the Land of Israel but also fight for it. The link goes further back than that to two of his great-grandfathers, both of whom had vital, active attachments to the Land of Israel. As a small child, Meir heard stories about his ancestors and the ideals that defined their lives. These influenced him profoundly.

Rabbi Meir Liven

Meir's maternal grandmother, Henya Trainin, was the daughter of Rabbi Meir ben Tuvia Liven, born in 1840 in Kreuzberg (Krustpils), in the Vitebsk area of Latvia. After studying at the Remaila yeshiva (rabbinical seminary) in Vilna, he was ordained by Rabbi Moses Abraham of Mir and by Rabbi Isaac Elchanan of Kovno. For most of his life, he was the rabbi of a synagogue in Vielike (Nowo Wielejsk), near Vilna. He published several books of sermons and essays and was active in Zionist causes. Family members recall that once he attended Theodore Herzl's Zionist Congress. The upheavals caused by the Communist struggle for

---

* The Irgun, or Irgun Tzva'i Leumi (National Military Organization), was also known by its acronym, Etzel. Founded in April 1931 as a self-defense group, it actively fought British rule in Palestine. The British government, which ruled Palestine under a League of Nations Mandate, was obstructing Jewish settlement and preventing entry into Palestine of Holocaust survivors, while imprisoning members of the Irgun who acted against them, and even passing death sentences.

1

power led him to flee in 1917 to far-off Sizran, on the Volga River near Samara, where he died in 1925 at age 85.

R. Meir Liven's love of the Land of Israel is expressed movingly in his book of sermons *Imrei Chemed*, published in Vilna in 1902. In a sermon titled "Praise of the Holy Land and the Hope in Our Hearts," he recounts the wonders of the Holy Land and expresses his longing to see it one day.[1]

Rabbi Baruch David Kahane

On his father's side, Meir descends from David Magid Hakohen, rabbi of Radomysl Wielki, northeast of Krakow, Poland. R. David studied under Rabbi Jacob Isaac Horowitz of Lublin, known as the Seer of Lublin because of his brilliance and visionary gifts. The Seer proclaimed R. David a true *kohen*, a direct descendant of the first *kohen*, Aaron, and always tried to stand opposite him during the priestly blessing in the synagogue.

R. David Magid Hacohen's grandson, Rabbi Baruch David Kahane (c. 1850-1925), was Meir's great-grandfather. R. Baruch David was a devoted follower of the Rabbi of Sanz, Rabbi Chaim Halberstam, better known as the Divrei Chaim. The Divrei Chaim had chasidim (followers) throughout Poland and even in the Land of Israel, mainly in Safed. The sole occupation of most of the Sanzer chasidim in Safed was studying Torah and Talmud. Their very reason for being in the Land of Israel was to reach a high level of holiness – attainable more readily in the Holy Land, where studying Torah has special attributes.

They were supported by a system of distribution of charitable funds known as *chalukah* whereby money was distributed according to community of origin. Thus, chasidim from Sanz in Poland were supported by funds from Sanz.

The Sanzer Rabbi selected trustworthy R. Baruch David to immigrate to the Land of Israel and supervise the distribution of *chalukah* funds to his followers. In 1873 R. Baruch David, his wife Rivka, and their four-year-old son Nachman settled in Safed, where their daughter Nechama was born. One of R. Baruch David's first accomplishments was rebuilding the Sanz community's synagogue and study hall in Safed. He made several trips back to Sanz to raise money and was respected for his generosity, integrity, modesty, and Torah knowledge. As he grew older, his son Rabbi Nachman made the journeys to Sanz, while he devoted himself to his studies. R. Baruch David published two oft-reprinted books concerning the laws, customs, and holiness of the Land of Israel: *Chibat Ha'aretz* (Love of the Land), in 1897, and *Birkat Ha'aretz* (Blessing of the Land), in 1904.[2] The title page of *Chibat Ha'aretz* proclaims that its purpose is "to arouse and strengthen love of the Holy Land."

Rabbi Nachman Kahane

R. Nachman Kahane, Meir's grandfather (1869-1937), married Pessia Faige, the daughter of his teacher, Rabbi Moshe Yehuda Tzvi Yavetz-Miller. To support his growing family, R. Nachman ran a prayer-shawl factory. One day, in a trusting way that reminds me of Meir, R. Nachman gave money to a traveler to buy wool for him in Damascus. The traveler absconded with the money and R. Nachman lost his entire investment.

R. Nachman was a devoted follower of the Sanzer Rabbi's son, Rabbi Yechezkel Shraga Halberstam of Shinov. When R. Nachman's prayer shawl enterprise failed, he followed the Shinover Rabbi's advice to lease an orchard in Kfar Hittim, near Tiberias (about twenty miles from Safed), and grow *etrogim*, the citrus fruit used during the Sukkot holiday. He did so with a partner, Yitzchak Loberboim. During the summer, R. Nachman would bring his *etrogrim* to the port in Jaffa to have them shipped to Poland and Russia in time for Sukkot. This seasonal occupation was precarious, with thievery from his orchard by local Arabs a constant problem, but at least he was able to devote himself to learning Torah most of the year.

During the harvest season R. Nachman lived in Kfar Hittim. One very hot night during the harvest of 1893, when he was about 25 years old, he decided to sleep in the cool orchard, while an Arab watchman stood guard against thieves. That night, the head of the neighboring Arab village came to steal *etrogim*. The Arab watchman attacked the thief, wounding him fatally. When he discovered he had killed the head of the village, he dragged the body to the place where R. Nachman was sleeping.

R. Nachman awoke to find himself surrounded by the Arabs of the village. This was the period of Turkish rule in the Land of Israel, so after the Arabs beat him soundly, they handed him over to the Turkish police. The police also arrested his partner Yitzchak Loberboim, manacled both of them hand and foot, and beat them to make them confess to the murder. Despite the beatings, they maintained their innocence. The next day, two mounted policemen accompanied them to the jail in Tiberias, ordering them to run before the horses all the way. They arrived in Tiberias exhausted but grateful to be alive. A local Jewish delegation tried to intercede on their behalf, but the city's Turkish governor refused to release them.

That night R. Nachman dreamed that a certain Reb Yitzchak promised he'd be freed in two days. This Reb Yitzchak was an elderly man who had asked to join R. Nachman's convoy of donkeys from Jaffa back to Tiberias earlier that summer. It had been a very hot day, and the frail old man succumbed to the heat and died. The superstitious Arab who owned the donkeys refused to allow R. Nachman to leave the corpse on his donkey and deserted R. Nachman by the roadside. R. Nachman lifted the corpse onto his shoulders and started to walk. Even though a *kohen* is forbidden to touch a corpse, he knew that the overriding precept is to see to a proper burial. However, the body was too heavy, and he could not continue. It was twilight and there was no help in sight.

Suddenly, two Arabs on donkeys came along. They, too, were superstitious and would not allow one of their animals to carry a corpse, so R. Nachman had to purchase the donkeys outright. He traveled slowly, lest the body fall from the donkey. Late at night he arrived in Tiberias, where the burial society gave Reb Yitzchak a proper burial. This was only one of R. Nachman's many acts of kindness and charity.

When R. Nachman's family in Safed heard about his imprisonment, his wife went straight to her son's *cheder* (school) and told the teacher what had happened. The teacher took the entire school to the synagogue of the Ari, the famed 16th-century mystic, where all the children prayed for R. Nachman's release. His father, R. Baruch David, an Austrian citizen, persuaded the Austrian consul to speak to the Turkish governor. His mother, Rivka, accompanied the consul to the jail but was not permitted to enter. A spirited woman, she climbed onto the roof of the adjacent building and – without regard for her own well-being – jumped into the prison courtyard. After she recovered from her fall, the guards took pity on her and allowed her to see her son and give him food and drink.

The Austrian consul spent two days and ten gold napoleons negotiating with the governor, and on the third day – as R. Nachman had dreamed – he was released. Many difficult months passed before his final acquittal.[3]

R. Nachman and Pessia Faige had eight children. The youngest of the five boys was Meir's father Yechezkel Shraga, born in Safed in 1905 and named for the Shinover Rabbi.[4]

Rabbi Yechezkel Kahane: Zionism and Community Service

At the end of World War I, when Yechezkel was only 13 years old, he traveled with his father to Galicia in southern Poland to enroll in a yeshiva there. It may seem harsh to send such a young boy so far from home, but conditions at that time in Palestine were unbearable. The war had cut off funds from Europe and the entire country suffered from food shortages and disease. R. Baruch David, whose wife's family in Europe supported him generously, sold his possessions in order to buy food for the poor of Safed.[5]

In Galicia, Yechezkel studied in a yeshiva headed by Rabbi Pinchas Bombach in the town of Oswiciem (later infamous under its German name, Auschwitz). He continued his studies at the Pressburg yeshiva in Hungary, where he was ordained by Rabbi Akiva Sofer. He remained in Europe for six years. When he returned to Safed in 1924, he discovered he could not earn a living there. People were so poor and conditions so primitive in Safed that some had never seen an automobile.

In 1925 he joined his two older brothers, R. Chaim and R. Levi Yitzchak, in America. He began calling himself Charles and enrolled in the Rabbi Isaac Elchanan rabbinical seminary on Manhattan's Lower East Side, where he received a second ordination. During this time, he supported himself by teaching in the afternoon synagogue school of Congregation Ahavas Torah in Williamsburg, where his brother Levi Yitzchak was rabbi.[6]

In 1930, R. Yechezkel became the rabbi of Congregation Anshe Sholom Avenue U Educational Center in Brooklyn, and in 1931 he married Sonia (Sara Chana) Trainin.[7]

Meir's mother Sonia arrived in the United States when she was about fifteen. She had already studied Latin, German, mathematics and other subjects at the *gymnasia* (high school) in Dvinsk (Daugavpils). Her father, Rabbi Baruch Shalom Trainin, son of Rabbi Dov Trainin of Dvinsk, was a brilliant Talmudic scholar and a student of the renowned Rabbi of Dvinsk, Rabbi Meir Simcha Hakohen, better known as the Ohr Samayach. R. Baruch Shalom also served as a member of the Ohr Samayach's rabbinical court, and Sonia recalled being dandled on his knee as a little girl. R. Baruch Shalom preceded the family to the United States, found a job as a rabbi in Plainfield, New Jersey, and then brought over his wife Henya with Sonia and her two younger brothers.[8]

Meir was born in 1932 and was named Meir David for his two great-grandfathers, Rabbi Meir Liven and Rabbi Baruch David Kahane. In 1943, when Meir was eleven, his father left the congregation on Avenue U and became rabbi of another Brooklyn synagogue, Congregation Shaarei Tefiloh, on West First Street at Quentin Road. The family moved to an apartment in a two-family house on West Second Street between Quentin Road and Kings Highway, where they were still living when we married. Their landlord, Michael Blan, held them in high regard and was very accommodating. They had the use of his garage for storing chairs for extra guests for the Passover Seder and other special occasions. R. Yechezkel was Shaarei Tefiloh's rabbi for almost thirty years, until July 1971, when he and Sonia moved to Israel.[9]

Meir's father was active in religious affairs. As a founding member of the Vaad Harabbanim (Board of Rabbis) of Flatbush, he sat on the kashrut committee, where he promoted far-reaching improvements in kashrut supervision. At one time he served as its secretary, and from 1950 to 1955 he was president of the Vaad.[10]

He also took part in an early effort to found a Jewish day school in the area. In those years, most Jewish children were sent to public schools and received a few hours of religious education in Talmud Torahs – afternoon synagogue schools. Typically, a Jewish child would take part in Christmas preparations in the morning and learn about Chanuka in the afternoon. The public school, where the child spent most of his day, was usually a stronger influence on him than the synagogue school. Not surprisingly, only the exceptional child remained religious. The rate of intermarriage was rising drastically, threatening Jewish life in the United States. The rabbinical and lay leadership realized that only Jewish day schools could save the American Jewish community.

In January 1945, R. Yechezkel was among the Flatbush area rabbis who founded the Rambam Yeshiva. He took an active part in its operation and was chairman of the Board of the Hebrew Department for ten years.[11] In 1945 Meir was already in eighth grade at the Yeshiva of Flatbush so he never benefited from his father's efforts.

After World War II, Rabbi Abraham Kalmanowitz sought R. Yechezkel's help in re-establishing the Mirrer Yeshiva in Flatbush. R. Yechezkel was astounded. "Why do you want to come to Flatbush? It's a *midbar*, a spiritual wasteland!" But R. Kalmanowitz assured him, "In twenty years it will be an oasis." He was right: By 1965, the area abounded in religious Jews, yeshivot, and synagogues. R. Yechezkel arranged temporary housing for the Mirrer Yeshiva at 1615 East Ninth Street in an unused building owned by the Rambam Yeshiva, and then helped find its permanent site on Ocean Parkway at Avenue R.

A citation he received in March 1960 from the Beth Jacob School of Bensonhurst and Flatbush reads: "… to our devoted friend Rabbi Charles Kahane in appreciation of his untiring efforts to help build Torah education in our neighborhood."

R. Yechezkel published several books. In 1935, two collections of his sermons appeared: *Natzionaler Religiezer Vort* in Yiddish and *Echo of Tradition* in English. An expanded Hebrew version, *Mishnah Yesharah,* appeared in Israel in 1973. It included Meir's bar mitzvah speech and a chapter on the Kahane family tree. In 1963 R. Yechezkel published *Torah Yeshara*, an innovative English translation of the Five Books of Moses. It is unique in that it incorporates the traditional Jewish commentaries essential for a true understanding of the text. In the latter two titles, he used the acronym "Yashar," composed of the initials of his name, **Y**echezkel **Shr**aga.[12] Yashar, which means honest and straight, typified his character. He was straight in all his dealings with G-d and man, and passed on those ideals to his sons, Meir and Nachman.

It was not only the example of R. Yechezkel's scholarship and community leadership that influenced the direction of Meir's life. It was also his active participation in Zionist causes. A long-time member of the religious Zionist Mizrachi

Organization of America, R. Yechezkel served on its executive committee for many years.

A major influence in Meir's youth was R. Yechezkel's support for the Irgun, an underground organization that fought British rule in Palestine. His involvement with the Irgun began early, with his admiration for its spiritual father, Zeev Jabotinsky, founder of the Zionist Revisionist movement.* Meir's mother Sonia recalled that Jabotinsky was in their home for a meeting with supporters in 1940, and when Peter Bergson arrived in the U.S. to enlist support for the Irgun, R. Yechezkel was among the first to join him.[13]

In January 1942 Bergson placed an ad in the *New York Times* headed "Jews Fight for the Right to Fight." It listed Rabbi Charles Kahane as a member of the Committee for a Jewish Army. Bergson's dramatic full-page ads were his trademark propaganda tool. One of them shouts in bold letters, "When the enemy's gun is leveled at the heart, the time for quibbling is past." This ad and others are analyzed in a master's thesis titled, "Propaganda Techniques of the Bergson Group 1939-48," by Charles Levine, who noted, "Charles Kahane ... had little expectation that his nine-year-old son, Meir, would be publishing similar ads three decades later as chairman of the Jewish Defense League."[14]

R. Yechezkel was also active on behalf of the Jews in Europe. The Germans tried to keep their systematic slaughter of the Jews in Europe secret, but by 1942 a few Jews who managed to escape from the extermination camps succeeded in getting the news out to the free world. On October 6, 1943, R. Yechezkel was among 500 Orthodox rabbis who converged on Washington, D.C., to ask the U.S. Congress to act against the slaughter. The names of those who took part in the pilgrimage reads like a "Who's Who" of Orthodox Jewry. In the front row of marchers were Rabbi Abraham Kalmanowitz and Rabbi Eliezer Silver. The marchers are pictured in a booklet published to commemorate the occasion.[15] Columnist Samuel Margoshes described the march:

> People stopped in their tracks to watch and follow a parade of a few hundred individuals sing Psalms on their way to the Capitol. Tens of thousands of passersby got to know, possibly for the first time, that millions of Jews were done to death in Nazi-held Europe, and that millions more are in jeopardy, and that the Jews of America, profoundly agitated by what is happening to their kin, are appealing to the government for help in saving their brethren. As the 500 rabbis moved along Pennsylvania Avenue, they certainly presented a picture

---

* Zeev (Vladimir) Jabotinsky (1880-August 4, 1940) was a journalist, politician and orator who promoted Jewish pride and encouraged the Jews of Europe to immigrate to Palestine. He organized the first modern Jewish fighting force, the Jewish Legion, in World War I. In 1923 he formed the Betar youth group and two years later, to amend Zionist ideology, he founded the Revisionist movement. See: www.csuohio.edu/tagar/tagar2.html.

which for its exotic quality was unprecedented even in such a cosmopolitan city as Washington. Passersby watched in wonderment and respect. The traffic stopped and here and there a burgher removed his hat. I myself saw many a soldier snap to salute as the oldest rabbis, remarkably reminiscent of the patriarchs of Doré's Bible, passed in review.[16]

R. Yechezkel also supported Betar, the Zionist youth group founded by Zeev Jabotinsky. He encouraged Meir to join and to attend Camp Betar summers. A camp brochure from those years lists Rabbi Charles Kahane as one of eight sponsors.[17] Meir's experiences in Betar made a lasting impression on him and had a strong influence on his direction in life.

Murder in Safed

Another major influence on Meir was the tragic murder by Arabs of four of his relatives on the road to Safed in 1938, when he was six years old. They were returning from a family wedding in Tel Aviv, where R. Yechezkel's oldest brother, R. Zundel Kahane, lived. Another brother, R. Mordechai, lived in Safed. R. Zundel's oldest daughter, Chaya, also lived in Safed with her husband, Tzvi Naftali Segal, who ran a grocery store there. The Safed branch of the family attended the wedding of R. Zundel's daughter Rachel to Chaim Paster in Tel Aviv on March 26, 1938, and then headed home.

But four of them detoured to Haifa: R. Mordechai's wife Tzippora and her three-year-old daughter Rivka, who went to collect Tzippora's mother, Basha Baral; and Tzvi Naftali and his son Baruch David, 12, who went to visit Tzvi's brother. Three days after the wedding, they were traveling in a *sherut* taxi* back to Safed when they were attacked by Arabs. Meir's aunt, Tzippora Kahane, her mother Basha, Meir's cousin Chaya's husband Tzvi Naftali, and her son Baruch David were killed.

Their murder was reported on page one of the *Palestine Post* of March 30, 1938:

> Four victims of yesterday afternoon's hold-up [sic] on the Acre-Safed road (near the Arab village of Sajur) were buried Tuesday in a common grave. All were members of one family.
>
> ... The victims were buried near the Jewish residents killed in [the Arab rioting of] 1929 and in 1936.
>
> ... Zvi Segal was found to have been hit by two bullets in the heart and two in the head; Mrs. Tsippora Kahane was hit in the chest; Mrs. Basha Baral, her mother, was hit several times in the head; and the boy was hit in the head.[18]

---

* A *sherut* taxi was used for inter-city travel. It held eight passengers who paid individually for their seats.

The daily *Ha'aretz* reported that apparently the Arabs piled stones on the road to stop the taxi and this enabled them to shoot into the car at close range. One passenger survived by fleeing from the car: Zeidel Heller of Safed hid until all was quiet, and then stopped a passing border police patrol. Another survivor, Shalom Bieber, saved his year-old son by lying on top of him, pretending to be dead. R. Mordechai Kahane's three-year-old daughter Rivka, shielded by her mother's body, was saved as well and was raised by her oldest sister, Bilha Vilner.

It is noteworthy that both newspaper reports refer to the Arab murderers as robbers and ascribe no nationalistic motive, whereas Jews all over perceived that Arab attacks on Jews were due to Arab nationalism – and history has shown this to be so. The report in *Ha'aretz* quotes a telegram sent by the Jewish community of Safed to the High Commissioner for Palestine, protesting the continued violence and terrorism: "... Your responsibility is to guarantee our safety.... We demand full protection of our persons and property." It ends with the cry, "... our situation is too difficult to bear." [19]

Those were indeed terrible times. For two years, Arabs had been rioting constantly and there were new acts of terrorism daily, killing women and children, burning communities, and molesting Jews on the highways. Yet the leadership of the Yishuv (the Jewish community in the Land of Israel) chose to exercise *havlaga*, self-restraint, lest Jews be accused of provoking the riots or of eschewing peaceful methods.

Now three young men acted to avenge this latest murder. Shlomo Ben Yosef, Abraham Shein and Shalom Djuravin decided to block the way to Rosh Pina to Arabs. At around noon on April 21, 1938, the three young men saw an Arab bus approaching, shot at it and missed. The Arabs reported the incident to the British authorities.

Ben Yosef, Shein and Djuravin gave themselves up within a few hours, so that innocent Jews would not suffer at the hands of the British. Although none of the Arabs were harmed, the British indicted the three on terrorism charges, determined to put an end to acts of Jewish self-defense. Shein and Djuravin were sentenced to life imprisonment and Ben Yosef, found guilty of firing into the air, was sentenced to death. Shlomo Ben Yosef was hanged in the Acre Fortress on June 29, 1938, the first Jew to be executed by the British.[20]

This was a significant turning point in modern Jewish history, and it was directly connected to Meir's family. Meir was deeply affected by it. The atmosphere in his home was one of deep concern for Jews and active involvement in Jewish communal affairs. Meir absorbed strong Zionist and religious ideals from his father – ideals that were reinforced by his schooling.

Chapter 2

Grade School (1937-1945)

MEIR WAS BORN on August 1, 1932 (28 Tamuz 5692), during the Great Depression, a period of economic collapse that began in 1929 and lasted more than ten years. Businesses failed and there was widespread unemployment. People lost their jobs, their homes, and their savings. In New York City in 1930 there were almost 6,000 unemployed men standing on street corners selling apples for five cents each. Although a rabbi's salary is usually much lower than that of his congregants, the very fact that Meir's father had a regular salary spared the Kahanes the despair of many less fortunate families. To have a steady job during the Depression years was to be rich! The family even had a live-in maid until Meir was nine. Until the age of six, when his brother Nachman (Norman) was born, he benefited from his parents' undivided attention. He learned to read early, and his favorite newspaper was the *New York Times*. A photo taken when he was about five shows a bright smile and a mop of dark curls.

The Yeshiva of Flatbush

Meir attended the Yeshiva of Flatbush elementary school, which emphasized the rebirth of the Jewish nation in the Land of Israel. The Jewish studies department concentrated on teaching the Hebrew language and the Bible. Only a few hours a week were devoted to Talmud study.

Meir recalled that when the school went over to using the Sephardic pronunciation of Hebrew, the principal, Rabbi Joel Braverman, went from class to class telling the children that they were going to stop using the Ashkenazic pronunciation and start speaking Hebrew like Israelis. His reaction, like that of the other children, was to laugh at the "funny" sound of Sephardic Hebrew. Rabbi Braverman strove to bring the best teachers to his school, many of them from the Land of Israel. Music teachers Moshe Nathanson and David Alster-Yardeni[1] taught Hebrew songs that inculcated admiration for the Israeli pioneers and the beauty of the Land of Israel. Meir's Hebrew teacher in fifth grade was Shlomo

Shulsinger, who was in the forefront of Hebrew language education in New York and founded the Hebrew-speaking Camp Massad. Shulsinger remembered Meir as a "quiet fellow."[2]

Meir received several prizes for excellence in his studies, which he treasured. One was a Passover Haggada. Over the years we acquired other Haggadot with more commentaries and fewer wine stains, but that was the one he used every year. Another prize was a brass Chanuka menorah (candelabrum). Although one of our wedding gifts was a silver menorah, he lit only the brass one all his life.

Also much used was the Bible he received for his bar mitzvah. The inscription (in Hebrew) reads: "... May the words of this book be on your tongue and in your heart always, and that will be our reward – The Teachers and Principals."[3]

Classmate Jerry Shapiro wrote:

> Meir, or Martin, as we knew him then, was what I believed to be my best friend for a number of years during our education at the yeshiva. Martin and I lived near each other, quite a distance from the yeshiva....
>
> On days when our school bus could not drive us to school down Ocean Parkway (the street upon which I lived), his mother would drive us to school. I was impressed by that, as in those days before World War II it wasn't that common for women to drive cars. Their car was a relatively old clunker, a Plymouth (as I remember it).
>
> What was Martin like in those days? I thought he was handsome, although perhaps not as handsome as his younger brother Norman. Martin was wiry and very quick. I mean his movements were fast, as was his thinking.... Martin was perhaps the smartest in the class, although that did change from year to year, but in the overall sense I thought he was about the smartest.
>
> For me, the most important characteristic was that he sang beautifully. We were both in the choir led by Moshe Nathanson. I don't know if that name is known in Israel, but he seemed to us to be quite an impressive guy. Both Martin and I enjoyed singing, in particular a song entitled *Chamisha* [Five]. Do you know it? "*Chamisha yatzu moledet livnot, chamisha.*" [Five went forth to build a homeland, five.][4] That's how it began, and I guess I haven't forgotten it.[*] I think we sang a few duets together, but my voice didn't compare to Martin's, in my estimation. His voice was high and clear. We really loved singing those songs. In fact, when I look back on my yeshiva education that is the part I remember best of all.
>
> At recess, which was an important part of the day, the boys would play some organized games, such as handball or punch ball.... We sometimes played at

---

[*] This was an early lesson for Meir, Jerry and their classmates about self-sacrifice for the sake of ideals. The song is about five Jewish workers who set out to work in the fields of Kibbutz Kiryat Anavim, near Jerusalem on November 9, 1937. They were encircled by an Arab gang, and after exchanges of fire, all five were killed and their rifles were stolen. Kibbutz Maaleh Hahamisha (The Hill of the Five) was named for them.

home, after school was over. I would ride over to his house, or vice versa, by bicycle. I don't remember very much about that, except that his mother was always very nice to me.

Jerry's insight into the influence of Meir's father is astute:

When we got older and Meir became famous, I marveled at his courage and his anger, but I was not really surprised. It was not out of keeping with his personality, which always seemed strong and independent. The Zionist education pursued at the yeshiva, in addition to his father's ideas, must have had a terrific imprint upon him, but I suspect that it was the latter rather than the former which was most important.[5]

Jerry recalled Meir's academic excellence:

Meir was extremely articulate, even at that young age, and he knew the answers to most of the questions – both in Hebrew and in English. He seemed to answer questions with great confidence, which is another characteristic of his that I now recall. I am certain that his marks were very good, surely much better than mine, but these things were not bandied about very much in those days.[6]

A classmate in fourth grade remembered him as one of the three top students. Meir was not only a scholar. Tall and slender, he was good at sports and had great verbal skills.[7]

Meir's mother kept his seventh grade report cards. His marks were excellent, with reading, literature, composition and geography his best subjects in general studies. In Jewish studies he received 90s in all subjects, with 99 in Jewish history, 96 in Rashi (a Bible commentary), and 95 in Hebrew reading, showing where his interests lay.[8]

Like every Jew of his generation, Meir was profoundly affected by World War II and the reports he heard and read about the concentration camps and the cruelties inflicted on the Jews. He recalled that one evening, when his parents were at a synagogue function, there was an air raid drill and the sound of the sirens frightened him very much. His brother Nachman related that Meir even kept a scrapbook of news clippings about the war.[9]

Bar Mitzvah

Meir's bar mitzvah took place in his father's synagogue (Congregation Shaarei Tefiloh) on June 16, 1945, just two months after the end of the war. In his bar mitzvah speech, he affirmed his commitment to the Jewish people and to the Torah. Though in Europe the murderers had destroyed millions of our people, and in America assimilation was "killing off" Jews just as surely, he was certain the Jewish people would overcome.[10]

Rabbi Irwin (Yitzchak) Witty was Meir's classmate at the Yeshiva of Flatbush and later at the Brooklyn Talmudical Academy. They were also in Bnei Akiva together. Of their elementary school years, Witty wrote:

> Meir and I ... sang together in the Yeshiva of Flatbush choir, and I remember vividly how he was chosen by the late Cantor Moshe Nathanson, our music teacher at Yeshiva of Flatbush, to be the soloist when we sang *Hallel* [a cantata written by David Alster-Yardeni for the graduation exercises]. I remember also that he sang in the choir that I organized and led at Brooklyn Talmudical Academy high school.
>
> He had a bell-tone, clear voice that was ... sweet and remarkably untainted by nasality. He would cock his head usually to one side as he sang, something that gave his cherub like face, piercing eyes, and curly hair a special cuteness.
>
> I attended his bar mitzvah ... and I have to this day vivid memories of a mass attendance at the event. Cantor Yaakov Koussevitzky was the officiant, along with a choir, the name of which I have forgotten. The cantor, who was a star attraction, and the choir eclipsed regrettably the Bar Mitzvah's performance, even if he was the rabbi's son.
>
> I recall that in grade seven or eight (more likely the latter), our class presented a play in Hebrew on Joseph Trumpeldor.[11] The production was staged in the form of a "shadow play" in which the student audience viewed what was being shown on stage through the medium of sheets where the curtain would normally hang. The appropriate lighting was used to create a dramatic shadow effect. It was, ironically, Meir who played the part of Trumpeldor and uttered the words that Trumpeldor immortalized: *"Tov lamut be'ad artzenu* [It is good to die for our country]."[12]

Baseball

Like yeshiva boys all over New York City, playing ball was an important part of Meir's life. He spent many hours playing stickball, a variation on baseball. Instead of a bat, the boys used broomsticks, and the bases were manhole covers, lampposts, and street signs. They were able to play in the middle of the street because there were not many cars on the roads in those days.[13]

He often played stickball with the non-Jewish boys on his street, but because he wore a yarmulke (skullcap), he was constantly harassed by them. Meir became a fierce fighter. As boys will, he liked to prove his prowess. Rabbi Yaakov Yellin, later of Jerusalem, recalled that one summer when they were 11 or 12, he and Meir faced off. Yaakov was bigger, but Meir got him down on the ground.[14]

Meir kept track of the New York teams – the Giants, Yankees, and Brooklyn Dodgers, and was able to rattle off scores and players' standings by heart. Unlike most Brooklyn boys, he was a Yankee fan. Meir loved to play ball. When we were first married, his cousin Shaul lived nearby, and the two played basketball every Sunday morning, while Shaul's wife Menucha and I prepared lunch. When Meir's Israeli cousins David and Tova Rotlevy visited the United States in the early 1960s, we took them to a baseball game at Yankee Stadium. Meir even wrote a sports column for a short while in 1963.[15]

Rabbi Kenny Cohen recalled a baseball story that Meir often told to demonstrate the self-discipline required of an observant Jew: At baseball games, where vendors sold snacks in the aisles, he sometimes had to pass non-kosher hot dogs to people sitting in his row. The hot dogs looked and smelled delicious and were tempting, but part of being an observant Jew was exercising self-restraint.[16]

Meir's elementary school years were tranquil and productive. In high school, as he matured and developed his talents, he began to show leadership qualities.

Chapter 3

High School (1945-1949)

MEIR'S HIGH SCHOOL years at the Brooklyn Talmudical Academy, popularly called BTA, were challenging. BTA combined the curriculum of an ordinary high school with extensive Jewish study, including Talmud. It was therefore a very long school day – from 8 A.M. to 6 P.M. – plus half-days on Sundays and homework. Nevertheless, he found time for Betar, the Zionist youth group he joined in 1946.[1] During free periods, Meir would talk to classmates about Betar ideology and lead them in singing Betar Hebrew songs.[2]

The Brooklyn Talmudical Academy

Classmate Rabbi Irwin (Yitzchak) Witty recalled:

> BTA was a new school. To be sure, it was a branch of the Manhattan Talmudical Academy [both sponsored by Yeshiva University], but, for all intents and purposes, it was an independent institution. It had an atmosphere of pioneering and newness. New traditions were being established. This provided room for many of us to exercise to the maximum every talent and untapped ability we possessed. Meir was no exception in this regard.
>
> There were a number of very fine teachers at that school in both Jewish and general studies.... Each in his own way had a lasting impact on the students who came in contact with him....
>
> But probably the most significant of the BTA influences stemmed from the student body. Those attending BTA in our day were students who came from an array of different yeshivot and day schools.
>
> ... One of Meir's difficulties at BTA was in fact the different elementary school backgrounds of the students. Most had come from schools where the study of Talmud was begun early and was emphasized throughout the course of study, whereas Meir came from the Yeshiva of Flatbush, where very little emphasis was put on Talmud study. While Meir breezed through most of his courses, and was well-known throughout the school because of his role on the school debating team, Talmud classes were a great challenge.[3]

Rabbi Abraham Zuroff, the administrator of BTA, concurred: "Meir's elementary school emphasized Hebrew language, and Talmud was taught there only one hour a day. The other elementary schools that fed BTA devoted several hours a day to Talmud. At BTA a lot of time was given to the study of Talmud. Rabbi Harold Kanotopsky taught the first year of Talmud in depth, emphasizing the concepts and significance of the subject matter as well as requiring a full knowledge of the early and later commentators. Meir and another boy who had come from the Yeshiva of Flatbush found the Talmud class difficult."[4]

Rabbi Witty went on to extol BTA's diverse student body:

> Among the students from these various institutions, there were individuals with gifted leadership skills. What I did not know at the time, but learned with the passage of years, was that a large percentage of the students ... were of superior intelligence and ability. The degree of talent that was available in the clusters of students with whom Meir, I, and others were involved was oftentimes overpowering.[5]
>
> ... The result was that the "cross-pollination" of ideas, personalities, and background enriched all of us, Meir included. There would be little wonder, then, that the years spent at BTA had an enormous influence on Meir, as I know they did on others of our generation.[6]

Meir did not confine himself to BTA and Betar activities. At 14, he found a summer job in a bookbindery, where he worked at a machine that punched holes for the binding threads. He used to recall this as an important experience that gave him an idea of the ordinary workingman's mentality.[7]

When he was almost 15, despite his parents' objections, Meir left the protected atmosphere of BTA and joined his friends from Betar at a public school, Abraham Lincoln High School (ALHS). He remained there for the February 1947 semester only. When he returned to BTA in September, he told Rabbi Zuroff that he hadn't felt at home at ALHS.[8]

According to Meir's BTA transcript, which includes marks from ALHS, his Regents scores were 78 in French; 80 in English (although his class marks in this subject averaged 89); 71 and 75 in plane geometry and algebra; and 84 in history, his special interest. He also earned a 95 in an economics course he took at Boro Hall Academy during his ALHS term. (Neither BTA nor ALHS offered the subject.) At ALHS he received a 96 in Hebrew. Allan Mallenbaum recalled, "We took Hebrew together for the Regents. The class level was beneath Meir's and he breezed through."[9]

Meir's marks in music, art and health ed – easy but not intellectually stimulating classes – were a passing 65, which lowered his average to roughly 78.9. ALHS had a good-sized track field and Meir devoted quite a bit of extracurricular time to track practice that semester, yet received a 65 in health ed there too.[10]

It's clear that Meir was capable of getting higher marks. Rabbi Zuroff said, "Meir's extracurricular activities, in school and out of it, were extensive and interfered with his studying. He should have gotten better grades." Meir's graduation yearbook lists him as a member of the debating team, the public speaking club, *Kolenu* – the school newspaper board, the library, the choir, the Hebrew club and as class secretary. Rabbi Witty wrote: "He was completely immersed in such disciplines as world history, Zionism, politics, and economics. That he was not always, because of his manifold extracurricular preoccupations, the stellar student he was capable of being, is something that I recall clearly."[11]

Other classmates recalled the pranks Meir played. Once he brought an alarm clock to school that had a ring similar to the school bell. He set it to ring ten minutes before the end of a biology class, and put it outside the classroom door. Sure enough, the teacher heard the bell and dismissed the class ten minutes early![12] Another time he, Irving Greenberg and others piled mattresses below their second-story classroom window. When their French lesson began, Meir cried out that the material was too difficult and he was ending it all. He climbed on to the windowsill and jumped, leaving the astonished teacher open-mouthed, but of course he landed on the mattresses unscathed. Meir told this story whenever he reminisced about his high school days. Classmate Rabbi Yitzchak Greenberg recalled it too and wrote, "Meir, with a handful of co-conspirators including me, was a continuous source of entertainment and dramatics both in class and out of class."[13]

Literary Editor of The Elchanite

At BTA Meir was known as Martin or Marty. Since it was customary in those years to give Jewish children English names, Meir's parents put the name Martin David on his birth certificate. In Betar, too, everyone called him Marty, although the name Meir was used in newsletters and other official Betar documents. It was only when he joined the Bnei Akiva youth movement in 1952 that everyone began to call him Meir.[14]

When Meir graduated from BTA in 1949, he was associate literary editor of the *Elchanite*, the class yearbook. A picture of him with the editorial staff shows a handsome young man with bushy eyebrows, wavy dark hair and an attractive smile. His personal yearbook entry reads: "Good-looking (so he says), intelligent, and possessing a grand personality (If you don't believe it, ask the man who knows – Martin Kahane), this baby is packaged for delivery to Israel. In the meantime, he's becoming a journalist to while the time away. He joined the Cherut movement to get out of school." The last sentence is a play on the Hebrew word for freedom, *cherut*, referring to his devotion to Betar, the youth movement of Israel's Herut (Cherut) party.

The front page of the yearbook's mock *Star Gazer* newspaper, dated twenty years in the future, features the headline, "KAHANE DEMANDS ASIA!" The accompanying article begins: "Martin Kahane, candidate for president on the Herut party ticket, today closed his campaign with a reaffirmation of his party's slogan, 'We must have a Jewish state on both sides of the Pacific...'" (This is a take-off on the Herut demand for a State of Israel on both sides of the Jordan.) Illustrating the article is a drawing of an auditorium with only three or four seats filled, captioned, "Kahane addressing usual overflow audience." The prophetic drawing looks like the Knesset on days when Meir's speeches there were boycotted.

Meir's talent for dramatic expression was apparent in his contributions to the yearbook: Two poems, "Mother of the Dead" and "Land," and a short story, "The Judgment," reflect the yearbook's dedication theme: "To the fallen heroes of Israel."

"Mother of the Dead" depicts the matriarch Rachel, who traditionally weeps for her children.

> *The graves lie quietly in the night,*
> *No noise, no sounds, but gentle peace,*
> *Sweet silence encompassing all of these,*
> *Who found and bled for good and right.*
>
> *No ordinary dead are they.*
> *These children ripped from mother's womb.*
> *For they have chose the book and tomb,*
> *And died – O G-d, so cold they lie.*
>
> *An eerie silence grips the land.*
> *The lambs, the wolves crouch fearfully,*
> *As stepping, gently, tearfully,*
> *Comes Mother Rachel with outstretched hand....*
>
> *This she hears: "O sweet Rachel,*
> *Your bitter tears have reached My throne.*
> *No more shall they roam; they have their home,*
> *And peace to our sons, Israel."*[15]

The Israeli War of Independence was still being fought during Meir's last year of high school, and he and his classmates, who in elementary school had mourned the victims of the Holocaust, now mourned those murdered in the fledgling State of Israel.

Stuttering

During his high school years, Meir began to stutter, or at least to become conscious of it. A classmate said he did not stutter when they were together in fourth grade; if he did she would have been aware of it, because her own brother stuttered.[16]

When Meir was 20 and attending the Mirrer Yeshiva rabbinical seminary during the day and Brooklyn College at night, he decided to do something about his stuttering. In July 1952 he enrolled in the (now defunct) Martin Hall Institute for Speech Disorders in Bristol, Rhode Island.[17] In a summary written for a therapist at Martin Hall, Meir related:

> When I was 9 years old my parents gave me a book for my birthday, titled *So to Speak: A Practical Training Course for Developing a Beautiful Speaking Voice*.[18] I did not know then why they gave me the book.
>
> In grade school I had no trouble. I recited in class and acted in plays. I recall going to the office, speaking to the principal, Rabbi Braverman, about skipping a grade, and to Mr. Hirsch about being the valedictorian. I was not afraid then.
>
> In high school I had no trouble, as far as I remember, during the first and second terms [the first year] – except that I would rather read [aloud] than speak in classes. I had trouble speaking in Rabbi Feivelson's class, and I think he expressed surprise, but I had no trouble speaking to kids or teachers informally.
>
> Once in class, Farber poked me to say I stuttered [in reading] ... even though I was better in reading than in talking.... [The teacher] definitely expressed surprise. I also had trouble in French class. (I think I was AFRAID.) I also had trouble in English at Lincoln giving reports.
>
> I spoke up in class, especially English ... recited, etc. I approached Rabbi Zuroff about a Begin meeting. I was definitely much better conversationally than now, and had no trouble speaking to girls. My friend Victor confirms this.

One of the most difficult things for a stutterer is making phone calls. Meir names the friends he phoned easily and those he was afraid to call. He has a fuzzy memory of being nervous about making calls for his father. He recalled a Betar meeting where he could not talk to two girls. He was afraid to speak up at the Betar convention, but he overcame his fear, and a friend assured him that he had not stuttered. In college, Meir's fear of stuttering became worse. He wrote:

> I did do some speaking in class ... though in History 1.1 I was afraid but wasn't BODILY afraid.... I was afraid to give a report in economic geography, and walked out of the Bible Hebrew class. I was deathly afraid of speech in my last term. In fact, I dropped a previous speech class when the teacher said I stuttered. I had bad trouble asking for transcripts. I showed a paper to the guidance counselor [instead of speaking]. I stammered controllably at interviews. I had trouble answering when attendance was taken. I was afraid to talk up in sociology.... When I was 19, I couldn't ask for a stapler at Macy's.

Some stutterers discover that they cease stuttering when they are distracted from their usual speech patterns. Almost any novel stimulus, such as tapping a finger, swinging the arms, or stamping a foot, can serve as a distraction (until the novelty wears off).[19] Meir's trick was to blink, as he did on various occasions in later years.

Meir was one of many young people from all over the United States who came to Martin Hall for its excellent speech training. The institute's method of relearning speech patterns helped him immensely. The program began with breathing exercises and proceeded through the diligent practice of sounds, words, and phrases. The students were also made aware of the psychological aspects of stuttering. In large letters, Meir wrote in his Martin Hall notebook: "If fear hits, stop. Say it slowly, long pause(s), but SAY IT."

During that summer at the institute, Meir was the only Orthodox Jew. Most of the students were not Jewish, and many had never met a Jew. Yet Meir did not hesitate to speak of his beliefs with them, as is evident from their messages to him in his speech notebook. At the back of the notebook, together with his menu plan (cornflakes, canned soup, sardines, tomatoes, cucumbers, oranges and apples), are end-of-term greetings such as, "To Kosher Boy: Best of luck to a guy with strong convictions," and, "To A Very Nice Guy: I hope that you reach your goal in speech and in going to Israel. I am very sure that you will ... "

At the peak of Meir's career as founder and leader of the Jewish Defense League, a reporter wrote: "At some time in his youth, he apparently forced himself to master a stutter; his tongue still falters occasionally, but the flow of ideas into words is remarkably fluent."[20]

Intent on mastering his stutter, Meir was on the debating team throughout high school. Rabbi Witty recalled:

> Meir was without question – as I look back on our school days together – a highly capable, probably even gifted student. He was especially talented in Jewish studies, no doubt an outcome of being raised in the type of rabbinic home in which he was reared. But what often surprised me was his inordinate knowledge of, and familiarity with, world affairs, current events, and what was transpiring in disciplines and study areas which I had taken always to be the province of adults.
>
> Despite his well-known speech impediment, he was amazingly articulate; his command of language and the ideas he offered were impressive.... [He had a] remarkable command of seemingly esoteric information about the Irgun, the Stern Group, and the entire political situation that surrounded the years of pre-state Israel.[21]

BTA had an important influence on Meir, but Betar, which was his personal choice, was even more important in determining the direction his life would take.

Chapter 4

Betar (1946-1951)

MEIR JOINED THE Betar Zionist Youth Movement[1] in 1946, when he was 14. Shmuel Kraushar, an older member, introduced Meir to Betar at Meir's father's request. Kraushar recalled that Meir liked Betar so much that he made the long trip to meetings at Kraushar's *ken* (chapter) in the East New York section of Brooklyn, though he had to change trains twice to get there.[2]

Later Meir joined the new Bensonhurst *ken* along with neighborhood friends Joseph Churba, Ralph Bieber, and Allan and Victor Mallenbaum. "We became seriously active when Tzvi Rintel and Dave Krakow came to our area to start the new *ken*," recalled Allan Mallenbaum. David Krakow tried to pinpoint the year. "It was probably in 1947," he wrote, "because that was the year I started a lot of new branches."[3]

What was it that drew Meir to Betar?

Activities of a Zionist Youth Movement

"The activities of Betar," reports Yitzhak Heimowitz, "consisted of meetings on Sundays, a rifle club, choir, and participation in public protests and demonstrations. There were social activities held on Saturday nights."[4]

"We had no music other than our voices," recalled Dov Troyansky. "Dancing consisted of the hora, since we had very few people to teach Israeli folk dancing. Only in the early 1950s did we begin to learn and teach folk dancing. We sang songs of Betar and other Hebrew songs..."[5]

Betar's *Tel Hai* newsletter of December 1947 announced a meeting of the pistol and rifle club. In March 1948, *Tel Hai* told of a boxing tournament and described a basketball match between the Bronx and Bensonhurst teams. An April 1949 Passover event included "a dramatic presentation about the Irgun, a movie on Eretz Israel, a performance by the New York choir, and Hebrew singing and dancing by all." In warmer weather, they took trips to the countryside.[6]

Meir took an active part in Betar sports. A report in *Tel Hai* about the Brooklyn basketball team said: "In its opening game, the team was sparked by Meir Kahane, high scorer with 17 points.... A smart display of freezing the ball by V. Mallenbaum, Kahane and Wallin was the deciding factor."[7]

Betar members were expected to have high moral and ethical standards: "A Betari is helpful to others. He is devoted to his friends. He loves the homeland and defends it. He is the first to volunteer in an emergency... He is trustworthy ... disciplined ... kind and courteous ... proud.... He helps the poor and the sick...."[8]

Members were urged to learn a trade or profession that would be useful for "the up building of our country." They attended lectures on Zionist and Jewish history and courses in military strategy, map reading, self-defense, and the Jewish underground in Palestine.[9] (From the time, two thousand years ago, when the Romans gave the name Palestine to Judea until the founding of the State of Israel in 1948, the Land of Israel was known as Palestine, and the Jews there were known as Palestinian Jews.)

Betar was similar to other Zionist youth groups: The dances, songs, and discussions gave the young people the feeling of being part of something larger than themselves, which was connected very specifically with Israel.[10]

Meir was often a soloist in the Betar choir. Arthur (Alter) Heller, another choir member, recalled: "There were two or three hundred Betar members in New York City; fifteen or twenty were in the choir. The choir would entertain on special occasions. Sometimes a program would be put on for parents, and the choir would sing. We also sang at what we called the Third Seder, during the intermediate days of Passover, and at the annual Chanuka party."[11] The *Tel Hai* report on the 1948 Chanuka party noted that Meir "gave a solo vocal rendition" and added, "The real gaiety began after the formal program; Betarim joined in Hebrew songs and dances that lasted until 2 A.M."[12]

Meir was again a soloist at the memorial service for Zeev Jabotinsky's widow. *Tel Hai* reported: "On December 24th, 1949, a Betar *misdar* [assembly] honored the recent death of the 'Mother of Betar,' Madam Hannah Jabotinsky. As the Betar members stood at attention, Meir Kahane chanted the beautiful and deeply moving *Kel Malei Rachamim* prayer."[13]

Singing patriotic Hebrew songs was one of Betar's most effective methods of inculcating ideology. For example, *Shtei Gadot Layarden* (The Jordan Has Two Banks) insisted that the State of Israel must include both sides of the Jordan River. Another song popular in Betar was *Alei Barikadot* (On the Barricades), written by Michael Ashbel, a Jew sentenced to death by the British. Great Britain, which ruled Palestine under a League of Nations Mandate, was obstructing Jewish settlement and preventing the entry of Holocaust survivors into Palestine, while imprisoning and even passing death sentences on members of the Irgun who acted against British rule. Ashbel's lyrics idealized self-sacrifice and military action:

> *And if on the gallows*
> *My life for my people I give –*
> *Weep not, for this is my fate.*
>   *On the barricades, on the barricades we'll meet.*
>
> *On the barricades for freedom we'll fight,*
> *Our gun barrels side by side,*
> *Our shots echoing each other.*
>   *On the barricades, on the barricades we'll meet.[14]*

Some Betar members tried to send arms to their brothers fighting in Palestine. In January 1948, four of them were arrested for attempting to ship 20,000 pounds of TNT and 154,000 detonators to the Irgun and accused of falsifying shipping documents.[15]

Most members supported their Jewish brothers in Palestine by holding protest demonstrations such as these against the British Mandatory government:

- On April 17, 1947, Betar youngsters stormed the British Consulate in New York City to protest the hanging of Dov Gruner and three other Jews in Palestine the previous day.[16]

- On September 10, 1947, 48 members took over the British Admiralty Delegation office in New York, to denounce British "pirates" who took Holocaust survivors off the refugee ship *Exodus* and interned them in Cyprus.[17]

- In March 1948 activists picketed theaters showing British films.[18]

- On Saturday night, September 20, 1947, Betar members held a "Monster Protest Demonstration" at the Seventh Regiment Armory at Park Avenue and 66th Street in Manhattan. The mayor of New York was hosting a ball there in honor of the visit of a fleet of the British Royal Navy. For Betar, these were the same British sailors who had intercepted the *Exodus* that July and kept Holocaust survivors from reaching Palestine. Betar flyers read: "The eyes of our brothers and sisters in embattled Palestine and in the European concentration camps are on you...."[19]

Jenny Marden described the "Monster" protest: "The police wanted to keep us on the far side of Park Avenue, very far from the armory where the ball was taking place. We linked arms to form a human chain and tried to break through the police lines to get to the other side. Then the mounted police came on horseback and kept us from getting closer."[20]

Lester Hering remembered the tactics of the mounted police: "They were all over the place and they succeeded in separating us into smaller and smaller groups with their horses until we finally dispersed."[21]

Meir recalled the Royal Navy protest as "an incredible riot."[22] In 1949, when he was almost 17, he took part in another memorable demonstration. Ernest Bevin, the British foreign minister, was arriving in New York on the *Queen Mary*, and many Jews came to protest at the pier. A Betar flyer proclaimed:

> By his orders the patriots of Israel were hung at Acre; the Displaced Persons on the ship *Exodus* were forced [to Cyprus]... The blood of Israel's patriots is on your hands, Bevin.[23]

About thirty members of Betar threw tomatoes and other vegetables at Bevin's car. Photos of the demonstration appeared in the *Daily News* centerfold. One photo shows Meir and his friend Joseph Churba, with two policemen close by. The policeman standing directly behind Meir is almost hidden in this picture, but the one at his side has a hand under Churba's arm. His thumb is pressed firmly into Churba's back, making a sharp indentation in the fabric of his jacket. Apparently, the policeman behind Meir is using a similar tactic, because the camera has caught both reacting to the sudden jabs. Meir's eyes are wide with shock and his mouth is open in a cry of pain. The pressure on his back has Churba wincing, his eyes closed and his teeth clenched.[24] Neither of them was arrested. Only three Betar members were arrested for disorderly conduct, and they got off lightly. Two, who had tomatoes in their pockets when they were arrested, received suspended sentences, and the charge against the third was dismissed.[25]

Leadership Qualities

Betar gave Meir an outlet for his many talents and provided a framework in which to develop his leadership ability. In February 1949 he was appointed to the Culture Department of Betar's New York City region. Among his duties: "library, Hebrew language lessons."[26]

That July, shortly before his 17th birthday, he was chosen to head Young Betar (ages 10-13) in Borough Park and Bensonhurst. "Meir was in charge of all activities of the youngest group of members in Brooklyn. He used to give talks at meetings and lead group singing," related Izzy Herman. "I would meet him when there were joint meetings in Manhattan."[27]

In August 1949 Meir spent three weeks at Betar's *Bet Sefer* (leadership school) in Livingston Manor, New York, "graduating" with a citation for outstanding work. During the summer of 1950, after almost a year of studying at the Mirrer Yeshiva in Flatbush and attending Brooklyn College at night, Meir again attended the leadership school at Livingston Manor.[28]

Izzy Herman recalled: "I was at the *Bet Sefer* in 1950 and got to know Marty well." Herman pointed out that Betar included observant and non-observant youngsters: "Marty talked a lot about a Jewish state based on Torah. I enjoyed hearing him and Yitzhak Heimowitz sing *zemirot* [Shabbat songs] Friday nights." Yitzhak (Elitzur) Friedman, who was also at the *Bet Sefer* that summer, recalled that Meir's piety was respected.[29]

David Silverstein was 11 when Meir was his group leader in Bensonhurst. He remembered Meir as more religious than the other Betar leaders.[30]

In December 1949 Meir became assistant editor of *Tel Hai*, which surveyed local Betar news as well as current events in Israel and in the American Jewish community. By March 1951, he was chief editor, further developing his writing talent.[31]

He was also a group leader. At the end of 1950 Meir organized a group of yeshiva students in Williamsburg into a Betar *kitah* (unit within a *ken*.) In March 1951, he became a *machoz* (district) leader of *Bnei Etzel*, the 15 to 18 age group. The other leaders of the *machoz* were Allan Mallenbaum, Israel (Izzy) Herman and Yitzhak Heimowitz.[32]

Meir also involved his younger brother, Nachman, in Betar activities. When he was thirteen, Nachman spoke at the opening session of Betar's national convention in February 1951 in Manhattan. His topic was the importance and growth of the youngest Betar group. Nachman recalled that Meir wrote the speech for him on the subway en route to the convention.[33]

This convention marked the beginning of the end of Meir's membership in Betar. There is no evidence that he remained in Betar after May 1951, and by the summer of 1952 he had joined Bnei Akiva, a religious Zionist youth group. In the interim, Meir tried to form a "religious Betar," which he called Tenuat Hatorah (the Torah Movement). No one I interviewed recalled more than a founding meeting at Meir's father's synagogue, but some Betar members felt threatened enough by this competition to want to "teach Meir a lesson." At a Saturday night gathering, they enticed him into a car and "kidnapped" him for the night. There were no hard feelings, however. In fact, one of the "kidnappers," Mordechai Dolinsky, co-founded the Jewish Defense League with Meir in 1968.[34]

Some former Betar members I interviewed said that Meir left Betar after the February 1951 convention because he was not elected *natziv* (head of American Betar). It seems more likely, however, that the influence of his friends Avraham Silbert and Baruch Gelfand, with whom he studied at both the Mirrer Yeshiva and Brooklyn College, moved him to join Bnei Akiva. Meir later told me that with the establishment of the State of Israel, Betar's main goal – supporting the Irgun – was no longer relevant. Now the challenge was to ensure the state's religious character, and that pointed him to Bnei Akiva.

Chapter 5
Approaching Maturity (1949-1956)

MEIR JOINED BNEI Akiva in mid-1952, while attending the Mirrer Yeshiva during the day and Brooklyn College in the evening. In Bnei Akiva, he was no longer in the minority. He was now part of a youth group whose members all observed Shabbat, prayed three times a day, and followed a religious lifestyle – and everyone called him only by his Hebrew name. Avraham Greenhouse recalled a Bnei Akiva leadership seminar Meir attended:

> I first met Meir in the summer of 1952 at the Bachad Farm School, where a seminar for leaders was being held. He came in mid-August, at the end of the summer. He was brought there by Avraham Silbert, who was his *chavruta* [study partner] at the Mirrer Yeshiva. I remember that I and others who had come earlier slept in a large tent. He and Avraham decided to sleep in a separate tent which, it turned out, was full of holes. In the morning Meir's face was full of mosquito bites. He and Avraham had been singing Zionist songs all night, keeping us awake, and we thought that it only right that Meir was all bitten up. Anyhow, he learned his lesson and the next night he and Avraham moved in with us for the remainder of the seminar.[1]

I myself had joined Bnei Akiva in 1950, when I was 12, with my classmate Batya Soller Tratner. Shabbat afternoon meetings focused on Jewish history, life in Israel, Judaism, and songs reinforcing religious and Zionist sentiments, as well as Hebrew vocabulary. We often danced the hora while singing, but unlike Betar, Bnei Akiva members formed separate dancing circles for boys and girls, in keeping with halakha, Jewish law. On Sundays we went on outings. In good weather, we would travel by ferry and bus from lower Manhattan to one of Staten Island's immense, grassy parks, where we'd play baseball, listen to talks about Israel, and sing Zionist songs. Singing created togetherness and instilled ideals. When I sang, "We have come to the land to build and be built," I imagined myself one day living in Israel and working the land. Having endured the taunts and threats of non-Jewish neighborhood kids, I yearned to live where Jews could protect themselves.[2]

26

Some evenings we stood on bustling Delancey Street,* holding an Israeli flag and chanting, "Israel needs your help! Give for Israel!" Sometimes we danced the hora and sang Israeli songs. Passersby tossed coins onto the flag spread between us. Other times we worked the subways. Going from car to car, one of the older boys made a short speech about our brothers and sisters in Israel, while we younger kids approached people with our *pushkes* (charity boxes), jangling them to draw attention. Attending the Bnei Akiva summer camp in Gelatt, Pennsylvania, strengthened my desire to live in Israel and my feeling of being part of something vital.

Within Bnei Akiva, Meir's leadership abilities were quickly recognized. In September 1953, he became head of the *ken* in the Brighton Beach section of Brooklyn, about an hour's walk from his home.[3] Miriam Brovender, a member of that *ken*, remembered Meir coming to Central Yeshiva High School for Girls in Brooklyn and declaring, "Girls, we have to go collect! Israel is in danger!" She and other members of the *ken* promptly left school and headed for the subways. *Pushkes* in hand, they exhorted, "Give to the only democracy in the Middle East!" And people gave.

When Miriam was in ninth grade, some *ken* members had a party at which boys and girls danced together. "Meir heard about it and called us to a meeting. He addressed us as adults and showed us where the *Code of Jewish Law* and other halakhic books expressly decreed that mixed dancing was not allowed. For me, that decided it. I always had the feeling that Meir truly believed in whatever he said. He did not condemn us, he talked to us seriously, and it made a tremendous impression on me."[4]

Meir also made a lifelong impression on Naomi Klass Mauer:

> The year was 1955. I was 13 years old and living in Manhattan Beach, Brooklyn. My two closest friends (Libby Goldberg and Sandy Singer) and I would spend Saturday afternoon walking the boardwalk in Brighton Beach. One Saturday, my mother went looking for us, inquiring of many people if they had seen three young girls. Someone directed her to a basement where a Jewish organization met. Perhaps we were there. And so it was that my mother found *Ken Sharona* of Bnei Akiva. She entered in the middle of a story. A handsome, dark-haired man had a large audience of youth spellbound. When the story was over he began to sing in a clear and beautiful voice. My mother didn't find us that Saturday afternoon, but she found something that was to play a significant part in my life.
>
> When I arrived home, she couldn't stop talking about the Bnei Akiva group and one of its leaders, Meir Kahane. She practically had to beg me to go there

---

* Delancey Street was a main thoroughfare of the Lower East Side, a predominantly Jewish neighborhood.

the following Saturday, but once was all we needed. I had never been part of an organization before. A new world opened up to me. And the dynamic young man making it all come alive was Meir Kahane. How can I describe him? To start with, he was very good-looking, but it wasn't just his actual features. There was a fire in his eyes, and there was a magnetism about him. He had a beautiful voice.... Many of the songs he taught us ... were about Israel, and I still sing some of them today. When he spoke, when he spoke about Israel, there was magic. He was captivating. You could hear a pin drop during his stories. And I always felt that if it wasn't Shabbat, and he told us to follow him to Israel at the conclusion of a story, we'd get up and go.[5]

Almost everyone I interviewed about Meir's years in Bnei Akiva recalled him teaching the song "*Heyu Shalom Moledet U'Zehava.*" The song is a farewell from a soldier in the Jewish Brigade, the Palestinian unit of the British army in World War II.[*] He must go to fight in Europe, but his heart will forever be drawn to the East, to the blue sky and sea of his beloved homeland and to his sweetheart, Zehava.[6] Together with this anonymous soldier, we in Bnei Akiva yearned to return home.

Like Betar, Bnei Akiva had rules of behavior. Among its "Thirteen Principles" were:

- The *chaver* [member] is loyal to the Torah of G-d, His people, land and language.
- The *chaver* loves work and dislikes idleness.
- The *chaver* sees the future of the Jewish people in the Land of Israel.
- The *chaver* respects his parents, teachers and leaders.
- The *chaver* is pure in his thoughts and actions.
- The *chaver* speaks the truth.
- The *chaver* loves nature.[7]

Most important was the *chaver*'s aim to live in Israel.

In October 1954, after a year of leading the Brighton Beach *ken*, Meir was appointed to the *hanhala artzit* (national board) and became the *mazkir* (director) of Greater New York's sixteen *kinim* (chapters). In addition to his administrative duties, he was responsible for the annual New York *neshef*, a dramatic and choral presentation for the entire New York membership. He also oversaw the leadership seminars held most summers. Rabbi Aaron Rakeffet-Rothkoff, a well-known lecturer and historian, attended the 1955 seminar and still has his "graduation" certificate signed by Meir.[8]

---

[*] The Jewish Brigade consisted of infantry, artillery and service units. Five thousand of its soldiers fought on the Italian front.

Elsie Gleich Dudowitz was the secretary-typist at the Bnei Akiva office in downtown Manhattan and worked closely with Meir when he was regional director. She wrote:

> Meir was in charge of all of the New York *kinim* – seeing to any problems they might have and also planning any citywide activities. He planned inter-*ken* activities, too.... I was also a member of the New York board and I was head of *Ken Mizracha* in the East Bronx, and so we worked together as "boss/secretary" [and] as equals....
>
> Meir was very efficient and did a great job balancing everything and everyone. He was very creative in his thinking and had a great sense of humor. He was very dedicated to his work and his ideals and was super to work with on all levels.[9]

Was Meir remunerated for this dedication? "Meir probably was paid some kind of salary," Dudowitz said, "since he had to be in the office pretty much every day, but I don't know how much." His predecessor, Yitzchak (Itchie) Fuchs recalled that he received $15 a week to cover expenses.[10]

A Future in Farming?

During the year that Meir was director of the New York area, an ideological crisis within Bnei Akiva came to a head. Bnei Akiva's aim had always been to prepare its members to live in Israel on a kibbutz. Upon graduation from high school, members went to a training farm in Jamesburg, New Jersey for half a year to learn about farm life, and then went to live on a kibbutz in Israel. I myself attended a summer program at the training farm in Jamesburg in August 1954. Besides crops, there were cows and chickens on the farm. I recall picking tomatoes and cucumbers and taking the cows out to pasture – a real adventure for a city girl.

In 1951, a group of Chicago boys decided not to go to the training farm after high school. They preferred to continue their yeshiva studies. Later, they agreed to go to the farm only if six yeshiva boys in Brooklyn would do so. But the Brooklyn boys decided to remain in their yeshiva. In Boston, too, some boys wanted to remain in yeshiva rather than go to the training farm. Boston leader Yossie Goldberg recommended that rather than leave the city to attend yeshiva, members be encouraged to study at a branch of Lakewood Yeshiva in Boston, thus remaining within the Bnei Akiva framework there.[11]

Other members aspired neither to yeshiva nor to the fast track (going to Israel directly after high school). For example, Moshe Soller studied agriculture at Rutgers University, believing he could benefit the fledgling State of Israel more as an agronomist than as a simple farmer. In April 1955 Shoshana Talansky wrote to Bnei Akiva's Israeli office suggesting that there should be two separate tracks:

one to attend the training farm and then join a kibbutz, and one to finish college before moving to Israel, "because a person who has only a high school diploma is not prepared to work at any really useful job."[12]

Enrollment at the training farm was declining steadily, and there were discussions about replacing the program with a work-study year on a kibbutz in Israel. In November 1954, in a last-ditch effort to save the training farm program, the national board voted to expel the six Brooklyn yeshiva boys. Meir was aghast and at the September 1955 national convention, he and Avraham Silbert led a move to reinstate these six formerly active members. It was a very close vote, but the yeshiva boys lost. Within a year, however, the training farm closed down, and from then on members spent the year after high school in Israel on a work-study program.[13]

This was one of many times when Meir acted decisively on his beliefs, defying the power structure and ignoring his own self-interest. Indeed, following the September 1955 convention, he was no longer the New York director nor was he a member of the national board. We became engaged in the fall of 1955, and Meir concentrated on his studies.

The Mirrer Yeshiva

In September 1949 Meir had enrolled at Brooklyn College, where he majored in political science and history. At the same time, with his father's encouragement, he decided to continue his religious studies at the Mirrer Yeshiva, which had recently opened near their home in Flatbush. Soon he was spending all day at the yeshiva and studying at Brooklyn College during the evening.

The Mirrer Yeshiva's recent history inspired awe in its young American-born students. The entire yeshiva in Mir, near Bialystok, on Poland's eastern border, had escaped the Holocaust en masse: With the outbreak of World War II in October 1939, they had relocated to Lithuania. When the German army was about to invade Lithuania, in June 1941, they traveled via the Trans-Siberia railroad across Russia and sailed from the port of Vladivostok to Japan, which had not yet entered the war and was one of the few countries open to Jewish refugees. They remained in Kobe, among some 2,000 fellow Jews who had obtained refuge there, until the fall of 1941, when all 250 students moved to Shanghai, a free city under international law, where many other Jewish refugees found a haven. In Shanghai, a synagogue seating exactly 250 was placed at their disposal, and they spent the rest of the war there. After the war, about half the students went to Israel and founded the Mirrer Yeshiva in Jerusalem. Over one hundred received visas to the United States, where they became the nucleus of the new Mirrer Yeshiva in

Brooklyn.[14] The American students referred to them respectfully as *"Alte Mir"* (The Old Mir).

Rabbi Moshe (Marcel) Blitz studied at the Mirrer Yeshiva in Meir's time and shed light on the experience: "The overwhelming majority of students were from the old European Mir. They were brilliant Talmudic scholars, world-renowned.... We Americans (at that time) were not great scholars, and we had plenty of trouble properly preparing for a class. We would go and ask very simple questions of the *Alte Mir*, sometimes only translations of Aramaic words.... Meir had a weak background in Talmud, so his father, of blessed memory, hired Rabbi Moshe Bunim Pirutinsky to study with him."[15]

Rabbi Pirutinsky recalled teaching Meir: "Almost fifty years have passed, but I recall Meir's diligence and his strong desire to increase his knowledge of Torah. His pleasant ways with friends and acquaintances are fresh in my memory."[16]

The yeshiva was headed by Rabbi Abraham Kalmanowitz, one of the Torah giants of the twentieth century. It was he who accompanied the students of the Mirrer Yeshiva to a safe haven in Lithuania in 1939. In 1940, he managed to get a visa to the United States and from there arranged for the yeshiva students' transfer to Kobe and Shanghai. He took the financial upkeep of the yeshiva upon himself for the duration of the war, and afterwards succeeded in obtaining visas for many of the Mirrer Yeshiva students to enter the United States. He re-established the Mirrer Yeshiva in Brooklyn in 1946. It was mainly due to his efforts that the entire yeshiva survived.[17] Rabbi Blitz commented:

> One thing that Rabbi Kalmanowitz admired and respected [about] the young Americans was our honesty and integrity. He knew where he stood with us. Another thing he liked about us was our knowledge of the Written Torah, the books of the Bible. Meir and I were well versed in Bible, while some of the European scholars were not.
>
> ... The fact that Meir was very much involved with the Zionist youth group Betar, and later [with] Bnei Akiva, made us personae non gratae with a large element in the yeshiva. Some even looked upon us as heretics because we went to college.
>
> In addition, Meir and I had great love and admiration for Rabbi Joseph Dov Soloveitchik of Yeshiva University and went to hear his lectures from time to time, especially his famous memorial lectures. This was frowned upon. Some students would go clandestinely. Meir and I, however, would go and advertise our going.[18]

Meir completed his tests for rabbinic ordination by Rabbi Kalmanowitz before we were married.[19] He proudly related the hardships involved in being tested by the rabbi. During the summer of 1955, one test was set for 5 A.M. in Sharon Springs in upstate New York, where Rabbi Kalmanowitz was vacationing. Meir and his friends Avraham Silbert and Baruch Gelfand drove half the night to arrive in time.

Gelfand related: "Rabbi Kalmanowitz was very tough on us. He asked very difficult questions and acted very dissatisfied. But later, he took us with him on fundraising visits to some of the wealthy residents of Sharon Springs, showing us off as prize students."[20]

Rabbi Avraham Lieberman recalled: "When Meir was studying for his ordination, Rabbi Kalmanowitz used to test on a few pages at a time, and usually two or three students were tested together. This made it easier on them, because if one was weak on a question, another would answer for him. But Meir often went in to be tested by himself. The students had to know the *Taz* and *Shach* commentaries by heart. This means that he knew the material thoroughly."[21] Here is Rabbi Blitz's account of the testing process:

> The tests were generally given between midnight and 2 A.M. [when Rabbi Kalmanowitz had time], usually on a one-to-one basis.... When it came to *Yoreh Deah* [laws of Kashrut], Rabbi Kalmanowitz was an expert. After all, he had been the rabbi of Tiktin in Poland, a city whose rabbis were always outstanding scholars. When he questioned you, you had to know the answers by heart. This was not an "open book" test.... You were expected to know the intricacies of Talmudic logic surrounding the ruling. But a major condition of ordination by Rabbi Kalmanowitz was the student's complete commitment to Jewish law. His students were permitted to become rabbis only in Orthodox synagogues, never in Conservative or Reform synagogues.
>
> It was on one of these occasions (in 1956), when I'd completed one of the tests at about two or three in the morning, that Rabbi Kalmanowitz asked me to dial a phone number for him in Washington, D.C. He wanted to speak to the archbishop of Washington. I said to him "Rebbi, do you know what time it is? After all, it's 2:30 A.M. I'm sure the man is sleeping – wait till the morning."
>
> His answer to me: "I desperately need him to help save Jews in Morocco.* I've been trying to contact him all day, and I was repeatedly told that he was in conference or out of the office. Now I know he's home, and this is a matter of life and death, so I must do what I have to do. I was instructed by the Chofetz Chayim [the renowned Rabbi Yisrael Meir Hakohen Kagan of Radun] that my mission in life is to save Jews, and nothing, including [social etiquette], will stand in my way."[22]

Rabbi Abraham Kalmanowitz: What a Dedicated, Bold Man Can Do

During the Holocaust, Rabbi Kalmanowitz expended superhuman efforts to obtain

---

* In 1956 Morocco cancelled all exit visas to Israel, and Jews throughout the world feared that Morocco's anti-Israel sentiments would cause harm to Moroccan Jews.

visas for European Jews to enter the United States. The U.S. Immigration Act of 1924 severely limited the number of immigrants from Poland and Russia. Rabbi Kalmanowitz became a frequent visitor to Washington, D.C., and gained access to heads of government in Washington by the sheer force of his personality. He alone acquired more than a thousand visas. Wartime regulations forbade communications and the transfer of funds to enemy territory. Rabbi Kalmanowitz developed a special relationship with Secretary of the Treasury Henry Morgenthau Jr. and other influential people, and through them, the State Department was persuaded to amend the regulations. As of December 1943 Americans were permitted to transfer funds to Jews in enemy occupied territory and to communicate with them.[23]

There is an anecdote told by students of the Mirrer Yeshiva that once Rabbi Kalmanowitz was in the waiting room of an important government figure in Washington. He had been waiting for several hours. Suddenly, he fainted – it is said that he could do this on demand – and caused a commotion in the waiting room. The VIP came out of his office to see what the commotion was about, and was so impressed with the depth of the Rabbi's feeling and concern for the refugees that he arranged for several visas. Rabbi Kalmanowitz epitomized the power of a determined individual. His methods set him apart from the ordinary rabbi and taught Meir that extreme situations demand extreme actions.

Another time, Rabbi Kalmanowitz was trying without success to make an appointment with Morgenthau. Finally, Morgenthau's secretary said he would be available only on Saturday, when Orthodox Jews do not write, travel, or phone. Yet in Jewish law, saving a life is more important than keeping the Shabbat. So this rabbi with a long beard and long black coat took a taxi from his hotel on the Shabbat – and received a promise of a number of visas. Rabbi Blitz recalled:

> Rabbi Kalmanowitz was tenacious. He wouldn't give up, and he came to be considered a nuisance by the authorities. At one point he was told in no uncertain terms, "Rabbi, this is it, we cannot give you any more visas." He pleaded and cried for just one more visa, and as a result of that plea he succeeded in bringing over Rabbi Aaron Kotler, who in turn helped rescue many thousands of Jews and raised up a generation of teachers that changed the face of American Orthodoxy.[24]

Writing in the *Jewish Press* in 1968, Meir paid tribute to his teacher: "Those who know of Va'ad Hatzala's work during the Hitler era know what anonymous and obscure people did.... Those who know of the work that men like the great departed Rabbi Eliezer Silver and the late Rabbis Abraham Kalmanowitz and Yaakov Griffel accomplished, know what dedicated, bold and unaffiliated men can accomplish."[25]

Our Wedding

Meir and I were privileged to have Rabbi Kalmanowitz preside at our wedding on 17 Sivan 5716 (May 27, 1956). The witnesses who signed our *ketubah* (marriage contract) were also prominent rabbis at the Mirrer Yeshiva: Rabbi Abba Berman had spent the war years in Shanghai and was one of Meir's teachers. Rabbi Tzvi Feldman was the *mashgiach*, spiritual mentor, of the yeshiva.[26]

Many of the wedding guests had never seen a wedding like ours. There was no ballroom dancing, only horas, with men and women dancing separately. The band had never played at such a wedding, so Meir gave them the music we wanted beforehand. Even so, as I started to walk down the aisle, the manager of the hall instructed the band, "Now play, 'A Pretty Girl Is Like a Melody.'" Fortunately, I heard him, and asked for the music we had selected. We walked down the aisle to religious music and after the ceremony, the band played Hebrew songs while family and friends danced lively horas.

Meir was influenced by his family, his schooling, and the youth groups he joined. But most of all, he was influenced by the Mirrer Yeshiva. The yeshiva provided the foundation for the direction he took in life. Imbued with the spirit of authentic Judaism, he devoted himself to instilling it in others.

Chapter 6

Courtship and Marriage (1954-1958)

RECEIVED WISDOM IS that a woman seeks a husband who is like her father. When I met Meir at a Bnei Akiva meeting in 1954, what impressed me was his idealism, so like my father's. Meir was director of the New York area and was also leader of my *chevraya* (citywide age group). At those Sunday evening *chevraya* meetings in midtown Manhattan, Meir would lead a discussion on Bnei Akiva ideals and sometimes he would teach a song. One Sunday evening, after such a meeting, Meir drove my friend Toby and me home, because "it was on his way." Our conversation in the car convinced me of one thing: I was barely inside the door when I announced to my parents, "I've met the boy I'm going to marry!"

From then on, I attended the weekly meetings without fail. Once, rather than miss a meeting, I turned down a date to go to the opera. After several months, Meir asked me to go out on a date.

I have always felt that Meir and I were fated to meet and marry. He was born on the 28th of the Hebrew month of Tamuz, and my birthday is 28 Adar. In Hebrew, every letter signifies a number, and 28 is the numerical value of the letters that spell the Hebrew word *ko'ach*, strength. Meir had to be strong to follow through on his ideals, and I had to be strong to follow him, especially as a "single parent" during the periods he was in prison. I was named for my grandmother's grandmother Liba, who lived to 105.[1] The knowledge that I was named for such a long-lived person encouraged me to deal positively with difficulties.

Our dates were usually at coffeehouses in Greenwich Village, where you could order a (kosher) soft drink and sit and talk. Meir liked to remind me that on one coffeehouse date, I began a sentence with the words, "When we are married...," saving him the need for a formal proposal. When Meir's best friend and yeshiva partner Avraham Silbert started seeing another Williamsburg girl, Shoshana Talansky, we sometimes double-dated at the movies, which were relatively clean in those days. Monopoly was one of our favorite pastimes. Sometimes just the two of us played; sometimes friends or family joined us. Combined with

35

lively conversation on a variety of subjects, it was a battle of wits and daring to see who could buy up more property and collect more rent without overspending and losing everything.

By June 1955 we were a "couple," but we spent the summer apart. Meir attended Martin Hall speech school in Rhode Island for a refresher course,* and I spent six weeks at the Bnei Akiva summer camp in Gelatt, Pennsylvania. For the first three weeks I worked in the kitchen, and then I was counselor for a group of 12-year-olds. I slept in their tent and took part in all their activities. Occasionally I gave them talks. It is said that the teacher learns best what he teaches, and to this day I recall my talk on Tisha B'Av, the day Jews fast and mourn the destruction of the Temples in Jerusalem. I spoke about a lamentation prayer that likens the sorrow over the loss of the Temple to the feelings of a bride awaiting a groom whose coming is delayed. Brides and grooms were certainly on my mind that summer!

Meir visited me at camp several times, traveling more than three hours each way. At the end of the summer, he formally asked my father for my hand in marriage, laying out his plans for our future: We would go to live in Israel, where his master's degree in international relations would qualify him for a job in the Foreign Ministry. Our engagement party was held in October 1955 and our wedding date was set for mid-May the following year. That year we had the first Passover Seder with his parents and the second one with mine. Flatbush, where Meir's parents lived, and Williamsburg, where my parents lived, are at opposite ends of Brooklyn. The walk from Flatbush to Williamsburg took three hours!

A Corsage of Red Roses

In keeping with the Bnei Akiva ideal to live the simple life in Israel, I refused a diamond engagement ring. However, Meir's parents were appalled at this flouting of convention, so he devised a way to satisfy their wishes. One day, shortly before our engagement party, he phoned me at work and asked me to meet him near my office, at Central Park. There, he hired a horse-drawn carriage whose driver wore a cutaway formal coat and top hat. Once the horses were prancing in the park, Meir opened the box he was holding, which held a corsage of red roses. Under the roses was a diamond ring. How could I refuse?

During the year we were engaged, I worked days and went to school evenings. My parents felt that since I was so young and had no experience of the "real world," I should get a job. I had learned touch-typing in ninth grade, after I received a typewriter as a graduation gift from my grandfather, and I improved

---

* See chapter 3 for more about Martin Hall.

my typing skill when I edited my grade school yearbook and co-edited the newsletter of the Bnei Akiva summer camp. Now, using that skill, I found secretarial work at the Youth Department of the Jewish National Fund (JNF) in Manhattan. The JNF, which raised money to plant trees in Israel, suited me because they closed early on short winter Fridays to enable the staff to get home before the start of Shabbat at sundown. One of my responsibilities was mailing out pages of "trees" and "leaves" to Jewish schools all over the city. Each student received a tree with blank leaves. For each five-cent donation, he would be given a leaf to paste onto his tree. The JNF offices were located in a brownstone in a posh section of the city. The Youth Department was on the top floor, and in nice weather I ate my brown-bag lunch on the roof, enjoying the great view of Manhattan.

I attended evening classes twice a week at Brooklyn College and twice a week at the Stern College Teachers' Institute. At Brooklyn College, I accumulated credits toward a bachelor's degree, taking the required courses in history, sociology, English, and so on. My teachers at Stern, Rabbi Abraham Shkop (Jewish philosophy) and Rabbi Chaim Levine (Jewish law), made a lasting impression on me.

Meir Completes His Studies

Meir had graduated from Brooklyn College in June 1954,[2] the year before we married. Majoring in political science and history, he'd attended only evening classes, spending most of his days at the Mirrer Yeshiva. To complete a B.A. in only five years of evening study – together with his responsibilities in Bnei Akiva – was quite an accomplishment. His college yearbook, *The Broeklundian*, identifies Meir on page 141 as "Martin D. Kahang," a common misreading of his signature. I became accustomed to receiving mail for Mr. Kahang, later one of Meir's alleged aliases listed by the FBI.

In October 1955, Meir began his law studies at New York Law School. After our engagement he began to teach at the Shaarei Tefiloh afternoon Hebrew school. He had great rapport with the children in the Hebrew school, who called him Rabbi Meir. His notebook of speech exercises tersely records his daily schedule the year we were engaged: "A.M.: law school, P.M.: work, evening: yeshiva." After we married, Meir added courses for his master's in international relations at New York University to his hectic schedule.

We planned to go to live in Israel as soon as Meir completed his law degree and his master's degree. Meanwhile, we needed a place to live. We found a three-room apartment in Flatbush, but Meir thought the rent was high – $65 a month. His uncle, Isaac Trainin, reassured him: "You're planning to go to Israel as soon as you finish your law and master's degrees. Five dollars more or less for a year doesn't amount to that much. Take the apartment!" So we did.

The apartment was on East 2nd Street near Avenue N, about a 15-minute walk from Meir's parents' home. It was the upper story of what had once been a one-family house. It had a living room, bedroom, and kitchen, with a porch where I grew geraniums. As a wedding present, Meir's parents gave us a custom-made, floor-to-ceiling bookcase covering an entire wall, with special shelves to hold the oversize volumes of the Talmud. The bookcase was so well made that I still have it, with some sections in my children's homes.

The first year we were married, I worked in a number of offices as a typist, and attended Brooklyn College evenings. One of my first jobs was as a receptionist, but the personnel administrator objected to my wearing a hat (I covered my hair after marriage for religious reasons), so I left. Winter was approaching, with its short Fridays. Fortunately, the Young Israel employment service helped observant Jews find jobs where they would not have to work on Saturdays and Jewish holidays and could leave early on Friday afternoons. Through them, I found secretarial work at a ball-bearings firm owned by religious Jews. The office was under the Manhattan Bridge. Real estate in New York City was so expensive that even the area under the bridge, where it sloped down from high above the river toward street level, was built up. The office was grimy from the greasy ball bearings and the exhaust from bridge traffic, but the black bean soup we ordered for lunch from a local kosher cafeteria was delicious. I even worked as a typist in the office of the Mirrer Yeshiva for a few months. Rabbi Kalmanowitz's wife, who came to the office from time to time, had a master's degree in library science. This may have influenced my decision to become a librarian.

In the evenings, Meir drove me to Brooklyn College in his newly acquired used car, a dark green Hudson. One of my courses was on the third floor of the psychology building, where the one and only elevator was reserved for teachers and handicapped students. After a second-month miscarriage, I applied for an elevator pass, citing medical reasons. The pass was given to me with the proviso that once I entered the third month of my next pregnancy, I would inform the school. In those days, women who were conspicuously pregnant were not allowed to attend college (or teach in public schools) lest they be a "bad influence" on young people!

At law school and at NYU, Meir met interesting people and brought some of them home. One was a law student named Roger who aspired to work for the FBI. He was a Christian and his wife was a former nun. Like us, they were newlyweds. When we visited their home, Roger spoke of someday living in Jerusalem. "But then," he quipped (aware that for Meir one of the advantages of living in Israel was sparing our children the yearly Christmas festivities), "my children will want to celebrate Chanuka!" Another guest was a Pakistani studing international relations with Meir at NYU. He came for dinner several times. This young Moslem would not eat pork, so our kosher home was exactly what he needed.

In February 1957, Meir received his LL.B. (law degree). Since we planned to live in Israel, he did not take the New York Bar exam. He received his M.A. that June. His thesis was titled "Israel's Concept of Aggression: An Analysis."[3] Meir expected this degree to secure him a job at the Israel Foreign Ministry.

The Martin Hall Speech School

We spent July and most of August in Bristol, Rhode Island, where Meir, who felt that his stuttering was returning, did another refresher course at the Martin Hall speech school. This was my first experience of small-town America. We had a room in a two-story hotel on Main Street, where all the town's stores were located. The shoe store across the street was owned by one of the few Jews in town. Kosher food was non-existent, but at the supermarket down the street I was able to buy milk, cheese, fruits and vegetables. We had come to Bristol with a large supply of kosher canned food: soups, tuna, salmon and sardines. We even had cans of meat that a butcher in Williamsburg had prepared for us. I cooked spaghetti and heated soup on an electric hotplate and washed dishes in a tiny sink in the corner of the room. Instead of a refrigerator, we had a picnic cooler with cans of chemical ice. The hotelkeeper did not object to our eating in our room and allowed me to refreeze the chemical ice in his freezer.

The only real problem was kosher bread. On Fridays, the supermarket carried Levy's Rye Bread, a so-called "Jewish" bread – but it had no kashrut certification! Fortunately, we had received a "wonder pot"* as a wedding gift, so I was able to bake bread on the hotplate. I even baked three separate *challot* for Shabbat by placing silver foil dividers in the dough.

Meir was fully occupied with his speech therapy, and I found something to do too. I was five months pregnant and needed maternity dresses. I bought fabrics and patterns on Main Street and finished two dresses – by hand – before we returned to Brooklyn. The baby was due in November, and we planned to move to Israel after the birth, so rather than renew our rental lease in Flatbush for a few more months, we moved in with my parents in Williamsburg. The evening before Tova was born, friends came to visit. Amid lively conversation, we played Monopoly. After they left, I couldn't sleep. It finally occurred to us that labor was starting, and we hurried to the hospital. A photo shows Meir, beaming with pride and joy, holding newborn Tova in his arms.[4]

---

* A "wonder pot" was a tube-center pan with a special bottom that distributed the heat and could be used for baking on an ordinary top burner. It was widely used in Israel because many Israelis did not have ovens.

Looking for a Job in Israel

In January 1958, Meir's friend Chaim Spring took his place teaching in the Hebrew school,[5] and Meir left for Israel to look for a job and a place for us to live. Meir's acute awareness of the magnitude of this step is reflected in a farewell letter to his parents: "Whatever I am, whatever I strive for, whatever ideals that I go to Israel to achieve, are the products of your teaching and training. The love of G-d and compassion for man that I hold to be more important than life itself – this I received from you."[6]

Travel by ship was cheaper than by plane, so Meir took a berth with Zim Lines, the Israeli shipping company. Years later he told Tova about an episode during the voyage, and she wrote the story (in Hebrew) in her eighth-grade yearbook.

> … One Shabbat, my father was resting in his cabin, which he shared with seven other passengers, among them a chasid and a non-observant Israeli. He was awakened when the secular Jew burst into the cabin angry, fuming, and cursing all religious Jews. The chasid had seen him smoking on the deck, and knocked the cigarette from his hand into the ocean. My father was saddened by the effect of the chasid's aggressive religiosity on the non-observant Jew.
>
> Then my father told me of another incident. When he was a yeshiva student, he took a walk with his rabbi. They sat down on a bench next to someone smoking. The rabbi realized he was a Jew and said to him, "Ah, my friend, you probably forgot that today is Shabbat." The man threw away his cigarette. My father learned from that rabbi that this is how to speak with non-observant Jews."[7]

In Israel, Meir stayed in Kfar Haroeh, near Hadera, with his good friend Avraham Silbert, who taught at the Bnei Akiva yeshiva there. Meir visited relatives around the country and spent several weekends in Tel Aviv with his uncle Zundel and aunt Gittel. He also caught up with our old friend Eliezer Waldman, who had moved to Israel the previous year and was studying at the Merkaz Harav yeshiva in Jerusalem. This yeshiva was founded by Rabbi Abraham Isaac Kook, whose writings about the Jewish people's destiny in the Land of Israel were the basis of the Bnei Akiva movement.[8] His only son, Rabbi Tzvi Yehuda, headed the yeshiva, and Meir very much wanted to meet him. Rabbi Waldman arranged it, and accompanied Meir to Rabbi Tzvi Yehuda's home in the Geula section of Jerusalem. When they met, Meir told Rabbi Tzvi Yehuda, "I have come to settle here." Meir used the Hebrew verb *lehishtake'a*, which was correct usage, but also connotes "sinking." Rabbi Kook replied, "In Israel we do not sink, we raise ourselves up."[9]

When Meir discovered that Foreign Ministry positions were reserved for Labor party faithful, he turned to Israel's Ministry of Religious Affairs, where he was told that Kibbutz Saad, in the western Negev, was looking for a full-time rabbi. He was invited to give a trial sermon on Shabbat, February 22.[10] Meir already knew one member of Kibbutz Saad, Rabbi Chaim Druckman, who had been in America as the Israeli emissary to Bnei Akiva. Rabbi Druckman, later the head of Yeshivat Or Etzion and a Knesset member, recalled Meir's inspiring trial sermon about the sabbatical year, when the land must lie fallow while the Jew devotes himself to spiritual matters.[11]

Back in Kfar Haroeh, Meir wrote to the kibbutz thanking the members for their warm welcome and for the enjoyable and uplifting Shabbat he had spent there.[12] However, all was not well.

Meir stuttered terribly in Hebrew. At the Silberts', he spent many hours a day doing the speech exercises he had learned at Martin Hall, hoping they would help him with Hebrew as they had with English. He tried very hard, but without success. At the end of March, he gave up and returned to the United States.

Meir wrote an emotional farewell to Kibbutz Saad: "I have not yet received a letter from you about my candidacy.... I must return to the U.S.A.... If the decision is to appoint me your kibbutz rabbi, I am more disappointed than you [that I cannot accept].... I am broken!"[13]

Meir came back to the United States in time to celebrate Passover, saddened but undefeated. We moved into a one-room basement apartment on East 45 Street near Kings Highway in Flatbush. There he renewed his efforts to overcome his stuttering with a strict daily regimen of vocal exercises. He found a summer job as the rabbi at Camp Hatikvah in the Catskills, and in late June we moved to the camp, where eight-month-old Tova spent her days in a playpen in the sun, surrounded by admiring young campers.

Meir had learned of an opening for a Hebrew-school teacher at the Howard Beach Jewish Center in Queens. Since the synagogue had no rabbi, he was interviewed by members of the Education Committee. He made such a favorable impression on them that they asked him to be the rabbi of the center.

From Camp Hatikvah, we moved to Howard Beach.

Chapter 7

The Howard Beach Jewish Center
(1958-1961)

MEIR ACCEPTED THE rabbinical position at the Howard Beach Jewish Center (HBJC) with certain conditions. He demanded Orthodox practices, even though none of the synagogue members were observant: a kosher kitchen, traditional prayers, and separate seating for men and women with a *mechitza* (partition) between them. Another condition was that the synagogue resign from the Conservative movement's United Synagogues of America.[1] Remarkably, the board of directors agreed to all these terms, perhaps because the salary Meir accepted was far lower than that of a Reform or Conservative rabbi. Robert Falk, the synagogue's accountant, replied to my query about Meir's salary: "I only know that it was very little and often wondered how you got along. The rabbi never complained."[2] At one point, Meir did try to supplement his salary by joining a stockbrokers firm, but the task of approaching investors aggravated Meir's stutter so he left it.[3]

Meir's salary could, no doubt, have been higher, but I never felt any lack. Fortunately, we did not have to cover certain expenses. For example, my mother brought us meat from her butcher once a week. Both sets of grandparents covered the cost of a baby carriage, crib, playpen and similar equipment, and other relatives and friends gave us their children's outgrown clothing. We lived modestly, glad that Meir had found this position.

One of Meir's first acts as the rabbi of the HBJC was to buy two sets of dishes for its kitchen – one for meat and one for milk. Then, to purify them, he and one of the older members of the synagogue, cantor Charles Prost,[4] drove to a nearby lake where they piled the dishes into a rowboat. Meir rowed out to the center of the lake, and they dipped each dish in the water, as required by Jewish law.

Membership Drive

Robert Falk recalled:

> The synagogue had a membership of 46 families. Because of Rabbi Kahane's

efforts, members would go out on Sunday mornings to visit new Howard Beach residents and invite them to join the synagogue. The results of this drive are best stated by quoting from a financial statement that I prepared, dated September 6, 1959: "A membership drive commencing in the fall of 1958 increased the membership body from 46 to 80 families as of June 30, 1959. Continued membership solicitation has raised this total to almost 100 families at the writing of this report." During this period the synagogue was freshly painted, and an attempt was made to raise a $25,000 mortgage from the Richmond Hill Savings Bank, which was moving into the area. Rabbi Kahane was the force behind these events.[5]

The synagogue occupied a three-story wood-sided building on a large corner lot facing Casino Park. The building was designed by the well-known architect Sanford White. It had a huge front porch with an overhead awning and another porch on the second story. In the 1920s, the building was sold to the Yokohama Bank and turned into the Japanese-American Club, serving the bank's Japanese employees. The Club closed following Japan's attack on Pearl Harbor, and the Howard Beach Jewish Center bought the building in 1942.[6]

In a *Jewish Press* article, Meir described Howard Beach as:

> ... a small Queens community lying off Jamaica Bay. For years it was a quiet, forgotten area abounding in swamps and desolate fields wherein roamed rabbits, pheasant, and wild birds. There were only a handful of Jews – perhaps 25 families – mostly elderly people lost in a sea of gentiles.
>
> Then came the postwar housing boom. In 1950 the first great housing development in the area – Rockwood Park – was built. As in so many other communities on Long Island, Jews began to migrate to the area.

Meir analyzed the motivation of Jews who joined the HBJC:

> They were young people from East New York, Bensonhurst, Brownsville, not in the least religious, who, had they stayed in Brooklyn, would have been, at best, cool to synagogues and to Judaism. In their new environment, however, they soon felt the need to find a little Jewish social security in the face of a strange world. This point must, of course, be stressed again. Theirs was not a "return to religion" but a need for Jewish togetherness, not a "yearning for G-d" but a fear of their boy Sammy coming home with one of the many Marys roaming the area.[7]

Though most of the congregants lived about a mile away in Rockwood Park, a new neighborhood of one-family homes, we rented an apartment near the synagogue[8] in the old swampy Spring Creek area, which abounded in mosquitoes. Once, on a warm day, I took baby Tova out for a stroll and she was attacked by what seemed like hundreds of mosquitoes. I went running back to the safety of our apartment! In a photo taken in that apartment, a very young and proud Meir is holding eighteen-month-old Tova.

Baruch was born in January, at a strapping 10 pounds. His *brit* (circumcision ceremony) took place in that apartment on a snowy morning. Both grandmothers did the catering, with the guests, mostly relatives, crowded into our tiny living room. Rabbi Moshe Bunim Pirutinsky, Meir's tutor at the Mirrer Yeshiva, was the *mohel* (circumciser).[9] Baruch was named for Meir's maternal grandfather, Rabbi Baruch Shalom Trainin.

That winter I hung Tova's and Baruch's diapers (no disposable ones in those days) to dry overnight in the steam-heated kitchen rather than out on the line, where they would freeze.

After a year, we bought a ranch-style house in the Rockwood Park section with a Federal Housing Administration 30-year mortgage. At 3% of the $15,730 sale price, the down payment was only $470, and the monthly payments were low.[10] The previous owners had carpeted the living and dining rooms, done the kitchen cabinets and breakfast nook (built-in seats around a pedestal table) in pink and black, and turned the basement into a recreation room. The unfinished attic became Meir's study. Best of all was the large, grassy backyard, where the children played on a swing set and rode their tricycles.

Educating the Congregation

Meir taught most of the classes at the synagogue's afternoon school, and the children responded to his sincerity. They came happily to classes, and he often invited them home to experience a "real" Shabbat. Our basement recreation room was where they spent Shabbat afternoons, listening to Meir's stories and singing Hebrew songs. Robert Falk recalled those afternoons: "My eldest daughter, Merryl, went to the Hebrew school. She was a member of the Shabbos club. On Saturdays, Merryl would walk from our house on 96th Street to your home in Rockwood Park. Her friend Agnes, a gentile girl, would tag along."[11]

Meir's achievements at the HBJC are detailed in its bulletin, the *Howard Beach Jewish Community Herald*:

> Months ago some of the more pessimistic were gloomily predicting that the Talmud Torah [afternoon synagogue school] would get no more than five children. Now we can boast of 25 hardy boys and girls divided into two classes. Our Sunday school has seventeen youngsters. Mrs. Chaya Reich is the beloved Sunday-school teacher. As for the Talmud Torah children, they are already busily teaching their parents the facts of Jewish life. With our membership drive going the way it is, Rabbi Kahane expects to have a grand total of 40 to 45 children by spring.

... The Adult Education Seminar under the guidance of Rabbi Meir Kahane is now in the second semester.... The courses so far have consisted of basic Hebrew reading and writing, conversational Hebrew, and Jewish history and philosophy. Several people who had absolutely no Hebrew background have learned to read like professionals (almost).... It took no longer than two to three months to master all the letters and combinations.[12]

Meir's installation ceremony took place on January 25, 1959, at the neighboring Ozone Park Jewish Center – the HBJC did not have a large enough auditorium. The bulletin reported, "More than 200 people attended to hear dignitaries from both religious and civic fields welcome the rabbi to his new post."[13]

In an *Our Rabbi's Message* in the bulletin, Meir marvels at

> ... all the wonderful changes that have occurred within our Center in such a remarkably short time: An unprecedented new membership success, the surprising growth of our Talmud Torah and Sunday school, the creation of an Adult Education Seminar, the formation of a youth group, and now, our new bulletin. There is a new feeling of accomplishment in the Center.... For not only materially and outwardly have we made gigantic strides, but more important, we have advanced spiritually – we have truly become a House of G-d. The creation of a completely kosher kitchen, the introduction of truly traditional services are manifestative [*sic*] of soul seeking, honesty and TSHUVA – a return to the true principles of Torah. May our Father in Heaven grant us the continued strength and courage to continue in the path that we have begun to blaze.[14]

Meir was outspoken in his insistence that only Orthodoxy was authentic Judaism. In a letter to the editor in the *Jewish Post and Opinion*, he referred to a recent *Post* article in which Reform leader Jacob Weinstein said he saw nothing wrong with interdating. "Why should we start to build walls around ourselves?" asked Weinstein. Meir answered:

> Having rejected the exclusiveness of Judaism, having rejected the distinctive ritual of the Jewish faith, clinging only to universal "ethics," subconsciously Jacob Weinstein sees no great difference between a Jew or non-Jew so long as both do not beat their grandmother. Intermarriage and assimilation to him do not convey the pain and sense of loss that the average Jewish parent feels. Glibly, he takes to task those who fear intermarriage by proclaiming that this means they are uncertain and afraid to trade culturally.... Were he a scholar in the tradition of the true rabbi, he would know of the countless discussions held by rabbis with pagans and churchmen.... Let us not confuse equality and love and tolerance with assimilation. Certainly we are prepared to live on the same streets as non-Jews. We shall surely go to schools with them. By all means we work side by side with them. We are commanded by G-d to love them, help them, build a better world side by side. However, respect for my fellow human being and his belief does not necessitate my destroying my own.... I, for one,

will continue to urge Jewish parents to guide and teach their children to reject that "first date," and I hope that this letter will succeed in some measure in opening the eyes of the average Jew to the subtle threat of the Reform version of Judaism.[15]

Blessing the Congregation

Meir devoted himself wholeheartedly to bringing authentic Judaism to Howard Beach. He taught Hebrew school in the afternoon and worked with the congregants in the evening. Mornings, however, were devoted his yeshiva studies. Since the Chaim Berlin Yeshiva on Stone Avenue in East New York was only a ten-minute drive from Howard Beach, he went there to study rather than make the longer trip to the Mirrer Yeshiva. He contributed an article on the halakhic question of two people claiming ownership of the same object to *Hapardes*, a rabbinic journal.[16] He also dealt with interesting halakhic questions that arose in the synagogue. For example, HBJC member Jimmy Cohen had lost a leg fighting in the U.S. Army and wore a prosthesis that was permanently attached to a shoe. As a *kohen*, a member of the priestly family, he was obliged to bless the congregation during holiday prayers. Yet a *kohen* must remove his shoes before delivering this blessing. Since Jimmy's shoes were permanently attached to his prosthesis, could he give the priestly blessing?*

Meir sent a *she'ela* (query) to Rabbi Moshe Feinstein, the preeminent halakhic (Jewish legal) authority in the United States, who analyzed the problem as follows: Ordinarily, if a *kohen* does not remove his shoes as required, people are likely to wonder why, and this would distract their attention from the blessing. But if they know about his disability, they will understand why he is keeping his shoes on, and it won't distract them. Furthermore, if he refrains from blessing them, they might question his lineage as a true *kohen*.

Another point Rabbi Feinstein made was that the *kohen's* fulfilling the commandment to bless the congregation is far more important than any fear of his shoes' attracting attention. Therefore, ruled Rabbi Feinstein, Jimmy Cohen should bless the congregation.[17]

This query was referred to by Rabbi Feinstein's son-in-law, Rabbi Moshe Tendler, in his eulogy of Meir in 1990. "Such was this man," he said of Meir.

---

* One reason for the removal of the *kohen's* shoes is that they may be muddy or otherwise dirty, making it disrespectful for him to bless the congregation while wearing them. A second reason is that an untied shoelace or torn sandal strap could delay his pronouncing the blessing, and people might think he is not blessing them because he is (for various reasons) a disqualified *kohen* (*Talmud Bavli, Sotah* 40a). In Israel, the *kohanim* bless the congregation at every morning prayer service, but in the Diaspora they do so only on holidays.

"His whole goal was always 'How do you make each Jew stand tall?' Nations of the world try to chop our legs down, but he wanted us to stand tall."[18]

Meir faced yet another halakhic problem. At age twelve, a girl attains "bat mitzvah," religious maturity, and is obligated to observe the commandments. A bat mitzvah celebration had been scheduled before Meir became the rabbi, and since some aspects of bat mitzvah celebrations in Reform and Conservative synagogues contravened Orthodox practice, Meir queried Rabbi Feinstein again. Rabbi Feinstein's response stated:

> This celebration is not a commandment, and therefore it should not be held during services. After the services, members may be invited to partake of a *kiddush* [collation], because it is like any celebration. The bat mitzvah girl may make a speech at the *kiddush* but not from the pulpit of the synagogue.
>
> However, since in this case the bat mitzvah has already been scheduled, if it is impossible to change the plan to have her speak from the pulpit without causing strife and disrespect for the rabbi, then the rabbi may agree that this time she speak from the pulpit, but at future bat mitzvah celebrations, practice will be in accordance with Jewish law.

Regarding the argument that such a celebration brings a bat mitzvah girl closer to Judaism and the commandments, Rabbi Feinstein disagrees. In his opinion, even a *bar* mitzvah ceremony (for a boy) – which is a commandment – should not be encouraged if attendees will drive to the synagogue or otherwise violate the laws of Shabbat, since experience has shown that such a celebration does not make a boy more observant.[19]

This was sadly true of Arlo Guthrie, son of the well-known folksinger, Woody Guthrie, and a resident of Howard Beach. Meir gave Arlo bar mitzvah lessons at the request of his mother, who was Jewish, but Arlo remained an unobservant Jew.[20]

Indeed, a one-time Jewish celebration does not have much Jewish impact, but Meir brought many children and their parents closer to Judaism by teaching them week after week. He wrote about himself and his work with the congregation:

> Rabbi Kahane had from the first maintained that a rabbi's function was not to lead services only; was not primarily to comfort mourners or address sisterhood meetings or represent the community at Memorial Day services. These were of course part of the job. But essentially the rabbi was a teacher, a guide, a leader. It was his function – if he believed in the ideology of Judaism – to bring that ideology to the people. In short, to bring the message of the Torah to the people by persuading them to observe the laws. Any goal less than this was hypocritical.

Working with Children

Meir regarded his work with youngsters as vital:

> Rabbi Kahane also understood that his greatest hope of success was with the children. And they adored him. By a combination of teaching, attending their youth gatherings, playing basketball and softball with them, and a sincere interest [in] and love for each child, the rabbi succeeded to a fantastic degree. Many children began to observe the Sabbath completely, to observe *kashrus*, to say the prayers and blessings daily, to wear the *tallis katan* [fringed garment], etc. He succeeded in registering several in yeshivas over the opposition of many members who resented the loss of synagogue revenue [from Hebrew school tuitions].
>
> He formed at his own expense a Shabbos club, meeting every Saturday afternoon at his home, where for the first time in their young lives – besides games and stories – the children sat at a shalosh seudos meal [the third and last festive meal each Sabbath] singing *zemiros* (Sabbath songs) and discussing aspects of the Torah.[21]

At Meir's suggestion, several children started attending the Tifereth Moshe yeshiva. The principal of the yeshiva, Rabbi Abraham Levin, accepted them at Meir's request despite the special instruction required to bring them up to par in Jewish studies. He even slashed their tuition. Rabbi Levin recalled:

> Reb Meir sent three or four boys from Howard Beach to Tifereth Moshe. None were from observant homes. Kenneth Bell was, I believe, a sixth grader, as was Marvin Lax. Michael Katz entered first grade in Tifereth Moshe and went on to the Talmudical Academy for high school. I became acquainted with Michael's parents... They held Reb Meir in very high esteem.[22]

HBJC president Victor Kirschenbaum was unobservant, but his dedication to the center reflected an affinity for Judaism that was not lost on his sons, Alan and Mark. They were among those influenced by Meir to become observant and even to live in Israel. Alan wrote:

> My memories of Meir and you (and all your family) were primarily during my teen years, when he (and your family life) made an important impression on me and provided the social and emotional support to become and remain religious.... The fact that I went to Yeshiva University and moved to Israel (1969) can be attributed in great part to both Meir's and your family's influence.... My mother [Belle] is now living in Eilat with my brother (and family)....[23]

Belle and Victor Kirschenbaum eventually embraced their children's religiosity, but in 1960 their immediate reaction was to get rid of the man who was causing their boys to demand a kosher kitchen and other changes at home. Meir described the bind in which he found himself:

... the most important of the rabbi's achievements in the end proved his undoing. The rabbi, of course, was no fool and understood that he must not plunge headlong into this. On the contrary, each lesson was followed by strict reminders that the child must never disobey his parents. Respect for parents was so emphasized that children were soon rising when parents entered a room and would not sit in their parents' seats without permission. The possibility of conflict in the home was thus carefully cut to a minimum. Even this, however, was not enough. More and more, a small but determined group led the opposition to the rabbi's teachings. From demands that the rabbi cease teaching the children observance, criticism actually spread to the fact that the rabbi's sermons dealt with such things as Shabbos and kashrus! The rabbi's fate was sealed when the president's son turned strictly observant. Despite the fact that the boy did not attend Hebrew school (he was 17), he was so impressed by the teachings of the rabbi that he began to observe the laws completely, even applying for the Jewish studies program at Yeshiva University.

With the president also turned against him, the rebellion spread. When the rabbi's contract came up for renewal, demands were served upon him that the center revert to Conservatism and that the board have the right to modify the teachings of the rabbi. The rabbi naturally refused.

On the night of March 3, [1960] a carefully planned meeting was scheduled to vote on this issue. That whole day, a tremendous blizzard swept the area, but despite demands by many members that the meeting be postponed, the board refused. The rabbi spoke long and impassionedly. Many members who were themselves not in the least observant supported the rabbi, decrying the disgraceful stand of the center. It was of little avail. As the clock turned midnight, the coach turned into a pumpkin. The synagogue voted to revert back.[24]

As rabbi, Meir was required to leave the meeting before the vote. Robert Falk, in a letter to me about Meir, recalled how Meir learned of the outcome.

On Thursday evening, March 3, 1960, although there was a blizzard, the synagogue was packed. My wife, Esther, called the rabbi after the meeting to express her sorrow. She did not know she would be the first person to call and break the news.

After Rabbi Kahane left, the synagogue fell apart. Those who voted for him quit. Those who voted against him quit. It was not until 1965 that the synagogue was rejuvenated.[25]

Meir believed his efforts had not been in vain:

Of course it is a tragic tale. It points up the illusion and shallowness of the vaunted return to religion among modern Jews.... [But] much good came from it. It enabled non-observant Jews to see that an Orthodox rabbi can be idealistic and a man of principle. It taught many people that Orthodoxy can be a living, vibrant belief.... Many homes will never be the same again, having brought kosher foods and Sabbath candles into their lives for the first time. Many children will ever look back to Orthodoxy as something wonderful and beautiful, unlike their parents, who as children came to hate it. Several children themselves have become observant and some attend yeshivas; from them will come observant adults who in turn will raise families, pious and G-d-fearing.[26]

When students and teachers at the Mirrer Yeshiva heard of Meir's dismissal from the HBJC because of his devotion to Orthodoxy, they were full of admiration. Rabbi Moshe (Marcel) Blitz wrote:

> ... Rabbi Abraham Kalmanowitz had a great love for Meir. I was told that when Meir gave up his rabbinical position in Howard Beach because the congregants found him "too religious" and Meir refused to compromise his Orthodoxy, Rabbi Kalmanowitz said to him: "Because you sanctified G-d's name in your refusal to modify Jewish law, your name and fame shall spread far and wide." His blessing was literally fulfilled beyond Rabbi Kalmanowitz's wildest imagination.[27]

A Wider Audience: The Jewish Press

Meir's HBJC experience inspired "End of the Miracle of Howard Beach," which he submitted to the *Jewish Press*. Although it was printed without his byline, this was his first article in the *Press*. He continued to write for the paper for 30 years, until his murder in 1990. In addition to a weekly column, he wrote feature articles and often news reports as well.

Meir's need for employment came at a fortuitous time. In February 1960, only one month before he submitted "End of the Miracle of Howard Beach," the *Jewish Press* had expanded from eight pages to twenty-four and needed more staff. Publisher Rabbi Shalom Klass, who knew Meir as the talented, reliable head of his daughter Naomi's Bnei Akiva *ken*, immediately hired Meir to be the associate editor.[28]

Meir sought another rabbinical position, not only to supplement his modest *Jewish Press* salary, but because as a congregational rabbi he could continue bringing people closer to Judaism. In June he was invited to deliver a trial sermon at Congregation Etz Chaim – South Shore Jewish Center in Woodmere, New York. Meir was not hired, but his host that Shabbat, Rabbi Binyomin Kamenetsky, remembered his sermon almost forty years later. He spoke of the spies sent by Moses to scout out the Land of Israel who failed in their mission because they focused on trivial matters. Meir made the telling point, said Rabbi Kamenetsky, that they should have concentrated on what was really important.[29]

Meir knew what was really important – studying Torah. When he learned about newspaper delivery franchises from Arnold Fine, editor of the *Jewish Press*, it seemed the ideal solution.[30] The work was concentrated into a few hours in the early morning, leaving the rest of the day free for study.

A Newspaper Route

The daily newspapers had a system of neighborhood franchises. Each franchisee paid the dailies a few cents per paper, then collected the regular price from subscribers in his area. Members of my family lent us $2,000 (which Meir repaid within a year) to buy the franchise in Laurelton, a twenty-minute drive from Howard Beach.

Meir would get up at about four in the morning, while it was still dark, drive to the distribution point near the Long Island Railroad station in Laurelton, and load his bundle of newspapers into his car. The number of newspapers he received depended on the subscriptions. One customer might subscribe to the *Daily News*, another to the *New York Times*, and yet another to the *Daily Mirror*. Some subscribed to more than one.

Sitting in the back seat of the car, Meir would fold the papers in half, roll them up, and fasten each with a rubber band, to give them shape for throwing. He worked with a list, tossing the papers onto customers' doorsteps or front porches. His ball-playing prowess came in handy, although sometimes a paper landed on a roof or a neighbor's lawn. Initially, he would open the car door, lean out and throw with his right hand, but eventually he became adept at using his left hand. If the subscriber's house was on the right side of the road, he lobbed the paper over the car roof.

Naomi Brody related: "One night I couldn't sleep and happened to look outside in the early hours of the morning. I saw Meir's car pull up, a left hand emerge from the driver's seat, and the newspaper thrown to the front door with an athletic throw."[31] Finished by 7:00 A.M., he was free to go to the yeshiva. His customers had their newspapers by breakfast and so did I – Meir always brought home several different papers.

Sometimes a customer did not find his newspaper on his doorstep. I often answered the phone only to hear, "Where's my newspaper today?" Bookkeeping was my job. At the end of every month, I billed each customer. In a ledger in which I kept track of subscribers, I also entered credits for vacation notices or non-deliveries. My aunt Louise Fruchtman did all the bookkeeping for her husband's lamp business, and my father was an accountant, so it was natural for me to handle the bookkeeping.

Meir's cousin Shaul Kahan bought a similar franchise to support his young family while attending law school. As observant Jews, neither one worked on the Sabbath, but newspapers had to be delivered seven days a week, including

Saturdays. In such cases, Jewish law permits employing non-Jews to work on Shabbat, with stringent halakhic stipulations.[32]

We were still living in Howard Beach, with Meir commuting to his newspaper route in Laurelton, when our daughter Tzippy was born. Meir had been in the hospital waiting room for hours. At four in the morning, I still had not delivered, and he had his own "deliveries" to make. My mother relieved him at the hospital, while my father stayed at home with Tova and Baruch. My brother Phil, then twenty, accompanied Meir to help him finish the route more quickly. When Meir returned to the hospital at 7 A.M. on that snowy day in February 1961, my mother greeted him with the news that he had a ten-pound baby girl. He went to see her in the "big children's" nursery and fell in love at first sight.

Two months later, in April 1961, we moved to Laurelton. Not only was Laurelton more convenient for Meir's work, it had a Young Israel synagogue and a vibrant Orthodox Jewish community.

Chapter 8

Newspapers (1961-1963)

Moving to Laurelton

WE HAD VERY little equity in the house we sold in Howard Beach, but our new home in Laurelton cost only $16,335, a bargain even then. At 3% of the sale price – thanks to another Federal Housing Administration mortgage – the down payment was only $490.[1] The house was sided with imitation-brick asbestos and had two stories. Downstairs were the kitchen, dining room, living room and a closed-in front porch, which was Meir's study. On the second floor were two bedrooms and a bathroom. The house was small, but the lot was large, with plenty of room for the children to play in the backyard. We had swings, a slide, and monkey bars, and the boys and girls on our block came to play in our yard. Our street had no other Jewish families, so our children played with our next-door neighbors' little boy Carlo and the children of an Irish Catholic family that lived across the street. The oldest daughter of this large family often baby-sat when we went out at night.

When the first Puerto Ricans moved in, our children were the only ones allowed to play with them, because the Italians and the Irish looked down on them. It was the same story with the first black family on our street, whose children were Baruch's and Tzippy's ages. Tzippy recalled some interesting conversations with her new playmate. Tzippy knew that Jews went to synagogue on Saturday and Christians went to church on Sunday. One Sunday, 6-year-old Michelle showed her some stickers she had received in church earlier that day. Knowing we weren't allowed to carry on Shabbat, Tzippy asked her friend in amazement, "How did you dare to carry on Sunday?" When Binyamin was born, it was little Michelle's turn to be amazed. "Is he Jewish too?" she wanted to know. And when some Irish children nabbed Baruch's yarmulke (skullcap), Michelle's father retrieved it for him.

One year, Meir took the children to the annual "Salute to Israel" parade in Manhattan. The kids came home waving small Israeli flags Meir had bought them.

The next morning, our light blue car had the word JEW painted on it in large black letters. After hours of scrubbing, I finally managed to remove all the black paint. I never felt the same about my neighbors again.[2]

Since he had to drive through Flatbush for his editorial job at the *Jewish Press*, the location of the Mirrer Yeshiva was now more convenient than that of the Chaim Berlin Yeshiva. Every morning after his newspaper deliveries, Meir went to study at the Mirrer Yeshiva. One of the facets of Jewish law that he was studying evolved into an article for *Hama'or*, an important rabbinic journal.[3] Rabbi Chaim Plato wrote: "I recall vividly Meir's dedication and punctuality when he had his paper route. I sat right near him in the Mirrer Yeshiva, and day in, day out, he would keep to his rigorous schedule."[4]

Meir drove a manual-shift Austin, which was handy for stop-and-go newspaper delivery, and I had a secondhand light blue Rambler for shopping and car pools. We lived modestly but comfortably on the income from Meir's newspaper route, occasional private Hebrew lessons, and the *Jewish Press*.

A Jewish Press Column

Meir's earliest writing in the *Jewish Press* reflected his preoccupation with Torah study. His first weekly column was *The Shiur* [Lesson] *of the Week*. Topics included the permissibility of delivering clothes to a laundry that would wash them on Shabbat, the lighting of Shabbat candles, and the blowing of the *shofar* on the High Holidays.[5] He wrote *The Shiur of the Week* under the pen name Hamaor Hakatan (the small light), a play on the name Meir, which means giving light.

He began to write another column, *A Small Voice*, under his own name at about the same time. The first few columns had the title *A Still, Small Voice*, a phrase from *I Kings* 19, in which the prophet Elijah hears the word of G-d: "... but the L-rd was not in the earthquake. And after the earthquake a fire; but the L-rd was not in the fire; and after the fire, a still small voice." From 1960 to 1962, *A Small Voice* dealt with topics such as South African Jewry, religious laws in Israel, the Eichmann trial, the *Bnei Israel* Indian Jews, Christian missionary activity among poverty-stricken Israelis, and freedom of speech for Nazis in the U.S.[6]

In *A Small Voice* of June 10, 1960, Meir attacked critics of David Ben-Gurion.

> No one can deny the tragedy inherent in the picture of a Jewish prime minister publicly contradicting the Bible... [But] among the voices of criticism raised were clearly heard those of the Scandal Mongers. They are the voice of those that are always ready to criticize the government of Israel.... Every sin and

every transgression is shouted forth, while the good is always interred in silence....

Meir then gave details of recent Israeli legislation that promoted adherence to Jewish law. For example, "The husband who defies the rabbinical court and refuses to grant a divorce to his wife will be jailed for contempt of court until he complies." This legislation freed many women from being *agunot*, chained to their husbands, a situation all too common among Jews in the United States. "Certainly there is much that is wrong with Israel today.... But there is much that is right with Ben-Gurion and with Israel also, and I would be more impressed with the tears of the Scandal Mongers if they acknowledged this.... "[7]

In a December 1960 column, Meir praised Rabbi Menachem Perr of South Ozone Park, Queens, for banning Saturday bar mitzvahs in his synagogue because so many Jews were desecrating Shabbat to attend them. "My world is divided into two classes – the talkers and the doers," Meir wrote. "... I have a weakness for the doers. I realize full well the importance of the critic, the role of the muckraker.... The doer, however, is not content with the discovery of wrong. He is bothered by it, he broods over it... His is the greater soul." Since the Torah is read not only on Saturday, but also on Mondays and Thursdays, Rabbi Perr ended desecration of Shabbat by having his congregation hold bar mitzvahs on civil holidays occurring on Mondays and Thursdays.[8]

In 1960 Jews in Rockland County, New York, fearful of "standing-out," tried to have the local zoning board refuse the application of chasidic Jews to build a community there. Of those who opposed the chasidic town of New Square, Meir wrote:

> It is the condition of man to be beset by fears and insecurities.... The frail thing that we call man shivers and shakes before every threatening wind that rocks his peaceful equilibrium, yearns for that peaceful and soothing calm.
>
> It is this yearning that is the father of submissive conformity, this need that gives birth to oppressive uniformity. He who clothes himself in the garb of the community ... he who mouths the words of village opinion – is assured that he is an accepted son in the World of Now.
>
> To be faceless is to be safe; to conform is to be acceptable.... One does not have to be a chasid or believe in chasidism or agree with its essentials to recognize that here is a spark of courage in a world devoid of such things. One does not even have to be courageous himself to perceive the act of bravery in this community of little men and women who want to live their lives as they see fit....[9]

Meir took an equally firm stand concerning women's apparel. On July 14, 1961, he wrote, "Increasingly, a small group of Beit Yaakov and chasidic women stands alone in the observance of the concept of *tznius* (modesty). They refuse to wear shorts or short-sleeved blouses ... [and] they increasingly earn the mockery and anger not alone of the irreligious – but of the nominally Orthodox woman, too. The minority is right! Let the women of Israel listen and take pride in this sublime challenge that is theirs alone to fulfill."[10]

Thanks to the *Jewish Press*'s growing circulation, Meir was reaching a large readership, and his decisive stance earned him many admirers. Not yet 30, he did not hesitate to address weighty questions of morality and communal responsibility. Upon meeting him, people often said, "I thought you were much older!"

A major issue of the day was government aid to parochial schools. Like many other Orthodox Jews, Meir felt the government should support all schools, not only public schools. However, the powerful American Jewish Congress and other Jewish Establishment groups considered the separation of church and state vital to safeguarding Jewish civil liberties, and ignored the financial difficulties of parents seeking to educate their children in Jewish day schools. In his articles in the *Jewish Press*, Meir was an outspoken proponent of federal aid to Jewish schools. On May 15, 1961, he was invited to debate the subject at the prestigious West Side Institutional Synagogue in Manhattan with another *Jewish Press* columnist, Dr. Jacob B. Glenn. The debate was moderated by the synagogue's rabbi, Rabbi O. Asher Reichel.[11] Shortly after the debate, Meir wrote to Rabbi Reichel:

> I have been informed by Rabbi Pinchas Stolper that you are looking for a youth leader for your congregation. I am at present devoting full time to learning, but rather than be supported by the public funds of a Kollel, I have bought a morning paper route. I find, however, that I must supplement this income. I have a great deal of experience with youth groups of all types and would bring this experience to bear in this position."[12]

Rabbi Reichel, favorably impressed, hired him to teach the synagogue's teenagers on Sunday mornings. The synagogue bulletin of October 1961 attests to Meir's success with the teenagers. "Don't miss our High School class which meets this Sunday at 10 A.M. with Rabbi Meir Kahane," it says. "Those who have been attending regularly sing its praises."[13]

At about the same time Meir started this teaching job, his name was removed from the *Jewish Press* masthead. Rabbi Klass wrote an editorial explaining that although Meir would no longer be the associate editor, he would continue his column:

> Rabbi Meir Kahane has decided to devote his entire day to studying in the yeshiva.... We take pride in the fact that a young rabbi, at a great personal sacrifice, has decided to devote his life to learning. Let us hope that others follow his example and make greater efforts to devote more of their time to the study of Torah.... We look forward to his growing into a scholar and leader of Israel.[14]

In November, Meir addressed the young adults of the West Side Institutional Synagogue's Sinai League on "Is Modern Orthodoxy Really Orthodox?"[15] This theme recurred in his writings and lectures. For him there could be no compromises in Judaism, be they Reform, Conservative, or "modern Orthodox." A Jew must observe ALL the laws of the Torah. Seeking to reach "the American Jew who has strayed from the fold," Meir wrote:

> In our struggle to preserve him for Torah and mitzvahs, we must understand what and who [the American Jew] is.... What motivates him in his religious feelings...? The image, the image of the American Jew, this is what we must define.... [But] as important as it is for us to understand the American Jew, it is of equal importance to comprehend exactly what HIS image is of us. What does he think when he hears the term Orthodoxy?

Orthodoxy was mistakenly associated with outdated rituals, he said, but it can be presented in a positive way.

> Distorted, we lament: wrong, misunderstood, the product of ignorance, but there it stands; our image in their eyes. Is all lost then? Most emphatically not.... Firstly, young [people] are idealistic. They search for idealism in a society that turns them into craven materialists. They hunger for truth and sacrifice.... We are the ones that can offer it....
>
> What is necessary is to establish a specially trained group of young Orthodox men and women with the proper traditional background, with a strong secular academic knowledge, and with ... rapport with the typical young American Jew. People with ... a deep knowledge of Torah. People who can at the same time discuss Plato and Keynes and Faraday and Marx as well. People who can prove themselves adept at the laws of Shabbos and dialectical materialism and the standings of the American League. People who can win the respect and admiration of the American Jew, who can force him to say, "It IS possible to be an Orthodox Jew in 1962!"[16]

Meir was, unwittingly, describing himself. He indeed brought many Jews back to Judaism. In a similar vein, "To Our Non-Orthodox Readers" proclaimed:

> The non-observant Jew knows. Deep in his heart he knows. He knows that the path [he treads] is a false one, that the Judaism he professes is a mockery.... His moment of truth lies within him. His is the power to call it into being. Let him but dig deeply into his Jewish resources and draw from them the traditional Jewish qualities of courage, determination and sacrifice. Let him seek out the traditional rabbi who will hold the lamp as he wends his way home....[17]

A 1962 *Small Voice* column had high praise for the National Conference of Synagogue Youth (NCSY), which was devoted to "gathering in the spiritual exiles among our people, [who] give their hands to the irreligious Jewish youngster and say, 'Come, my son, taste and see how good is the L-rd' (*Psalms* 34:9)." He wrote: "Last year I was asked to participate as an advisor to the annual convention of the NCSY.... Words are too poor to describe the scene as children from irreligious homes gathered in a synagogue ... joined in *Kabbalas Shabbos* (Friday night prayers) ... at first awkwardly, and later with sureness and confidence. The Sabbath Queen herself tapped her toes in happy rhythm."[18]

In contrast, Meir mocked the Conservative and Reform movements in his December 1962 satire "*Mai* Chanuka?" ("What Is Chanuka?")

> If I were a Reform or Conservative leader, I would do my utmost to abolish all traces of Chanuka.
>
> ... It is the irony of Chanuka that is most striking. Picture the community gathered for the Chanuka pageant. The spiritual leader of the Temple rises and speaks of the great events in those days at this time. How a small band of noble Jews arose and fought for their beliefs, fought to preserve the Judaism that was theirs.
>
> The congregation thrills to the tale of men who gave their lives rather than sacrifice the laws of G-d....What bravery, what courage – what foolishness!
>
> Yes, yes, what foolishness! What should a man who loves his bacon and eggs think of the man who died rather than let the flesh of the swine cross his lips? What else should the one who desecrates the Sabbath willingly think of the fool who died so that he might never violate even one of its laws? What should the spiritual leader who looks upon the Torah as a mixture of pagan myth and rabbinical fraud REALLY think of those men who died thinking that this was really the word of G-d?
>
> Chanuka is NOT a holiday of national liberation. It is NOT a day commemorating political events. For many years the Jews accepted political subjugation at the hands of the Greeks without a murmur. It was only when their religious beliefs were trampled that they rose up.
>
> ... It appears now that these simple, naive, misguided people died needlessly.... CHANUKA BECOMES ONE GREAT MISTAKE.
>
> And so, if I were a Reform or Conservative leader I would try to bury this ghost. I would try to flee from the tormenting questions that are implicit in this festival. The question: How do Jews who reject the laws that the Maccabees died for, celebrate their martyrdom? ... The question: To the non-Orthodox Jew, what in the world is this Chanuka?[19]

Martin Keene: Sportswriter

Meir's early morning routine of delivering newspapers came to an end on December 8, 1962, when newspaper workers declared a strike, shutting down nine New York City dailies for almost four months.[20] At first we thought the strike would be brief and would not affect the newspaper delivery service. As the weeks passed, we realized we were in for a long, difficult period. Yet this apparent setback gave Meir an opportunity to write for a larger audience than that of the *Jewish Press*.

The *Jewish Press* had begun as a by-product of the *New York and Brooklyn Daily*, published by Rabbi Shalom Klass and his father-in-law, Raphael Schreiber, at their printing press in the Coney Island section of Brooklyn. The mainstay of the *Daily* was legal notices (such as stockholders' meetings), which were required by law to be announced in a newspaper. The *Daily*, with its small circulation, attracted such ads because of its low rates. As the strike continued, Klass realized people were starved for newspapers. If he filled the *Daily* with interesting articles, he could expand its print run. Thus, Meir began writing for the paper on a variety of subjects, using the pen name Martin Keene.

Always a sports fan, Meir contributed many excellent sports stories. His style and delivery were lively, but most telling was his philosophical undertone. Consider these excerpts:

EDDIE DONOVAN: ONCE A WINNER

When you're a winner, it's good to be alive; the loser can take it or leave it. The winner notices the bright sun of the day, the loser turns up his coat against the wind. The winner finds it easy to laugh; the loser's dressing room is a place of silent men who dress hurriedly as if eager to escape from the scene of their crime.

The Knicks* have been losers for so long they have almost come to expect defeat. Tradition, either of success or [of] failure, is an intangible thing, not to be lightly discounted. Some teams go out knowing they'll take it; others walk out dragging an invisible ball [and] chain behind them. Winning can become a habit; losing a form of addiction. The Knicks have been hooked for a long time now....

[Eddie] Donovan is a fine coach, a man who knows basketball.... In a sense Donovan is a misfit on the Knicks; he has the habit of winning. Earlier this season he sat in shocked disbelief as the Knicks went through the motions in a 40-point loss. It was too much; he left the bench and walked the streets of Detroit for hours....[21]

THE YANKEES: CAN THEY WIN IT AGAIN?

Great buildings go up knowing that they will someday be razed, and even Orphan Annie's sun must set someday.... They don't play punch ball anymore, and whatever happened to the Packard?**

They had to stop DiMaggio's streak someday, and Andy Bathgate couldn't

---

* Knicks, short for Knickerbockers, a New York basketball team.
** The Packard automobile was manufactured from 1899 to 1949.

tip them in every game. The best of them have to slip from the top someday and this could be the beginning of the slide for the Yankees.

Somewhere along the line a lot of New Yorkers began to see something wrong with the Yankees' winning all the time. Perhaps it has to do with our economic tendencies toward distribution of the wealth; perhaps with our penchant for democratizing everything, including talent....[22]

YOU'RE HARRY GALLATIN

You're Harry Gallatin, coach of the St. Louis Hawks, and your team is in Madison Square Garden playing the Knicks. There are eight seconds to go in the game and you're down, 102-101. Their center Gene Conley has just missed a foul shot, and with silent prayer you're on your feet shouting for time.

Now your players are around you, sweaty, breathing heavily, the weariness and strain showing on their faces. You know you have eight seconds, enough for one play. What are you going to call for?

You're Harry Gallatin, who played ten seasons in the NBA, nine of them for the very team you're trying to beat tonight. You were never a great scorer, but in the clutch they never made them better....[23]

In "Still Dreaming: Mets Squeeze Yanks 1-0," Meir begins: "Don't wake me yet, Mother, the dream is too beautiful. Yesterday at St. Petersburg, the New York Mets continued to look like the New York Yankees, as they won still another one...."[24]

One of Meir's sports articles even merited a nomination for the Grantland Rice Memorial Award for outstanding sportswriting, "Jack Molinas – A Story of Man's Self-Destruction."

The man who loses his life at the hands of others is not as shocking a figure as the one who ends it himself. The individual who was born with two strikes against him is not as tragic a soul as the one who had all the gifts and squandered them....

Jack Molinas could have become a good basketball player; he chose to become a criminal. He could have been an attorney; he chose to become a salesman of corruption. He might have treasured honesty and decency; instead his greed for money and the things it could buy perverted his sense of values and caused him to sell his soul.

I come neither to pity Molinas, nor to kick him while he is down. He deserves neither.

It would be wrong to leap on his fallen body because – as with most that slipped – it is not a bad man with whom we deal, but a weak one.

Molinas is an all too vivid product of a society that even in sports has elevated money, materialism, and kicks to the throne of glory. We pay lip service to Boy Scouts and give the scholarships to the hotshots....

Cheating has become a thing condoned, and among too many the only thing that matters is that you got what you were after.

It is not Molinas the individual that we hit, but Molinas the symbol of the easy buck; Molinas who represents the cynical corruption of youth; Molinas who cheapens the sport that gave him all; Molinas who took youngsters and destroyed their characters.

Molinas was convicted on clear-cut evidence of bribing college youngsters. He was a willing agent of a machine which fixed games in 22 states....

Every Molinas is a threat to us as decent and upright men.... Every Molinas causes us to become suspicious of a missed basket, a traveling violation, a wild pass.... He, and we too, had better do some deep soul-searching.[25]

Crime in New York City

Meir's sense of social justice and his concern about his changing hometown led to a series of articles in the *Daily* about teenage gangs, whose victims were often elderly Jews in New York City's poorer neighborhoods. In "The Teenage Gangs Must Be Wiped Out," the first in the series, Meir declares:

The editors and reporters of this paper are not fuzzy-cheeked innocents who are jolted by every act of violence that occurs in our city. This latest incident, however, is not an isolated thing. It is part of a growing – and alarming – pattern of youth crimes, which increases yearly in brutality as well as in numbers.

We are not prepared to nod philosophically and say that youth problems have always existed. We cannot concur with those who quote voices of the past lamenting the morals of THEIR youth as proof that nothing has changed.

For something has changed. Certainly, youth has troubled civilized nations from time immemorial. However, we flatly declare – and know that our readers will agree – that the amount of youth crimes and anti-social acts has achieved proportions unheard of in the past, and that furthermore the SERIOUSNESS of these crimes is something that civilized nations have never seen before.

In speaking to many people, we are struck over and over again by one comment: "It used to be that kids would fight or steal and that would be it. Today, though, there are youngsters who think nothing of stomping on a victim, burning him, killing him."

Quantitatively and qualitatively then, the incidence of youth crime has grown, and the mayor and all citizens are shocked.... We are worried because our youth [are] our future, and the way that they think and act and are shaped will indicate the way that the voters of this nation will tomorrow decide to steer the ship of state....

In New York City we have gangs. What is a New York gang? Not just a group of kids that hang around a candy store; our gangs mean a lot more than that. A gang here is a formalized thing. It has a leader, it has a cabinet, it has a foreign minister. Most important, it has a territory – a part of a neighborhood, perhaps your very own – which is its own. It runs it; it dominates it; it keeps out "undesirables."

And so, knowing all this and being worried and afraid, and knowing that millions of other New Yorkers are frightened and confused, we at the *Brooklyn Daily* are ready to do something. Beginning tomorrow, this paper will begin a comprehensive series on general youth crime in New York and on the gangs in particular. Our purpose is not to sensationalize. It is to give you a complete survey of the problem of youth crime; the number of crimes committed; how the gangs work; which city agencies are dealing with the problem in what way.

SWAMP US WITH MAIL! Tell us of incidents; complain, threaten, suggest. But above all – don't just sit there. Let us move in on this problem – now![26]

In "The Street Gang and the Police Department," Meir follows a patrol car, then talks with the gang members police apprehended. "The Teenage Gang and the Youth Board" deals with the city's efforts to funnel teenagers into non-violent, non-criminal activities. And the institutions designed to house young arrestees are the subject of Meir's tenth article in this series: "A Teenage Gang – An Arrest Is Made."[27]

Not all of Meir's assignments were so serious. When Cassius Clay,* the boxer with a talent for self-promotion, was to be introduced to the New York press by way of a poetry-reading contest, Meir covered it:

Cassius Clay came to town yesterday in preparation for his fight next week with Davy Jones, and if he is nothing but a great wind, let us remember that winds also make headlines when they are big enough.... He proceeded formally to introduce himself:

"I'm Cassius Marcellus Clay. I am the world's most outspoken fighter as well as the boldest, the fastest and the prettiest."

... Obviously a gentle man, the self-effacing one was provoked to justifiable anger only once, when asked by a boorish reporter:

"If you beat Jones...."

His mother's pride stared coldly at the oaf and verbally thrashing him, thundered:

"If I beat Jones? Mister, you are talking to Cassius Clay, the greatest fighter in the world! I do not know what the word 'if' means. He MUST fall – and in six."

Meir described the Greenwich Village coffeehouse where the press conference was held:

The Bitter End is a Village attraction euphemistically called by its proprietors a coffeehouse-nightclub.... It is a walk-in whose walls exhibit odd lithographs and whose floor is dotted with coffee tables. A small 8 x 12 [foot] stage stands

---

* Clay changed his name to Muhammad Ali in 1964, when he joined the Nation of Islam.

before a red brick wall, flanked by a mournful piano whose musical efficacy stands in *prima facie* doubt.

On its east wall are etched sentences prefaced by the introduction "Proverbs." They reflect the general atmosphere of the place, calling out such wisdom as "He who bestirs himself is lost," "Cold meat lights no fire," and "Elephants are contagious."[28]

At the Bitter End, Meir saw posters about comedian Woody Allen, and he was curious, so we went to see Allen perform that Saturday night. Meir appreciated Allen's humor, as well as Allen's novel approach to his Jewishness. As Gerald Mast put it: "It isn't simply that Allen looks odd or funny in comparison to everyone else.... Allen's clownship is more dependent on what he is rather than how he looks, how he thinks rather than how he appears. And what Allen is, is Jewish. Woody Allen is the first great American clown for whom being Jewish was not simply a hereditary accident but a way of life...."[29]

Allen's humor uncannily expressed the American Jewish condition. Allen personified the paradox of the Diaspora Jew, who is part of the surrounding culture yet always different, and therefore fearful and ingratiating. Allen's novel presentation of this paradox enhanced Meir's growing awareness that the status of the American Jew warranted further study.

On April 1, 1963, after almost four months of intensive negotiations, the newspaper strike finally ended.[30] Without its captive audience, the circulation of the *Daily* dropped back to what it had been, and Meir resumed writing for the *Jewish Press* only. His writing for the *Daily* had opened up new vistas, but he was not interested in journalism *per se* as a career, nor did he go back to delivering newspapers. Instead, he turned to political research.* However, the insights he gained during this period, especially on the increasing crime and violence in New York City, were to influence the direction he took in the future.

Orthodox Jews in Israel

Meir's *Jewish Press* columns during the second half of 1963 shed light on contemporary events. As always, he did not hesitate to chastise his fellow Jews, even the Orthodox:

> *Chametz*, leaven, is not a thing relegated to food alone. It is to be found conspicuously in the soul of man. For as leaven in food ... causes it to swell and ferment, the *chametz* that is found in each man [causes him] to ... become swelled and fermented by forces of pollution. Last week, a group calling itself the United Rabbinical Supervisors of America [was] found guilty in Queens Criminal Court of laxity in kashrus supervision.... Any attempt to bury this

---

* See chapter 10.

story will only implicate Orthodoxy as accessories to the crime.... We deal here with a serious case of communal *chametz*. It must be diligently searched out; it must be nullified ... driven from our house and possession.... The house of Orthodoxy must forever be pure....[31]

Meir supported the zealots in Israel who acted to save Jews from conversion to Christianity:

It is easy to condemn the "zealots" who attacked the Christian missions in Israel last week. It is certainly much easier than to condemn ourselves for turning from our minds the thousands of Jewish children that the "zealots" seek to save from the shadow of the cross.... The law [halakha] is clear. In order to rescue a Jew from forced conversion one may – indeed he is ordered to – violate the Sabbath.[32]

However, he decried zealots who threw stones on the Sabbath.

Several buses came into Jerusalem last Sabbath, buses bearing Christian pilgrims who had come to see their holy places. The carrier was owned by a Jewish company, Hamekasher, and because of this, Orthodox Jews ... rioted and stoned the buses, causing substantial damage.

I put it to you that the sanctity of the Sabbath was not lifted one whit by this action. I submit that there was little rejoicing before the throne of the Almighty as the stones smashed windows. I know that because of this sad event the gulf between the religious and irreligious in Eretz Israel widened and the poison that has seeped into their relationship spread.

There are numerous things about the Eretz Israel of our day that pain the heart and outrage the soul of the religious Jew.... Its Sabbath is not the Sabbath of Torah; its kashrus is not the kashrus of our rabbis; its youth is not the youth that Judaism desires. There are things that Eretz Israel possesses that are not pleasant to us, and I fear that in the future there will be worse things. I fear that Reform and Conservatism will invade the Holy Land and deform it, and already their temples are beginning to grow. I fear that the marriage and divorce laws will become a burden to many and they will demand and institute civil marriage....

Meir foresaw a collapse of the religious status quo, and suggested a way to deal with it.

But the steps of stones are not the proper steps, nor is the path of insult and rioting and hatred the proper path. Whoever thinks that these will persuade Israelis to return to G-d is incapable of understanding human beings.... That can be done only through the building of schools and yeshivas to capture the souls of the youth. That can be done only by the formation of religious groups that will participate in sympathetic dialogue with the irreligious.... By explaining what Torah really is; by answering misconceptions and confused images of religion.[33]

Chapter 9

The Young Israel of Laurelton
(1961-1967)

WHEN WE MOVED from Howard Beach to Laurelton in 1961, we joined its only Orthodox synagogue, the Young Israel, led by Rabbi Eliahu P. Rominek. We were part of that warm Jewish community for eight years, and we made lasting friendships.

Teaching the Youth

On Shabbat afternoons, encouraged by Rabbi Rominek, Meir taught teenagers and young adults a class on the laws of Shabbat, and he even found time to teach the younger children. Binyamin Dolinsky, our son Baruch's friend, remembered Meir studying with the two of them between afternoon and evening services when they were both about eight.[1]

The boys' day school, the Yeshiva of South Shore, held classes on Sunday mornings, but the girls' schools did not, so Meir taught the girls the Shabbat laws on Sundays at the Young Israel. Some girls kept their coats on during the class because they knew he disapproved of their miniskirts. Malka Parnes marveled at Meir's dedication: "One Sunday there was a terrible downpour. Jack [her husband] thought it was important for Mindy to attend classes, so he drove her to the Young Israel. It turned out that she was the only girl who showed up for classes that day. Even though she was the only student, Meir gave the lesson. If she could make the effort to come, he could make the effort to teach her."[2]

One girl in the community, Helen Gluckman, was born with cerebral palsy. Her parents sent her to a non-Jewish special needs school but wanted her to have a good Jewish education as well. When she was ten years old, they hired Meir to give her lessons. He taught her to read Hebrew, pray, and understand the prayers. He told her about famous rabbis' self-sacrifice for their ideals and instilled in her a love for Torah and Eretz Yisrael. "At the beginning I cried because I did not know Hebrew and wanted to talk with G-d," Helen reminisced. "Rabbi Kahane told me G-d understands all languages. He worked with me for hours and hours until I was able to pronounce words. And always with patience and kindness in his eyes, especially his eyes. He saw my potential. He said I would be very religious one day." Helen graduated from high school with honors, then studied in Israel, first at Bar Ilan University and then at the Neve Yerushalayim seminary. She married and had five children; all of them are Orthodox.[3]

Many boys who attended Meir's Shabbat classes moved to Israel. Avraham Ben Yochanan of Alon Shvut, a settlement south of Jerusalem, recalled: "I and my best friend, Lee Weinblatt, were sixteen years old when you came to Laurelton. We sat on the same bench as Meir in shul [synagogue], right next to him. I prayed from the same kind of siddur [prayer book] as Meir – the *Tikkun Meir*. We went to the class that Meir gave in shul on Shabbat afternoon for high school and college-age boys on laws of the Shabbat. Meir also studied Gemara [Talmud] with me and Lee in shul during *seuda shlishit* [the third Shabbat meal]. This went on even while I was in graduate school."[4]

Elliott Horowitz of Jerusalem recalled: "Meir gave a *shiur* [class] to teenagers before the afternoon service on Shabbat. He lectured on a variety of subjects, among them *Pirkei Avot* (*Ethics of the Fathers*). Most of the *shiurim* turned into group discussions of the problems bothering the youth.... Meir understood that the young people of our synagogue could go either way, but if they had a strong enough Jewish education, they would remain religious."[5]

Meir felt obligated to draw these kids closer to Judaism, keep them observant, and deepen their understanding of Jewish law. To keep them from secular revelry, he even held late-night classes on Christmas and New Year's Eve, which almost all the Young Israel's teens attended.[6] Meir always urged both the youngsters and their parents to live a full Jewish life in Israel. Thirteen Laurelton families, an impressive number, moved to Israel in the early 1970s when we did.[7]

"Meir was not a racist," insisted Horowitz, noting that several times Meir brought a black man to synagogue.[8] This man was Chakwal M. Cragg, editor and publisher of the *African Israelite* and head of the Union of Ethiopian Hebrew Congregations, who had contacted Meir at the *Jewish Press* regarding the Ethiopian Jews in New York City.[9] Whenever Cragg was our Shabbat guest, Meir made every effort to put him at ease. Once, I served watermelon for dessert. Because of the stereotype that blacks are especially fond of watermelon, Meir was sensitive to the possibility that Cragg might be insulted that I'd chosen that dessert. So he made a point of thanking me profusely for serving his favorite dessert.

Horowitz recalled Meir's ability to relate to others: "One Sunday morning, one of the Young Israel's neighbors was complaining loudly about the synagogue's noisy Little League baseball team. Exercising quiet diplomacy, Meir apologized and calmed him down."[10] Ben Yochanan recalled how Meir taught them to be sensitive to the needs and feelings of others:

> Meir taught us *ahavat Yisrael* and *ahavat habriyot*, love of fellow Jews and love of fellow human beings. One day he challenged us – asking what we are doing to justify our existence. I was sort of shocked and I said, "I give some charity, I don't bother anyone, I pray every day." Meir rejected this and demanded that we actually do something.... As a result of Meir's *shiur*, Lee [Weinblatt] became a volunteer at a local hospital. I went every Wednesday for an entire semester to Metropolitan Hospital, working alternately in the children's ward and the psychiatric ward.[11]

"When Renah and I decided to become engaged," wrote Ben Yochanan, "first we went to tell our parents, and right after that we came to your house to tell Rabbi Kahane." Renah recalled, "Meir danced like crazy at our wedding."[12]

Meir's rapport with youth was partly due to his natural charisma, but he also worked hard at it. Elliott Horowitz remembered that whenever Meir drove by and saw any Young Israel boys playing football, he stopped and joined them.[13] Recognizing this chemistry, Fred Horowitz and other parents encouraged their children to attend Meir's classes.

Fred Horowitz even hired Meir to tutor his son Elliott, ten and a half, in Talmud, beginning in the fall of 1963. At the Yeshiva of South Shore, Talmud was taught in the early grades, but Elliott went to the Yeshiva of Central Queens, where they started Talmud only in the sixth grade. Sunday mornings Meir and Elliott came back from synagogue together and, after a breakfast of scrambled eggs, they studied at our dining room table. Fred Horowitz recalled, "Elliott would rather study with Meir on Sunday mornings than go to Boy Scouts."[14]

Elliott still has the Aramaic dictionary Meir had him compile during their two years of study. Many years later, when studying Talmud with his own son, Elliott remembered Meir's body language while teaching: he walked to and fro, punching his right fist into his left palm for emphasis or tossing a ball. Most important, he made sure Elliott understood every single word of the text.

When Elliott was twelve, and again when he was thirteen, he came with us to Brooklyn for Yom Kippur services at the Mirrer Yeshiva. Meir always preferred to pray there on the High Holidays, because the services were especially meaningful and inspiring. It was also an opportunity to spend the holidays with our families, since both lived near the yeshiva. It was Elliott's first experience in a *yeshiva gedola*, a post-high school yeshiva. Elliott recalled that Meir brought his own *shtender*, a floor stand on which to lean and rest his prayer book. Elliott later acquired his own *shtender*, which he keeps at his seat in the synagogue to this day. He recalled that although Meir was not yet a public figure, the students at the Mirrer Yeshiva admired him. Most read his *Jewish Press* column, *A Small*

Voice, and knew he was delivering newspapers in order to continue his Torah study. Elliott subsequently spent many a Yom Kippur at the Mirrer Yeshiva.

When Elliott was in ninth grade at the Yeshiva High School of Queens and not "applying himself," his parents followed Meir's advice and transferred him to the Mirrer Yeshiva High School for a while. Elliott still has the book Meir inscribed to him then, the ethical classic *Mesillat Yesharim* (*Path of the Just*).

Meir helped Elliott with his February 1966 bar mitzvah speech, contributing a quote from the late U.S. President John F. Kennedy: "The strength of democracy is not merely in observing the laws we happen to agree with, but in observing the laws we disagree with." Elliott correlated this idea to Jewish law, saying, "This is the main difference in theory between the observant Jew and the non-observant Jew. The non-observant Jew (i.e., the Conservative or Reform Jew) keeps those commandments that suit him.... If he wishes to travel on Shabbat, he travels on Shabbat. If he likes the holiday of Chanuka and not Sukkot, he celebrates only Chanuka. On the other hand, the observant Jew ... keeps the commandments whether he likes them or not."[15]

This theme dominates Meir's writings: Judaism is not man-made; one may not choose which laws to obey and which to ignore. When Conservative and Reform rabbis do so, they worship not G-d, but man.[16]

The Young Israel Community

Meir elevated everyone, not just the young. In fact, he revolutionized Simchat Torah* celebrations at the Young Israel. He danced as they danced in the Mirrer Yeshiva – with his entire being, with wild abandon, hugging the Torah, our life-blood. He even brought an extra shirt with him, because the one he wore was soon drenched. His joy and enthusiasm were contagious.[17] Meir would climb on a chair, crouch, then jump up and sing out his signature song, the Yiddish *Tzu Vemen*, with the congregation shouting out the chorus exuberantly.[18] In 1968, when he announced that he was leaving Laurelton to take a pulpit in Rochdale Village, everyone's first reaction was, "But who will lead our Simchat Torah?" Meir replied, "No one is indispensable" (a motto I've recalled many times since). Many former Laureltonians remember him first and foremost for his Simchat Torah antics.

Bob Perlman remembered something else as well. As the *gabbai***of the Young Israel, Perlman kept a folder handy with transliterations of the blessings

---

* Simchat Torah celebrates the completion of the annual cycle of weekly Torah readings and the start of a new cycle.

** The *gabbai* is a member of the synagogue who assists in the running of services. One of his functions is to call upon congregants to recite the blessing before and after the reading of the Torah portions.

said before the Torah reading for those who did not know Hebrew. "Whenever Meir was called to the Torah," Perlman said, "he made a point of opening the folder and making the blessing from it, so that others who needed to use it would not be ashamed."[19]

One beneficiary of this sensitivity was Bert Zweibon, later co-founder of the Jewish Defense League. Zweibon wrote about meeting Meir:

> As you know, I was not raised *frum* [observant]. In 1963, for reasons not here germane, I began the "road back" by going to the Young Israel of Laurelton one Saturday morning.
> ... My fear was being called to the Torah, as I would have to read the *brochos* [blessings] out loud. As matters turned out, I was summoned, and since I did not know [the blessings] by heart as everyone else did, and my Hebrew was poor, I read them from an English transliteration.
> That afternoon at the *mincha* service, Meir was called first to the Torah. He stood there making it obvious he was simulating the reading of the *brochos* from the transliteration. It was his way of covering me. I did, and still do, appreciate that kindness.[20]

Meir's kindness and thoughtfulness extended to the most mundane situations. Once, before I learned to drive, he took me to a shoe store. The salesman brought pair after pair of shoes for me to try on. None were comfortable, and I wanted to try a different shoe store. Meir insisted I buy a pair of shoes in that store, "because the salesman worked so hard."

Education remained Meir's priority. Irwin Benjamin recollects Meir's convincing him to enroll his children in the Yeshiva of South Shore and Torah Academy for Girls (TAG), where our children studied: "I discussed the question with Meir as we circled the block over and over again. What convinced me was my feeling that Meir was *emes* [truth] inside and out. Meir said to me that rather than send the children to a MODERN Orthodox Jewish day school, it would be better to save my money and send them to public school. He changed our lives. Our children became very observant and I and Barbara followed suit."[21]

Toby Fink told a similar story: "Sheldon and I sat with Rabbi Kahane in his small study, and he convinced us to send our children to the more 'religious' schools. I'll always be grateful to him for his good advice."[22]

Rabbi Binyomin Kamenetsky, head of the Yeshiva of South Shore, told me: "Rabbi Kahane urged many people to send their children to our school. He would say, 'I went to the Yeshiva of Flatbush and I know what is missing in that kind of education.'"[23]

On January 30, 1965, the Young Israel of Laurelton Teenage Group sponsored a dinner in Meir's honor. The handwritten mimeographed invitation specified the entrance fee: TEENAGERS $4.00 PER PLATE; ADULTS $5.50 PER PLATE.

Along with the invitation, social chairman Irving Kreisler and co-chairman Hy Bieber* enclosed a letter urging attendance: "[Rabbi Kahane] is devoted to our shul and especially to our youth.... The only way to show our respect and appreciation is by attending...."[24]

The letter bore the Young Israel motto:

To the Youth Belongs the Future
To the Jewish Youth Belongs the Jewish Future

This was the philosophy behind the formation of the Young Israel movement in 1912. Instead of services dominated by elderly, European-born Jews, Young Israel synagogues chose young people to lead the prayers and to recite the blessings at the Torah reading. Young Israel introduced melodies into services, removed commercialism, and offered lectures in English rather than Yiddish. Young Israel helped save a generation of Orthodox youth.[25]

In keeping with the movement's emphasis on youth, the Young Israel of Laurelton held a teen *minyan* (prayer group) upstairs. Meir often prayed with these youngsters to show their importance.[26] Indeed, the future of Judaism depended on them.

Our Children's Education

Our children's upbringing reflected Meir's emphasis on a strong Torah education. He taught them to read Hebrew from the age of three, and they would sit wide-eyed as his stories from the Bible and the Talmud made Judaism come alive. His tales about the deeds of famous rabbis emphasized virtues such as kindness, humility and truthfulness. They sat next to him in the synagogue every Shabbat morning, learning to participate in the prayer service.

As a little girl, I too went to the synagogue with my father, while my mother stayed at home with my baby brother. I would sit next to my father, and he would tell me when to sit and when to stand and would help me find the place in the prayer book. Tova and Tzippy sat next to Meir in the synagogue until they were able to pray unaided in the women's section.[27] Meir impressed on our daughters that their Jewish obligations and spiritual growth were as important as those of their brothers. It seems to me that the feminists who seek to share in traditionally male synagogue functions are women who lack a sense of the importance of their own role.

---

*Hy (Chaim) Bieber had been in Betar with Meir and was to be among the earliest members of the Jewish Defense League. On June 25, 2005, his grandson, Corporal Avi Bieber, made history as the first soldier to refuse to take part in evicting the Jews of Gush Katif from their homes.

Once Tzippy could walk the distance to the synagogue,[28] I joined them eagerly, participating in prayers and, when the children played outdoors, chatting with other young mothers. These Laurelton women became my good friends. Nursery schools were not as commonplace as they are now, so the children stayed home with me until they started kindergarten. Several times a week I took the children to play with their Young Israel friends. Mina Krumbein had children of comparable ages, and we soon set up a mutual baby-sitting arrangement. We were all members of the synagogue sisterhood, which met once a month and sponsored occasional lectures and luncheons.

There were no Jewish day schools in Laurelton, so the children went to school in Far Rockaway. The girls went to Torah Academy for Girls (TAG) and Baruch went to the Yeshiva of South Shore-Toras Chaim. The school day was long because they had Jewish studies as well as the subjects taught in public schools. The trip from Far Rockaway to Laurelton took about half an hour, and since they were the last ones on the school bus route, they arrived home only at 5 P.M. In addition, the boys studied half a day on Sundays. The city did not provide transportation on Sunday, so I carpooled with other Laurelton parents.

In the summer of 1966, when Tova had just finished second grade, Meir and other parents of second-graders hired a young rabbi, Rabbi Bloch, to teach the children during the summer vacation. Baruch, the only first-grader in the group, recalled that their textbook was *Peninei Hadat* (The Pearls of Religion).[29]

When Binyamin was born, Tova was almost nine, Baruch seven and a half, and Tzippy five and a half. They were happy to have a baby brother to even out the girl-boy balance in the family. The *brit* (circumcision ceremony) was held at the Young Israel of Laurelton on October 10, 1966, with Rabbi Moshe Bunim Pirutinsky performing the circumcision.[30] At the breakfast, catered by our friends Lou and Dotty Schwartz, Rabbi Binyomin Kamenetsky, head of the Yeshiva of South Shore, spoke and gave our family a beautiful blessing: He related the Talmudic parable about a traveler who sat beneath a fruit tree on a hot day and addressed the tree, "How may I bless you? With sweet fruit? With shade? You already provide sweet fruit and shade. Therefore my blessing is that all your offshoots be as you are."[31] This parable reflected the rabbi's esteem for Meir, who was well known by then for championing authentic Judaism.

Our synagogue also showed its esteem for Meir by honoring him at its tenth annual dinner on May 27, 1967. The dinner journal had this message from Rabbi Eliahu P. Rominek: "[Meir's] devotion to our youth and willingness to sacrifice time and energy for their spiritual welfare has made a tremendous contribution to our development. His unique ability to share the wisdom of Torah with modern youth has left an indelible impression on the minds of our children and has contributed immeasurably in making our Young Israel into a center of Torah learning for old and young."[32]

Queens College

Back in 1964, when Tzippy was three and was attending a play group three afternoons a week at the Young Israel, I had resumed my college education at nearby Queens College so that eventually I could supplement the family income. I took a reduced course-load because of my responsibilities at home, and completed my bachelor's degree only in 1970. Fortunately, my parents were willing and able to baby-sit when my college courses extended past the children's school hours.

In September 1966, when I was pregnant with Binyamin, I was certain I would have to miss the fall semester at college. But Lizbeth Goldschmiedt, a Young Israel member, encouraged me to approach the dean for permission to begin the semester late. She explained that since the city colleges were free, many students never bothered to graduate, so it was in the school's interest to help those who wanted to complete their degrees.[33] She was right. After the dean's secretary questioned me and calculated that I had not violated college rules by attending classes past my fifth month (women who were conspicuously pregnant were not allowed to attend), I received permission to begin the semester late.

I took my biology textbook to the hospital with me. In those days, new mothers stayed in the hospital almost a week, so I had plenty of time to catch up on the material I was missing, while my mother and mother-in-law cared for Tova, Baruch, and Tzippy.

After completing the basic liberal arts courses, I chose to major in early childhood education, planning to teach kindergarten or first grade. I enjoyed the courses very much, but in my senior year I switched to English literature, because education majors were required to do a semester of full-time student teaching. That would have kept me away from home more hours than my mother could handle.

The June 1967 Six Day War, with its miraculous victories, rekindled our desire to live in Israel. I sought a profession that would be suitable to practice in Israel and decided to become a librarian.[34] I received my master's degree in library science from Queens College in August 1971, just before we left for Israel, and later worked at the National Library in Jerusalem for 27 years.

Chapter 10

Political Research (1963-1965)

WHILE TEACHING HIGH school students Sunday mornings at Manhattan's West Side Institutional Synagogue, Meir renewed his friendship with Brooklyn buddy Joseph Churba, who was living in Manhattan while working on his doctorate in political science at Columbia University.[1]

The Center for Political Studies

They were both concerned about the political situation in the United States and how it affected the Jews and Israel. In 1964, in an effort to influence American policy to benefit both American Jews and the State of Israel, they set up the Center for Political Studies in Washington, D.C.[2] Meir began to commute to Washington, remaining there two or three days at a time. He suggested that we move there, but I was reluctant to make the changes in my life such a move would have required. By 1967 he was no longer working in Washington and I was glad we had not relocated.

When Meir was in Washington, I had to cope with three small children by myself. I vividly recall how it was during the power blackout of November 1965. For 13 hours, New York and seven other states on the Eastern Seaboard were without electricity. Meir phoned to find out how I was managing. I explained that the children were in the bathtub and I was using Shabbat candles for light. He apparently heard only part of what I was saying, because he asked in amazement, "What are the candles doing in the bathtub?"

My parents lent me a hand at least once a week. To make her trip from Brooklyn to Queens easier, my mother learned to drive at age forty-five, inspired by my mother-in-law's driving skill. My father would travel by train and bus from his accountancy job in Manhattan and take the children out to ride their bikes in the park. In winter, they belly-whopped happily down the snow-covered slopes on the sleds he bought them. He also attended to carpentry, electricity and plumbing repairs.

In Washington, Meir obtained government funding for various research projects. In 1974 Meir told interviewer Hyman Frank about one of those projects:

> I remember one request for a research study from Senator Javits. They were fighting on Cyprus even as now, with the Turks and the British and the Greeks in a triangle of bloodshed. Senator Javits wanted research studies from the Greek point of view.[3]

Another project concerned the John Birch Society. This ultraconservative, anti-Communist, anti-Semitic group was gaining support all over the country. During the 1960s it had about 100,000 members and extended its influence through a chain of 400 bookstores. Meir had written about the danger to Jews posed by the Birch Society in 1963.[4] He told Dr. Frank:

> The F.B.I., to [its] credit, was intensely worried about the Birchers. They sensed a threat to the democratic structure. They asked our group to research the Birchers and find out whatever we could about them: where they were getting their money, who their backers were, their philosophers, their writers and what constituted their appeal in their mushrooming growth.
>
> ... The fact that the Birchers, and others of their ilk, could thrive during a period of relative prosperity (actually it was an affluent period) made me worry: What would happen during economic depression when a scapegoat is needed for the hardships and deprivations of the masses?[5]

In a project funded by a "law enforcement wing of the government," Meir joined and infiltrated the Birch Society. In a 1972 radio interview, he said: "I spent almost two years with them trying to find out their sources of income, which I did."[6]

Honest Observant Jews

Since Meir's work in Washington occupied him only two or three days a week, he resumed work as an editor at the *Jewish Press*. His name appeared on the masthead as editor from August to December 1964, and again from April to July 1965. While he was editor, original news stories appeared on page one, and numerous editorials bore the imprint of his style. His lasting innovation, dating from this period, was the introduction of a table of contents.[7]

Meir's *Small Voice* column was widely read, and many synagogues and communal groups invited him to speak. To encourage this, he placed an ad informing "all organizations, synagogues and social groups" that he was ready to speak before them. "Why be burdened with dull & uninteresting meetings?" said the ad. "To arrange for an exciting and informative evening, write to: Speakers Bureau c/o the *Jewish Press*."[8]

Among the groups Meir addressed was Yavneh, a nationwide association of Orthodox Jewish college students. On February 16, 1964, he spoke at Yavneh's Leadership Seminar at New York University. His speech typified his ongoing demand that the Orthodox Jew live up to his commitments:

> In this country we are developing a non-Torah Orthodoxy.... For us Shabbat is not particularly difficult to observe, and kosher food is relatively easy to obtain and quite inviting. However, there are main areas of halakha that are [ignored] without any qualms, such as mixed dancing, mixed swimming, modesty.
>
> Are we being honest observant Jews? That is the question that should concern us. What is our rationale for areas of halakha [violated]? Do we set aside time for learning Torah?[9]

Save Soviet Jewry

Later that year Meir spoke twice before Yavneh's Hunter College downtown chapter. One of his topics was "The Plight of Soviet Jewry."[10]

Glenn Richter, national director of the Student Struggle for Soviet Jewry, recalled: "Since the early 1920s, the Jews of the West had almost no contact with Jews in the Soviet Union. The reign of terror initiated by Joseph Stalin cut them off completely. During the Stalin period, 1922-1953, anyone who even whispered a word of disagreement with the Kremlin disappeared. Even under Khrushchev, they continued to suffer discrimination, and the Cold War prevented Soviet citizens from openly contacting Americans. Although the State of Israel (up to the Six Day War) maintained diplomatic relations with the Soviet Union, Israel was very cautious about publicizing the plight of Soviet Jews. In 1962, Israel's secret Soviet Jewry department, Lishkat Hakesher, leaked information to the writer Moshe Decter, who published a groundbreaking article in *Foreign Affairs* magazine in January 1963.[11] Decter told of the subtle policy of discrimination against Jews in employment, education and other sectors of public life. "They are allowed neither to assimilate, nor live a full Jewish life, nor to emigrate, as many would wish, to Israel or any other country where they might live freely as Jews," he wrote.[12]

Thus it was that in 1963 newspaper reports about the persecution of Soviet Jews increased. Some concerned the difficulties they had in baking matza (unleavened bread) for Passover, when Jews may not eat ordinary bread. A Jewish baker who sold matza for Passover was imprisoned for "profiteering." After Soviet officials had agreed to accept matzot from American Jewish organizations, twenty tons of matzot remained undelivered in Soviet customs houses. Jews who registered with the Soviet authorities to receive matza were subject to official observation by the Soviet police. One Jew, convicted of currency speculation, was sentenced to death by firing squad for this infraction.[13]

An overview in the *American Jewish Year Book* said:

> By mid-1963 ... Jewish cultural institutions, forcibly padlocked by the Stalin regime, remained closed.... Unlike other ethnic and national minorities in the Soviet Union, Jews remained deprived of schools, publications and theaters. Synagogues were being closed ... the ban on the production of religious articles continued, baking and distributing matzot were forbidden or hampered, and the training of religious leaders was made impossible.... Jews were being used as scapegoats for the Soviet Union's economic problems. A discriminatory application of heavy penalties, including death, for alleged economic crimes was bolstered by a propaganda campaign in the [communist] party provincial and national press to vilify Jews, Judaism and the synagogue, and exacerbate popular anti-Semitism.[14]

Meir called for protests against the Soviet Union. In 1963, in one of his first articles about Soviet Jewry, he wrote:

> Silence is not always golden – sometimes it is criminal. This being true, American Jewry must stand condemned for the crime of silence.... While you read this, two and a half million Jews in the East lie condemned to a spiritual death.... They cannot train *shochetim*, kosher slaughterers, they cannot learn circumcision, they are harassed [for] any manifestation of Sabbath observance....
>
> And of course it will be protested: "But what can we do? How can our protests and cries help the Jews of Russia?" To this we can only say: If a finger hurts, it may be of little benefit to cry out in pain. However, if one does NOT cry out, one thing is certain: It does not hurt. If it did, we would be marching at this moment around the Soviet consulate.... We would cry out, boycott, protest, hold sit-ins in the Soviet Washington Embassy, constantly keep the problem on the front pages....
>
> Let [Torah Jewry] take the lead in a campaign to re-awaken pain. Let us formulate a program of bold, CONTINUOUS protest. By so doing we will give new heart to the Russian Jews who feel today that their brothers in the West have forgotten them....[15]

The Student Struggle for Soviet Jewry (SSSJ), organized by Jewish college students in 1964, began to hold public protests regularly. Jacob Birnbaum, the driving force behind SSSJ, wrote to me: "During the early period, I was searching for young potential leaders, and our mutual friend Morton Dolinsky brought Meir to my attention. On October 18, 1964, I organized an important rally on the Lower East Side with the participation of President Johnson's personal representative and Senators Jacob Javits and Kenneth Keating.[16] Despite [Meir's] reluctance on account of his speech impediment, I insisted that he speak. Though this first speech was halting, he became very committed and excited."[17]

Meir promoted the rally in his *Jewish Press* column, praising the "group of young college students that were doing something about the situation.... Only SSSJ has not been afraid to openly picket and openly cry out.... Russian Jewry has a great ally in our Father in Heaven. On earth, it has none better than these dedicated young men and women."[18]

However, as early as May 1964, in a major article titled "Save Soviet Jewry," he deemed peaceful picketing insufficient:

> They are murdering the ancient faith of three million Jews in the Soviet Union today and we shut our ears to the cries of our brethren.... They are killing our brothers in Russia today and we go about our business.... They have locked the doors of 350 synagogues until today there are only 94 to serve all Jewry, and they have arrested rabbis and lay leaders. They outdo the Nazis who took only our bodies, and seek to rob us of our souls. Who cries? Who acts? ... You ask: What can we do? Is there anything that can possibly be done to save the Russian Jews from spiritual extinction?

Meir presented the solution:

> There is a possible answer – one that has been briefly skirted by a group that calls itself the Student Struggle for Soviet Jewry ... [which] picketed the Soviet Mission to the United Nations two weeks ago. It is this group alone which appears to understand the one and only possible way to move the Russian behemoth, as [SSSJ] took to the streets and the subject of Russia's Jews made headlines for the first time ...
>
> The idea of Jewry moving the Soviet government is one that is so far-fetched as to be audacious. What logical human being can conceive of a handful of American Jews moving a nation of 200 million that possesses atomic arms? What possible weapon do we have to move this mountain?

He introduced the idea of taking advantage of the current Soviet need to develop friendly relations with the United States.

> The only weapon – aside from our Father in Heaven – lies in the poisoning of the atmosphere between the United States and Russia. In a time when the Soviets, wracked by economic problems at home and challenged by China for the leadership of the communist world, desperately need friendship with the United States.... If we can challenge this era of good feeling ... it is possible that the Soviets will consider it not worth the bother of persecuting their Jews at the risk of a reversal in foreign policy. If there is a hope, this is the only one. How can it be achieved? By reaching the American people, by having the story of Russian Jewry hammered home to them constantly.... Picketing is a good thing but hardly enough.
>
> How many headlines does a peaceful picket line make? ... We MUST make headlines and they are made only by audacious and dramatic activities. If need

be, these activities cannot be confined to sweet respectability and legality....
A sit-in inside the Soviet Mission; the disrupting of a United Nations session
at which the Soviet delegate rises to speak – these are some of the ways that
the entire nation will certainly hear of the plight of Soviet Jews. It is not a
pleasant task, but this is not a job for people who fear getting their hands
soiled. Soviet Jewry will not wait upon respectability and gentility.

Uncannily, Meir foresaw the results of such audacity:

It will mean condemnation from the "respectable" elements within Jewry who
fear more for their own image than for Soviet Jewry. The struggle for Palestine
was made infinitely more difficult because there were Jews who refused to act
like "gangsters" and use force. In the end, the minority that was unafraid to
fight [the Irgun] was proven correct and it was their way that won the day.

The Negro ["black" was not yet in use] for 100 years in America was
enslaved and persecuted and stepped upon. I put it to you that the radical
groups such as CORE and SNIC* did more with their sit-ins and street demonstrations than all the respectable Negro organizations combined.

I do not preach violence for its own sake or unless absolutely necessary. I
only decry those who would tie our hands and limit us to respectability. We
have a great weapon in anti-Communism and should not be hesitant to use
it....[19]

Years later, one college student compared the results of SSSJ protests with the
outcome of Jewish Defense League activities: "I remember walking for hours on
end in a picket line about two blocks from the Russian consulate with 100 students from SSSJ. We would get, if we were lucky, a two-sentence news item on
page 32 of the *Times*. Then one morning Meir's boys struck simultaneously at
three Russian installations in New York City – Tass, Intourist, and Aeroflot, leaping aboard a Soviet plane that had just landed at Kennedy Airport. This issue was
finally on the front page. From then on Soviet Jewry was a top issue and the pressure built until they began to free the Jews. I believe Meir was responsible for
the release of tens of thousands."[20]

Who recalled in 1969 that Meir had formulated this successful strategy back
in 1964! However, "Man proposes and G-d disposes." Only after he had founded
the Jewish Defense League and attracted a large following, was Meir able to
implement his ideas.

The War in Vietnam

In 1965 Meir made another attempt, together with Joseph Churba, to influence
American politics. That year, Churba received his Ph.D. and set up the Institute

---

* CORE: Congress on Racial Equality. SNIC: Student Non-violent Committee.

for Research in Foreign Affairs in Washington. Interviewed in the *Jewish Press*, Churba explained the Institute's activities:

> We receive requests from U.S. government agencies such as the State and Defense Departments, from Senate and House committees; from specialized agencies of the United Nations; and from business.
>
> We are presently doing a lengthy study of the problem of aggression and its place in international law. As you can tell from the news from Vietnam, the classical methods of aggression, the formal declaration of war, [are] a thing of the past. New methods such as [those] of guerilla warfare, economic blockade, hostile propaganda, [and] the aiding by a supposedly "neutral" power of guerilla bands are the common practice today. Do these constitute formal aggression sufficient to justify unlimited acts of self-defense? The question is a practical one and we are preparing a thorough study of it.[21]

One of the institute's projects was the patriotically named July Fourth Movement. The movement was formed to counteract widespread opposition, especially among college students, toward U.S. involvement in the war in Vietnam.

Meir's support for American involvement in the Vietnam war was based on Jewish self-interest: First, Jews dominated the anti-war effort, causing the Christian "silent majority" to accuse American Jewry of being unpatriotic. Second, if the United States adopted a policy of isolationism and abandoned its allies in Vietnam, that policy could lead to abandonment of its ally in the Middle East – Israel.[22]

Meir and Joe invited students to join the July Fourth Movement in an ad in the *Herald-Tribune*, a conservative New York City newspaper that supported the war. The ad appeared on June 29, 1965, and on July 4 itself, the *Journal-American* – another conservative New York City paper – published an interview with Meir and Joe about the organization. For the interview, Meir used the name Michael King, so as not to involve the *Jewish Press* with which his name was closely associated. He told the interviewer that the movement was founded to give the numerous college students who supported U.S. participation in Vietnam a chance to be heard.[23]

The July Fourth Movement collapsed after several months because of lack of funds,[24] but Meir continued to point out the folly of Jews who opposed involvement in Vietnam in articles in the *Jewish Press* and the *New York and Brooklyn Daily*.

In "The Old Man and the Sea," for instance, Meir compared aged pacifist Norman Thomas' opposition to the war in Vietnam to his condemnation of U.S. involvement in the war in Europe: "It was 1939 and already Austria and Czechoslovakia were prostrate beneath the heel of Hitler, [when Norman Thomas said,] 'the war in Europe is not our war ... [it is] a war of imperial capitalism.' ... and the old man continues his babblings thirty years later in magnificent obliviousness to his unbroken record of error...."

His political commentary was not limited to the war in Vietnam. In "Mother's Day in Alabama," Meir denounced the racist southern states where blacks couldn't vote, sit in the front of a public bus, or even eat ice cream in the same store as whites. After civil rights activist Viola Liuzzo, mother of five, was murdered in Anniston, Alabama, he wrote: "[On Mother's Day] in New York they sent flowers, in San Francisco they sent cards, in Kansas City they had dinners, and in Anniston they honored dear old Mom with a rip-roaring parade of the Ku Klux Klan in honor of three men indicted for the murder of Viola Liuzzo."[25]

In December 1965 Meir wrote to a number of newspaper syndicates, hoping to gain a wider readership for his "political column ... appearing for the last three years in the *New York and Brooklyn Daily*." Afterwards, he sent out a collection of *Small Voice* articles, hoping to find other newspapers that would carry his writing. He was unsuccessful in both cases.[26]

To Study and Learn

Meanwhile, Meir's *Jewish Press* column, renamed *Hashkafa* (Viewpoint), dissected Jewish life in the United States, tackling such topics as sending children away from home to yeshiva boarding schools, the education of Jewish women, and summer vacations that contradict the Jewish values imparted by yeshivas during the school term.[27]

Meir continued lecturing to Jewish groups on a variety of topics. His talk to the Yavneh chapter at the Polytechnic Institute in Brooklyn was part of a series on "The Philosophy and Relevance of Prayer." Another speaker in the series was Dr. Philip Birnbaum, whose translated and annotated prayer books became best sellers.[28]

Meir's *Hashkafa* column of April 2, 1965 shows his continued focus on bringing Jews closer to Judaism. In it he wrote about the success of Yeshiva University in meeting this challenge:

> It is precisely because of the general apathy on the part of traditional Jews to the wanderings of their non-observant brothers, that the existence of an institution like the Jewish Studies Program at Yeshiva University is so vital and heartwarming.... At this institution [are] young men ... [whose] backgrounds are devoid of parents who taught them the meaning of kashrus or the beauties of Shabbos.... Their families do not know what possessed them to suddenly become religious, but in each of their cases, something did. A feeling of lack in their lives, a chance meeting with an individual who inspired them, some such occurrence. But in nearly every case, the initial spark of Judaism, the initial return, would have faded because of the lack of opportunity to study and learn....[29]

Chapter 11

Chronology of a Miracle (1967-1968)

The Six Day War

ON JUNE 27, 1967, right after the Six Day War, Meir made his second trip to Israel – this time by plane. The *Jewish Press* gave him a press card to "cover" the war. In just under two weeks, he gathered enough material for a series titled *Chronology of a Miracle*, which appeared weekly from July 14, 1967, through January 14, 1968. Its scope is indicated by its sub-title: "A step-by-step account of all the events that led up to the Israeli-Arab war and a detailed description of the war itself, its miracles and stories." *Chronology of a Miracle* lent "human interest" to the call-up of Israeli soldiers:

> ... Mobilization, the amazing Israeli process that turned the mass of civilians into a disciplined army and the country into a huge armed camp within 48 hours.
>
> ... Civilians eagerly participated: One reservist, who had given his wife the exact location of his camp (Israelis are usually fanatically close-mouthed about anything military) was ordered home. The whole day and the next night he sat outside the camp refusing to leave. The C.O. finally relented and allowed him to stay. For the next week he refused to answer any questions whatsoever, not even the correct time.[1]

With the signing of a pact between Hussein of Jordan and Nasser of Egypt on May 30, 1967, Israel was surrounded on all sides by the hostile armies of Egypt, Jordan, Syria and Lebanon. Meir wrote of that period:

> The Hussein-Nasser pact was a signal for wild exultation throughout the Arab world.... There was a contagious air of excitement.... The people seemed animated and stimulated and loudspeakers installed on lampposts at major intersections interspersed crashing martial music with news and exhortations....
>
> Sixty-five-year-old Um Kulthoum, the favorite singer of the Arab world, captured the fervor of the Arabs as their armies stared across the Israeli border

and their leaders flew all over the area in excited consultation. She had a new song composed for her which, sung over Cairo's Voice of the Arabs ... became an immediate favorite:

> *We are going back by force of arms.*
> *We are going back like morning after the dark night.*
> *Army of Arabism, may Allah be with you.*
> *Oh, how great, splendid and brave you are.*

Children heard the songs and were excited by them. One eight-year-old son of a wealthy family who attended an English [language] school came home with new recitations: "Palestine, you are our hope. We are your fighters. We have sworn to drive the hated enemy from your soil." It was a lesson in civics that was being more than matched throughout the Arab world....[2]

Naomi Brody of Laurelton relived the feeling among Jews then: "It was about two weeks before the Six Day War. The Gulf of Eilat had been blockaded, the United Nations 'Peacekeeping Force' had pulled out, and Israel appeared in imminent danger. I had been walking around for days with a feeling of impending doom."[3]

Fred Horowitz recalled sensing the threat of another Holocaust. In Israel, there were contingency plans to turn Tel Aviv's Meir Park into a cemetery. The threat was a constant topic of conversation at the synagogue.[4]

"Meir spoke at the Young Israel's annual dinner [May 27, 1967], which was in honor of you and Meir that year," wrote Brody. "He spoke quietly, reassuringly, saying that G-d said He would never abandon the Jewish people.... I walked out of that dinner feeling calmer than I had in days."[5]

Meir's optimism was vindicated. World Jewry witnessed wonders. Meir was especially moved by my father's brief description of the marvelous events: "Thirteen Arab and Moslem nations threatened to destroy Israel. Thank G-d, in one week Israel captured Sinai, Old Jerusalem, [the] Western Bank of Jordan and part of Syria, a miracle far above Chanuka and Purim."[6]

In August 1967, as a step towards moving to Israel, we sold our house on 133rd Avenue and rented an apartment on 139th.[7] It was close to JFK International Airport and some incoming flights were routed directly overhead. If the children were playing in the backyard when a jet came in for an earsplitting landing, they ran for cover.

The Jewish Stake in Vietnam: Religion under Communism

Between April 7 and June 2, 1967, Meir wrote a series of *Jewish Press* articles titled "The Jewish Stake in Vietnam," arguing that Jewish support for U.S. intervention in Vietnam would counteract American anti-Semitism and help Israel. In

July, New York Congressman Abraham Multer inserted the entire series into the *Congressional Record*. Multer introduced the series into the *Record* with these words: "Mr. Speaker, the Jewish stake in Vietnam is a very vital one, for wherever communism gains control, the Jew is denied his religious freedom.... Meir Kahane ... has written a thorough and informative series...."[8]

The Jewish Stake in Vietnam was also the title of a book written jointly by Meir and Joseph Churba and published in 1967. The chapters dealing with Vietnam's foreign relations were clearly authored by Churba, while Meir – using his own name and the pseudonym Michael King – contributed the chapters on the dangers of communism for Israel and for the Jews.[9]

Meir points out in the book that the leftists opposing U.S. participation in the Vietnam War were also anti-Israel and pro-Arab. He warns that U.S. isolationism would reduce America's support for Israel, and he documents the anti-Israel, pro-Arab stance of China and other communist countries backing the Vietcong. To illustrate the anti-religious policies of the communists, he included a 30-page chapter about communist Russia's suppression of religion, especially Judaism. Detailing the plight of Soviet Jewry, he begins with the Yevesekzia, the Jewish communists:

> Armed with instructions by the Communist government to eliminate religious "superstition," they hastened to sequester synagogues and convert them to Komsomol (Communist Youth) clubs. Rabbis and teachers who broke the law by secretly teaching children religion and Hebrew were caught and arrested. (No minor child may be taught religion in the Soviet Union.) The religious schools were shut, and the great Russian Judaism began to dry up at its source – the child and his studies.
>
> ... As the years went by, the Yevesekzia grew even more vicious. Its schools, lectures, forums, newspapers, and books mocked Jewish laws and customs and distorted Jewish history. Wedges were deliberately driven between children and their parents and grandparents. The new generation was being ripped from the bosom of its heritage. Not only religion but Zionism too was brutally hunted down. Show trials of Zionists accused of "imperialist conspiracy against the state" were held. Hebrew, the language of "rabbinism" and "imperialist Zionism," was strictly forbidden. In addition, there began a campaign to blacklist all former petty traders and artisans as "bourgeoisie" – a list that included the vast majority of the Jews of the Soviet Union. Because of this, more than sixty per cent of all Soviet Jews were "declassed," meaning that they were last on the list for food, clothing, employment, housing – everything.
>
> ... All religious education is still prohibited to any Jew below the age of 18, while at the same time he is forced to attend classes in atheism that are compulsory in all Soviet schools. One can imagine the heartache of Jewish parents who see their children cut off forcibly from their G-d and their faith....

The persecution of Jewish religious institutions has been systematically stepped up in recent years. In June and July of 1961, six lay religious leaders in Moscow and Leningrad were secretly arrested, and synagogue presidents in six major provincial cities deposed. The arrested leaders were held in prison until October of that year and then secretly tried, convicted of alleged espionage and sentenced to lengthy prison terms. When a storm of protests arose, *Trud*, the trade union paper, published a vicious article accusing the religious leaders of being agents for the Israeli secret service and tools of the American intelligence system.

... But perhaps the act of religious faith that has come most under attack by the Kremlin commissars is the simple one of eating matza (unleavened bread) on Passover. Perhaps it is because the Communists realize that Passover commemorates a redemption from slavery, the molding of Jewry into one people, the beginning of an unbroken chain of nationhood, the linking of all Hebrews including those in the free world with those subjugated behind the "Iron Curtain." It is precisely this consciousness, this identity, this unity, that the Soviets are desperately trying to shatter.... And so, Passover – and matzas in particular – were targeted for attack and eventual oblivion.

Then Meir introduces a poignant tale written by Shelomo Ben-Israel of the *Jewish Daily Forward*, about his visit to the Soviet Union:

... Many of the older Jews cling to their faith with a strength that surpasses all understanding. Once, in a synagogue in another Russian city, I heard a tremulous voice behind me. "Reb Yid, don't turn around. Keep your eyes on your *siddur* [prayer book] and pretend you hear nothing. I have to talk to someone." Out of the corner of my eye I saw an old man, his face covered by the prayer shawl draped over his head.

Leaning against his lectern, he spoke in a voice choked with tears. He had lost his whole family – his wife, his children, his relatives, all except one son, who now had a young son of his own, named Volodya [diminutive of Vladimir]. Until he was five, Volodenka [another diminutive of Vladimir] had accompanied his grandfather to synagogue. When he started school, his teacher forbade the students to attend church or synagogue, but the boy was so devoted to his grandfather that he went anyway, until one day a classmate reported him. The teacher punished him, humiliated him in front of the class, and issued a stern warning. Since then, Volodenka has not dared to go to synagogue.

... The years passed. Six months ago, eight gentile boys attacked Volodenka and beat him up, shouting, "*Zhid!* Let's kill the dirty *Zhid!*" Since then, the boy has been full of fears. He clings to his grandfather and begs the old man to explain why he is Jewish and why the others hate him for it. The old man would have liked to teach his grandson Jewish history, Hebrew and the Bible, but the boy's father would not permit it, afraid that if word got out, he might lose his job, or worse. Soon Volodenka will be 13 years old, and the grandfather is desperate. "'Volodenka,' I said to him," the old man wept, "'I'll give you anything you want. Just come to shul with me.' But Volodenka won't do it."

The lectern behind me shook with the old man's sobs. Suddenly he leaned forward. "I beg of you, dear friend," he whispered, "when you go back to the free world, don't hold your peace. Stir up the people, turn the world upside down if you must, but help us! Help me so that my Volodenka will remain a Jew."[10]

Two years later, when the JDL was gaining support and Meir was speaking before many audiences, he would tell the moving story of Volodenka.[11]

In 1966 Meir again turned to the *Jewish Press* for additional income, since government funding for political research had dwindled. This time, his title was associate editor.[12] Between 1966 and 1968 he also "moonlighted" as a High Holidays rabbi and cantor, usually in an outlying Orthodox synagogue. His High Holiday prayer book is replete with his notations for prayer melodies. During those years, the children and I spent Rosh Hashana with my parents and Meir's in Brooklyn. We spent Yom Kippur with cousin Menucha Kahan, whose husband Shaul also took a seasonal rabbi-cantor position.

The year Meir served at Congregation Adas Israel in Fall River, Massachusetts, he led the *shacharit* prayers and blew the *shofar*, and was also in charge of the junior congregation.[13]

In 1967 he spent the High Holidays in Richmond, Virginia, at the Beth Israel synagogue. His host, Rabbi Abraham Goldreich, the synagogue's youth director, recalled Meir's sermon about Jewish education, in which he pointed out that most afternoon synagogue schools not only don't teach, but even "turn the children off."[14]

Despite the sharp drop in government spending for political research, Meir and Joseph Churba tried once more to enter the field. Churba spent a Shabbat at our home and spoke at our synagogue's *Oneg Shabbat*. On Saturday night he and Meir approached congregant Fred Horowitz about underwriting a research firm. Horowitz agreed to lend them $5,000 for startup expenses, and Consultant Research Associates was formed. An application for New York State certification dated November 23, 1966, lists the partners as Horowitz, Churba and Martin Kahane. There is no evidence that the firm was active, and Meir and Churba had no contact after 1967.[15]

Meir considered the loan of $5,000 from Horowitz a personal debt and sent payments whenever he could. "He continued sending checks, even from prison," recalled Horowitz. "When I visited Meir in prison in 1975, I told him that I took that debt as a business loss and that I absolved him of the debt. Meir said to me, 'It doesn't matter what YOU THINK I owe you. It's what I THINK I owe you.'"[16]

Giving Charity

Meir's generous donations to charity deeply impressed Horowitz: "Someone came to the synagogue and spoke from the pulpit to appeal for funds for Pe'ilim [an anti-missionary organization in Israel]. Meir was the first to announce his pledge, with a donation of $50. By starting out with a high amount, he made others follow his example."[17]

Meir also supported Or Chadash, a religious school for Sephardic girls in Kfar Hasidim, east of Haifa. Founder Rabbi Moshe Tanami wrote:

> In 1967, around Chanuka, I traveled to the United States to raise funds for Girls' Town-Or Chadash. It was Pe'ilim that suggested I contact Reb Meir.
>
> He was very aware of what was happening here in Eretz Yisrael. We spoke of the problems facing the young Sephardic girls in northern Israel in those days. Due to the economic hardships their families faced, every income from all members of the family, no matter how young, was a matter of survival. As a result of this economic pressure, many young girls were dropping out of school at the age of 14 and going out to work. These naive young girls would meet boys at their place of work [and] strike up an innocent relationship, only to find out that they were Arabs. By that time it was too late and they were forced into marriage and living in Arab villages.
>
> When Meir heard these stories, he understood all the ramifications and said: "If you are dealing with preventing this problem, I want to help you." He asked for details of the girls in the institution and promised to find people who would sponsor a girl and contribute $500-$600 a year towards a scholarship.
>
> He supported close to ten girls a year, which was a significant undertaking in those days. He raised the money and gave it to me personally or through his brother, Nachman, who lived in Israel. In addition, Meir introduced me to many affluent people, which was most encouraging as I began working on setting up a fundraising base in the States.[18]

Once, at our Shabbat table, Rabbi Tanami told us how he combed the Central Bus Station in Tel Aviv for girls who seemed lost, trying to get to them before the pimps did. Meir took him to our neighbors in Laurelton and even acted as his translator.

Charity was an essential part of Meir's life. He scrupulously recorded his income, so he could tithe it as required by Jewish law. Meir even maintained a separate checking account into which he deposited that 10 percent – and some-times more – as soon as he received his paycheck. Meir taught our children to give charity as well. For every dollar they received as a gift or earned by baby-sitting, ten cents went into the charity box.

Escape from the Soviet Union

In December 1967, to increase his *Jewish Press* salary, Meir launched another column, *Israel Through Laughter and Tears*, using the pen name Meir Hacohen. He wrote this column regularly until the end of 1978, culling human interest stories from Israeli papers. One brief, bittersweet vignette was "Wait Till I Put on My Hat."

> Yoel is three years old and his parents are not observant. His grandfather, however, is a religious Jew and out of honor for him, the parents always have Yoel wear a *kippa* (skullcap) when they visit.
>
> One evening last week, the phone rang in Yoel's house and the youngster ran to pick it up. It was his grandfather. "Wait a minute, Saba (Grandfather)," he said. "Before I talk to you, let me get my *kippa*."[19]

Meir's articles during the first months of 1968 dealt with a variety of subjects: Israel and the U.N.; terror attacks in Israel; the communist threat to the U.S.; the racist views of black teachers in New York City schools; the war in Vietnam; and growing anti-Semitism in America.

A recurring topic was Soviet Jewry. One *Israel Through Laughter and Tears* column, subtitled "Boris Comes Home," profiled Israel's new Russian immigrants,[20] while a feature article, "Light in the Soviet Darkness," poignantly described the plight of the Jews in Russia:

> For ten years Emma Davidowitz had waited to get out of the Soviet Union and go to Israel. Ten long years of applications, rejections, persistence and finally – the precious documents were granted her. She was an old woman, bent and lined with suffering under the Nazis and the Communists, but the long journey was now at an apparently happy end. And then – all seemed threatened. War had broken out between Israel and the Arab states and no one knew what was happening.
>
> ... Together with an old friend, Emma took the train for the long journey to Moscow. All day and night they rode without eating and, finally, they reached the capital.
>
> They arrive only to find the Israeli Consulate closed, because the Soviet Union had cut ties with Israel. At the Dutch Embassy, which is handling Israeli affairs, they learn that since they must travel through Poland and Czechoslovakia, they must obtain transit visas from those countries.
>
> ... Darkness had already fallen and they would have to wait till morning.
>
> Where would they spend the night? They were strangers and they did not have the proper papers required to register in a hotel. There was only one place to go – the synagogue.
>
> In the synagogue stood a man. "Who are you?" he asked. "What do you want?"

"We want to see the rabbi."

"He is sick. I am the president. What do you want?"

Emma thought for a moment. Presidents of synagogues in Russia were, as a rule, government informers. But there was no choice. She told him why she was in Moscow, and said, "We must have a place to stay tonight."

The man shrugged. "I can do nothing. I have no place for you."

"In that case," said Emma, "we shall stay here all night."

The man saw that he had a tough nut here. Going to the phone he began to make calls. Everyone refused; fear rules Jews in Moscow. Finally, one old woman agreed to take them for the night.

Arriving at the house they found the old, bent woman, half blind. She refused to speak a word to them. Emma sat on a chair and once when she walked to the window, her hostess suddenly broke her silence:

"No! The neighbors will see you!"

At five in the morning Emma left and went to the Czech Embassy.... A day of frantic attempts finally produced a visa from the Hungarian Embassy and Emma headed home. She would sell all her possessions and leave. And then, the rumors began.

The Soviets were going to cancel all existing exit visas!

Emma was frantic. Taking a few possessions and a few rubles she ran for the train. She must escape; now! From Kovno to Vilna to Budapest to Vienna to Rome. There was the plane for Israel, for freedom. Emma Davidowitz had escaped. Just in time.

Meir underscored the severity of the situation:

And behind her she left more than three million other Jews. They are Jews without yeshivas, schools, tefillin, circumcision, Hebrew books.

This is the crux of the Soviet Jewish problem. Religion. It is a religious problem. A regime devoted to the extermination of the Word of G-d attempts to put an end to Jewish consciousness, to the Jewish faith.

The question remains: Is there nothing that can be done?

Many answer that the Iron Curtain divides us from our Russian brethren and there is no hope of piercing it. With sad hearts they say that our brothers are doomed to spiritual death.

It is not true. Most believe it because they truly know of no way to help. Others say it because this serves as a rationale for inaction. The fact remains that things can be done and are being done on behalf of Soviet Jewry.

... There are things that are being done at this very moment in Russia in the field of Torah, education, circumcision, prayer. For the most obvious reasons, these things cannot be spelled out, but this in no way negates their reality or their importance. It is work that is not being done by leading Jewish groups. The history of Hatzala – saving Jewish lives during the Holocaust – has been proof that such things are usually not done by the Establishment but rather by individuals and small, non-prestigious groups.

Meir's description of one such small group, and the great deeds accomplished by singular men, hinted at the direction his own life would take:

> Those who know of Vaad Hatzala's work during the Hitler era know what anonymous and obscure people did. Surely it was not the famous and prestigious leaders of the American Jewish Congress, the American Jewish Committee or B'nai B'rith who rescued those pitifully few who escaped from Hitler.
>
> Those who have read the sainted Rabbi [Michael Dov] Weissmandl's book, *Min Hameitzar*,[21] know of the perfidy and inaction of the Establishment. Those who know of the work that men like the great departed Rabbi Eliezer Silver and the late Rabbis Abraham Kalmanowitz and Yaakov Griffel accomplished know what dedicated, bold and unaffiliated men can accomplish.
>
> ... Those who seek to learn about SOME of the facts and SOME of the accomplishments [in helping Soviet Jews] are invited to contact Al Tidom, 60 East 42 Street, N.Y.C. It is a group that does things for our Russian brothers....[22]

Of course, Meir could not reveal all he knew about Al Tidom, which smuggled prayer books, tefillin, and other religious articles to Jews in the Soviet Union. He was in close touch with founder Rabbi Harry Bronstein, with whom he shared a deep concern for Russian Jews.[23] Because both were widely known as champions of Soviet Jewry, they were summoned to testify on June 19, 1968 before a Congressional committee, the House Committee on Un-American Activities, about the persecution of Jews in the Soviet Union.[24] Meir's detailed testimony fills seventeen pages in the committee's report. He and Rabbi Bronstein urged the United States government to voice strenuous protests to the Kremlin on behalf of Soviet Jewry. Their complete testimony was reprinted in the *Jewish Press*.[25] Indeed, the *Jewish Press* played an important part in publicizing the plight of Soviet Jews.

Chapter 12

The Jewish Defense League Is Born
(1968)

Urban Violence

THE *JEWISH PRESS* was flooded with calls and letters about crimes committed against Jews and Jewish institutions. Women's purses were snatched in broad daylight, men were mugged for their watches and wallets, Jewish storeowners were held up, knifed, and sometimes murdered, Jewish teachers were assaulted in the public schools. Jewish cemeteries were desecrated and synagogues defaced.

The change in New York City was dramatic. Violence was rampant, and because of New York's demography, much of the violence was committed by blacks and a large percentage of their victims were Jews. Unscrupulous real estate dealers, known as blockbusters, convinced frightened Jews to move from crime-ridden neighborhoods and sell their homes to blacks at a loss.

New York City was typical of cities all over the United States. The migration of blacks from the rural South seeking jobs in cities in the North had led to "white flight" from the inner cities. Wealthier Jews moved to the suburbs, leaving poorer Jews behind.

In 1967 and 1968, blacks rioted in over 150 cities in the United States. Their growing militancy, a response to decades of slum housing in congested ghettos, low-paying jobs and unemployment, included unprecedented expressions of overt anti-Semitism.[1]

Government officials hoped to solve the problem by giving blacks and Puerto Ricans preference in college admissions and in municipal employment, including teaching jobs in the public schools. This policy amounted to discrimination against Jews, whose advancement was based on merit.[2]

The members of our synagogue discussed the situation extensively. In May 1968, Meir, Bert Zweibon and Morty Dolinsky decided to do more than talk: They formed an organization to protect Jews against violence and discrimination.

As *Jewish Press* editor Arnold Fine related, "Meir came into the *Jewish Press* one day and asked, 'Could one of the linotype guys set some type for me?'"[3]

A few days later, on May 24, 1968, an ad appeared in the *Jewish Press*:

We Are Talking of
JEWISH SURVIVAL!

Anti-Semitism is exploding in the United States.

Revolutionary leftist groups – hostile to Israel and Jewishness – are capturing young people's minds and destroying law and order.

Right-wing extremism is growing at an alarming rate.

Anti-Semitic Black racists are battling for control of cities.

America is being divided and the democratic fabric ripped apart.

Your child or loved one is a target.

Jews in America and all democratic-loving people face the gravest dangers.

Only an informed and active public can take proper steps to combat this.

ARE YOU WILLING TO STAND UP FOR
DEMOCRACY AND JEWISH SURVIVAL?

JOIN AND SUPPORT THE JEWISH DEFENSE CORPS

DOING THIS YOU WILL:

Receive classified monthly briefings on events within the extremist world.

Be invited to attend regular closed meetings at which you will be briefed on and discuss these problems with experts in the field.

Participate eventually in concrete countermeasures.

Receive invitations for your children to attend meetings where they will receive warning briefings on dangerous groups in their schools and areas.

ABOVE ALL –

You will help us infiltrate and expose extremist groups,

provide speakers on campuses and publish informative material.

Join now! We are talking of Jewish Survival. Show this to your friends.[4]

Ads in the *Jewish Press* reached a wide public. Its circulation was on the rise, with advertising keeping pace. With a readership of 136,000 in 1968,[5] the popularity of the paper was to be an important factor in the Jewish Defense League's success. Through the *Jewish Press*, Meir's ideas reached many people. He used news stories as well as his column to inform readers of JDL activities.

Meir presided over the first meeting of the new organization on Tuesday evening, June 18, the day before his trip to Washington to testify on Soviet Jewry. People who had responded to the ad in the *Jewish Press* received invitations to "an information and briefing meeting of the Jewish Defense League (Corps)."

Shortly before this meeting, the group had been renamed the Jewish Defense League. As Meir explained in all sincerity to a reporter from the *Newark Star Ledger*, "We feel it would be wise to change 'Corps' to 'League.' 'Corps' might be construed as being too militant and we are totally dedicated to legal means."[6]

On July 30, Bert Zweibon, an attorney, filed a Certificate of Incorporation for the JDL. The organization's declared purpose: "To combat anti-Semitism in the public and private sectors of life in the United States of America...." The officers were Meir Kahane, Morton Dolinsky, and Bertram Zweibon (in that order), all of Laurelton. Meir was national director and Zweibon was "general counsel." [7] Dolinsky moved to Israel soon afterward and took no active part in the group.

Black Anti-Semitism

The JDL's first demonstration took place August 5, 1968. It protested the appointment of John F. Hatchett as director of the Afro-American Student Center at New York University (NYU). Hatchett had been fired from the New York City school system for taking children on an unauthorized trip to see a white-hating play.[8] And the *New York Times*[*] had quoted him as saying, "Richard M. Nixon, Vice President Humphrey and Albert Shanker are all racist bastards...."[9] An example of Hatchett's virulent writing against Jewish teachers appeared in the November 1967 issue of the *African-American Teachers Forum*: "Jews dominate the educational bureaucracy of the New York Public School system.... [This] phenomenon spells death for the minds and souls of our black children."[10]

Hatchett's article was condemned as "racist" and "anti-Semitic" by the Synagogue Council of America and other Jewish organizations a month after the JDL demonstration, and only in January 1969 did the American Jewish Congress issue a press release that stated in part: "An editorial in the *African-American Teachers Forum* charging Jews with responsibility for 'stifling' the education of black children [is] a vicious piece of racism.... [Publication of] the malign ignorance of John F. Hatchett is an obvious and calculated attempt to stoke the fires of racial hatred and religious tension that are already burning in our city...."[11]

The *Newark Star Ledger* reported on the JDL demonstration: "Meir Kahane led some 15 protesters yesterday in Washington Square Park [opposite NYU].... The [JDL] members, appearing much older than the usual Greenwich Village protesters, chanted: 'No Nazis at NYU, Jewish rights are precious too.'"[12]

Most of the early JDLers were Meir's age (36) or older. Among them were merchants whose stores in "ghetto" areas were being robbed by blacks. There

---

[*] The *New York Times* is considered the official and authoritative reference for modern events. See: http://en.wikipedia.org/wiki/The_New_York_Times

were also many teachers whose jobs were threatened by school decentralization programs. Decentralization, which would give local school boards hiring and firing privileges, was aimed at appeasing black militants. Many teachers had also suffered physical and verbal anti-Semitic abuse by blacks.

The *Star Ledger* continued:

> Despite heckling from students in the Square, Kahane and his group continued their protest for nearly an hour before quietly breaking up and leaving.
>
> Kahane intends to pursue his protest in other directions. "We are asking NYU alumni to stop contributing to the school. And we've written to the government to see what steps can be taken to cut off federal funds.
>
> "We formed basically to do the job which the Anti-Defamation League should do but doesn't."
>
> Kahane feels that anti-Semitism and extremism of the Right and Left are increasing in this country and are a threat to American Jews. "There is a need for law and order," Kahane said, "otherwise, democracy has no future."[13]

Meir blamed New York City's problems largely on Mayor John V. Lindsay. When the *Jewish Press* printing plant was firebombed early one Tuesday morning in July, the paper noted: "The Coney Island area has been swept by sporadic rioting and looting since last Friday.... Mayor Lindsay has tied the hands of the police."[14] Since April, Meir's articles in the *Jewish Press* had charged that the mayor was to blame for the city's crime, racial division, and rioting. In October, citing crime statistics, Meir wrote:

> John Lindsay is one of those who attempts to deprecate the cry of an anguished citizenry for law and order.... But no amount of demagoguery ... can conceal the fact that crime and terror have taken control of the streets.
>
> In June, reported robberies showed a 70% increase over the corresponding 1967 figure. In the first five months of the year, police department figures showed ... every ten hours one could expect one murder, two rapes, 30 assaults, 54 robberies, 32 car thefts, 120 burglaries and 150 thefts. Total crime soared an astonishing 25.4% over 1967....
>
> But we need no figures, we need only ask the merchants ... as more and more stores close as robberies and assaults become part of the normal scene.... We need only ask the children who are robbed as they walk to school....
>
> When the Afro-American Teachers allowed Hatchett to write his Streicher-like* article, [Lindsay] never opened his mouth against Hatchett.... He never demanded they be expelled from our schools. Never has he attacked Herman Ferguson, the Black Hitler who will be teaching in a New York City school and will be principal of an Ocean Hill–Brownsville school as soon as

---

* Julius Streicher was a prominent Nazi in Germany in the 1930's. He edited *Der Stuermer*, a daily whose anti-Semitic propaganda incited the German population against the Jews.

he escapes the annoyance of a conviction for a conspiracy to murder.... Lindsay
has kept silent.... His silence has meant an assent to their obscenities...

In July, days and nights of rioting took place on the Lower East Side of
Manhattan with residents throwing bricks, bottles and trash cans at Tactical
Police. A week earlier, Coney Island was the target of four nights of rioting and
looting. Policemen were beaten and Molotov cocktails were thrown. On July
20, youth went on a firebombing spree in the Morrisania section of the Bronx.

[The same day], 500 youth ... attacked people and smashed cars at City
Hall....

Following the assassination of Dr. Martin Luther King, Jr., [on April 4,
1968] hundreds of stores [were] sacked or vandalized in Harlem, and dozens
in Brooklyn's Bedford Stuyvesant section.... Lindsay worked desperately and
successfully to kill all news of the true extent of the riot....[15]

Meir was not alone in criticizing the mayor. In October, at Brooklyn's East
Midwood Jewish Center, other Jewish leaders voiced dissatisfaction. A study by
Frederick Siegel supports Meir's view. It found that during Lindsay's tenure as
mayor, robberies in New York City increased fivefold between 1962 and 1967
and then doubled between 1967 and 1972. Siegel ascribes Lindsay's support of
the "rising tide of black radicalism that he embraced without understanding" to
narrow political motives. "Even after a series of citywide teacher strikes," writes
Siegel, "Lindsay refused to enforce the law, so it was left for the state education
commissioner to depose [black racist school principal Rhody] McCoy."[16]

As early as March, Meir's four-part *Racism and Subversion in New York City*
series in the *Jewish Press* had documented black anti-Semitism in the schools.[17]
In May he wrote about school decentralization:

Eventually a decentralization plan will pass and create a number of autonomous, independent school boards. They will have the power to fire those teachers they see fit to dismiss (and let no one be fooled by vague promises of due
process) and they will have complete power to hire those teachers they so
desire...

What will happen is that accused Communist Black Nationalist Herman Ferguson ... will become principal of Brownsville Intermediate School 55 and
begin teaching his "Black survival curriculum" that stressed a pledge of allegiance to the red, black and green flag of Black Nationalism. The pledge would
be from LeRoi Jones, anti-Semite and racist, who [wrote]: "Look at the Liberal
spokesman for the Jews clutch his throat and puke himself to eternity....
Another bad poem cracking steel knuckles in a Jew-lady's mouth..."

What will happen is that white teachers will be gradually eliminated from
Black areas almost entirely and hiring and firing will be based purely on race
rather than merit.

... In the past weeks the maddest scenes in the mad New York school farce have been played. The Brownsville area governing board, proposed fiefdom of Herman Ferguson, in complete illegality, suddenly fired 19 teachers and administrators.... The reason was clear. The teachers were almost all white....

Lindsay, the *New York Times* [editorial] and all the other liberal lemmings hysterically urged capitulation to Black racism....[18]

In June, hate sheets threatening physical violence against white teachers were distributed in many schools. Meir quoted the texts of several in his feature article, "Racist Leaflets in N.Y. Schools Warn White Teachers to Leave."[19]

The teachers union called three strikes between September and November to protest the unjustified firing of 19 white teachers. The city's 55,000 teachers and 1.1 million pupils stayed at home for 36 days. After the strike, to protest the longer school day imposed to make up time lost, black high school students rampaged through schools and subways for four days. Teachers and policemen were injured and some 132 arrests were made.[20]

The JDL Manifesto

An overview of the Jewish Defense League's approach to these and other problems is contained in *A Manifesto*, a four-page flyer bearing the league's first logo: the letters JEDEL imposed on a Star of David within a shield.

The *Manifesto* typifies Meir's early rhetoric:

America has been good to the Jew and the Jew has been good to America. A land founded on the principles of democracy and freedom has given unprecedented opportunities to a people devoted to those ideals....

The dream that is America, that saw the eager eyes of millions in the Old World turn to it, is in immense danger today, and all the citizens of these United States face the consequences of the collapse of that dream....

America finds itself suddenly threatened by the clear and present dangerous alliance of political extremism and racist militancy....

Crime in the streets spills brazenly into the homes.... Civil disorder, contempt for police authority, denial of responsibility.... All this is aided and abetted by foolish groups who rationalize the tragedy and shortsighted politicians who give aid and comfort to it by pronouncements of surrender to criminality....

The Black Nazi Front consigns all whites to the depths but the Jew has a special role; he is a special devil ... the Jewish teacher, the Jewish merchant, the Jewish landlord are the recipients of special vituperation....

The *Manifesto* defines the Jewish Defense League, initially shortened to JEDEL:

JEDEL is NOT a racist organization. JEDEL is neither Right nor Left in its philosophy. JEDEL rejects all hate and illegality....

JEDEL works to fight the revolutionary Left – so hostile to Jewish continuity and the State of Israel....

JEDEL combats the cancer of Right Fascism which would plunge the country into a repetition of the Nazi nightmare and the Jew into the gas chambers.

JEDEL stands up to the Black Nazi whose hatred of the white man is compounded by anti-Semitism.

JEDEL believes firmly in law and order ... [and] backs the police forces....

JEDEL has as its special project the youth of this country – Jewish youth in particular....

JEDEL will bring to them the facts and truths of the horrors such groups would impose on them.

How does JEDEL propose to work?

JEDEL will bridge the information gap that keeps the public ignorant of the true extent of the extremist danger by speaking at every synagogue ... and public gathering place.

JEDEL will speak on every university and college campus as well as at high schools to reach the young before they are ensnared by the extremists.

JEDEL will work actively in the courts to strike down all discrimination....

JEDEL will work to defeat politicians who bow to extremists....

JEDEL will demonstrate with legal militancy, with fervor and passion, so that the government shall see that the voices of law and order are powerful and meaningful....

JEDEL will help to establish legal, responsible neighborhood groups where crime is rampant and where the police have been unable to assure the citizen's safety....

This is JEDEL. It is an idea whose time has come. Shouldn't you be part of it? Remember, we are talking of the future of America. Remember, we are talking of Jewish survival.[21]

The motto "Remember, we are speaking of Jewish survival" was featured on JDL's office stationery, along with the biblical verse, "A time to keep silent and a time to speak up" (*Ecclesiastes* 3:7).

Many of the ideas in the *Manifesto* recur in the 14-page booklet *The Jewish Defense League: Aims and Purposes*, also published during its first year. The cover of *Aims and Purposes* features a picture of a child raising his hands at German gunpoint, captioned NEVER AGAIN! The dedication page states:

DEDICATED TO

THE SIX MILLION

WITH OUR PLEDGE:

NEVER AGAIN!

Allan Mallenbaum, the JDL's first administrative director, takes credit for the slogan "Never Again!" which became the JDL's rallying cry.[22] Meir explained:

"Never Again was never meant to declare that a Holocaust would never occur again. That is an absurd proposition to state, for so long as one gentile lives opposite one Jew, the possibility of a Holocaust remains.... [It meant] that as long as anyone attempted to repeat that Holocaust, never again would there be that same lack of reaction, that same indifference, that same fear."[23] In a short introduction to *Aims and Purposes*, Meir wrote:

> The appearance of the Jewish Defense League on the American scene has brought forth a remarkable reaction. In the brief period of its existence, JDL has caused immense controversy.... There are those who idolize it; there are those who fear it – few ignore it. The Jewish Establishment has – almost unanimously – decried it, and the campaign of slander and libel these groups have mounted against JDL is reminiscent of similar campaigns against other heroic groups.
>
> In the belief that an informed public will rally around the cause of JDL, we have published this booklet to clearly state the ideology of the fastest growing Jewish organization in America. The answers given here will go far to dispel the crude and malicious attacks upon the Jewish Defense League.[24]

Like the *Manifesto*, this booklet did not mention the plight of Soviet Jewry, which later became one of the JDL's main issues.

The Jewish Defense League was gaining members at an unprecedented rate and was gradually becoming financially stable. Eventually, it began to demand all Meir's time and by June 1969 was paying him a salary. But meanwhile, our personal finances were shaky, with Meir's *Jewish Press* position only part-time. In March, Meir wrote to the director of the National Conference of Synagogue Youth, Rabbi Pinchas Stolper, his former classmate, seeking a job as a youth leader: "... Because of a complete freeze of government contracts (due to the [Vietnam] war) ... I am now in New York almost permanently and I very much need a boost in my income."[25]

However, NCSY had no openings for him. For a while, he drove a taxi. He enjoyed playing the role of the traditionally talkative New York cabby, telling me about his conversations with passengers. Then, in the fall of 1968, he took on two positions – as a yeshiva high school teacher and as a synagogue rabbi.

Chapter 13

Teacher and Rabbi
(September 1968–June 1969)

MEIR TOOK ON two new jobs in the fall of 1968, both in Jamaica, only a few miles from Laurelton. He taught at the Yeshiva High School of Queens and was rabbi of the Traditional Synagogue of Rochdale Village.

Yeshiva High School of Queens

At the Yeshiva High School of Queens (YHSQ), Meir taught Jewish philosophy in the boys' school and Jewish law in the girls'. Susan Friedman recalled:

> Rabbi Kahane was an extraordinarily charismatic teacher. I still remember some of his stories and anecdotes. I recall that he told stories in conjunction with the lessons. Two stories in particular stand out.
>
> One was about the purchase of a car that was needed to go to Canada [for a Bnei Akiva convention] and back. Meir only had money for an old, beat-up car. The person selling the car claimed it could go to Canada and back many times. Unfortunately, I no longer recollect much else about the car. I just know that the class was rolling with laughter as the anecdote was told.
>
> The other story was about how you proposed to Meir. You were someplace where you were served bad coffee. You said that when you and Meir married you would serve better coffee – or something to that effect. Again my memory fails me when it comes to further details. I just know that Meir held our attention as a class and part of his technique was a superb ability to tell mesmerizing stories.
>
> He also spoke very movingly about the importance of Jews' feeling each other's pain and as parts of a whole. It is now over 25 years since I graduated high school. I can still remember vividly how he told us that the plight of the Soviet Jew and of the Syrian Jew is our plight. The love of Eretz Yisrael was another of his recurrent themes. A year or two later I heard Meir speak at Queens College. He was trying to promote aliya [immigration to Israel]. He

told us about your parents' aliya and of the feeling of joy and wonder expressed
by his father-in-law at being able to walk around on the hills of Yerushalayim.

Susan recalled Meir's increasing involvement with the Jewish Defense
League.

> When Meir ... was making the newspapers on a regular basis, ... he dropped
> all classes except for my class, the seniors. He taught us until the end of the
> fall semester, and in February 1969 a different teacher was hired and we lost
> our by now famous teacher.[1]

Netty Gross said, "He was a great teacher; held the kids' rapt attention. He
was interested in teaching, and less in details. He gave everyone A's. This was
an unusual experience for these kids, whose motivation wasn't to learn necessarily but to get high grades."

Gross recalled that Meir spoke at several YHSQ assemblies held at the boys'
school, a few blocks away from the girls'. Because of the Jewish Defense League,
when she thinks of Meir she thinks of the danger of travel in that neighborhood.
Most of the residents were black, and muggings of whites were common. She and
other girls traveled to school by subway, and she remembered how a classmate
was viciously attacked.[2]

Meir stood out among the teachers at YHSQ, said Stuart Cohen.

> He told the class, "If you're going to the ... movies, take off your yarmulke
> [skullcap]." This was a very unique way of teaching the idea that you are
> looked at as a representative of Klal Yisrael [the Jewish people] by non-Jews
> when you wear a yarmulke.
>
> His classes were thought-provoking and different. He would tell the stu-
> dents, "If you feel that you can't behave and contribute ... go to the library..."
> He said if you get caught in the library and are asked why you are there during
> class, he would cover for you. It made him stand out in what was then a school
> with a very cold and *yekish* [pedantic] attitude toward its students.
>
> He was able to connect with students in the way that good teachers can. My
> first contact with JDL was hearing him speak at a shul in Queens and signing
> up for membership....[3]

Larry Dub was in Meir's ninth-grade class: "In class one day, one of the boys
mentioned the JDL, but Rabbi Kahane said, 'Today we're learning Jewish philosophy!' Then he told us about the Maccabees, who believed you solved problems
by destroying your enemies, not dialoging with them."[4] Jerry Ganger recalled that
Meir would talk about JDL at the end of class, urging students to come to demonstrations.[5]

Joel Silber vividly remembered a heated discussion about charity. When Meir
told the boys that according to Jewish law a person may not donate more than 20

percent of his income, they argued that one should be allowed to give more than that if he wants to. Clearly, Meir had succeeded in conveying the importance and beauty of giving charity.[6]

The Traditional Synagogue of Rochdale Village

Since Meir had only about twelve teaching hours a week[7] and was not yet receiving a salary from the JDL, our income still needed a supplement. Despite his unfortunate experience as a rabbi in Howard Beach, he took the pulpit at the Traditional Synagogue of Rochdale Village.[8]

Rochdale Village was a cooperative housing project comprising 20 high-rise apartment buildings, with 294 families in each, widely spaced over what had once been the Jamaica Race Track. It was built in 1963 by a consortium of the Amalgamated Clothing Workers and other labor unions, whose members were mostly Jewish.[9] It was pure coincidence that Meir had saluted the Rochdale Village synagogue in his column back in 1965:

> There was a groundbreaking ceremony in Queens recently…. What makes this news is that the new synagogue is a traditional one, in a brand-new development, in an area where there are no other synagogues. We salute the residents of Rochdale Village on their choice of a traditional synagogue in the face of what surely must have been tremendous pressure to do otherwise.[10]

Synagogue president Ralph Weinstein recalled:

> Our temporary synagogue had burnt down, and a local politician, Eddie Abramson, let us use his storefront on New York Boulevard for Sabbath services and for bar mitzvahs. (Our permanent building was finished in November 1968.) Every Friday morning a group of us would move the Aron Kodesh [ark of Torah scrolls] from a Rochdale Village apartment to the store, setting up the chairs for [the] Sabbath. Every Sunday morning we moved it back to Rochdale. I remember the first Sabbath the Rabbi came to us, he walked from Laurelton – over three miles. When the services were over, at least a dozen youngsters walked him back home.[11]

The walk from our home in Laurelton to Rochdale Village took just under an hour. At first Meir walked both ways every Shabbat morning, but within about a month we moved into a fifth floor apartment there. Our apartment was owned by the synagogue and we paid the co-op's monthly management fee of $180.35 plus $7 for parking.[12] Living on the fifth floor had its drawbacks, especially on Shabbat when we did not use the elevator, but the apartment was sunny and comfortable. There were three bedrooms and we created a small study for Meir in the living room by using his bookcases as a room divider. The children continued in the same schools and traveled on the same school bus as their Laurelton friends, but the ride was now longer.

In January 1969, Baruch invited his Laurelton friends to our new home for his tenth birthday party. An unusually heavy snowstorm during the party made travel impossible, and the eight young birthday guests became overnight guests. Somehow I found them all pajamas, blankets, and beds. (I am still quite proud of my resourcefulness.) In the morning, two fathers trudged through the waist-high snowdrifts to escort the boys home. It was a birthday party to remember! It was a memorable snowstorm for Meir too. He was speaking that evening at a synagogue in the Bronx and was marooned because of the snow. He spent the night at the home of Joy and Alfred Amsel, who lived near the synagogue.[13]

After the synagogue's Selection Committee chose Meir as rabbi, the membership met October 3, 1968, to ratify their choice. During the meeting, Meir spoke briefly on – not surprisingly – Jewish education. The recording secretary noted some of his points: "A Talmud Torah [afternoon school] is the most important part of the synagogue. A high school for teenagers is very important. Rabbi Kahane stated that Jerusalem was destroyed because of lack of learning Torah. Adult education is also very important. Many Jews age thirty, forty and older are greatly in need of a basic Hebrew education."[14]

Meir signed a one-year contract. The 1969/70 synagogue budget lists his salary as $11,000 annually.[15] Weinstein wrote: "We were a new congregation in a lower middle-class community. We could not afford to pay a high salary. Rabbi [Irving] Halberstam of Brooklyn had recommended Rabbi Kahane. When I mentioned to [Rabbi Kahane] that we could not pay him a salary commensurate with his experience, he said that was not important as he was writing for the *Jewish Press* also."[16] In fact, Meir considered himself very lucky to find an Orthodox rabbinical position in New York City. He could continue to lead the JDL, and Rochdale Village was only half an hour's drive to the *Jewish Press* offices, to our children's schools, and to our parents.

The synagogue had a membership of about 300 families.[17] The *Messenger*, the synagogue bulletin, ran Meir's tongue-in-cheek account of his efforts to recruit new members.

> [One was the] neighbor who would join in the twinkling of an eye but for the crass materialism of the synagogue, its pecuniary gall, its base preoccupation with dues, tickets and donations.
>
> "Look, Rabbi, I simply can't afford luxuries like a synagogue right now what with all the obligations I have, like the car payments and Judy's guitar lessons and the new furniture and the weekly poker game with the boys – you know, Rabbi, charity's gotta begin at home and I'm tired of always being asked by all those people who probably pocket half the money anyway, and it was nice

meeting you anyhow and don't be a stranger because I'm a Jew right down to my toes, so anytime you people need something stop by but please no money, well, goodnight..."

Other neighbors were like this one:

"Rabbi, on my honor, the wife and I have been meaning to join a synagogue since we moved in three years ago, but we just can't get settled. Look, give us a little more time to get organized, get things out of the way, let the boy start school, the girl [get] married, my business straighten out, [let me] ease myself gently out of some of my other organizations; just a little while to get settled and we'll join. That's a promise; someday. Goodnight, it was an honor to meet you..."[18]

The *Messenger* indicates some of Meir's educational activities:

The Hebrew High School (boys and girls, age[s] 13-16 years old) meets on Tuesday nights and Sunday mornings for prayers, discussions and breakfast, from 9 to 11 A.M....

Adult education courses are being held at our Synagogue every Monday evening beginning at 8 P.M. under the leadership of our rabbi, Meir Kahane. Join Now!...

At the March 4th Sisterhood meeting Rabbi Kahane gave a stimulating talk about Customs and Preparations for Passover....

Starting on Sunday March 9, 1969 Rabbi Meir Kahane will be available for Mechiras Chometz [Sale of Leaven before Passover] on Sunday morning at the Synagogue. For afternoons and evenings during the week, phone the Synagogue at 525-1451.[19]

The handwritten minutes of the November 26, 1968, synagogue meeting offer a more informal description that sheds light on Meir's educational aims.

The Talmud Torah [afternoon school] has between 110 and 120 children. The Rabbi stated that all children will be taught to read the *siddur* [prayer book]. All children are obligated to attend Junior Congregation services.

The President announced that Sabbath services of the congregation are well attended. About 200 people attend both *minyans*, prayer groups. The High School meets every Sunday morning. Members and parents are invited to observe the teaching.

As always, Meir stressed the importance of a Jewish education for girls.

Our first *Oneg Shabbat* [Sabbath party] will begin on December 13th. During the course of the *Oneg Shabbat* there will be an opportunity for Bas Mitzvahs to be held.* Rabbi explained that a Hebrew education for girls is as important as an education for boys.

---

* Meir innovated this way of celebrating bat mitzvahs within the requirements of Jewish law.

Adults who never had an opportunity to learn to read Hebrew could now do so.

> An adult education class will be held each Monday night to teach Hebrew reading. It will also teach siddur reading, and we will learn why we say certain prayers and their meanings.
>
> Rabbi has excellent communication with young people. Sabbath clubs will be set up for children ages 7-10 and 10-13. Rabbi usually invites children to his home to learn the meaning of the Sabbath.[20]

As he had in Howard Beach, Meir invited children to our home on Shabbat. Among them were the children of Ralph Weinstein, who recalled:

> ... I was then in my forties. The Rabbi instilled in me a love of Israel, love of Yiddishkeit [Judaism], Jewish pride and identity. What he instilled in me and my late wife Claire we passed on to our children, who in turn have passed on to my grandchildren.
>
> With the young people in our Synagogue he worked to instill Jewish pride and identity, becoming Shomer Shabbat [Sabbath-observant], observing Kashruth, and encouraging them to pursue their Jewish education. In spite of his busy schedule (he was then starting up the JDL), he always had time for our young people. I remember, he would play basketball with them. The Rabbi was an amazing man – a man for all seasons – a renaissance man who could recite a portion of Gemara as easily as reciting the batting averages of the New York Yankees.[21]

When Meir became the rabbi of the Traditional Synagogue, the Jewish Defense League was only a few months old. By the time he was officially installed as rabbi at a ceremony on January 26, 1969, several JDL demonstrations had made the news. Speakers at the installation dinner referred to him as the "well-known writer and leader."[22] During Meir's tenure at the Traditional Synagogue, the JDL gained momentum as anti-Semitic violence rose alarmingly.

Chapter 14

The Jewish Defense League Responds (November 1968-June 1969)

Arson and Vandalism

TYPICAL OF THE upsurge in anti-Semitic incidents in 1968, was this one, reported in the *Jewish Press*: "A group broke into Public School 288 in the Coney Island section of Brooklyn and refused to leave.... Assistant Principal Arthur Finkelstein was warned that as a 'dirty Jewish pig' he was 'going to be sent home in a pine box.'"[1] In one week alone, the *New York Times* carried five reports on anti-Semitic incidents:

- November 25: Bronx synagogue fire.
- November 26: Suspicious fire at a Bronx Hebrew school.
- November 27: Ten synagogues vandalized in the past three months.
- November 28: Yeshiva of Eastern Parkway in Brooklyn destroyed by fire.
- November 29: Young Israel synagogue in Jackson Heights burglarized.[2]

Halloween Eve, on October 31, was traditionally a time for mischief – and sometimes for anti-Semitic acts. That year, teens firebombed Yeshiva Torah Vodaath in Brooklyn. The American Jewish Congress reacted with a press release requesting a police probe. But members of the Jewish Defense League had prepared for Halloween Eve. They did not issue a press release; they acted. The *Jewish Press* reported:

> Thirty-five members of the Jewish Defense League staked out on Halloween night prevented a gang of vandals from repeating last year's desecration of the Montefiore Cemetery in Queens....
>
> First they informed the police of their intention. The leader, Hy Bieber, said, "We were not there to deliberately look for trouble. This is not the purpose of our organization. We were merely determined to prevent a repetition of last

year's disgrace when police were unable to prevent hoodlums from desecrating a Jewish cemetery."

The group declared that as it waited, close to 150 youths, many carrying wine bottles, approached and stopped when they saw the Jewish Defense group. "We were polite but firm," said Mr. Bieber. "We made it very clear that there would not be one tombstone overturned. They appeared puzzled, and hung around for a while, but they left quietly."[3]

This article is unsigned, but it was surely written by Meir. It is an example of how he used the *Jewish Press* to publicize the JDL. During this period, Meir wrote on a variety of subjects: preparations for Rosh Hashana in the Israeli army, the Jewish right to Judea and Samaria, the financial sacrifices made by rabbinical students' wives, and the stereotype that all slumlords are Jewish.[4]

His articles in September and October, "Delaware Police Find Army of Racist Militant Weapons" and "Arab Students Hail Black Militants," were a warning that extremist groups posed a serious threat to American Jews. In November, he launched a new weekly column, *Spotlight on Extremism*, detailing the activities and literature of right- and left-wing extremists. Whether they were white supremacists, blacks, or Trotskyites, they all hated Jews and Israel.[5]

Through his *Jewish Press* articles, Meir gained prominence and was invited to speak to many groups about the JDL. An October 1968 photograph shows him at the rostrum of the Young Israel of Hillcrest, looking very young at age 36, wearing a dark suit and tie. Murray Schneider recalled, "I wrote to Meir at the *Jewish Press,* inviting him to speak at my synagogue in the Bronx. He arrived by subway. He was just what the audience needed." On February 23, 1969, he was one of the speakers at a symposium on "Responses to Current Expressions of Anti-Semitism" held at the Rochdale Village Community Center.[6] Meir's speaking engagements were a major source of JDL funds.

Anti-Semitism in the Public Schools

At the beginning of 1969, the JDL held several demonstrations. The first was a protest against Leslie Campbell, a black anti-Semitic teacher. On December 26, 1968, on the Julius Lester radio program on WBAI-FM, Campbell read a poem that began:

> *Hey, Jew-boy, with that yarmulke on your head,*
> *Pale-faced Jew boy – I wish you were dead.*[7]

The teachers union filed a complaint to the Federal Communications Commission against the radio station and a member of the Board of Education called for Campbell's dismissal, but Meir protested more vigorously. When Campbell held a rally at Public School 30 in Rochdale Village on January 16, JDL members came to picket. They distributed a flyer that presented Campbell's "unbelievably racist record." For example, in September 1968 Campbell spoke to a group of two hundred black children in their school cafeteria about white teachers: "These teachers are your enemies. You are not to listen to them.... You are not to talk to them. When the police leave, we will get them." In November 1968, he wrote the lead article in the *African-American Teachers Forum*, referring to whites as devils: "All devils must go ... put the devils out of our schools."[8]

Sy Polsky came to the demonstration because he had read about Meir and thought he made sense. Polsky recalled that they heckled Campbell during his speech, risking a physical confrontation with his supporters.[9] Ralph Weinstein described the scene: "Campbell was well over six feet tall with a huge Afro hairdo, dressed in a dashiki. Two of his henchmen stood on the auditorium stage while he proclaimed that his people were going to take over the school system."[10]

The JDL protest made the front page of the *Long Island Press*. Meir, Murray Schneider, and others were pictured holding placards saying: "The Jewish Defense League Fights Anti-Semitism," "Afro-American Racist Teachers Must Go!" and "Schwerner and Goodman* Didn't Die For This."[11]

Bertram Zweibon, the attorney who co-founded the JDL, attacked Campbell through the courts. On January 22, he was granted a show-cause order directing the Board of Education to prove why Campbell, as well as Albert Vann, another anti-Semitic teacher, should not be dismissed. However, two days later, a higher court reversed the order.[12]

On January 23, Meir and Zweibon were invited by City Councilman Julius Moskowitz to take part in a press conference to protest the inflammatory anti-Semitic statements made by Leslie Campbell and Albert Vann. The next day a report on the press conference, with a photo of Meir, appeared on page three of the *Daily News,* the most widely read newspaper in New York City.[13]

Soon afterwards, another guest on Julius Lester's WBAI radio program declared, "Hitler didn't make enough lampshades."** Meir immediately sent an urgent letter to the JDL membership:

> We are planning to demand that WBAI-FM immediately cancel the Lester show.... Bring down every neighbor, relative and friend you have. Get on the phones now and call.... Bring down entire crowds of people.... We will meet [at the station, 30 East 39th Street] at 1 P.M. sharp. Please be there with everyone you can dig up.[14]

---

* Michael Schwerner and Andrew Goodman, young Jewish activists for black civil rights, were murdered by white supremacists in Mississippi on June 21, 1964. The JDL favored civil rights for blacks and opposed only black anti-Semites.

** The skin of Jews murdered in the Nazi death camps was used to make lampshades. See: http://www.scrapbookpages.com/dachauscrapbook/DachauTrials/IlseKoch2.html

On January 30, over 200 Jewish Defense League supporters picketed WBAI, while proponents of Julius Lester's "freedom of expression" marched across the street. The *Daily News* reported:

> At least five persons were taken into custody and 75 cops were called to the scene when the rival picket groups clashed. Police eventually closed [the street] to traffic....[15]

Polsky recalled: "It was a blustery January afternoon. Some of us even tried to enter the broadcasting station from the roof. The police intercepted us but no arrests were made."[16]

Meir titled his article on this episode "Freedom of Lampshades." He wrote:

> Two lines of demonstrators marched outside WBAI last week. One demanded that men be given the right to advocate the making of lampshades from Jews.... WBAI's right to incite to hate is linked with that of teachers to do the same.[17]

Meir continued writing about anti-Semitic black teachers and rioting students. His article, "The Face of Fascism," was about the take-over of Cornell University by rifle-toting militants:

> For 36 hours they broke the law while the lemmings who preside over the school ... allowed this incredible assault on democracy and society.... No concession is meaningful to [one who is] driven by self-hate and self-destruction to destroy all others with him.[18]

Anti-Semitism continued to spread. These incidents were reported in the *New York Times* in January 1969:

- January 3: Five small fires, apparently set by arsonist, cause damage to Manhattan Beach Jewish Center.

- January 4: Shaaray Tefila Synagogue in Far Rockaway destroyed by fire. Local Jewish Community Council president, Rabbi Rubin R. Dobin, cites series of anti-Semitic incidents, plans round-the-clock guard for section's 15 congregations. N.Y. Board of Rabbis' Gilbert Klaperman asks Mayor Lindsay to increase police surveillance, holding Manhattan Beach and Shaaray Tefila fires more than coincidence.

- January 7: Fire in Jewish Orthodox house of worship, Upper West Side of Manhattan. Employees report seeing two Negro teenagers running from building.

- January 21: Two suspicious fires at Magen David Congregation, Bensonhurst, Brooklyn.[19]

The reactions of public figures the same month underscored the gravity of the situation:

- January 5: New York State Human Rights Commissioner Robert J. Mangum has staff begin probe of 14 recent incidents of fire and vandalism at New York City Jewish institutions.

- January 7: American Jewish Congress executive Will Maslow scores U.S. Negro leaders for allegedly ignoring black anti-Semitism.

- January 17: Report to Mayor Lindsay says ... threats used by black extremists during last year's school decentralization dispute were aimed at Jews.

- January 21: American Jewish Congress Women's Division head Mrs. Elinor C. Guggenheimer denounces Lindsay's ineptness in handling racial tensions between Negroes and Jews.

- January 23: B'nai B'rith Anti-Defamation League issues a report on crisis-level anti-Semitism emanating from N.Y.C. school dispute.

- February 3: The B'nai B'rith Anti-Defamation League and New York Board of Rabbis call for lifting station WBAI's license to broadcast.

Jews fared no better in other U.S. cities:

- One Friday night in February 1969, three blacks – one with a gun – walked into a Philadephia synagogue and demanded money from the congregants, most in their 60s and 70s. Orthodox Jews do not carry money on the Sabbath, so the trio beat up Hymie Oppenheim and Nathan Lazarowitz.[20]

- In June, Jewish shopkeepers in New Orleans were boycotted. They were rumored to be drugging and kidnapping women customers to sell them into white slavery.[21]

- In July, an acid bomb was thrown at Rabbi Gerald D. Zelermeyer after his synagogue in Boston's Mattapan section refused to sell its property to blacks. Rabbi Zelermeyer said blockbusters were trying to panic Jews into fleeing the neighborhood.[22]

- In August, gravestones were toppled at the Ansonia-Derby Hebrew Cemetery in Hartford, Connecticut.[23]

Many JDL chapters were set up as a result of these and other incidents. Because the Jewish Establishment did not respond to their needs, people increasingly looked to the Jewish Defense League for solutions. According to a November JDL newsletter, there were chapters in Philadelphia, Cleveland, Boston, Chicago, Detroit, San Francisco, Los Angeles, and Montreal, totaling almost 7,000 members. The newsletter was summarized in an American Jewish Committee internal report on the Jewish Defense League labeled "Not for publication or distribution."[24] The Jewish Establishment was keeping a close watch on the JDL!

Meir's First Arrest

Meir was arrested for the first time on February 26, 1969, when he and other JDL members assembled at the main office of the New York City Board of Education to protest the continued employment of Leslie Campbell and Albert Vann. After they refused to leave the premises, Meir and eight others were arrested by the police.[25] The case was dismissed, but the arrest attracted media attention. An interview with Meir appeared in the *Manhattan Tribune*:

> Rabbi Kahane believes the city has lost its balance.
> Militants in the black community and the New Left, he says, are the only voices heard. The League's job, as Kahane sees it, is "to convince city officials that the pressure is not all from one side."
> And Rabbi Kahane is ready to print leaflets, shout at reporters, form a group of vigilantes, demonstrate in the streets – even start his own riot if he has to – to make a point.
> ... Dues are $10 a year and the absence of heavy financial backing is reflected in the three-room headquarters at 156 Fifth Avenue, south of 20th Street. The offices are furnished sparsely, white paint is peeling from the walls and high ceiling.
> ... The 36-year-old rabbi talked to [the reporter] after returning from Eastern District High School in Brooklyn. Some 200 rampaging students had succeeded in closing the school in an effort to force the transfer of the dean of boys, Dideon [sic] Goldberg.
> ... Members of the Jewish Defense League are taking judo and karate lessons ... [and] patrolling the streets of Brooklyn and other boroughs during peak crime hours. In cars equipped with two-way radios, the vigilante group is ready to answer emergency calls to the League's headquarters or to move in on muggings or other crimes that might be seen on patrol. Baseball bats and similar "legal" weapons are used, Rabbi Kahane said.[26]

Baseball Bats and Lead Pipes

The *Manhattan Tribune* profile was another step in publicizing the JDL. But what really put the League on the map was its response to black militant James Forman. Forman was going from church to church, demanding half a billion dollars as reparation for his people's suffering. On May 4, 1969, Forman disrupted a service at New York City's Riverside Episcopal Church to read his manifesto from the pulpit. His audacious behavior made headlines.[27]

A few days later, Manhattan's Reform Temple Emanu-El received a warning that Forman planned a "performance" during its Friday evening services on May 9. Some forty JDL members gathered outside the synagogue on Friday afternoon, armed with baseball bats.[28]

Sy Polsky recalled a JDL press release that said: "In the eyes of the non-Jew, Temple Emanu-El represents Judaism. It is a *chillul Hashem*, a desecration of G-d's name, to tolerate blackmail or any crime against Jews. Jews came here long after the black slaves were freed. Jews owe Forman nothing."[29]

Pictures of JDL activists armed with baseball bats and lead pipes appeared in the next day's newspapers. Even *Time* magazine ran a photo of them over a story about the JDL. Joe Alster notes that Forman never came: "He was afraid to show up when he heard we were there."[30] Sol Raffalow sent a letter of support to the *New York Times* that said, in part:

> The sight of those stalwart and courageous men standing guard in front of Temple Emanu-El on Fifth Avenue in Manhattan recently must have been a reassuring sight to many Jewish people of this city.... Had there been a German Jewish Defense League [during the Holocaust] we Jews would have won the admiration of the world instead of earning the contempt of [our] enemies as they slaughtered us mercilessly. The Jewish Defense League may not be all things to all men, but to me they represent strength – not weakness, courage – not cowardice....[31]

Meir capitalized on the Temple Emanu-El episode and the JDL's fearless image with an ad in the *New York Times* picturing six JDL youngsters holding numchucks (karate sticks).* The headline read: "IS THIS ANY WAY FOR A NICE JEWISH BOY TO BEHAVE?" The answer:

> Maybe. Maybe there are times when there is no other way to get across to the extremist that the Jew is not quite the patsy some think he is.... Maybe nice Jewish boys do not always get through to people who threaten to carry teachers out in pine boxes and to burn down merchants' stores.... Maybe – just maybe – nice people build their own road to Auschwitz.
>
> ... Nice Jewish boys – or any nice boys – should not be forced out of their jobs by hoodlums. Nice Jewish boys should not be victims of quota systems and reverse discrimination in schools. Nice Jewish boys should not be forced to pay a penny to extortionists for crimes they never committed. Nice Jewish boys should not be the victims of a do-nothing city, state or federal government....

At the bottom of the ad – signed, "Meir Kahane, National Director, and Bertram Zweibon, General Counsel" – were coupons to fill out and send in along with contributions and membership applications.[32]

---

* *Nunchaku*, or *numchucks*, are pairs of 12- to 14-inch hardwood sticks joined by a short length of rawhide, cord, or chain. They generate tremendous momentum when swung rapidly, and are now illegal in New York and other states. They are pictured at www.nunchaku.org.

Many people sent contributions, but the ad also sparked some negative reactions. In a report the very next day in the *Times*, the Jewish Establishment was said to have reacted with "a strong rebuke," while the Anti-Defamation League accused the JDL of "imitating the mindless tactics of racial hoodlums." At the same time, the *Times* report gave the JDL publicity. It identified Meir as the rabbi of a synagogue in Rochdale Village and noted that the JDL, which claimed a membership of 5,700, was making a major bid for new members.[33]

The ad inspired articles in Jewish newspapers all over the United States and even in Great Britain, where the *Jewish Chronicle* quoted Rabbi Wolf Kelman, executive vice president of the Conservative Rabbinical Assembly: "It behooves the main-line Jewish organizations to deal with the genuine anxiety that Jews feel in New York." The *Jewish Chronicle* quoted Zweibon, too:

> We are not vigilantes. We don't go out to apprehend anyone. We protect Jewish life and property. When someone attacks you, you fight back. That's the law. When someone comes to kill you, you have the right to defend yourself.[34]

The major Jewish organizations did not categorically reject black demands for Jewish reparations, and the extortion attempts multiplied. In St. Louis, blacks made demands at Yom Kippur services at three synagogues, threatening attacks unless payoffs were made. Black Muslim Muhammed [sic] Kenyatta targeted the Main Line Reform Temple of Wynnewood, Philadelphia – and was invited to speak there. At the urging of Rabbi Harold Novoseller, head of the Philadelphia JDL, eighty percent of the audience walked out.[35]

The JDL's response to the Jewish Establishment's criticism of its methods was succinctly phrased in a *New York Times* report: "The league regards its readiness to use force in certain situations as one of its virtues."[36]

Leaving Rochdale Village

The JDL was demanding more and more of Meir's time, and he had little to spare for his rabbinical duties in Rochdale Village. Yet he was so well liked that the board voted to hire an assistant rabbi and retain him as the rabbi on a part-time basis.[37] I was using the family car once or twice a week for shopping and other errands, but Bert Zweibon thought Meir needed a car at his disposal every day, so he gave me his old Buick. It was hard to start in cold weather, but I learned to open the hood and jiggle the butterfly in the carburetor to get it going.

The media discovered that the public was interested in interviews with Meir and stories about the Jewish Defense League. Meir's picture appeared in newspaper after newspaper, and he was soon recognized on the street. As his fame increased, many JDL members wanted him to have a bodyguard. Almost every day, the media reported senseless, vicious attacks against whites by blacks. Meir's supporters were concerned that many blacks perceived him as anti-black, although in every interview and lecture he insisted that he was not against blacks; he was only against anti-Semites. His supporters' concern was heightened by the fact that Rochdale Village where we lived was a mostly white enclave in a black neighborhood. Once, coming home from the Jamaica shopping area, I was the only white person in a long line of commuters waiting for a bus to Rochdale Village.

Hy Bieber, built like a wrestler, tried over and over again to persuade Meir to allow him to accompany him wherever he went. Once, Meir set up an evening meeting at our home with Bieber. Meir was late arriving and Bieber was worried and fretful. He calmed down only when Meir arrived home safely. Meir adamantly refused to have a bodyguard. He had complete trust that G-d would protect him in his efforts to help His people.[38]

However, the day came when we were indeed threatened by blacks. Almost all the news stories about Meir included the fact that he was a rabbi in Rochdale Village. It wasn't difficult to find out where he lived.

One Sunday afternoon in June while we were eating, there was a knock at the door. Baruch went to ask who it was. "We wanna speak to the Judge," he was told. I looked through the peephole and saw three tall black men. We talked a bit through the door. A neighbor later told me there were two others – one near the staircase and one near the elevator. The children looked out and saw two more waiting near a car. Meir wanted to talk to them face to face, but I was so terrified that I would not let him open the door. Eventually they left, but from that day on, until we moved to Brooklyn in August, JDL members slept in our house. In the morning, they accompanied the children in the elevator and waited with them until the bus to their day camp arrived. In the afternoon, they escorted them back home from the bus.

The next day, June 30, just before a board meeting at the synagogue, Meir asked President Max Kolker to come to our house. According to the minutes of that meeting, Kolker told the board: "Rabbi Kahane, with tears in his eyes, told me he must leave – he can't stay here – he is afraid for himself and his family. Rabbi Kahane is leaving us immediately."[39]

Shortly after that frightening visit, I removed the name "Kahane" from the brass frame on the door. Underneath was the name of the previous tenants, Mandel. From then on I used that name. When we moved to the Flatbush section of Brooklyn in August, we did not use an ordinary moving company. Our furniture was moved by JDL members, in a van owned by Ari Calderon, in order to keep our new address a secret. I even put the name "Mandel" on the door of our new apartment and ordered a phone line for "Abraham Mandel." Of course, the phone company wanted an employer to confirm that "Mandel" could pay his bills. The switchboard operator at the *Jewish Press* may have found my request odd, but she agreed to tell the phone company that the paper employed one Abraham Mandel.[40]

I was not sorry to move to Brooklyn, though it meant driving back and forth to Queens College to complete my college degree. Living near my parents meant they could baby-sit more easily when I had late classes. For Meir, living in Brooklyn meant a shorter commute to the JDL office in Manhattan. Within a few months, the children adjusted to the new neighborhood and their new schools. The most difficult adjustment in school was Baruch's. Meir had chosen Yeshivat Torat Emet for him because of its excellent reputation, despite the fact that they studied Bible and Talmud in Yiddish. Baruch had to learn a new language as well as keep up with the material covered in class. It took Baruch about six months to feel comfortable in Yiddish.

After the episode in Rochdale Village, our address in Brooklyn remained a closely guarded secret among JDL members. Only when I began writing this book did I discover that this secrecy had hindered the FBI's investigation of Meir.* It took several months until their agent discovered our address through the Semel grocery store in Borough Park, which often delivered to our home.[41]

---

* The FBI (Federal Bureau of Investigation) is the principal investigative arm of the U.S. Department of Justice. It investigates specific crimes assigned to it and provides other law enforcement agencies with cooperative services such as fingerprint identification, laboratory examination and police training. See: www.fbi.gov/aboutus/faqs/faqsone.htm.

Chapter 15

Camp Jedel (1969-1971)

Learning How to Fight Back

DURING THE SUMMERS of 1969 through 1971 our family spent weekends at the Jewish Defense League's Camp Jedel, in Woodbourne, New York. Meir led the singing and spoke on Torah topics at Shabbat meals and on Sunday he would lecture on Zionism, Jewish history and religion. Sunday night we would return to the city. During the week, the children attended day camp while I continued studying for my master's at Queens College. Meir drove to and from camp several times a week to give classes and informal talks.

Campers between the ages of fourteen and eighteen rose early for a regimen that included four hours of karate training a day; two hours of weapons training, including rifle practice; one hour of close-order drill; and four hours of classes in Jewish history and other subjects, including the history of anti-Semitism.[1] The campers discovered that Camp Jedel's main purpose was ideological. Samson Levine wrote:

> In the summer of 1969 I went to Camp Jedel solely for karate, which I loved.
>
> To be fully honest, I was also motivated by events of the Six Day War. There was a heightened awareness of politics and the Jewish place. I was just old enough to give blood, and I did. I grew up with the idea that Jewish kids were the patsies, victims, intellectuals, and generally ordinary people. The Six Day War changed that for me....
>
> During my time in Camp Jedel, I received massive amounts of indoctrination as well as karate. I remember getting up at six and davening [praying] and doing karate before breakfast. Then breakfast and lectures, followed by lunch and more lectures. Afterwards, more karate and dinner.... Then a campfire, where there were more lectures as well as sing-alongs with Palmach, Irgun and Betar songs.[2]

Another camper declared: "A person who only knows how to fight, but not how to talk, can only be considered a GOON!"[3] Jan Geliebter detailed the camp's daily routine:

> Karate, a crash course taught by experts, is divided into two sessions, both two hours each: one in the morning and the other in the afternoon. In two months, don't expect to become a black belt, but you learn enough to hold your own when you need it.
>
> At 9:30 the camp is separated into two groups; one is assigned to firearms training while the other is offered close order drill. At 11:00, the groups switch. One o'clock is … lunch.
>
> At 2:30 it's back to karate. From 4:30 until 6:00 free time or a lecture.… After supper, Mincha [afternoon] prayers are said, and the seminar follows the evening prayers.
>
> The seminars, actually the most important activities at JEDEL, usually cover such topics as JDL philosophy, Jewish heritage, extremism on the Right and Left, Zionist history and Soviet Jewry.
>
> I have gone to Camp Jedel both summers of its existence. [This was written in June 1971.] I am not a karate expert nor am I a sharpshooter. There is, however, one change which Camp Jedel has burned into me: I am damn proud to be a Jew.

Not all campers were observant. Geliebter wrote:

> Orthodox practices are optional; the Shabbat, however, must be observed by all.[4]

Karate teacher Marty Lewinter recalled, "Rabbi Kahane never said a bad word about those of us who were not observant. He welcomed all sincere volunteers, religious or not."[5]

Camp Jedel reflected Meir's Camp Betar experience, where military training combined with courses in Jewish history and culture. A *Jewish Press* ad for the camp said:

This Camp is NOT for FUN & GAMES!

This camp is for young Jewish Men & Women who feel pride and strength in their people.…

[Campers] will be privileged to undergo a program of:

1. Intensive physical training and self-defense preparation
2. Seminar training in the understanding of extremist groups, the history of Jewish resistance and pride, and training in leadership and in countering the extremist left and radical right on college campuses and high schools.[6]

A photo of the campers doing karate kicks accompanied a feature article in the *National Observer*. Bert Zweibon told the *Observer*'s reporter how the camp started:

> The rabbi came up with the idea in May, the next day he ran an advertisement in the *Jewish Press*. Within a week we had about 30 young men who had sent in their $150 for the eight weeks.
>
> But we didn't have a camp. We didn't have any money.... But Meir was ecstatic. He's a little like Moses with his faith. He believes that if something needs doing, you have to start and G-d will help you find a way. You know, the Red Sea didn't open up for Moses to walk through until [Nachshon] took the first step into the water....

The *National Observer* quoted karate teacher Marty Lewinter: "The kids learn fast because they are dedicated. All of us had someone among those six million during World War II who walked quietly into German gas chambers. We won't just walk in again. Never again." Lewinter added, "A Jew can't just keep his nose in his books and mind his own business anymore. People won't let you."

The article presented the JDL's philosophy in a nutshell, citing one of Meir's favorite lines: "To turn the other cheek is not a Jewish tenet." Said Meir, "When the Black Panthers* say, 'Jew, you gonna be burnt out,' what are the alternatives? The police can't watch every store, [so] we put an armed man in there with the merchant." Echoed Zweibon, "We organized to make it clear that if the Jew is kicked, he will kick back."[7]

JDL members contributed their time and effort to the camp. Bob Duchanov brought food supplies from the Pioneer Country Club, where he worked. "Mrs. Gartenberg gave me food for the camp with a full heart," he recalled. On Thursday evenings, Mal and Yetta Lebowitz collected food for the camp from shops in their Brooklyn neighborhood; one bakery always gave them *challah* and cake for Shabbat meals. This was important because camp fees ($150 in 1969 and $300 in 1970) did not cover even basic costs.[8]

Two high school teachers ran the 1969 camp. Dave Sommer, 31, had joined the JDL at its inception and often spoke to groups on its behalf. Sy Polsky, 25, joined in January 1969. That summer, Sy was camp administrator and taught riflery.[9]

Lillian Kaufman was camp mother in 1969, and by 1970 became Sommer's co-director. She planned the meals, ordered the food, and ran the canteen. Kauf-

---

* The Black Panthers, founded in 1966 by black Americans, espoused violent revolution as the only means of achieving black liberation. Jews were often the object of their violence. See: "Black Panthers," *American Jewish Year Book*, 1972, pp. 124-125.

man had joined the JDL after she and her husband attended a demonstration at the end of 1968.[10]

Devotion to the JDL's ideals enabled this staff to weather many crises. For instance, in keeping with the camp's military regimen, the campers wore army fatigues and slept in tents. Initially, they ate from mess kits, until sloppy dishwashing resulted in a diarrhea epidemic. Though the use of mess kits cut costs, the camp promptly switched to paper plates. Although Meir left the running of the camp to the staff, he was sometimes called upon to attend to special problems, such as an appointment with the local Board of Health on July 16.[11]

The enrollment at Camp Jedel reflected the success of the JDL. There were thirty-seven campers in 1969 and sixty in 1971. In 1972, when our family was already living in Israel, Meir held a leadership training course in Jerusalem instead of the camp. After that, Camp Jedel reopened for only two more seasons, once in 1975 and again in 1981, years when JDL was revitalized.[12]

But those early years were special. Sommer recalled Meir's close bond with the campers:

> I can still picture Meir playing football with the boys in the pouring rain, and him shouting, "It isn't raining! Remember, it isn't raining!" They didn't hesitate to tackle him. My most vivid memory is the faces of the boys as they listened to him speak about Jewish history. They sat as if [in] a trance. How they loved those lectures and how they adored the man teaching them! It was truly something to see.[13]
>
> Friday night, the singing in the dining room, the *ruach* [spirit] was great. Meir would tell stories, teach songs. Once Meir brought a survivor of the Holocaust to camp. He entranced the campers with the story of the Warsaw ghetto uprising.[14]

Journalists were intrigued by the notion of Jewish boys learning to fight. Reports about the camp included pictures of the boys at karate or rifle lessons, dressed in green army fatigues with the JDL blue and white sleeve patch. Articles appeared in numerous newspapers and magazines, including the *Times Herald Record*, *Newsday*, the Yiddish *Day-Jewish Journal*, *Time* magazine, and even Israel's prestigious *Ha'aretz* daily.[15]

Sommer said: "The media printed whatever we told them. I had a gentle German shepherd. I told the reporters it was a fierce guard dog. They printed it. During the summer of 1969 a local TV channel broadcast a long report about the camp. All of us went into Woodbourne to watch it."[16]

Education Is Our Favorite Weapon

At the JDL's second annual international convention, camp director Russ Kelner spoke about plans for the 1971 season:

> Our purpose is to train young Jews from all over ... so we can build a network of leaders. For this aim, we need guts and sacrifice. The day begins with rigor and effort and packs three days into one. Training is coupled with learning.
>
> Education is our favorite weapon.... The camp will be conducted extensively by youth, for youth, to produce genuine Jewish leaders and warriors.[17]

The camp had a well-stocked library. Campers were assigned books such as *Treblinka* by Jean-François Steiner, *The Palestine Underground* by Y. Borisov, and a book that accuses the Jewish Establishment of doing too little to aid Hitler's victims, *While Six Million Died* by Arthur D. Morse.[18]

The JDL anthem, a Hebrew song written by Meir, was sung at the nightly lowering of the Israeli and American flags.[19] An English translation by Meir read:

> *From the diary of a people, oppressed, humiliated and saddened,*
> *From nights of tears and blood,*
> *There appeared a generation – noble, self-sacrificing and beloved,*
> *There arose a Jew, lofty and upright.*
>
> *Hear, O L-rd, our oath,*
> *To slaughtered brethren and lonely widows;*
> *Never again will our people's blood be shed like water,*
> *Never again will such things be heard in Judea.*
>
> *Not for us is the man fearful and faint of heart,*
> *We have not been conscripted into a generation crooked and tortuous;*
> *We all stand in the valley of pain,*
> *All of us are brothers – the Children of Israel.*[20]

At flag raising every morning, campers recited the Jewish Defense League Affirmation:

> With love of my people and pride in my heritage, I hereby affirm my readiness to sacrifice my time, my energy and my very being for their defense. I affirm my total allegiance to the instrument of that defense, the Jewish Defense League. I affirm my allegiance to the group, to my brothers and sisters and to my commanders. I accept total discipline to their commands with faith in their judgment, their aims and their abilities. I pledge to my people to be faithful to their survival. Never Again![21]

On Sundays the children and I would go with Meir and the campers to nearby Jewish resorts, where campers staged karate exhibitions and Meir would speak. On July 20, 1969, during Meir's talk at a nearby Jewish camp, counselors and campers kept leaving the room a few at a time. Soon the message being whispered from one to another reached me, and I too stepped out – to see the first televised footage of American astronauts on the moon!

The last karate exhibition and lecture of the 1969 season took place in Fallsburg, New York, on August 31, 1969, at the annual convention of college-age Young Israel members. Speaking of the controversial appearance of JDL members with clubs and pipes at Temple Emanu-El, Meir told the audience: "We told our boys to look like *shkotzim* [roughnecks]. We weren't concerned with the Jewish reaction. We just wanted the goyim [gentiles] to know that the Jews are ready to defend themselves." His talk sparked a lively discussion. As always, his rapport with young people was remarkable.[22]

As it turned out, activities at Camp Jedel led to jail terms for two people: Dave Sommer and Meir.

Sommer and two other JDL members had driven to Woodbourne one summer day to buy extra rifles for camp classes. Whimsically, they gave the dealer false names, unaware that it was illegal to buy weapons under an alias. A year later, during JDL's 100-Mile March to Washington in August 1970, a policeman confiscated the guns and made a routine check of the serial numbers. Sommer's case came to trial in 1972. He received a stiff punishment, part of the government's crack-down on the JDL. He was sentenced to nine months in prison and forced to disassociate from the JDL.[23]

Meir's prison sentence was also the result of ignorance of the law. Meir had demonstrated the use of explosives at camp in August 1970, unaware that it was illegal to do so without a special license. In fact, his demonstration had taken place in front of someone he knew was a police informer. When he was brought to trial in 1971, he said, "We had no idea that it was illegal to explode a bomb on our own property and in a classroom atmosphere."[24]

Everything Meir did was of interest to the authorities. An FBI report noted that on July 16, 1969, Meir bought twenty-five shotguns from Center Firearms in Manhattan and had them shipped to the camp.[25] Meir's awareness that the JDL was being examined under a microscope was confirmed when an anonymous sympathizer sent him an Anti-Defamation League memo headed "Confidential." It suggested possible legal violations for which the JDL could be prosecuted. Some examples listed in the memo: JDL's certificate of incorporation did not empower it to run a camp or provide weapons training. It may be illegal to wear uniforms similar to those of the U.S. Army, to parade in public as a military company, and to transport weapons without permits. The memo concluded with a recommendation that the Attorney General ensure JDL compliance with the law concerning tax deductions for charitable organizations.[26]

From Theory to Practice

In August 1969, carrying only legally registered weapons, campers went to Passaic, New Jersey, to protect Jews. Puerto Ricans in Passaic were protesting poor housing conditions with a wave of vandalism, looting, and shooting. On August 3, in a hail of rocks and bottles, police arrested over one hundred people. After the fourth night of rioting, local merchants, whose businesses had suffered major damage, called in the Jewish Defense League. Marty Lewinter recalled:

> Rabbi Kahane asked me to take a small group of volunteers to Passaic to guard a fur factory owned by a Holocaust survivor who had called him for assistance. The city had admitted its inability to protect merchants after nights of riots and looting.
>
> Rabbi Kahane was grim when he instructed me to make sure this merchant and his property were not harmed. I was to prevent a recurrence of Kristallnacht. I will remember this till the day I die. My parents lived through Kristallnacht in Vienna.
>
> We brought shotguns with us and stood guard all night long but "luck" prevailed and the rioters avoided our block. I believe that word leaked to the organizers of the "spontaneous" riots that we were well-armed. Some neighborhood residents must have seen us bring the shotguns into the factory.[27]

The *New York Times* noted: "Some city officials are pleased that League members are at the scene, because of the inability of police to protect all businesses. They suggest that some outside peace-keeping force might prove beneficial." But Jewish Establishment leaders were critical of JDL's involvement, arguing that the unrest in Passaic wasn't a Jewish problem.[28]

Meir countered in a *Jewish Press* column that the rioting in Passaic was indeed a Jewish problem because the stores smashed, burned and looted were owned by Jews; the riots in Passaic were aimed at Jewish slumlords. He pointed out that there were no riots against black slumlords: "In the Bronx, there is a slumlord named James Meredith, and in the Bronx they will not riot," he wrote. He accused Jewish bureaucrats with no economic stake in the area of ignoring fellow Jews' needs.[29]

Another call for help was made to JDL later that month. The *Jewish Press* reported:

> Three young hoodlums who had allegedly terrorized a bungalow colony of predominantly chasidic Jews were placed under citizen's arrest this week by six young members of the JDL, who had staked out the area at the request of the owner of the resort....
>
> Six of the JDL men were dispatched Sunday night where they waited in heavy wooded covering. At two o'clock in the morning, a car stopped and three young men, aged 17-22, got out and began overturning garbage cans. Three of

the staked-out watchers jumped out of the woods and announced that the three were under citizen's arrest. They attacked the JDL people. In the fight, the three local residents were subdued and held until the police arrived. The three arrested men were taken into the local hospital for treatment of minor wounds inflicted by the JDL defenders.[30]

Such incidents impressed grassroots Jewry – but not the Jewish Establishment. The ordinary Jew was heartened by Meir's efforts to change the image of the Jew from a weakling to a fighter, but the heads of the established Jewish organizations, who never had to walk alone at night in a rough neighborhood, had other concerns. Their priority was to maintain social and business connections with wealthy upper-class non-Jews. Meir was spoiling the respectable image they worked so hard to promote.

Chapter 16
The JDL Confronts Its Critics
(May-December 1969)

ESTABLISHMENT JEWS STRONGLY opposed the action taken by the Jewish
Defense League against James Forman. A sermon by Rabbi Maurice N.
Eisendrath, president of the Reform movement's Union of American
Hebrew Congregations, attacked the presence of armed JDL members at Temple
Emanu-El. The *New York Times*' report on the sermon included Meir's response:

> We are a group that believes that Jewish defense is not a thing to be ashamed
> of, and men like James Forman unfortunately understand the language of bats
> and chains far more clearly than sermons by Rabbi Eisendrath.[1]

Attacks on the JDL continued. An editorial in the *New York Times* "deplored"
the Jewish Defense League, particularly its contention that Jews owed no reparations to blacks. Then the National Jewish Community Relations Advisory Council, a coalition of nine national Jewish organizations, denounced the JDL. The
council condemned Jewish extremist groups that threaten "violent and coercive
tactics" in defense of "Jewish security and Jewish interests." The *New York Times*
observed, "The statement did not name the Jewish Defense League, but seemed
to be directed at it."[2]

Meir responded with an article in the *Jewish Press* of July 11 titled "From a
Jewish Father, to My Dear and Beloved Children." It defined Meir's basic beliefs:

> The past few weeks must have been puzzling ones for you, and the months
> ahead will be even more confusing. You have become aware of a raging con-
> troversy over an organization you know I am deeply committed to. You have
> heard me speak about and seen me act with the Jewish Defense League and
> now you see the abrupt rise of a chorus of angry protest and loud condemna-
> tion.
>
> ... And so you hear we are "extremists" and "vigilantes" and "racists" and
> "un-Jewish." Of course, you know the truth.
>
> ... My children, great events necessitate great men. The great landmarks of

history were erected by the few men of vision, the minority of courage, the handful who understood and were ready to sacrifice timidity and fear upon the holy altar of idealism. And added to the massive obstacles in their way and the heavy burden on their backs, there has always been the further opposition of the many – the timid, fearful many.

Do not let such things deter you. We, who are in the mainstream of Jewish tradition, know the words of our sages well: "Where there are no men, endeavor to be a man!"

Meir expressed a basic tenet of Jewish thought:

The Jew has never followed the lead of the majority. Had he done so, he would long since have perished. The Jew was first known as the "Hebrew," which as you know is the "Ivri" in the holy tongue. Why "Ivri"? Because the word is derived from the Hebrew "*ayver*," or "side," and from the days of our father Abraham, the Jew was prepared to stand alone on one side although the entire world stood on the other.

To be alone and right is not a sin, but to stand with the many in cowardice is a crime. So choose loneliness if need be; accept the taunts and anger and the vilification because that is your obligation. Truth, not popularity; principle, not timid retreat. This is the Jew, this is the mainstream.

There is a time for all things – a time for soft words and a time for strangled cry; a time for moderation and a time for vigor. To turn the other cheek is not a Jewish concept.[3]

Responding to P.L.O. Attacks

Jews throughout the world were alarmed by the growing number of bombings and killings by the P.L.O., the Palestine Liberation Organization, at El Al offices and Israeli embassies in European cities.[4] Meir, who felt the pain of ALL Jews, not only those in New York City, announced a "Support for Israel" rally. It was to take place on September 4 at noon in New York's garment district, where many Jews worked.

A press release issued on August 27 promised that at the rally Meir would reveal "means of dealing with possible Arab attacks on Jewish property in the United States." Two days later, the P.L.O. hijacked a TWA plane bound for Tel Aviv and forced it to land in Syria. The hostages, many of them American Jews, were forced to remain for hours in the desert, and even after most were released, those with Israeli citizenship were detained in Damascus. On the day of the hijacking, the P.L.O. office in New York City was raided. Meir appeared on WNEW TV and said that the Jewish Defense League assumed responsibility for the raid. The hijack, which aroused the anxiety and anger of many, became the focus of the well-attended "Support for Israel" rally.[5]

An all-out campaign against Arab delegations in the United States was next on Meir's agenda. He sent letters to the United Nations missions of Syria, Jordan, Lebanon, Iraq, and the United Arab Republic (Egypt), with copies to the press, saying:

> The two Arab terrorist gangs, the Popular Front for the Liberation of Palestine and Al Fatah [groups within the P.L.O.] have declared war on world Jewry and threatened Jewish lives and property throughout the world. The Jewish Defense League has announced it will respond to this declaration of war in kind.
>
> These gangster groups could not survive without the support of your government, which allows them to carry out their operations on and from your territory.
>
> ... We hold your government, its installations and personnel directly responsible for any act of terror committed by these gangster groups, and declare that you are legitimate targets for legitimate retaliation.[6]

Bert Zweibon told the *New York Post*, "We did not send any warning to the P.L.O., because we want the boss and not the hireling."[7]

The JDL announced a Torchlight Parade on Saturday night, September 20, which would start out from the United Nations Plaza. The marchers would stop at each of the Arab delegations to the U.N. in Manhattan: the Jordanian, Syrian, Algerian, Egyptian, Lebanese and Iraqi Missions. At each one, a formal announcement of its responsibility for any act of Arab terror would be made, followed by the singing of the Israeli national anthem, *Hatikvah*.[8]

An Arab threat to abduct wealthy Jewish contributors to the United Jewish Appeal added momentum to the planned march. An ad in the *Jewish Press*, headlined "There Will Be No Arab Terror Here!" called on readers to attend the protest march. In bold letters it proclaimed:

> FORGET ABOUT YOUR TV SET AND MOVIE...
> STAND UP FOR JEWRY AND AMERICA!

A mail-in coupon at the bottom of the ad stated: "I will be with you on September 20th to stand up for Jewry and America. Enclosed is $__ to help you in OUR fight."[9]

Media reports on the "threatening" letters to the Arabs provided additional publicity for the Torchlight Parade.[10]

Two days before the parade was to take place, two FBI agents visited Meir, who had signed all the letters. They expressed their "concern" about his "threats to foreign nationals" and warned Meir that his communiqués might be unlawful. He countered that they had been phrased under advice of counsel so as not to violate any laws. The Jewish Defense League, he said, would not violate the laws of the United States, because to do so would cause the JDL to lose the sympathies of the American public. Meir told the agents that if the attorney general thought the letters were illegal, a federal judge would have to decide. The next day the FBI agents presented these facts to Assistant U.S. District Attorney Andrew M. Lawler, Jr. Because of the "non-specific nature of the threats," Lawler decided not to prosecute.[11]

The march was a resounding success. The *New York Times*, noting that there were about five hundred marchers in the Torchlight Parade, reported: "Rabbi Meir Kahane, leader of the League, said the march had been designed as a warning 'that we hold [the Arab states] responsible for any acts of terror against Jews in this country, as Jews,' and also to condemn Arab terrorism against Israel."[12]

Associate Editor, Jewish Press

A few days later, Meir, as associate editor of the *Jewish Press*, was invited to a dinner hosted by Mayor Lindsay in honor of Israel's visiting prime minister, Golda Meir. Lindsay, aiming at the "Jewish vote" – New York's two million Jews – in the upcoming mayoralty election, even greeted Golda Meir at the airport.[13]

Meir and I were among some 1,400 Jewish notables at the fete, held at the Brooklyn Museum. Since it was the Sukkot holiday, the dinner took place on the museum's rooftop to allow for eating in a *sukkah*, a thatched-roof structure in which Jews are to dwell during this holiday. The gourmet kosher cuisine – my first exposure to boned Cornish hen and artichoke hearts – cost the city about $25 per person, over $10 more than the usual tab.[14] The weather was perfect, and the sight of the artfully lit tables placed among the potted trees on the roof was enchanting.

During this period Meir wrote regularly for the *Jewish Press*. In addition to his column, *Spotlight on Extremism*, many news stories were followed by his analysis, headed "Commentary." His June 20 Commentary column, "On the Nature of Anti-Semitism," declared no anti-Jewish attack too small to be ignored: "Being silent only guarantees its further spread." An August article decried reverse bias in medical schools, which discriminated against whites and, ultimately, against Jews. On September 26, 1969, in his article "Color It Lindsay, Lindsay and the Jews," Meir urged Jews not to vote for Lindsay in the coming election because his policies were harming Jewish interests.[15]

After a Christian tourist set fire to Jerusalem's Al Aksa Mosque in August, and the Israeli government apologized profusely, Meir wrote "No Apology Necessary." And his continued concern about P.L.O. terror attacks is evident in the news feature, "U.S. Churches, Refugee Group Supporting Al Fatah Operations," which documents "charitable" institutions' aid to the Palestine Liberation Organization.[16]

In an article about Tisha B'Av, commemorating the destruction of the Temples in Jerusalem, he wrote that this year "our tears must run" for oppressed Soviet Jews as well as for the Temples. He told of a Jewish engineer, Boris Lvovich Kochubievsky, a *refusenik*, who, after his request to immigrate to Israel with his wife had been refused, was arrested in Kiev on charges of "spreading fabrications slandering the Soviet state and its social system." But, wrote Meir, Kochubievsky's only crime was asserting Israel's right to self-defense in the Six Day War.[17]

In "I Spent a Night in Canada Last Week," Meir wrote about his appearance on a Canadian television program called *Under Attack*, in which public figures replied to questions posed by a panel of college students. "The Jewish students on the panel," he wrote, "denounced JDL for violence while cheering the pacific Black Panthers.... [They attacked] the State of Israel for being a tool of United States imperialism.... [The panelists represent] the long-haired alienation from everything Jewish." Meir described their reaction to his response:

> Unused to hearing a Jew in public stand tall and unapologetic, [they] listened in amazement at phrases like "Jewish power" and "the Zionist dream" and "Jewish might." They listened in surprise, and when the show was over, they did not go home. They remained and asked to discuss this strange Jewishness more and more and more. And not till 4 A.M. did they leave the home of Rabbi Rosensweig of Waterloo [near Toronto], where we sat (G-d bless his understanding wife) till late and talked of Jews and Jewishness.

Meir was concerned about the influence of the New Left on young Jews such as these.

> Can these Jews be saved? I do not know. I do not know if the sins of their parents, which have doomed them to bitter reaction against their heritage, can be overcome. I do not know if we are too late to feed them the life-giving elixir of Jewish pride they were never allowed to taste. I do not know if the harm done them by fearful and timid Jewish leadership can be undone.
> But hope there is. For these are good and decent and intelligent youngsters who want to be Jewish and ... the JDL preaches a philosophy that strikes some instinctive response in them.... To the Jewish youngsters whom I met and with whom I sat till early into the morning I can only say: Thank you for the experience. You will yet be better than your elders and your timid leaders. Stand tall and say NEVER AGAIN.[18]

Campaigning Against Mayor Lindsay

On his return to New York City, Meir embarked on an intensive campaign against the reelection of John Lindsay.* In addition to his *Jewish Press* articles explaining why Jews should not vote for Lindsay, he placed a two-column full-length ad in the *New York Times* of October 6 headed "The Jews of New York City Cannot Afford Four More Years of John Lindsay." The text charged that the city's racial situation had deteriorated to the detriment of the Jewish population, largely because Mayor Lindsay avoided showdowns with militants. The ad blamed Lindsay for the erosion of Jewish rights and the rise in crimes against Jews, and called on them to vote against him.[19]

Early the next morning, telegrams were sent to the major television, radio and news agencies inviting them to a press conference at JDL headquarters the same day. The telegrams said only: "JDL launches major campaign to defeat Lindsay. Charges and program presented at press conference Tuesday, Oct. 7, 10 A.M., 156 Fifth Avenue, Room 323."[20]

Media attendance at the press conference was good. Meir told the reporters that at every one of Lindsay's meetings with Jewish groups, a JDL Truth Squad would distribute "documented material reminding New York Jews of the disastrous decline in the Jewish position under Lindsay." There would be motorcades and rallies in major Jewish neighborhoods, all geared to the overall theme "We remember – do you?" Anti-Lindsay literature would be given out in the millions to the Jewish residents. Dave Sommer recalled: "The Lindsay 'Truth Squad' was usually made up of Meir, myself, Bert Zweibon, Marty Lewinter, and a bunch of kids."[21]

The next day, the *New York Times* reported the JDL's contention that Lindsay was indifferent to anti-Semitism. The same news item carried Lindsay's response that the JDL's charges were "unfair." That afternoon's *New York Post* carried a scathing attack on the JDL's anti-Lindsay campaign by columnist Pete Hamill. Meir shot back with a letter to the *Post* that began, "I leave the smears to Mr. Hamill." He reminded Hamill that he himself had criticized an anti-Semitic remark made by Lindsay in his March 27 article in the *Village Voice*.[22]

Lindsay's campaign team acted swiftly to counteract the JDL. On October 9 they circulated a strong condemnation of the JDL signed by former Supreme Court justice Arthur Goldberg on behalf of the leaders of more than three hundred Jewish organizations. Meir's call for Jews to vote on the basis of Jewish interests had offended the liberal Jewish Establishment, which denied the existence of a "Jewish vote."[23]

One day later, perhaps because of the Establishment's overwhelming condemnation, perhaps because of pressure on Rabbi Shalom Klass from his most important advertiser, Meir was fired from the *Jewish Press*. Meir's October 10 articles were the last to appear in the *Jewish Press* for some time. His dismissal merited

---

* See chapter 12 for more about Mayor John Lindsay.

a mention in the *New York Times*, which included his avowed intention to continue working against Lindsay.[24] By now, Meir was receiving a salary from the JDL, but his dismissal meant the loss of a platform as well as the loss of a job.

In response to Arthur Goldberg's condemnation, the JDL scheduled a press conference for October 10 at the Overseas Press Club to "present a detailed rebuttal and exposé of the political machinations associated with the Lindsay-Goldberg attack." Meir prepared a press kit that included eight flyers and pamphlets explaining JDL opposition to Lindsay. According to the *Jewish Defense League Newsletter*, hundreds of thousands of copies of the flyers and pamphlets were distributed throughout the city. The press kit included Meir's *Jewish Press* article "Twenty Questions for Lindsay," American Jewish Committee press releases about one of Lindsay's friends, black anti-Semite Jesse Gray, and the JDL's ideological brochure *Never Again*.[25]

The media gave this press conference, too, wide and generally fair coverage. One of the largest radio stations, WCBS, gave Meir an opportunity to rebut an editorial to be aired October 14 and 15. Meir's reply:

> We deplore the tragic public attacks on the Jewish Defense League by powerful Establishment forces.... JDL has NEVER been and never WILL be a racist group. JDL has NEVER and WILL never disrupt the rights of John V. Lindsay to speak in a synagogue or anywhere else. JDL is NOT a vigilante group that heedlessly takes the law into its own hands. Such charges are the product of fear. They are lies.
>
> The Jewish Defense League was formed because the people of New York have been given over to extremism, to racial hatred, to crime, to reverse discrimination and quotas – while John Lindsay and city government watch in apathy and indifference....
>
> We promise the people of New York City – the ones who live and suffer here – that we will not be frightened by the attacks of the wealthy and contented forces that have learned nothing from history. To them let us pledge, "Never Again."[26]

On Sunday morning, October 19, a motorcade of cars covered with anti-Lindsay banners drove through the popular Jewish shopping district on the Lower East Side. The motorcade was organized by Roz Nesis, head of JDL's Anti-Lindsay Committee. A 45 rpm record cut by Nesis, Ballad of Fun City, was played over loudspeakers. The song, set to the tune of *Those Were the Days, My Friend*, began:

> *Once upon a time there was a city,*
> *Where the people all would safely walk,*
> *Before the advent of Sweet Prince John Lindsay,*
> *Oh, what a city was that Old New York.*
> *   Those were the days, my friend....*

Then Fun City Mayor came upon us;
We've lost our starry notions since that day.
Four years filled with racist crime and chaos –
Let's bring back the time of which we say
  Those were the days, my friend....

The flip side of the record, titled "Questions for Mr. Lindsay,"[27] was a talk by Meir that was probably similar to the speech he gave at a rally after the motorcade. A press release announcing the rally referred to Meir's dismissal from the *Jewish Press*. It said that at the rally he would "... unveil charges that Lindsay has been attempting to buy Jewish votes.... The JDL offices have been besieged by angry inquiries concerning Lindsay's involvement in the firing of Rabbi Meir Kahane from his post as associate editor of the *Jewish Press* and the sudden shift in the policy of the paper to one progressively more favorable to Lindsay."[28]

At this point, Meir placed the July *Jewish Press* article, "To My Dear and Beloved Children," as a three-column full-length ad in the *New York Times*. In addition to the personal credo quoted at the beginning of this chapter, it clarified the JDL's actions against John Lindsay and spelled out the charges against him:

> Do not confuse the voices you hear with those of the common people.... Those who live in the safety of a fine neighborhood do not ask for JDL help. But the Crown Heights Jewish Community Council, when faced with naked threats, called upon a Jewish group for help and protection this year. That group? Spell it JDL.
>
> Nor are any of our critics unfortunate enough to be the dean in a high school in Brooklyn whose life and job were both threatened by hoodlums while the authorities sat by silently. To whom did that dean turn? The call went to JDL and thirty-five "vigilantes" protected him.
>
> ... New York City and ALL its citizens are in the midst of a terrible crisis today. That is the result of a fearful and meek mayor.... But – as always – for the Jew there is something special.
>
> The truth cannot be ignored. There is the beginning of a special crisis for Jews in New York City. There is open anti-Semitism. There is indifference to this on the part of the government.... There are teachers in the New York City public school system who teach hatred of Jews. There are Jewish merchants who are at the mercy of the haters....
>
> The danger is compounded by the image of the Jew as an easy mark, as a "patsy." It is doubly complicated by the refusal of leadership to escape from its paralysis of will. It is triply escalated by the vilification of those who care and prepare to act.
>
> This is why we fear John Lindsay. This is why we hope that he will give up the reins of government.[29]

The November issue of the *Jewish Defense League Newsletter* summed up the events of October: "We placed two large and expensive ads in the *Times* that have produced a major reaction.... We received enthusiastic responses from readers of the ads – including many non-Jews – who wrote us beautiful letters and contributed funds."[30]

In mid-October, administrative director Allan Mallenbaum introduced JDL's famous logo: a clenched fist imposed on a Star of David. Mallenbaum wrote, "I used my business connections to get a commercial artist [Jack Schecterson] to design the logo and a new letterhead."[31]

Two weeks after Meir's dismissal from the *Jewish Press*, a front page "Statement from the Publisher" explained why he was no longer writing for the paper. The statement began with a quote from Isaiah 1:2, "Children have I raised and brought up, and they have rebelled against Me," alluding to publisher Rabbi Shalom Klass' fatherly affection toward Meir. Klass attacked Meir's "campaign of vilification against Mayor John Lindsay." He wrote: "Honest dissent is the democratic way, but to use vilification is to use the very tactics the JDL has always condemned and ... is contrary to our Torah." Then Rabbi Klass added another reason for sacking Meir: "At a staff meeting he was given the option of working for the *Jewish Press* full time or resigning. He resigned in favor of the JDL, for a person can't be in two places at the same time, especially if he is a national director of an organization...."[32]

The next issue of the *Jewish Defense League Newsletter* blasted Rabbi Klass for firing Meir "under pressure from the mayor's office," claiming that the *Jewish Press* had "seen a spectacular growth in the last year, due directly to the fact that Meir Kahane's exposés have brought it many non-Orthodox and even non-Jewish readers...." Meir's duties as associate editor were detailed: "For the record, it should be known that Rabbi Kahane was the one who wrote and edited ALL the news stories in the paper, including ALL of pages 1, 2, and 3 (except for the main headline, which was the publisher's province) including any editorials on those pages. He ALSO wrote the *Tales of the Midrash and Gaonim*, despite the fact that they appeared under another name."

The newsletter's editor, who was not named, concluded angrily: "In view of his invaluable work for the *Jewish Press*, Rabbi Kahane would not, could not, have been fired if not for the Lindsay offer ... to build the paper a brand-new building.... The major culprit is not the *Jewish Press* but a mayor who initiates offers aimed at buying an election...."[33]

These allegations were repeated in Robert I. Friedman's book, *False Prophet*. Marvin Schick, Lindsay's advisor for Jewish affairs in 1969, gave his version of the affair in a 1990 article refuting those allegations against Rabbi Klass. Schick, who was present at the 1969 meeting between Lindsay and Klass, wrote:

Klass made a strong plea for city assistance to yeshivas. When Lindsay responded sympathetically, Klass said he would consider a *Jewish Press* endorsement if the mayor would put the views he had just expressed into a letter. I drafted the letter the same day or the next, and I believe that the *Jewish Press* cited it in an editorial. Kahane was not only not the subject of the meeting, I am certain that he was not fired "within hours" of Klass' leaving Gracie Mansion [the mayor's residence]. What apparently happened is that sometime later Klass and Kahane argued over the Lindsay endorsement and the JDL leader was then fired.

In fact, Klass did not endorse Lindsay or any other candidate. Instead, he printed "Letters of Intent" submitted by both John Lindsay and Mario Procaccino, pledging to support yeshivot. Schick explained that the *Jewish Press*'s move to a new building had nothing to do with Meir's dismissal.

... Even before the Gracie Mansion meeting, Joe Brovich, managing editor of the *Jewish Press*, told city officials that the newspaper wanted the city's help in finding another Brooklyn location. The *Jewish Press* was located in Coney Island in a building that the city had condemned as part of an urban renewal project. There was no mention of this request at the Lindsay-Klass meeting. Long after the election, city officials identified the former Transit Authority substation as a possible site, among others, for the newspaper.

... Friedman has written inaccurately on matters that I know about from personal experience.... Contrary to Friedman's suggestion of a super-sweetheart deal, the property had been abandoned for several years; there was no interest in it by any other business or party; ... the annual rent was $30,000; and the building was in disrepair and required a considerable investment of at least several thousand dollars to make it minimally usable by the newspaper. These funds did not come from the public treasury, but from what was then a small weekly.... Klass had to go into considerable debt to renovate a building that his newspaper did not own.

Schick presents a plausible explanation of the move of the *Jewish Press* to a different site. Considering the fact that Rabbi Klass did not endorse Lindsay outright, Schick's report seems more accurate than that of Robert I. Friedman, whose book is full of factual errors.[34]

Lindsay won the election on November 4 with 41.8 percent of the vote, probably because the votes against him were split between two other candidates, Mario Procaccino and John Marchi. It is uncertain whether depriving Meir of his *Jewish Press* platform played a part in Lindsay's reelection, because Lindsay and Procaccino each received about 44 percent of the votes cast by Jews.[35]

Operation Hagana

After the election, the Jewish Defense League turned to other matters. Space was rented in midtown Manhattan for the JDL's youth movement, where Alex Sternberg led karate classes. JDL's emphasis on youth was reflected in the formation of JDL chapters on fifteen college campuses in the United States and Canada.[36]

Operation *Hagana* (Defense) was launched. It organized night patrols in dangerous neighborhoods to protect people walking on the street and to guard Jewish shops and homes against theft and vandalism. On foot and in cars, JDL members armed with bicycle chains and baseball bats patrolled three Brooklyn neighborhoods and Manhattan's Lower East Side.[37]

Meir continued to attract media attention and was invited to participate in radio and television programs and speak to groups. He appeared on TV in Philadelphia and Hartford, and in November made his fourth appearance on the Barry Farber radio program, where he and JDL administrator Allan Mallenbaum debated Murray Gordon of the American Jewish Congress and Dr. Samuel Silver of Temple Sinai in Stamford, Connecticut.[38]

During the last two months of 1969 Meir was invited to address several synagogues and Jewish groups, including an audience of 250 in the East Flatbush section of Brooklyn; the Adult Education Club at the Young Israel of Chomedy, near Montreal; and the eight hundred-member Brith Sholom Lodge at Congregation Beth T'fillah in the Overbrook Park section of Philadelphia.[39] Meir's speaking dates during this period are not fully documented. However, his appearance in Chicago on Saturday night, November 22, was reported in detail by Rabbi Irving J. Rosenbaum in his *Jewish Sentinel* column.

> The affair extended into the post-midnight hours, partly because the rabbi's plane was delayed, but mostly because the 400 or so people who jammed the hall were eager to hear everything he had to say....
>
> As for me, I must say that I believe he is far more correct in diagnosing the situation of America's poor and lower middle class urban Jews than are the major Jewish organizations which are so quick to condemn him. I believe he has a far better grasp of the temper, the fears, the frustrations, the hopes and aspirations of America's Jews than does the entrenched leadership.... It is time the major Jewish organizations began to think seriously about the issues raised by the JDL and stop believing that by calling it names they can make it disappear.
>
> Any Jewish speaker who can keep 400 of his peers (and especially this one) awake, eager, excited and interested until past midnight ... must have something important to say!

Rabbi Rosenbaum alluded to the campaign of vilification against the JDL by the Jewish Establishment in his description of the audience: "... I did not see nasty, brutish, sick, irrational people.... They looked like nice Jewish boys, girls, men, women, parents and grandparents.... It was a reasonably representative gathering of committed American Jews."[40]

Next on Meir's itinerary was Boston, where "white flight" had left poor and elderly Jews the victims of black violence. This was especially so in neighborhoods such Mattapan, Roxbury and Dorchester. On November 30, Meir spoke in Boston at a JDL meeting attended by the local press and by a representative of Mayor Kevin White's office. Among the speakers were elderly, harassed residents whose tales of neighborhood violence added up to a nightmare. At the meeting, Meir announced the formation of a local anti-crime patrol.

The *Jewish Defense League Newsletter* reported: "Within a day, Mayor White announced that the area would be saturated with police. The promise was kept and for the first time in years, police with dogs blanketed the area. Full credit was given by the papers to the JDL."[41]

Alan Mandel, who joined the Boston chapter that evening, recalled that after the first few days of "police saturation," JDL patrols took over. Mandel wrote:

> Before I knew it, I was in charge of JDL patrols. I started by defining the problem and organizing as I was trained to do in the army. We had vehicle patrols with radios and legal weapons, dog patrols and, most important, high visibility in the neighborhoods and in the media. We raised money for the equipment. Every element of the "real" Jewish populace was involved: toughs from the streets with "professionals" from the nearby suburbs.
>
> Besides patrols, we filled classes with lessons on basic self-defense for men, women and children. Reb Meir loved what I had set up in Boston, and even had me come down once to lecture at a JDL convention in New York.[42]

About a month later, Meir spoke in the Boston area again, in the deteriorating town of Newton. Despite well-publicized condemnations of JDL by Boston's Jewish Establishment, the JDL gained a strong foothold in Newton. Approximately three hundred people came to hear Meir at Congregation Beth El-Atereth Israel on Sunday, December 14. Mandel told them that since the JDL's civilian patrols had begun in the Dorchester-Mattapan neighborhoods, Police Commissioner Edmund McNamara had announced a 50 percent drop in crime there.[43]

The JDL of Boston reacted to Establishment criticism with a press release citing praise for the organization from such prominent personalities as the Bostoner Rebbe, Rabbi Levi Yitzchak Horowitz ("The JDL has made a positive response to problems of Mattapan and Dorchester"), Rabbi Mordechai Savitsky ("... only the Jewish Defense League has taken positive steps to reduce the threats to the lives of residents in Dorchester and Mattapan"), Reconstructionist Philip Perlmutter (" ... by all traditions of grassroots American history, the actions were understandable and necessary"), and Massachusetts State Representative John

Saltonstall, Jr. ("JDL is not a vigilante group, it is a responsible answer to the crime that plagues our city").[44]

Meir had learned to expect opposition from Jewish organizations that ignored the growing violence against Jews in depressed urban areas. Rabbi Emanuel Rackman, Provost of Yeshiva University, pointed out that the established organizations "were fearful of new approaches and unwilling to change programs to cope with new needs." In his address to the National Convention of the Union of Orthodox Congregations, Rabbi Rackman said there was a need for self-defense groups. Regular police protection had been shown to be inadequate and American cities were becoming "jungles." "Self-defense is not illegal," he said. "In many instances the Jewish Defense League has demonstrated its ability to be the instrument presently required by the Jewish community," he admitted.[45]

A Caring Father

Two family vignettes from this period shed light on Meir's sensitivity to the needs of his own family, in spite of his time-consuming devotion to the growth of the Jewish Defense League.

In November, Meir took the family to the theater to see *Fiddler on the Roof* in honor of our daughter Tova's birthday. *Fiddler* was one of the few plays Meir agreed to attend because its subject was a traditional Jewish family, whereas most Broadway shows were immodest and/or immoral. During *Fiddler*'s wedding scene, however, men and women danced together.[46] Meir's first reaction was to walk out angrily, but I pulled him back into his seat, giving him a minute to reflect. In the end, rather than ruin Tova's outing, he stayed for the rest of the show.

Tova recalled another illustration of her father's empathy:

> Shortly after we moved to Brooklyn, when I was about twelve, one of my friends in Laurelton invited me to a slumber party. It was mid-winter, and the weather was terrible. There had been a heavy snowfall all day, and it kept coming down. Abba [Dad] told me that driving to Laurelton would be very difficult. But twelve-year-olds feel everything keenly. I was very, very disappointed. When he saw how important it was to me to go to the party, he decided to take me in spite of the difficult drive. He had to drive through continually falling snow and take a roundabout route because some roads were closed. It took over two hours, but he did it for me.[47]

Meir's sensitivity was not limited to his own family. He was equally sensitive to the suffering of his fellow Jews. Lecturing on the plight of Soviet Jewry, he often said, "A good Jew is one who feels the pain of his fellow Jew." In December 1969, Meir initiated a series of public protests that brought their plight before the world and eventually enabled countless Jews to leave the Soviet Union.

Chapter 17

Publicizing the Plight of Soviet Jewry (1969-1970)

T HE TIME WAS ripe to act on Meir's prophetic 1964 article, "Save Soviet Jewry."

> ... Wracked by economic problems at home and challenged by China for the leadership of the Communist world, [the Soviet Union] desperately needs friendship with the United States.... If we can challenge this era of good feeling ... it is possible that the Soviets will consider it not worth the bother of persecuting their Jews....
>
> We MUST make headlines and they are made only by audacious and dramatic activities. If need be, these activities cannot be confined to sweet respectability and legality.... It is not a pleasant task.... This is not a job for people who fear getting their hands soiled.[1]

When Meir wrote these words, few were willing to "get their hands soiled." Members of the Jewish Defense League, however, had learned not to be obsessed with being "respectable." Their protests against anti-Semitic teachers at school board meetings had turned into fistfights. They had clashed with rival picketers outside radio station WBAI. They had confronted the Black Panthers at their headquarters in Harlem. They had done so because of Meir's teachings on the love of fellow Jews, and since they knew this rule applied to all Jews, everywhere, they were ready to act on behalf of Soviet Jewry.[2]

Meir was able to summon large numbers of people to demonstrations even when the platform of the *Jewish Press* was closed to him. The JDL office sent out mass mailings and used a system of phone chains to inform members of activities. One observer said, "They work very efficiently on the phone and they have people responsible for mustering units of several dozen men."[3]

The First 100-Hour Vigil

Beginning in December 1969, Meir led a series of protests that attracted the media and publicized the persecution of Soviet Jewry, especially of *refuseniks*,

135

those Russian Jews seeking to immigrate to Israel. *Refuseniks* were harassed, intimidated and fired from their jobs. One *refusenik*, Dov (Boris) Sperling, spent two years in Soviet prisons and nine years in social and economic limbo before obtaining a permit to leave the Soviet Union.[4]

Meir's accomplishments on behalf of Soviet Jewry and the rationale behind his actions are detailed fully in his book *The Story of the Jewish Defense League.*[5] The present work does not duplicate *Story*. It has new material based on archival sources and interviews with people who participated in JDL activities.

Such was the reputation of the JDL, that when Meir announced a December 25 demonstration outside the Soviet Mission to the United Nations in Manhattan,[*] Soviet ambassador Jacob Malik requested extra police protection. Police rules forbade demonstrations on the block of the Soviet Mission, East 67 Street between Third and Lexington Avenues. Nevertheless, seventy-one JDL members gathered on the sidewalk in front of the mission. Enraged, Malik summoned the police and threatened an official protest to President Nixon, but the demonstrators dispersed before the police could move against them.[6]

Two days later, taking advantage of the mid-winter school vacation, the JDL called a 100-Hour Vigil. It began Saturday night, December 27, and was to end one hundred hours later, on December 31. Letters to members and to public figures called on them to attend the vigil: "At a time of year when religious feeling and the freedom of worship is manifest, let us remember those who are in religious chains...."[7]

The vigil began on Saturday night with the demonstrators behind police barriers on Third Avenue. The Mission, about a third of the way down East 67 Street, was visible from that corner. On Sunday morning, about sixty young people suddenly broke through the barriers in an effort to reach the mission. Police quickly turned them back and one was arrested, but Meir negotiated with the officers, who finally permitted twenty demonstrators past the barriers. This was the first time demonstrators were allowed on the same block as the mission.[8]

On Monday afternoon, December 29, Meir and others left the picket line and, in closely coordinated raids, they invaded three Soviet installations in New York: the Tass news agency, the Intourist bureau, and the Aeroflot airline.

Coordinating the raids was not a simple task, especially for people who had no experience in operational planning. Samson Levine, who invaded Tass with Meir, wrote: "I was told to be at a certain place at a certain time. We were to pick up a team and go over to Rockefeller Center, where we were to make a phone call to time our coordination with the two other events. We hadn't worked out any

---

[*] The Soviet Mission to the United Nations, 136 East 67 Street, was the major Soviet installation in New York and the target of most of the protest demonstrations on behalf of Soviet Jews.

code system! I called to see if the Aeroflot plane had landed, as that was our cue. I asked Bert if 'the bird was at the pet shop.' He responded with something like 'chickens are at the butcher.' It took one or two back-and-forths until I was sure he was saying 'yes' and we could proceed to Tass."[9]

The protesters spray-painted slogans such as "Let My People Go!" and *"Am Yisrael Chai* (The Jewish People Lives)" on office walls and on an Aeroflot plane that had just landed, and two activists handcuffed themselves to its nose wheel. All together, fourteen people were arrested. Charges included assault, disorderly conduct, and criminal trespass.[10] In most JDL arrests, people were held in jail only a few hours or overnight before being released on very low bail. However, when the cases were heard in court, the sentence could be severe. It is a measure of their devotion to the cause of Soviet Jewry that JDLers were ready to be arrested.

The media reacted as Meir had hoped. Newspapers in the United States, Europe, Canada, and Israel covered the coordinated raids and Meir was interviewed on radio and TV.[11] A press release on JDL stationery, featuring the organization's new logo – a clenched fist imposed on a Star of David – stated:

> Our attacks upon the institutions of Soviet tyranny in America represent the first step in our campaign to bring the issue of oppressed Soviet Jews and other religious groups to the attention of an apathetic public and an indifferent news media.
>
> ... The organized persecution of Soviet Jewry is a fifty-year-old night-mare.... We have ... tried the traditional methods of diplomacy. They have failed to open the gates. There is little remaining for us to do but heed the requests of the Russian Jews themselves who have commanded us to shake the world.
>
> ... Our actions yesterday were only the start of a campaign to prove to the Soviets that their oppressive policies are not worth the price that angered Americans will extract from them.

The press release went on to describe police rules that prohibited pickets from marching directly outside the Soviet Mission. Often, they were not even allowed on Lexington or Third Avenues but were stopped as far away as Park Avenue. Earlier, JDL had brought suit demanding the revocation of those rules, but it was dismissed on grounds that the rules were "reasonable safeguards." Now JDL intended to appeal that decision.

> At the same time we serve notice on the police that we are moving through the courts to put an end to their unconstitutionally imposed ban on picketing in front of the Soviet mission....[12]

The next day, after Jewish Defense League members had marched peacefully near the mission for three days and nights, the police – perhaps because of the three-pronged raid on Soviet offices – revoked the JDL's permit to hold a march on Tuesday night. Nevertheless, the protest took place as planned. It began with a rally at the United Nations' Dag Hammarskjold Plaza, where the protesters issued a demand to expel the Soviet Union from the United Nations for human rights violations. From there, the crowd marched to the mission, about twenty blocks away.

That evening NBC covered both events. The broadcast showed Meir addressing the rally at the U.N. plaza, calling for all Jews in the city to take to the streets and demonstrate for the cause of Russian Jews. He called for one million people to march on the Soviet Mission. Then the footage showed Meir moving into the crowd to lead them up Third Avenue. Carrying signs, posters and Israeli flags, and chanting "Let My People Go," the protesters confronted the police. While JDL leaders were negotiating with the police, the protesters rushed their lines, and the police began making arrests. Twenty-seven persons were arrested for "obstructing traffic."[13] One demonstrator later wrote about the arrests:

> ... The TPF [New York City's brutal Tactical Police Force] inflicted a broken finger and battered arm on Rabbi Kahane, and three broken ribs and a skull injury on 75-year-old Dr. Zucker, a man whose white hair belies his fighting spirit. When we refused to disperse and insisted on our constitutional rights, we were attacked, beaten and arrested at random.
>
> ... For some of us, this night ended with our arrest.... After being arrested and beaten by the TPF, I was brought into the 19th Police Precinct,* where I witnessed horror upon horror being inflicted upon our fellow Jews for the crime of demanding those rights.... I saw a 68-year-old man assaulted by those creatures in blue and sustain a shoulder injury. When some of us tried to help this man, we were pulled by our hair, threatened with bodily injury, and, most significantly, called Kikes, Hebes and Jew-bastards....[14]

Meir was charged with inciting to riot. One headline read, "JDL Rabbi Hits Cops in Row on Picketing." Freed on parole on his own recognizance, he told reporters that Mayor Lindsay's office bore ultimate responsibility for the confrontation with police and for injuries to three persons, because police orders to rescind the JDL's permit to demonstrate had come from above. That day, the chief rabbi of Moscow, Yehuda Leib Levin, denounced the JDL's acts.[15] But Meir was certain that just as city officials were under pressure from the State Department to prevent JDL demonstrations against the Soviet Union, Rabbi Levin's denunciation was issued under duress.

Meir's arrests generated a series of court cases. One case had to do with the raid on Tass. Together with Samson Levine and Abraham Muallem, Meir had

---

* The Nineteenth Precinct Police Station was conveniently located right near the Soviet Mission, at 153 East 67th Street.

been charged with harassment, criminal conspiracy, criminal trespass, and criminal mischief. Levine recalled that, fearing the worst, they calmed their nerves in court with *Daily News* word jumbles and *New York Times* crossword puzzles. In court on February 9, 1971, something unusual occurred: The jury failed to reach a verdict. The judge declared a mistrial, and a second trial was scheduled for March 30. This time the jury deliberated for seven hours and informed the judge, once again, that they were hopelessly deadlocked.[16]

Levine explained: "The jury members saw our cause as being against the 'evil empire, Russia' – which forbade all religious practice – and sympathized with the non-conventional methods we had learned from opponents of the Vietnam War."[17]

Meir called the third trial, set for June 28, "the third act of a farce entitled 'JDL at the Soviet Tass News Agency.'" He wrote: "Following two hung juries, [which] would have normally seen the state drop the case, we were informed that New York City was going to prosecute this a hundred times if necessary, no matter what the cost."[18]

Disrupting Soviet Performances

Pressure from officialdom and denunciations by fellow Jews did not put an end to Meir's activities on behalf of Soviet Jews. He turned his attention to Soviet cultural events in America. In the era of *détente* (easing of political tensions), these cultural events were intended to promote American good will toward the Soviet Union – good will that was vital to Soviet foreign policy. Meir initiated an effective tactic: disrupting the performances of visiting Soviet musicians and dancers. His aim was to arouse public attention so as to pressure the Soviet Union into changing its policy of persecuting Jews.[19]

At Soviet performances at Brooklyn College in January 1970 and at Carnegie Hall in February, JDL members distributed flyers at the entrance that said "Don't Go In! Music Doesn't Make Barbarians Civilized" and "They Also Played Music at Auschwitz." Other JDLers sitting in the audience interrupted the concerts by shouting slogans like "Let My People Go!"[20]

These noisy demonstrations made Meir a widely known figure, and he was invited to address many groups. In lectures to Jewish groups throughout the United States, Meir stressed the importance of disrupting Soviet cultural performances. In September he told a Cleveland audience about vigorous disruptions of the Moiseyev Dance Troupe's appearances in Chicago, New York and Philadelphia. The performance in Chicago was cancelled after someone in the audience threw a tear gas bomb, forcing the audience of 3,500 to evacuate the hall.[21]

During the Moiseyev's performance in Philadelphia, demonstrators sounded a buzzer, let mice loose in the auditorium, and threw leaflets into the audience. The local JDL newsletter reported, tongue-in-cheek: "Idle rumor had it that these acts were committed by members of JDL but no charges were pressed against those caught." Rabbi Harold Novoseller, leader of the Philadelphia chapter, explained to reporters that the spectacle was meant to "alert an apathetic public, both Jewish and non-Jewish, to the fact that Jews in the USSR are permitted no cultural freedom." The increasing demonstrations led Sol Hurok, an impresario who specialized in arranging the U.S. visits of Soviet performers, to offer the JDL $5,000 to discontinue its protests![22]

March and April were marked by a series of protests to help former *refusenik* Yasha Kazakov obtain emigration permits for his parents in Russia.[23] JDL called a "Day of Solidarity with Soviet Jews" rally on Sunday March 29. In an ad in the *New York Times* urging Jews to attend the rally, Meir wrote:

> In 1943, when we learned about Auschwitz – we did nothing. Our leaders went to President Roosevelt and asked him to bomb the rail lines carrying the cars packed with Jews to the gas chambers. He refused. We did nothing.... OUR SILENCE HELPED TO SEAL THEIR DOOM....
>
> In 1970, when we know of the national and spiritual destruction of Soviet Jewry... Where are the huge protests? Where are all the demonstrators who bleed for every people, every cause, every group – except the Jew?
>
> We, by our silence, doom the Soviet Jew. We, by our apathy, shed his blood.
>
> We reject respectability. We will do what must be done. We wish to shake the world and spotlight the Soviet Jewish problem so that the United States government will be forced to demand justice for people if the Soviets want the West's friendship.
>
> Some day, your children or grandchildren will ask you: "What did you do for Soviet Jews?" What will you say?[24]

Meir's eloquence was effective. The weather that day was bitterly cold, with snow, sleet, and a biting wind. Yet fifty people, huddled under umbrellas, attended the protest.[25]

Freedom of Religion

Meir was well known by now for his struggle against the religious persecution of Jews in the Soviet Union. On April 12, the St. George Association organized a "Day of Mourning" for the persecuted Russian Orthodox Church in the Soviet Union, and invited Meir to address the assembly. The televised program included a prayer for the millions of victims of communism.[26]

The following week Meir and fifteen JDL members staged another protest. It was the eve of Passover, the festival commemorating freedom from Egyptian slavery. One participant wrote:

In Russia it is a crime to celebrate Passover and hold a Seder. Therefore JDL decided to hold a public Seder on Russian soil [i.e., across the street from the Soviet Mission].... We set up a table, wine and matzos for the Seder. The youngest among us, Rabbi Kahane's son, Baruch, asked the Four Questions [adapted from the Seder service]:

Why is the Soviet Jew different from all free Jews? In all other lands, we are permitted to practice our religion, but in the Soviet Union we cannot.

In all other lands, our children may study the Jewish heritage many times over, but in the Soviet Union they may not study it even once.

In all other lands, our people are permitted to leave and join their relatives, but in the Soviet Union they must remain against their will.[27]

After this Seder, Meir and several others managed to position themselves in front of the Mission and quickly chained themselves to the gates. Since protests were not permitted near the Mission, police arrived quickly with clippers and cut the chains. Meir, the only one arrested, was charged with inciting to riot.[28]

Understanding the Media

Meir recognized the importance of publicity in pressuring the Soviet Union, and he understood what motivated the press. In a press release about the Seder, for instance, Meir spelled out its newsworthiness: "JDL assures you that this story of significance to Passover, the Jewish commemoration of freedom from bondage, and to the current world political situation, WILL BE OF HIGH NEWS CONTENT."[29] His success was confirmed by his denigrators: "The papers are again filled with reports of JDL-provoked hysteria before the Soviet U.N. Mission...."[30]

In May, fifty JDL members took over the Park East Synagogue on East 67 Street, directly across the street from the Soviet Mission. From its upper balcony overlooking the Mission, they unfurled huge banners decrying the plight of Soviet Jews and shouted through bullhorns, "Let My People Go" and other slogans. The takeover continued for nine hours while synagogue officials debated the wisdom of calling the police. When the police finally came, the JDLers left voluntarily and there were no arrests. The demonstration garnered a mention in the *New York Times* and a provocative caption in the *Daily News*: "Jewish Group Taunts Reds."[31]

In June 1970, about thirty JDL members invaded the Manhattan offices of the Communist Party newspaper *Daily World*, accusing the paper of failing to report the plight of Soviet Jews. Later that month, twenty-seven JDL members were arrested after storming through the offices of Amtorg, the Soviet trade organization, protesting the recent arrest in Russia of twenty-one Jews who had applied for exit permits. Meir, interviewed about the violent protest, roundly condemned the Soviet government for recent raids on the homes of Jews who had applied for exit visas.[32] Several days later, Meir's eloquent reply to criticism of the JDL was published as a letter to the editor in the *New York Times*.

> ... For fifty-three years there has been an agreement to try the respectable way. The result has been the almost total decimation of the Jewish community within the USSR from a religious and national standpoint. Those who oppress people and refuse to allow them democratic dissent can hardly have the right to complain when others employ against them the only actions that may bring salvation to those whom they oppress.[33]

A JDL booklet, *The Plight of the Soviet Jew: The Destruction of Soviet Jewry 1917–1970*, was distributed at Meir's speaking engagements and at Jewish Defense League meetings. Composed partially of Meir's earlier writings, it chronicled the Soviets' systematic elimination of Jewish religious and civil rights.[34]

The JDL's anti-Soviet acts drew an official reaction. In July, the American ambassador to the United Nations, Charles Woodruff Yost, summoned Meir to his office. He requested an end to anti-Soviet activities because they were harming friendly relations with the Soviet Union and he feared they might lead to Soviet retaliation against the American Embassy in Moscow. Meir left the meeting smiling, reassured that attacking détente was an effective means of pressuring the Soviet Union to cease its oppression of Jews.[35]

During the same period, Rabbi Moshe Feinstein, the most highly-regarded Orthodox rabbi in the United States, expressed opposition to JDL activities lest the Soviets retaliate by oppressing their Jews even more. The editor of the *Jewish Defense League Chapter Bulletin* pointed out that Rabbi Feinstein had not issued a Jewish legal ruling. He had merely repeated a message from the chief rabbi of Moscow, Yehuda Leib Levin, delivered by Rabbi Pinchas Teitz of Elizabeth, New Jersey, who often visited Russia.[36] Clearly, Chief Rabbi Levin's statements were dictated by Soviet officials.[37]

August 1970 saw further activities for Soviet Jewry. The first one, photographing diplomats at the Soviet Mission, is documented only by a press release: "Personnel and all others entering or leaving the premises will be photographed.... The project ... will begin on August 5th, at 10 A.M. The news media is invited to attend."[38] The media was invited to the second activity, a ceremony to rename the intersection near the Soviet Mission, at the corner of Lexington Avenue and East 67th Street. City officials were also invited to participate. The *Jewish Defense League Newsletter* reported that on August 11, JDLers gathered at the intersection and draped a new street sign reading "Square of Oppressed Soviet Jewry" over the city's stanchion.[39]

100-Mile March

The main event of August was a week-long 100-Mile March for Soviet Jewry. The march began on Sunday, August 16, in Philadelphia at the Liberty Bell, symbolic of the basic freedoms lacking in the USSR. It proceeded through Delaware and Maryland, culminating in a rally at the White House the following Sunday. A photograph of Meir speaking in Independence Park at the start of the march shows him dressed in olive green army fatigues standing before a microphone, with a mixed crowd listening intently. Near him are some of the marchers, also dressed in army fatigues. A reporter crouches before him, a microphone in his upraised hand.[40]

All the major television networks covered the march, and Philadelphia newspapers featured pictures of young marchers in army fatigues assembling in military formation. NBC TV showed the ranks of young men in army fatigues listening to Meir speaking about discrimination against Jews in Russia and demanding action against Soviet tyrants. Meir made such a strong and persuasive case for the aims and tactics of the Jewish Defense League that contributions poured in from all parts of the country.[41]

One youngster described the march:

> We had a state police escort, with two U-Haul trucks and a refrigerator truck for supplies. Sunday night we slept in a meadow near the Valley Forge firehouse. Reveille was at 3 A.M. so that marching would be done during the cool morning hours. Monday night was spent in another field in Edgewood, Maryland, loaned by a Congressional candidate named Anderson.
>
> Members of the Jewish community, and also non-Jews, extended personal hospitality so the girls could shower. We lit bonfires and had a *kumsitz* [a communal singing and storytelling session]. When we awoke we found that morning dew had drenched our sleeping bags and turned the field into mud. All three trucks got stuck and had to be tugged and rocked by about eighty-four valiant marchers singing the "Volga Boatman." We marched along the highway, carrying the Star-Spangled Banner and the Israeli flag, singing songs of Betar, the Irgun and the Palmach. The marchers displayed *hadar* [dignity and pride] at all times, in behavior and dress and strict clean-ups of rest areas, and in warm community feeling, cooperation and sharing.[42]

The marchers were observed by the FBI when they camped in Baltimore on Tuesday and in Wheaton, Maryland, on Thursday. The FBI reported that in Wheaton, Meir addressed a rally in the parking lot of the E. Brooke Lee Junior High School, where he said, in a plea for contributions, "You can't bribe a KGB agent with a quarter."

The marchers' arrival in Washington on Friday is also documented by the FBI: They headed for the Soviet Embassy but were stopped by police on M Street NW.

Only a delegation of three was permitted to present a petition at the embassy gate. When the embassy representative refused it, Meir read the petition to the crowd, then threw it over the embassy fence. The petition protested the oppression of Soviet Jews and Soviet aggression in the Middle East. It stated:

> Our demonstrations, our occupations of your offices, our harassment of your so-called cultural troupes has still not moved you. Like some modern-day Pharaoh, your hearts are hardened. It is obvious that more plagues must be visited upon you. It should be clear to you, by this time, that we are quite serious in our warnings. Let our people go![43]

Meir asked me to be with him for Shabbat, so I traveled to Washington by train, leaving the children with my parents. I arrived on Friday morning in time to accompany Meir to the local NBC television station for an interview that was aired on the *Today* show. The broadcast showed the march toward the Soviet Embassy and the refusal of the Soviet representative to accept the petition held out by Meir.[44]

The marchers spent Shabbat in the social hall of the Shaare Tefila synagogue in Silver Spring, while Meir and I were guests of his supporters, Howard and Helen Vogel, in the capital.[45] The conversation that Shabbat revolved around the growing violence by blacks in northwest Washington, where most of the capital's Jews lived.

On Sunday, August 23, the marchers and local supporters held a rally in Lafayette Park opposite the White House, where Meir was the featured speaker. An FBI observer summarized Meir's speech: "He made two main points: Freedom for Jews in the Soviet Union and a change in U.S. foreign policy towards Israel, which would provide more arms to Israel to help her defeat Egypt and the Soviets in the Middle East." The fact that Meir spoke not only about Soviet Jewry, but also about U.S.-Israel relations, points to the fact that JDL was never a "single-cause" organization. Even while the plight of Soviet Jewry was at the top of JDL's agenda, Israel's welfare was an important concern as was protection of Jews from violence in U.S. cities.

The FBI observer also noted Meir's statement that the JDL was committed to continuing harassment of the Soviets in the United States, and "this may include following some of them around." The tactic of following Russian diplomats as they left the Soviet Mission and shouting epithets after them was implemented only from January 1971. It is interesting that Meir thought of it more than four months earlier.[46] It proved to be a highly effective tactic.

The rally in Lafayette Park brought to a close the week-long 100-Mile March. Meir summed it up in an interview on Israel radio with its Washington correspondent, Ram Oren. One week later, *Izvestia*, the official Soviet newspaper, charged that United States officials had failed to protect Russian diplomats and citizens in the U.S. from "Zionist thugs" who disrupted cultural performances and invaded Soviet offices in New York. *Izvestia* stated that the Kremlin regarded the JDL's acts as harmful to the friendly ties between the two countries.[47] This, of course, was Meir's objective. He reasoned that the Soviets would grant Jews religious freedom and permit them to immigrate to Israel rather than jeopardize the USSR's friendship with the United States. Events proved him right.

The Leningrad Eleven

The JDL's activism also inspired Soviet Jews themselves. Yosef Mendelevich recalled: "When we read about JDL 'hooligans' in Russian newspapers, we realized there were Jews in the free world ready to do more for us than just sign petitions. The feeling that we were no longer alone in our struggle gave us courage."[48]

With that courage, Mendelevich and ten fellow Jews had attempted on June 15, 1970, to escape from the USSR by hijacking a 12-seater plane from Leningrad airport. The eleven were apprehended before the plane left the ground and trial was set for December.

While other Jewish organizations tried to help the Leningrad Eleven with peaceful pickets and "quiet diplomacy," the JDL's dramatic protests drew instant media attention to their plight. On November 23, a JDL member drove a car onto the sidewalk of the Soviet Mission. The driver, Marilyn Betman, recalled: "Our plan was simply to drive the rented car into the driveway of the Soviet Mission and to sound the horn as a disturbance. Unfortunately, the police overreacted, smashing the car and dragging us from the vehicle.... [I was] jailed for the night and released the next day on bond." NBC TV showed the car's shattered windshield while a voiceover by Meir spoke of the eleven Jews on trial in Russia on trumped-up charges.[49]

Two days later, pipe bombs exploded at the Aeroflot and Intourist offices at 5 A.M., causing only slight damage. An anonymous phone call to news agencies – concluding with the JDL slogan "Never Again" – described the bombing as a protest against the upcoming Leningrad trial. This was widely reported in the media together with Meir's dramatic presentation of the plight of the Leningrad Eleven and the oppression of Soviet Jewry.[50]

The Soviets reacted shortly afterwards. Charging that U.S. officials had failed to stop "provocation by Zionist thugs," Soviet authorities cancelled the Bolshoi Ballet's 1971 U.S. tour – a page one story. Meir considered this a great victory.[51] A *Daily News* editorial headed "Bye-Bye Bolshoi" indicated that the JDL was influencing public opinion. The *News* said:

The Kremlin could stop virtually all attacks on its agents and properties ... by simply adopting a policy of treating Jews inside Russia with common, everyday decency and tolerance....[52]

The verdicts of the Leningrad Eleven were announced on December 24, 1970. Two, Edward Kuznetsov and Mark Dymshits, received death sentences, and the rest were given long terms in prison camps.[53] The JDL planned a second 100-Hour Vigil.

On December 27, Meir addressed 2,400 people at Hunter College. The *Daily News* reported: "Speaking in a staccato style that electrified the audience, Kahane said: 'Three million Jews in Soviet Russia are being ripped from us now. It is our obligation to break any and every law to save them.'" About six hundred people readily followed Meir from Hunter College to the Soviet Mission to begin the second 100-Hour Vigil.

Earlier, JDLers had taken up positions across the street from the mission, occupying the balcony of the Park East Synagogue. They threatened that if the Leningrad death sentences were carried out, Russian diplomats would be killed. Using a bullhorn, they repeatedly shouted, "Two Russians for Every Jew."

As the marchers neared the street of the mission, Meir urged them forward. They surged past the police barricades. In the violent clash between helmeted cops and the pushing, shoving, screaming mob, traffic was blocked on Third Avenue for about ten minutes. In the crush, some demonstrators were pushed through the display windows of a department store. Meir and nine of his followers were arrested. As JDL member Barbara Ginsberg wrote, "No matter what, Meir always went first and that was the reason we followed him."[54]

The next day, Meir was paroled and he returned to the vigil.[55] Yitta Halberstam described it:

> The vigil is in its third day. It is 10 o'clock in the morning. As I walk toward the site of the vigil, numbed by the harsh, biting winds which sweep past me, I wonder: Will anyone be there in this icy weather? Could anyone have possibly stayed the night, as pledged, in this nipping cold? I reach the vigil site and look on in astonishment. Some 15 youngsters, faces reddened, huddled in their parkas, are marching in a bedraggled-looking circle, calling out to the few who will stop to listen, "Please save Soviet Jewry!"
>
> Their voices are tired and faint and very young. Amazed to find that the vigil was not abandoned, I asked, "Have you been here all night?" They nod in assent. "But how could you? It's so cold."
>
> "It is colder in Russia," one very young boy declares.[56]

With the end of the vigil came the good news that the Leningrad death sentences had been commuted.[57] One newspaper columnist credited the JDL:

> Rabbi Meir Kahane led a series of turbulent demonstrations.... Hundreds of JDL youngsters maintained day and night vigils and thus helped to stir up the

conscience of America.... There was danger in delaying vigorous actions of protest. Those condemned to death in Leningrad might have had their sentences executed the next day.... Let us acknowledge the fact, although it may be unpopular to say so, that it was the Jewish Defense League that acted promptly in the first few highly critical days after the death sentences in Leningrad were announced and thus served as the catalytic agent which spurred the momentum of nationwide protests against the Soviet travesty of justice.[58]

The following week, the *Jewish Press* carried Meir's article "Reflections on a Vigil." There he congratulated all the Jewish organizations that had contributed to the cancellation of the Leningrad death sentences but added, "It is militant pressure that causes 'moderates' to take action."[59]

Chapter 18

Branching Out (1970)

Two Old Desks

THE JEWISH DEFENSE League's demonstrations made a strong impression on Geula Cohen, an Israeli columnist who often wrote about Soviet Jewry. During a visit to the United States, Cohen stopped in at the JDL office. She found a small, narrow room, with desks, chairs and floor piled high with flyers and newsletters. Attention-getting posters that said "Be Relevant" and "Never Again" adorned the walls. In the room were young men and women, some typing on typewriters, some folding piles of flyers, others stuffing them into envelopes, one talking on the telephone. She wrote, "Amid the confused disorder, something is happening. There's a feeling of a lack of professionalism, but these people care about what they're doing."[1]

One person in the office who cared about the JDL was Meir's mother, Sonia, who was proud of him and wanted to help. When she was close to 60, she traveled into Manhattan by subway twice a week. She would open the mail, send receipts for donations, type membership invoices and help stuff envelopes for mass mailings. Renee Brown recalled that she was always sweeping up papers, trying to keep the cluttered office clean.[2]

Other reports on the JDL office also remarked on the volunteers and the clutter. In an article about the JDL in *Midstream*, Kenneth Braiterman wrote:

> The outer office is full of kids; JDL has no clerical staff except for these young volunteers. Some of the kids look like typical long-haired radical-liberal college students. Others look like super-ethnic refugees from some yeshiva. Others look like kids I remember from my own Zionist youth movement wearing those Israeli-style knit yarmulkes no bigger than a fifty-cent piece that are held on with a bobbie pin.

Braiterman described the office – in a low-rent area of Manhattan – in greater detail:

The outer office contains one long cardboard-top table, two old desks painted dull yellow, and a couple of metal bookshelves. Every flat surface in the outer office is covered with stacks of mimeographed flyers and assorted clutter. Each desk contains a phone which rings incessantly and an ancient typewriter, the kind you see in the old movies about the city room of a crusading newspaper...."

The cracked plaster walls of Meir's small inner office, Braiterman noted, were covered with maps, schedules and pictures of Zeev Jabotinsky.[3]

Interviewing Meir for the *Manhattan Tribune*, Joel Griffith wrote:

Soon Rabbi Kahane rushes out of his office, shakes my hand shyly, and rushes back in beckoning for me to follow. The rabbi is 37 years old and has a handsome, Semitic face with white skin, bluish jowls and jet-black eyebrows. Seated behind his battered dark wood desk, he seems a little nervous and the side of his face tics occasionally. But his manner is cooperative, earnest...."

Griffith found the office "cluttered and unpretentious; on one wall there is an oil painting depicting the Wailing Wall of Jerusalem, on the opposite wall a poster exhorting members to attend the Shori Dojo (Japanese for "school of victory") karate school."[4]

Most JDL activities in 1970 originated in this office. Among those detailed in *The Story of the Jewish Defense League*:

- Protests against Leonard Bernstein's January fundraising for the Black Panthers, avowed anti-Semites opposed to the State of Israel.[5]

- Campaigns in February, March, and November to impel the Federation of Jewish Philanthropies of New York to fund Jewish education and other Jewish causes.[6]

- A May 7 visit to Black Panther headquarters in Harlem.[7]

- Responses to anti-Jewish policies in universities.[8]

- Aid to Jews in the Williamsburg section of Brooklyn on June 28, following three days of escalating assaults by roving bands of black and Puerto Rican youths, after a Jewish motorist accidentally injured a black girl.[9]

- The arrest of JDL members Avraham and Nancy Hershkowitz on September 27 as they were boarding a plane to London at Kennedy Airport. They were found to have concealed weapons and were suspected of planning a revenge hijacking of an Egyptian airliner in London. Avraham was convicted only of falsifying information on his passport application.[10]

- Measures to reinstate Dr. Arnold H. Einhorn as head of the Department of

Pediatrics at the Albert Einstein College of Medicine, after he was dismissed in November because of threats by black activists.[11]

Much of JDL's success was due to Meir's perceptive, intuitive grasp of what interested the media. However, much depended on how the media presented the story. A letter from Samuel Shoshan, JDL's director of public relations, to George Sharman, head of Channel 5 TV, about JDL's visit to Black Panther headquarters, makes this clear:

> You reported the Jewish Defense League picketing the Black Panthers' head-quarters in Harlem, showed the police keeping the two groups separated and also illustrated the reason for JDL being there by Rabbi Kahane's brief address to the Panthers while standing on a truck. It all came across the screen as an informative and objective report.
>
> On the other hand, Roger Grimsby, on Channel 7, opened up with the neg-ative comment "Someone thought it would be a good idea to go up to Harlem," while the screen showed only police pushing, etc. One never found out why JDL went to picket nor about their decrying the Panthers' virulent anti-Semitism. The whole tone was one of scoffing....[12]

Helping Any Jew Anywhere

Media reports on the JDL had a positive tone after the New York gravediggers union went on strike in January 1970. When the union refused to allow any buri-als, Orthodox Jews immediately went to court, because Jewish Law requires bur-ial within three days. Since this was a question of religious liberty, the New York State Supreme Court ordered the gravediggers union to permit the burial of Orthodox Jews without delay. However, their graves had to be dug either by fam-ily members or by volunteers.[13]

Since the JDL's objective was – in Meir's words – "to defend ALL Jewish rights, no matter what is involved," he announced that they would provide vol-unteers. Digging in frozen ground was very hard work for the young JDL volun-teers. They knew that many elderly Jews needed their help, but after a while the boys begged off. JDL office manager Avraham Hershkowitz asked girls to replace them, embarrassing the boys into resuming their duties.[14]

In one case, the JDL was summoned when the caretaker of a cemetery pre-vented sons from burying their father. A photo of two husky JDL gravediggers appeared on the front page of the *Daily News* and the story was featured on local TV news and in a national Jewish newspaper.[15] When the strike ended in mid-March, more people had heard of JDL and the JDL gained a reputation for helping any Jew, anywhere. Avraham Hershkowitz recalled:

I was on duty in the office when a woman called. She had already called the police and then the Jewish War Veterans. It was midnight and the woman was in a panic. She lived with her elderly father, a Holocaust survivor, in a poor neighborhood in the Bronx, and often drug addicts stole from them. She had come from work and found her father with stab wounds and his head in the oven with the gas on.

She called an ambulance, and automatically a police car came with it. The neighbors who had stabbed her father phoned her and said, "You called the cops – we'll get you for that." The police told her to move out of the neighborhood.

I got some people with shotguns and rifles to stay with her that night, so the neighbors would see that she had protection. Whenever she left the house they would escort her with rifles for the neighbors to see. Finally, one of the JDL men who was a real estate agent found her an apartment in a different neighborhood.[16]

Janice Stern told me why she joined JDL:

My mother lived on Sea Breeze Avenue in Brooklyn. Neighborhood black kids would run through the halls shouting threats at the Jewish residents, and they'd steal their social security checks from the mailbox. I called the police who said they couldn't do anything against shouts and threats. Then I called a friend of mine, Hermione, who had joined JDL, and she set up an appointment for me with Meir. He sent some guys who waited for them in the hall, and when they came running through the halls shouting, they beat them up and threatened them, and that kept them from ever again terrorizing my mother's building. That's when I joined JDL.[17]

Mirage Fighter Planes for Israel

JDL members' willingness to aid any Jew, even a stranger, stemmed from Meir's emphasis on *ahavat Yisrael*, loving one's fellow Jews and taking responsibility for them. This was the reason JDLers traveled to Washington in February to demonstrate against visiting French President Georges Pompidou. They identified with their Israeli brothers, to whom France had refused to deliver the Mirage fighter planes Israel had already paid for.[*] Simcha Mallenbaum wrote:

The bus [chartered for the trip to Washington] had to be supplemented by a caravan of private cars hastily assembled when so many showed up that there was S.R.O. [standing room only] on the bus....

---

[*] France's refusal to deliver the planes was due to an international embargo that was nominally an effort to reduce military escalation of the Middle East conflict, but it was Israel that was primarily hurt by it.

> At noon we waited outside the National Press Club, where Pompidou was scheduled to speak.... As he got out of his limousine, we began to chant, "Down with Pomp! Down with Pomp!" In a few minutes, the police arrested as many of us as they could.[18]

Meir had driven to Washington earlier with Mal Lebowitz, in order to meet with the chief of police and go over the ground rules of demonstrations. Mal recalled:

> We were told that demonstrators were not allowed within five hundred feet of any foreign dignitary. We ended up in jail, twenty-eight of us, about half adults and half kids. I spent about three hours in a cell with Meir.
>
> An official comes over – "Rabbi, we have sixteen juveniles here. If you promise to get them out of Washington by five o'clock, we'll release them in your custody." Meir says, "No." I looked at him and I said, "Yes." Finally, he agreed. The official starts to walk away. We look at each other. I call him back. – "You just released sixteen kids into the custody of the Rabbi. It's going to get a little crowded in this cell, don't you think?"[19]

The *New York Times* report on Pompidou's visit to Washington noted: "... Minor protests by pro-Israeli groups resulted in twenty-eight arrests, including that of Rabbi Meir Kahane." The police charged them with disorderly conduct and breach of the peace and released them all. The final disposition of the case was the forfeit of the ten-dollar collateral paid by each one in order to be released on his own recognizance.[20]

The principle of *ahavat Yisrael*, which includes self-sacrifice on behalf of other Jews, was an important feature of this demonstration. "Some of us had gotten up at three or four o'clock Tuesday morning," Mallenbaum wrote, "... and we didn't get home until early Wednesday morning. All of us had missed a day of work or school."[21]

Meir taught the importance of *ahavat Yisrael* in his writings and at JDL meetings and seminars. [22] First and foremost, he was an educator. That's why the JDL maintained a Speakers Bureau. To quote the *Jewish Defense League Newsletter:* "As part of our program to educate the public, the JDL Speakers Bureau has started a speakers training program to train future JDL speakers. In order to become a speaker, a person must undergo an extensive period of training...."[23] Many people I interviewed for this book recalled that Meir's seminars had inspired them to be good Jews.

Reaching Young Jews

For Meir, the education of young Jews was paramount. To counteract the growing trend of assimilation on college campuses, where Jewish youth were joining anti-Jewish and anti-Zionist leftist groups, he made JDL campus activities a priority.

All Jewish leaders were acutely concerned about this trend. The *American Jewish Yearbook* reported on "... the alienation from the Jewish tradition of many bright, socially conscious young people who joined the New Left movement ... [which is] generally anti-Israel [and] anti-Zionist...." A blatant example was Abbie Hoffman, a Jewish leftist student leader who said, "I support the Palestinians. They are the victims of the Middle East conflict."[24]

By November 1969, the JDL had twenty-four chapters operating in colleges and a membership drive under way in junior high and high schools, "so that JDL will be THE counterforce to the radical groups that are almost unopposed at present in weaning away Jewish youth to their cause."[25]

By autumn 1970, there were chapters at New York University, Pace College, Columbia University, the State University at New Paltz, Long Island University, the Fashion Institute of Technology (FIT), and on all campuses of the City University of New York. Outside New York, there were chapters at Northwestern University, the University of Arizona, the University of Michigan, UCLA, and at two Montreal colleges.[26]

Since November 1969, JDL Youth had its own office in Manhattan at 440 West 42nd Street, near Tenth Avenue. This was a loft that also housed the karate school, Shori Dojo, run by Alex Sternberg, age 21. The youngsters were given responsibilities and lived up to them. At 17, Izzy Danziger was in charge of "Jewish Defense League Rifle Range No. 4," which opened in the Williamsburg section of Brooklyn in October. The *Jewish Defense League Newsletter* was edited by high school and college students and, at Meir's initiative, a representative of the youth movement took part in JDL board meetings.[27]

During this period, there was an effort to formally organize JDL into two groups named Oz (Hebrew for "strength"). The younger JDL members who knew karate and could take part in street fighting were in Oz-A. Adults and other young people who picketed and took part in demonstrations were in Oz-B. In 1972, Oz-A became the "*Chaya* Squad," so called because a *chaya*, a "wild animal" in Hebrew, was someone who would cast off the "wimpy" Jewish image and act like a wild animal when he was called on to protect other Jews.[28]

At the beginning of September, JDL's youth movement held a week-long leadership training seminar on the grounds of Camp Jedel. To ensure attendance, the JDL subsidized the seminar, charging participants only $10 for the week. There were three ninety-minute lectures each day. Two of Meir's were "An In-Depth Study of the Radical Organizations of Today" and "The Current Jewish Organizations: What Are They and What Do They Stand For?" Bert Zweibon spoke about becoming a public speaker and campus activist. Dov Sperling, a Russian Jew who had immigrated to Israel, spoke about how to free Soviet Jews. Other topics were "The Jewish Claim to Israel" and "How to Combat Arab Propaganda." Karate and riflery classes were mandatory. Riflery was taught by Seymour Charnoff and karate by Alex Sternberg. All the arrangements for the leadership training seminar, including the lectures, were made by JDL's Youth Board.[29]

To strengthen JDL's educational aspect, Meir wrote *The Jewish Defense League: Principles and Philosophies*, a 24-page booklet that emphasized five values:

- *Ahavat Yisrael*, including a "pledge to help all Jews, wherever they may be, at all times."

- *Hadar Yisrael*, Jewish dignity and pride; an assertion of "immense pride in our Jewish heritage."

- *Barzel Yisrael*, literally "the iron of Israel," or physical strength: "Only Jews can help Jews. The NEW JEW will rely on himself to earn the respect of others by increasing his own self-respect through physical strength, courage and self-knowledge."

- *Mishma'at Yisrael*, self-discipline for the sake of Jewish unity.

- *Bitachon*, faith in the indestructibility of the Jewish people, based on the "incredible history of the frailest of peoples and the Heavenly promise to the first Jew, Abraham."[30]

Holocaust awareness was intrinsic to the JDL. This is expressed eloquently in the introduction to *Principles and Philosophies*:

> We are a generation that lives in the memory and in the shadow of the six million. The destruction of one-third of our people, the Holocaust that occurred such a brief while ago, is a great trauma for us, a blow that irrevocably influences our lives and our thinking....
>
> From the bitter memories of a people grown sick unto death of suffering, from the tear-stained pages of Jewish history ... arises the new generation. Listen as this New Jew recalls his ancient and proud past and swears to his G-d, to himself and to his enemies – "Never Again!"

The second part of *Principles and Philosophies* was headed "Putting Ideology into Practice." It discussed physical attacks on Jews, reverse discrimination, changing neighborhoods, crime, and poverty. It pointed out the negative factors in America, such as the growing economic crisis and extremist anti-Jewish groups, and maintained that the only option for American Jews was aliya, to immigrate to Israel. (Within a short time, aliya was featured in all Meir's talks.)

The booklet concluded: "The fight for the mind and allegiance of the Jewish youth is one of the primary aims of JDL. Ideologies and movements, foreign and destructive to Jewry, vie with each other for Jewish youth.... Only through a maximum Jewish education can we hope to keep our Jewish youth.... JDL believes in the necessity for establishing unique Jewish schools with programs similar to those given at JDL camps."[31]

Meir's lifelong effort to set up a formal educational framework was formulated as early as 1970. He envisioned a Jewish Identity Center: "... Its purpose is to instill Jewish pride, nationalism, culture and tradition into young Jewish boys and girls." It would be "open to Jews of all ages regardless of religious background and will concentrate on courses involving Jewish nationalism, history, tradition and culture, modern-day problems (Israel-Arabs, Soviet Jewry), and the crisis for Jews in America."

Part of the center would be Yeshiva Torah Ve'Oz (The Yeshiva of Torah and Strength), a "rabbinical military school" for college-age Jewish youth. "The military school," Meir wrote, "will train young men for the rabbinate with the traditional Talmudical courses supplemented by Jewish history (with emphasis on Jewish resistance), laws concerning Eretz Yisrael (the Land of Israel), as well as courses in karate, drill, and other weapons of self-defense."[32] In November 1970 the *Jewish Press* carried an advertisement for the Jewish Identity Center and a feature article about Yeshiva Torah Ve'Oz. In the article, Meir wrote that a primary purpose of the JDL was to educate first-rate leaders who would work with Jewish youth in high schools and on campuses.[33]

One method Meir used to instill Jewish pride was teaching about Jewish heroes, such as Dov Gruner, a member of the Irgun.* On April 23, 1946, during British Mandatory rule in Palestine, Gruner took part in an attack on the British police station in Ramat Gan. He was charged with firing on – not killing – a policemen. He was sentenced to the gallows and was hanged April 16, 1947.[34] The *Jewish Defense League Newsletter* reported: "JDL dedicated the Jewish month of Cheshvan (November-December) to the memory of Dov Gruner, who gave his life so that there could be a Jewish state. During Cheshvan, Rabbi Kahane lectured on many college campuses about Dov Gruner and Jewish pride.... Audiences were attentive and most people were moved by the self-sacrifice of this great Jew.... Most JDL college chapters have observed Dov Gruner month with special 'learn-ins' during which Dov Gruner and other Jewish heroes and martyrs were honored by speech and song."[35] Flyers announcing Meir's talk about Gruner on November 12 at Brooklyn College proclaimed:

> Dov Gruner month will serve as the start of a great campaign to educate Americans as to the truth of the Jewish national claim to Israel ... while winning back thousands of young Jews whose ignorance of this phase of Jewish history has led them to echo radical leftist and Arab stupidities....

---

* A pre-state military unit. See Glossary.

The Irgun, Sternists and Hagana are a proud chapter in Jewish history, a time when Jews told a world that had kicked the Jew for two thousand years and capped it with the horror of Auschwitz: We have had enough! We are going home![36]

Meir had been speaking since the beginning of the year on college campuses. The February 18 issue of the *Long Island Press*, featuring a picture of him in a suit and striped tie, reported: "Yesterday Rabbi Meir Kahane spoke to 200 Queens College students.... At the end of his prepared talk he answered questions for 30 minutes. He said, 'We are not racists. We believe in the equality of all men ... that men are created equally bad or good. We'll fight the bad guys and help the good ones.... We aim to protect our Jewish brethren.... We have to have respect before we can have love, and the only way to get respect is to earn it...'"[37]

Under FBI Scrutiny

Soon the FBI was keeping track of Meir's speaking engagements. He was under investigation because "... the White House and the attorney general have an interest in Kahane's activities, since he and JDL have attempted to disrupt U.S.-Soviet relations...." The investigation, which began in June 1970, was indirect. Reports were received from informants and some phone calls were monitored. Meir was interviewed directly by FBI agents only three times: on September 18, 1969, when he sent letters to Arab diplomats; on September 29, 1970, after JDL members Avraham and Nancy Hershkowitz attempted to board a plane while carrying weapons; and on September 11, 1972, in Tel Aviv, concerning threats to kidnap Soviet diplomats.[38]

Sometimes, FBI informants did more than just submit reports. One tried to turn people against Meir when he spoke at the Jewish Community Center in St. Louis during the summer of 1970. He said Meir was a "con man" and was using the JDL to get together sufficient funds to get him and his family to Israel, where they could "live in style."[39]

The FBI files on Meir were labeled "Internal Security – Nationalistic Tendency." The FBI was, of course, exaggerating the danger posed by Meir's activities. Said Bert Zweibon, "We have come to the point where the FBI has seen it necessary to destroy us. Not because we are subversive to the government. But because ... we have hit the Soviet nervous system ... a flea attacking an elephant. But that flea made that animal squirm. JDL was put on page one for championing Soviet Jewry. Because of this, the government has unleashed a campaign in full power to silence us."[40]

Meir often joked about being under FBI surveillance. "Speak into the sugar bowl, please," he would say to guests. When he wanted to speak to someone privately, he would ask him to step outside.

FBI reports were an important source of information for this book, especially regarding Meir's speaking engagements. When Meir spoke at the American University in Washington on October 13, the FBI reported in typically stilted style that thirty-five youths attended his two-hour talk in which he urged Jewish unity and the formation of a JDL chapter on campus.[41] The FBI counted about sixty-five people in attendance at his talk at the Hillel House of the University of Missouri at Columbia some two weeks later. The FBI summary of his speech said, "Kahane compared the present conditions in the United States to conditions present in Germany before World War II. Kahane claimed Jews will be blamed for the Vietnam War. Jews must overcome their 'respectable hang-up' and resort to means which have helped blacks in America to achieve their goals. Kahane stated the Jewish future in the U.S. is hopeless. Kahane, who is planning immigration to Israel in September 1971, stated he hoped all American Jews will go to Israel."

The FBI report included the information that Meir rented a two-door Ford Galaxy from the Hertz rental agency at St. Louis' Lambert Field airport for the drive to the University. The Hertz employee described Meir as wearing "a gray flannel jacket, a white shirt and a black rabbi-type hat." Meir stayed in room 203 at the Downtowner Motor Inn in Columbia and departed at 5:45 A.M.[42] An early departure hour was usual for Meir. He preferred to arrive back in New York early because he had so much to do.

On November 1, Meir spoke at Williams College in northwestern Massachusetts. The college paper reported on some of the issues he discussed:

> "If you think 'to turn the other cheek' is in the Bible, you're absolutely right, but you've been reading the wrong Bible." With these words Rabbi Meir Kahane, the leader of the Jewish Defense League, summarized the motivating concepts behind his organization.
>
> ... The Jewish Defense League (JDL) came into being to fill "a vacuum" in [American Jewish] leadership.... He told of the situation existing in 1943 when the American Jewish community learned of the existence of Hitler's "death camps." The leaders went to President Franklin Roosevelt, demanding that the United States bomb ... the rail lines leading to them.... Roosevelt denied this request.... Rabbi Kahane contends that these Jews should have gone beyond their "respectable" protests of sermons and pamphleteering. They should have gone into the streets and brought dramatic attention to their plight.
>
> ... The Soviet Union, according to Kahane, has been perpetrating a program of "national and cultural genocide" for the last 53 years.... It is this situation the JDL hopes to cure by awakening the world to this ... problem.[43]

A month later Meir was in Los Angeles, speaking at UCLA, a bastion of left-wing students. He had been invited by Associated Students chairman Bob

Elias, who wrote: "I had read about him in *Esquire* and was excited, so I invited him to come to UCLA. I remember a lot about his talk that day."[44]

Some points in Meir's hour-long talk were quoted in UCLA's *Daily Bruin*:

> "People who call us un-Jewish are those whose Jewish education has been arrested somewhere around age 13," Rabbi Meir Kahane, head of the Jewish Defense League (JDL) in New York, told a capacity audience in Haines Hall 39 yesterday.
>
> "There is a crisis for Jews in this country – a danger because Jews are the main target of the radical right and the blacks, and Israel has become the target for the New Left," Kahane said.
>
> "The Jewish leadership in this country is bankrupt," he said. "It doesn't do enough for Soviet Jews, for Jewish education or for Israel. Jewish priorities are all screwed up."
>
> Kahane told of the assistance given by the JDL when trouble erupted in the poor, integrated Williamsburg neighborhood of New York City last June. "A Jewish truck driver accidentally ran over a young black girl and the neighborhood blacks began three days of street fights against the Hasidic Williamsburg Jews," he said.
>
> "The Jews called the JDL," Kahane said, "which came to fight with bottles, bricks and chains and restored peace. JDL is not a respectable group," Kahane said.…[45]

An audio tape of this speech has more on the subject of being respectable, especially concerning the Jewish Establishment's obsession with respectability during the Holocaust. "Blacks," Meir said, "faced with inequality in education and in employment, faced with rules about where they could sit on a bus – to their credit – they went into the streets, and they marched in the streets and they sat in the streets and they chained themselves to buildings. They were beaten and they came back again and again – and they won. When it was a question, not of seats on a bus, but of Jewish lives, why didn't Jewish leaders do the same? … Because Jews have a hang-up. It's called respectability.… 'That's not any way for nice Jewish boys to behave,' they say."

Meir concluded his speech with the words, "If all the Jewish respectable groups were laid end to end there'd be no end to them."[46] This line was repeated by Meir at countless lectures for many years, and it was usually greeted with appreciative laughter and applause.

The *Jewish Defense League Newsletter* said of that talk: "The students not only listened attentively, but responded to his remarks with great enthusiasm and applause." The *Newsletter* continued: "That same day Rabbi Kahane flew via Air West to Tucson and spoke at 8 P.M. to students at Hillel House at the University of Arizona. The rapport with these students was extremely gratifying."[47] An FBI report on the Tucson visit says that Meir spoke "to about thirty students about the aims of JDL, criticizing Jewish leaders for not instilling pride in their heritage in youth and for not protecting Jews from anti-Semitic violence."[48]

On December 10, Meir was back in Manhattan, speaking at City College. A picture on the front page of the college newspaper, *Observation Post*, shows him at the podium in a typical pose – his right hand hooked to the back of his belt, his left hand gesturing with pointed finger. For Meir, it was important to speak at colleges like this one, where the danger to the young Jews exposed to leftist philosophies was most acute. All too often, the Jewish leftists were the most fervent pro-Palestinians, accusing Israel of cruel oppression.

Meir's 90-minute speech was marred by heckling and fighting in the audience. First, a leftist heckler called out *"Sieg Heil"* and a JDLer picked up a chair and tossed it at the heckler. Meir resumed his speech but was soon interrupted when two students stood up and unfurled a handmade version of the Israel flag with a swastika superimposed on the Star of David. JDL members lunged for them in a renewed outbreak of fighting. College guards intervened to separate the two factions. Later, radicals took up a chant of "Long live Al Fatah – Off JDL." Meir's response was quoted in the college newspaper:

> The State of Israel is our state; the Land of Israel is our land. It's time to stop apologizing. I want each and every Jew here to understand that your future lies in the State of Israel. It's your job to go there, live there, and fight for the State of Israel.[49]

Chapter 19

Spreading the Message (1970)

A Dramatic Speaking Style

MEIR'S SPEECHES DREW large crowds of all ages. Many organizations and synagogues sought him out. A confidential report of an Establishment group, the American Jewish Committee, revealed: "Rabbi Kahane, generally conceded to be an emotional speaker, is said to have more than five speaking engagements a week, during the course of which he seeks to recruit members and solicit funds."[1] The aim of Meir's talks was not only to enlist new members and raise money. His primary purpose was to educate – to transmit his ideas and ideology.

The *New York Times* described his dramatic speaking style: "In his speaking dates throughout the country, Rabbi Kahane starts in a quiet voice, explaining his view of anti-Semitism in the United States. His voice rises to a homiletic crescendo. By the time he ends his address, his voice is booming, 'Never Again.'"[2]

A complete record of Meir's 1970 speaking engagements does not exist. My information about his talks is derived from newspaper clippings, his correspondence with the Jewish Welfare Board Lecture Bureau, which arranged some of his lectures, and FBI reports which I received under the Freedom of Information Act.[3]

In February 1970, when Meir spoke at Temple Beth Emeth in Philadelphia, a police report to the FBI noted that "approximately 250 people were observed entering the building" and that Meir spoke about "participation of young people in the JDL, the plight of Soviet Jewry and the need for more militancy in the Jewish community." During the next three months, Meir spoke at numerous synagogues, mostly in the greater New York area.[4]

In May, Meir addressed a huge audience in Montreal. This extraordinary turnout was due in part to the city's French separatist movement, which had encouraged a spurt of anti-Semitism in Quebec province. Milton Winston had this to say about Meir's talk there:

The appeal of the militant Jewish Defense League was demonstrated here when 1,200 local Jews chose attendance at a JDL rally rather than the Federated Zionist Organization of Canada's Israel Independence Day celebration that same evening.

The rabbi suggested that the "hang-up" of the Establishment was its concern about respectability: "Sometimes you have to go beyond respectability. We are learning defense techniques to change the image of the Jew as a patsy.

"... Jews should take to the streets ... and answer violence with violence. The world must be shaken," the founder of the JDL emphasized. "We are a people sick to death of being martyrs. It is not a Jewish concept to turn the other cheek.... It is a Jewish concept to live.

"... To the JDL there is nothing more sacred than peace; but it must be a two-way street."

To a standing ovation, the lawyer-rabbi pledged, "Never Again." He warned his audience that although "we need you; you need us more.... Support us, back us, join us."

The program for the evening included a karate demonstration....[5]

Seymour Lecker of the JDL Montreal chapter related: "When JDL was just starting up in Montreal, the rabbi came to speak with us and give us encouragement and direction.... Most of the early JDL activists in Montreal were not religious. But the rabbi accepted us, because, he said, it is important that every Jew in the world feel at home in the JDL. As a direct result of that talk and that attitude, JDL went on to become, two years later, the largest Jewish youth group in Montreal."[6]

In October, on the last day of Sukkot, Meir spoke at a synagogue in Borough Park, where he was enthusiastically received. A week earlier, the JDL had marched in the neighborhood to protest the disruption of Yom Kippur services at the Adath Sochochow synagogue by fifty young Puerto Ricans. After the hoodlums heaved a garbage can through the window, several congregants went out to repel them and were pummeled, receiving cuts, bruises, and bloody noses. By the time police came, the attackers had fled and there were no arrests. The lack of police protection and the widespread incidence of crime led Brooklyn borough president Sebastian Leone to decry the appalling fact "that people are afraid to leave their homes to attend religious services for fear of purse snatchers and assaults."[7]

From Boston to Los Angeles

The widespread of assimilation of American Jews, and Meir's efforts to counteract it, are revealed in an anecdote by a member of the Boston chapter. "Once Meir was invited to speak in a small town in Massachusetts, probably Brewster, home of many upper-class Jews. The meeting was held at the home of the president of the town's largest congregation. When Meir talked about assimilated Jews who name their children Christopher and Scott and send them to Catholic schools, one listener stood up and snapped, 'Rabbi, don't insult us. You know our host has two children named Christopher and Scott, and the public schools here are so bad that we have to send our children to private schools, and the only private schools are Catholic schools!' "[8]

Meir was always ready to debate JDL detractors. On October 25, he took on Will Maslow, executive director of the American Jewish Congress, at Adath Israel Synagogue in Trenton, New Jersey. An FBI report summarized: Maslow favored established procedures to obtain police protection, while Meir "made an emotional appeal to the pride of Jews to take steps to protect themselves...." On November 15 at the Suburban Temple in Wantagh, New York, Meir debated Rabbi Samuel Silver of Temple Sinai, Stamford, Connecticut. The topic: "Jewish Defense: How Militant?"[9]

Close to eight hundred people came to hear Meir speak on November 4 at Temple Emanuel, the largest synagogue in Providence. Speaking on "A New Approach to Anti-Semitism," he urged the audience to join the local JDL chapter.[10] On November 27, the Subversive Unit of the Chicago Police Department advised the FBI that Meir had been invited to speak in Chicago. An FBI agent who came to hear him counted approximately 350 people in the audience. He used Meir's own words in a summary of the talk, beginning with comments on President Roosevelt's failure to bomb the railroad tracks to Auschwitz:

> ... The JDL is taking to the streets now to prevent a repetition of what happened then. Three thousand Jews in the Soviet Union want to be free, and we should do everything to help them. If it takes a bombing to put them on page one, FINE.
>
> Jews have a hang-up about "Love." The Jews seem to think that the whole world must love us. More important is respect.... JDL believes that the time has come to have Jewish pride.... Stand up and fight! Jewish problems must come first! ... No anti-Semitism has ever been caused by a Jew who has fought back.[11]

Early in December, Meir spoke in Los Angeles for the first time. So many came to hear him at the Century Plaza Hotel that the audience overflowed into the lobby. Ninety people joined the Los Angeles chapter that evening.[12]

Back in New York on December 8, Meir addressed the Jackson Heights B'nai B'rith Harvest Lodge. The lodge members chose to invite him in spite of the B'nai B'rith leadership's opposition to the JDL. To be sure of enough seating for the large crowd that was expected, the Lodge rented a hall at the Sheraton Laguardia Hotel in Jackson Heights.[13]

Later that month, the JDL's First International Leadership Conference took place in Boston. The sessions were held at two synagogues: Beth Pinchas, whose rabbi was the Bostoner Rebbe, Rabbi Levi Yitzchak Horowitz, and Beth-El Atereth Israel, whose rabbi was Abraham Koolyck. On the final day of the conference, the media reported that the Soviet Union had cancelled the Bolshoi Ballet's U.S. tour because of JDL "hooliganism." That made the conference newsworthy, and Meir's closing address calling for the liberation of Soviet Jews was reported in the *New York Times*.[14]

For several years, Renee Brown arranged Meir's speaking engagements. A member of the JDL's first executive board, Brown wrote:

> I did not have to initiate the speaking engagements. I responded to requests from the people who handled speaking engagements for their organizations – synagogues, men's clubs, women's groups, and youth groups (Meir would speak at colleges and yeshivas without a fee. He wanted very much to speak to the youth).
>
> As Meir became more renowned, the requests to hear him steadily increased. He was invited to speak all over the country – Florida, California – as well as Canada....
>
> For out-of-town engagements, I would have the host organization pay for the airline ticket, have someone meet Meir at the airport, and arrange overnight accommodations. I would also suggest private fundraising parties. If there was a JDL chapter in the city, its members would generally arrange everything.[15]

To counteract Meir's popularity, the Jewish Establishment embarked on a campaign to discourage Jewish groups from inviting him to speak. The Union of American Hebrew Congregations (Reform) sent member congregations a seven-page report. It said: "... The JDL presents a distorted, paranoid view of America divided along religious, ethnic and racial lines.... We suggest that you reject appearances by JDL spokesmen in your congregation.... Print a repudiation of JDL in your congregation's bulletin.... Oppose them publicly in every way.... Urge any Jewish organization to which you belong to publish a statement of repudiation of the JDL."[16]

Rabbi Kurt Klappholz, writing in the *Bulletin of the New York Board of Rabbis*, denounced "self-appointed Jewish defense groups that appear on the scene who allege to speak for the entire Jewish community while they actually only echo sentiments of a small segment of Jewry." (Ironically, that's precisely how Meir characterized the Establishment organizations.) At the same time, Rabbi Klappholz acknowledged that the JDL was filling a void. He conceded the need to train "young Jews in self-defense methods to protect themselves against street attacks." Describing the problem of "people in urban centers being afraid to walk the streets by night," while "the rise of anti-Semitism among radical groups intensifies the Jewish problem in our cities," Rabbi Klappholz lamented that "our Jewish organizations have yet to devise an effective plan to deal with those aggravated conditions."[17]

Meir took the Jewish Establishment's opposition to him seriously. He believed he had to convince Jewish leaders to support such things as Jewish education and the struggle for Soviet Jewry, because they had the means and the status to do so. Meir charged that only wealthy Jews criticized the JDL. "How can a rich Jew or a non-Jew criticize an organization of lower and middle class Jews who live daily in terror?" he demanded. "The Establishment is scandalized by us, but our support comes from the grassroots."[18]

Grassroots Support

When Meir placed an ad in the *New York Times* requesting support for Operation Hagana, which would set up street patrols to prevent crime and violence, it was the lower and middle class grassroot Jews who responded:

- A Manhattan manufacturer of ladies' handbags wrote: "I am a concerned Jew, active in my community in Jewish affairs, and I do believe in your work and your continued existence. Please accept my check as a contribution from one concerned Jew to many others who have the courage of their convictions."

- A Brooklyn Jew wrote: "It was with a great sense of relief that I read your advertisement in the *New York Times*. Many of us would be glad to contribute money and ideas in an effort to solve this problem...."

- The program chairman of Jewish War Veterans' Stein-Goldie Post 552 wrote: "We give a damn for Jews and Americans always! On behalf of our commander Jerry Leitner, and the members of our JWV post, please accept $18 for Operation Hagana."

- "I strongly support your courageous stand and action," wrote a Bronx doctor. "You deserve the support of all Jews for your brave and dedicated work. Those who condemn you do so out of fear. These weaklings are willing to avoid confrontation by giving in to outrageous demands of hoodlums. Without your strong and dedicated leadership and action we could almost step back into the age of pogroms."

- A short letter from a Columbia University student said: "I heard Rabbi Kahane speak here last month. Please accept this money and use it for Operation Hagana. [signed] A Brother."[19]

Meir showed one reporter $10 and $15 checks and told him: "Though no group can claim to speak for all Jews, I think we can speak for the grassroots

Jew."[20] In keeping with the modest means of this constituency, JDL dues were low – $18 for new members and $10 for renewals – and the organization had to struggle to survive.

Fortunately, many members contributed not only their time and money, but also their services. Thus, the *Jewish Defense League Newsletter* offered "a special thanks and heartfelt note of appreciation to Morris Drucker, who has worked tirelessly to supply us with millions of pieces of printed matter AT HIS OWN EXPENSE." Another *Newsletter* thanked Irving (Ari) Calderon "for his donation of the IBM Selectric typewriter on which this stencil is being cut," adding, "We could use one or two more of them!" And Stanley Schumsky wrote to Meir in November 1969: "I am deputy chairman of the Brighton Beach chapter. I wonder if I could be of greater help.... Being in my own business, I do have some time to spare, and do not have to account to anyone for my time."[21]

Regardless of financial limitations, Meir's policy was to proceed with important projects – such as Camp Jedel and the 100-Mile March – and trust in G-d to help him raise the required funds. In October 1970 it was suddenly necessary to raise bail money for Nancy Hershkowitz, who had been arrested with her husband Avraham on September 27 on suspicion of planning a revenge hijacking. Everyone felt the urgency of protecting this young pregnant woman from the harsh conditions of prison. People gave generously. One *Jewish Press* ad alone netted $9,000 of the required $25,000 and she was finally freed on October 14, 1970. In a talk at Temple Emanuel in Providence, Meir said the JDL's annual budget was $70,000.[22] This figure may have included chapter budgets, but it implies that the JDL, for all its limited cash flow, was active.

New chapters were formed in 1970 in Los Angeles, Milwaukee, St. Louis, Chicago, San Francisco, Albuquerque (New Mexico), and Bergen County (New Jersey). All these locales were experiencing the violence – both general and anti-Semitic – that had led to the formation of JDL in New York City. In Chicago, there was an added factor, as Louis Shoichet wrote: "Chicago is the only city where American Nazi Party members can march down the street in Nazi uniform."[23]

The challenge of keeping chapters, and even individuals, in ideological agreement is evident in Meir's March 1970 letter to Marilyn Betman of Detroit.

> I have just received your letter advising us that you are in the process of organizing a group to be named the Jewish Defense League of Detroit.
>
> While I have no doubt that you may be working towards the same goal, I wish to inform you that the Jewish Defense League's name cannot be used by any group which is not sanctioned by our national organization. We have no intention of allowing our name to be used by potential kooks or racist groups, thus smearing our entire organization.

... If you are interested in becoming a part of the Jewish Defense League movement, let us know. [signed] Meir Kahane, National Chairman.[24]

Meir issued guidelines to ensure that all chapters followed JDL ideology:

JDL is a disciplined, centralized organization.... We are able to guarantee that no change in our philosophy and policy takes place. There are those individuals who would take a violently militant stance and those who would turn us into a carbon copy of other Jewish groups. Such changes would be disastrous, and will be impossible under our present [centralized] structure.

Through it [centralized organization], we are able to swiftly eliminate racists and unstable individuals who might drift in. Neither type has any place within JDL.

Through it, we insure the swift mobilization of members to demonstrations and other activities.

Through it, we eliminate internal politics and personal, petty quarrels.

... All final decisions come from our national office, which consists of an executive board, which works in consultation with a National Committee.[25]

Meir was often called upon to referee quarrels among the leaders. He urged them to rise above pettiness and concentrate on constructive activities for the sake of their common goal.

On Sunday, July 28, JDL's First International Convention was held at the Hotel New Yorker in Manhattan, with more than 150 delegates from JDL chapters all over the United States and Canada. Meir gave the keynote address, Bert Zweibon was the moderator, and Murray Schneider discussed finances. Delegates Alan Mandel of Boston, Arnie Mintzberg of Montreal and Ben Pomerantz of Philadelphia described the activities of their chapters. Meir was reelected national chairman and Russel Kelner of Philadelphia was elected to the national executive board, in an effort to transform the JDL into a truly national organization.[26]

Chapter 20

Time to Go Home (1970)

Spotlight on Extremism

S
HORTLY AFTER MEIR was dismissed from the *Jewish Press*, he sent samples of his column *Spotlight on Extremism* to a number of Anglo-Jewish newspapers. In his covering letter, he wrote, with a touch of irony: "... My ten-year association with the *Jewish Press* of Brooklyn was terminated rather abruptly recently. Because of this I have decided to syndicate my column *Spotlight on Extremism*."[1]

Only the bimonthly *California Jewish Record* of San Francisco was interested, offering to pay him $7.50 per column. Its January 16, 1970, issue advertised the new column with a reprint of *Newsweek*'s "The Jewish Vigilantes." "Cheers for the Panthers" appeared in the *Record* on January 30 with the byline "Meir Kahane, the 'Vigilante' Rabbi." However, the February 13 issue carried a large notice that *Spotlight* had been pre-empted by the "Who is a Jew?" controversy, and the March 17 *Record* featured instead a front-page reprint of the *Jerusalem Post*'s "The JDL: Heroes or Hooligans?" Meir's column never appeared in the *Record* again.[2]

The meager response to his syndication offer led him to publish *Spotlight on Extremism* privately, as a biweekly newsletter. Aside from hoping to supplement his modest JDL salary, Meir thought it was important to inform American Jews about anti-Semitic radical groups so they could protect themselves. To this end, he subscribed to numerous extremist publications – right-wing and left – produced in the United States and abroad. He also collected newspaper clippings about the groups.[3] He urged JDL members to subscribe to the newsletter for news of radical groups and samples of their anti-Semitic literature. Meir placed this ad in the *Jewish Press*:

> If you miss reading Meir Kahane
> DON'T!
> Subscribe today to his exciting newsletter
> *Spotlight on Extremism* at only $4.50 a year.[4]

Spotlight made its debut in January 1970 as a biweekly. In April, with number 8, it became a monthly and then there were longer gaps. Number 11, the final issue, appeared in November. Its eight pages included a front page article naming Communist Party members running for office in fifteen states. Inside were articles on two radical organizations, the Weathermen and the SDS (Students for a Democratic Society), as well as the lengthy "Hanoi: Zionists and Imperialists," fifth in the newsletter's *Moses vs. Marx* series. It also ran a story by Meir about Israeli soldier David Uzan, who was killed in 1967 at the Suez Canal. The story featured Uzan's last letter to his mother, affirming his sincere belief in the justice of Israel's struggle against the Arabs.

At $3.75 for an annual subscription and only twenty-five cents per issue, *Spotlight on Extremism* needed many more subscribers than it had to cover its printing costs, and Meir was forced to discontinue it.[5]

In addition to Meir's early efforts to syndicate *Spotlight*, he sought freelance writing jobs. Again only one newspaper responded: the weekly *Times of Israel*, published in Los Angeles and Tel Aviv. Meir's "Mr. Bernstein and the Panther," about Leonard Bernstein's fundraising for the Black Panthers, ran in the February 20 issue. Enclosing a $20 check for the article, publisher Stanley Goldfoot wrote, "We would like to have something by you every week." However, Meir's byline did not appear again until June.[6]

In May, putting a good face on it, Meir told a *New York Times* reporter that "he left his job as a columnist for the *Jewish Press* to devote most of his time to organizing new JDL chapters."[7] As it happened, less than a month later, Meir was again writing for the *Jewish Press*.

Return to the Jewish Press

His return to the *Press* was probably due to Rabbi Klass' esteem for Meir and for the JDL. Rabbi Klass once said to me, with a grin: "If there's no news to print, Meir goes out and makes news." An indication of the reconciliation was Arnold Fine's July column in praise of the JDL:

> Say what you will – the JDL and their membership have served a valuable purpose to the Jews of New York City. Although many say, "I agree with them in principle but not their tactics...." – some argue: When was the last time you saw a "principle" stop a riot? You may disagree with the JDL if you please, but accept the fact that they have a record of accomplishment... It is apparent that the JDL has made an impression on the Russians. And we'd like to feel that the Russians are in for a great many more surprises.[8]

Meir wrote for the *Jewish Press* until his death in 1990. On August 21, 1970, his column *Israel Through Laughter and Tears* resumed, and his new column *Is-*

rael News Analysis was launched.[9] *Analysis* focused on Israel's foreign policy and international problems. Topics included American pressure on Israel to accept the Rogers Plan, Third World countries' opposition to Israel in the United Nations, civil war in Jordan, Soviet hostility to Israel, Israeli foreign policy in Africa, the religious *Kulturkampf* in Israel, and Arab propaganda against Israel on college campuses. Meir's words remain as relevant as ever.

Meir's first article to appear in the *Jewish Press* after the hiatus was "Time to Go Home," which urged Jews to immigrate to Israel. Of the fledgling Jewish state, Meir wrote:

> ... that which we yearned for, that for which we prayed and wept and sat upon the cold stones each ninth of Av [the day of mourning for the First and Second Temples]. Here it is – at long last – the thing for which our grandfathers would rise in the middle of the night and shed hot tears to implore the Almighty for its merciful return.
>
> And here we sit, knowing that the dream has become a reality, seeing the vision become realization and casting – instead – our lot with the Nazis and Cleavers* [black anti-Semites] and New Left! How sad for us and woe to a people that cannot learn from its own bitter history. It is time to go home.[10]

Jewish Pride

In his lectures, Meir often cited the words of the Gerrer Rebbe on the Midrash that G-d gave the Torah to the Jews, not atop a lofty, majestic mountain, but at Mount Sinai, a modest peak barely more than a hill, to teach us to be humble. The Rebbe asked, "If so, why was the Torah not given in a valley?" And he answered, "To teach the Jews not to be overly humble!" This parable is the central theme of "The Way of the Mount," which appeared in the *Jewish Press* in August. Decrying misplaced humility, Meir declared: "Jewish rights are not cheap and Jewish defense is not wrong."[11]

"Time to Go Home" and a number of other *Jewish Press* articles written after June 1970 were reprinted (with Meir's byline) in the *Times of Israel*. One was "Beat Me Again." With a strong dose of sarcasm, it assailed Jews who supported the Jew-hating Black Panthers.

> By all means let us attempt to overlook the article in the April 25th issue of *Black Panther* which dropped its farcical argument that it was not anti-Jewish but only anti-Zionist by attacking those well-known "Zionists," Jerry Rubin, Abbie Hoffman and William Kunstler. Let us not be too pained by the statement: "It was a Zionist judge, Judge Friedman, who sentenced Huey P. Newton

---

* "Cleavers" refers to Eldridge Cleaver (1936-1998), the spokesman of the Black Panthers, a militant, leftist, anti-Establishment black-nationalist group.

to jail. It was a Zionist judge, Judge Hoffman, who allowed the other Zionists to go free but has kept Bobby Seale in jail."

"The one-eyed bandit of Tel Aviv, Moshe Dayan, must be hunted down and killed." Let us chalk such statements up to youthful exuberance and rhetoric. Does the cartoon in the *Panther* issue of April 11 showing a pig labeled "World Zionism" being fed a bottle of dollars by "U.S. Imperialism" trouble you? Let us not be overly SENSITIVE. Do Eldridge Cleaver's comments last winter that "Zionists, wherever they may be, are our enemies" cause you some little discomfort? Let us rather show our tolerance and understanding for Mr. Cleaver and be big enough to overlook his nasty words, undoubtedly spoken in unmeant anger. Are we tempted sometimes to question our support for the Panther freedom fighters merely because they attack Jewish merchants, embrace Al Fatah and do all manner of things that seemingly menace Jews? Let us overcome this childish temptation and realize that oppressed peoples have reason to overdo their attacks and that we, as a moral and suffering people, must learn to accept a little bit of anti-Semitism for the general good.

Indeed, it is time for all Jews to consider membership in JAM – Jewish Association of Masochists. It may not be easy to pass the stringent requirements which call for an ability to be insulted and berated while smiling; beaten and kicked while shouting happily: "Beat me again, again."[12]

In November Meir wrote "Freedom of Filth," concerning the deteriorating moral fiber of America, and "Next Year in Jerusalem – Maybe," condemning the materialism that keeps Jews in America. In December, prior to the 100-Hour Vigil, he wrote two articles about Soviet Jewry: "Blueprint for Soviet Jewry" outlined the actions necessary to help the Jews in Russia and explained why such efforts would succeed. "Confession" urged American Jews to repent for their inaction during the Holocaust by working vigorously on behalf of Soviet Jewry.[13]

Jewish Education

In "Jewish Money," Meir revealed the state of organized Jewish charities in America, and reiterated the importance of Jewish education:

> ... Federation, a highly organized modern-day version of *tsedaka*, charity, that bears no resemblance whatsoever to the original warm and moving concept, is an autocratic, undemocratic corporation run by a small group of wealthy, assimilated Jews with few ties to the Jewish community and little understanding of the needs of the little Jew. Not elected by the Jewish community, they are accountable to no one and channel the funds received by the Federation into institutions and areas that are alien to real Jewish needs.
>
> In an era when the greatest of problems remains the alienation of Jewish youth from their people and heritage, and when this phenomenon is traceable

directly to the primitive state of Jewish education in America, these arrogant men refuse to allocate more than a pittance of their huge sums to that education.

At a time when the Jewish youth can look forward only to the farce of the afternoon Hebrew school, which leaves him looking upon Judaism as a travesty dreamed up by a bar mitzvah caterer, ... the Federation refuses to understand the need for a maximum Jewish education.... [He] goes into his university and contrasts his farcical Judaism with the depth shown him by agnostic professors, leftist movements and radical causes – a thing that is the direct cause of the phenomenon of Jewish participation in the extremist camp – Federation allows the Jewish day school movement to remain an unwanted stepchild, plagued by absurdly low salaries for teachers and cramped buildings at best.

The reason is, of course, simple. The autocrats of Federation are assimilated Jews who frown upon Jewish education and long for Jewish "integration."... They are opposed to maximum Jewish education, per se. It is TOO JEWISH.

And so, these people ... continue to guarantee the destruction of the Jewish future. Funds for community centers that cater to a majority of non-Jews are always available.... Money for hospitals whose clientele is predominantly not Jewish can always be found....

But funds for Jewish education, the heart of Jewish survival, are *verboten*....[14]

Meir did more than write about this problem. He led several noisy, well-publicized demonstrations and sit-ins at the offices of the Federation of Jewish Philanthropies in Manhattan, demanding that they fund Jewish education. In November 1970, after five disruptive demonstrations, a court order barred JDL from Federation headquarters. However, Meir's campaign proved so effective that in 1971, at the annual meeting of the Council of Jewish Federations and Welfare Funds in Pittsburgh, Council president Max M. Fisher urged fellow Jewish leaders to "re-examine their obligations to the day schools, [which hold] one of the very best answers to further Jewish continuity."[15]

Preparing for Aliya

One axiom in JDL's *Principles and Philosophies* was that a Jew must live in Israel. In January 1970 a young JDL member told a reporter: "Rabbi Kahane is going to Israel in two years, and so are we." He added: "When Rabbi Kahane moves to Israel ... he will come to the States every other month." Meir's plan to continue working with the JDL after his move to Israel was announced at JDL's second annual convention. When reporters asked him how the JDL would function without him, Meir said: "We don't have lifelong, professional leaders. I will make aliya [go to live in Israel] and others will take my place. They will make aliya, and others will replace them. The JDL is not dependent on a 'Goldmann'* who refuses to leave the stage."[16]

Ever since my teen years in Bnei Akiva, I had aspired to live in Israel. When Meir's brother Nachman and his wife Faige moved there in 1962, we vowed to join them as soon as we could. Nachman wrote that a building was going up in his neighborhood with a fifth-floor apartment available for $25,000. I told Meir I was hesitant about living on the fifth floor and wanted to see the neighborhood myself, so during college intersession, I flew to Israel.

It was a cold, rainy day in February 1970 when I was met at the airport at dusk by Faige and her adorable children. We drove to Jerusalem with a taxi driver who had never heard of Itri,** the new neighborhood where she and Nachman had just moved. Theirs was the only completed building, perched on a hillside near a mud-covered road. The closest grocery store and bus stop were in the Mattersdorf neighborhood, a fifteen-minute walk away. There was a bus stop a bit closer, but getting there meant climbing up a steep dirt path – later replaced by a staircase of 118 steps – an ascent of about seven stories. To the north, beyond a series of hills and valleys, was the city of Ramallah. Its lights twinkled at night, and on a clear day we could see its radio antenna, the tallest in the Middle East.

I started apartment hunting in the Bayit Vegan neighborhood where my childhood friend Batya Soller Tratner lived. But in contrast to Itri, alone on a hilltop, Bayit Vegan, with its closely built housing, seemed overcrowded. I liked Itri's wide-open spaces. I also found old friends from Bnei Akiva living there. Because the neighborhood was so new that it lacked basic services, such as shops and buses, the apartments cost less than elsewhere in Jerusalem. A flat under construction on the ground floor of Faige and Nachman's building was especially inexpensive because the back rooms, the bedrooms, were partially under ground. In the original plans, this was to have been a shop, with the back rooms used as storerooms. When the contractor realized it would be a long time before a store in this neighborhood would be commercially viable, he decided to construct an apartment instead. Priced at $18,500, the down payment was only about $6,000. I phoned Meir. "It sounds good to me," he said. "I trust your judgment. Sign a contract."

One of my friends in Itri warned me that this apartment would get very little sun because the kitchen and living room faced north, and the bedrooms, which faced south, had only small windows close to the ceiling. "So what!" I thought. "Who needs sun?" Coming from the United States, where fuel and electricity

---

* Nahum Goldmann was president of the World Jewish Congress for almost twenty years.
** Itri is an acronym for Israel Torah Research Institute, a Jerusalem yeshiva founded by Rabbi Mordechai Elefant. The construction of buildings in this previously uninhabited part of Jerusalem was a project of the yeshiva.

costs were lower, I was unaware that Israelis depend on the sun for warmth during the winter and light during the day. I also discovered during our first winter there that with the bedroom walls encased in earth, rainwater seeped in. Fortunately, the contractor was able to fix that.

I visited old friends in Israel during my trip. Many lived in Jerusalem, but I also traveled to Beersheba with Faige and Nachman and spent Shabbat with Avraham and Shoshana Silbert on the campus of Ohel Shlomo, the Bnei Akiva yeshiva that Avraham headed. On Sunday morning, Faige and the children boarded the bus with me to visit the historic Jewish town of Hebron, recaptured during the Six Day War. Jews were living in Hebron in an IDF military compound built in the 1930s by the British mandatory government. Among them were more old friends from Bnei Akiva: Rabbi Eliezer Waldman, later the head of Yeshivat Nir Kiryat Arba and a member of Knesset, and Miriam Beinhorn Levinger, whose husband, Rabbi Moshe Levinger, was largely responsible for the construction of Kiryat Arba, a populous town bordering on Hebron. Chaim Mageni, formerly a youth leader in Laurelton, who was an inspiring tour guide, lived in the compound, too.[17]

I looked forward to making aliya and living in Itri. I was glad my children would be near their cousins. For me, playing with my cousins was a happy childhood memory: My mother's parents lived in Williamsburg, as did most of her ten siblings, married and single. Almost every Saturday afternoon we would visit them, walking half an hour across the Williamsburg bridge from our home on the lower East Side. At dusk, we children played hide and seek in the darkened rooms while the men said the evening prayers in a large room fitted out by my grandfather as a synagogue.

Signing the contract for our new apartment was a momentous step. I returned to New York, and we began making plans for the day we would move to our new home in Jerusalem.

A year later, in January 1971, it was Meir's turn to fly to Israel. Turbulent JDL protests against the death sentences of the two Leningrad Jews who had attempted to hijack a plane to Israel had played an important part in commuting their sentences, and Soviet activists in Israel had asked to meet with Meir.

Chapter 21

The Authorities React (January 1971)

A Visit to Israel

I N THE EARLY hours of January 1, 1971, after the JDL's highly successful 100-Hour Vigil for Soviet Jewry, Meir flew to Israel to meet with fellow activists. Ever since Geula Cohen's visit to the JDL office the previous year, she had urged this meeting for the good of Soviet Jewry. "Meir's name," she said, "was a byword among aliya activists in Russia." In Israel, she introduced him to Herut party leaders such as Amichai (Giddy) Paglin, Yitzchak Shamir, Shmuel Tamir, and Dov Shilansky.[1] In later years, leftists claimed that at these meetings Meir became a tool of the Israeli right-wing. This is patently ridiculous. Meir acted independently long before he met with them, as well as afterwards. The fact is that both sides saw these meetings as politically useful. Herut wanted to co-opt this famous American Jew to their ranks, and Meir wanted the public acceptance Herut could provide.[2]

Meir's reputation had preceded him: Israelis admired his bold activities on behalf of Soviet Jewry and in defense of American Jews. The Israeli media had covered his activities throughout 1970.

In May, after Arab terrorists murdered nine Israeli children in Avivim, JDLers took over the New York offices of a P.L.O.-related group and severely beat three Arabs. The JDL response was widely reported in Israeli newspapers. An editorial in *Yedioth Ahronoth* commented: "Rabbi Meir Kahane is an innovator; he's not a typical *galut* [Diaspora] Jew." *Hatzofe* applauded the JDL's retaliation and quoted a *New York Times* article about Meir's speaking engagements throughout the United States and the formation of JDL chapters in many cities.[3]

In September, *Ma'ariv* featured the JDL in "The Hagana, American-Style," and in October, Israeli radio's prime-time news program broadcast an interview with Meir concerning a bombing of the P.L.O.'s New York headquarters.[4]

On the day of his arrival in Israel, Meir's speech at the 100-Hour Vigil was broadcast on Israel's TV news. During his visit, Meir gave interviews to Israel radio news, the *Jerusalem Post*, *Yedioth Ahronoth*, and *Ma'ariv*. The articles detailed JDL activities and ideology and told of Meir's plan to move to Israel within the year. The media were so positive towards Meir that the reporter for *Yedioth Ahronoth* concluded his interview with the words: "I was happy that we would be gaining a new Israeli citizen and wished him and the Jewish people good luck."[5]

Uri Dan, in *Ma'ariv*, reminded his readers that it was the JDL pipe bombs at the Soviet Aeroflot and Intourist offices in Manhattan that had focused media attention on the plight of the Leningrad hijackers. Dan's observations on Meir's appearance are interesting: "His knitted black *kippa* blends in with his short black hair," he wrote, since Meir's *kippa* was often not visible in photographs. He commented on Meir's youthful appearance: "He looks more like a student than like the head of a dynamic, innovative organization."[6]

There were feature articles on Meir and the JDL in the weekend magazine sections of *Al Hamishmar* and *Ha'aretz*. "Rabbi Kahane's 'Jewish Panthers'" in *Al Hamishmar* described the karate school, the summer camp, and the Temple Emanu-El protest. Meir's article "Time to Go Home" in Hebrew translation was printed at the end of the article. The feature article in *Ha'aretz* declared Meir "the most famous Jew in America."[7]

JDL Harassment of Soviets Must Stop

Upon his return to New York on January 8, Meir initiated a series of daring acts that again brought the Soviet Jewish question to the fore in the media. One was a tactic he had conceived more than four months earlier: the harassment of individual Soviet diplomats by following them as they left the Soviet Mission. JDLers walked behind them holding signs that said, "We are following a Russian swine who oppresses Jews," and shouting epithets in Russian such as, "Go Home" and "Freedom for Jews." One reporter described the harassment of a Russian by six JDLers:

> He entered a Woolworth's. They followed him. He sat at a lunch counter and ordered a soft drink. They sat on stools beside him or stood behind him. This time they kept up a fairly loud commentary in English, as though they were talking to one another.... They made such comments as:
> "Give the Russian whatever he wants. Give the Russian everything he has coming to him.... I remember those brave Russian soldiers when they came into Hungary.... Don't forget the Russians in Czechoslovakia. They were brave too.... You can always tell a Russian by the yellow streak down his back."[8]

This tactic was roundly condemned by the Jewish Establishment, but when the cars of American reporters in Moscow were vandalized, the American public was angry at the Russians. Columnist Max Lerner said: "At first I thought that the prize for using exactly the worst means for achieving their ends should be awarded to the JDL ... But now that the Russians have retaliated by thinly disguised official vandalism against innocent American correspondents in Moscow, I must grudgingly award the prize instead to the Soviet government.... No Americans can expect the American Jews and their friends to be silent about the Soviet treatment of their fellows."[9]

The State Department, fearful of escalating anti-American sentiment in the Soviet Union, brought its full influence to bear, and during the coming months government agencies took vigorous steps to suppress the JDL. On January 12, police came to JDL headquarters and arrested Meir for missing a preliminary hearing on January 7, while he was in Israel – an unusually severe reaction to a minor infraction. He had sent a telegram to his lawyer Bert Zweibon to inform the court, but it arrived after the scheduled hearing.

A few hours later Meir was out on bail. He immediately called a press conference in the pressroom of the criminal court, declaring that he would not bow to pressure. Going straight from jail to the press conference, Meir looked understandably unkempt. A *New York Times* reporter pointedly described Meir's appearance as "unshaven." The unflattering photograph taken on this occasion was later used by many newspapers. The *Times* reporter accompanied Meir back to the "crowded, cluttered Jewish Defense League headquarters on West 42nd Street," where Meir told his supporters that this was just "the start of a campaign to stop us," but he was determined to continue. To point up the State Department's part in his arrest, he said: "The cries of three and a half million Soviet Jews are far louder than the bleatings of Foggy Bottom [a nickname for the State Department]."[10]

Meir's arrest for failing to appear in court garnered wide newspaper and TV coverage, including three Israeli television news clips, a mention on Israel radio, and a *New York Times* profile, "Spearhead of the JDL."[11]

Gabe Pressman interviewed Meir that day for NBC TV. Meir was shown walking through the halls of New York's Federal Courthouse surrounded by JDL members and reporters, saying, "When the federal government wants someone, they get them, but the JDL will never be stopped.... The harassment of Soviet officials will continue as long as there remains a Jew in Russia that wants to leave. U.S. government pressure will have no effect. Media attention is the only way to help Russia's Jews."[12]

Years later, leaders of the moderate Student Struggle for Soviet Jewry (SSSJ) confirmed the importance of attracting media attention. Glenn Richter, national director, wrote: "Rabbi Kahane propelled the issue of Soviet Jewry into the headlines in a way we, with our less confrontational demonstrations, could not.... I've been often asked if JDL tactics for Soviet Jewry helped or hurt.... Certainly, do-nothingness was disastrous, quiet diplomacy largely ineffective, and public pressure ultimately successful." Jacob Birnbaum, founder and national coordinator of SSSJ, likewise conceded, "[Rabbi Kahane] did heighten mass awareness of the plight of Soviet Jewry in a way that would not have occurred otherwise."[13]

On NBC's *Today* show the next morning, Meir was outspoken. "Anyone who thinks that we who have heard the cry of three and a half million Jews will be stopped ... really does not understand the psyche of Jews who were born in an era of Auschwitz. We lost six million Jews twenty-five years ago. We have no intention of losing three and a half million more to national genocide.... There is not the slightest doubt that after 53 years, the Soviet-Jewish issue is now on page one. It is THE story. That must help."[14]

By the second week in January 1971, Meir had several court cases pending. In one he was charged with first-degree riot and resisting arrest during the demonstration on December 27, 1970, outside the Soviet Mission. First-degree riot was a felony carrying a maximum penalty of seven years in prison! Another trial, scheduled for January 19, concerned a riot charge following his December 29, 1969, raid on the Tass offices. A third case, stemming from the December 30, 1969, demonstration at the Soviet Mission, was to come before a six-member jury to be impaneled February 9.[15]

Grand Jury Indictments

Then, on January 13, the New York County district attorney made a dramatic announcement: He was going to present a grand jury with four indictments against key JDL members. They were charged with damage caused to two Soviet agencies, Amtorg and Intourist, and with an alleged attack on Dr. Mohammad T. Mehdi. Meir was surely apprehensive, because only major crimes were brought before a grand jury.

He called a press conference that afternoon at Zweibon's law office to announce that he was relocating to Israel in August and that Zweibon would be the new JDL national chairman. There was speculation that this move was intended to dissociate the JDL from Meir's possibly illegal activities.[16] An interview Meir gave that evening reveals something of his state of mind. *New York Post* reporter Fern Marja Eckman wrote:

> With the news crackling around his handsome head like bolts of lightning, Rabbi Meir D. Kahane was a tired man. He sank into a chair and leaned back. "I'm exhausted," he said. "Totally exhausted."

He looked wilted. His short, black hair was neat under the dark yarmulke but his eyes were bloodshot, his white shirt with button-down collar was slightly rumpled and there was a hint of sag in his facial tone.

... Tensions were quickening between the U.S. and the Soviet Union, which gratified Kahane. But Mayor Lindsay had ordered a crackdown on the JDL.... Kahane faced imminent grand jury action on four anti-Soviet and anti-Arab incidents.

... Far from buckling under this pressure, Kahane functioned smoothly if wearily. For the next hour and fifteen minutes ... the rabbi remained gracious, mild, and unhurried as he responded to questions.

Periodically Zweibon and another associate burst into the office to announce, "We're late," and "I have to make a train," and "We have an appointment, LET'S GO." But Kahane stilled these strident interruptions without raising his voice.[17]

The next day, January 14, the JDL again made headlines when, at 6:30 in the morning, someone hurled a brick from a speeding car, smashing the display window of Aeroflot's Manhattan office. Interviewed on NBC News, Meir denied JDL responsibility for the incident and focused on the Soviet-Jewish issue. "If the United States' foreign policy is to buy peace over the bodies of Jews, then the end product will be dishonor to the United States, with no peace." He noted that letters and speeches by Jewish leaders had achieved nothing. Meir called Jewish critics of the JDL "finks" who worried what non-Jews thought of them. "The goals of the JDL," he said, "are to force Jews to empathize with the pain and distress of Russia's Jews and to establish a sense of pride in Jews." He pointed out that Russian Jewish children were forbidden to learn about Jewish culture and history. "Only outrageous actions can keep the question on the front page," he insisted.[18]

The *National Observer*'s Mark R. Arnold summed up: "JDL's campaign of harassment set off a string of events that subjected Soviet-American relations to new, worrisome strains." Arnold provided an interesting description of Meir. "For all his impassioned rhetoric and the intense, we-mean-business image he projects on television, Rabbi Kahane seems somehow miscast in the role of a militant leader. In three hours of conversations with this reporter, he was consistently soft-spoken and restrained, giving an impression of essential shyness and modesty that was reinforced by his slight build and the trace of a stammer." Similarly, reporter Michael Pousner remarked on Meir's "lean, neat appearance and placid features ... far from a firebrand."[19] Indeed, Meir was by nature quiet and retiring. He often said that he worked hard at projecting an aggressive image in order to intimidate his opponents.

The January 13 indictments against key JDL members signaled the beginning of a concerted government effort against the JDL. On January 15, Meir and other JDL activists received subpoenas to appear before a grand jury, while three other

members were indicted in federal court in Manhattan on charges of using fictitious names to purchase rifles.[20]

That same day, Meir called a press conference. For the third time in four days,
he was on TV. NBC TV showed him sitting at his desk at JDL headquarters, with
JDL banners and posters on the wall behind him. While the camera panned the
reporters assembled in the room, Meir denounced the indictments as an effort to
pressure the JDL to cease harassing Russian diplomats. Not only would this harassment continue, he vowed, but it would intensify.

Meir told NBC reporter Jack Paxton that President Nixon must exert leverage
on Russia to allow open emigration and warned that Nixon would suffer in the
1972 elections should he continue to ignore Russian Jewry. He further asserted
that the JDL was trying to salvage American honor and pride by fighting Russia's
treatment of Jews.

Meir then read a cablegram from recent Russian émigrés in Israel, which had
been sent to American Jewish leaders. It said, "... We are convinced the League's
policy and activities are most effective. The Soviet government should be brought
to understand that the liberation of Soviet Jews is preferable to endless international complications." One signatory, Dov Sperling, said the JDL's methods were
forced on them by the Russians themselves, who ignored all other kinds of protest.[21]

On January 18, Meir and seven others were indicted in Manhattan Supreme
Court on charges including assault, incitement to riot, rioting, criminal mischief,
unlawful assembly, and burglary, with the assistant district attorney promising
more to come. Meir was indicted on three counts: rioting, inciting to riot and
unlawful assembly, stemming from demonstrations on December 27 and December 30, 1970. The defendants all pleaded not guilty and were released on bail
pending trial April 12.[22]

Meir's release on $2,500 bail was granted only after he agreed to limit dem-
onstrations to designated areas. Zweibon, who had represented him in court, told
Daily News reporters that this restriction violated the First Amendment. Meir
labeled the indictment a "continuation of the plot hatched in Washington." The
JDL quickly organized a show of support at a press conference at the Overseas
Press Club. Jews who were not members of the League spoke in its defense.
Rabbi Julius Neumann, formerly a member of the city's Human Rights Commission, said, "We are truly witnessing a miracle when a handful is able to pierce
the Iron Curtain." George Meissner, an attorney and vice president of the International Organization for Repatriation of Russian Jews, blasted what he called
Mayor Lindsay's "crackdown" on the JDL.[23]

On January 19, Meir was in court again, this time on charges of criminal conspiracy, criminal trespass, and criminal mischief committed during the December

29, 1969 raid on Tass.* Unlike previous hearings, arraignments and other courtroom procedures, this was his first actual trial.[24]

Before entering the courtroom, after eleven days of harassing Russian diplomats, Meir announced to reporters in the corridor that there would be an "indefinite moratorium" on this tactic. In *Story of the Jewish Defense League*, Meir said
that the moratorium was intended to give the Jewish Establishment time to use
JDL acts as a bargaining lever to help Soviet Jews. He hoped the leaders of the
Jewish Establishment would say to Washington, "Unless you can persuade the
Russians to make concessions, these militants will gain more adherents and their
violence will continue."[25]

The following day saw a new JDL tactic: a boycott of U.S. companies doing
business with the Soviet Union. The *New York Times* even listed a JDL phone
number that gave out the names of the firms being targeted.[26] Meir explained the
boycott in a *Jewish Press* article:

> The Soviet Union's drive for Western dollars and trade is clearer today than
> ever before as news items explode all about us, telling of business contracts and
> trade agreements between the Soviets and the West. The Mack Truck Company
> contracts to build a huge factory for the Russians, and the trade missions, with
> United States Department of Commerce blessings, roam the Kremlin's corri-
> dors. This need of the USSR for American trade and dollars gives us a splendid
> opportunity to attack the Soviets at their jugular and draw from them conces-
> sions on Soviet Jewry.[27]

The JDL held a number of demonstrations and sit-ins at firms doing business
with the Soviets, including the Mack Truck Company. A series of protests against
Mack proved so effective that it cancelled its planned factory in the USSR. To prevent similar harassment by JDL members, a Soviet delegation that arrived in the
United States to promote the Yak-40 aircraft avoided all publicity and fanfare.[28]

The Soviet government's December cancellation of the visit of the Bolshoi
Ballet encouraged the JDL to step up its campaign against Soviet cultural
exchange. On January 21, they held a sit-in at the Columbia Artists Management
office in Manhattan, which was bringing the Siberian Dancers and Singers of
Omsk to Carnegie Hall at month's end. The performance, which Columbia Artists
refused to cancel, was interrupted when ten open bottles of ammonia were placed
throughout the auditorium. A week later, Soviet officials cancelled all concerts
planned for February and March.[29] This signaled a further deterioration in
American-Soviet relations. However, the U.S. State Department, whose policy
was to maintain friendly relations with the Soviet Union, had already begun to
exert the full force of its influence against the JDL.

---

* See chapter 17 for the conduct of the Tass case.

Behind the Scenes: The State Department

Behind-the-scenes pressure by the State Department was evident as early as January 12, when Meir was arrested for the minor infraction of missing a preliminary hearing. That same pressure was probably responsible for a change in the media. For example, at the beginning of January a *Daily News* editorial was heartily in favor of the JDL:

> The Kremlin tyrants are making scapegoats of the Jews in Russia just as the old czars did. But the reaction of Jews ... is something to behold. Rabbi Meir Kahane and his Jewish Defense League in New York City are swearing vengeance on Soviet nationals and property alike.... It may be that, in turning on the Jews, world communism – or at any rate the Russian part thereof – has most obligingly signed its own death warrant.[30]

Only ten days later a *News* editorial declared that "JDL actions will only worsen the plight of Soviet Jews." A defamatory article about Meir, full of half-truths and innuendos, appeared in the *New York Times*, while *Time* and *Newsweek* focused on the JDL and the Soviet-Jewish issue in negatively slanted articles. The barrage of negative publicity even led eight JDL chapter chairmen to announce their resignation. Pressure from the timid American Jewish Establishment and the U.S. State Department caused a shift of official opinion against the JDL in Israel, too, with the Israeli government condemning its "acts of terrorism." *Yedioth Ahronoth* echoed this position in an article headed "Moscow Liable to Harden Its Stance Because of League Violence."[31] The State Department aimed to destroy public trust in Meir so as to defeat his efforts to harm détente.

The *Jewish Post and Opinion*, noting the attacks on Meir, offered a supportive editorial: "What is being done today [for Soviet Jews] by the organized Jewish community is ten years and more late, and still is a halting program.... Only as recently as last year, the American Jewish Conference on Soviet Jewry ... opposed such a minuscule program as sending greeting cards to individual Russian Jews on the grounds that this might aggravate the situation." Support also came from *Yedioth Ahronoth* columnist Dr. Israel Eldad, who wrote in an open letter: "Don't be daunted by the Israel government's statement against your blessed acts for Soviet Jews."[32]

Meanwhile, the legal cases against Meir mounted, each threatening a jail sentence. For the rest of 1971, Meir appeared in court frequently.

Chapter 22

The Brussels Conference
(February-May 1971)

Serious Charges

O N FEBRUARY 22, 1971, Meir was in court on charges stemming from the demonstration at the Soviet Mission on December 30, 1969. In his testimony before a six-man jury he explained that he had attempted to cross a police barricade only after he was denied access to the Park East Synagogue to pray. The next day, after deliberating three hours, the jury dismissed the charge of resisting arrest but found him guilty of disorderly conduct. This was the first time Meir had been convicted of any crime. He quipped to reporters, "It was a fair trial, a fair jury, a fair judge – and a bad verdict."[1]

Sentencing took place April 13. Aware of the altruistic nature of Meir's crime, Judge Irving Lang fined him $500 (or 90 days in jail), noting that "civil disobedience, whether directed at the Vietnam War, the draft, or integration in the South, has become commonplace in society."[2]

Meir still faced other charges, including one of felonious riot at the Soviet Mission on December 27, 1970, punishable by up to seven years in prison. Meir's appointment book for 1971 is filled with brief notations of court appearances, sometimes even two a day. On March 3 he was fined $100 in Brooklyn Criminal Court in connection with his arrest in Williamsburg on June 23, 1970. The entry for March 19 says "probation," indicating either a hearing or a report. On March 30 he was in court for the Tass case that resulted in a deadlocked jury, as did the April 26 Tass retrial. April 27 and May 7 saw further court appearances, probably procedural hearings.[3]

Suddenly, without warning, on May 12 Meir and six other JDL members were arrested. Agents of the Treasury Department's Bureau of Alcohol, Tobacco and Firearms found Meir at a meeting in Bert Zweibon's law office and took him straight to the Federal House of Detention in Manhattan. The seven were charged with "conspiracy to violate the federal Gun Control Act of 1968," a crime that carried a maximum penalty of five years in prison. Meir's offense was that he had demonstrated the detonation of explosives at Camp Jedel in August 1970. He had done so in the presence of someone he knew was a police informer, unaware that even in a classroom atmosphere a special license was required to detonate explosives.[4]

The next day, all seven were arraigned in federal court in Brooklyn. The bail set by U.S. Magistrate Max Schiffman was extremely high: $25,000 for Meir and $10,000 for Hy Bieber and two others. Three were released on personal bond. The rest were overwhelmed by despair. Who would guarantee such large sums?

Early that the morning, a JDL member had come to our home to get Meir's *tallit* and *tefillin* so that he could recite the morning prayers in the lockup. At first I refused to hand them over. Meir had never before been kept in jail more than over night, and I had to be persuaded that he really was not coming home that morning. I sincerely believed he would be released quickly. And indeed he was. A guarantor was found in the person of Joseph Colombo, an alleged Mafia figure. Attorney Barry Slotnick, who represented Meir, recalled how Colombo became involved:

> I met Meir as a result of an introduction by my uncle Rabbi Harry Hurwitz, who suggested that Meir needed a good lawyer. I informed him that I did not represent people who were charged with disorderly conduct, which, of course, was Meir's essential arrest. But I did tell Meir that if there was ever anything more serious, to give me a call, and lo and behold, on May 12, 1971, he called.
>
> The night before Meir was arraigned in federal court, I was to have dinner with [my client] Joe Colombo. As a result of Meir's call, I told Colombo that I had to cancel dinner and gave him the reason why. He showed up the next morning in court to post bail for Meir.[5]

On May 27, Meir and the other defendants were officially indicted. They were accused of "conspiring to make, receive and possess explosives and firearms without written application to the Secretary of the Treasury ... without paying tax ... and without registering them...." Among the charges were procuring dynamite; possessing firebombs, Molotov cocktails, and underwater fuses; transporting gunpowder between states; discussing and attempting the manufacture of explosives; and demonstrating the detonation thereof.[6] The trial was set for July.

Meir was denounced for associating with Joseph Colombo, but in articles in the *Jewish Press* and in numerous interviews, he argued that it was a question of mutual aid. The JDL legitimized Colombo's Italian-American Civil Rights League, and Colombo's group picketed the Soviet Mission alongside the JDL. "I'll march with anyone if I think I can help a Jew," Meir wrote. "On Italian-American Unity Day, June 28, 100,000 people will be at Columbus Circle. I'll speak on Soviet

Jewry and get these people, whom Nixon depends on for support, to help us with Soviet Jewry...."[7]

As a sign of their friendly relationship, Joseph Colombo invited Meir to play golf on June 7 in Eastchester, New York.[8] Meir had played miniature golf once or twice but never the real game, so he did not have the requisite cleated golf shoes.* Colombo insisted on buying him a pair. When he came home from the golf course with those spanking-new white shoes, I looked at his worn everyday ones and said, "What a pity to leave these new shoes in the closet." I dyed them black and unscrewed the metal cleats, and Meir had a useful pair of shoes. Four-and-a-half-year-old Binyamin appropriated the metal cleats for playing jacks, and when we flew to Israel in August, he had them in his pocket, to the great interest of El Al's security personnel.

Bennett Levine recalled that golf game: "Meir and I had a court appearance that morning about the 1970 riot, and then we drove up to Westchester County to play golf with Joe Colombo. They gave Meir white golf shoes, and he was ripping up the golf course. I don't think he hit the ball once. He said to Joe, 'Let's play stickball – that's my game.'"[9]

Meir's relationship with Colombo was short-lived – a matter of six weeks. On June 28, Colombo was gunned down. He did not die, but remained in a coma for the rest of his life. The shooting occurred at the start of Italian-American Unity Day ceremonies in Manhattan, where Meir was to speak. When I heard the news on the radio, my first thought was that he could have been on the podium alongside Colombo and injured as well. Then I reminded myself that Meir's habitual tardiness would have kept him from arriving so early. Thankfully, I was right. The Unity Day program continued as scheduled, and Meir was shown on television addressing the crowd, encouraging friendship between Italians and Jews.[10] Bennett Levine recalled:

> Meir was driving over to Columbus Square for the Unity Day rally by himself. I was on my way there when I heard the news flash on the radio. Somehow I found Meir in the confusion there. He had a speaking date that evening and asked me to sit in the hospital with Colombo's family to represent JDL. Outside the hospital, there was a reporter from the *New York Post*. I told him I was there to represent the JDL, to show solidarity with the family after the terrible event. When he asked my name, I gave my Hebrew name. The next day, my mother phoned me: "What were you doing with Joe Colombo!"

Levine was not brought up as a religious Jew, but today he and his family are all observant. He sent his children to Jewish day schools and they gave their children the same education.

---

* Golf shoes have half-inch metal cleats, or spikes, screwed into the soles of the shoe to provide traction on the grassy turf of the golf course.

It started when Meir had a speaking date way upstate.... We took turns driving and took one motel room. When we got up in the morning, he *davened* (prayed) and asked me if I wanted to put on *tefillin*. I said, 'I really don't know how.' He said, 'I'll show you,' and he helped me put them on, and then he said, 'See, you didn't die from it.'

Levine put in a great deal of time for the JDL.

Meir was calling on me day and night. I said, 'Meir, I have a business.' He said, 'You save Jews, and G-d will take care of the business.' And I thought he was crazy. But there were no problems with my customers, everything went smoothly. It was absolutely amazing.[11]

Soviet Jewry Can't Wait!

Despite the imminent threat of imprisonment, Meir continued to work on behalf of Soviet Jewry. He saw the arousal of public opinion as the only way to end Soviet oppression of Jews. Less than a month after his January 18 indictment in Manhattan Supreme Court for rioting, incitement to riot, and unlawful assembly, he led the JDL in a noisy protest. On Sunday evening, February 14, at "a raucous rally" at Hunter College, Meir announced the end of the moratorium on harassment of Russians, because "the U.S. government has capitulated to Soviet pressure." He exhorted supporters, "Tonight we will go back to the Soviet Mission. We will ask the police to let us demonstrate in front of the mission, and they will say no. I want you to go out there and sit down and wait to be arrested for disorderly conduct."

Shouting slogans such as "Two, four, six, eight, let our people emigrate!" the "noisy but peaceful demonstrators" partially blocked traffic, while police allowed only twelve pickets to parade outside the mission. No one was arrested, but the next day mission secretary Vladimir Federov filed a complaint against Meir, charging harassment and verbal abuse. Summoned to the Nineteenth Precinct police station, Meir told reporters waiting there that the JDL was resuming its harassment campaign because the mistreatment of Jews in the Soviet Union had dropped from public sight.[12]

That evening Meir appeared on the David Susskind TV show with representatives of the Jewish Establishment, to discuss tactics on behalf of Soviet Jewry. A viewer wrote: "... Mr. Susskind repeatedly implied that there were no apparent gains from the actions taken by the JDL because the Russians were [already] allowing 1,000 Jews each year to immigrate to Israel. At this rate it will take 3,000 years to free our three million brethren.... Mr. Susskind, we can't wait!"[13]

The JDL's success in bringing the oppression of Soviet Jews before the general public was surely behind the decision of the Jewish Establishment to hold an international conference on Soviet Jewry. The World Conference of Jewish Communities on Soviet Jewry was to open in Brussels on February 23, 1971, with representatives from Jewish communities all over the world. Its avowed aim was to improve the lot of the Jews in the Soviet Union. The American Jewish Conference on Soviet Jewry, the Establishment's umbrella organization, sent delegates who were prominent in all walks of American life, including film director Otto Preminger and playwright Paddy Chayefsky. Among the Israeli delegates was the head of the Herut party, Menachem Begin.

Up to then, the activities of the American Jewish Conference on Soviet Jewry* had consisted of issuing statements of protest addressed to the Soviet government and organizing mass meetings of American Jews – activities which had been largely ineffectual.[14] Meir feared that the conference would do no more than adopt resolutions which would perpetuate such activities. He wanted to persuade the delegates to follow his strategy of actively threatening Soviet interests in order to pressure them to give Jews freedom of religion and freedom to emigrate. Since the Establishment was opposed to Meir's methods, he had not been invited to the conference, but he decided to try to speak at Brussels anyway.

On the day the conference opened Meir had to be in court, so he flew there the next day with Sam Shoshan.[15] Bert Zweibon had arrived in Brussels a day earlier to lobby delegates to allow Meir to address the assembly. Zweibon recalled that when Meir arrived, he went directly to the conference hall and sent a note to Rabbi Herschel Schachter, chairman of the American Jewish Conference on Soviet Jewry, requesting permission to address the delegates. While awaiting an answer ... he was recognized by reporters, who began interviewing him.[16]

After a short time, a note came from Rabbi Schachter refusing Meir's request. Meir informed the reporters that he was going to his hotel because he had not come to disrupt the conference, and invited them to a press conference that afternoon. Before he could turn around to leave, he was seized by Belgian police and arrested as an "undesirable."

Israeli correspondent Edwin Eytan reported: "There was pandemonium in the hall when the delegates heard of the arrest." Menachem Begin, of the Herut party, who favored allowing Meir to speak, accused the conference leaders of the un-Jewish act of denouncing Meir to the Belgian police. Otto Preminger, addressing the assembly that evening, said that the way Meir had been treated was

---

* The American Jewish Conference on Soviet Jewry, a sponsor of the Brussels conference, was formed by the Jewish Establishment in 1964. In 1971, after the Brussels conference, it was replaced by the National Conference on Soviet Jewry.

"exactly as contemptible and wrong as what the Nazis and the Soviet Communists have done."[17]

At 9 P.M., the police took Meir to the airport. The *Daily News* described his deportation: "Like the western sheriff who avoided a particular problem by putting the bad guy on the six o'clock stage, Belgian police escorted Kahane up the ramp of a London-bound plane."[18]

The conference's closing session issued a declaration appealing to international opinion to urge Soviet authorities to allow Soviet Jews their own cultural and religious life and the right to emigrate, and it denounced the "alleged Soviet policy of suppressing historic Jewish culture and religious heritage." Not exactly a media event. Yet Meir's deportation from Brussels catapulted the Soviet-Jewish issue onto the front page of major newspapers throughout the world, including Vienna, Amsterdam, Antwerp, Paris, London, Cologne, Hamburg, Rome, and even papers in Buenos Aires, Sao Paulo, and Rio de Janeiro.[19]

The Paris *Herald Tribune* pictured Meir on page one, standing outside the conference hall. It reported: "Rabbi Kahane was as peaceful as possible.... Calm and smiling, he left the hall, saying that he did not come 'to destroy the conference' but wished only to assert his democratic right to speak." A *Yedioth Ahronoth* cartoon, captioned "A Strange People," depicted a Russian official looking on, smiling gleefully, as Meir is booted out by the conference.[20]

Columnist Max Lerner put it this way:

> In one sense Rabbi Kahane has succeeded: he said it had been his purpose and that of the JDL to get the plight of the Soviet Jews off the back pages and get it on page one, and with the help of the Russian government he has done it... [by their] continued discrimination against Jews in Soviet life.
>
> ... Had I been at the Brussels meeting I should have added my voice to the minority of delegates that strongly opposed Kahane's tactics but was willing to have him appear and address the conference. What danger did he represent that warranted banning him by the conference leaders, and that warranted detaining him by the Belgian police? If the conference is on the track of the right policies it could have tolerated a challenge....[21]

TV news programs showed Meir arriving in Brussels and later boarding the flight out. On February 25 he was shown landing at JFK and telling reporters at a hastily convened press conference that the Soviet Union was guilty of Jewish genocide. That evening, on NBC-TV's *Sixth Hour News*, he debated Arnold Forster of the B'nai B'rith Anti-Defamation League. Meir maintained that he had a moral right to attend the Brussels conference and announced to viewers that on March 21 thousands would take part in a JDL demonstration for Soviet Jews at the White House.[22]

Sit-Down in Washington, March 21, 1971

Prior to the rally in Washington, JDL members picketed at the United Nations on March 10 to show solidarity with 150 Riga *refuseniks* who were courageously holding a sit-in at Moscow's Supreme Soviet building. The Fast of Esther fell that day, so they held a hunger strike as part of their protest. As night fell and the Purim holiday began, they read the Scroll of Esther, recounting the fall of ancient despots. Police blocked off a lane of traffic on First Avenue for the demonstrators. This solidarity protest drew all the media, and television coverage included an interview with Meir on Israeli news.[23]

On March 14 demonstrations for Soviet Jewry took place at seven state capitals: Boston, Providence, Albany (where Meir spoke), Trenton, Harrisburg, Springfield, and Sacramento. Simultaneously, recent Soviet émigré Yosef Schneider, sitting in a small prison-like cage outside the White House, began a week-long fast on behalf of *refuseniks* in Russia. His fast was to end on Sunday, March 21, the day of the mass rally in Washington.[24]

Meir promoted the rally in Washington at every speaking engagement, and on Friday, two days before the rally, he placed a large ad in the *New York Times*. It showed a pile of corpses in concentration-camp garb beneath an inch-high headline "THIS IS THE PRICE OF SILENCE." The text said:

> Because of that silence, six million died. Never Again!!
> Today, when Soviet Jewry is crying out for freedom, we look back over the decades of silence we were guilty of and we say:
> Never Again can we be silent in the face of another Jewish tragedy!
> Never Again can we continue the shameful lack of action on their behalf.
> Never Again can the world be permitted to ignore their problem.
> Come with us to the White House, Sunday, March 21, at 12 noon.[25]

Thanks to vigorous promotion, some 2,500 demonstrators came to Washington. The day began with a rally near the White House. Speakers, including Meir and student activist Yossi Templeman, urged participants to sit down in the streets of Washington and exercise their right to engage in non-violent civil disobedience, even if it meant being arrested. Meir said, "Thirty years ago [during the Holocaust], we Jews sat on our apathy. Today we're sitting in Washington."

Chanting "Freedom Now!" they marched from the White House to an intersection near the Soviet Embassy and sat down in the middle of the street, blocking traffic. Meir was arrested first. Approximately 1,000 others followed him, led one by one to waiting police buses. As Meir had instructed, they offered no resistance. Those over 18 were charged with disorderly conduct and released in lieu of $10 collateral.* Washington's Assistant Police Chief George R. Donahue told report-ers, "I can't remember when we made more arrests at once."

An hour and a half after the sit-down began, the intersection was clear. Larry Topf, 17, of the Bronx said, "Everything worked out the way we planned. There was absolutely no resistance. It was 100 percent non-violent."[26]

Washington Post reporter Carl Bernstein quoted one patrolman who, as he led a young man away to be arrested, whispered to his sergeant, "I kind of hate to do it; these kids are different." Bernstein pointed out that "the determined army of Jews who sat down in the streets near the Soviet Embassy bore few resemblances to demonstrators with whom Washington police are more accustomed to dealing. Yesterday, there were no ... shouts of 'off the pigs,' no chanted obscenities, no thrown stones."[27] Dr. William Perl, head of the JDL Washington chapter, recalled:

> Chief of Police Jerry V. Wilson ordered the demonstrators to get up and move. Hardly anybody did so. Wilson came over to me. Apparently he thought I would function as a mediator, because the Washington JDL was relatively law-abiding. It never happened that one of our people resisted arrest or fought with policemen. He said to me, "Please tell Rabbi Kahane that you have achieved everything you could (plenty of publicity with hundreds of feet of tel-evision coverage). If your people get up at the next warning, there will be no arrests and no fines."
>
> I knew, of course, that Rabbi Kahane would not accept this offer, but I gave him the message. His answer was, "We will all sit here until everyone is arrested, or until the last Jew who wants to leave the Soviet Union has left."
>
> The newspapers reported that close to 800 were arrested, but they figured only the adults. All the juveniles were arrested too, but they were released with-out any processing. [The total including juveniles was 1,347.] Later, friends in the USSR wrote that the news of 800 people arrested for a demonstration sounded like a riot to them. Actually, everything was very peaceful and disci-plined.[28]

Another participant, Bobby Rosenberg, wrote:

> At 2:40 P.M. Officer Herman C. Schroeder arrested me for obstructing a public highway. "Kid, you could get three months in jail and a $1,500 fine for this," Officer Schroeder says to me.
>
> I believe him. I get this queasy feeling in my stomach.
>
> "How old are you, son?" he asks.
>
> "Seventeen, sir," I answer.
>
> ... I'm taken to jail with another fifty people. We sing songs and yell, "Never Again!" whenever the cops bring in some new people.

---

* Collateral is a form of bail. It is returned when the arrestee comes to court, and becomes a fine if he does not. Since it would cost more than $10 to travel from New York to Washington, it was, in effect, a fine.

... And when it was all over, what had we accomplished? We were major news on all the networks. We received favorable publicity from all the media.[29]

The arrest of close to 1,000 people was truly newsworthy. NBC TV news showed Meir addressing the demonstrators and sitting in the street with them, singing and shouting slogans. Israeli television aired similar footage and also showed demonstrators being herded onto buses, while Israeli radio reported on the high arrest rate.[30]

For Meir, the highlight of this demonstration was the commitment of young Jews to a Jewish cause. He compared them to their contemporaries, such as Jerry Rubin and Abbie Hoffman, who supported leftist causes, "going to Cuba to cut sugar and to Hanoi to embrace the George Washingtons of North Vietnam." Meir wrote of the leftists' "mass flight from their heritage," their "total lack of pride, the inferiority complexes, the revulsion against the suburban type of Judaism, the self-hate [and] ignorance...." He saw reason for optimism:

> ... When thousands can come to Washington and hundreds upon hundreds demand arrest; when row after row of proud young Jews – some with yarmulkes, some with long, shaggy hair – march together for their people 5,000 miles away; when long lines of young Jews – some religious, some totally removed from religion – can stride together and cry, "We are Jews, we couldn't be prouder, and if you can't hear us we'll shout a little louder!" there is hope.

Meir spelled out the way to bring Jews back to Judaism:

> It was not speeches and programs that won them back and not sermons and YMHA basketball leagues. It was not the huge and ornate temples or the Jewish hospitals funded by Federation. It was not the pap that is given them in the after-school-hour religious schools or the interfaith services at the local synagogue. It was nothing that we GAVE them; rather, it was what we TOOK from them.
>
>   If you want to win back Jewish youth, do not offer them things – demand it of them. Demand sacrifice – real sacrifice. Insist upon idealism.... Show them the way up the mountain, but walk there first – before them – and they will climb with you to the heights....[31]

Commitment to Jewish ideals brought at least one young couple together. "I met my wife because of the March 21, 1971, demonstration in Washington," wrote Charley Levine. "Shelly was photographed for a Jewish newspaper as she was being arrested at the rally. I saw the photo and said to my college roommate, 'Why can't I ever meet pretty, committed girls like this one in the photo?' A week or so later, I met her and felt I knew her already because of the newspaper photo!"[32]

"The Rabbi Seems to Pick Up All the Marbles!" was the title of an editorial by Philip Hochstein in the *American Examiner–Jewish Week* of Washington, in which he analyzed the local Jewish organizations' boycott of the March 21 rally:

> There have been far bigger Jewish demonstrations in Washington before, but none have come out with a greater aura of moral victory than Kahane's. His few thousand participants seemed like a Gideon's army against the background of an ill-advised condemnation by the Greater Washington Jewish Community Council.
>
> ... Kahane was able to belie the accusation that he countenanced violence by making quite a show of non-violence and even friendliness toward the cops. All in all he harvested the all-time record for the most urbane and friendly protest confrontation with the police in the history of the nation's capital!
>
> The Establishment has not yet learned to reckon astutely with the phenomenon of television.... It is by no means clear that Kahane understands this medium any better but he obliges swiftly and with intuitive effectiveness. [Television] craves action personalities. The free-wheeling Kahane was made to order for television news programs.
>
> Kahane is now three distinct public personalities rolled into a single body. Out of the Brooklyn backlash he became the militant defender of Jews against Negro toughs.... Out of the travails of Russian Jews sacrificing themselves for their Jewish identity he became the hero of great numbers of affiliated and non-affiliated Jews.... Out of the Brussels conference he became a world figure, thanks to Establishment bumbling.
>
> ... The Establishment leaders, who had labored many years to counter defamation and protest for Jewish rights with almost total selfless modesty, felt incensed that this man was projecting a false image of the American Jew as a militant leader of backlash. There followed a vigorous publicity campaign within the Jewish community and Jewish press to read him out of the community.[33]

Hochstein's analysis is significant because it explains why the Anti-Defamation League of B'nai B'rith secretly provided the FBI with information about JDL members. This collusion was made public in April 1971, after classified files were stolen from the FBI office in Media, Pennsylvania, by the Citizens' Committee to Investigate the FBI. A group named Resist distributed copies to newspapers in order to publicize how the FBI's broad investigative powers threatened political freedom in America. They found that forty percent of the documents involved political investigations while only one percent pertained to organized crime.[34]

Resist sent Sam Shoshan, JDL's public relations officer, a copy of an FBI memo which said that Samuel Lewis Gaber of the Philadelphia ADL had briefed FBI Special Agent Edward A. Smith about Russel Kelner, Benjamin Pomerantz, and Irving Sheinman, members of the JDL's Philadelphia chapter.[35]

Since informing on a fellow Jew is forbidden by Jewish law, JDL made much of this revelation. Meir wrote bitterly:

> It is not an isolated phenomenon. Jewish underground soldiers were kidnapped by Jews in Palestine and handed over to the British. Kapos and Judenrats in Eastern Europe did their dirty work well during the Holocaust. The Anti-Defamation League is in fine historical company.[36]

Mel Ziegler, writing in *New York* magazine, expressed similar sentiments about the ADL. In researching his article "The Jewish Defense League and Its Invisible Constituency," Ziegler requested background material from the ADL and discovered that "ADL analysts grind out an increasing volume of memoranda which assesses many aspects of the JDL operation, from chapter meetings (some of which ADL appears to have infiltrated) to the sources of its funds." After assessing this material, Ziegler concluded: "The Anti-Defamation League does indeed know a lot about defamation."[37]

Despite the opposition of the Jewish Establishment, people were interested in what Meir had to say. On a radio program billed as a round-table discussion of Judaism and Zionism, Meir debated Abbie Hoffman and Paul Krasner, professed leftists, and Dr. Mohammad T. Mehdi, an Arab spokesman. The sparks flew![38]

Local Defense

The JDL continued to act on local issues as well as on behalf of Jews in other countries.

In the Dorchester neighborhood of Boston, a gang of young hoodlums assaulted a Jewish home with rocks and a firebomb. It was the final incident in a long campaign of terror designed to drive these last remaining Jews on the block out of the neighborhood. Appeals to the police brought no relief. As the situation escalated, JDL members began to arrive. Only when police were told that JDL was going to bring more forces into the area, did the police agree to guard the house through the night. A JDL flyer said, "The fear of a riot brought action; the suffering of a Jewish family did not. The *Boston Globe* was called at the height of the incident and flatly refused to send a reporter. The story was not newsworthy enough, it seems."[39]

Some JDL activities did not reach the mass media because of their modest character. A JDL newsletter reported: "In the Fort Greene area [of Brooklyn] ... there are still small pockets of elderly Jews who cannot afford to move from their rent controlled apartments.... In order to help these isolated Jews and protect them from harassment, JDL has helped them get a large hall to meet and *daven* [pray] and picks up worshippers and returns them to their homes daily."[40]

However, one response by the JDL to attacks on Jews was widely reported. On April 12, after an escalation in the number and severity of attacks on Jews in Borough Park, the JDL held a rally in the district's Public School 103. Meir announced to the audience of three hundred that his organization would begin nightly patrols and "smash heads" if necessary. After his talk he led the crowd on a march to the Borough Park police station to demand protection. This event was covered by local newspapers, two local television stations, and the Associated Press. Meir assured the *Daily News* that JDL patrols would be coordinated with the police. NBC TV news showed the JDL Auxiliary Police Force receiving instructions. Its leader told a reporter that if a member of the force suspected a crime and the police did not respond, he would make a citizen's arrest.[41]

A week later, the JDL took part in Manhattan's annual Salute to Israel Parade, in which thousands of Jews parade up Fifth Avenue to mark Israel Independence Day. The *New York Times* reported: "In the march also were some 500 members of the militant Jewish Defense League, headed by Rabbi Meir Kahane, who paused in front of the reviewing stand to sing *Hatikvah*, Israel's national anthem. Then, with a shout of 'Never Again,' the unit, wearing blue berets and insignia, moved on."[42]

Sy Polsky described the JDL's enthusiastic reception: "Our contingent of 300 at 57th Street was well over 1,500 by 86th Street. As JDL marched, it [received a] continuous ovation from those Jews who recognized in their hearts that the JDL belongs to them.... [There were] hundreds of people leaping over the barricades to join a group which has been castigated at every turn by its more established brothers."[43]

The JDL again turned to local Jewish defense when Meir spoke at Brooklyn College's May 4 Soviet Jewry Day. After addressing the crowd, he learned that black students had recently broken open the jukebox in the Student Center canteen and destroyed its only Jewish record, *Bashana Haba'a* (Next Year), a popular Israeli song.

Meir and a group of students decided to visit the scene of the crime. According to one of them, "We went into the section of the canteen where the blacks congregated and we began to sing the song. The blacks walked out after a few minutes, mimicking our singing. They soon returned with more blacks and started throwing chairs. I myself had heard rumors that there was racial animosity there, but the ensuing riot came as a shock. It was brief, but bloody. Meir Kahane had to be held back by his followers to prevent him from joining in the brawl."

JDL members went back the next day and staged a march down Campus Road. Yossi Templeman told the crowd, "We will not stand for any racism. The Student Center will not be limited to any one type of person.... We will not be intimidated. If any Jewish brother is attacked, we will fight back. Never again!" All the local media covered the story. Meir was barred from campus by a court order, but that did not harm his popularity: At the Bellmore Jewish Center in Long Island that evening, he spoke to an overflow crowd.[44]

The following week, to show that he wasn't anti-black, and in a gesture reminiscent of his pact with Italian Americans, Meir met in Harlem with Dr. Thomas Matthew, head of NEGRO – the National Economic Growth and Reconstruction Organization. Matthew told reporters that the proposed alliance between his organization and the Jewish Defense League was prompted by recent clashes between black and Jewish students at Brooklyn College. And Matthew wanted to help Soviet Jews. That summer, he traveled to Russia with an eleven-man delegation. He appealed to Premier Aleksei Kosygin to allow the group to visit the capital of the Jewish Autonomous Region, Birobidzhan, saying that he'd promised Rabbi Meir Kahane he would investigate the status of Soviet Jews.[45]

Soviet Jews were the focus of a demonstration in April organized by the Student Activists for Soviet Jewry (SASJ), the JDL group, led by Yossi Templeman. It took place on Passover and was named "Ten Plagues." Templeman recalled: "Meir had the idea of bringing 'plagues' on the Soviet oppressors like the Ten Plagues inflicted on the Egyptians to force the release of the Israelites. And so was born the idea of hitting the Russians with frogs and – because of the scarcity of locusts – with mice." Shouting "Let My People Go," the students let loose frogs and mice at two Soviet offices in New York City. First, some fifty frogs hopped out of flight bags in the Aeroflot ticket office, and roughly thirty minutes later, fifty mice invaded the reception area of Amtorg, the Soviet trading agency. A police sergeant said of the frogs: "They were jumping up and down and getting everybody jumping with them." The mice were not recovered.[46]

Iraqi Jews Jailed

A week later, on April 20, a JDL demonstration was held for Iraqi Jews. Thirty-eight Iraqi Jews, including women and children, had been jailed, and there was reason for deep concern. Only two years earlier, nine Iraqi Jews, falsely accused of spying for Israel, had been executed in the main square of Baghdad. Five hundred protesters gathered on April 20 at the Iraqi Mission to the United Nations. Standing on a car roof, Meir warned that if one Jew was hanged in Iraq, one Iraqi diplomat would hang in New York. Suddenly, about 75 of the demonstrators crashed through the police barricades. In the scuffle, three policemen were knocked to the ground and slightly injured. Meir and six others were taken to the Nineteenth Precinct police station on East 67th Street. Meir was accused of over-turning police barricades and encouraging others to follow him and was charged with second-degree riot (a serious misdemeanor), disorderly conduct, and resisting arrest.[47]

A hearing on this case on August 10 proved highly traumatic for me. I went to court that day because Meir's aunt had died and we planned to pay a condolence call after the hearing to her sons, Rabbis David and Solomon Kahane. The courtroom was tiny. I arrived in the middle of the hearing and took the only available seat in the first row. A policeman rose to testify about Meir's conduct at the demonstration. He was asked whether the person who had pushed him was in the courtroom. The policeman, towering above me on the witness bench, raised his arm, pointed his finger at Meir and said loudly and angrily, "That's the one who pushed me." It may seem an overreaction, but I felt personally threatened. The experience was so frightening that it was the last time I went to a trial of Meir's.[48]

Fortunately, Judge Edward Pincus dismissed the riot charge on grounds of insufficient evidence and the jury acquitted Meir of the two other charges, disorderly conduct and resisting arrest.[49]

Chapter 23

Proud Sons of the Maccabees
(April-July 1971)

J DL MEMBERS WERE encouraged by recently released statistics revealing that
the number of Jews allowed to leave the Soviet Union in the first three
months of 1971 was almost 1,400 – three times higher than the average of
past years. This wave of emigration was unprecedented in the 53-year history of
the Soviet Union.[1] JDLers were convinced that it was their turbulent demonstrations that made the difference. It was a constant challenge to keep the media
focused on the cause of Soviet Jewry and, at the same time, limit JDL activities
to those which would not endanger anyone.

On Thursday, April 22, a bomb in an attaché case exploded at Amtorg, the
Soviet-American Trading Company office in Manhattan. Warning phone calls to
Amtorg and to the AP and UPI news agencies ensured the evacuation of personnel from the office, and there were no injuries, but the blast blew a hole in the
stairwell and littered Amtorg's reception area with debris.

Later that day, speaking to students at Princeton University, Meir said, "We
don't do such things. But we applaud those who take any action which is aimed
at keeping the Soviet Jewish problem on page one and before the conscience of
the world."[2]

After the bombing, Moscow sent a strongly worded protest to the U.S. government. American officials told reporters that "it had been virtually impossible
to convince Moscow that the U.S. government was not able to control private
groups."[3] In the Soviet Union, a tight rein was kept on all dissident groups, but
in America, where there were safeguards on personal freedom, the government
was unable to put an end to violent anti-Soviet activity so quickly. In the long run,
however, they did so by using "due process of law" and the judicial system to
imprison the leadership.

Harsh Sentences

The government's strategy of putting an end to JDL activities by jailing its activists was apparent from the harsh sentence imposed on Avraham Hershkowitz, who had been arrested at Kennedy Airport for carrying concealed weapons. On April 23, after he had been found guilty on only one charge – that of falsifying his passport application – he was sentenced to five years in prison. In March Meir had written:

> Avraham Hershkowitz is a 26-year-old Jew who has been in prison for six months. He is not there because he robbed money or assaulted someone; he is not a common criminal. He is there because the government alleges that he attempted to avenge attacks against Jews and was seized boarding a plane with explosives. In the end, the charge was dropped and Hershkowitz remains in [jail with] an incredible $50,000 bail merely for alleged violation of passport regulations.

The religious needs of Jewish prisoners in New York were officially under the jurisdiction of the Board of Rabbis, an organization of Orthodox, Conservative and Reform rabbis. Meir believed that the Board had not done enough to provide kosher food for Hershkowitz while he was in a Manhattan jail.

> Rabbis, what are you so busy with? ... What have you done that keeps you from getting around to helping Avraham Hershkowitz?
> The Board spends its time preening itself and using its offices for status and prestige.... It could not get kosher food for a young Jew; ... it could not care about a fellow Jew.[4]

Within one week after sentencing, Hershkowitz was suddenly transferred from the Manhattan House of Detention to the Federal Penitentiary in Lewiston, Pennsylvania. Meir demanded that the Board use its position to ensure that he be permitted to function as an Orthodox Jew in Lewiston penitentiary. To emphasize the urgency of Hershkowitz's needs, JDL members invaded the offices of the New York Board of Rabbis on April 28, causing damage. In an unexpected move, the Board of Rabbis filed a complaint with the police and twenty-three youngsters were arraigned the next day in criminal court. Repeated efforts to persuade the Board to withdraw the complaint failed, and the case came to trial in June. The youngsters were found guilty of criminal trespass and sentenced on January 31, 1972. Most of them only had to pay fines of $100 and $200, but two were sentenced to three months in prison.[5]

Demonstrating for Soviet Jewry

Despite the constant threat of legal penalties, the JDL continued to initiate activities that would draw attention to the oppression of Soviet Jews.

On Sunday, May 2, about three hundred people staged a demonstration at Dag Hammarskjold Plaza near U.N. headquarters, and then marched toward the Soviet

Mission. Near the mission, at the major intersection of Third Avenue and 67 Street, they sat down in the street, obstructing traffic, chanting "Let My People Go" and "Am Yisrael Chai" (The People of Israel Live) for about an hour before police began taking them into custody. Seventy-seven people, mostly teenagers, were arrested on charges of disorderly conduct and "obstructing governmental administration." The demonstrators did not resist arrest. For lack of space in the stationhouse, forty-nine of them were temporarily imprisoned at the site in a detention pen hastily constructed of police barriers.[6]

Mal Lebowitz recalled the sit-down. "My daughter Sandy was standing on the curb and a cop was jabbing a club into her chest and there was a crowd behind her. There was nowhere she could move back. Sandy says to the cop, 'Stop pushing me.' She got arrested. Yetta says, 'Why are you arresting my daughter?' The cop says to her, 'You're under arrest.' I didn't see this. I had left the camera in the car. I came over to them to ask them for the keys to the car. The cop says, 'You're under arrest.' So there we are, sitting in the arrest bus. Meir saw us, laughed, probably said to himself, 'The crazy Lebowitzes got arrested again.' I came into the police station. It was on West 20 Street. Someone recognized me – a cop we knew from way, way back. His father and my father were *landsleit*, from the same town in Europe. He got all of us out of there in record time."[7]

Among the spirited songs JDLers sang at demonstrations was this one:

> *We proud sons of the Maccabees*
> *Stand up for Jewish rights.*
> *Bar Kokhba's blood fills our veins;*
> *We fear no mortal's might.*
>
> *In Warsaw's ghetto we arose*
> *For an heroic stand,*
> *And then we blew the British out*
> *Of our Holy Land.*
>
> *You tyrants listen everywhere:*
> *Don't trample Jewish rights.*
> *For when our brothers are oppressed –*
> *The J-D-L WILL FIGHT!!!!!!*
>
> *"Never Again, Never Again" is our cry.*
> *"Never Again, Never Again" we vow.*
> *For we will do what must be done,*
> *And we will do it NOW!!!!!!!!!*[8]

"That was a great song at demonstrations right before the crowd would charge the cops," recalled David Fisch. "With the words THE J-D-L WILL FIGHT!!!! or sometimes WE WILL DO IT NOW!!!! people would charge the police, surge into the street for the sit-down, or just shout their heads off. It became a wonderful way to get the crowd in synchronization for the big moment of the demo. If the demo was not going to be violent or even a sit-down, it would be the build-up to the loudest possible chanting of the evening, so it would be reserved for the moment that the TV cameras were rolling, or whatever. If the song did not have the last sentence, it would not have been remembered. But the build-up at the end of the third stanza to THE J-D-L WILL FIGHT!!!! really was cool."[9]

On June 10, there was another major demonstration for Soviet Jewry. It followed a rally earlier in the evening at Hunter College auditorium, where Meir had exhorted the audience of about three hundred people to "do something nice for Soviet Jewry. If we do something for them, we save ourselves." From Hunter College, he led them in a march toward the Soviet Mission. At the intersection of Lexington and Third Avenues, more than two hundred people sat down in the street to protest the police barriers that kept them from picketing closer to the mission. They blocked the intersection at Third Avenue and 67 Street for twenty minutes and then about seventy-five helmeted men from the Tactical Police Force moved in among the singing protesters. Meir and 125 others were arrested and loaded into city buses and patrol wagons. The protesters were taken to four different police stations where they were all charged with disorderly conduct and released on personal recognizance.[10]

A spate of court appearances marked the month of June. Meir's appointment book shows him in court on June 4, 7 and 14 in a case related to a charge of "riot." On June 3 and 18 he was in court on a charge of chaining himself to the gate of the Soviet Mission during the April 1970 "Seder," and on June 23 (and again on July 9) there was a hearing relating to the demonstration at the Iraqi Mission.[11]

Neither the ever-present threat of a court case that could result in a prison sentence nor his most recent arrest on June 10 dissuaded Meir from calling another demonstration in Washington on June 27. This rally had a smaller attendance than the one in Washington on March 21, when close to 1,000 had been arrested for sitting down in the street, but it garnered a good amount of media attention.

This time, instead of a mass sit-down, Meir planned to test two local ordinances. One prohibited demonstrations within 500 feet of a foreign mission and the second prohibited "bringing a foreign state into disrepute."

Most of the protesters arrived Sunday morning on buses that left New York City at 7 A.M. Wearing symbolic handcuffs and lapel pins that said "Free Soviet Jews," they congregated in a park near the State Department. Meir, in handcuffs, spoke to the group from the hood of a parked car. Charlotte Levin, secretary of JDL's Washington Chapter, recalled: "He jumped up onto our Dodge Dart (and left slight dents in the metal!) and gave a very rousing speech from there." An amazing picture shows Meir in midair, jumping onto the hood of the car with his handcuffed wrists held high.[12] This was not the only time Meir had jumped onto the hood of a car, but it was the only time he did it while handcuffed. Levin said of his agility, "I once saw him take off on a dead run from a standstill at a big demo in New York. He was so fast, even his bodyguards didn't see it."[13]

NBC News broadcast part of Meir's speech. He called for the suspension of all talks with the Soviets, demanded that the Department of Commerce deny export licenses to any American business that traded with them, and urged that all sports and cultural exchange programs be stopped until Soviet Jews were given freedom.[14]

From the park, Meir led about three hundred protesters in a ten-block march toward the Soviet Embassy. When they were stopped by police two blocks from the embassy, Meir walked through police lines to the gate of the embassy to test the ordinance against demonstrating within 500 feet of a foreign mission. Then he tested the ordinance that prohibited "bringing a foreign state into disrepute." Standing at the gate, he shouted, "The Soviet Union is a tyranny and the Soviet Union stinks." One by one, JDL members approached the gate of the embassy and shouted the same thing. Thirty-seven of them were arrested with Meir. Meir wrote: "I could think of no [words] more elegant or more calculated to get me arrested.... I told the small army of newsmen following me that the Soviet Union must be brought into disrepute for its treatment of Jews."[15]

A photograph of Meir taken at this demonstration was used for the cover of *Story of the Jewish Defense League*. It shows him wearing a short-sleeved white dress shirt with open collar in the Washington heat, tie-less, the perennial ball-point pen showing from his shirt pocket. His handcuffed wrists are held at chest level, a black police officer is close behind his left shoulder, while a news-man holding a television camera can be seen in the distance behind his right shoulder. A charcoal drawing based on this photo, with Meir's handcuffed wrists prominently displayed, was used throughout the 1970s on posters and in ads announcing his speaking engagements.[16]

Media coverage of this completely non-violent demonstration was extensive. NBC News showed Meir telling the police, who demanded that he move away from the Soviet Embassy gate, that he had a right to criticize the Soviet Union and shout out its "disrepute." The footage then showed Meir being escorted by policemen to the waiting van as the JDL protesters shouted "Freedom Now" in the background. The *New York Daily News*' editorial page, in its "Guest Editorial" section, featured Meir's statement, "The Soviet Union is a tyranny and the Soviet Union stinks."[17]

The next day Meir taped a debate for the David Frost show on "How to Deal with Anti-Semitism in the Soviet Union." The other two participants were Dore Schary of the Anti-Defamation League and Professor Hans Morgenthau, international relations scholar. The program was aired on July 9. A supporter who viewed it wrote: "In your simple, honest, sincere manner you outshone the hypocrite Dore Schary." [18]

Speaking About JDL Ideology, January-June 1971

The sincerity that Meir projected contributed to his popularity as a speaker, but a key factor was media exposure. Invitations to speak increased as his media exposure grew, and he drew large audiences because people had heard so much about him. As a result, he had the opportunity to impart his ideas to a vast number of people.

On January 21 Meir flew to Toronto with Dov Sperling. They appeared there together at two universities: York University and the University of Toronto. One student paid tribute to Meir:

> He spoke to two packed lecture halls and stirred hundreds of Jewish students. Rabbi Kahane introduced many students to militant Judaism and to a Jew who is proud of his heritage and is willing to fight for it.... Probably the greatest accomplishment of Rabbi Kahane's visit was the focusing of attention on the Soviet Jewry issue. Hundreds of students heard Rabbi Kahane and Dov Sperling, a Russian Jew, speak on this topic. It is rather ironic that it took Rabbi Kahane to bring a Soviet Jew to Toronto. No other organization has done this.... Perhaps the "Establishment" could learn a few lessons from Rabbi Kahane. At least he gets something done. [19]

Another student wrote:

> ... Perhaps the most profound effect the meeting with Kahane had on me was that for a few brief hours, I felt I was unequivocally a Jew, a feeling which has not overly possessed me as of late.... Rabbi Kahane has so far been, in the cold facts of political realities, a remarkable success.... The harassment of Soviet government officials has had a real effect on Soviet-American relationships, the kind of effect which could force the two superpowers into some sort of deal which would allow more Soviet Jews to immigrate to Israel.... [20]

Meir's entire address, verbatim, was printed in Toronto's Jewish students' newspaper. This excerpt expresses an important aspect of his philosophy:

> We have another hang-up – our Jewish leaders do. It's called love. Now love is a great thing, but the kind of love that they're talking about is the almost frenetic desire to have the world love us and therefore make sure that what you're doing doesn't lose you the sympathy of the world.

At Beirut airport* Israel lost the sympathy of the world – of that there's no doubt! The UN blasted Israel 15 to 0. That's quite a score. They lost the sympathy of the world that they had so laboriously gained a week earlier with the death of a Jew at Athens airport.

If you want to win sympathy, that's the way to do it. One Jew dead – sympathy! Two Jews – more sympathy! Six million Jews – sympathy, plaques, monuments, eulogies, *Kaddish*, *Yizkor* [memorial prayers] – all over the world!

The late prime minister of Israel, Levi Eshkol, once held a press conference following a condemnation of Israel by the U.N. – we forget which one. And he said, "You know, had we lost the war, the eulogies over Israel would have been among the most beautiful of all time. Parliaments would have risen for two minutes of silence all over the world. So instead," he said, "this time we figured, let's live. So we fought and we won and they condemn us for it. We prefer it that way."

And that's the way it has to be! ... No more *Kaddish*; no more *Yizkor*. LET'S LIVE![21]

In January Meir also spoke at Dickinson College in Carlisle, Pennsylvania (to an audience of eight hundred), at the Herzlia Academy in Winnipeg, and at synagogues in New Jersey and New York.[22] He made a number of TV appearances during this period, one of them on a local channel in Baltimore, to which he took our son Baruch. Baruch recalled how fascinating it was to be in a TV studio for the first time. Another TV appearance was in Philadelphia, and on January 29 Meir flew to Dayton, Ohio, for a live broadcast of the nationwide Phil Donahue TV show, answering questions posed by the audience. In June, he spoke to callers on the Bob Grant radio program in New York.[23] His ability to think on his feet and his snappy responses helped put his ideas across to a wide public. Meir expressed himself clearly and succinctly at the Bronx High School of Science:

"If someone calls you a Jew bastard, hit him so hard he'll never do it again. You know what you'll get? Respect! ... Moses did not make a study of the root causes of the Jewish problem in Pharaoh's Egypt – he smote the Egyptian!"[24]

The controversy surrounding Meir is reflected in Liz Berney's reminiscence about his talk in White Plains on February 21:

I recall that the head rabbi at the Reform synagogue in White Plains, the Jewish Community Center (J.C.C.), Rabbi Maurice Davis, kept railing against Meir and telling us not to listen to him because he was a hatemonger, etc.... Of course, that made me even more interested to hear Meir when he came to speak at the Hebrew Institute [of White Plains] breakfast.

---

* In December 1968, in response to the hijacking of Israeli planes, Israeli paratroopers captured Beirut airport and blew up fourteen planes. Nobody was hurt.

My first impressions were that Meir seemed so young – he had thick black hair at the time – and that he sounded so reasonable and soft-spoken – not at all what his "bad press" said.

... I went back to the class I was in at J.C.C. and told the whole class how reasonably and intelligently Rabbi Kahane spoke. Another kid in the class said he heard Meir on the radio and had the same impression. We almost caused a revolution over there.[25]

The primary aim of Meir's talks during February and March was to promote attendance at the mass rally for Soviet Jews in Washington on March 21.[26]

At a synagogue in New Rochelle, Meir urged the overflow audience: "We don't ask you to break windows or throw bombs. We do ask you to go to Washington and sit down in the streets. There will be banner headlines around the world," he promised, "if a hundred thousand Jews demonstrate in the streets."[27]

Meir was well received when he spoke at a meeting of the Revisionists in New York, urging them to come to the rally in Washington. The newsletter of the Revisionists reported: "Surprise guests were leaders of the JDL, Rabbi & Mrs. Meir Kahane, Mr. & Mrs. Bertram Zweibon, and Mr. & Mrs. Irving Calderon. Rabbi Kahane and Mr. Zweibon addressed the gathering and received a standing ovation."[28]

At the end of February, Meir concentrated on audiences in the greater Washington area. He hoped they would make up the bulk of the crowd at the rally in March. His appearances were described on page one of the *Washington Post*:

Meir David Kahane ... drew standing-room-only crowds and standing ovations yesterday at appearances at two Washington suburban synagogues.

Kahane spoke to more than 500 persons at Agudas Achim in Alexandria and to more than 300 at Har Shalom in Potomac. The second audience was so reluctant to let him go that he missed his 4 P.M. plane back to New York.

He told both audiences ... "The essence of Judaism is spiritual, and I say violence is evil when it is not necessary. But the spirit cannot exist without the body, and to protect a Jew's body, a Jew's fist is sometime required."

The *Washington Post* noted that "Kahane, 38, the small, dark, soft-voiced leader of the Jewish Defense League, faced not a single clearly hostile questioner...."[29]

But at talks that month at two universities, he faced very angry hecklers. At the State University in Buffalo on February 4, the hall was jammed with leftist Jewish students chanting "Ho, Ho, Ho Chi Minh, Palestine is going to win," "Down with Israeli fascism," and "End Zionism." Meir recalled, "... I stood on the platform and told them that I would remain there all night but they would never get me to cancel the speech." Then, at Colgate University in Hamilton, New York, he got into a shouting match with a Palestinian exchange student. It ended when Meir snapped, "I'm not a college president. Nobody shuts me up." Meir also spoke in February at Syracuse University, at Staten Island Community College, and was the guest speaker at a concert at Brooklyn College.[30]

At McGill University in Montreal in March, there were hecklers too. There, Jewish students clashed with members of the Maoist Student Movement who interrupted Meir's speech. Later that month, while he was speaking at Pembroke College, Brown University, not only were there hecklers, but a bomb threat was phoned in. The university's security staff asked the audience to leave the hall, but they stayed when Meir persuaded them the threat was phony. (He proved to be correct.) As he continued to speak, Maoists in the audience started to heckle him. They were forcibly removed from the hall by Jewish students.[31]

However, audiences were politely attentive when Meir returned to Washington. On March 16, he spoke at three universities in the area urging students to attend the March 21 rally at the White House. In a talk at the University of Maryland before seven hundred students, he said:

> There are other things Russia wants more than to keep its Jews. They have a problem. It's called China. Russia has an army on the Chinese border that costs billions and billions of rubles.
>
> ... Russia also wants consumer goods, trade and peaceful co-existence with the West. They will release their Jews if it will solve their other problems.

He told the students about Jews who confront anti-Semitism daily:

> In Brownsville, a predominantly black area in Brooklyn, New York, there are more than two thousand Jews over 65 on welfare, who are so terrified they don't even go out of their homes more than twice a week to buy food.
>
> When JDL formed a patrol to allow these people the elementary right to walk in the street, what is the word we get? "Vigilantes." Do you know who calls us vigilantes? All the Jewish leaders who don't live in Brownsville.[32]

Later in the day, Meir spoke to students at American University and at George Washington University. The GW student newspaper reported:

> Rabbi Meir Kahane ... told a Tuesday afternoon GW audience that American Jews should "bury their complexes and believe that Jewish is beautiful."
>
> "... G-d forbid we should sit in the streets," Kahane declared in tones laced with sarcasm, "nice Jewish boys shouldn't do such things!"
>
> Kahane pleaded for Jews "to stop worrying about what non-Jews think. We've got to get rid of that complex. A decent non-Jew knows that when someone beats you, you beat him back. That's moral. That's sanity."
>
> "The fact is," he told the polite, attentive audience, "that when the chips are down, you know who's going to fight for the Jew? Only the Jew, and it's about time we understood this."

... This new militancy has already caused repercussions in Soviet-American relations, Kahane claimed: "Only the militant Jews have pushed the Soviets against the wall. And all of a sudden, Nixon, who loses no sleep over Jewish problems, but plenty of sleep over Nixon problems, is losing sleep."[33]

Meir's talks to the general public included a speech on March 15 in downtown Montreal. Bryna Weinberger recalled the large turnout:

> I have one personal memory of seeing Rabbi Kahane speak.... The day had brought a vicious snowstorm. Driving was treacherous and a heavy snowfall had accumulated during the storm. The radio and television had been warning people to stay off the roads due to poor visibility and very bad driving conditions. If not for my friend and her husband, I would not have ventured out that night. I was sure we would be the only three in attendance.
>
> Many arrived late, but the hall was soon filled to capacity, with many people standing and many who had to remain at the door, straining to hear and to see, but unable to come in due to lack of space. The speech was enthralling, captivating and fascinating....[34]

Meir often attracted very large audiences. That March in New Jersey he drew "Yom Kippur-sized" audiences in Glen Rock, Fair Lawn, Livingston and New Milford. In New Milford, where more than seven hundred people came out to hear him, Meir answered the charge that JDL's militancy was "un-Jewish."

> All Jews celebrate Chanuka and honor the Maccabees. We go to Massada and our hearts swell with pride. These were not apostles of non-violence. The Bible says, "There is a time for war and a time for peace," and sometimes – after all else has failed – violence is necessary.... To turn the other cheek is not in OUR Bible.[35]

Meir's last address that month, at Congregation Shaaray Tefila in Far Rockaway on March 28, 1971, took place only a week after the arrest of almost 1,000 Jews at the demonstration for Soviet Jews in Washington. Meir drew an overflow crowd. Many people had to be seated in the smaller auditorium downstairs and listen to him over the public address system.[36]

The speech was recorded for posterity by an enterprising supporter, Isaac Hager, who released it as an rpm (gramophone) record titled *Never Again*, packaged in a bright blue cover bearing JDL's logo, a clenched fist imposed on a Star of David. Meir's voice in the recording was light and youthful. His speech began with the story of Volodenka,* who personified the religious oppression of Soviet Jews. Meir explained how American Jews could help them by taking advantage of the Soviet Union's need for an alliance with the United States. In just under an hour he also spoke of the plight of Jews in America's inner cities, the tactical

---

* See chapter 11 for the story of Volodenka.

use of violence, Jewish pride as an antidote for intermarriage and assimilation, and the beauty of Judaism.[37]

On March 31 Meir flew to Los Angeles, where he spoke at six synagogues (Orthodox, Reform and Conservative) to audiences averaging seven hundred people. He also spoke on five college campuses, and there were press conferences and parlor meetings as well. An FBI informant reported on his talk at UCLA's Student Union Hall: "At one point an agitator sought to disrupt the speech, but was put in his place when Kahane shouted, 'Sit down, Arab!'"[38]

Taking advantage of President Nixon's presence at the "summer White House" in nearby San Clemente, Meir announced an all-night vigil there to demand Nixon's intervention on behalf of Soviet Jewry. Buses carrying about eighty participants left from JDL's Fairfax Avenue headquarters at 9 P.M. on April 5. Meir lectured most of the night on Jewish history and religion, with Rabbi Zvi Block of Los Angeles giving a lecture as well. "The Rabbi spoke all through the night, surrounded by a group of young people," recalled Sherri Okin. "He wove a web of Judaism under the stars that night in San Clemente."[39]

The Los Angeles chapter was growing and active. It had a total membership of approximately 750, with about 200 actively participating members. Their plans included a demonstration at the Wilshire Ebell Theater to protest the performance of Moscow's Borodin String Quartet scheduled for May 12. As Meir was leaving for the airport at noon on April 7, they held a demonstration at the May Company department store to protest the tours to the Soviet Union that its travel department was arranging. Sherri Okin recalled the May Company protest.

> I, my son Jan, and Sy Gaiber sat down in front of the doors. We didn't let anyone into the store. Such a thing had never happened before. The police even called in helicopters. We were only about twelve people, but they stopped arranging tours to the Soviet Union![40]

Later that April and at the beginning of May, Meir spoke at several universities: in Detroit at Wayne State University and the University of Michigan; at Boston's Northeastern University and at Princeton University. At Wayne, he told an audience of three hundred: "No one is going to help a Jew except a second Jew. In the past we marched for anyone. For Vietnam and civil rights we were right out in front. But when a Jewish problem came up, we marched and no one came." He spent much of his two-hour appearance answering hostile questions from campus radicals who sympathized with the Arabs.[41]

On one occasion Meir's return flight was due to arrive at JFK on Friday afternoon.* A slight delay in take-off put the time of his arrival only an hour

---

* This occurred at the end of March or the beginning of April when sunset, signaling the onset of Shabbat, was around 6:00 P.M.

before sunset, the start of Shabbat, when observant Jews do not travel. Irving Calderon, who lived near the airport, met him as planned. They realized that Calderon would not return home before Shabbat if he drove Meir to Brooklyn. At Meir's insistence, he took him only as far as the Queens-Brooklyn border, and then, with Meir's money and suitcase in his car, drove home, leaving Meir to walk the rest of the way on foot.

It was almost time to light the Shabbat candles, and Meir was not yet home. I was worried, but realized there was nothing I could do. I lit the candles, said the *Kiddush* (the Shabbat blessing over wine), served the children their meal, and just waited and waited – trying to push away the dreadful thoughts.

Finally, at 9:30 there was a knock at the door. It was Meir! It had taken him almost three hours, passing through some rough neighborhoods on the way, but he was home. He could have spent the Shabbat with the Calderons, but he wanted to be home with his family. His article "To My Four Children" expresses his profound devotion to them and his concern for their future.

> ... I stand in your room, your little bedroom, with lights dimmed. All is still where you lie so quietly and your eyes are closed and you do not even realize that I watch you and think.
>
> We brought you into this world; the Almighty, your mother and I. We were the three partners in your creation. Sometimes, when I am alone with my thoughts, a sadness envelops me and I wonder how this can be done? I look out the window of the world and see the abominations that go on, the evils swirling throughout, the savages that pass for men, the heartaches that none can escape.
>
> ... I see all this in the world; that world that I helped bring you into, that world that I must thrust you out to, that world which screams and snarls and will seek to devour your bodies and extinguish your souls and I become a despairing man.
>
> It is the Almighty alone who knows the answers. Wisdom and understanding are His and ours is but to obey.
>
> ... And because, some day, you will ask: Father, what is the reason? I must be able to answer you. I must be able to look at you and say: Bless G-d for all that is your lot. As you bless Him for that which you consider good, so shall you fervently bless Him for all that you consider lacking in good.
>
> Know and understand this, my children. Man was not created for happiness, at least, not the happiness that we understand. Man was not created to live free from tragedy and heartache. This is not his lot. It is not laughter that you must strive for, but duty; not joy, but goodness; not security, but holiness.
>
> ... Man was created so that he might reach the heights of perfection that exists within him, so that the perfect ideals of Love, of Goodness, of Justice combining to form the ultimate state of Holiness, might be taken from the realm of the transcendental, from the place of the theoretical, and brought to the living, actual reality.

But what greatness lies in this life! What splendor, what permanence, what truth! Yes, this is the word. Truth. What ugliness is that life which is falsehood. What a sordid thing is that existence based from beginning to end upon lying vanities, dying superficialities.... And so, bless G-d and thank Him for allowing you to live this life. And having done so, proceed to live it as He would have you do.

Love all. With tenderness look upon all that you see: the frail flower, the frightened dog, the desperate man. Love them all and let this love lift you to the heights of holiness.

My children, there are many who exist; there are few who live. It is for you to grow, to mature and to choose life.[42]

Against a background of the stormy, tumultuous events that made up Meir's life, this article shows his deep concern for our children and his steadfast commitment to the ideals of Judaism, a commitment that permeated and motivated all he did.

The Jewish Establishment Censures the JDL

Perhaps because of his great success in drawing crowds, in April there were two attempts to prevent him from speaking. The first was a bomb that went off at the West Orange (New Jersey) Jewish Center on April 18, the night before he was scheduled to address its Men's Club. The bomb shattered windows and caused extensive damage to parts of the building. Officials of the Center announced that Meir would speak there instead on May 2. A large demand for tickets for May 2 was reported.[43]

The second attempt was a bit more civilized: When his address at the Beth Jacob synagogue in Columbus, Ohio, was announced for April 27, the local Anti-Defamation League did everything it could to block his arrival and tried to muffle all the publicity. Beth Jacob's rabbi, David Stavsky, received "continuous harassment with threats to both himself and his synagogue.... Two wealthy members of the local Jewish community told Rabbi Stavsky, 'If you don't cancel Kahane, we will cut you off.'" However, he did not yield, and more than six hundred people came to hear Meir. This was not forgotten: When Meir came to Columbus again on February 21, 1990, and again sparked a controversy, supporter Larry Pollack pointed up the existence of a double standard in the advocacy of freedom of speech by liberals:

Almost 20 years ago, the largest crowd ever to assemble for a speaker in the Columbus Jewish community came to hear Rabbi Meir Kahane.

You don't have to agree with all of Kahane's views to attend. Listen to his ideas and then challenge him during the question period if you want to. But most important, decide for yourself. Don't let the double standard of liberal tolerance decide what you can and cannot be allowed to hear.[44]

Naphtali J. Rubinger analyzed the efforts of the Jewish Establishment to prevent Meir from speaking.

> It is the right of every Jew to support or oppose the JDL ... or some aspect of their program.... Any Jewish agency that seeks by means of subtle coercion and slander to deprive other groups of the Jewish community of a fair hearing, as was done in Springfield, Massachusetts and Toronto, Canada, violates the most sacred obligation of public trust.
>
> ... I charge that the Jewish Establishment, including the Anti-Defamation League, American Jewish Committee and the American Jewish Congress have been engaging in a vicious campaign of slander and vilification against the Jewish Defense League.

Rubinger offered an explanation:

> ... The JDL brings into focus the vacuum that has been created by the radical shift in the Negro revolution from a non-violent confrontation to a more militant and aggressive attack upon the *status quo*. Add to this the growing affinity between Black nationalism and Arab anti-Zionism, and we have a situation with which the [Establishment] has not been able to cope.
>
> The idiom, the technique and the underlying philosophy of the so-called experts of the National Community Relations Advisory Council are still of the 1930, 1940 and 1950 vintage. There are paradoxes which the Jewish agencies find difficult to handle....[45]

The Jewish Establishment's difficulty in coping with new realities may have been the underlying reason for their opposition to Meir and the JDL. But when the Omaha Community Relations Committee censured the JDL, the reason they gave was that the JDL's use of violent means was "un-Jewish."[46]

Members of the Jewish Establishment voiced this reason over and over. Meir refuted it in his article "On Violence:"

> ... No knowledgeable Jew denies that peace is the ultimate ideal, just as he must admit that, until that utopian era, we must continue to abide by the Talmudic axiom: "He who comes to slay you – slay him first." (*Berachot*, 58)
>
> ... From the days that our father Abraham went to battle against the four kings in order to save his nephew Lot, to the moment that Moses smote an Egyptian rather than create a committee to study the root causes of Egyptian anti-Semitism; from the Maccabees ... to the students of Rabbi Akiva who were sent from their studies to fight in Bar Kochba's army ... Jewish leadership has taken an active and violent part in the struggle for freedom.[47]

Mickey Gerelick, the editor of the Omaha *Jewish Press* also thought that violence was sometimes a good thing:

> ... There were thousands of Jews who went silently and non-violently to the gas chambers in Germany. Is non-violence always the best policy?
>
> It is commendable for ADL to support "the law of the land" but there would be no Jews alive today had we not broken the laws of Pharaoh, the Philistines, Antiochus....[48]

A rethinking of the Jewish Establishment's attitude toward the JDL was suggested by an editorial in the *Jewish Post and Opinion:*

> ... Whether the rank and file of the Jewish community, not those who control it, hold the same view, is questionable. Wherever Meir Kahane has appeared he has been greeted with large and enthusiastic crowds. His message strikes a responsive chord in young Jews unlike anything in recent years except the Six Day War, and both have an underlying thread of similarity...."[49]

In May, Meir's speaking engagements in Cherry Hill, New Jersey, and Norfolk, Virginia, were cancelled. This time it was not because of pressure from the local Jewish Establishment, but because Meir was arrested on May 12 on a major weapons charge and was held overnight.[50]

Among Meir's speaking dates in May was one in Toronto, where the JDL chapter held a farewell dinner in honor of his coming move to Israel.[51] Wherever he went, he urged Jews to move to Israel. To students at the University of Illinois at Chicago on May 6, he said, "America could turn out to be another Germany. They thought it couldn't happen there, but it did.... Israel is the only place for Jews today."[52]

Aliya was one of Meir's topics at his monthly lectures to JDL members. He also lectured informally at meetings of the leadership, to sharpen their understanding of JDL's concepts and purposes. Meetings lasted late into the night.[53]

In March, JDL rented space at 4002 New Utrecht Avenue in Brooklyn. The location was ideal for the nucleus of activist members. There were karate lessons every night and a weekly seminar every Tuesday night. The Jewish Identity Center that Meir had envisioned almost a year earlier became a reality in September. There were courses on the American Jewish Community, World Jewry, Jewish History, Israel and Zionism, Jewish Traditions and Culture.[54] An indication that JDL also served as a social club is the announcement that only those registered for karate, the Jewish Identity school or gym would be allowed to remain in the lounge after 7 P.M. The social aspect was important, said board member Murray Schneider. As he put it, "at the Identity Center, Jewish boy meets Jewish girl."[55]

For most young members, JDL's social aspect, its camaraderie, was a factor that enhanced both their commitment to its ideals and their vigorous enthusiasm at demonstrations.

Chapter 24

Aliya: Our Family Immigrates to Israel (July-September 1971)

Writing a Best Seller: Never Again!

I N APRIL 1971, in addition to all his other activities, Meir began work on a book about JDL's aims, principles, and philosophies, which would be called *Never Again!* It was published in October 1971 by Nash Publishing of Los Angeles and was Meir's best-selling book: 10,000 copies in hardcover and 100,000 copies in paperback.[1] Edward L. Nash recalled how he made contact with Meir.

> When I was in publishing, most of our books were searched out by me or my editors. We were too new, too small and too controversial to get submissions from the big agents. Usually, and in Meir's case, we were the ones who suggested writing a book.
>
> JDL was of special interest to me because of boyhood memories of running a gauntlet of anti-Semitic bullies (in the Bronx) who gathered around our Hebrew school. My personal defining moment was when I turned on one such bully in school and out of sheer anger beat him so badly that he never taunted me or any other Jew again. You can understand why I would seek out your late husband as a proud addition to our list.[2]

Meir's files include several letters from Nash. In the first, dated April 20, 1971, Nash wrote:

> I'm sorry you were unable to make the appointment at the St. Moritz Hotel last Saturday evening, as set up by Mr. Avram of your office. I had postponed my return to Los Angeles in order to see you, as I am sure that we could work out a mutually profitable deal for writing a book about the JDL position.
>
> I was prepared to offer you an advance of $10,000, payable one-third on signing, one-third on manuscript completion, and one-third on publication,

against a royalty ranging from 10% to 15% and one-half book club, foreign and paperback proceeds....

Such a book could help give you not just worldwide publicity for your movement, which you already have, but worldwide intellectual support. It would be bought and read by thousands of potential supporters and contributors ... and would help provide an income to offset the great personal expenses you must be incurring.

Our firm is relatively new, but very well established, particularly in terms of successfully promoting books nationally. Our recent successes include *How to Parent, Psychology of Self Esteem, Witness to Evil* and, coming soon, *Between Man and Woman.* Our company is ... sympathetic with your position.

I know you are busy, but one well-written, well-promoted book, with a title such as *Never Again*, could accomplish many goals for your cause. Would you please call me at (213) 272-9624 so we can discuss this and get started in time for publication this fall.[3]

As to the choice of the title, Nash recalled, "The title *Never Again!* suggested by us was an obvious one at the time. The book was not only about the Soviet Jewish problem, but about the need for Jewish pride and resistance."[4]

Nash's letter convinced Meir that it was worth his while to phone Los Angeles. Two days later Nash wrote again:

I'm delighted you called.... Please look over the enclosed contract.... The return contract will be accompanied by a check for $3,333....

I get to New York about once a month.... I'd like to review our publicity and advertising plans with you.

All of us are looking forward to making this book one of the big successes of the year, not only for the money it will make but because of the support it will give to your program.[5]

A week later, Nash wrote: "It's very important that we get the agreement signed.... We also need biographical data...."[6] He attached a form headed "Author's Biography." On the line "Marital Status and Number of Children," I wrote OMIT, because of my constant concern for privacy. Indeed, the book jacket had no data about the family.

Unfortunately, Nash found it difficult to fulfill the financial aspects of the contract. Not only did he not send $3,333 with the return contract, but on May 3 he wrote, "We'll get the first installment of the advance out to you within ten days, as provided in the contract." Then on May 19 he wrote:

I'm sorry for the delay in your initial check. I have been in somewhat of a cash bind because of seasonal problems, but we do plan to get the check out before the end of this month.... I thought it might be better to send you a postdated check to avoid the delay of processing and mailing the check. I have made it out for May 29, just 20 days from now.

In the same letter, Nash wrote: "I have been concerned over the news of your various arrests, and I hope that ... this will not delay your manuscript."[7] Had Nash realized the full extent of Meir's frenetic schedule, he would have wondered how Meir could find time to write a book in the first place. However, Meir did find time to write and he completed the manuscript in record time.

An enthusiastic telegram from Nash attests that Meir sent him the manuscript of this 287-page book at the beginning of June. The telegram, received at the JDL office on June 16th, said: "Manuscript received better than anything we could have hoped for. It is a beautiful as well as important work. Aiming for September publication. Congratulations on a great writing job."[8]

Sentenced to Federal Prison

Perhaps one of the reasons Meir worked overtime to complete the manuscript in June was the seriousness of the court case that was to be heard in July. At a pre-trial hearing on July 6 in Brooklyn Federal Court, U.S. District Attorney Joseph W. Ryan told the court that most of the charges against Meir and the other defendants, including possessing and detonating explosives, were based on information supplied to the District Attorney by policemen who had infiltrated the JDL and by Gilbert Laurie, the man who sold dynamite to the defendants. They would be the key government witnesses.[9]

However, additional evidence against the defendants might be gleaned from their own conversations! The government had disclosed that it had used electronic listening devices on telephones in the JDL office and in members' homes at the end of 1970 and the beginning of 1971, and had done so without first obtaining a court order.[10]

Tapping JDL phones should have aroused the ire of the liberals, who always opposed government encroachment on civil rights, but none spoke up. One editorial said, "Short-cuts taken by the Department of Justice ... against black extremists suspected of criminal conduct have been fought to a standstill by liberal defenders of civil rights, and Jewish organizations have commendably been on the side of the libertarians. Sadly [they] have not been greatly concerned with the constitutional rights [of] Jewish militants...."[11]

The primary purpose of this pre-trial hearing was to determine whether information obtained by the government through wiretaps on JDL telephones could be presented at the trial. Attorneys for the JDL defendants demanded they wait for a Supreme Court decision on the admissibility of evidence gained from the wiretaps. The presiding judge, Jack B. Weinstein, refused to postpone the trial, but said he was working under the assumption that the wiretaps were illegal. Meir told reporters after the pre-trial hearing, "This is the start of a massive effort to crush me." He charged that the government was knuckling under to pressure from Moscow by "rushing" into the trial without waiting for a Supreme Court decision on the wiretaps.[12]

U.S. District Attorney Robert Morse and the attorneys representing Meir and the twelve other defendants – Barry Slotnick, Bertram Zweibon, Nathan Lewin, Robert Persky, Stanley Cohen and Harvey J. Michelman – held lengthy pre-trial negotiations. On July 9 they came to an agreement that Meir, Hy Bieber, and Stuart Cohen would plead guilty, and all the charges against the remaining defendants would be dismissed. In addition, the defendants would withdraw the motion concerning illegal wiretapping by the government. Meir, Bieber and Cohen each faced a maximum penalty of five years in prison and a $10,000 fine.

To cover legal costs, the JDL *Newsletter* requested contributions to the Legal Defense Fund, which were "totally tax deductible." Even though most of the lawyers gave their services to JDL *pro bono*, there were many incidental court costs the lawyers could not be expected to assume. Ads for contributions to the Legal Defense Fund, such as one headed "Fair Trials for Jews," appeared in the *Jewish Press*.[13]

Following his agreement to enter a guilty plea, Meir explained to reporters at the courthouse that he had pleaded guilty on one count in order to have the charges against ten of the defendants dropped. He had set off an explosive at the League's camp the previous August without filing the required application or paying a $200 tax. His purpose had been to show the campers the type of bomb described in pamphlets of the radical right and left. (To make the bomb, he followed directions on the back page of the Black Panthers' newspaper.)[14] He did not know that it was illegal to explode a bomb on private property and in a classroom atmosphere. Had he known, he would certainly not have done so in the presence of someone whom he knew to be a police informer.[15]

On July 12 Meir held a news conference at JDL's Brooklyn headquarters on New Utrecht Avenue. The fact that he was facing a jail term had brought the reporters to Brooklyn, but Meir placed the emphasis of the news conference on the plight of Soviet Jews. When asked if he or his followers would use explosives in the future, he said that he would not use them against Americans, but he declared, "We would not hesitate to use these methods [against Soviet installations in this country] because it is a tyranny that does not allow any form of protest."

One reporter asked him if he would consider imprisonment a form of martyrdom that would help Soviet Jews. He shook his head and said, "Jail isn't a nice place for a nice Jewish boy or for anybody and I don't want to go there."[16]

Meir declared in his *Jewish Press* column a week before sentencing that no matter what sentence was passed on him personally, the struggle for Soviet Jewry would continue.[17] An advertisement in the same issue proclaimed, "On Friday,

July 23rd, at 9:30 A.M. they will sentence Rabbi Meir Kahane. His real crime: His love for Soviet Jews and his disruption of Soviet foreign policy." In large letters, the ad said

PACK THE COURTROOM

Supporters held an all-night vigil outside the courthouse to be sure of seats and were seen on television reciting the morning service in prayer shawls and phylacteries. The three hundred seats in the courtroom were quickly filled and many had to stand outside.[18]

Before he pronounced sentence, District Court Judge Jack B. Weinstein asked Meir if he had anything to add to attorney Barry Slotnick's defense. Meir's words to the court were recalled by Dov Hikind, who participated in the all-night vigil outside the courthouse. Hikind expected Meir to express remorse and to request mercy, as defendants are wont to do. To his amazement, Meir took a different tack.[19]

Meir explained to Judge Weinstein the concern for Soviet Jewry that motivated him and admitted his fear of a possible jail sentence. He concluded his address to the judge with words that were so moving that Hikind – and many others – recalled them years later.

> I am not happy being here, even though you are only a judge of flesh and blood. I do not look forward to being put in prison, although that may very well be, but some day I will have to face a second Judge, and with Him there will be, I believe, a great many souls. And I believe those souls stand by His side and when every Jew comes, they have a question that they pose to the soul that has just arrived, and that question is, "Where were you when we cried out?" Those are the souls of the Jews of Eastern Europe's Holocaust and they will also be the souls of the Jews of the USSR. I want to be able to say I was there and I did what I could. I have tried to do what I can and whether I go to prison or I do not, I am going to continue doing what I have to do and I only hope that the members of the Jewish Defense League and all Jews, no matter what happens this morning, will do what they have to do. Thank you.[20]

When Judge Weinstein handed down a five-year suspended prison sentence, Meir's supporters were so relieved he wasn't going to prison, they shouted for joy. Later, they carried him out of the courtroom on their shoulders, singing. Footage of Meir being carried aloft by his supporters was on television, together with clips of his comments on Judge Weinstein's decision.[21]

Meir's sentence included five years on probation and a $5,000 fine. Hy Bieber and Stuart Cohen each received a three-year suspended prison sentence with three years on probation. Bieber was fined $2,500 and Cohen $500. The terms of probation provided that the three "must have nothing to do with guns, bombs, dynamite, gunpowder or any other weapons." Judge Weinstein warned: "If the terms of probation are violated, the suspension of the sentence will be revoked and jail for the full term imposed can result."[22] Judge Weinstein explained his decision:

> There was no proof that [Kahane's] activities had directly led to any physical damage.... In view of the factual ambiguity, the defendant's good background as a teacher, father and husband, his lack of any substantial criminal record, the fact that he appeared to be motivated by consideration of the welfare of others rather than self, and the recommendations of authorities that probation be utilized in such circumstances, the court sentenced the defendant to five years probation.[23]

The State Department, which had been monitoring the trial, was satisfied with the decision. By using the courts to weaken the JDL, they expected to achieve their goal of improving relations with the Soviet Union. The American ambassador to the U.N. sent a cable to the Secretary of State in Washington:

> We are pleased with sentence which more severe than expected. Asst. U.S. Attorney Thomas H. Pattison believes JDL violence now far less likely and JDL potential for causing serious harm to Soviet personnel sharply reduced.[24]

Meir told reporters afterwards: "I did not ask for leniency. I stuck to my principles." Straightaway, he outlined plans to organize rifle practice for Jewish self-defense. Since it was legal to own unconcealed weapons, such as the .22-caliber rifle, the motto of the campaign was "Every Jew a .22." Meir reasoned that the terms of his probation – not to have anything to do with firearms – applied to him alone and did not limit the JDL in any way.[25]

Every Jew a .22

The rifle practice campaign was given impetus by the cruel, senseless slaying of Brooklyn candy store owner Beno Spiewak on August 20. This was the latest in a rash of robberies, muggings, and killings in the East Flatbush section of Brooklyn. Meir announced that JDL would organize patrols there and help residents of East Flatbush arm themselves with .22 rifles.

Right from the start there was speculation: Was Meir violating probation by promoting the legal purchase of rifles? Would the "Every Jew a .22" campaign put him in prison? Attorney Barry Slotnick invoked Meir's right to freedom of speech.[26]

The government was keeping close tabs on Meir. A probation report noted that Meir was present at a Brooklyn press conference on August 5 where JDL spokesman Eli Schwartz announced that the League had purchased .22-caliber rifles from registered gun dealers and had sold them to area residents. The report also noted that on August 29 Meir was "heard endorsing" Larry Fine, national director of the JDL, who urged the crowd to fill out applications for gun permits at a JDL rally at Tilden High School in Brooklyn.[27]

The rally at Tilden High School, which focused on Jewish self-defense, was called to protest the slaying of Beno Spiewak and the rising crime and violence in the East Flatbush section. The *Daily News* reported that "more than 1,500 East Flatbush residents roared their approval as Meir outlined his plan to turn back the tide.... He addressed the crowd for nearly twenty minutes, stopping frequently for outbursts of cheering and standing ovations."[28]

The motto "Every Jew a .22" drew the wrath of the Jewish Establishment. Even the *Jewish Press* editorialized: "Putting a gun in the hands of every Jew implies that law and order has broken down in this country – and nothing could be further from the truth!" [29] Meir responded in his column:

> "Jewish youth, learn to shoot." So wrote the late, great Zeev Jabotinsky in an essay that has to rank as one of the most brilliant and prophetic writings of modern Jewish times....
>
> If Jewish neighborhoods are prey to muggers and rapists and robbers because it is well known that Jews and Jewish homes have no guns – let it be changed. If Jews are victims of hoodlums and hooligans because the Jew is not one who is armed and dangerous – let it be different. If the Jewish image is one of fearful timidity ... let the voice of Jewish strength [go forth] from every Jewish neighborhood and home. If there is a difference in the level of crime and violence in an Italian neighborhood as compared with the Jewish one, the difference is that within the mind of the hooligan; one has the shadow of the gun while the other is filled with peaceful ignoramuses.[30]

Meir emphasized two related concerns in his speech at Tilden High School – crime in schools and blockbusting. Regarding the first, he told the audience that JDL members would visit "local high school principals to warn them that JDL will step in if they are lax with hoodlums in the schools...."

Crime in city schools was not limited to New York City. It was a nationwide plague. A report from Los Angeles that year said, "... Black high school students at Fairfax High School demand money from Jewish students under threat of physical harm.... Students are afraid to walk in the halls or enter the restrooms alone because they will get beaten up."[31]

Meir spoke of another acute problem in East Flatbush – blockbusting. In New York and other cities, real estate dealers known as "blockbusters" took advantage of increasing crime in neighborhoods. They persuaded frightened homeowners to sell at low prices to dealers, who would then demand inflated prices from black families needing better housing. Meir urged the audience not to allow unscrupulous real estate dealers "to capitalize on recent killings and muggings by getting home owners to sell their property at a loss."[32]

The formation of the Council of Oppressed Jewish Neighborhoods was Meir's solution to deteriorating neighborhoods and the related problem of Jewish poverty. At JDL's annual convention, he said:

> ... Poor Jews in crime-ridden neighborhoods are afraid to leave their homes to shop – a matza serves in place of bread, for it keeps longer.... Close to two hundred thousand Jews comprise the third-largest poverty group in New York City.[33]

Part of the council's activities would be to influence local politics.

> Jews will be informed on a neighborhood level for whom to vote.... When Jews vote in that little booth, they will know whom to vote for. JEWISH POWER is the name of the game. With it, we will be saved. Without it, we would be destroyed.[34]

In the *Jewish Press,* he called on neighborhood representatives to attend the opening conference of the council on June 20:

> There is only one answer and that is for the Jewish masses to take matters into their own hands.... This Conference will deal with practical steps to form a Jewish power base in urban neighborhoods. It will be the beginning of efforts to publicize the problems, come up with our own solutions, and expose ... our do-nothing Jewish organizations.[35]

The cover of a four-sided flyer publicizing the conference shows a boarded-up storefront, a rubble-strewn yard, and a windowless apartment building facade. The conference, held at Congregation Adath Jeshurun in the Bronx, set up a group named the Jewish Neighborhood Action Council, headed by Nat Rosenwasser. In a neighborhood meeting sponsored by the council in Brighton Beach in August, Meir called for the establishment of a citizens' patrol to prevent crime. Nat Rosenwasser told a reporter who had come to the meeting, "We want to convince Jews in areas like this that they don't have to move out to put an end to their problems."[36]

On August 27 Meir led a takeover of New York City's Human Resources Administration. Claiming discrimination against poor Jews, the protesters blocked and barricaded doors. Meir, invited in to the assistant commissioner's office, said that Jews constituted 12 percent of New York's poor but received less than 2 percent of anti-poverty funds. Officials agreed to set up a committee to meet regularly with the JDL and its affiliate, the "National Jewish Power Council."[37]

Throughout this time, the JDL continued to focus on Soviet Jewry. In Washington, D.C., Meir and twenty JDLers staged a sit-in at the office of Senator Edward M. Kennedy to demand that he take a stronger stand against the repression of Russian Jews. Kennedy, who was attending a session of the Senate, remained on the Senate floor for almost four hours. When he finally returned to his office, he engaged in "a friendly debate" with Meir. Meir told Kennedy that just as he fights American sugar deals with South Africa because of its racial policies, he should call for economic sanctions against the Soviet Union because it deprives Jews of their elementary liberties. Meir asked Senator Kennedy to oppose Department of Commerce trade licenses for Russian business deals. A UPI photo shows Meir talking to Kennedy in his office, with several young JDLers and reporters looking on.[38]

A September 9 Soviet Jewry rally in New York was advertised under the heading "Largest Rally Looms."[39] It began with about two hundred people picketing near the Soviet Mission. Suddenly, a group of them surged toward the police barricades and tried to climb them. Police kept pushing them back. After about an hour, they sat down in the intersection, blocking traffic. When they refused police orders to disperse, 34 (mostly youngsters) were carried to police vans and taken to jail.[40] A JDL bulletin described police brutality: "Beatings were inflicted on two demonstrators by TPF officer badge no. 17345, while another officer, badge no. 26330, drew his revolver at a demonstrator who offered no provocation of any sort." An impartial report of the New York Bar Association later confirmed that one officer pulled a gun, many used their nightsticks as clubs, and mounted police used their horses to drive the demonstrators away. The report emphasized the large number of policemen on hand, "in excess of one hundred ... several of whom wore black mourning bands on their badge numbers, making identification difficult."[41]

Leaving the Exile

The September 9 rally was held without Meir. He had taught JDLers the basics. From now on, they would continue to act even while he was in Israel. Plans were made for a September 11 *selichot* prayer meeting, a September 16 "black umbrella" demonstration against appeasing the Arabs, and a rally for Soviet Jewry by women and children in several American cities on September 24. To protest Soviet support for the admission of Communist China to the United Nations, JDL youngsters in New York City stole a Soviet flag from the display at Rockefeller Plaza and diverted the police by burning a plastic replica nearby. Another protest against admitting Communist China took place the next day, September 20, Rosh Hashana, when Washington JDLers blew a shofar in a noisy protest at the Russian Embassy.[42]

Meir's move to Israel was accompanied by an emphasis in JDL on aliya, immigration to Israel. This was not new. In all his talks Meir urged American Jews to move to Israel. In his article "Time to Go Home," he warned that the attitude toward Jews in the United States was changing; that their lives were in danger. It ended with the words, "... Woe to a people that cannot learn from its own bitter history."[43]

In April 1971, when he wrote "And One More," economic difficulties in the United States were growing. He enumerated the danger signs for Jews:

> Governments speak of huge layoffs and breadwinners are confronted with the unique prospect of unemployment.... The cities stand under massive, cross-country threat of bankruptcy.... And the sudden economic crisis is heightened by the psychological fact that for 25 years we have lived a relatively good life and have come to look upon [it] as that which is our due.
>
> ... And so, in this year of 1971, as unemployment and fear reach the highest peaks since 1938 and when ... many millions of white, blue-collar workers face bleak and painful economic futures, the Jew must once again consider what may lie before him. People who are frightened of their economic future are desperate people and desperate people are dangerous.... Desperate people are people who hate ... and all their antagonism against minorities and racial groups; all their insecurities and their pent-up rage over a world they dislike and cannot understand; all these are thrown into the witches' brew from which comes forth an explosion. That explosion means the destruction of democratic civilization and the substitution of a brutal, tyrannical totalitarianism. America ... is in great danger and the Jew in the greatest of perils.
>
> ... I only know there are people who speak of gas chambers and of Jewish traitors and elimination of the Yid. I only know that millions of desperate people are listening to them with greater acuteness than before. I only know that the German [Final Solution] was not an aberration and that the gas chambers are not a thing indigenously European.
>
> ... I only know that Jews are fools to risk my being right. I only know that we have a land where Jews are free of this and I add one more warning to those of the past. Jew, go home. Go back to Israel. Please.[44]

This was his theme when he addressed the national convention of the Zionist Organization of America in Pittsburgh on September 5. It was the first time he had been invited to speak before a Jewish Establishment organization, and although he was aware that his message would not be well received, he urged them to adopt a program promoting the immigration of Jews to Israel. He argued that American Jews were faced with the possibility of another Holocaust because of deteriorating conditions in American society.[45]

The Establishment reacted harshly to Meir's warning. Columnist Ernest E. Barabash, while agreeing that violence and discrimination against Jews in America existed, argued, "... democracy and freedom are still strongly rooted in the judiciary, executive and legislative branches.... The prospect of a Holocaust will become real only in the [unlikely] event of an overthrow of the democratic system of government...."[46] To answer those who insisted "It can't happen here," Meir wrote "The Courage to Fear," a lengthy exposition of his reasoning, which appeared in the *Jewish Press* in three installments. It concluded:

> There is only one solution to Jewish physical survival. Go home, Jew, go home to your own land. It is difficult? True – but it is infinitely superior to what may await us in the exile.[47]

Meir's departure for Israel on Sunday, September 12, was another opportunity to promote aliya. An ad headed "Jew – Go Home!" announced the day's program. In the afternoon, Meir would address supporters at a mass aliya rally at the Manhattan Center. At 5 P.M. there would be a musical program, "Jewish Is Beautiful," billed as "a night of Jewish soul music." Afterward, everyone would accompany Meir to the airport for a mass farewell.[48]

Almost seven hundred JDLers took part in the farewell to Meir. One participant wrote: "Our Reb took leave of us this day. [Many young JDLers called Meir *Reb,* a term of respectful endearment, short for Rabbi.] ... At 5 P.M. the Jewish soul rally, Jewish Is Beautiful, was celebrated in true Israeli vein, and the Reb joined with many JDLers in dancing the Hora.... Shalom, dear Reb – we all wish you *hatzlacha*, success. Although you are scheduled to alternate between Israel and the U.S., we will sorely miss you during your absence."[49]

That evening Meir was escorted to the El Al terminal at JFK airport by a large group of supporters. TV news reports showed him carried aloft on their shoulders as they sang and danced at the terminal.[50]

During a stopover in London the next day, Meir was received at Heathrow airport by members of the Committee for the Release of Soviet Jewish Prisoners, led by Barbara Oberman. At a press conference at the airport, he told reporters of plans to coordinate demonstrations: "We must escalate the forms of protest here and make sure that when there are protests in America, the same thing happens in Europe at the same time."[51] Then he led a demonstration at London's Soviet Embassy. Many American papers carried a UPI photo of him displaying a letter he was delivering to the Soviet ambassador, with picketers behind him carrying placards. The placards bore pictures of Leningrad hijacker Silva Zalmanson, 28, who was wasting away of tuberculosis at the Potma labor camp in Siberia. The finale to his four-hour London visit was his speech at a rally at Speakers' Corner in Hyde Park, which some recall to this day.[52]

Meir's arrival at Lod Airport on September 14 was a media event. Pictures taken at the airport show him surrounded by newsmen and microphones.[53] In an interview broadcast that evening on Israel TV he was asked, "Will you want to make Israel the base for anti-Soviet activities?" He began to reply in Hebrew, and apparently found it difficult to express himself because he said, "Let me say this in English. I want to make this clear. This is a very important question." He said:

To turn the struggle for Soviet Jews into a struggle between Israel and the Soviet Union can only hurt Israel and can only hurt Soviet Jews. The struggle for Soviet Jews must come from Jews of the Western countries, America, England, and so on. I think you can have protests and demonstrations and rallies here – these things should be held here, but to turn Israel into the center can only play into Russian hands.

To the question, "Do you think that your struggle up to now was beneficial to Soviet Jews?" Meir replied:

I don't think I should be the one to answer that. I think that if you go to the Soviet Jews here, you'll find that the great majority will say that if not for these protests and if not for the JDL taking this problem from the back pages to page one, they would not be here. This is a problem that is now fifty years old, and for all those fifty years there was silence, and because there was silence, the Russian Jews stayed [in Russia]. Suddenly there is anger and there are protests and there is militancy, and this year suddenly thousands upon thousands of Russian Jews arrived here. There is no question that this helps."[54]

During the entire interview, Meir's cousin Baruch David Kahane, the son of Zundel, could be seen behind him. Known by his nickname, Budik, he had come to the airport with other relatives to welcome Meir.

Reunited in Israel

Our family's aliya began on July 3, 1971, with the departure of Tova, 13, and Baruch, 12. Since they would be starting high school in September, we thought it best if they improved their Hebrew during the summer.[55] Our parting at the JFK airport was emotional. Israel was very far away then. The flight took much longer than today, and long-distance phone calls were very expensive. We asked a stewardess to keep an eye on them, but Tova told us later that she was too busy with a group of noisy teenagers.

Meir and I remained in the United States with Tzippy and Binyamin so I could complete my master's in library science at Queens College. I also found part-time work as a stenographer to help pay for our moving costs, including a new refrigerator and washing machine suitable for the Israeli climate and electrical system.

Nachman and Faige, Meir's brother and sister-in-law, welcomed Tova and Baruch into their home. Nachman registered them for an *ulpan*, a Hebrew language school. They soon left the *ulpan* because they already knew the Hebrew grammar being taught. Instead, they concentrated on learning spoken Hebrew. Every day, Tova took her little cousins out to the playground, where other girls her age were watching their younger siblings. At first they spoke too rapidly for her to understand, but her ear quickly became attuned. Nachman teamed Baruch up with a young scholar, Rabbi Meir Gershon, who gave him Talmud lessons in Hebrew, and by September, Baruch felt at home with the language.

At the end of July, after a rousing send-off from their congregation, Meir's parents moved to Israel. They had purchased an apartment in Jerusalem's Kiryat Moshe section several years earlier, and now that Meir was making the move, they decided the time had come to do the same. Tova and Baruch were happy to have their grandparents nearby.

School started on September 1 for Tzippy and Binyamin, but Meir had been invited to address the Zionist Organization of America – his first address to a major American Jewish organization – on September 5, and then there was the JDL farewell "aliya rally" for him on September 12. So I flew to Israel with Tzippy and Binyamin on August 22, and Meir joined us three weeks later. Tzippy already knew Hebrew quite well, and a neighbor's daughter helped her with homework for a while until she was able to manage on her own. Binyamin, in kindergarten, learned Hebrew easily, as young children do.

We were part of a great wave of immigration to Israel following the euphoric victory of the Six Day War.[56] I loved life in Israel. My parents, who made aliya one year later, received euphoric letters from me that first year. "You can send a six-year-old on a city bus alone without worrying," I marveled. "When a woman has a baby carriage, she enters through the back door of the bus and passes the fare to the driver. The passengers pass the fare from one to another until it reaches the driver. There is no fear that someone will steal the fare – or the change the driver passes back to her. There is always someone who will help carry the baby carriage on and off the bus."

My parents did not need my letters to convince them to come to Israel. They had always loved the Jewish homeland. During their 1968 visit, my father underwent emergency surgery at Hadassah hospital. He often said that the view of the Judean hills from his hospital bed nourished his soul and restored his health.

When Meir finally joined us in our new home in Jerusalem, it was only a week before Rosh Hashana. That Shabbat was our first together in almost a month. I had missed our Shabbat meals, with Meir leading the singing of the *zemirot* (songs). We had special Friday night traditions, handed down in Meir's family from father to son, following the customs of Sanzer chasidim.

An example of this is the song *Shalom Aleichem*, sung Friday night to welcome the angels who accompany Jews home after prayers. The last stanza, marking their departure, begins with the word *tzet'khem*. Meir's custom was to say the word *tzet'khem* followed under his breath immediately by the word *uvo'akhem*, calling for their speedy return.[57]

After *Shalom Aleichem*, we always said the prayer *Ribon Kol Ha'olamim*, declaring G-d's glorious attributes, thanking Him for His compassion and good-ness and asking Him to bless us with a myriad of blessings. This was chanted to a traditional Sanzer melody, as was *Eishet Chayil*, a canticle lauding the woman who is the mainstay of the home. The highlight of the song was the verse "Charm is false and beauty is vain / A G-d-fearing woman – she shall be praised." At the first words, Meir used to wave his hand in a deprecatory motion, and then he would point to me with a smile as he sang, "A G-d-fearing woman – she shall be praised."

Still following the chasidic custom of his father's home, we then sang *Atkinu Seudata* and *Azamer Bishvachin* to the Sanzer melody. We often had youngsters with no religious background as guests for the Friday night meal, and I used to sympathize with them having to wait through all those songs, and then Meir's chanting of the *Kiddush* (the special Shabbat blessing over wine), and the hand-washing ceremony, until we finally sat down to eat.

During the three Shabbat meals Meir led the family in singing the traditional *zemirot*, Shabbat songs. At *seuda shlishit*, the third meal, which we ate as the sun was setting and the Sabbath was drawing to a close, we sang somber, pensive songs like *Bilvavi*, set to soft, plaintive melodies. The words of *Bilvavi* – "In my heart I shall place ... an altar to G-d's glory.... and for a sacrifice I shall offer Him my one and only soul" – expressed Meir's devotion to the Torah and was one of his favorite songs.[58]

Since ours was a new neighborhood, there was no proper synagogue building. The neighboring yeshiva, Torah Ohr, gave the residents an upper floor to use, and that was our synagogue. The High Holiday prayers that year were especially inspiring.

Our first Yom Kippur in Jerusalem was an eye-opener for Meir. He had become accustomed to going to the center of town late Friday afternoon, before Shabbat, to buy newspapers. It was very important for Meir to keep up with cur-rent events, and he often bought three or four different papers. That year, Yom Kippur began on Tuesday night. On Tuesday afternoon, Meir went to town to buy papers, unaware that every Jew, observant and non-observant alike, held the holy day in such awe that all stores closed by 2 P.M. "It's like a ghost town," he exclaimed joyfully when he returned empty-handed.

During the intermediate days of Sukkot, with the children on vacation, we were able to take a trip together. Meir rented a car and we traveled north to Safed, to see where his family had lived. On the way, we stopped in Tiberias. We visited the tomb of Rabbi Meir Baal Haness, waded in the Kinneret, the Sea of Galilee, and ate its famous St. Peter's fish, known locally as *musht*.

In Safed we stopped at a small grocery to buy cold drinks. We asked the eld-erly shopkeeper if he knew where Meir's father had lived. He remembered the family, especially Meir's uncle Mordechai. He pointed us toward the small lot where the family's house had stood before it crumbled and had to be pulled down. We also went to the Sanzer *kloiz*, the synagogue built by Meir's great-grandfather, and recently refurbished by his cousins, the children of his uncle Zundel. We climbed up to the Crusader fortress in the highest part of Safed and then wandered through the Old Town's narrow, winding streets where we stayed at a small two-star hotel. Our room had its own toilet – a great luxury. There was even a showerhead in the tiny room. To work it, you pulled a chain, and the water drained away through a hole in the floor. Breakfast was included, and no one minded when we took extra rolls and cheese to make sandwiches for lunch.

We drove to Haifa to visit Morty and Gloria Dolinsky. Morty, Meir's Betar buddy, had been one of the Laurelton founders of JDL but went to Israel on aliya soon after it was founded. In Haifa we learned that Israelis like to be helpful. To find the Dolinskys' home, we asked several passersby how to get to their street. Everyone pointed out the way, even people who had no idea where it was!

A highlight of the Sukkot holiday was Meir's visit to the *sukkah* of Rabbi Tzvi Yehuda Kook, head of the Merkaz Harav Yeshiva. Rabbi Tzvi Yehuda was the spiritual leader of the myriads who followed the ideology of religious Zionism propounded by his late father, Rabbi Abraham Isaac Kook. A student who was in the *sukkah*, Nachum Rakover, recalled that Rabbi Tzvi Yehuda invited Meir to accompany him to the Western Wall. Before they went, the rabbi asked another student, Rabbi Yaakov Filber, to bring his camera, and they were photographed together in the *sukkah* and again at the Western Wall. Rabbi Yosef Bramson pointed out that Rabbi Kook did not like to be photographed, but he admired Meir so much that he actually requested it![59]

Meir's awe and wonder at being in Israel were expressed in a *Jewish Press* article that he wrote on his arrival.

> I sit here, Home. It is night and the stars twinkle with a fierceness and a multitude of heavenly lights such as I have not remembered for many years. Across the valley sleep the hills of Benjamin and the lights of Ramallah shine directly across from me as to the left I strain to see Nebi Samuel, the grave of the Prophet Samuel. The night is totally quiet, carrying with it a stillness, not born of the fear of other urban areas where people cling to their dwellings in the concrete jungle, but rather, the gentle, peaceful quiet that affords tranquility to the soul and pause for thought to the mind.
>
> I am home in Jerusalem and inside sleep my children whom I have returned with me. Tomorrow they will go to school, climbing the hills that forever bear the footprints of those who preceded them here so many years ago – their ancestors. They will walk the hills of Jerusalem, tread its streets, mingle with their brothers and sisters from Riga and Casablanca, pray at the Wall and shyly

– and then not so timidly – touch its craggy surface, add their lip prints to those who preceded them for twenty centuries and then joke in Hebrew with the bus drivers, drink their Jewish grapefruit juice as they read their Jewish newspaper and exult in their Jewish city.[60]

Meir's plan to spend every other month in the U.S. would cut into his already limited time with the children. He was acutely aware that the more time he devoted to the JDL, the less remained for his family. At the Shabbat table, he often spoke to the children about the importance of working for the Jewish community. He admitted that he was spending less time with them, but stressed the need for self-sacrifice on behalf of the Jewish people and how privileged they were to live in Israel.

Chapter 25
In Israel and America
(September-November 1971)

MEIR WAS NOT going to be idle in Israel. Back in July, a JDL office had been opened in Jerusalem by Neil Rothenberg, a JDL youth leader, and Yosef Schneider, a Russian émigré.[1] Meir defined the role of JDL in Israel in a *Jewish Press* article:

> People ask: "What purpose is there for JDL in Israel? Are there troubled neighborhoods? Is there anti-Semitism?"

JDL's role in Israel would be educational, he explained.

> The *Galut*, the Diaspora ... has bred in the Jew inferiority complexes, physical fear and mental abnormalities.... It is totally possible to be a Sabra [native-born Israeli], a genuinely free soul, and nevertheless be beset with all the complexes and problems of a *Galut* Jew.
>
> ... What must concern us is the Sabra who IDEOLOGICALLY proclaims himself an Israeli first and a Jew second.... When the son of the mayor of Jerusalem writes a book and candidly states his Israelism over his Jewishness as he sits next to his non-Jewish wife, we are faced with a serious problem.[2]

In an interview in August, Meir's father explained it this way: "Meir wants to save Jews – not only their bodies, but their souls as well."[3]

The JDL in Israel soon became known as Haliga (the Liga), short for Haliga Lehagana Yehudit (JDL in Hebrew). Instead of the American pronunciation of Kahane (ka-HAN-ee), Israelis used the Hebrew pronunciation, ka-HAN-ah.

The Unity of the Jewish People

The social gap in Israel between Ashkenazim (Jews of European descent) and Sephardim (Jews from North Africa and Middle Eastern countries) was another problem to tackle. Meir's interview with Shimon, a Sephardic Jew, points up its seriousness.

"... My family came from Morocco and spent seven years in a *maabara* (transit camp) here. There was a tent and then a hut and finally we managed to get a three-room apartment for nine people."

... Twenty-one-year-old Shimon sat bare-chested in the hot printing shop where he works for 600 IL ($143) a month. His words, spoken directly and pointedly, clearly brought into focus the growing tragedy and danger of internal friction and hostility that threatens Israel today. Here was not a Black Panther* speaking (Shimon spoke with contempt of the Panthers, whom he described as criminals who had never served in the army) but he, nevertheless, echoed almost all of the arguments that the Panthers had brought into the open.

The oppressive practice of selling homes rather than renting makes it almost impossible for young Israelis to have their own places after marriage.

... "Why can we not have the same custom as in America?" Shimon demanded to know. "There you can rent an apartment and you can pay the rent on the salary you earn. This is why I want to leave Israel and go to live in America...."

The lack of adequate, cheap living space is indeed the greatest impetus for an emigration from Israel that remains one of the closely guarded skeletons in the Israeli closet. The frustration that grips low-income Israeli families ... is compounded [as new apartments] are given to Soviet immigrants or to Americans who have money. Worse, the frustration becomes bitterness when the poor, like Shimon, picture the situation's genesis as being in discrimination against them because they are Sephardi Jews.

... "We even suffer in the army. Most Sephardim have many children while many Ashkenazim have only one or two. The law says that if a boy is an only child he is not allowed to be sent to the front. So who are most of the soldiers on the borders? Sephardim!"

... The intercommunal strife that has grown into such aberrations as the Panthers threatens Israel with a socio-economic crisis. The fact that the rich are mostly Ashkenazim and the poor, Sephardim ... [make these] words of Shimon ring ominously: "Unless something is done there will be civil war here."[4]

Meir's goal was equality for every Jew in Israel. The day he landed at Lod airport as a new immigrant, he told an interviewer that his main concern was the unity of the Jewish people, and this remained his ideal.[5]

Soviet Jewry continued to be a primary concern. Meir used the brief time between Rosh Hashana and Yom Kippur to focus on the plight of Silva Zalmanson, one of those who had attempted to hijack a plane in Leningrad in June 1970. Zalmanson was serving a ten-year sentence in a forced labor camp and

---

* The Black Panthers of Israel were Sephardic Jews who had attracted media attention by their violent demonstrations. They believed in communist class theory and blamed Sephardic poverty on Ashkenazic capitalists. For the Marxist ideology of the Israeli Black Panthers, see: www.marxist.com/MiddleEast/israeli_black_ panthers.html

was in very poor health. Meir called a press conference in Jerusalem on September 27 with her uncle, Avraham Zalmanson, who lived in Bat Yam. Her uncle told reporters she had tuberculosis, had developed ulcers in prison, and was dangerously ill. Meir declared: "If anything befalls Silva Zalmanson, two Russian diplomats will be executed.... In return for every Jew harmed in Russia, two Soviet citizens around the world – an eye for an eye, a tooth for a tooth." This provocative announcement was reported in news media throughout the world.[6] Meir began to plan for a major rally in the States in November at which Silva Zalmanson's plight was to be the focus.

Meanwhile, Meir met with Geula Cohen and other members of the Herut party, who were still interested in co-opting him to their party. Cohen invited him to a Herut event where he was photographed shaking hands with Rabbi Mordechai Peron, Chief Rabbi of the IDF. Meir also met twice with the minister of immigrant absorption, Natan Peled. He prepared a memo for Peled detailing plans for a community for American Jews in Neve Yaakov, a new suburb of Jerusalem. The new community would have eight hundred apartments, a shopping center, schools, a synagogue, and a center for summer visitors.[7]

The editor of *Yedioth Ahronoth* who interviewed Meir during this period was impressed with his sincerity:

> We sat over a cup of tea in a Tel Aviv café and spoke – or more precisely, he spoke. It was easy to listen, because he speaks quietly, often in understatement, not as people would imagine. His speech is more English than American. Without raising his voice, without exaggeration, without anger, without using his hands; and he continuously indicates his admiration for people who do not agree with him, "They're good people but they don't understand the problem," he says. And you can feel that it pains him.[8]

Writing for the Jewish Press

Our main income during those first years in Israel was Meir's *Jewish Press* salary.[9] Sitting at the typewriter in his small study in our new home and writing his articles, his two index fingers would fly over the keys. Then he would go over what he had typed, revising and correcting. His heavily crossed-out text, replaced by handwritten words, led Rabbi Klass to complain that his copy was difficult to read. *Jewish Press* editor Arnold Fine once wrote to Meir (this was when type was set manually), "Please try to get a typewriter ribbon – or send us the carbon and you keep the original. The copy is so poor, it takes hours to set and no one wants to set it until everything else is set. Please try for better copy."[10] When Meir wrote about current events, there was a problem of timeliness, because mail from Israel to the United States took at least ten days. Knowing that his articles would appear two weeks, or even three weeks later, he did not write about late-breaking stories, but confined himself to ongoing events.[11]

Many of Meir's articles for the *Jewish Press* used data from his personal clippings file. Every morning he would go through the major Israeli newspapers, cutting out articles that interested him. Any article that had information he might want to refer to in the future, went into his file cabinets. The clippings folders · were arranged under topics such as American Jewish leadership, assimilation of American Jews, intermarriage in Israel, morality in Israeli society, religion in Israel, Islam, intellectual anti-Semitism, peace plans, Arab nationalism, U.S. foreign policy, and Soviet Jews.[12]

One of the articles Meir wrote during this period concerned a seventy-year-old Jew named Meyer Lansky. He was allegedly a gangster who had come to Israel to avoid criminal prosecution in the United States. The Israeli government refused to renew his tourist visa, and Lansky had appealed to the Supreme Court. Meir wrote, with some irony:

> I have read a great deal about him, and from all I have read he is a scoundrel, a gangster, a hoodlum.... I have no way of knowing the truth about Meyer Lansky, but I will accept the veracity of the news media accounts, based on my own long personal experience that newspaper, television and radio people would never lie.

Meir accused the government of non-Jewish political and moral considerations. What bothers them, he wrote, is whether Israel "will become a haven for Jewish criminals" and "What will the anti-Semites say?" Meir held that the government's ultimate guide should be halakha, Jewish law.

> ... It is not within the moral or even legal power of a Jewish government to refuse entry to [any] Jew into Eretz Yisrael, the Land of Israel, the Jewish State.[13]

This was an unpopular stance, and Meir could have declined to deal with the issue. But he felt an obligation to point out that Jewish law forbids the exclusion of any Jew from the Land of Israel.

A new *Jewish Press* column was introduced by Meir at this time: *Exposing the Haters.* Rabbi Klass did not want an author's name to appear more than once in an issue, so Meir wrote it under a pseudonym, David Borac. David, Meir's middle name, was a logical choice. The name Borac is more difficult to understand. It may be the acronym of *Ben Rav Cahana,* Hebrew for "the son of Rabbi Kahane."[14] *Exposing the Haters* appeared for the first time on October 8, 1971.[15] As in *Spotlight on Extremism,* Meir made use of the extremist literature he collected. His aim was to show American Jews that there were dangerous groups in the United States, in order to convince them to immigrate to Israel. In one column he wrote of the American Nazi party's popularity:

> Groups of Nazis have sprung up in various parts of the country from Connect-
> icut to Seattle. In Bridgeport, a Nazi bookstore operates openly, while in
> Seattle the Nazis ran a candidate for the local Board of Education who, openly
> using a swastika and without funds of any kind, garnered five percent of the
> vote. In several cities, recorded messages operated by the Nazis spew forth
> their hate to all who dial the number. Professional Nazi watchers admit that
> Nazi numbers have grown in every city and that many of their new members
> are veterans of various branches of the armed forces.
>
> What accounts for the upsurge in Nazi fortunes? ... The bitterness and frus-
> tration engendered by the Vietnam fiasco that saw the U.S. lose more than
> 50,000 troops ... the collapse of long-held moral standards and the rise of a
> youth culture whose permissive attitude towards sex and drugs frighten and
> horrify an older generation; growing racial tensions and direct confrontations
> between blacks and whites on bread-and-butter issues like housing, employ-
> ment and school busing and, above all, the worsening economic crisis – have
> all played into the hands of Nazis.
>
> ... [Matt] Koehl [head of the National Socialist White People's Party] has,
> shrewdly, played upon all of these factors. He has used the grievances of the
> whites to turn them to the Nazi platform of anti-Jewish and anti-black think-
> ing....[16]

Exposing the Haters often quoted directly from the haters' newspapers. One such paper, *Thunderbolt,* said, "Our solution is to ultimately expel the Jews and confiscate their wealth."[17]

At the end of his first month in Israel, Meir put into practice his plan to spend alternate months in the United States. The day before he was to fly to the United States, October 13, he made two public appearances in Israel. In the afternoon, he led a demonstration at the American Embassy in Tel Aviv to protest the pro-Arab policies of Secretary of State William Rogers. Members of the DOV student group, led by Meir's supporter Shimon Rachamim, joined the Liga protesters, who carried Hebrew placards that said, "Never Again, Rogers," "Abba Eban, Fifth Column," and "With a Friend Like Rogers, Who Needs Enemies?" Media coverage included an interview on NBC News in which Meir declared that the Rogers Plan gave Russia increased control over the Suez Canal and was bad for both Israel and the United States.[18]

In the evening, Meir spoke at the local movie auditorium in Dimona, a town in the south where a community of about four hundred self-styled "Black Hebrews" from Chicago had settled during the previous two years, saying they were one of the lost tribes. They refused to abide by regulations and did not recognize the Israeli government's authority, claiming that blacks were the "true

Jews." A capacity audience gave Meir a rousing welcome, and cheered when he said, "I am not against these people because of the color of their skin ... but because they deny us the Divine right to our country."[19]

Covering this event for NBC TV news, Reporter David Burrington asked Meir how he felt about racism. Meir replied, "All men are created equal but some are good and some are bad.... If there's any racism here, it comes from the blacks!"[20] It was the fear of being labeled racists that kept Israeli officials from dealing with the serious problems caused by the blacks in Dimona, but Meir was not one to allow epithets to keep him from expressing his beliefs.

Stopped at Montreal Airport

The next day, on the heels of a spurt of media attention, Meir arrived in New York. After a restful weekend with my brother and sister-in-law in Brooklyn, Meir boarded a Sunday evening flight to Montreal, where he planned to confront visiting Soviet premier Alexei Kosygin. He told reporters he would do his utmost to disrupt Kosygin's visit. Not unexpectedly, he was stopped at the airport. When he declared his refusal to leave Montreal and his intention of beginning a hunger strike for Soviet Jewry at the airport, he and five other JDL members were taken into police custody and jailed overnight. Meir was kept in handcuffs until he boarded the return flight on Tuesday morning, October 19. A UPI wire photo shows him at Kennedy airport, exiting the TWA terminal, flanked by three New York policemen. On his face is a barely suppressed grin of satisfaction at the police and media attention he has aroused.

From the airport, Meir went straight to a press conference at JDL's Manhattan headquarters, where he told the press of his frustration at being prevented from greeting Kosygin. He vowed that he would bring the plight of Silva Zalmanson and Soviet Jewry to page one.[21]

Later that day, the JDL executive board held its first meeting since his arrival from Israel. Meir told them about his meetings with Natan Peled at the Immigrant Absorption Ministry and about plans to encourage American Jewish aliya (immigration) to Israel by building a JDL *kirya* (neighborhood) and establishing a JDL kibbutz. "In time," he said, "Kiryat JDL will become a thriving community of houses, shopping centers and schools. An average four-room apartment will cost about 90,000 lirot [about $21,500]."

Meir invited board members to visit JDL headquarters at 26 Ben Maimon Street in Jerusalem and reported, "We are now in the process of negotiating for a building in the heart of Jerusalem for an Identity Center for Jewish youth." Courses would include Judaism, Jewish History, Jewish Nationalism and Physical Training, with an option for rabbinical studies. To promote the program, he said:

"During my stay in New York, I will make it a point to visit youth everywhere ... to familiarize them with ... opportunities for aliya [and] our ID/Jerusalem program...."[22]

JDL's finances were also on the agenda. Some expenses had been detailed by JDL's treasurer, Murray Schneider in June:

> Demonstrations and phone bills cost money, and expenses are sometimes exorbitant. Telephone bills often run to around $2,600 and an ad in the newspaper costs $3,000 to $4,000. When our boys meet with trouble, we must raise bail. Our members are not millionaires. Most of them are working people, and people must be paid back. Money comes from dues, speaking engagements, donations, but not enough. The ID [Jewish Identity Center, Brooklyn] rent is $750 per month.[23]

Fundraising in August had focused on the legal costs:

> ... We require $8,000 to liquidate the fines set. Otherwise the Rabbi, Bieber and Cohen ... face jail for their non-payment. It is therefore incumbent upon us all to raise as much money as we can.... The Legal Defense Fund is totally tax-deductible. Do your part to keep the "JDL Three" away from a prison term....[24]

The meeting concluded on an optimistic note: With Meir back in the United States, the many speaking engagements that had been arranged for him that month were "a sure-fire means of restoring rapidly waning [funds]."[25]

Never Again! Fresh Off the Press

Meir's arrival in the United States coincided with the publication of his first book, *Never Again!* On October 20, with the book fresh off the press, Meir appeared on Barry Farber's midnight to 2 A.M. radio show to publicize it. He presented a copy to Farber with "the ink still wet on its pages."[26] Holding the volume in his hand gave Meir a tremendous sense of accomplishment. Now people would have his entire philosophy within reach, not only the one-minute sound bites in the media. When he returned to Israel, he proudly presented copies to all the family. It was gratifying for me to read his dedication in my parents' copy: "To Mom and Dad, With all my love and thanks for their daughter." A quarter-page ad placed by the publisher in the prestigious *New York Times Book Review* featured the book's cover and said, "You don't have to agree with Rabbi Kahane. But you must admit he has something to say. Something IMPORTANT. At least listen to him."[27]

A book review of *Never Again!* by Robert J. Milch in the *Saturday Review* was harshly critical of this "first comprehensive exposition of [Kahane's] thinking," but conceded, "... he knows how to touch the nerve ends of even the most blasé Jewish reader. 'When there is a Jewish crisis, when the Jew is up against the wall of history,' [Kahane] asks, 'who will fight for him and how many strangers will be at his side in his hour of need?' As the past has shown all too often, the Jew usually does stand pretty much on his own. There is no convincing response to Kahane's grim question." Nevertheless, Milch did not accept Meir's comparison of contemporary America to Weimar Germany.

Readers who disagreed with Milch wrote to the *Saturday Review* from California and Connecticut. One wrote, "Rabbi Kahane has issued a long overdue rallying cry for action. He wants Jews to stop being like milk." Another stated, "Rabbi Kahane merely proves that democracy is no guarantee of Jewish survival. This may be unpalatable, but facts are stubborn things."[28]

A review in the *Chicago Sun-Times* agreed that Meir's "critique of the organizations and their leadership has much validity...."[29] And a New Jersey newspaper quoted this passage from the book: "Assimilation is the subtly raging soft disease that ... threatens us with oblivion. That which the Church could not do and which the Cossacks could not achieve and that in which Auschwitz failed, is being accomplished by the sweet smell of assimilation. There is no greater problem facing the Jew today...."[30]

Not surprisingly, two communist publications carried negative reviews: Moscow's Yiddish monthly *Sovetish Heymland*, and the Communist Party's *Daily World*. Jim Bishop, a non-Jew whose column was syndicated throughout the United States in almost 5,000 newspapers, contended that Meir's premise, "Jewishness is all," was wrong. "All of us are Americans first," he maintained.[31]

With the book's publication, Meir was to have received the remaining third of the advance fee. It was not paid until four months later, in February 1972. Although *Never Again!* sold more copies than any of Meir's other books, and was published in softcover as well, by September 1972 he owed the publisher $4,700 because advance royalties exceeded the percentage due him on sales![32]

However, *Never Again!* was important, not for the income it might earn, but because it was a tool for spreading Meir's ideas. He promoted the book at his numerous speaking engagements that fall.

On October 28, an audience of six hundred attended a debate between Meir and Rabbi Samuel Silver at Temple Sinai in Stamford, Connecticut. The temple paid JDL $500, sure that admission fees would cover the fee, since earlier debates between Meir and Rabbi Silver had attracted large audiences. The debate was broadcast live on WSTC, the local radio station, giving Meir an opportunity to explain his ideas to a wide audience.[33]

This successful talk in Stamford was arranged by Sam Shoshan, a resident of the town, but not all Jews were happy to host Meir's talks. Almost two months earlier, when Shoshan arranged for Meir to speak at the nearby Norwalk Jewish Center, the Center charged a $225 rental fee payable in advance and demanded that all press releases clearly state that the Center was not sponsoring the talk.[34]

A reporter for the *Hudson Dispatch* described Meir's two-hour talk on Saturday night, November 6, to an audience of four hundred at the Englewood Jewish Center in New Jersey. Meir urged the audience to seriously consider immigrating to Israel, "to enjoy the luxury of living as a majority rather than a minority." Meir reminded them that "Jews are getting out of the Soviet Union because militant Jews in the United States went to the streets and forced moderate Jews to do what they would not have done otherwise."[35]

Meir sometimes spoke to three groups in one day. On Sunday he might be at one synagogue for a morning brunch, at another in the afternoon, and at yet another in the evening. On weekdays, he might speak to college or high school groups during the day and at a synagogue in the evening. For example, on October 29 he spoke at HILI high school, Queensborough College and the East Nassau Hebrew Congregation in Syosset. On November 2 he spoke at Cooper Union College and at Adelphi University during the day and at Stern College in the evening. He was also invited to speak at the prestigious Yale Political Union in New Haven.[36]

Seventy-Nine Arrested for Silva Zalmanson

Meir's speaking dates during this period, especially those before young people, were aimed at urging people to attend a major demonstration planned for November 7 in Manhattan, which would focus on the plight of Silva Zalmanson, a courageous and sympathetic figure who had taken part in the attempt to hijack a plane at Leningrad airport on June 15, 1970.

Pointing up the plight of one individual was an effective way to dramatize the oppression of three million faceless Jews, said Meir, as he detailed plans for the mass rally on her behalf.[37] Meir recalled the trial of the Leningrad Eleven:

> We will behold, again, the trial in Leningrad with Silva and her husband, Edward Kuznetsov, and all the rest, and weep as she is sentenced to ten years of murderous imprisonment in the Potma labor camp. We will hear the death sentences pronounced on Kuznetsov and Mark Dymshits and hear Silva Zalmanson cry out: "I am a Zionist!"[38]

In Zalmanson's address to the court after sentencing, her courage and her love of Israel were evident:

> ... Israel is a country with which we Jews are tied spiritually and historically.... The dream of uniting with our ancient Homeland will never leave us.... Our

dream of life in Israel far transcends the fear of the pain that could be caused to us. By our departure we were causing no harm to anyone....[39]

Meir began a round of talks at colleges to draw people to the demonstration for Silva Zalmanson. At Brooklyn College, on October 27, the walls of Boylan Hall were covered with posters reading "Silva Zalmanson Must Live." A report quoted Meir's words to the capacity crowd:

"It is up to us to make [Zalmanson's] name as well known as that of Angela Davis,"* he declared. "She is half deaf, suffers from a heart condition and tuberculosis and receives only 200 grams of food per day."

... Sharply criticizing Jewish apathy, he reminded the audience that an earlier generation of Jews had failed to meet its responsibility. "We had it in our hands to save over one million Jews at Auschwitz, but ... the United States... could not bomb the rail lines ... because of 'technical difficulties.' ... It was Jewish reaction which was wrong. Nowhere was there raised the voice of non-violent civil disobedience.... So what if they had gotten arrested. You can survive an arrest, believe me!" Laughter resounded through the hall at this remark.

He reminded the audience:

Don't think it can't happen here! It is! ... Our country is Israel. So, walk tall, walk straight, walk proud, and walk Jewish! Make the sacrifice. Be a good Jew.

Calling for massive participation at the rally on November 7, he said:

You don't have to be violent. Spend twenty-four hours a day on behalf of Silva Zalmanson – non-violently.

At the question-and-answer period that followed, the questions were on a wide range of topics. One student asked, "Why did Israel vote yes on the Albanian resolution (to expel Nationalist China from the U.N.)?" Meir's reply was refreshingly frank:

I was stunned, too. But I don't know. Mr. Eban and I are not on speaking terms. But, remember, Israel is not a sacred cow. Most of the things about it are beautiful. Some are not.

The reporter described Meir's departure from Brooklyn College:

... Rabbi Kahane [was] ... followed by a block-long stream of supporters... As the marchers reached East 26th Street, a car pulled up and the rabbi got in... As the car drove off towards a scheduled rally at Flatbush Yeshiva ... the trail-

---

* Angela Davis was a black radical activist accused of murder and kidnapping in 1970. Liberals took up her cause and she was acquitted in 1972.

ing throng moved virtually en masse to Bedford Avenue to board city buses to the Rabbi's next appearance.[40]

The success of the rally for Silva Zalmanson would depend on how it was promoted. In talks at "countless colleges and yeshivot," Meir urged young people to take part in it.[41] But his talks were not limited to describing the plight of Zalmanson. In his speech at Queens College, quoted verbatim in the *Jewish Journal*, he pointed out the hypocrisy of liberal Jews, who opposed JDL "violence."

> "I was in a synagogue in Forest Hills praying, when a member of the congregation approached me and said: 'Rabbi, if they build a low-income housing project around here, do you think you can blow it up?'" After the audience's laughter subsided somewhat, Kahane seriously admonished this "Forest Hills Jew" for being against violence with regard to Soviet Jewry, but condoning it in response to a "real, serious problem" – open housing. In Kahane's words, "The lambs turned into lions," and he disgustedly labeled them "racists."
>
> The JDL, according to Kahane, has no sympathy for Jews "whose Jewishness is based on racism." Rather, the rabbi said, "A good Jew is one who feels the pain of a second Jew."
>
> Specifically, Kahane referred to Silva Zalmanson, a young Jewish girl suffering the freezing winter of a Siberian labor camp.... "[She] works twelve to fourteen hours a day and with her heart ailment probably won't survive the first two out of her ten-year sentence."[42]

At Long Island University he noted that earlier that day he had arranged extension of bail for JDL member Isaac Jaroslawicz, accused of shooting into a window of the Soviet Mission.[43] Asserting the innocence of 18-year-old Jaroslawicz, Meir told his audience they had to feel the pain of Soviet Jews and come to the demonstration. "I could wear three yarmulkes," he said, "and I still wouldn't be Jewish if I didn't have a feeling for the pain of a second Jew."[44] He reminded the students that the rally for Silva Zalmanson was on a Sunday, when schools were closed and there were no competing demands on them.

Meir's round of talks to college students bore fruit. About one thousand people turned out for the rally on November 7. One photo in the *Daily News* centerfold shows a large, enthusiastic crowd, singing and clapping hands, sitting down at the busy intersection near the Soviet Mission. Another shows police packing youth into paddy wagons. That day, seventy-nine young people were arrested for blocking traffic on behalf of Silva Zalmanson and Soviet Jews.[45]

The U.S. Department of State took note of this. Concerned that the JDL campaign for Silva Zalmanson would harm America's relations with the Soviet Union, its policy makers took steps to help her. A State Department memo dated December 4, 1971, shows the effectiveness of Meir's efforts.

... With the return of Rabbi Kahane from Israel in October, the JDL has increased the level of its activity in New York.... We have investigated a number of means for protecting the Soviets and inhibiting JDL actions against them.

... A suggestion has been made to the Soviets that special treatment be given the case of Silva Zalmanson, who ... is reported to be in ill health. Rabbi Kahane has threatened that two Soviet diplomats would be killed should Miss Zalmanson die in prison...[46]

In his talks to promote the November 7 demonstration for Silva Zalmanson, Meir spoke on other topics as well. At Yeshiva University, he urged support for Senator Henry Jackson as the Democratic Party's presidential nominee. Jackson should be preferred, he said, because his congressional amendment had tied special trading status for the Soviet Union to their emigration policy for Jews. Meir put it simply: "Jews should decide any issue on whether it is good for the Jews or bad for the Jews."[47]

Speaking in Belle Harbor, New York, to the Rotary Club, a group that included non-Jews, Meir pointed out that America's own self-interest should determine its foreign policy. He said that the United States should help Israel maintain her strength in the Middle East, because without Israel, Russia would dominate the Indian Ocean and the Persian Gulf, and NATO's military capability would be lost.[48]

Meir's article that week in the *Jewish Press* advised the Israeli government to take a firm stand in the face of Egyptian President Anwar Sadat's demands that Israel withdraw from the liberated areas. He wrote:

... Secretary of State Rogers is embarking on a flurry of activity aimed at pressuring Israel and Egypt into accepting a partial settlement.... The fact is there are no Phantom jets being shipped to Israel and there will be none unless Israel agrees to an interim settlement.

... There is no doubt that [a partial withdrawal] would do nothing to appease the demand of Sadat for a total withdrawal.... Capitulation of Israel to American pressure for a partial settlement could prove disastrous ... [It] will have gained Israel nothing and merely given the wolves something more to howl about as they sense fear and retreat.

What Israel should be saying now is that a partial withdrawal will never satisfy the Arabs or their Soviet allies and that world and Western guarantees are poor staffs upon which to lean....[49]

One week before Meir's return to Israel, he flew to Los Angeles where he was scheduled to speak at synagogues and college campuses as well as on television and radio programs.

Arriving at Los Angeles airport on November 10, he addressed a press conference that had been arranged by local JDLers. The highlight was a letter from prisoners who had taken part in a violent rebellion at the Attica maximum security prison that September. The New York State Militia had been called out to quell it, and the bloody four-day confrontation, in which forty-three were killed, had been at the top of the news for days.[50]

Meir showed reporters a letter signed "Brother Herbert X. Blyden, Minister of Information, Attica Liberation Faction."

> To Rabbi Kahane: Shalom! I have read with interest your efforts to secure the release of Silva Zalmanson from her incarceration in the U.S.S.R.
>
> I am illegally imprisoned and am in addition faced with confinement in Rockefeller's maxi-maximum concentration camp for "Attica" when in effect the whole world knows that he is responsible for the massacre.
>
> I speak for the survivors of "Attica 9-13-71" and if at all possible please try and arrange to have the "Attica Liberation Faction" members transferred to whatever socialist country will accept us, preferably in exchange for incarcerated people in those countries. I, for example, would gladly go in exchange for Miss Zalmanson if you could set it up....[51]

Meir told reporters he planned to ask California's Governor Ronald Reagan to mediate this prisoner exchange.[52] This piquant announcement was the kind of story the media loved. The publicity it generated helped the synagogues that had invited him attract large audiences.

From the airport Meir went directly to the Rambam Torah Institute to speak to students. In the evening he spoke at the Young Israel synagogue to an audience of about one hundred. On November 11, after several daytime radio interviews, he spoke at Temple Akiba in Culver City.[53]

At noon on Friday, November 12, he spoke at the Student Center of Pierce Junior College in Woodland Hills, and that Saturday he led an *Oneg Shabbat* for JDL members at their headquarters at 7456 Beverly Boulevard. After a speech Saturday night at Congregation B'nai David,[54] he was interviewed on the late-night Regis Philbin TV show, *Target*. An informant who viewed the program took notes for the FBI.

First, Philbin asked whether JDL was opposed by most Jewish organizations because it uses violent means. Meir replied that the Establishment organizations did not represent the Jewish masses, they represented the wealthy Jews – who "abhor" violence – "until it serves their purpose." Meir told Philbin about the wealthy Jew in Forest Hills who suggested Meir blow up a proposed housing project for blacks in his neighborhood.

Philbin fed questions to Meir that allowed him to expound on JDL philosophy. He asked whether Soviet Jews are allowed their own culture and language, and although he took Meir to task for harassing innocent Soviet diplomats, he gave Meir the opportunity to describe the cultural and religious oppression of Soviet

Jews and show that the harassment campaign had placed the spotlight on the Soviet Jewish issue.

To Philbin's query, "Is it true you feel like the place for all Jews to go to is Israel?" Meir answered, "This is a great country, but we are a minority here. It is tough to be a minority. It is a myth to call this country a melting pot.... The incredible rise of ethnic feeling the last decade has polarized this country.... The first target of the extreme left and the extreme right will be the Jew. I don't want to gamble."

It was a successful TV appearance. Philbin even showed Meir's new book, *Never Again!* to the viewers and informed them where Meir would be speaking that week.[55]

On Sunday afternoon Meir officiated at the wedding of Bob and Rochelle Manning. "He married us at the Young Israel on Spaulding and Melrose, and we went to hear him speak that night at Temple Isaiah on Pico," recalled Bob. The FBI report said that Meir was well received at Temple Isaiah and that an enthusiastic listener made a donation of $100 during his speech. The report listed the FBI file numbers of JDL members who accompanied him, among them Al Epstein and Bob Manning.[56]

On Monday, November 15, Meir flew to Denver to speak at the University of Colorado. The student group that had invited him, American Students for Israel, paid the JDL a fee of $750 that included Meir's travel costs.[57]

He flew back to Los Angeles the next morning, arriving in time to speak at noon to a group of about one hundred and eighty students at the Valley Junior College in Van Nuys. After two afternoon radio interviews, he went on to speak at Temple Beth Shalom in Long Beach. Meir had originally been scheduled to speak that evening at Temple Solael in Canoga Park, but the rabbi there cancelled the engagement.[58] In contrast, Rabbi Philip Schroit, of Congregation B'nai David, where Meir had spoken Saturday night, was firmly supportive. Rabbi Schroit later recalled:

> I found pride in him being at my shul. It was a pleasure to take the flack from those who tried to dissuade me from allowing him to speak in our shul....[59]

One listener sent Meir a letter that showed him that his efforts to reach Jews in Los Angeles had been worthwhile:

> ... I still can't get your words out of my mind.... I awoke out of a restless sleep with phrases like "Jewish education" and "Volodenka" running through my thoughts.
>
> I am one of those Jews of whom you spoke who fights diligently for every group and every cause and every injustice, but never for Jews.
>
> ... I want and need so much to be a Jew. I need that "substance" of which you spoke.... It is only recently that I have begun to believe in God again....

Your words do not fall on deaf ears. They have made a difference in my life, and for that I thank you.

... I am enclosing $5 to help you in your court fight, or should I say OUR court fight. [signed] Marsha Wernick.[60]

Meir's November trip to Los Angeles was far less successful than his visit in April. The FBI informant reported that audiences were much smaller and less money was raised during this trip. There are several reasons for this. For one thing, many Jews in Los Angeles had heard him speak only half a year earlier and had satisfied their curiosity. For another, Meir had not recently attracted the wide media attention that had drawn large crowds in April. In addition, the Jewish Establishment had increased their pressure on synagogues not to grant Meir a platform.[61]

Continuous efforts by the Jewish Establishment to prevent him from being heard were hurting. "Over and over again," he wrote, "the words are thrown up to us: But why is it that all the major Jewish leaders oppose you?" His reply is prophetic:

... The man whose views have been rejected by a majority of his fellows is hardly necessarily false. History is filled with examples of men and women who stood alone and shouted forth their disagreement with the majority, who rejected the dogmas and sacred cows of their times and who, in the end, were proven correct.

... If we believe that we are right, let us go forward. Greatness and truth are born within men who are not intimidated by their lack of numbers and by the prestige and wealth of their opposition.

If you believe you are right, go ahead. March forward and do what you must. In the end you will be proven correct and your people will acknowledge their debt to you. That time may come after you are gone but that is of little consequence.[62]

Chapter 26

On Three Continents
(November-December 1971)

Why Jewish Defense

MEIR RETURNED TO Israel in mid-November. A week later, the *New York Times* Sunday magazine carried an eight-page piece by Walter Goodman titled "Rabbi Kahane Says, I'd Love to See the JDL Fold Up. But" This in-depth interview gave Meir an excellent opportunity to present his ideas. Of JDL's aims, he said:

> When people think of Jewish defense, they automatically think of physical assault. And that's not what we meant.... If tomorrow morning, all anti-Semitism were, by some miracle, erased, the Jews of this country would still face decimation through assimilation, intermarriage, alienation from their heritage.... The Jewish Defense League came into being to physically defend Jews. It also came into being to go out among Jews and instill within them a feeling of Jewish pride, to defend the Jews from simply fading out....

In reply to a pointed question, Meir replied:

> ... I know very, very well that there is a potential for crude racism among Jews, as among anyone else. My whole life I've given over to fighting the hatred and bigotry of people against Jews, and I see no difference between that and the bigotry of Jews toward other people.

Ironically, in later years Meir's opponents accused him of racism for pointing out that Israel's Arab population posed a danger to the State of Israel. He explained: "Racism means the absolute and permanent relegation of one race or people or color to a position of inferiority, whereas Judaism decrees that all who wish to convert ... become Jewish and equal to every other Jew.... Judaism, Zionism, proclaim not the racism of the Jews, but his *havdala*, his separation and difference, a status that is not biological but ideological."[1]

JDL's strategy to help Soviet Jews, Meir explained to Goodman, was to focus world attention on their plight by doing "outrageous things." He hoped that such tactics might spur established Jewish groups into more aggressive action and would, in view of its great need for détente with the United States, force the USSR to make some concessions to its Jews.

Goodman raised the oft-repeated argument that the JDL's use of violence was "non-Jewish." Meir's response was detailed:

> First of all, what has to be gotten clear is our concept of violence – and in a greater sense, the Jewish concept of violence.... So many of the leaders of secular Jewish groups are people with tragically little knowledge of what is Jewish....
>
> The Jewish concept of violence is that it's a bad thing – but sometimes necessary.... At Chanuka time, every member of the American Jewish Congress ... takes his little child by the hand to honor the Maccabees. Who are you honoring here? You're not honoring people who picketed.... We are links in a chain with the Irgun, the Maccabees, with all the Jewish groups who used violence for a Jewish cause.
>
> ... If you're dealing with ... someone like Sonny Carson ... He takes over the Crown Heights Jewish Corporation and he sits there and he makes demands. He starts pounding on that desk. Now, how do you get Sonny Carson out, especially when the Jews are terrified? They're afraid to call the police. They're afraid to do anything.... Now what do you do with Sonny Carson – a hoodlum, a vicious anti-Semite, a racist? ... You can sit down with the president of First National City ... you can sit down with him and you discuss and debate.... You don't sit down with Sonny Carson. Sonny Carson does not listen. With Sonny Carson, you walk in and you say, "Sonny, baby, you gonna get out? Or do we have to cut you up?" And he says, "Now man, now sit down, let's talk."
>
> ... Now we're speaking Panther to Panther. So we have a mystique – "Jewish Panthers." We never deny that, even though it's not true.... If the Panther thinks we're Panthers, so, beautiful. It helps Jews.... It hurts us among Jews. The Jewish middle class doesn't like to think that there are Jewish Panthers so they don't give us funds.

Goodman described Meir's appearance and manner:

> ... a slight, dark, handsome man in a blue suit and white shirt open at the collar. He wore a black wool yarmulke. He is barely 40, yet the soft gestures, the head-nodding, the weary, knowing air give him the aspect of a much older man, or a man in an old tradition. His accent, however, is contemporary New York.
>
> On the platform, his right hand pounds away, but his voice scarcely rises. That afternoon in October,[*] his message was simple: He wanted us to attend a

---

[*] This refers to a demonstration for Silva Zalmanson at the U.N. on October 25, 1971.

larger rally to be held in a couple of weeks ... near the Soviet Mission. He told us that when Jews were at last allowed to leave Russia ... the J.D.L. would go down in history along with other admirable groups that had been defamed in their time.... There was passion, if not volume, in the delivery. When he was done, he became the center of a group of boys and neighborhood men, answering their questions patiently, softly, wearily.

When Goodman first met with Meir back in January, JDL headquarters were located in mid-Manhattan. The rooms were "... all pipes, wires, wooden slats, creaking floors, mezuzas and ragged posters on unpainted plaster ... [one] large dusty room, which managed to look both bare and cluttered ... cardboard boxes, mail sacks, beat-up chairs, collection cans and cockeyed files."[2]

By the time the *Times* article was published in November, JDL headquarters had moved to 4002 New Utrecht Avenue, Brooklyn. The article features a picture of Meir sitting at his desk in Brooklyn. Behind him, spray-painted on an unplastered wall, are the words "Office of the Reb" and a small framed picture of Zeev Jabotinsky.[3]

It was a coup to be featured in the highly regarded and widely read Sunday *New York Times*. The article gave Meir an opportunity to explain his views on Jewish self-defense, Soviet Jewry, the alliance with Joseph Colombo, assimilation and intermarriage, and the concept that "Jewish is beautiful." Media attention always improved attendance at his speaking engagements – it would have been helpful if the article had appeared at the beginning of Meir's trip instead of a week after his departure for Israel!

Meir's departure was duly noted by the U.S. State Department in a telegram to American embassies in Tel Aviv and Moscow and to the American ambassador to the United Nations. It demonstrated that the U.S. government would have preferred to see Meir in prison rather than disrupting relations with the Soviet Union. The telegram said:

> Department understands from New York police that JDL chairman Kahane departed U.S. for Israel on or about November 17. Expected to return December 26. Department would appreciate full reporting on Kahane's activities while in Israel, particularly on actions which might constitute violation of his probation status. Please slug messages "For Eur/Sov." [Signed] Rogers.[4]

Stopover in London

Meir's return flight to Israel included a stop off in London on Thursday, November 18. He was delayed at London airport by immigration officers for over an hour while they carefully read all his papers. He told them that he had been invited to speak to Jewish youth about Soviet Jews and was eventually given a visa to stay until Sunday afternoon.[5]

Like the Jewish Establishment in America, the Board of Deputies of British Jews feared that Meir's methods would draw too much attention to their Jewishness. In an effort to counter the Board of Deputies' opposition to him, Meir's hosts in London, Cecil and Barbara Oberman, arranged for Meir to meet with British Chief Rabbi Emanuel Jakobovits and accompanied him to the rabbi's office.[6] The meeting was of no avail, for the Board of Deputies issued a statement condemning Meir. Barbara Oberman, who headed the Committee for the Release of Soviet Jewish Prisoners, firmly believed, like Meir, that the way to help Soviet Jews was to demonstrate in the streets. The Committee had arranged for Meir to speak on Thursday evening at Central Hall in Westminster. Despite the Board of Deputies' condemnation, five hundred people came to hear him. Afterwards, he met informally with young people, urging them to take a more radical stance and to set up a branch of the Jewish Defense League.[7]

He spent Shabbat at the home of the Obermans and attended services at the Dunstan Road synagogue with them. A few minutes after the Sabbath ended, a spontaneously organized meeting was held in the Oberman home. Sitting on the floor cross-legged, Meir appealed to the one hundred and fifty young people packed into the parlor, to "use their feet" for Soviet Jews. A reporter noted, "When he speaks to young people he talks emotively and with a sense of urgency.... He understands one vital point. That young people demand creative flair in their Soviet Jewry drive. And it has to be done not with violence, but with anger."[8]

Sonja Cohen Illouz recalled a meeting on Sunday morning:

> I have a recollection of a very warm casual group, definitely completely mixed ages and styles of people, your husband in his shirt sleeves as opposed to a formal attire, and maybe a cardigan.... We all sat around him, some on the floor, and we listened, drinking in his every word, and discussing plans for the next "move," so to speak. I was certainly captured from that time on, and became devoted to the cause.[9]

By the time Meir left for Israel on Sunday afternoon, he had accomplished much in London: He had planted seeds for a JDL chapter there and had inspired British Jews to take an active stance for Soviet Jewry.

Jews in Arab Lands

Meir returned to Israel in time to celebrate our daughter Tova's fourteenth birthday, and then quickly turned his attention to a campaign in Israel on behalf of Jews in Arab lands, especially in Syria, Iraq, and Egypt.

In Syria, where there were approximately four thousand Jews, the situation of the Jewish community was precarious. Jews were required to carry special identity cards and they were subject to frequent curfews. They were barred from employment in government enterprises and certain professions and were denied bank credit. They could not travel farther than four kilometers (2.5 miles) from their homes and were not allowed to emigrate.

Secret police officials supervised every Jewish gathering, including weddings and synagogue services. Many young Jews fled the harsh conditions with the help of smugglers who helped them cross the border. Every night at 9 P.M. each Jewish household had to report the absence of any member to the authorities. If one was missing, members of the family were subjected to questioning as possible accomplices in his escape.[10]

Meir explained his decision to start a campaign to publicize the plight of Syrian Jews in his weekly column:

> It was at my first appearance on an Israeli campus, at the Hebrew University, that I first heard the question, "Why is it that you have not done for the Jews of Syria the same as you did for the Jews of Russia?" ... That question was echoed at every other place at which I spoke in Israel.... The premise of the Israeli government and Establishment groups in the United States that action against the Syrians would lead to retaliation against Syrian Jews was rejected by a surprisingly large number of Israelis.
>
> ... There will be little tangible salvation for the oppressed Jews of Damascus and Aleppo so long as Jews in the world fear to react.[11]

Meir called a rally at the Western Wall on December 2, 1971. Shimon Rachamim, who organized it, recalled the three guest speakers: David Sitton, chairman of the Committee of Sephardic Jews in Jerusalem, and Menachem Yedid, Herut Member of Knesset, were both born in Aleppo in Syria. The third, Dr. Israel Eldad, was a fiery right-wing orator.[12]

Meir was the featured speaker. He told the crowd, "What we did for Jews in Russia we will do for Jews in Arab countries – harassment in New York, in London, and even in Damascus."[13] At the end of December, when Meir arrived in New York, he made Syrian Jewry his priority.

Two Days in Paris

In mid-December, at the request of French Jews who wanted to start a JDL chapter, Meir flew to Paris for a two-day visit. One of his hosts, Mrs. Lilliane Setbon, arranged a meeting for him with Nobel prize winner René Cassin, a leader of the French Jewish Community. At prayers in the synagogue he was introduced to the chief rabbi of France, Jacob Kaplan. These meetings were duly noted by the

American Jewish Committee ("His visit was a quiet one....") and by the FBI ("Subject arrived on December 15.").[14]

Meir was unable to converse freely in French – his three years of high-school French was not enough for that. Instead, he spoke in Hebrew or English, with his hosts translating his words into French when necessary. Because of this, only the local Jewish press was invited to a press conference about his plans for a JDL branch in Paris. He told the reporters that a JDL branch in France would make life uncomfortable for Soviet and Syrian diplomats. At the same time, he assured them that JDL would not use violent or illegal tactics in France. In reply to a question from Edwin Eytan, the Paris correspondent for *Yedioth Aharonoth*, he said that a refusal by the French government to permit a JDL chapter would only serve to attract more members. No JDL chapter was formed, but about 30 members of Herut who met with Meir that day started a group named Massada, and from time to time there were reports in Israeli newspapers about JDL-type activities in France.[15] Probably because of his difficulty with the language, Meir did not visit Paris again.

Just before Meir's return to Israel, *Ma'ariv* published an article whose headline proclaimed that Meir's actions for Soviet Jewry had improved their situation in the USSR. Jews interviewed in three Russian cities told reporter Shmuel Halperin that the improvement in their conditions was mainly due to Meir's activities.[16]

But for Meir, a mere "improvement of conditions" was not sufficient. In an article written soon afterward, he called on Jews to step up the protests:

> The fact that nearly 14,000 Jews have arrived in Israel from the USSR in 1971[17] and that between 35-40,000 are expected in 1972 has clearly underlined the potency of Jewish struggle when accompanied by courage and self-sacrifice.
>
> ... Joy at the apparent change in heart of the Soviet government tends to give birth to a feeling of relaxation and confidence that victory has been won. This in turn leads to arguments that further protests and demonstrations are, therefore, no longer needed.... It is clear that Soviet need for a détente was the major reason for its shift of policy.... A much larger flow of Jewish immigration is the direct result of Jewish militancy.... It would be foolish and disastrous to stop now....
>
> In the months of late spring and summer of 1971, when the post-Leningrad period saw a fall-off in Jewish protests, the Soviets lowered the rate of emigration.... And we cannot forget the group of Soviet Jews that remains not only in the vast prison that is the USSR but in the smaller prisons within that prison. The tens of Soviet Jewish political prisoners are not sharing in the emigration and for them, if not for the others, the protests and militancy must be continued and enlarged.

It is inconceivable that Silva Zalmanson, Raiza Palatnik and all the others should be forgotten.... The time to scream louder and march with angrier steps is precisely now, when the Soviets have shown they are weak and open to pressure. No one knows for sure what tomorrow will be.[18]

Another article Meir wrote while he was in Israel dealt with one of his major concerns – the international campaign to force Israel to return the land liberated during the Six Day War. In a two-pronged argument, he cited a principle of international relations: "Conquest consists of the appropriation of property ... and ... vests the whole rights of property and sovereignty over such territory in the conquering state."[19] He also cited international relations in practice:

... [When] in the Far East, the Soviets seized the Kurile Islands ... what did *Pravda* say on September 2, 1964? Listen:

"A people which has been attacked, has defended itself and wins the war is bound by sacred duty to establish itself in perpetuity a political situation which will insure the liquidation of the sources of aggression.... No territories are to be returned as long as the danger of aggression still prevails."

And, yet, this is the state [the USSR] that has the gall to demand that Israel return the land liberated four years ago!

... And over and above all this lies the central fact that the land liberated is JEWISH LAND. The West Bank and Old Jerusalem and the Golan Heights are all part of ancient Eretz Yisrael. When, in 1947, the Jews agreed to accept a United Nations Partition Plan that gave them a pittance of Eretz Yisrael ... it was done only in the hope that the Arabs would ... give peace in return. The partition plan was ... shattered and abrogated by their 1967 calls of "throw the Jews into the sea."

... The 1949 boundaries are dead, murdered by the Arabs. The land liberated by Israel in 1967 is Jewish land both by historical right and the right of self-preservation. On the latter, there should be no argument. The Russians have provided the precedent and the logic.[20]

Meir used every opportunity to spread his ideas. His appointment book indicates that he spoke that winter at Churchill House in Haifa's Technion on December 22 and at the B'nai B'rith Center in Tel Aviv on December 25.[21] Although no other speaking engagements are entered in his appointment book, it is likely that there were others. Meir was not in the habit of noting everything in his appointment book. He entered only distant dates that he might forget, or very important events.

As 1971 drew to a close, Meir's plan to spend alternate months in Israel was working. He had been in Israel from September 14 to October 14 and now again, from November 17 to December 26.

JDL Youth Show the Way

When Meir arrived in the United States on December 26, he made Syrian and Iraqi Jewry his priority, as he had promised. At a rally in front of the Syrian Mission to the United Nations, he announced that the league was beginning a "campaign of harassment" against the mission. Its switchboard would be jammed with calls, the mission visited and its members followed. George Tomeh, Syria's chief delegate to the United Nations, charged that two intruders, a youth and a young woman, forced their way into the mission's offices, sprayed a Star of David on the door and on the glass front of a cabinet holding Syrian art treasures and littered the floor with leaflets bearing the slogan "Never Again." Meanwhile, demonstrators outside the mission distributed leaflets to passersby denouncing the mistreatment of Jews by "Syrian butchers." Tomeh hastily summoned a meeting of a U.N. committee to complain about insufficient police protection. Appearing on CBS TV, Meir declared that in order to obtain freedom for Syrian Jews, the JDL would use the same tactics as they had used against Soviet diplomats. JDL followed up with several rallies for Syrian and Iraqi Jews and organized protests in New York and Washington in January and at Red Cross and United Nations installations in Israel later that year.[22]

On the American political scene, preparations had already begun for the November 1972 presidential elections, and Mayor John V. Lindsay was seeking the Democratic Party nomination. Meir publicly endorsed Senator Henry Jackson because he had introduced legislation (the Jackson amendment) that made trade benefits for the Soviets dependent on their fair treatment of Jews. He began a campaign against Lindsay's nomination. "During Lindsay's six years in office," Meir said, "the city was wrecked by him." If his performance as New York City's mayor were to be repeated on a national scale, "it would spell out disaster."[23]

After several speaking engagements in New York City, Meir carried his drive against Lindsay to Miami, arriving there on January 13. Nat Rosenwasser, who had flown to Miami earlier in the week to set up speaking engagements, met Meir at the airport accompanied by reporters from "four or five TV channels, the *Miami Herald*, the *Miami Star* and local radio." Meir reminded the audiences in Miami how Lindsay had ridden roughshod over Jewish civil rights in New York City, and when Lindsay arrived in Miami the following week to campaign for the Jewish vote, he was met by picketers who carried placards in English and Yiddish recalling his disastrous handling of New York City's problems. In Boston, too, JDL members followed Lindsay with placards proclaiming him "the man who destroyed New York City."[24]

Meir's first meetings on this trip to America were with the youth. JDL's Brooklyn headquarters on New Utrecht Avenue had become the focal point of youth activities, with a core of young members who prided themselves both on their physical courage and on their understanding of JDL ideology. The group that met regularly for physical training was called the *Chaya* squad. Meaning "wild animal" in Hebrew, a *chaya* was someone who would cast off the "wimpy" Jewish image and act like a wild animal when he was called on to protect other Jews. At the same time, the core group prided themselves on a thorough understanding of Meir's *Jewish Defense League: Principles and Philosophies,* especially the five principles, *Ahavat Yisrael, Hadar Yisrael, Barzel Yisrael, Mishma'at Yisrael,* and *Bitachon.* An exam on the five principles was noted on their calendar for February 6.[25]

In addition to physical training and lectures, the group's busy calendar included a demonstration at Governor Rockefeller's office to promote the exchange of Silva Zalmanson for Attica prisoners, a demonstration at Carnegie Hall to protest the appearance of the Bolshoi Ballet Company, a rally for Syrian Jewry, and a demonstration for Jewish poor. In Torrington, Connecticut, they disrupted a performance of the Osipov Balalaika Orchestra by rolling uncapped bottles of ammonia down the aisles of the theater.[26]

JDL chapters outside New York were active too. In Washington, D.C., two young JDLers were arrested for assaulting a Soviet diplomat. The Cleveland chapter picketed Park Synagogue because its confirmation class was going to see the movie "Jesus Christ Superstar." A concert of the Russian cellist Mstislav [*sic*] Rostropovich at Symphony Hall in Newark was picketed by the Northern New Jersey Council of JDL. In Philadelphia, JDL members demonstrated when a synagogue was vandalized in the Logan section, where many poor elderly Jews lived.[27]

On Greatness

Meir had to appear in court twice during this winter visit: on January 6 for invasion of the Tass offices in December 1969, and on January 10 in connection with the December 1970 demonstration at the Soviet Mission. Neither hearing resulted in a verdict. Meir later wrote home about the Tass case:

> My trial for the Tass sit-in [his terminology] has apparently been dropped since the Soviets have suddenly refused to testify. I can only assume that they don't believe that they can win after two previous [deadlocked jury] trials.[28]

The threat of a prison sentence was always present at Meir's appearances in court, but he continued to act on his beliefs. Meir expressed the rationale behind his untiring struggle for Jewish ideals in an article in honor of Chanuka, the holiday that stands for the struggle of "the few" against "all logic of numbers and power." The lesson of Chanuka, wrote Meir, is that a Jew must "act according to his conscience, no matter what the majority says and no matter what the consequences."

This was a rule that Meir followed without hesitation. His article "On Greatness" was an expression, both to himself and to the world, of his conscious decision to act on his beliefs despite opposition and personal discomfort or danger. "On Greatness" concluded with these words:

> Greatness is the ability to perceive what is important and what is not, what is eternal and what is temporary. Greatness yearns for mountains, not valleys, and understands how brief the candle of life is and how important it is to use it to light the world. Greatness is the possession of "the few" because it is acquired only through dedication, pain and sacrifice. It is understood by the *navon* [one who has understanding] and not by those who are merely wise. It is that which lifts man from the merely human to the heights of sublime near-divinity. It is understood by "the few" to whom we owe the very fact of Jewish existence and who have created history in their own lonely image.[29]

Only a few of Meir's public appearances during this trip are on record: Temple Adath Yeshurun in Syracuse, the East Nassau Hebrew Congregation in Syosset, the Long John Nebel late-night talk show, and a parlor meeting in the home of Mr. and Mrs. Charles Schreiber.[30]

Most of his time was devoted to organizing a conference that would promote American Jewish immigration to Israel. By the time he returned to Israel on January 19, 1972, he had laid the groundwork for a Mass Aliya Conference in New York in May.

Chapter 27

The World Zionist Congress, Jerusalem (January-February 1972)

A Forum for Promoting Aliya

AN IDEAL FORUM for Meir to promote the immigration of American Jews to Israel would be the 28th International Congress of the World Zionist Organization (WZO), opening in Jerusalem on January 18, 1972. In mid-December, Meir wrote to the WZO, requesting delegate status in order to speak at the upcoming Congress:

> It is with deep regret that I note that the Jewish Defense League has not been granted delegate status to the forthcoming Congress. I assume that the official reason given to the press will be that JDL is not a member of the American Zionist Federation, a fact that is true only because the federation has refused to accept JDL as a member despite applications that go back two years to February 1970.
>
> While I might ordinarily hesitate in making this a public issue, I must do so at this time because of what I believe to be a critical time for the Jews of the United States. It is my sad belief that the sands of time are running out for both the American democratic system and the Jews of America. I fear that the political, socioeconomic and racial upheaval in the United States portends a tragedy for the American Jew that will escalate into a Holocaust.
>
> There is precious little time and what must be done is to educate the American Jew to the dangers as well as begin a concrete program of planned aliya. The World Zionist Organization at its congress must take the lead in this...
>
> I am formally asking, at this time, for both formal Jewish Defense League delegate status (we seek a minimum of three seats) and the right to speak to the delegates on the above topic. I sincerely hope that the JDL, a far larger group than most Zionist groups in the United States, will be granted the democratic right of representation and we will be spared a repetition of the shameful Brussels incident.

He sent copies of this letter to the media and it was summarized in the *Jerusalem Post*.[1]

When Meir left Israel on December 26, he told reporters at Lod airport that he would take part in the Congress "with or without permission." While he was in the States, the Congress organizers announced the distribution of the ten seats assigned to non-political groups. They gave four to the Israeli Student Association, three to Zionist youth groups, one to the United Sephardic community and two to officials of the Congress, completely disregarding Meir's request.[2]

There were probably two reasons for the Establishment's refusal to give Meir a platform to expound on his dark vision of the future of Jews in the United States. One was the belief that Jews ought to move to Israel for positive motives, not negative ones. The other was the fear that if Meir was given the floor at the Congress, his dark vision might be interpreted by non-Jews as disloyalty to America and the result might be an anti-Semitic backlash.[3]

A week before the Congress opened, Meir's *Jewish Press* article gave the reasons he wanted to speak there.

> America is today a troubled land. Torn by racial passions and hatreds, we find white pitted against black in anger over the busing of children to achieve integration, violence over changing neighborhoods and housing patterns, competition for blue-collar and low-level white-collar jobs, and tensions and fighting between races in schools and the armed forces....
>
> The frustration of the average American as he watches social, moral and ethical values that he has long cherished, mocked and changed is evident to all.... He seeks to lash out and erase those whom he believes have been responsible for the social revolution – the Jew.
>
> ... Demagogues, haters and fascists are to be found in the United States in abundance. Forget their numbers at present. Consider rather their recent growth and their capacity to grow tremendously in an era of violence, frustration, anger, bitterness, fear and hate.... They speak openly of gas chambers and of eliminating Jews.... Is America so different? Was Weimar Germany different? Were there not Jews in the latter who were just as sure that they had found Nirvana as there are in the United States? ... What happened before can happen again and, indeed, is beginning to happen already. The answer – the urgent answer – is to evacuate the American Jew and bring him home.
>
> The World Zionist Congress stands in a unique position to seize the time.... It is in its hands to place upon the agenda a resolution calling for an emergency conference of American Jewish communities and organizations to plan a massive, organized propaganda campaign to explain the threat to the American Jewish future and to plan for a practical, mass aliya to the Land of Israel.
>
> ... Once, decades ago, the great Zeev Jabotinsky called out to his brothers, "Jews, a fire is burning! Eliminate the exile before it eliminates you." Jewish

leaders destroyed him and, by doing so, helped to destroy those whom he sought to save. G-d forbid that it should happen again...[4]

When the Congress opened on January 18, Meir's supporters distributed reprints of this article to the delegates. Meir, who had scheduled an important fundraising event for January 17 at the home of Charles Chanover in Brooklyn, arrived in Israel only on January 19. He told reporters who greeted him at the airport that he would either be allowed to speak at the Zionist Congress or would go to jail in the attempt. "I have no choice," he said, "I must warn of the holocaust that threatens American Jews."[5]

The next morning, *Jewish Press* columnist Menachem Israel was at the Jerusalem International Convention Center, awaiting Meir's arrival. He wrote:

> ... [There was] an excited spirit of anticipation as to whether the "Jewish Establishment" would indeed repeat the rebuff it had handed to maverick Kahane last year at the World Conference on Soviet Jewry at Brussels.
>
> ... Reporters and cameramen huddled at the entrance to the hall, where the third day of the Congress was scheduled to begin. They braved unusually cold weather to be on the scene for an expected attempt to bar Rabbi Kahane's entry. The JDL leader and his small entourage arrived only a few minutes later than publicized, and the scene was set for a confrontation. Plenty of police and even a couple of armed soldiers were conspicuously present.
>
> ... But the Zionist leadership had decided to change the Brussels script, and a confrontation was postponed. Jewish Agency [officials] Moshe Rivlin and Mordechai Bar-On met Kahane outside and tried to make a deal with him, even offering to let him address a committee. When Kahane refused, he was conducted into a brief meeting with Congress leaders. Word quickly spread throughout the hall and to the ever-growing ticket queues outside that the entire Congress would vote on Kahane's right to speak.
>
> ... Kahane ... entered the hall to a thunderous reception of applause and booing....

As they had at Brussels, the Herut party delegates presented a motion that Meir should be allowed to speak. Before the vote was taken, Lydia Slovin spoke on the Herut motion.

> ... She spoke in glowing terms of Kahane's efforts on behalf of Russian Jewry and appealed for him to be given an opportunity, as a proven Zionist, to address the Zionist Congress. [Chairman Aryeh] Pincus' reply ... focused on the need to uphold parliamentary procedure...

The vote was by a show of hands, with delegates holding aloft their credentials.

... The overwhelming vote to deny Kahane the right to speak had been a fore-gone conclusion; all that was in doubt was the reaction of Kahane and his supporters. The answer to this came with the conclusion of the voting: Kahane and his group marched out of the hall in protest.

The scene that followed may best be described as parliamentary pandemonium. While Pincus futilely tried restoring order ... the hall emptied. An atmosphere bordering on riot prevailed as Kahane conducted an impromptu press conference in the lobby and heated debates raged all about him on the justice of the Congress' decision.

When the dust had finally cleared, it was apparent that Jerusalem had joined Brussels as another milestone in the meteoric career of an activist who is already being widely spoken of as a Herut candidate* for the Israeli Knesset in the next national elections.[6]

An American Embassy official covering the Congress for the U.S. State Department reported that Meir "walked out dramatically, followed and surrounded by media representatives." In the lobby, the embassy official listened to Meir's statements to the journalists and then sent a cable to the State Department summarizing what Meir said about the need for American Jews to immigrate to Israel. The cable described Meir's plan to hold his own congress, a mini-congress.[7]

Israel radio reported that as Meir left the hall, he announced that he would appeal the Congress' decision to the court of the Zionist Organization. The next day, his lawyer filed a complaint with the court requesting invalidation of the delegate elections in the United States because of the unfair exclusion of the JDL.[8]

Reporter Mati Golan visited the JDL's temporary Congress headquarters in a two-room suite at the King David Hotel and described the scene:

> The place is buzzing. The rabbi and his aides are preparing newspaper ads for the "mini-congress" planned for Monday evening [January 24]. The telephones don't stop ringing. One aide informs the rabbi that the court of the Congress is sitting Monday night. Going to the phone, the rabbi angrily reminds Rivlin he had promised the court would sit on Sunday. Finally, Rivlin promises they will sit on Monday afternoon. The rabbi tries to calm his aides, who want all day Monday free for the mini-congress.
>
> People are constantly coming. They want to hear firsthand what the television, radio and newspapers have repeated tens of times.

Meir explained to Golan why he was using the King David Hotel as his headquarters:

---

* There was a good deal of speculation about Meir joining the Herut party. There were similarities between Meir's ideology and that of the Herut party, and his appointment book lists many meetings with Herut leaders. For example, during the week after the Congress, Meir met with Menachem Begin (January 23), Amichai (Giddy) Paglin (January 25), and Geula Cohen (January 30).

"A man from Canada gave me this suite of rooms. I have a modest, retiring wife who is not ready to turn our home into a meeting place, and in another hour I am going home to her and my four children."

Golan described Meir:

... Rabbi Kahane's smooth, youthful face is pale in contrast with his jet-black hair. The black *kippa* he wears is obscured by the black of his hair – it is almost invisible. His lowered eyes and apologetic smile convey a shyness difficult to understand in the face of all the publicity. Nevertheless, the man radiates vitality and dynamism, and above all, sincere honesty and belief in all he says.[9]

As expected, on Monday the court of the World Zionist Organization rejected Meir's appeal, and he went ahead with plans to hold his own mini-congress at the Central Hotel that evening. Our son Baruch's bar mitzvah was being celebrated that week, so newspapers featured this event together with reports on the mini-congress. One photo showed Meir and Baruch at the Western Wall, both wearing *tefillin*, Meir beaming with pride.[10]

A report on the mini-congress said that the hall, seating one thousand, was packed. There were men and women, boys and girls. Some wore yarmulkes and some young men had long hair. Speaking alternately in Hebrew and English, Meir said "Jews in America simply do not want to believe my warning." During the question-and-answer period, Aaron Perl, who said he was a correspondent for the Mutual Radio Network, attacked Meir for "looking for anti-Semites under every rock." When the audience heckled him, Meir took the microphone and said, "At this congress, everyone has a right to speak!" Portions of the proceedings were broadcast on Israel radio and TV. Riding on the wave of publicity, Meir placed an ad in the Hebrew papers reading: "The Congress did not want to hear us, but maybe you do. Join us! Membership dues – 20 lirot; Soldiers – only 10 lirot."[11]

Bar Mitzvah Lesson

Grandparents, aunts, uncles and friends joined us for the entire Shabbat on January 29 to celebrate Baruch's bar mitzvah. After the Friday night meal, Meir left our guests for a few hours to walk to the Beit Haam auditorium in downtown Jerusalem. He had been invited to appear at the weekly "Jerusalem Vocal Newspaper," a kind of "Meet the Press" event that conformed to Shabbat law. There was no entrance fee and there were no microphones. As the organizers had expected, Meir drew a crowd that completely filled the 700-seat auditorium. Replying to questions posed by Yoram Ronen, Zvi Kessler and Mati Golan on the panel of journalists, Meir spoke about Syrian Jews and emphasized the importance of aliya for American Jews. In reply to the oft-posed question whether JDL's stance might be harmful for Jews, he said, "No anti-Semite was ever created by a Jew standing up and fighting for himself."[12]

At the synagogue on Shabbat, Baruch led the prayers and read *Beshalach*, the weekly Torah portion. On Saturday night, we had a party for him in our four-room apartment. In order to have more room for our guests, we set up tables and chairs in the children's bedrooms, piling all their furniture in our bedroom. With the extended Kahane family from all over Israel and political acquaintances like Geula Cohen, it was so crowded that at one point it was impossible to pass trays of food around!

Meir's *Jewish Press* article, "To Baruch on His Bar Mitzvah," expressed the ideas Meir worked all his life to instill in our children and in all Jews.

> ... The foundation of foundations is the knowledge that man was placed upon this earth for a purpose and that the achievement of material and transitory happiness is NOT the reason for existence. We live in an age when man roams wildly about his earth seeking happiness, gratification and pleasure. Such people are thirsty men who are given salt water to drink. Their momentary satisfaction is followed immediately by an even more unbearable need for water than before and their lives are a continual cycle of yearning, wandering and searching in vain for a thing that, in reality, does not exist.
>
> Not mere happiness, but holiness — this is the goal. And this is what you set off to reach as you shut behind you forever the doors of childhood and venture out into the cold winds of manhood. The winds will howl in the inky, dark streets of life. On all sides are dangers and terrors and people will clutch at you and try to bring you down.... My heart is not happy when I think of my young son thrust into such a world but I know that this is the way of the world and this is how it must be....
>
> It is only the discipline and the willpower of Torah law that will assure your acquisition of holiness and it is only the study of Torah that will give you the knowledge and insight into that law. There is nothing truer than the words of the rabbis who said that the ignorant can never achieve that perception and sudden flash of intuition, that momentary glimpse of truth. I do not want you to become a rabbi but I pray that you become a scholar....
>
> Above all, love your fellow Jews and do not search out some secluded corner where you will seek your own personal growth. Too many scholars turn their backs on the world and become merely men of selfish holiness. Never become a recluse, insensitive to the needs of the world. Never acquire the arrogance of the scholar who sneers at those who are less learned or less pious. Achieve greatness but always remember how small you are.[13]

In the midst of the celebration of Baruch's bar mitzvah, crushing news came from America: JDL members had been accused of causing the death of a young woman. On January 26, incendiary bombs went off in two offices that specialized in arranging visits of Soviet performers: Sol Hurok Productions and Columbia Artists. Minutes before the fires started, the Associated Press and NBC News received calls declaring that the fires were set to protest the "deaths and imprisonment of Soviet Jews." The calls concluded with the JDL slogan, "Never Again!" An employee in Sol Hurok's office, Iris Kones, age 27, died of smoke inhalation.[14]

Meir's immediate reaction on hearing the news was, "It's an insane act!" He told reporters, "It isn't the first time our slogan has been used. Anyone could use our slogan. I know our group wouldn't do this. I think the people that did this are insane." JDL spokesmen also denied any connection with the firebombs. The New York Police Department formed a special squad to find the perpetrators, and half a year later, three young JDLers were arrested for the Hurok fire. Meir, who was in the United States then, worked unceasingly on their behalf.[15]

Meanwhile, the Zionist Congress episode, which put Meir in the public eye, had led to a flurry of invitations to speak. Meir's appointment book shows speaking engagements at Kibbutz Netiv Halamed-Heh, Kibbutz Bror Chayil, Kibbutz Gezer (three non-religious kibbutzim), Misdar Jabotinsky (an organization of Revisionists), a Bnei Akiva group, the Bar Ilan High School in Tel Aviv, a parlor meeting in Netanya, and an informal meeting at the Hebrew University.[16]

Kibbutz member Oscar Zimmerman remembered Meir's speech at Bror Chayil. He recalled that Eli Argaman, a member of the kibbutz, met Meir when he was in America as an emissary to the Hatzofim youth group there. Argaman admired him very much and it was he who brought Meir to the kibbutz. "Rabbi Kahane spoke about JDL's accomplishments. It was an impressive talk," Zimmerman said.[17]

When Meir went to speak at Kibbutz Gezer, he invited me to go along. Located on the old Tel Aviv-Jerusalem highway, near Ramle, it was not far from Jerusalem. As we drove there, Meir told me an interesting fact about Gezer. It was the only one of the non-religious kibbutzim that had a kosher kitchen. The explanation may be that many of Gezer's founding members were American and did not have the vehement anti-religious stance of their Israeli counterparts. However, because of their liberal mind-set, many raised objections that evening to Meir's insistence that Jews, because of their religion, are different and have a special role to fulfill in this world. Meir's passionate advocacy of the "specialness" of Jews was the reason leftists gave for their animosity toward him, claiming that it negated the principle of the equality of all peoples. Meir maintained that the real reason for their animosity was their rejection of the authentic Judaism he represented.[18] Throughout his life, the left attacked him with all the means in their power, including slanted media reports.

The Jewish Identity Center, Jerusalem

Meir remained in Israel until February 14. In addition to speaking to groups and writing articles for the *Jewish Press*, he worked on two new booklets. One was the *Jewish Defense League Movement Handbook*. The first 33 pages were a reprint of the ideological material in *Jewish Defense League: Principles and Philosophies*, but it had 30 additional pages of practical guidelines for JDL activities, suggestions for programs at chapter meetings, rules and organizational structure. The last section, headed "Proper Procedure Following an Arrest," had practical and legal instructions for anyone who might find himself in that situation.[19]

Printing the booklets was a complicated procedure. Since Morris Drucker printed for the JDL at cost, the booklets were printed in New York, but this meant that the galley proofs, corrections, and revisions of the manuscript had to go back and forth between continents by mail. The booklet ended up with page numbers like 3A, 39A and even 57A and 57B. Even minor revisions or corrections were sent by mail, because international phone calls were prohibitively expensive in those days.

In a letter to Bennett Levine, who was his liaison with Drucker, Meir wrote, "If you have not finished giving the revised handbook to the printer, please add to page 3A at the very beginning [the following]:"

> The Jewish people is a religio-nation that came into being at Sinai. It is a special people with a special heritage and teaching, whose destiny it is to live in and to create within the Land of Israel a society of holiness and greatness that will be an inspiration and example to the world.[20]

The term "religio-nation" had important ideological significance. How frustrated Meir must have felt when the *Handbook* came off the press, and he found that it had been misprinted as "religious nation."

The second booklet, called *The Jewish Identity Center in Jerusalem, Israel*, described the philosophy and aims of the educational center Meir planned to open in Israel. It described the need for such a center:

> If all anti-Semitism could be made, by magic, to disappear, the American Jew would still face a problem of survival. The disease of assimilation and alienation of Jewish youth from its heritage and people is often spoken about, but its full gravity and danger are not comprehended by most of us. We face the problem of young Jews by the hundreds whose lack of Jewish identity and pride and whose Jewish rootlessness combine to drive them into foreign fields and hostile ideologies.
>
> ... At the same time, in Israel, the ironic growth of a similar Jewish identity crisis has arisen to plague the state with young Jews who identify with the state

but not the Jewish people and whose alienation from Jewish heritage and tradition has now been joined by weakening of ties with their fellow Jews in exile.

The booklet went on to describe the structure and aims of the Jewish Identity Center. It would have three units – Yeshiva Torah Ve'Oz, the Jewish Identity Leadership School and an Institute for Jewish Studies – with one aim: "To produce a Jewish scholar-activist," who will be taught "to go out to the young Jews – not to wait for them to come to him. He will be a teacher, guide, leader and brother."[21] In his article, "Do Not Sin Against the Child," Meir blamed the Jewish Establishment for "their disgraceful loss of our Jewish youth."

> Decades of a powerful commitment to "melt"* ... led to efforts to "modernize" Judaism.... [They] did away with the essentially separatist philosophy of Judaism.... [and] turned Judaism away from sacrifice, rigorous study and a strong emphasis upon Jewish nationalism [to] a Judeo-Christian American version of a community center where basketball replaced substantive Torah learning; the bar mitzvah took the place of commitment to ritual observance; ... bagels and lox became the major form of Jewish identification....
>
> We gave them a ritual that catered to status and obscene ostentatiousness and called it the Judaism of our fathers; we told them to be liberals and revolutionary fighters for all other people without ever teaching them the history and glory of their own, and expected them to grow up to be proud Jews. Little wonder that they – sensitive and understanding the fraud and meaningless sham – forsook their faith and their people.[22]

In Israel, too, the youth lacked Jewish identity:

> In their ignorance of the overwhelming odds that faced a Jewish minority which possessed neither government nor army, the Sabra grew to disdain his fellow Jews.... In his preoccupation with his own problems and interests, he began to look inward rather than outward, forgetting that, but for the Jew in the Exile who had been his ancestor and grandfather and father, neither he nor the state would have come into existence.
>
> ... In its most extreme form, the new non-Jewish outlook was represented by the Canaanites, a small group of intellectuals who created their own myth of an Israeli people whose links were with the non-Jewish peoples of the Middle East rather than with their Jewish brethren in the Diaspora.
>
> ... Thus, a total rejection of religion as a *galut* [diaspora] creation. Thus, a call for limiting aliya until things become better for the Sabra himself. Thus, polls that find, over and over again, the young Sabra student asserting his Israeliness over his Jewishness.[23]

---

* America has been called a melting pot, with the waves of immigrants and their diverse cultures and traditions melting into the American culture.

Meir saw the root of the problem on American campuses, and presented a solution:

> While leftist groups had their ideologically trained leaders full-time in schools winning over young people to their causes, Jewish identity had no such leaders.... The obvious, desperate need is for YOUNG JEWISH LEADERS who are attuned to the youths and who will spend their time on campuses and in cities, working, teaching, and ideologically influencing Jewish youth.... Until we have such people, we will continue to lose the battle for our Jewish youth.
>
> ALL people at this school would go there for one purpose: to become superbly trained, articulate and dedicated Jewish leaders who would obligate themselves for two years to work totally and constantly in schools, campuses and streets.[24]

Meir attended to the logistics of the school. First, there was the need for a building. Among the officials he approached for assistance was minister of defense Moshe Dayan, who scheduled a meeting with Meir on January 30, 1972, and followed up with a short handwritten note: "... At present we do not have an empty building; all the buildings in our possession are occupied and crowded." Aware that Meir was working to bring Americans to settle in Israel, he added, "In any case, if large groups of young people come here from the United States to settle permanently, I am sure that you will find open hearts and full cooperation." At the beginning of February, Meir applied for a permit from the Ministry of the Interior to open a public institution. The permit for "Yeshiva Torah Ve'Oz-Jewish Identity Center," which was to open in Jerusalem in July, came through on June 17.[25]

The next step was recruitment. Meir placed an ad in the *Jewish Press* calling on young American Jews to sign up for the leadership training school planned for that summer in Jerusalem. Flyers about the school were distributed wherever young people congregated. Meetings with prospective candidates were scheduled for February 27 and 28, when Meir was in the United States. Meir delegated administrative responsibility for the schools to young JDL members, but he promoted enrollment vigorously in person whenever he spoke to groups in the U.S.[26]

Christian Missionaries in Israel

Before Meir left for the States on February 13, he gave practical expression to his long-time concern about the influence of Christian missionaries on Jews. In 1962 he had written about indigent Jewish refugees from Algeria in the slums of Marseilles, Paris and Lyon, who were offered financial benefits if they would send their children to the Christian missionary schools.[27] When we arrived in Israel in

1971, a similar problem existed: Poor Sephardic Jews, tempted by promises of economic well-being, were enrolling their children in Christian schools.

One aggressive missionary group was headed by Emma Berger, a German Christian from Stuttgart. She had founded a sect of fervent believers and in 1963 led some of them to Israel, where they founded a commune called Beth-El in Zichron Yaakov. In 1972 they were still acquiring property there.[28]

On February 10, Meir called a press conference to announce a demonstration against Emma Berger's sect in Zichron Yaakov. JDL members and young people from local schools would take part, he said. The demonstration was not only against the Zichron Yaakov sect, but also to protest the Knesset's failure to pass legislation forbidding missionary activities in Israel. Meir believed that Christians should not be permitted to spread their religion in Israel, and that the Knesset should enact a law against it. He pointed out: "Greece, Switzerland, Italy, India and other nations that are not less democratic than ours have laws against missionaries."[29]

A police permit was obtained for February 13 at 4 P.M. Although Meir did not take part in the demonstration because he was flying to the States that day, about two hundred protesters, many of them from nearby religious high schools such as Midrashiat Noam, were there. They sang *Am Yisrael Chai* (The Jewish People Lives) and carried placards that said, "Emma Berger: Follow the Templars!"* and "Never Again!" The media, including cameramen from German TV, were present in force, and the problem of Christian missions in Israel was brought to the attention of the public.[30]

This was the first of a number of anti-missionary activities initiated in 1972. On May 3, a demonstration was held at the Knesset to demand legislation against Christian missionaries. In response to flyers distributed in Jerusalem, tens of protesters gathered at the Knesset, where they presented a petition for the passage of anti-missionary laws to Herut Knesset Members Menahem Yedid and Matityahu Drobles, who went out to meet them.[31]

In the ensuing years, Meir campaigned actively for legislation against Christian missionaries in Israel.

---

* The Knights Templars were 12th-century German Christians who arrived in the Holy Land during the Crusades but soon returned to Germany.

Chapter 28

Next Year in Jerusalem
(February-May 1972)

On the College Campus

MEIR RETURNED TO the United States on February 14 and resumed his round of speaking dates, many at universities. Craig Aranoff, a student at the University of Pennsylvania, reported on a typical campus talk:

"Nowhere in the 613 laws of the Torah does it say, 'Thou shalt be a doctor, lawyer or a CPA.'"

The audience laughed. The speaker didn't smile.

"Every Yom Kippur millions of Jews, led by their rabbis, shout forth a massive lie: 'Next year in Jerusalem.'"

The Jewish audience laughed; the Jewish speaker somehow seemed to miss his own jokes.

"American Jews have taken a magnificent culture, heritage, history, faith and traded it for bagels and lox."

Laughter.

"King David would have made a lousy member of B'nai B'rith."

Laughter.

"Someday they'll engrave on the tombstones of all the 'leaders' of American Jews: 'Shh! He did things quietly – behind the scenes.'"

Laughter.

"It was not the military-industrial complex that created Israel..."

Laughter.

"... it was Jewish blood!"

Meir Kahane is a very funny man. He knows how to make people – well, he knows how to make Jews laugh. But his humor is the type that relies upon incongruity and sarcasm, on people laughing at themselves. It's that strange kind of humor, like the humor of Lenny Bruce, that mixes people up – that sometimes has them laughing when things really aren't very funny, and that sometimes leaves them strangely silent when things really are.

... Kahane spoke in Irvine Auditorium at the University of Pennsylvania on Thursday evening, March 2. The 200 people there didn't fill the place well. A lot of Jewish students on campus didn't go to hear him.

... "I shudder at the picture of rabbis using violence," he said with tongue in cheek. "That's no way for a nice Jewish rabbi to act. Moses would have been a terrible rabbi. When he saw the Egyptian beating the Jew, he killed the Egyptian."

The folks that stayed away missed a good show.

"Israel just spent four days breaking international law – thank G-d."

Hilarious.

"Violence is a bad thing that's sometimes necessary. I wish things could be done in nicer ways. I wish you could sit down and talk things out like gentlemen – decide things the way you do here at Ivy League schools."

Rabbi Kahane is not a comedian. He didn't come to tell jokes. The rabbi is a teacher, a leader, an activist, a Zionist, and maybe, as he was alleged to be, maybe he's a bomb maker.

But he didn't tell his audience to make bombs. He didn't tell his audience to kill two Soviet diplomats for each Jew that dies in Soviet hands.

He taught a history lesson about Jews who broke the law in Mississippi, but who didn't fight to save Jews.

"We didn't do for ourselves what we've done for any other people. This is why JDL was founded – so this should never happen again."

And the rabbi preached.

"The time to bury respectability is now ... respectability keeps us silent."

And he explained.

"People who are opposed to violence are people with no problems. JDL's strength is in those areas where life is a nightmare of poverty and crime. Where you can't go out on the streets even in the daytime. Where a trip to the supermarket is an adventure – sometimes you make it, sometimes you don't."

Believe it or not, laughter followed that one too. Kahane must be a very funny man to make that funny.

And he talked about Israel, about American Jews going there.

"The only reason American Jews will go to Israel is fear," he said. But American Jews aren't afraid.

"The Jew is blamed for racial problems, radical politicians, LSD, pornography, and on top of everything else, the economic crisis.... Groups who talk of gas chambers are growing.... It can happen here.

"There is an ultimate solution to the Jewish problem: A Jewish state."

Applause.

... "Can you imagine the joy of longshoremen cursing in Hebrew?"

Laughter.

... Kahane is a very funny man. If you ever get a chance, catch his act. It won't leave you laughing.[1]

Meir certainly had good rapport with his audiences and was a talented speaker, but it wasn't only talent. It was a matter of hard work, of expending effort and energy. Meir worked hard to counteract the leftist influences that pervaded American colleges and universities and to draw Jewish students all across the country closer to Judaism. At each talk he called on students to attend the JDL school for Jewish leadership in Jerusalem and to plan for aliya (immigration) to Israel.[2]

However, his talk to students at Hofstra University on February 22 had a different emphasis, coming as it did in the midst of a campus furor over the right of David Kerr, the head of a Nazi group on campus, to hang a swastika from his dorm window. Kerr had also placed an ad saying, "Hitler was right!" in the campus newspaper two weeks earlier. At first, the university administration upheld Kerr's right to display the Nazi flag, despite vigorous campus and community protests. But when Hillel director Rabbi Leon Wolf refused to cancel Meir's speaking engagement, scheduled months earlier, the university administration, fearing violence on campus if the flag was not removed before Meir's arrival, forced Kerr to take it down. Instead, Kerr hung a sign from his window that read "Free Speech to Nazis."

Meir referred to this sign in his talk. He said that Auschwitz, Belsen and Buchenwald were "the fruits of free speech granted to Nazis in the 1920s." A news report said, "He hammered away at the comparison between the Kerr incident and Hitler's rise to power, warning students not to 'laugh off' the self-proclaimed Nazi's activities." To the overflow audience of 1,200 students he said, "The solution to the David Kerr problem is short, simple and easy. Some will say that to physically beat David Kerr is not the Jewish way. But," he continued, "If it had been done in Germany, there would not have been a Hitler."

One reporter noted a habit of Meir's that will bring a smile of recognition to those who knew him:

> Kahane's hand quickly lifted the black yarmulke a few inches off his head and dropped it into place again. In almost the same motion, the hand brushed the hair off his forehead and returned to his side in time to emphasize a point with a gesture. It was a nervous habit repeated many times, but always followed by a point driven home.[3]

Meir told the audience that not only neo-Nazis hated Jews. He showed the audience a leaflet distributed that very day at Hofstra by the leftist "Free Angela Davis Committee." He charged that Angela Davis and the Black Panther Party, who maintained they were "only" anti-Zionist, were, in fact, anti-Jewish. "They call Jerry Rubin, William Kunstler and Abbie Hoffman Zionist pigs," he said.

This was clearly ridiculous, because those three Jews were outspoken anti-Zionists. "If they are Zionists, I'm a Bulgarian!" declared Meir.[4]

Shortly after this, Meir wrote about anti-Semitism masquerading as anti-Zionism:

> It has long been one of the tenets of the Arabs in their struggle against Israel that they are not anti-Jewish, but only opposed to Zionism. This particular theme, which has since been picked up by other haters of the Jewish people, including the communist and fascist worlds, has been effectively used to dupe a great many people, including Jews themselves. It has led to proposals that Israel make "accommodations" and that the whole concept of a Zionist state be scrapped in order that the Arabs and Jews might dwell happily together in some sort of bi-national or multiracial Palestine.
>
> ... It is vitally important that young Jews, and Israelis in particular, have some knowledge of the depth of anti-Jewish hatred on the part of the Arabs and realize, too, that this is indeed hatred of JEWS and not only of Israelis. Indeed, the penchant of Islam for oppressing ALL minorities that are non-Moslem or non-Arab has been evidenced a hundred times over, not the least in our time. The Negroes in the Sudan, the Kurds in Iraq, the Coptic Christians, the Biafrans – all are mute testimony to their savage intolerance and hatred of non-Islamic peoples.
>
> ... The pat excuse that "we are only anti-Zionists" has now become endemic to all Jew-haters. It was seen clearly in Poland in recent years, in Czechoslovakia in 1968 and in all the right-wing fascist literature in this country. Zionism becomes a code word for Jews and we run a great risk if we forget it.[5]

He spoke in the same vein later that day, when he addressed an audience of about two hundred and fifty at Long Island University's campus in nearby Greenvale. A report on this talk featured his call for students to enroll in the leadership-training program.

> "The place for you is not here, but in Israel," he said. The school will train tomorrow's leaders. They will become revolutionaries of the mind rather than of the gun. They will go through a long and difficult course and when they finish they will return to America to each campus that has a large Jewish population and will stay there for two years, teaching Jewish pride. "When they finish," says Kahane, "you will see a change. You won't know it's the same place."[6]

Meir was trying to make American Jews recognize that phenomena like the Nazi group at Hofstra were signs warning them to move to Israel. Even the Anti-Defamation League reported on "a marked increase during the past two years in the scope of American anti-Jewish incidents, organizations and publications," but the ADL did not see them as the urgent warnings Meir did.[7] This report on Meir's warnings to a Philadelphia audience reflected that urgency:

... a massive, emergency aliya. This is Rabbi Kahane's latest mission to American Jewry, and he has been criticized seriously for the "scare" tactics involved.

... "You try to tell yourself, 'I'm like every other person here in America,'" Rabbi Kahane said, "but in the back of your mind you know you're not. Jews have a habit of not wanting to see things. We hope they will go away.

"... In the end, the solution to the 'Jewish problem' is a Jewish state. The Jews in exile always have suffered. And with the Panthers and Nazis around, let's not take any extra chances.

"We always say 'Next Year in Jerusalem' and then go back to our homes. We have prayed for Zion – now it's here! El Al is waiting to take you there... The time is now. Come home. Think of making your life in Israel – if not for yourself, for your children and grandchildren."[8]

Meir's enthusiasm for his plan for mass aliya shows clearly in a letter home:

... the mass evacuation of a Jewish neighborhood to Israel. This last is a really revolutionary concept and we have chosen areas like the East Side, the Rockaways, Bronx.... I am thinking of an aliya not in terms of thousands – but tens of thousands and more.[9]

Aliya was his theme when he spoke at synagogues that wintry March in Oklahoma, Texas, Massachusetts, Indiana, Arizona and New York. Riding on the wave of Meir's popularity, the Harry Walker lecture agency arranged some of his talks during this period.[10]

The day Meir spoke in Des Plaines, a suburb of Chicago, a late winter snowstorm made roads almost impassable, but more than a hundred people trekked bravely through the sleet and snow to hear him.[11] The next day he flew to Texas, where the weather was balmy, but the audience was turbulent. A local newspaper described his talk at Hebrew House, a residence of the University of Texas at Austin.

Kahane spoke over the boos and shouts of "racist" from pro-Arab students and members of the Young Socialist Alliance who carried signs urging support for the "Arab revolution." Verbal barrages launched alternately by pro-Jewish and pro-Arab students often stopped Kahane's talk.

... At one point, a pro-Arab student came to the edge of the stage and attempted to challenge Kahane. Other students persuaded him and a small crowd gathering at the edge of the stage to disperse, but one student shoved Kahane, who had left the podium to talk to the crowd. A brief shoving match ensued before relative calm returned to the area and Kahane continued with his speech.

One pro-Arab student asked Kahane why Palestinian refugees should "have to live like dogs for 22 years in refugee camps."

Kahane said, "That's a good question, but it is being asked of the wrong people. Had the Arabs done for their refugees what we did for ours, there would be no refugees. If the Arabs had agreed to partition, there would be an Arab state and a Jewish state. You caused the Arab refugee problem, not us."[12]

A student newspaper reported:

Kahane spoke of the [leftists'] desire to create a "democratic, secular, multiracial Palestine," saying:
"When they have a democratic, secular, multiracial Syria, then we'll talk about a democratic secular, multiracial Palestine...." Kahane described the Zionist movement as "the National Liberation Front of the Jews."
In answer to questions concerning oppression of other minority groups and nationalities, Kahane stated, "First we'll save the Jews, then we'll go together and save the world."[13]

Another report said:

Rabbi Kahane spoke quietly and logically. His effect on the students was evident in the exchange of Letters to the Editor in the student newspaper long afterward.[14]

"My friend Ed Fagan and I worked to bring the Rabbi to Austin," recalled Michael Abramowitz. "The campus, the largest in Texas, had over 40,000 students at the time, and the atmosphere toward Israel and Zionism was very negative. The left controlled student government, and oil was king, so anyone (i.e., Israel and Jews) who got in the way of the business of oil was the enemy. As always, the Rabbi was brilliant, bringing at least a thousand students out to hear him. With all the heckling, he was in perfect control of the situation."[15]

After that tempestuous afternoon in Austin, Meir flew to Phoenix, where he arrived in time for an evening speaking engagement at Arizona State University at Tempe. The audience at that talk, which was sponsored by the Hillel Union of Jewish Students and the university's sociology department, listened decorously. A report quoted Meir's warning of the rise of anti-Semitism in America: "We should never assume that it will NOT happen here.... Decent people become indecent people when they are unhappy and frustrated." On the apathy and alienation of Jewish students, he said, "The time has come for Jewish pride and knowledge. Jewish money must go for Jewish education."[16]

Potma Prison

The plight of Soviet Jews was always an important issue for Meir. A report published in March described their suffering and their courage:

Nineteen prisoners in Camp 19 of the Potma prison in Soviet Mordovia – ten of them non-Jews – went on a hunger strike of indefinite duration starting last Saturday over the issue of admittance of visitors. The mother of Boris Penson was denied permission to see him.... The sources also report that in Kovno, Lithuania, the Deputy Mayor in charge of cultural affairs denied a group of Jews a license to teach Hebrew at the local synagogue, saying it was to be used only for prayer. Sixty-five Jews signed up for the classes....[17]

Meir wrote an article that month focusing on a Soviet-Jewish heroine:

Her name is Raiza Palatnik and the world hardly knows of her. If her name had been Angela Davis, we would have seen masses of humanity – a great part of which would have been undoubtedly Jewish – prepared to mount the barricades on her behalf. But Raiza is not Angela Davis, she is only Jewish and the Jewish leftists have no time for her, particularly since she is a Zionist.

Raiza Palatnik is a Zionist and also a prisoner in the concentration camp of Dnieproderjinsk, in the Ukraine....

... The Six Day War sparked wild emotions within her and a desire to leave for Israel. She applied to the Jewish Agency in Jerusalem with a request to search for her relatives in Israel, a precondition to any possibility of aliya. It was enough to get her a visit from KGB, the Soviet Secret Police, who searched her house for six hours in October, 1970. Found were such "subversive items" as literature on Israel, a copy of the Declaration of Human Rights and her type-writer.... She was charged with ... keeping and distributing material that con-tained slander against the regime.

The trial was held in June 1971, and in her final statement, Raiza Palatnik took her place among the ranks of the stubborn, determined Jews thanks to whom we still exist as a nation. Standing before a judge whom she knew had found her guilty even before the court proceedings had begun, Raiza Palatnik spoke – not to him, but to her fellow Jews in the Soviet Union and to the world:

"Why am I on trial? I am being tried because all my life I have deeply felt my Jewishness, because I dared to participate in the rebirth of the national con-sciousness of the Jews in the USSR who wish to immigrate to Israel.

"... I dare to hope that the day will come when I shall be able to realize my constant dream and go to the country whose achievements have all been created by the hands of my people, the country I consider as my only Homeland..."

Raiza Palatnik is, today, ill. Terribly so. Her condition is so grave that there are genuine fears for her very life. Her family fears that she will be unable to survive the remaining time in prison that she still faces....[18]

To publicize the plight of Palatnik and all Soviet Jews, Meir devised a new ploy. On March 6, he called a press conference in Washington, D.C., and announced that he was applying for a visa to travel to the USSR. He was planning, he said, a fact-finding mission so as to be able to inform President Nixon "exactly what is happening to Jews in the Soviet Union" before the President's departure on May 22 for a summit meeting in Moscow. Meir told the newsmen he planned to visit Jewish communities in Kiev, Odessa, Moscow, Leningrad and Riga as well as the Potma labor camps where Jews were imprisoned and the Chernyakovsk special psychiatric hospital where many Jewish dissidents were sent.[19]

Dr. William Perl, head of JDL's Washington chapter, recalled this ploy:

> Rabbi Kahane arrived from New York with several supporters. They had come in two cars.
>
> We had informed the police and the media that Rabbi Kahane would ask for a visa to the Soviet Union (which of course we knew he would never get).
>
> But those who came with him, plus about a dozen from Washington, had obtained in the preceding weeks in several visits of two or three or one person, visa applications.
>
> On the form a question read, "Do you have relatives in the Soviet Union?" Another question was, "Do you have friends in the Soviet Union?" At your husband's [Meir's] suggestion, we all wrote that we have three million relatives in the USSR and that the majority of them were our friends.[20]

Accompanied by a number of reporters and cameramen, Meir approached the Soviet Embassy, visa application in hand. As everyone expected, he was not allowed even to enter the embassy. He was stopped at the six-foot-high iron gates before he could submit his request, but he accomplished what he had set out to do: A photo of him at the gates of the Soviet Embassy appeared on page one of the *Washington Post* and reminded the public of the oppression of Soviet Jewry.[21]

President Nixon's planned bridge-building visit to Moscow in May worried Meir and other Jewish activists. It could lead to beneficial trade agreements with the Soviet Union, and they feared that once the Soviets achieved this, they would further curtail Jewish emigration. Meir met with JDL leaders in Washington to plan a demonstration for Soviet Jewry outside the White House on the day President Nixon was to leave for the USSR. Nixon had to be reminded that Jews were prisoners there. Meir wrote home:

> I am writing you this from Washington, where we are making plans for a great Soviet Jewish Day on May 22, the day that Nixon leaves for Moscow. We are closing down Jewish schools and businesses and hoping to have thousands of Jewish people sitting down near the White House while Nixon is leaving by helicopter for the airport.[22]

Later that month, an op-ed article by Julius Gottesman, founder of the JDL chapter in the Bronx, appeared in the *New York Times*. It maintained that the League's militant tactics had accomplished more than anything the Jewish Establishment ever did to help Russian Jews. Gottesman cited the improvement in Soviet treatment of Silva Zalmanson after Rabbi Kahane's warning of possible retribution and the recent increase in emigration of Soviet Jews.[23]

Shanker Boycotts Kahane

In mid-March, Meir spoke at a number of synagogues and schools in the New York area, including the schools he himself had attended, the Yeshiva of Flatbush and Brooklyn Talmudical Academy.[24] On March 19, Meir was to be the guest speaker at the 45th annual luncheon of the Jewish Teachers Association – a token of appreciation for aiding embattled Jewish teachers during the New York school crisis of 1968-1969. Albert Shanker, head of the teachers' union, refused to honor Meir and announced that he would not attend.

Defending Meir's appearance, the president of the Jewish teachers group declared, "Whether we agree or disagree is not important.... The important element is that all shades of opinion should be respected." Nevertheless, when Meir approached the lectern, Rabbi Harold Gordon, executive director of the New York Board of Rabbis, left the dais in protest and other notables left with explanations that they had to leave for other meetings. The Israeli consul, who was to have received an award on behalf of Golda Meir, did not attend at all. However, the audience of 1,200 gave Meir a standing ovation when he approached the lectern and frequently interrupted him with applause during his talk. He said that Jews must use their "political and economic power" to protect Jews, and he defended the merit system in hiring teachers.[25]

One teacher, Stanley Marlin, responded to the controversy over Meir's appearance:

> We've had our share of broken noses and bloodied heads since decentralization and local school boards have come into power. The JDL has stood only to help us avoid such incidents, and nothing else. The ovation Rabbi Kahane received at the luncheon should make it clear to our union leaders that many of us accept his principles and are not at all dismayed by his ability to produce a forceful hand when such is required....[26]

Two days after his talk at the teachers' luncheon, Meir flew back to Israel. His letters were always full of longing for home. At the end of February, he had written:

> "I miss you, I miss you, I miss you, and the children, but mostly you."[27]

It was good to have him back in Israel.

The day after he returned, he went to see the place his brother Nachman had found for the Jewish Identity Center. It occupied the upper two stories of a three-story building that had formerly housed the Zion Hotel. Though it was small, it had enough space for the classrooms and dorms needed to house the leadership training school that was to open in July. More important, it was centrally located in downtown Jerusalem, just off Zion Square, at 10 Dorot Rishonim

Street. Meir immediately signed a lease for the key-money rights* with Mr. Yitzchak Bivas.[28]

Meir remained in Israel for a little over a month, writing, meeting with supporters, and speaking to groups. His appointment book indicates talks at high schools in Jerusalem and Tel Aviv, and *Yedioth Ahronoth* reported on a speech he gave to the lawyers of the Tel Aviv Bar Association. *Yedioth Ahronoth* also printed an article by him arguing the urgency of American aliya.[29]

This Great Country

That month in Israel, Meir concentrated on preparing for the Mass Aliya Conference to be held on May 7 in New York City. In a letter to Sam Shoshan, he wrote, "A fair-sized ad for the conference should go into all the Anglo-Jewish papers and the *New York Times* if possible." Meir's five-page handwritten letter included the wording of the ad, with exact indications of which text to print in bold and which in capitals. At the end, he sketched a coupon to be printed below the text for donations to cover the ad's cost. Aware that an ad in the widely read, prestigious *New York Times* would cost several thousand dollars, he wrote, "I am writing to several people to try to borrow money for the ad. Meanwhile, contact Marty Rosen in the office and ask him if he can get the money for two weeks. We'll pay it back from the ad."[30]

A few days before he was to arrive in New York, the quarter-page ad appeared in the *Times*.

Block letters cried out:

> G-D BLESS THIS GREAT COUNTRY. MAY IT NEVER HAPPEN HERE!
> BUT, CAN ANYONE SAY THAT IT CANNOT?

The ad continued:

> America has been good to its citizens and there is no other power on earth that can compare to it in its tolerance, compassion and freedom.... But that which was, will not always be. Jewish history has a monotonously tragic precedent of ultimate disaster for the Jew.
>
> It can't happen here! So they said in Weimar Germany, a land with a Jewish foreign minister, with Jewish wealth and influence. Of all the countries in the world it could not happen in cultured and civilized Germany. But it did!
>
> ... We love America but in the end, the place of the Jew is in the Jewish state. We love America and as long as we live here our loyalty is to her, but we feel, in the marrow of our bones, that it is time to go home.

---

* Key-money transactions were for two-thirds of the value of the property.

On Sunday, May 7, at 8:30 A.M. an historical all-day Emergency Aliyah Conference will take place at the McAlpin Hotel, 34th Street and Sixth Avenue, in New York City. Rabbi Meir Kahane will speak on the immediate need to return to the Jewish Homeland.

The purpose of the conference will be to create a private, permanent, non-political MASS ALIYAH organization, which will think in terms of bringing masses of Jews to Israel. There are Jews who love America, but who see a change and who know that only a Jewish State guarantees safety from the cancer of assimilation and the spectre of a holocaust. To be a majority in one's land is to be normal....[31]

An image of a Jew at the side of a wall bearing the graffiti *Jew Go Home* headed the ad. It was created by Sam Shoshan, who recalled, "I took a cement block and painted on it *Jew Go Home*. I took a wooden doll I had at home, of a Jew in chasidic dress, set up the lighting and photographed it. I showed it to Meir and he loved it."[32] The ad was reprinted and widely distributed as a flyer with the heading, in Hebrew letters, *Mene Mene Tekel Upharsin*, the historic code for impending danger.[33]

The *Times* ad aroused the condemnation of Establishment Jews around the country. On the heels of the furor over the ad, Meir flew to America on April 27 to promote the Mass Aliya Conference.

Chapter 29

The Mass Aliya Conference
(May-June 1972)

Talk Under Fire

ON APRIL 28, when Meir arrived in New York, he learned that members of the Jewish Establishment in the greater Washington area were trying to cancel his April 30 speaking engagement at Congregation Beth Sholom in Potomac, Maryland. A report in the *Washington Post* headlined "Kahane Talk Here Sunday Under Fire" named the Jewish leaders who were urging the rabbi of Beth Sholom, Rabbi Mitchell S. Wohlberg, to cancel Meir's talk because of the ad he had placed in the *New York Times* on April 24. They were vehemently opposed to his call for American Jews to immigrate to Israel.

Rabbi Wohlberg told the *Washington Post* reporter he believed that Meir had a right to be heard, and that a large portion of the Jewish community supported him. In fact, as of noon Friday, more than seven hundred people had bought tickets to Meir's talk. Many years later Rabbi Wohlberg wrote, "I remember the day very well.... I believe over 1,000 people were in attendance that Sunday and your husband really received a hero's reception.... It was really a great day, long to be remembered."[1]

On the Shabbat before the Mass Aliya Conference, Meir spoke at the Young Israel of West Hempstead, as the guest of the Levine family, whose son, Samson, was an active member of JDL. The synagogue bulletin's report on Meir's talk had the usual obligatory reservation, together with sincere praise:

> He gave of himself freely and generously during the entire time he spent in West Hempstead. Though speaking on *Shabbos*, a day of rest, he still managed to activate quite a few brain cells amongst his listeners. We truly saw the dedication and spirit of this controversial, unusual and charismatic individual.
>
> ... Regardless of one's personal feelings towards the JDL, we can still admire Rabbi Kahane's total devotion, sincerity and dedication to the cause of world

Jewry. To paraphrase one of Rabbi Gold's sermons, the long view of a historical moment or person may be necessary to put an event or an individual into proper perspective. The tabulations are still coming in...[2]

The Mass Aliya Conference opened on Sunday morning, May 7, with the media in attendance. Speakers included Bert Zweibon, Moshe Amirav, James Rapp, and Eli Schwartz, but it was Meir's talk that was quoted in the *Daily News*:

"For the American Jew, just as for any other Jew, there is only one home – one permanent safeguard – the land of Israel," Kahane told a conference of about 500 delegates at the McAlpin Hotel yesterday. Then he instructed aides to collect $10 apiece from each delegate to pay for setting up "an American Jewish national organization to begin the job of immediate mass returns to Israel." Each person was instructed to take material back to his synagogue and start signing up people to move.

"The American dream is coming to an end for the Jew," Kahane warned his audience of men, women, small children and youths. He told them that the crises facing the American public in general "are making the ground fertile for Jew-hatred."

"The Jews will ultimately bear the brunt of America's failure in Vietnam," he contended.

"That humiliating defeat" he said, "is going to let loose a flood of hatred. Fifty thousand American boys died for nothing – and I mean nothing. And someone is going to pay for it."

Remarking on the prominence of Jews in the anti-war movements, Kahane said, "We will yet pay for our Jerry Rubins and Abbie Hoffmans. Don't underestimate the patriotism of the American people. They'll see Rubin and they'll see the Jew."

He reminded the audience of Hitler's talk of a "stab in the back" after Germany's defeat in the First World War. "The myth of the stab in the back is with us again," he warned.

... He reminded his listeners that "the German Jews in 1920 lived well and much longer in Germany than we have lived in this country.... Germany was a good country to the Jewish people."

But the Jews were still exterminated, he said. "Don't believe the myth that Germans are different from any other kind of people," he admonished.

"When Germany started persecuting the Jews," he said, "she had undergone a humiliating defeat, just as we have. Someone had to be the scapegoat. The most logical one is the Jew."

Kahane said that in the first phase of the mass "return" to Israel, "we will take a minimum of 5,000 families."[3]

On May 11, Meir tried to speak about aliya at the biennial convention of the American Jewish Congress in Cleveland. He was refused entry by Arthur J.

Lelyveld, AJC president. The *New York Times* reported Lelyveld's declaration that the delegates at the convention "disagree utterly" with the "hysterical" opinion that Jews in the United States face a new holocaust.[4]

Two weeks later, the *New York Times* – on its prestigious op-ed page – published Meir's reasoned appeal to Jews to move to Israel. Titled "A Call for Mass Emigration to Israel," Meir prefaced it with the words:

> I love the United States and believe that it has, in the past, succeeded in building a political model of freedom and democracy that – with all its faults – has given its people and the world goodness, decency and liberty.[5]

The *New York Times Index* summarized Meir's article:

> ... Rabbi Kahane's article warns that the most critical Jewish issue of the next decade is the physical survival of the American Jewish community. He argues that the abatement of open hatred to the Jew is not due to any permanent change in reality but rather the result of two temporary phenomena. He contends that the holocaust of World War II created a "temporary embargo" on anti-Semitism, and proposes, in addition, that the economic boom thrust the "good life" upon America and allowed it to "wallow" in prosperity and consumer luxuries previously undreamed of. He holds that the period of economic boom has ended, and anticipates that many people, in frustration and bitterness, will turn to demagogues and racists who will promise them the "good life" in return for their liberties and at the price of a scapegoat, which he fears will be the Jew. He asks why Jews should "gamble again" and declares the answer is immediate mass emigration of American Jews to Israel....[6]

This essay brought the topic of American aliya to the attention of millions, especially when the *Times* published reactions to it. Morris B. Abram, of the American Jewish Committee, feared a possible misunderstanding by non-Jews:

> I must point out that [Rabbi Kahane's] views are shared by a very small minority of Jews, at most. Despite the strong and proper interest of most Jews everywhere in the state of Israel, the vast majority of the world's Jewish population continues to opt for life in countries other than Israel.[7]

A popular Jewish commentator, Harry Golden, argued that another Holocaust could not happen in America, because "Hitler had to abolish the Weimar Constitution and create new laws at Nuremberg before he could do any harm to Jewish population."[8]

A powerful Establishment group, the National Jewish Community Relations Advisory Council, issued a sharp repudiation of Meir's stand. It denounced "alarmist assertions" that a massive wave of anti-Semitism was likely to confront the American Jewish community and called them "irresponsible and reprehensible," adding that at no time and in no place in modern history have Jews as a group been more secure than in the United States. It admitted that there had been overt manifestations of anti-Semitism but claimed that they had been largely confined to some militant Negro groups and extremists of left and right.[9]

All this brought the issue of the aliya of American Jews to the forefront. One observer credited Meir's public relations technique.

> As these things go, Rabbi Kahane, whose masterful use of modern public relations and propaganda technique is a case study in itself, will probably enjoy a greater reception for his words and opinions than will both Rabbi [Joachim] Prinz and Elie Wiesel....[*]
>
> Rabbi Kahane has had the best of it in the press. Having won a good foothold and headlock on Jewish public opinion in America by convincing those easily persuaded that leaders of historical and well-established Jewish agencies defaulted on their responsibilities during the Hitler era and continue unto this day blind to reality, he has now talked himself and his devotees into believing that a new wave of anti-Semitism is about to engulf the Jewish community of America....[10]

Severe Probation Conditions

Meir faced two court hearings during this trip. The first, on May 2, was serious. The U.S. Probation Office in Brooklyn contended that Meir's advice to Jews to arm themselves for self-defense was a violation of the terms of his probation. Although the "Every Jew a .22" campaign began in August 1971, Meir was charged with probation violation only in March 1972.[11] In the interim, as their correspondence shows, the State Department was working to prove that Meir had indeed violated probation. For example, a letter from the State Department to Secretary of the Treasury John Connally expressed concern that the U.S. Probation Office in Brooklyn did not have "the personnel or facilities to ... demonstrate a violation to the satisfaction of the Court," and requested help from the Treasury Department's firearms division in monitoring Meir's activities.[12]

At the hearing on May 2, James F. Haran, Chief U.S. Probation Officer, said, "Rabbi Kahane's actions reflect a deliberate course of conduct which is totally antithetical to both the spirit and the letter of his probation terms." Meir's reaction was: "The government is trying to muzzle me. They won't be able to muzzle the JDL." Fortunately, Judge Weinstein held that Meir's acts provided insufficient grounds for revocation of probation and imprisonment. However, he issued an order severely amending the terms of Meir's probation. Meir was forbidden to participate in any meetings concerning weapons. He was forbidden to transmit to

---

[*] Joachim Prinz, 1902-1988, was president of the American Jewish Congress. Elie Wiesel, born in 1928, well-known activist and writer, won the 1986 Nobel Peace Prize.

the press decisions made by JDL or others concerning weapons. He was not allowed to be present in any room or vehicle where weapons were displayed or carried, unless by law enforcement officials, and more.[13]

Meir's second court hearing concerned the 100-Hour Vigil in December 1970. Charges were riot in the first degree, unlawful assembly, and inciting to riot. The case was heard before Judge Harold Baer in New York County Supreme Court on May 30, 1972. Meir pleaded guilty to inciting to riot and received a probationary sentence.[14]

Back to the Campus

Meir continued to focus his energy on the importance of aliya for American Jews in the months and years to come – indeed, to his dying day, literally. Now, he turned his attention to recruiting students for the leadership training school that was to open in Jerusalem in July.

His talk at Boston University on May 10 apparently bore fruit, because he went there again on May 14 with his fare charged to the budget of the leadership school.[15] At the University of Rochester, where nearly six hundred students came to hear him, a student newspaper recorded his favorite argument for militancy: "Everyone celebrates Chanukah. It's a nice, easy holiday to celebrate. Can you imagine telling stories of the Maccabees who PICKETED the Greeks to death?"[16]

After a number of speaking dates in New York and Boston,[17] and after informing his probation officer of his itinerary, Meir took off on May 17 for a five-day visit to Los Angeles. His probation officer informed the FBI, and as a result, the FBI monitored Meir's entire West Coast visit. Teletype instructions to the FBI's Los Angeles office said:

> Offices are requested to follow Kahane's activities through established sources and report any statements of Kahane which advocate violence or the use of firearms, explosives, etc.
> ... Los Angeles and San Francisco should endeavor to determine the amount of stipend Kahane will receive for his appearances at colleges in the respective areas.

The government was looking for any legal malfeasance by Meir, be it a violation of his probation conditions concerning weapons or tax evasion by not reporting his income. They sought a reason to send him to jail and thus put an end to his activities against the Soviet Union.[18]

An unexpected benefit of FBI surveillance was that it provided a record of Meir's speaking engagements in Los Angeles. Eighteen JDL members met Meir at Los Angeles International Airport. One of them, Abe Epstein, drove Meir to California State College in Los Angeles, where he was scheduled to speak at King

Memorial Auditorium. However, the person who was supposed to handle the arrangements had done nothing. He had not reserved the auditorium, had not obtained a permit for Meir to speak, and had not arranged advance publicity. Finally, Meir received permission to speak in a classroom. Although only 15 students came to hear him, he spoke for over an hour.[19]

The next day, when he spoke at the University of California at Santa Barbara, proper arrangements were in place. He told the students about the school in Jerusalem where young Jews would be trained in speaking, organizing and recruiting, and would return to their campuses to teach others what they had learned. His talk in Santa Barbara and at other schools had results: Three students from Los Angeles attended the school in July. FBI files include not only a report on Meir's talk, but also photocopies of a check stub made out to Meir for $250 and of a letter of thanks from Barbara Javor, chairperson of the Associated Students. Javor wrote, "Your message reached many ears which were formerly deaf, but perhaps now will be opened."[20]

On Shabbat afternoon, Meir held a "rap session" with JDLers at the Rambam Torah Institute and on Sunday, before his flight, he attended two house parties. Fifteen to twenty people accompanied Meir to the airport in the evening, where they sang and danced in the boarding area. Meir urged them to go to San Francisco the next day to demonstrate at the Soviet consulate there, because President Nixon was departing that day for a state visit to the USSR.[21]

Simultaneously, a large JDL demonstration was to be held in Washington to demand that Nixon use his visit to persuade the Soviets to allow Jews to emigrate. The JDL appeal to members to come to Washington read:

> ### A Call for Amnesty and Exodus
> No school, no work! Come to Washington!
> President Nixon has an historic opportunity to raise the issue of Soviet Jewry in the Kremlin. If the Kremlin wants a détente, it must give something in return. The President must ask that they "Let our people go" and that they grant amnesty to Jews imprisoned because of their desire to live in a Jewish State.[22]

The Firearms Division

State Department officials were truly worried that the JDL would jeopardize President Nixon's May 22 trip to Moscow. At their behest, Secretary of the Treasury John Connally had assigned thirty men from his department's firearms division to New York to monitor JDL use of firearms. Connally reported to the State Department that these men were working closely with the U.S. Secret Service, the New York City Police Department and the FBI.[23]

The State Department's concern was surely exaggerated. The May 22 demonstrations did not even attract much media attention. Nevertheless, they were noticed, because Meir was invited to discuss the Soviet Jewish issue three days later on the Dick Cavett TV show. This was a coup for Meir – the Cavett talk show was broadcast nationwide by ABC. However, the American ambassador to the United Nations, George Bush, was scheduled to be on the Cavett show the same evening, and he refused to appear with Meir. There was no doubt which of the two men had more prestige – Cavett cancelled the invitation to Meir. This led to even greater media exposure, because Meir did not accept the cancellation quietly. He and thirty JDL members staged a sit-in in the lobby of the Manhattan theater where the Cavett show was aired, delaying taping of the show for an hour and a half. The incident ended with a tentative agreement that Meir would appear on the show in June.[24]

Ambassador Bush later explained that representatives of established Jewish organizations had advised him not to appear together with Meir. The *Cleveland Jewish News* printed a report on this incident, with an editorial comment.

> The basic myth still abides ... in Jewish circles that "leaders" speak for the true sentiments of the people.... [Rabbi Kahane has] a good deal of "grass-roots" support from many Jews....[25]

Meir appeared on the Dick Cavett show on June 7. A letter he received afterwards attests to the impact of his outspoken approach.

> Last week I caught the Dick Cavett show.... I was astounded.... I wished it would have never ended. I am now a more enlightened Jew. I am one of three Jews out of a student body of 65,000 at Alabama State University in Jacksonville. I come from Henderson, Kentucky – 30,000 population, 6 Jewish families. Please send me more information. [signed] Clarence Mann.[26]

On Sunday morning, June 11, Meir participated in the annual convention of the North American Jewish Students Network, where he led a workshop about the JDL. A report said participants aired grievances against the strategy of the JDL and "Rabbi Kahane, an excellent speaker, found himself hard pressed to answer many of the questions being fired at him. Many leaving the hall were vehemently against Kahane's politics." However, wrote the reporter, "... others were influenced and began to explore their own political stands." Network was an affiliate of the World Union of Jewish Students, which, Meir wrote, was controlled by leftists.[27] That was why it was important to speak with the students, share his ideas with them, and urge them to attend the school in Jerusalem. Meir was to return to Israel shortly after the convention, to prepare for the opening of the leadership training school.

His departure was delayed when, on June 16, the New York Police Department arrested three JDL members for firebombing the offices of Sol Hurok the previous January and causing the death of an employee. Meir immediately called a press conference on behalf of the three young men. He said they were "absolutely innocent, nice Jewish boys." Brought before a judge, the three entered pleas of not guilty. The judge ordered them held in jail until trial and set bail at $35,000 each. Again, Meir called a press conference. His first priority was to raise bail to keep them out of prison. He decried the outrageously high bail and called on Jewish organizations to raise money so the boys could be released immediately. It might be months until the case came to trial and their innocence could be proven.[28] Many good Jews responded to Meir's plea for bail money, but he was sorely disappointed at the lack of response from Jewish organizations. He wrote:

> Bearing in mind that under the American system of jurisprudence – so vaunted by liberals and respectable Jews of all kinds – all people are presumed to be innocent until proven guilty, and that the mere fact of an arrest has no bearing whatsoever on the ultimate verdict; bearing in mind that Jewish law knows of no greater obligation than the one known as "pidyon shvuyim" or redeeming of prisoners; bearing in mind that these three are people who have a long record of doing things for their people while so many others did nothing; bearing in mind that for so many arrested "heroes" of other faiths, colors and creeds – the Berrigans, Angela Davis, the Panthers – Jews gave money and raised money; bearing in mind all these things, surely one would have imagined that Jews, Jewish organizations and Jewish leaders would have seen to it that these three young Jews would have been given the bail needed to release them from Federal prison. Surely, one would have thought that the three would not have had to remain for four days without kosher food and tefillin and in the company of bank robbers, heroin smugglers and other such unsavory types.
>
> ... Surely, in an affluent, involved Jewish community, that kind of bail money could have been raised in a matter of minutes. If only someone had cared...[29]

Sheldon Davis, one of the three accused of the Hurok bombing, later wrote to me: "The issue which taught me to show the greatest respect for your husband was when he refused to leave the United States to be with you and your children in Israel until he had raised bail for me."[30] Meir succeeded in raising bail for all three young men, and they were spared the hardship of a year in prison. Legal proceedings ended in June 1973 with a dismissal of the case due to insufficient evidence.[31]

Looking back on the Hurok firebombing, one thing stands out: JDLers were accustomed to acting on their own, without consulting Meir. Hy Bieber told me, "People did things on their own without Meir saying so and without checking with Meir." Shlomo Russ, in his account of Sheldon Siegel's actions following his arrest for the Hurok bombing, wrote: "Siegel did everything without Meir's knowledge or assent."[32]

What motivated young Jews to protest the oppression of Soviet Jews with explosives? Samson Levine, arrested in May 1972 as he and three others were putting together a bomb, explained:

> ... There was a great pull to be involved. I felt relied upon. As for the total motivation, it is impossible to separate my own personal history (... extended family killed during the Holocaust, distant cousins coming to live with us...) and feeling responsible for my Jewish brethren. Of course, I would be remiss if I left out how I was caught up in the eloquence of Meir. Tie all this in with the environment of the 1960s, with the prevailing attitude that "we can change the world." I wanted to do this for my fellow Jews. During the '60s, the end did justify the means.[33]

Meir was aghast at the loss of life in the Hurok bombing. Alan Rocoff speculated, "After the death of Hurok's employee, Meir was subconsciously closing down American JDL."[34] Journalist Walter Ruby believed that JDL "fell off rapidly after the Hurok bombing due in part to ... the depletion of JDL's funds and the arrest of many of its leaders."[35] The factors that led to the eventual decline of the Jewish Defense League were many, and we will examine them in the course of this book.

Living in the Holy Land

Probably one factor that led to JDL's decline in the States was Meir's campaign to encourage American Jews to move to Israel. Of course, his own aliya meant that Meir was spending less time with the JDL. But more important, Meir's stance was unpopular. American Jews wanted to stay in America. They did not want to uproot themselves and move to an unknown place. Meir understood this, but he was concerned with the ultimate good of the Jewish people, not only the good of JDL. An article he wrote during this period to promote aliya presented a powerful exposition of the religious dimension of living in the Holy Land.

> The People of Israel and the Land of Israel stand in unique unity ... for the Jewish people and the Jewish faith from its very beginning, Eretz Yisrael – the Land of Israel – has remained central to Judaism as a place where a Jew was COMMANDED to live.... The Rabbis declare that settlement in Israel is "equal to all the commandments of the Torah" (Sifre, Re'eh, 60).... "It is better to lodge in the deserts of Israel than in the palaces of other countries," state the Rabbis. "A man should forever live in the Land of Israel, even in a city that has a majority of gentiles, rather than live outside the Land, even in a city that

has a majority of Jews, for he who lives in the Land of Israel is considered as having a G-d, while outside the Land is considered as not having a G-d" (*Talmud Bavli, Ketubot* 110b).... The religious obligation of a Jew to go live in the Land of Israel is clear and unchallengeable....

For two thousand years the Jew bombarded his G-d with pleas, entreaties, tears, promises, repentance, threats, recriminations, and yet more tears. HOME, was his persistent and nagging plea to his Maker. When shall we be allowed to go home?

Even the Almighty can endure just so much. The unceasing persistence of a Jew can wear down Omnipotence and at last He consented. In a drama unrivaled in the history of Man, a people that had begun its long journey into Exile twenty centuries earlier, returned.... Can one really grasp the magnificence and impossibility of it all? Can one appreciate our fortune in having – for some inexplicable reason – been chosen as the generation to behold that which all the prophets of old never saw? ... [36]

Meir reminded Jews that anti-Semitism had many faces. At the end of May, news came from Israel of a massacre at Lod airport. Three Japanese gunmen opened fire in the arrivals area, killing 26 and injuring many others. Meir analyzed the massacre:

... Over and over one heard puzzled people questioning the logic and sense behind the fact that Japanese perpetrated the act.

... The Japanese who shot down innocent people at Lydda [Lod] were dedicated Marxists who see the Arab struggle and the "progressive" battle as one and the same. They were trained by Arabs just as the first Fatah terrorists were trained by North Vietnam and China. We can expect to see more Arab-Communist cooperation as the months go by.

In America this trend will manifest itself in terms of Leftist demonstrations against Israeli offices, picketing of UJA and Israel Bonds dinners, raising money and volunteers for the Arab cause and the like.

... The foolish Radical Jews ... will have to learn that they are Jews before they are Leftists.[37]

A New Book

Aliya was so important to Meir that he devoted an entire book to it: *Time to Go Home.*[38] The book, completed in June 1972, showed the reality of Jew hatred in America; the likelihood that the current social, economic, political and psychological crisis in America would set off another Holocaust; and the rise of hate groups and their motivations. *Time to Go Home* concluded with a practical program for American aliya and ended with the words, "Home. It calls us. Let us return."

On June 19, shortly before he returned to Israel, Meir asked his lecture agent Harry Walker to help him find a publisher for the book. Walker advised Meir that his contract for *Never Again!* gave Nash Publishing the first option of publishing *Time to Go Home.* "If he wants to exercise that option," wrote Walker, "he takes your manuscript and your book on the same terms as your first contract, namely $10,000 advance."[39] A week later, Ed Nash wrote, "At this moment, it is very likely that we would want to exercise our option and we are simply awaiting the manuscript."[40]

Meir wanted the book published as quickly as possible. He sent Walker a telegram instructing him to send the manuscript to Nash.[41] Two weeks later, on July 19, Walker informed Meir that Nash had agreed to publish *Time to Go Home,* adding:

> We have a standard 10% commission, which is standard with all literary agencies in America and a modest legal fee for Alan Schwartz.... When Alan read the terms of your original contract he was flabbergasted. The modest fee for his services will be worth it.[42]

Meir was annoyed. He could have negotiated with Nash without Walker's help. Now, he was losing $1,000 because he had to give Walker a 10% commission on the advance from Nash, and he had to pay an unspecified fee to Walker's lawyer as well. This ended Meir's connection with Walker.

Several months earlier, Ed Nash had asked Meir to write a foreword to another book he was publishing: a new edition of *The Revolt,* a book about the Irgun by its commander, Menachem Begin. For Meir, who admired Begin, it was an honor to write the foreword. For Nash, Meir's foreword was a way to sell more books. The front of the book jacket bore the words: "Foreword by Rabbi Meir Kahane, founder of the Jewish Defense League and author of *Never Again!*" The back of the book jacket featured this excerpt from Meir's foreword:

> Israel owes its life to the fact that a handful of modern-day Maccabees rose up, determined that the Jewish homeland would live again. It exists because many of these young Jews fell on the field of battle against the British. It came into being because young Jews went to the gallows and, in turn, showed the enemy that Jews could not only be killed but could kill in return. The British imperialists were forced out of the land of Israel because of the Jewish Resistance movement led by the Irgun and Lechi. This is their story as told by the man who led the forces of Jewish freedom. If today the State of Israel stands tall and proud and prepared to fight for its existence without fear or hesitation, it is because of the spirit of the New-Old Jew. That spirit is the story of *The Revolt.*[43]

Nash believed that Meir's name had selling power when he featured it on the cover of *The Revolt.* That same belief motivated him to publish *Time to Go Home.*

Meir, who felt it was urgent to persuade American Jews to settle in Israel, pressed Nash for an early publication date, but Nash replied:

> As far as fast publication goes, the soonest the book could be brought out by any publisher is February or March. "Fall" catalogs already printed go through January and the next season is not until then. Salesmen have already started their rounds, using the new catalog, and there is no way to get national distribution until next season.
>
> We can bring the book out earlier, if you would like, and make preview copies available through JDL or some other organization, but there is no way to effectively get national coverage in bookstores.[44]

In August, after Begin's *Revolt* was published, Ed Nash promised early availability for *Time to Go Home*:

> I am sending you two copies of *The Revolt* ... We are planning to set the official publication date for *Time to Go Home* as March 1973, with the book shipped to bookstores in January and available [to you] for use in December.[45]

But Nash's letter to Meir at the end of October was less promising.

> Keep in mind that the advance we have paid you is against all income, including your 50% share of the paperback income. As neither the paperback nor the hardcover [of *Never Again!*] did well, I would not count on more than a couple of thousand dollars at most.
>
> The hardcover book [*Time to Go Home*] will be available this month as you requested. How many do you want to order and where do you want them sent?[46]

The last sentence in this letter was a harbinger of things to come. It appears from this, and from later correspondence, that Nash expected bulk sales to the JDL to make the publication of *Time to Go Home* profitable for him. On November 27, Nash wrote:

> ... We reserved the copies of *Time to Go Home* that you wanted for personal use in connection with your lectures. The books are ready for shipment.... We have entered an order for 2,500 copies which we are holding out for you. We are awaiting shipping and billing instructions.[47]

A second, harsher letter from Nash to Harry Walker referred to Meir's "book order:"

> ... The books were ordered on [Meir's] instructions and we are now attempting to get the money from JDL. If we get it we will remit the [royalties due].[48]

By this time, Meir was facing indictment in Israel and the Israeli government had confiscated his passport.[49] He could not travel to America and had to conduct all his affairs by mail. Meir usually did not keep carbon copies of the letters he wrote, but developments can be inferred from the letters he received from Nash. In Nash's next letter to Meir, there was a severity that was to become more pronounced in future communications.

> I have not received the reply re the books shipped to JDL and not paid for. Our records indicate that you told us to ship the books, meaning you are responsible for the payment. It would be easier if you could help us to get JDL to pay the bill or return the books. I'd appreciate your help in this.
>
> I will be sending you royalty statements at the end of the year as required by your contracts – returns [unsold books] were rather substantial.[50]

Royalty statements had not yet arrived when this letter came in February 1973 from Nash's assistant:

> [Edward Nash] has had a severe case of the London flu and has been out of the office for several weeks.
>
> In his absence, royalty accounts are being handled by our parent company, BFL Communications, 50 Liberty Street, Freeport, New York.... Mr. Robert Brown will be in touch with you.

Meir sent the letter back with a curt handwritten note on it dated February 11, 1973:

> Spare Mr. Brown the trouble. I have asked my attorney to begin legal proceedings. [signed] Meir Kahane.[51]

His note must have had an effect. A check stub in Meir's files dated March 6, 1973, shows a payment of $2,000 for "royalties on account" for *Never Again!*[52]

Meir may have achieved a victory in being paid the royalties due him, but he still had the questionable shipment of books to deal with. Perhaps unaware that Meir was not allowed to leave Israel, Nash's credit manager addressed a letter to him on March 27, 1973 at JDL's Brooklyn headquarters demanding payment:

> Your past-due indebtedness: $11,925. Our records show that the above balance is still due us....

Meir was facing two court cases in Israel when he received this letter. He had been accused of attempting to smuggle arms out of Israel, and letters he had sent to Israeli Arabs suggesting that they emigrate were said to be unlawful. He surely did not need another problem. He sent the letter back to the credit manager with an angry note at the bottom of the page:

> This joke is getting to be very unfunny. Our pending lawsuit will be even funnier.[53]

Now Meir started keeping carbon copies of letters he wrote in connection with Nash. On May 2, he wrote to Steve Smason, a JDL leader in Los Angeles, asking him to bring suit against Nash in Los Angeles.

... Please, Steve, have Steinberg file suit for all the money owed me. In addition I want it made clear that until September I do not pay taxes [in Israel] on money earned and after that I do, – 60% of the amount. I want this to be part of the damages. In addition I ask you again to please get an injunction against Nash selling my book...

... I enclose the bill from Nash, which is now $19,875. Please get those crooks now! [54]

Shortly afterwards, a check arrived for $3,623.21 for royalties earned to March 31, 1973. The check, dated May 8, bearing Nash's Los Angeles address, is signed by Robert Brown. I endorsed it and deposited it on June 20 because Meir was in jail then.[55]

On July 6, 1973, Meir was released from jail. He wrote a long letter to Nash Publishing, detailing the royalties due him for *Never Again!* He also requested "exact statements on time." Concerning *Time to Go Home*, he wrote:

Furthermore, I have had no statement sent me concerning my other book, *Time to Go Home* ... Are you planning to sell the paperback rights and if so, when? I do know that a little bit of advertising in the Jewish media would produce a great many sales and I suggest you do this...

Then he referred to the fictitious book order:

I would also like to have extra copies of *Never Again!* which I MIGHT be interested in buying. I emphasize that this is not an offer, since I do not want to repeat the unfortunate insistence by Mr. Nash that I had ordered books when I never did. I simply ask if you have any and if the price is right, I might order quantities.[56]

Clearly, Nash never had any written order from Meir for thousands of copies of *Time to Go Home*, and when he saw he could not intimidate Meir, he stopped dunning him. Since the book did not sell well, Nash tried this ploy to cover his costs. Supporter Rabbi Kenny Cohen recalled, "*Time to Go Home* did not sell. Jews did not want to read about aliya. I bought a copy marked down from $7.99 to 99 cents!" A softcover edition appeared only in 1975.[57] The book probably sold poorly because its warning, like the warnings of the prophets, made Jews feel uncomfortable. Reuben Gross pointed this out in his book review:

Time to Go Home is a plea for aliya. But it is not another of the usual pieces of Zionist propaganda. It is a stark statement, "It can happen here – and most probably will happen." The very idea will cause many to recoil and denounce the author as an alarmist and charlatan.

... Anticipating the outcry his book is bound to stir, Rabbi Kahane points out not only that Jeremiah was thrown into the pit for telling the unpleasant truth, but that closer to our time, Jabotinsky was called a fool for crying out in the 30s "Jews, get moving. There is no time. A fire is burning, get out."

... Considerable patience is not required to read this book. Rabbi Kahane's writing combines first-rate journalistic fluency with a touch of rabbinic rhetoric and well-organized forensic persuasiveness."[58]

The *Chicago Sun-Times* carried a review of *Time to Go Home* by Roy Larson, the paper's religion editor. He agreed with Meir that the lower socioeconomic class was liable to become a danger to democracy: "He is more right than far-right when he warns of the dangers of romanticizing the New Populism." Larson reinforced Meir's appeal to Jews to consider their own future: "Rabbi Kahane sounds pertinently prophetic when he points out how vacuous moral appeals can be which fail to take seriously the factor of self-interest." He concluded: "Rabbi Kahane cannot be summarily dismissed as an enemy of the people because of his shrill warning against totalitarianism. It isn't always better to be sanguine than sorry."[59]

On June 22 Meir returned to Israel and began preparations for the leadership training school.

Chapter 30

The Leadership Training School (July-September 1972)

TWENTY-FIVE STUDENTS signed up for the summer Leadership Training School – twenty men and five women – most of them from New York and Los Angeles.[1] The school occupied the upper two stories of a three-story building that had formerly housed the Zion Hotel. It was in downtown Jerusalem, just off Zion Square. The classrooms and dining room were one flight up, the men dormed on the top floor, and the women lived in a nearby apartment.[2]

Non-Stop Lectures

Meir gave two or three lectures daily and arranged for several outstanding people, some of them Irgun veterans, to teach as well. Dr. Israel Eldad and Dr. Joseph Nedava lectured on Jewish history, and attorney Dov Shilansky taught about the Holocaust, with special emphasis on the Irgun's work in Europe. Attorney Shmuel Tamir, Amichai (Giddy) Paglin, and David Niv also lectured, but the star, as far as the students were concerned, was Aharon Pick, who – lecturing non-stop – led them on unforgettable weekly tours throughout the country, with a week-long trip to the Sinai at the conclusion of the course.[3]

David Fisch recalled:

> The program was extraordinary, one of the best experiences in my life, even as I look back twenty-five years later. Many anticipated a Camp Jedel in Jerusalem, but it was not so. Rather, it was books and classes and note taking and leadership training and *tiyulim* [hikes].
>
> Dov Shilansky taught a class on the Holocaust. After eight weeks, only in the final class, did we learn his story, who he was, what he had done in the 1950s, etc.
>
> We had a history instructor, a professor [Dr. Joseph Nedava]. He was scholarly, in an intellectually academic way. His classes were not all that ideological, just good Jewish history.

Amichai (Giddy) Paglin made a strong impression:

> We had a guest lecture or two (maybe three) given by Giddy Paglin, in which he spoke of the Irgun days and told us about bombs that he made, how they worked, where they were placed, etc. That was another mega highlight and a big psyche. As in: Wow! Holy smokes, this is the guy that blew up the King David Hotel, and he's telling us about how they got the milk cans into the basement! Wow!

Meir's classes were the basis of the course. Fisch wrote:

> Meir taught two or three classes daily. One was on "Organization" – how to organize a demo, how to draft a press release, etc. I remember his three principles:
>
>   (1) Initiate (nowadays, we speak of being "proactive" rather than reacting); (2) Do not let "them" force you to react to their agenda; and (3) Be Creative. For instance, if Joachim Prinz urges Israel to give up land, go to his front lawn with shovels, dig up his lawn, and announce to the media that JDL is implementing phase one of Rabbi Prinz's moral call by giving up his land.[4] That kind of stuff.

Some of the course materials were photocopied texts that Meir had selected.[5] In addition, Meir's lectures were taped, transcribed and run off on a mimeograph machine, so the students could review them. Seymour Lecker recalled those lecture notes: "Meir's lectures were wonderful. After they were transcribed, Meir would go over the transcriptions, correcting errors."[6]

One transcription reveals Meir's broad knowledge and captures his classroom style wonderfully:

> … So what happens is that the Marxist Jew … a fellow who was born Jewish and is now a Marxist, says, "My interest lies … with the Polish worker, the Irish worker, the Puerto Rican worker, the black worker, all workers, against all bosses, including Jews."
>
>   I gave you yesterday among the notes, and I don't know if you read those notes yet, but among those notes, on page 18, there was a remarkable statement by Pavel Axelrod, the most famous of the Russian-Jewish anarchists – he was of the Narodnik movement in Russia, and it's on page 18 – we don't have to waste money on tape for this.

On another topic Meir said:

> … Does anyone know who this fellow is, Art Waskow? In 1968, when riots ripped Washington, after Dr. King was shot, and Jewish stores were – Jews were literally wiped out in Washington – Art Waskow suddenly appeared with a group of people in synagogues and temples, demanding backing for the riots. A group called "Jews for Urban Justice.…"

... *Doreinu*, a Jewish student newspaper in Maryland.... they discuss a speech on October 8, 1970 ... featuring Arthur Waskow.... He spoke about Palestinian rights, Israeli government repression.... He attacks Israel as a terrorist country, as an oppressive country, one that persecutes and massacres Arabs and commits genocide.... When *Doreinu* questioned Waskow as to support of terrorist attacks on Israeli civilians, such as the school bus massacre, bombs in marketplaces, he says, "I don't support, but I don't reject the attacks.... If the attacks by the Palestine Arabs against Israeli fascists are part of a world attack by oppressed peoples against fascists, then I'm for that."[7]

In his lecture "Jewish Basics," Meir spoke about the practical aspect of the concept of *hadar*, Jewish pride.

The Jew who allows himself to be dishonored is opening the way to eventual physical assault upon himself. Therefore, it's more than just, "Don't be so sensitive when you're called a kike." More than that. It's more than just sensitivity. It is a very practical realization and a practical knowledge that the goy is pushing you, he wants to see how far you'll be pushed.[8]

Fisch recalled another type of course given by Meir:

Once weekly, Meir taught us Irgun and Lechi* songs. Most of us never before had heard him sing, so that was a surprising side for us. I learned all the songs and still remember the lyrics to every one. That, too, is a lasting legacy of that summer.

We had a guest lecture about the pre-state underground one time by David Niv, who actually wrote one of the songs, *Hem Lo Yishberu Otanu* [They Will Not Break Our Spirit]. After the lecture, he mentioned to us that he had written a song, and I volunteered to him that I think we know the song. He figured, how can a bunch of American kids know my song? Like, after all, this is not Elvis stuff. So we all sang it, and he was very, very – very – deeply moved.

Hikes were the highlight of the camp experience for Fisch.

The main thrill, for me, other than getting to know Meir and to experience the side of him rarely seen – classroom teacher – was going on *tiyulim* [hikes].

Aharon Pick did the *tiyulim*. He was a blast. First the look – we all saw him as sort of a missing link, with the very thin body, large ears, always eating bananas. He led us on *tiyulim* through all the regular places, but he made them very right-wing, psyching on us all the time. We went to Hebron, Gaza, four days in the Sinai, the Banias, Massada, etc. For instance, on the Massada *tiyul*, he just ragged and ragged on the fat-cat Americans who take the cable cars up. Not us. Nope. We would climb. And not just climb, but *davka* especially on the snake path. He had us climbing all over the place. Anything that could be

---

*Lechi is the acronym of Lochamei Cherut Yisrael, a pre-state military unit founded in 1940 to fight British rule in (then) Palestine.

climbed, we climbed. And he would climb in those ragged, torn sandals, while we would *schvitz* [sweat] in our fine American-issue hiking boots, etc.[9]

Marilyn Betman recalled the hikes:

We pretty much traveled throughout the country from top to bottom. We climbed Massada, visited the Golan Heights, camped out in the Sinai desert, and went snorkeling.[10]

Avraham Hershkowitz, who had been "deported" to Israel as a condition for release from prison, was the school's administrator. Hershkowitz lived in the leadership school building with his wife Nancy and baby Leah and took care of building maintenance, hired the cook and ordered the food. He was also responsible for payments to the lecturers and for arranging their transportation to Jerusalem. Each Shabbat, he would take the boys to a different synagogue.[11]

Fisch recalled the synagogues and an adventure:

One Shabbat we *davened* [prayed] at the Etzel*-Lechi *shul* off Jaffa Street, where the *gabbai* [sexton] made a long speech after *davening*, praising Meir and calling him all the great Biblical praises – next in the chain that traveled through Jabotinsky.[12] Another Shabbat we went to the Italian Synagogue on Hillel Street.

Another Shabbat we went to this *shul* in East Jerusalem. We had been told the story of how, in 1948, when Jordan took that section of the city, the *shul*'s Arab caretaker had sealed off the building and secretly had locked all the *sifrei Torah* in a room for safety and protection – and then, after the liberation and reunification in 1967, the Arab's son showed up with the key, opened the door, and all the *sifrei Torah* had been preserved perfectly. So, all psyched up, we walk to *shul*, and along the way, in East Jerusalem, some Arab kid on a balcony spits *garinim* [sunflower seeds], and the next thing you know, one of our students was in a fistfight with the Arab kid, bloodying him up and everything. The cops came, separated us, etc. We go to *shul*, *daven*, have a nice time, and later learn from Meir that the Arab kid that got beaten up was the grandson of the original Arab caretaker who had helped preserve the *tashmishei kodesh* [holy articles].

Meir tried to discourage the boys' rough behavior. He was concerned about the reputation of the JDL in Israel. Fisch recalled:

One night, the boys got rowdy and had a dormitory water-balloon fight. It was quite an evening. (I have this broad grin as I think back.) Anyway, at 6 A.M. the next morning, Meir comes into my room, wakes me up, cajoles me into going into his office, and tells me that it has been all over the news all evening

---

* Etzel is the acronym of Irgun Tzva'i Leumi, also known as the Irgun, a pre-state military unit that fought British rule in (then) Palestine during the 1930s and 1940s.

and morning that a ruckus happened at the JDL building at the Zion Hotel. He told me that, look, he was trying to create an organization in Israel that would have a better reputation than the one in America, and he would not allow this program to ruin that. He told me to tell everyone when they awoke that we had spoken and that he did not want to know what had happened, who, what, when, where, etc., but if anything – anything – like it ever happens again, he would instantly cancel the program and send us all home. So we behaved ourselves better thereafter....[13]

It was clear to Meir that Fisch was good leadership material – just the person he needed to run the JDL office in New York. By the end of August, he wrote to Bert Zweibon, "... An executive director to be in the office every day ... is essential. David Fisch is ready to do the job and he is quite good.... and his price is minimal." When Meir's passport was confiscated that October, and he was not allowed to leave Israel for almost two years, it was fortunate that Fisch was already in place at the New York headquarters.[14]

Audiences in Israel

That summer, the Zionist Organization of America (ZOA) held their annual conference in Israel. At their conference in Pittsburgh in 1971, Meir had been given an opportunity to address the delegates, and they agreed to give him the podium again in Israel. Not only that, but they gave him a block of tickets for the opening session at the Jerusalem International Convention Center on Thursday, July 13. I accompanied Meir to the opening session, and the entire student body of the leadership school came as well.[15] In an ad in the *Jerusalem Post* the day the conference opened, Meir called on the delegates to adopt an emergency evacuation plan for American Jews and to form aliya groups in every community. In large block letters, it cried out:

> What are you as Zionists doing about immediate plans for permanent aliya? What are you doing about plans to help move the mass of American Jews home before they go under beneath a wave of assimilation and physical holocaust?... Make no mistake. What happened in other exiles can and is beginning to happen in America. The time to leave, the time to return home, is NOW and you, Zionists of America, are people from whom we, the Jewish people, have a right to expect leadership....[16]

Meir's speech at the conference session on Sunday in Tel Aviv was quoted in the Hebrew press. Noah Kliger of *Yedioth Ahronoth* wrote, "Rabbi Kahane's words – despite the fact that not all present agreed with them – were greeted with prolonged applause, and many rushed forward to shake the hand of the 'fighting rabbi,' as he is called." Meir's photo in *Yedioth Ahronoth* and *Ma'ariv* showed him wearing a short-sleeved, open-necked white shirt and, because it was the three-week period of mourning for the destruction of the Temples, he had a beard, short and black – no gray as yet! Meir's participation in the conference was noted on Israel TV news. But the picture flashed on the screen showed not Meir, but Rabbi Kalman Kahana, member of Knesset for Poalei Agudath Yisrael – perhaps because of the beard! [17]

During the week of the ZOA conference, Meir's article, "The Wandering Jew," appeared in the *Jewish Press*. He wrote about the Jews who move from neighborhood to neighborhood, seeking safety.

> I once met a Jew from Montreal. He was a survivor of Auschwitz who had gone through the seven circles of Hell. In Montreal he had become very wealthy. Suddenly, the French separatist movement threatened his economic future if not his physical safety. He told me he was thinking of moving. I looked at this survivor of the gentile hell in Europe and the budding victim of its fury in Montreal and asked him where he contemplated going:
>
> "Toronto...," was the answer. And after that Vancouver, no doubt, and after that Australia. Any place but not the one logical, sane place. Home. Eretz Yisrael. [18]

Meir was invited to speak before various groups that summer. His appointment book shows two speaking dates in Netanya – before a Bnei Akiva group and at the Ohel Shem auditorium – and one just outside Netanya, in Moshav Azriel, a farming village that borders on the Arab town of Taibe.[19] He probably had other speaking dates, but he was not in the habit of noting everything in his appointment book. For example, he did not note an invitation to speak before a group of American youth. Charley Levine, who arranged that talk, recalled an interesting aspect of Meir's character:

> Both Shelly [later his wife] and I coincidentally ended up in Haifa in the summer of 1972 at a special leadership training seminar of the WZO [World Zionist Organization] – designed for a select crew of about 25 or so key student leaders from all over the world. As it turned out, the vast majority were left-wingers. Shelly and I were annoyed by the steady stream of similarly inclined speakers and put up a fuss to invite another voice, e.g., Rabbi Kahane.
>
> Grudgingly, the organizers okayed it as long as Shelly and I would handle all the nitty-gritty details. We were a little crazy, and actually hitched a free ride to Jerusalem on a Rakah Communist Arab bus heading for a demonstration for Biram and Ikrit at the Knesset.*
>
> We found your husband in town, and joined him in a rental car for the shlepp up to Haifa as dusk settled in. He was driving around the outer service

---

* Biram and Ikrit were villages on the Lebanese border in which Arabs wished to resettle. The demonstration took place on August 23, 1972. See text below.

road of Hebrew University [Mount Scopus campus] which was under construction at that time. A large exposed manhole loomed ahead and we suddenly roared over it with a jangle. (I still think of that whenever I pass by that road and the now paved-over cover.) We only made it another 20 minutes or so farther north, into Ramallah, when the car started emitting strange noises and eventually smoke.

It was before the Intifada, but IDF presence was light and it was obviously a hostile environment. Rabbi Kahane was adamant: Despite the smoke (and eventually some licks of flame), he absolutely refused to abandon the car. He felt he had a responsibility to the rental company. So we searched back and forth for a parking spot and finally found one. We went to a little Arab kiosk and joshed with the owners, bought some soft drinks and made a call. Eventually, Shelly and I somehow caught a bus back to Haifa, and the Rabbi stuck around with the car till the rental company sent a tow truck.

Charley concluded sadly:

We never managed to have that speech before our group.[20]

Nakam: Reacting to a New Wave of Soviet Persecution

Never for one moment did Meir forget the Jews in Russia. The Soviets had embarked on a new wave of persecution against Russian Jews who applied for visas to Israel. One was *refusenik* Vladimir Markman, who had just been sentenced to three years of hard labor in Sverdlovsk on charges of "hooliganism" and "engaging in anti-Soviet propaganda."[21]

Meir planned a protest at the Finnish Embassy in Tel Aviv. (Ever since the Soviet Union had broken off diplomatic relations with Israel after the Six Day War in 1967, Finland had represented Soviet interests in Israel.) On August 9, about twenty members of the Liga – JDL's nickname in Hebrew (*Haliga Lehagana Yehudit* was a mouthful) – sat-in at the Finnish Embassy in Tel Aviv. They occupied the embassy offices, hung the Israeli flag from the embassy's balcony and displayed slogans such as "Let My People Go" and "Russians to Russia; Jews to Israel." The protesters refused to leave and had to be forcibly removed by the police. Two weeks later, twelve Liga members held a ten-day hunger strike near the Red Cross offices in Tel Aviv, demanding that the Red Cross act on behalf of oppressed Soviet Jews.[22]

The Soviets had recently found a novel way to prevent Jews from emigrating. They levied an "exit tax" that was equal to the cost of the free higher education the Jew had received. The exit tax (or "diploma tax") ranged from $5,000 to as much as $30,000. One *refusenik* told the newsmen that the exit tax would doom thousands of Jews to years of waiting as "unsold slaves" until ransom money

could be raised abroad. Paulina Korenblit, wife of Russian Jewish prisoner
Mikhail Korenblit, said that a good engineer earns 200 rubles ($243) monthly at
most and "families would have to literally go without food for years to accumulate the money to pay for the exit visas."[23]

On August 16 Meir was one of the speakers at a joint rally in Tel Aviv protesting the exit tax.[24] In America, Establishment Jewish groups joined the cry
against the "extortionate ransom tax." They called on Nixon to deny trade concessions to the Soviet Union until exit taxes were cancelled.[25] Meir wrote:

> World Jewry has mounted an enormous campaign to arouse world opinion and
> one is struck by how far, under the original prodding of militants, we have
> come from our former state of apathy and fear of "noise-making."
>
> ... The ransom is not the end but only the beginning.... The Russians are
> now waiting to see the full extent of world and Jewish reaction.... It is time for
> Jews to begin thinking along the lines of a direct assault on American-Soviet
> détente.[26]

Following his own recommendation to threaten American-Soviet relations,
Meir tried a new tactic. He called a press conference in Jerusalem on August 21
and announced that he "had heard a rumor" that Jewish Defense League members
in the United States were planning to kidnap Soviet diplomats. They would go
ahead with this plan if the USSR would not abandon, within one month, its policy
of levying taxes on Jewish intellectuals going to Israel, he said.

At the press conference, Meir read from a letter he had written to Secretary
of State William Rogers to let him know of the danger:

> I need not tell you what an assault upon a Soviet diplomat in the United States
> would do, nor how relatively simple such an act is.... The best prevention is
> obviously quiet and firm action by the U.S. to persuade the Soviet Union to
> change its policy.
>
> Let us join together in preventing any insane acts of fanaticism that could,
> in an instant, wreck all that you, the President and Mr. Kissinger have worked
> so long to achieve.[27]

Meir's avowed concern for better U.S.-Soviet relations was clearly ironic, but
his warning was taken seriously. The FBI immediately issued a directive to their
field offices:

> In view of subject's published statements that JDL would kidnap and hold for
> ransom Soviet diplomats, it is imperative that this matter be afforded preferred
> supervisory and investigative attention.
>
> Subject is scheduled to return to U.S. from Israel mid-October.... New York,
> as office of origin, remain aware of Kahane's location on day-to-day basis upon
> his return to United States and set out leads for similar coverage to offices in
> whose territories he is scheduled to make future appearances.[28]

On August 25, a Liga member phoned the U.S. Embassy in Tel Aviv and said that Meir wanted to meet with the ambassador on August 28 at 3 P.M. (Meir was planning to be in Tel Aviv that day for a wedding.)[29] The caller was told the ambassador was out of the country, but Meir could be received at that time by an "appropriate" officer. An FBI memo issued the next day reported on the meeting. Meir was received by Munro P. James, the embassy's administrative officer, and Edward S. Walker, a political officer. He explained to them that "some Jews feared that the exit tax was the prelude to show trials and the restoration of Stalinist persecution of Jews." Since in the past, he said, "the Soviets had responded to international pressure when it was in their interest to do so, he hoped the U.S. government would take action to convince the Soviet Union that it was in their interest to let Soviet Jews emigrate freely."

Meir told the embassy officers that he had been misquoted when it was reported that he called for the kidnapping of Soviet diplomats. He had only warned that there were some Jews who might do so. He said that someone had come to him the previous week and informed him that there was an underground Jewish group in the U.S. called Nakam [Hebrew for vengeance], which would kidnap a Soviet diplomat within two weeks. He had never heard of this group and he did not know the man who came to him and could not contact him. The man spoke good Hebrew but did not appear Israeli or American. "Kahane declined to describe him," the report continued, "and said, 'I hope he does not do it and if he does, I hope he does not get caught.' Kahane said he did not think the man was a crackpot or a crank."

Afterwards, at a previously scheduled press conference, Meir told reporters what he had told the embassy officers, and the next day the media carried reports on the kidnap threat of the mysterious Nakam organization. In an interview with reporter Bill Branigan broadcast the same day on ABC-TV, which was excerpted on Israel TV, Meir explained how interfering with the Soviet Union's desire for détente would help Jews. It is clear that Nakam was invented by Meir to draw public attention to the plight of Soviet Jews. Nevertheless, the FBI took precautions: A cable marked "urgent" instructed FBI offices throughout the United States to notify the Secret Service and law enforcement authorities of the threat that Soviet diplomats would be kidnapped within the next two weeks.

In a cable to the American Embassy in Tel Aviv, the FBI instructed the Legat (Legal Attaché, the title of FBI special agents abroad) to interview Meir "penetratively," without disclosing his status as an agent. The directive added, "Legats frequently conduct such interviews in the Embassy, since this is U.S. soil."[30]

On September 5, a hand-delivered letter from the U.S. Embassy arrived at our home in Jerusalem.

I would appreciate it if you have the opportunity to come to the embassy in the near future to further discuss matters which you raised during our meeting August 28.

Please give the bearer of this letter a time and date for a meeting or telephone me at the embassy, Tel Aviv, (03) 56171, ext. 265.

[signed] Edward S. Walker, Jr.

Second Secretary of Embassy[31]

A meeting was set for September 11, at 3:30 P.M., and a demonstration to protest the exit tax was scheduled outside the embassy for the same time. Before entering the embassy, Meir spoke to the demonstrators through a bullhorn, urging them to continue to act against the punitive tax. As some 50 demonstrators marched outside carrying placards, some in Russian, calling for an end to the tax, Meir entered the embassy.[32]

Inside, Meir was interviewed (in Walker's presence) by two men introduced only as "officials of the U.S. government." The FBI report stated:

> Although subject was penetratively interviewed for one hour, subject maintained that he did not know the identity of the individual who advised him of the organization Nakam and refused to further identify him even to the extent of bluntly refusing to answer questions with regard to the unidentified individual's physical description.

Regarding other members of Nakam, Meir said, "I don't know who they are and if I did I wouldn't tell you." He told them that the ultimate objective of Nakam was to secure the freedom of Soviet Jewry by threatening détente. The report continues:

> Although at no time did Legat and Assistant Legat indicate they were Bureau agents, subject, at close of interview, stated he heard about a year ago of two FBI agents being present in Israel. He smiled, made no further comment, and no comment was volunteered on part of Legat and Assistant Legat or Walker.[33]

This was Meir's third direct interview with the FBI.[34] He was fully aware that his every deed was observed by the Bureau, but he continued to act according to his conscience.

Biram and Ikrit

The idea that the Land of Israel was designated by G-d as the Jewish home was an axiom that Meir taught by various means. At times he "reacted" to current issues to get the idea across, and at other times he was "proactive." That summer, he had an opportunity to use both methods.

A controversy currently in the news in Israel concerned Christian Arabs who had been expelled from their villages, Biram and Ikrit, near the Lebanese border, during the 1948 War of Independence. They had been compensated with other lands within Israel, but wanted to return to Biram and Ikrit. However, the Israeli government maintained that Israel's security did "not yet allow re-establishment of Arab villages near the border." Archbishop Joseph Raya, their principal spokesman, was to lead them in a mass demonstration in Jerusalem on August 23. He planned to carry a large wooden cross on his back down the Via Dolorosa to arouse support from Christians all over the world. Israeli leftists, who sided with Raya, had succeeded in arousing doubts and misgivings among many moderate Israelis. Meir wrote:

> A campaign was mounted against Golda Meir, the army and the government portraying them as coldly calculating, heartless, racist and imperialistic creatures.... Archbishop Raya announced he was planning to carry a cross on his back from the Old City's Via Dolorosa and from there throughout the world.... The Archbishop's meaning was clear. The Jews were at it again. Yet another crucifixion.[35]

On August 15, at a question-and-answer evening at the Beit Haam auditorium in Jerusalem, Meir announced that the Liga would hold a counterdemonstration against Archbishop Raya the following Wednesday. He told the audience that Raya had written a slanderous report on the condition of the Christians in Israel – most of whom were Arabs – accusing the Israeli government of oppressing Christians. Meir said the Liga demonstration would not be violent: It would attempt to counter Raya's propaganda by distributing flyers detailing the cruel treatment of Jews by Christians during the past thousand years. The *New York Times*, reporting on the march of "about 3,000 Arabs and Jews" from the Old City across downtown Jerusalem to the office of prime minister Golda Meir, noted the presence of Meir and "a handful" of his followers. The report summarized Meir's speech to a crowd at Jaffa Gate: Israel had the right to preserve its security against neighbors with whom she remained at war and who threatened to eradicate her.[36]

Several months later, Meir had the opportunity for a direct debate with Archbishop Raya at Kibbutz Amir in the Upper Galilee. There, Meir contended that the government was correct in not allowing the villagers to return to Biram and Ikrit because "the younger generation of Arabs is not loyal to the State of Israel."[37]

The Right to Return to Hebron

At the same time, Meir embarked on a campaign for the right of Jews to return to Hebron, which was historically Jewish. Over 3,000 years ago it was King David's capital. Only recently, in 1929, Jews abandoned Hebron's old Jewish quarter after a bloody riot in which Arabs massacred sixty-seven Jews and wounded many others. Arabs now occupied the homes of the eight hundred Jews who had lived there. After the 1967 Six Day War, when Israel recaptured Hebron, a group of Jews went to settle there. They were housed in the Israeli military compound until 1971, when a new Jewish town bordering on Hebron, Kiryat Arba, was built.[38] But Jews were not permitted to live in Hebron itself. Meir believed Jews should have the elementary right to return to the Jewish homes in Hebron and live there.

Meir's first step was to send a telegram to the mayor of Hebron, Sheikh Mohammed Ali Ja'abari. He informed Ja'abari that he and his followers would arrive in Hebron on Sunday morning, August 27, to begin arrangements for the return of Jews to their homes and for the return of their property. Of course, he also sent copies of the telegram to the media.

Mayor Ja'abari, who claimed to support co-existence between Arabs and Jews, appealed to the Israeli government to prevent Meir's arrival, declaring that he would not be able to prevent violent demonstrations by the Arabs of Hebron. To avoid Arab unrest, minister of defense Moshe Dayan issued an order keeping Meir and his followers out of Hebron. However, they succeeded in circumventing the army's roadblocks. Some went by car early in the morning, when the main roadblock on the southern outskirts of Bethlehem was manned by only one soldier. Others went by Arab buses and taxis, and some spent Shabbat in Hebron. Meir drove through the roadblock by pretending to be an American tourist. He donned sunglasses and a baseball hat, and when he was stopped, he asked in English, "Is this the way to Beersheba?" The soldier waved him through.

David Fisch recalled:

> Meir had three of us, including me, dress as American tourists – floppy rainbow hats, dangling cameras, Bermuda shorts, really ridiculous stuff – and take a ride to Hebron on an Arab bus line. We did. We got into the city, really close to Ja'abari's house (i.e., just short of the front door), and handed a letter to the guy guarding the door. I don't know what was in the envelope, but it got the guy really frenzied. There were a million soldiers, and they seized us and put us on a bus out of Hebron.[39]

The letter that was presented to Ja'abari was in English. It said:

> To the Honorable Sheikh Ja'abari, Mayor of Hebron, City of the Patriarchs:
> We are here to discuss repatriation of the former Jewish residents to the Jewish city of Hebron, whose Jewishness dates back to Abraham our father.
> We are also interested in receiving your reply to the ugly rumors concerning your participation in the Hebron riots of 1929, in which scores of Jews were massacred, as well as the part you played in the slaughter at Gush Etzion [the Etzion Bloc] in 1948.
> [signed] Yitzhak Ben Avraham
> Hebron Chapter Chairman.[40]

About 60 Liga members assembled in the plaza outside the Cave of the Patriarchs. A photo in *Yedioth Ahronoth* shows Meir with Yosef Schneider and other supporters, singing and clapping hands. In a *Ma'ariv* photo, Meir stands with several supporters at the top of a hill, the houses of Hebron spread out below them.

Reporters who came to cover the story asked Meir if Liga members could live together with the Arabs of Hebron. Meir promptly replied, "What a question! The Arabs couldn't wish for better neighbors!"

Referring to the historic Jewish quarter of Hebron, Meir told the reporters: "There's a Jewish quarter here, but no Jews yet. Ask the leftists who think the Arabs should return to Biram and Ikrit why they aren't demanding the return of the Jews to Hebron!"

Army officers approached Meir quietly and invited him for a talk in the nearby Settlers' Restaurant. There he received orders to leave Hebron with his followers.[41]

Back in Jerusalem he held a press conference.[42] He maintained that expelling him from Hebron was a violation of his civil rights. He announced that he would apply for a court order that very day to allow his group into the Jewish quarter of Hebron. Attorney Meir Schechter immediately applied to the High Court of Justice for an order *nisi* calling on the defense minister to show cause why Meir should not be allowed to "tour" the old Jewish quarter of Hebron.

Justice Moshe Etzioni's decision, given the next day, denied Meir's request.[43] But Meir had succeeded in making the Hebron issue an important news story. His demand for the return of Jews to Hebron and the restoration of their property was carried by all the Israeli media. *Ma'ariv* carried this insightful commentary by Yizhar Arnon:

> The Hebron massacre took place when I was a child. I have vague memories of postcards with the pictures of the victims, but in later years there were no reminders of the massacre. In grade school and in high school there was no mention of it, and in the course of the years it was forgotten by most of the population.
>
> When Hebron was liberated in the Six Day War I thought to myself, "Now the victims of the massacre will see justice done." But after 43 years they were forgotten, and there were even many who were opposed to "stealing" Hebron from the Arabs. Rabbi Meir Kahane has done us a favor by reminding us that Hebron is not only an Arab city, it is first a Jewish city.
>
> ... Try as I can, I cannot think of when anyone, in the past 40 years, or even the past 20 years, has raised the subject of the Jews who were massacred in Hebron. It is not enough to write about them in the weekend newspaper, when

the reader is drinking a cup of tea and nodding off. Rabbi Kahane is to be praised for putting the massacre at the top of the news.[44]

Meir's campaign in Hebron made waves. A letter to the editor in *Ma'ariv* asked, "Why can't Mayor Ja'abari be interviewed about his past? Why can Mayor Kollek be interviewed but not Mayor Ja'abari?" To Jewish visitors, Sheikh Ja'abari made a point of denying all involvement in the 1929 massacre of Jews.[45]

Meir continued his campaign for a Jewish Hebron. He called a prayer meeting for 10 A.M. on the eve of Yom Kippur, September 17, in Hebron, calling on the public to join him in prayers for the return of the refugees to Hebron. In mid-September, flyers asked witnesses to come forward to testify at a public trial against Ja'abari to be held September 28 at Beit Agron in Jerusalem. The flyer featured a 1948 photo of the sheikh reviewing a line of soldiers of the Arab Legion. In order to seek out witnesses for the trial, Avraham Hershkowitz and others went to Hebron, where they were detained by soldiers.[46]

On September 22, in an unusual step, the government issued an injunction ordering Meir and 19 other members of the Liga to stay out of Judea, Samaria and Gaza. The purpose of the order was to prevent them from carrying out "any activities liable to disrupt order or endanger security in those areas."[47] The Ja'abari trial was "postponed," because the Association of Journalists, whose headquarters was Beit Agron, refused to rent the hall to the Liga, but Meir had made his point.

> I say that Hebron is not the real issue, but rather the right of Jews to create a *Jewish* state in THEIR Eretz Yisrael is the real issue. The Arab has NO RIGHT to Haifa and Jews DO have right to Hebron because it is part of Eretz Yisrael.[48]

Chapter 31

Counterterror
(September-October 1972)

Pressure on Israel to Cede Lands

THE HEBRON OFFENSIVE was an indication that Meir was concentrating more and more on issues in Israel. The question of retreating from the areas won in the 1967 Six Day War was a vital issue. He perceived that Israeli public opinion and the Israeli government were being manipulated to succumb to international pressure to give up the liberated lands.

A Hebrew translation of his article, "No Illusions, Please," urging Israelis to stand up against international pressure, was printed in September in *Yedioth Ahronoth*. Still true today, it said in part:

> Time is always on the side of the tenacious; conversely it is the enemy of the weary. The constant and never-ending struggle tends to erode the determination to achieve total victory and pushes tired men into the search for solutions and compromises that are often more the product of the desire to rest than that of common sense.
>
> ... It is precisely such a thing that is occurring today in the Land of Israel. Perhaps it is common to all peoples; perhaps it is more so with us Jews, the inability to withstand victory.
>
> ... Forgotten are the pledges to throw us into the sea, wash Tel Aviv clean with Jewish blood and eliminate the gangster-state of Israel.... What were the demands in THOSE days when there were no June 5, 1967, borders to which to return? If all the Arabs seek now is our retreat to the borders of those days, what were the Arabs marching to war about THEN? Forgotten is the reality of Arab refusal to recognize a State of Israel that is even one dunam square. Forgotten is the never-changing reality of "Hebronism."
>
> ... What is "Hebronism"? It is the Arab policy of extermination of the Jew who seeks to live in his own land. It is the reality of that summer day of 1929

that saw men, women and children slaughtered in the streets, homes and shops of Jewish Hebron.

... We are inundated with all kinds of illusions and delusions. Let us return this land or that land and we will have blessed peace. Let us not dare to settle Jews in the Land of Israel lest it anger the Arabs and jeopardize blessed peace. Let us make partial and semi-partial and total and semi-total agreements that call for compromise and we shall have blessed peace.... Let us not dare to bomb terrorists lest we hit innocent civilians; let us be "better than they are" – thus gain blessed peace.

... What is there within us that makes us misunderstand and underestimate the Arab? ... What Jew does not, after all these years, recognize that the Arab is a proud nationalist, incapable of compromising on that which he considers to be his land, and who mistakes every Jewish kindness for weakness to be exploited?

What kind of Jew? I will tell you. A Jew who lacks Jewish pride himself and so cannot understand the Arab kind.

... If we hope to survive in the literal sense of the word, let us not succumb to the siren call of easy answers and the tempting promise of "peace." Above all, let us, please, have no illusions! The Arabs intend to wipe us out; we must be strong enough to stop them.[1]

Proof of the Arabs' intentions had been given only the week before. On September 5, Arab terrorists murdered eleven Israeli athletes at the Olympic games in Munich. Meir felt deeply the humiliation of Jews being held hostage and killed in cold blood. In New York, JDLers demonstrated at the U.N. missions of the Arab countries that "harbor, train and finance" the P.L.O. terrorists. Five Jews were arrested after throwing a bottle of black paint at the building of the Iraqi Mission to the U.N.[2]

The Only Solution to Terror

But demonstrations against Arab terror were not enough. Meir believed that only counterterror could succeed in stopping terror. He wrote:

Let us not underestimate the importance of the psychology of combatants in this deadly war of terror. The terrorists' "exploits," despite the fact that they were soaked in innocent blood, are nevertheless psychological victories that raise up from the dust the victory-poor Arabs. They also remind the world, long after it has gotten over the shock of the Munich victims, of the topic "Palestine."

... And together with this, there is the problem of the nations of the world who also suffer because of "those Israelis." In Paris, the Masons receive a threat after they send a message of condolence to the Israeli branch.... A German weekly retracts an article unfavorable to the terrorists, again after threats.

Air travelers throughout the world are forced to undergo lengthy searches that delay flight schedules and infuriate the passengers with the usual result – they direct their anger at the root of the whole mess: the Israelis.

... It is imperative to eliminate – immediately and permanently – the terror plague.... It is obvious that the conventional methods of attack such as a sweeping operation for two days in Lebanon or air attacks on the terrorist bases do not begin to solve the problem and that we must arrive at the decision to use unlimited counterterror; to strike directly at Arab leaders and to bring terror into the streets of Cairo, Damascus and Tripoli. Only this will bring an end to the criminal Arab attacks.

... And as for the argument that the State [of Israel] dare not be dragged into the sensitive matter of terror lest that effect on world public opinion be negative ... I suggest a number of replies that Israel might take to her critics:

1) Just as the Arab states openly support the terrorist with money, training, guidance, false papers, materials, bases and sanctuaries – so do we support our own "unofficial" terrorists...

And if this is, perhaps, too strong a reply for the "moralists," I suggest the following one:

2) We, the State of Israel, solemnly and categorically condemn all actions by Jewish counterterrorists. We understand, however, the root causes of their actions – frustration and bitterness – and so long as the Arabs continue their activities we will be unable to put a stop to them.

... The time is not too late to set up such a group.... "Thou shalt not stand idly by thy brother's blood."[3]

A Crate of Weapons

Meir's appointment book shows that he met on September 11 with Amichai (Giddy) Paglin, a key strategist in the pre-state Jewish underground. Subsequent newspaper reports indicate the significance of the meeting: On September 14, a crate packed at a factory owned by Paglin was opened by authorities at Lod airport. Addressed to a European capital, it contained weapons allegedly intended for use against terrorists in Europe. Avraham Hershkowitz, who delivered the crate to the airport, was arrested. Amichai Paglin was questioned by the police, and on September 19, the day after Yom Kippur, Paglin, too, was arrested.[4]

As soon as he heard of Paglin's arrest, Meir called a press conference in Tel Aviv for that afternoon. He declared that Avraham Hershkowitz, the Liga employee who had been arrested, did not know what was in the crate he was told to deliver to the airport. Then, Meir openly and candidly disclosed the plan to ship arms abroad to enable Jews overseas to fight terrorists. Meir called on Jews around the world to "help in setting up a counterterror organization that would teach the Arabs that Jewish blood could not be shed freely." An employee of the

Israel Embassy in London had been killed by a bomb that very day! "[This] will not be the last drop of Jewish blood spilled by those psychopathic killers," Meir said and added, "They are capable of throwing a bomb into a synagogue in Los Angeles or Hong Kong."[5] His firmly stated point of view that terror must be fought with terror catapulted Meir into the center of the controversy over how Israel should cope with the rising tide of Arab terrorism.

The Liga distributed a Hebrew flyer calling openly for counterterror, proudly admitting that it was the Liga that sent the crate of arms to attack Arab embassies and offices in the United States and Europe. The flyer proclaimed: "Jewish blood is not cheap."[6]

This could not go unnoticed by the police. Meir was told to come in for questioning on September 21, but before reporting to the police station, he held a press conference to fully explain his stand. Never before had the Liga broken the law, he said, and now it was only because there simply was no other way to fight terror except by counterterror. The government's policy in dealing with Arab terror overseas was misguided. Its hands were tied by its fear of what the nations of the world would say. This was bad, because the government was endangering not only Israelis, but Jews all over the world. The government should rightfully turn a blind eye to the Liga's acts, because only a non-governmental group can use counterterror, and it is difficult to procure arms overseas. He told the reporters that the previous day police had come to the Jewish Identity Center with a search warrant and had confiscated most of the documents there.[7]

Now, almost daily, there were news reports of Liga members being detained for questioning about the arms shipment and more reports when, one by one, they were released. Yosef Schneider, Liga administrative director, was arrested on suspicion of delivering the crate to the airport with Hershkowitz but was soon freed. There was also extensive media coverage of the investigation of Paglin, a prominent figure, of whom Meir later wrote, "The fact that Paglin, a quiet factory owner for 25 years, agreed to help JDL attests both to his appreciation of the group's purpose and his fear of Arab acts in the future."[8]

On September 22 a concerted government offensive was launched against Meir. The minister of police, Shlomo Hillel, declared in a radio interview that antiterrorist underground activities directed from Israel would not be tolerated. He recommended that the government consider outlawing the Liga. "This is not Brooklyn; we will not import foreign ways," he said. Deputy prime minister Yigal Allon, in a TV interview that evening, echoed Hillel's sentiments.

A few days later, a vitriolic attack on Meir and the Liga was published by Amos Shapiro in *Ha'aretz*. Shapiro called Meir a fascist, an epithet derived from the brutal Fascist party that ruled Italy from 1922 to 1943. Meir was certainly not a fascist. It was simply an epithet used to besmirch political opponents. Shapiro, echoing Shlomo Hillel, demanded that the Liga be declared illegal. A reply to Shapiro by attorney Aharon Papo said that what troubled Shapiro was not any "danger" posed by the Liga, but rather the Liga's ideology, which was diametrically opposed to Shapiro's. "It is no coincidence," wrote Papo, "that those who attack the Liga are those who want to give rights to the Arabs that will destroy the State of Israel."[9]

Since the maximum term for illegal possession of arms was seven years in prison, Meir tried to work out an agreement with the government. On September 24 Meir requested a meeting with the minister of justice, Yaakov Shimshon Shapira, and suggested a deal: Drop all charges, particularly against Hershkowitz and Paglin, in exchange for a full disclosure of all details. Paglin, who was not cooperating with the police investigation, was opposed to the deal, and so was the government.[10]

The government's next step was to blacken the name of the Liga. Media reports said that phone calls were received by *Ha'aretz, Davar, Al Hamishmar* and the Polish-language *Nowiny Kurier* newspapers, threatening, "Your people are in danger if you go on publishing articles against the Liga." Terming these reports "provocation" and a "transparent effort to defame me," Meir said sarcastically to reporter Shabtai Portnoy, "I might be a fascist, but I'm not stupid!" The next day *Ma'ariv* told of another attack on Meir: Yehiel Leket, head of the Young Leadership faction of the Labor Party, declared that Meir, who had admitted to being a fascist, must be vigorously fought.[11]

Meir was worried. Political leaders, the police, and the media were against him, and he could be arrested at any time. Perhaps by forming a political party he could fight back, but this was not an easy decision. Meir had repeatedly stated that he had no intention of entering Israeli politics.

In January, when a reporter suggested that Meir run for the Knesset, he had said: "Never! It would destroy the League. Now we do things because they're right, but if you are a party you have to worry about votes and then you don't follow your conscience because you are afraid of losing votes."[12] As recently as August 30, he had replied to a letter from the well-known Nazi-hunter Tuvia Friedman:

> In reply to your letter of July 25, I thank you for your suggestion, but I have no intention, as I have publicly announced, of political activity or of running for the Knesset.[13]

Now, however, the Liga secretariat decided that the best way to fight the leftists who were trying to destroy the Liga was to form a political party and run for the Knesset.

The Liga Becomes a Political Party

To formally announce the Liga's political aspirations, Meir called a press conference on September 27 in Tel Aviv at Beit Sokolov, the headquarters of the Journalists Association. Yoel Lerner and Yosef Schneider, members of the Liga secretariat, spoke first. Lerner read from a prepared press release in Hebrew and English that stated that the Liga had at first believed that its goals could best be accomplished by remaining apolitical, but recent events had shown otherwise. Meir told the reporters that the government's campaign against the Liga had begun with orders forbidding its members to enter Judea, Samaria and Gaza, and had been followed by the minister of police talking of outlawing the Liga and by hostile articles in newspapers. There were even attempts to frame the Liga for bomb threats against newspapers, while in fact there were phone threats to bomb Liga headquarters.

In reply to reporters' questions, Meir said he believed he had enough public support to elect several Knesset members. He would attract voters who were "frustrated by the absence of a fighting opposition for the past ten years or more." He declared that in the future, the Liga's counterterror activity would not be based in Israel. He strenuously denied the existence of an underground. Pointing to the members of the secretariat sitting at the dais, he exclaimed, "What underground! All our names and addresses are public knowledge!"[14] Lerner recalled that the hall was crammed with newsmen and TV cameras from all over the world. Meir's parents were there, too, and Lerner thinks this was when Meir's father coined the phrase "Mama Liga"* for Meir's mother.[15]

All this took place during *chol hamo'ed*, the intermediate days of Sukkot, when observant Jews do not shave. The pictures that accompanied reports of Meir's Knesset announcement showed him with the stubble of a beard – not a very flattering image – and that is also how he appeared that evening on Israel TV. Looking thinner than usual, but quite self-confident, Meir told interviewer Menashe Raz that he had applied for Israeli citizenship and he expected it to be granted automatically. He was entering politics, he said, because he feared that without a Knesset seat, the Liga would cease to exist.[16]

Now, the opposition to Meir became more intense. Newspapers reported that police had searched the homes of Liga members in the Tel Aviv area. Left-wing Knesset Member Shalom Cohen demanded an urgent Knesset debate on the Liga's illegal activities. Another left-wing Knesset Member, Uri Avneri, opposed granting Meir Israeli citizenship. When Meir first came to Israel, he had applied for temporary resident status rather than for new immigrant status (which auto-

---

* Mamaliga is a cornmeal dish popular among Eastern European Jews. It is also a popular food in Italy, where it is called polenta.

matically grants Israeli citizenship), because he was planning to travel to America every other month. Since Knesset candidacy required Israeli citizenship, he now applied for new immigrant status. He expected to be granted citizenship shortly, because the rule was that citizenship was automatically granted within three months of the application. Now, Avneri demanded that Yosef Burg, minister of the interior, deny Israeli citizenship to Meir.[17]

In addition, there were demands that the police get to the bottom of the "arms smuggling," and Paglin's lawyer asked why his client had been arrested while Meir, who had admitted publicly to the plot, was still free. A cynical reply to this question was given by one of *Ma'ariv*'s senior reporters, Shmuel Shnitzer. He wrote that the police knew full well that Meir could not possibly have anything to do with an underground. It was simply against his nature to be secretive. "Without press conferences and media interviews he could not exist," said Shnitzer. "The whole incident has been blown up out of proportion." Paglin's lawyer, Shmuel Tamir, thought so too: "Everyone knows there is no underground. I'm sure our Intelligence Branch knows everything going on in the Liga."[18]

Police officer Rav Pakad (Major) Moshe Katz simply told reporters, "We cannot arrest Rabbi Kahane because we have no proof of his direct involvement, although we suspect that he may have given moral support to the others. If we had proof, we would arrest him immediately."[19]

Meir's Knesset candidacy aroused media interest. *Yedioth Ahronoth* published an editorial by Dr. Herzl Rosenblum, opining that Meir had an excellent chance to be elected. A few days later, Rosenblum wrote about the Kremlin's campaign against Zionism. Their claim that Meir Kahane was "Zionist number one" was a move, he editorialized, which would surely give Meir more votes.[20]

"The rabbi has become a celebrated figure here in recent weeks," wrote a *New York Times* correspondent who interviewed Meir on September 29. Referring to the media tumult around the Hebron visit and the arms shipment, Meir told him: "We've gotten a million dollars worth of publicity from this thing. The government has made a big mistake by going after us this way. It has made us seem like a big, important organization, which we are not – yet."[21]

Meir told *Ha'aretz* reporter Mati Golan that he had decided to run for the Knesset because he had come to the realization that a vision cannot be implemented without strength, and strength depends on political power. "I think," he said, "we can bring a new spirit to the political picture and change things." He criticized public apathy, which might allow the Mapai party to remain in power "for another hundred years."* Had he considered joining the Herut party? asked

---

* The Mapai party, later the Labor party, in coalition with other parties, had been running the government since the State was established in 1948.

Golan. "No!" said Meir, "I'm very disappointed by them. Herut is to be blamed for the absence of a strong opposition party here."

Meir told Golan that the arms shipment affair had succeeded in arousing public demand for a new approach to fighting terror. Golan asked, "When you claimed responsibility for the shipment, you said you had been mistaken. What was the mistake?"

Meir replied, "We thought the government would realize the importance of an organization that could act against Arab terror outside Israel. We hoped they would agree to train our people overseas, or at least, that the authorities would look away. This is a Jewish problem, not just an Israeli problem. If the government does not adopt our plan, a Jew in Los Angeles could be murdered. The minister of police accuses me of irresponsibility, but I say it is the government that is irresponsible. It should set up a secret organization in all the world capitals where terrorists have acted.... When Arab countries see that their embassies and offices are objects of counterterror, they will stop allowing terrorists to train in their countries.... Our mistake was in thinking there were smart people in the government who would understand the need for our actions and look away."

"What will you do now?" asked Golan, and Meir replied, "I'm waiting for them to come to arrest me. It's clear that they will."

"I get the impression you want to be arrested," said Golan.

Meir replied, "Your impression is wrong. Look, I have to leave the country on Sunday, I have important things to do in New York. You were probably never in prison. It's not pleasant. It's a waste of time. But if they arrest me, it will only help me. I'll only profit from it. But I'd rather not have that profit!"[22]

Two days later, on Sunday morning, October 1, at 7:30 A.M., four policemen came to our home and took Meir to a detention center south of Tel Aviv for "questioning." There was speculation that his arrest was prompted by his publicly announced plans to fly to America for a two-month trip, since there was no logical reason to arrest Meir now, three weeks after he had disclosed the facts surrounding the arms shipment. In fact, the police did not specify the charges against Meir at any time. In those years, Israeli law provided for 48 hours of administrative detention before formal charges were required, and this period could be extended by court order.[23] I wasn't certain when I would see Meir next.

It was Yosef Schneider's turn to be arrested after Meir. On October 2 he was ordered jailed for eight days for allegedly organizing the smuggling attempt. A newspaper report that day had disturbing news: In a search of the Liga office, the police had taken lists of members' addresses as well as the file of incoming mail.[24] This was bound to discourage people from joining the Liga or even from writing letters of encouragement. No one wanted his name connected with an "illegal" group!

Police efforts to interrogate Meir in jail were futile. *Ha'aretz* reported that he refused to cooperate. During questioning, he perused a page of Talmud and suggested the investigators study it with him. A brief item on page one of *Ma'ariv,* confirming that Meir was studying Talmud instead of answering investigators' questions, said that he would probably be brought before a judge that afternoon.[25] But next to that brief item was a larger one, headed "I Worked for the FBI."

With uncanny timing, a six-page article about Meir and the JDL had just appeared in America in *Playboy* magazine. "I Worked for the FBI," with excerpts from the *Playboy* article, filled most of *Ma'ariv*'s front page on October 2. The next day, excerpts also appeared in *Ha'aretz* and *Davar.* [26] Although *Playboy* was known for its risqué pictures, its essays and literary selections were considered superior. Meir explained why he gave an interview to such a magazine: "*Playboy* has five million readers, many of them Jewish. At least once in their lives they ought to hear things that are different from what the Establishment rabbis say."[27]

The *Playboy* article, a well-researched, wide-ranging exposition, was written by Walter Goodman, whose study of Meir and the JDL had appeared in the *New York Times* the previous November. Again, Goodman gave Meir the opportunity to expound on JDL ideology. One thing Meir said to Goodman explains the intensity of his beliefs:

> We have a tremendous thing about love in this country [America]. Everybody has to love everybody. Well, I believe that there is a certain importance to hate. One has to hate injustice. You've got to burn it out of the human condition.[28]

In an Israeli Jail

From his cell in the lockup, Meir wrote a letter to prime minister Golda Meir. Handwritten in Hebrew, his four-page letter said the members of the Liga desired only to work for the good of Israel. "Why fight the Liga from within," he asked, "when both the Liga and the Government should concentrate on fighting the Arab enemy from without?"

His letter ended with the biblical verse that was the logo on the Liga's stationery: *Umi Ke'amkha Yisrael Goi Echad Ba'aretz* –"Who is like Your people Israel, one nation in the Land" (*II Samuel* 7:23). In a play on words, this verse can also be understood as "the only nation in the Land [of Israel]," stressing the exclusive Jewish right to the Holy Land.

Meir's letter to the prime minister was delivered to her on Tuesday morning, October 3, by attorney Meir Schechter, who told reporters that he hoped the letter would clear up any misunderstanding.[29] But it did not help. Later that day, Meir was brought before a judge. When the prosecutor told him that Meir still refused to cooperate with the investigators, the judge extended his detention to Friday,

October 6. Meir was permitted to speak with reporters before returning to the lockup. He was described as calm and smiling as he gave interviews to foreign and local newsmen.[30]

Despite Meir's detention, the Liga continued to hold anti-Soviet protests. The day of the court hearing, October 3, a demonstration against the exit tax was held at the American Embassy. An ad said: "We call on the Government of Israel and all the nations of the world to protest the exit tax, to protest the slave-trade." An agreement was pending to sell U.S. surplus wheat to Russia. It was wheat the Soviets needed badly. The United States had the power to pressure the Soviets into canceling the exit tax by threatening to withhold the wheat. "The U.S. must not sign the wheat deal!" proclaimed the ad. Demonstrators stood opposite the American Embassy holding placards in Hebrew and English calling for the abolition of the "head tax." One sign said, "Our Brothers in Russia Are the Slaves of the 20th Century." Another said, "We Won't Allow Another Holocaust."[31]

By Friday, October 6, Meir, Schneider, Hershkowitz, and Paglin were free on bail.[32] A memo from the New York office of the FBI to its "legal attache" at the American Embassy in Tel Aviv said, "Radio newscasts today in New York City report that Kahane was released on bail of ten thousand dollars equivalent [i.e. 40,000 Israeli lirot] and his passport taken to prevent his departure from Israel." The memo requested, "Furnish full particulars." It reminded the agent in Tel Aviv that a conviction in Israel on a weapons charge could be enough reason to find Meir guilty of violating the conditions of his 1971 probation. "Kahane's probation officer is interested in information which can be used to seek revocation of Kahane's probation."[33]

The United States government was marshalling forces against Meir, but after five days in jail he was undaunted. The *New York Times* reported:

> Rabbi Meir Kahane emerged from his first stay behind Israeli bars beaming. He said his treatment in jail was extraordinary. "I can't speak too highly of the police, their sympathy and their attitude," he said.[34]

Passport Confiscated

Meir told reporters that he was going to court on Sunday to regain his American passport, which had been confiscated by the police when he was arrested. He had speaking engagements scheduled in the United States, and he was ready to agree to any conditions to assure the court that he would return to Israel to stand trial.[35]

When Meir's request for his passport was denied by a lower court, attorney Meir Schechter submitted an appeal to the Tel Aviv District Court. Judge Elisha Sheinboim agreed to return the passport for one month for travel to Europe only, not to the United States. The judge reasoned that Meir's involvement in the arms shipment might be construed as a violation of the conditions of his probation, and he might be imprisoned in the United States and be unable to return to Israel to stand trial. To guarantee Meir's return to Israel, he ordered him to post a IL100,000 [$24,000] bond in cash and a IL50,000 [$12,000] lien on our apartment. Both sides were dissatisfied with this decision. Meir did not want to be limited to Europe and the prosecutor did not want to return the passport. The case went to the Supreme Court, and on October 15, the day before Meir's scheduled speaking engagement in San Francisco, Judge Haim Cohn decreed that because of the seriousness of the crime, Meir must remain in Israel until the end of the legal proceedings.[36]

The October 15 court decision to confine Meir to Israel meant that he would not be able to lead the Jewish Defense League in the United States in person. Nat Rosenwasser wrote: "The JDL cannot remain without a leader. It would be terrible without you. You must come back."[37]

During the first half of 1972 Meir had been in the U.S. twice, from February 15 to March 27 and from April 28 to June 22. JDL members had undertaken many activities in Meir's absence and they could continue to do so, guided by his *Jewish Press* writings and by letters from him. One Miami activist recalled, "We followed the ideas he advocated in the *Jewish Press*. He was the driving force without being there. We couldn't pick up a phone and call him to ask him what to do."[38]

The JDL gained members that year, both in the United States and other countries. In reaction to local anti-Semitism, groups started up in England, South Africa, Australia, and France.[39] Barbara and Chaim Ginsberg of New York's Nassau County joined because of the violence and crime in their area, with overt anti-Semitic incidents. Barbara wrote:

> My house was the place that was called when there was an anti-Semitic incident. Whenever I called the police, their answer was, "There aren't enough policeman to send out." But when I said, "Okay, JDL will go to that synagogue, yeshiva or house," it was funny – immediately they found enough policemen to go.[40]

Among the 1972 activities of JDL chapters throughout the United States were these:

- On January 26, after Jewish members of a New York City school board were threatened, JDLers came to a meeting of the school board. A violent fight broke out, in which JDLer Garth Kravat threw a piano at attackers.[41]

- In March, a member of the Washington, D.C., JDL chapter crashed a formal reception and poured blood over the head of a Soviet diplomat.[42]

- When a Soviet ship docked at Miami at the end of March, JDLers picketed on the pier while a seaplane they hired flew overhead carrying a large banner that read, "Exodus for Soviet Jews."[43]

- The Michigan chapter of JDL sponsored a "Crush American Nazism Day" on March 26, to bring attention to the startling rise of Nazism in America.[44]

- In April the Philadelphia chapter undertook a campaign to enlist the aid of the Quakers in their city on behalf of Jews in Arab countries, but were eventually rebuffed. Later that month led by Ed Ramov, they held a well-publicized demonstration at the headquarters of a Nazi group in their city.[45]

- The Atlantic City chapter announced that because of the high crime rate, JDL members would "walk the streets and escort elderly persons to and from supermarkets, synagogues, and other destinations."[46]

- In July, JDL responded to a plea from Jews in Brooklyn's Crown Heights section, who had been threatened with violence if they would take part in local community elections. The presence of the JDLers enabled Jews to vote, win seats and gain a voice in local affairs.[47]

- On August 2, two JDL youngsters bought tickets to a performance of the Ukrainian Dance Company at New York's Metropolitan Opera House. Fifteen minutes into the performance, they rushed up to the stage and threw bags of blood at the dancers. Other Soviet performances were disrupted in 1972 by members of JDL's New Jersey and Chicago chapters.[48]

- JDLers occupied President Nixon's re-election campaign office in Manhattan on October 18 and dumped boxes of Wheaties cereal on the floor to protest the recent sale of U.S. wheat to the USSR.[49]

- JDLers in Washington, D.C., using false invitations, gained admittance to a gala at the Soviet Embassy. White-haired chapter chairman William Perl chained himself to a heavy, four-foot candelabra, while the others shouted, "Get the Jews out of Russia," and tossed leaflets decrying the "Great Russian Wheat Steal."[50]

The Jewish Identity Center Offers Courses

When Meir found himself "grounded" in Israel in mid-October 1972, he concentrated his efforts on the Jewish Identity Center school. In August, he had held a press conference about the school, which was to open in October. Flyers and newspaper ads outlined the school's programs.[51]

For full time students, there would be yeshiva studies as well as general Jewish studies. Part-time students would have afternoon and evening classes in general Jewish studies, such as the history of Zionism, geography of Israel, Jewish philosophy, the Holocaust, and the revolt against the British. Shimon Rachamim arranged for Geula Cohen, a *Ma'ariv* columnist who had been a radio broadcaster for the pre-state underground, and Bezalel Landau, writer for the daily *Hamodia* and prolific author, to lecture on Jewish history and Zionist history.[52]

Meir invited visiting American students to take classes. A flyer distributed at locations where they congregated listed the courses: Halacha, Jewish beliefs, Jewish identity, Talmud, Mishnah, Jewish problems in our times. The classes, "conducted in an informal manner," would be held from Sunday to Thursday, 2:30 A.M. to 10:30 P.M.. The flyer pointed out:

> Many Jews come to Israel in order to discover just what it means to be a Jew. Our intention is to give you a positive meaningful Jewish identity.[53]

But enrollment was low and tuitions did not cover even basic costs. Unable to go to America to raise funds, Meir was forced to sell the lease on the Jewish Identity Center building back to the Zion Hotel management.[54]

Members of JDL's executive board in America were dismayed at the turn of events and began to quarrel among themselves. A few of them questioned Meir's use of the proceeds of the sale of the lease. In a letter of resignation to the board dated November 28, 1972, Meir wrote:

> More than four years ago I had a dream of an organization that would bring physical and spiritual redemption to the Jewish people. That dream, in order to succeed, required people of greatness. Step by step I made efforts to drag JDL people and other Jews to that greatness. When I demanded that we move from neighborhood patrols, alone, also to the fight for Soviet Jewry – there were people who complained that this was not our purpose. When we moved from there to aliya, there were those who said that THAT was not our purpose. When I tried to create a school for Jewish leaders who would be better than the little people with no vision who opposed it, that was also NOT our purpose.
>
> Four years of fighting with many people is a tiring amount of time. I am no Moses or Samuel who gave of themselves to their people and then were accused of stealing, personal desire for honor and all the rest. G-d can barely survive Jews; I am not G-d.
>
> My reputation has been dragged in the mud on a personal basis by all kinds of people. Heaven knows that I couldn't care less when that comes from outsiders but I cannot see how it is possible to continue when that comes from within the organization, since that destroys my greatest value to JDL – the faith of people in me.
>
> Those who imply that I have taken money for myself; those who say that I politicized JDL in Israel for myself are wrong, but that is not enough. The fact that they say it and are believed by our own members makes my own value so much smaller.

I will not deceive you. I am tired. I am tired of fighting small people without the help of a few great ones. I hereby tender my resignation from the American JDL and from all international bodies of the organization....[55]

Meir's resignation was not accepted by the board.[56] Most of the members of the board knew that Meir was always scrupulous in his use of public funds. They realized that only by vacating the Jewish Identity Center building was Meir able to realize the donors' intent – the promotion of JDL ideology. Proceeds of the sale enabled Meir to continue to expose the public to his ideas. Instead of limiting himself to the Jewish Identity Center, Meir would direct his educational program to the Israeli public at large, as part of his election campaign.

Chapter 32
The Jewish Character of Israel (October 1972-March 1973)

A Mezuza on Damascus Gate

AS HE HAD done in Hebron, Meir sought concrete ways to illustrate that the Land of Israel was Jewish and that the Jewish people must proudly declare their sovereignty over it. Shortly after announcing that he would run for the Knesset, he decided to affix a *mezuza** to the Damascus Gate, one of the gates in the wall surrounding Jerusalem's Old City.

The idea came to him one Friday evening on his return home from prayers at the Western Wall. As he passed through Damascus Gate, he noticed that at the side, where a *mezuza* should have been, there was only a cleft in the stone. Just as every Jewish home, office, store and public building is supposed to have a *mezuza* on each of its doorposts, so must there be *mezuzot* on all the gates of a walled city such as Jerusalem's Old City. In fact, after the Six Day War, *mezuzot* had been affixed to all the gates, but Arabs had removed the one on Damascus Gate. Replacing the *mezuza* would reaffirm the Jewish character of Jerusalem and all of Israel.

That Saturday night, October 14, 1972, Meir had been invited to present the Liga platform to students at Bar Ilan University. The Liga platform, he said, stated that all the lands liberated during the Six Day War were part of the Land of Israel and should be formally annexed, with full rights of settlement for Jews. The Liga's principal aim was to promote and preserve the Jewish character of Israel, he declared, and to that end, Liga members were going to hold a public ceremony to affix a *mezuza* on Damascus Gate. The next day Meir formally notified Jerusalem mayor Teddy Kollek of his intention.[1]

---

* A *mezuza* is a parchment on which texts from Deuteronomy are inscribed. The parchments are rolled up in cases that are attached to the doorframes or gateposts of homes or buildings.

In the *Jewish Press*, Meir explained why the Israeli government "preferred not to notice" the disappearance of the *mezuza* from Damascus Gate:

> The Israeli government has followed a careful policy for more than five years of not "aggravating" the Arabs. This has involved Israeli refusal and failure to assert Jewish rights as well as a willingness to, de facto, accept Arab demands that run counter to those Jewish rights. Part of that policy includes the refusal to allow Jews unlimited settlement anywhere in that part of Eretz Yisrael liberated after 1967; refusal to allow Jews more than minimum rights at the Cave of the Patriarchs in Hebron; refusal to allow Jews to live anywhere except in certain parts of the Old City of Jerusalem; and, of course, refusal to declare that the liberated areas of 1967 are part of the Jewish State.

With remarkable foresight, Meir prophesied the consequences of this policy.

> ... [This] tells the world and, worse – Israeli Jewish youngsters – that these rights in truth do not exist. Should we, in the future, decide to demand them, we will find our own credibility attacked and opposition intense from our own people who will justly ask: "But if we really are entitled to these things, why did we not demand them earlier and why did you stop those who did demand them?" ... All the sensitive and liberal Jewish youth of Israel, its intellectuals, its writers, its professors, will rise up and say: But we have no right to keep that land because it is not ours and the greatest proof is your own refusal to declare it ours from the very first day.
>
> ... No matter what the clever propagandists say, the Arab is NOT equal in Israel so long as Israel remains true to the Zionist dream that created it as a JEWISH state....
>
> The Arab knows this and his placid acceptance of Jewish rule is not an indication that he is happy and has made his peace with the situation. It simply means that five years is a very, very short time in the Middle East; that the Arab is making money now; that a generation of young Arab intellectuals who place nationalism and ideals over that money has not yet fully ripened; and that we face a terrible Northern Ireland-type confrontation in the years to come. And on the Arab side will be ranged thousands of Jews who will back the Arabs....

Meir underlined the motive for replacing the *mezuza* on Damascus Gate.

> And that is the heart of the JDL intention. Not only the affixing and the stamping of a *mezuza*, but a fixing and stamping of the word "Jewish" on the city of Jerusalem. Jerusalem is not an Arab-Jewish city. It is a city where Jews and Arabs live, but the city is Jewish, the sovereignty is Jewish...[2]

To show public support for the plan, supporters circulated petitions addressed to the Ministry of Religions and the Municipality of Jerusalem stating, "We, the undersigned, request that *mezuzot* be affixed to all the gates of the Old City of Jerusalem."[3] Meir publicized the plan at a press conference at Beit Sokolov in Tel

Aviv. The *mezuza* issue drew many newsmen and gave Meir an opportunity to present the Liga platform to a large audience. Reports noted that he called for full Jewish sovereignty over all parts of the Land of Israel, with the rights of Arabs limited to their rights as individuals. He called attention to the fact that Arab universities in Judea, Samaria and Gaza were a danger to the State because they encouraged the national aspirations of the Arabs.

At the press conference Yoel Lerner reported that he had applied that morning for a police permit to hold a public ceremony at Damascus Gate. He displayed a large, beautifully embellished silver *mezuza* which members of the Liga would place on the Damascus Gate on Monday, October 30, at 4 P.M.[4]

As expected, the police refused the Liga's application to hold the ceremony. Meir's next step was an appeal to the High Court of Justice. He requested that the court issue an order to the police to allow the ceremony to be held as planned. A hearing was scheduled for October 29 before a three-judge panel. Meir's argument to the court was two-pronged: First, the government was not actually opposed to having a *mezuza* on Damascus Gate – after the Six Day War the government itself had affixed one there. Second, this was a matter of freedom of religious expression. He added that one of the principal aims of the Liga was to perpetuate the Jewish character of the State of Israel in public places, and that a *mezuza* was an important expression of this.[5]

The High Court refused Meir's appeal on the grounds that a public ceremony to place a *mezuza* on the Damascus Gate would cause Arab rioting. Nevertheless, on October 30 at 4 P.M. a lively crowd assembled near Damascus Gate. They were joined by a large contingent of police. There were many more policemen than participants, recalled Yoel Lerner. A photo shows Meir holding a discussion with several police officers, surrounded by young supporters listening attentively, as Arab stall keepers look on. News reports said that the participants, led by Meir, approached the gate singing and dancing, and as Meir was about to affix the *mezuza,* Police Chief Avraham Turgeman swept it from his hand. Meir and nine other participants were taken into custody. Brought before a judge, they were charged with disturbing the peace and were released on bail.[6] One newspaper photo showed Meir with a policeman on each side, linked arm-in-arm. This unusual image of a rabbi in police custody was reproduced as a Liga election flyer with the provocative heading "Wanted: Is This the Way a Rabbi Should Act?"[7]

The entire affair was given wide media coverage in Israel and, most important, even the briefest reports stated that the purpose of affixing the *mezuza* was to emphasize the Jewish character of Jerusalem. On December 11, when the case came to court, Meir was fined IL100 ($24) and ordered to post a IL2,000-bond to ensure good behavior for one year. The light sentence, explained Judge Moshe Shalgi, was due to the defendant's good intentions.[8]

The FBI was interested in the *mezuza* affair because Meir's arrest might furnish a reason to revoke his probation and imprison him. An FBI cable sent to the legal attaché at the U.S. Embassy in Tel Aviv referred to efforts to revoke Meir's probation:

> U.S. Attorney, Southern District of New York, is interested in pursuing possible revocation of subject's federal probation.... He was arrested in Israel for his possible participation in a JDL plot to smuggle weapons out of Israel for use against Arab terrorists. Our New York Office is currently conducting an intensive investigation of that matter insofar as it pertains to Kahane. We are closely following subject's activities and travels. This matter is of obvious interest to our continuing investigation of subject as well as to his Federal probation officer.[9]

Arab Terror

At the end of October, the Munich massacre of September was again headline news when Arab terrorists hijacked a West German airplane over Turkey. By threatening to blow it up, they gained the release of the three terrorists jailed in Germany a month earlier for killing eleven Israeli athletes. Israel reacted with an indignant protest at Germany's "ignominious" capitulation to the Arab terrorists.[10]

But Meir, given the prestigious platform of the *New York Times* op-ed page, argued that those who expect the nations of the world to join together to stop Arab terrors are "fools." He wrote that the real culprits are NOT the Germans who released three Arab terrorists, but those in the Israeli government who reject the idea that only Israel can defend the interests of Jews. In a three-column article topped by a photo of a masked Arab guerrilla in Munich, Meir wrote:

> Those who were responsible for attempting to ship arms from Israel in order to begin a worldwide counterterror movement understood full well what was happening.

He highlighted the role of counterterrorism.

> It is up to the Israeli government to mount a merciless, cold-blooded campaign against Arab targets all over the world. It is up to the Israelis to understand that they remain the trustees of the Jewish people throughout the world, and that if a Jew is a target of Arab terror – because of Israel – then the Jewish State is obliged to come to his defense, too. It is time for Israel to quietly train Jews all over the world in methods of defense and in counterterror. It is up to Israel to do for Jews what Arab states do for Arabs.[11]

Meir continued to hold public meetings to get his ideas across. His lecture at Jerusalem's Beit Haam auditorium on October 26 on "the problems of the State and the solutions of the Liga," was followed by a question-and-answer session.[12] Meir had found that the lively give and take of question-and-answer sessions brought audiences to a better understanding of his ideas.

To promote the right of Jews to settle freely in all parts of the Land of Israel, he announced a meeting in November to organize new settlements in Judea, Samaria and Gaza. An ad about the meeting proclaimed, "The Land of Israel belongs to the Jewish people forever! Be part of its resettlement...." A mimeographed flyer headed "The Liga and Settlements in the Land of Israel" listed the following objectives:

1. Resettlement of all parts of the Land of Israel that were liberated in 1967.
2. Promoting the settlement of new immigrants in the liberated areas.
3. Settlement as a housing solution for young couples.
4. Improving relations between all segments of the population by settling them together.[13]

In November Meir spoke at a number of schools, three of them Tel Aviv public high schools. The general public also showed an interest in his ideas. He was invited to address the Tel Aviv Lodge of Freemasons, the Tel Aviv Junior Chamber of Commerce and groups in private homes. On Saturday night, December 2, I accompanied him to a parlor meeting in Herzliya where he was received enthusiastically. There is only a partial record of Meir's speaking engagements during this period. Meir did not enter every one in his appointment book. I found six speaking engagements in November in other sources; only one of them was listed in the appointment book.[14]

Arab Emigration

Meir's most significant talk during this period was on November 29 at the Technion, Israel's technical university in Haifa. His presentation of the Liga's platform drew media attention when he outlined his plan to encourage Arab emigration from Israel. *Ha'aretz* quoted him:

> "We must find ways," he said, "to persuade the Arabs that it would be best for them to emigrate to one of the neighboring Arab states, rather than continue to live under Israeli rule." He explained, "As long as they are a large minority here, we will not be able to achieve peace with them."
>
> "This could be accomplished," he said, "by setting up a fund to compensate them for the lands and property they would leave behind."[15]

In his *Jewish Press* article, "Facing Up to the Arab Presence," Meir detailed the Liga's platform: immediate annexation of all the liberated areas, which are "historically part of Eretz Yisrael, ripped away from us by conquerors who exiled us," and the opening of a national fund "with an initial sum of IL100 million for the purpose of urging and aiding Arabs to immigrate to other lands." To those who wanted to be rid of the liberated areas because of the large Arab population there, he presented a history lesson.

> If any part of the Land of Israel is Jewish, it is surely that which is today known as the West Bank. It is here – under its more proper historical names of Judea and Samaria – that the Israelites of the Bible found their setting. What student of the Bible does not perk up his ears when he hears the name Hebron? It was here that Abraham, Isaac and Jacob created a Jewish people; it was here that the Judges ruled and it was here that Saul, David and the kings who followed them welded together the first Jewish commonwealth. If these lands are not Jewish, surely the new cities of Tel Aviv, Kiryat Gat, Haifa, Savion, and Netanya are not! If Jews have no claim to the former, they certainly have none to the latter.[16]

In another article, "What Palestinians?" Meir enlarged on the origin of the name "Palestine."

> In the year 135, the Judean fortress of Betar fell to the Roman legions of the Emperor Hadrian.... The name of Judea – the home of the Jewish people – was changed to Palestine. Had Hadrian suppressed his desire to erase the memory of the Jews and their state and not done this, it is conceivable that the Jews of Israel would today be faced with the "JUDEAN TERRORISTS."
>
> ... There never was and there is not now such a thing as a Palestine people or Palestine state. The Land of Israel, *Eretz Yisrael*, is the land of the Jewish people in all its historical boundaries.
>
> We live in a fool's paradise. Despite pious hopes, there will not be any peace between Jews and Arabs so long as there remains a Jewish state of any kind, regardless of what concessions we offer.... To the Arabs, all of the land is "Palestine" and there is no difference between the soil of Hebron or the coastal villas of Herzliya and Savion.
>
> ... The present hazy and irresolute Israeli stand on both the borders of Israel and the Arab population (on both sides of the 1967 cease-fire line) only leads to corresponding confusion and doubt in the minds of the youth of Israel as to the propriety of their government's moral and ethical stand. It increases their questioning of Israel's right to remain in the territories liberated in 1967, the legitimacy of a Jewish state AT ALL, and of the relations between Israelis and World Jewry.
>
> ... A well-conceived and well-financed plan to persuade the Arabs (through financial aid and all other assistance) to leave the Land of Israel must be undertaken. In the end, this last point – no matter how unpleasant – is the only hope for averting a second Cyprus or Northern Ireland.[17]

Terming the situation a "time bomb," Meir wrote that almost half a million Arabs – 17% of the total population – currently lived in pre-Six Day War Israel.[18] Regarding the million Arabs living in the liberated territories, he wrote:

[We must] disabuse ourselves of the illusion that the demon of Arab demography will be disposed of by getting rid of the liberated lands.... Indeed, I hasten to add, the Arabs within what is known as "the Green Line" (pre-1967 Israel) will pose a far more dangerous and explosive threat to Israel than those of Hebron and Gaza.

... The Arabs of Israel are a group whose population grows at a much higher rate than the Jewish one and their percentage of the total population of Israel grows greater with each decade.

The new generation of Israeli Arabs is not more well-disposed to the Jews.... The growing number of educated Israeli Arabs, those entering both secondary schools and universities, will never create a more moderate and compromising Arab but precisely the opposite. Every example of history shows that revolutionaries come not from the numb and dumb peasant and oppressed classes but specifically from the intellectual middle or upper classes, or the sons of the oppressed classes who have escaped into the new, rarified atmosphere of the university. It is the new, educated Arab generation that is infinitely more dangerous; that is unwilling to accept its status as a something-less-than-first-class citizen and will resort to ever-growing protest and revolt.

... The revolutionary left, liberals of all kinds and anti-Semites in general, will seize upon the "plight" of the Arabs to raise an international hue and cry of world-wide protests on behalf of the Arabs. This will hurt, to an as yet unknown degree, financial support for Israel both from foreign governments as well as private supporters – including Jews.

... The best partial solution, the most humane in the long run and the safest for the Jews, is ... [the] urgent creation of an Emigration Fund for Peace (Keren Hagira Lema'an Hashalom).

The majority of Arabs will not agree to leave Israel under any circumstances, but sizeable numbers — more than we think — will, IF THEY ARE GIVEN SUFFICIENT INCENTIVE. It is up to those who wish to save Israel from a disastrous crisis to furnish that incentive.... Integration is not always the answer.... Attempts to integrate the Arabs of Israel can be successful only at the price of a unique JEWISH state.... [We] need a PRIVATE body of wealthy and influential Jews to set up the machinery for an ongoing emigration fund with an initial capitalization of at least 20 million dollars.

... These same people should also begin the task of contacting governments of states that are underpopulated or in need of manpower ... this fund would do more to solve the Middle East problem than all the United Nations plans yet created.[19]

Two days after Meir's talk at the Technion about the emigration plan, he was invited once again to take part in the "Jerusalem Vocal Newspaper" panel at the Beit Haam auditorium in Jerusalem. Another guest speaker that evening was Yehiel Leket, secretary of the Labor Party's "Young Leadership," who was fiercely opposed to Meir's ideas.[20] Sparks flew that Friday night!

In 1975, Leket, then Director of the Israel Aliyah Center in New York, recalled that "debate." In a letter thanking Meir for sending him a copy of *Time to Go Home*, he wrote, "... When we appeared at Beit Haam in Jerusalem in December 1972, the difference in our opinions was clear. However, what we have in common – love of the people of Israel and the land of Israel – is more important. There are no differences between us on the subject that most concerns us both: the connection between the Jews and their land."[21]

Indeed, it was Meir's *ahavat Yisrael*, love of the Jewish people, that motivated him to pursue the Arab emigration plan. He wanted to prevent a destructive religious and national war in Israel like the one then raging in Northern Ireland. In mid-December, he mailed letters both to Israeli Arabs and to Arabs of "the territories" offering them financial benefits if they would emigrate. The letters said:

> It is obvious that the Jewish citizens of the State of Israel will never agree to give up the Land of Israel or to split it or divide it. There is no possibility of a withdrawal from the territory of Israel which was liberated in 1967. Therefore, since we respect the Arab nationalist feeling, we realize that an atmosphere of eternal tension between the Jewish majority and the Arab minority might arise such as that in Northern Ireland. In the cause of peace and brotherhood, it would be advisable to take steps to prevent this danger. It is preferable that every nation should live in its own country, and not under the jurisdiction of another nation. Therefore, we are raising an emigration fund for this purpose, which will help every Arab who is willing to leave the country. If you are willing to emigrate, we ask you to notify us:
>
> a) The number of people in your family, so that we can work out a plan of payment to each family according to its size;
> b) If you are willing to sell your dwelling to a Jew, and if so, when?
> c) To which country would you like to immigrate? ...
> Sincerely yours,
> The Jewish Defense League in Eretz Israel
> POB 7287, Jerusalem

A press release containing this text in Hebrew and English was sent to the media. The Hebrew version, accompanied by reporter Ziva Yariv's angry comments, was printed in full in *Yedioth Ahronoth* on December 21.[22]

Coincidentally, that same day the media reported that Meir had been granted Israeli citizenship. Only a week earlier, Meir had appealed to the Supreme Court, maintaining that the delay in granting him citizenship would thwart his plan to run in the November 1973 elections. Before the appeal could be heard, the Ministry of Interior ruled in his favor. Its spokesman explained that "such requests generally take months to handle" and said they had never intended to deny his request. The spokesman added that Meir "posed no threat to public safety" despite ongoing legal proceedings against him for the arms shipment. Meir assured reporters that if he had not turned to the Supreme Court, his request would still be lying on some bureaucrat's desk.[23]

Two weeks later, the letters to the Arabs were again in the news. Reporter Gabi Baron revealed his discovery that there was no money in the emigration fund. Baron claimed that without cash, Meir's emigration plan was not practical.[24] But Meir had never said there was money in the fund. He had specifically written in the letters to the Arabs, "We are RAISING an emigration fund...." For Meir, the first priority was to bring serious public attention to the problem. He wrote:

> [We must] not persuade ourselves that [the problem] does not exist or that it is not as bad as some people make it out to be or that it will get better or that it will eventually disappear of its own accord. Not by illusions or patently impossible brotherhood hopes will this problem be solved. It will be begun to be solved by squarely facing a number of realities....[25]

Only a few days later, the letters made headlines again when Druze citizens of Israel who had also received the letters protested furiously. The Druze had defected from Islam in the tenth century and formed a separate religious community. As early as the 1948 War of Independence, they allied themselves with the Jewish state and became one of the few minority groups serving in the Israeli army. Arabic-sounding names had been taken at random from the phone book, but Meir had not meant to send the letters to Druze citizens. He immediately issued a public apology.

A *sulcha*, a reconciliation meeting, was arranged for January 7, 1973 at the Haifa office of Druze attorney Kamal Kassem. Yoel Lerner and Shimon Rachamim accompanied Meir to Kassem's office and found the press there in full force. Among the thirty or forty Druze notables who attended were Sheikh Jaber Mu'adi, Israeli deputy minister of communication; Sheikh Kamal Tarif; Amal Nasir-el-Din, later a member of Knesset (Likud, 1974-1988); and Sheikh Hatam Halabi, who arranged the *sulcha* and later supported the Liga's campaign for the Knesset. The parties to the *sulcha* shook hands, embraced, and toasted each other with glasses of fruit juice. Meir is pictured in *Yedioth Ahronoth* shaking hands with Mu'adi and smiling broadly. Meir repeated the Liga's plan to finance Arab emigration and told reporters that the Liga had sent out about four hundred letters and had received some replies from interested Arabs. He was depending, he said, on public figures and wealthy individuals to support the emigration fund.[26]

On the train ride back to Jerusalem, Meir discussed the meeting with Lerner and Rachamim. The majority of the Druze representatives had expressed an affinity with the Jews, but Meir was troubled by the words of a young Druze speaker who had declared that the younger Druze identified themselves more closely with the Arabs than with the Jewish state.[27]

Neither Offensive Nor Insulting

The news the next day was ominous. Meir was to be prosecuted on criminal charges for the letters sent to Arabs. He was charged with violating the Law of Sedition, which stated, "It is a criminal offence to publish material likely to promote feelings of ill will or hostility between different sections of the population." The maximum penalty was two years imprisonment.[28]

Meir reacted with a quarter-page ad in *Ma'ariv* on January 11, 1973, addressed to prime minister Golda Meir. In it, he maintained that it was absurd to accuse him of sedition or any illegal act – his words were neither offensive nor insulting. He presented logical reasons for promoting Arab emigration, and he protested the government's official condemnation of his plan. He argued that Golda Meir herself had violated the Law of Sedition: "Regularly, you reject the annexation of the liberated areas on the grounds that 'Israel cannot take in any more Arabs.' What do you think the Arab citizen of Israel feels when he hears that?" Meir asked. In light of Golda Meir's own statements, charging him with sedition was hypocrisy, he said.[29]

That day, he held a press conference at which he announced that he would continue to send letters to Arabs. His message was broadcast on Israel TV news that evening.[30] Coverage of the press conference in *Yedioth Ahronoth* began with the words "Rabbi Meir Kahane has an answer to every question" and continued:

> ... He can't understand why the prime minister and the minister of finance can express their fear of the growing numbers of Arabs in Israel, but when he translates this into action, they want to take legal steps against him.
>
> "There is a large and growing minority here," he said, "which hates us and will in the not-distant future cause us many difficult problems. If we don't act today," he warned, "it will be too late." He cited Canada and the French separatists of Quebec, Cyprus and the Turks, England and the Irish, to show the magnitude of the danger.
>
> He is not worried about the lack of money in the emigration fund. "The project will, in the future, be taken over by the government," he said. But meanwhile he has a problem with the police. Two days ago, for example, he was brought to Jerusalem police headquarters for questioning.
>
> "Rav Pakad [Major] Levi wanted me to sign a statement saying that I refused to reply to his questions. However, the document had the words 'conquered ter-

ritories.' I was ready to sign if he would change those words to 'liberated territories.' Rav Pakad Levi refused to change the wording, so I did not sign, nor did I answer questions.

When I returned from the investigation, I gave instructions to send out more letters. The letters have nothing wrong in them. They do not offend, they do not insult, they are not illegal. But even if I have to sit in jail, I will not cease to encourage Arab emigration. It is a question of life and death for the future of the state of Israel."[31]

After thirty-five Arabs sent back forms indicating an interest in emigrating, a meeting was scheduled for January 23 with three *mukhtars* (heads of villages) in the Galilee.[32] Funding the emigration plan was still a major problem. Meir could not go to America to raise money for it because he was not allowed to leave Israel due to the legal charges connected with the September arms shipment.

One of the Arabs who replied to the letters was Emmanuel Khoury, a Christian Arab from the village of Fassuta in the western Galilee. Khoury, who came to our home once or twice, agreed with Meir's ideas and, for a salary, undertook to persuade other Arabs to emigrate. A U.S. State Department report described Khoury as Meir's "legman, trooping from village to village, explaining the emigration idea and talking about resettlement in the U.S., Brazil, Canada, New Zealand, and Australia." He was pictured with Meir in *Yedioth Ahronoth* at a joint press conference at the end of January. Khoury was quoted as saying he believed that Arabs should emigrate because "this is not our land."[33]

Meir's emigration campaign was causing discontent among some Israeli Arabs, something the government wanted to avoid at all costs. To put a stop to Meir's activities, and to show Israeli Arabs that the government did not in any way support his plan, he was summoned to Jerusalem Magistrate's Court on February 4, 1973. He and Yoel Lerner, who had typed the Hebrew letters to the Arabs, were arraigned and charged with violating the Law of Sedition. Meir was released on IL5,000 ($1,200) bail, with no date set for a hearing of the case.[34]

Converting Jews to Christianity

Only a few days later the Liga was in the news again, when four of its members were arrested. They were suspected of setting a fire at the International Centre for Holy Scriptures on the Mount of Olives in Jerusalem, the main printing and distribution point for missionary literature. Eyewitnesses reported that a group numbering five to seven persons masquerading as visitors entered the Center, overturned a kerosene-fueled space heater, and set fire to several copies of the New Testament.

Meir held a press conference at which he denied any "official connection" between his organization and the fire. He said, however, that the arsonists were "good Jews" and added that the Liga does not rule out acts such as setting fires, should the Knesset fail to legislate against missionary activity. He cited the halakha that laws of the Torah may be violated to combat those who proselytize Jews.[35]

Meir's statements at the press conference were broadcast on Israel radio and were widely covered in the press, because the arson on the Mount of Olives was a reaction to a serious ongoing problem. Since the 1967 Six Day War, missionaries had converted between 5,000 and 6,000 Israelis a year to Christianity. In the previous year the government had expelled several missionaries who had acted illegally, but there were approximately one thousand still residing in Israel. Religious affairs minister Zerach Warhaftig advocated legislation to prohibit proselytizing, but the Cabinet, which feared the displeasure of Christian countries, would not act. A report in the *International Herald Tribune* said:

> ... Rabbi Meir Kahane staged a one day hunger strike yesterday at the Western Wall to protest missionary activity.... "I don't like soul snatching," Rabbi Kahane told newsmen. "Whether you lose a Jew in Auschwitz or through conversion, it's still a soul lost to our people."[36]

In America, too, missionaries were tirelessly trying to convert Jews to Christianity. Meir wrote of the dangers posed by one group, Jews for Jesus:

> Some time ago, full-page advertisements appeared in New York, Los Angeles and Miami showing a group of smiling, happy people obviously at peace with themselves and the world. Above their heads hovered the caption "Why Are All These People Smiling?"
>
> The answer was happy, smiling and to the point. All the above were Jews who had found Jesus.
>
> ... It is heartwarming and inspirational to consider that all Christians have now reached that level of holiness, piety and goodness so that nothing is left for Christian sects to do but to recruit Jews...
>
> Unfortunately, large numbers of Jews – youth in particular – are potential victims of the smiling zealots. Thanks to the bankruptcy of the Jewish Establishment and the modern Jewish institutions that have done so much to replace substantive Judaism with the bagels-and-lox brand, Jewish youth finds itself wandering, lost and without ideological and spiritual moorings.... Most of our youth finds itself ignorant of Jewish tradition, ...alienated from their people and heritage, searching for something to fill their empty lives, and easy prey for every ideology that appears to offer some alternative to that emptiness.
>
> The phenomenon on the college campuses known as "Jesus Freaks" ... is but another one of the desperate fads that sweep over a hungry youth.... It will have stolen from us Jewish souls....[37]

Jews for Jesus was especially aggressive in Israel. They offered money and housing to prospective converts and were successful in recruiting adherents – twenty adherents a month in Jerusalem and twenty a month in Haifa, many of them visiting American Jews. Ironically, the converted Jews who were sent by Jews for Jesus to proselytize were taking advantage of Israel's Law of Return and making use of the financial benefits given to Jewish immigrants.[38]

When Bill Perl, the head of the JDL chapter in Washington, D.C., visited Israel, Meir took the opportunity to promote the campaign against Christian missionaries as well as to work toward implementation of his plan for Arab emigration. A two-part press release invited newsmen to a press conference to meet Perl. The first part said:

> [We] take great pleasure in inviting you to meet Dr. William Perl, head of the United States Committee on Middle East Emigration, who has arrived to discuss practical efforts to implement Arab emigration from Israel for those who so desire. Dr. Perl, a retired U.S. Air Force Colonel and former head of the illegal aliya to Palestine in Vienna for the Revisionists in the 1930s, will meet with Arabs who wish to emigrate and will return to the United States to work on visas and fundraising.
>
> Dr. Perl will meet the press at 10 A.M. at Beit Sokolov in Tel Aviv. Afterwards, he will accompany Rabbi Meir Kahane and Emmanuel Khoury on a day-long visit to Arab villages in the Galilee.

The second part of the press release introduced a new group, "Christians for Moses." Satirizing Christian missionaries' rhetoric of "love" and "saving lost souls," Meir wrote:

> The JDL will also present at the same press conference a young member of the JDL-sponsored Christians for Moses which will begin to work immediately to convert young Christians in Israel to Judaism. These young people, former Christians who have adopted Moses and Love, will be found at Church services, foreign embassies and wherever lost Christians gather, to save them.[39]

The press conference was covered in several newspapers, as well as on Israel radio. Noah Kliger of *Yedioth Ahronoth*, wrote:

> Since his aliya to Israel, Rabbi Kahane has accustomed us to surprises. Now he has come up with two surprises in one. Yesterday in Tel Aviv, he presented Dr. William Perl, head of the United States Committee on Middle East Emigration. Dr. Perl said that financing the emigration of Arabs is being presented to American Jews as a business deal. His committee is selling shares in a firm named New Horizons for two dollars each. Through New Horizons, Jews will acquire and invest in the properties of the Arabs who emigrate. Emmanuel Khoury is to leave shortly for the United States to promote the sale of shares.
>
> Like a magician pulling rabbits out of a hat, Rabbi Kahane pulled another

surprise out of his hat yesterday – an organization called "Christians for Moses." This organization was created only a few days after Israel was overrun with advertisements of "Jews for Jesus." Present at the press conference was the head of Christians for Moses, John Cummings, and two of its active members, Peter Simpson and Don Thompson. Cummings, age 20, who was born in Utah, came to Israel to study theology. After two years of study, he suddenly realized that the true prophet was Moses and that Moses should replace Jesus as the leading figure in Christianity. He quoted from the Bible to prove that it is forbidden to listen to the preaching of those who believe in Jesus. Peter Simpson, age 19, came to Israel from Los Angeles about three months ago and met Cummings at the Western Wall. He immediately realized the truth of Cummings' ideas: "I read the Bible and saw clear proof that Moses was the true prophet."[40]

Meir campaigned against missionaries in the *Jewish Press*, too. He urged readers to write letters to the Israeli government demanding a law against missionary activity. Protesting the imprisonment without bail of Liga people charged with anti-missionary attacks, he appealed to his readers: "If you are coming to Israel, help us hand out Christians for Moses literature at hotels."[41]

It was Easter, and Jerusalem hotels were crowded with Christian tourists who had come for the holiday. Meir and his supporters distributed flyers to them headed "Christians for Moses Begins Its Campaign to Save Christian Tourists."

Again imitating the idiom of Christian missionaries, Meir endeavored to show Christians how it felt to be the object of proselytizers. At the same time, he wanted government ministers to understand the ramifications of their refusal to ban missionary activity. Perhaps a threat to tourism, so vital to the country's economy, might sway them. The flyer said:

> With the approach of the Easter season, concerning the false Jesus, "Christians for Moses" has begun its mission to save Christians in the Holy Land. Enclosed is a copy of a sample booklet that is being distributed to Christian tourists in hotels, churches and on tours. Please note that the missionary activity of our group is perfectly legal and has been protected by such great men as justice minister Shapiro and foreign minister Eban.
>
> Initial reaction from Christian tourists has not been a very happy one, and we hope that this anger will not affect tourism to Israel. In any case, we have directed their reactions to the Ministry of Tourism, which, we are sure, will be delighted to know that Christians react quite the same as Jews do when THEY are given missionary booklets....[42]

Meir had put it succinctly at his press conference with Dr. Perl: "We will give the Christian missionaries a dose of their own medicine and act precisely as they do on the Mount of Olives and in Jaffa. Maybe then the authorities will reach the conclusion that missionary activity of any sort should not be permitted."[43]

Meanwhile, Khoury had been working on persuading Arabs to emigrate. He arranged a meeting in Fassuta between Meir and the heads of Arab clans from the north: Haifa, Nazareth, Kafr Kana and Gush Halav (ancient Gishala). Meir told the clan leaders that he had no enmity toward Arabs or their cultural heritage. He was motivated solely by a deep conviction that they could never feel themselves equal citizens in a Jewish state and that they would always be strangers in it. He maintained that throughout history two different peoples had never lived in one state in peace and friendship. His listeners had many questions: When could they leave? To which countries could they go? How would they change the Israeli currency into dollars? Will they be equal citizens in their new homes? Meir had an answer ready for each question, wrote reporter Menachem Rahat.[44]

For Dr. Perl, who had returned to the States, Meir had good news. He wrote: "Brazil has agreed to give visas to skilled workers or those with $25,000. This shows that a direct request to the embassies under the New Horizons label works!" He added that Khoury was to arrive in the United States on April 1 to promote the project. But Khoury was refused a visa to America, and in May, when an attempt was made on his life, he stopped working for Meir.[45] Still, the concept of New Horizons was attractive. In April and May, many letters arrived from Jews who were interested in buying Arab property in Israel.[46]

Criminal Indictment for Incitement

On April 29, 1973, Meir and Yoel Lerner were formally indicted and charged with incitement under the Sedition Act. Meir noted that the new District Court for Jerusalem, where the case was being tried, had been erected on Salah a-Din Street, which was part of Jordan prior to 1967. "This Israeli court in East Jerusalem is a hundred times more of an incitement to the Arabs!" declared Meir. He pointed out: "Regularly, Golda Meir and her cabinet ministers reject the annexation of the territories on the grounds that 'Israel cannot take in any more Arabs.' What do you think the Arab citizen of Israel thinks when he hears his own prime minister say that? Why is that statement less offensive than our emigration fund?"[47]

Lerner recalled the outcome of the trial: "The letters we sent could not be defined as 'incitement' because all they said was, 'We respect the Arab national consciousness and suggest you leave in order to prevent a deterioration here to a Northern Ireland or a Cyprus.'" The case was heard in fits and starts. Finally, at a hearing on May 5, 1975, Judge Ezra Hadaya demanded that the prosecution show intention to incite. Uzi Hason, the government prosecutor, requested an adjournment. Clearly, Meir and Yoel had not intended to incite, and the court never reconvened on this matter.[48]

Typically, Meir had yet another solution to the demographic problem presented by the growing Arab population:

> Less than thirty years ago the Holocaust ripped from us six million Jews, a third of the entire nation. Among them were millions of young people and children who, had they lived, by this time would have produced millions more. We lost not only a vast quantity, but a vital quality. The smallest of peoples became smaller yet, the weakest, weaker yet.
>
> ... And we lose countless more each year through assimilation and intermarriage. The answer? Have more Jewish babies.... Drop the sterile, depressing and suicidal *Playboy* concept of life and return to an understanding of what a beautiful thing the Jewish family life, center of life, center of woman's and man's existence, is; and have more Jewish babies.
>
> The Land of Israel stands today magnificent in size and opportunity. The moment has come to fill its empty fields and barren mountain sides, to close the gaps in its security and defense, to populate the land that is ours and that never dare be returned. How? By having Jewish babies and having them grow up to be men and women who will spit in the eyes of a world that thinks that it can wipe us out. In memory of the little babies who burned in Auschwitz, let us have little babies in Jerusalem. To replace the little boys and girls who perished in Treblinka and Warsaw, let us have strong little Jewish boys and girls in Tel Aviv and Hebron and Golan and Rafiah.[49]

In the following months, Meir continued his efforts to bring Jewish ideas and ideals to the fore.

Chapter 33

Don't Trust Brezhnev!
(March-June 1973)

The Liga Prepares

IITH THE TERMINATION of the lease on the Jewish Identity Center building, Meir sought office space for the Liga in the same area. Zion Square was centrally located in downtown Jerusalem, near numerous bus lines, convenient for members and visitors. He quickly found rooms on the top floor of 38 Jaffa Road, only one block away from the square, in a building that had two floors of office space over a row of ground-level stores.[1]

In Tel Aviv, Meir rented another centrally located office for the Liga at 83 Dizengoff Street. It became the focal point of activity for members who lived in the populous Gush Dan area around Tel Aviv and attracted students from nearby Tel Aviv University. It was a modest office: a simple desk, a few chairs, faded walls. A large blue poster with the Liga's logo, a clenched fist within a Star of David, dominated the room. Other posters bore the slogans *Ahavat Yisrael* (Love of the Jewish people), *Hadar Yisrael* (Jewish pride), and *Never Again!*[2]

The Liga began to prepare for the elections. Its first newsletter, *Kol Haliga*, March 25, 1973, reported that Yosef Schneider had resigned and Shimon Rachamim was now the *mazkir*, administrative director. Tzippy Levine was chairman of the Tel Aviv branch, and there were branches in Haifa, Beersheba, and Ashdod. At a board meeting on April 2 Meir was named Liga chairman and planning began for the Liga's national convention in June. Delegates to the convention were chosen at a meeting at ZOA House in Tel Aviv on April 24, where Meir spoke and led a discussion on ideology and aims.[3]

It was also in April that Meir changed his name officially from Martin to Meir. This had to be done because the Ministry of the Interior policy was to register a new immigrant under the name that appeared on his passport. Anyone who wanted to Hebraicize his name had to file a special application to do so. When we came to Israel, I considered changing my name to Ahuva, the Hebrew translation of my Yiddish name Liba, but Meir preferred the name Libby, so I avoided the bureaucratic hassle of a name change. Meir, however, had to run for the Knesset under the name on his identity card. Since he had been known as Meir since he was twenty years old, it was natural for him to make it official.[4]

Meir's appointment book for this period no longer exists. Letters of thanks in his files indicate only a few speaking dates, but there were probably more. In February he spoke at the ORT high school in Ramat Gan and to residents of Kfar Hittim near Tiberias. In April he lectured at Kibbutz Rosh Tzurim in Gush Etzion and at the Segula girls' high school in Kiryat Motzkin. In May and June he spoke to high school students at the Bnei Akiva yeshiva in Kiryat Shmuel and before a Poalei Agudah group in Bnei Brak.[5] The media noted his participation in a panel discussion on the David Frost TV show taped in Israel. At issue was the shooting down of a Libyan passenger plane that had "strayed" into Israel's air space on February 21. When the show was broadcast in Israel on March 11, 1973, it aroused the anger of leftist Israelis because almost all the panelists agreed that Israel was justified in shooting down the Libyan plane. Uri Avneri, an extreme leftist who had been on the panel, complained, "Frost edited out everything I said, but allowed Rabbi Meir Kahane and right-wing Knesset member Shmuel Tamir to have their say."[6]

Nixon and Brezhnev: Crucial Time for Soviet Jewry

Meir took every opportunity to express his opposition to Israel's Communist Party, Rakah, for supporting the Soviet Union despite the oppression of Jews there. When Rakah sponsored a press conference in Tel Aviv in mid-April to introduce a delegation from the Soviet Union, Meir saw a chance to dramatize his stand. He donned a long black wig and thick eyeglasses, flashed his *Jewish Press* journalist's card, and was admitted to the press conference. He approached one of the visiting communists and spilled a drink over his head. In the free-for-all that ensued, his glasses fell off, his wig slipped, and his true identity was revealed. This ploy brought attention to the contemptible behavior of Rakah members who honored the oppressors of Soviet Jews.[7]

On May 3, as the June 18 state visit of Soviet prime minister Leonid Brezhnev to the United States drew near, Meir placed a quarter-page ad in *Ma'ariv* addressed to prime minister Golda Meir. In it, he pleaded that she warn American Jewish leaders not to trust Brezhnev. Although he had announced that he was canceling the ransom tax on Jewish emigrants, his sole interest was to further détente and gain trade benefits with the U.S. He could not be trusted to allow free Jewish emigration in the future, said Meir. American Jewish leaders were in a quandary:

Should they continue to support Senator Henry Jackson's amendment making trade benefits dependent on free Jewish emigration? Should they follow Nixon's view and cease to support the Jackson amendment? Should they trust Brezhnev? They looked to Israel for guidance. "Mrs. Meir," the ad said, "Tell them not to trust Brezhnev. Tell them to support Jackson. Do not remain silent!"[8]

Meir was convinced that this was a crucial period for Soviet Jewry. He wrote:

> The President of the United States, in an extraordinary appearance, has met with the leaders of American Jewry and asked them to trust his way of achieving emigration for Soviet Jews. His way is the way of quiet diplomacy and trust in the word of Leonid Brezhnev.... Two oral communications, supposedly received from the Soviet leader, declared that the ransom tax on Soviet Jews had been suspended.... Mr. Nixon now asked the American Jewish leaders to cease their attacks on the administration's bill to grant the Soviet Union important trade concessions [and to cease their support for Senator Henry Jackson's amendment].
>
> ... Richard Nixon's greatest dream [is] to go down in history as the man who achieved détente with the Soviets and brought peace to the world in our time.... [He] and his Jewish advisor [Henry Kissinger] have persuaded the Soviets that it is imperative that they agree to suspend the tax, for only in this way can men like prestigious Congressman Wilbur Mills drop their opposition to the trade concessions.
>
> ... The Soviets not only have no intention of permanently reverting back to the days before the ransom tax, but intend to pay the Jews back for all the humiliation ... as soon as all the concessions have been granted and the détente between the United States and the USSR is firm and unbreakable.
>
> ... Now is precisely NOT the time to cease the pressure; now is the time to increase it and to stop, at all costs, the drive for détente.... Now is the time for daring attacks upon Soviet officials and offices, now is the time for any and every act that will pluck from the eager hands of the Russians that which they most want.
>
> ... For everything there is a season, and the season for saving the Soviet Jews is drawing to a close. We have little time left and we must gain more time.... Will we have the courage to strike at the Russians with all deliberate violence...?[9]

A definitive article by William Korey in the *American Jewish Year Book* described the quandary of American Jewish leadership in the face of Nixon's opposition to the Jackson amendment. Korey argued the folly of depending on Soviet promises and demonstrated that Jackson's legislation provided the only assurance that the Soviets would continue to allow emigration.[10]

Unfortunately, the majority of Establishment Jewish organizations, at Nixon's urging, rejected the Jackson amendment. Meir's distrust of President Nixon's declarations of support for Soviet Jewish emigration was proven correct. It was not long before Nixon was quoted as saying, in reference to Soviet Jews, "The United States cannot make its policy hostage to any one group."[11]

Meir believed that only the cancellation of Brezhnev's visit could save the situation. He reasoned that State Department officials would cancel Brezhnev's visit if they were convinced there was a real danger to his life.

To that end, he published in a press release part of the text of a speech he was going to give at a Torah dedication ceremony in Jerusalem on May 17. He also sent the release to the *Jewish Press*, and in his covering letter to publisher Shalom Klass he said, "We must do something about the Brezhnev visit which Soviet Jews here fear will mark the end of Soviet Jewry. Because of this, I have sent you hastily the enclosed brief article. I implore you to print it IMMEDIATELY. Do not let these Jews down."[12] The press release read in part:

> Where are the young Jews in America? ... Where are the Jews bursting with rage who will use force against Soviet diplomats so as to prevent the visit of Leonid Brezhnev to the United States, and thus prevent a détente which will mean the end of Soviet Jewry? ... Now, before Brezhnev arrives and accomplishes détente.
>
> And if not now, when? And if not a Soviet diplomat, then who? The answer is clear, Brezhnev himself![13]

This letter was stopped by the Israeli postal censorship, and the article was never published in the *Jewish Press*, but the text was later quoted by the U.S. government to show that Meir had violated his 1971 probation conditions.[14]

Another eloquent expression of the urgency Meir felt at this juncture was his article "Day of the Holocaust and the Bravery," which appeared on May 25. It ended with these words:

> ... If we hope to save the Soviet Jew before the gates shut and the long night begins, it is up to the small bands, the individuals, to smash the détente by themselves.... If détente becomes a hard reality, Soviet Jews are doomed....
> For a while, there was a nice "clean" way, the way of Jackson. Now that is finished, done with. The only way left is the dirty way, the way of violence, the kidnapping of Soviet diplomats in the United States, the attack on an installation, the destroying of the coexistence that the Soviets want and need so badly – just a little more badly than does Nixon. Only if they fear the loss of their so-much-needed détente will the Russians be forced to concede their Jews.
>
> We have had enough holocausts. Today, the survival of the Soviet Jews depends upon bravery. Where are they? Where are the Jewish brave ones who will risk all and do what has to be done?[15]

Meir's effort to create the impression that Brezhnev would be harmed in America was probably behind an anonymous tip to the police that two explosive devices had been hidden at JDL headquarters in New York. The caller warned that the bombs would be planted at the Russian or Iraqi Missions to the United Nations during Brezhnev's visit.

Of course, when FBI agents and local policemen arrived with a search warrant, they found no bombs, but ransacked the office and took files. David Fisch, JDL director, held a press conference which attracted many newsmen and was widely reported. Fisch accused the FBI agents of wantonly damaging equipment and illegally confiscating files. He said the raid had "just radicalized people" and declared that the JDL was more determined than ever to protest Brezhnev's visit. Another JDL member commented: "This was an obvious attempt to terrorize the JDL prior to the Brezhnev visit."[16]

Others besides Meir were worried about the effect Brezhnev's meeting with Nixon would have on the Jackson amendment. Glenn Richter, national director of the Student Struggle for Soviet Jewry (SSSJ), recalled: "We supported the refuseniks and dissidents who called for linkage between trade and emigration, e.g., the Jackson amendment."[17] On Sunday, June 17, as final preparations were being made for the June 18 summit meeting with Brezhnev, nearly 10,000 American Jews gathered near the White House in a demonstration sponsored by the Establishment's National Conference on Soviet Jewry. In New York, about eight hundred people protested at the Soviet residence in Glen Cove on June 20, while others held a 16-hour vigil at the Soviet Mission in Manhattan. JDLers who took part continued the vigil late into the night. They splattered red paint on the building to symbolize "the blood of Soviet Jews that is being spilled in Russia," and late that same night, a Soviet diplomat's car was firebombed.[18]

Si Frumkin, of SSSJ in Los Angeles, recalled their demonstration on June 20, prior to Nixon's meeting with Brezhnev at the summer White House in San Clemente: "We had about one thousand people who took buses and cars to the 'Candlelight Caravan for Brezhnev.' On June 23, the day of the meeting, we took two moving vans filled with balloons to San Clemente. We sent up balloons bearing banners reading 'Brezhnev: Let the Jews Go.' Several dozen banners were lifted by six or seven balloons each."[19]

Anxious to take part in the American demonstrations against Brezhnev, in May Meir had renewed his efforts to get his passport back from the Israeli police. Attorney Meir Schechter filed an appeal for its return, pleading that a trip to the United States to take care of business affairs was essential for his client's livelihood. Nine months had passed since Meir's passport had been taken from him, and because of the heavy caseload in the courts, it was likely that another eight or nine months would pass before the case of the weapons shipment would be heard.

An FBI report dated June 1 referred to Meir's appeal to regain his passport:

"In all probability, Kahane is returning to the United States to provide leadership to JDL as well as to incite terroristic and harassing actions aimed at Leonid Brezhnev during his visit to the United States commencing June 18, 1973.... Request probing search of Kahane's baggage when he enters this country."[20]

The FBI report assumed that Meir's appeal for the return of his passport would be successful. However, at the court hearing, the State attorney argued forcefully against its return. Meir issued a press release accusing the Israeli government of following the wishes of the Americans, who did not want Jewish protests during Brezhnev's visit. He also announced two demonstrations for the return of his passport: On June 3, JDLers in New York were going to demonstrate at the Israel Consulate, while on June 4 he himself would begin a hunger strike in front of the Mashbir department store in downtown Jerusalem. Meir's protest was of no avail. On June 4 Judge Haim Dvorin handed down his decision denying Meir's appeal. The reason he gave was that Meir "might organize disturbances in the U.S. during Brezhnev's visit there" and this was liable to "seriously embarrass authorities there."[21]

Meir's intense fear that a successful U.S. visit for Brezhnev would be catastrophic for Soviet Jews led him to urge JDLers in America to undertake extreme actions that might force the Americans to cancel Brezhnev's visit out of fear for his safety. Meir wrote to a JDL member:

> I suggest: 1) An immediate kidnapping and/or shooting of a Soviet diplomat... 2) A very QUICK request by a high school group for a Soviet speaker to explain the Russian side of the argument can be made ... you will know exactly when and where the Russian will be. 3) A bomb at the offices of Occidental Petroleum to warn Armand Hammer and any other people against any deals with the Russians.... 4) Take over a house at the back of the Soviet Embassy in Washington and fire shots into it.... 5) A building in Washington was used by the Iraqis as their embassy before they broke off diplomatic relations. Perl knows where it is. It is still officially theirs and an explosion there would be excellent.... This is urgent for the survival of these Jews or else I would never ask you to risk things."[22]

This letter, like his letter to the *Jewish Press*, was intercepted by the authorities. Meir was aware that the *shabak* (Israel Secret Service) had infiltrated the Liga, and he knew that there was postal censorship. He had mentioned several times that the government was tampering with his mail.[23] Perhaps he wanted the authorities to read his letters. As he later explained, the primary intention of his letters was to bring about the cancellation of Brezhnev's visit.

Meir was detained for questioning on June 3, but no reason was given for his arrest. News reports attributed it to the sedition charge for letters he had sent to Arabs. Then, on June 5, he was taken before a judge who ordered him held in

Jerusalem Central Prison for 48 hours – over the *Shavuot* (Pentecost) holiday – without telling him the reason. Minutes after his release on June 7, he was again taken before a judge and ordered held for fifteen days. His attorney was told only that the judge's decision was based on secret information submitted by State Attorney Gabriel Bach. The judge ordered that the charges remain secret, and only much later did Meir learn that his crime was "conspiracy to influence to violent action against Brezhnev."[24]

In Jerusalem Central Prison

Meir's stay in Jerusalem Central Prison was far from pleasant. The prison was only a lockup, designed for short-term prisoners, with primitive living conditions. The floors were rough cement, difficult to keep clean. Each cell had a "toilet" – a hole in the floor – and a "shower" – a shower head above the hole which gave cold water only. Both were in a closet-sized compartment with no door.[25] Among the things Meir needed from home were toilet paper and bed sheets. He also lacked basic religious needs. In one letter he wrote, "I need the wine and *havdalah* candle and matches before Wednesday because I didn't make *havdalah* last week."* And because of the unsanitary conditions, he asked for "that anti-fungus medicine."[26]

The family was able to visit and to exchange letters. On the envelope of one of Tzippy's letters (she was twelve), she wrote: "To the police: Do not read this, there are secrets here." In the letter, which Meir saved, she wrote, "On Shabbat, we went to the Schwartz family in Moshav Chemed." She enclosed her report card for him to sign, and, because he had described the giant roaches in jail after his first arrest in October 1972, she added, "I hope the bugs aren't too bad..." Tzippy recalled bringing sandwich cookies, Meir's favorite, when she visited him at the Jerusalem lockup.[27] After one of my visits, as I was leaving the prison, a policeman, whom Meir had pointed out once as "Arkadi," fell in step with me and said, "Your husband is causing you problems, eh?" Taken aback, I replied, "No, it's the police who are causing me problems!"

Meir wrote several letters home from Jerusalem Central Prison. During the first week, in a combined letter to the four children, he explained why he was in jail:

> Thirty years ago [during the Holocaust] no one did what had to be done for Jews and if someone had, he would have been condemned. Today, when Soviet Jews are faced with a catastrophe and the Israel government knows of it and sells them out for Nixon's favors, we cannot be quiet. It is the tragedy of the

---

* If for some reason one cannot perform *havdalah*, the ceremony formally concluding Shabbat, on Saturday night, it may be performed as late as Tuesday evening.

state of Israel that it is so un-Jewish that – at Washington's pressure – it arrests a Jew for doing what it should have done.

In any case do not worry. All important things are achieved through *yisurim* [suffering] and I always hope that I will DO and not only SAY what should be done. I will be home soon, with G-d's help, and until then, remember what is important and what is not.[28]

He also sent lighthearted letters to the children. He asked me, "Did Binny like the story about the chicken? I am writing him another one – about a tea kettle that didn't know how to whistle."[29] Meir kept his sense of humor, despite all: "Tell the children I'm the champion fly-swatter in prison."[30] There was a bright side to Meir's imprisonment – he had time to study Bible and Talmud. Years had passed since he was able to devote most of the day to study. Now he had the opportunity to return to it, and it gave him a feeling of joy. In an article datelined Jerusalem Central Prison, June 1973, he wrote:

... Only the study of Torah is that mitzvah that grips the Jew and binds both time and his conscious mind. It holds him for hours and he is keenly aware of his plunge into the sea of holiness. This is a unique difference, one that leaves its indelible mark upon his soul and his mind. This is the mitzvah that, more than any other, changes the Jew, shapes him, leaves him a genuinely different person each evening from the one who entered the House of Study that morning. Torah study is not only a mitzvah that is different from all the others in form; it is something else in quality and in substance.

But there is something else. There is still something else that emanates from the essence of Torah study and I had begun to forget. I had begun to forget how SWEET – how genuinely sweet it is to struggle over a difficult Talmudic concept and then, having wrestled with it, grappled in hand-to-hand combat with it, wracked one's brains, sweated and concentrated on it with an energy that blotted out all other consciousness – suddenly UNDERSTANDING! Suddenly, as if a great light shone in his mind, illuminating the shadows and doubts, the Jew grasps the difficulty, solves the problem; UNDERSTANDS! He jumps up from his chair and begins, happily and excitedly, to pace the floor with a warm feeling of satisfaction at having wrestled with a difficult problem – HAVING WRESTLED WITH THE TORAH ITSELF AND EMERGED VICTORIOUS, TO THE DELIGHT OF THE VANQUISHED LAW!...[31]

His next letter to the four children reminded them to study Torah and pointed out the difference between the government of Israel and the State of Israel.

Just a brief word to make sure that you are devoting MUCH time to *Torah* and giving more *kavana* [thought and feeling] to all your *mitzvot*....

What you should never forget is that we love the Land of Israel and the State of Israel, and they are separate from the government. What is happening in my case is the struggle over the question whether Israel will be a JEWISH state or a state with Jews. As to what the answer will be, lies the future of this country.

Not many children can say that their father is sitting in jail charged with the crime of fulfilling the mitzvah: "Do not stand idly by your brother's blood."[32]

So do not worry and remember the letter that the Vilna Gaon wrote to his family when he left them to go to Eretz Yisrael.

"I ask you to refrain from becoming sad, as you truly promised me, and not to worry. Besides, what is there to worry about? It is common for men to leave their wives in order to travel and wander destitute for years to make money. But I, thank G-d, am traveling to the Holy Land – which everyone longs to see."[33]

And so I say: I praise G-d, because I am jailed for the "terrible crime" of *ahavat Yisrael* [love of fellow Jews].[34]

The Liga Holds a Convention

On June 7, the judge had ordered Meir held for fifteen more days, until June 22. This presented a serious problem, because the Liga's national convention at the Jerusalem International Convention Center had been scheduled for June 12. The convention was a major event in the Liga's campaign for Knesset seats and Meir's speech was to have been one of the main attractions. Now, with Meir in prison, what would Liga leaders do? Accusing the government of arresting Meir in order to obstruct the convention, they declared that it would be held nonetheless. They called on the public to come and show their support for Meir, who was holding a hunger strike in his prison cell.[35]

All that week, Meir smuggled letters out of jail. In small, closely spaced writing he sent Shimon Rachamim detailed instructions for the convention. Rachamim was to see to it that press releases were distributed to newsmen at Beit Agron and Beit Sokolov every day for three days prior to the convention. Flyers publicizing it should be distributed on the streets and in mailboxes. On the morning of the convention, Rachamim should speak personally with a few selected reporters such as Noah Kliger and Shmulik.[36] Perhaps Aryeh Julius could drive them to the convention in his car, he suggested.

A table should be set up no later than 7 P.M. at the entrance to the convention hall where delegates could find paper and pens, he wrote. Forms should be distributed to all participants to indicate what they could do to help in the campaign, including space for their names, addresses and phone numbers. Be sure to call for the forms to be handed in before the convention begins, he added. A booklet outlining the Liga's election platform had been given to a printer a few days earlier. It, too, should be on the table outside the hall. The delegates were to voice their approval of the party platform at the convention.[37]

The booklet was Meir's new book, *Ha'etgar: Eretz Segula* (*Our Challenge: The Chosen Land*), a dramatic presentation of his ideas. It was to have been completed in time for the convention but it was not. Meir instructed Rachamim to put copies of its cover on the walls and announce that orders would be taken. At the low price of three lirot a copy (less than a dollar), participants should be urged to order multiple copies for their friends and family.

Finally, on the day of the convention, he wrote to Rachamim: "Please make these points in your speech tonight: My imprisonment is another effort to break me. The audience must be told the reasons I am in prison and they must understand that even if I did promote acts on behalf of Soviet, Iraqi and Syrian Jews, as charged, that is no crime! And remember, the only way to ensure my release from prison is for all those in the audience to work for my election to the Knesset!" Meir himself had taped a speech which was played to the audience. His voice, because of his hunger strike, was hoarse. Among his topics were the education of Israeli youth and the emigration of Israel's Arabs.

One of the speakers at the convention was Emmanuel Khoury, who told the audience that Arabs in Israel did not have equal rights and that emigration was the best and most humane way for them to express their nationalism.[38] Recently freed Prisoner of Zion Boris Kochubievsky delivered a moving tribute to Meir for all he had done for Soviet Jews. Dr. Israel Eldad, *Yedioth Ahronoth* columnist and professor of Jewish history, said it was a disgrace that the government had jailed Meir. There was no logical reason to do so except to break Meir's spirit. He declared that it was important to continue to help Russian Jews by supporting Senator Jackson's amendment. The next day Meir wrote to Eldad, thanking him for his readiness to speak up, especially in contrast to the silence of the rest of the right-wing camp. "My spirit is unbroken," he wrote to Eldad. "When I get out of prison, I will continue my struggle against the enemies of the Jewish people, from within and from without.[39]

One of the main attractions of the convention was the talk given by Meir's father, Rabbi Yechezkel Kahane, who made it clear that his pride in Meir's accomplishments was not dampened by his distress at Meir's imprisonment. "The Liga is like Titus' mosquito," he said. "It constantly pecks at the conscience of traitors to Jewish ideals." He brought other historical parallels: "The biblical reign of King Achav and Queen Jezebel, which was outwardly a period of peace and plenty, was in reality a corrupt dictatorship. Only the prophet Elijah, putting his life in danger, had the courage to speak out against Jezebel. Meir is like Elijah, and he is also like Rabbi Shimon Ben Shetach of the Second Temple period, who spoke out against the evils of the assimilated ruling class." He compared Meir to Aaron, the high priest, who was instructed to light the candelabra in that week's biblical portion: "You, Meir, are the match; you are the spark, you are the torch that is a light to your nation."[40]

Meir's letters to Rachamim before the convention touched on other concerns. It was clear to him that he would not be allowed to travel to the United States in the near future to raise money for the election campaign. Rabbi Aryeh Julius, who had been working on the campaign at the Liga's Jerusalem office, was, in Meir's words, a "brilliant speaker" and his English was excellent. (He too spoke at the convention.) "It's very important for Aryeh Julius to go to the U.S. on June 20 for a month," wrote Meir. "He should be able to raise enough to cover his salary and then some. Call my brother Nachman – he has connections with the Rejwan Travel Agency. They will sell him the cheapest possible ticket and will wait for payment until Julius returns with money." Meanwhile, he wrote, "Aryeh and Avraham [Hershkowitz] should work on arranging dates and places" for speeches by various Liga speakers in all parts of Israel beginning August 1.

Meir's letters also showed his concern about Liga finances. Expenses included rent for office space and salaries to several people. Even some of the youngsters who distributed flyers were receiving hourly fees. Yitzchak Bivas, of the Zion Hotel, had not yet paid all he owed for the Jewish Identity Center property. Meir wrote to Rachamim, "Keep reminding Bivas that he still owes 7,000 lirot. Have Schechter demand that Bivas pay up – this is the sum due after deductions for the telephone bill!"[41]

Détente Must Be Smashed

On the day of the Liga convention, confined to his cell, Meir wrote another letter. His determination to do all he could to prevent the strengthening of détente represented by Brezhnev's coming visit to Washington, led him to write to a JDLer in America:

> Please send the following message to the press – if a press conference would be effective, even better – and if you could seize the office of the International Red Cross or some Russian office (Tass?) and hold it until the press arrives (announce that you have seized the place to read a special message from me and then you will leave), THAT WOULD BE BEST.

The message was:

> From prison in Jerusalem I speak to the Jews of the United States in particular, but to all those of the free world.
> A successful trip of Leonid Brezhnev leading to the achieving of a firm, stable détente is a disaster to the Free World as it will give the Soviets the technology, trade dollars, and disarmament it needs, not for peace – but for eventual world domination. Détente along these lines must be smashed!

For Jews there is an even greater, immediate danger! ... The moment he
achieves his détente ... we will have mass arrests, show trials and physical
assaults on Soviet Jews.

... Mild, calm protests – even made up of large numbers of people – will
not bother Brezhnev or President Nixon. They will only give us the ILLUSION
that we have done something.

And so I plead with American Jews by their hundreds of thousands. Do not
allow the shame of Jewish apathy and failure to act in the 1940s to be repeated
today. Do whatever you think is necessary to smash détente. Do not be afraid.

Similarly, how much longer can we watch quietly as Iraqi Jews are murdered
in cold blood and Syrian Jews live in hell? Should the Iraqis and Syrians be
allowed to calmly and happily stroll through life? I beg of you to consider these
questions and reach the necessary conclusions....

Then Meir added:

If you do seize an office – PLEASE do it with sense and SECURITY. Everybody
including the police knows everything before it happens. Look the office over
carefully; choose 5 big guys carefully; keep your mouths shut; and grab it.
Don't phone at all to people who will take part in it. AND BURN THESE
PAPERS except for my message [to the press].

Meir addressed the letter to one of the younger members, but mailed it to
Gene Singer, an adult member, to hand-deliver. This letter, too, was intercepted
by the *shabak*. Handwritten and dated June 12, 1973, the text was later neatly
typed for presentation as evidence in court.[42]

Rabbi Julius made plans for a June 19 flight to the States, where supporters
had been alerted to arrange speaking engagements for him. The day before he was
to leave, he was in the office on Jaffa Road when police arrived with a search
warrant. Meir's period of detention was almost over, and the prosecutor needed
more evidence against him in order to extend it. According to the search report,
the police took a four-page mimeographed copy of a speech by Meir as well as
membership lists.[43] How could membership lists be used in evidence against
Meir? This was simply a way to discourage new members. People might not join
the Liga if there was a likelihood that their names would end up in the hands of
the police!

On June 20 Meir was again brought before a judge in Jerusalem District Court
for an extension of his detention. Attorney Meir Schechter argued that he should
be freed because the police had not yet revealed details of the charges. But the
judge was convinced by State Attorney Gabriel Bach's contention that Meir's
release might hinder the investigation, and ordered him held for another ten days.[44]

Supporters were bewildered by the high-handedness of the Attorney General
and the court. They were distressed that Israelis, who were always quick to con-

demn any act against civil liberties, did not protest Meir's arbitrary imprisonment. A telling cartoon was published in *Ma'ariv* after Meir's detention was extended. It showed two longhaired men holding placards that protested the imprisonment of well-known Israeli draft-dodger Giora Newman. They are looking on as a huge hand labeled "the Establishment" grasps a figure that resembles Meir. The caption says, "Don't get excited! It's only Rabbi Kahane."[45]

From his prison cell, Meir smuggled out an article with instructions to me about typing it and sending it to the *Jewish Press.*

> Dear Lib, Here is the article. It is essential that it be typed (original and 3 carbons). Give it to your friend [to type] and keep 1/3 to 1/2 [to type] yourself so that it can be ready by Saturday night. I understand Naomi [Rabbi's Klass's daughter, who would hand-deliver it to the *Jewish Press*] is leaving Sunday. In any case, it MUST be ready, so that you can proof-read it and put in the necessary corrections of mistakes made by your friend and go personally to Naomi.... Please. If necessary, take off time from work but it must be ready for her. WHEN YOU CALL HER BY PHONE, DON'T SAY YOU HAVE SOMETHING FOR HER FATHER. [Meir was certain our home phone was tapped.] Get me one of the carbons, give one to Yoel [Lerner] to translate to Hebrew QUICKLY and hide one.[46]

Meir feared the police would search our home as they had searched the office. The article, "Eretz Yisrael and the Burning Fire," was powerful. It expressed his belief in Israel, but decried the Israeli Establishment.

> ... I love the Land of Israel; I love the State of Israel – I am horrified and repelled by those who hold the reins of power in Israel.
>
> But I do not mistake one for the other. I do not confuse the Land that is holy and the State that is divine, with the governing clique made up of people steeped in assimilation, non-Jewish values and influences, and a lust for power that has been theirs for FORTY YEARS, a record unmatched in any democratic society.
>
> I sit here and contemplate what "the people of the land" – the government of Israel – has done to me. They have arrested me in cooperation with the gentiles; they have charged me with the crime of urging Jews to act violently against the Soviets and Iraqis; they have silenced the press – ordering a blackout on the case, and they want the trial to be held behind closed doors; they told me that I threaten the good relations of Israel with the United States; and they intend to ask the court to sentence me to a five year prison term....[47]

In a letter home to bolster our spirits, Meir wrote:

> As you know, I received 10 more days, which means until next Friday.... I ask you all to please be strong and carry on the way a real strong Jewish family does. *Ivdu et Hashem besimcha* [Worship G-d with joy] and with the knowl-

edge that [He] always sends *yisurim be'ahava* [suffering with love] for which we are richly rewarded in the world to come.... Above all, have faith in G-d, especially when things are not quite rosy. I will be with you soon, with G-d's help, and we will go to Netanya [for a summer vacation]....

Only his postscript expressed the mundane aspect of being in jail: "I will need some underpants and a towel; also wine for Shabbat, 2 candles; also drinks; shirts."[48]

At the top of the letter, Meir cited a verse from the Book of Jeremiah with the prophet's message to his chief disciple, Baruch (*Jeremiah* 36:5). Whimsically, he inserted our other children's names in the verse: "And Jeremiah commanded Baruch (and Tova and Tzippy and Binyamin), saying: 'I am detained, I cannot go to the house of the L-rd.'" It is likely that Meir selected this verse not only because of our son Baruch's name and the fact that he, like Jeremiah, was in jail, but also because he felt a special affinity with Jeremiah, who had been imprisoned for his unpopular prophecies. Many years later, in "Fire in My Bones," he expressed that feeling:

In 1973 I was arrested by the totalitarians of Israel and placed in a solitary cell for 31 days. In my anger and bitterness, I paced my cell and said to myself that I was finished with helping Jews and working to warn them when they – in response – tried to kill the messenger. I angrily said, "Let them save themselves!"

And I sat on my cot and opened a *Tanach* (Bible) swiftly and bitterly. And it opened to a page in Jeremiah, chapter 20, in which the bitter and disgusted Jeremiah, faced with the enmity and hatred of Jews, cries out in his anger and determination to cease his mission.

And then I stared at the words that shot out at me from the page to which I had turned by sheer "chance," so to speak, and it read,

"And if I say: I will not make mention of Him nor speak anymore of His name, there is in my heart as it were a burning fire shut up in my bones and I weary myself to hold it in but cannot."

And I sat on that cot, staring at those words on a page I had turned to without thinking. And I sat for many minutes, not moving. And I knew then that I could never hold back the fire in my bones.

The article concluded:

And so, I will continue. But not because I know that I will win. I will continue – as Jeremiah – because I cannot do anything else.... Jeremiah continued and never was supported. And he failed.

One reader wrote: "I wept when I read your column.... Please don't despair. Jeremiah did not fail."[49]

Meir felt the loss of his liberty deeply. In a *Jewish Press* news item, he wrote:

> We tend to think of a police state as a formal, communist or fascist country. It could never happen in our beloved Israel. But the specter of the government calmly disregarding all civil rights, including wiretapping and intercepting mail WITHOUT A COURT ORDER is a daily occurrence here. I do not know whether I will be able to get articles out to you or for how long...[50]

There was a legal basis for these undemocratic procedures. In 1948, the Emergency Defense Regulations enacted by the British mandatory government became, like all mandatory law, part of Israeli law.[51] But protest was still permitted. Liga leaders called a press conference on June 28 at Beit Sokolov in Tel Aviv to protest the injustice of Meir's detention. Yoel Lerner charged that Meir was being detained at the behest of the U.S. State Department to prevent him from embarrassing Nixon during Brezhnev's visit. Meir's father bitterly denounced Israeli authorities for jailing his son two days before the Shavuot festival. "Nobody raises his voice against a detention which is of a political nature," he declared. "No one cries out when a Jew is arrested in Israel!"[52]

Indicted for Conspiracy

On June 29 Meir was indicted on conspiracy charges in the Jerusalem District Court. The prosecution charged that between May 24 and June 12 Meir had sent four letters and a telegram to the United States in an attempt to conspire with the recipients and others to commit felonies. The letter dated June 12, sent while he was in detention, was said to have been smuggled out of jail by a visitor. The alleged felonies were: 1) the abduction of foreign officials in the U.S.; 2) the bombing of, and shooting at, foreign embassy buildings; 3) setting fire to buildings of American companies that traded with the USSR. "These acts," said the indictment, "were designed to harm Israeli interests with regard to relations between Israel and the United States." The law prohibiting "criminal conspiracy to harm Israel's relations with a foreign country" carried a maximum penalty of seven years in prison.

Meir explained to the court that he had sought to disrupt the Brezhnev visit because he feared that improved American-Soviet relations would jeopardize Soviet Jews. He said that the letters he sent to the United States were part of an operation to discourage the visit of Brezhnev there. "We saw in this visit a decided danger to the future of Jews in Russia," he said. He denied any intent to commit murder, but said "there was a need to kidnap a Russian diplomat for 24 hours and for shooting into a Soviet building." The plan was "to release the diplomat after 24 hours, without any demands being made. Our aim was simply to have the visit canceled." He said he would plead guilty to the facts but innocent to the charges, because the facts did not constitute a crime. In his request for release on bail, Meir told the court that he could now promise that he would not repeat his actions because Mr. Brezhnev had returned to the Soviet Union. Attorney Schechter reminded the judge that Meir had always honored his commitments. Nevertheless, Judge Avinoam Eden denied bail, ordering Meir kept in custody until the end of the trial, which was to begin on July 20. Now that he was officially indicted, he was transferred from the Jerusalem lockup to Kfar Yona (Ashmoret) Prison, near Netanya.[53] He wrote home: "... I am not in isolation and really can walk around pretty much as I please.... I eat only eggs and cheese.... I hope the trial will start within 10 days."[54]

American Jews responded to a plea in the *Jewish Press* urging readers to write letters of protest to the Israeli ambassador in Washington, Simcha Dinitz. So many wrote to him, that the embassy sent out a printed form letter.[55] Sam Shoshan wrote to the Israel Consul General in Chicago: "Rabbi Kahane's civil rights are being violated. As you can see, I am taking this Israeli mini-Watergate to the public media, the result of which may be that only our '*sonim*' [enemies] will benefit.... [This] has all the trappings of a political trial.... You should alert those in power that persecuting Kahane will work against the interests of the world Jewish community."[56]

Letters of protest in the Israeli press were published only after Meir had been granted bail. A group of former Prisoners of Zion published an open letter in *Ma'ariv* demanding Meir's freedom. "We are not members of the Liga," they wrote, "and we do not always agree with its activities, but we cannot remain silent in the face of the harsh treatment of Rabbi Meir Kahane.... This man devoted all his life to Soviet Jewry.... His acts encouraged us in our struggle.... We hope Jews in Israel will rise up and protest his shameful imprisonment." Among those who signed were Ruth Alexandrovitch, Grisha Feigin, Vladimir Frumer, Yasha Kazakov and his father Yosef, David Markish, Raiza Palatnik, Leah Slovin, Dov Sperling, and Michael Zand.[57]

Letters to the Editor in *Yedioth Ahronoth* also expressed dismay at the injustice. One decried the apathy of the public to Meir's month-long imprisonment. "If a rabbi in the Soviet Union were imprisoned, Israel would protest vehemently," wrote Moshe Stein of Herzliya. Aharon Yazdi of Tel Aviv claimed that if it were a leftist who had been imprisoned under such circumstances, there would have been countless protests.[58]

The injustice of keeping Meir in prison without bail for such a long time aroused Meir's cousin, prominent Tel Aviv attorney David Rotlevy, to join attorney Meir Schechter in filing an appeal for bail to the Supreme Court. They maintained that Meir was not guilty of conspiracy because the letters – which were seized by the police – had not reached their destinations. The family rejoiced when Justice Moshe Landau granted bail, even though it was high: 100,000 lirot ($24,000). Meir's parents, who were present in the judge's chambers during the proceedings, put up half of it. Upon his release, Meir received a check for 83 lirot (about $20) from the Israel Prison Service. He cashed the check but kept the stub, labeled "Prisoner Release," as a souvenir.[59]

At the trial on July 20, Meir entered a plea of "not guilty." Although he admitted to writing the four letters and one telegram on which the government had based its conspiracy charges, he maintained that their contents did not constitute a crime. The Attorney General did not present the prosecution's case until almost one year later, on March 12, 1974. This time frame was considered reasonable by his lawyer.[60] In the interim, Meir was not permitted to travel to the States. With elections set for mid-October, he looked forward to three months of campaigning in Israel.

Chapter 34

Our Challenge
(July-September 1973)

The Party Platform: Ha'etgar

I N JULY, RELEASED from prison but compelled to remain in Israel for the Brezhnev letters trial, Meir turned his attention to the Knesset campaign. The publicity engendered by his month-long imprisonment in June actually helped his campaign for the Knesset by bringing his name before the public repeatedly. To maintain media interest – and more important, to publicize his ideas – he called a press conference at Beit Sokolov in Tel Aviv on July 16, one week after he was freed. His press release announced that he would speak about his arrest and would also reveal facts about Christian missionaries who preyed on new immigrants at the Carmiel immigrant absorption center. At the press conference he pinpointed the real issue: "Is Israel a state of the Jews or a Jewish state?" His answer: "At present, Israel is a Western state of people speaking Hebrew, but when the Liga has Knesset representation, it will be able to accomplish its primary aim of assuring the Jewish character of the state. We, the extremists, will push the moderates to action." He told the press about his new book, *Ha'etgar: Eretz Segula* (*Our Challenge: The Chosen Land*), which presented the Liga's platform. "It will be printed in ten thousand copies," he said. And it was.[1]

Meir began writing *Our Challenge* in English in October 1972, right after he announced that he was running for the Knesset. His schedule in Israel was flexible, so he was able to devote most of his time to writing. He completed the book sometime in December or January, and gave it to Yoel Lerner to translate into Hebrew. When Lerner was imprisoned for anti-missionary activity in February, Aryeh Julius completed the translation. (Meir had been in Israel only one year, and his Hebrew was not yet polished enough to write an entire book.) *Our Challenge* was published in English only in April 1974, but the early publication of the Hebrew version, *Ha'etgar*, was important, because it presented the Liga's platform for the elections that were to take place at the end of October.[2]

The book defined the problems facing the Jewish state: the loss of religious values, the grave socio-economic gap, and friction between religious and irreligious Jews. In *Ha'etgar* Meir offered a plan to infuse Jewish youth with an iron-clad sense of identity to make them impervious to modern Western influences and strong enough to overcome the weariness of an interminable struggle with the Arabs. He presented a program that would convince the Arabs, both in the liberated territories and in "little Israel," that their own interests would be best served by immigrating to other countries. He maintained that the State of Israel's foreign policy should include its role as the guardian of all Jews throughout the world. The government must realize that there are no permanent allies for Israel among the other nations. Jewish interests come first, no matter what the world may say. He wrote:

> The great tasks of our day are ... to define clearly and precisely the purpose and destiny of the Jewish people.... Our State must not seek merely to be like all the rest, but a distinctively Jewish one. The Jewish people stands or falls on the knowledge that it is NOT like other people....[3]

Ha'etgar was printed at the Hebron Press. The printing plant was located in Kiryat Arba, where it provided employment for residents. Yehoshua Ben Zion, one of the owners of the Hebron Press, agreed with Meir's ideas and liked the way he promoted them. Ben Zion personally underwrote the entire cost of printing the 183-page, softcover book, and by the end of July 10,000 copies were ready.

The book was priced at three lirot, on par with the price of books in Israel at that time. It was available at Liga branches and at public meetings and was sold by the Steimatzky bookstore chain. Every Liga campaign flyer and newspaper ad featured a mention of *Ha'etgar*. One ad for the book proclaimed:

Just Published!
Rabbi Kahane's New Book *Ha'etgar*
Presenting the Problems of the Jewish People
in Our Times and Explaining the Philosophy of the Liga[4]

Autographed copies were distributed at election rallies, many as gifts. Moshe Lebowitz, a native of Safed, recalled that at a 1973 election rally in his home town, he received a free autographed copy of *Ha'etgar*, which he still has.[5]

After the elections, Shoshana Mageni sent Meir this assessment of the book:

> Ever since reading *Ha'etgar*, I've been amazed as events have proven, over and over, the extent of your foresight. You have a lot to contribute to the Israeli

scene, if only as a catalyst.... It may take a while to get used to the Israeli mentality, but you have definitely touched a responsive chord.

... Besides the general need for spreading Jewish values, I think the most important problem you could tackle now is, once more, the problem of "Who is NOT a Jew" – the question of Arab residents of the State of Israel and your program for its solution.... The best thing is to take one issue and get people first to think about it.... Stepping on toes, even intellectual ones, gets action – You've already proven that.[6]

Meanwhile, Meir had found a publisher in America for *Our Challenge*. Benton Arnovitz, a book editor, recalled, "I had been interested in Meir's work, and contacted him while I was at Macmillan, asking him what book-length writing he might be engaged in. He offered me the manuscript of *Never Again!* and I proposed it to management.... It was vetoed.... When I moved to Chilton, I kept in contact with Meir, and he offered me *Our Challenge*."[7]

In June, while Meir was in jail, a telegram from Arnovitz arrived: "... If these terms are satisfactory for *Challenge* please wire approval and I will send contract. $2,500 advance against royalties of 10% on our net receipts on first 10,000 copies sold, 20% thereafter." This telegram bears Meir's handwritten notation to me, "Please wire immediately: Offer Accepted."[8]

Correspondence with Arnovitz was another indication that the government was tampering with Meir's mail. When two weeks had gone by and the contract had not arrived, Meir told me to contact Arnovitz. He replied in a telegram dated July 11: "Contracts mailed to you on June 11, duplicates coming by air. I need to have Meir's signature on them to send the check. Please return them quickly." The duplicate contract arrived, Meir signed it, and I mailed it. On July 25 Arnovitz wrote, "Here is your copy of the countersigned contract. The check will be along in two or three days." Regarding the contract he wrote, "I can't imagine what happened to the first set I sent you early in June. Do the postal authorities open your mail?"[9]

Delays in our mail delivery continued. On August 20, Arnovitz wrote: "The advance check was sent airmail on July 26th to 13 Sorotzkin Street. If it's still not arrived by the time this letter reaches you, please cable me and I'll have it cancelled and will send you another." He sent this letter to our Post Office box, 15027, thinking the address might make a difference. The check arrived in mid September, over six weeks after it had been sent. On September 21 Arnovitz wrote: "I'm glad the check finally arrived. I've never had such problems before with mail to Israel." After that, he followed Meir's advice to send letters to my parents' Jerusalem address.[10]

In September Arnovitz wrote to Meir about promoting the book in America: "May I ask if you're planning to be back in the States this spring? I would like to set our promotion and publicity people to work, and tie-ins with your campus or other appearances would be excellent. You'll see the book is now scheduled for March publication."[11]

Meir was not happy about the distant publication date. In November he wrote to Arnovitz:

> With the outbreak of [the Yom Kippur] war it appears clear that the subject of Israel will be the main international topic for many months. At the same time, the growing pressure on Israel by the whole world, including the United States, to withdraw from the liberated lands will escalate. Now, or as close to 'now' as possible, AND NOT IN MARCH 1974, is the time to publish my book.[12]

Meir was disappointed when Chilton's marketing manager replied in December that they could not change their production plans: "We are now drawing up plans for the promotion of your new book *Our Challenge*," he wrote. "Keep in mind that we expect to have the books off press by the first few days of March at the earliest, plus an added 40 to 50 days for distribution and reception of the books at the bookseller level." He asked Meir to inform him of a two to three week period in late April (or a similar period) when he would be available for a promotion tour that would include TV talk shows.[13] Meir would have been delighted to be able to give him a firm date for a promotion tour, but in December he had no way of knowing when he would be allowed to leave Israel.[14]

Meir was also unhappy about the book's jacket. The contract stipulated that the author did not have to approve jacket, art, flap copy nor blurb.[15] When Meir received a copy of the jacket, he was distressed to read the inside flap, which began:

> OUR CHALLENGE is not a Jewish MEIN KAMPF, though some readers are sure to think so. But it is nothing less than a battle plan for the creation on the ancient model of a new Jewry and the reshaping of Jewish destiny. This is a rallying call to pride in self and pride in one's people – and will shock Jewish assimilationists and many gentile observers to the core.

Meir sent the book flap text back to Arnovitz. He circled the words MEIN KAMPF and above them he wrote, "This is **bad**!" In his reply, Arnovitz reminded Meir how difficult it had been to get mail to him:

> Let me say at the outset, that the jackets are already printed with the original copy and that bound books are due in about one week.... You may know though, that while it is not usual industry practice to clear jacket copy with an author, I did several months ago send that material to Shifra [Hoffman]. After consulting with a number of her/your colleagues, the consensus was that it was excellent and effective selling copy. They did ask that one line in the fourth paragraph be changed, and I amended it accordingly. Getting mail to you from

here was particularly difficult at the time, you'll recall, and sending the copy to your New York associates seemed a sensible courtesy.

The sentence in the fourth paragraph had been: "... may call to mind, for those who want to find a connection, another speaker in another day." It was changed to: "... plans which he is attempting to put in practice have resulted in his being brought to trial by the Israeli government."

Arnovitz's reply to Meir continued:

> ... As evidence of the value I place on our relationship, however, I am prepared to see the jacket flap copy amended, consistent with effective selling, for second and future printings of the book if you still desire that after you have had an opportunity to gauge the sales response on the first printing. All I can do for the present is say I'm truly sorry.[16]

To show Meir how Chilton was working to promote *Our Challenge*, Arnovitz enclosed a pre-publication review from *Publisher's Weekly*, which gave April 15 as the publication date. It said:

> ... [Rabbi Kahane] here sets forth his concept of [Israel] as the Biblically ordained realization of the ancient Jewish dream. Kahane's passionate assertiveness, which at times seems self-righteous truculence, stems from his total commitment to a vision which is ultimately a mystique – the vision of Israel as *Eretz Yisroel*: the Chosen People in their Chosen Land, fully sovereign and defining their lives by the most sacred traditions and beliefs of historical Judaism....[17]

Chilton also had the book reviewed in the prestigious *New York Times Book Review*. However, the reviewer, Arthur Waskow, did not give the reader any information about the book's content. Instead, he declared that Meir's ideas were completely negated by the universal ethic of the Bible and expounded on his own leftist ideas.[18] In contrast, a review by Rabbi Isaac L. Swift stated: "Some of his diatribes – especially where they concern Israeli youth – should be taken seriously by all who cherish the State of Israel and 'pray for the peace of Jerusalem.' That some of his political suggestions are unrealistic ... need not diminish our ungrudging recognition of a serious mind grappling with problems of serious magnitude."[19]

A mixed review by Professor Arnold Ages noted:

> Whether or not one agrees with Rabbi Kahane's thesis, and there are many who will take violent opposition to it, his candor on the question of the Arabs in Israel is refreshing.... Kahane feels that Israel's future depends ultimately on the spiritual regeneration of the Israelis.... If this return to mitzvah Judaism is not accomplished, there is a danger that Israel's people will slip into the quagmire of leftist ideology which inevitably saps the life of a nation. Kahane points

to the treason of Udi Adiv (convicted of conspiring with the Arabs in 1972) as an example of what happens to Jews who have lost their pride in their people and their land.[20]

To promote the book, Chilton sent pre-publication galley proofs to librarians' journals. The evaluation in *Kirkus Reviews* began:

> When it comes to righteous wrath, Moses has nothing on Rabbi Kahane. The militant leader of the Jewish Defense League damns the "assimilationist rot" contaminating both young Israeli leftists and the children of Jews in the Diaspora. Strident and uncompromising, he hammers away at his fundamentalist precepts: divine ordinance guides Jewish destiny.... The Arabs are bent on the destruction of Israel; not an inch of the territory conquered in 1967 must be surrendered: only armed might can insure the political survival of the Jewish state. "Concessions? Compromise? Moderation? Foolish exercises in self-delusion and self-destruction." The Arabs within Israel should be encouraged to get out; they are an internal "time bomb." Education and prosperity will only make them more bitter and extreme....[21]

Choice, a journal for librarians, stated simply:

> ... This slim volume presents Kahane's views in their bluntest expression. He believes the Emancipation to have been a failure, trusts only Jewish self-defense, and predicts a coming wave of anti-Semitism in the U.S. Repudiated by the government of Israel and by large sectors of American Jewry, Kahane yet deals with real problems and issues.[22]

One Chilton press release enthusiastically proclaimed: "Jewish Defense League's leader issues a rallying call to Jews the world over ... a battle plan for the reshaping of Jewish destiny through the creation of a new Jewry on the ancient model."[23] Despite their promotion efforts, the book did not sell very well, and in 1978 Chilton offered to sell Meir the remainder overstock at a 70% discount on the list price of $7.95. In July 1974, Arnovitz wrote to Meir: "The response to *Our Challenge* has been very strange indeed. There's been outright hostility from some of the paperbackers (liberal Jews who tout freedom of the press)." Later, he explained this to me: "So many folks who are engaged in bookselling lean to the left. Meir's message (or the message they imagined he was offering) often was anathema to them. And if too few of them would stock the books, possible purchasers had no opportunity to buy them."[24]

A Book of Jewish Press Articles

Our Challenge was not a bestseller, but Meir saw its modest sales as a way of spreading his ideas. With that in mind, he thought of publishing a collection of his *Jewish Press* articles. As he wrote to Shifra Hoffman, a JDL member who had volunteered to help him, "I do not know when I will get back to America, but it appears to be a long time now, and the only way I will be able to speak to American Jews will be through my writings."[25]

Many people told Meir that they looked forward each week to reading his *Jewish Press* column. Some even said they bought the paper only because of his column. To test the waters, he put a notice at the end of his columns in April and May, that said: "If you are interested in a book of selected articles and essays by Meir Kahane that have appeared over the past ten years in the *Jewish Press*, write to Meir Kahane, P.O. Box 15027, Jerusalem. Send no money. Simply say you would be willing to purchase a copy for under $5."[26]

He called the book *Meir Kahane: Writings (5731): Selected Writings by Meir Kahane from the Year 5731 (1971-72)*. It included not only articles written in 1971 and 1972, but a good number from earlier years – even two that he wrote in 1960. He began to select articles for this volume a short time before April 1973, when he first mentioned it in his *Jewish Press* column. He added distinctive titles for articles that had originally appeared in his columns without headings and gave the clippings to the Michlol typesetting service in Jerusalem.[27] In June, while in jail for the Brezhnev letters, he sent me the introduction to bring to Michlol.

> Here is the introduction to the *Jewish Press* articles book (written with incomparable modesty). Please type it and insert it where it should go (wherever you think). Did you get the paper with the diagram for the other pages to be included? They were written under difficult conditions.[28]

Meir's reference to his "incomparable modesty" reflected the fact that he himself wrote the "Publisher's Introduction." It began:

> This first volume of selected writings by Rabbi Meir Kahane is also the first effort to get into book form all of the ideas and thoughts in pen of the man who is easily the most controversial, exciting and charismatic Jewish leader of our times. His major ideas and expositions are at variance with every Establishment Jewish leader one can think of, but none can deny that he has succeeded in capturing minds and hearts and in being loved (and hated) as none of the other leaders have.

One purpose of the book, it continued, was "to give the reader pause to ask himself: 'If he [Meir] was so right in the past, perhaps he is also right in the unpopular things he says concerning the future?'" The introduction also outlined plans for future volumes: "We already have begun work on the next volume ... to cover the writings of 1972-73, again with many others from distant [earlier] years."[29]

From Michlol, the material went to the Hebron Press where the plates were to be prepared. Another letter from jail in June reveals Meir's eagerness to see the book in print.

> Please make sure Weiss [Moshe Weiss, of Hebron Press] gets the *J.P.* [*Jewish Press*] articles and starts work on them immediately. Did Weiss start the Hebrew book [*Ha'etgar*]? Tell Shimon [Rachamim] to see Ben Zion immediately Sunday and get money for Weiss.[30]

In October, the Hebron Press shipped the plates to Morris Drucker in New York for printing and in November, when printing was completed, Meir informed his *Jewish Press* readers how they could order it.[31]

Once the volume for 5731 was in print, Meir looked for a commercial publisher to print the volumes for 5732 and 5733. He tried to sell the idea to the Chilton Book Company:

> A great many readers of my regular column in the *Jewish Press* have pushed for years for me to put out a book(s) containing my writings. I have done so, and the first such book, *Meir Kahane Writings: 5731* (writings for the years 1971, 1972) will be on the market in softcover within a month. It was published by myself because demand made it possible.
>
> I have two other books all ready to be published (*Writings 5732; Writings 5733*)... There is a special market for these books aside from the general Jewish and non-Jewish market, that is, the *Jewish Press* readership.... I emphasize again to you the built-in market that you have with the *Jewish Press* which has a paid circulation of 140,000, mostly fanatical fans.[32]

Chilton was not persuaded. As Arnovitz later explained, "Collections are notoriously bad sellers, and I could not interest my firm in publishing a book that would not sell."[33] Meir realized he would not find a commercial publisher. To save money he had the 1972 and 1973 articles printed in one volume. It included articles written through September 1973 and was titled *Meir Kahane: Writings (5732-33): Selected Writings by Meir Kahane from the Year 5732-33 (1971-73).*[34]

Arnovitz was right. From the start, *Writings 1971* was a "bad seller," even though a commercial distributor, Bookazine, was handling sales. Meir connected with Bookazine through JDL member George Torodash. Torodash had contacted Meir's Betar friend, Zvi Kraushar, who worked at Bookazine, and Kraushar persuaded his boss to take 1,000 copies. In February 1974, Shifra Hoffman reported: "Kraushar says *Writings* are moving slowly." JDL could not help much either: "Russ Kelner says that since the treasury is low, he cannot order by volume," wrote Shifra. In April she wrote, "Kraushar said he sold about 50 books of *Writings* and promised to mail me a check at $2.50 a book." Many copies of *Writings 1971* were still unsold in 1977. When *Kahane: the Magazine of the*

Authentic Jewish Idea (launched in April 1976) was temporarily discontinued in September 1977, the subscribers were informed: "In lieu of the forthcoming issues we owe you, we are taking the liberty of sending you Rabbi Kahane's *Writings 5731* to compensate for the unexpired portion of your subscription."[35]

However, in 1973 Meir believed that books of his articles were an important project. It was a way for his ideas to reach American Jews. In October 1973, he thought of another book for American Jews – a history of the Jewish Defense League. He was certainly the most qualified person to write it! It would be not only a history of events, but also an exposition of JDL philosophy. In October, to find a publisher, he sent a mimeographed letter to the leading New York publishing firms. Since it would be more impressive if the offer came from an agent, the letter was signed by Rabbi Aryeh Julius, who was working on the election campaign. It requested an advance of $15,000, six times as much as Meir had received for *Our Challenge*:

> The name, Jewish Defense League, has become a household word.... The phenomenon of a militant, radical Jewish group and its exploits against the Soviets, Arabs and anti-Semites have made it the most controversial group in the world.
>
> I have been asked by Rabbi Meir Kahane, the founder and head of the JDL, to offer you the option of publishing his official "Story of the JDL," the first such book on the market and the one which will include the real facts concerning JDL's controversial and exciting activities.
>
> The terms of the contract include a $15,000 advance against royalties plus royalties of 10% on the first 10,000 copies sold and 20% above that.[36]

Replies from a number of publishers arrived in November. Some rejected the idea out of hand. Viking Press: "I'm sorry, but we can't express any interest in seeing Rabbi Meir Kahane's manuscript." Atheneum Books: "The book about which you have written does not seem likely for Atheneum." Alfred A. Knopf Publishing: "We do not think it a possibility for our list." Prentice-Hall: "The project falls outside the areas of our ... publishing programs and we feel the market is too limited."

Other publishers expressed interest in seeing the manuscript. Delacorte Press: "We would very much like to see your work." Little, Brown and Company: "We would be glad to see your official story of the JDL ... send the manuscript." McGraw-Hill: "When you have a substantial portion of the manuscript completed, we would certainly be interested."[37] The most interesting reply came from Charles Scribner's Sons:

> Dear Rabbi Kahane, I don't feel we can really discuss a contract or an advance for your new book unless we have a comprehensive outline or a manuscript in hand.... There are limits to what we can do without a formal book proposal.

There's one more thing I'd like to add – about the work you're doing and the position you've taken. As I don't need to tell you, it scares most Jews, but that doesn't make it any less valuable. I don't know how to reconcile the fact that I disagree with a lot of the things that you're doing, yet at the same time, deep in my heart, I'm glad you're doing them. I think a lot of Jews feel that way too.

[signed] Norman Kotker, editor, Charles Scribners' Sons.[38]

Kotker's reply was gratifying on the one hand and frustrating on the other. It was typical of so many Jews. They supported Meir "in their hearts" but did not give him the financial support that was so vital for him to continue his work.

Fundraising for the Elections

Meir's first feelers for *Story of the Jewish Defense League* (eventually published in 1975) were sent out in October 1973, in the midst of the Knesset election campaign, precisely because he needed funds for the campaign. He hoped to find a publisher whose advance on the book would supply those funds, but was unsuccessful. In an article explaining why he was running for Knesset, he referred to people like Norman Kotker:

... worst of all – [are] the people who listen, cheer – and go home. It is they, especially, who have helped dig the grave of the Jewish Defense League in the United States, and their silent support will forever be the silent funeral for the group that tried to save them.

If he were elected to the Knesset, he wrote, "[I would] be received in the United States with open doors by the same people who, in the past, refused to be seen with me. It makes no sense ... but that is the nature of man." He explained what he needed from American Jews:

... The support of the ordinary Israeli for the League is impressive. But we will be unable to translate this vocal support into votes unless we have funds to reach him with ads, posters and personal appearances.

... In order to have any kind of a chance in the election, we need a minimum of $25,000, a sum that I know covers the kitchen expenses of any one of hundreds of temples; a sum that any given ten Jews regularly lose on a Las Vegas weekend junket; a sum that is given without a second thought to the vast wasteland that is known as the American Jewish Congress.[39]

But Meir's supporters were not wealthy people, and fundraising was a constant struggle. A ten-dollar contribution from each reader was the modest aim of a *Jewish Press* ad in June:

> ### Kahane to the Knesset
> The Jewish people need Kahane whether it's in Israel or America because
>   he tells it like it is and how it should be.
> We desperately need money for the campaign. For a $10 contribution you
>   will receive the book for Jewish survival, *Never Again!*
> No contribution too large. No contribution too small.
> Please make a generous contribution to "Kahane to the Knesset '73"
>   so Rabbi Meir Kahane can be the moral conscience of Israel.[40]

Rabbi Aryeh Julius agreed to travel to the United States to raise money for
the Knesset campaign. An ad in July, before Meir's release from prison,
announced: "Rabbi Kahane, now in prison incommunicado, feels that this incar-
ceration is a deliberate attempt to keep him out of the Knesset race. Representing
Rabbi Kahane in the U.S. is Rabbi Aryeh Julius ... to raise funds for the Rabbi's
election campaign...[41]

The ads were composed by Hilton Goldman, chairman of the Kahane for
Knesset Committee in America. Goldman, a New Jersey lawyer, was the driving
force in fundraising for the election campaign. In telegraphic style, Goldman
reported to Meir on Rabbi Julius' activities:

> Rav Julius is leaving for the [West] Coast on the 16th, a cocktail party, some
> synagogue appearances, to San Diego, Chicago, etc., to return the end of the
> month. He's off to the mountains today – just left him.[42]

Earlier, Rabbi Julius had appeared on the Barry Farber radio show, had
addressed JDL members at the home of Liz Greenbaum in Brooklyn, and was the
guest of Rabbi Herzel Kranz at the Silver Spring Jewish Center. On July 2 he
attended a meeting of JDL's executive board to urge them to support Meir's election effort. Many board members were afraid of depleting JDL's meager resources,
but Rabbi Julius' efforts were successful. The board agreed to send out an appeal
to the membership for funds for the Knesset campaign.[43]

In the mailing to JDL supporters, Goldman, writing over Meir's signature,
pointed out that the JDL in America would benefit from Meir's election to the
Knesset:

> The JDL past is a glorious one of fighting for and achieving Jewish rights. But
> past memories are not enough to solve present and future problems.
>   The hard fact is that only JDL representation in the Knesset will assure the
> movement the strength and prestige it needs to help JDL in America and Jews
> wherever they live in the world.
>   Frankly, our chances of being seated are excellent. The support of the people
> here [in Israel] is obvious; but to translate that support into votes requires

MONEY. The election is only a few months away and we still have many miles to travel.

I now turn to you as one who has shown your love of Jewry and support of our program in the past. For the sake of the movement both in Israel and America, I urge you to give as much as you can today and invite you to help celebrate our mutual victory by having lunch with me this Autumn in the Knesset.

[signed] With Love of Israel, Meir Kahane

A note to me at the bottom of this printed letter made it clear that Goldman had composed this letter. He wrote: "On reflection, I think that my ploy [lunch in the Knesset] beats Bill Clinton's 'coffee in the White House.'"[44]

Two fundraising parties were organized by Goldman at Café Yaffo, in Manhattan. An invitation to the first, on August 8, indicates that the charge per person was a mere $10, but after a "stirring speech" by Dr. Morris Mandel, people probably opened their pockets and donated additional sums. Dr. Mandel, a *Jewish Press* columnist, was a featured speaker at Meir's fundraising dinners throughout the years. His emotion-laden words never failed to arouse listeners to contribute generously to the cause. The dinner was so successful that Goldman put an ad in the *Jewish Press* the very next week for a second event on September 12:

> WE'RE SORRY!
> You weren't able to get a table at our dinner August 8th ...
> But the demand was so great that we were S.R.O.
> BY POPULAR REQUEST:
> A second evening for
> KAHANE TO THE KNESSET...
> Delicious Glatt Kosher Dinner and Entertainment
> Featuring Outstanding Israeli Artists.
> $10.00 per person.[45]

Dr. William Perl, the newly elected JDL national chairman, spoke at the dinner on September 12. A report on his speech hailed Perl's "knowledge and enthusiasm" and expressed hope that he would bring "new national unity to the JDL [and] give a tremendous boost to the organization." Repeating Goldman's prediction, the report ended on the hopeful note that "our organization will gain strength after the election of Rabbi Meir Kahane to the Knesset."

There was an added impetus for JDL to aid the election campaign: Special funds were distributed to the affiliates of Knesset parties. "If we enter the Knesset," wrote Meir, "the foreign branches of JDL automatically get Jewish Agency and World Zionist Organization funds."[46]

Goldman's innovative methods included this message to JDLers all over the United States: "Enclosed is a copy of a highly successful fundraising ad placed in New York's *Jewish Press*. It is requested that this ad be placed in a Jewish newspaper in your area most likely to attract a pro-Kahane readership.[47]

The ad Goldman enclosed said:

> RABBI MEIR KAHANE
> SPEAKS FROM ISRAEL
> ON "WHY KNESSET?"
>
> Now you can receive a compelling message recently recorded in Jerusalem by the most dynamic Jewish leader on the world scene, AND at the same time aid the JDL Knesset Campaign.
>
> For every contribution of at least $10, you will receive FREE a compact cassette recording running approximately 30 minutes and be able to hear Rabbi Kahane address the pressing issues confronting the Israeli electorate and Jews throughout the world in 1973.[48]

Meir also used his *Jewish Press* column to attract potential contributors. In one he wrote:

> ... Meir Kahane, has begun taking street walks and going into neighborhoods and homes.... Rabbi Kahane shakes hands and knocks on doors to introduce himself to startled Israelis.... Will it work? According to JDL secretary Shimon Rachamim, "It worked for Kennedy – why not here?"[49]

American supporters sent lapel buttons and stickers. Gene Singer designed, produced and shipped tens of thousands of buttons to Israel. One said, *Kahana Laknesset – Lo Lakeleh* (Kahane to the Knesset – Not to Jail). Another said, *Hatzba Kahana* (Vote for Kahane). Shmuel Knopfler designed the stickers. In September he wrote, "Bumper stickers on the way."[50]

Singer recalled his support for Meir:

> Meir was responsible for me becoming a real Jew. I first heard him speak at the Bialystoker synagogue [on Manhattan's Lower East Side]. From then on I put all my artistic efforts into JDL. I designed buttons, New Year cards, signs. I was self-employed, in a hardware business. I would run out in the middle of the day to do what had to be done. In the summer of 1973 I was on tour in Israel. Shifra Hoffman was in Israel too and arranged a meeting for me with Meir. I was already a follower of Meir's, but not on an active basis. I promised Meir I would help with his campaign. I returned to the United States and met with Hilton Goldman. We worked on the campaign with a vengeance. My only concern was to do all I could for the Jewish people.[51]

With the help of his American supporters, Meir began an intensive election campaign in Israel.

Childhood

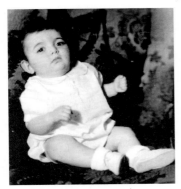

Meir, about three months old.

With mother, about four years old.

Family wedding, 1943

Meir, age 11, at his maternal uncle's wedding. Front row, left to right: brother Nachman, grandmother Henya Trainin, Meir, grandfather Rabbi Baruch Shalom Trainin. Back row, left to right: parents Rabbi Charles (Yechezkel) and Sonia (Sara Chana) Kahane, Isaac and Frances Trainin, Meir Dov Trainin.

Quest for Knowledge

Graduation from Brooklyn Talmudical Academy High School, June 1949. *Chapter 3.*

Graduation from Brooklyn College, June 1954. *Chapter 6.*

Mirrer Yeshiva

Rabbi Mordechai Ginsberg teaching Talmud at the Mirrer Yeshiva, Brooklyn, NY., *circa* 1950. Meir is second from the left. *Chapter 5.*

Wedding Day
Brooklyn, N.Y., May 27, 1956

Preparing the *ketuba* (marriage contract). Left to right: Rabbi Menachem Zev Friedman, Libby's grandfather; Rabbi Abraham Kalmanowitz, head of the Mirrer Yeshiva; Meir, in formal attire. *Chapter 5.*

Meir and Libby after the wedding ceremony, with friends and Libby's brother, Shraga Blum, in formal white jacket. *Chapter 5.*

First Newspaper Photo

At demonstration against British Foreign Minister Ernest Bevin, Manhattan, March 30, 1949. Left to right: Meir, Joseph Churba, unidentified demonstrator. *Chapter 4.*

First Car

Meir with the dark green Hudson, Brooklyn, NY., 1955. *Chapter 5, end note.*

First-Time Father

Meir brings Tova home from the hospital. Brooklyn, N.Y., November 1957.
Chapter 6.

First Trip to Israel

In his bunk aboard the Israeli ship SS *Zion*, January 1958. *Chapter 6.*

The Jewish Defense League
Spreading the Message

Speaking at the Young Israel of Hillcrest, Flushing, NY., October 1968, five months after the formation of the JDL. *Chapter 14.*

Courtesy of Dr. Mattis Yellin

Arriving via Texas International Airlines for a speaking engagement at the University of Texas, Austin campus, March 15, 1972. *Chapter 28.*

The Jewish Defense League
Picketing Anti-Semites

In a picket line at Public School 30, Rochdale Village.
From left to right: Meir, Murray Schneider, unidentified
JDL members. *Chapter 14.*

The Jewish Defense League
Sit-In for Soviet Jewry
Park East Synagogue, Manhattan, May 20, 1970

Meir lecturing to sit-in demonstrators in the sanctuary of the Park East Synagogue, which
faced the Soviet Mission to the United Nations. *Chapter 17.*

Meir reads from his notes at a lecture to sit-in demonstrators at Park East Synagogue. *Chapter 17.*

Meir gazing down at the Soviet Mission to the United Nations from a balcony of the Park East Synagogue, opposite the Mission. *Chapter 17.*

100-Mile March for Soviet Jewry

Meir speaking in Independence Park, Philadelphia, at the start of the march to the White House, Washington, D.C., August 16-23, 1970. *Chapter 17.*

Demonstration for Silva Zalmanson, Soviet Prisoner

Meir, wearing astrakhan hat, leading a mass sit-down at the intersection near the Soviet Mission to the U.N. Over 60 JDLers were arrested for blocking traffic, Sunday night, November 7, 1971. *Chapter 25.*

The JDL Draws Media Attention
to the Plight of Soviet Jewry

Meir is interviewed on Channel 7 (ABC-TV) after a demonstration for Soviet Jews. Photographer: Heshel Kupchin.

Sudden Arrest

Suddenly arrested after several attention-getting JDL demonstrations, Meir waits to be brought before a judge, Manhattan, January 12, 1971. To Meir's right: attorney Bertram Zweibon. In the background: photographers and reporters. *Chapter 21.*

One Thousand Arrested for Soviet Jewry,
Washington, D.C., March 21, 1971

Meir urges demonstrators to sit down in the streets of Washington for Soviet Jewry. Near him a young man wears backpack with a portable loudspeaker. *Chapter 22.*

Salute to Israel Parade
Manhattan, April 25, 1971

JDL Marchers, enthusiastically applauded by parade spectators, gather in Central Park. Meir, wearing "I Put On Tefillin" button, speaks to the media. *Chapter 22.*

After the parade, Meir signs autographs. *Chapter 22.*

Aliya to Israel

Family portrait before our departure for Israel.
Meir and Libby with four-year-old Binyamin.

JDLers give Meir a joyous sendoff at JFK airport,
September 12, 1971. *Chapter 24.*

Arrival in Israel
September 14, 1971

Reporters board airport bus to interview Meir. *Chapter 24*.

Meir is surrounded by reporters at the airport. *Chapter 24*.

Two Russians for Every Jew

Press conference with Avraham Zalmanson, uncle of Silva Zalmanson, Jerusalem, September 27, 1971. The world media featured Meir's warning that two Russian diplomats would be executed if Silva Zalmanson's harsh prison conditions led to her death. *Chapter 25*.

Meetings

Greeting Rabbi Mordechai Peron, Chief Rabbi of the IDF. Second from left: Geula Cohen. Tel-Aviv, October 1971. *Chapter 25*.

With Rabbi Tzvi Yehuda Kook
Jerusalem, Sukkot, October 1971

In Rabbi Kook's *sukkah*. *Chapter 24.*

At the Western Wall. *Chapter 24.*

Protesting the Rogers Plan

Demonstration against ceding lands liberated by Israel during the Six Day War. American Embassy, Tel Aviv, October 13, 1971. *Chapter 25.*

Promoting Aliya

Surrounded by reporters after being refused the right
to speak about aliya at the World Zionist Congress,
Jerusalem, January 20, 1972. *Chapter 27.*

Bar Mitzvah

With Baruch, almost age 13, as he puts on *tefillin* at the
Western Wall, January 24, 1972. *Chapter 27.*

Biram and Ikrit

Meir leading a demonstration against the settlement of Israeli Arabs in border areas. Jaffa Gate, Jerusalem, August 23, 1972. *Chapter 30.*

A Mezuza on Damascus Gate

Meir is arrested for attempting to affix a *mezuza* to a gate of the Old City of Jerusalem to show the Jewish character of the State of Israel. Jerusalem, October 30, 1972. *Chapter 32.*

Candidate for the Knesset, 1973

Meir, with attorney Meir Schechter at his side, holds a press conference on September 21, 1972, to counter charges of illegal acts. One week later, Meir forms a political party to fight the suppression of his ideas. *Chapter 31*.

An informal meeting following Meir's presentation of his party's platform at a press conference, Beit Sokolov, Tel Aviv, July 17, 1973. Left to right: Meir, heroic *refusnik* Grisha Feigin, and Liga member Shimon Rachamim. *Chapter 34*.

Election Day

With Sam Shoshan outside our neighborhood polling station.
The background: a sweeping view to the north. Jerusalem,
December 31, 1973. *Chapter 35.*

One Hundredth Anniversary

The Kahane clan marks 100 years since Meir's great-grandfather, Baruch
David, arrived in Safed in 1873. Meir, standing, with his cousins, left to right,
Yair Rotlevy, Chaim Paster, Baruch David (son of Zundel) Kahane. Jerusalem,
December 1973.

Passport Confiscated
While Awaiting Trial

Bent over a large volume of the Talmud in a low-ceilinged van, on a hunger strike for the release of his passport, Tel Aviv, February 5-14, 1974. Chapter 36.

Kach Movement Is Formed, 1974

Meir presents the goals of the newly formed Kach movement at a press conference, Beit Sokolov, Tel Aviv, July 16, 1974. *Chapter 39*.

Returning to the United States

After almost two years in legal limbo, Meir receives a suspended sentence and his passport is returned to him. He holds an impromptu press conference at JFK airport, August 14, 1974. *Chapter 39.*

Speaking from an impromptu platform at a street rally against Secretary of State Henry Kissinger's Middle East policy, Garment Center, Manhattan, August 28, 1974. *Chapter 40.*

Speaking Informally

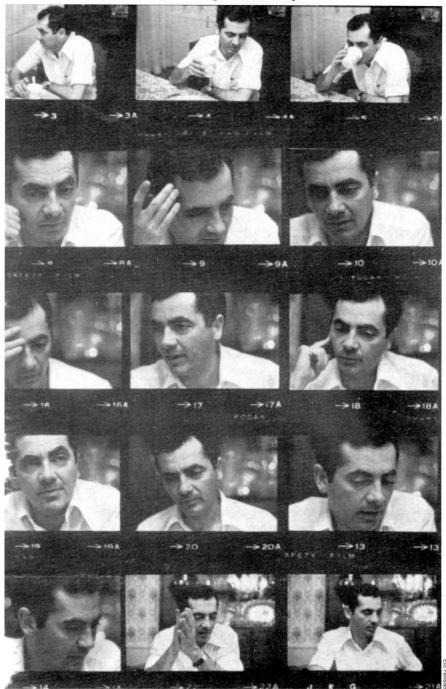

Meir is captured on film during an interview following a lecture at the Pickwick Jewish Center, Baltimore, September 14, 1974. *Chapter 40.*

Sentenced to Prison

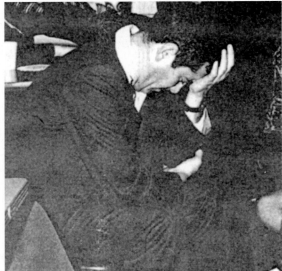

Deep in thought at a JDL farewell event before the start of his federal prison term. Cafe Yaffo, New York, March 15, 1975. *Chapter 42.*

Held at a Halfway House in Manhattan

The U.S. Bureau of Prisons refuses to give Meir kosher food in Allenwood Federal Prison. Held in a halfway house in Manhattan while the kosher food issue is decided by the courts, Meir uses his lunchtime furlough to speak at an outdoor rally, May 11, 1975. *Chapter 44.*

Kosher Food for All Jewish Prisoners

Meir speaks at a synagogue during his evening furlough, ignoring halfway house rules in order to pressure the Bureau of Prisons to expedite legal proceedings on the kosher food issue. [October] 1975. *Chapter 46.*

Nachum Bar Berel

Five days before the Court of Appeals decision guaranteeing Meir kosher food at Allenwood Federal Prison, Meir speaks at Grand Central Synagogue, Flushing, New York, November 22, 1975. *Chapter 46.*

Torah Dedication Ceremony
Allenwood Federal Prison
Montgomery, Pennsylvania, January 11, 1976

Meir, in his prison uniform, holds a canopy over the Torah scroll. Left to right: Meir, Dr. Hillel Seidman (holding the Torah scroll), Mordechai Pollan. *Chapter 47.*

Meir shows a Jewish prisoner the place in the prayerbook. Left to right: Rabbi Herzel Kranz, Rabbi Abraham Yeret, unidentified prisoners, Meir. *Chapter 47.*

Meir is held aloft during a dance with the Torah. *Chapter 47.*

Dancing with the Torah. Left to right: Rabbi Abraham Yeret, Rabbi Moshe Blitz, Meir, Abe Friedman, Shlomo Thaler. *Chapter 47.*

Rally at Carnegie Endowment Center
Manhattan, January 31, 1976

Pensive at the speakers' dais, one day after his release from Allenwood Prison. *Chapter 48.*

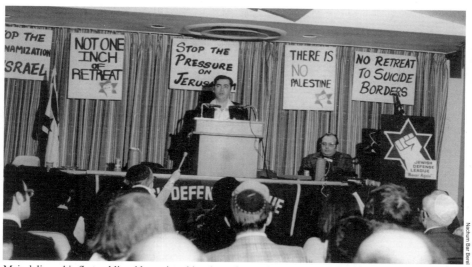

Meir delivers his first public address since his release from prison. Behind him is an array of posters calling on the Israeli government to remain in the liberated lands. Seated at the dais: Mal Lebowitz. *Chapter 48.*

Departure for Brussels and Israel

JDLers proclaim Meir's right to speak at the Second World Conference for Soviet Jewry in Brussels. KLM terminal, JFK airport, February 18, 1976. *Chapter 48.*

Jerusalem: Home at Last

Meir is greeted by daughter Tzippy on his return to Israel, February 19, 1976, after almost a year in prison in the United States. The sign on the door says, "Baruch Matir Asurim [Blessed is He Who Frees Prisoners.]" *Chapter 48.*

The Election Campaign
(July-December 1973)

Reaching the Voters

THE ELECTION CAMPAIGN was under way. Meir made a concerted effort to reach the voters. He used wall posters, flyers, and newspaper ads, and made many personal appearances. He targeted the religious and traditional population, including the Sephardim, who were traditional in their religious outlook, but whose younger generation was being influenced by non-religious and even anti-religious schools and the media.

One flyer contained a succinct expression of the ideas in the first three chapters of *Ha'etgar* (*Our Challenge*): *Am Segula*, a chosen people; *Eretz Segula*, a chosen land; and *Medinat Segula*, a chosen state.

> **A Chosen People:** Our children are in the streets, ignorant of their religious and national heritage, the product of an educational system empty of content, a pale imitation of Western culture. They lack pride in the destiny and distinctiveness of the Jewish people. The "rational" socialist government has deleted any hint of Judaism's elevated, holy aims from their education and produced "Israelis" instead of Jews. Our youth is overrun with doubts. Is it not necessary to protect them – our future – so we won't lose them?
>
> **A Chosen Land:** On the strength of G-d's promise to our Fathers, which gave us the right to this country, we returned to our Holy Land, the place of our nation's history. And what happened? We hear chatter about demography from Oxford-educated diplomats who fear what "the nations" will say. A Jew is not even permitted to buy land and to live in our cities – Hebron, Shechem [Nablus], Bethlehem. Is it not necessary to protect our country spiritually, so we won't lose it?
>
> **A Chosen State:** For 2,000 years we dreamed of a Jewish state, and the *Mapamniks* [socialists] founded a state of Jews which aspires to be a Western state. Jews in Syria and Iraq are being murdered, but the State of Israel does nothing for them because they are not its citizens. This is a Western concept!

The Jews of the Soviet Union cry out, but our government says it is forbidden to anger President Nixon. Is it not urgent to declare that our State will protect all Jews, wherever they are? Is it not necessary to protect this state spiritually, so we won't lose it?

The flyer concluded:

> The Liga is not here for physical defense, but for spiritual defense.
> We are going to the Knesset. Come with us.
> Do we have a chance? Sure we do!
> Kahane to the Knesset – Not to Jail. Vote Liga.[1]

Every flyer had a tear-off coupon at the bottom, where a supporter could indicate what he could do for the campaign. The coupons were useful both for feedback and for expanding the Liga's mailing list, and Meir aimed to include a coupon on every flyer.[2]

Another flyer dealt with the social gap between established Ashkenazim and newly arrived Sephardim. It asked:

> How Do We Overcome the Gap? After the way of the Labor party has failed, and *Gahal* [Menachem Begin's opposition party] has no answer, this is the Liga's solution:
>
> EDUCATION TO JEWISH VALUES. Jewish values promote *ahavat Yisrael*, love of one's fellow Jew. In Torah observant communities, interaction between Ashkenazim and Sephardim is good.
>
> OPEN THE LAND OF ISRAEL TO RAPID JEWISH DEVELOPMENT. A dispersal of the population, with newcomers and old-timers living and working together in all parts of the land, will reduce the tension between the two sectors, because people who work together for the same cause grow closer.
>
> GUARANTEED EMPLOYMENT AND DECENT MINIMUM WAGE. It is the right of each citizen to earn honorably according to his ability. Society must find jobs for all; in a country where new settlements are being established, unemployment does not exist.
>
> ENCOURAGE MEETINGS BETWEEN ASHKENAZIM AND SEPHARDIM. How will we get to know each other and different customs, how will we learn to respect one another, if we don't meet? We will strive to interact with our brothers at work, in the army, in education, in entertainment and in every other aspect of life.[3]

A four-sided *Daf Hasbara* (Information Page) included Professor Ehud Sprinzak's assessment of Meir as "an outstanding leader, with organizational abilities, courage, ability to innovate, and an excellent feeling for public relations. He is not anti-democratic and there are no fascist elements in his ideology."[4]

Yet another flyer featured a photo of Meir after he was arrested for trying to affix a mezuza to Damascus Gate, flanked on each side by an Israeli policeman.[5]

> **WANTED!**
>
> Beware! This man is dangerous!
> He's wanted by the KGB, the FBI, and Israeli government officials.
> Accused of:
> - Helping Soviet Jews
> - Helping Jews of Arab Countries
> - Activities Against Missionaries
> - Suggesting Emigration of Arabs
> - Putting a Mezuza on Damascus Gate
> - Running for the 8th Knesset

Election rallies were an important feature of the campaign. Meir had been making public appearances for some time. A rally at the end of July, aimed at a specific audience – young religious people – was held in Jerusalem at the Tel Talpiot hall.[6] In August, Meir held an outdoor rally in Haifa. He was supposed to speak in the public square in front of a synagogue, but some members of the synagogue who opposed him locked the gates to the square. Since he had a permit for an outdoor meeting, he remained outside the gates and, standing on a table, spoke to an audience of three hundred. A report on the rally appeared in *Ha'aretz*. The people who locked Meir out were the ones who made this election meeting newsworthy![7] In Tel Aviv that month, Meir spoke of the establishment of the State of Israel as a sanctification of G-d's Name:

> ... The Name of G-d is profaned and spat upon by taunting, laughing and mocking gentiles when the people of G-d, the people chosen by Him, that is identified with Him, that carries His zeal into ideological battle, is beaten, defeated, scorned and humiliated. The humiliation of the Jew is the humiliation of G-d; the desecration of the Jew is the profaning of G-d, his Maker.
>
> ... Every pogrom is a desecration of the Name. Every Auschwitz and expulsion and murder and rape of a Jew is the humiliation of G-d. Every time a Jew is beaten by a gentile, this is the essence of *chillul Hashem*, the desecration of G-d's Name.
>
> ... The State of Israel came into being not because the Jew deserved it, but because the gentile did. It came into being not because the Jew was worthy of it, but because the Name of G-d had reached its fill of humiliation and desecration.... Israel came into being because Israel is the essence and the apex of *kiddush Hashem*.[8]

Continuing to proclaim that Israel did not need foreign allies – certainly not an ally like the United States, which was urging her to cede territories – he held a press conference in August at which he announced that the Liga was organizing a mass petition against withdrawal from the liberated territories. The petition was headed, "We, the undersigned, proud Jews, sure of the eternal nature of the State of Israel, demand from the government not to withdraw from even one inch of the Holy Land. G-d will be with us if we remain faithful to Jewish destiny."[9]

Several public appearances by Meir in September are on record. A talk on the lawn of a Petach Tikva condominium was reported in *Yedioth Ahronoth* after some neighbors called the police, claiming he was disturbing them. The residents who had invited him maintained that the meeting had been quiet and orderly and that it was wrong of the police to stop Meir from speaking. The residents had a democratic right to hear him. At a public meeting in Bnei Brak he was received enthusiastically. A Ponevezh Yeshiva student wrote, "Your appearance gained many adherents." He also spoke at an Ezra youth group seminar. A letter of thanks from Meir Gross remarked, as many did, on Meir's indisputable sincerity. "Words that come from the heart penetrate the heart," he wrote.[10]

At a talk in Jerusalem in September, Meir analyzed the effect of the American withdrawal from Vietnam on Israel:

> The fools reign today in America.... They are thundering down the trail of iso-
> lationism, of coexistence, of blurring the truth of Communist tyranny....
> [Nixon], who knowingly signed away southeast Asia and American commit-
> ments, will be prepared to do the same to Israel tomorrow in response to pres-
> sure from the same fools who would rather buy "peace" for themselves than
> think of the sanity of Israeli retaliation and self-preservation.... Let us not lean
> too heavily on the "broken reed" that is ANY alliance with ANY nation.[11]

In a speech in Rehovot that month, he pointed to the widespread assimilation of Jews in Israel, despite the fact that "in a Jewish state with a Jewish majority there is no anti-Semitism and no stigma to being a Jew." He explained why the problem existed in Israel:

> A Jewish State does not eliminate assimilation when the same non-Jewish con-
> cepts, ideals and goals remain imbedded in the Jew.... And from the assimila-
> tion of [Western] ideas and concepts and the jettisoning of Jewish values and
> practices, MUST come intermarriage and apathy to any concept of a particular
> Jewish identity.[12]

Imaginative newspaper ads kept the Liga, and Meir, in the public eye. Many were reprinted as flyers. One ad announced a prize in the form of a coffin, sym-
bolizing the spiritual death of Israeli youth. On September 3 it would be presented to Teddy Kollek, mayor of Jerusalem, for promoting mixed Arab-Jewish summer camps and to Yigal Alon, minister of education, for encouraging cultural assimilation in Israeli schools. Meir told newsmen that the camps were "part of a plot for the spiritual destruction of Israeli youth." When he and Liga members went

to present the coffins, police arrested them for illegal assembly and took them in for questioning.*

Another ad accused Moshe Kol, who had headed Youth Aliya from 1947 to 1966, of forcing immigrant children, especially Yemenites and Moroccans, to stop observing the mitzvot. The ad announced that the Liga planned a public trial that would bring to light Kol's soul snatching and asked people to come forward to testify. Meir pointed out: "Today, Kol denounces 'religious coercion,' but when he had the power, he coerced children from religious homes to become irreligious."[13]

Liga ads and flyers featured the Hebrew letters *kaf-kaf*, which would officially identify the Liga on Election Day. Each party was assigned one or more letters, which were printed on paper slips the size of playing cards (7 cm x 10 cm). At the polling station on Election Day, the voter would go into a private booth where the slips were displayed, choose the slip marked with the letters of his party, and place it in a plain white envelope, which he would drop through the slot of the ballot box.

Shimon Rachamim, who was number two on the Liga list of candidates, recalled:

> Meir chose [the letters] *kaf-kaf* because it would remind the voters of Kahane and Knesset. On July 9 I wrote to Judge Haim Cohn, chairman of the Central Elections Committee, and asked him to approve our letters in advance. I explained that as a new party, our letters would not be officially approved until the committee met on October 2 to confirm our candidacy, and since the elections were to take place on October 30, we would have very little time to publicize our letters. In my letter, I gave four possible letter combinations and purposely reversed the order of our preference. The order of preference I gave was *gimel-lamed, lamed-yud, kaf,* and *kaf-kaf.*
>
> On July 24 Judge Cohn wrote that the letters *gimel-lamed, lamed-yud,* and *kaf* were unacceptable because they "could be mistaken" for other parties, "but there is no reason not to approve *kaf-kaf.*" At the same time, Cohn noted that the final decision would be made by the Central Elections Committee. Relying on Judge Cohn's words, "no reason not to approve," all our ads and flyers from the end of July through the end of September had the letters *kaf-kaf* in large bold print.
>
> And then came the blow. Two months of efforts to prepare the public to recognize our letters in the voting booth came to naught when the Central Elections Committee met and decided that the letters *kaf-kaf* were legally unacceptable. They said that the Elections Law required that a party's letters be made up of two DIFFERENT Hebrew letters. I was present at the committee meeting

---

* Summoning police to break up a small demonstration and prevent freedom of expression is reminiscent of the totalitarian tactics of the Soviet Union.

as an observer. I stood up and showed them Judge Cohn's letter approving *kaf-kaf*. I asked how Cohn had not known of this law.[14]

A news report indicated that the Elections Committee members were aware of the personal opinion of their chairman but had decided to override it. On October 4, attorney Meir Schechter presented a petition to the Supreme Court to nullify the Elections Committee's decision, but it was rejected on procedural grounds: First, the Liga had to present an appeal to the Elections Committee, and only if it were refused could they petition the Supreme Court.[15]

The Liga did not have enough time to follow this procedure, said Rachamim.

> An appeal to the committee would have meant a decision only 20 days before Election Day, so we decided to change the party's letters to *kaf-kaf sofit*. We prepared large rubber stamps which said, "New letters: *kaf-kaf sofit*," and stamped it in red ink over the letters *kaf-kaf* on all the existing flyers and wall posters.[16]

The Yom Kippur War: Election Day Is Delayed

Little did Rachamim know that they would have two more months to campaign. Only two days after their petition to the court was rejected, on October 6, Yom Kippur, the holiest day of the Jewish calendar, Egypt and Syria opened a coordinated surprise attack against Israel. The equivalent of the total forces of NATO in Europe were mobilized on Israel's borders. On the Golan Heights, approximately 180 Israeli tanks faced an onslaught of 1,400 Syrian tanks. Along the Suez Canal, fewer than 500 Israeli defenders were attacked by 80,000 Egyptians. Thrown onto the defensive during the first two days of fighting, Israel mobilized its reserves and eventually repulsed the invaders and carried the war deep into Syria and Egypt. The Arab states were swiftly re-supplied by sea and air from the Soviet Union, which rejected American efforts to work toward an immediate cease-fire. As a result, the United States belatedly began its own airlift to Israel. Two weeks later, Egypt was saved from a disastrous defeat by a cease-fire imposed by the U.N. Security Council,* which had failed to act while the tide was in the Arabs' favor.[17]

In mid-October, with a large part of the population in the army, the decision was made to postpone Election Day to December 31.[18]

This meant the public had another two months to learn to recognize *kaf-kaf sofit* as the Liga's identifying letters. In fact, the letters *kaf-kaf sofit* were even

---

* On October 22, the Security Council adopted Resolution 338 calling for "all parties to the present fighting to cease all military activity immediately." The vote came on the day that Israeli forces cut off and isolated the Egyptian Third Army and were in a position to destroy it.

better than *kaf-kaf* because they spelled out the word *kach*, meaning "thus." Soon, the Liga was using the slogan *"Rak Kach,"* which could be understood in two ways: as "[Vote] Only *kaf-kaf sofit.*" or as "Only Thus." The words *Only Thus* had a special meaning for Israelis, because this had been the slogan of the Irgun, the pre-state Jewish underground, whose posters featured the words "Only Thus" over an upraised arm holding a rifle. Meir had always admired the Irgun, and he was proud to use its slogan.

The postponement of Election Day due to the outbreak of the Yom Kippur War meant that Meir needed more funds to campaign for an additional two months. He wrote to Sam Shoshan:

> The war was a tragedy for the country and has hurt us badly, too. We were moving forward with tremendous momentum and had worked out a budget that would have survived the election date. Now with an extra nine weeks added, the advertisements and speeches that were so effective will be forgotten and there is hardly any money left. Please keep this in mind when you speak to people and try to raise more money for us. It would be a tragedy to lose now when we are so close.[19]

In a letter to Hilton Goldman, his distress was obvious:

> Last Sunday we ran out of money. With a total of 11,000 lirot on account at the newspapers for advertising (which will carry a total of three big ads in the two evening newspapers), there is no money left for campaigning, posters, salaries or debts.
>
> Because of this, we have cancelled all plans to campaign, and I will make no appearances after Wednesday since we must cancel all our contracts for meeting halls. Our staff is being let go on the 15th [of November] and I regret to say that all your efforts and those of the people who did so much have failed because of the war which forced us to go an extra nine weeks with not a penny to pay for it.
>
> I want you to know, because I get reports of glowing optimism from America from people who thought that $13,000 was the next thing to the Messiah. Please inform our active workers now, so as to spare them the shock when we fail to make it in December.... I send you my deepest thanks for all you have done.[20]

It was at this time that Meir tried to raise money for the campaign by seeking a publisher who would advance $15,000 for his book on the history of the JDL. But no publisher was willing to sign a contract without seeing a manuscript.[21] The difficulty of fundraising from "grassroots" Jews is evident in this letter from Bill Perl:

> At this time you have in Jerusalem a check (bankers draft) for $500 from the
> Washington chapter. Largely from us officers and from JDL funds. I sent it the
> same way I did with some remittances before, via Libby.
>   ... Mr. Fox and his Florida group met for about three hours with JDL mem-
> bers re campaign.... Meir, you should not think that the JDL here is not trying
> to raise funds. Ours are not well-to-do people. For Mr. Fox, the sums Hilton
> raised at two cocktail parties are peanuts.

Perl assured Meir of JDL's support:

> The [JDL] board is fully, absolutely and unconditionally behind you in your
> election bid. One or two of the board ... are concerned about cutting off our
> local funds if we press [members] too hard for the campaign, BUT these are
> only two out of eight board members....[22]

Meir resolved to carry on. He flooded the popular evening papers *Yedioth
Ahronoth* and *Ma'ariv* with ads; he rented halls in every town to speak to the voters. Toward the end, when the checks from America did not suffice, or did not
arrive in time, he even took personal loans. David Fisch recalled that Meir borrowed $100 from him, "much as the state of Israel tries for grants and gifts via
the UJA, then borrows via Israel Bonds to fill the gaps." When, in January 1974,
Meir sent him a check to repay the loan, he did not cash it. "I probably preferred
keeping the check as a souvenir, what with it bearing his autograph and such,"
he wrote. In the meticulous accounting Meir kept of his loans and repayments, he
noted, "David Fisch tore up my repayment to him!"[23]

Bright sky blue and white Liga wall posters, featuring the party's letters, were
plastered on the walls of every town. Unlike wall posters in later election campaigns, Meir's portrait was not their main feature. Several of the posters
announced local election rallies. Some had a minimum of text, while a few were
mostly text, usually enlargements of newspaper ads.[24]

Failure to Strike the First Blow

Another effect that the Yom Kippur War had on the election campaign was a
shift in the theme of Liga ads, posters, and speeches. Now, they featured Meir's
strongly held views on the conduct of the war. A short time after Israel was
attacked, it became clear that Israeli intelligence sources had known that Egypt
and Syria were poised to attack but had not taken preemptive measures for fear
of "what the nations would say." That fear, said Meir in a speech in Jerusalem
on October 20, had cost hundreds of soldiers' lives. He explained the fundamental
misconceptions underlying the government's failure to strike the first blow:

> People who see the Jew as like all other nations understand that without Phan-
> toms [fighter planes], the State will be destroyed. And so, they lean upon the

giver of Phantoms and find it necessary to obey his requests – even at the cost of Jewish territory or lives. In order not to displease the giver of Phantoms, the practical men accede to the request of the giver and do not strike a preventive blow that would spare the lives of hundreds of front-line soldiers. They accede to the request to compromise on territory and believe that some particular gentile states are true and permanent allies.

Hopefully, this war will teach us several lessons. One, that the Arabs are not total incompetents and cowards, and that the Jew is not a superman. That the fear that swept over the Arabs in 1967 and 1956 and 1948 was not a thing created by man but was put into the enemy by the Jewish G-d of History. Two, that one does not sacrifice Jewish lives in order to show the goy that we are truly pious saints who do not start wars and so that the giver of the Phantoms can be satisfied. Three, that the universal alliance against Israel should teach us that there are NO permanent allies for the Jew.[25]

He voiced his criticism of the government's conduct of the war in a half-page ad in *Ha'aretz*, headed "A Victory for the Arabs." He maintained that Israel should not have agreed to the U.N. cease-fire on the very day that IDF forces encircled the Egyptian Third Army and were in a position to destroy it. The ad's closely written text said in part:

By accepting a cease-fire, the government lost the chance to completely vanquish the Arabs and gave Sadat the victory he wanted from the beginning. The war was a political means to convince the Americans to pressure Israel to secede, to concede and in the final analysis, to commit suicide. Its aim was to force a political solution to the conflict rather than a military one. U.S. Secretary of State Kissinger was in favor of forcing a political solution on Israel. America's aid to Israel was in her own self-interest. America is our temporary ally, not our friend.

The ad detailed the Liga's principles:

To ignore U.N. resolution 242 regarding the liberated territories.
To immediately react to any breach of the cease-fire.
To follow a policy of deterrent actions, with no fear of the world's reaction.
To announce: We do not recognize a Palestinian people and our boundaries are based primarily on Divine Word and only secondarily on security needs.
To resist any foreign pressure.

Meir ended the ad on a prophetic note:

In the coming years, Israel will stand alone; now is the time to urge immigration from the West and the Soviet Union.
To return to true Judaism and have no fear.[26]

On November 4 Meir led a demonstration at the U.S. Embassy in Tel Aviv charging that Nixon was selling Israel out. The demonstrators protested the refusal of the Egyptians and Syrians, in a breach of the Geneva Convention, to release Israeli POWs until Israel would agree to change the cease-fire lines in a way that would be detrimental to her. Meir and his supporters held banners that declared, "No Negotiations Until Our Prisoners Are Released." A flyer they distributed said, "We will not allow any Israeli government to sit and negotiate ad infinitum while our soldiers are prisoners.... We will not allow the government to follow a course that is less than that of a final smashing of the enemy's bones." When they demanded to meet with Ambassador Kenneth Keating and refused to leave the embassy building, the police were called. Meir and nine others were taken away in a police van "for questioning." Meir was released in time to speak that evening at a major election rally at the Jerusalem International Convention Center. Yet another demonstration led by Meir, urging the government not to give in to Egyptian demands, was held at the Knesset in November. Its slogan was "There will be no surrender agreement."[27]

A speech Meir gave at a rally in Tel Aviv on November 7 defined his attitude toward Israel's dependence on America. The text of the speech was given in his article, "The Nuisance."

> A few days ago, the prime minister of the Jewish State [Golda Meir] was in Washington. A reception was held in her honor and she rose to speak. And the prime minister of the third Jewish Commonwealth that rose from the ashes of Auschwitz and the depth of the Exile, that overcame her enemies yesterday and in 1967, and in 1956 and in 1948 and throughout two millennia of gentile efforts to exterminate the Jew, said: "I hope that we are not becoming a nuisance to the United States." A nuisance! Like some pauper standing humbly and shamefacedly at the open door of the wealthy Baron, seeking alms....
>
> The prime minister of Israel is normal. She belongs to the camp of the sane, the practical, the rational, the logical. That is why she agreed to a cease-fire that saved the Egyptians – who had bloodied us – from a total destruction that the Israeli army was at that moment readying to deliver unto them. This is why she allows the supply of food, water, blood and medicines to the trapped Egyptian Third Army when instead she might use them as the greatest card in the world for the freeing of our Jewish prisoners. All these she did and does because she is rational, not mystical; logical, not a mad dreamer. Because she and her defense minister told the people and the world that Israel, the pauper, needs Washington, the Baron; that Israel cannot survive without American help; that Israel must have a friend who will give her arms and protect her against the Russians.
>
> ... If one looks at the world in a certain way, there is no arguing with the lady, and no matter how one's insides crawl at that sight of the crawling Jewish

prime minister, and no matter how one thinks that her outstretched hand is frighteningly reminiscent (no, exactly the same!) of the ghetto Jew who sought the aid of the local baron or prince or king so that his life and property might be saved from the hands of the *muzhik* [Russian peasant], one must agree.

... [But] I put it to you that the Jew has never been [a man of logic and a rational being] and that if he had been, he would not be alive today, he would not have survived the impossible nightmares that strangled him for two millennia. I put it that Jewish survival and redemption are proof eternal and ultimate that the world is not governed by logic, by sanity or by man. It is controlled and decreed by G-d....[28]

One can only imagine how Meir felt when this article was rejected by the *Jewish Press*. Editor Arnold Fine explained to Meir:

The present policy of our paper is pro-Nixon and pro-Golda.... The articles you have sent condemning Golda would short-circuit a goodly part of our circulation if they got into print. I can readily understand your motivation, and in some sense agree with you. But you and I are not the *Jewish Press*. On the pro-Nixon issue, we get letters ten to one applauding that stand. We get occasional criticisms, but they are few. Why antagonize Nixon when Israel needs him?

I hesitate to edit your copy (although I do) because I know you are writing from the heart, but you place not only me, but Sid [Shalom Klass] and the entire staff of the *J.P.* in jeopardy. At the present time the fuel shortage here is getting so acute, we are concerned with getting each issue out. The paper shortage almost completely halted publication. We are at the whim and whimsy of the very barons you write about. I feel we can be cleverer than they by not using direct inflammation....[29]

After the Yom Kippur War, the Arab oil-producing states stopped shipping petroleum to the United States because it had supported Israel. The result was a shortage of oil, including fuel for automobiles. It was not uncommon in the United States to see long lines of cars waiting for gas, and many blamed the Jews for the situation. The fuel shortage gave rise to anti-Semitic and anti-Israel expressions such as bumper stickers that said, "We can do without Jews. We can't do without oil." American Jews were frightened. It was only in August 1975, well after the end of the Arab oil embargo, that the *Jewish Press* dared to print "The Nuisance."[30]

At the beginning of the Yom Kippur War, Meir wrote a booklet, *Netzach Yisrael Venitzchono* (Jewish Eternity and Triumph), which defined the war as a lesson in national identity. Excerpts were printed on wall posters, in flyers, and in ads. The English version appeared in the *Jewish Press*:

... Each of us, every human being who enters the world, must know exactly who he is, why he is. A person who does not know how to identify himself, has no roots and no sense of direction, does not know from whence he came and where he is going. He cannot know how to act and how to react; he can only thrash about wildly; frustrated and lost in ordinary times and frantic and desperate in days of crises.

... And what is true for the individual is, similarly, true for a people. A nation, too, must have a sense of identity and purpose, or it has no reason for calls to loyalty, fealty, martyrdom and sacrifice in the name of that nation. Man, the individual, and Man, member of the greater community known as the nation, must know who he is or life has no purpose or great reason to continue.

... In these days of historic destiny, when war and violence threaten us from all sides and our enemies thirst for the destruction of the Jewish state and people, the categorical imperative for the Jew is to KNOW HIMSELF, to understand the greatness and uniqueness that is inherent in him as an individual and as a people, to appreciate from whence he came and to what glorious and unstoppable destiny he marches.

... The Jew is like no other people on earth. He can neither be like the goyim nor amongst them. He is special, unique, chosen. He is the Chosen people of G-d with a special destiny, mission and task. There is nothing the gentile can do to oppose this and there is nothing the Jew can do to escape from it, even should he be so foolish as to attempt to retreat from his greatness as the people of G-d.[31]

The entire text appeared as a full-page, densely printed ad in both *Ma'ariv* and *Yedioth Ahronoth*. The cost of the ad in *Yedioth Ahronoth* alone was 3,307 lirot (about $785). It was expensive, but Meir felt it was important to get his ideas across to the serious voter. Supporter Yehoshua Ben Zion disagreed. The day the ad appeared, he sent a letter to Meir: "In my opinion, the small ads, for example the one with the picture of Begin [which declared that Menachem Begin needed Meir's support in the Knesset], are more effective than the long ones, such as the one published today in *Ma'ariv*. The public does not read long ideological ads."[32]

A Rally Against Henry Kissinger

For Meir, ideological ads were important, but action was important, too. Henry Kissinger was coming to Israel to urge the government to participate in a "Middle East Peace Conference" in Geneva. Meir placed an ad calling for a mass rally against Kissinger at Lod airport:

This Sunday, December 16, at 9 A.M.
Everyone is coming to Lod airport to give Henry Kissinger the reception he deserves....

Kissinger is going to Geneva to force our government to commit suicide.

ISRAEL WON'T GO TO GENEVA WITHOUT
The release of our prisoners of war
The release of the Jews held in Syria and Iraq
The retrieval of the bodies of all our fallen soldiers
from Egyptian territory
This Sunday No One Studies and No One Works.
A person who does not sacrifice something for his country,
does not deserve a country – and soon will not have one!

The ad concluded in large letters:

NOT ONE INCH
The Liga Is the Alternative
ONLY THE LIGA – ONLY KAHANA – ONLY *KAF-KAF SOFIT*[33]

As the demonstration got underway, participants were confined by police to the diplomatic parking lot. They carried black umbrellas, signifying that Kissinger's program was comparable to Chamberlain's appeasement of Hitler in 1939, and held up placards calling on the Israeli government not to take part in the peace conference until all prisoners of war and all Syrian and Iraqi Jews were released.

Meir, portable microphone in hand, urged the crowd to ignore the police barriers and march from the parking lot. When he and about fifteen young men pushed through the barriers, they were stopped by police with steel shields. Meir was thrown to the ground. A photo shows him lying on the ground, surrounded by policemen. Meir seems to be out of breath, and the faces of onlookers in the photo show alarm and concern. The demonstration ended with the arrest of Meir and others who crashed the barriers. Later he said to a reporter, "Yes, we failed to wake the people up – there were not thousands there, only hundreds."[34] However, the demonstration of hundreds was widely reported and called attention to Meir's views on concessions to Egypt.

That evening, Meir was scheduled to speak at the Orly movie house in nearby Lod, but because of his arrest, his brother Nachman spoke instead. Meir was kept in jail for forty-eight hours. Afterwards, he appeared at a press conference at Beit Sokolov, where he spoke of leading demonstrations against Kissinger in America. After his election to the Knesset in two weeks, which he said was a certainty, the police would have to return his passport to him, and then he would be able to bring the facts about Kissinger's program before the American public.[35]

Meanwhile, Meir did all he could to run a successful campaign despite financial limitations. Young volunteers did much of the office work and distributed flyers on street corners and at rallies. At the start of the campaign, the Liga tried to save money by using public areas for election rallies, rather than renting halls. Form letters were sent to local councils and municipalities requesting permits to hold rallies in parks and public squares. One, to the Ashkelon municipality, said, "As part of our election campaign we wish to conduct an election rally on September 9, 1973, at 8 P.M. in Gan She'on Hashemesh, at Kikar Tzefania near Bet Rachman." There is no reply on record, but there are many indications that most election rallies had to be held in rented halls. An invoice dated October 1 for 150 lirot (about $35) for the use of a meeting room in the Mitzpor Hotel in Safed is one sign of this. An election meeting on December 1 in Ramat Gan was held in a synagogue hall,[36] but as Election Day drew near, more and more rallies were held in movie theaters, wedding halls and hotels.

Ads announcing Meir's talks appeared almost daily. From December 10 to December 16, he spoke at the Yarkon movie house in Rosh Ha'ayin, the Hadarom hall in Rehovot, the Rachel movie house in Ashkelon, the Pe'er hall in Ramle, the Gil hall in Petach Tikva, and in Kiryat Arba. Meir's schedule from December 17 through December 23 included a rally at the Jerusalem hall in Bnei Brak, the pool in Dimona, the Pe'er hall in Beersheba, the Pninat Hadar hall in Rishon Letziyon, the Mitzpor Hotel in Safed, the Chen hall in Netanya, and the Ron Hotel in Tiberias. One check stub dated December 5 for 5,000 lirot (about $1,200) says only *Ulamot* (meeting halls). The larger halls, such as Beit Sokolov and Jerusalem International Convention Center, charged 600 lirot (about $140) for each meeting.[37]

Another expense involved the Liga branches that were opened in town after town to reach the voters more directly. Costs included rent, telephone, electricity, local salaries, leasing cars and more. The monthly rent for the Jerusalem office was 900 lirot (about $215); in Tel Aviv it was 1,000 lirot (about $240). Of course, in the smaller towns the rent was far less, and in most cases it was only for the months of September through December. Printing was another expense, although many flyers were mimeographed in-house. The invoices from one printer, Dfus Igra, came to 10,000 lirot (about $2,400) just for November and December. Newspaper ads were a tremendous expense. The invoice from *Yedioth Ahronoth* for ads in December alone was 68,607.36 lirot (about $16,335).[38]

Despite their cost, Meir placed newspaper ads almost daily. Their content was similar to the content of the flyers. Most explained the Liga's ideology, while a few were aimed at specific sectors of the population. One ad, meant for Agudat Yisrael voters, criticized their candidate, Rabbi Menachem Porush, a deputy mayor of Jerusalem, for allowing the distribution of free Christmas trees in Jerusalem. An ad aimed at Likud voters bemoaned the fact that the Likud was not loyal to the ideals of Zeev Jabotinsky. Another, aimed at Mafdal voters, religious Zionists whose spiritual leader was Rabbi Tzvi Yehuda Kook, bore a photo of

Meir with Rabbi Kook at the Western Wall. The text quoted Rabbi Kook's dictum on not giving up any part of the Land of Israel as the basis for the Liga's motto, "Not One Inch." Another ad, designed to draw right-wing and religious voters, had a photo of Meir, shouting, at the demonstration against Kissinger. The text said, "What's the difference between an Opposition of tired politicians and the Liga? The 'nationalists' (Likud) and the religious (Mafdal) stayed home. Only the Liga demonstrated against Kissinger."[39]

The campaign among Soviet immigrants was supervised by Yosef Schneider, number three on the Liga list. It was assumed that Russian Jews would show their gratitude to Meir for all he'd done for them by voting for him. Many did, but many voted for the parties that would give them jobs.

As Election Day drew close, ads were aimed at persuading voters that the Liga had a good chance to get in – that a vote for the Liga would not be "wasted." One ad, headed "15,000 Citizens Declared Their Support for Kahane," listed about seventy of the "15,000 names on record at the 26 branches of the Liga throughout the country." The ad included an impressive list of branches – each with address, phone number and contact person – in Jerusalem, Tel Aviv, Haifa, Ramat Gan, Bnei Brak, Beersheba, Netanya, Petach Tikva, Rosh Ha'ayin, Givatayim, Hadera, Kfar Saba, Kiryat Ono, Hod Hasharon, Herzliya, Safed, Tiberias, Carmiel, Bat Yam, Holon, Ramat Pinkas, Bet Dagon, Lod, Dimona, Ashkelon, and Eilat. Each corner of the ad had the letters *kaf-kaf sofit* in large, bold print.

Meir also had an opportunity to reach voters via radio and TV. Prime air time on the state-run stations was given over to electioneering during the month preceding Election Day. Since air time was apportioned according to the number of seats a party already had in the Knesset, new parties were given only a few minutes. The Liga had three TV spots and five radio spots. Ads announced the hours when the Liga would be broadcasting.[40]

The TV spots were prepared with the help of a professional filmmaker, Dov Lederberg, who recalled that they decided that Meir would stand before a *shtender*, a wooden lectern. Meir felt comfortable with it, and it was a nice touch. Meir had prepared what he would say, and Lederberg filmed him and edited the film afterwards. The allotted ten minutes were divided into three segments, which were broadcast directly from the film. Although it was a low-budget job, the TV presentation alone cost close to $1,000. The radio spots cost much less. Meir recorded the messages at home and they were broadcast directly from a tape cassette he supplied to the radio station.[41]

The Education of Israeli Youth

Meir's concern about the values being taught to Israeli youth came to the fore shortly before the elections. In a letter to the editor of *Yedioth Ahronoth*, he wrote that Israeli youth lack a feeling of belonging to the Jewish people, and the result is that they "sympathize with" the enemy. This was due to the education they were receiving, he said.[42] An example of this was a memo to teachers from the Ministry of Education about preparing pupils psychologically for the proposed withdrawal from liberated territories. Meir placed ads saying:

High School Students:
Oppose the Brainwashing and the Betrayal of the Land of Israel by the
Ministry of Education...

Against: Teaching Pupils to Accept Withdrawal.
For: A Greater Land of Israel
           A United People
           Judaism in the Educational System.

Come Demonstrate at the Ministry of Education Tomorrow, December 6
In Jerusalem (3 P.M.) and in Tel Aviv (5 P.M.)
BRING YOUR PARENTS[43]

In mid-December, Meir spoke to secular high school students in Kiryat Motzkin about Jewish history and destiny. His words were received with enthusiasm. These were the youth, he said, who would benefit if the Liga was elected to the Knesset. An ad addressed to the religious public, describing his talk to the secular students, declared that putting Judaism into the schools would be the Liga's priority. The ad concluded:

FOR THE SAKE OF OUR CHILDREN,
Give Kahane the strength
To begin to make this
A CHOSEN STATE.
We Are the Alternative![44]

Yedioth Ahronoth published an op-ed article by Meir on the same topic. In Meir's opinion, the blunder of the Yom Kippur War paled in comparison to the real failure of Israel – its educational system. He wrote:

Since I came to Israel, I have met with young people several times a week. Usually I am invited to speak at a school. I talk about my ideas, but more important, I listen to the young people and try to understand them. I find the most basic values replaced by complete nihilism, because of the education they receive.

When I sat in prison, I got to know the "marginal" youth, most of them Sephardim, part of a people who maintained a glorious Jewish tradition throughout 2,000 years of exile. Their schooling in kibbutzim of the Shomer Hatzair deprived them of their tradition and left them empty. But are the wealthy youth of North Tel Aviv any better? They have no values either. It is a generation that does not know who they are or what they are. What does this have to do with the Yom Kippur War? The blunder of the war was not in the number of soldiers lost, but in the heavy cloud of depression that descended on the nation, in the absence of a belief in the eternity of the Jewish people and its Divine origin.[45]

On December 23 Meir joined the residents of Shalhevet, a settlement near Abu Rodeis in the Sinai, at a press conference in Tel Aviv. Under the pact with Egypt, the Abu Rodeis oil fields (which produced 55% of Israel oil needs) were being ceded to Egypt, and Shalhevet was going to be evacuated. Meir came to protest the evacuation with Aryeh Baruch and Mario Kogan, who chaired the Liga branch in Shalhevet.[46]

In a press release about the protest for Shalhevet, he wrote:

> The JDL has, from its inception, represented the idea that the Jewish people all over the world constitutes a single and indivisible entity.... The Land of Israel ... is the property of the entire Jewish people, those who reside in it and those who have not yet returned home. No power on earth ... has the legal or moral right to give up any part of the Land of Israel.
>
> ... We call upon the government of Israel to recognize its position as trustee and not owner of the land. It is because of this that we gather here to protest the liquidation by the government of Israel of the Jewish settlement of Shalhevet.... This is a betrayal of Zionism and a betrayal of the Jewish people....[47]

The JDL has, from its inception, represented the idea that the Jewish people all over the world constitutes a single and indivisible entity. There is one Jewish people and one Jewish homeland— the Land of Israel.

That land is the property of the entire Jewish people, those who reside in it and those who have not yet returned home. No power on earth within or without the people, no Knesset and no government of Israel has the legal or moral right to give up any part of the Land of Israel which is the property of the Jewish people throughout the world.

Draft of press release about the evacuation of Shalhevet, a Jewish settlement in Sinai

That day he also appeared before students at Bar Ilan University, and the next day he spoke in Netanya. On December 25 he spoke at a rally at the Lachish Hotel in Kiryat Gat, and on December 26 he spoke in two different towns – at 6 P.M. at the Paz movie house in Netivot and at 8:15 at Bet Hatarbut in nearby Ofakim. With Election Day drawing close, he held two large rallies on December 27. He spoke at the Magdiel movie house in Hod Hasharon at 6.30 P.M., and from there he went on to Bnei Brak where, in a bid for the religious vote, he held a rally at the Wagshal hall. His last rally in Jerusalem, on Saturday night, December 29, also appealed to the religious voter. Held in a religious neighborhood it was advertised on large posters pasted up around town. In sky blue letters on a white background, they announced that Meir would speak on "A True Peace – How?"[48]

Several American supporters who had worked on fundraising for the election campaign came to Israel at the end of December to share the excitement of the final days of the campaign and, hopefully, to celebrate the victory. A letter written by Samuel Shoshan to his wife Renah is an indication of the high spirits that prevailed.

> Sunday [December 23] ... I went to Safed and Tiberias with Meir for evening rallies. Past midnight we decided to stay in Tiberias. The drive up there from Jerusalem was at 80 miles an hour.... Meir's small car flies at those speeds and the roads are terrible.... Still confident even though polls say he won't get elected....
>
> This morning I saw Tzvi Rosenberg [Shoshan's uncle] to see if he would give us 5,000 pounds [lirot] (about $1,200) for a full page ad on Friday. Couldn't convince him, but he gave us 500 pounds and he and his whole office will vote for Meir.
>
> This evening I am joining Meir at his rally in Kiryat Gat. Nat Rosenwasser is also coming.... Arranged interviews for Meir with UPI, AP, Bruno Wassertheil (CBS radio), Terence Smith (*New York Times*) etc.[49]

Hilton Goldman recalled:

> I arrived in Israel a few days before the delayed elections. Gene [Singer] and I spent Friday night at your apartment in Kiryat Itri. I still remember little Baruch and Binyamin sitting on the floor in the living room polishing their shoes with liquid wax before Shabbos![50]

The Final Vote

The closing polls forecast one Knesset seat for Meir. Alan Rocoff, a young JDLer who had come from America to help in the elections, recalled:

> I came just for the campaign. I used to drive the Reb. Everyone thought he could win. The night of the elections, I dropped him off at your house. I forgot

something and went back to the office. It was 3 A.M. The phone rings. It was Bruno Wasserteil [CBS radio]. He wants a victory statement.[51]

When the final votes were tallied, the Liga received 12,811 votes. This could have been enough for one seat (0.81% of the total vote), but the rule was that to enter the Knesset, a new party had to have at least 1% of the vote (15,360 votes). The next day, when *Yedioth Ahronoth* reporter Gil Sadan interviewed him, he found that Meir was looking at the vote realistically and was not deluding himself that the soldiers' vote, as yet uncounted, could make a difference. Recalling the enthusiasm of the crowds at every election rally, Meir could only attribute his failure at the polls to the conservative nature of the Israeli electorate. An Israeli who had voted all his life for one party felt a kinship to it. Psychologically, it was difficult for him to vote for a new party.[52]

Twenty-five years later, Rabbi Aryeh Julius analyzed the conduct of the campaign:

> Some voters wanted to vote for the Liga but were afraid their vote would be wasted because Meir might not get the minimum needed for a seat. Meir placed an ad in both *Ma'ariv* and *Yedioth Ahronoth* for four days running during the week before Election Day. It said that the Liga already had enough committed voters for two seats, so no votes would be "wasted."
>
> This was a mistake. People wanted Meir to get in, but they didn't know who the others on the list were. "No problem, Meir will get in, so you don't have to vote for the Liga," was what people understood from the ads.[53]
>
> The campaign was not run correctly for Israel. We did not even have poll watchers. That meant that in all the polling stations the representatives of the other parties could (and did) throw the Liga votes into the garbage. In Jerusalem, the Liga received 2 or 3 votes per polling station. At the polling station in Bayit Vegan, where I was in charge, the Liga received 45 votes. We had done door-to-door canvassing for weeks, and on Election Day we watched the polls until midnight.
>
> There should have been poll watchers all night at all the polling stations. In later years, Meir told me that the ads were a waste. Meir had a knack for writing ads, but did not know the Israeli mentality.[54]

Shimon Rachamim agreed that there was probably cheating in counting the results. "The Liga had too few poll watchers at the individual polling stations where the counting was done."[55]

Meir pointed to yet another reason for the Liga's failure to get enough votes:

> Anyone who has been here on Election Day knows that the party will hire taxis – pick the people up at their homes, take them to the polling places, give them a copy of the ballot, an exact duplicate of the ballot, and say, "Don't do anything – here is the ballot, this is an envelope – just drop it in the box!"[56]

At a press conference on January 7, Meir told newsmen that despite his election defeat, he was going to go forward: He would try to get his passport back so he could lead protests in the United States against Kissinger's plans.[57] A few days later, he placed an ad announcing that he was going to continue to actively promote his ideas:

WITH THANKS!!!

To the 12,811 civilians and soldiers who voted *kaf-kaf sofit*,
To all the volunteers who gave their time and effort for the Liga list,
... The campaign is not ended. It has only begun. We are organizing to meet great challenges.
Adults – We will be happy to come to your home to talk about the Liga's ideas.
Youth – If you are a high school, yeshiva or university student, invite Rabbi Kahane to speak in your school.

Join the Liga and Become an Active Member: Take Part in the National Challenge.[58]

The year 1973 ended with Meir very active and highly visible on the Israeli scene. Although he had not attained a seat in the Knesset, his frequent personal appearances made him a "real" person to a large number of people all over Israel, while the ads and flyers explaining his ideas had promoted his point of view.

After the elections Meir made a valiant effort to regain his passport. He felt strongly that in America he could work effectively toward his goals. There, demonstrations against Kissinger would have more influence, and there he could reach the hearts and minds of American Jews.

Chapter 36

A Passport to America
(November 1973-February 1974)

I F MEIR HAD succeeded in his bid for a seat in the Knesset, his passport would have been returned to him as a matter of course and he would have been able to travel to the United States. There, his ability to influence Jews was proven. There he could best work against Kissinger's pressure on Israel to retreat from the Sinai Peninsula.

On the other hand, in America he could be sent to prison. The five-year suspended sentence handed down by Judge Jack Weinstein in July 1971 was conditional on Meir's not having anything to do with firearms or weapons of any kind. This included speaking or writing about weapons or even being in a room where people were discussing weapons. The September 1972 weapons shipment and the June 1973 Brezhnev letters, urging the use of explosives, could certainly be considered violations of probation and could lead to his imprisonment.

A Plea to Judge Weinstein

One solution was to press for an early termination of his probation period. Therefore, in November, in the midst of the election campaign, when his probation had two and a half more years left to run, Meir began to work toward having it terminated. In a letter to supporter Dr. Hillel Seidman of New York, a journalist who was prominent in Jewish public affairs, he wrote, "Please do all you can to persuade [Judge Weinstein] to cancel the period of the probation." He enclosed a letter for Seidman to give the Judge "only if all other efforts do not succeed."[1]

The letter to Judge Weinstein said:

> I write you this letter after a great deal of soul-searching and because I know how vital it is for me to be able to return to the United States to speak to Jewish youth during this troubled period that will be more troubled yet.
>
> I am asking you as a judge and as a Jew to end my probation period which has now run about 2 1/2 years. This will guarantee my ability to return to the

U.S. and work in the areas of youth, Jewish identity and Israel which at present are vital for our people's existence.

Because I feel so strongly about this, I am prepared to make a personal pledge to you that I will have, personally, nothing to do with explosives or illegal firearms despite my belief that for others, in some cases, their use is justified. I MUST return to America to build a strong Jewish youth and I ask you to help in this.[2]

Meir's friend and supporter, attorney Reuben Gross, wrote to Judge Weinstein requesting a discussion of Meir's case. Weinstein jotted his reply at the bottom of Gross' request: "Court will hear this matter at 10 A.M., November 21." On a copy he sent to Meir, Gross wrote, "Say *Tehillim* [Psalms] for me that day." In his statement to the judge, Gross pointed out that any violence in which Meir may have been involved was within the American mainstream. This is how he put it: "... force has a legitimate function in creating public policy since this country was born in a revolution against a tyranny that was mild by modern standards...." To Meir, Gross summed up the outcome of the hearing: "Judge Weinstein cannot do anything on an informal application." A news report the next day said that a formal petition to the court would be filed shortly.[3]

The case was scheduled for January 2, 1974. At the hearing, James Haran, the chief probation officer, submitted a report that implied that Meir had violated the terms of his probation. It said:

> ... The probationer has been arrested on a number of occasions in Israel for offenses which could constitute probation violations. However, since the probationer is not yet permitted to leave that country, nor are witnesses available to travel to the United States prior to the conclusion of the cases in Israel, violation proceedings have not been initiated at this time."

Gross sent Meir a copy of Haran's report with the comment, "You'll see what we're up against – but still trying."[4]

After the elections and prior to a decision from Judge Weinstein about the termination of his probation, Meir again petitioned the Jerusalem District Court for the return of his passport.[5] At the same time, he urged his supporters in America to put pressure on the Israeli government to return it by holding public demonstrations and using personal influence.

Meir wrote to JDL Chairman Bill Perl:

> You must begin a concentrated and CONTINUING campaign to get the Israeli government to give me back my passport.... The things to emphasize are the following:
>
> 1) It has been a year and a half that I have not been allowed to leave the country. Paglin, the other main defendant, has left FIVE times.

2) The judge ruled on the last two appeals that there are no reasons for not returning the passport. That is, he has no fear that I will not return, but he accepts the argument of the prosecution that I am going to America to make speeches and lead demonstrations that are against the interests of the Israeli government.

This is the kind of reasoning that the Soviets use to prevent people like Sakharov and Solzhenitsyn from leaving.*

... I will go on a hunger strike here at the same time, so I must know when you are planning the first big protest.

In a postscript, Meir wrote, "Congressman Mario Biaggi [who backed JDL in the past] should be asked to head a Committee for the Return of Meir Kahane."[6]

Don't Muzzle Kahane

On January 8 Bill Perl reported to Meir that JDLers had demonstrated at the Israeli Consulate in New York. "It's hard to get people at this time to demonstrate against Israel," he wrote, referring to the impasse in negotiations between Israel and Egypt. "But we did demonstrate at the Israel Consulate with signs, 'Don't Muzzle Kahane,' preparatory to your possible hunger strike next week."[7]

In response to Perl's reluctance to demonstrate at the Israeli Consulate Meir wrote:

> I certainly realize that there are many Jews – including myself – who do not like to demonstrate against Israel.... The principle is cited in the Biblical verse, "Thou shalt not revile a leader of the people" (*Exodus* 22:27). The Talmud immediately comments on this, and conditions it on the assumption that "he acts in accordance with the good of the people" (*Bava Batra* 4a).
>
> In other words, the protest against the government's incredible actions should not be based simply on its injustice but because – especially in these times of crisis – when the fate of Israel and of the Jewish people hang in the balance, and the government has capitulated out of fear, there is a desperate need for me to be able to get back to America.

Meir's next sentence is the key to understanding why he was so impatient to return to the United States.

> It is America where the battlefront is, not in Israel where the people are petrified and fatalistic....

Meir suggested only "silent demonstrations – totally silent, candles and night

---

* Solzhenitsyn and Sakharov were well-known in the West for speaking out against Soviet repression. Alexander Solzhenitsyn was "expelled" from the Soviet Union on February 13, 1974. Andrei Sakharov was stripped of all his privileges in 1968 and was exiled to the closed city of Gorky in 1979. He was only allowed to return to Moscow in 1986.

long vigils outside the Israel Embassy and consulates in New York and other cities...."[8]

Perl's reply was disappointing: "We here have problems with demos: All want you back, but demonstrations against Israel would tear our little group to pieces."[9]

Meanwhile, Meir's supporters in America tried "influence" to help him regain his passport. A JDL delegation was received on January 6 at the home of American Orthodoxy's most important rabbi, Rabbi Moshe Feinstein. Samuel Sternfeld described the meeting:

> Mal [Malcolm Lebowitz] started off the conversation by stating how great an honor it was just to have the *zechus* [privilege] to be in the same room with so great a personage. Reb Moishe then asked the specifics of the charge against you ... then turned to one of his *gabo'im* [assistants] and said: Call Shlomo Levine [at the Israeli mission to the U.N.] ... Reb Moishe was very firm with Mr. Levine, saying that your presence in the U.S. at this time was of the greatest necessity, and as such your passport should be returned to you. Mr. Levine ... promised to look into the matter.[10]

Dr. Hillel Seidman organized a delegation of influential people that met with Israel's ambassador to the U.N., Yosef Tekoah, asking him to intervene for the return of Meir's passport.[11] A Yiddish article by Seidman in English translation was printed and mailed to JDL's entire mailing list. Members were asked to post it in their synagogues and to organize mass petitions. Seidman wrote:

> One person whose absence is deeply felt in America is Meir Kahane.... The multitude of invitations extended to him to lecture on college campuses where his appearance and voice was a turning point for influencing our youth back to Judaism.... If Jews seek today to defend their neighborhoods; if Jews support the Jackson amendment ... it is because of Rabbi Meir Kahane.[12]

After many false starts, Bill Perl made contact with Congressman Biaggi. He reported to Meir:

> Last Tuesday, I met here in Washington with Mr. Biaggi.... I suggested that Mr. B. write either to Golda or to the Attorney General.... He said that first he has to write – would write – to Mr. Dinitz [Simcha Dinitz, Israel's ambassador to the U.S.], explaining to him the bad impression such muzzling must create in the U.S. public...[13]

Another letter from Perl indicated that there were serious problems within JDL – still another reason for Meir to go to America quickly. Perl wrote to Meir:

> I resigned as National Chairman.... JDL has an enemy – the readiness to fight to the death anyone in the JDL whom one dislikes.... The air is loaded with tension, hostility and distrust. This is not the atmosphere in which I can work successfully.... I told the Jewish Telegraphic Agency that "directing out of Wash-

ington an organization that has most of its members in New York is so costly and complex a process that this decision was imperative." I am worried about JDL-USA as one large national organization, but not at all worried about the ongoing and continuing activities of the chapters: Washington, D.C., Philadelphia, Miami, Los Angeles, San Francisco, etc.

He reassured Meir, who continued to ask for demonstrations on his behalf:

> There will be actions for you re your passport, but no major demonstrations. Only Sam and I and (somewhat halfheartedly) Nat were for the kind of demo which would include wide publicity.[14]

By mid-February it was clear that there would be no early termination of Meir's probation period. Meir received a letter from Probation Officer James Haran dated February 14 saying that although Gross' motion had been withdrawn, Haran was interested in a statement that "we were informed was signed by you on October 23, 1973, pledging an intention ... to refrain from any further activity espousing weapons, force, violence and the like. We are interested in your own evaluation of this change of posture as well as in the steps you have taken to implement these changes thus far, such as by public addresses, editorials and so forth." Haran added a procedural directive: "We are also enclosing a supply of report forms to be mailed on the first of each month for the time you remain in Israel."[15] When Meir returned to the United States, he would be required to visit his probation officer in person once a month.

With his probationary term still in force for the full five years, through July 22, 1976, Meir could be sent to prison at any time if the U.S. Probation Office could prove that Meir's writing about rifles and explosives were a violation of the terms of his probation. It was a gamble, but Meir continued his efforts to regain his passport in order to travel to the United States because, as he had written to Perl, "It is America where the battlefront is."

The *Jewish Press* remained an important vehicle for Meir to disseminate his ideas, but not everything he wrote was printed. Publisher Rabbi Shalom Klass answered Meir's complaints about censoring his articles:

> You forget that we are publishing a paper in the U.S., not in Israel. Hundreds of anti-Semites and Arabs receive the paper every week. To attack the Israeli government and its politicians would only give ammunition to these haters. In an Israeli paper it's very good, but not here in America. Also, many lukewarm supporters of Israel would soon become disillusioned with Israel if they read how bad some of the things are over there.
>
> ... Israel hasn't the industrial capacity to fight a war alone regardless of how good an army and air force it has. This is similar to Mordechai who remained in Persia as the prime minister instead of answering the call of Ezra and

Nechemia and following them to Israel.... He did more good in advising and influencing the king than being in Israel at that time.

I believe that it was only one or two articles we ever edited which were hitting Nixon, etc. You use the word censorship. I think you are unfair and I have treated you very well. I've been sending you $150 every week for an average of only two or three articles and many weeks for no articles at all because they didn't arrive, such as this week, January 11. Your articles first arrived on Wednesday and we go to press on Tuesday.

Klass' next pronouncement was unexpected:

All I need is one or two columns or articles from you a week, for which I'll pay $25 per article or $50 a week. No one else in the paper has more than two columns and we have so many more columnists than any other paper. So starting next week you can send me any two columns as you suggest, not the political ones.[16]

Imagine Meir's consternation when he read this last paragraph. He still had so many personal election loans to repay! Now it was even more urgent for Meir to travel to the United States. Indeed, when he finally returned to New York half a year later and was able to speak with Klass face to face, the pay cut was rescinded. With the play on words he so liked to use, Meir wrote to me:

I got the raise back from Klass.... He has agreed to give me carte blanche and he put my "Open Letter to Ford" on page 3. He changes strangely or maybe he stranges changely.[17]

Hunger Strike

Meir's petition to the Jerusalem District Court for the return of his passport, which he had presented right after Election Day, was heard on January 27. In a press release informing the media about the hearing, Meir wrote:

Rabbi Kahane intends to travel to the United States to warn Jews of the dangers of remaining there and to urge them to move to Israel. He also plans to organize demonstrations against Secretary of State Henry Kissinger's pressure on Israel to withdraw from the liberated lands. He intends to promote his book, *Our Challenge*, which presents his arguments against such withdrawal. Its publisher, the Chilton Publishing Company, has arranged a series of radio and TV appearances for Rabbi Kahane to promote sales of the book. If the court again refuses Rabbi Kahane's request, Liga branches all over Israel and the United States will hold stormy protest demonstrations and will turn to Amnesty International to protect Rabbi Kahane's elementary civil rights of freedom of speech and freedom of travel.[18]

The District Court refused Meir's petition for his passport. Now he applied to the Supreme Court. While it deliberated, Meir went to the U.S. Embassy in Tel Aviv. He prepared a press release saying: "Rabbi Meir Kahane has an appointment on Thursday, January 31, at 10 A.M. at the American Embassy to demand that the United States lodge a stiff protest with the Israel government concerning the actions against Rabbi Meir Kahane, who is a United States citizen as well as an Israeli." The press release also announced Meir's intention to begin a hunger strike the following week if the passport was not returned.[19]

The American Embassy in Tel Aviv kept the State Department informed.

> Meir Kahane appeared at the embassy on January 31 to request our intervention with the government of Israel.... Kahane said that his lawyer had made several attempts to have Tel Aviv District Court release his passport so that he could travel to the United States but has thus far not been successful.[20]

In response to Meir's request, U.S. Consul General Larry Roeder wrote to Israel's attorney general Meir Shamgar.

> Rabbi Meir Kahane recently called at the Embassy and stated he had been unable to get his U.S. passport from the Tel Aviv District Court. He asked for the Embassy's assistance.
>
> ... Under our regulations, a United States passport is considered the property of the United States government and not of the individual holder. It would therefore be appreciated if you would return Mr. Kahane's passport to the Embassy.
>
> ... Since Mr. Kahane is still a citizen of the United States, we must upon request provide travel documentation to Mr. Kahane, irrespective of whether his passport is returned or not.
>
> If the Government of Israel has prohibitions against him departing Israel, we would appreciate being informed of said prohibitions, so that we may advise Mr. Kahane.[21]

The next day, the U.S. Embassy reported to the State Department that on February 5 the High Court in Israel had rejected Meir's appeal. "Today, starting at 9 A.M.," continued the report, "Kahane began a hunger strike in a jeep [actually, a van] across the street from the embassy. Placards in Hebrew on the side of jeep state: 'Kahane is deprived of free speech and travel' and 'Wants to go to U.S. to work against Kissinger withdrawal plan.'"[22]

Meir told a reporter, "I will hunger strike until I get my passport back." In a paraphrase of Patrick Henry's "Give me liberty or give me death!" Meir said, "Give me my passport or give me death!" So that he could continue the hunger strike for many days, Meir drank one glass of fruit juice each morning and night.[23]

Liga members distributed flyers in English to passers-by and to the press that said:

In October 1972, the government of Israel – under American pressure – took away the passport of Rabbi Meir Kahane, following his arrest with Irgun hero Amichai Paglin on charges that they planned to act against Arab terrorists after the Munich massacre. Since then Paglin has been allowed to leave the country numerous times, while Rabbi Kahane has been refused this elementary right.

The reason is clear. It is not the fact that he faces trial, because not only has Paglin been allowed to leave but the prosecutor and judges have said, time and time again, that Rabbi Kahane is an honorable man who will appear for trial.

The reason is clear from the statements by the prosecutors that Rabbi Kahane intends to go to America and speak and demonstrate on issues that in their view will hurt Israeli relations with the United States.

... Rabbi Kahane wants to go to the U.S. to speak and to organize large and LEGAL DEMONSTRATIONS. He believes that Henry Kissinger is a danger to the existence of Israel and that the government of Israel, frightened and confused, has collapsed completely before Kissinger. Since it is obvious that in Israel the people are stricken dumb with apathy and silence, the place to fight against the policy of retreat is in America.

Rabbi Kahane has the power to organize the American Jews against the policy of retreat – this is what the American and Israeli governments know and this is why they fight bitterly to keep him here as a POLITICAL PRISONER.[24]

An editorial by Herzl Rosenblum in *Yedioth Ahronoth* supported Meir's contention. He asked, "If the attorney general can take someone's passport to 'prevent them from harming Israel,' why weren't the passports of Vilner and Machover [Israel Communist Party members Meir Vilner and Moshe Machover] taken from them to prevent them from damaging Israel's reputation overseas? Meir Kahane is not likely to flee to avoid his trial," wrote Rosenblum. "It is unjust for the government to retain his passport."[25]

A photo in *Ma'ariv* showed Meir standing near the van he was using for his hunger strike. Its sides were plastered with posters explaining his demands. Another photo showed Meir inside the van, sitting on a makeshift bed. Unable to sit upright in the low-ceilinged van, he is bent over a large volume of the Talmud. On a small table near him is a book given to him by a supporter. Titled *Fasting Can Save Your Life*, it maintains that periodic fasting is healthy.[26] Physicians were on hand at all times to make sure that Meir showed no ill effects from fasting.

On the sixth day of his hunger strike, Meir left his vigil at the U.S. Embassy to take part in an Emergency Aliya Conference at ZOA House in Tel Aviv. The main speaker was Dr. Victor Ratner, formerly a Zionist leader in Great Britain. A press release announced that Meir would speak at the Emergency Aliya Conference, "notwithstanding the fact that he is in the sixth day of a hunger strike on the issue of the confiscating of his passport."[27]

Ratner, who had contributed generously to the Liga's Knesset campaign, followed Meir's advice to keep quiet about their friendship. A month later, when Ratner announced a day-long conference on aliya at the Sheraton Hotel in Tel Aviv to launch the Habayta organization, no one recalled that Habayta had been founded by Meir in 1972. The World Zionist Organization helped publicize Habayta, and Ratner received letters from Labor party leaders Moshe Dayan and Shimon Peres regretting that they could not be at the opening session.[28]

Meir continued his hunger strike for ten days. On February 13, Rabbi Aryeh Julius made inquiries at the American Embassy and was told that a new passport would be issued to Meir "on the condition that the Israel government inform us that the present passport will definitely not be returned at this time." On February 14, after this stipulation (leaked by Julius) was noted in *Ha'aretz*, Meir entered the U.S. Embassy and filled out a passport application form. Ambassador Kenneth Keating reported: "Kahane indicated to consular officer that he had called off his hunger strike, as he is now satisfied that he will receive a U.S. passport."[29]

Only now, on February 15, did state attorney Gabriel Bach reply to Larry Roeder's letter of February 5:

> Rabbi Kahane has serious charges pending in the District Court of Tel Aviv (156/73) and Jerusalem (167/73) and is prohibited from leaving the country as part of the conditions of his release on bail. In October 72 the Tel Aviv Magistrate ordered his passport to be deposited at Police Headquarters. Passport will be returned upon completion of the proceedings in the above criminal cases.[30]

Upon receipt of this letter, Consul John H. Adams wrote to Meir:

> The embassy has now received a letter from the state attorney which indicates that your present passport will only be returned after completion of proceedings currently pending against you in the District Courts of Tel Aviv and Jerusalem. Under the circumstances, the embassy is prepared to issue you a new passport upon payment of the required fee of $10 (IL 42)."[31]

In keeping with instructions from the State Department, the embassy issued a full validity passport to Meir on February 21, 1974. However, Meir still could not travel to America. Ambassador Kenneth Keating explained this in a telegram to the State Department: "Israel National Police informed our legal attaché on February 15 that a stop order has been placed at all international ports in Israel to prevent Kahane from leaving.... Kahane is required, as an Israeli citizen, to have an Israeli passport in order to depart Israel. Possession of a U.S. passport clearly will not assist him in his efforts to depart Israel for a speaking tour in the U.S."[32]

Although the hunger strike did not enable Meir to travel to the United States, it served to bring Meir's name before the Israeli public once again. One thing is certain: Meir could not have held the hunger strike without the help of Liga members, who prepared the van, stayed with him around the clock, distributed flyers, and attended to all the tasks involved in it.

The Liga at Work

In January, immediately after Election Day, Liga members convened to discuss future aims and activities. At one point, while composing a Declaration of Principles, some members raised the question of the movement's affinity to halakha, Jewish law. Meir said that halakha was a basic principle of the Liga, but there was no need for the declaration to state whether its binding authority would be, for example, the Chief Rabbinate of Israel or Agudat Yisrael rabbis. Attorney Rachamim Cohen, who was not personally observant, pointed out that a member need not be observant but he must agree to the supremacy of halakha.

Everyone agreed with Meir's proposal that the Liga should make education and outreach to youth its priority. Yoel Lerner was chosen to chair the Education Committee and plans were made for a weekly lecture series: Shimon Rachamim and Moshe Potolski would lecture in Jerusalem, and attorney Moshe Simon would give lectures in Tel Aviv when a new office was found. The Liga could not longer afford the rent for the Dizengoff Street office.[33]

Funding was becoming a serious problem. On January 27, at another meeting of the Liga, Meir told the board members that they could not depend on aid from the JDL in America. They would have to economize: The new office in Tel Aviv would be manned only by volunteers and would have no telephone. Telephone costs, he said, were outrageous. The Jerusalem office would henceforth severely curtail telephone calls.[34]

It was increasingly difficult to cover the monthly rent for the office on Jaffa Road. Avery Gross, whose father Reuben was our neighbor on Sorotzkin Street, recalled: "Meir had to vacate the office he had in town. He was a bit despondent about it and this was evident in his face. He was waiting for a bus in front of our house when my father happened to come out. He saw that Meir was troubled and asked what the problem was."[35]

The next thing Meir knew, Reuben Gross had contracted to lease a "key-money" apartment and presented him with a sub-lease. It was a ground floor apartment at 31 Ussishkin Street, in a pleasant, tree-shaded neighborhood that was close to the center of town and near several bus lines. It had one large room where lectures could be held, and two others for office work. Best of all, the rent was very low. Gross later notified Meir: "The rental, if you can afford it, you can pay to the sellers. If you can't afford it, we'll try to raise it by some other means."[36] Neither of them could have foreseen then that the Ussishkin Street office would be the headquarters of the Liga, and later of the Kach Party, until Meir's death.

Meir continued to give public lectures in January. Despite the cost, the Liga rented a hall at ZOA House in Tel Aviv for a public meeting on the topic, "What Do the People Expect From the Eighth Knesset?" Shimon Rachamim and attorney Moshe Simon spoke about Liga policy, while Meir emphasized the urgency of the release of his passport. On Saturday night, January 26, Meir was invited to Ramat Gan to speak at a meeting of Gesher, an organization that worked to bridge the gap between observant and non-observant Jews. "Your talk presented the listeners with new points of view and gave them a positive challenge," said Gesher's letter of thanks. Students at Hebrew University who were JDL supporters arranged for Meir to speak there. He gave one such lecture on January 31 at the Canada Building on the Givat Ram campus.[37]

The students and other Liga members agreed with Meir that Christian missionaries had no place in Israel. In the pre-dawn hours of February 11, while Meir was holding his hunger strike in Tel Aviv, three Christian institutions in Jerusalem were firebombed: the Baptist House on Narkis Street and two on Neviim Street, the Swedish Theological Institute and the House of Zion, a Christian bookstore. Twelve persons were arrested, including two Liga members. A Liga spokesman told newsmen: "We do not support violations of the law, but we look upon acts to counter Christian missionary work as a religious commandment." Meir later told reporters that the Liga had not authorized the arson, but added that "a number of those arrested happen to be our members and I am proud to have such members."[38]

Four people were convicted and served time in jail. Rabbi Aryeh Julius recalled, "There was a scoundrel, later exposed as a swindler, who incited others to set fire to the missionary offices during Meir's hunger strike.[39] One of those who served time recalled: "We acted impetuously. Somebody suggested it and we followed. Meir did not know anything about the plans, but he kept in touch with us while we were in jail and helped with lawyers."[40]

When Meir assumed the burden of raising money for the legal defense of the JDLers who had been arrested, he was already hard-pressed to pay attorney Meir Schechter, who was representing him in the Brezhnev letters case. He appealed to supporters in the States for donations and even for personal loans. A typed letter to Nat Rosenwasser, with Nat's name handwritten at the top, was probably sent to other supporters as well. It said:

> I know how much you helped in the past and I'M DEEPLY GRATEFUL but –
> with the fact that I and other JDL people face trial and have never received one
> penny from the official JDL in the United States.... With nearly $7,500 in debts
> hanging over us; with the knowledge that I must be able to win my case so I

can get back to America and lead the fight there – knowing all this and knowing that so few care, I turn to you and ask: at least loan us the money we need and I will personally assume the obligation. I hope I am worth that much to you.[41]

With the issue of Christian missionaries at the top of the news, Meir initiated an effort to enlist yeshiva students for practical, non-violent anti-missionary activities. Supporters distributed flyers calling for yeshiva students to attend a conference at the Tel Talpiot hall Saturday night, February 23, to form an umbrella organization, *Ha'irgun Hame'uchad Neged Hamisyon* (The Union of Anti-Mission Organizations).

A press release announced that the Union of Anti-Mission Organizations had lists of Jewish children in missionary schools in Israel and names of indigent Israelis who had been offered large sums of money if they would convert and leave Israel. It also had data on wealthy Christians in Europe who helped the missionaries buy up land in Israel. The new umbrella organization aimed to bring the extent and seriousness of the problem before the public and to help the Israelis who had been approached by missionary workers.[42]

On February 24, one day after the anti-missionary conference, a meeting of the Liga leadership was held. Once again, Meir stressed the need to economize. He explained that due to the current strife within JDL in New York, there had been a drop in contributions and the organization in America was not sending funds to Israel. The Liga would now have to depend on donations from individual supporters.[43]

Together with financial difficulties, Meir had to deal with the uncertainty of his impending trial for the Brezhnev letters. In a letter to Bill Perl, Meir expressed optimism about the Brezhnev trial:

> My trial date for the Brezhnev case has been set for March 10 and 12. It should be over within a day or two since I have admitted the facts – with pleasure and pride – and denied any guilt. It is a gamble. If I am found guilty I could sit in prison. On the other hand, I may get a suspended sentence. Hoping for the best, therefore, I may be in America by the middle of April.[44]

Despite his outward optimism, Meir had good reason to worry. The outcome of the trial was critical. Even if he were not sentenced to prison, the wording of the judge's decision was important. His ruling could determine whether an American court would consider the letters he had written, urging the use of rifles and explosives, to be a violation of the conditions of his probation.

Chapter 37
On Trial for the Brezhnev Letters (March 1974)

MEIR'S TRIAL IN connection with the Brezhnev letters opened on March 10, 1974, in Jerusalem District Court. He was charged with attempted conspiracy and efforts to harm Israel-U.S. relations and Israeli interests. As evidence, the prosecution introduced four letters and a telegram that Meir had sent to JDLers in New York prior to the visit of Soviet premier Leonid Brezhnev to the United States in June 1973. The letters suggested kidnapping and shooting a Soviet diplomat in Washington and bombing Soviet and Iraqi buildings there. One letter recommended bombing the New York offices of the Occidental Petroleum Company as a warning to its president, Armand Hammer, not to conduct business with the Soviets as long as they forbade emigration of Jews to Israel. The telegram suggested they do "anything necessary" to upset the Brezhnev visit.[1]

Meir's motive in urging these attacks was to make the Americans fear for Brezhnev's safety. He hoped this fear would lead to the cancellation of Brezhnev's visit to the United States, because he believed that such a visit would cement beneficial trade relations between the Soviet Union and the United States. He foresaw that once the Soviets achieved this, they would curtail Jewish emigration. Meir's fears proved to be well grounded. News reports in March 1974 told of an abrupt decline in the number of Jews leaving the Soviet Union. Their number dropped to about 2,000 per month in January and February, compared with the final months of 1973 when as many as 4,500 Jews left in one month. In addition, there was a rise in the denial of exit visas. In March 1974, seventeen Soviet Jews who had been denied exit visas were arrested when they tried to deliver a letter of protest to the headquarters of the Communist Party.[2]

Prior to the trial, to bring his position before the public, Meir sent a mimeographed letter to newspapers. He maintained that he was not guilty of "attempted conspiracy" because there was no overt act.

The letters never reached their destination, having been intercepted here in Israel, thus leaving the prosecution with the question: How can it be sure that the conspirators would have agreed to the proposal? In addition, there was no act taken by anyone to begin to implement the plan, something that is indispensable under the law of conspiracy.

Regarding the second charge against him – "harming Israel-U.S. relations and Israeli interests," Meir wrote:

[Israel's] efforts to try Rabbi Kahane stem from its fear of offending the United States and the Soviets, something that has been true for many years. Rabbi Kahane will bring many Soviet Jews who are now in Israel, plus Americans who were active in the struggle for Soviet Jewry, to testify concerning the refusal of the Israeli government to help Soviet Jewry during all the years after Stalin until our day, when it has fought the Jackson amendment.... This is a shocking and tragic and – until now – untold story which Rabbi Kahane intends to expose.

He explained why he had recommended that someone shoot into the Iraqi embassy building, vacant since the 1967 Six Day War when Iraq severed diplomatic relations with the United States.

... Concerning the Iraqis, the previous month a Jewish family of five in Baghdad had been murdered in cold blood, making at least nineteen Jews who had been either murdered or were missing in Iraq. The reign of terror that had begun in 1969 with the public hanging of Jews in Baghdad showed no signs of letting up and the remaining five hundred Jews lived in fear of their lives. All civilized protests had, apparently, no effect on the Iraqis.

The Kastner Case

To bolster his position, Meir introduced the historic 1954 Kastner case, which he said was similar to his, especially concerning the role of the ruling party in Israel.

During the Holocaust, Rudolf Kastner, a Jewish Agency official in Hungary, made a deal with the Nazis for himself and some 1,600 Hungarian Jews to escape to neutral Switzerland. In Israel in 1954, a fellow Hungarian Jew, Malkiel Greenwald, published a booklet accusing Kastner of withholding information from other Jews in Hungary regarding the Nazis' annihilation plan. Greenwald believed that if the Jews of Hungary had been aware of the danger they were in, they would have acted more vigorously to save themselves. He maintained that because of Kastner's duplicity, 450,000 Hungarian Jews were gassed at Auschwitz. The Israeli government sued Greenwald for libel on behalf of Kastner, then a government official. Meir declared:

> [The 1954 Kastner trial] exposed the role of the Jewish Agency, then the governing body of the Jewish community in Palestine, composed of the same parties that still control the Israeli government, in deliberately concealing the news of Holocaust. [The Jewish Agency betrayed] hundreds of thousands of Hungarian Jews [who could have escaped to Palestine] for fear of offending the British mandatory power.[3]

Meir said the same thing at a press conference on March 5, prior to his trial. In his case, he said, Israel was fearful of offending America. He maintained that his trial was a political one, dictated by American pressure and Israel's deference to that pressure. He brought another parallel with the 1954 Kastner case: Kastner initiated it as a libel case against Malkiel Greenwald, but the focus of the trial changed and turned Kastner into the defendant, arousing Israeli public opinion to a feverish hatred of Kastner. Meir said that in this trial, where he was the defendant, he would turn the tables and make public his accusations against the Israeli government.

This trial would give him an opportunity that many Soviet Jewry activists had long awaited. It would provide a platform for him to reveal how Israeli government officials had hindered the Soviet Jewish struggle – because they feared to endanger diplomatic relations with the Soviet Union (which in any case were severed by the Russians after the Six Day War). Among the experts Meir planned to call as witnesses to Israeli government hobbling of Jewish activism in the Soviet Union were foreign minister Abba Eban, Shaul Avigur, head of "Nativ," the Israeli government agency in charge of Soviet Jewish affairs, and Yoram Dinstein, an authority on international law.[4]

Two days before the trial opened, Meir placed an ad in the Israeli press, explaining that the aim of the Brezhnev letters had been to protect Soviet Jews from the adverse effects of a pact between the United States and the Soviet Union. His defense would be to expose how the Israeli government had hampered the struggle of Soviet Jews for freedom. The ad said:

> On Shushan Purim the "1974 Kastner Case" will take place. Rabbi Meir Kahane is on trial for trying to save Soviet Jewry by violent methods.... This trial will give Rabbi Kahane the opportunity to inform world Jewry of the terrible facts about how the Israeli government hindered Soviet Jewry's struggle for freedom. Soviet Jews who wish to testify at the trial are asked to call attorney Meir Schechter.[5]

A Trial Behind Closed Doors

The trial opened on Sunday, March 10, with Judge Yaakov Bazak presiding. A photo taken that morning shows a smiling Meir accompanied by attorneys Meir Schechter and David Rotlevy. The prosecutor, state attorney Gabriel Bach, presented the letters that had been stopped by the postal censor as evidence that Meir had conspired to bombings, kidnapping and murder. When Meir was called to the stand, he admitted that he had sent the letters, but said that they did not represent a crime. Then he began an attack on the government's policy on Soviet Jewish emigration. He was immediately interrupted by Bach, who produced an affidavit from prime minister Golda Meir, which said that disclosures of the government's actions concerning Soviet Jewish emigration would be a breach of the Official Secrets Act and could hurt Israel's foreign relations.[6]

After reading the prime minister's affidavit, Judge Bazak ordered the court cleared of spectators. The trial continued behind closed doors. The prosecutor called two witnesses to testify: the police officer who had interrogated Meir in June 1973, and an employee of the postal censor's office who described how he had discovered the letters. Attorney Meir Schechter told the judge he wished to summon foreign minister Abba Eban to testify that Meir's disclosures were not likely to violate the Official Secrets Act. Bach voiced an objection to this, which Judge Bazak accepted. After ruling against calling Eban as a witness, the judge adjourned the trial until Tuesday, March 12, 1974.[7]

Judge Bazak's decision to hold the trial behind closed doors did not come as a surprise to Meir. In June 1973 he had written to Shimon Rachamim from Jerusalem Central Prison: "Work to make sure my trial is not behind closed doors ... Demand from Begin, Tamir and the other politicians to make strong protests against any attempt to try me behind closed doors." A month later, in July 1973, he informed the readers of the *Jewish Press*, "They have silenced the press – ordering a blackout on the case, and they want the trial to be held behind closed doors..."[8]

Julie Thornberg recalled, "When the decision was made to try Rabbi Kahane behind closed doors, we immediately printed flyers to publicize the facts. We flooded the streets with the flyers. To me it seemed a very 'American' way of reacting." One flyer, headed "Why is Golda Afraid of Kahane?" gave the story of Yasha Kazakov as an example of the Israeli government's hobbling of Soviet Jewish activism. When Kazakov had first gone to America in December 1969 to enlist public opinion, the Israeli Consulate in New York leaked stories that he was a Soviet spy and most of his sponsors cancelled his speaking dates. The flyer proclaimed that the government feared Meir's revelations: "They're Afraid of a 1974 Kastner Case!" Two young women who distributed flyers near the courthouse were arrested, and when Meir went to the police station to have them released, the police threatened to charge him, too, for distributing material too close to the courthouse.[9]

Meir placed an ad in the *Jewish Press* calling on American Jews to protest: "Rabbi Meir Kahane was interrupted in his defense," it said. "Civilized justice is to give every defendant an opportunity to defend himself. Not to allow a defendant to defend himself is also a violation of halakha." Readers were asked to send letters to Judge Bazak saying, "I want Rabbi Meir Kahane to be given a fair trial, or dismiss all charges against him."[10]

The *Jewish Press* rallied to Meir's support with an emotional editorial signed by Irene Klass, the publisher's wife, titled "I Remember Meir:"

> I remember the first time he came to us twelve years ago. He was slim even in those days and handsome. But it was not just the physical beauty of his face that caught your eye and held it! There was a certain brooding quality about his eyes as though he carried the weight of the world on his shoulders. If ever a human being felt the pain and anguish of his brothers, it was Meir Kahane. This feeling, which one Jew is supposed to have for another, was to lead him into avenues even he could not have foreseen.
>
> ... Meir joined our staff and began "telling it like it is." Thousands of young people were influenced by his themes. "Jewish is beautiful" he reminded them, and many a young Jew walked with his head a little higher. For he had given them back their Jewish identity. For this alone he deserves NOT TO BE FORGOTTEN.
>
> ... Now he is in danger and we must come to his aid.... Jewry owes a debt of gratitude to Meir Kahane that can never be fully repaid. The least we can do is show him we care. Let us send letters, petitions (telegrams and phone calls if you can afford it) to the Israeli government asking for leniency on Meir Kahane's behalf. He would do more than that for us."[11]

In reaction to the denial of his basic, democratic right of freedom of expression, Meir announced that he would not take part in the trial. His supporters distributed mimeographed sheets in Hebrew and English to the press and to the public headed, "Rabbi Meir Kahane's Statement to the Court Explaining His Refusal to Participate Further in the Proceedings of His Trial." His statement to the court said:

> I love and respect the Jewish State of which I am a proud citizen and I would like, too, to respect its laws and courts. But any law and any government must earn the respect of citizens by respecting the rights of those citizens, and a state is not the ruthless master, but rather the servant of its citizens. This, unfortunately, is not true in Israel today, and my case is a flagrant and frightening example of this tragic fact.

I was arrested by the Jewish State and kept in isolation for a month for attempting to fight for Soviet and Iraqi Jewry who both faced physical extermination – as the Israeli government suddenly became Brezhnev's keeper. I attempted to do that which I have done for years, that which the Israeli government both refused to do and also fought, damaged and harmed – the fight for Soviet Jewish freedom to emigrate to Israel. I willingly admitted this and looked forward to a free and open trial in which I could explain the entire background of the Soviet Jewry issue – and the totalitarians demanded that I be silenced and barred from speaking.

It is vital that this entire story be told – in order to show that the real motivation of the Israeli government in bringing me to trial was to curry favor with the Nixon administration and not anger the Russians ... and – above all – in order not to have the glare of publicity force change in the policy of the leaders of the government.

In a free society, A TRULY FREE SOCIETY, this right would have been unquestioned, respected, and I would have been allowed to present my testimony and call my witnesses. If the State differs with those witnesses or that testimony it has the right to challenge, cross-examine and call its own witnesses. This is what is done in a free society.

Instead, the prosecutor – a functionary who is at the beck and call of the few, totalitarian-minded who have run Israel for so long that it has become, for them, a private domain – brings into court a frightening and pathetic document signed by the prime minister herself, ordering me not to give testimony based on facts, dates and people; not allowing Soviet Jewish immigrants to testify and commanding the court not to hear all this.

... If there is a problem of security here, it stems only from the threat to it by an arrogant, power-intoxicated clique that has run the government and the people of this country not for 25 years, but for 50 years, and which – thanks to a people that is so apathetic and indifferent to its own fate – believes that there is nothing that it can do which will cause it to lose power.

... I want the Jewish world to remember what happened during the Holocaust period of Kastner and what is happening today with Soviet Jewry, as the Israeli Labor leaders bow to Nixon pressure and attempt to weaken the Jackson amendment ... and refuse to aid Soviet Jewish activists. I want the whole world to know this, NOT BECAUSE I WANT TO HURT ISRAEL – I STAND SECOND TO NONE IN MY LOVE FOR THE COUNTRY TO WHICH I CAME TO LIVE FROM A LAND OF COMFORT. I want rather to do this because the State of Israel is being corrupted and destroyed by the signers of totalitarian orders and the destroyers of individual liberties of those who defy them.

The totalitarians are not used to genuine opposition in this country. In general, people here are docile, cowed, frightened or bought, and the opposition itself is a pale caricature of the term. Let it be known that there are some who are different. I therefore am respectfully refusing to participate in the proceedings in which I cannot present my case to the world and which, for me, became a mockery and a "lynch."

I fully expect the government and the court to punish me stiffly and savagely – this is the way of the people who run the State. So be it. But the Jews of Israel and the world must know the truth....

Meir declared that he would be in the courtroom the next morning "in order that no one might say that I failed to appear" but he would refuse to participate in the proceedings.[12] At the request of Meir's attorneys, Meir Schechter and David Rotlevy, Judge Bazak recessed the trial to enable them to go to the Supreme Court for a ruling on the secrecy (closed-door) order. This was the first time in the history of Israel that the Supreme Court was asked to rule on a secrecy order in a case in a lower court. Attorney Meir Schechter told reporters he would argue that "secrecy" should apply only to cases involving espionage or a clear danger to the state.[13]

While the Supreme Court deliberated, Meir took advantage of a convention of Reform rabbis in Jerusalem to publicize what the Israeli government had done to hamper the Soviet Jewish struggle. On March 13, he issued a press release announcing that he was asking the CCAR, the Central Conference of American [Reform] Rabbis for the opportunity to address their convention. He wished to speak to them on the question of emergency aliya for American Jews and on the question of holding a trial behind closed doors. "I know," he wrote in the press release, "of the liberal spirit of the CCAR, and they will surely find time for me." While waiting for their invitation, which he did not really expect, he distributed flyers outside their convention hall:

> Will Those Who Bled for Selma Keep Quiet About Golda?
> You, Reform leaders, who waxed so indignant about black civil rights in Selma, Alabama; who figured so prominently in the fight for Mexican grape pickers in California and who thundered from the pulpits about Vietnamese victims in Hanoi –
> You went to jail in Selma, Alabama – Where is your voice at the outrage committed by Golda in Jerusalem!

The flyer went on to give an example of the testimony Meir would have presented in court:

> From the testimony of Binyamin Gur, May 17, 1973: "After visiting my relatives in the USSR in 1966, I went to Shaul Avigur (head of the government office on Soviet Jewish affairs that reported directly to the prime minister). He told me: 'We are not interested in a conflict with the Soviet Union because of a few people that we or their relatives desire to bring to Israel.'"[14]

The next day, March 14, a mimeographed press release in Meir's handwriting, the top half English and the bottom half Hebrew, was placed in reporters' pigeonholes at the Beit Agron Press Center in Jerusalem. It announced the topic of his press conference that day: "The Testimony I Planned to Give and Golda Stopped."[15]

At the press conference, Meir's supporters distributed a three-page "Declaration to the Court" in Hebrew and English, which he had written in June 1973 while in Jerusalem Central Prison. A moving expression of his beliefs, it began:

> I am a Jew, and I consider that to be the most important thing in the world. I do not say this out of some kind of foolish secular nationalism or chauvinism; I do not repeat what a Bulgarian or a Pakistani or a Frenchman would say about his own nationality; there is nothing sacred about nationalism at all ... But to be a Jew is not the same as being a member of any other nation, and it has nothing to do with nationalism. To be a Jew has a special, unique meaning ONLY because there is a G-d and He has chosen us as His special, unique and particular people – over and above, separate from all the others.
>
> ... And from this central concept stems a sacred commandment, a holy obligation.... "Thou shalt not stand idly by thy brother's blood." This is not a request or a call for charity – it is a demand, an obligation.
>
> ... I am charged with writing letters urging the commission of violent acts against the Soviets and Iraqis in an effort to save the Jews of those countries. I admit without hesitation to writing those letters and I have left it to my learned attorneys to argue the legal question of whether letters which never reached the parties for whom they were intended, or even the country to which they were sent, can constitute a crime. What I wish to discuss here is the far more important question of why I wrote those letters, so the world will understand what is at stake here and what must be done in the future so that we not stand someday as those Jews of 30 years ago – the generation of the Holocaust – and be found guilty with them of treason to the Jewish people.

Meir spelled out the logic behind JDL acts for Soviet Jewry and the logic behind his actions, and then summed up:

> I am not a criminal and I believe that there is not a Jew in the street who thinks that I am. I am, however, a Jew who believes in the Divine mission of the Jewish people – the Chosen of G-d – and in the obligation, from which there is no escape, to love and to hear the cry of a fellow Jew in distress.
>
> ... I do not want to go to jail and I do not seek to be a martyr. Yet I rejoice that I have had the opportunity to love my people even at the risk of jail and I have not proven faithless to the task.[16]

At the same time, Meir issued an invitation to newsmen to a press conference at our home on March 17, where he would show them the actual order from Golda Meir prohibiting free speech and testimony.[17] The next day, because of the official news blackout on the trial, Rabbi Aryeh Julius was arrested for bringing an ad about the trial to the offices of *Ma'ariv*. Incensed at this totalitarian tactic, Meir announced that he would read the "criminal" ad at the press conference. The arrest of Rabbi Julius aroused Meir to issue an emotional "Statement to the Press:"

> I weep for Israel, the people of Israel, and the Jewish people. This is a State that was a dream and is turning to ashes. The leaders who allowed hundreds of boys to fall last Yom Kippur because of their fear of offending the gentile ... followed in the footsteps of the totalitarian Soviets.... How many crimes have been committed in the name of security! ... They arrested our people for placing ads in the newspapers and for handing out leaflets to protest their policies.
>
> ... I intend to violate the Soviet-type law of Golda Meir in every way. I have handed out literature, I will hand it out. I have told people what the Israeli government has done against Soviet Jews and will do so. A law is not holy simply because it is there. A law can smack of tyranny and this one stinks of it to high heaven.
>
> ... It is a tragedy of Israel that the press is a pale caricature of what a press in a free country should be. There is no initiative, no courage, no drive to expose. All these create the elements of a totalitarian state....

Meir feared the worst:

> ... They can silence me with a bullet (and how many others have gone that way) but short of that, let them know that I am continuing to speak to people here and give them the facts.

He went into hiding so he would be sure to be present at the press conference.

> I am now in an undisclosed place because I want to be free for my press conference, which I called for this coming Sunday, March 17, at 8 P.M. at my home, 13 Sorotzkin Street in Jerusalem. I shall at that time give facts and dates and places concerning the treason of the Israeli government vis-à-vis Soviet Jewry.[18]

Since the printed word was the only ammunition Meir had, he distributed yet another multi-page mimeographed "Declaration" at the press conference at our home. There were two versions: *The Chosen State* in English and *Medinat Segula* in Hebrew. He had originally written this, too, in prison in 1973 following his arrest for the Brezhnev letters.[19]

Media Blackout

However, none of Meir's statements to the press found their way to the public. Since there was a court order barring the press from the courtroom, it was illegal to print anything Meir said or wrote about the case. The government censored all reports filed to newspapers outside Israel, too. In New York, Shifra Hoffman phoned Murray Zuckoff of the Jewish Telegraphic Agency to ask him to print Meir's *Declaration*. She reported to Meir: "Zuckoff checked with his Jerusalem correspondent and was told that Prosecutor Bach stated that since there is a court order barring the press, JTA would be held in contempt if they print anything sent to them by you."

Shifra asked Gene Singer and Hilton Goldman to join her at a meeting in Zuckoff's office. He advised them: "If your material were to be published in a paper like Brooklyn College's *Hatikvah* or the East Side chapter's *Hadar*, then JTA could reprint it as a quote and bypass the ban." Shifra promised Meir to "get it together and start the ball rolling."[20]

A few protests against holding Meir's trial behind closed doors did appear in Israeli newspapers. On March 20, a letter to the editor in *Yedioth Ahronoth* denounced the government's refusal to allow Meir to testify about Israel's policy on Soviet Jewish emigration:

> Holding a closed trial reminds us of the Jewish Establishment in the free world in the 1930s and 1940s, which remained silent during the Holocaust. A discussion of a subject as important as Soviet Jewish emigration must be held openly, not secretly.
>
> There are many who contest the government's policy on Soviet Jewish emigration and even say that it represents the government's greatest failure, greater even than its blunder in the conduct of the Yom Kippur War.
>
> Without agreeing with Rabbi Meir Kahane's activities in Israel, we are obliged to state that the Jewish Defense League played an important part in the struggle for freedom for Soviet Jews. We say that his trial must be conducted in open court.

The letter was signed by twenty Soviet Jews who had immigrated to Israel after leading the struggle in Russia. Among them were Ruth Alexandrovich, Yasha Kazakov and Leah Slovin.

This was followed by an editorial in *Yedioth Ahronoth* that asked, "Why forbid Kahane to testify on the Israeli government's policy on Jewish activism in the Soviet Union? ... Where are the freedom and the logic?" The next day, the Maoz organization of new immigrants from Russia, headed by Golda Yellin, collected over 1,000 signatures on a petition calling on the High Court of Justice to open Meir's trial to the public. It said that holding Meir's trial behind closed doors reminded them of Russia, where all political trials were closed to the public.[21]

Nevertheless, the High Court of Justice denied Meir's request for an open trial.[22] While he awaited Judge Bazak's verdict, Meir turned his attention to other issues. For example, when newspapers reported that courses in Christianity were being given at Denmark High School, a secular public school in Jerusalem, he distributed flyers to the students suggesting they learn more about their own religion. The flyers asked, "What do you know about Judaism? Have you learned *The Kuzari?*"

"If you want to know about Christianity," he wrote, "Here is a short lesson as an educational service of the Liga: During the Holocaust, Rabbi Michael Dov Weissmandl, who had escaped from a death train, managed to arrange a meeting with an important official of the Catholic Church, the Nuncio of Hungary, the Pope's personal ambassador to Hungary. The Rabbi begged him to save innocent Jewish children. The reply of the Nuncio: 'There are no innocent Jewish children. All Jewish blood must be spilled.'" Meir sent copies of the flyer to the press, recommending that the school concentrate on what is good and beautiful in Jewish tradition.[23]

Discord in the JDL

Despite problems within the JDL, there were many members sincerely devoted to its ideals. Since Meir's last trip to the States, they had continued JDL activities.

- In February 1973, ten JDL members held a sit-in at the offices of the World Council of Churches in Manhattan. They asked the Council to demand that President Nixon 1) suspend all dealings with the Soviet Union until Jews there were permitted to emigrate freely, 2) issue a demand for freedom for Syrian and Iraqi Jews, and 3) sell Council holdings in companies that deal with Syria, Iraq or the Soviet Union. The sit-in lasted over 24 hours and ended when the Council's representative agreed to hold "serious discussions" on JDL demands.[24]

- JDL members in Miami dressed in prison stripes picketed a performance of the Bolshoi Ballet to protest the imprisonment of Jews in Russia.[25]

- In August, JDLers in Los Angeles and San Francisco splattered local offices of Standard Oil with red paint to protest its pro-Arab stance.[26]

- The Philadelphia JDL branch presented a petition to the editor of the *Jewish Exponent* that read, "We petition you to regularly publish the editorial commentary of Rabbi Meir Kahane." They recommended that chapters in other cities approach their local Anglo-Jewish paper with similar petitions.[27]

- In October, after Arab terrorists took Austrian hostages, Chancellor Bruno Kreisky gave in to their demands and closed the transit station at Schonau, Austria, for Jews immigrating to Israel. Since the Soviet Union had severed diplomatic relations with Israel in 1967, planes taking Jews out of the

Soviet Union could not land in Israel. The transit station in Schonau was vital for Soviet Jews. JDLers throughout the United States protested. In San Francisco, JDLers held a sit-in at the office of attorney Paul Eisler, Austria's honorary consul there, while JDLers in Los Angeles, holding (unloaded) semiautomatic rifles and wearing Arab *kafiyas* on their heads, picketed the Austrian Consulate. Several JDLers in Washington unfurled a Nazi flag in front of the Austrian Embassy and urged passersby to boycott tourism to Austria. After picketing the Austrian Consulate in New York, about 75 JDLers tried to force their way through the gates, "injuring a police officer and breaking at least one window."[28]

- At the onset of the Yom Kippur War, JDL members demonstrated in a number of cities.[29]

- Four Brooklyn synagogues and yeshivot were vandalized after the start of the Yom Kippur War. Garth Kravat, head of JDL security, announced, "We are going to patrol this area in cars and on foot for as long as is necessary."[30]

Despite these activities, the JDL was not functioning properly. In December 1973 David Fisch had written to Meir, "The infighting here is unbelievable. There are so many factions of 4 or 5 people." At that point, Dr. Perl had resigned as national chairman because of the "tension, hostility and distrust."[31]

Formal Resignation

Meir realized that it was impossible for him to run JDL from Israel. On April 16, 1974, right after Passover, he called a press conference to announce that he was resigning from the JDL to devote himself to the Jewish Identity Center. He told reporters that JDL had too few active members and the entire burden of fundraising and organization had fallen on him and taken up the time he wanted to devote to teaching. He had become bogged down in fundraising and petty organizational matters for the JDL. "Freed from the burdens of petty problems, I will be able to devote all my time to the Jewish Identity Center, speaking, writing and teaching all Jews," he said.[32]

A Jewish Telegraphic Agency report in the *Jewish Press* quoted Meir as saying that he was resigning because there was "too little of the right people, too little talent and too little money" to carry out the JDL program. The JTA report, referring to dissension within the JDL leadership, added, "According to reliable sources, Kahane believes that the JDL is presently laden with many 'provocateurs' allegedly planted by various opposing bodies to hamper its activities."[33]

Since Judge Bazak had not handed down his decision in the case of the "Brezhnev letters," there was speculation about the timing of Meir's resignation.

David Fisch told the JTA reporter that Meir's resignation had nothing to do with a deal with Israeli authorities. Bill Perl voiced his thoughts about such a deal when he wrote to Meir, "Why you resigned I do not know. Of course, I knew that you had thought of it before.... I personally hope you had at least as one reason, a chance to beat the prison sentence." Perl added, "If this was so, this would be for me GOOD news, a patriotic act. The Jewish people need you, Meir, free...."[34] Columnist Dov Genachowski was cynical: "He says he's fed up with fundraising, but maybe he's also fed up with the law courts. Meir Kahane is still the same Meir Kahane. The Liga has a new name [the Jewish Identity Center] and nothing more."[35]

A thoughtful analysis of Meir's resignation by Marvin Schick said:

> Meir Kahane's resignation as chairman of the JDL was not totally unexpected. The JDL has been drifting for some time and it has been beset by internal leadership problems and financial difficulties.... It is apparent that [Rabbi Kahane] grew tired of the organizational bickering and the financial burdens with which he had to cope as head of the JDL.
>
> ... With few exceptions, it takes a great deal of money to run an organization. Established groups have fundraising apparatuses and dinners and other events, which ensure that the money keeps on coming in. Indeed, some of our best-known groups devote more to raising money than to assisting Jews. In the case of JDL, fundraising was very ad hoc and very much on the shoulders of Rabbi Kahane.... What is clear is that each year, a new, sustained effort would have to be made to raise money and this proved too difficult to achieve.
>
> ... Kahane, in a sense, has contributed himself to the JDL's predicament.... He is a talented writer, speaker and organizer, with an extraordinary public relations sense. I do not intend to suggest only surface qualities, for Kahane also possesses a first-rate mind. The problem was that with regard to its other leaders, JDL was not blessed with an abundance of talent, though a couple of them were fairly effective. All in all, too much of the JDL rested on Kahane, and once he decided to move to Israel, there was no one to replace him.[36]

Meir "became tired of begging for money" but he did not become tired or disillusioned about his own program – the JDL ideology. Meir made it clear to all that he would continue to advance the JDL ideology through the Jewish Identity Center in Jerusalem.

Chapter 38
The Jewish Identity Center
(March-June 1974)

MEIR'S RESIGNATION FROM the JDL meant he could devote more time to spreading his ideas. He announced that the Jewish Identity Center would be the focus of his activities.

From now on, I will act within the framework of the Jewish Identity Center. The Center, at 31 Ussishkin Street in Jerusalem, will hold lectures, offer courses and initiate discussion groups on Jewish identity. It will publish books and booklets and will send lecturers to every school or group that requests it. It will be the intellectual bastion of Jewish thought."[1]

He told a *Yedioth Ahronoth* reporter: "The JDL is not a 'holy cow.' It is a means, an instrument for transmitting ideas. Now I will devote myself to teaching Jews, especially the youth, the truth and the challenge of their Jewishness." *Ma'ariv* quoted Meir on the need for the Jewish Identity Center: "We live at a time when dark clouds threaten the Jewish people in Israel and throughout the world. The present leadership is bankrupt. The Jewish Identity Center will function as a 'think tank' which will discuss and analyze current problems and suggest solutions."[2]

The courses offered to the public were similar to those given at the Jewish Identity Center in September 1972. The course schedule for April 28 through June 27 listed classes in Hebrew and English on Bible and current events given by Rabbi Aryeh Julius and by Meir. On Monday and Thursday evenings Meir taught a Bible class in English, followed by a course called "Problems of Our Times," and on Saturday nights he spoke on current events.[3] In time, the daily classes were discontinued, but Meir continued to give Saturday night lectures at Ussishkin Street for the rest of his life. Saturday night was a good time to speak to tourists because they were usually free then. A handwritten, mimeographed flyer announcing "This Saturday night and every Saturday night – Rabbi Meir Kahane

Speaks," was handed out at hotels and on the streets of downtown Jerusalem regularly, beginning in 1974. Many young people who visited Israel went to hear him and came away with a broader understanding of Judaism and Israel. Baruch Ben Yosef and Menachem Gottlieb were two who attended the Saturday night lectures during the summer of 1974 and gained new insights into Meir's ideas.[4]

Chillul Hashem: The Desecration of G-d's Name

Meir's talks to tourists emphasized the importance of American Jews settling in Israel. Flyers for his speech on April 2 said his topic would be "Jew Get Out." In May, his article about American aliya was distributed at hotels. It said:

> ... In the newspapers of the eve of Yom Ha'atzma'ut [Israel Independence Day], there appeared a remarkable advertisement we would do well to ponder. "A Message of Solidarity from American Jewry to the People Dwelling in Zion." It was signed by all the major Jewish organizations in the United States.
> ... They – secure and safe, assured and stable; reaching out their hands to us – beleaguered and insecure, unsure and besieged, the endangered people dwelling in Zion.... The concern is genuine and their illusions concerning their own position and future frighteningly blind and unseeing.
> ... Jew! Your vision is failing, your perspective is all wrong! ... It is not the Jew of Israel who stands under the threat of destruction and is in need of help to save him from a holocaust. Quite the opposite. It is you, who think that the fleshpots of Long Island and Highland Park and of Beverly Hills and Miami are immutable and unshakeable and permanent. It is you, who are fated to be physically assaulted and psychologically shattered. It is the Exile of America that is trembling and unstable...[5]

Meir maintained that American Jews were those who were really in danger, despite the fact that the "Message of Solidarity from American Jewry" was written after a devastating terrorist attack in Kiryat Shmonah, a town close to the Lebanese border. Shortly before dawn on April 11, 1974, three P.L.O. terrorists had infiltrated the town and entered an apartment building. They broke into apartment after apartment, threw hand grenades, and fired at the occupants with Kalashnikov automatic rifles. By the time Israeli soldiers caught up with them, they had killed eighteen men, women, and children, and wounded many others. This opened a new era in Arab terror. Until then, the P.L.O. had attacked El Al terminals and other Israeli installations in Europe, with few attacks within Israel's borders. This was the first in an onslaught of terror attacks by the P.L.O. within Israel itself.[6]

For Meir, one such attack was one too many. He told Gil Sadan of *Yedioth Ahronoth* that terrorists must be stopped by any means, including counterterror. If this was done the right way, even the Arabs would demand that the P.L.O. be destroyed. Through the Jewish Identity Center, he said, he would seek ways of convincing the Jewish people of the need for an uncompromising policy that would ensure national security. Sadan, who interviewed him at home, described how Meir worked. Our dining room table was piled high with newspaper clippings, and the telephone was disconnected because Meir was busy writing and did not want to be disturbed.[7]

The article Meir was working on when Sadan interviewed him may have been "*Chillul Hashem* – The Desecration of G-d's Name,"[8] which he distributed at a press conference a few days later. In it, Meir wrote that the P.L.O. attack in Kiryat Shmonah represented an appalling national humiliation and as such, it was a terrible desecration of G-d's name. Several months earlier, Meir had written:

> Every time a Jew is beaten by a gentile this is the essence of *chillul Hashem*, the desecration of G-d's Name.[9]

This was a recurring theme in Meir's philosophy and a prime motivation for his belief that determined action had to be taken to put an end to terrorist attacks on Jews. Together with his article "*Chillul Hashem*," Meir gave newsmen an outline of a five-point counterterror program titled "*Rak Kach* (Only Thus)." Meir chose Dir Yassin, a former Arab village near Jerusalem's Givat Shaul neighborhood, to hold a news conference on counterterror, because in 1948, at this site, Irgun and Lechi fighters "had acted against Arab terror with imagination and effectiveness." A UPI wire report cited Meir's reasoning: "Terror cannot be stopped by the moral means which we Jews have always used." It summed up Meir's five-point program in one sentence: "The Jewish counterterror group would use the same means as the Arabs, against the same kind of targets."[10]

Reporter Gil Sadan presented the five-point program in *Yedioth Ahronoth*:

1) The establishment of a worldwide Jewish anti-terror organization that would train Jews to prevent terror and retaliate for terrorist acts.
2) It would open an offensive of terror against civilians in Arab countries in order to bring the masses to demand that their governments expel Palestinian terrorists under their protection.
3) If Arab terrorists took hostages in order to demand the release of their compatriots in Israeli prisons, the terrorists named would be executed immediately. If the hostage takers did not specify names, the same number of terrorists in prison as those demanded for release would be executed immediately.
4) In the case of any terrorist act against Jews, one thousand Arab families would be expelled from the liberated territories.
5) Since it is impossible to change the nationalist feelings of Israeli Arabs, they should be encouraged to emigrate and be given funds to aid their resettlement in Western countries.

Meir told Sadan: "The Israeli government should finance a counterterror group, just as Arab terrorists are financed by the Arab countries."[11]

Less than one month later, terrorists again infiltrated from Lebanon and held a group of high-school students hostage in the town of Maalot, before killing twenty-four and injuring almost eighty. This vicious attack shocked world Jewry. In New York, over 10,000 protesters demonstrated at U.N. headquarters and at the Lebanese Consulate. An Arab spokesman, M. T. Mehdi, claimed that JDLers attacked him as he was walking on East 42 Street after a press conference. Meir repeatedly advised counterterrorism: "The Arab in Damascus, Beirut and Tripoli must learn that as long as his government aids the terrorists in any way, he runs the risk of being blown to bits by bombs in his marketplace, bus and streets."[12]

In April Meir was drafted. Since he was forty-two years old, he was not given the same basic training given to eighteen-year-old conscripts, nor was he expected to serve in the regular army. Instead he was assigned to serve in *Haga* – Civilian Defense. In later years, he was assigned, at his request, to the regular army, but at the time, even the "tame" service in *Haga* was an eye opener for him. *Haga* duties were assigned to older men or men with large families, and their schedules were arranged to allow them to be home most evenings. This arrangement allowed Meir to continue to write and hold public meetings while serving.[13]

Waiting and Writing

This was also a period of waiting – waiting for Judge Bazak's decision in the Brezhnev letters trial. Meir used the time to publish a newsletter and several ideological booklets, all in English, under the auspices of the Jewish Identity Center.

He published the newsletter, named simply *Meir Kahane News Letter*, twice a month. It was aimed at supporters in the United States as well as English-speaking supporters in Israel. Meir promoted it as "Nothing fancy, nothing slick – just the incisive and deep insight you have come to expect." Mimeographed on folio leaves, it had ideological articles and reports on current events. The first newsletter, dated April 26, 1974, had excerpts from the recently published *Our Challenge* and a review of the Brezhnev letters trial titled "A Secret Trial in Israel." It also had Meir's article about the Kiryat Shmonah massacre, "*Chillul Hashem*," with his five-point program for counterterror, "Only Thus!" These two were the texts he distributed to reporters on April 22 at Dir Yassin. His article, "The Chosen State," which he had distributed in March at a press conference as a "Supplementary Declaration to the Court," filled the last fourteen pages of the newsletter.[14]

In the current events section, under the heading "Henry and Nancy," Meir reported:

> Having heard Golda Meir bemoan the rate of intermarriage and assimilation in the United States, to have [her] suddenly send a telegram of congratulations and an invitation to visit Israel to Henry Kissinger [a Jew] and his *shiksa* [non-Jewish] bride, at first glance did seem surprising.... We had simply forgotten, momentarily, that same *galut* complex known as "We-need-Kissinger-and-America-so-let's-not-anger-them." ... Last Wednesday [April 24], we came to the U.S. Consulate in Jerusalem to honor Henry with our first annual "Intermarriage of the Year" award.[15]

There were few paid subscribers to the *Meir Kahane News Letter*. Its third issue, May 24, 1974, noted that their number "had risen to 26." The sixth issue, July 5, 1974, announced:

> ... The newsletter will be discontinued as of this issue. As with so many other things, the people who agree with it and claim to see a need for it, refused to subscribe or to support it and the "circulation" remained ridiculously low, so that it becomes financially far more logical to return the money paid by the few subscribers rather than continue to pay the expenses of continued publication."[16]

Meir had more success with a booklet format. The Jewish Identity Center published four booklets in 1974. One was a collection of articles titled *Letters from Prison*. Most of them were written by Meir while he was in prison in June 1973 on the Brezhnev letters charge, but two were written in October 1972, when he was jailed on suspicion of involvement in the weapons shipment.[17]

One article, an eloquent expression of the beauty of Torah-true Judaism, was in the form of an exchange of letters with a prisoner whom Meir had met briefly at the Federal House of Detention in Manhattan. More than a year after that meeting, the prisoner had written to Meir:

> ... that hectic night in Federal Detention headquarters when you and your friends were booked in that crowded interview room ... I was that short, fat, fortyish inmate interviewer-typist.
>
> You may not recall it, but those few minutes of contact and talk affected me deeply. Later, after having time to think ... I became aware of the deep contrasts and contradictions, as well as the lack of spiritual moral commitment in my life.... Perhaps I might profit from a return to the roots which my mother cut herself off from when she married a gentile, the root and soil to which I have only been "socially" exposed to, as my family sought to deny their heritage.

Meir replied:

> ... I will try to tell you what I have tried to tell so many other Jews who are products of people and institutions that both ran away from and distorted eve-

rything strong, vital and beautiful in Judaism. I may not in the end give you encouragement, but I will certainly give you that message of Judaism that kept our people alive and relevant down to the decadent fraud of our times.

Let me start off by saying that there is a Jewish Destiny. It is one that exists whether we like it or not. Whether we cling to it or not is irrelevant to its existence and eventual fulfillment. The Jew has a past with a definite starting point: he has a commitment that gives a reason for being – both as a human being and as a separate Jewish entity; he has a goal and a future that will be no matter what. Only those who know and believe this will find the answer to the question that so agonizes so many: Why be a Jew!? Only those who cling to this distinct destiny and who practice their specific and exclusive Judaism have any conceivable logical and intellectual reason for remaining proud and exclusive Jews.

... The very different and special laws that define the conduct of a Jew as an individual and as a nation, we call the Torah. It is this Torah that the Jew carried with him into exile and into suffering; into pogroms and Crusades and Inquisitions and not least, into Auschwitz. It is the Torah that he studied on bitter cold wintry nights in Russia and on stifling summer days in Yemen. It is this Torah that turned his poverty-stricken hovel into a palace every Friday night when the Sabbath meant more than an occasion to exhibit an obscene $10,000 ritual of bankruptcy called a Bar Mitzvah. It is this Torah that made the Jewish family a warm and close unit where respect and love dwelt in necessary harmony. It was this Torah that turned out youngsters whose passion in life was not drugs and kicks and violent sadism but the famous "*kometz, aleph – aw.*" And it was from the little Torah "cheder" (school) that scholarly giants of the earth came forth to teach sweet morality and true goodness...

... I am enclosing a list of books that I hope to obtain for you. Read them and know that they constitute only the most modest beginnings. When you are released from prison, I hope that you will find it possible to come to Israel and study in either the JDL school, which caters in particular to those Jews with little background and who are searching for their past and future, or other schools of that kind here. In any case, I enclose my address in Israel ... and pray that G-d grant you the strength and the insight to reach out and to find yourself.[18]

Another booklet appeared in June: an overview of Meir's philosophy titled *The Jewish Idea: A Jewish Program for Jewish Survival.* It incorporated the ideas in his 1971 *Principles and Philosophies* and his 1972 *Jewish Defense League Movement Handbook,* as well as the concepts about Jewish destiny and the Jewish state that he had presented in *Our Challenge.* In his introduction, Meir wrote:

... The Jewish Idea – Torah – has become narrowed, limited and emasculated. That magnificent totality is unrecognizable. On the one hand is the Jewish "nationalist" who either rejects or limits the "religious" sphere. On the other hand is the "religious" Jew who narrows Judaism into its "religious" aspect and concept and not for him are such "non-religious" matters as political questions, oppressed Jews, the Land of Israel and its borders, social and communal problems, etc.

Both of these Jews stand together in the same error. Both narrow, diminish and misshape the Jewish Idea.

... A great overview of the Jewish Idea is necessary in order that we may see it in its entirety.... The mitzvot are bricks – bricks that are part of a structure. To look at an individual brick is to see nothing; to see it as part of a building is to see a great structure and overall plan. To observe mitzvot separately and individually, as individual bricks, is to go without plan and knowledge of ultimate purpose and Destiny. It is to turn Judaism from a great idea into "folklore."

Meir gave an example of the complexity of Judaism:

The Jew always works on two parallel levels. He does not merely trust in miracles and suffice with prayers but rather prepares for battles by all natural means. At the same time he realizes that not with his strength or the power of his arm alone can victory ever come.

He also pointed out:

We must never fear to be alone, for that is the Jewish blessing that has saved the Jew from assimilation and that is what will make the final miracle and the Jewish victory all the more great and astounding.[19]

Meir expanded on the latter idea in a booklet published a month later, in July. Its title, *Numbers 23:9*, referred to the Biblical verse "... Lo, it is a people that shall dwell alone and shall not be reckoned among the nations." Meir endeavored to persuade Jews that Israel should not depend on allies; that when Israel is isolated, with no allies, the Almighty comes to His people's aid.

To be alone, a curse? Precisely the opposite! To be alone is the salvation of the Jew and the sanctification of G-d's name. "Assyria will not save us..." (*Hosea* 14). ... If we understand this, we – ourselves – will bring the redemption and salvation. [20]

The fourth booklet printed at this time was *Madmen and Murderers*. The words of the title had been used by Rabbi Michael Dov Weissmandl to describe the Jews who were silent during the Holocaust. Meir used the same words to describe American Jews who were silent while Nixon and Kissinger pressured Israel to give up land. He wrote:

Jew!! Madman! Murderer! How long will you sit silently and allow the cold hands of pressure to close about the Jewish throat of Israel.... If the toadies and vestrymen who pose as Jewish leaders in the United States ... calm and soothe your nervous brow and declare that your instincts of danger are wrong, how long will you continue to be madmen and murderers and listen to them?

... Who will save us? ... Surely not the government of Israel, the government of the Yom Kippur War blunder.... The budding new prime minister, Yitzhak Rabin [who became prime minister in April 1974 after the resignation of Golda Meir] tells a settler of Kfar Etzion ... "It is not so terrible to give Etzion back to the Arabs and visit there with a Jordanian visa!"

... Jews of America! The battlefront is not here in Israel but there in the United States.... Drop everything else that you are doing! ... Organize yourselves, get out into the streets, sit down, take over offices, awaken the American people, turn to the gentile and shout that the Middle East is NOT A JEWISH ISSUE but part of the same bankrupt madness of [Nixon and Kissinger]. That détente is death for freedom and that Israel is being sacrificed on its altar....[21]

Madmen and Murderers, unlike the other booklets, was printed by Meir's supporters in the United States.[22] Its back page was used for ads. A subscription to the *Meir Kahane News Letter* was advertised at $11 or 20 lirot. An order form listed Meir's publications and their prices: *Writings 5731 / 5732-33* ($5.00 each), *Never Again* ($3.00), *Time to Go Home* ($4.00), *Our Challenge* ($7.95), *Letters from Prison* ($1.50) and *Numbers 23:9* ($1.00). The *Jewish Press* also carried ads for *Letters from Prison*, the newsletter, *Writings 5731 / 5732-33* and *Never Again.*[23]

Seeking a Publisher for *The Story of the Jewish Defense League*

Meir also advertised the as yet unpublished *Story of the Jewish Defense League* in the booklets. During January and February 1974, in addition to reorganizing the Liga and conducting a hunger strike to regain his passport, Meir had worked on *Story* intensively. In February, after completing the first five chapters, he sent the manuscript to publishers who had expressed an interest in his proposal. In his covering letter he wrote:

> Gentlemen, Please find enclosed the first five chapters of the manuscript, *The Story of the Jewish Defense League* ... The remaining chapters are undergoing revision and typing. (I am at the moment in the midst of a hunger strike in an effort to make the Israeli government return my passport, so I am somewhat hampered.)

He outlined the remaining chapters:

> Chapter 6: "Is It Good for the Jews?" The JDL break with Jewish dedication to outside philosophies and universalist concepts that saw Jews go against Jewish interests on behalf of others; the fight against Mayor Lindsay and our call for a Jewish vote; the problem of quotas and reverse discrimination; Jewish

poor; the reasons for our working together with Joe Colombo; Leonard Bernstein and the Panthers; our stand on Vietnam.

Chapter 7: "Jew Hatred: Auschwitz, USA?" A hard look at anti-Semitism in
the United States from the Right, Left and Blacks; the economic, social, political and racial roots of another Auschwitz; the danger of Populism; our attitude
toward free speech and Nazis; our call for an immediate evacuation of Jews to
Israel and the Jewish reaction to it.

Chapter 8: "JDL – What Now?"[24]

The response was disappointing. McGraw-Hill wrote, "We do not feel that it
fits into our present publication plans."[25] Little, Brown and Company replied,
"We were certainly fascinated, angered, excited and often encouraged by your
account of the JDL's history.... [However] Little, Brown is simply not good at
marketing books of this sort...."[26]

When *The Story of the Jewish Defense League* was published by Chilton in
May 1975, it followed the above outline, with the addition of a ninth chapter. But
in the early months of 1974, while Meir worked on chapters six, seven and eight,
he was still seeking a publisher. The ads on the back pages of the booklets said,
"The JDL Story ... To be published this year. SEND NO MONEY. Simply check if
interested in purchasing this book for $7.95." Meir hoped that if the response was
good, it would encourage his supporters to raise money for the book's publication. At this point, he despaired of finding a commercial publisher. He had written
to his key supporters:

> I hope that you will appreciate the fact that there is nothing without an Idea and
> that the idea is meaningless unless it is known, and it can never be known
> unless it is disseminated. Thus, the importance of printing and distributing my
> writings.
>
> The reason why I place such emphasis on the JDL story is that it is necessary
> for people to get a reminder, an overview, of what JDL did in order that they
> back it in the future.... The setting up of an investment group for profit is the
> best way to get people to back the book. If some people gamble on stocks and
> others in Las Vegas, surely some will understand that it is important to "gam-
> ble" on Jews. TIME IS ESSENTIAL.[27]

Reflecting optimism that he would be allowed to leave Israel soon, the ads on
the back pages of the booklets were headed "RABBI KAHANE MUST BE HEARD!"
and told readers how to arrange for Meir to speak in their homes or at their synagogues or clubs.

The back page ads also solicited contributions. "I am interested in helping
Rabbi Kahane's teachings spread to youngsters and other Jews. I enclose ____ to
help in this work," said one ad. Another ad said, "The idea is the greatest of
weapons. Help spread the idea. Make out your check to Jewish Identity Center

(tax deductible) and mail to Eugene Singer, 577 Grand Street, New York, N.Y. or J. Blum [my father], 8 Reines Street, Jerusalem."[28]

During this period, Meir also tried to raise money by writing for Anglo-Jewish newspapers in the United States. Gabriel Cohen, publisher of the *Jewish Post and Opinion* in Indianapolis, replied to his proposal with good humor, "Of course, I have read some of your columns in the *Jewish Press*... You would be able to buy a good meal in Israel for the $10 a week that we can offer...."[29]

Meir continued to use his weekly column in the *Jewish Press*, "Exposing the Haters," to persuade Jews to move to Israel by revealing the existence of dangerous Jew-haters in America. In one column he cited the assertion of the extreme right-wing National Youth Alliance that the "international gang of Zionists was responsible for the oil shortage." In another column he described the dispute over school integration in San Francisco and how "thirty uniformed, swastika-wearing Nazis came down to attend a Board of Education hearing on the matter." When Jews protested against the "Call-a-Nazi" phone service, local media supported the Nazi right to "freedom of speech." Meir subscribed to right-wing newspapers to keep abreast of this kind of information. In April he wrote to Shifra Hoffman, "I used to get Nazi-type literature regularly but my subscriptions ran out. Could you please subscribe to the following for me...."[30]

Meir also wrote feature articles for the *Jewish Press* under the name Meir Hacohen. They were popular treatments of Israeli current events that conveyed Meir's point of view. In "Fear on the Heights," he presented interviews with Golan Heights settlers who described how hard they had worked to establish farms there. He sympathetically portrayed their fears that Kissinger's pressure on the Israeli government would mean an evacuation of Jews from the Golan and the destruction of all they had built. Another feature article, "The Last Long Day," dealt with the government's failure to prepare for the Yom Kippur War. Using their own words from the *Knesset Minutes*, Meir showed Labor party ministers arguing among themselves about their responsibility for the debacle and discussing which of them had to resign from office.[31]

No to Nixon and Kissinger

Meir continued his campaign against Kissinger with a new emphasis: "Our target," he wrote, "must be the American non-Jew ... [and our] theme that Nixon-Kissinger policy is against the interests of the United States. The basic anti-Soviet theme must be used and Israel portrayed as the main bastion of militant anti-communism in the Middle East."[32]

Establishment Jews in America also voiced opposition to Kissinger. Hans J. Morgenthau, the political scientist, maintained that Kissinger's Middle East policy was too dependent on the questionable peace commitment of Egypt and questioned American reliance on a United States-Soviet détente at the expense of Israel.[33]

Meir called on Americans living in Israel to work against Kissinger. In a small ad in the *Jerusalem Post*, he invited United States citizens to attend the founding meeting of "Citizens for Jackson and Against Kissinger" at ZOA House in Tel Aviv on April 30. The group would support Senator Henry Jackson in his bid for the Democratic party's nomination in the 1976 presidential elections, while at the same time pointing out the danger posed by Henry Kissinger. A press release about the meeting declared:

> [Edward Kennedy] is the only serious contender who stands in the way of Senator Jackson at a time when America must have the kind of leadership that only Jackson can give. Kennedy, with his bankrupt illusions of détente and neo-isolationism, will be a tragedy for America, the free world, Israel and Jewry. Because of this, we have decided to begin now – while Kennedy is still unsure of the public reaction, to campaign both for Jackson and against Kennedy.[34]

Fifty people, including *Ma'ariv* reporter Inge Deutschkron, came to the meeting. Meir told her, "If only they would give me back my passport, I would go to the United States to stop Ted Kennedy."[35]

Several days later, Meir led a demonstration at the U.S. Embassy in Tel Aviv to mark Kissinger's arrival in Israel. A newspaper photo shows demonstrators holding placards that say "Israel Is Not for Sale!" and "No!" while Meir, holding a portable microphone, addresses the crowd. Afterwards he was permitted to present a petition to Ambassador Kenneth Keating. Flyers invited the public to join the "No to Nixon and Kissinger" movement at meetings on May 8 at the home of Mr. and Mrs. Thornberg in Tel Aviv or on May 9 at the Jewish Identity Center in Jerusalem.[36]

Meir also worked to attract Israeli youth. A Hebrew flyer headed, *Young Jew – Young Jewess*, said:

> Depression, worry, doubts, despair surround us as individuals and as a group in the State of Israel today.
>
> Our right to the Land of Israel – all of it – on the basis of G-d's covenant with His people who upheld his Torah throughout the generations – has reached a crisis point.
>
> The concept "Not One Inch" was not invented by Kahane, but by the Arabs, AND THEY ARE RIGHT! If there is a "Palestine" – there is no Israel. If we have no right to live in Shechem and Hebron, in the Golan and in the Jordan Valley – we certainly have no right to Tel Aviv, Beersheba, Jaffa, Ramle, Lod and Savion....[37]

A New Tactic: Civil Disobedience

Meir's struggle against Kissinger had reached a critical phase. He decided to follow the example of the American civil rights movement. His next flyer declared that only a program of civil disobedience could succeed.

> Demonstrations, public meetings, brilliant speeches, petitions and shouting – all these are great, but they will not put a stop to the retreat from our Land. The government and "High Commissioner" Kissinger disregard all these and ignore our protests. The time has come to act!

The public was invited to take part in discussions on "Civil Disobedience – Yes or No" in Jerusalem on May 14 and in Tel Aviv on May 20.[38]

In his newsletter, he wrote:

> [Ordinary protests] will never persuade a government that is both under strong and merciless pressure from Washington and which has key figures in it who, for the sake of "peace," are willing and eager to give up parts of the Land.
> ... The only way to persuade the government to stand firm and save the State is to frighten it and prevent it from mad concessions.... The time has come for a genuine national debate on the question of "Civil Disobedience – Yes or No?"
> ... Whether Gandhi had the right to peacefully refuse to obey the law in the struggle to create a free India or whether Martin Luther King had a right to lead thousands in civil disobedience on behalf of civil rights for Blacks were matters of debate ... [by] many people who were committed to the rule of law but who recognized that there are times when the law must be set aside in order to defend freedom and liberty.
> Surely, it is not out of place to begin discussing in serious terms, whether the cause of EXISTENCE is not also a legitimate arena for civil disobedience.[39]

Meir was optimistic about the civil disobedience tactic:

> ... [What if] huge numbers of Jews refusing to pay taxes, sitting in at pre-determined government offices, demanding to be jailed and knowing that there are not nearly enough jails to hold them all – and all this before the eyes of the world press...
> ... The government would not only be unable to retreat, but it would be given an invaluable political card and opportunity to tell Kissinger: "You see, we are prepared to concede, but what can we do? Look at 'them' out there. They will not let us."[40]

A newly established group, Gush Emunim, which looked to Rabbi Tzvi Yehuda Kook for spiritual guidance, was much admired by Meir. The group repeatedly took to the streets to protest against Henry Kissinger during his "shuttle diplomacy" visits to Israel. Gush Emunim's primary goal was to settle in all parts of the Land of Israel liberated in 1967, including areas with a dense Arab population. One such place was the area adjoining Shechem (Nablus).* (Meir always transliterated the name of the city as "Shchem," which is closer to the Hebrew pronunciation, but I have adopted the more widely used spelling, "She-chem.") On June 5, the anniversary of the Six Day War, 150 settlers – men, women and children – set up camp near Shechem. Hamdi Kan'an, former mayor of Shechem, called on the Arabs of his city to be ready for a "violent struggle" if the settlers remained. Yitzhak Rabin, prime minister since April, declared that settlement in the liberated lands was a matter of government policy, and not for individuals to decide on their own. When the settlers refused to leave, Rabin ordered the army to evict them forcibly.[41] Meir wrote:

> ... The effort at settlement was a great step forward.... It is to be hoped that such things will continue and people will be prepared to fill the jails until there is no more room, and that which the people's will was able to do in Northern Ireland, total strikes and non-violent shutdown of the country, can force the pit-iful government here to allow Jewish settlement in Eretz Yisrael....[42]

Meir expounded on the ideology of civil disobedience and its application to settlement in all parts of the Land of Israel in an article titled "On Law and Order in Israel."

> ... The very foundation of democracy is the concept that the majority decision, correct or foolish, must be accepted by the minority and that change can only be brought about by elections and orderly process. If, today, one group disre-gards the law, tomorrow a second one will and the order and stability of society will break down into a jungle of anarchy.
>
> ... The question of the right of the state to demand obedience from a citizen who, in turn, replies that on certain matters his conscience will not permit him to obey that state, is at least as old as the story of Socrates. Certainly, those who are acquainted with Thoreau and his concept of civil disobedience and who watched as Martin Luther King willfully disobeyed the laws of a democ-racy are familiar with the dilemma.
>
> ... Indeed, many who today anguish over the "threat to democracy" posed by the settlers of Samaria were themselves ardent admirers of both the law-defying Reverend King and the demonstrators who defied the laws of the United States to protest what they considered to be an illegal and immoral war in Southeast Asia [Vietnam]. But why go further than Israel itself and the incident in 1956 at Kfar Kassem when, as the Sinai War broke out, a group of Israeli Arabs unwittingly broke the curfew and were shot down by Israeli sol-diers following orders of their commanders. The state – cheered on by the very

---

* During the Roman conquest of the Holy Land (for about 500 years beginning in 63 B.C.E.), Shechem was called Neapolis ("New City"). Nablus is the Arab pronunciation of Neapolis.

circles who today fume over Samaria – put on trial soldiers who had merely followed orders. The argument was that a soldier has an obligation to refuse to follow an immoral order.

... The question of law and order in Israel is not the same as a similar problem in the United States or France or Italy or Australia. Just as the Jew is different and unique, so is the question of law and order in the Jewish state unique and different.

... The Jewish concept of government is clear: The government exists to serve the state. The state exists to serve the people. The people exist to serve G-d.

... When the government demands that a Jew disobey a [Divine] law – he must disregard the illegal order. When the government refuses to allow a Jew to obey a legal obligation – he must defy the illegal attempt [of the government]. Settlement attempts in Eretz Yisrael are in the highest tradition of Jewish obedience to law and order.... For the sake of the Jewish people and the Jewish State, [Jewish] law and order must be preserved.[43]

Meir was angry at the army's removal of the Gush Emunim settlement attempt near Shechem, and in particular at the government's surrender to the threats of the mayor of Shechem. "Arab arrogance," wrote Meir, "is a direct byproduct of Jewish softness and stupidity."[44] Meir sent a letter to Hamdi Kan'an, Shechem municipality, with copies to the mayors of Ramallah, Tulkarem and Jenin, and, of course, to the press:

I was shocked to hear your audacious comments on the Jewish settlers who wish to return to the land of their fathers in the Jewish city of Shechem.... Your threats against the legal owners of the land of Israel are insufferable, and we demand an immediate apology to the settlers.

We are holding an emergency meeting at the Beit Agron Press Center in Jerusalem this Wednesday, June 12, at 7:30 P.M. to discuss what steps to take regarding your insult to Jewish sovereignty. You are invited to come to apologize....[45]

Meir's supporters distributed a flyer inviting the public to hear him speak at Beit Agron. The flyer reminded the public that it was Yitzhak Rabin who had given the orders in 1948 to shell the *SS Altalena*, causing the death of sixteen innocent Jews, and now Rabin was giving orders to forcibly evict Jews from Jewish land. The flyer proclaimed that submission to the threats of the mayor of Shechem was a *chillul Hashem* and the first step in conceding Judea and Samaria to the Arabs.[46]

Two weeks later, Judge Bazak handed down his verdict.

Chapter 39
Building and Rebuilding
(June-September 1974)

A Suspended Sentence

MEIR'S TRIAL FOR the Brezhnev letters resumed at the end of June. Judge Bazak was to hand down his verdict on June 27 and pronounce sentence on June 28. In "Finally, A Verdict," Meir commented on the coming trial and invited the public to attend.

> ... In the District Court in East Jerusalem, Judge Yaakov Bazak will finally end the process of "Israel-is-Brezhnev's-keeper" and pass sentence. The maximum sentence on the two charges is 12 years, and while no one expects that the government of Israel will be able to jail me for 12 years, there is little doubt that I will get some prison sentence.
>
> ... The end of the trial is in as outrageous a circumstance as the rest of it. It was a full SIX WEEKS ago that the trial ended, a trial which in actual time in the courtroom took only two days. There were a total of THREE witnesses (none for the defense) and the defense refused to present any counter evidence in objection to the closed-door order by Premier Golda Meir. Despite this, and despite the fact that the judge could have reached a decision in a week, there was again a slow and deliberate delay calculated to keep me tied up as long as possible.
>
> ... The public is invited to the court on Salah-el-Din Street, at 9 A.M.[1]

Newspaper photos of Meir entering Jerusalem District Court show him looking calm and optimistic, wearing a short-sleeved, open-necked white shirt and tan cotton pants. In court, Judge Bazak pronounced Meir guilty of conspiracy to harm Israel's foreign relations, but innocent of conspiracy to commit violence. At sentencing the next day, he imposed a two-year suspended sentence. The judge noted that it was difficult to deliver a verdict when the defendant's aims are lofty and his intentions good. He said the sentence was a light one because the letters Meir

sent had been intercepted, and even if they had gone through, there was no certainty that the recipients would have carried out Meir's instructions.[2]

I was relieved that Meir would not have to serve time in prison, and I was glad
that he had been found innocent of violent acts. I hoped this verdict would mean
that the U.S. Probation Office would not consider Meir's espousal of the use of
weapons in his letters to be a violation of the terms of his probation.

But Meir was not satisfied with the verdict.

> I have been asked whether I am happy with the suspended sentence I received
> last week. The answer is no. I should not have been tried in the first place for
> a "crime" that was based on helping Jews, and I still await an answer from
> Judge Bazak to the question I asked in court: Why is Israel furious at the fact
> that Germany puts Beate Klarsfeld on trial for the admitted attempt to kidnap
> a German for good reason and then puts me on trial for the same thing – when
> it involves Russians?
>
> Finally, I am not happy that not a word of my statement in court was carried
> by any of the pitiful sheets that pass for newspapers here. No, I am not happy.[3]

Meir's "unhappiness" with the Israeli press was not new. In May, following
a summary hearing in court to schedule the verdict, Arye Avneri of *Yedioth
Ahronoth* had interviewed Meir. The article was a long one, dealing with a variety
of topics, but I will not quote from it, because on the clipping in Meir's files are
Meir's handwritten words: "Incredibly garbled and untrue statements!"[4] Throughout his life, the Israeli press often presented Meir's ideas in a garbled fashion. It
left him feeling frustrated, but he did not allow it to defeat him.

He was encouraged by the reaction to talks he gave during this period. After
one lecture at the Ramot Shapira Educational Center in Bet Meir he was invited
back to give another. The students and teachers of the Mitrani High School in
Holon thanked him for his "fascinating talk," and the Netanya branch of the
Association of Americans and Canadians in Israel welcomed him warmly. In
Kiryat Shmuel, where he spoke at a Bnei Akiva yeshiva, "both teachers and students were greatly impressed by his words." He also spoke at two parlor meetings:
at the home of Sara and Dudu Taubman in Rishon Letziyon and at the home of
Lanny and Evelyn Yellin in Jerusalem. The Yellins thanked Meir for his "pro-
vocative analysis of current challenges facing Jewry here and abroad."[5]

Jews in Jericho

In the wake of the shameful removal of the Gush Emunim settlement near
Shechem, Meir devised a plan for Jewish settlement in Jericho. He pointed out
that no Jew had thought of settling in this part of the Land of Israel. It was
Judenrein, he wrote, and explained the urgency of settling there: "The completion

of a substantial portion of a new defense line west of Jericho makes it clear that Israel and Jordan have agreed to an initial withdrawal. This area is the first that will be given to King Hussein...."[6]

Meir's plan to establish a yeshiva and a settlement in Jericho to prevent ceding it to Jordan was put forward by Rabbi Aryeh Julius. Meir saw to it that his name did not appear in any of the yeshiva's flyers, press releases, or correspondence, since that might cause the government to oppose the plan. A June 20 report in *Yedioth Ahronoth* told of students from various yeshivot in the country who wanted to establish a settlers' yeshiva in Jericho. The group had written to prime minister Yitzhak Rabin and other officials for help in establishing a yeshiva in Jericho that would preserve the "wholeness" of the State of Israel as well as its Jewish character.[7]

The name chosen for the yeshiva, Aderet Eliahu (Elijah's Cloak), indicated its connection with Jericho: It was near Jericho that Elijah the Prophet tossed his cloak to his disciple Elisha, as he was taken up to heaven in a fiery chariot. Newspaper ads read:

We proudly announce the establishment near Jericho of
Yeshivat Aderet Eliahu
(Elijah's Cloak; see II *Kings* 2)
and a settlement being built around it.

– If you have finished high school and wish to learn Torah in historic Eretz Yisrael, enroll in the Yeshiva.

– If you are a Jew who wishes to ensure that no part of the historic Land of Israel will be given away, join the new settlement.

– If you are a new immigrant who wants to find the Land of Israel you came for, join us.

– If you think it's a wonderful idea but cannot come yourself, HELP US. WE NEED, IMMEDIATELY, THE FOLLOWING ITEMS: Cots; mattresses; sleeping bags; religious books; a Torah scroll; tables; chairs; a generator; cables; one 800-litre water tank; two 220-litre water cans; jerry cans; rubber hose (30 meters); gas stove (large); large gas balloon; small and large flashlights; gas "lux" lamp; two refrigerators; hammers (5 kg.); sheets; kitchen utensils of all kinds; food of all kinds.

– We are accepting students for the rest of the summer, for the whole year, or even for a week at a time.[8]

Meir did not want to see the army forcibly evicting settlers in Jericho. In a July 3 letter to supporters in America, he described his plan to prevent the removal of the Jericho settlement.

To keep the government from dragging us away as they did last month in Shechem, we are holding a memorial meeting in two weeks, on July 17, for Dr. Martin Luther King and his mother [Alberta King] and inviting Ambassador Keating and other dignitaries to establish the Mrs. Alberta and Dr. Martin Luther King, Jr. Institute in Human Relations. At the meeting I will announce that it will be located in Jericho and I will speak about King's great contribution – civil disobedience to immoral laws. This will place the government in a difficult position in dragging us away.[9]

At a July 16 press conference, Meir revealed his connection with the settlement effort in Jericho. He told newsmen that the new settlement in Jericho would house the Martin Luther King, Jr. Institute on Human Relations. He had sent telegrams announcing the founding of the Institute to Americans connected with King, such as Martin Luther King, Sr., Governor Jimmy Carter of Georgia, and Vernon Jordan of the Urban League. The Institute's aim, he told the press, was "to tumble the walls of hatred and honor those who stood for disobedience, non-violent, to immoral laws."[10]

A New Political Party: Kach

It is very likely that the establishment of the Institute on Human Relations in Jericho received media coverage only because, at the same press conference, Meir announced that he was forming a new political party, to be called Kach, Hebrew for "Thus." The name Kach was already associated with Meir: In the election campaign only half a year earlier, the letters *kaf-kaf sofit* spelling kach had been the Liga's letters and the Liga's slogan had been *Rak Kach*, Only Thus.[11]

Meir explained to supporters in America why he was forming a political movement:

> We are announcing the formation of a new organization to be known as Kach – Thus.... It will be JDL carried to its ultimate and necessary logical conclusion. It will be a vital Jewishness with added Judaism, for in the end, without the latter there is nothing. Rallies and *chayas** are excellent ... but they are only temporary things, and the real truth and permanence is Judaism.... JDL failed because it did not have the Judaism that was the idea, the cement.[12]

The press conference on July 16, its purpose announced in detailed press releases, was well attended. With Shimon Rachamim and Rabbi Aryeh Julius sitting alongside him, Meir told reporters that Kach's basic ideology was the same

---

* The JDL *chaya* squad, initiated in 1972, fought anti-Semites. A *chaya*, meaning "wild animal" in Hebrew, was someone who would cast off the "wimpy" Jewish image and act like a wild animal when he was called on to protect other Jews. See chapter 26.

as that of the Liga, but emphasized that Kach would be a protest movement. They planned a settlement in Jericho, he told them, and if the army would come to remove them, they would protest according to the principles of non-violent civil disobedience. He also said that he intended to run for the Knesset again. Lengthy manifestos in Hebrew and English explaining the movement's principles and programs were distributed to reporters. They presented the concepts of the chosen people, the chosen land and the chosen state featured in the 1973 election campaign.[13]

The historic importance of the establishment of the Kach movement is reflected in the inclusion of photos of the press conference on the website of Israel's National Photo Collection. The photos show Meir with a 10-day beard – it was the mourning period for the destruction of the Temples, when observant Jews do not shave. He is wearing a short-sleeved, open-necked white shirt, and his usual small appointment book and slips of paper are sticking up from his shirt pocket. On the table before him a microphone is held in place in an empty water glass. His arms are folded and his elbows rest on the table as he leans toward the microphone. His mien is serious and subdued. The photos show him speaking calmly. Only in two of them is he gesturing with his hand, pointing his index finger to make a point, and even there, his elbow rests on the table.[14]

The establishment of Kach was widely reported. Jay Bushinsky, a correspondent based in Jerusalem, gave the details in a special broadcast on New York's WINS radio. Kach would protest Kissinger's pressure on Israel because it was forcing Israel to adopt a suicidal policy of retreat. Kach would also campaign to get more American Jews to settle in Israel. Bushinsky noted Meir's legal problems: the two-year suspended sentence handed down by an Israeli court for having acted in a manner harmful to U.S.-Israeli relations and the five-year suspended sentence issued by a U.S. court for violating weapons laws.[15]

Rebuilding the JDL in America

After sentencing by Judge Bazak on June 28, Meir did not leave the country immediately, because most Americans would be on summer vacation. "July-August is a waste, since no one is around at this time," he wrote to supporters. "I will therefore arrive, please G-d, around August 15. Please get speaking dates on campuses and in synagogues. I will be there until November 1." He wrote to them of his plans for rebuilding the JDL in America:

> I want to revitalize JDL when I get back to the U.S. I want JDL to be the arm of Kach in the Exile. I want JDL to take the last step it never took and restore it to the active group it has ceased being. I have written to [the board] asking that a convention be held (one has not been held now in four years) at which

I will present the program and at the same time offer the names of people I think should be on the new board. I want the convention for the weekend of September 7-8, and if the board refuses (I have given them a time limit for reply), I will call a conference that weekend of 50-100 people from all over the country and organize a group known as JDL-KACH. In any case, I hope you will agree to serve on the executive board.[16]

Meir also sent a long letter to the general JDL membership:

... Six years ago, I formed the JDL and this year I resigned from it as my way of protesting what has happened to it.... There is not a single area of Jewish need – Jewish identity, patrols, defense, aliya, oppressed Jews, in which one can find a semblance of an imaginative ongoing JDL permanent program.

Worse, one of the great principles of JDL – *Hadar*, personal behavior that is exemplary and proud – is frighteningly lacking, and no group which has people whose major thought is simply fighting and beating people can survive, let alone attract good, talented people.

A group is like a person. Each person must grow throughout his life, reaching new heights, new insights and understandings. Once, JDL did that. From local defense it was taken to the heights of Soviet Jewry – and how many members objected to this! It branched out into aliya and how many objected to that! When I was in the U.S., I was able to overcome the objections and make JDL grow and become greater than it was. The final step – and without this there is no truth and no future for JDL or Jews – to bring JDL up to JUDAISM and to make Jewish identity in the full substantive Jewish sense meaningful, was not in my power to achieve because of the fact that I was detained in Israel for two years and unable to return.

In Israel, I have announced the formation of a movement to be known as Kach – Thus. It is JDL in its total and final stage of progress. I enclose a brief pamphlet explaining it. I hope to be back in the U.S. in August. A convention of JDL, which has not been held for four years despite my pleadings, will be held. (It will either be called by the executive board or by me.) At that convention I will put this program before the members and present an executive board that will return JDL to its former pride and make it a responsible, stable and talented group of people prepared to sacrifice for Jews. Should the members approve this, JDL will keep its name in the Exile and become the arm of Kach there. Should the members not approve, Kach will be formed in the Exile and will begin the job of doing for Jews that which the JDL once did.[17]

In March, Meir had written to Sam Shoshan about what he wanted to do when he came to America.

It is vital that I appear before youth, synagogues, *goyim* [non-Jews], and on TV and radio. Kissinger is a disaster for us, the Arab terror must be met, and there is no American aliya.

I enclose an example of an itinerary of an Arab propagandist. I hope that you can be the coordinator of such a thing for me. If you work with people like Shifra Hoffman, my sister-in-law Shelley Blum, Hilton Goldman and other key JDL people in New York and other cities, plus using your own contacts and ingenuity (as well as working with Chilton Publishing, which has already tried to get things set) it can be quite successful....[18]

Letters were sent to synagogues throughout America saying: "Dear Community Leader, Rabbi Meir Kahane will be returning to the United States in 1974 for lectures and speaking dates.... We are now taking requests for speaking dates for the 1974-75 year. We suggest you contact us immediately to book a speaker you will long remember. [signed] Shelley Blum."[19]

Sam Shoshan, Hilton Goldman, and others arranged speaking dates for Meir, and his ten-week trip looked to be a hectic round of speeches and rallies in New York, Baltimore, Chicago, San Francisco, and other U.S. cities.[20]

At the end of July, with his plane ticket ready and his U.S. passport in hand, he wrote to Gene Singer and to Sam Shoshan: "I am planning to leave on August 12. If I make it past passport control, someone will phone to let New York know and you can contact the press." His fear that he might be stopped at the airport was well founded. Just before departure, he was taken off the plane by police and forbidden to leave the country. He told reporters at the airport that the ban was to keep him from getting to America, where he intended "to arouse United States Jews to angry protest" against Secretary of State Kissinger's policy in the Middle East.[21]

Apparently, the records of passport control at the airport had not been updated after the Court lifted the 22-month-old ban preventing Meir from leaving Israel. However, the next day, they allowed Meir to depart. His supporters, who threatened to demonstrate at the Israeli Consulate in New York to protest the ban on his departure, turned out en masse to greet him at Kennedy airport. At an impromptu press conference, Meir said, "It's about time the myth of Kissinger as a savior is punctured. I think that Kissinger's general policies of détente with the Soviet Union have seen U.S. military power dropped and have caused the sacrifice of people behind the Iron Curtain." A photo of Meir's arrival is captioned: "Rabbi Meir Kahane arriving at JFK is met by more than 100 JDL members carrying Israeli flags and signs." It was an auspicious beginning for his visit. In his first letter home, Meir wrote:

When I arrived at Kennedy airport and got off the plane, I saw three plain-clothesmen trying to look inconspicuous. When they saw me, one introduced himself and flashed his badge. I was convinced that I was being arrested, but they were only there to get me through passport control and customs quickly.[22]

In another letter home, Meir wrote of his plans to revitalize JDL.

> I miss you all very much and for me, being in America is like being in Galut [Exile] twice over...
>
> The JDL at my direction has called a convention for September 8 over the objections of the Board and Bert [Zweibon]. I am calling for a broadening and uplifting of ideology with Judaism and Jewish nationalism as the twin goals. In addition, the crazies must go.[23]

Meir's reference to "the crazies" followed alarming reports he had been receiving, such as this letter in July from Dr. William Perl, explaining his resignation:

> ... I suppose you know what is going on in the New York JDL.... [In January, I was] pressured to appoint Jack [not his real name] and two more people I did not know to the board. I told them that ... I do not trust Jack as a person.... They insisted.... Finally, I gave in. At the next meeting I saw what had happened. I counted and saw that these people had the majority. They wanted to go out and beat up one of our BEST members, for nothing, so I resigned.[24]

Similarly, Sam Shoshan reported, "While [I was] in Israel, the 'Young Turks' made a *putsch* on the Board.... The Board as now constituted is now brawn with little brains."[25]

JDL's Queens coordinator sent a graphic description of the situation to youth coordinator Sammy Hirschman:

> A few months ago Jack was put on the Board of Directors. He started [making] physical threats to many JDL members.... Two weeks ago he came to a *chaya* workout with three guys and four guns.
>
> At the [fundraising evening] at Westbury, Sandy Goldstein was put up against the wall and almost beaten up because Jack wanted the money donated that evening.
>
> ... Nat Rosenwasser quit as vice-chairman of JDL, Fay Lloyd resigned from the Board, Lorraine Schumsky quit as Brooklyn coordinator. Everybody else is scared that Jack will either shoot them or blow their homes up or burn their cars.
>
> ... Dave Fisch left two weeks ago.... Russ Kelner also left.... All that will be left soon will be Jack and his animals.... I think this information ... should be given to Meir.[26]

David Fisch issued a press release that said, "... the people who comprise the present Executive Board are ... motivated, as I see it, by something completely foreign to that which I – and, I believe, Meir Kahane – have been committed.... The present Executive Board has continually refused to call a Convention to face the scrutiny of the JDL membership.... [It] has never been ratified by the organization's membership...."[27]

Barbara Ginsberg recalled, "There were a lot of people in JDL who were just there for the kicks, not for the ideology. Jack was one of them, 25 years old, working for his father, a Jewish hoodlum. He didn't kill, he didn't steal, but a hoodlum.... Meir said he doesn't want that kind in the JDL. They will as soon beat up a Jew as an anti-Semite."[28]

In reaction to Meir's call for a JDL convention on September 8, the existing Board of Directors called a meeting on September 4. Only Bert Zweibon and several teenagers were present. The first motion, passed unanimously, was to expel most of the adults from the Board of Directors, including Gene Singer, Barbara Ginsberg, Mal Lebowitz, Charles Cohen, Stanley Schumsky, and Max Lidz. The group also sent out letters and placed an ad in the *Jewish Press* announcing that JDL was NOT holding a convention on September 8.[29]

A confrontation between Meir and Bert Zweibon had been brewing for some time. In the early days of JDL, Bert's talents as an attorney had complemented Meir's charisma and innovative imagination. However, when Meir moved to Israel and Bert became the head of JDL, a rift developed between them. Bert accused Meir of undermining JDL by shifting his emphasis from America to Israel. When Meir's passport was confiscated in October 1972, Bert went so far as to squelch a *Jewish Press*-sponsored letter writing campaign to pressure the Israeli government to return the passport. Meir, unable to travel to America, was dismayed at JDL's stagnation under Bert's leadership and demanded his resignation. In early 1974, when Meir tried to have his probation period terminated, he was forced to turn to individual supporters because the JDL board, under Bert, did nothing to help him. By the time Meir returned to the United States, he was determined to wrest the leadership of JDL from Bert.[30]

Meir placed an ad in the same *Jewish Press* issue that had the ad "No Convention." Meir's ad said: "Pursuant to the by-laws of the Jewish Defense League, the official National Convention will be held on September 8 at the Belmont Plaza Hotel." It was signed by the chairmen of chapters in Philadelphia, Northern New Jersey, Providence, Los Angeles and Washington, D.C., as well as chapters in the greater New York area. The ad said, "Only paid-up members will be permitted to vote. Back dues will be accepted at the convention." In large letters, it announced, "Invited Guest Speaker, Rabbi Meir Kahane."[31]

The printed program of the day-long convention said that Meir would speak at 9:30 A.M. on JDL ideology, followed by lunch and *Mincha* prayers. On the afternoon agenda were talks about JDL by Mal Lebowitz, Nat Rosenwasser, Paul Smith, and Joy Greenblum. Chaim Ginsberg would chair the nominations and elections, and Hilton Goldman would install the new Board of Directors. Masters of Ceremony Stanley Schumsky and Morty Lloyd would conduct a financial appeal, and after dinner Meir would speak on "Kissinger: Bad for America and Israel." At 7 P.M., the participants would rally at the U.S. Mission to the U.N. to protest American pressure on Israel to withdraw from the liberated lands.[32]

After the convention, Meir sent a letter to the membership.

> After more than two years of struggle, I have finally been able to return to the U.S. to continue the work that has to be done.
>
> ... I found when I returned [that] ... into JDL had come certain elements whose conduct, language and character were the antithesis of everything that HADAR, Jewish Pride, was meant to be. Threats and physical force against Jews, filthy language, and the concept of JDL as some kind of street gang were never the things JDL was meant to contain AND THEY NEVER WILL BE.
>
> ... [This] drove many good members out.... Despite ... the demands of the chapter chairmen and the vast majority of members, the Board refused to call a convention DESPITE THE FACT THAT THE BYLAWS OF JDL CALL FOR AN ANNUAL ONE AND NONE WAS HELD SINCE 1971.
>
> When I returned ... I met with chapter chairmen and coordinators, and a call went out for a convention, pursuant to the bylaws. The convention was held, attended by more than 250 people, the vast majority valid dues paying members of JDL. The Board that the convention chose is the Executive Board of the JDL....
>
> The JDL will again be what it once was, and it is being built again on the basis of STRENGTH WITH SANITY, MILITANCY WITH NORMALCY!
>
> ... There is a new office and it is the only office of JDL. It is located at 1133 Broadway (corner 26th Street), Room 1026. The office will be run by the finest administrator JDL ever had, Russ Kelner, a man who quit in disgust last year and comes back to make JDL what it once was.[33]

An ad in the *Jewish Press* featured the new slogan that disassociated JDL from people who sought violence for its own sake. In an ad headed "A Message to the Jewish Community," Meir wrote:

> JDL will never give up its daring and militant posture
> But we move to the mature days of
> STRENGTH WITH SANITY AND MILITANCY WITH NORMALCY.[34]

The remainder of Meir's ten-week stay in the United States was a busy round of speaking engagements and rallies. He concentrated his efforts on convincing people that Kissinger's policies were bad for Israel and bad for America and on convincing Jews that they should settle in Israel.

Chapter 40
Speaking to American Jews
(August-October 1974)

MEIR WANTED TO make the most of his first trip to America after more than two years. His stay in America this time was going to be a long one – ten weeks, far longer than his month-long trips in 1971 and 1972. It would include the entire three-week High Holiday season: Rosh Hashana, Yom Kippur and Sukkot.

He tried to make up for his long absence from home with frequent, often humorous letters. He wrote one letter during a stint on the Long John Nebel radio show, probably during breaks for commercials.

> At this minute, a bomb threat was phoned in and four cops are crawling on all fours. The bomb is due to go off at 4:30. It is now 4:31. Obviously a Jewish bomb.[*]
>
> This letter will show no continuity because I must stop to answer questions. I am now answering people who phone in. One said that he is married to a *shiksa* [non-Jewish woman] for 40 years and is living "in bliss." I asked him where that is – "probably near Paramus?" John Nebel thought that was funny but the caller didn't.
>
> Well, to continue, I stayed at your brother's bungalow [for Shabbat]. It rained and their new dog had to be brought into one of the two rooms (guess which one). He is a big German shepherd (but not as big as the cop who is under the table now looking for the bomb.)[1]

One of Meir's first meetings in New York was with Benton Arnovitz of the Chilton Book Company. They had been in touch about publishing *Story of the Jewish Defense League*, and before Meir left Israel they had agreed on terms. The advance Arnovitz offered was disappointing, but it was the best Meir could get: two payments of $1,250 each. What was more important to Meir was that the book be published, because it would be a means of teaching people not only WHAT JDL had done, but WHY. Publication was scheduled for March 1975.[2]

---

[*] "Jewish bomb" refers to jokes about "Jewish time," i.e. not punctual.

Meir's second letter home described what he had been doing and what he planned.

> I finished a hectic weekend speaking in synagogues. We are preparing for a JDL convention which will broaden the ideology and change the leadership.
>
> On Wednesday [August 28], a big anti-retreat rally will be held in the Garment Center as a prelude to one on September 8 at the U.N. and September 15 at Kissinger's home.
>
> The Jewish Identity Center office was opened here ... and it will not only deal with the leadership training school in Israel but also teach-ins and seminars in colleges here and printing of identity literature.[3]

In another letter, he went into greater detail about the Jewish Identity Center:

> I am working on many projects of Jewish Identity including a weekly radio and TV show, publications, teach-ins, "drop-in" centers for information and classes, etc.[4]

A flyer for the anti-retreat outdoor rally at the Garment Center said, "Kahane Is Back and the Fight Against Kissinger Has Begun." A report described Meir speaking "while standing on top of the trunk of a car ... dressed in a gray suit with an Israeli-style open collar white shirt.... A lunchtime crowd of nearly two hundred applauded warmly when he said, 'There will be no peace with the Arabs no matter how much the State of Israel gives back.'"[5]

In another letter home, Meir set out what he hoped to accomplish during this trip.

> In general, the goals here are: To stop the pressure on Israel, to promote aliya (particularly religious), to get the *Yericho* [Jericho] project going, to bring back youngsters for the school and, above all, to get across my ideas through speaking and writing.[6]

Speaking engagements and media appearances were very important for spreading Meir's ideas. At the beginning of his visit he placed an ad in the *Jewish Press* that said: "Rabbi Meir Kahane is back! Synagogues, organizations and others who wish to invite Rabbi Kahane for speaking dates, please call immediately..."[7]

Meir's talks usually drew large crowds, despite some opponents. One opponent urged the cancellation of Meir's speech in his neighborhood with this "logical" argument: "Now he is on a mission to destroy Kissinger ... which will further divide and confuse the masses of our people everywhere in this sensitive period of Jewish survival."[8]

Meir kept us informed about his speaking schedule and about cancellations too.

In the last few days I spoke at three shuls, the Yavneh convention [where his speech was said to be "the most provocative, challenging aspect of our convention"], and the Young Israel Intercollegiate Conclave. I also was cancelled on three radio and TV shows as "too controversial" which is a sign that the anti-Kissinger drive is beginning to take.

The hotel where the JDL convention is to be held (September 8) also cancelled, but we came down and persuaded them to change their mind – they did not relish the idea of a convention in their lobby.

... It is very difficult to get people for the yeshiva in *Yericho* but I am still working on it. This Shabbat I am to speak in Long Beach and Hillcrest and the Yankees are ½ game in first place.[9]

A newspaper report on his efforts for the yeshiva in Jericho said, "In building a yeshiva in Jericho, a heavily Arab populated area, Rabbi Kahane hopes to begin a trend that will ensure Jewish continuance in controversial sectors – that is, establishing a Jewish Center of Learning to proclaim that this place belongs to Israel and no one else."[10]

Kissinger and American Foreign Policy

In August, Meir had formed a new group named SOIL, an acronym for Save Our Israel. Its aim was to keep Israel from ceding any of the liberated lands. Meir advertised the group as "a non-violent activist movement for the totality of the Land of Israel." He emphasized that it would be non-violent because he wanted to attract people who were wary of the JDL and at the same time avoid those who were seeking violence. Dov Hikind, who had shown administrative skills in preparing for the 1972 summer leadership school, was appointed to head SOIL, and office space was rented for it. The rallies against Kissinger that autumn were held under SOIL auspices.[11]

A major rally was planned for Sunday, September 15, at Kissinger's home in Washington, D.C. An ad in the *Jewish Press* informed New Yorkers that buses would be leaving for Washington from Brooklyn, Queens and Manhattan at 8 A.M. The ad began:

> Why Do Jews Always Wait Until the Knife Is on Their Throats?
> We march on Washington to:
> Stop the pressure on Israel to give up land
> Stop Kissinger's choking of the Jewish state[12]

Speaking dates were arranged for Meir in the greater Washington area so he could urge local people to participate in the rally. On Friday he spoke to students at the University of Maryland at College Park, and on Saturday night he spoke at the Pickwick Jewish Center in Baltimore. He was also interviewed for the *Baltimore News American*, and on Sunday morning Baltimoreans learned of the demonstration and why it was being held. Meir told the reporter:

> [Kissinger] is a threat to the United States and to world peace. [He] is a liability, not an asset. The Israelis knew on Thursday before the Saturday attack of the Egyptians that it was coming. It was no surprise as everyone believes. Kissinger prevented Israel – forbade it – from striking a preventive blow. He said, "Don't fire the first shot. The world will not stand for it."
>
> Now I have come to the United States to awaken American Jews to the danger that is Henry Kissinger and his foreign policy.
>
> ... President Ford is a man who would like to be elected president in 1976. If he sees angry protests by Jews in key states, if Jews fail to contribute their money, if he sees his self-interest suffering, Ford's self-interest will lead him to drop Henry Kissinger.
>
> It's time for Jews to let the President know.... Look at the lobbies. Everyone has one. Look at the black caucuses. They looked out for black interests and voted accordingly. Farmers do the same.
>
> Jews, on the other hand, have always done the incredibly stupid thing of turning away, of avoiding a fight. Our yardstick should be what is good for our interest.[13]

To augment the number of demonstrators against Kissinger, Meir banded together with other groups that were suffering from Kissinger's policies. He wrote home:

> We are in contact with the Greeks [of Cyprus] who hate Kissinger now, as well as the Cubans and the European captive nations. They will attend the rally ... on September 15....[14]

The five-page FBI report on the demonstration named the co-sponsors of the demonstration as the Cypriot American Association, the Free Cyprus Committee and the American Ukrainian Society. Another FBI report indicated that Meir's talks at the University of Maryland and at the Pickwick Jewish Center, as well as those at the demonstration, were audited by an FBI agent who was listening for possible violations of the "special conditions" of Meir's federal probation. Fortunately, the agent did not observe any violations. However, the risk of being found guilty of probation violation was always with Meir, and he was clearly aware that he was under FBI surveillance. In a report on the demonstration, Meir wrote, "We were accompanied by a small army of secret service men and police."[15]

The FBI report described the demonstration: Shortly after 1 P.M., a group of about seventy-five people assembled in the park opposite the Kissinger residence at 4220 Nebraska Avenue NW. At about 3 P.M., two buses arrived from New York City with an additional one hundred people. The demonstrators carried placards with slogans such as, "Kissinger Is Choking Israel" – "Kissinger, Don't Help Moscow Kill Ukrainians" – "Kissinger, Cyprus Isn't Your Pawn" – "Kissinger, Hands Off Israel."

A public address system for the speakers was set up in the park. The master of ceremonies was Rabbi Moshe (Marcel) Blitz of the Pickwick Jewish Center. When it was Meir's turn to speak, he expressed the hope that the coalition of sponsoring groups would impress upon President Ford the fact that Kissinger was a liability to him and to the United States. Handouts distributed at the demonstration included a *Jewish Press* article by Meir titled "An Open Letter to the President."

> ... Mr. President, As an American, raised in common sense and direct, uncomplicated truths of humanity, what should Israel do when, after [the Arabs were] beaten on the battlefield, they attempt to use the political arena to force Israel to retreat to lines that will make the next war suicidal? What would you do for America or for your family? Would you trust those who swore ... to destroy you? Would you give back land that keeps the enemy 12 miles from your heartland and minutes from your major cities? Would you gamble with the lives of the American people? I know you would not.
>
> ... I appeal to you to reconsider carefully your announcement that you will continue the Middle East foreign policy that has been shaped by your Secretary of State, Henry Kissinger.[16]

The media covered the demonstration extensively. Israel TV showed the demonstrators at Kissinger's residence, and a photo in *Newsday* captioned "Anti-Kissinger March" showed Nat Rosenwasser marching with a large banner that said, "JDL – Never Again." The *Baltimore Sun* quoted from Meir's talk at the demonstration:

> Kissinger is bad because he sold Israel down the river, forcing them to yield gains made in last year's Yom Kippur War without offering any real security guarantees in return.
>
> For America, Kissinger is a calamity because the fundamental and sole achievement of his foreign policy is détente, and détente is an illusion.... The United States has given all (our grain, our technological know-how and our military superiority) while the Soviets have reciprocated with exactly nothing.[17]

After the demonstration, Meir remained in the Washington area. On Sunday evening he spoke at the Silver Spring Jewish Center on "Kissinger and the Future of the Jewish People."[18] The next day was Rosh Hashana eve. Since he had a speaking engagement at George Washington University on Thursday, the day after Rosh Hashana, he spent the holiday in Baltimore, at the home of Rabbi Blitz.[19]

Aliya: Bring Them Home

The subject of aliya was also on Meir's agenda during the Washington visit. The *Baltimore News American* quoted his "quiet but fervent" words:

> The State of Israel came into being by the hand of G-d, a decree of G-d, and it will not be wiped away. But the Jew outside Israel is in Exile. The greatest danger is not to the Jew in Israel but outside. When we have an economic set-back, people become angry and bitter and frightened and they look for a scapegoat.... The Germans were just ordinary people, nevertheless they did what they did. It could happen here.... It was not because the [German] people were bad, but they were frightened people. When times are bad, it brings out the worst....[20]

He appealed to the Jewish students at George Washington University: "If you love the children that you will yet have, you will bring them home ... to grow up with their own culture, language, people – a majority." He reasoned that if the liberated lands were settled by Jews, the jurisdictional disputes would be weighted in favor of Israel. "Israel cries out for Jews ... there's plenty of land ...," he said.[21]

Meir referred to the aliya of America Jews in a letter he wrote to Tova on the flight from Washington to New York.

> Just a note to let you know that I am sending you and Tzippy a salamander. Please let me know if it arrived and there is no need to thank me. [The girls had written to him of their horror at finding a salamander in their bedroom.]
>
> I know how busy you are and really am impressed by the quality and quantity of the studies. I hope you get enough rest.

He wrote, with a hint of sadness, of the realities of persuading Jews to leave America to settle in Israel.

> The family here, i.e. Shragi, etc. [my brother's family], is fine and they may have been a little moved towards aliya. It is very difficult for American Jews to give up their roots and good life, and since they neither understand that we are in the era of *chisul hagola* [the liquidation of the Exile] and do not have the greatness to pick themselves up, there will never be a mass aliya willingly.
>
> I spend most of my time speaking on campuses and in synagogues (usually two dates a day) and it is very hectic. I have little time for writing (this is written on an Eastern Airlines plane from Washington) but the major effort is to get "the idea" out to Jews. [22]

A letter home after the Washington visit was somewhat subdued.

> I am exhausted from a trip to Washington and Baltimore, which went over as well as might be expected. I stayed in Baltimore at the home of Moshe Blitz, with whom I learned in the Mir [the Mirrer Yeshiva]. He is a rabbi there, *lo*

aleinu. [Roughly translated: "G-d save me from such a fate." Meir had been a pulpit rabbi twice and it did not suit him.]

There were many clippings in the papers (some enclosed – please save) and the *Baltimore Jewish Times* had a very hostile editorial which naturally publicized the whole campaign. We can always count on them![23]

Meir returned to New York to a busy round of speaking dates. On Shabbat afternoon, September 21, he spoke at the Washington Heights Congregation, and that night he led marchers from U.N. headquarters to the major Arab missions in Manhattan chanting, "Not One Inch." On Sunday he spoke at the Oakland Jewish Center in Bayside and on Monday at Brooklyn College. The college newspaper reported that Meir "blasted Kissinger" and told the Jewish students, "G-d is liquidating the Exile – it's time for you to go home!" Negating violence for the sake of violence, he stressed that today's JDL represents "strength with sanity and militancy with normalcy." The words of one student echoed the sentiments of many Jews:

> I respect the man. I wouldn't join the JDL; but there has to be somebody to go out and take action. It's a good feeling knowing that he's there. Where would we be without him?[24]

The High Holidays: Reevaluating Aims

It was the eve of Yom Kippur, and Meir wrote separate letters to each of the children. To Tzippy, he wrote:

> It is now a few hours until Yom Kippur, and my heart goes out to you with the hope that the year brings us the insight and understanding to know how to bring peace and redemption for ourselves and the world, swiftly and without tragedy.
>
> ... I want to take this opportunity to tell you how much pleasure and pride I have in you and what a wonderful daughter of Israel you are. Keep up your honesty and sincerity, learn well and do mitzvot. If you hold on to the tree of life and truth that is Torah, you will be happy and contented. Lead and do not be led; be strong and swift to do what is right.[25]

A few days later, on October 1, the week-long holiday of Sukkot began and he wrote home about it. He joked about the choir at the hotel prayer service and, always thinking of the children's education, ethical and religious, he detailed the use of Binyamin's birthday check.

> Dear Lib, It is now *motza'ei yom tov* [the second day of Sukkot] and I am at the Colony Hotel in Atlantic City as a guest of Morris Mandel. (He made an appeal for us here.) ... Mandel has agreed to be active for the school as well as raise money for it. There was a choir here for the services, and I was able

to bear it until *kedushah*, when they repeated *"matai"* ["when"] 26 times and I wondered when, indeed, it would end.

Over the past few days I spoke twice on the East Side, in New Hyde Park, Bellmore, Rego Park, Miami and Rutgers so that I am on the go constantly.

... I miss you and will be back soon.

P.S. Here is a 25 lira [about $6] check for Binny's birthday. Let him give *ma'aser* [ten percent for charity] on the whole thing and then give him two lirot to spend [and put the rest into his savings account].[26]

The Sukkot holiday was also the subject of a letter that my parents wrote to Meir. Meir was so moved by my father's words that he kept the letter in his files.

We were over at your house the first night of Sukkot and, of course, I slept in the *sukkah* with the boys. It was most enjoyable, with Binny [age 8] singing "Elka, Elka"* at the top of his voice.

... Today Libby was working and I took the two boys for a hike. There had been some question of my canceling out my "clients"** but Baruch wouldn't hear of it, so I went on my route first.

We took bus 35 (that's a new bus line) to Ramot and started hiking in the hills. Baruch goes right up the mountain sides like a goat, Binny scrambles after, and I had to follow. Although we could see the buildings of Itri [our neighborhood], we were all alone as far as we could see.

I was thinking of the *Hashgacha Pratit* [Divine Providence] that I have; that 55 years after I went through the cholera and hunger in Vilna in 1919, I was racing my grandchildren up the Judean mountains.[27]

During the High Holiday period, Meir reviewed and reevaluated his aims and came to a decision about his role in the future. He wrote to supporters in Israel, among them Julie Thornberg and Shimon Rachamim:

... I have made a decision. It is now clear to me that most of my influence, and the best chances for reaching our goals, is in the U.S. and I am convinced that my best work is here. I have speaking engagements almost every day, sometimes twice a day. I am loaded with invitations to speak.

I see that it is not possible for me to be involved in public affairs and politics in Israel. On the contrary, all my time in Israel must be devoted to writing and preparation for the work in the Exile. If I can succeed in properly preparing the programs while I am in Israel, I will be able to easily, quickly and efficiently accomplish them here. In short, I am setting aside all my concerns in Israel, including the Kach movement, and devoting my time to the success of the tasks

---

* The song "Elka" was taught to the children by Meir's father. It was based on a humorous event in the Kahane family in Safed.

** My father, a volunteer at Shaarei Zedek hospital, had a daily schedule of visits to elderly men (his "clients") who were homebound or handicapped.

here: aliya, struggle against retreat, Jewish identity, and so on. The building on Ussishkin Street will be used for lectures and leadership training. If I succeed in this, it is enough!

He added: "I was unable to recruit enough students for the yeshiva in Jericho. I suggest you give the money we raised for this purpose to Chanan Porat's settlers."[28]

A mass settlement attempt was organized by Chanan Porat and other Gush Emunim leaders at the end of the week-long Sukkot holiday, on the night following Simchat Torah. They called it Operation *Hakafot*.* About 5,000 people, including Tova and Baruch, managed to evade army roadblocks and spread out across Judea and Samaria to those points where Gush Emunim maintained that settlements should be established. Since the operation was meant to publicize the right of Jews to the entire Land of Israel, not to settle immediately, the participants did not get into a serious collision with the army.[29]

Meir was proud that our children had taken part. He wrote to Baruch:

> I heard of your efforts and *mesirut nefesh* [self-sacrifice] on behalf of Eretz Yisrael and our people. I thank G-d for having given me such a son and wish you strength all the days of your life for your people.
>
> Do not be discouraged by the disorganization. It is not easy for Gush Emunim with the little money and police spies everywhere. But for what they are doing, they merit their place in *Olam Haba* [the World to Come].[30]

Throughout the holiday period, Meir continued his hectic pace. On September 30, to point up the fact that Kissinger's policy was endangering Israel's very existence, he led a group to U.N. headquarters to present John Scali, the American ambassador to the United Nations, with an "Auschwitz booklet." On October 6, after a speech at the Café Yaffo Convention Hall, he led a march on the Syrian Mission to protest the mistreatment of Syrian Jews. That month he was also a guest on the Barry Farber radio program and debated Balfour Brickner on national TV.[31]

On October 10 Meir spoke to "a huge crowd" at Queens College. The enthusiastic audience "interrupted [him with] applause and laughter several times." His talk was mainly about Kissinger and the need for American aliya, but the college newspaper chose to quote these words:

> "To be a Jew means that there is a Divine truth, that our great grandparents were willing to die at the stake so their children would be – Jews for Jesus?"

---

* Operation *Hakafot* took place at night, after Simchat Torah, the holiday of *hakafot*, dancing around the synagogue with Torah scrolls. In Israel, on that night it is customary to have *hakafot sheniyot*, a second round of dancing with Torah scrolls, in public squares. Since *hakafot* means "going around," Operation *Hakafot* could also be understood as "going around" army roadblocks.

he said, his voice building and shrinking at the last two words. In one hour, he denounced American Jewry for assimilating, its leadership for "sitting on its apathy" and Kissinger for "selling Israel short" during last year's Yom Kippur War.[32]

Afterwards, he flew to Binghamton University in upstate New York. In the audience of several hundred there were many foreign students, including Arabs. A newspaper report on the question-and-answer period after his speech related:

A Jordanian student said, "There will not be peace as you say, and because of people like you who see human beings not as human beings, but as blacks or Arabs or Jews."

"Don't give me this garbage about human beings," Rabbi Kahane retorted. He pointed out the fact that Arab countries had mistreated Jews long before the State of Israel was established and that now Arab countries say they only want back the territories they lost to them in the wars. "I don't trust you," he said. "If that's all the Arabs wanted, they had the territory once, why did they go to war?"

The report gave another example of Meir's swift, sharp retorts to hecklers.

A mimeographed sheet refuting the rabbi's position was distributed by "Jewish socialists." When Rabbi Kahane referred to them as ignoramuses, one of them stood up and identified himself as a "supposed ignoramus."

"Not supposed" was Rabbi Kahane's quick put-down.[33]

Most Jewish speakers at universities and colleges were careful not to offend anyone, so Meir's outspoken frankness made him a popular campus speaker. Students also enjoyed informal conversations with him. Jonathan Libber recalled Meir's talk that year at the University of Maryland.

What made it so memorable was that after his presentation, a group of us went with him to the only kosher restaurant in the area to *shmooze* [talk]. While I always respected Rabbi Kahane's leadership, I was struck at this *shmooze* by what incredible insight he had into the political situation and human nature.[34]

On Saturday night, October 12, Meir's talk at the Bergenfield-Dumont Jewish Center in New Jersey drew an audience of over three hundred. A local newspaper summed up his talk: "Speaking with verve and wit, his tie-less white shirt open at the collar, [he said] 'To be a Jew means to observe Jewish law strictly.' He said that implies universal Jewish emigration to Israel, a ban on intermarriage, and a defense of Jews everywhere." The enthusiastic audience, encouraged by Seymour Berkowitz, head of the Teaneck-Englewood JDL chapter, "pledged $500 to the Jewish Identity Center and gave hundreds more in cash."[35]

On Sunday, there were two events in Philadelphia. In the afternoon Meir led a rally at City Hall, where he spoke on "Kissinger: A Threat to the U.S. and World Peace." A reporter described him "standing atop a speaker's platform made from a piece of board balanced on top of several metal milk cans.... The rabbi's shout of 'Not one inch of retreat' was echoed by a part of the crowd."[36]

The second event in Philadelphia brought home to Meir once again the power wielded by the Jewish Establishment. He was to speak on Sunday evening at the Society Hill synagogue in central Philadelphia, and Samuel Bortnick of Philadelphia JDL had submitted an ad about the speech to two Jewish newspapers in the city.

The *Jewish Exponent*, published by the Federation of Jewish Agencies of Greater Philadelphia, refused to accept the ad because the Federation's president, Samuel Feldgoise, "does not agree with the philosophy of the JDL." When a reporter questioned Feldgoise, he replied with a sweeping defamation. "I rejected the ad because they are people you don't want to do business with." Fortunately, Philadelphia – unlike most cities – had a second, independently published Jewish paper, the *Philadelphia Jewish Times*, which accepted the ad and placed it on page one.[37] Meir had to contend with the Jewish Establishment's defamation and obstructive tactics throughout his life, but he did not cease to seek ways to spread his ideas.

Two days later Meir was in San Francisco, where he spoke at Veterans Auditorium on Tuesday and at Oakland Auditorium on Wednesday. Arriving on Tuesday morning, October 15, he held a 9 A.M. press conference at the San Francisco Press Club to publicize his speeches and also appeared on NBC TV's "Tomorrow" show. He wrote home:

> I can't wait to get back and miss you all very much. I am writing this from San Francisco, where I have spent the whole day with the press, TV and radio, and will speak *be'ezrat Hashem* [with G-d's help] tonight at Veterans Auditorium.[38]

Leftist protesters from the nearby University of California at Berkeley learned of his speech from the media and distributed flyers outside the auditorium. One flyer was headed "Meir Kahane Is Under Indictment for Sedition in the State of Israel." Meir told the audience, "JDL has a bad image, which is good. Jews generally have a good image, which is bad. I'm not in the business of being loved."[39] Afterwards, Meir was interviewed for the *Daily Californian*, a Berkeley student paper. The result was an in-depth article that focused on his campaign for American Jews to settle in Israel.

> "When times are good, they hate Jews quietly. When times are bad, they hate Jews loudly. When times are critical, they hate Jews violently. We're moving towards a violent hatred of Jews because this country is facing the kind of crisis that is inherent in its system."

So said Rabbi Meir Kahane ... during his visit to the Bay area last week....
Kahane speaks energetically, emotionally, with frequent gestures and a ripe
New York accent.

"My survival outweighs everything," Kahane said slowly, his hand slapping
the desk with each word. Then he leaned back and added, almost in a whisper,
"Don't tell me to be more moral than everybody else. I'm tired of it. I'm sick
of it.

"The Jewish spirit is a great, great thing," Kahane said, "but no Jewish spirit
can survive without a Jewish body. The Jewish body has got to come first. All
the great Jewish spirit of Eastern Europe is dead, because there are no Jewish
bodies there."

... The solution for American Jews lies in Israel, Kahane contends, for two
simple reasons: "First, it is a commandment of the Torah. And second, they're
going to kill you here."

The rabbi shrugged his shoulders as if acknowledging an obvious fact.[40]

Meir's next speaking date was in Chicago on Saturday night, October 19. The
evening was sponsored by the Religious Zionists of Chicago and arranged by RZ
members Esther Friedman and Norbert Rosenthal. JDL public relations director
Sam Shoshan, who lived in Chicago, helped. He organized a "small coffee and
cake gathering" after the public lecture for "a select group of influential members
of the Jewish community" to meet Meir personally at the home of Mr. and Mrs.
H. Persky. The invitations specified, "No solicitation of funds. Our purpose: To
dispel ill-founded myths." This was an effective way to encourage future support.
Posters and ads in local papers publicized Meir's talk on "The Real Henry
Kissinger." They all made the point that this would be Meir's only appearance in
Chicago. [41]

The *Jewish Post and Opinion* reported that more than nine hundred people
came out to hear him. "[They] filled the seats of Congregation Ezras Israel, lined
the walls standing up, filled an outer hall, and even the staircases leading up to
the hall." A *Chicago Tribune* reporter estimated the audience at one thousand.[42]
With a professional like Shoshan on the job, it was no wonder that the turnout
was so large.

Meir's host that Shabbat, Norbert Rosenthal, wrote: "... Everyone appreciated
your entire stay in Chicago, from dinner Friday evening through your warmth that
permeated our home and children over Shabbat; your inspiring messages to Bnei
Akiva [youth group], and finally the informal, intimate get-together at the
Perskys'."[43] Over the years, Meir spent Shabbat with many different families in
different cities. Their recollections were similar to Rosenthal's. They all told me
of his warm rapport with their children and of how he imbued the Shabbat with
spirituality.

Echad: A Rally Against Retreat

Meir was back in New York on Sunday morning for two important events: The founding conference of a new organization – *Echad* ("One") – and a rally against retreat at the Israeli Consulate.

A week earlier, Meir had written to me of his plans: "I am also on the verge of welding together members of many nationalist groups under one roof of an organization to be called 'Echad.'" A flyer for the new organization read:

ECHAD
A historic founding meeting will be held at Convention Hall, Café Yaffo
October 20, 1974 at 2 P.M.
The conference will be followed by a huge rally
at the Israeli Consulate at 4 P.M. to protest
American pressure on Israel and to cry out, Not One Inch!

The flyer went on to explain the need for Echad.

> The greatest danger to the Jewish people does NOT come from non-Jewish enemies, but from within ourselves.
>
> The tragedy of Jews who think alike and who agree on almost everything, but who nevertheless refuse to join together is the greatest curse and tragedy in our times!
>
> Enough of disunity! Enough of the petty and foolish splits and obstacles to Jewish unity.
>
> ... You can remain a member of the organization to which you now belong, while at the same time coming together with members of other groups who agree on a common nationalist program.
>
> Whether you are a member of Betar, NCSY, Young Israel, Yavneh, the Jewish Defense League, Masada, Bnei Akiva, Hamagshimim, Noam or any other Jewish group which is nationalist, respectful of Jewish tradition and Zionist, OR SIMPLY A JEW WHO IS UNAFFILIATED, now you can join together for the maximum Jewish power to help our people and land![44]

The conference would contribute to the success of the rally planned for the same afternoon, because the founding members would all attend the rally. Coming ten days after the inspiring Operation *Hakafot*, the demonstration at the Israeli Consulate would cry out against retreat and would demand the right of Jewish settlement in all parts of the Land of Israel.

This was the first time Meir had called a rally at the Israeli Consulate. In fact, the consulate occupied offices in the same building as Israel's Mission to the U.N. – 800 Second Avenue. Until now, JDL flyers always named the Israeli Mission to the United Nations as the site of protests, because of a self-imposed taboo by pro-Israel groups not to demonstrate at the Israeli Consulate. Meir thought that the urgency of the present situation justified the change.

To promote attendance at the rally, Meir used his column in the *Jewish Press* that Friday to urge New Yorkers to be there.

> ... Nothing the Arab enemy has done to the Jew is so painful as that which the Jewish brother has done. No picture of Arab guns and planes could ever be so agonizing as the picture of Jewish soldiers ordered by the Jewish government of Israel to drag away young Jews who sought to go home, to return to the Biblical soil of the Land of Israel, to settle the lands of Samaria and Judea. That which the Almighty in his miraculous generosity gave us in 1967, the government of Israel – frightened and totally lacking in understanding of the era of the beginning of the redemption in which we live – is prepared to give back.
>
> ... No Knesset in the world and no cabinet has the legal or moral right to break the sacred law that declares that every Jew has the right – nay, obligation! – to settle anywhere he chooses in the Land of Israel....
>
> May every Jew in New York who does not attend the demonstration of support for the Jews who settle the land, know that he helps to bring about the tragedy and destruction upon Israel.... The date is Sunday, October 20th and the time is 4 P.M. and the place is the Consulate of Israel, 800 Second Avenue, New York City. There is nothing more to say. Go and do.[45]

The demonstration was a resounding success. Over 1,000 people attended. They dumped soil in front of the Israeli Consulate to "shame" the government into allowing Jews to settle in all parts of the Land of Israel. In his speech, Meir told of his pride in his children, who had marched in "Operation *Hakafot*" in Israel. He pointed out that the Land of Israel does not belong to the State of Israel but to the Jewish people. He said that American Jews were obligated to help Israel financially, but at the same time they had a right and an obligation to demand that the government refuse to comply with Kissinger's plan to cede land to the Arabs.[46]

The next day Meir had two speaking dates. "Go Home Before You Can't Go Home" headlined a report on his talk at Lehman College at noon. In the evening he lectured at Congregation B'nai Jeshurun, a Conservative synagogue in Manhattan. When Meir was invited to take part in B'nai Jeshurun's lecture series, he gladly agreed, because it would enable him to reach Establishment Jews. His was the first lecture in a series that included speakers Emil L. Fackenheim, Isaac Bashevis Singer, Abba Eban, and Senator Hubert H. Humphrey. He was so well received that he was invited to give a series of four lectures the following year.[47]

Two days later Meir was in Miami Beach, where Morton Maisel and other supporters had arranged a hectic schedule for him. On Wednesday, October 23, he spoke at noon at the University of Miami's Hillel House; from 3 P.M. to 6 P.M.

he answered questions from callers on the Bill Smith radio show; and in the evening he spoke at the Nautilus Auditorium on "Kissinger and Israel." The next day he spoke at Dade Junior College (North), led a demonstration at the Greater Miami Jewish Federation to demand funds for Jewish causes, and was guest speaker at City Hall Auditorium in North Miami Beach. There was a $1.50 admission fee at his talks to the public, but there was no charge for students, because it was so important to Meir to reach out to the youth.[48]

Meir returned to New York for his last weekend in the United States. On Saturday night, October 26, he spoke to four hundred people at a JDL fundraising dinner in Long Beach and on Sunday morning he spoke at a walkathon for the Jewish poor in Manhattan. A photo in the *Daily News* showed him on the speakers' dais at City Hall, chatting with Congressman Mario Biaggi.[49]

In the afternoon, before his flight back to Israel, he led a rally whose theme he would be promoting on his return to the United States in mid-January – support for the settlers of Judea and Samaria. The motto of the rally was "The Land of Israel is ours, all of it, forever. There is no Palestine and there is no Palestinian people!"[50]

Chapter 41

The Motive: Patriotism
(November 1974-February 1975)

RETURNING TO ISRAEL on October 29, Meir could look back on a successful trip with a measure of relief. He had not been charged with probation violation while he was in the United States, and perhaps this was no longer a serious threat. In Israel, however, he faced two court appearances shortly after he arrived. The first case concerned the 1972 weapons shipment. At sentencing in Tel Aviv District Court on November 17, Judge Hadassah Ben-Itto gave Meir a two-year suspended sentence. In her decision, the judge said she was taking into account the argument that the accused had acted not for personal gain, but out of patriotism.[1]

The second case, heard in December, was one of several hearings on a charge of incitement. This charge stemmed from letters Meir had sent to Arabs in December 1972 suggesting they emigrate from Israel. The case was heard intermittently and was finally discontinued in May 1975, when the prosecution could not show intention to incite.[2]

Thoughtful, Inspired Articles

In November and December, Meir concentrated on completing the manuscript of *Story of the Jewish Defense League* and continued to write for the *Jewish Press*. At the end of 1974 the *Jewish Press* had a circulation of 194,000, with readers all over the United States. With a readership far higher than any other Jewish newspaper in America, the *Jewish Press* enabled Meir to reach a wide audience.[3]

In addition to his regular columns, "Israel Through Laughter and Tears" and "Exposing the Haters," he wrote a number of serious, thoughtful articles. Addressing the increasing number of Soviet Jews – as many as 40% – who received permits to emigrate and had opted to remain in Western Europe rather than continue on to Israel, Meir wrote:

> You will run from Belgium and from West Germany and from America because the Jew has no place in the Exile. Israel is the Jewish State and it was created

447

so that the Jew would not have to run…. Stop running and be part of the Divine Jewish destiny.[4]

To encourage American Jews to settle in Israel, he wrote of the demand of Ismail Fahmy, Egypt's foreign minister, to put an end to aliya.[5] Tongue in cheek, he wrote of the "irresistible opportunity for the *am keshei oref*, the stiff-necked people of yore, to bristle and say, 'Fahmy demands an end to aliya? No anti-Semitic goy is going to tell us what we can do and cannot do! We are going to make plans to move to Israel immediately.'"

Meir's constant warnings of American anti-Semitism were borne out that November by a blatantly anti-Semitic statement made by an important American military leader, General George S. Brown. In a lecture at Duke University, Brown declared that Jews controlled American newspapers and banks. Jewish organizations united to demand his resignation, and Brown issued a public apology. Meir's reaction was to call for an emergency aliya program.[6]

Meir also urged American Jews to give more charity in order to hasten the redemption from the Exile. In "Bashan," he wrote:

> The redemption of Israel from the Exile is dependent upon the Jew returning to the quality of kindness and mercy – just as was his failure to do so responsible for his Exile…. The giving of what one has – both time and money – to a second Jew, makes the two one.
>
> … There has grown up a myth in the United States. It says that American Jews are vastly charitable, generous and kind. Perhaps; perhaps in relationship to the gentile, the Jew gives more money to charity or to public activities, [but] … how many throw away in one weekend in Las Vegas or the Bahamas more money than they give to the needy in three years?[7]

"One Little Word" expressed Meir's conviction that the problems of the State of Israel were due to its leaders' lack of faith in G-d.

> A nation that does not believe in G-d must, per se, trust in man. A government that has no faith in heaven lifts its eyes unto Washington. Leaders who cannot mention the one little word [G-d] that promises redemption and victory look about them and, seeing the vast armies, the huge sums of money and the awesome weaponry of the enemy, become paralyzed with indecision and confusion…. And so, Israel becomes a lackey, a vassal, forced into concession after concession … its sovereignty circumscribed by the ally it needs. The paradox is that the men who rejected G-d for "freedom" become – through that rejection – vassals, subjects and political protectorates.[8]

Another article, "It Has Only Begun," was also critical of Israeli government leaders – for their refusal to implement plans for counterterror.

... Indeed, the miracle is that until now the Arabs have been so inept and timid in their terror. What we are seeing now, however, is an expansion and an escalation that will see horror in the cities of Israel.... The Arabs will begin to get non-Arab volunteers to come to Israel and commit acts of terror for them; we will see more sophisticated and powerful weapons of terror; we will see terror carried out against Jews in the Exile, too....[9]

Unfortunately, this warning proved to be prophetic.

During those two months in Israel, Meir gave several lectures. On December 10 he spoke on "Jewish Pride and Responses to Anti-Semitism" at the Institute for Youth Leaders from Abroad in Jerusalem. A week later he spoke at ZOA House in Tel Aviv to a group of American immigrants on the need for an emergency aliya organization. Referring to the demand by Egyptian foreign minister Fahmy that Israel freeze its population and ban immigration for fifty years, he said that Arab leaders are moving to demand Israel's retreat to 1947 borders in exchange for recognition of Israel. "The joker is that this 'Israel' will be an impossible state, a state as tiny as it is weak and defenseless." He added, "Premier Rabin, who has said that he will never negotiate with the P.L.O. because it does not recognize the State of Israel's right to exist, will be hard put to explain why he will not negotiate with them now.... The Israeli government [must] say that there is no Palestine at all..."[10]

The next day, December 19, Meir spoke at Bar Ilan University's Student Union building in a noon hour Hyde Park-style open discussion. "Come, listen, and ask," said posters. Meir called on the students to take an active part in opposing "Kissinger-Nixon-Ford" policies in the Mideast. He said that Israel was on the verge of a huge concession in the Sinai and that the government was leading the country to "tragedy."[11]

Meir's campaign against Kissinger was interrupted when he was called up on December 22 for five days of reserve duty at the *Haga* civil defense training center at Nes Tziyona. Part of the course was learning how to rescue people trapped in buildings that were burning or had collapsed. When he came home at the end of the course, he spoke admiringly of the technical abilities of his fellow trainees.[12]

Christians for Zion

As soon as he returned from reserve duty he resumed his work against Kissinger by forming a new group: Christians for Zion. Taking advantage of the increase in Christian tourism during their December holiday season, he called a meeting of Christians for Zion for Saturday night, December 28. Meir's ad in the *Jerusalem Post* said:

CHRISTIANS FOR ZION!

We are seeking Christian believers in the Biblical prophecies of the return of the Jewish people to Zion as a precondition for the final redemption. We want to form "Christians for Zion," a group that will work to guarantee United States support for no territorial concessions by Israel and to explain to United States Christians why the Divine Will is that Israel be unconditionally supported.

IN THIS HOUR OF TRAVAIL FOR THE JEWISH STATE, when the United States and the Christian world look upon oil and other material factors as their primary interests, it is vital that we speak of THE REAL CHRISTIAN INTEREST IN THE MIDDLE EAST, THE REALIZATION OF GOD'S FINAL REDEMPTION THROUGH TOTAL SUPPORT FOR THE JEWISH STATE IN ZION.[13]

In a *Jewish Press* article, he urged Jews to enlist Christian Americans on Israel's behalf.

> It is the clear task of American Jews to work to persuade the fundamentalist Christian community, whose members number in the millions, to organize an active and politically militant "Christians for Zion."
>
> It should be a group based strictly on Christian self-interest which would give political muscle to its religious beliefs by making it clear to President Ford that his support in the Bible Belt – without which he is a clear loser in 1976 – will vanish unless he takes a firm stand on behalf of Israel and ceases American pressure. The fundamentalists believe that those who oppose Israel are doomed ("Blessed is he that blesseth thee and cursed is he that curseth thee," *Numbers* 24:9). This belief must be imparted to Ford and the political threat made a clear and present one. That is the language that the President understands....[14]

There Is No Palestinian People

November marked a turning point in the international community's official attitude toward the P.L.O., led by Yasser Arafat. Arafat, who was responsible for the murder of countless Jews in Israel and outside it, was invited to address a meeting of the United Nations on November 13.* In a rally called by an enraged Jewish Establishment on November 4, close to 100,000 people protested the United Nation's invitation to Arafat.[15]

On November 12, the day Arafat arrived in New York, the JDL scheduled an afternoon press conference at its headquarters. JDL Director David Fisch, who

---

* An Arab League summit meeting in Rabat, Morocco, in October 1974, recognized the PLO as the "sole legitimate representative of the Palestinian people." Previously, many Arab countries, especially Jordan, had opposed independent Palestinian political action. The Arab League decision led the U.N. to grant the PLO "observer status."

was to officiate at the press conference, took part in an impromptu demonstration that morning and was arrested, so instead, administrative director Russel Kelner greeted the press. He surprised everyone when he placed a .38-caliber revolver on the table in front of him and, with cameras rolling and mikes open, announced JDL's intention to assassinate Arafat: "We have trained men who will make sure that Arafat and his lieutenants do not leave New York alive.... We plan to assassinate him." Under a catch-all federal law that prohibited broadcasting a threat across state lines, Kelner was jailed and held on bail of $10,000.[16]

Gene Singer recalled how he raised the money to get Kelner out of jail.

> I went to Abe Lebewohl, owner of the Second Avenue Deli. Abe loved JDL. It was Friday afternoon. Abe took a paper bag, took me to the bank nearby, got out the money and put it into the paper bag for me and pushed me into a cab. I presented the money at the police station. Until all the procedures were completed it was already Shabbat, so Russ and I had to walk from Chambers Street to my home on Grand Street. Abe never asked for the money, but he got it back after the trial."[17]

Arafat spoke at the U.N., and the delegates gave him a standing ovation. Barely a week later, "Palestinian" infiltrators from Jordan killed four Jews in the border town of Beit She'an.[18] Meir declared that United Nations' recognition of a "Palestinian people" could not change the facts. In "A Different Jewish View: There Is No Palestinian People," he wrote:

> ... There is no "Palestinian people" and there is no "Palestine." The lands that today constitute the State of Israel, Judea, Samaria (the West Bank), Gaza and the Golan are parts of the Land of Israel, the sole land of the Jews.
>
> ... There can be no "Palestine," a name that was invented by the Romans to symbolize the end of the Jewish people, for that would be to diminish and to force back the miracle of G-d and to go against the Divine era of redemption. There can be no "Palestine," for if there is, then there is no Israel.
>
> In all this we DIFFER FUNDAMENTALLY with the official stand of the government of Israel which ... recognizes a "Palestinian" people after years of refusing to do so, ... [and] believes that peace with the Arabs by concessions is possible...
>
> We ... maintain that the government of Israel, through its shortsighted, timid and vacillating policy, not only destroys the vision and the dream of redemption, but brings potential disaster down on the heads of the Jewish people.[19]

Enthusiastic agreement with Meir's analysis was expressed by the editor of the *B'nai B'rith Messenger*, who editorialized:

> In the days before the State of Israel, each November, Palestine Day* was com-

---

* Palestine Day, also called Balfour Day, commemorated the Balfour Declaration, issued November 2,

memorated. And when we spoke of Palestinians and the press wrote of Palestinians, it was the Jew who was being described.

Through the millennia it had been the Jew who cared about Palestine.... Suddenly we awake to a new nightmare, the rewriting of history.... Suddenly the interloper – the alien Arab – has become the Palestinian in this new perversion of history....

When Kahane speaks of the Jewish claim to the land, he speaks in the same spirit as the prophets [in] these blunt words: "There is no Palestine or Palestinian people. There are Arabs who trespassed on Jewish land...."[20]

Further support for Meir came from a series of articles about him in the *Jewish Press*. Written by columnist Dr. Hyman Frank, the series presented an extremely favorable portrait of Meir. It began: "Although in his early forties, his name is known in every capital of the world...."[21] The eighteen weekly installments, titled "Inside Meir Kahane," appeared from October 1974 through February 1975. Dr. Frank's supportive series surely influenced readers in Meir's favor. It may have contributed to the large number of speaking engagements that were booked for Meir's trip to America in mid-January. On that trip, Meir also planned to lecture regularly at the Jewish Identity Center (J.I.C.) in New York City. An ad placed in mid-January invited people who wished to study national-religious ideas to register for Thursday night classes at the J.I.C.'s *Chug*, the Circle.[22]

When Meir arrived in New York on January 17, plans were already in place for a large rally to mark "There Is No Palestine Day" on Sunday, January 19. Similar rallies were to be held simultaneously in other cities. In Washington, D.C., for example, demonstrators spray-painted the United Nations Information Office with the words, "There is no Oz. There is no Palestine."[23]

Extensive preparations were made for the New York rally. JDL members contacted other organizations, such as Betar, to attract a large number of demonstrators. They placed ads in the *New York Times* and on the radio, not only in the Jewish papers. As a result, more than five hundred people showed up at the Diplomat Hotel and heard Meir's rousing speech. Urging unlimited Jewish settlement in all parts of the Land of Israel, Meir said, "If Jews have no right to Hebron and Nablus, then they have no right to Tel Aviv. Our ancestors did not live on Dizengoff Street." Baruch Ben Yosef recalled, "That speech was the best one I ever heard. It riled everybody up."[24]

From the Diplomat Hotel, the crowd was to march first to the U.S. Mission to the U.N. to protest American pressure on Israel and then to the Soviet Mission to protest Soviet repression of Jews. Before setting out on the march, Meir led the audience in reciting the oath "If I forget thee, O Jerusalem..." When the marchers, walking in a heavy rain, reached the intersection near the Soviet Mis-

---

1917, promising British support for a Jewish national home in Palestine.

sion, they stormed the police barricades, and in the clash several demonstrators and policemen were injured and had to be hospitalized. A lawyer who was with the demonstrators charged the police with "excessive violence." This did not end the demonstration. Inspired by Meir's moving words at the Diplomat Hotel and despite the pouring rain, about one hundred of the marchers sat down at the intersection and blocked traffic for half an hour. A picture in the *Daily News* shows youngsters sitting on the shiny wet asphalt. When a police van arrived, many of the demonstrators ran away, but Meir and forty-six others were taken to the police station and given summonses for disorderly conduct.

As Meir walked out of the police station with a summons to appear in court on January 30, he told a reporter, "We stormed the barricades. For the first time, we wanted to do something a little radical to wake up American Jews."

Unfortunately, the general press ignored the theme of "There Is No Palestine" and reported that the rally was for Soviet Jewry. This was probably because early that morning, at 3 A.M., two .22-caliber bullets fired from a nearby construction site pierced windows at the Soviet Mission. No one was injured and damage was minimal, but the Soviets protested angrily. New York Mayor Abraham Beame called it an act of "wanton terror," and the FBI was called in to investigate. An anonymous phone caller told the UPI news agency that the shots had been fired because of "the repression of Jews in the Soviet Union" and used the JDL slogan "Never Again!" This surely led the authorities to associate the shooting with Meir and gave them an added reason to seek to impose sanctions on him. One news report noted that Meir "risks a revocation of the suspension of a five-year sentence he received in 1971." An FBI report with Meir's itinerary for February and March was sent to branch offices in Baltimore, Boston, Chicago, Washington and other cities directing them to monitor his activities.[25]

Meir appeared in court on January 30 to answer his summons for disorderly conduct at the "There Is No Palestine" demonstration. While waiting for his case to be called, he wrote a letter to me. In it, he assured me, "It is not a very serious charge at all." But when he was called before the judge, he found that the charge had been changed from disorderly conduct to unlawful assembly, a misdemeanor punishable by imprisonment. The fact that the charge was changed to a misdemeanor did not augur well for Meir's future. A news item about it in the *Jewish Press*, probably written by Meir, protested that the change in the charge was unfair and unjust and claimed that it was intended to put an end to Meir's demonstrations against Kissinger.[26]

Nevertheless, Meir continued to lead protests against Kissinger's policies as he had been doing since January 22, when he protested the Reform rabbinate's silence on American pressure on Israel with a 24-hour hunger strike at Manhattan's Temple Emanu-El. On January 23, he led JDLers in picketing the offices of the B'nai B'rith and the American Jewish Committee to urge them to take a stand against Kissinger. Later that week he appeared on Long John Nebel's midnight to 6 A.M. radio program, where he had the opportunity to explain his views. On February 2, JDLers demonstrated in New Rochelle at the home of Arnold Forster, an official of the Anti-Defamation League, urging the organization to protest Kissinger's policies.[27]

A memorable demonstration was held on February 3 at the home of Reform Rabbi Joachim Prinz, president of the American Jewish Congress, who had stated that Israel should give up land. Meir wrote home, "... We are going to visit Joachim Prinz's home ... and dig up his lawn so as to let him know what losing territory means." JDLers dug up soil from his lawn as "a symbolic territorial concession by Prinz to the Arabs." They chanted, "Hell, no, we won't go. The land is ours, and the Arabs know."[28]

CAIR: Committee Against Israeli Retreat

During this period, Meir set up a new group that would concentrate on protests against retreat: the Committee Against Israeli Retreat (CAIR). Flyers and ads announcing JDL activities to protest retreat during this period were signed by CAIR. It was a name that conveyed their purpose far more effectively than the name JDL. One CAIR flyer said:

ISRAEL GO UNDER? G-D FORBID!
The survival of Israel compels us to speak out against the tragic policies of
the Israeli government that lead the State to disaster!
... For the sake of the Jewish State,
the present government and policy must be changed, and the American Jew
has the right and obligation to take the lead in this.
If you care – join CAIR.
... Join us in proclaiming to the government of Israel: NOT ONE INCH![29]

Another CAIR flyer read:

WANTED! A New Firm Israeli Government That Will Tell the World:
Hell, No – We Won't Go – from the liberated Lands of Eretz Yisrael!
Join us in working for:
Immediate reunification of the liberated Lands with the State of Israel.
Immediate unrestricted Jewish settlements in any part of the Land of Israel.[30]

Even Israeli doves were worried by Kissinger's demands for retreat. In a *New York Times* op-ed article in February, Hebrew University professor Yirmiyahu Yovel wrote that Kissinger's step-by-step program could be meaningful only as a gradual move toward peace. But he had grave doubts about Kissinger's policy because it lacked clarity: It did not spell out a comprehensive peace formula. At the same time, it burdened Israel with almost the full price of the interim agreement. In America, too, there were Establishment Jews who expressed opposition to Kissinger's pressures. For example, Hans Morgenthau, a prominent political scientist, maintained that Kissinger's Middle East policy was too dependent on the questionable commitment to peace of Egypt's President, Anwar Sadat.[31]

Meir continued to concentrate his efforts on swaying both Jewish and non-Jewish public opinion against Kissinger's policies. The danger of Kissinger's policy was only one of his topics when Meir spoke at synagogues and universities during that period. During the first three weeks of this trip he spoke at two or more synagogues each Shabbat. On January 26, he spoke at Syracuse University. His concluding words, "Jewish is beautiful. Go to the Jewish state and live – in the land of Israel," drew a thunderous ovation, as nearly all the two hundred fifty people in the audience rose to their feet.[32]

When the Zionist Organization of America (ZOA) invited Meir to speak at the Beth Israel synagogue in Worcester, Massachusetts, on February 3, there was considerable opposition. An ad announcing his talk included a rebuttal to those opposed to the invitation: "We believe Worcester's Jewish community has the intellectual capacity to listen, question and to make up their own minds."[33]

After the talk in Worcester Meir wrote home:

> ... I am now in Boston at Arnie Hoffman's home, having spoken in the area last night. There was a huge debate all week with people angrily phoning the ZOA (my sponsor) to demand that I not speak. One person offered to buy $150,000 worth of [Israel] bonds if I was cancelled, but the Bonds chairman said no (too cheap an offer). In any case, I spoke, and as usual, three things happened: It was the largest crowd in the history of Worcester Jews; they gave me a standing ovation; they walked away feeling good and will do nothing else.

Meir was aware that most people were conservative and would not take the actions he urged, even when his ideas were received with enthusiastic applause. Nevertheless, he continued to urge aliya, with an emphasis on current economic difficulties that he predicted could lead to Jew hatred in America.

> ... The economy here is so bad that unemployment has reached a national average of over 10%. Business is terrible and economic depression is around the corner. There is not a person in any audience who publicly disagrees with me when I speak of the possible holocaust....[34]

A report on Meir's talk at Worcester's Clark University later the same night pointed up Meir's special rapport with young people.

> ... Following the presentation at the Beth Israel synagogue, Rav Kahane, at the spontaneous invitation of Clark Zionist Alliance members present, visited the C.Z.A. office [in] Wright Hall. During the late night visit, Rav Kahane addressed a group of approximately thirty students in an informal question-and-answer period ... [revealing] the man's devotion to his cause.[35]

Violation of Probation

On his previous trip in the fall, Meir had not been charged with probation violation, and he may have felt confident that the threat had passed. But it had not. On February 7, James Haran, Chief U.S. Probation Officer, applied to Judge Jack Weinstein to have Meir's probation revoked for violating the conditions that forbade him to be directly or indirectly involved with any kind of weapons. Haran maintained that Meir's two convictions in Israel, one for planning to ship arms from Israel to Europe for counterterror and one for urging the use of firearms and explosives to discourage Brezhnev's U.S. visit, were clear proof that Meir had violated the conditions of his probation. The reason Haran had not applied for revocation of Meir's probation earlier was that he was waiting for sentencing in November in Israel on the arms shipment charge. It certainly strengthened Haran's hand to be able to show that Meir had been convicted, albeit with suspended sentences, in cases involving weapons not once, but twice. Judge Weinstein ordered Meir to appear for a hearing on February 21.[36]

The news broke on February 8, the day before the JDL's scheduled convention to elect officers. Barry Slotnick, who had agreed to represent Meir *pro bono* at the probation violation hearing, delivered a speech at the convention. He pointed out that Meir knew he faced possible imprisonment in the United States but returned nevertheless. Slotnick's speech was quoted by Meir in his article "Why I Came Back."

> My attorney, Barry Slotnick, last week spoke at the convention of the JDL and gave the parable of the Jew, taken from the ghetto and placed on the transport to the death camp. Through fortune he manages to escape from the train carrying him to his death and he returns to the ghetto to warn the others. That Jew, said Slotnick, did not have to go back to the ghetto – he could have saved himself. The question with each of us – and indeed it is the yardstick of every Jew – is, "How can anyone ever be that Jew who saved himself and lived contentedly while the ghetto was being liquidated."

The second part of "Why I Came Back" may have been what Meir said in his own speech at the convention about the threat of being imprisoned.

> Many people have asked me why I risked returning from Israel for the visits that I make. Not a few have turned to me in these days and said, "You were

safely in Israel, out of reach of the United States government. You know that the federal government wants you out of the way and that the possibility of their moving to put you in prison is very high. Why did you not remain in Israel? Why did you come back?

... I would like to clarify why I left my wife, whom I love so much and who has been so magnificent in her understanding, and my four children whom I love as any father, and risked the hearing that is scheduled, as well as the possible consequences that might flow from it.

I believe that the Jewish people stand today in an era such as they have not encountered since the days of their creation as a people.

Meir detailed the dangers facing the State of Israel and American Jews, and continued:

I see these things and I see that others do not. I see the response that must be given and I see that others do not. Why did I come back? TO CALL OUT THE WORDS THAT MUST BE SPOKEN AND TO CRY OUT THE MESSAGE THAT MUST BE HEARD. I came back because I love Jews and I see the Holocaust that need not be....[37]

In the two weeks prior to the hearing before Judge Weinstein, Meir continued to lead protests against Kissinger's policies. On February 10, to coincide with Kissinger's arrival in Israel for talks with Israeli government leaders, he again led a sit-in at Manhattan's Temple Emanu-El to protest "the failure of American Jewish groups to mobilize protests against the Ford-Kissinger strangulation of Israel." Meir and six others were arrested for trespassing, and the event was well covered by the media. Meir said this of Kissinger's policy: "We are watching planned genocide by the Arabs, aided by an American policy that forces Israel to concede vital territory."[38]

A rally at the Israeli Mission to the U.N. was set for February 12, Lincoln's Birthday, a school holiday. It snowed heavily that day, but there was a good turnout anyway. Photos show the demonstrators with the snow coming down, holding up handwritten placards declaring, "Not One Inch" and "Shechem Is Jewish – Settlement Now." On February 13, the JDL picketed President Ford when he arrived in New York to speak at a Republican Party fundraising event. That evening Meir appeared on TV to explain his opposition to Kissinger's Middle East policies.[39]

Meir wrote about the events of February 13 to his parents and tried to dispel their concern about the coming court hearing.

There is quite a snowstorm outside and President Ford is coming to New York where we will protest, following which I will be on television.

> It is difficult to wake up Jews when they do not know that they are asleep. They are, though they think they are not, to paraphrase Descartes.*
>
> Don't worry about me – everything is fine.[40]

Ten days later, on Washington's Birthday, Meir led a demonstration at the Syrian Mission to the U.N. to protest pressure on Israel to cede the Golan Heights to Syria. He noted the significance of Washington's Birthday: "Israel, like the U.S.A., is here to stay, and will not surrender one inch of land to foreign rule."[41]

To counter the U.S. Probation Office's arguments in the upcoming hearing, Meir and his supporters started a letter-writing campaign and arranged for important public figures to testify on his behalf as character witnesses. Meir wrote home:

> I don't want you to worry about the hearing; it will be fine. There are millions of people here working on this, getting out letters, and there will be many witnesses, including Soviet activists from Israel, as well as Elie Wiesel.[42]

The letter-writing campaign was soon underway. An editorial in the *Jewish Press* urged readers to write to Judge Jack Weinstein to ask that he "deal with leniency and fairness with the man who, in the eyes of so many Jews, has done things for his people at great personal sacrifice."[43] Some letter writers sent copies to Meir. George Torodash, himself a probation officer, wrote:

> ... The Rabbi's major "offenses" appear to be the attempts to protect his people throughout the world.... Any attempt to place this man in confinement with the most degenerate elements in our society is a negation of the democratic ethic.[44]

A letter from Benton Arnovitz expressed an idea that is significant to this day.

> ... Nuremberg** is ample precedent that moral law has judicial standing over statute law.... Let the rabbi go free.[45]

JDL member Saly Zloczower wrote to the judge:

> ... This man is imbued with *ahavat Yisrael*, the love of one Jew for another. This inspiration led him to return from Israel to the United States in order to arouse the Jews in this country out of their lethargic mood.... We do need someone to sound the alarm.[46]

Zloczower received a reply from Judge Weinstein, which may have been a form letter. It included information about the hearing. "... I appreciate your having taken the trouble to write. On February 21, at 10 A.M., in Courtroom 10 of this courthouse, there will be a hearing...."[47]

---

* French philosopher Rene Descartes said, "I think, therefore I am."

** The Nuremberg Laws of 1935 legalized anti-Semitism in Germany and paved the way for Germany's systematic slaughter of Jews during the Holocaust.

A news item in the *Jewish Press* asked people to come to the courthouse:

> Massive State Department pressure to attempt to stop JDL's increasing efforts against American policy in the Middle East is seen as the background behind the sudden government move to revoke the probations of Rabbi Meir Kahane and send him to prison.
>
> ... A hurriedly organized Committee for Kahane called for Jews to write urgent letters to Judge Jack B. Weinstein, Brooklyn Federal Court, 225 Cadman Plaza, asking him to show mercy for the man who has sacrificed so much for his people. It also asked hundreds to show up for the hearing on Friday, February 21, promptly at 9.30 A.M.....[48]

Character Witnesses Testify

About two hundred and fifty people packed the courtroom. More than fifteen U.S. Marshals were on duty and, in an unusual precaution, everyone had to pass through an elaborate electronic weapons-detection system. The evidence presented by U.S. Attorney Thomas Pattison included the official Israeli court records of Meir's two convictions in certified translation, as well as photographs of the weapons in the arms shipment case and photocopies of the four letters and one telegram written by Meir about Brezhnev's U.S. visit. All these documents were supplied by Israeli officials at the request of the U.S. State Department.[49]

Many character witnesses appeared in court on Meir's behalf. Among them were Rabbi Fabian Schonfeld, president of the Rabbinical Council of America; Rabbi Benjamin Blech, president of the Council of Young Israel Rabbis; Rabbi Moshe Tendler, prominent rabbi and professor of Talmud and of biology at Yeshiva University; Rabbi Nachman Bulman, of the Young Israel of Far Rockaway; Rabbi Abraham (Avi) Weiss, of the Hebrew Institute of Riverdale; Dr. Samuel Korman, vice-president of the Greater New York Conference on Soviet Jewry; and Leah (Lydia) Slovin,* Soviet Jewry activist in Russia and in Israel.[50]

Meir wrote home about the hearing.

> The hearing was packed, and the witnesses that came to testify for me included Leah Slovin, the Russian activist who came over [from Israel] especially for the trial. She said that I was the drummer in the orchestra for Russian Jews and that my imprisonment would be a blow to Soviet Jewry.[51]

---

* Leah Slovin related how Meir helped her "force" the Soviets to allow her 19-year-old daughter Ruth to join her in Israel: "I visited many countries, I made appeals, I demonstrated, I was interviewed on radio and TV, to no avail. Finally, I announced that I would hand the case over to Meir Kahane and let him deal with it 'in his own way.' Within eight weeks my daughter was in Israel with me."

The transcript of the hearing quoted another character witness, Rabbi Avi Weiss, who took up Slovin's metaphor.

> ... There really is an orchestra, and the moderate is heard better after someone blows the trumpet ... we are speaking now of a person who really sounded the trumpet, a person who said something has to be done....[52]

Meir was not speaking of actual explosives and weapons in the letters he wrote, Rabbi Weiss said, explaining Meir's rhetoric.

> My own feeling is, and this is very personal, that when Meir Kahane writes letters and says he wants guns sent here and guns sent there, that really is an attempt to dramatize the situation and to galvanize the community.[53]

Meir's lawyer, Barry Slotnick, implied that Meir knew his letters would be opened by the censors and asked Judge Weinstein to consider Meir's intentions and "to go through a realization of some letters that were sent that reached military censors pursuant to a mail watch, and to think in his own mind, Did Rabbi Meir Kahane, sitting in Israel, know about mail watchers on him? Did he know about military censors?"[54]

Finally it was Meir's turn to testify on his own behalf. His testimony was taken down by the court stenographer and later printed verbatim in the *Jewish Press*. The following is an excerpt:

> Your Honor, I think it's very, very difficult for us to simply look at these letters and these documents without going back and seeing exactly what the context was at that time. I'd like to share with you those days, both the days of the guns case and the days of the letters case.
>
>   In September 1972, I was in Israel, along with 2.8 million Jews, and everyone was excited over the fact that the Israeli team was in Munich, Germany, when suddenly the news came over the radio of the capture of Israeli athletes.
>
>   I don't believe people in this country realize what a trauma that was.... Suddenly so many people there who had always said, "How could the Jews of Auschwitz go quietly," suddenly saw a picture of Israeli athletes going in a sense quietly to the airport.
>
>   ... At 2 A.M. the news broke that they were all killed. I cannot possibly – there are no words to describe the agony and the frustrations and the fury and the tears that gripped Israel on that day, and I can't tell you the mass hysteria that gripped that country when those bodies were brought back.
>
>   ... I said, "This has been a great victory and perhaps the first great victory for the Arab terrorists, and we will see in the days to come many such things."
>
>   ... The solution is to convince the host country that it is to their interest to remove the terrorists, and so this entire thing did not involve a decision to ship arms to this country, but rather to Belgium, for an assault upon the embassy of

that [Arab] country which financed those terrorists, so as to convince the hand which gave the funds and the support that it would be cut off.

In a sense, Arafat was created that day, and because no one else did what we wanted to do, there was a Maalot and a Kiryat Shmonah and all the others that will yet be.

The letters – all of the violence that JDL and other people have used against the Soviet Union – I have said many, many times and written many times, was not a mindless violence or a heedless violence. It was a lesson in political logic, in which we knew that if the Soviet Union would ever achieve a détente which would be irreversible, the Soviet Jews would be doomed.

The only leverage that we ever had was preventing them from getting a détente, and when in 1973, as they moved closer and closer to it, and as Senator Jackson's attempts – and he understood this – as his efforts to prevent a détente without a price being paid by the Soviets, as that hung in the balance and Brezhnev was coming here, we knew that he would convince the American people to have a détente and that the Soviet Jews would be doomed, and we are beginning to see that now.

... When I came back now and there was a riot at the Soviet Mission and I went around from place to place to galvanize Jews against Kissinger and against American foreign policy, that was the moment. That was the moment when it was ruled that I would be brought here.

The [Brezhnev] letters trial was last June, and the government had sufficient opportunity ... and they didn't move.

This is a political trial in that sense. I didn't have to come back here. Attorneys wrote me, "Don't come back, you're taking a great risk. The government will attempt to put you in prison." I have a wife and I have children and I love them as any husband, as any father.

I came back here because I believe that I say the kind of things that others don't say and that have to be said, and I took that risk in August and again now.

... So I can only end by saying that I don't envy you, Your Honor. I did what the government says that I did and I violated probation, and you will have to do what you have to do and do it with a good conscience and know that that which I did, I did with a good conscience.[55]

Judge Weinstein replied, in handing down his decision:

The law compels, as you recognize, Rabbi Kahane, this Court to do now what it must do. Were it to fail to punish you, the probation system could not effectively continue.

It was in recognition of the many good works that you have done, your role as a father and a husband and as a teacher, that on two prior occasions this Court bent the law in your favor.[56]

Judge Weinstein showed leniency this time, as well. He reminded Meir, "... You are now subject to a penalty of five years in prison." But he did not sentence him to the full five years. Instead, he said:

> In view of what has been said here today and in view of the fact that almost four years of probation have already passed, I sentence you to one year of incarceration, in full satisfaction of the probationary period.[57]

Meir was released in his own recognizance and gave his passport to Barry Slotnick as assurance that he would not leave the country. Judge Weinstein gave him five days, until February 26, to put his affairs in order before beginning his prison term, and then granted him another three weeks to allow him to fulfill his schedule of speaking engagements. At the end of that time, on March 18, instead of using his return ticket to Israel, he was to turn himself over to U.S. marshals, to be sent to an as yet unnamed minimum security prison.[58]

Meir's speech – his testimony on his own behalf – encouraged his supporters, who raised him aloft and carried him out of the courtroom on their shoulders. A photo shows him with fist raised, smiling broadly.[59] That same day he wrote to the children, after one of those rare occasions when he splurged on what was then an expensive luxury – an international phone call:

> My dear children, It was wonderful to hear your voices this week and I am only sorry that I will not be able to see you for a while. But the time will pass quickly, and with the aid of G-d we will be together again before you know it.
>
> I know that each of you will learn from this the lesson that I try to teach you so often, that without *mesirut nefesh* [self-sacrifice] the Jew is not a complete Jew and can never fully reach *kiddush Hashem* [sanctification of G-d's name]. It is not difficult to TALK about sacrifices, but so many people are not prepared to act upon their words.
>
> ... The government has made me a martyr, and this will be a great opportunity for JDL to help Jews if they can seize it.
>
> I do not have to add that I know that you will listen carefully to your mother during the next months and will love and respect each other. There is no greater joy in life than to be strong enough to do that which is right.
>
> Until we meet again, I send you all my love.[60]

To me, he wrote:

> My Darling Libby, It was wonderful hearing your voice last night and I know that you will be the magnificent wife you have always been while this minor problem is gotten out of the way.
>
> ... I enclose a copy of the speech I made [in court]. All in all, it was almost worth it! I love you very much and I know, again, that you understand exactly what has to be done. I will probably begin my sentence on March 16 or 17. Until we meet again – VERY SOON, Love, Meir.[61]

At first, Meir considered appealing Judge Weinstein's decision to a higher court. But, as he wrote to me:

> I will definitely not accept bail without permission to go to Israel since that could mean a long period of waiting HERE and then going to jail. This way I will get it over with quickly, will be a "martyr" ... and also have a much better chance for a reduction of sentence from Weinstein. [62]

In another letter, he tried to reassure me:

> It is not so terrible because I have a good prison and good conditions, and there is a big campaign to get a modification of the sentence. [63]

Another letter writing campaign was under way. This time it was to urge Judge Weinstein to reduce Meir's sentence. An editorial in the *Jewish Press* said:

> ... The government's blatant effort to silence the voice of a man who has been a thorn in their side was, unfortunately, successful.... We call upon our readers to mount a massive letter-writing campaign to Judge Weinstein. Under the law, he has the power to modify the sentence within 120 days of sentencing.... [64]

Moshe Brodetzky, president of the Council of Orthodox Synagogues of Greater Washington wrote to the judge, "... We are confident that you will find the strength and the wisdom to substantially reduce this sentence...." [65]

A letter writing campaign was also under way in Israel. Meir's brother Nachman told reporters that "friends and relatives would flood the Federal Court with letters." [66] Nachman also made direct appeals to public figures. One, Rabbi Tzvi Yehuda Kook, wrote:

> Every moral human being can see and feel the injustice perpetrated with regard to this illustrious man, whose strength, abilities and life are dedicated to the hallowed struggle for the freedom and honor of the Jewish people. [67]

A letter written by two members of the Tel Aviv Bar Association, Max Seligman and Meir's cousin David Rotlevy, said:

> Rabbi Kahane is a true patriot of Israel, and in all of his public activities he has been imbued at all times with a burning desire to advance the vital interests of Israel.... Whatever may have been the irregular acts which he has committed, he is not deserving of the harsh punishment of imprisonment.... [68]

Judge Weinstein replied to every letter. Meir wrote, "Judge Weinstein said he receives an average of 40-50 letters a day." [69] Perhaps that is why it was not until June that he replied to my letter:

> ... I know how difficult incarceration is for members of a prisoner's family. Unfortunately, I am not in a position to do any further in this case.
>
> I am enclosing a copy of my opinion in your husband's case. [70]

There was no sign that the letter writing campaign was influencing Judge Weinstein to modify his decision, and Meir prepared to turn himself over to prison authorities on March 18. I wanted to be with him at this difficult time, but he did not want me to come to America. He wrote:

> Dear Lib, I hope you understand why I do not want you to come to America. Aside from there being no point to it, the children need you there and I want to put into practice the concept that the Jew has no place in the *galut* and that there is no reason for him to leave *eretz Yisrael* unless there is the direst of circumstances, which this is not.

He explained very logically, "I miss you very much but I will not miss you less if you come here for a week." As always, his thoughts centered on the children.

> I received a very nice letter from your father who wrote that Nachman asked Baruch what he thought of the whole thing and Baruch said, "My *Abba* [father] is a soldier. He is not afraid." That makes the whole thing worthwhile.
>
> I am writing to Binny to learn a *pasuk chumash* [Bible verse] by heart every day and after that a *mishna* [verse of the Oral Law] a week. I want Baruch to teach him the *mishna* every Shabbat, so make sure that both do it and that Tzippy tests Binny.[71]

After sentencing, Meir maintained a hectic schedule of speaking dates and demonstrations in an attempt to accomplish as much as possible during the extra three weeks Judge Weinstein had granted him.

Chapter 42

Of Prisoners and Free Men
(February-April 1975)

Jewish Power Day

MEIR TOOK FULL advantage of the three-week extension granted by Judge Weinstein to fulfill his scheduled speaking engagements. On February 24, the day before Purim,* Meir led JDL youth in a gathering billed as "Jewish Power Day." First, to mark the Fast of Esther, they fasted and said Psalms together. Then, in keeping with the Purim holiday, which commemorates the day that Jews fought back, they discussed a plan to raise a volunteer army to fight for Israel. The press was invited to "Jewish Power Day" to learn more about this.

Meir explained that the volunteer force of young people between the ages of seventeen and thirty would be trained in Israel that summer to constitute a reserve fighting force. They would return to their homes in the United States, but would be ready to rush back to Israel for front-line duty in the event of a war in the Middle East. He showed them membership cards that said, "[Jacob/Judith Doe] has registered for training with the Volunteer Forces for Israel and has affirmed his/her commitment to respond when called to defend Eretz Israel [the Land of Israel]." He said that JDL members would begin recruiting in various parts of the city that same day.[1]

When about twenty recruiters camped outside the headquarters of the Palestine Liberation Organization in Manhattan that afternoon, the media converged on the spot. Meir admitted to a reporter from the *New York Post* that the volunteer force had no approval from the Israeli government, but was sure that Israel would not reject their offer. A flyer handed out by the recruiters said, "Hear how you can be part of a unique training program for Diaspora Jews who will be

---

* Purim commemorates the deliverance of Jews from Haman's plot to exterminate them, as recorded in the biblical Book of Esther. It is preceded by a fast day, the Fast of Esther. The Book of Esther is read on Purim after evening prayers and after morning prayers.

on call to report for combat duty in Eretz Yisrael [the Land of Israel], if, G-d forbid, the Arabs should wage conventional war against our brethren."[2]

Shifra Hoffman wrote to me about the reading of the Scroll of Esther that evening.

> A group of us gathered together with the Rabbi to hear the reading of the *Megillah* [the Scroll of Esther]. It was attended also by some of our children, and I could not help but notice as Meir scooped up the youngest one and lovingly placed him on his lap. How he must have wanted to have his own children at his side and enjoy briefly the levity of this happy time together with them and you.[3]

Meir's letters home show that he missed us very much, but being far apart was the reality of his life, so he made the best of it. One week after Purim, on March 6, Meir was again on the Long John Nebel radio program. Fortunately, an audio tape of this session exists. Nebel's first question was to ask why Meir did not plan to appeal Judge Weinstein's verdict. Meir replied frankly, "I did it. I did what they said I did. I can't come to an appeals court and say I've been wronged by the lower court." In addition, if he appealed and lost, which he thought likely, the long appeals process would increase the time he'd have to be away from his family. Meir explained why Judge Weinstein had sentenced him to prison. "You stop terror by counterterror. You make the personal lives of the terrorists dangerous.... I tried to do it myself [by shipping weapons to Europe] and was arrested. I received a suspended sentence, but that act violated the terms of my probation here." If the Israeli government had adopted his counterterror plan, he maintained, "There would not have been a Maalot or a Kiryat Shmonah or what happened yesterday."

He was referring to the March 5 attack on the Savoy Hotel. Eight Arab terrorists, arriving by sea, had infiltrated the Savoy Hotel on Tel Aviv's shorefront and killed four Israelis before they were overpowered by IDF soldiers. A surviving terrorist said they had been trained in Syria and had embarked on their mission from Lebanon. Meir told Nebel's listeners what he had said at a press conference earlier that day: The only solution to Arab terrorism was counterterror. Israel must respond in kind against the civilian population of Syria and Lebanon, the countries that trained and supported Arab terrorists. An outcry from the Arab civilian population was the best way to effectively end Arab governments' support for terror.[4]

Among Meir's scheduled speaking engagements in February and March were several arranged by an Establishment group, the Israel Aliyah Center, a branch of the Jewish Agency. Meir's impassioned promotion of aliya had come to their attention. A letter he received from Shalom Inbar, the director of the Brooklyn office, said:

I attended a gathering which you addressed on your last trip to the States....
As an Aliyah representative, I was very impressed with your desire to promote
Aliyah. I would like to have you address clubs and large audiences....[5]

Meir was amused by the fact that the Establishment, which usually opposed
him, was going to sponsor him. He wrote home, tongue in cheek, "The Aliyah
Department ... asked me to speak under their sponsorship. They said that Sapir
[Pinchas Sapir, head of the Jewish Agency] himself cleared it. The Aliyah situation must be terrible." In another letter, he sent clippings and wrote, "I enclose
living proof that the Aliyah Department of the Jewish Agency really sponsors
me."[6]

Many of Meir's speaking engagements during this period were billed as his
"last appearance before imprisonment" and drew large and sympathetic audiences. On Sunday, February 16, Meir addressed an audience of three hundred at
Temple Beth El in Asbury Park, New Jersey. "He delighted them with his sharp
wit while stressing the urgency of the crisis situation facing Jews here and in
Israel," said one report. On Thursday he spoke at a high school in Hewlett, New
York, where his talk had the students "thinking and questioning," and the following Shabbat he spoke at the "White" *Shul* in Far Rockaway. Rabbi Ralph
Pelcovitz wrote, "The huge outpouring of people last Friday night who came to
listen to your address bears testimony to the fact that your message to *Klal Yisroel*
[the Jewish people] is one that is eagerly awaited and certainly strikes a responsive chord in the hearts of your listeners."[7]

A reporter who heard Meir speak a week later at the Madison Jewish Center
in Brooklyn on February 26 wrote, "Relentlessly assaulting the consciousness of
his audience with indictments for apathy in the face of mounting dangers ... it was
a rapt, at times stunned, audience that hung on every phrase...." The reporter
described Meir's appearance as "hardly the prototype of the firebrand crusader,
given his mild, clean-shaven and conventional appearance." After Meir's talk,
denim-jacketed JDL members passed around a hat for contributions and distributed petitions calling for a firmer stand on the liberated areas.[8]

Meir spent Shabbat, March 1, in Maryland at the home of Rabbi Herzel Kranz,
and spoke at his synagogue, the Silver Spring Jewish Center, to "a hushed audience of three hundred." On Saturday night a cheering audience of "a few hundred
people" heard him speak in nearby Hyattsville, where he shared the podium with
Reverend Harrison Valentine, an enthusiastic Christian supporter of Israel. Reverend Valentine drew prolonged applause when he cited the Biblical prophecy
that Israel would occupy the territory stretching from the Nile in Egypt to the
Euphrates in Iraq.[9]

On Sunday morning Meir flew to Albany. The Aliyah Department was sponsoring his talk at an Aliyah Expo at the State University. Flyers about the Aliyah

Expo said Meir would be the special guest speaker, and experts and display desks would offer information about study programs, kibbutz programs, housing, employment, financial aid, and summer programs. Afterwards, Meir spoke at a synagogue in Albany to members of the AACI, a Jewish Agency aliya group.[10]

To Help Us Open Our Eyes

Back in New York on Monday, he was again sponsored by the Israel Aliyah Center when he spoke at the Brooklyn College Walt Whitman auditorium. Larry Gordon was in the audience:

> Recently I spent a couple of hours with Rabbi Kahane.... Till then, I honestly thought Meir Kahane and the JDL were finished.... I listened quietly to what he had to say and came away overly impressed. His attitude, disposition and sincerity are genuine. There is nothing plastic about him; he is not trying to convince us of anything. All he is aiming for is to help us open our eyes as to what is actually going on.
>
> ... To the audience of about 800, Kahane expresses his anger over an incident which appears in today's *Times*, namely the arrest of sixty young Israelis by their own soldiers for attempting to establish permanent settlements on the West Bank of the Jordan River. "If they have no right to be on the West Bank," he says, "then they have no right to be in Tel Aviv."
>
> ... Kahane subscribes to the belief that Israel should have no qualms about talking to the P.L.O. "If they could talk to Syria, they could talk to them."
>
> ... Why, he asks, hasn't any Israeli representative displayed the boundaries as they exist in the Bible? Within this context he demands to know why not one Israeli official has ever made mention of G-d. "They wouldn't have to worry about American popular opinion swaying towards the Arabs if the Israelis would say this is the way it has to be because the Bible says so." He reminds his audience that most of the American people are believers in the Holy Scriptures.[11]

A second report on his appearance at Brooklyn College showed the wide range of topics Meir covered in his talks.

> "I don't only speak of the cancer of intermarriage that rages throughout this country," he said in this BC lecture on Monday. "I speak of all the Bernies [Jewish boys] who run around chasing Bridget [non-Jewish girls]."* ... He suggested Jewish education as the one weapon that would keep young Jews proud of their heritage.[12]

---

* *Bridget Loves Bernie* was a 1970s TV series about the marriage of a gentile woman and a Jewish man, based on *Abie's Irish Rose*, a 1920s long-running play. Because of its connotation, Meir used the names Bernie and Bridget when he wrote and spoke about assimilation and intermarriage. See chapter 45, "What Makes Bernie Run?"

That afternoon Meir flew to Brown University in Providence, Rhode Island, where he was scheduled to speak at 8 P.M. Meir made this observation to the audience of two hundred at Brown:

> ... American hopes for a peaceful settlement are futile. Kissinger's demands for Israeli concessions will prove so "outrageous," even the most "dovish" of Israeli leaders will be dissuaded...[13]

After his talk he stayed to speak informally with students, and in the early morning hours, after five hours of questions, answers and discussions, he was interviewed for the Brown college paper, which quoted his forthright statement.

> We (the Jews) are right, and they (the Arabs) are wrong; and there is no reconciliation possible. I don't have to be offered part of my country. It's that simple. Everyone has a right to his own country. But they don't have a right to Israeli lands. It isn't their country.[14]

On March 4, Meir was in Buffalo for an evening appearance at the State University. To an overflow crowd of about one thousand students he spoke of the folly of territorial concessions.

> The tragedy of the Middle East is that it is not a question of giving back lands and having peace or not giving them back and having war. The Arabs say they want back Sinai and the Golan Heights. What did they want when they had them in 1967?[15]

Turned On to Jewish Pride

In a letter to the children about his appearance in Buffalo, Meir spoke of how difficult it was for him to be away from them.

> I am writing this from Buffalo where I spoke at the University under the auspices of the Jewish Agency Aliyah Center. (I sent Ima a whole bundle of items.) There were about 25 anti-Israel leftists (mostly Jewish, of course) and it was very enjoyable playing with them to the delight of about 1,000 students who were truly "turned on" to Jewish pride. My only regret about having to go to prison for a while is that I will not be able to be with you or to appear on campuses to speak to Jewish youth.
>
> Which brings me to something I want to mention. The most difficult and potentially tragic part of any public figure is the fact that he spends so much time away from his own family. Foolish people point and say that he worries about other children but not his own. I know that you – as *bnei Torah* [knowledgeable observant Jews] – will not make that mistake. I know that you will understand that I love you more than anything and not for one moment have neglected your welfare and education. But you, thank G-d, have grown to be

normal and healthy Jews because of the family and schools which were so carefully worked out for you. The others [American youth] do not have that.[16]

Leftists again handed out flyers against Meir when he spoke the next day at
Cornell University in Ithaca, New York. There he said to a packed auditorium,
"Go home. There is no future for Jews in America."[17] He flew back to New York
City for the next meeting on his hectic schedule, an aliya event advertised in the
Jewish Press:

> A New Life in Your Own Settlement in a New Area of Israel
> Young Jews 18-30:
> Join the JDL Aliyah Group
> Learn More from Rabbi Meir Kahane and Officials of the Jewish Agency
> Thursday, March 6, 6 P.M., JDL Training Center, 227 W. 29 Street, N.Y.C.[18]

On Shabbat, March 8, Meir spoke in Monsey, New York, at Rabbi Moshe
Tendler's synagogue, the Community Synagogue of Monsey. That Shabbat he was
the guest of Rabbi and Mrs. Tendler, and on Saturday night he drove to
Grossinger's Hotel in Liberty, New York, where he was to speak Sunday morning
at a "JDL weekend." Lorraine Schumsky, who organized the weekend, recalled:

> It was a great financial success, that's for sure – a large JDL turnout, many
> rooms rented. MK was his usual dynamic speaker.... The regular Grossinger's
> guests crowded into our hall bringing the audience to around 500 or more peo-
> ple, and they gave and gave $."[19]

Meir's perspective on intermarriage and assimilation was emphasized in a
report about his talk at Hunter College in Manhattan on Monday at noon.

> He cited the major Jewish organizations ... as the ones responsible for so many
> of the problems facing Jews in America today.
> ... "They went around banging a large pot, which they called the melting pot,
> and they said to the Jews in America, MELT!" The result, according to Kahane,
> is that Jews today march for every cause except Jewish ones. "They march for
> Blacks and Puerto Ricans and Jesus and Trotsky and Arafat and grapes and let-
> tuce [i.e., the fieldworkers], but never Jews. Judaism has as much relevance to
> American Jews as the color of their hair."
> Rabbi Kahane stated that the one vehicle for instilling Jewish knowledge and
> pride in young Jews, full time Jewish education, was severely frowned upon by
> Jewish leadership groups. "Let's send our kids to public school," said Kahane
> sarcastically, "We want our children to meet everybody."
> "Now," he said, "those same groups are spending hundreds of thousands of
> dollars to find out why the intermarriage rate is so high!"[20]

Late Monday afternoon Meir flew to Milwaukee for a speaking engagement
sponsored by the Zionist Organization of America. Pickets outside this time were

not leftists, but neo-Nazis. Wearing helmets and swastika armbands, they marched outside with placards that said "Save U.S.A. from Jewry" – "Smash Jewish Dirt League" – "No More Arms to Israel" – "Kike Kahane Traitor to America," and more. To a supportive, enthusiastic audience of five hundred, Meir said that allowing Nazis to walk around freely is like "spitting on the graves of six million Jews." He said that the way to deal with Nazis, when the police are not around, is to "break their heads."[21]

In nearby Chicago the next evening, March 11, Meir spoke at Temple Beth El of Rogers Park to about two hundred people. Among his topics was American pressure on Israel to give up the Sinai.

> No concessions on the part of Israel will bring peace. The Arabs are not inter-ested in peace. Egypt does not want the Sinai back. It already got the Sinai back once – every grain of sand in it – and it still wanted something else. It wanted to destroy any Jewish state, anywhere, in any shape or form. Let's not forget that. Let's not give an inch. [22]

Similar sentiments were voiced by my father, Jacob Blum, in a letter to the editor of the *Reader's Digest* that month. The *Digest*, a magazine with a circula-tion of 20 million, had published an article urging Israel to cede the Sinai.

> Since when was Sinai a part of Egypt? Egypt, Syria and Jordan attacked Israel in 1948 when they figured that Israel was as helpless as a newborn babe, and grabbed whatever they could. Through a miracle, Israel was able to fight them off in 1948, and through another miracle, was able to get the areas back in 1967. In 1973 Egypt and Syria attacked with overwhelming forces in an attempt to annihilate Israel. Through a miracle again, Israel was able to stem the attack.
>
> The Arab nations even now refuse to sit down and negotiate with Israel. Their only cry seems to be, "Step back so that it will be easier for us to try to overrun you." Instead of depending on Mr. Griffith's promises, Israel prefers to depend on the G-d of our ancestors who has promised us this Land...[23]

After speaking in Rogers Park, Meir spent the night at the home of Sam and Rena Shoshan in nearby Skokie and then caught an early morning flight to Bos-ton. His talk at the Massachusetts Institute of Technology (MIT) in Cambridge was sponsored by the Israel Aliyah Center and the Zionist Organization of America.

An audio tape of Meir's talk at MIT shows the wide range of subjects Meir would cover in each speech. He urged a return to Judaism and decried the alien-ation of young Jews from everything Jewish. He compared the Jewish Establish-ment's inaction during the Holocaust with JDL's forthright acts on behalf of Soviet Jewry. His appeal to the audience to stymie President Ford's foreign policy by working for the presidency of Senator Henry Jackson drew prolonged applause. He described JDL patrols in crime-ridden areas with dry humor. "When they caught a mugger in action they took out a Torah and taught the mugger a lesson, 'Thou shalt not steal.'" Meir's quips were scattered throughout his speech, drawing hearty laughter and frequent applause.[24]

He wrote to the children about his lectures.

> I am writing this from Chicago where I have arrived from Milwaukee and from which I go to Boston and on and on.... People are listening to what is said and I can see in the faces of many in the audiences that they are hearing – for the first time – something that promises to give their lives Jewish meaning and challenge. And so it is worth it.
>
> The Jewish Agency is already unhappy with sponsoring me because I do not only speak of aliya, but of the Judaism that they do not represent and of the truth and principle that they do not stand for. I see that the only way to speak is to talk of *emuna uvitachon* [faith and belief] and the fundamental, real Judaism that we would imagine would drive away the Jews who do not observe. The truth of the matter is that [it] is especially THAT Judaism which they never saw that can attract them, since all the others they have already seen, already known to be fraudulent and already rejected.
>
> Take care of yourselves, keep learning and doing....

His letter to me went into more detail concerning the Jewish Agency's sponsorship.

> Tomorrow night in Boston I speak under the sponsorship of the Agency that spent a huge amount of money to advertise me and is now sorry since I have been speaking not only on aliya but bitterly attacking the government. Yadlin tried to cancel me, but it is too late. Nevertheless, the honeymoon is over, as the government would rather see the state harmed than the party.[25]

The JDL Bids Farewell

The week preceding March 18, when Meir was to begin his prison sentence, was filled with activity. On March 13, after a rally at the Egyptian Mission to the U.N. at 5 P.M., he spoke on aliya at the JDL Training Center. A flyer said, "Come and find out what is awaiting you in Israel."[26]

On Shabbat he was the guest of Rabbi Avi Weiss and spoke at his synagogue, the Hebrew Institute of Riverdale. His letter home about the question-and-answer period there shows his broad understanding of international politics.

> The Shabbat before going to prison I spoke in Riverdale and someone asked for a "rational" answer to those who ask why America should support Israel. I told him that America's main Arab allies – the Shah, Feisal, etc. – are all feudal monarchs, reactionaries, whose base of support is weak and unstable. They will

be overthrown as were Haile Selassie and King Idris (Libya) and their places taken by either anti-American leftists or anti-American nationalists.

So yesterday Feisal was killed.[27]

On Saturday night Meir spoke first at the Julia Richmond auditorium on "Jewish Is a Complete Identity" and then at JDL's farewell event for him at Café Yaffo. Hilton Goldman, who chaired the well-attended party, wrote: "It was in the upstairs party room and approximately 400-600 people crowded in." A newspaper photo shows a weary Meir seated off to the side, probably during someone's speech. His eyes are closed and he is bending forward, his elbows on his knees, the palm of one hand cradling his forehead.[28]

Meir delivered the keynote address at a convention of CAIR (Committee Against Israeli Retreat) at the Hotel Diplomat on Sunday morning. This was followed by a "Youth Farewell to Meir Kahane," and at 2 P.M. Meir led a rally at the Israeli Mission to the U.N. to support the West Bank settlers. A flyer said, "Jews arrested for inhabiting Jewish land?! NO WAY!"[29]

Before reporting for prison on Tuesday morning, March 18, Meir took part in one last demonstration, a sit-in at the Israeli Consulate that began on Monday. A photo shows Meir in a dark raincoat sitting Indian-style on the floor together with some young people, the boys sporting Afro-type hairdos. Two hold handwritten placards that say "Hebron, Samaria Are Jewish" and "Jewish Settlement Now."[30]

The American ambassador to the U.N. reported the dry details in a telegram to the State Department in Washington.

> At 10 A.M., March 17, 1975, approximately 20 pickets, representing the Jewish Defense League, conducted demonstration outside Israel Consulate General, 800 Second Avenue. At 11:15 A.M., while demonstration continued, Rabbi Meir Kahane, accompanied by 6 supporters, entered 14th floor foyer to present demands and conduct sit-in.

New York Police gave the State Department the list of demands presented to Consul General David Rivlin:

a. "Not one inch" of territorial concessions in present negotiations being mediated by Secretary Kissinger with the Arabs and the Israeli government.

b. Immediate reunification of liberated lands with State of Israel.

c. Immediate unrestricted Jewish settlement in all liberated lands.[31]

During the long hours of the sit-in, the demonstrators sang, chatted with officials and listened to lectures. One of Meir's talks later appeared in a *Jewish Press* article by him. It was an account of two fathers whose sons had been killed in the Yom Kippur War. One father was so devastated that he committed suicide, but the other channeled his sorrow into action:

... [He] threw himself into the struggle against the surrender of Jewish land. He is Yitzhak Gazit, who placed an ad last week in an Israeli newspaper that [said], "This land is ours. It is not only the inheritance of our fathers, but also of our sons who paid on its behalf the full price.... Despite this you are prepared to surrender it to an enemy in return for a few foolish words, worthless, which even the enemy is unwilling to express, let alone write down...."[32]

Meir said the sit-in would continue until the Israeli government agreed to their demands or until they were arrested. The State Department telegram quoted a police source that explained the consulate's reluctance to have them arrested: An arrest would enhance Meir's image as a martyr and be valuable publicity for the JDL. The telegram continued:

JDL maintained level of approximately 15 sit-ins overnight.... Building is open all night and elevator service is maintained. Sit-ins have come equipped with juice, milk, cookies and other snacks and move about freely...[33]

Meir, however, did not remain overnight; he left for a speaking engagement at Baruch College at 5 P.M. At 8:15 the next morning he returned, accompanied by media representatives, to bid farewell to the fifteen sit-ins. A newspaper photo shows him shaking hands with the protesters before departing to surrender to U.S. marshals."[34]

From a Cell in the Federal Courthouse

Reporters awaiting Meir's arrival at the Brooklyn Federal courthouse noted that he was coatless and carried only a brown paper shopping bag of Hebrew books and pamphlets. Meir told them that he would spend his time in prison studying the Torah and said, "I'm going to write articles and do a lot of reading." Asked why no appeal had been filed to postpone his imprisonment until after the Passover holidays, his lawyer, Barry Slotnick, said: "The rabbi is determined to get this over with.... The sooner he goes in, the sooner he goes back to his wife and four children in Israel." This echoed Meir's letter to me, "... I will get it over with quickly..."

Passover was only a week away. Slotnick asked Judge Weinstein to allow Meir to begin his sentence at the West Street Federal Detention Center, where he would have "better access to kosher food during Passover." Instead, Weinstein directed that Meir be sent to an unnamed "community treatment center," where he would be free to leave for kosher meals and religious services. He would stay there until the end of Passover, April 4, and then would be sent to the minimum security prison in Allenwood, Pennsylvania.[35]

From his cell in the courthouse, Meir wrote home:

> I am writing this from a cellblock in the Federal Court House in Brooklyn. I have just begun serving my sentence, having left the Israeli Consulate, where the sit-in is going into its second day. Radio, TV and newspapers are now picking it up well....
>
> I am being taken from here to 210 W. 55 Street, a hotel that is used for addiction treatment, so that I have my own room, my books and typewriter. I can leave for all meals and [prayer] "services." I will probably spend *Pesach* [Passover] with Shelley and Shragi or at least with some Orthodox family.
>
> On April 4, I will be going – almost certainly – to Allenwood, where the Watergate people are sent. Again, there is a court order for me to have books, *tefillin* [phylacteries], shaver and typewriter there. All I will not have is you.[36]

Weinstein's order specified that Meir could bring books, typewriter, electric shaver and phylacteries and that he was to be allowed to leave for all meals and religious services. It added, "On April 4, 1975, he is to be transferred to a minimum security institution, with the right to have his typewriter and books ... [and] ... electric shaver and phylacteries.... In view of the fact that Rabbi Kahane is a practicing rabbi, if there is no minyan (quorum of 10 men), he is to be reasonably allowed to attend services."[37]

Although Slotnick was defending Meir *pro bono*, there were other expensive fees: depositions, court reporters, travel, investigation of witnesses, transcripts, and payments to associate attorneys. Between February and April, ads were placed to raise money for legal costs. One in the *New York Times* read:

Slotnick referred wryly to his *pro bono* status in a note to Meir.

> Please find check for $5.00 from a Mrs. H. Behrensohn of Flushing, N.Y. So
> that there will be no question with regard to my receipt of further checks, I
> would greatly appreciate it if you would, somehow, indicate that my services
> are rendered out of a love of Zion, rather than for remuneration. Not only do
> I represent you for nothing, now it costs me a dime [for postage]![39]

Meir's next letter home was written from the community treatment center (a
halfway house for prisoners about to be released). He described his daily schedule
there:

> Very interesting place. Samples of graffiti range from "dullard" to clever.
> Sample 1: "Do not urinate in hallway ... it is selfish, ignorant and unhealthy."
> Sample 2: "Clifford Irving was unraveled here. Howard Hughes was knot."
>   Actually things here are not bad. I leave for "prayers and meals" from 6:30
> A.M.-10 A.M.; 12-1 P.M.; 6 P.M.-9 P.M. I spend a great deal of time learning
> and writing and the rest in the JDL office directing things (it is only five blocks
> away). At this moment, I am waiting to learn what happened at the Israeli Con-
> sulate. The sit-in was in its fourth day when we heard of the arrest of the
> settlers at Rabin's home. So they blocked the elevators and stopped all busi-
> ness. Rivlin (the Consul General) promised a press conference with JDL at
> 3:30. It is now 5 and I don't know what happened.[40]

Although Meir wrote to me that he was still directing JDL, he was clearly limited by his imprisonment: He could not know the outcome of the sit-in because
he was allowed out only for meals and prayers.

In "Of Prisoners and Free Men," datelined "Federal Prison, New York, March
25, 1975," Meir discussed the concept of freedom and the essence of the
approaching Passover holiday.

> ... How many prisoners walk the streets of the world seemingly free, and how
> true it is that one can find within the cells and behind the bars of prisons men
> who are truly and totally free! And how odd that there are people who sadly
> shake my hand and murmur their regrets that I am in prison, when they daily
> walk the streets with countless ordinary people who are in the most abject kind
> of slavery, weighed down by the shackles and chains that keep them prisoners
> doomed to indeterminate sentences that never will end.
>   ... I smile a pitying smile at those who fear the prison of mere walls. For
> there are men behind those walls who are free men, men who have done exactly
> what they want to do, men who have acted out their ideals and truths and who
> laugh at the wardens who seek to imprison them. How can one be imprisoned
> when his mind is free and his soul clean and satisfied? ... "There is no free man

except one who occupies himself with the study of Torah" (*Avot*, 6:2). So do the rabbis speak as they lay down the Jewish definition of freedom and slavery.

Note carefully what they say: "One who occupies himself with the study of Torah" – and of course, the study of Torah has merit only when it leads to its practice.... A Jew is a free man when he has a sense of values that consigns the foolishness of money and status and honor to the junk heap of the slave mart.... A Jew is free when he has a sense of values that cries out to him, "Far more important than life is how one lives it!"

The Jew who is so weak and bound by his animal body that he is incapable of disciplining himself through the prohibitions against eating non-kosher food – is a slave to his own body. The man who is unable to abstain from work and the siren song of material pursuits on the Sabbath – is a man who serves a sentence in an unseen penitentiary....

But the Jew who makes his body bend to his will is a man who has no chains on his arms. The Jew who hears the cry of fellow Jews and casts off from himself the vanities and nonsense of money and sterile status ... and leaps into the waters of duty – this is a man who has come out of Egypt.

For that is the essence of Passover, to come out of the land of Egypt.... It is the ultimate imperative for the Jew to ... flee the slavery of a world of animal materialism and climb the Sinai of men of free spirit.... One casts off his chains, one escapes from prison, by becoming the servant of G-d. By doing that which a Jew is obligated to do....[41]

On the eve of Passover, Meir sent us an update.

It is now *Erev Pesach* [Passover Eve] so this will be the last letter till after the *chag* [holiday]. I will be leaving here *be'ezrat Hashem* [with G-d's help] in an hour to be at Shragi and Shelley's until *motzei Shabbat* [Saturday night]. Then I will be off again the last two days [of Passover], and I will be allowed to go by myself to Allenwood on April 7.[42]

With Meir in federal custody, two cases pending against him were adjourned: one for his part in the melee on "There Is No Palestine Day" on January 19, 1975, and one for trespassing at Temple Emanu-El on February 10, 1975. Another case, concerning a December 1970 charge of inciting to riot, was closed on May 20, 1975, since Meir was already in prison.[43]

During the intermediate days of Passover, Meir was again directing JDL. To coincide with a two-day Gush Emunim march throughout Samaria, which aimed to dramatize the call for free settlement in Judea, Samaria and Gaza, JDLers held a rally and a sit-in at the Israeli Consulate in New York. A news item in the *Jewish Press* said:

... from his New York City prison, JDL head Meir Kahane appealed to Jews to turn out by the thousands.... A special tape recording by Kahane will be read at the rally, and demands will be made that include unrestricted Jewish settlement in all parts of the Land of Israel, immediate reunification of Judea, Samaria, Gaza and the Golan Heights with the State of Israel, and a new government of national unity based on the principle of "not one inch of concessions."

This JDL sit-in at the Israeli Consulate ended with the arrest of ten JDLers who refused to leave. Their arrest drew American media attention to the march in Israel that culminated that day with the arrival of over 20,000 Israelis in Sebastia, the site of the ancient Israelite city, Samaria.[44]

The children and I took part in that two-day Passover march. We slept at the side of the road, shivering in sleeping bags that were not warm enough for those cold nights, and ate from the two-day supply of food in our backpacks. Our matza sandwiches broke from being squashed in the backpacks, but we also had boiled potatoes, hard-boiled eggs and soft "cookies," a concoction of dates, bananas, and crumbled matza based on a recipe I found in the *Jewish Press*. Tzippy wrote to Meir about the hardships of the march, and Meir replied:

> I know that the march was not easy, but as I wrote to Binny, "Three things are acquired through suffering: Torah, the Land of Israel, and *Olam Haba* [the World to Come]." You can tell your children that you marched for Eretz Yisrael Hashelema [the complete Land of Israel].[45]

Passover ended and Meir made preparations for his move to the prison in Allenwood, Pennsylvania. Two days before he was to leave New York, the U.S. Bureau of Prisons informed Judge Weinstein that it would be "too complicated" to give Meir kosher food in Allenwood.

Chapter 43

The Right to Kosher Food in Prison (April-May 1975)

A T MEIR'S SENTENCING on February 21, Judge Weinstein included a provision for Meir's religious needs:

> He is to be placed in an institution and in a setting so that he can obtain ... kosher foods and [comply with] other religious requirements that he may reasonably have.[1]

At sentencing, the attorney for the Bureau of Prisons did not oppose this order. Now, almost two months later, on April 4, as Meir was preparing to depart for the Federal Prison in Allenwood, Pennsylvania, the Bureau of Prisons suddenly announced that it would be "too complicated" to give Meir kosher food there.

While Meir's attorney, Barry Slotnick, petitioned Judge Weinstein to find the Bureau of Prisons in contempt of court for ignoring his order, Meir called a press conference at the halfway house. Meir declared that he had a constitutional right to a prison diet according to his religious beliefs. He vowed to fast totally if he were transferred to Allenwood prison without being granted kosher food. This was an historic struggle for the right of all Jewish prisoners to be served kosher food, he said. Not only that. Since Judge Weinstein's order had provided that Meir be allowed to attended services, Meir maintained that religious rights included facilities for prayers with a *minyan* (quorum) and a *Sefer Torah* (Torah scroll), and if this were not possible, Jews should be allowed supervised furloughs over the Sabbath to the nearest synagogue of their choice. Meir also told reporters about a JDL event that would take place shortly and proclaimed, "I'm running JDL from prison!"[2]

In his *Jewish Press* column, Meir urged readers to attend the upcoming JDL event he had described to reporters.

> I ask you Jews for a going-away present ... a little bit of yourselves. On April 13, there will be a huge Solidarity Day March for Soviet Jewry [sponsored by

the Jewish Establishment]. You and 100,000 Jews will be there. I ask you to make it a different day than it was last year.... At the end of the program thousands of Jews will march to the United States Mission to the U.N. to shout forth their angry cries of "Never again a Munich, Never again another Holocaust, Not one inch of retreat." They will sit by their thousands in the streets of New York.... Give me a going away present. Be there....[3]

An ad said: "Gather at U.N. Plaza and sit down on First Avenue singing and shouting for the Jews of Israel and the Soviet Union. Turn Solidarity Day into a meaningful thing."[4]

Flyers urged, "... Be there. Sit there. Be part of history. Make this part of the biggest arrest in New York history. Do not be afraid. There will be no violence. But you can be part of history."[5]

Many Jews responded to Meir's appeal. They staged a one hour sit-down at 45 Street and First Avenue, completely blocking traffic, to protest American pressure on Israel to cede lands. A total of 133 were arrested on charges of disorderly conduct.[6]

Kosher Food for Richard Huss and Jeffrey Smilow

In response to Barry Slotnick's petition against the Bureau of Prisons, Judge Weinstein issued an order extending Meir's stay in Manhattan. The order delayed his transfer to Allenwood for three weeks to allow Slotnick and federal attorneys time to prepare and submit legal briefs on the question of kosher food there.[7]

Coincidentally, there was another case pending at this time about kosher food in federal prison. That case concerned Richard Huss and Jeffrey Smilow, JDL members who had been given one-year sentences for contempt of court in June 1973 because they refused to testify against a fellow Jew. Meir wrote about Huss and Smilow and the fight for kosher food:

> The struggle here is not for kosher food for MYSELF. It is not for any SPECIAL privilege.... This fight will continue until a court ruling is handed down establishing the constitutional right of every Jew who so wishes, to have kosher food regardless of cost or problems for the prison. Indeed, it will go beyond food, and seek to establish a general network of basic, constitutionally guaranteed rights including the right to proper prayer and observance of Sabbath and religious holidays, as well as time for religious study....
>
> ... And in particular, I want to fight for two young men in prison who are Jewish, and who can walk out free men tomorrow and who do not, and because of this they become more heroic with every passing day.
>
> They are named Rick Huss and Jeff Smilow. When first faced with prison, one was barely 16 and the other not quite 18. Both were charged with no crime. Both were arrested and threatened with prison ... because [the U.S. govern-

ment] claimed that the two had evidence concerning the Hurok bombing, and Washington told them: Inform or go to jail.

Each and every day, Jews pray to G-d, and in the central part of the prayers, the *Amidah* or *Shmone Esray*, they say: "And may the informer have no hope." Indeed, informing on a Jew is among the most heinous of crimes and the halakha (Jewish law) allows the death penalty to be meted out to such a person!

Yet how many Jews, even religious Jews, would do what these two very young Jews did? ... How many would have stood before an angry, assimilated Jewish judge and tell him – to his fury – that Jews do not inform!

... We will yet win the battle of kosher food and other rights for Jewish prisoners.... The fight for the rights of Jewish prisoners is a mitzvah. The fight for the rights of young Jews such as Rick Huss and Jeff Smilow is an honor.... [8]

Meanwhile, Huss and Smilow were eating fresh fruits and vegetables and canned sardines. Their request for cooked kosher food was being heard by Judge Thomas P. Griesa at the U.S. District Court for the Southern District of New York. Since Judge Weinstein was a federal judge for the Eastern District of New York, their decisions would be completely independent of each other.[9]

In a letter home, Meir gave the details.

Well, things never get boring. My stay in New York was extended indefinitely because the government refused me kosher food in Allenwood. Judge Weinstein therefore ordered briefs on the subject and will issue a decision.

This is important, because while I could have gotten kosher food eventually (with *protektzia* [pull]), I want ALL Jewish prisoners to get kosher food as a RIGHT. We had a big press conference in prison here, and I was on all the channels.

Pesach was fine. I spoke at the Sephardic shul in Borough Park and it was packed.[10]

Not only had Meir informed reporters that he was directing JDL during this time, he was even giving public lectures in Borough Park! Meir was purposely disregarding the rules of the halfway house, which forbade "conducting outside business." He was aiming for a court decision that kosher food was the constitutional right of all Jewish prisoners.

It was not long before the media reported his disregard for the rules. The *Daily News*, the most widely read newspaper in New York City, published a biting report:

Federal prisoner Meir Kahane calmly strolled out of his West Side digs at 7 A.M. yesterday on his way to business, which he said included "directing the activities of the Jewish Defense League."[11]

An editorial in the *News* the next day said:

> Rabbi Meir Kahane ... continues to lead a charmed life as far as the U.S. law is concerned.
>
> ... Kahane, by his own admission, is right back coaching his JDL followers, brazenly defiant and totally unrepentant.
>
> With that attitude, and his penchant for making trouble, Kahane belongs in jail.[12]

One reporter asked Matthew Walsh, supervisor of the halfway house, whether Meir was spending his time on other activities. Walsh replied, "We can't follow him. That's not part of our program. We have to take his word."[13]

Meir used the pages of the *Jewish Press* to rebut the *Daily News* story. He maintained that the government planted the story to intimidate Judge Weinstein into sending him to Allenwood federal penitentiary without delay. His rebuttal of the "tissue of lies, distortions and half-truths" in the *Daily News* story said:

> The "luxury hotel," is one that every visitor would far more likely describe as little more than a flophouse. It is a cheap West Side place with roaches and vermin all about. It is a prison where I must check in and out of only because there are no kitchen facilities and ALL THE PRISONERS there eat out.... The statement attributed to me that I could eat vegetables for a year was actually one that said, "The government would like to send me to Allenwood and make me eat vegetables for a year."
>
> I was ordered by Judge Weinstein to be sent to the Allenwood prison on April 7, and it was because of the government that the transfer was stayed.... On April 4, the U.S. government formally told Judge Weinstein that it would REFUSE TO OBEY HIS ORDER that I be given kosher food! ... That men who are sworn to uphold the law – to tell a federal judge that they would ignore his order is shocking.... Had the government obeyed the court order in the first place ... I would long since have been in Allenwood. I am, of course, grateful for the spite and stupidity of the Justice Department for granting me the opportunity to broaden my fight into one for kosher food for ALL Jewish prisoners as a matter of RIGHT.
>
> Finally, as to my continued efforts to direct the JDL: The Jewish people face a critical era unparalleled in their history. I will continue to do all in my power to help them whether I am in Manhattan, in Allenwood or in a maximum prison in Atlanta....[14]

Meir sent me the *Daily News* clippings with this analysis:

> As you can see from the enclosed, the government has leaked the story to the press and is trying to get me to Allenwood. They have foolishly refused to give me kosher food and now are sorry for it, because Weinstein will undoubtedly rule on my motion that ALL Jews get kosher food.[15]

Meir's fight for kosher food was supported by five prominent Orthodox rabbis, Moshe Tendler of the Community Synagogue of Monsey and professor at
Yeshiva University, Shlomo Riskin of the Lincoln Square Synagogue, Saul Berman of Stern College, Avraham Weiss of the Hebrew Institute of Riverdale, and
Reuven Grodner of the Young Israel of Scarsdale. On April 22, to dramatize the
issue, they went to the Federal House of Detention in Manhattan with individually
packaged frozen kosher meals for the prisoners there. However, the warden
refused the meals as "a matter of prison policy." The rabbis then went to the halfway house, where they joined Meir at a press conference to explain that since
kosher food was a fundamental tenet of Judaism, they were offering to provide
it for Jewish prisoners at no charge until a Federal court would rule on the issue.[16]

Non-Jews also supported Meir's fight for kosher food, because it was part of
his right to freely practice his religion – a right guaranteed by the First Amendment of the Constitution of the United States. Former U.S. attorney general
Ramsey Clark, at another press conference on Meir's behalf, said, "It is sad that
at this late date in our nation's history, it is still necessary to get a specific court
order to gain elementary religious rights.... I hope the government will move mas-
sively now to assure complete religious freedom within correctional facilities."

Clark's statement was made at a press conference sponsored by the Rabbinical
Council of America, and chaired by its president Rabbi Fabian Schonfeld. Rabbi
Sol Roth, president of the New York Board of Rabbis, told the press that the
Board planned to file a brief with the court supporting Meir's efforts to obtain kosher food. A letter from Congressman Edward Koch to Norman Carlson, director
of the Federal Bureau of Prisons, was read out. Koch wrote, "What is particularly
distressing to me is that ... even if the prisoner wishes to pay to have kosher food
sent in to the prison, authorities will not permit it."[17]

Prison officials claimed they could not supply kosher food because of the
elaborate procedures involved in its preparation. Since there were only twelve
Orthodox Jews in the entire federal prison system, the question had not yet been
dealt with seriously by the courts. On this point, Ramsey Clark maintained that
it was not a question of the number of inmates involved. The very fact that they
were a small and weak minority in the prison system, he said, made it imperative
that their case be heard. Regarding the constitutional right to freedom of religion,
he said, "The United States was founded on the concept of religious freedom, yet
two hundred years later, prisons are still denying basic religious rights."[18]

The case was heard on April 24, with U.S. Attorney David Trager arguing
only that Judge Weinstein did not have the jurisdiction to impose special prison
conditions. Attorney Barry Slotnick represented Meir, with attorney Dennis Rapps
of COLPA (National Jewish Commission on Law and Public Affairs) assisting
him. Testifying on Meir's behalf were Rabbi Moshe Tendler, Rabbi Henry

Siegman of the Synagogue Council of America, and Rabbi Solomon Shapiro, chaplain of Kings County Hospital. Rabbi Shapiro pointed out that hospitals, air-lines and hotels routinely provide frozen TV-style kosher meals and disposable utensils for religious Jews, without significant added expense.[19]

Rabbi Tendler, head of Yeshiva University's biology department and an expert on Talmudic law, testified as to the importance of keeping kosher in Jew-ish law. His moving testimony was cited verbatim in Judge Weinstein's decision:

> If all [an Orthodox Jew] had was non-kosher food to eat, he would have to wait until ... competent medical authorities [determine] that he is in danger of dying. Then and only then, could he partake of non-kosher food [according to Biblical and Rabbinic law].
>
> ... Up until forfeiture of life, man must forfeit everything he has, company of his wife and children, his entire wealth, to enter into the realm of the most poverty-stricken, rather than transgress the Kashruth laws.
>
> He is to allow himself to be subjected to torture, to physical torture, to mutilation rather than consume [non-kosher] food.
>
> I hope that impresses the Court with the fact that we are not dealing with a frivolous notion. It is not a question of a special dietary requirement of white wine with fish or red wine with beef. We are talking about a critical need of the Jew to relate with his G-d in a series of instructions that have been our mark of distinction from the days that we left Egypt so many thousands of years ago.
>
> ... At no time is he exempted. From the day he is born ... until the day he dies ... he is governed by Jewish law.[20]

A *Daily News* report on the hearing has two pictures of Meir, side by side, captioned "Meir Kahane (left) before he gave up to authorities, and 20 pounds lighter (right) in Federal Court yesterday." Contributing to Meir's haggard appear-ance in the more recent picture was his thin beard, grown because it was the *sefira* period, between Passover and *Shavuot* (Pentecost), when Jewish law pro-hibits shaving. After hearing the arguments and testimony, Judge Weinstein asked both parties to provide additional briefs to satisfy technical legal questions, reserving decision until after he received the briefs. Meanwhile, Meir, "gaunt and 20 pounds lighter," remained at the halfway house.[21]

Meir was optimistic that Judge Weinstein's decision would be in his favor. At the same time, he realized that if the Bureau of Prisons agreed to give him kosher food, he would be transferred immediately to Allenwood Federal Prison in Penn-sylvania. He wrote to me:

> You will be getting this after my phone call to you, so much of it is repetitive but I love talking to you anyway. I miss you and the children very much and can't wait to get back. As of this moment, Weinstein is on the verge of handing down a decision in my favor and it will be rather historic.
>
> However, I may be moved then to Allenwood.[22]

The Halfway House

He was moved, meanwhile, along with the entire population of the halfway house, to another address in Manhattan. It was only two days before Judge Weinstein was to hand down his decision. Meir wrote:

> The whole prison was transferred today to a hotel on West 54th Street at Broadway (Bryant Hotel). It is quite a comfortable place, with private bath, carpeting, etc. I have three restaurants where I eat free of charge [Meir was given $4.00 a day to buy food], so I "suffer" in silence.[23]

In another letter, he described the "new" halfway house.

> I am on the sixth floor of the Hotel Bryant, a place with a relatively nice past and a mediocre present. Room 602 will go down in infamy. I share it with a fellow (Jewish) about 55, bald (with a toupee), quiet and clean. He replaced a fellow who was in for two nights (for fraud). He replaced a Puerto Rican who drank, smoked marijuana and was very polite when I came in. (When I *davened* [prayed] he would freeze and not move till I finished). Anyhow, he escaped. There are two beds. I have a desk, typewriter, books, files, a little ice chest, EVERYTHING EXCEPT YOU!!!
>
> The guards here range from mediocre to mediocre. I am in a constant battle with them over hours but I take my hours the way I want to.[24]

Later, Meir wrote:

> I now have two black roommates. One wants to go to Israel and open a beauty salon.[25]

An overview of the halfway house appeared in an article by Yitta Halberstam about Meir's current predicament.

> Once an elegant residential hotel for physicians, the 72-year-old Bryant Hotel is currently in a state of sad disrepair. With its faded, threadbare carpeting, chipped paint, cracked ceilings and general haggard air, it now attracts ... assorted transients. The motley population uses the hotel as a temporary base and valiantly ignores its creaking elevator, dim lighting and vermin invasion.
>
> What would be another undistinguished has-been hotel in a city with many, Hotel Bryant is unique because of the double life it leads. Unbeknownst to residents, several floors of the hotel have recently been rented to the Federal Bureau of Prisons and converted into a halfway house for Federal prisoners. The hotel has judiciously kept the identity of the new tenants under wraps, and unenlightened residents ride the elevator with convicts who are completing the last phase of a long prison sentence.

The article spoke of the many people who visited Meir in the halfway house.

> ... Bob Hauser, case manager at the halfway house, similarly marvels at Kahane's ceaseless productivity. "He's always busy. When he's not receiving

the steady stream of visitors who have descended here en masse since his arrival, he works quietly in his room, either reading or writing."[26]

A Constitutional Right

On May 7, two weeks after the hearing, Judge Weinstein handed down a 48-page ruling that upheld Meir's right to kosher food in prison.

> ... prisons could purchase, under their normal food requisitioning procedures, pre-prepared, frozen, foil-wrapped kosher meals accompanied by disposable eating utensils; they are readily available.... While the cost of these dinners would be somewhat higher than regular prison fare, the government does not contest the fact that only in the order of a dozen persons would have to be provided with such food, so that costs would not be significant.

He concluded:

> ... No irresolvable conflict exists between the rights of the defendant and the practical needs of the correctional institutions.
>   ... Defendant is constitutionally entitled to an order accompanying his sentence that allows him to conform to Jewish dietary laws.... The minor practical problems presented can be easily met if the government tries in good faith to do so.
>   ... The defendant may be sent to an institution suitable to his needs and the requirements of the correctional service. The Director of the Federal Bureau of Prisons is directed to take precaution to accommodate the defendant's religious requirements....[27]

Meir was jubilant. He wrote to me:

> ... I won the kosher food case and it was a great victory. The news media – especially TV – made a big thing of it. I don't know what is next, but it has to be good.[28]

Photos taken at a press conference at the halfway house after the decision show Meir wearing a light-colored suit jacket and dark pants, with a month-and-a-half old *sefira* beard.[29] At the press conference, attorney Barry Slotnick told reporters that it was unlikely that Meir would be transferred to Allenwood prison soon, because the Bureau of Prisons would probably try to overturn Weinstein's decision in a higher court, rather than give him kosher food in Allenwood. Slotnick was right. It was not long before the prison authorities filed a notice of appeal.[30]

An appeal by the Bureau of Prisons to a higher court stood a good chance of success, because only two days earlier Judge Thomas P. Griesa had denied the request of Richard Huss and Jeffrey Smilow for kosher meals. In his decision,

Judge Griesa said that supplying kosher meals to Jewish prisoners would involve "special treatment" and be more expensive. He maintained that the boys' current diet of fruits, vegetables, milk, boiled eggs, and canned sardines, supplemented by vitamins, was nutritionally sufficient. Observers commented that behind Griesa's reasoning was his thinly concealed belief that a convicted criminal is not morally capable of religious devotion.[31]

However, Judge Griesa's decision had no bearing on Judge Weinstein's decision because they presided in different districts. A conflict between federal judges in different districts could be settled only by a court of appeals. Until then, both rulings were valid.[32]

Meir wrote a letter of encouragement to the two boys, to which Smilow replied:

> Me and Rick received your letter. We are both doing fine and things are as good as can be expected under these conditions.
>
> As you know, prison life can be very depressing at times. Your letter was very inspiring and made me and Rick feel much better than we were feeling in the last few days. Being so far from home, we don't hear much and the few letters that we get are very comforting.
>
> A person must learn from every experience in life, every event has a meaning. This whole court case and this imprisonment has strengthened one of my beliefs very much. That is, that there will never be any other home for the Jewish people except Eretz Yisrael. This should be a sign to every Jew that we are always outsiders in every country. Even those who try to conform to the ways of this land will always be looked upon as an outsider, as a Jew. I have seen this more in prison than anywhere else. All Jews who refuse to realize this are living in prison. I may be here now, but I look forward to the day when I will raise my family in Eretz Yisrael.[33]

The Shuva Aliya Movement

Waiting for the Bureau of Prisons to present its appeal against Judge Weinstein's ruling, Meir embarked on a series of JDL activities with fervor. JDL's newly formed aliya movement, Shuva (Return), became his first priority. Office space was rented, and Cheri Feldman was appointed Shuva's director. She set about organizing groups of American Jews who would make their homes in Israel together, while Meir took steps to acquire land for them in the Galilee area. He wrote home:

> The Shuva aliya group is beginning to pick up steam and I have written to Ari Calderon to please start working on 1) the mayor of Hatzor and 2) the Jewish Agency for land in the Southern Golan or the Galilee for a settlement.
>
> There will be two *garinim* [settlement units], the first in Hatzor, for married

"bourgeois" couples and the other for a settlement (kibbutz or *moshav shitufi* [cooperative farm]).[34]

Ari Calderon, an early member of JDL, who lived in Israel, contacted officials in the Galilee for Shuva. Inspired by Meir's teachings, Calderon had moved to Israel with his growing family in 1973. He recalled: "Before I heard the Rabbi speak, I was a Jew without a soul, without an identity, without a connection to our people, with no sense of religion. The Rabbi motivated me to be, first of all, a better person. I started to think Jewish, to act Jewish, and to have a closer connection to our faith and people. My family and I became 'Shomer Shabbat' [Sabbath observers] and we began to love who we were."[35]

Meir inspired many people as he had inspired the Calderons. His genuine sincerity also led people to support him financially. He wrote:

> ... Our [JDL] office (three rooms which are used also by Shuva and CAIR) is paid up for six months by a new *nadvan* [donor]. He is also paying the weekly salary of a secretary and executive director, phone bills, etc.[36]

Meir advertised Shuva, as well as his Thursday evening seminars, in a *Jewish Press* ad which referred to him only as "a prominent rabbi from Israel:"

> BEGIN A NEW LIFE IN ISRAEL
> The Jewish Defense League and Rabbi Meir Kahane
> announce the formation of two aliya groups: Garin A and Garin B
> Meeting Monday May 5, 7:45 P.M., 227 West 29 Street.
>
> The Jewish Identity Center resumes Thursday evening seminars,
> May 8, 7 P.M., 227 West 29 Street
> A prominent rabbi from Israel will officiate.[37]

At first, ads for Meir's other public appearances in May also referred to him obliquely, because he was forbidden to conduct outside business while he was in the halfway house, and he feared that the *Jewish Press* would not accept ads that used his name. One ad referred to him as a "prominent JDL speaker" and another as a "prominent Israeli speaker."[38]

Then, in an innovative step to attract more people to his talks promoting aliya, and without coordinating it with the authorities, Meir decided to hold seminars at the halfway house. An ad on May 30 announced:

> A limited number of people
> will be accepted to a series of seminars
> by Rabbi Meir Kahane on aliya.
> ... at the Manhattan Federal Prison where Rabbi Kahane is confined.
> ... Contact Shuva, tel. 691-7753 or JDL, tel. 255-0211.[39]

The following week, Meir inserted a small news item in the *Jewish Press* that said that the seminars would begin on Wednesday, July 11, and that "all who wish to attend must make reservations by contacting the Shuva aliya movement." This did not sit well with the prison authorities, but they could not punish him by sending him to prison (as they could other halfway house residents) because Weinstein's court order required them to keep him at the halfway house until there was a ruling from the Court of Appeals. The only sanction halfway house authorities had was to recommend that he not be given "good time," the five days a month he could accumulate toward an earlier release date.[40]

Meir also publicized the seminar classes in his pseudonymous *Jewish Press* column, *Israel Through Laughter and Tears*.

> In an imaginative effort to promote general aliya as well as to gain members for its *garinim* [settlement groups], Shuva arranged for a series of seminars on aliya to be given by Meir Kahane in his Manhattan prison. The response was so enthusiastic that Rabbi Kahane is now thinking of having one seminar in the evening too, since the others are held in the afternoon when many people cannot make it.[41]

Meir's *chutzpa* (impudence) was intentional. More than a month had passed since Judge Weinstein had ruled that he must be given kosher food in federal prison. The Bureau of Prisons had filed a notice of appeal to contest that ruling and Meir was prodding them to expedite the appeals process because he was confident that the Court of Appeals would rule that kosher food was a constitutional right for all Jewish prisoners.

He called Shuva seminars in prison because he sincerely believed that it was dangerous for American Jews to remain in the United States. Seminars at the halfway house would attract people who might not attend an ordinary gathering. Meir thought Shuva could succeed where the Establishment's Israel Aliyah Center had not because Shuva's emphasis was different. He explained Shuva's rationale:

> Aliya is alive in the U.S. – but barely. Over and over again the JDL has pointed out that no amount of persuasion that uses positive arguments will create meaningful aliya, since no example in Jewish history can be found of mass aliya from affluent countries.
>
> To seriously believe that hundreds of thousands of American Jews will leave familiar surroundings and culture, high living standards and the life they have always known, for Arab hostility, inflation, economic insecurity, and a strange cultural, social and political environment, is to be less than realistic.
>
> It is only fear of persecution and physical threats that has at any time brought large numbers of Jews to the Land of Israel, and the announcement last week of a new aliya movement, known as Shuva, was an encouraging sign.

... Shuva is ready to risk the wrath of a great many groups by speaking the "unspeakable" and saying: The potential for a terrible holocaust in the United States is real and it is time for the Jews to come home to Israel – to save their lives.[42]

Articles by Meir explaining why American Jews should go to live in Israel were distributed as Shuva flyers. Among them were "Galut Realities and Galut Mentalities" and "A Jew Dies in Brooklyn." Their theme was that the United States was no longer a safe place for Jews.[43]

Meir wrote home in June:

Our two *garinim* are coming along nicely and we will build the *shikun* [housing project] in Safed and the *moshav shitufi* [agricultural cooperative] probably near Gush Etzion.[44]

However, Cheri Feldman's negotiations with the Israel Aliyah Center for apartments in the Galilee town of Safed fell through. A letter arrived in October from Safed saying that there were not enough apartments for thirty new families in Safed. "It would be best to go to Kiryat Arba, since there they are followers of Rabbi Kahane" said the letter. In December, Meir wrote to me, "Our settlement site was changed to Kiryat Arba."[45]

Ever inventive, Meir devised a new way to publicize his ideas about aliya. At the end of May, he had the *Jewish Press* run a "Letter to the Editor" attacking his own stand on aliya. He signed it "Melvin Gresham" and in it he presented reasons why Jews should NOT go to live in Israel. "Gresham" reasoned that Jews should stay in America because they could do more to help Israel that way. Jewish youth were needed in America, asserted Gresham, to deal with Jewish problems there. He wrote, "This is not Germany – there could never be a Holocaust in America."

Many readers sent heated letters to the editor refuting Gresham's arguments and explaining why American Jews should indeed move to Israel. Meir filed the page of letters with a note: "All the aliya letters here came in response to a phony letter against aliya I put into the *J.P.* [*Jewish Press*]." The replies gave Meir the satisfaction of knowing that his aliya campaign was bearing fruit.[46]

AJAF: American Jews Against Ford

As always, Meir sought to deflect American pressure on Israel to cede lands to the Arabs. He conceived of threatening the incumbent president, Gerald Ford, with a loss of votes in the coming presidential elections if he continued to pressure Israel. Meir formed a new organization, American Jews Against Ford (AJAF), which had no official connection with the JDL. The declared aim of AJAF was to campaign against the reelection of President Ford in order to prevent Israeli retreat from Sinai. An ad in the *New York Times* about AJAF began:

> For the sake of the United States, the free world, and Israel
> PRESIDENT FORD MUST GO
> With respect and honor for the office of the Presidency,
> but with a terrible sense of fear for the future
> of the United States and the free world,
> we call for a change in administration in 1976.

The ad explained the danger to the free world and the danger to Israel: Ford supports "false détente which threatens the entire free world as it strengthens the Soviet Union by giving it the technology, trade, and credits it so badly needs." The false détente has "weakened both NATO and American military might." In addition, Ford is "strangling Israel ... attempting to force it into concessions that would threaten its very existence." He is also "attacking the Jackson amendment that is the great hope of free emigration from the USSR."

AJAF plans detailed in the ad included gathering signatures on petitions against Ford's reelection and enlisting volunteers who would "knock on doors, stuff mailboxes and distribute literature." AJAF would also work with Christians:

> [AJAF will make] a serious effort to reach the Christian fundamentalist Bible community, to impress upon them the Biblical axioms that make the final redemption conditional upon the prior return of all the Jewish people to Israel and the resurrection of the Jewish state from the hands of its illegal conquerors.

Yet another aspect of AJAF's program was to support "political efforts to persuade a strong rival within the Republican party to run against Mr. Ford."

Meir sent me a copy of the ad, which cost over one thousand dollars, with a note: "[It] was paid for by Gary Ratner of Chicago (I met him at the Tel Aviv Hilton in 1973)."[47] Meir also wrote about funding for the AJAF office.

> Our AJAF office will open *be'ezrat Hashem* [with G-d's help] this week thanks to a contribution of $2,100 from a fellow whom I may have written about. A ... fellow who is a Breslever chasid, member of Mapam, with a beard and *tzitzit* who goes to David's Conservative shul. There are many other facets to him, but that is enough for now.[48]

When some Jews criticized the AJAF ad in the *Times*, Meir said they were "people who live in constant fear of offending 'the ruling power,' [who] murmur, 'Let us not offend Ford, since he can harm Israel.'" Meir pointed out: "The fact that such an attitude has always guaranteed Jews being hurt makes no impression on these people, since what is really at the bottom of their concern is fear ... of what such bold attacks will do to the Jewish position in the United States and more specifically, to THEM."[49]

Meir composed several AJAF flyers and an eight-page leaflet, *Ford Must Go.* These were distributed on street corners, at Meir's lectures, and at peaceful AJAF demonstrations. A petition was circulated that said, "We the undersigned hereby pledge to vote against President Gerald Ford in 1976 ... unless the U.S. ceases pressure on Israel to withdraw ... and President Ford dismisses Henry Kissinger." The petition was also printed in *Jewish Press* ads that concluded: "Sign the names – Mail them back – Ask for another petition – Help us with $."[50]

Addressing Christian Fundamentalists

Another strategy was to stress Ford's Christian beliefs and his pragmatic interest in the votes of the Christian fundamentalist community. In his *Jewish Press* column, Meir wrote, "It is not that the United States grants Israel favors when it supports the Jewish state, but rather that the very existence and survival of the United States is dependent on its support of Israel." He cited the biblical verse, "And I will bless them that bless thee, and him that curseth shall I curse" (*Genesis* 12:13).[51]

Meir was given the opportunity to address a Christian audience when *Newsday,* the widely circulated Long Island daily, accepted his op-ed article for their "Viewpoints" page. In it he told American Christians why they should oppose Kissinger's policies.

> ... The ultimate interest of America and its Christian citizen is to make absolutely sure that both individual and country will be able to satisfactorily answer the awesome question, "Did you aid or prevent the coming of the Kingdom of Heaven?"
>
> ... The final redemption and the Kingdom of Heaven with their era of eternal peace are inexorably tied to the Jewish people ... to the return of the Jewish people to its land, the ingathering of the exiles, the resurrection of the Jewish state.
>
> ... The Jewish people WILL come back to Zion and the land WILL be Jewish in its entirety – that is certain. The only question will be whether the United States and the Christians within it will understand their role and obligation in this magnificent and incredible era of the beginning of the redemption....[52]

Newsday printed another op-ed article by Meir two months later, after Israel and Egypt had agreed to Kissinger's plan for Israel to cede the Sinai to Egypt. Since the agreement had to be ratified by Congress, Meir argued that Congress should vote against it purely on the basis of America's own interests, but he also reasoned that it was a prescription for Israeli disaster.

The recently signed Sinai retreat will lead to war and tragedy.... What Israel did – as it collapsed before the Ford-Kissinger pressure – was to give up two vital passes (Gidi and Mitla) ... whose ridges enabled them to be defended with relatively small forces. Losing the passes means that many more troops – perhaps as much as a division more – will have to be deployed and the added days of military service each year only deepen the morale problem for Israel reservists.

... Losing the oil fields means that Israel gives up fully 65 per cent of its domestic needs [and has] an ever greater dependence on the United States.... There are so many things wrong about this agreement to retreat! There are so many questions that are obvious and which have no answers to them. What if Congress balks at giving Israel all that Kissinger promised? What if the legislators listen to their constituents and ask why the cities face bankruptcy with no federal relief available, while Israel receives billions?

What possible value is there to an agreement Egypt refuses to negotiate face-to-face? ... Why the secret clauses? What value is there to Egyptian concessions that they cannot publicly declare? ... And what meaning is there to the vaunted Egyptian (secret) pledge to refrain from hostilities for three years when it will be up to HER to decide whether Israel "began the hostilities?"

The agreement included stationing American technicians in a no-man's land in Sinai between the Israelis and the Egyptians, where they would operate electronic monitoring posts to observe troop movements. This, Meir said, would be a catastrophe, and Congress should not approve the plan.

... Fortunately, the plan is truly a bad one for American interests. One of the great concerns that has been voiced ... by the president is that a Middle East war might lead to an American-Soviet confrontation. There is nothing more likely to lead to such a clash than the introduction of American personnel into the region. Out of American interests, if nothing else, the plan should be defeated....[53]

In another appeal to Christian fundamentalists, Meir organized "a coalition of politically concerned Jewish and Protestant clergymen ... to lobby against the White House's erosion of Israel's security and Biblical integrity..." He issued a press release saying that the clergymen oppose the commitment of American technicians, and will offer incontrovertible arguments that President Ford's plan to reduce the borders of Israel is contrary to Divine Biblical decree. The clergymen would hold a press conference at the offices of AJAF on September 2, and Meir would participate.[54]

Meir was again disregarding prison rules with his public announcement that he would attend the AJAF press conference on September 2.[55] Four months had passed since Judge Weinstein's ruling extending Meir's stay at the halfway house until he was given kosher food at the federal prison in Allenwood. After all that time, the Court of Appeals had not yet heard the Bureau of Prisons' brief contesting that ruling. Meir hoped his blatant disregard of halfway house rules would speed up the appeals process. He was confident that the Court of Appeals would decide that kosher food was a constitutional right for all Jewish prisoners.

But Meir's primary reason for taking part in the AJAF press conference was to do his utmost for the security and welfare of the State of Israel. He urged supporters to press their congressmen to vote against the clause in the Sinai agreement that called for American technicians to man surveillance posts: "If Congress will not agree to this clause, then the entire agreement will fall. We must dedicate ourselves to that task."[56]

Chapter 44

Public Lectures (June-August 1975)

THE NEW GROUPS, Shuva, AJAF and CAIR, were considered standing committees of the JDL, like its Speakers Bureau, Oppressed Jewry Committee and Legal Committee. Meir's connection with them was made clear at a fundraising event in June. The invitation to the event said, "... Every evening I am allowed out of prison for three hours for dinner and prayers. On Tuesday, June 17, I am skipping dinner and will instead plead to you for your support." Pledge cards handed out at that event said:

> I pledge that Israel will live, and hereby contribute $ ___ to that end. I wish my donation to be used in the following critical area:
> ___ CAIR Committee Against Israeli Retreat
> ___ AJAF American Jews Against Ford
> ___ SHUVA Aliya Movement
> ___ J.I.C. Jewish Identity Center[1]

Each of the groups occupied its own space in an office building at 1133 Broadway, but JDL had the largest area. Like earlier JDL headquarters, it was utilitarian, stripped down to basics. A contemporary writer described it:

> ... A tiny anteroom: a desk, a mimeograph machine on a table with stacks of white and pink paper; raw wood shelves piled with handbills and newspaper reprints. On the wall opposite, an almost closed door with a [JDL] poster taped to it.... the shabby, cluttered office with its wall maps of the city and the world, a blackboard easel, stacks of books and papers, cartons.[2]

Enthusiasm and Efficiency in the JDL

Russel Kelner directed the JDL office in New York. Formerly director of JDL in Philadelphia, his move to New York, at Meir's urging, coincided with Meir's return to the States in August 1974. Kelner ran the office with energy and efficiency. He instituted a system of coding flyers that made them easy to store and retrieve. For example, in the code N-PS-275-1, N stood for national office, PS for *Pidyon Shvuyim* [freeing prisoners], 275 for February 1975, and 1 indicated that this was the first document under code N-PS for that month/year.[3]

Kelner prepared a mimeographed diagram headed "Telephone Squad Schematic: JDL Phone Chain" for summoning members to activities. It said, "The chain must never be broken. If the person called is not in, skip his/her name and continue the chain. Make that person's calls for him. Some Jewish life may depend on your call."[4]

To promote efficiency and accountability, he made demands on the members:

> A committee report must be submitted by each committee chairman every week.... Include:
> A. Copies of letters and other matter produced by the committee, for central filing in the National Office.
> B. Information to be filed in central information files (e.g. intelligence on anti-Semites, names of new volunteer lawyers, names of potential donors, PR contacts in the media, charts on leaflet distribution points, resource information, etc.)[5]

Kelner was meticulous about detail. Preparations for the JDL convention included the exact time allotted to each speaker. At the "Solidarity Sunday" parade for Soviet Jewry, he assigned exact parade positions to each member. Kelner's letter to Abe Levine said, "... The JDL position in the parade is Section F ... Your personal position is number 54..."[6]

JDL youth and their education remained Meir's priority. Besides karate lessons, the newly opened JDL Training Center at 227 West 29 Street offered courses on personalities in Jewish history, the Bible and the Hebrew language. Teenager Joy Greenblum, who was in charge of the educational program, maintained a library with a good selection of books on the course material.[7]

JDL continued to hold demonstrations for Soviet Jews. On July 15, the day of the joint U.S.-Soviet launch of the Apollo-Soyuz space mission, JDLers burned an eight-foot high cardboard rocket model outside the Soviet Mission to the U.N. They protested the détente symbolized by the joint mission and charged the Soviet Union with imprisoning 250 Jews for wanting to immigrate to Israel. Later that month JDLers staged a sit-in at the Finnish Consulate in New York to protest a meeting of the European Security Conference in Helsinki, which was about to legitimize Soviet hegemony over Eastern Europe and much of Central Europe.[8]

Abe Levine recalled a spontaneous JDL demonstration:

> It was *chol hamoed* Pesach [the intermediate days of Passover], rainy and cold. Around ten o'clock at night, I get a call from Charlie Cohen – "I just saw on TV that the Russians will not allow the Jews into the synagogue in Moscow and

we're having a demo at two o'clock." I said, "Okay, I'll be there at two o'clock tomorrow." He said, "No, two o'clock tonight."

There must have been fifteen or twenty people there. Someone threw paint at a policeman. They arrested us all. We had nothing to eat, because it was Pesach. My two boys came to take me out of jail. Ironic – a switch.[9]

Most JDL members were not wealthy, and JDL fundraising efforts did not keep pace with expenses. There were some "big" donors, such as those who underwrote the costs of reprinting *Time to Go Home* and renting office space, but costs always exceeded income. The following letter to supporters is an example of Meir's constant concern with fundraising:

During the six years of our existence we have never known how to ask for money to sustain ourselves and keep our organization alive.

... We have a backlog of unpaid bills in excess of $54,000.... We are asking you to help us in this financial emergency.

Particularly in these times, it is necessary for Jews to be well informed and prepared to act when forces threaten the peace and stability of our people.

... We appeal to you. Please help us to help Jews![10]

Meir saved this reply from one contributor:

Enclosed find my contribution of $100 as MY investment in Jewish survival under your superb leadership and guidance.

I, for one, Rabbi, recognize your devotion and many sacrifices on behalf of all the Jewish people. Please accept my sincerest thanks for your untiring efforts in your search for security and well-being of our people.[11]

JDL women worked at fundraising, and even held their own protests. Yetta Lebowitz recalled:

Once, Alexander's Department Store was selling pocketbooks made in one of the Arab countries. Three of us went in and started to drop them on the floor.[12]

We all became very good friends, and we felt WE WERE DOING something. We had a rummage store on Grand Street and we ran booths at flea markets in Flatbush to raise money for JDL.[13]

Camp Jedel: Jewish Minds to Match Jewish Fists

The successful reopening of Camp Jedel in 1975, after a hiatus of four years, was largely due to Meir's uninterrupted presence in New York, which attracted numerous young people to JDL. Members of the executive board undertook to find a campsite and entered negotiations to purchase the former Camp Aishel in the Catskills. When they realized they could not afford to buy, they rented the grounds of the former Camp Da-Ro in New York's Hudson Valley.[14]

To cover camp expenses, Meir sent this entreaty to supporters:

> ... The JDL has been in existence for six years. We have never enjoyed the financial support, nor the financial security, of our most prestigious organizations. We need the support of people who feel as we do...
>
> We have a training center where we train our young people and ... a summer camp ... where our youth will be physically and mentally trained with an intensity to match the crisis we are facing as Jews. We train them so that their Jewish minds will match their Jewish fists.
>
> We have begun classes in ideology, Jewish history and Jewish nationalism, and this summer the Jewish Identity Center will be operative on the premises of Camp Jedel. These carefully selected young people, after completion of our leadership training program, will become the leaders needed to teach our people on college campuses how to debate the leftists, Arabs, radical rightists and other groups that threaten Jewish survival.
>
> ... We ask you to arrange gatherings of friends at your home and we will send a spokesman for the camp to explain the program.
>
> ... Please do not fail us. Donate generously. Without your support we will fail. By helping us you are helping Jews.[15]

The camp was advertised in JDL publications and in flyers distributed at demonstrations and lectures. A *Jewish Press* ad about the camp was headed "Learn Jewish Pride and Leadership." A drawing showed youngsters doing karate exercises alongside a young man with a book open before him. The campers would receive "intensive physical training in self-defense and seminar training in the understanding of extremist groups, history of Jewish resistance and Jewish pride, countering the extremist left and radical right on college campuses and in high schools." The ad called the camp "the proudest and most unique camp in America." One flyer with a similar text specified: "Young men age 13-21. Eight weeks in the Catskills, $500. Glatt kosher."[16]

Camp Jedel of 1975 was different from the camps held in 1969, 1970, and 1971, where all campers participated in all activities. This time, there were two separate groups. One, attended by high school-age teenagers and led by Garth Kravat, emphasized physical training, karate and rifle practice. The second, for college-age youth, directed by David Fisch, was the Jewish Identity Center, where campers attended ideological and academic lectures. About twice a week, Kravat led Fisch's group in rifle practice and Fisch gave lectures to Kravat's group. The entire camp had meals and prayers together and all attended flag raising, where they sang *Hatikvah* and the JDL anthem.[17]

To recruit campers for the leadership training section, Fisch sent a four-page letter to selected JDL teenagers.

This "form" letter, which is being sent to only 20 people, is my best way of asking you to make a major decision – one which will affect your life and, per-haps, the lives of hundreds of young Jews you will meet in the future.

... We have run only one such school before; that was in the summer of 1972.... I went... The school changed my life. It taught me a lot and trained me in JDL leadership.... Do yourself a favor, and maybe do a generation of your brothers and sisters a favor.[18]

A flyer for the program, headed "Young Revolutionaries Wanted On Cam-pus," listed the qualifications required for admittance to the program:

1. Their intelligence must be high and their grades very good.
2. Their leadership potential must be such that they will, with training, be capable of leading and commanding a following.
3. Their agreement with the basic ideas of Rabbi Kahane and the Jewish Identity Center.
4. Their solemn pledge that after the course, they will undertake to work in their schools or elsewhere to spread the Jewish Idea as they have learned it so as to create proud, knowledgeable and activist Jews.[19]

Campers came from all over the United States: Los Angeles, San Francisco, Chicago, Miami, New Jersey and Connecticut – and even from Great Britain. Dan Gottlieb of Miami recalled that after he heard Meir speak in Miami and read *Never Again,* he tried to set up a JDL chapter at the University of Miami but failed. He used to buy the *Jewish Press* regularly in Miami to read Meir's col-umns. He read about the camp and signed up. The leadership training he received at the camp made a real difference for him. When he returned to Miami after attending the camp, he set up a JDL chapter on campus. It was very active in Soviet Jewish affairs and in urging the local Jewish Federation to budget money for Jewish education. Another camper from Miami, who worked side by side with Dan, was Menachem Gottlieb (no relation). Menachem recalled that he was in the physical training program of the camp for four weeks and moved over to the J.I.C. leadership part for the last four weeks. "The lectures were excellent."[20]

Looking back on the leadership course, Fisch wrote:

The Jewish Identity Center consisted of eight hours of lectures daily – in Jewish history, Bible, Halakha [Jewish law], JDL ideology, leadership/activism train-ing, etc. There were book reports, heavy nightly readings in the library, exten-sive written exams, etc. None of the karate stuff – just classes and, perhaps, some riflery.

That program was a highlight in my life. The graduates were everything that Meir hoped for/dreamed of – but never expected. We graduated real JDL lead-ers, who could read, think, make trouble creatively, etc. Several went back to their campuses or cities and made everyone crazy.

If we had followed up three years in a row, we would have had something extraordinary.[21]

Funds for the camp were in short supply. The *Jewish Defense League Bulletin* noted: "Despite a valiant effort by Garth Kravat to cut red tape and procure food and supplies within just a couple of weeks before the opening, the program is running at an impoverished level. Donations of food and ammunition are desperately needed."[22] David Fisch wrote about the meals solicited for the campers by JDL members.

There was a kosher Chinese restaurant in Brooklyn – Shang Chai – that donated dinner one night each week. They had a once-weekly "All You Can Eat" smorgasbord. They donated the leftovers to us and someone would drive it in. It was unbelievably great stuff.[23]

Yetta Lebowitz recalled:

We used to collect food for the camp on Thursday nights. Shang Chai gave us all their leftovers and we got cake and *challah* [a special Shabbat bread] from a bakery on Avenue P.[24]

Mealtime at camp was a time for lively singing. Campers sang Betar songs such as *Song of the Parabellum* and *The East Bank of the Jordan*, as well as popular Israeli songs such as *Jerusalem of Gold*. These, together with the JDL anthem, were printed in the *Camp Jedel Songbook: Songs from the Underground, Camp JEDEL and Other Fun Songs*.[25]

David Fisch recalled "KGB Night," a way of teaching campers to empathize with Soviet Jews:

… In the middle of the night, we would rush into a bunk of four or six people, wake them all up, and pick on one. We'd look at the victim, speak in Russian accents, and accuse the kid of having Hebrew books. I was surprised at how effective this corny exercise was. Some kids denied having Hebrew books in order to stop being roughed-up. When they would be left alone and the "KGB" would go to the next kid in the bunk and accuse him of having Hebrew books, some bunks evolved into, one-by-one, denials of having Hebrew books. Others stood up [to the pressure]. At 3 A.M., we debriefed and talked about the experience and what it must be like to be a Soviet Jew.[26]

Baruch Ben Yosef recalled an incident that brought the camp publicity:

At a certain point, the locals began driving by at night, shouting out "Kill the Jews" or something of the sort. Several [campers] were upset that nothing was being done to stop it, so they took the initiative and set up an ambush.[27]

Fisch, who came on the scene in its midst, recalled:

I was in the library of the J.I.C. section, supervising nighttime study hall, when

I heard the noise. By the time my crew got to the front, we saw four teens on the ground, arms pinned behind their backs.... We let them go after they were roughed up, and they were warned not to come back.

Next day, the media came down. It hit the *Poughkeepsie Journal* Sunday paper; the AP or UPI spread it cross-country, and then everyone wanted to come down. The camp got lots of coverage, and I did two radio talk shows.[28]

A reporter from the *Poughkeepsie Journal* interviewed campers:

... One of the participants,[29] Ellen Greenblum, 16, said.... "I'm here to learn to defend myself better and to be able to defend Jews in the streets." ... Andy Green [Baruch Ben Yosef], 16, of the Bronx, said he planned to live in Israeli-occupied territory west of the Jordan. "The West Bank belongs rightfully to the Jews," he said. "The Arabs have no right to the land." [30]

At the end of the program, members of the leadership training course returned to their communities to practice what they had learned. In Miami, Dan Gottlieb and Menachem Gottlieb put their leadership training to immediate use. They demonstrated at the Greater Miami Jewish Federation headquarters to demand more funding for Jewish education. A September news report said:

Several young Miami Jews, dressed in traditional white Yom Kippur gowns, symbolically reenacted a famous biblical battle in front of the Greater Miami Jewish Federation headquarters Sunday, chanting about discrimination against Jewish education. Dan Gottlieb said, "Without Jewish education we don't survive."[31]

Another report pictured Dan chained to the doors of the Miami Jewish Federation while Menachem held a poster that proclaimed, "Yeshivas Must Survive."[32]

Camp Jedel graduates in New Jersey cut gasoline pump hoses at ten Gulf Oil service stations in the North Jersey area. A caller told the AP news agency that they were protesting donations by the Gulf Oil Company of $50 million dollars over the last three years to Arab propaganda efforts.[33]

Among the protests held by camp graduates in New York were these:

- A sit-in September at the offices of New York's Senator Jacob Javits, demanding that he vote against Kissinger's plan to send American technicians to the Middle East as part of Israel's surrender of the Sinai.[34]

- In December, JDLers followed U.N. personnel shouting "Free Syrian Jewry." They demanded the United Nations "do for the oppressed Jews of Syria that which they are doing for the so-called Palestinians."[35]

- They continued to protest the oppression of Soviet Jewry. At the premier performance of the Moscow Circus in December, JDLers shouting "Never Again!" threw eggs and paint on stage. A few days later, at a hockey game between the New York Rangers and the Soviet Army team, they threw eggs onto the ice, interrupting the game for a short time.[36]

Not A Model Prisoner

Contrary to halfway house rules, Meir continued to lecture to the public. If he were a model prisoner, the Bureau of Prisons might allow his term to expire without dealing with the kosher food issue, so he continued to prod them to expedite the appeals process. He knew that a victory in the Court of Appeals would mean his transfer to Allenwood Federal Prison, but his primary aim was to achieve a court ruling that kosher food was a constitutional right for all Jewish prisoners.

Every Thursday evening, during his supper hour leave, Meir gave Jewish Identity Center seminars and in July and August he advertised:

> Invite Rabbi Meir Kahane to speak in your home
> The most exciting Jewish ideological voice of our time
> Speaking on Aliya and the Jewish future in the United States.[37]

He also spoke at synagogues and colleges during his brief leaves. His lecture on June 9 at the Young Israel of Ocean Parkway in Brooklyn was scheduled to begin at 7:45 P.M. Metropolitan coordinator Berryl Septimus informed JDL members: "Rabbi Kahane is allowed out of prison for his meals. He must be back at 10 P.M. We would therefore appreciate it if you would be there on time, as the Rabbi will be having his dinner with us." On Shabbatot, he was invited to the homes of people who lived within walking distance of the halfway house, and was often invited to speak at their synagogues. On Shabbat, June 14, he spoke on "The Importance of Jewish Activism" at the Lincoln Square Synagogue and its rabbi, Shlomo Riskin, invited him to his home for the Shabbat meal.[38]

At the end of June he named some of the Orthodox Jews who lived near the halfway house in Manhattan and hosted him on Shabbat. Some of them did not agree with all his views, but invited him to their homes because of the respect they had for his devotion to Jewish causes and to fulfill the precept of hospitality.

> Betty [wife of his cousin Rabbi Solomon Kahane] got out of the hospital and I still eat there off and on ... also at [Rabbi Shlomo] Riskin and [Rabbi Haskel] Lookstein and [Jacob and Claire] Dienstag (regards) and others.[39]

Although he was trying to make good use of his time, Meir wanted to be free. On June 2 he wrote home, "We are filing a motion for reduction of sentence this week. I will let you know." According to the rules of federal criminal procedure, a judge could reduce a sentence within 120 days after sentencing. Meir had been sentenced on February 21, so on June 11 attorney Barry Slotnick presented a Motion for Reduction of Sentence. It was heard on June 17.[40]

At the hearing, Weinstein was visibly moved when told that Meir had received a letter from his eight-year-old son asking him to run away and come home. But he rejected Slotnick's motion to reduce Meir's jail sentence so he could return to his family in Jerusalem. He had no authority to change the sentence because the matter was now before the Second Circuit Court of Appeals.[41]

Meir was not granted a reduction of sentence, but he would soon be technically eligible for parole. He wrote:

> The Judge has refused to act on my application.... Meanwhile, we have applied to the Parole Board for a reduction and I will let you know what happens there.[42]

Meir's yearning to come home is evident in a letter to the children.

> This week marked the fourth complete month of my imprisonment and the sixth month that I have been away from you and I miss you so very much. What is more, I really do not know when I will be able to come home because I do not know if I will get parole before the sentence ends....[43]

In an unsigned news item, Meir asked readers of the *Jewish Press* to write letters to the U.S. Board of Parole.

> On July 17, Kahane became technically eligible for parole and the government has vigorously recommended that he be kept in jail. An Emergency Committee for the Parole of Meir Kahane has been formed and its officials have asked all who can to write to the U.S. Board of Parole ... pointing out that Kahane is a political prisoner and has already been separated from his family for half a year.[44]

One week later, a notice in the *Jewish Press* said that the Parole Board hearing on Meir's case would be held during the week of August 25. It, too, requested readers to write letters asking for clemency for him. The hearing was inconclusive: The Parole Board gave Meir a score of 9 points out of 11 on the objective standard test, but handed the case over to the Regional Parole Board because his "situation is so controversial."[45]

One of the reasons for the parole board's indecision may have been Meir's participation, shown on TV, in a JDL demonstration against Arab terror on July 8. Meir surely could not keep still after a terrorist bomb exploded in Jerusalem's Zion Square on Friday, July 4, at the height of the pre-Sabbath shopping rush hour. It was Jerusalem's bloodiest terrorist incident since the founding of the State, killing fifteen and injuring more than seventy. Meir wrote to the children:

> We are all shocked at the bombing and I only regret that the government did not do the two things I called for, and for which I am in prison – counterterror and Arab emigration. Had they done so, a great many Jews would be alive and well today.[46]

The JDL issued a press release announcing a prayer vigil at the El Al offices in Manhattan on July 8 at 12 noon, during Meir's lunch break. "Rabbi Meir Kahane will lead the service and outline the JDL program," said the announcement. The press release included Meir's oft-repeated message that only brutal counterterror could be effective against Arab terror. The quiet prayer vigil turned into a loud protest march through Manhattan's streets and was fully covered by the media. "On 7-Hour Furlough, Kahane Leads Protest," said one headline.[47]

The U.S. Bureau of Prisons Acts

The next day, July 9, Meir received a memo headed *Revised Sign-In/Sign-Out Schedule*. It reduced his daily free time from 7½ hours to 4½ hours. Before mailing it to me to place in his files, Meir wrote at the top of the memo, "I took part in a demonstration against Arab terror and it was on TV and in the papers. The government was angry and limited my hours. I still do mine...."[48]

In a letter to Matthew Walsh, director of the halfway house, he protested the reduction.

> In reference to the change in my hours, I bring to your attention the fact that during the summer, the sun sets between 8 and 8.20 P.M. The afternoon and evening services are, therefore, sandwiched between that period. Thus, between services and the need to eat and travel to a kosher restaurant, there is a minimum of 2½ hours needed.
>
> This is therefore a formal request for 2½ to 3 hours time off in the evening.[49]

Matthew Walsh replied:

> Your request is denied. Your repeated disregard for curfew limits and your failure to abide by agreement necessitated closer restrictions on your time. You are now being allowed 1½ hours in the evening and I consider that sufficient time to eat.[50]

Angrily, on July 14 Meir wrote to Walsh:

> While you, regretfully, have the legal power to make decisions regarding prisoners in your jurisdiction, I find the tone of your reply to my request of July 10th totally unacceptable both in itself as well as against the contemptuous reply background of our conversation on the eve of the holiday of Shavuot when you evidenced total disregard for Jewish religious criteria.
>
> At that time you told me – in response to my statement that restaurants would be closed for the holiday – that "you can eat hardboiled eggs." Now, you totally overlooked my statement that 1½ hours of free time in the evening could not possibly serve both for prayer and travel to eat in a kosher restaurant with a reply that ignored the part of prayer.

> Both in the reply and general tone of your conversation I detect more than a little anti-Semitism and I want you to know that I am not prepared to allow the matter to rest.[51]

Meir's breaks for meals and prayers were recorded daily on the "Resident Check Out/In Sheet." A member of the staff had to initial the hour Meir left, his destination and the time he expected to return.[52]

Meir put a news item into the *Jewish Press,* which reported that since his hours outside the halfway house had been cut, he did not have enough time for prayers. It said, "Kahane deliberately disobeyed the new guidelines, claiming they were illegal, and was cited a number of times for 'violations.'"[53]

Meir's attorney, Barry Slotnick, filed a motion in federal court to hold the Department of Justice and various officials at the halfway house in contempt of court. Slotnick said that the Bureau of Prisons had "willfully committed an outrageous violation of law in its arrogant refusal to obey a direct court order stating that Rabbi Kahane be given sufficient time for both eating and prayers."

Meir said he did not intend to comply with the "illegal" rules and he continued to take the same amount of time as he had before, despite numerous reprimands. He said, "Walsh will learn that Jews will not be easily intimidated."[54]

Meir's conflict with the authorities interested the media. Reporters even phoned the halfway house to set up interviews with him. One message slip, dated August 4, said, "... Mr. Gil Fox, WINS Radio ... asked that you return his call by 11 P.M." Another, dated August 5, said, "Herb Young, WPIX News ... wants interview."[55]

Meir suspected that they were opening his mail at the halfway house. On August 4, he advised me to address my letters to my brother's home. A few days later, he wrote:

> I am in a battle with the government which wants to send me to Allenwood because I am organizing and doing things. I will send over various clippings to let you follow the "exciting" battle. As always, it is a good sign that we are getting under their skin.[56]

The government was not long in acting. On August 4, U.S. Attorney David Trager called a press conference to announce that he had petitioned the Court of Appeals to override Judge Weinstein's ruling guaranteeing kosher food. At the hearing, scheduled for August 12, he would ask the court to send Meir to Allenwood prison immediately. Trager told reporters that Meir "checked in late eighteen times in two weeks.... He comes and goes as he pleases, in violation of the rules of the halfway house."

Trager showed reporters the affidavit submitted by Matthew Walsh, halfway house director:

[Kahane] has continuously refused to comply with our sign-out request, asserting travel congestion as his excuse for daytime lateness, but offering no excuse for tardy evening arrivals.

During a two week period, Kahane checked in late eighteen times.... Without any advance warning, Kahane holds news conferences at the center and conducted a seminar there.[57]

Meir responded at a press conference on August 7 at Gefen's Dairy Restaurant, a kosher restaurant where he frequently ate. A photo taken there dramatizes Meir's loneliness. It shows Meir before the reporters arrived, seated at a table by himself, surrounded by empty tables. At the press conference, Meir said, "The obvious reason for the government's agitation is the increasing success of my activities along with other Jewish activists." He freely admitted that he used his meals and time off to plan demonstrations and activities.[58]

Attorney Barry Slotnick told the *Jewish Press* that the government had successfully denied other Jewish prisoners the right to kosher food and was eager to do the same to Kahane. He urged readers to attend the hearing at the Federal Courthouse in Manhattan on August 12 at 9:30 A.M.[59]

To Meir's great relief, the Court of Appeals referred the matter back to Judge Weinstein, and Weinstein reaffirmed his original order for Meir to remain in New York until he could be guaranteed kosher food in Allenwood.[60]

Meir continued to be absent from the halfway house for more time than he was allowed. An Incident Report on August 13 said, "He signed out at 7:30 A.M., should have been back by 9. As of 10:30 A.M., he has not contacted the Center. Put on A.W.O.L. status." On August 27, he received a similar Incident Report: "Signed out at 7 A.M. to return at 8.30. As of 9.50 A.M., he has not contacted the Center. A.W.O.L. status."[61]

Congressman Mario Biaggi tried to help. He wrote to U.S. Attorney General Edward Levi, complaining about prison officials' harassment of Meir.

... When he engaged in criticism of the administration, prison officials arbitrarily and unilaterally cut the time for prayer to four and one-half hours. This is not sufficient time for him to complete his services. Thus he has now been returning to his cell late and is being noted as being in violation of regulations.

... He was never late under the seven and one half hour rule, but now he is always late. Thus, when it comes time to consider him for parole ... he will have a series of violations that will jeopardize his parole and early release.[62]

The High Holidays were early that year. When Meir received a furlough to spend them at my brother's home, his instructions were specific. He could leave the halfway house just before sundown and had to return shortly after sundown. The application said: "September 5, 4 P.M. to September 7, 10 P.M. [Rosh Hashana]; September 14, 4 P.M. to September 15, 10 P.M. [Yom Kippur]." On the

Sukkot holiday, he walked to the Fifth Avenue synagogue, about a mile away. Since most of its members lived in apartment houses and could not build their own *sukkot*, they built a large *sukkah* at the synagogue and invited Meir to partake of the catered meals with them.[63]

Meir's use of this *sukkah* led to another Incident Report. It said, "Scheduled to return at 8:30 P.M., did not return until 10:55 P.M. He said he attended a religious ceremony of holiday of Tabernacles [Sukkot]. Admitted he did not inform staff in advance and failed to request extended curfew."[64]

On August 12, immediately after the decision of the Court of Appeals, Meir wrote home:

> I have won the court fight. The government moved to have Weinstein's decision on kosher food struck down for lack of jurisdiction and they lost – again. So the kosher ruling stays, and so do I, in New York.
>
> Of course, all these victories do not compensate for the fact that I cannot be home with you. But that will come, soon enough, *be'ezrat Hashem* [with G-d's help].
>
> ... I feel well enough and eat green vegetables every day. Maybe that is why I am getting fat. I miss you so much that I sometimes get depressed.

There were other problems at the halfway house: Some of the residents took things that were not theirs. Meir wrote:

> ... Please URGENTLY contact Eisenbach and say that the tickets from KLM and Sabena (Sabena was the substitute) were stolen from my room. Please have him do something immediately and have HIM personally write to me to let me know what I should do.[65]

Meir's letter to our son Baruch about his "victory" had a different emphasis:

> I have just won another round in my continuing struggle with the government that wants to send me away to Pennsylvania. I only wish that I could do as much "harm" as they think I can. The Sinai retreat is apparently definite and the pity is that even those who oppose a retreat from [other parts of the Land of Israel] do not realize the tragedy and *issur* [prohibition] of a retreat in the Sinai. Any retreat before *goyim* [non-Jews] which is brought about because of fear and weakness is a *chillul Hashem* that desecrates the great *kedusha* [holiness] of the Six Day War.... Jews pay for their sins by suffering the NATURAL CONSEQUENCES OF THEIR ACTIONS. In this case, the retreat will weaken us terribly and make the next war and suffering that much worse.[66]

Meir wrote many letters to the children that year. They were full of love and his concern that they grow up to be good Jews.

Chapter 45
A Prisoner Writes
(February-December 1975)

Letters to the Children

THE CHILDREN WERE always in Meir's thoughts. In his frequent letters to them he sought to impart Jewish values and concepts. He emphasized the importance of Torah study and discussed episodes in Jewish and Zionist history to give them a sense of Jewish national identity, and he taught them moral lessons.[1]

Meir's pedagogic bent is especially apparent in his letters to our youngest, Binyamin, age nine. He always wrote to Binyamin in Hebrew because Binyamin's school did not teach English. It was only in seventh grade that he learned to read and write English. In one letter, Meir wrote:

> I was happy to hear that you are such a good pupil and that you recite Psalms every Shabbat. If you recite Psalms with deep faith, you can bring the Messiah sooner. Together with this, you must give charity every morning when you wake up. The Messiah will come because the Jewish people give charity.
>
> I am working here to prevent a retreat from parts of our land because it is forbidden to give any part of the Holy Land to non-Jews and because it is a desecration of G-d's name.
>
> Now, I want to ask you some questions [on the Book of Judges], and we'll see if you can answer them:
> 1) What was the name of the High Priest when Samuel [the Prophet] was young?
> 2) What clothes did the High Priest wear?
> 3) How did the High Priest die?
> 4) What was the name of the first king and from what tribe was he?
> 5) What happened to the Jews in Yavesh Gil'ad?

The letter ended with the reminder, "Be a good boy and listen to your mother."[1]

Meir's next letter praised Binyamin's correct and precise replies to the questions, and asked him to write a composition on charity. "After that," requested Meir, "write a composition on 'Why I Should Love the Creator.'" Meir explained, "When I receive the compositions, I'll give you a mark, and we'll have a 'school' where I am the teacher and you are the pupil." He urged him to memorize verses of the Bible:

> I hope you are learning verses from the Bible by heart, because a boy your age can easily learn things by heart, and what you learn by heart when you are young, you will never forget.

He went on:

> I want to tell you a story that can teach you something important:
>
> One cold, wintry day, a poor man came to the home of the rabbi of his town. "I'm so very cold," he cried. "My wife and children are freezing and I don't have money to buy wood to heat our house." (In those days they did not have central heating like we do.) The rabbi was very moved by the poor man's words and decided to go to one of the rich men in the town to ask for money for this unfortunate man. The problem was that this rich man was very stingy and never wanted to give charity even though he had a lot of money. But the rabbi decided to try.
>
> As he walked to the home of the rich man, the cold was intense and it was snowing so heavily that he could hardly see two feet ahead of him. Several times he fell in the deep snow. Finally he arrived at the home of the rich man, completely frozen and covered from head to toe in snow.
>
> He knocked and the rich man opened the door. He was amazed to see the rabbi out in such terrible weather. "Come in, honored rabbi," he said. But the rabbi did not enter. He stood outside and started to speak: "How do you do, Reb Asher. (That was the rich man's name.) I came to ask for a donation for a poor Jew who does not have enough money to buy wood to heat his home."
>
> "Okay, okay," said Reb Asher, his teeth chattering from the cold. "But we can talk about this inside. Honored rabbi, please come in."
>
> But the rabbi did not move. He continued to stand outside in the snow and the wind and the cold and said, "The poor man is so unfortunate. His home is so cold, and his little children are shivering."
>
> "Honored rabbi," begged the stingy rich man, "I understand, but why do you have to tell me all this outside, while both of us are freezing? Please come in. The cold is killing me."
>
> "No," said the rabbi. "Only this way, when you are shivering from the cold, can you begin to understand the problem of the poor Jew. If we were inside, in your warm house, you would not be able to feel the pain of the poor man."
>
> And now, since you are a smart boy, you can understand the point. Every Jew must try to FEEL the pain of his fellow Jew even if he himself is content

and untroubled. I hope you will always fulfill the commandment to love your
fellow Jews as yourself and try to feel the pain of your fellow Jew.[2]

Another letter to Binyamin taught a similar lesson, but had an added dimension.

> Once, some Jews boarded a ship to sail to a distant country. Suddenly, a few
> of them noticed that another Jew was banging at the bottom of the ship with a
> hammer. "What are you doing?" they shouted at him.
> "I'm making a hole in the ship," he answered.
> "What! Do you want to sink us all?"
> "What do you care?" he asked them. "I'm making a hole on my side, not
> on yours."
> "Fool!" they cried out. "Don't you understand that when you make a hole
> on your side of the ship, the entire ship will sink!"

"What is the lesson?" asked Meir, and he answered:

> Every Jew must imagine that he is on a ship. If one Jew is in trouble – if there
> is a "hole" in the ship – the others must not leave him to suffer, just because
> he's on "the other side," because otherwise, the whole ship will sink. What is
> more, if one Jew sins, we must admonish him and teach him Torah, or G-d will
> punish us all.[3]

These stories succinctly expressed the principle that motivated Meir throughout his life. He took to heart the rule "Every Jew is responsible for all other Jews"
(*Talmud, Shvu'ot 39a*). He did all he could to help a Jew who was in trouble, and
he did not hesitate to admonish and reprove his fellow Jews.

In a letter on Binyamin's ninth birthday, Meir explained his absence from
home:

> In answer to your question about when I am coming home, it is hard to know.
> I hope it will be very soon, but you have to understand that it is not a simple
> matter. I'll explain, and since you're already a big boy, you'll surely under-
> stand.
> There are two types of prisoners. One is a real criminal, a thief, a robber,
> etc. On the other hand, there are people who violated non-Jewish laws because
> they wanted to fulfill the Commandments of the Torah. I wanted to help our
> Jewish brothers in Russia who are oppressed by the non-Jews there, and the
> only way was *la'asot shefatim* [harassing the Russians]. And, in fact, we were
> successful in pressuring the Russians and forcing them to let thousands of Jews
> leave Russia. But the American government found me guilty of violating its
> laws and sent me to prison. You must realize that this kind of imprisonment is
> actually an honor.
> If you think a bit, you'll be able to count several great Jews who were
> imprisoned, or whom non-Jews killed because they stood up for principles. For

example, our father Abraham, who was cast into the fiery furnace; Jeremiah the Prophet, who was thrown into the pit; Rabbi Akiva, who was imprisoned because he taught Torah; and many more.

With a little patience, you'll see that the time will pass quickly, I'll return home, and we'll play together.[4]

He praised Binyamin for the excellent report card he sent him (VERY GOOD in every subject) and again wrote about the importance of learning Torah:

When you light the Chanuka candles, remember why the Maccabees fought the Greeks: because Antiochus did not allow the Jews to keep the Commandments. How? By outlawing the learning of Torah. He knew that if the Jews would not learn Torah, they would not know how to keep the Commandments. The lesson is clear. Every Jew must learn and learn and learn Torah until his entire soul is filled with the words of the Torah....[5]

Learning Torah was the major topic in Meir's letters to Baruch. He urged him to devote himself to it. On Baruch's sixteenth birthday, he wrote:

... You, with your G-d-given head and talents, DARE NOT escape from the task that you must undertake. Your job and role in life is to be a *talmid chakham* [Torah scholar] of the highest possible magnitude so as to speak the ideas which I have tried to give you and which the Jewish people must hear and thus avert tragedy. I cannot do what you can do because I am not the Torah scholar that you can and must be.

This is why it is so important that you dedicate your life to this role and this is why I spend so much time seeking the best possible ways for you to learn more and better. A private *rebbe* [teacher] who is good is the only way to advance. Remember, your life is not yours alone, but belongs to the Jewish people.[6]

And in another letter:

Keep learning.... Every day that you "bank" away your deposits of learning will draw a kind of interest. And perhaps that kind of *ribit* [interest] is allowed and we find a *remez* [hint] of it: "These are the things that have no measure ... and learning Torah is equal to all of them" (*Mishnah, Pe'ah* 1:1).[7]

And again:

The more I write and speak, the more I regret every minute that I wasted time not learning Torah. It is vital that you FILL yourself with Torah so that you will know what to say and write.[8]

In another letter, he referred to Baruch's response to his suggestion to hire a *rebbe*, a private teacher, and to his study schedule.

I think that you are right about waiting until I get back to see about the *rebbe*. You have a fine schedule, but do not take too much on yourself, and I think that rather than just going over the *shiur* [lesson], you should go ahead each day and learn it yourself and then in the third *seder* [study session], go over what was learned in the *shiur*. In this way you 1) use your head to figure out the *gemora* [Talmud portion] 2) go over it again and 3) do not try to learn too much by adding a third *gemora*. Also, it is VERY IMPORTANT that you rest during the afternoon because otherwise your learning and health will both suffer.[9]

To share our Chanuka celebration, Meir phoned home, only to find that Baruch was taking part in another settlement attempt. He reminded him what his priorities should be.

When I phoned last night, I heard that you were at Sebastia. I am very proud that you are doing what you do, but do not let it interfere with your learning. You have the ability to help the Jewish people to understand what Sebastia is, and not only to settle there yourself.

He shared his thoughts about the fate of Israel and American Jewry.

It is a pity that the Jew really does not understand what is happening. The U.S. is ready to recognize the P.L.O.; the pressure is pushing the Israelis into recognizing the "nice" Palestinians; the economy is tragic and still everyone speaks of *realpolitik*. The words of Isaiah are true: "Who is blind, but My servant? Who does not hear, as the one whom I send with news? ... Who among you will hear this? Who will listen and hear in the future? Who let Jacob be taken? Who gave Israel to robbers? Was it not the L-rd?" (*Isaiah*, 42:19-24)
    And in America the Jews sit on a volcano that is already smoking and they see nothing. In prison here, I get a good opportunity to see the *tipus* of the *goy* [the nature of the non-Jew]. The guards [at Allenwood Federal Prison] are small and petty ignoramuses whose highest form of culture is hunting. They are cruel and hateful and they treat the prisoners with no sympathy, taking out their own frustrations on them. The kind of mentality that created a Nazi era exists in the tens of millions here, and the Jews sit calmly, waiting to go under.
    KEEP LEARNING.[10]

In August, Meir was thinking about Baruch's future.

I think that you should give some deep thought to learning a *miktzo'a* [profession or a trade], which will allow you to have a *parnassa* [livelihood] with ample time to sit and learn. Your obligation to sit and learn and to grow into a halakhic leader is clear.... I think that you should think of 1) what you enjoy doing 2) is there something in that field that will allow you to work just enough to eat and live modestly 3) and if so, how do you begin learning it. ANY kind of work that is honest is good.[11]

Meir was constantly aware of his responsibility to teach the children to be good Jews. Before Rosh Hashana, the time of spiritual introspection, he wrote to Baruch:

> Another month is gone, and while it means that I am one month closer to coming home, it also extends the time that I have been away from all those I love. In any case, I want – in *chodesh Elul* [the month of Elul, preceding Rosh Hashana] – to do what every father should. You know, the wife of Rav Chaim Brisk once explained the function of a *rebbetzin* [rabbi's wife]. "The rabbi's function," she said, "is to give *musar* [teach morals] to the community. But who gives HIM *musar*? That is the job of the *rebbetzin*." I suppose that this is the job of a father too, to give *musar* to his children.
>
> No one needs *musar* more than the one who is growing up, leaves his childhood, and starts to become a man. Every child is pure and innocent, and in the child, *emuna* [faith] is clear and there are no *sefekot* [doubts]. But the teenager becomes "sophisticated," and suddenly things are not black and white. He, more than anyone, needs a *chodesh Elul* for *cheshbon nefesh* [spiritual self-examination] and to replenish *emuna*. *Chodesh Elul* tells him that he is not as wise or sophisticated as he thinks, that while he acquires greater knowledge and experiences, that is not the same as wisdom and truth. So with *chodesh Elul* again with us, use it to get a glimpse again of the pure *emuna* of a child which all of us once had.
>
> I, myself, regret that I cannot give you what other fathers do – give you my time always. I hope you know that it is not because I love you and the family less, but rather because I love you more. SOMEONE must do these things and the sacrifice is the price that must be paid. My *nachat* [satisfaction] is that you have grown up to be a *ben Torah* [person devoted to Torah] and a *yerei shamayim* [G-d-fearing person]. This is to the credit of your mother, above all.[12]

Meir expressed the same sentiments about introspection, adolescence and his obligations as a father in letters to Tova and to Tzippy. He often sent almost identical letters to each of the children, repeating the same news and sentiments, because he wanted them to know that he cared about each one individually.

He also wrote some letters to all four.

> Someone is leaving for Israel tomorrow, so I don't have time to write you individually this week.... Now, Tova, I hope you are finally finished with the *shiga'on* [madness] known as *bagrut* [matriculation exams]. I understand you will be going soon for preparation for your *sherut le'umi* [national service]. I wish you well and am sorry I will not be there to kiss you goodbye. You are doing *avoda kedosha* [holy work]....

Tzippy – wonderful report card and term paper. I wish you would stop saying that you were surprised you did well and similar nonsense. You have wonderful qualities, and appreciate yourself.

Baruch – Point the rifle in the right direction.* Never believe anything you read in the papers.

For Binyamin, he wrote a short note in Hebrew and ended with a question from the Book of Samuel 1: "Who had six fingers?"[13]

Another letter written to all four together was in Hebrew, so Binyamin could read it too. He addressed it "To the children of *mishpachat hamelech* [the 'melekh' family]." In parenthesis he explained that *melekh*, Hebrew for "king," was an acronym for Meir and Libby Kahane. He wrote:

I haven't gotten mail from you for two weeks. I hope you haven't already forgotten your father!

As always, he shared his ideas with the children. He told them what he had learned from chapter 20 in Ezekiel:

I drew an important lesson from this chapter: Even after a great miracle is attained, through which G-d's name is sanctified and exalted, there is still the danger of *chillul Hashem* if there is a "retreat" that blurs the victory and makes it seem that it was temporary and achieved by natural means. This is a clear warning to those who wish to give up the liberated lands, which means retreat from the great victory in the Six Day War by which G-d's name was sanctified and exalted.[14]

Meir appreciated the children's letters. He wrote to me:

I received a long letter from Tova and she was very articulate and interesting.[15]

In October, he jokingly observed:

Tova wrote me two letters and thank G-d, she is becoming an Israeli. (She forgot how to spell in English.)[16]

Meir tried to make his letters home cheerful. Tzippy, not realizing that his aim was to keep us from worrying about him, asked him in one of her letters if he was "having a good time." His reply defined the Jewish view of "happiness."

I am not really having "a good time" here. It is just that it could be worse.

I want to emphasize to you the importance of being *same'ach bechelkekho* [satisfied with one's lot], because a person is her own worst enemy by making herself miserable. You, who have the right values in life, and know what is important and what is *hevel* [nonsense], can never be unhappy because you know that material things are not worth getting unhappy about.

---

* Baruch was patrolling for the *Mishmar Ezrachi* (Civil Guard) with other students of Yeshivat Merkaz Harav.

The trouble is that most people LOVE themselves and don't LIKE themselves. The difference is that a person who loves himself is always wrapped up in his problems. He is the center of the universe. That is bad because such a person is never happy. A person who likes himself, however, knows what he SHOULD do, and then, when he lives that kind of life – even though it is hard – he takes pride and happiness in himself. He LIKES himself.

You have so many things to be happy about. You have health. You have all your limbs. You have sanity. You have a loving family. You have a good school and training. You have enough to eat. You have clothing. You have all the things that hundreds of millions of people do not have. That alone should put a smile on your lips all day.

And when you add the fact that you are a *bat Torah* [learned in Torah] and know what holiness is and you have the opportunity to do *mitzvot* [the Commandments], you should be singing all day. As far as asking whether life can be free from *tzarot* [troubles], the answer is: People only have *tzarot* if they look at them as *tzarot*. Others never have *tzarot* because they have a smile on their lips all day. I miss you and love you.

Meir commented on another statement of Tzippy's:

Really, there should be no material in Torah that is boring, since all Torah should be learned *lishma* [for its own sake]. But in practice, there is obviously material that is more interesting, which is why we ask G-d every day: "*Veha'arev ... divrei Toratecha* [Make the words of Your Torah pleasant.]" I enjoyed the *d'var Torah* [homily] very much and I am happy that you get enjoyment from something "good."[17]

Meir remembered what it was like to be an adolescent. He wrote to Tzippy:

I have not heard from you for such a long time, I hope nothing is wrong. I always look forward to your letters but I know that you are probably very busy. I imagine that you are such a young lady already, that I will be overwhelmed when I see you. I also know that it is not easy to be 14, and I did not love it when I was that age. But time is very fleeting, and if I had a choice of being 14 or 43, I suppose I might think twice.[18]

Indeed, Meir, at 43, was doing some hard thinking. He was drawn in two directions. He wanted to act on behalf of the Jewish people, but at the same time, he was worried that his long absences from home were harming the children. Midway through his imprisonment, he wrote a long letter to the children expressing his inner conflict:

This week marked the fourth complete month of my imprisonment and the sixth month that I have been away from you, and I miss you so very much. What is more, I really do not know when I will be able to come home, because I do not know if I will get parole before the sentence ends. I am, of course, not a "good" boy, and I do go to the JDL office, organize rallies, have pushed the Conference of Activists, CAIR, AJAF, Christians for Zion and so on and am writing and saying those things that must be said. Obviously this does not endear me to the authorities, and I have regular run-ins with them.

As with everything else, I am torn by two opposing drives. One is to be home with your wonderful mother who is such an *aishet chayil* [woman of valor] and such a magnificent wife to me, as well as to be with you who give me such *nachat* [joy]. On the other hand, the tragedy of the Jews here ... must be met. ... The ideas and programs that I have must be implemented, and who will do it?

I apologize to you for not giving you what other fathers give their children, and I only hope that the ideas and training that I did give you allow you to understand. You know, I am sure, that all that I do is because I love you, and that if I did not do these things, I would not be the kind of father you could respect.[19]

This inner conflict remained with Meir for the rest of his life, but it was especially sharp that year, when he was away from the family for almost twelve months.

A Prolific Writer: Assimilation and Other Timely Topics

Meir had plenty of time for writing that year and thought of several new projects.

As he had in the past, he sought to write a weekly column for newspapers other than the *Jewish Press*. Back in March, over the signature of Sheila Lidz, he had sent letters to editors and publishers of Anglo-Jewish newspapers in America that said:

On March 18, Rabbi Meir Kahane is scheduled to begin serving a year's sentence in federal prison. His voice will not be stilled, because from prison will come forth a regular series of writings on the Jewish problems of our time. We believe that message should be heard by your readers in what will undoubtedly be the most dramatic column you have ever carried.

"A Letter from Prison" will be the title of the column that will reach you every week from federal prison and which will contain the kinds of ideas and concepts that are not heard from other Jewish leaders.

... There is no set charge for the column. You may run them gratis or, if you wish, send a check for whatever amount to the Jewish Identity Center, a non-profit, tax-deductible school for the training of young Jewish leaders on campus.

The columns will be sent to you weekly, and we hope that you carry them. Should you decide to, we would appreciate your adding us to your subscription list, so that we may have copies.[20]

There is no evidence in Meir's files that any newspaper ever printed his "Letter from Prison" column. However, during the early part of his detention at the halfway house Meir wrote many articles, probably with that column in mind.

His long article "What Makes Bernie Run?" – widely distributed as an eight-page booklet – reflected his ongoing concern with American Jewish assimilation and intermarriage. It was a topic that was part of all his talks. The article is an incisive analysis of the problem and presents a definite solution:

> ... What makes Bernie run after Bridget? What makes Bernie run away from Judaism and cut the chain of generations? What makes Bernie run away from the Judaism that his great-grandfather clutched at the risk of loss of happiness, material wealth and, so often, [his] very life? What makes Bernie run?
>
> This is the question that makes the American Jewish Establishment frantically set up committees, study groups, surveys and commissions.... The answer is obvious: The very same Establishment groups ... marched down the American road with a melting pot under their arms, beating it over and over again and shouting forth the Eleventh Commandment to the American Jew: Thou shalt melt!
>
> Thou shalt melt, thou shalt integrate, thou shalt amalgamate, thou shalt be an American as all others.
>
> ... They raised high the banner of the public school and fought, with a zeal no one knew they possessed, the one weapon that might have given Bernie knowledge and a sense of pride and roots.... They declared a holy war against the Jewish Day School, the parochial school, the yeshiva.... The yeshiva threatened them with too much Jewishness! What would the gentile say if Jews were too Jewish, if they looked and behaved differently, if their profile was not properly low? How did one mix easily with gentiles in the non-kosher country clubs they were so eager to join; how did one assimilate if Jews did not learn to drop the embarrassing customs, habits and old ritual baggage?
>
> ... The Establishment groups and leaders who took a Judaism of particularism, of separatism, of uniqueness ... and created an American brand that leveled all uniqueness, "proved" that Jews and Christians were no different, and eliminated every logical and moral reason to be different. They created Bernie; they made Bernie run.
>
> And who else made Bernie run away from Judaism? ... The temple, where the Jew can create any kind of religion that he cares to and call it Judaism.... The temple rabbis ... who take a Judaism of Divinity and truth and go about Reconstructing it and Reforming it and making a mockery of Conserving it.... The temple rabbis ... who took the real and awesome Jewish G-d of history Who made man and created all and Who rewards and punishes, and exchanged Him for a "god" who is the "spirit within man," indistinguishable from indigestion.... The temple rabbis; they created Bernie, they made Bernie run.

And who else made Bernie run away from the embrace of Judaism into Brigitte's waiting arms? The parents, the good Jewish parents ... whose credo is upward and upward in wealth and status and who created a comfortable Judaism that would accommodate their needs.

... If Bernie was sent to that vast cultural wasteland known as the "religious" or "Hebrew" school.... If he came home and mentioned something about Sabbath observance or a ban on ham and bacon, his parents smiled and told him, "We aren't sending you there for that." ... They defrauded themselves ... and thought that Bernie would grow up to be as fraudulent, hypocritical, materialistic, and disgusting as they. But he did not.

They thought that Judaism was a faucet that could be turned on and off at will. They wanted to give up the uncomfortable and inconvenient things but still keep the "important" things, like marrying a Shirley. Bernie was honest. He took the whole thing and junked it.... He married Bridget to the wailing of his parents...

... The hypocrisy is nauseating and amusing at the same time.... What is a nice Jewish girl like my mother? One who desecrates the Sabbath like my mother? So does Bridget. One who eats non-kosher food like dear Mom? So does Bridget. One who comes to synagogue three times a year to parade about in our version of the Easter parade? Bridget has the real thing."

Of course, what Bernie is really saying – no, CRYING OUT – is ... Why is it important to be a Jew? What difference does it make? Why not knock down the barriers between religions, nations and groups once and for all?... Why be a Jew!

It is an agonizing cry from the souls of tens of thousands of young Jews who assimilate, integrate and disappear into the outer space beyond Judaism.... It is asked by young Jews who have seen the emptiness and vapidness of the "Judaism" they grew up with....

... Judaism lives or dies on the unique fact that G-d Revealed Himself at Mount Sinai and gave the Jew a truth that no one else has. Judaism lives or dies on the fact that the Bible and the Talmud, with their laws, commandments, statutes and ordinances were Divinely Revealed and that the only way to holiness and true goodness comes from the observance of Torah laws.... Jewish is beautiful if you do not play games with it – or with yourself....[21]

At the end of May, Meir submitted this article, together with twenty others that he had written at the halfway house, to the Bertha Klausner Literary Agency, hoping that Mrs. Klausner would find a publisher. He gave this collection the same title he had used in 1974 – *Letters from Prison*, but it was never published.[22]

The articles in the 1975 collection are among Meir's most thought-provoking writings. All but one eventually appeared in print. Meir was so prolific during this period that several articles datelined "Federal Prison" were not printed in the *Jewish Press* until the following year. Even "What Makes Bernie Run?" which was datelined "Federal Prison, April 29, 1975" appeared in the *Press* only in July 1976.[23]

One article in the *Letters from Prison* collection that was not published in the *Jewish Press* was "On the Beach." Datelined Federal Prison, April 8, 1975, it was a dark vision of the future that showed how a policy of retreat could result in disaster. Meir wrote it as an imaginary newspaper report, with a fictitious future dateline, "Washington, June 23, 1976."

> With the fall of Tel Aviv two days ago, panicky refugees fleeing from the south have driven the population of Haifa upward by almost half-a-million. The approaching Syrian-Iraqi-Pakistani forces have surrounded Haifa on three sides, and only a narrow strip remains connecting Israel's last free port with the shrinking coastal strip that still remains in Jewish hands. Earlier in the day, in the first official comment on the fall of Tel Aviv, Secretary of State Elliot Richardson said: "The President and myself consider the fall of Tel Aviv an immense tragedy. Rest assured that the United States will use its good offices to guarantee that humanitarian treatment will be afforded the survivors."[24]

There is no doubt that Rabbi Klass refused to print this bitter satire and he apparently brought Meir around to his point of view. When *Writings 5734-5-6* was published in 1977, it included fifteen of the articles from the *Letters from Prison* manuscript, but it did not include "On the Beach."

In the halfway house, Meir continued writing his two pseudonymous *Jewish Press* columns: *Israel Through Laughter and Tears*, under the name Meir Hacohen, and *Exposing the Haters*, under the name David Borac. To gather material for his articles, especially for *Exposing the Haters*, Meir was assisted by JDL supporters. For example, an organization named Americans for Middle East Neutrality aimed to prevent an Arab oil embargo on the United States by lobbying for an American foreign policy in favor of the Arabs. At Meir's request, Abe Levine replied to their ad in the *Village Voice* in order to receive their publications.[25]

Newspaper and magazine clippings were important source material for Meir. He went through them regularly and expanded his clippings collection during this period. He arranged the clippings under subjects such as Intellectual Anti-Semitism, U.S. Public Opinion, Israel – Religion, Intermarriage – U.S.A, Soviet Union – Israel, International Isolation [of Israel]. Whenever he found someone traveling to Israel, he would send me an envelope of clippings. In one letter he wrote, with emphasis, "Please make sure that you SAVE EVERYTHING I SEND YOU."[26]

On May 30 Meir began a new column under his own name, "The Week That Was." In August he changed its name to "The Activist's Column" and kept that name for almost two years.[27] The first "Activist's Column" expounded on a familiar theme:

> The name of G-d is permanently linked to the name of Israel, and thus the SHAME of G-d is permanently linked to the shame of Israel. Whether the L-rd is truly Omnipotent or impotent is gauged and judged by His seeming ability or inability to bring victory and triumph for His people Israel over their enemies.[28]

Several of Meir's 1974 booklets were reprinted in 1975. In May he sent me *Numbers 23:9* in its new, smaller format. Other booklets reprinted in New York were *Madmen and Murderers* and *The Jewish Idea: A Jewish Program for Jewish Survival*. The back page of *Madmen and Murderers* featured the newly devised logo of the Jewish Identity Center, a charcoal drawing of a torch being handed on: one hand extending the torch and another hand reaching out to take it.[29]

Intent on promoting aliya, Meir wanted to reprint *Time to Go Home* as a pocket book, in order to distribute it widely and inexpensively. The Hebron Printing Press, which had printed *Ha'etgar* and prepared the plates for *Writings*, submitted a cost estimate for printing and binding 5,000 copies at $2,550. To encourage the export trade, the Israeli government offered tax and currency benefits which made it possible to print more cheaply in Israel than in America, including shipping costs. Even Morris Drucker, who printed for the JDL at cost, could not do it more cheaply. There was one requirement: "In order to begin, we must have an official order from a publisher, printer or bookstore in the U.S."[30]

At the beginning of March, Meir raised part of the cost of printing and made arrangements for an official order to be sent to the Hebron Press. He wrote to me:

> Please check with the Hebron Press to see if they received a check for $1500 from a man named Carlitz in San Francisco towards the book *Time to Go Home*. Let me know by return mail. Also ask them to rush the book job and mail us some sample copies.
>
> Ask them also if they received an official order from Rabinowitz Book Store. We ALSO sent an official order from the Jewish Identity Center, so if they got the Rabinowitz order, let them use that. If not, let it be the J.I.C. Please send me back all the information so that it reaches me by March 17.[31]

On March 18, from his cellblock at the Federal Court House, he wrote:

> Tell Weiss [the manager of Hebron Press] that if he is willing to wait a few weeks AFTER THE BOOKS HAVE BEEN SHIPPED to get his $500, then he should do all the extras. If not, just the parts that need not be reset. URGE HIM to take my word on the $500, but we must get the books first. Let me know.[32]

The "extras" Meir wrote about were probably the eleven pages that were added to the paperback edition as an epilogue. Its text, from his booklet *Numbers*

23:9, begins: "We live today in the final era, in the footsteps of the Messiah" and concludes with the words "... for the exile is doomed, while the 'dangers' facing Israel can never destroy the State because of G-d's vows and the Jewish destiny."[33]

Meir was anxious to see the paperback in print. In almost every letter home he asked me to phone the Hebron Press. In May he wrote, "Get Hebron Press moving and persuade him to set the type for EVERYTHING. He already got $2,550; we will pay him the rest. But have him HURRY."[34]

Ten days later he wrote, "What is with Hebron Press and is he putting in the extra work I sent him several months ago?" At the end of May he sent $450 and wrote, "This is for the Hebron Press.... Tell them to rush the books." Then, "Tell Hebron Press that we are very anxious for the books."[35]

At the end of June, he received a sample copy and wrote: "You should owe Hebron Press about $50 now. Tell him to rush the books and not to worry about the payments." And again, pleading, "Please have the books shipped by sea, but quickly." As it turned out, because of a shortage of money, the plates of *Time to Go Home* were prepared in 1975, but the actual printing was delayed until 1976.[36]

The Story of the Jewish Defense League Is Published

The Story of the Jewish Defense League finally came out in May 1975, while Meir was at the halfway house. Benton Arnovitz sent a copy to him with a note: "Here is the very first copy of your new book. I trust your warders will let you have it. The *New York Times Book Review* has just phoned to request a copy."[37]

Meir was quite pleased with his new book: "I just received the very first copy of the JDL *Story*. It looks quite good and I think it may sell." Then he sent me copies for the family: "Here are two more JDL *Story* books. I sent you two others and Chilton should have sent five. Divide them thusly: Two for the house, one each for the children, one for my parents, one for your parents, one for Nachman." He was also pleased with the June 8 book review in the *New York Times* and with the fact that on June 16 the *Times* had published an article by him on its op-ed page. He wrote home:

> This week I had uncharacteristic treatment from the *New York Times*. First, a very interesting book review (after the obligatory criticism, a very good review, indeed). Then, my op-ed page article appeared with an unexpected picture and in the middle of the page.[38]

Meir's op-ed article "So Easy to Forget" was prominently placed on the editorial page, under a large drawing showing a Jewish refugee wandering near a withering tree-candelabrum. In the article, Meir berated those who were ready to agree to compromises with the Arabs and charged them with "forgetting" how the

Arabs had attempted to eliminate Israel. The *Times* paid $150 for this article.[39] Meir would gladly have paid THEM for the opportunity to present his ideas to their readers.

Herbert Gold's critique in the *New York Times Book Review* began, as Meir wrote, with "the obligatory criticism," but went on to express support for the League's premises.

> Rabbi Meir Kahane's new book ... gets at a truth about contemporary Jewish experience which is generally missed by both the non-Jewish popular mind and the established Jewish organizations.... Jews are still oppressed by prejudice in the old ways, and now have the new ways to contend with: programs to give special job and educational preference to non-white minorities, at the expense [of Jews].
>
> ... If you break a neighborhood with welfare cases and drug users, it is likely to be an "ethnic" neighborhood – Italian or Jewish, most often. The easy liberals who preach integration ask others than themselves to pay the price of past injustices.
>
> ... [Kahane] is capable of a shrewd public relations humor, as when he demanded additional hiring of Jewish players by the Mets.... Pickets carried signs: "Merit, shmerit, we want our quota.... So what if I can't hit, I'm motivated.... The hell with second base. No more tokenism. I want to pitch." At these moments he is almost lovable.
>
> At a deeper level, he speaks for those Jews in crisis, trapped in decaying neighborhoods, and speaks with the authority of need. There are poor and oppressed Jews, and the downtrodden often grate on the nerves of the rest of us, as the Jewish Defense League grates.
>
> ... Rabbi Kahane perhaps deserves ... the scorn heaped upon him by the Jewish Establishment. And perhaps they deserve having to cope with this peculiar rabbi who preaches karate for Jewish leaders.[40]

Ads in the *Jewish Press* promoted the book, and to pique people's interest, Meir wrote pseudonymously:

> ... Rumors are that the famous producer and composer Leo Fuld is actively negotiating for [*Story of the* JDL] to be made into a movie. Peter Falk is the man Fuld wants to play the lead.[41]

The book was seen as a significant contribution to American Jewish historiography. Several reviews contained interesting insights:

Lenora Berson in the *Philadelphia Inquirer*:

> The problems that Kahane points out are real. They also are not exclusive to Jews, but are shared by other white working class ethnics.... This is not a pleasant book to read, but it does offer a revealing insight into the rage that is boiling up from the lower middle class and could well destroy our democracy.[42]

Donald L. Wolberg in the *Minnesota Daily:*

> Kahane understands that ... in order for him to gain and focus attention on an
> issue, he must be outrageous. In a society where outrage after outrage has
> escalated ... Kahane realizes that he must be bold.... Thus [the JDL] goes eye-
> ball to eyeball with the Black Panthers ... the Soviets become uneasy.... The
> system responds and people begin to listen to his line.[43]

Ron Mehler in the *Wisconsin Jewish Chronicle:*

> He is almost universally condemned by Jewish leaders, but many of them, while
> still condemning Kahane, now agree with some of the stances he took five years
> ago.... His documentation is devastating and his sincerity rings true throughout
> the book.[44]

A reviewer in the *Detroit Jewish News* wrote: "In his book, he gloats about
incidents in the history of the Jewish Defense League that have turned the tide
of history." Then, to explain Meir's stubbornness despite the opposition of the
"majority," the reviewer quoted from Meir's June op-ed article in the *New York
Times:* "Strong and tenacious people know that there may never be an end to the
struggle and the sacrifice, but they also look about and see what their refusal to
surrender has accomplished."[45]

In October, Meir thought of a new project – a book about the Six Day War.
He wrote:

> Dear Lib, ... You recall I started something in the *Jewish Press* in 1967, after
> the war, called "Chronology of a Miracle." I think that for the tenth anniversary
> year, it would make a great book and would remind Jews of the miracle of 1967
> and what could have been in 1973 and today....[46]

He listed source material for me to find at the National Library: newspapers,
transcripts of radio broadcasts and publications of the Foreign Ministry.[47] In an
ad in the *Jewish Press* he asked readers to send him synagogue bulletins and other
Jewish communal literature written during the weeks preceding the war.[48]

However, Meir never wrote a book about the Six Day War. More pressing
issues captured his attention.

Chapter 46

Stop Israel's Retreat from Sinai!
(September-November 1975)

Conference of Jewish Activists

IN MID-MAY MEIR wrote to me about yet another new organization he was starting.

> We have managed to break out of the isolation and become the "organization that came in out of the cold." I persuaded various activists to meet and got them to agree to the formation of an umbrella group to be known as the Conference of Presidents of Major Jewish ACTIVIST Organizations (an obvious counter to the "Presidents Conference" of Rabbi Israel Miller). A number of groups have agreed to participate along with JDL. They include SSSJ, Betar, plus Rabbi Steve Riskin, Rabbi Avi Weiss (who are forming a big group of Y.U. and Stern people), and many local Young Israel groups and regional Jewish organizations. It gives us a respectable platform, and they accepted our program, which is really JDL without violence.[1]

Earlier, JDL had applied for membership in existing umbrella groups – the Conference of Presidents of Major American Jewish Organizations, the American Zionist Federation, the National Community Relations Advisory Council, and the National Conference on Soviet Jewry – and had been rejected. A JDL spokesman said, "These are not private clubs, but public Jewish organizations that represent the community. We, as a national Jewish organization, have an absolute right to sit with all the others, regardless of whether our ideology meets with their approval or not." When the umbrella groups did not respond to JDL's bid for adjudication in a rabbinical court, JDL threatened to bring a suit against them in civil court – but did not do so.[2]

Instead, Meir devoted all his energies to establishing the new activist umbrella group. On May 20 he wrote, "I am getting ready to leave now for a meeting with the representatives of the activist groups to plan a convention. I will let you know, *be'ezrat Hashem* [with G-d's help], how it goes."[3]

Meir was able to attend the meeting by skipping his supper. The minutes of a meeting of the group reveal how it planned to gain support.

> The meeting was called to order at approximately 8 P.M. with Dr. Samuel Korman, Vice-President of the Greater New York Conference on Soviet Jewry, presiding.
>
> ... Elly Rosen (Director, Association of Jewish Anti-Poverty Workers) proposed that in the statement on American Jewish needs, the second paragraph should be amended so that the phrase "to move [indigent Jews] to more secure areas within the Jewish community," would be followed by the phrase "and develop aliya programs for them." This resolution was accepted by acclamation.
>
> ... Toby Willig (president, Emunah Women) proposed that a committee be set up to inform Jews of elections for school boards, poverty programs, and the like.
>
> ... Rabbi Kahane proposed that a date be set now for a convention to take place in not more than two weeks from today. Rabbi [Avi] Weiss objected on the grounds that more groups must be brought into the organization first to prevent its being labeled a JDL front.
>
> ... It was finally agreed to hold a convention on Monday, June 30, at 5:30 P.M. at Lincoln Square Synagogue. (Sandwiches will be served.) Various people agreed to contact other organizations to get them to come to the convention. (Shirley Korman: Hapoel Hamizrachi Women; Sam Korman: Orthodox Jewish Scientists; Rabbis Riskin and Weiss: RCA [Rabbinical Council of America] and RZA [Religious Zionists of America] and its affiliates; Alex Friedman and Sam Korman: Young Israel.) A convention committee was appointed to deal with the question of whether the media should be invited, whether the convention should be open to the public, and any other matters which might arise concerning the convention. The members of the committee are Rabbi Steven [Shlomo] Riskin, Rabbi Avi Weiss, Bobby Brown, Alex Friedman and David Fisch.[4]

An ad invited the public to the founding convention of the Conference of Presidents of Major American Jewish Activist Organizations on June 30 at the McAlpin Hotel. The ad presented the principles of the new group: Federation funds for Jewish education and Jewish poverty; large-scale demonstrations against the anti-Israel foreign policy of Ford and Kissinger; an onslaught on false détente in order to free Soviet Jews; unrestricted settlement in all parts of the Land of Israel; an aliya campaign based on the threat of anti-Semitism; cessation of Israel-Arab talks until Syrian Jews are free. Charter members of the Conference included Betar, the Association of Jewish Anti-Poverty Workers, the United

Zionist Revisionists, Young Israel, the Jewish Defense League, Bnei Akiva, Yavneh, Noar Mizrachi, the Student Struggle for Soviet Jewry, and the National Conference of Synagogue Youth.[5]

The convention was a resounding success, with almost four hundred participants. Congressman Mario Biaggi, the guest speaker, received an overwhelming ovation when he referred to Henry Kissinger as "cunning" and "dangerous" and told the audience to be strong and stand firm against his pressure. Meir, whose release time from the halfway house began only mid-way through the convention, arrived in the middle of Biaggi's speech. As he went up to take his seat on the dais, he received a standing ovation from the crowd and shook hands warmly with Biaggi.

When it was his turn to speak, he proposed:

> ... a great convocation of Jews before the United Nations on Tisha B'Av[*] as the day draws to a close. There, wrapped in *tallit* and *tefillin*, let thousands of Jews gather to hear a special reading from the Torah – from the chapters that speak of the Divine grant of *Eretz Yisrael* [the Land of Israel] to the Jewish people.... The issue must, at last, be placed in its proper context, so that Jews and non-Jews alike will understand. The struggle over Israel is a RELIGIOUS one.... Let these words be affirmed by the Jewish people as they sanctify the name of G-d by crying, "Not one inch!"

Meir's proposal was approved unanimously.[6]

Jewish Press readers were informed that a group called Friends of Jewish Activism had been set up to enable individuals to support the Conference of Activists. "It has a four-room suite in room 1214 at 156 Fifth Avenue, and mail has been pouring in." A memo from Meir said that rent for the office of the Activist Conference was $300 monthly, the phone bill was $400, and as of July 9 ads had cost $1,200. Concerning the Tisha B'Av prayer rally, he wrote, "We still need a *Sefer Torah*, truck and stand, food, speakers, and people to give out flyers."[7]

In his next letter home, Meir wrote about the rally on Tisha B'Av, which would be called Sanctification Day.

> The Activist Conference is moving nicely, and we expect to meet with leaders of the Young Israel, R.C.A. [Rabbinical Council of America], OU [Union of Orthodox Congregations] and other Orthodox groups about joining the Activist Conference.
>
> On Tisha B'Av we expect a great turnout for our Sanctification Day at the U.N. It is absolutely imperative that the world know that the return of the Jews

---

[*] Tisha B'Av, a fast day, commemorates the destruction of the Temples in Jerusalem. It is on the ninth day of Av, which fell that year on August 17.

to Eretz Yisrael and their military victories are a *kiddush Hashem* [sanctification of G-d's name] and the beginning of His *malkhut* [dominion].[8]

Sanctification Day was publicized by flyers, press releases, ads, and mailings. One flyer read:

> The Jews of New York will gather at the United Nations, symbol of the nations of the world who wish to blot out Israel's name, and proclaim:
> ### SANCTIFICATION DAY
> Thursday, July 17, 1975, Tisha B'Av, 7 P.M.
> ... The rise of the Jewish State is not a political event, but a religious miracle decreed by the L-rd, the Jewish G-d of Israel.
> The Arab-Israel dispute is a dispute between the L-rd and the nations that know Him not.
> We will gather for the *Mincha* afternoon prayers with *tallit* and *tefillin*... Refreshments to break the fast will be served.[9]

A similarly worded mailing to synagogues requested:

> Dear Rabbi, ... This will be a historic moment of Sanctification of the Name of G-d. We urge you to announce it from your pulpit...[10]

Meir publicized the event in his column and he inserted a news item in the *Jewish Press* that bluntly expressed the religious theme:

> ... For the first time, we will take the issue of the land of Israel, the Mideast conflict, and the Arab-Israeli problem and put it into its proper context. Not a political issue, not a diplomatic one, not that of Israelis and Arabs. This is a RELIGIOUS question, a question of the truth of Judaism as opposed to those of the other faiths and ideologies.[11]

The publicity campaign was effective. Despite the severe thunderstorms that day, more than five hundred people gathered at U.N. Plaza and listened to a message from Meir that said:

> ... Standing at the site of the headquarters of the nations of the world, the United Nations, we read to them and to ourselves the reminder of the origin of the Jewish claim to Israel: ... the proclamation of the Jewish people as the special and chosen people of G-d; and the Biblical Divine boundaries of the Land of Israel.
> We proclaim, too, the ultimate vengeance of the L-rd upon those enemies of the Jewish people who knew Him not. We will then conclude with readings from the prophets Isaiah, Jeremiah and Ezekiel foretelling the return of the Jew home and the efforts of the nations to forestall that return – in vain, because of the awesome power of the L-rd, G-d of Israel.[12]

The ceremony concluded with the singing of *Ani Ma'amin.** The Activist Conference basked in the success of its first public demonstration.[13]

March on Washington

Only a few days before Tisha B'Av, Meir had written to me:

> I am into half a dozen things here and have no real help. Everything I have been saying is so true, and the Jewish leadership is so blind ... while the "good Jews" do not have the necessary resources or talent.

Indeed, Meir almost single-handedly accomplished tasks for which most organizations required a professional staff of speechwriters, researchers, public relations experts, and fundraisers. He was involved in American Jews Against Ford, Committee Against Israeli Retreat, Shuva, the Activists Conference, the fight for kosher food in jail, and more. His letter continued:

> Tisha B'Av is our effort to get the real issue, *Yediat Hashem* [recognition of G-d], out into the open, and we are trying to get a huge demonstration with a sit-down in Washington.[14]

To protest the plan for Israel to cede Sinai to Egypt, the Activists Conference planned two demonstrations after Sanctification Day. In Israel, too, there were vigorous protests against Kissinger's plan. One report said, "Thousands of Israeli demonstrators against Kissinger staged a series of street confrontations that were characterized by observers as the worst violence in the State's history." Baruch Kahane recalled a Gush Emunim demonstration that blocked traffic on the main Jerusalem-Tel Aviv highway.

> We met at an apartment near the main highway, at the entrance to Jerusalem. Someone was stationed in another apartment, on the top floor of the tall building at 11 Nissenbaum Street. When he saw Kissinger's motorcade arriving from Lod, he hung a sheet out the window, and we ran into the road and lay down. Police came and told us to get up. When I didn't move, they sprayed tear gas on my face and carried me to the side of the road.

Police removed some demonstrators with such force that they had to be hospitalized.[15]

Meir wrote, "There is still time to stop Israel's retreat from Sinai." He urged his readers to attend a protest in New York on August 17 and to make plans to be in Washington on October 5. An article about the August 17 demonstration pleaded, "Give up a summer Sunday as Ford and Kissinger prepare to give up

---

* The hymn *Ani Ma'amin* is an expression of complete faith in the coming of the Messiah.

Israel."[16] In a letter home, he was optimistic about the upcoming rally in Washington:

> Last Sunday [August 17] was a successful rally at the U.N., and the October 5 Washington rally seems to be on its way to being big. There are ads in subways, and we feel that events will "conspire" to move many Jews into our camp.[17]

The use of the unwieldy name, Conference of Presidents of Major American Jewish Activist Organizations, led to the threat of a lawsuit from the original Conference of Presidents of Major American Jewish Organizations. They protested the "widespread public confusion resulting from the persistent use of a name ... deliberately similar to our own." Meir's reply in the *Jewish Press*, titled "What Confusion," declared that no one could possibly confuse the two groups: "... One issues press releases and the other acts..."[18]

The October 5 rally, marking the second anniversary of the Yom Kippur War, was preceded by an intensive publicity program. This was the first time Meir used poster ads in the subways. Shlomo Thaler recalled that there were also ads in buses, and estimated the cost at a few thousand dollars. Ads in the *Jewish Press* reached many potential participants, but subway ads reached a wider audience. Posters, made up according to the specifications of the Transit Authority, were placed in subway stations in Jewish neighborhoods. In blue on white, the colors of Israel's flag, the posters proclaimed:

> American Pressure Is Destroying Israel's Security.
> It is up to you to change U.S. policy.
> What will you tell your children if you remain silent?
> Buses will be leaving from all parts of Greater N.Y.[19]

Ads were even placed in the general press to reach as many people as possible. One, in the *New York Post*, called on New Yorkers to attend a rally at the Diplomat Hotel on August 27 to learn more about the October 5 march on Washington.[20]

The date of the rally coincided with the start of Congressional committee hearings on the Interim Sinai Agreements. Meir wrote to Congress, requesting an invitation to testify before the committee. Then he wrote to Matthew Walsh, director of the halfway house:

> As you know, the United States Congress is holding hearings on the important question of American personnel being sent to the Sinai. This question, as well as that of the entire Sinai agreement, is critical.
>
> I am formally requesting permission to travel to Washington to testify.... Furloughs are usually granted in the event of an emergency and I can think of

no greater one than this which holds within it the terrible potential for "death in my family" – the Jewish people.[21]

Walsh's refusal was brief: "I respect your concern, but do not find that your purpose warrants furlough."[22] Afterwards, Meir received this invitation to testify before the committee:

> The Committee on Foreign Relations will hold public hearings beginning 10 A.M., Thursday, October 2, ... on the Interim Sinai Agreements of September 4, 1975.
>   Pursuant to your request, the Committee will be glad to receive a statement from you at that time.... [signed] John Sparkman, Chairman, Committee on Foreign Relations, U.S. Senate.[23]

Since Meir could not be there, Shlomo Thaler, as vice president of the Conference of Presidents of Major American Jewish Activist Organizations, testified instead. He recalled that he compared the present conflict to the story of the baby that King Solomon wanted to divide between two mothers. He told the senators, "Israel is the baby we've been carrying in our bosom for 2,000 years. We will not give it up."[24]

Meir used every opportunity to persuade people to participate in the Washington rally. Since young people were more likely to take part, he made a special effort to reach them. At Queens College on September 25, he told students that the Sinai Pact "was signed with Kissinger's fingers on Israel's throat; no one wanted it." He urged them to attend the rally to "let President Ford know that the 'leading' Jews do not accurately represent the Jewish community.... Ford understands the language of votes, and when he sees that a large number of Jews are determined to defeat him in 1976, he will, most assuredly, re-evaluate the pact."[25]

On October 1, Meir urged students at Yeshiva University and at Stern College for Women to attend the rally in Washington. A report on his impromptu talk at Stern College said:

> On October 1, [during his] one-half hour out of jail, Rabbi Meir Kahane made a special, unscheduled appearance at the Stern dormitory.... [He] questioned the total silence on the part of American Jews. Before the signing of the Sinai pact, there were no demonstrations in America, Kahane charged.... Kahane urged us to participate in the October 5th march in Washington.... He reminded us of the *mitzvah*: "Do not stand on your brother's blood."[26]

Flyers, stickers and weekly ads in the *Jewish Press* also publicized the "March for Israel." One flyer read:

Silence Kills!
... We Are Silent No Longer!
On Sunday, October 5th, at 2 P.M. American Jewry is going to the
  White House in Washington to tell President Ford –
... Stop choking Israel!
Jews from all over the country will gather by their thousands to
  "REASSESS" Mr. Ford's candidacy in 1976.

The flyer included a coupon for bus reservations. The round trip fare was $10 for students and $13 for adults.[27]

An ad in the *Jewish Press,* clearly composed by Meir, began:

Daddy, where were you when they tried to destroy Israel?
That is the question your child will ask you some day.
What will your answer be?[28]

The *Jewish Press* accepted ads for the October 5 protest in Washington against the Sinai pact, but because the American Jewish Establishment supported the pact, Rabbi Klass, the publisher, refused to print any more articles by Meir opposing it. Meir wrote home:

> We have been the only group to oppose the Sinai Pact and we sent lobbyists to Washington to oppose the sending of Americans to Sinai.
> I had a fight with Klass about censorship, and he agreed finally to put in a column with a disclaimer. Nu![29]

A few days later, he wrote again about the article with Klass's disclaimer, attributing it to Establishment pressure.

> Klass is under great pressure to censor my articles. I had a big battle with him, which I won. So he put in a ridiculous disclaimer.[30]

The article in question was "A Retreat from More Than Sinai." One week after Israel signed the Sinai Interim agreement, it appeared in the *Jewish Press* with a disclaimer at the top that said, "The views expressed in this article are solely those of Rabbi Kahane." Meir wrote:

> The capitulation by Israel to United States pressure this week was more than a retreat from Sinai. It was retreat from the Divine miracle of the Six Day War. It was retreat from the magnificent Jewish destiny that began to unfold in 1948 with the rise of the Jewish State from the ruins of centuries.
> ... What to do? There is still time.... There is still time for two things that are indispensable for Jewish victory.... The first is *tshuva*, true repentance, and it begins with actions that show that we truly, truly believe. It begins with a determination to stand firm before the puny armies of Man.

> ... And the second is to ... prevent Congressional approval of the accord that
> calls for United States personnel to man surveillance posts. If Congress will not
> agree to this clause, then the entire agreement will fall. We must dedicate our-
> selves to that task.

Meir listed the names of the most influential congressmen on the foreign
affairs committees of the Senate and the House, and urged his readers to bombard
them with letters against the presence of American personnel in the Middle East.
He noted that in Israel, the hawks, who bitterly opposed the agreement, and the
doves, who welcomed it, agreed on one thing: "There was a terrible choking
United States pressure."

However, Rabbi Israel Miller, chairman of the Establishment's Presidents
Conference, did not agree with them. After a meeting with Henry Kissinger,
Miller stated, "Nothing is being imposed on Israel."[31] Meir wrote angrily:

> ... What Miller does ... is to assure the Jewish lambs of America that they need
> not and, indeed, SHOULD not protest and condemn Ford and Kissinger. He lays
> the groundwork for the next round of tragedy, as Ford and Kissinger confi-
> dently march forward, convinced that the pliant beasts of burden that make up
> the Jewish leadership are well in hand. What a wondrous thing is the American
> Jewish community! Where before were so many sheep led by donkeys?[32]

There was positive feedback to Meir's efforts to promote the rally in Washington. For example, a letter to Meir from Dr. Irving Moskowitz said, "We must
not abandon those [in Israel] who oppose concessions, and every rally will rein-
force their determination to stay firm. I am enclosing a check for $250 to help
you in your efforts."[33]

Meir was optimistic about the rally's success. In a letter home, he outlined the
plans for the day.

> This Sunday, the March on Washington takes place. There will be a major
> sit-down, and we expect at least several hundred arrests. I will not be there, but
> a speech will be read at the very end of the formal rally, and I have taped a
> 30-second exhortation to be played right before the sit-down.[34]

The message from Meir was mimeographed and distributed at the rally.

> ... From my prison in New York I salute you, who are the cream of American
> Jewry; you, who have rejected the silence and timidity and apathy of others.
>   ... Once again, potential tragedy of epic proportions faces the Jewish people,
> and once again, silence – timid and frightened silence – on the part of Amer-
> ican Jewish leadership.
>   ... 1975 is not 1943, and I pray that you are better Jews that those of a gen-
> eration ago. Beautiful Jews, rise this day to greatness. Give of yourselves for
> the State that lay in ruins for two thousand years and for which we waited so
> long. Where are the Maccabees of today? Where are the descendants of Bar

Kochba? Come, show Ford and Kissinger that the Jews of the post-Auschwitz generation are prepared to GIVE OF THEMSELVES. March to the White House with song and dignity. March PEACEFULLY but with determination.... March to the White House so that tomorrow the papers and news media of the world will carry this prominently, and Gerald Ford will think again. I promise you that tomorrow you will carry yourselves with pride and will be able to hand down to your children a memory that will be a blend of pride and awe.

He concluded:

... Be great, be Jewish, truly Jewish. March to the White House. March with heads high and songs on your lips. The people of Israel and all the world is looking at you, and you will be telling them: Am Yisrael Chai![35]

The next morning, the *Washington Star* reported:

Eighty-five demonstrators from a nationwide Jewish organization were arrested in front of the White House yesterday after a demonstration against Ford administration policies in the Mideast.

... Arrests were made after the group – the Conference of Presidents of Major American Jewish Activist Organizations – refused to leave the sidewalk in front of the White House when their demonstration permit expired.

... The group opposes the use of American technicians to monitor the ceasefire and contends that Israel is being sold out under the agreement.

... Following the six hour protest, more than 600 protesters chanting "No Technicians, No Retreat" and "Bury Kissinger, Not Israel" moved across to the White House and waited there until their permit expired. At about 7 P.M., police told the group to disperse and then arrested those who refused.[36]

The *Jewish Week* estimated the crowd at one thousand and reported that 108 persons were arrested. Its front page featured a photo of the protesters sitting down in front of the White House. An Associated Press report on the demonstration appeared in the *New York Times*, the *New York Post*, the *Springfield* (Missouri) *Leader-Press*, *Ma'ariv* (Tel Aviv), and other newspapers.[37]

It is significant that Meir worked tirelessly to promote the Washington demonstration against the retreat from Sinai even though he foresaw that the struggle was doomed to failure. More than a month earlier he had written to Baruch that he knew the Sinai was lost.

This is just a short letter because I am so busy with trying to arouse Jews – not against the Sinai retreat, that is lost, but against the future *chillul Hashem*. It is important to say over and over again that the REAL tragedy is not just the pragmatic military danger, but the failure of the Jewish people to understand the era of *kiddush Hashem* [sanctification of G-d's name] and the *ge'ula* [redemption]. The retreat from *emuna uvitachon* [faith and belief] is the greater part of the retreat from Sinai.[38]

The demonstration in Washington was important because it gave Meir an opportunity to publicize and promote the basic principles of *kiddush Hashem,* faith, and belief.

The Rules of the Halfway House

Before and after the October 5 demonstration in Washington, Meir spoke at many New York-area synagogues and colleges during his mealtime furloughs.

Abe Levine, chairman of JDL's Speaker's Bureau, placed an ad in the *Jewish Press* in October that said, "The Jewish Speaker's Bureau is pleased to announce that Rabbi Meir Kahane is available to speak in your synagogue or home."[39]

In a mailing to chapter chairmen, Levine wrote, "Rabbi Kahane has urgently requested that all JDL members help in obtaining speaking engagements for him." Meir's files, including a list of his speaking engagements compiled by Abe Levine, indicate that Meir spoke to many groups in October and November.[40] He spoke at high schools and colleges and ads were placed in the *Jewish Press* listing his talks at synagogues in the New York City area.[41]

On October 9, the *Daily News* reported that Meir was to give a series of four lectures at B'nai Jeshurun, a Conservative congregation in Manhattan. Its rabbi, Dr. William Berkowitz, told the *News* reporter that Meir had been invited to teach a four-session course on Jewish activism at the synagogue's Institute of Adult Jewish Studies, because the Institute "believes in having different points of view expressed."[42] The *Daily News* report came to the attention of Matthew Walsh, the director of the halfway house, who wrote to Meir:

> I am advised that there was an article in one of the local papers last week to the effect that you will be teaching or lecturing at a local institution commencing next week.... Please be advised that you do not have permission to do so.
> ... I again remind you that the periods allotted three times a day away from the center are authorized solely for the purpose of providing you sufficient time to take your meals. While in our custody, you are not permitted to carry on outside business activities or engage in any form of activity not specifically approved by the staff of this facility.[43]

The very day that the *Daily News* report appeared, October 9, was the day scheduled for the Court of Appeals to hear the appeal of the Bureau of Prisons. There was no way of knowing when they would hand down their decision, so Meir continued to give his scheduled lectures. His regular Thursday night seminars at Congregation Zichron Moshe were openly advertised in the *Jewish Press.* One ad announced that his next weekly seminar at Congregation Zichron Moshe would deal with training in the use of legal firearms.[44]

He even planned a street corner rally on October 19 in the Crown Heights section of Brooklyn, where many chasidic Jews lived. He called on the chasidic community "to take up arms against the criminal element that has been terrorizing local Jews," and to promote aliya. As far as Matthew Walsh was concerned, Meir should not have been engaging in this "outside business." Three days before the rally, Meir received a memo at the halfway house asking him to return a call from Mr. E. Kelly of the New York Police Department. On the memo, which Meir saved, he wrote:

> When the police heard we were to rally in Crown Heights for "Guns for Jews," they tried to get me to "cool it."

Despite pressure from the police and from some Jews in Crown Heights to cancel the rally, it was held as scheduled.[45]

The next day, October 20, Meir traveled to Syosset, Long Island, where he ate, prayed, and spoke to an audience at the East Nassau Hebrew Congregation. He signed out at 7 P.M. and was due back at 8:30 P.M., but returned at 11:20 P.M. The Incident Report on this infraction resulted in a decision to withhold Meir's October "good time," the five days a month he could accumulate toward an earlier release date. A newspaper report on Meir's speech in Syosset noted that Meir was allowed an hour and a half each evening to get kosher food but was running two hours late that night. "I'm always late," he told the reporter, making his disregard for the rules quite clear.[46]

The U.N. Votes: Zionism Is a Form of Racism

Since the early 1970s, a bloc of nations hostile to Israel had formed in the United Nations. This bloc was responsible for Yasser Arafat's invitation to speak before the U.N. General Assembly the previous November and for a subsequent General Assembly resolution recognizing the "national rights of the Palestinian people." In October, the bloc initiated a debate on Zionism in the U.N.'s Third Committee. As a result, the General Assembly was scheduled to vote on a resolution against Zionism in November. Chaim Herzog, Israel's ambassador to the United Nations, had publicly criticized the Jewish community in October for failing to speak out during the bitter committee debate. In an ad in the *New York Times* on November 10, the day of the crucial vote, Meir saluted Herzog for "lashing out" at the Jewish Establishment's passivity, and announced a November 15 JDL demonstration supporting Zionism.[47]

The U.N. General Assembly vote was 72 to 35 in favor of the infamous "Zionism is racism" resolution. Jews all over the world were alarmed. They realized that the vote was not only anti-Israel, it was a manifestation of blatant anti-Semitism. The very next day the Jewish Establishment held a rally in New York that was attended by more than 100,000 Jews.[48]

An editorial in the *B'nai B'rith Messenger* cited Meir's words about the Establishment's rally:

> Rabbi Meir Kahane's ... reflections following the 100,000-plus rally in New York ... are indeed worth repeating.... We must respect Meir Kahane's ability to reach into problems.... Kahane writes:
>
> "I stood ... with all the others at the great rally for Zionism and listened to the speakers, all the Jewish leaders who poured forth wrath upon the nations. I listened and listened and waited to hear one little word that is the key to knowing what Zionism is all about, to the inevitable victory of the Jewish people. One little word that not one speaker mentioned.
>
> "One little word, whose absence precisely symbolized the reason for Jewish distress today, whose disappearance from the lexicon of Jewish leaders is the exact reason for their bewilderment, confusion and helplessness....
>
> That word, says Rabbi Kahane, is "G-d."
>
> "To people who cannot speak the one little word, Zionism becomes, at best, the national liberation movement of the Jewish people, indistinguishable from Canadianism, Swedenism, Bulgarianism or Zimbabwenism. And that is false, for Zionism is nothing of the kind. Zionism is part and parcel of the one little word, and the Jew who utters the latter knows the true definition of the former.
>
> "... Zionism is the Jewish destiny, the destiny proclaimed by the L-rd, G-d of Creation and History ... based on a Divine grant."

The editorial concluded:

> Meir Kahane has spoken well.
>
> Indeed, he – not the Establishment – has supplied the answer to the Arab claim that "Judaism is not Zionism" and "Zionism is not Judaism."
>
> They are one and the same.
>
> It may well be, if the Establishment will not harken to Rabbi Kahane, that they might do well to remember the words of the theme to the motion picture *Exodus*, "This is my land. G-d gave this land to me."
>
> And that is what Israel and Zionism are all about.[49]

In response to the "Zionism is racism" resolution, Gene Singer produced buttons saying "I Am A Zionist." JDL members proudly wore the buttons and photos of Meir show the button pinned to his lapel.[50]

Two public addresses by Meir were openly advertised in the *Jewish Press* for the weekend after the "Zionism is racism" resolution. One was at a JDL rally on Saturday night, November 15, at U.N. Plaza. Its slogan was advertised as "Listen U.N., We Are All Zionists." The second was at an "Open Jewish Youth Conference" on Sunday afternoon. An ad for the youth conference said: "Listen to the sane, militant program to help Jews when no one else is. Listen to Rabbi Meir Kahane and speak with him."[51]

Meir continued to address many groups during his mealtime breaks, sometimes twice a day.[52] On November 9 he spoke at the Young Israel of Borough Park, where members of the audience described their suffering at the hands of neighborhood muggers. In response, he led a crowd of over two hundred on a "March for a Safe Neighborhood" to the predominantly Hispanic area of Borough Park. There, they shouted slogans such as "If Jews Are Hit, We'll Hit Back" and "Every Jew a .22." Two days later, synagogues in Borough Park were firebombed, and police told reporters that Meir had sharpened the tensions between the Jews and Hispanics. Meir called a press conference to deny that the JDL's presence had caused the tensions. He said that criminals prey on Jewish areas because Jews have been "patsies" for two thousand years. He wrote:

> Over the past weeks and months the phones at the JDL offices rang daily and the subject was, invariably, the same: Borough Park. A mugging, a robbery, an attack, threats, a fire.... JDL came into Borough Park not as a whim; not on its own, not by the decision of outsiders, but because of the frantic calls of many small Jews who were suffering....[53]

The episode in Borough Park was followed by a disclosure in the *New York Times* about Meir's violation of prison rules.

> Rabbi Meir Kahane ... regularly stays out in the evenings long after his 8:30 P.M. curfew and prison officials say there is nothing they can do to stop him.
>
> The rabbi ... has been lecturing in synagogues around the city in the evening when he is supposed to be incarcerated in the Community Treatment Center, which is run by the Bureau of Prisons in a hotel on West 54th Street. According to the director of the Treatment Center, Rabbi Kahane is often in "complete violation of the rules that are imposed on him."
>
> Rabbi Kahane, an Orthodox Jew, is serving his term in the hotel because he cannot obtain kosher meals in prison. In May, Federal Judge Jack B. Weinstein ruled that the Bureau of Prisons could not deny the rabbi observance of the dietary laws of his religion. The case is now under appeal. As a result of the decision, Rabbi Kahane is allowed out for prayer services and for three one-and-a-half-hour meal periods a day. He is given $4 a day to cover the cost of food and he eats at kosher restaurants or is invited into friends' homes.
>
> But prison officials say that although Rabbi Kahane regularly stays out late, there are no sanctions they can impose on him except to deny him the five days a month he could accumulate toward his release for good behavior.
>
> If other residents of the halfway house, who are prisoners undergoing rehabilitation, violate rules, they can be sent back to prison. But unless the decision by Judge Weinstein is reversed, prison officials say Rabbi Kahane must remain in a facility where kosher food is available to him.

"Well, I tell you very frankly that he is in complete violation of the rules that are imposed on him, but under the existing court order we have no alternative but to keep him here," a spokesman for the Correction Center said.

The Court of Appeals heard the Bureau of Prisons' arguments on October 9, but it had not yet issued its decision.

U.S. Attorney David Trager said in an interview that "we're at a sort of legal impasse and there is very little we can do but wait to hear on the appeal."[54]

The *Times* report aroused public indignation. New York City's Human Rights Commissioner, Eleanor Holmes Norton, sent a letter to Judge Weinstein complaining of Meir's "serious abuse of special privileges."[55] As a result, Judge Weinstein ordered that a U.S. marshal accompany Meir whenever he left the halfway house. This was put into effect immediately – wherever Meir went, two federal marshals (not one) went with him.[56]

Meir wrote home:

The government finally cracked down on me after 8 months, and now I go to *shul* and eat ONLY with 2 marshals. They chauffeur me around. The point is that I have no choice now but to be good.... I can't wait to get home.[57]

In another letter he mentioned the marshals again:

I love you and the days are getting down to the time when I will come HOME.... Best regards from Marvin and Jimmy – my marshals.[58]

On November 17, Meir again tried to attain a measure of freedom: With eight months of his sentence behind him, he applied for placement in the Bureau of Prisons' Work Release program. This would have allowed him to spend the entire day at work, and only return to the halfway house to sleep. On the application form he gave the name of his employer as the *Jewish Press* and the name of his supervisor as Rabbi Shalom Klass. His case managers replied severely:

You have repeatedly demonstrated a lack of responsibility in conforming to your curfew limitations, which would preclude the treatment team in granting your request for work release.[59]

Meir could hardly have expected to have his request granted, because he had been provoking the prison authorities all along, giving public lectures, leading rallies, and returning late from his mealtime breaks. This was deliberate. He could have spent his time quietly at the halfway house, eating at kosher restaurants, and, eventually, he would have been released. But his aim was kosher food as a constitutional right for ALL Jewish prisoners, not only for himself. He did all he could to prod the Bureau of Prisons to expedite the appeals process even though it meant he might be sent to Allenwood.[60]

Meir's continuing activism refuted conjectures that his imprisonment meant the end of JDL and the end of his public activism. In February, after his sentencing, the *Jewish Post and Opinion* had predicted: "The end of his career as an activist and the submergence of the Jewish Defense League as a factor in Jewish life was seen as Rabbi Meir Kahane was sentenced to a year in prison." A *Chicago Tribune* journalist also foresaw the demise of the JDL: "... The Jewish Defense League has been having rough times because of dissension and defection, and there's doubt it can last through Kahane's scheduled year in a federal penitentiary."[61]

The successful demonstration in Washington on October 5 was only one of many projects that proved the vitality and vibrancy of both Meir and the JDL.

Chapter 47
At Last: A Court Decision
(September 1975-January 1976)

Democracy for Jews

AFTER THE SUCCESS of the demonstration in Washington in early October, Meir gave all his attention to another cause: Democracy in Jewish Life (DIJL, pronounced DYE-jel and sometimes written DIJEL). DIJL was a call for open, popular elections to leadership positions in the established American Jewish organizations. Meir maintained that the leaders holding office did not represent the thinking of the majority of Jews in the United States, and they should be replaced by people who did.

Meir had first written about the campaign for Democracy in Jewish Life in his *Jewish Press* column back in July, after JDL's application to join the Presidents Conference was rejected.[1] His next column was titled "Who Elected Them?" He wrote:

> The idea broached here last week for a desperately needed revolutionary change in the tyranny of the present Jewish leaders has received enthusiastic support.... Rabbis and other Jewish leaders who seek more information on a preparatory conclave immediately after the holidays should contact DIJL, 156 Fifth Avenue, Room 1214, New York City. [This was also the address of the Conference of Activists.] You can also ask for a speaker who will appear before your group to explain the plan.[2]

Meir was optimistic about DIJL in a letter to me that month.

> I am busily working on Democracy in Jewish Life, which could be the key to getting our program moving. We will be having the synagogues serve as polling places, and two months before the elections all Jews will register in a synagogue and get the literature of the groups running. They will then vote for the party of their choice. We are convinced that with a three-month speaking campaign tour by the Activist Conference, we can get a large percentage.[3]

Meir's pamphlet *Democracy in Jewish Life* was mailed to over three thousand rabbis and Jewish leaders. It detailed the undemocratic methods used to select officials in Establishment groups and pointed out that even within the umbrella groups there was a lack of equity. Some organizations were large and some small, some prestigious and some utterly unimportant.

This was especially true of the Conference of Presidents of Major American Jewish Organizations, which was looked upon by the non-Jewish world as the spokesman for the American Jewish community. The pamphlet said, "On every sensitive issue involving Israel or the Soviet Union or Syrian Jewry ... it is the Presidents Conference that is called upon to testify before Congressional committees.... The Presidents Conference and its chairman, Rabbi Israel Miller, meet with Kissinger on vital issues.... It is not composed of elected individuals, but of various organizations.... Such an arrangement automatically excludes all the millions of Jews, the MAJORITY of American Jewry, who do not belong to these groups."[4]

Meir's arguments were confirmed by others: The President of the American Jewish Congress, Rabbi Arthur Hertzberg, admitted that the voice of the majority was not given due weight. "The bulk of American Jews take a harder line than the Jewish Establishment," he said. In addition, a study prepared for the World Jewish Congress found that those who determined the policies of the Jewish Establishment were a small number of wealthy Jews.[5]

Meir placed an ad in the *Jewish Press* in August to promote the DIJL campaign.

In This Bicentennial Year, Let Us Have Democracy in Jewish Life:
... Who elects the people who make policy for the Jewish community? Can you choose them? Can you reject them?

The fact is that on both a national and local level you have no say. There is a feudal oligarchy composed of the wealthy and privileged which is self perpetuating, which bars democracy, and which is responsible for disaster upon disaster.

...We are organizing committees for democracy in every Jewish community. We want you to join them and work for a ... "parliament" of U.S. Jewry elected directly and openly on the basis of "one Jew, one vote."[6]

Meir wrote home again about DIJL in September:

We will be placing an ad ($5,000) in the *Times* explaining the idea and announcing a Preparatory Conference. We have invited EVERY rabbi, synagogue and sisterhood president; every editor and publisher in the Anglo-Jewish field; intellectuals and writers, etc. Local committees are being formed to spread the idea and to get one synagogue in each community to serve as a polling place. If we succeed in this it will be a great victory on every issue. If we fail – it will be bad.[7]

In his next letter he outlined his plan to raise money for the project.

This Thursday night is a meeting of potential local committee chairmen for Democracy in Jewish Life. I sent out 2,500 letters asking for $100 each and we are preparing a half page ad in the *New York Times*.[8]

The half-page ad in the *New York Times* introducing DIJL to the general public was headlined: "Jewishness Without Representation Is Tyranny." This play on the slogan of the American Revolution (Taxation Without Representation is Tyranny) conjured up an image of the despotism that existed in Jewish communal life. Addressed "to the American Jewish community," the ad said:

... What is most clear, and beyond debate, is the fact that those who speak for American Jewry are people who have never been elected to do so.... The American Jewish community does not enjoy that elementary democratic privilege of direct election of its representatives that it demands for any Third World victim of colonialism.
... We believe that elementary justice and fair play, as well as the survival of the American Jewish community, demand that a historic change take place.
... We are organizing committees for Democracy in Jewish Life in every Jewish community.
... These local committees, working strictly in their own neighborhoods, will ... arrange for speakers to address local synagogues and centers to explain the project [and] persuade one or more local synagogues to agree to serve as registration and election centers.
... We call upon you to contact us immediately and help form a local committee in your area.[9]

On the day the ad appeared in the *Times*, October 14, Meir held a press conference at the Summit Hotel in Manhattan to give the DIJL idea optimal publicity. He told reporters that the existing umbrella Jewish organizations were "tyrannical and feudal baronies that bar any minority views and any opportunity for the American Jewish masses to decide vital issues that affect their own future and survival." He outlined voting procedures and announced a national preparatory conference to be held on November 24 at the New York Hilton.[10]

To promote the idea of "one Jew, one vote," Meir spoke to various groups during his mealtime furloughs. Ever the optimist, Meir wrote of the project, "It is an exciting concept and one which may do that which everything else failed to do."[11]

The idea of democracy appealed to people. Many recognized the truth of Meir's premise, but called his plan impractical. Rabbi Emanuel Rackman, provost of Yeshiva University, writing in the *Jewish Week*, commended the idea, but called it unworkable and naive. He claimed that the Establishment leaders and their umbrella group, the Presidents Conference, had their hands on the pulse of the "overwhelming majority of Jews, who approved their actions."[12]

In a rebuttal that Meir sent to the *Jewish Week*, he said, "If Rabbi Rackman and the Establishment groups believe they represent most Jews, let them put this to the test and run for office."[13]

Meir outlined the proposed election procedures:

> ... For two entire months, so that every Jew will have the opportunity to register, registration will be open. As each Jew registers, he will receive the basic platform and program of every major Jewish group and any other slate that care to run (anybody can create a slate by getting 500 people to sign a petition).... ALL major Jewish groups will be on the ballot, regardless of choice (there are states in this country that have a similar provision; see, for example, Oregon) since we want a truly representative election and do not wish to give the Establishment an opportunity to invalidate the election by refusing to participate and then claiming they were not represented.... The election will be held under the auspices of a non-Jewish, non-partisan group, such as the Honest Ballot Association.[14]

Marvin Schick, writing in the *Jewish Press*, opined that if elections were to be held, the activists would win. This fear, he said, gave the Establishment a special incentive to oppose the idea.[15] Support for the DIJL idea came from the Zionist Organization of America. Its president, Rabbi Joseph Sternstein, called for abolition of the Conference of Presidents of Major American Jewish Organizations, charging the group with being "constrained by the Israeli government." He said the Conference should have rallied American Jewry against the Israeli-Egyptian interim agreement, terming it a "one-sided, discriminatory agreement." Philip Klutznick, a cofounder of the Conference of Presidents echoed Sternstein's charges and suggested that the conference be replaced by a new group that would be "more reflexive of the mood and sense of American Jewry."[16]

Meir announced street corner rallies in various New York City neighborhoods to publicize the preparatory conference. The rallies would be held at 1 P.M., Meir's lunch hour. He placed ads about the conference in Anglo-Jewish papers and called a press conference at the DIJL office on November 10 at 9:30 A.M., during his breakfast break.[17]

The much-publicized DIJL preparatory conference was held as announced at the Hilton on November 24. Charlie Cohen recalled: "About two hundred people came, and a man from B'nai B'rith sat in the back taking notes. The Establishment was really worried about DIJL!"[18]

In a letter to Tzippy that night, Meir had only this to say:

> Today was a lovely day. It began by my getting trapped in an elevator with
> seven other people. We climbed through the top trapdoor, and it was more fun
> than hamsters.[19]

Disappointed at the low attendance, Meir – who was surely accompanied by
federal marshals Marvin and Jimmy – said to the audience, "That this room is not
filled is an indictment not of Jewish leaders, but of the sheep who are being led
to slaughter and are allowing themselves to be led." He urged the audience to collect at least 250,000 signatures on the DIJL petitions. He said that "unless the
quarter million figure was reached, the election would not be accepted by the present Jewish Establishment." He also suggested that JDL, which had initiated the
move for popular Jewish elections, not lead the DIJL drive. He said, "Take DIJL
out of JDL and give it up to respectable people, so that it will be accepted by the
general Jewish community." Among the "respectable" speakers at the conference
was Rabbi David Hollander, president of the Rabbinical Alliance of America,
who said that the main issue was the "principle that people have no right to speak
for the Jewish community without having a mandate from the community."[20]

The conference concluded with the appointment of a committee, but it made
no concrete progress. This may have been due to Meir's transfer to Allenwood
prison three days after the conference. Perhaps the plan was bound to fail. One
study pointed out: "... The majority is apathetic: While the well-to-do may control
the organizations, they also pay the lion's share of the bill. As long as they keep
on paying, few will protest.... Very few are really interested in altering the status
quo...."[21]

Transfer to Allenwood Federal Prison

On November 26, two days after the DIJL conference, the Court of Appeals
handed down its historic ruling that kosher food in prison was a constitutional
right. It was a victory for Meir, but the decision paved the way for his transfer
to Allenwood Federal Penitentiary in Pennsylvania.

Back in September, Meir's attorney Barry Slotnick had foreseen that the court
would rule in favor of Meir's right to kosher food.[22]

His optimism was based on the fact that on August 12, when the Bureau of
Prisons petitioned to transfer Meir to Allenwood immediately because of his
violation of rules, the Court of Appeals had upheld Judge Weinstein's ruling guaranteeing kosher food.[23]

The U.S. Court of Appeals heard the Bureau of Prisons' appeal on October
9, five months after Weinstein's ruling. The Bureau's main argument was that

Judge Weinstein's court lacked jurisdiction; he had no authority to rule on the matter of specialized diets in the prison system. The decision handed down on November 26 by a three-judge panel of the Court of Appeals for the Second Circuit ruled that Judge Weinstein did have proper jurisdiction but modified Weinstein's conditions.

> The use of frozen, prepared foods, while perhaps helpful, is not constitutionally required if another acceptable means of keeping kosher is provided. We therefore modify the order to require the provision of a diet sufficient to sustain the prisoner in good health without violating the Jewish dietary laws, without otherwise mandating specific items of diet.[24]

Both sides hailed the decision as a victory: Meir, because now all Jewish prisoners were entitled to kosher food, and the Bureau of Prisons, because they would be able to serve him foods that were on hand in the prison kitchen, like fruit, vegetables, eggs, cheese, tinned fish, and other items that did not require special kosher processing. The court specifically ruled that they did not have to serve Meir fresh meat or even kosher TV dinners that had been guaranteed by the original Weinstein order.

Meir was ordered "forthwith" to the Allenwood Federal Penitentiary in Pennsylvania and was immediately taken there. According to his *Inmate Personal Property Record*, among the things he took with him were: "1 overcoat, 1 typewriter, 1 shaver, 6 boxes of candles, 1 spice box, 1 candle holder and $2.02."[25]

In Allenwood, he was shocked to discover that no provision had been made to give him kosher food. The assistant superintendent at Allenwood, Carroll H. Shade, said he had no court order for a special diet. Perhaps the Bureau of Prisons thought that once Meir was under their jurisdiction, he could be cowed into submission. Not Meir! He demanded to speak to his lawyer, Barry Slotnick.[26]

It was Thanksgiving Day, and Meir reached Slotnick in the middle of his Thanksgiving dinner. Meir told him he would go on a hunger strike until he was given kosher food, and asked him to go to court immediately about this blatant disregard of the ruling of the Court of Appeals. Since it was Thanksgiving Day, Slotnick had to phone Judge Weinstein at his home, interrupting his dinner as well, to begin the process of filing an application to hold the Bureau of Prisons in contempt of court. Meir also called the JDL office to have them publicize his hunger strike. The AP wired the news to papers throughout the country. Their report, "Rabbi at Allenwood on Hunger Strike," appeared in a local Pennsylvania paper as well as in the *New York Times* and other papers.[27]

Judge Weinstein acted quickly. The next day, a Friday, U.S. Attorney David G. Trager and Edward S. Rudofsky, Assistant U.S. Attorney, were present in Weinstein's courtroom. Slotnick said, "I am asking for the Court at this time to do whatever possible to make sure that this man, who has not eaten in over twenty-four hours, be provided food through the prison system and not be provided with apples and oranges." Although Weinstein no longer had jurisdiction and Slotnick would have to follow through in a court in Pennsylvania, Weinstein suggested that – to avoid a citation for contempt of court – U.S. Attorney Trager inform the prison superintendent of the court order. Trager followed Weinstein's advice. His telex to Allenwood said:

> Rabbi Kahane should be furnished with new plates and utensils (disposable plastic ware and paper goods will more than suffice) and a new pot and pan, and should be permitted to prepare his own meals, which may consist of the following items: raw fruits and vegetables, eggs, tinned fish, cheese, milk, juice. If Rabbi Kahane requests a particular brand of food, every effort should be made to provide him with the requested item insofar as this is possible within budgetary limitations. Furthermore, if Rabbi Kahane finds that any other item of food available in your commissary meets his requirements and standards, he is, of course, free to partake.[28]

When prison officials in Allenwood received Trager's telexed order on Friday, they arranged for separate cooking utensils and a special kosher nook in the prison kitchen. Meir broke his fast.[29]

Allenwood was a minimum security prison. In Meir's words:

> ... It is in the heart of Pennsylvania and the scenery is beautiful if you are a deer. There are no walls or fences and anyone could walk out at any time. The prison sits on 4,000 acres but there are only a few buildings which house about 430 inmates. The dormitories have no bars or doors that are locked. They are large dormitories in which sleep about fifty prisoners. I have my own bed, desk, two closets and typewriter (by court order), shaver (court order), books and everything else.[30]

There were no walls, but life in prison was hemmed in by rules. There were rules about work assignments, the use of public telephones, the visiting room and more. "Personal Grooming" rules specified clean uniforms and prohibited beards. Soiled clothing could be exchanged for clean items from Monday to Friday; sheets and pillowcases only on Thursday. Lights-out in the dormitories was at 10:30 P.M., but inmates could use the television room or reading room after that hour. Prisoners were counted six times a day, once at 12:30 P.M. at their work assignment, and then at 4 P.M., 10 P.M., 12:15 A.M., 3:15 A.M. and 5:15 A.M. in the dormitory. At each count, prisoners had to be at the specified place. A prisoner who disobeyed the rules could be transferred to a high security prison where there was less personal freedom.[31]

Of the inmates at Allenwood, Meir wrote: "The prisoners sent here are almost all charged with non-violent crimes ... such as embezzlement, stock fraud, income tax evasion and violation of FHA regulations. These 'Jewish' crimes account for most of the older Jewish prisoners being here, while the younger Jewish prisoners are mostly charged with gambling and narcotics violations."[32]

In his first letter home, Meir recapped his early days at Allenwood.

> ... The prisoners were all waiting for me and the Jewish prisoners (there are 38 of them) greeted me royally (more of that later). Naturally, the officials in prison are the lowest of the low, and the next day I was told that they knew nothing of a court order and there was no kosher food. I immediately called New York [i.e. the JDL office] and told them to call the press and tell them I was on a hunger strike. At the same time I told my lawyer to get a writ of contempt against the government and the prison officials. The next day, Friday, the press kept calling up, and the officials got more and more nervous.
>
> Finally, the U.S. Attorney called up to say that Weinstein was prepared to hold them all in contempt and they gave in. They bought me special pots, silverware, a hot plate and food. I have fresh vegetables, eggs, fish [canned sardines], matzas, drinks and next week we should get meat. Needless to say, the Jews were delighted, but even more – all the prisoners love it when the officials get defeated and I became a camp hero.[33]

Nevertheless, Meir's diet was limited. Besides having no meat, he was not eating cheese, canned soups and bread because they did not have the required kashrut certification. The prison superintendent, Eldon Jensen, refused to buy kosher brands because of "budgetary limitations." He also refused to allow Jewish organizations to donate kosher TV dinners.[34] So Slotnick petitioned the U.S. District Court in Lewisburg, Pennsylvania to hold Norman Carlson, director of the U.S. Bureau of Prisons, in contempt of court because he had ignored the court order directing that Meir receive a healthy diet.

The case was argued on December 12 before Judge Michael Sheridan in Lewisburg, Pennsylvania. When Superintendent Eldon Jensen took the stand, he made it clear that he was unwilling to comply with the order of the Court of Appeals. Under questioning by Slotnick, Bureau of Prisons Chief Dietician Norma Jacobson admitted that Meir's present diet was "less than satisfactory." The judge called a short recess, after which prison representatives, afraid of being cited for contempt, said that an immediate study was being made in Washington for the purpose of providing a varied and complete kosher food menu to Orthodox Jewish inmates.[35]

Meir went public with a December 16 press release condemning prison officials and demanding equal rights for Jewish religious practice.

> ... This is more than a question of a dull diet. It is a question of a dull, petty tyrant (and Jensen is only one of so many in the system) who is incompetent.... He not only seeks to defy the courts on the issue of kosher food – to which he

brings a measure of his own primitive anti-Semitism – but takes pleasure in denying privileges … despite general Bureau policy. The result is a total failure of rehabilitation, because Jensen and all the Jensens produce bitter, frustrated and angry prisoners.

 … I intend to carry this fight against Jensen in general and on the kosher food issue in particular, all the way through administrative and court channels. I intend to press for general reforms on behalf of all the prisoners here, as well as equal rights for Judaism, including a room for a synagogue (there is a complete church); shelves for Jewish books and religious supplies; a Torah scroll and phylacteries; nightly study groups (the Christian Yokefellows have this) and other basic religious rights.

Meir aimed to use the power of publicity to achieve these things. At the end of the press release, he wrote:

 … The press is invited to come to Allenwood for personal interviews and is reminded that it is their right.[36]

Learning, Teaching, Writing

Meir found his niche at Allenwood giving classes to Jewish prisoners. He wrote home:

Jewish prisoners have a Friday night service (Reform) which is run nicely (in a manner of speaking) by an inmate. I now give them regular classes which they really enjoy and they keep asking for more. I have a number of Protestants who want to come to an Old Testament class of mine and someone asked me about conversion. I spend my time learning, teaching, writing, and doing two hours a day "work" in the kitchen.[37]

In a letter detailing his daily routine, Meir joked about his work assignment.

My daily routine (in general) is as follows: Wake up at 5:30 to learn *Tanach* [Bible] and *Chumash* [Pentateuch]; 7 A.M.: *Daven* [pray] and eat; 8-8:15: Wash the kitchen windows; 8:15-11:30: Learn and write; 11:30-12:15: Eat; 12:15-12:30: Wash the kitchen windows; 12:30-3:30: Learn and write; 3:30: Mail call; 4-5: Eat; 5-5:15: Wash the kitchen windows (by this time you may have gathered that we have the cleanest kitchen windows in the system). Night: classes or helping prisoners with writs, complaints, etc.[38]

There was more about his work assignment in another letter in which Meir's sense of humor took over:

I have had a sweet job in the kitchen that involves perhaps 15 minutes a day of cleaning the windows. This week, disaster loomed as they asked me to clean the toaster. The possibilities were frightening. What would they ask me to do next? But G-d is good. As I was wheeling it in, it suddenly tipped over and broke. They decided that I should stick to what I was doing.[39]

Meir did not want his parents to worry about his diet. He wrote to them:

> I eat well. My average menu is as follows: Breakfast: orange, Wheatena or other hot cereal, cold cereal, bread and butter or jam or peanut butter, milk. Lunch: Varies: Example: Three eggs, mashed potatoes, soup, bread, etc. milk. Supper: Example: Tuna casserole (with noodles and green peas), soup, bread, etc., grapefruit and milk. I really have the run of the storerooms.[40]

Meir asked for donations of prayer books and other religious articles in a *Jewish Press* column:

> ... There are more than 40 Jewish prisoners in this institution.... The disgraceful fact is that the Jewish organizations ... prefer to make believe [Jewish prisoners] do not exist.
>
> The irony is that there are few Jews with such an objective opportunity to return to Jewish values and tradition. They have the time – unfortunately – that is presently utilized in card playing or other wastes or simply watching the hours and weeks pass by.
>
> Having been arrested and sentenced to prison has caused many such people to rethink their values and they are in a position to be guided and directed – if. If there were only Jews, organizations, rabbis who cared enough.
>
> ... The rabbis? What in the name of Heaven has the Synagogue Council of America done for Jewish prisoners? Did they fight to get them kosher food? Did they work out a library system whereby Jewish religious and cultural books of many and varied descriptions would be available? Did they move to have a Jewish chaplain in every prison...?
>
> When I arrived at Allenwood ... I found a prison where there was no kosher food; no Sabbath morning service; no library; no regular classes and only by the dint of "good fortune," a Friday evening service and *Oneg Shabbat* because one of the prisoners – on his own – had pushed for it and led the ritual.
>
> And for the fat and contented who will quickly say that they tried and it is not possible to have these things, let me say that one week later we had gotten: ... a Sabbath morning service; regular classes, and permission to have *tefillin* brought in.
>
> We can use *tefillin*, Orthodox prayer books (in English and Hebrew), Hertz *chumashim*,* English Bibles and other religious and Jewish books.... Send all books care of Reverend Harold Washburn, Chaplain. [Washburn was the Protestant chaplain. The prison did not have a full-time Jewish chaplain.] ... With

---

* This refers to an edition of the Pentateuch (first five books of the Bible) with an English translation by Rabbi Joseph Herman Hertz. Portions of the Pentateuch are read aloud during the Shabbat synagogue service.

G-d's help, I will be leaving soon, but the others remain and there will be others who follow them. Who knows? It might be someone you know or love. Or it might just be a Jew. [41]

One Jew, moved by Meir's cry, responded immediately.

As a Yeshiva University student, I will do everything in my power to see that you get the things you need, even a bunch of guys to come down and spend the Sabbath with the men there, if you suggest.[42]

An official of the Synagogue Council of America wrote to Meir:

I would like you to know that in response to the request of Shmuel Knopfler, [we have] sent twenty-five copies of a Hebrew and English *Tanach* [Bible] and the same number of copies of an English *Shulchan Aruch* [Code of Jewish Law].[43]

A few days later, Meir wrote that they were deluged with gifts of books but were given no shelf space or room for them.[44] He put the Hebrew-English prayer books to good use at Friday evening and Shabbat morning services. He even typed up a page of instructions so those who knew no Hebrew could participate. Using carbon paper, he made several copies. Instructions said, for example: "Page 237 – Cantor reads first sentence in Hebrew. Page 238 – Congregation together Psalm 95, cantor reads last line in Hebrew. Page 266-274 – RISE. Amida, silent meditation."[45]

Meir turned his legal knowledge and writing ability to good use: "I constantly file writs and complaints for the other prisoners who really are not treated fairly," he wrote.[46] A plea for clemency that he wrote for Robert Owen, a prisoner from West Virginia, said, "I was convicted in your court of Interstate Transportation of a Stolen Motor Vehicle. I never committed the act.... I pleaded guilty at the advice of counsel." The letter explained that a woman helped by Owen at an Alcoholic Center offered to let him use her car and then she said he stole it.[47]

Many prisoners asked him for advice.

The Black Muslims came to me about their own demands for kosher food and a possible hunger strike, and the Italian prisoners who are labeled "Special Offenders" (Mafia), something which is illegal by court ruling, have also come for help.[48]

Always ready to help others, Meir asked me to help, too.

Some of the prisoners really take their imprisonment hard, and one – a former lawyer – was just turned down for parole and was shattered for two days. He is a widower, and his 17-year-old son is running around with a bad crowd.

I am trying to get NCSY [National Council of Synagogue Youth] in Baltimore to get in touch with him, but I would also like to get him to go to the

Hebrew University or another such school. He graduates in May. Could you IMMEDIATELY rush information about the foreign students program.[49]

Meir's letters home did not speak of how difficult the stringent prison regime was for him. He shared only good news with us: For example, he wrote with satisfaction that his article about the U.N.'s "Zionism is racism" resolution had been reprinted in the *B'nai B'rith Messenger*, a national Jewish weekly.

> On the heels of the *B'nai B'rith Messenger* (Los Angeles) picking up my article on Zionism (I mailed that to you), the *Jewish Post and Opinion* reprinted it in full (I will mail that out).[50]

This encouraged Meir to write a rebuttal to an anti-Israel article in the *New York Times* by Joseph Alsop, a leading syndicated columnist. Alsop severely criticized Israeli "intransigence" and claimed this was harming relations with Washington. Meir countered by stating that Washington's policy was and always had been the Rogers Plan, which called for total Israeli retreat from the land liberated in 1967, and that nothing short of this would satisfy Washington. He added that American interests – from the political-economic standpoint – were at odds with those of Israel.

Meir declared that American policy was irrevocably doomed to be anti-Israel, no matter what Administration would take office. He warned Israel, therefore, to adopt a firm policy of "saying no to America now." He contended that Israel should begin immediate settlement of all the liberated lands and annex them to Israel. To reduce Israel's dependency on the United States, Israel should "create non-conventional weapons." In conclusion, he wrote that the major argument that the Americans might understand was the Christian one: The Christian American should be told that his interest on Judgment Day – his ultimate interest – was to stand by the Chosen People of G-d.[51]

When Meir learned that his reply to Alsop had been accepted for publication in the prestigious magazine *American Zionist*, he wrote home proudly:

> The *American Zionist* is printing the full text of my answer to Alsop. The *New York Times* wrote that they would have printed it, but the article by Alsop [which began "Dear Amos"] was to a real "Amos" and he wants to reply. We are making a booklet of my answer also.[52]

Meir's article was directed particularly to those who determined Israeli foreign policy. In a letter to Liga activist, Shimon Rachamim he noted, "I am writing a letter to the *New York Times* about the poisonous article by Joseph Alsop. It is an answer to the government of Israel, too."[53]

At the end of November, Meir learned that there was a good chance of his early release from prison. He wrote:

... The officials want to get rid of me – send me back to New York – because they are afraid of my influence on the prisoners.... I may get out of prison sooner than expected because of their desire to get rid of me. They may give me back all my time off ["good time"] that I lost. So you see, crime does pay.[54]

He was right. They gave him thirty-five days of "good time." His full term was to expire on March 15, 1976, but with "good time" his release was advanced to February 9. In mid-January, Meir wrote home joyfully that he had received "extra good time," and would be released even earlier – on January 30, 1976.[55]

Meir had many visitors at Allenwood. It was one hundred eighty miles due west of New York City, more than a three-hour drive, but that did not discourage his supporters. So many of them wanted to visit that they arranged a roster. Shifra Hoffman recalled that she had to wait a few weeks for her turn. On December 7, Meir wrote, "Shragi and Shelley [my brother and sister-in-law] will be coming up to visit me next week."[56] Meir's visitors often hand-delivered the articles Meir wrote for the *Jewish Press* during this period. Sheila Lidz sent me a short note after she and her husband Mickey visited him:

Meir looks good. He's anxious to be home, but feels very productive in what he is doing at Allenwood.[57]

At the end of December, Meir wrote to the children of his success in returning Jewish prisoners to Judaism:

There is more progress here. Two men are about to ask for kosher food. This morning three more started putting on *tefillin*, and one stopped smoking on Shabbat.[58]

A Torah Dedication Ceremony in Prison

Meir's most memorable accomplishment was a public ceremony held at Allenwood prison to dedicate a Torah scroll. He explained the ceremony in his invitation to Congressman Mario Biaggi:

One of the most important moments for any congregation is the dedication of a Torah scroll which is brought into the synagogue with immense joy.[59]

Meir started to promote the Torah dedication shortly after his arrival in Allenwood. Stanley Schumsky, president of the Young Israel of Coney Island, arranged to donate a Torah scroll from his synagogue, and a bus was chartered to bring New Yorkers to the ceremony.[60]

Meir wrote home about the Torah dedication:

... I had the carpentry shop build an *aron kodesh* [ark or closet to hold Torah scroll] and we got a *Sefer Torah* [Torah scroll]. We will have a big ceremony on January 11 with the Torah brought in, a band, singing and dancing, as well as guest rabbis and lay leaders. The Jewish prisoners love it and they really feel more Jewish.[61]

The prison superintendent, who had been opposed to holding the ceremony, finally agreed to it.[62] He issued a memorandum that said:

The service of dedication will take place in the main dining room from 1 P.M. to 3 P.M. The Jewish residents are playing host to about 100 outside guests, who will participate in the service of dedication.

Prior to the service, a select group of about 25 people, residents and guests, will carry the Torah in a procession through the compound. The group will walk from the Dining Room past Dorms 7&8, 5&6, 3&4 and return to the Dining Room. The group will not enter the dorms.

Following the Service of Dedication, refreshments will be served in the dining room.

Visitors of the Jewish residents will be allowed to participate in the service.

Arrangements are under the supervision of Rabbi Abraham Yeret.[63]

Since only one hundred guests would be allowed into the prison for the ceremony, there were no ads in the *Jewish Press*. Only active members and public figures were invited. Among the guests were many New Yorkers as well as people from Philadelphia, Baltimore and the Washington, D.C., area. Barbara Ginsberg wrote, "That Sunday, it snowed; in fact it was a bad snowstorm. We all went regardless." Fay Lloyd sent a honey cake with her husband, and there were "loads of cake" and refreshments.[64]

The printed program of the ceremony shows methodical planning: The ceremony began in the dining hall, with the singing of the American and Israeli national anthems. There were "welcoming remarks" by Jewish prisoners and prison officials, including the Protestant chaplain, Rev. Harold Washburn. In a "service of dedication," Stanley Schumsky presented the Torah scroll to Rabbi Abraham Yeret, prison rabbi.[65]

Then the procession through the snow-covered grounds began. The Torah was carried under a canopy held up by four men, surrounded by guests and inmates singing lively Hebrew tunes. A mimeographed song sheet, handwritten by Meir, was distributed. It had the words of the Hebrew songs in Latin characters, so those who did not know Hebrew could sing along. The songs included *Hoshee'a Es Amecha*, *Tzion Halo Tishalee*, and *Od Yishama*. Photos show Richard Rolnick holding a corner of the canopy, with the Torah scroll held first by Dr. Hillel Seidman and then by Larry Dickter.[66]

Back in the dining hall, Rabbi Herzel Kranz delivered a sermon and there was more singing and dancing. Meir gave the closing speech. His theme was that a prisoner may lose his freedom, but he does not lose his constitutional rights.[67]

Photos of Meir show him dressed in a khaki prison uniform, his hair neatly combed. In one, he is dancing with a black prisoner; in another, he is attending to the reading of the Torah. In yet another, he is placing the Torah in the ark that was built for it by the prison's carpentry shop. A photo of Meir delivering the closing speech shows him with fist extended to emphasize his words. These photos and others appear in a souvenir journal commemorating the event, *Allenwood Prison Torah Dedication.*[68]

Stanley Schumsky recalled:

> The service that day was conducted by Rabbi Meir Kahane and he honored me with an *aliya* [blessing over the Torah].... It was very inspiring.... The Torah was marched through the grounds with cheering, singing and *simcha* [joy]. And tears... To see the rabbi in prison uniform was sad and disturbing to all.[69]

"It was an exhilarating experience," said Rabbi Herzel Kranz. "The warden sat quietly on the side, not saying a word. There were about forty Jews there and lots of blacks and Hispanics. The black prisoners were full of enthusiasm. They cheered, 'Right on, Rabbi,' and danced with the Torah, too. Meir made a speech about the constitutional rights of prisoners."[70]

Richard Rolnick, then a medical student, held one of the corners of the canopy. "It was an incredible experience!" he wrote. "Even in jail the rabbi was a force to be reckoned with."[71]

Meir later wrote home:

> We had a truly beautiful dedication of the *Sefer Torah*. Dr. Seidman said it was the most unforgettable thing he ever saw, and he has seen many things. The gentiles were tremendously impressed, and at the end, when I spoke, I mentioned all the changes that had to be made in prison – with the Superintendent there, to the frenzied delight of the prisoners. The dancing and singing was like a wedding and it was just wonderful.[72]

Three weeks later, Meir was released from Allenwood Prison. The Jewish prisoners showed their appreciation for Meir's efforts in a farewell letter to him:

> Dear Meir, ... You've been with us for but a short while, but your contribution has been overwhelming.... You've touched us all, both as a group and as individuals.... We've all grown by your presence, and hopefully we will all be better men and much better Jews for having known you.... Be well, have a safe journey to your loved ones and our country of Israel.[73]

Chapter 48
A Free Man
(January-February 1976)

MEIR PREPARED FOR January 30, the day of his release from Allenwood. He sent his manuscripts, typescripts and letters back to Israel with a note that showed how seriously he regarded his responsibility as the family breadwinner: "I want you to take care of them," he wrote, "because many of these things have value and can be sold in the event of need."[1] We did have a steady income, though. Meir continued to write for the *Jewish Press*, and I had a regular salary from the National Library in Jerusalem.

My job at the library was not only a second salary; it was interesting and challenging work. In December I set up an exhibit at the library to mark 150 years since Mordecai Manuel Noah, a prominent American Jew, devised a plan to create a refuge for the poverty-stricken, pogrom-ridden Jews of the Russian Empire. In 1825, he purchased a tract of land in upper New York State for a Jewish colony to be called Ararat. When the project failed, Noah realized that only the land of Israel could be a homeland for Jews. He lectured and wrote on the need for such a homeland, expressing ideas that preceded those of Theodore Herzl.[2]

Meir was glad I was keeping busy.

> ... I know how lonely you must be, but if you have a little patience, you will realize that the time is almost over and I will be home before you know it. I am glad that your job is so satisfying and that certainly helps.[3]

When he received the catalog of the exhibit, he wrote, with his usual touch of humor:

> That was really an impressive thing about M. Noah. Have they found his ark yet? But seriously, it was very well done.[4]

The terms of Meir's release from Allenwood Prison included the condition that he remain in New York for a two-week probationary period, under the supervision of Dr. Hillel Seidman.[5] In mid-January, as soon as he learned that he could not leave for Israel until February 15, he began to make plans to put those two weeks to good use. A schedule of lectures was arranged for him so he could speak out against the "unbearable pressure" on Israel from Washington and the "retreat in panic from one policy stand after another" by Israeli leaders.[6]

He wrote home:

> ... While waiting for the probation to end, I have a busy schedule.... I will be on two big TV shows and will speak for aliya and against giving up land.[7]

A Voice of Compelling Persuasion

Meir's first public address was on Saturday night, January 31, at the Carnegie Endowment Center. An ad in the *Jewish Press* featured its theme, "Treachery in Washington, Confusion in Jerusalem." Afterwards, Meir led the audience in a march to the Statler Hilton hotel where prime minister Yitzhak Rabin was speaking, to protest the Rabin government's policy of concessions.

In a photo taken at the Carnegie Endowment Center, Meir's face is fuller than before. He gained weight in Allenwood because he was less active – he did not have to walk long distances to meals and speaking dates there! He made up for it in a burst of activity during the next two weeks, with a hectic schedule of speaking engagements in synagogues and schools. He spoke every day, and sometimes twice a day.[8] After a talk in Lakewood, New Jersey, he received an encouraging letter from one of his listeners, George Topas.

> ... I am sure that most of the people that came to hear you in Lakewood found your words enlightening and inspiring.
> ... Some people who had expected a "rabble rouser" were surprised that instead of "lightning and thunder" (associated with the story of Elijah) they heard "a still voice" of compelling persuasion which appealed more to the intellect than emotion. It is a historical fact that Truth, although abused and maligned, has survived rising and falling civilizations.[9]

An audio tape of Meir's two-hour talk at the Dix Hills Jewish Center on February 2 attests to his tone of "compelling persuasion." His voice was firm and his flow of words was unhesitating as he spoke of American Jewish life, Soviet Jewry, and the situation in Israel. He presented a dire picture of the problems facing Jews: The rate of intermarriage in America was growing, and the arms strength of the Arab countries surrounding Israel was increasing.

But, he assured his listeners, who had come out despite a severe snowstorm, there is a Divine promise that the State of Israel will never go under. He beseeched them: "Become better Jews. Become traditional Jews. Come to live in

Israel." He quoted from a poignant letter he had received from my father, describing a hike in the hills of Benjamin with our two sons:

> As I watched them running up the hills, I thought how fortunate I was and how G-d had been good to me, because fifty years ago, in the city of Vilna, I almost died of influenza as a child, and now I was in the Land of Israel with my grand-children.

"It's hard to live in Israel," Meir said, "but it's worth it. And when you come, come to visit me." His next words, "You don't have to have my address – just ask any policeman," were greeted with a burst of laughter. Prolonged applause followed his upbeat conclusion: "It's hard to be a Jew, but in the end, Jewish is beautiful."[10]

At his talk in Highland Park, New Jersey, he "implored the hundreds of Jews who jammed the temple to go home to Israel. 'If you stay here,' he said, 'you'll die.'"[11]

Because of Meir's vigorous promotion of aliya, he was invited to speak at the convention of the Association of Americans and Canadians for Aliyah (AACA), sponsored by the Israel Aliyah Center and the Jewish Agency. Yaakov Zev, an American-born Israeli who had been sent to the Aliyah Center in New York to promote aliya, told me:

> I tried all kinds of ways to get people to make aliya. It was an educational process. Meir was one of the best known proponents of aliya at that time, so I invited him to speak at the aliya convention at a hotel in Lido Beach. I invited him for Saturday night, when the attendance would be augmented by people who had not been at the hotel for Shabbat.

But the Jewish Agency was run by Labor party supporters who did not like Meir's outspoken criticism of the policies of the Labor-led Israeli government.

> All hell broke loose. I got phone calls from all the important people in the Jewish Agency urging me to cancel Rabbi Kahane, and I had a lot of trouble from Yehiel Leket. I got all kinds of threats, but the board of the AACA backed me. Besides that, I had no plans to remain at the Aliyah Center, so I had nothing to lose. There was a very large audience.[12]

Meir's talk, summarized in a news report, spoke of things that most aliya emissaries did not mention. He inspired and challenged his listeners.

> ... Rabbi Meir Kahane, the leader of the JDL, stressed that a strong Jewish commitment was the major component of successful aliya. "Without an understanding of Judaism and Jewishness," he emphasized, "there will be no [voluntary] aliya." Tracing the trend of aliya throughout Jewish history, Kahane pointed out that the majority of Jews in the *galut* (exile) never wanted to leave it, no matter how difficult life there was, to come and live in Israel.

According to him, the only way aliya will become meaningful and life in Israel a reality is when Jews realize two things – an awareness and acceptance of their own Jewishness and the fact that anti-Semitism always lies under the surface, waiting for the proper conditions to erupt.

Kahane bluntly told the audience that aliya was extremely difficult, and despite the vast advances Israel has made, life there remains very hard. However, he emphasized, no matter how difficult life was in Israel, Jews must realize that life outside of Israel was impossible for them. He said that each Jew must realize that problems do exist in Israel but that it is each Jew's responsibility to come to live in Israel and solve those problems.[13]

Meir analyzed the "frantic efforts to bar me from speaking" by Jewish Agency people.

[They are] desperately frightened of hearing Jewish truths that will shake the very foundation of their philosophies and existence and that will make them question the essence of their reason for being.... [They] fear that my ideas and words may open the eyes of the Jewish masses and persuade them that their present leaders guide the nation to disaster.[14]

Meir expressed those fearful truths, such as the foolishness of making territorial concessions and recognizing a "Palestinian people," when he spoke at Yeshiva University on February 5. A report said:

... The Rabbi spoke to the crowd of more than two hundred people about a wide range of pertinent topics, including the survival of both Jewry and the State of Israel.

... [He] attacked those Israeli leaders who advocate compromise, and declared that attempts to buy peace with land are "insane." The Arabs are committed to Israel's complete destruction, he said, although they disguise themselves as moderates. "What did the Egyptians want in the Six Day War of 1967, when they possessed every grain of sand in the Sinai?" the angry Rabbi asked.

Kahane criticized many Israeli leaders, including prime minister Rabin, for his acknowledgement of a "Palestinian people." ... It is obvious, Rabbi Kahane pointed out, that the detached individual who views the Arab-Israeli conflict will respect Yasser Arafat and the P.L.O. rather than the pliant and ostensibly weak Israelis.

Meir concluded his talk at Yeshiva University with a reminder that Soviet Jews were still oppressed. Soviet anti-Semitism had increased sharply after the 1973 Middle East war, and the dissemination of anti-Semitic literature had "reached a new high" since the adoption of the United Nations resolution equating Zionism with racism. Intimidation and harassment of Jews seeking exit visas were also on the rise. Meir reminded his audience that it had been JDL's methods that brought about a breakthrough for Soviet Jews in 1971.[15] Since then, the

Establishment organizations had taken up the fight, but Meir argued that their methods were ineffectual. In fact, the number of Jews leaving the Soviet Union had fallen off drastically. Statistics showed that of the approximately three million Jews there, 31,000 Jews were allowed to leave in 1972 and 35,000 in 1973, but only 20,000 in 1974 and 13,000 in 1975.[16]

Brussels II: The Second World Conference on Soviet Jewry

The following week, just when Meir was to return to Israel, the Second World Conference on Soviet Jewry was opening in Brussels, with 1,200 delegates from 32 countries attending.[17] Meir made plans for a stopover in Brussels on his way home. After the wide media coverage of his attempt to speak at the First World Conference on Soviet Jewry in Brussels in 1971, Meir hoped that a second such attempt would again draw media attention to the plight of Soviet Jews.

While still in Allenwood, Meir had begun to publicize his demand to speak at the Brussels conference. He explained to readers of the *Jewish Press* why it was important for him to be a delegate at the conference.

> ... Why do I want JDL to be represented there? I could say that common justice demands that the group which did more for the Soviet Jews than any other and which pushed all the others (that will be sitting there so grandly) into doing that which they would otherwise not have done, SHOULD BE THERE....
>
> But the major reason is that I have something to say that will not be said by the others ... and this is the gist of it:
>
> It was the Jewish militants who understood, long before even Senator Jackson, that the Soviet Union would not be persuaded to modify its policy on Soviet Jewry by quiet diplomacy.... It was JDL that understood that the Soviets would compromise on Jews if their major interest was threatened.
>
> It was the JDL that attacked that major interest – détente – by assaulting Soviet offices and officials, thus causing a crisis in Soviet-American relations, a crisis that neither country wanted and that was only relieved as the Soviets gave in and allowed Soviet Jews to leave in numbers never dreamt of...
>
> ... Senator Jackson used the same political leverage by tying Soviet economic interests to emigration of Jews. Had the Jewish Establishment totally supported Jackson and had the assault on détente continued, many more thousands of Jews would have gone free, and détente would have been, still, a weak and fragile thing.
>
> The Jewish Establishment threw away the opportunity won by the JDL ... and deserted Jackson who was forced to compromise on his amendment. When the Soviets saw that, they realized that if they turned stubborn, the entire amendment would eventually go under.
>
> The Jewish Establishment has joined the chorus of blind fools who blame Jackson's strength for the Soviet toughness when the truth is quite the opposite.

> IT WAS THEIR WEAKNESS THAT FORCED JACKSON TO COMPROMISE and
> that killed the era of Jewish strength won by JDL.
>
> ... Now wheat and all the things the Soviets desperately need must be denied
> them ... unless the Soviets allow a mass outpouring of Soviet Jewry. This is
> what I want to say from the platform to world Jewry. It is up to the masses to
> write to the National Conference on Soviet Jewry and to demand my right to
> speak.[18]

On January 22, several JDLers took over the New York City headquarters of
the National Conference on Soviet Jewry, a sponsor of the Brussels conference.
They demanded that Meir be invited to address the delegates at the conference,
and evicted the office personnel. Police were called in and forcibly removed the
protesters. The arrest of seven JDL demonstrators made this a newsworthy event,
and the general public learned of Meir's demand to speak in Brussels.[19]

From Allenwood prison, Meir wrote to Anglo-Jewish newspapers throughout
the United States to enlist support for his right to speak at the conference. His letter, mimeographed and mailed out by the JDL office staff, was published in the
Jewish Week as a letter to the editor.

> Five years ago, in the midst of the struggle for Soviet Jewry, when Jewish
> Defense League efforts had forced the issue on to page one of the world press,
> I and the JDL were not allowed to participate in the Brussels Conference. That
> conference, itself born of the catalytic efforts of JDL, saw such well-known
> "fighters" for Soviet Jewry as Paddy Chayefsky, Otto Preminger and Arthur
> Goldberg invited, while those who had been in the forefront were barred.
>
> More. When I arrived in Brussels, I was arrested by the Belgian police and
> expelled – at the request of the Jewish leaders.
>
> Today, some 100,000 Soviet-freed Jews later, but at a time when the Jewish
> Establishment, through myopia and timidity, has allowed détente to reach a
> point where the very physical existence of Soviet Jewry can be threatened, they
> meet again to discuss their sterile and unimaginative plans.
>
> Once again I have been barred, and once again, as I leave prison, I will fly
> to Brussels to present a dynamic and real program. The question is: Will I be
> again arrested and expelled at the request of the Jewish leaders?
>
> ... I ask you to take an editorial stand and your readers to write letters to
> the National Conference on Soviet Jewry in New York. Having barred us from
> joining their group, they now bar us from Brussels because we are not members
> of their group....

A supportive "Editor's note" followed Meir's letter, but it had some reservations – probably because the *Jewish Week* depended on the Jewish Establishment
for subsidies.[20]

> We supported Kahane's request to be heard at Brussels last year [*sic* – it was
> actually five years earlier] and we think it would be wise to give him the floor

this year, but we do not think he is any less a "feudal baron" than those to whom he applies this epithet. Jews who give their energies to Jewish causes do not deserve name-calling. Kahane is self-appointed to no less a degree than other leaders.[21]

Meir believed that the subsidized funding of most Jewish newspapers by local Jewish Federations resulted in a lack of freedom of the press. In a January 16 *exposé*, he noted that the *Jewish Week*, like most other local Jewish newspapers, was "given over to self-serving statements and laudatory news concerning individuals and events tied to the Federation." In addition, he said, "the subsidies guarantee that no significant editorial criticism of the Federation will appear in print." For example, the *San Francisco Jewish Bulletin*, the only Jewish newspaper in San Francisco, was instructed by the local Jewish Welfare Federation to refuse an ad criticizing the Federation for not paying enough attention to Soviet Jewry.[22]

However, the independently owned *B'nai B'rith Messenger* published an editorial fully in favor of inviting Meir to speak at the Brussels conference.

> As the curtain prepares to rise on Brussels II on February 17, there is one bad scene we would not like to see repeated. There is too much at stake in the ever-worsening plight of Russian Jewry to play this tape all over again. Enough of reruns.
>
> Remember five years ago? That's when Rabbi Meir Kahane, the militant head of the JDL, asked for the floor at Brussels I. Instead he got the barroom bounce and a jail cell.
>
> It was the start of the martyrdom of Meir Kahane. He became a symbol for young activists – and some old activists as well. It was indeed his shining hour. And it was for the "organized" Jewish community assembled ostensibly to cry out for freedom, a shabby performance.
>
> At this stage, we are about to see a confrontation II at Brussels II. Kahane, in a letter to the editor, says he'll be out of his Federal jail and in Brussels for the conference. What's more, he wants the floor.
>
> And once again, it looks like he'll get the heave-ho.
>
> ... Frankly, Meir Kahane is entitled to be heard in any conference on Soviet Jewry. It was Meir Kahane, whether the Establishment likes it or not, who shook up the struggle for Soviet Jewry and gave it life when it was stagnating with pleas for prayers and symbolic seats at the Seder. Nice gestures but no action.
>
> ... Frankly, we would like to see the planners put aside their prejudices for one hour and ... hear him out.
>
> We should not be confronting one another. We should save our confrontations for the Russians.[23]

Another independent publisher, Gabriel Cohen, wrote a favorable editorial in the *Jewish Post and Opinion*:

... Because it would be the democratic way, we believe that Rabbi Kahane and the JDL should be permitted, if not invited, to attend the sessions and participate in them. The views and programs of the JDL can be repudiated by the Brussels conference, that is its prerogative, but unless those views are heard, the conference will be an unbalanced one – mostly representing the Jewish Establishment whose position remains unchallenged, an unhealthy aspect of any condition where decisions are involved.

We know that Nahum Goldman differs with the Establishment on its analysis – not its activities – of the Russian Jewish problem, yet he most certainly will be welcome, if not already scheduled as a speaker. This same extension of courtesy should be made to the JDL and Rabbi Meir Kahane.[24]

In a press release, Meir presented Gabriel Cohen's words "permitted, if not invited" as a possible compromise. That is, Meir and the JDL delegation would not be officially invited to the conference, but would be "allowed" to attend. But the National Conference on Soviet Jewry refused to consider this.

The press release also announced a rally at the Belgian Mission to the United Nations on February 12 at noon. JDL demonstrators would demand that the Belgian government allow Meir to enter Belgium, and Meir would announce his "exact plans for Brussels" to the press.[25]

People sent letters and telegrams to the National Conference on Soviet Jewry supporting Meir's participation in the World Conference. A petition signed by prominent Jews said: "If the conference is to truly be a reassessment of the past and a guide for the future, all groups identified with the struggle of Soviet Jewry, including the JDL, should be admitted and allowed to express their varied points of view." It was signed by public figures such as Dr. Hillel Seidman, Dr. Alexander Temkin, Glenn Richter, Otto Preminger, Dr. Samuel Korman, Rabbi Elyakim G. Rosenblatt, Esther Jungreis, Rabbi Shlomo Riskin, Rabbi Benjamin Blech, and Rabbi Avraham Weiss.[26]

It was fortunate that Sam Shoshan, who had accompanied Meir to Brussels in 1971, would be his traveling companion now, too. Shoshan traveled to Europe often on business; he was familiar with the roads and knew many European languages. He was certain that if Meir flew to a Belgian airport, he would be stopped by customs authorities, because he had been expelled from Belgium in 1971. So Shoshan suggested flying to Amsterdam and making the two-hour drive to Brussels in a rented car.

This plan was not kept secret. JDL distributed a press release that said, "Rabbi Kahane is leaving for Belgium on Royal Dutch Airlines (KLM) Tuesday, February 17, 9:15 P.M. He will hold a press conference that day, Tuesday, at 4 P.M. at the Women's National Republican Club, New York City."

The press release included the ten-point program Meir would present at the Second World Conference on Soviet Jewry and announced a JDL rally before

Meir's departure at the KLM terminal at Kennedy airport.[27] A *Jewish Press* ad announced:

The Brussels Conference Has Barred Kahane
Kahane Is Going to Brussels Anyhow
Rally at Kennedy Airport to Support Rabbi Meir Kahane's Right to Speak
Tuesday, February 17, 1976, 7:30 P.M. sharp, KLM Terminal.[28]

Snapshots of Meir and his supporters at the rally show Meir wearing a dark suit jacket over a beige sweater, with a maroon necktie closing his usually open shirt collar. One supporter holds a placard that says, "Protect Rabbi Kahane's Right to Speak." A news item noted the noisy chants and bullhorn protests of the JDLers at the airport.[29]

Sam Shoshan recalled his trip with Meir. He was certain that Interpol would be informed of Meir's flight number and destination.

> At Amsterdam's Schiphol airport, Interpol was waiting. There was someone walking in back of us, about a hundred paces behind. We could easily spot him because wherever we made a move, he made a move. We could have taken the train from Amsterdam to Brussels, but Meir would have been easily stopped at the border if we went by train. I said to Meir, "Okay, let's rent a car," and, of course, we spoke loudly, to make sure the Interpol man overheard us.
>
> We walked over to Avis and rented a car. I drove in the direction of Brussels and we noted that we were being followed. Just before the Belgian border, I exited the highway at high speed and drove to the nearest town. I parked the car in an underground garage there and we went out at the back exit. We had shaken off our trackers. We flagged down a taxi and arranged that for a $100 bill he would drive us to Brussels. Back on the highway, approaching the border booth, I told Meir to hunker down as if he was sleeping. I knew there were only cursory inspections at this border, like the U.S.-Canada border, and that taxis go through easily. The border guard waved us through.
>
> But the police were waiting at the Palais de Congres. I guess they figured we must be on our way when they lost us, and all they had to do was to wait for us at the conference hall.[30]

As soon as Meir appeared in the lobby of the hall, he was surrounded by reporters and conference security men, who had been on the lookout for him all day. According to newspaper reports, one security man began to shout repeatedly, "You are not a delegate." Meir retorted, "I am a Jew, I am a Jew!" There was a five-minute confused struggle. Police formed a cordon around him. He went limp and slipped to the floor in the midst of the crowd. Police picked him up by both arms and legs and dragged him to a waiting police wagon. An Associated Press photo shows him being carried out, completely surrounded by policemen. Meir's eyes are closed, in the classic posture of limp civil disobedience. The photo appeared in countless newspapers that day.[31]

Many expressed their dismay at Meir's ouster. One was a Russian Jew who addressed the conference the next day. Shoshan wrote to Meir about him.

> Gary [Ratner] tells me that at Thursday afternoon's session, a man who recently got out of the Soviet Union addressed the conference and deplored what had been done to you. He said that as long as you were there, you should have been allowed to speak. He reminded the audience that the purpose of the conference was for Jews to be able to speak freely and that this same freedom was denied to you. Gary says that he got the loudest applause during that afternoon session.[32]

An indignant letter appeared in Philadelphia's *Jewish Exponent*.

> ... It was a dastardly thing I saw on television and in the newspapers the other day, of Rabbi Kahane being pushed to the floor and dragged out of the Brussels Conference on Soviet Jewry.
> Golda Meir said, "He was not invited to the conference, hence the ejection." Well, as a diplomat and as a Jew, she has come down in my estimation.
> ... Shame on all the Jewish people at the conference and especially Golda Meir for her lack of wisdom and discretion against a holy and dedicated rabbi.
> [Signed] Madeline P. Becker.[33]

A strongly worded letter to the editor of *Jewish Week* said:

> ... Maybe they were afraid to let the world hear a Jew who stands erect and doesn't worry about what "they" will think. For shame, that the same people who deplore Israel's treatment in the United Nations will treat a fellow Jew in an even more cavalier manner. [Signed] Judith Ratner.[34]

Glenn Richter, national director of the Student Struggle for Soviet Jewry, returned from the Brussels conference greatly disappointed. He wrote:

> ... Little opportunity was officially made to deal with real issues, among them the new, highly arbitrary regulations denying exit to those whose leaving would be "damaging to the public morale," the imprisonment of young Jewish men who reject the punitive Soviet army draft, the balance between the revival of Jewish life in the USSR and the need for aliya, *noshrim* (those emigrants who do not go to Israel), the question of whether to help emigrants who do not wish to go to Israel or who leave the Jewish state, and the pains of absorption in Israel and elsewhere in the West.
> Kahane's forcible ouster diverted attention away from Soviet Jews' plight; he could have better been co-opted into the gathering.[35]

An editorial in the *B'nai B'rith Messenger* was scathingly critical of the conference's organizers.

... The conference sponsors knew he was coming. He had made no secret of it. They knew he wanted to provoke an incident if he could not speak. Yet, they opted to repeat their mistake of five years ago. While they were making speeches he was making the headlines and the TV screens.

... Many of those who denied him the right to speak because they don't like his militancy (now their excuse is that he is a felon), are the very same people who spoke out so strongly for dissent in America during the turmoil of the sixties....

... The spectacle of a conference protesting the mistreatment of Jews and decrying Moscow's heavy-handed tactics acting like the Kremlin itself is hardly a picture for the world to applaud.[36]

Meir called the conference organizers "the arrogant feudal barony that controls world Jewry."[37] The ostensible reason they gave for refusing to admit him this time was that he had committed felonious crimes. Every delegate received a page detailing Meir's conviction for violating the Federal Gun Control Act, his involvement in a plot to smuggle arms from Israel to Europe, the "inflammatory" rally he led in Borough Park, and his imprisonment in Allenwood.[38]

Meir gave the true reason they refused to let him speak.

... They, ... knew that Soviet Jewry faces a threat to its freedom and physical survival unmatched since the days of Stalin. They knew this and determined to do nothing.... [They] made a planned decision that no concrete program would be adopted, ESPECIALLY NOT THE ONE THING THAT ALL KNOW WOULD SHAKE THE RUSSIANS AND FORCE THEM TO MAKE CONCESSIONS – A DETERMINED ATTACK BY WORLD JEWRY ON DETENTE.

... I came to Brussels knowing that the Israeli government and its sheepish world Jewish followers were determined that no such concrete program be adopted lest Gerald Ford and Henry Kissinger grow angry and threaten Israel with all manner of sanctions....

... And what I know, the Jewish leaders know, and THAT is the reason why I was prevented from speaking. NOT the nonsense of my "violence."[39]

Home!

The Belgian police held Meir incommunicado in a jail in Brussels overnight. The next day, February 19, he was taken to Brussels airport and put on a plane for Israel. When I heard this on the radio, I checked the arrival times of flights coming in from Belgium and decided to go to the airport to meet him. Tzippy and Binyamin came home from school in time to go to the airport with me. It was a tearfully happy reunion.[40]

Afterword

In the ensuing years, Meir devoted himself to teaching and influencing American Jews through his writings and lectures. However, he realized that the destiny of the Jewish people was mainly dependent on events in Israel, and he entered the Israeli political arena.

After his unsuccessful bids for election to the Knesset in 1977 and 1981, he gained a seat in 1984 and was one of the Knesset's most active members. During this time, five of Meir's books were accepted by American publishers. One of them – *Why Be Jewish? Intermarriage, Assimilation, and Alienation* – influenced many American Jews to live fully Jewish lives. Some even went to live in Israel because of that book.

I hope to discuss the events of 1976 to 1990 in a sequel to the present book and would appreciate personal recollections and documents concerning those years. Please send them to P.O. Box 39020, Jerusalem, or to 1412 Avenue M #2387, Brooklyn, New York 11230. E-mail messages can be sent to: mrslkahan@yahoo.com.

Notes

Abbreviations

FBI U.S. Department of Justice. Federal Bureau of Investigation. Files are from the Washington, D.C., office unless otherwise noted.

RZ Archives Rabbi Meir Kahane Collection, Archives for the Research of Religious Zionism, Bar Ilan University (Ramat Gan, Israel)

RZ Archives, Appendix Copies of documents collected after Rabbi Meir Kahane's death

YU Archives Jewish Defense League Collection, Yeshiva University Archives (New York, New York)

JNUL Jewish National and University Library / National Library (Jerusalem, Israel)

JNUL Archives: Archives and Manuscript Department of the JNUL

Introduction

1   Yair Kotler, *Heil Kahane* (New York: Adama, 1986); Robert I. Friedman, *False Prophet* (Brooklyn, N.Y.: Lawrence Hill, 1990). Book reviews pointed out their faults:

Heil Kahane: "It suffers from a wearisome ill-tempered tone and insufficient documentation," said *Publishers Weekly* (January 17, 1986, p. 58). The reviewer in *Library Journal* (April 1, 1986, p. 146) wrote, "Kotler's distaste for Kahane and all he stands for prevents any semblance of objectivity."

False Prophet: The *New York Times Book Review* (May 13, 1990, p. 18) called it a "remorseless polemic ... ranting in heated and melodramatic prose." A review in *Hadassah Magazine* (January, 1991, p. 43-44) said, "There isn't even an attempt at balance or perspective."

See index for examples of inaccuracies in these books.

Chapter 1

1   Entries on R. Meir Liven in biographical dictionaries: Shmuel Noah Gottlieb, *Ohalei Shem* (Pinsk, 1912), p. 123; Ben Zion Eisenstadt, *Dor Rabanav Vesofrav* (Vilna, 1901), pt. 3, p. 23. Gottlieb gives his birth date as 1840; Eisenstadt as 1845. Gottlieb's date is accepted by the Institute for Hebrew Bibliography, Jerusalem.

Interview with Sonia (Sara Chana) Kahane, January 3, 1997, Jerusalem.

Books by R. Meir Liven at the JNUL are: *Imrei Chemed* (Vilna: 1902), 152 pp.; *Chasdei Avot* (Vilna: 1909), 67 pp.; *Rosh Amir* (Vilna: 1869), 26 leaves. The text of *Imrei Chemed* can be viewed on the Internet at www.hebrewbooks.org.

Praise of the Holy Land...: "Drush Hamechaber Beshevach Shel Eretz Hakodesh Vetikvateinu Bilvaveinu," *Imrei Chemed* (Vilna: 1902), pp. 6-10.

2   Baruch David Kahana, *Chibat Ha'aretz* (Jerusalem: 1897), 77 pp.; *Birkat Ha'aretz* (Jerusalem: 1904), 89 pp. Reprints: Jerusalem: 1968 and 1982; Monroe, N.Y.: 1993; Safed: 1996; Ashdod: 1997. Both books can be viewed on the Internet at www.hebrewbooks.org.

Biographies: "Baruch David bar Levi Yitzchak Kahana," in: Meir Wunder, *Me'orei Galicia: Encyclopedia of the Scholars of Galicia* (Jerusalem: 1986), vol. 3, pp. 325-328, and Yechezkel Shraga Kahane, *Mishnah Yesharah* (Jerusalem: 1973), p. 128.

A detailed biography of R. Baruch David is found in the introduction to the enhanced edition of his book *Chibat Ha'aretz* (Safed: 1996), pp. 19-33.

See also: "R. Baruch David," in Dov Berish Gottlieb, *Darkhei Av* (Jerusalem: 1991), pp. [162-175].

R. Naftali Wachstein, in his [as yet unpublished] book, *Mamlekhet Kohanim*, describes previously unknown documents that indicate that R. Baruch David was the great-grandson, rather than the grandson, of R. David Magid.

Seer of Lublin: Letter from Rabbi Chayim Y. Rubin of Congregation Avenue U Educational Center, Brooklyn, N.Y., to Libby, December 12, 1997, in RZ Archives. Rabbi Rubin's wife was a descendant of R. Baruch David.

R. Baruch David's wife Rivka was the daughter of R. Shraga Feitel of Kishinev. Their children were named Nachman and Nechama, meaning "comfort," because children born previously died young. Nechama married Shlomo Leider, and their descendants have published biographies of R. Baruch David. See above: *Chibat Ha'aretz*, 1996, and *Darkhei Av*.

3   For further details, see introduction to *Chibat Ha'aretz* (Safed: 1996), pp. 34-45, and *Mishnah Yesharah*, p. 130 (see note 2).

The distance from Safed to Tiberias is 36 kilometers (about 22 miles). The trek probably took about seven hours.

Halakha concerning a *kohen* and dead bodies: *Shulchan Arukh, Yoreh De'ah* 374:1.

Austrian citizenship: The Austro-Hungarian Empire included Galicia and other parts of southern Poland. The Ottoman Empire allowed foreign citizenship. See: en.wikipedia.org/wiki/ Capitulations_of_the_Ottoman_Empire.

4   See note 2, *Me'orei Galicia*, vol. 3, p. 327.

In Meir's passport applications, his father's date of birth appears variously as April 6, 1907, April 6, 1908, and 1905. According to one application, his father arrived in the United States in 1923 and was naturalized in 1929 in New York City. Passport applications in RZ Archives, folder 582.

5   Chanoch Zundel Kahana, *Zikaron Ledor Acharon* ([Tel Aviv]: 1955). Typescript, in RZ Archives, Appendix.

6   Interview with R. Solomon Kahane, son of R. Levi Yitzchak Kahane, June 24, 1998, New York City. He also related that the Lubliner Rabbi, Meir Shapiro, founder of the Daf Yomi daily Talmud study program, prayed at the Ahavas Torah synagogue (on Bedford Avenue near Rutledge Street) when he came to America and was very fond of Yechezkel.

In 1932 Levi Yitzchak became rabbi of the prestigious Congregation Anshei Brisk, the "Clymer Street Shul," in Williamsburg. A family history is included in his book of sermons and essays, *Mas'at Beit Halevi* (New York: Pardes, 1936), 140 pp.

7   The Avenue U Jewish Center is at East 9th Street between Avenues T and U. The name Congregation Anshe Sholom is from the journal of its fifth annual banquet, February 17, 1934, in JNUL Archives, folder ARC 4=1748.

The family lived near the synagogue, at 717 Avenue T.

8   In Meir's passport applications, his mother's date of birth is given variously as January 2, 1912 and December 31, 1912. According to one application, his mother arrived in the United

States in 1926 and was naturalized in 1932. Passport applications in RZ Archives, folder 582.

Rabbi Baruch Shalom Trainin's ordination certificate was signed by Rabbi Meir Simcha Hakohen, Rabbi Yisrael Avraham Aba Krieger, of Kashedar (Kaisiadorys), and Rabbi Meir Yitzchak Goldberg, of Vitebsk.

Rabbi Meir Simcha was rabbi of Dvinsk (Daugavpils) for forty years, up to 1926. He began publishing his *Or Sameach* commentaries in 1902.

See also note 1, interview with Sonia Kahane.

Sonia's brother, Rabbi Isaac Trainin, supplied the vital statistics of their parents: Baruch Shalom Trainin, 1882-1946; Henya Trainin, 1887-1967.

[9] In the journal issued for the congregation's testimonial dinner on October 15, 1961, R. Yechezkel wrote that this was his eighteenth year as its rabbi. Congregation Shaarei Tefiloh souvenir journal, 1961, in JNUL Archives, folder ARC 4=1748.

Shaare Tefiloh's address was 1679-83 West First Street, Brooklyn, N.Y. 11223.

[10] A plaque on the wall of the Kahane home had the dates of R. Yechezkel's presidency of the Vaad Harabbanim.

[11] Rambam Yeshiva, Articles of Incorporation and Certificate of Incorporation, January 1945, in RZ Archives, Appendix.

Graduation certificate signed Rav Yechezkel Kahane, June 1953; photo with other members of the Board of Education, in RZ Archives, Appendix.

[12] Yechezkel Shraga Kahane, *Natzionaler Religiezer Vort* [National Religious Words] (New York: Pardes, 1935), 127 pp., in JNUL. The full text can been seen under Kahana at: http://www.hebrewbooks.org.

Charles Ph. Kahane, *Echo of Tradition* (New York: Pardes, 1935), 88 pp., in JNUL.

Mishnah Yesharah, see note 2.

Yechezkel Shraga Kahane, *Torah Yesharah: A Traditional, Interpretive Translation of the Five Books of Moses* (New York: Solomon Rabinowitz, 1963-1964), 2 vol., in JNUL.

The commentary (indicated by italics here) enriches the text. For example: "Therefore the Almighty led them round about the way of the wilderness, *to mislead Pharaoh so that the Egyptians would be defeated by the Red Sea*" (*Exodus* 13:18); "... they borrowed of Egypt jewels of silver and jewels of gold and raiment... and they spoiled Egypt, [and] *thus they recovered what they had left in Egypt*" (ibid. 12:35, 36). The commentaries cited for each verse are listed at the end of each volume. Other examples are given in reviews of the work: Richard F. Shepard, "Rabbi Publishes New Bible Study," *New York Times,* June 21, 1964, p. 88; "Torah Yesharah: A Torah-True Translation," *Jewish Press*, May 17, 1963, p. 9.

[13] Interview with Meir's mother, Sonia (Sara Chana) Kahane, January 3, 1997. Jabotinsky was in the U.S. from January to April 1935 and from March 1940 until his death on August 4, 1940. E-mail from Amira Stern, archivist, Jabotinsky Archives, January 26, 2003.

Peter Bergson spent the Holocaust years in the United States recruiting support for military activities against the British who ruled Palestine then. His real name was Hillel Kook, but he used a pseudonym rather than exploit the fact that his uncle was the chief rabbi of Palestine, Abraham Isaac Kook.

[14] "Jews Fight for the Right to Fight," [ad] *New York Times*, January 5, 1942, p. 13. This was a full length, 7-column wide ad.

"When the Enemy's Gun..." [ad] *New York Times*, April 21, 1942, p. 17. The ad, four columns wide and the full length of the page, was signed Committee for a Jewish Army. Among the signatories were Ben Hecht, Lowell Thomas, generals and political figures; the name Charles Kahane did not appear.

Charles Jacob Levine, *Propaganda Techniques of the Bergson Group, 1939-48* (Master's thesis, University of Texas, 1974), 180 pp., in Jabotinsky Archives, file *kaf* 8-39. Levine documents Rabbi Charles Kahane's participation in a meeting led by Bergson. See pp. 31-32, pp. 104-105.

[15] "The Washington Pilgrimage," *Report of Activities and Financial Statement, Emergency Committee to Save the Jewish People of Europe* ([New York]: 1943), pp. 10-12, in Jabotinsky Archives, file *chet* 11-11/2. See also: www.wymaninstitute.org/special/rabbimarch.

[16] Samuel Margoshes, "News and Views," *The Jewish Day (Der Tog)*, October 10, 1943, p. 1; "Rabbis Present Plan to Wallace," *New York Times*, October 7, 1943, p. 14; both in Jabotinsky Archives, file *chet* 11-11/2.

Margoshes referred to the popular Bible illustrations by Gustave Doré (1832-1883) that depicted the patriarchs with long, flowing beards.

[17] The brochure proclaimed that the camp provided "kosher food, a Jewish cultural atmosphere, sports, and a choral group" for boys and girls, 6 to 14. *Jewish National Youth Summer Camp* [brochure], in Jabotinsky Archives, file *bet* 16-7/5.

[18] "Funeral of Safed's Road Sacrifices," *Palestine Post*, March 30, 1938, pp. 1, 2. In August 1929, Arab gangs massacred 63 Jews in Hebron, 30 in Jerusalem, six in Tel Aviv, six in Haifa and five in Safed. The Arab riots between 1936 and 1939 resulted in the deaths of over 400 Jews.

[19] "Zeva'a Bederekh Tzefat-Ako [Atrocity on the Safed-Acre Road]," *Ha'aretz*, March 29, 1938, p. 1.

[20] Ben Yosef was born in 1913 in Lutsk, Poland. In 1937 he went to live in the Betar settlement at Rosh Pina, not far from Safed. See: "Ben Yosef (Tabachnik), Shelomo," *Encyclopedia Judaica* (Jerusalem, 1971), vol. 4, p. 571. See also: "Shlomo Ben Yosef," www.etzel.org.il/english/people/shlomo.htm.

Chapter 2

[1]   E-mail from Bebe Levitt, Librarian, Yeshiva of Flatbush, June 3, 2003. Moshe Nathanson is credited with writing the popular Hebrew folksong *Hava Nagila*.

[2]   Interview with Shlomo Shulsinger, November 1986, Jerusalem.

[3]   The Hebrew inscription in the bar mitzvah gift from the Yeshiva of Flatbush:

תשורת חן, חן, מתנה למזכרת אהבה וחבה לתלמידנו המצוין מאיר כהנא ליום היכנסו לגיל של מצוות ברית
שלש עשרה. מי ייתן והיו דברי הספר הזה בפיך ובלבך עד עולמי עד. והיה זה שכרנו! המורים ומנהלים של
הישיבה דפלטבוש.

[4]   *Chamisha* (music by Mordechai Zeira, words by Shin Shalom). English translation: Max Helfman, *Israeli Songs in Settings for Voice and Piano* (New York: Brandeis Youth Foundation, 1949), in JNUL, Jewish Music Department, Meir Noy Collection.

[5]   Letter from Dr. Jerry L. Shapiro, San Francisco, to Libby, July 15, 1997, in RZ Archives, Appendix.

  Flatbush Forum, the alumni newsletter of the Yeshiva of Flatbush, kindly publicized my request for recollections about Meir, and Shapiro responded.

[6]   Letter from Dr. Jerry L. Shapiro to Libby, August 5, 1997, in RZ Archives, Appendix.

[7]   Interview with [name withheld], February, 1997, Jerusalem.

[8]   Copies of seventh grade report cards are in JNUL Archives, folder ARC 4=1748.

[9]   Meir also compiled a scrapbook about sports, especially baseball. A lifelong archivist, he kept extensive files, which assisted me in writing this book.

[10] Meir's bar mitzvah speech was printed in Hebrew in: Yechezkel Shraga Kahane, *Mishnah Yesharah* (Jerusalem: 1973), pp. 88-89.

Meir's bar mitzvah party was celebrated before his thirteenth birthday (28 Tamuz fell on July 9 that year) because most of the congregants left the city during the summer.

[11] Joseph Trumpeldor (1880-1920) was killed while defending Tel Hai, a settlement in northern Galilee. He is best known for his dying words, "Never mind, it is good to die for our country."

[12] Letter from Rabbi Irwin E. (Yitzchak) Witty to Libby, December 5, 1997, in RZ Archives, Appendix.

Classmate Marcia Wilk Greenwald recalled that Meir sang a solo in the graduation cantata. E-mail from Alumni Organization, Yeshiva of Flatbush, June 3, 2003.

[13] For more on yeshiva boys of that era and ball-playing, see Chaim Potok, *The Chosen* (New York: Simon and Schuster, 1967).

[14] Interview with Rabbi Yaakov Yellin, June 1998, Jerusalem. This took place at a summer day camp in Flatbush.

[15] See chapter 8 for Meir's sportswriting.

[16] Phone interview with Rabbi Kenny Cohen, September 24, 1997.

Chapter 3

[1] See chapter 4 for Meir's Betar experiences.

[2] Letter from Rabbi Irwin (Yitzchak) Witty to Libby, December 5, 1997, in RZ Archives, Appendix.

[3] Letter from Rabbi Irwin (Yitzchak) Witty to Libby, March 19, 1998, in RZ Archives, Appendix.

[4] Interview with Rabbi Abraham Zuroff, February 1, 1997, Jerusalem.

Rabbi Zuroff also related: "The other boy's father transferred him to our sister school, Manhattan Talmudical Academy, where there were two tracks: one that emphasized Talmud and one that emphasized Bible."

Rabbi Zuroff was also interviewed by Robert I. Friedman, who slanted Rabbi Zuroff's words to imply that Meir was a poor student, uninterested in Talmud studies. (*False Prophet*, p. 31.)

[5] Several of Meir's classmates were to play important roles in Jewish communal affairs: Rabbi Pinchas Stolper headed the National Conference of Synagogue Youth (NCSY) and the Union of Orthodox Congregations. Rabbi Irwin E. Witty was the executive director of the Board of Jewish Education in Toronto and later the director of the Coalition for Jewish Learning in Milwaukee. Rabbi Irving Greenberg was rabbi of the Riverdale Jewish Center, headed CLAL (the National Jewish Center for Learning and Leadership), and in 1995 became president of the Jewish Life Network.

[6] Letter from Rabbi Irwin (Yitzchak) Witty. See note 3.

[7] New York State law allowed young people to work for wages only after age 14, and even then they needed their parent's signed agreement.

[8] See note 4.

The school year then was divided into "terms" similar to the fall and spring semesters at universities. Meir enrolled in AHLS for his 4th term.

[9] Interview with Allan Mallenbaum, May 18, 1998, Jerusalem. Mallenbaum was, like Meir, a member of Betar.

[10] Talmudical Academy, Brooklyn, [*Transcript of High School Record*] Martin D. Kahane, September 1945-June 1949, in RZ Archives Appendix. The transcript covers only general subjects,

not Jewish ones. Thanks to Rabbi Melvin Davis, Yeshiva University Registrar, for locating the transcript.

[11] Letter from Rabbi Irwin (Yitzchak) Witty to Libby, January 15, 1999, in RZ Archives, Appendix.

See also note 4.

Meir's personal entry in his graduation yearbook, *The Elchanite* (Brooklyn, N.Y.: 1949), in RZ Archives, Appendix.

[12] Phone interview with Irwin Pechman, May 1, 2006.

[13] E-mail from Rabbi Yitzchak Greenberg, June 6, 2006. He also wrote, "Let me only add that our pranks were within the parameters of what rambunctious teenagers do."

[14] Meir officially changed his name from Martin to Meir in 1973. See chapter 33, note 4.

[15] Meir's poems, story and personal entry in *The Elchanite* (Brooklyn, N.Y.: 1949) in RZ Archives, Appendix. Meir's graduation picture is in the photo section of this book.

[16] Interview with [name withheld], February 1997, Jerusalem.

[17] The Bristol Chamber of Commerce put me in touch with Professor Wendell B. Pols, reference librarian at the city's Roger Williams University, who directed me to material about the speech school. Letter from Wendell B. Pols to Libby, February 12, 1997, in RZ Archives, Appendix.

[18] Elizabeth Ferguson Von Hesse, *So to Speak: A Practical Training Course for Developing a Beautiful Speaking Voice* (Philadelphia: Lippincott, 1959).

[19] Gerald Jonas, "The Disorder of Many Theories," *New Yorker*, November 15, 1976, p. 137.

Copies of pages from Meir's speech notebook are in RZ Archives, Appendix.

[20] Walter Goodman, "Meir Kahane: A Candid Conversation with the Militant Leader of the Jewish Defense League," *Playboy*, October 1972, pp. 69-78, in RZ Archives, folder 484.

There were periods when Meir did not stutter at all. One was during our engagement and early married years, after he had gone to Martin Hall, and another was from about 1969 to 1972, when the Jewish Defense League was at its pinnacle.

[21] See note 2.

Rabbi Zuroff also remarked on the anomaly of Meir's stellar role on the debating team despite his often severe stutter. Interview with Rabbi Abraham Zuroff. See note 4.

Chapter 4

[1] The Betar youth movement was founded by Zeev Jabotinksy in 1923. "Betar" is a Hebrew acronym for Brit Trumpeldor (Trumpeldor's covenant). See Trumpeldor, chapter 2, note 11.

[2] Phone interview with Shmuel Kraushar, January 24, 1999. Kraushar's father worked at *Hadoar*, a Hebrew weekly to which Meir's father subscribed, and they became friendly.

Meir had to take the train at Kings Highway and 15th Street to Prospect Park, then take the shuttle one stop to the Botanical Gardens and switch there to the New Lots train.

[3] Interview with Allan Mallenbaum, May 18, 1998, Jerusalem; letters from David Krakow to Libby, March 31, 1997, and July 9, 1999, in RZ Archives, Appendix.

Mordechai (Motel) Kreiner opined that Meir joined Betar after September 1947. (Phone interview with Kreiner, April 5, 1997.) However, a *ken* opened near Meir's home early in 1946: "With the return of veteran Betarim from the U.S. armed forces, *kinim* [chapters] have been started in Brownsville, East New York and Bensonhurst." *Betar*, May 1946, in Jabotinsky Archives, file no. bet 16-8/8.

[4] Letter from Yitzhak Heimowitz to Libby, January 26, 1997, in RZ Archives, Appendix.

[5] Letter from Dov Troy (formerly Troyansky) to Libby, November 10, 1998, in RZ Archives, Appendix.

Later, Betar purchased music records to help teach Hebrew songs. *Hamadrikh* [the Betar leaders' guide], April 1947, in Jabotinsky Archives, file kaf ayin 1-262.

[6] Pistol and Rifle Club: *Tel Hai*, December 4, 1947. Boxing: *Tel Hai*, March 16, 1948. Drama: *Tel Hai*, April 8, 1949, pp. 1, 2. Trips: *Tel Hai*, April 20, 1950. In Jabotinsky Archives, file bet 16-8/4, 8/5, 8/6.

[7] *Tel Hai*, March 14, 1951, in Jabotinsky Archives, file bet 16-8/6.

[8] *Structure and Law of Betar Hatzeira* (New York: Netzivut Betar U.S.A, 1947), pp. 2-3, in Jabotinsky Archives, file bet 16-8/15. See also *Hamadrikh*, p. 14 (note 5).

[9] *Betar*, May 1946, in Jabotinsky Archives, file bet 16-8/8.

[10] Dan Alter, *Playing Utopia: Habonim Summer Camps in America* (Master's thesis, Graduate Theological Union [Berkeley], 1997), p. 6.

[11] Phone interview with Arthur (Alter) Heller, July 8, 1997.

[12] *Tel Hai*, December 31, 1948, p. 2, in Jabotinsky Archives, file no. bet 16-8/4. The party was held on December 26th.

[13] *Tel Hai*, December 29, 1949, in Jabotinsky Archives, file no. bet 16-8/5.

[14] Michael Ashbel, "On the Barricades," in Itzhak Gurion, *Triumph on the Gallows* (New York: 1950), p. 82.

Hebrew lyrics and music at http://www.betar.org.il/world/music/songs/barikadot.htm.

Ashbel's death sentence was commuted to life imprisonment in July 1946, but he was wounded during the Acre prison breakout on May 4, 1947, and died of his injuries.

[15] *Tel Hai*, January 15, 1948, in Jabotinsky Archives, file bet 16-8/4.

[16] "Office of British Consulate Here Stormed by Group of Young Jews," *New York Sun*, April 18, 1947, in Jabotinsky Archives, Lester Hering Collection, file bet 16-23/1/1; "British Consulate Is 'Invaded' Here," *New York Times*, April 19, 1947, p. 8.

[17] "Zionist Youths 'Seize' Admiralty Office Here," *Daily News*, September 11, 1947, in Jabotinsky Archives, Lester Hering collection, file bet 16-23/1/2; "Exodus Protest Is Staged in City," *New York Times*, September 11, 1947, p. 3.

British sailors boarded the *Exodus* on July 18, 1947.

[18] *Tel Hai*, March 11, 1948, in Jabotinsky Archives, file bet 16-8/4.

[19] "Zionists, Police Clash," *New York Times*, September 21, 1947, p. 11. An action-packed photo, hand-dated September 22, 1947, unidentified newspaper, is captioned, "Cops Battle Pickets at Anti-British Demonstration," in Jabotinsky Archives, Lester Hering Collection, file bet 16-23/1/1.

[20] Phone interview with Jenny Marden, November 11, 1999.

[21] E-mail from Lester Hering, March 6, 1999.

[22] FBI file 105-207795, memorandum, January 21, 1972, p. 1, in RZ Archives, Appendix. The quote is from a transcript of an interview with Meir on Israel radio's English language program, January 17, 1972. In other interviews, he dated the Bevin demonstration as 1947, probably confusing it with the Royal Navy protest.

[23] "By His Orders..." flyer, March 30, 1949, in Jabotinsky Archives, file bet 16-8/3.

[24] "Vote of No Confidence," *Daily News*, March 30, 1949, centerfold. The photo of Meir, captioned "Line of Attack," is in the photo section of this book.

[25] "Bevin Greeted Here By Barrage of Fruit," *Daily News*, March 31, 1949, pp. 2, 52; in

Jabotinsky Archives, Lester Hering Collection, file bet 16-23/1/4; "Bevin Picketed by 500 on Arrival; 3 Held as Vegetables Thrown," *New York Times*, March 31, 1949, pp. 1, 3.

Harvey Hirsh, 17, Robert Newman, 19, and Lester Hering, 20, were arrested at this demonstration. *Tel Hai*, April 22, 1949, in Jabotinsky Archives, file bet 16-8/5.

26 "Circular 1," Young Betar, Machleket Tarbut (Culture Department), February 17, 1949, signed Pinchas Stolper, in Jabotinsky Archives, file bet 16-1/4.

27 "[Regional] Circular 1," July 27, 1949, signed Alter [Arthur] Heller, regional head, in Jabotinsky Archives, file bet 16-1/4.

Phone interview with Israel (Izzy) Herman, April 2, 1997.

28 Citation for outstanding work: *Tel Hai*, October 13, 1949, in Jabotinsky Archives, file bet 16-8/5.

See also note 27, Herman.

29 Letter from David Krakow to Libby, June 3, 1997, in RZ Archives, Appendix. Friedman's wife related this to Krakow.

See also note 27, Herman.

30 Phone interview with David Silverstein, February 1997.

31 The Jabotinsky Archives' last issue of *Tel Hai* with Meir as assistant editor is dated April 20, 1950. The next issue found in the archives, March 14, 1951, names Meir as editor. See: Jabotinsky Archives, file bet 16-8/6.

32 "In Williamsburg, Rosh Kitah [group leader] Meir Kahane has organized a group of Yeshiva Torah Vo'daath students..." *Tel Hai*, December 3, 1950 in Jabotinsky Archives, file no. bet 16-8/6.

Machoz leader: *Tel Hai*, March 14, 1951, pp. 1, 2, in Jabotinsky Archives, file bet 16-8/6.

Thanks to Yitzhak Heimowitz for information about Betar's various age groups and their names.

33 *Tel Hai*, February 16, 1951, in Jabotinsky Archives, file bet 16-8/6; interview with Rabbi Nachman Kahane, October 16, 1999, Jerusalem.

34 Two of the "kidnappers," Yitzhak Heimowitz and Izzy Herman, told me that Meir remained friendly for many years afterward. Dave Krakow also maintained that Meir held no hard feelings. He and fellow Betar alumni heard Meir speak many years later at Fairleigh Dickinson University "and afterwards reminisced with him about Betar. He was clearly happy to see us and asked to be remembered to Troyansky and other Betar friends...." Letter from David Krakow to Libby, December 24, 1998, in RZ Archives, Appendix.

Chapter 5

1 Letter from Avraham Greenhouse to Libby, January 20, 1997, in RZ Archives, Appendix.

Bachad, an affiliate of Bnei Akiva, is a Hebrew acronym for Brit Chalutzim Dati'im (covenant of religious pioneers). The farm school program was known as *hachshara* (training), because it trained members for work on Israeli agricultural settlements. The farm was in Jamesburg, New Jersey.

2 I had a good Hebrew background, having attended Jewish day schools – first the Beth Jacob School of the East Side, then Central Yeshiva High School for Girls in Brooklyn. Even during tenth grade, when I went to Hunter High School, I attended Beit Midrash Lemorot, an evening Hebrew high school on the Lower East Side. Hunter was a girls' school with stringent entrance requirements and an enriched curriculum. It was a coup to be accepted, but it was no place for a religious girl like me. Between classes the girls spoke about the dances they had attended, and

when committees met Sunday mornings in someone's home, I ate my hard-boiled eggs, while my classmates ate non-kosher cold cuts. I looked forward to seeing my Bnei Akiva friends on weekends, and after one year I joined them at Central.

My Hebrew was good enough to read texts on my own. When I was about 14, my father told me that *Ein Yaakov* (a Talmudic anthology) had interesting stories. When I took it off the shelf one afternoon, it fell open to a philosophical discussion of why good people may suffer, while the evil prosper. The book resolves this with the assurance that, although G-d's ways are inscrutable, in the world to come everything will be put right. The world we live in now is only a preparation for the really important world, the world to come. We must be righteous in this world in order to prepare ourselves properly for the next.

3 See membership list, October 8, 1953, in Zionist Archives, file S32/113.

The walking distance from Meir's home was an important factor, since the group met regularly on Shabbat, when travel is prohibited by Jewish law.

4 Phone interview with Miriam Koenigsberg Brovender, January 30, 1997.

5 Letter from Naomi Klass Mauer to Libby, March 1997.

6 The lyrics of *Heyu Shalom*, also known as *At Eretz Sheli*, are in *Belahav Hazemer: Shirei Betar Veshirim Lekhol Et* [songbook] (Tel Aviv: Betar, 1969), p. 57, in JNUL, Jewish Music Department, Meir Noy Collection.

A recording in the National Sound Archives, Jerusalem, no. K-4041 (1951), credits the words to Yaakov Orland and the music to Shmuel Preshkow.

7 Moshe Weiss, "Hashomer Hadati – The Forerunner of Bnei Akiva," *Jewish Press*, March 24, 1995, p. 48.

8 Meir's appointment in: *Decision*, national Bnei Akiva convention, Gelatt, Pennsylvania, September 2-6, 1954. Meir's duties in: *Minutes*, national board meeting, October 21, 1954, p. 1, in Zionist Archives, file S32/671 and in RZ Archives, Hapoel Hamizrachi-U.S.A. collection, folder 101.

The sixteen chapters are listed in Zionist Archives, file S32/113.

Aaron Rakeffet-Rothkoff graduation certificate in RZ Archives, Appendix.

9 Letter from Elsie Gleich Dudowitz to Libby, May 21, 1997, in RZ Archives, Appendix.

10 Phone interview with Yitzchak Fuchs, February 1997.

11 Boston: *Minutes*, national board meeting, March 28, 1955, in Zionist Archives, file S32/111.

Chicago: Report on the national Bnei Akiva convention in Rolling Prairie, Indiana, September 4, 1951, in Zionist Archives, file S32/671.

12 Letter from Shoshana Talansky (Silbert) to Mordechai Eliav, director, Bnei Akiva section, Jewish Agency for Israel, Jerusalem, April 17, 1955, Zionist Archives, file S32/112.

In another letter in this file, written in June 1955, Talansky urged: "Isn't it better for a member who wants to go to Israel as a teacher to do so after two years, after he prepares as a teacher, because he feels he can do much more for the state of Israel as a teacher?"

13 *Minutes*, national board meeting, October 25, 1954, Zionist Archives, file S32/111. Pinchas Spielman, Bnei Akiva's Israeli emissary, spoke of the urgent need to attract members to *hachshara*, the training farm in New Jersey.

Bnei Akiva Presidential Newsletter, November 5, 1954, in Zionist Archives, file S32/671. The six members expelled were students at the Chaim Berlin yeshiva.

Reports on the closing of the training farm in: *Yediot* (newsletter of Bachad and Bnei Akiva of North America) no. 53, October 1955, in Zionist Archives, file S32/111.

The September 1955 convention and the issue of the yeshiva boys is discussed in: Jerome

Fuchs, *A Sociological Analysis of a Zionist Youth Movement: Bnei Akiva of North America* (Master's thesis, New School for Social Research, 1960).

From 1956 on, Bnei Akiva members spent their first year after high school in Israel, at Kibbutz Yavneh, working and studying.

In 1957, Deanna Mirsky was expelled from Bnei Akiva because she did not attend the post-high school program in Israel. She had received a full scholarship to the Cooper Union School of Art and to qualify she had to complete one year there first. She went to Israel in 1958 and worked at Kibbutz Shluchot, where she painted murals for their 10th anniversary celebration.

The convention in September 1955 was held at the Bnei Akiva summer camp facility in Bronte, Ontario, a suburb of Toronto. Shortly before the convention, Meir bought a used car, a dark green Hudson, to drive the two of us to Canada. My parents did not think such a long car ride was appropriate for religious reasons, since we weren't married yet. Instead we went by air shuttle, my first plane ride!

A snapshot of Meir posing with the Hudson is in the photo section of this book.

[14] "Kalmanowitz, Abraham," *Encyclopedia Judaica* (Jerusalem: 1971), vol. 10, column 718; Yechezkel Leitner, *Operation Torah-Rescue* (Jerusalem: Feldheim, 1987).

[15] Letter from Rabbi Moshe (Marcel) Blitz to Libby, November 18, 1997, in RZ Archives, Appendix.

[16] Letter from Rabbi Moshe Bunim Pirutinsky to Libby, March 1998, in RZ Archives, Appendix. Rabbi Pirutinsky wrote *Sefer Habrit* (New York: 1973), an important book on circumcision. When our sons were born, we were honored that Rabbi Pirutinsky traveled from Brooklyn to Queens to circumcise them.

[17] *Encyclopedia Judaica*. See note 14. This entry also relates that Rabbi Kalmanowitz (1891-1964) was chosen to be the Rabbi of Rakov (in White Russia) when he was only 22. He helped many Jews who had been arrested by the Bolsheviks and was himself imprisoned in Minsk for a time. In 1926 he was chosen to head the Mirrer Yeshiva, and in 1929, he became the chief rabbi of Tiktin (Tycocin). He was an important member of the Vaad Hatzala which rescued many European Jews during the Holocaust.

See also: Aaron Rakeffet-Rothkoff, *The Silver Era* (Jerusalem/New York: Feldheim, 1981), pp. 201, 206.

[18] See note 15, letter from Rabbi Blitz.

Meir entered the Mirrer Yeshiva in 1949 and joined Bnei Akiva in 1952.

Blitz recalled that in 1954 a benefactor of the yeshiva complained there was not enough Zionism there. Rabbi Kalmanowitz replied, "That isn't true. We have the head of Bnei Akiva in this yeshiva."

Evenings, Meir attended nearby Brooklyn College, a branch of the City University of New York. In 1951, he applied to Yeshiva University, where students could study for rabbinic ordination while earning a college degree. His father, himself a graduate of Yeshiva University's rabbinical seminary, probably felt it would be simpler for Meir to complete his college courses there. Meir was admitted for the September 1951 term, but after a day or two he returned to the Mirrer Yeshiva. Meir's Yeshiva University application, admittance forms and correspondence, in RZ Archives Appendix. Thanks to Rabbi Melvin Davis, Yeshiva University Registrar.

[19] Meir's ordination certificate, dated July 4, 1957 (almost a year later), in RZ Archives, Appendix.

See photo section of this book for a picture of Meir at the Mirrer Yeshiva.

[20] Interview with Baruch Gelfand, May 8, 1999, Jerusalem.

[21] Interview with Rabbi Avraham Lieberman, June 18, 1998, Brooklyn.

[22] Letter from Rabbi Blitz to Libby, November 18, 1997, in RZ Archives, Appendix.

See: "Morocco – Emigration," *American Jewish Yearbook*, 1957, pp. 355-356. Rabbi Kalmanowitz brought many young men from Morocco, Algeria, and Tunisia to study at the Mirrer Yeshiva in America. He founded Otzar HaTorah, which opened Jewish schools in Morocco and Teheran. Many North African graduates of the Mirrer Yeshiva returned to teach there. See note 14.

[23] The Immigration Act of 1924 annual allowance was 598 immigrants from Poland, 344 from Lithuania and 2,248 from all of European and Asiatic Russia. Since the law allowed 34,000 immigrants annually from Great Britain, the low quotas from Eastern Europe were clearly not due to fear of overpopulation.

See note 17, Aaron Rakeffet-Rothkoff, p. 210.

[24] Letter from Rabbi Blitz to Libby, September 8, 1997, in RZ Archives, Appendix.

As longtime rabbi of the Pickwick Jewish Center in Baltimore, Rabbi Moshe (Marcel) Blitz arranged speaking engagements for Meir in Baltimore and often spoke out on Meir's behalf. (See: Marcel Blitz, "In Defense of Rabbi Kahane," *Baltimore Jewish Times*, February 6, 1976, p. 7, in RZ Archives, folder 93.) The Jewish Establishment's opposition to Meir led to the termination of Rabbi Blitz's contract in 1986. Meir tried to help him in this struggle but to no avail. (E-mail from Rabbi Blitz, December 1, 1998.)

[25] Meir Hacohen (pseudonym of Meir Kahane), "Light in the Soviet Darkness," *Jewish Press*, April 26, 1968, p. 14, in RZ Archives, folder 595.

Biography of Yaakov (Jacob) Griffel: Friedenson, Joseph, *Dateline Istanbul* (Brooklyn: N.Y.: Mesorah, 1993).

[26] Our *ketuba* was witnessed by Rabbi Abba Berman (Abba Mordechai bar Shaul Yosef) and Rabbi Tzvi Feldman (Tzvi bar Avraham Shmuel).

See photo section of this book for two wedding pictures.

Chapter 6

[1] Ashkenazic Jews do not name their children for someone living, so until my generation, no one could be named for this Bobba (Grandma) Liba.

[2] Meir's college graduation picture is in the photo section of this book.

[3] Meir attended New York University's Graduate School of Arts and Science from September 1956 to June 1957. Frank Cruz, registrar, confirmed the dates and the title of Meir's thesis: *Israel's Concept of Aggression: An Analysis*. He suggested that Bobst Library might have a copy of it. E-mail from Frank Cruz, Registrar, New York University, May 17, 2006.

The thesis was not found in the Bobst Library nor was it located elsewhere in the university. E-mail from Andrew H. Lee, Librarian, Bobst Library, New York University, June 7, 2006. It is not found in Meir's files.

Dates of attendance at New York Law School, October 1955-February 1957, and details of master's degree in: FBI file 105-207795, report, February 8, 1971, p. 2, in RZ Archives, Appendix.

See also: "In Memoriam... Rabbi Meir Kahane '57..." *In Brief* (New York Law School), Winter 1991, p. 19. Date of enrollment confirmed by e-mail from Denise Tong, New York Law School, March 26, 2007.

[4] A snapshot of Meir with baby Tova is in the photo section of this book.

[5] Interview with Chaim and Rachel Spring, February 5, 1997, Jerusalem.

The date of Meir's trip to Israel was given erroneously as 1963 in Robert I. Friedman's *False Prophet* and in several newspaper reports.

[6]   Letter from Meir to his parents [January 1958], in RZ Archives, Appendix.

[7]   Tova Kahane, "Tova Chokhma Miklei Krav [Wisdom Is Better Than Weapons of War]," *Reflections '71* (Brooklyn, N.Y.: Prospect Park Yeshiva, 1971), unpaged. The title of the essay is from *Ecclesiastes* 9:18.

A snapshot of Meir in his bunk on the SS *Zion* is in the photo section of this book.

[8]   Rabbi Abraham Isaac Kook, a prolific author, left Europe in 1904 to be the chief rabbi of Jaffa. He was the Ashkenazic chief rabbi of Palestine from 1921 until his death in 1935.

[9]   Interview with Rabbi Eliezer Waldman, January 4, 1997, Kiryat Arba. He related: "At that time there were only two 'Mizrachi-type,' Zionist yeshivot in all of Israel: Merkaz Harav, with 30 students, and Kerem Beyavne, with 40. Today, from that modest beginning, there are dozens of yeshivot, with thousands of students, that follow the philosophy of Rabbi Abraham Isaac Kook."

[10]   A letter introduced Meir as "a young man of 22 who studied at yeshivot in the United States and arrived only recently in Israel. He is ready to come to your kibbutz for Shabbat to speak whenever you wish." Letter (Hebrew) from Rabbi Dov Katz, Ministry of Religious Affairs, to Religious Council, Kibbutz Saad, February 4, 1958, in Kibbutz Saad archives; copy in RZ Archives, Appendix.

On December 12, 1998, Kibbutz Saad archivist Sarah Hamel kindly sent me copies of all the correspondence in the kibbutz archives pertaining to Meir's candidacy. The February 4 letter was reproduced in the kibbutz newsletter *Amudim*, November 1994, p. 47.

[11]   Phone interview with Rabbi Chaim Druckman, July 11, 1997.

[12]   Letter (Hebrew) from Meir to Yaakov Drori, Executive Secretary, Kibbutz Saad, February 23, 1958, in Kibbutz Saad archives; copy in RZ Archives, Appendix.

[13]   Letter (Hebrew) from Meir to Yaakov Drori, Executive Secretary, Kibbutz Saad, March 23, 1958, in Kibbutz Saad archives; copy in RZ Archives, Appendix.

Chapter 7

[1]   "End of the Miracle of Howard Beach," *Jewish Press*, March 18, 1960, pp. 3, 12, in RZ Archives, folder 594, reprinted in *Beyond Words*, 1:3-8. The article was bylined "Staff Writer" but it is clear that Meir wrote it: The typescript was found in his personal files, with the handwritten corrections typical of him. Typescript in RZ Archives, Appendix.

Meir served as the rabbi of HBJC from September 1958 to March 1960.

[2]   Letter from Robert Falk to Libby, September 19, 1997, in RZ Archives, Appendix.

[3]   Max Zweibel, a friend of my uncle Julius Friedman, introduced Meir to his firm, the First Financial Corporation. A photocopy of the firm's file card on Meir, dated October 29, 1959, is in RZ Archives, Appendix. Thanks to Zweibel and to Hilton Goldman for the file card.

[4]   A photo of Charles Prost and his elderly father, Solomon Prost, in cantors' robes, with Meir in prayer shawl and *kittel* (white robe) appeared in a local newspaper. Clipping, undated but probably before the High Holidays, 1959, newspaper not named, in RZ Archives, folder 59.

[5]   Letter from Robert Falk, June 11, 1997, in RZ Archives, Appendix.

[6]   "The Mettco Club," *Forum – Howard Beach*, centennial souvenir edition, June 13, 1997, p. 10. Courtesy of Robert Falk, September 19, 1997. This notes that Meir had been rabbi of the Jewish Center. The article is also on the Internet.

The address of the HBJC was 96-01 165th Avenue. Casino Park is now called the Frank M. Charles Memorial Park. In 2002, the HBJC moved to 162-05 90th Street.

7 "End of the Miracle of Howard Beach." See note 1.

8 Our address was 88-20 164th Avenue.

9 See chapter 5 for more about Rabbi Pirutinsky.

10 Our house was at 158-25 91st Street. The date of sale was September 25, 1959, and the price was $15,730. See: Deed Book of the City of New York, no. 7191, p. 625, October 8, 1959.

The Federal Housing Administration offered special mortgages to encourage home owning. The down payment of 3% of sale prices on FHA mortgages is indicated in the Code of Federal Regulations, 203.18.

11 See note 5.

12 "Talmud Torah & Sunday School," *Howard Beach Jewish Community Herald*, February 1959, p. 3, in RZ Archives, Appendix.

13 See note 12, the *Herald,* p. 1. Among the speakers were Rabbi Moshe Max of the Queens Jewish Center; Rabbi Samuel Wolkin, Union of Orthodox Rabbis; Rabbi Abraham Scheinberg of the Hebrew Alliance of Brighton Beach; and Meir's father. Rabbi Samuel Landa of the Ozone Park Jewish Center gave the invocation. State Assemblyman Jack Fox and State Senator Irving Mosberg attended.

Alex Hirschensprung, president of Congregation Shaare Tefiloh, Meir's father's synagogue, placed an ad in a Yiddish paper congratulating Meir's parents on the installation of their son, "an idealist whose fiery *Yiddishkeit* [Judaism] burns in his heart." Clipping, newspaper unnamed and undated, in RZ Archives, Appendix.

Mrs. Belle Kirschenbaum sent me photos taken at the installation ceremony. They show Meir, his father, synagogue officials Victor Kirschenbaum and Leo Skloot, Rabbi Samuel Wolkin, Rabbi Samuel Landa, and Charles Prost. Copies in RZ Archives, Appendix.

14 "Our Rabbi's Message," see note 12, the *Herald*, p. 2. The same page lists the members who worked on the bulletin: Editor: Howard Nussbaum. Contributors: Rabbi Kahane, Alan Kirschenbaum, Leonard Falitz, B. Falitz, M. Venikoff, R. Falitz, Leo Skloot, Victor Kirschenbaum, Irving Weber.

This was probably the only issue of the *Howard Beach Jewish Community Herald* to be published. I did not find it in any library or archive. I searched: OCLC FirstSearch, Queens Borough Public Library, Jewish Theological Seminary Library, Yeshiva University Library and Archives, New York Public Library, American Jewish Historical Society (now the Center for Jewish History) and Hebrew Union College.

15 Meir Kahane, "Letter to the Editor," *Jewish Post and Opinion*, July 17, 1959, p. 11.

16 Meir Kahane, "Bedin Mamon Hamutal Besafek [On the Question of Property of Disputed Ownership]," *Hapardes* (Brooklyn) 32:2, November 1957, pp. 31-32.

17 Rabbi Moshe Feinstein, *Igrot Moshe, Orach Chayim* II: 32. Printed edition: New York: 1964, vol. 2, pp. 209-211.

Meir's *she'elot* (queries) in Rabbi Feinstein's responsa, *Igrot Moshe,* can also be accessed through Bar Ilan University's computerized *Proyekt Hashut* (*Responsa Project*).

Rabbi Feinstein's eminence in halakha was emphasized in an obituary by Rabbi Moshe Weinbach, dean of Ohr Somayach Institutions, Jerusalem. See: Moshe Weinbach, "Moshe Feinstein: A Rabbi's Rabbi," *Jerusalem Post*, March 25, 1986, p. 3.

18 "Excerpts From the Eulogy Given at Rabbi Kahane's Funeral by Rabbi Moshe Tendler, Shlita," *Haraayon – The Idea*: *The Newsletter of Yeshivat Haraayon Hayehudi*, February 1991, p. 4, in RZ Archives, folder 821.

This eulogy was given at the Young Israel of Ocean Parkway, Brooklyn, New York, December 6, 1990, before Meir's body was flown to Israel for burial.

[19] Rabbi Moshe Feinstein, *Igrot Moshe, Orach Chayim* IV:36. Printed edition: Bnei Brak: 1981, vol. 4, pp. 47-48. See also: *Igrot Moshe*, computerized edition, note 17.

[20] At the time, Meir told me that Mrs. Guthrie had phoned the HBJC and asked him to teach her son. Meir's bar mitzvah lessons to Arlo Guthrie are noted in Tom Tugend, "Woodie Guthrie's Jewish Legacy," *Jerusalem Post*, December 2, 2004, p. 24.

[21] "End of the Miracle of Howard Beach." See note 1.

[22] Letter from Rabbi Abraham Levin to Libby, December 24, 1996, in RZ Archives, Appendix.

Tifereth Moshe was located at 83-06 Abingdon Road in the Kew Gardens section of Queens, about half an hour's drive from Howard Beach.

Meir wrote a tribute to Rabbi Levin, who "planted" the Tifereth Moshe yeshiva in the "barren soil" of Kew Gardens, "land of Conservatism and home of Reform." See: Meir Kahane, "A Tree Grows in Queens," *Jewish Press*, December 2, 1960, p. 16.

[23] Letter from Alan (Avi) Kirschenbaum to Libby, January 2, 1997, in RZ Archives, Appendix.

[24] "End of the Miracle of Howard Beach." See note 1.

[25] See note 5. Falk wrote that upon examining his 1960 appointment book, he found that the storm was so severe that he did not go to work the next day. The blizzard was page one news. See: "Nation Battered," *New York Times*, March 4, 1960, pp. 1, 15.

[26] See note 1.

[27] Letter from Rabbi Moshe (Marcel) Blitz to Libby, September 8, 1997, in RZ Archives, Appendix. The blessing in Hebrew is: "Shimkha yelekh misof ha'olom ve'ad sofo."

For more about Rabbi Abraham Kalmanowitz, see chapter 5.

[28] The first 16-page issue of the *Jewish Press* was dated January 29, 1960. By February 26, the *Press* had 24 pages. E-mail message from Naomi Klass Mauer, January 15, 2003.

[29] Interview with Rabbi Binyomin Kamenetsky, June 23, 1998, Woodmere, New York. Rabbi Kamenetsky headed the Yeshiva of South Shore – Toras Chaim, which our son Baruch attended through sixth grade.

[30] Letter from Arnold Fine to Libby, April 1997, in RZ Archives, Appendix.

[31] Letter from Naomi Brody to Libby, February 15, 1997, in RZ Archives, Appendix.

[32] Interview with Shaul Kahan, July 3, 1999, Jerusalem. "I bought the franchise through a business broker. I signed agreements with the *Times* and the *News* that included other morning newspapers, such as the *Daily Mirror*. At that time, no one else could deliver newspapers in your area."

Chapter 8

[1] *Deed Book of the City of New York*, April 25, 1961, lists the date of sale as April 21, 1961, and the sale price as $16,335.

Our address was 222-13 133 Avenue.

See chapter 7 for information about Federal Housing Administration mortgages.

Yair Kotler falsely wrote that we bought the house in Laurelton with $10,000 that Meir received as compensation from the Howard Beach Jewish Center (*Heil Kahane*, p. 24). Robert Falk, the accountant for the HBJC wrote: "... If he received any money it might have been an adjustment on his weekly salary for those days worked prior to the firing. [It would have been]...

impossible for the Center to raise $10,000 to pay Rabbi Kahane." Letter from Robert Falk to Libby, February 26, 2007, in RZ Archives, Appendix.

New York State law does not require compensation for "at-will" employees.

2 In August 1967, we sold our two-bedroom house on 133 Avenue in Laurelton and moved to a three-bedroom rented apartment on 139 Avenue (see chapter 11). An FBI informant inaccurately attributed our move to "paint smeared on subject's car." See: FBI file 105-207795, report, December 21, 1970, p. 2, in RZ Archives, Appendix.

3 "Chotam Beveged Lehotza'at Shabbat [Carrying on the Sabbath: The Question of a Garment With a Sha'atnez Seal]," *Hamaor* (Brooklyn) 13:6, April 1962, pp. 13-15, in RZ Archives, folder 1215.

4 Letter from Rabbi Chaim Plato, head of the Radin Yeshiva, Netanya, to Libby, January 1998, in RZ Archives, Appendix.

5 Laundering: Hamaor Hakatan [pseudonym of Meir Kahane], "Shiur of the Week," *Jewish Press*, May 13, 1960, p. 21. This is the earliest *Shiur of the Week* column I found.

Candles: Hamaor Hakatan [pseudonym of Meir Kahane], "Shiur of the Week," *Jewish Press*, July 1, 1960, p. 5, in RZ Archives, folder 598.

Shofar: Hamaor Hakatan [pseudonym of Meir Kahane], "Shiur of the Week," *Jewish Press*, August 12, 1960, pp. 9, 12, in RZ Archives, folder 594.

6 "About South African Jewry," *Jewish Press*, May 20, 1960, p. 9, in RZ Archives, folder 596.

This is the earliest *Small Voice* column I found. The choice of the word "small" in both of Meir's early columns is intriguing. The *Small Voice* column ceased in 1964.

"Religious Crisis in Israel," *Jewish Press*, June 16, 1961, in RZ Archives, folder 596.

"Eichmann," *Jewish Press*, April 12, 1961, p. 16, reprinted in *Writings 5731*, p. 95.

"The Bnei Israel," *Jewish Press*, October 13, 1961, p. 11, reprinted in *On Jews and Judaism*, pp. 4-7.

"In the Shadow of the Cross," *Jewish Press*, March 9, 1962, p. 12, reprinted in *On Jews and Judaism*, pp. 8-10.

"Death of Freedom," *Jewish Press*, July 20, 1962, p. 9.

7 "A Small Voice," *Jewish Press*, June 10, 1960, p. 18, in RZ Archives, folder 594. Meir himself castigated the Israeli government severely in later years. However, his criticism was voiced as a loyal citizen of Israel.

For the dispute referred to see: "Ben-Gurion Stirs Biblical Dispute; Foes Seeking to Overthrow Premier for Challenging Scriptures on the Exodus," *New York Times*, May 18, 1960, p. 43; "Hadati'im Haleumi'im: Lo Nigrom Lemashber Memshalti Biglal Hashkafa Pratit Shel Ben Gurion [Religious Zionists: We Will Not Cause a Government Crisis Because of Ben Gurion's Private Views]," *Ma'ariv*, May 18, 1960, p. 1.

8 "Bar Mitzvah," *Jewish Press*, December 30, 1960, in RZ Archives, folder 596. Rabbi Perr's synagogue, Congregation Sons of Israel, was in Ozone Park, New York. Thanks to Irma Sragg for this information.

9 "New Square," *Jewish Press*, March 10, 1961, in RZ Archives, folder 596.

New Square is an anglicized form of Skvera, a village in the Ukraine where the Skver chasidic dynasty had its roots. In 2005, New Square had a population of 7,000.

10 "The Minority Is Right," *Jewish Press*, July 14, 1961, in RZ Archives, folder 596.

11 *West Side Institutional Review*, May 12, 1961, p. 1, in RZ Archives, Appendix.

12 Letter from Meir to Rabbi O. Asher Reichel, June 8, 1961, in RZ Archives, Appendix.

Rabbi Pinchas Stolper, Meir's former classmate, was then Director of the National Conference of Synagogue Youth (NCSY).

[13] *West Side Institutional Review*, October 20, 1961, in RZ Archives, Appendix.

[14] "Talmud Torah Keneged Kulam [Learning Torah Is Equal to All]," [editorial] *Jewish Press*, August 11, 1961, p. 5.

[15] *West Side Institutional Review*, November 3, 1961.

[16] "Images," *Jewish Press*, June 15, 1962, pp. 6, 20, in RZ Archives, folder 592.

[17] "To Our Non-Orthodox Readers," *Jewish Press*, October 5, 1962, p. 13, in RZ Archives, folder 596, reprinted in *On Jews and Judaism*, pp. 14-16, and in *Beyond Words*, 1:70-73.

[18] "The Brightest Jewel," *Jewish Press*, December 14, 1962, p. 22, in RZ Archives, folder 596.

Meir's inspiring talk at the 1961 convention was recalled by Rabbi Avraham Goldreich, then an NCSY regional director. Phone interview with Rabbi Goldreich, April 24, 2001. The National Conference of Synagogue Youth (NCSY) is a project of the Union of Orthodox Jewish Congregations of America.

[19] "*Mai Chanuka*," *Jewish Press*, December 28, 1962, pp. 22, 24, reprinted in *Writings 5731*, pp. 50-52.

A later version, with references to the Jewish Defense League, was "Down With Chanuka," *Jewish Press*, December 15, 1972, pp. 30, 37, reprinted in *Writings 5732*, pp. 150-152, in *Beyond Words*, 1:356-360, and in *Kahane: The Magazine of the Authentic Jewish Idea*, January 1977, pp. 18-19; November-December 1987, p. 3-4; and November-December 1989, pp. 3-4.

"Down With Chanuka," was also printed as a half-page ad in *Kingsman* (Brooklyn College), December 14, 1973, in RZ Archives, folder 1206.

A Hebrew translation by Moshe Potolsky, "Hal'a Chanuka," appeared in *Kach: Bit'on Tnuat Kach*, December, 1985, pp. 5-7, and in *Kohen Venavi* [Selected Articles] (Jerusalem: Institute for Publication of Writings of Rabbi Meir Kahane, 2001), vol. 1, pp. 22-25.

[20] "Strikes Shut All Major New York City and Cleveland Newspapers," *World Almanac*, 1964, p. 86. The International Typographical Union feared job losses due to the introduction of automated presses. When other craft unions honored the picket lines, the newspaper publishers had to stop publishing. This was the longest newspaper strike on record in New York City, lasting 114 days. It ended on April 1, 1963.

[21] Martin Keene [pseudonym of Meir Kahane], "Eddie Donovan: Once a Winner," *New York and Brooklyn Daily*, February 4, 1963, p. 30, in RZ Archives, folder 591.

[22] Martin Keene [pseudonym of Meir Kahane], "The Yankees: Can They Win It Again?" *New York and Brooklyn Daily*, January 24, 1963, p. 30, in RZ Archives, folder 591.

[23] Martin Keene [pseudonym of Meir Kahane], "You're Harry Gallatin," *New York and Brooklyn Daily*, February 15, 1963, p. 28, in RZ Archives, folder 591.

[24] Martin Keene [pseudonym of Meir Kahane], "Still Dreaming: Mets Squeeze Yanks 1-0," *New York and Brooklyn Daily*, March 19, 1963, back page, in RZ Archives, folder 591.

[25] Martin Keene [pseudonym of Meir Kahane], "Jack Molinas – A Story of Man's Self-Destruction," *New York and Brooklyn Daily*, January 25, 1963, p. 37, in RZ Archives, folder 591.

The Grantland Rice Award, named for sportswriter Grantland Rice, was under the auspices of the Sportsmanship Brotherhood of New York in the 1960s. I did not find any report about the recipient of the 1963 award, nor could I locate the Brotherhood's archives.

William Harper, author of *How You Played the Game: The Life of Grantland Rice* (Columbia, Missouri, 1999), referred me to Rice's papers at Vanderbilt University. Archivist Kathleen I. Smith found no records about the award after 1955.

[26] Martin Keene [pseudonym of Meir Kahane], "The Teenage Gangs Must Be Wiped Out," *New York and Brooklyn Daily*, January 14, 1963, p. 4, in RZ Archives, Appendix.

[27] Martin Keene [pseudonym of Meir Kahane], "The Street Gang and the Police Department," *New York and Brooklyn Daily*, January 24, 1963, pp. 4, 6, 27, in RZ Archives, folder 591.

Martin Keene [pseudonym of Meir Kahane], "The Teenage Gang and the Youth Board," *New York and Brooklyn Daily*, January 25, 1963, pp. 4, 14, 36, in RZ Archives, folder 591.

Martin Keene [pseudonym of Meir Kahane], "A Teenage Gang – An Arrest Is Made," *New York and Brooklyn Daily*, January 29, 1963, p. 4, in RZ Archives, folder 591.

[28] Martin Keene [pseudonym of Meir Kahane], "A Poet Comes to Town," *New York and Brooklyn Daily*, March 8, 1963, back page, p. 22, in RZ Archives, folder 591.

Meir wrote about Clay's victory over Davy Jones the following week. See: Martin Keene [pseudonym of Meir Kahane], "Cassius Clay: Down From Olympus," *New York and Brooklyn Daily*, March 17, 1963, p. 33, in RZ Archives, folder 591.

[29] Gerald Mast, "The Neurotic Jew as American Clown," In: *Jewish Wry: Essays on Jewish Humor*, ed. Sarah Blacher Cohen (Bloomington: Indiana University Press, 1987), pp. 125-140.

[30] See note 20.

[31] *"Chametz,"* *Jewish Press*, April 12, 1963, p. 3.

[32] "The Attack on the Missions," *Jewish Press*, September 20, 1963, p. 12.

[33] "Not the Way," *Jewish Press*, August 2, 1963, p. 8.

Chapter 9

[1] Meir taught the laws of Shabbat from *Mishnah Brurah – Hilchot Shabbat*. He used the same text for the girls' lesson on Sunday mornings.

Phone interview with Binyamin Dolinsky, July 4, 1997. His father, Morty Dolinsky, was one of the three founding members of the Jewish Defense League.

Phone interview with Gloria Podzeba, December 2, 1996; phone interview with Malka Parnes, November 20, 1996.

Meir liked to tell a similar story about Zeev Jabotinsky: Once, only two people showed up to hear Jabotinsky lecture, but he spoke as if the auditorium were full.

[2] Interview with Helen Gluckman Meir, January 6, 1997, Jerusalem. At the time of the interview, her oldest daughter had married a rabbinical student.

[3] Phone interview with Avraham Ben Yochanan, January 11, 1997. According to Ben Yochanan's sister, Meir was a role model for him and for Weinblatt. Interview with Gita Jochnowitz Hoffman, January 7, 1997.

[4] There were two kinds of prayer books in the synagogue: *Daily Prayer Book* with an English translation by Philip Birnbaum (New York: 1949) and *Tikkun Meir* edited by Meir Chinsky (New York: 1937). E-mail from Avraham Ben Yochanan (formerly Jochnowitz), July 10, 2003.

[5] Interview with Elliott Horowitz, February 13, 1997, Jerusalem.

[6] Letter from Lisbeth and Martin Goldschmiedt to Libby, January 14, 1997, in RZ Archives, Appendix.

[7] The thirteen Laurelton families who moved to Israel are the Brown, Friedlander, Hershberg, Hillson, Horowitz, Kessler, Kreisler, Neimark, Parnes, Perlman, Podzeba, the Schwartz and Solomon families. Later, children of the Bieber, Feigenbaum, Grunstein, Harris, Jochnowitz and Zigelman families also settled in Israel.

[8] See note 5.

[9] Chakwal M. Cragg, "Letter to the Editor," *Jewish Press*, October 16, 1964, p. 4. See also: *African Israelite* 1 (1955), in JNUL, call no. PB13019=2.

[10] See note 5.

[11] See note 4, e-mail from Ben Yochanan.

[12] Phone interview with Renah Ben Yochanan, January 11, 1997.

[13] See note 5.

[14] Interview with Fred and Edith Horowitz, December 7, 1996, Jerusalem.

[15] See note 5.

See also: Elliott Horowitz's bar mitzvah speech, February 1966, in RZ Archives. Horowitz is a professor of Jewish history at Bar-Ilan, has been a visiting professor at Harvard and other universities, and is the author of many scholarly works.

Horowitz recalled that Meir's set of folio-size volumes of the Talmud were the first he had ever seen actually used, not just on display. When he paid a condolence call after Meir's murder, his saddest moment was seeing those volumes on the shelf.

[16] This theme is discussed in Meir Kahane, *The Jewish Idea* (Jerusalem: Institute for Publication of the Writings of Rabbi Meir Kahane, 1996), vol. 1, chapter 5.

[17] See note 5.

[18] Letter from Naomi Brody to Libby, February 15, 1997, in RZ Archives, Appendix.

[19] Phone interview with Robert Perlman, November 20, 1996.

[20] Letter from Bertram Zweibon to Libby, undated, received September 1997, in RZ Archives, Appendix.

Newcomers are often summoned to recite the blessing on the Torah as a welcoming gesture.

Zweibon told an interviewer that he became Orthodox at the age of 33 because of a visit to the concentration camp at Dachau. See: May Okon, "Never Again! Slogan of Jewish Defense League Is at Heart of Its Militant Activities," *Daily News*, [undated], reprinted as a four-sided flyer, in RZ Archives, folder 60A.

Bertram Zweibon, a founder of the JDL, should not be confused with his cousin, Herbert Zweibon, associated with Americans for a Safe Israel.

[21] Interview with Irwin Benjamin, January 2, 1997, Jerusalem.

[22] Interview with Toby Fink, June 29, 1998, Brooklyn, N.Y. This interview took place at the home of Mina Krumbein while I was in the United States to attend a dinner marking the 30th anniversary of the founding of Jewish Defense League.

[23] Interview with Rabbi Binyomin Kamenetsky, June 23, 1998, Woodmere, New York. Part of the yeshiva's uncompromising religious education was its innovative methodology for Bible study, in which students translated the Hebrew text into English rather than into modern Hebrew or Yiddish, for optimal understanding.

[24] Letter from Irving Kreisler and Hy Bieber to Young Israel members, January 1965, in RZ Archives, Appendix. The letter notes: "This affair is going to be highlighted by a professional band and a catered rib roast dinner."

[25] Amos Bunim, *A Fire in His Soul: Irving M. Bunim, 1901-1980: The Man and His Impact on American Orthodox Jewry* (New York: Feldheim, 1989), pp. 27-28.

[26] See note 5. According to our son Baruch, Meir attended the Shabbat morning prayers in the main synagogue and then joined the teenagers for the *musaf* (additional) service.

[27] During the *shiva* (mourning period) for Meir, one visitor remarked on how devoutly Tova's daughters prayed in synagogue, even the younger ones. She replied, "My father took me with him to *shul* and taught me how to pray, and my husband took my little girls with him and taught them how to pray."

28 According to halakha (Jewish law), one may not carry (or push a baby carriage) outside the home on Shabbat, so I stayed home with her until she was able to walk the distance.

29 Joseph Epelboim, *Peninei Hadat* [*Pearls of Religion*] (Brooklyn, N.Y.: A.L. Frankel, 1957), 272 pp. This abridgement of the *Shulchan Arukh* [*Code of Jewish Law*] for children was first published in Kishinev in 1938. A recent printing is Jerusalem: Mifal Torah Veda'at, 1986.

30 Rabbi Moshe Bunim Pirutinsky had also been Baruch's circumcisor. See chapter 5 for more about him.

31 See note 14. The parable is in *Talmud, Tractate Ta'anit* 5b.

32 *Tenth Annual Journal Dinner in Honor of Rabbi and Mrs. Meir Kahane, May 27, 1967-Lag Ba'omer 5727,* (Laurelton, N.Y.: Young Israel of Laurelton, 1967), p. [5], in RZ Archives, Appendix.

33 Queens College, part of the University of the City of New York (CUNY), was free of charge for all New York City residents. I had accumulated 16 college credits at Brooklyn College (also part of CUNY) during our first year of marriage, and Queens College accepted them all.

34 Meir and I planned to move to Israel in the summer of 1971, but I wasn't sure I'd finish my courses by then. I wrote to the School of Library Science at the Hebrew University of Jerusalem about continuing my library studies there. Dr. Yaakov Rothschild, head of the school, advised me to complete my degree at Queens, so I took a full schedule of courses each term, including the summer session.

Chapter 10

1 Churba completed his doctorate in 1965: Joseph Churba, *U.A.R. – Israel Rivalry Over Aid and Trade in Sub-Saharan Africa, 1957-1963* (Columbia University, Department of Public Law and Government, 1965). Summary in *Dissertation Abstracts.*

From 1972 to 1976, Churba was the Air Force's top Middle East intelligence expert. He was dismissed when he publicly criticized the Chairman of the Joint Chiefs of Staff, General George S. Brown, for saying that Israel was a military burden for the United States. Churba was an adviser to the Arms Control and Disarmament Agency in 1981 and 1982. Until his death at age 62, he was president of the International Security Council, a Washington-based research institute. See: "Joseph Churba, Intelligence Aide Who Criticized General, Is Dead," *New York Times*, April 28, 1996, p. 38.

See also notes 21 and 24.

2 *Biographical Data* (New York: Jewish Defense League, [1970]), 1 p., in RZ Archives, folder 733. This sheet lists Meir as "Director of the Center for Political Studies, a private research firm in Washington, DC, from 1964 to 1967."

3 Hyman S. Frank, "Inside Meir Kahane," *Jewish Press*, November 1, 1974, pp. 24, 27. This is part 4 in the series: Hyman S. Frank, "Inside Meir Kahane," *Jewish Press*, October 18, 1974-February 7, 1975, 18 parts, in RZ Archives, folder 80. Parts 1-6 reprinted in *Beyond Words*, 2:51-70. The "Inside Meir Kahane" articles appeared under the heading of Dr. Frank's column, *Bury My Heart in Jerusalem.* Excerpted with the permission of Gloria Frank Simon.

4 "The Communists," *Jewish Press*, August 15, 1963, reprinted in *Writings 5732*, pp. 202-204.

Another indication of Meir's interest in the Birch Society is their 1964 ad in his files: *Los Angeles Times*, September 27, 1964, in RZ Archives, folder 326.

Meir later wrote: "Is the John Birch Society Anti-Semitic?" two parts, *Jewish Press*, February 3, 1967; February 10, 1967; "Commentary," *Jewish Press*, August 9, 1968; "Jews and the John Birch Society," *Jewish Press*, October 3, 1969, p. 20.

[5]   See note 3, "Inside Meir Kahane," November 1, 1974, part 4, p. 24; November 8, 1974, part 5, p. 47.

[6]   FBI file 105-207795, Memorandum, January 21, 1972, p. 2, in RZ Archives, Appendix. This report contains a transcript of Meir's 14-minute interview on Israel radio's English language program broadcast in January 1972.

[7]   Meir's name appeared on the *Jewish Press* masthead from August 7 to December 11, 1964 and from April 2 to July 2, 1965. The gap may have been due to an intensive period of research in Washington.

Previously all news stories were from the Jewish Telegraphic Agency wire service. When Meir was the editor there were many unsigned news reports written in his style.

[8]   "Jewish Speakers Bureau," [ad] *Jewish Press*, October 2, 1964. p. 21. The ad was 2 columns wide by 2.5 inches.

[9]   *Minutes*, Yavneh Leadership Seminar, February 16, 1964, in RZ Archives, Appendix.

[10]   *Jewish Collegiate Observer*, November 1964, p. 3, in JNUL, call no. PB5655=2X. Meir lectured on October 14 and November 9, 1964.

[11]   E-mail from Glenn Richter, April 7, 2006. Richter was national director of the Student Struggle for Soviet Jewry.

Lishkat Hakesher was later named Nativ.

Another source of information about Soviet Jews during this period was the series of booklets *Jews in Eastern Europe* published by Emanuel Litvinoff in London from 1959 to 1974. Litvinoff probably received information from Lishkat Hakesher.

[12]   Moshe Decter, "The Status of the Jews in the Soviet Union," *Foreign Affairs*, January 1963, pp. 420-430.

See also: "Soviet Union," *American Jewish Yearbook*, 1960, pp. 257-264.

[13]   "Sentencing of Jews for Matzoth Hit in U.S. Senate," *Jewish Press*, July 25, 1963, pp. 1, 3; Irving Spiegel, "Matzoh 'Waste' Is Laid to Soviet," *New York Times*, April 13, 1964, p. 3 (Jewish organizations had spent over $100,000 for the undelivered matzot, including $20,000 for Soviet customs duties); Irving Spiegel, "Curb on Matzoh in Kiev Charged," *New York Times*, March 14, 1965, p. 20; "Soviets Sentence Rabbi to Death for Speculation," *Jewish Press*, September 6, 1963, p. 3.

[14]   "American Response to Soviet Anti-Jewish Policies," *American Jewish Year Book,* 1965, pp. 312-313. Excerpted with permission.

[15]   "The Generation of Cain," *Jewish Press*, May 31, 1963, p. 19, reprinted in *Beyond Words*, 1:79-81.

This represented a change from Meir's earlier point of view. In 1962 he wrote that American Jews should not demonstrate for Soviet Jews, in keeping with the stand of the *gedolim*, the important rabbis. See: "Of Mice and Men," *Jewish Press*, June 22, 1962, pp. 6, 10 (written in response to a letter to the editor, *Jewish Press*, June 8, 1962, pp. 4, 21).

This change in Meir's point of view can be explained by the fact that it was only in January 1963 that all the facts about the terrible oppression of Soviet Jews reached the West.

[16]   Other speakers at the rally were Rabbis Hershel Schachter, Shlomo Riskin, and Irving Greenberg. See: "Student Struggle for Soviet Jewry Announces Crisis Protest Rally for Russian Jewry," [October 18, 1964], four-page handout on tabloid newspaper stock, in RZ Archives, folder 714B.

[17]   E-mail from Jacob Birnbaum, December 17, 2000.

[18]   "Students, Russians and You," *Jewish Press*, October 2, 1964, reprinted in *Writings 5731*, p. 15.

[19]   "Save Soviet Jewry," *Jewish Press*, May 22, 1964, p. 25, reprinted in *Beyond Words*, 1:91-95.

[20] Letter from Avraham Ben Yochanan (formerly Jochnowitz) to Libby, January 11, 1997, in RZ Archives, Appendix. The strikes at Tass, Intourist and Aeroflot took place on December 29, 1969. See chapter 17.

[21] Hayim Yerushalmi [pseudonym of Rabbi Chaim Uri Lifshitz], "A *Jewish Press* Profile: Dr. Joseph Churba," *Jewish Press*, March 19, 1965, p. 5.

Rabbi Chaim Uri Lifshitz's byline appears on this interview, but the style and content suggest that Meir wrote at least part of it. For instance, the explanation of the Institute's work seems to be based on Meir's master's thesis, *Israel's Concept of Aggression: An Analysis*, noted in chapter 6.

The Institute's stationery with the address 2029 Allen Place NW (Tel. 483-7791) is found in RZ Archive, folder 1004. Meir's files have blank stationery for another research institute in Washington: Institute for Political Analysis, 422 Washington Bldg, Washington, D.C. 20005, in RZ Archives, folder 596.

A search by Infocus Research Services, Rockville, Md., found Institute for Research in Foreign Affairs only in the 1965-66 Washington, D.C., phonebook, but at a different address from that in Meir's files.

I found no documentation about the Institute's research projects. I asked several federal government agencies for information about contracts with Meir, Churba and/or the various research firm names from 1963 through 1967. None were found by any government bodies. The only records found by the FBI were those concerning Meir as head of the JDL.

My efforts to locate the papers of Joseph Churba were unsuccessful. A search conducted March 31, 2006 in ArchivesGrid, ArchivesUSA, the National Union Catalog of Manuscript Collections, and the National Inventory of Documentary Sources did not locate a repository of Churba's papers. Thanks to the New York Public Library's Manuscripts and Archives Division and the archivists at St. John's University for this search.

Churba's family informed mutual friend Charles Cohen that they did not have his papers. His associate, Sol W. Sanders, informed me that Churba discarded many of his records "without mercy." E-mail from Sanders, May 29, 2006.

[22] A fallout of anti-Semitism arising out of the heavy involvement of Jewish youth in campus revolutions was reported in: *News: Yeshiva University*, March 21, 1969, p. 1, in RZ Archives, folder 499A.

See also: "Student Activism, New Left and Anti-Semitism," *American Jewish Yearbook*, 1969, pp. 72-75. The article noted, "... the continued presence of Jewish students in the ranks of the protesters was noted as a possible impetus to anti-Semitism.... Of the... identifiable radicals on the most active campuses, probably one third to one half were Jews."

See also: Meir Kahane, "Johnson, Jews and Vietnam," *Jewish Press*, May 17, 1968, pp. 15, 45.

[23] Guy Richards, "'July 4th Movement' to Stress Our Revolt," *New York Journal-American*, July 4, 1965, p. 5I, in RZ Archives, Appendix.

[24] Joseph Churba, *The Washington Compromise* (Lanham, Md.: University Press of America, 1995), p. 13. This is autobiographical.

[25] "The Old Man and the Sea," *Writings 5731*, pp. 79-80. Dated November 29, 1965.

"Mother's Day in Alabama," *Writings 5731*, pp. 67-68. Dated May 15, 1965.

These did not appear in the *Jewish Press* and the reference librarian at the Brooklyn Public Library did not find them on these dates in the *New York and Brooklyn Daily*.

[26] Letter from Meir to newspaper syndicates (regarding his political column), December 5, 1965, RZ Archives, folder 1008.

King Features Syndicate replied: "Thank you for giving us an opportunity to peruse your book, *A Small Voice*, but columns such as it contains would not fit in here at the present time." Letter from Kings Features Syndicate to Meir, November 15, 1966, in RZ Archives, folder 1008.

[27] "Hashkafa," *Jewish Press*, April 9, 1965, pp. S1, S19; May 14, 1965; May 21, 1965, pp. 23, 30, all in RZ Archives, folder 596. The April 9 column was reprinted in *Beyond Words*, 1:107-114.

[28] *Jewish Collegiate Observer*, December 1965, p. 3, in JNUL, call no. PB5655=2X. Thanks to Rachel Steiner for a mimeographed notice of this lecture, in RZ Archives, Appendix.

[29] Meir Kahane, "Hashkafa," *Jewish Press*, April 2, 1965, p. 15, in RZ Archives, folder 596.

Chapter 11

[1] "Chronology of a Miracle," *Jewish Press*, October 13, 1967, p. 9.

[2] "Chronology of a Miracle," *Jewish Press*, October 6, 1967, p. 16. The same indoctrination characterizes the Arab world today, while Israeli children are taught that peace is paramount.

[3] Letter from Naomi Brody to Libby, February 15, 1997, in RZ Archives, Appendix.

[4] Interview with Fred and Edith Horowitz, December 7, 1996, Jerusalem.

[5] See note 3.

[6] My father kept a record of his daily Talmud study (*daf yomi*), in which he also noted important family and world events. This excerpt was written in June 1967. He placed the pages on which he wrote at the end of each Talmud volume. Meir saw this page and asked to keep it in his personal files, where I found it.

[7] Our new address was 233-20 139 Avenue.

[8] Meir Kahane, "The Jewish Stake in Vietnam," *Congressional Record*, July 18, 1967, pp. H8895-H8901, in RZ Archives, folder 714b.

Originally: Meir Kahane, "The Jewish Stake in Vietnam," *Jewish Press*, ten parts, April 7, 1967 – June 9, 1967, in RZ Archives, folder 597.

For Meir's views on American involvement in the Vietnam War, see also *Story of the Jewish Defense League*, pp. 184-185, 239.

[9] Meir Kahane, Joseph Churba, and Michael King, *The Jewish Stake in Vietnam* (New York: Crossroads Publishing Co., 1967), 224 pp.

Meir used the pseudonym Michael King in his work with Joseph Churba so as not to involve the *Jewish Press*, with which his name was closely associated.

The book's dedication reads: "To the enslaved Jews of Russia, with fervent prayer for redemption."

I did not discover who funded the publication of *Jewish Stake in Vietnam*. There is no information in Churba's autobiography, *The Washington Compromise* (see chapter 10, note 24) and no book publisher named Crossroads was found in the Library of Congress online catalog.

The Jewish Stake in Vietnam is in the New York Public Library and in the JNUL.

[10] *The Jewish Stake in Vietnam*, pp. 25-55.

See also: Shelomo Ben-Israel, *Russian Sketches: A Visit to Jews Without Hope*. Translated from the Yiddish by Gertrude Hirschler (New York: American Jewish Committee, 1967), 55 pp. Excerpted with permission.

[11] One such lecture, at Congregation Shaaray Tefila in Far Rockaway on March 28, 1971, was released by Hager Records as an rpm record titled *Never Again*, now in JNUL National Sound Archives.

[12] *Biographical Data* (New York: Jewish Defense League, [1970]), 1 p., in RZ Archives, folder 733.

[13] Interview with Shoshana Weinberg, formerly of Fall River, Mass., February 26, 2004, Jerusalem.

[14] Phone interview with Rabbi Avraham Goldreich, April 24, 2001. The rabbi of the synagogue in Richmond had left and the congregation had not yet replaced him. Rabbi Goldreich recalled Meir's kindness in bringing him a silver *atara* (*tallit* collar) from New York.

[15] Report supplied by the Intercounty Clearance Corporation, February 26, 1998. Consultant Research Associates' mailing address is given as 509 Fifth Avenue, New York City (a maildrop). There is blank stationery for the firm in RZ Archives, folder 596, but no record of its activities in Meir's papers.

There is no reference to this firm or earlier firms in Churba's autobiography. In it, he wrote that he had no contact with Meir after 1967. See chapter 10, note 24, *The Washington Compromise*, p. 17.

Churba's Shabbat in Laurelton was recalled by Elliott Horowitz. Interview with Horowitz, February 13, 1997.

[16] See note 4. Horowitz told author Yair Kotler (*Heil Kahane*, p. 73) the same thing, but Kotler wrote only that Meir had borrowed money from Horowitz, not that he was repaying it. This is a sample of the inaccurate, slanted reporting in Kotler's book.

[17] See note 4.

[18] Letter from Rabbi Moshe Tanami, May 15, 1997, in RZ Archives, Appendix. Translated into English by Laya Zryl.

In 1966 Meir set up a charitable foundation in memory of Estelle Donna Evans, who had worked with him and Churba until her suicide that August. The fund raised money for poverty-stricken Israelis through ads in the *Jewish Press*. Meir sent the contributions to his brother Nachman for distribution in Israel, following in the tradition of their great-grandfather Baruch David Kahane who distributed charitable funds in Safed from 1873 on.

[19] Meir Hacohen (pseudonym of Meir Kahane), "Israel Through Laughter and Tears: Wait Till I Put on My Hat," *Jewish Press*, April 26, 1968, p. 28.

[20] Meir Hacohen (pseudonym of Meir Kahane), "Israel Through Laughter and Tears: Boris Comes Home," *Jewish Press*, March 1, 1968, pp. 19, 30.

[21] Michael Dov Weissmandl, *Min Hameitzar* (New York: Emunah, 1960), [252] pp. Reprinted: Brooklyn, N.Y.: 1997.

[22] Meir Hacohen (pseudonym of Meir Kahane), "Light in the Soviet Darkness," *Jewish Press*, April 26, 1968, p. 14, in RZ Archives, folder 595.

[23] Rabbi Harry Bronstein regularly wrote about Russian Jewry in the *Jewish Press* and his organization, Al Tidom, raised funds for its activities through ads in the *Jewish Press*. One Al Tidom ad appeared in the *Jewish Press*, March 19, 1968, p. 30.

[24] Both Meir and Rabbi Bronstein received a "Command to appear before the Committee on Un-American Activities of the House of Representatives, on June 19, 1968." In RZ Archives, folder 595.

This was Meir's only appearance before a Congressional committee. E-mail from Infocus Research Services, February 28, 1997. Inaccuracies in both Yair Kotler's *Heil Kahane* (pp. 24-25) and Robert I. Friedman's *False Prophet* (p. 88) refer to Meir appearing before more than one Congressional committee and infer that his testimony was about leftists and neo-Nazis.

See also: Hyman S. Frank, "Inside Meir Kahane," *Jewish Press*, part 5, November 8, 1974, p. 47. Details in chapter 10, note 3.

25 *"Jewish Press* Writers Testify on Soviet Anti-Semitism," *Jewish Press*, July 5, 1968, pp. 20, 42; July 12, 1968, pp. 2, 3; July 19, 1968, pp. 23, 27, in RZ Archives, folder 595.

Meir's testimony appears in: House Committee on Un-American Activities, *Anti-Semitism in the Soviet Union: Hearings before the Committee on Un-American Activities*, 19th Cong., 2nd sess., June 19, 1968. (Washington, D.C.: U.S. Government Printing Office booklet no. 27-407-O), pp. 2202-2206; 2220-2233.

Rabbi Harry Bronstein's testimony appears on pp. 2206-2220.

See also: "Persecution of Jews Described to House Panel," *New York Times*, June 20, 1968, p. 16.

A good overview of the plight of Soviet Jewry is: "Soviet Union, Antisemitism and Discrimination," *American Jewish Year Book*, 1971, pp. 405-409.

Chapter 12

1 "Intergroup Relations and Tensions in the United States," in *American Jewish Year Book*, 1968, pp. 233-245, 247.

See: http://en.wikipedia.org/wiki/Blockbusting.

See also: Adam Gopnick, "Improvised City," *New Yorker*, November 19, 2001, p. 91. Gopnick wrote: "The city changed fundamentally in 1969 [to a place of] violence and despair."

2 Richard Reeves, "The City's Troubles," *New York Times*, October 18, 1968, p. 50, in RZ Archives, folder 1029.

3 Letter from Arnold Fine to Libby, April 1997, in RZ Archives, Appendix.

4 "We Are Talking of Jewish Survival," [ad] *Jewish Press*, May 24, 1968, p. 33.

5 *Ayer Directory*, 1969, p. 701.

6 Martin Gershen, "New Organization Protests Against NYU Official," *Newark Star Ledger*, August 6, 1968, in RZ Archives, folder 683A. Excerpted with permission.

7 Jewish Defense League, Certificate of Incorporation, approved September 25, 1968, in RZ Archives, Appendix.

8 Meir Kahane, "The Death of Indignation," *Jewish Press*, two parts, August 30, 1968, p. 12; September 6, 1968, p. 16, in RZ Archives, folder 595.

9 Charles Grutzner, "Hatchett Brands Nominees Racists," *New York Times*, October 9, 1968, pp. 1, 37, in YU Archives, folder 6/3. Albert Shanker, a Jew, was head of the teachers' union. See chapter 28, note 25.

10 John F. Hatchett, "The Phenomenon of the Anti-Black Jews and the Black Anglo-Saxon," *African-American Teachers Forum*, November 1967, in RZ Archives, folder 63.

11 Synagogue Council of America, "News," press release, September 3, 1968, in YU Archives, folder 11/5; American Jewish Congress, "News," press release, January 7, 1969, in YU Archives, folder 6/3.

12 See note 6.

13 See note 6. See also: "Demand Ouster of Anti-Semite," *Jewish Press*, August 9, 1968, pp. 1, 33, in RZ Archives, folder 683A, and *Story of the Jewish Defense League*, pp. 91-94.

14 *"Jewish Press* Printing Plant Bombed," *Jewish Press*, July 26, 1968, p. 1, in RZ Archives, folder 596.

15 "Lindsay," *Jewish Press*, October 25, 1968, pp. 19, 34, in YU Archives, folder 7/9.

16 Martin Gershen, "Feud Between Lindsay, Jewish Leaders Expands," *Staten Island Advance*, October 17, 1968, in RZ Archives, folder 1029.

Frederick F. Siegel, *The Future Once Happened Here: New York, D.C., L.A. and the Fate of America's Big Cities* (New York: 1997). See pp. 4, 40, 44. Siegel was professor of history at New York's Cooper Union College and wrote several books.

[17] "Racism and Subversion in New York City," *Jewish Press*, four parts, March 8, 1968, pp. 2, 14; March 15, 1968, pp. 5, 39; March 22, 1968, p. 27; March 29, 1968, p. 39, in RZ Archives, folder 595.

[18] "School Decentralization," *Jewish Press*, May 31, 1968, p. 45, in RZ Archives, folder 594.

[19] "Racist Leaflets in N.Y. Schools Warn White Teachers to Leave," *Jewish Press*, June 14, 1968, pp. 1, 2, 28, in RZ Archives, folder 596.

[20] "High School Students Rampage," *World Almanac*, 1970, pp. 902, 905; "New Chaos in the Schools," *New York Times*, December 3, 1968, p. 46, in RZ Archives, folder 1029.

[21] [Meir Kahane], *Manifesto* (New York: Jewish Defense League, [hand-dated 1969]), 1 folded four-sided folio sheet, in RZ Archives, file 482.

This has the league's name in Gothic letters and its address, 156 Fifth Avenue. The league stayed at this address until September 1969.

[22] E-mail from Allan (Eliyahu) Mallenbaum dated March 29, 1998. Mallenbaum, Meir's Betar friend, worked as administrative director of the JDL from October 1969 to March 1970. Interview with Mallenbaum, May 19, 1998, Jerusalem.

The first to use the slogan in a speech was Bertram Zweibon. See: *Story of the Jewish Defense League*, p. 95.

[23] *Story of the Jewish Defense League*, p. 5.

[24] [Meir Kahane], *The Jewish Defense League: Aims and Purposes* (New York: Jewish Defense League, [1969]), 14 pp., 28 cm., in RZ Archives, Appendix, and in JNUL, call number S2=2003B6891.

[25] Letter from Meir to Rabbi Pinchas Stolper, March 7, 1968; National Conference of Synagogue Youth, "Placement Application," [submitted by Meir Kahane], [1968], both in RZ Archives, Appendix. Thanks to Rabbi Yehuda Ginsberg of the NCSY for photocopies of the letter and the placement application.

Chapter 13

[1] Letters from Susan (Chaya Sara) Hartenbaum Friedman to Libby, January 2, 1997, and December 1, 1999, in RZ Archives, Appendix.

Spectrum 1970, the yearbook of the Yeshiva High School of Queens, notes: "Rabbi Kahane left the school in January [1969] to devote his energy to JDL." *Spectrum 1970*, p. 118, in RZ Archives, Appendix. Thanks to Elliott Horowitz for a photocopy of this page.

[2] Phone interview with Netty Gross, November 15, 1998. She was in ninth grade that year, as was Frimette Roth, who recalled that Meir taught their class the laws of Shabbat. Interview with Roth, July, 2002, Jerusalem.

[3] E-mail from Stuart Cohen, June 22, 1999.

[4] Phone interview with Larry Dub, January 9, 1997.

[5] Interview with Jerry Ganger, November 7, 1998. Ganger was in tenth grade that year.

[6] Phone interview with Joel Silber, May 19, 2003. Silber was in tenth grade that year.

[7] Meir taught freshmen through seniors, boys and girls. Some interviewees recall that he taught once a week and others twice a week, so I estimate that he taught about 12 hours a week.

8   The Traditional Synagogue of Rochdale Village was located at 165-27 Baisley Boulevard in Jamaica, Queens. Its Hebrew name was Emunat Avoteinu (the Faith of Our Forefathers).

9   E-mail from Arieh Lebowitz, Jewish Labor Committee, December 1, 1997.

The consortium of labor unions that built Rochdale Village was the United Housing Foundation. Since union members, most of them Jewish, were among the first to learn of the building project, they signed up for the apartments early. But there were also non-Jews, such as our black next-door neighbors.

Many residents of Rochdale Village were elderly tailors and seamstresses who had arrived in the United States in their teens and whose mother tongue was Yiddish. Wherever I went in Rochdale Village, I heard people speaking Yiddish, and I thought intolerantly, "So many years in the country and they haven't learned English yet!" Only as a newcomer in Israel did I appreciate how much more pleasant it is to converse in the language you know best.

10   "Hashkafa," *Jewish Press*, April 23, 1965, p. 10, in JNUL.

11   Letter from Ralph Weinstein to Libby, August 11, 1997, in RZ Archives, Appendix.

12   We lived at 163-15 130th Avenue from October 1968 to August 1969.

Apartment fees are given in synagogue records, note 14.

13   Joy Amsel is the sister of Malka Parnes, formerly of Laurelton. Interview with Malka Parnes, June 26, 2006, Jerusalem.

14   *Minutes*, Rochdale Village Traditional Synagogue meeting, October 3, 1968, in RZ Archives, Appendix.

Rabbi Hayim Schwartz, executive director of the Rabbinical Seminary of America (Forest Hills, N.Y.) sent me these minutes. He wrote: "Some years ago, the deteriorating conditions for Jews in Rochdale Village forced the *shul* to affiliate with our Yeshiva Chofetz Chaim in order to survive. We have repaired and maintained the building, and it is currently being used as a day care center for local residents. I spent considerable time perusing the old records of the *shul*. I selected and photocopied those items I thought you would find of interest." Letter from Rabbi Hayim Schwartz to Libby, April 9, 1997, in RZ Archives, Appendix.

15   Budget 1969/70, Rochdale Village Traditional Synagogue, in RZ Archives, Appendix.

A newspaper report said Meir's annual salary was $9,200. See: "Controversial Rabbi Resigns Rochdale Village Synagogue," *Long Island Press*, July 3, 1969.

16   See note 11.

Rabbi Irving Halberstam was a friend of Meir's father. He is mentioned in the synagogue minutes. See note 14.

17   FBI New York office file 157-5767, report, October 14, 1970, p. 3, in RZ Archives, Appendix. A report in the *Long Island Press* (see note 15) put the membership at 340 families.

18   "From the Rabbi," *Messenger* (Traditional Synagogue of Rochdale Village), March-April 1969, p. 3, in RZ Archives, Appendix.

Thanks to Murray Schneider for sending me this issue.

The *Messenger* of March-April 1969 is labeled volume 5, no. 2, but I did not find any issues in any library or archive. I searched in: OCLC FirstSearch, Queens Borough Public Library, YIVO library, Tamiment Archive at Bobst Library, United Housing Foundation archives, Yeshiva University Archives. It is not found in the Synagogue's archives either.

19   "Synagogue News," see note 18, *Messenger*, p. 8.

20   *Minutes*, Rochdale Village Traditional Synagogue meeting, November 26, 1968, in RZ Archives, Appendix.

21   Letter from Weinstein, see note 11.

[22] A report on the installation dinner said: "Rabbi Eli P. Rominek of the Young Israel of Laurelton and Rabbi Abraham Chinitz [of Yeshiva Torah Vodaath] spoke eloquently of the abilities and scholarship of this well known writer and leader. Rabbi Charles Kahane spoke movingly of the honor and pride he felt in his son...." See note 18, *Messenger*, p. 8.

See also "Traditional Synagogue Installs New Rabbi," *Jewish Press*, February 21, 1969, p. 31, reprinted in *Beyond Words*, 1:147.

Chapter 14

[1] Meir Kahane, "Anti-Poverty Group, Extremists Get Into School, Cops Back Down," *Jewish Press*, November 1, 1968, pp. 1, 3, 36, in RZ Archives, folder 595.

[2] The *New York Times Index*, 1968, under "Jews – United States – Anti-Semitism."

[3] American Jewish Congress, "For Immediate Release" [begins:]... today asked police commissioner..." press release, November 8, 1968, in RZ Archives, folder 050A.

[Meir Kahane], "JDL Guard Cemetery on Halloween," *Jewish Press*, November 8, 1968, p. 2, in RZ Archives, folder 63.

Since Montefiore Cemetery was near Laurelton, many members of the Young Israel of Laurelton took part in this activity. Meir also promoted patrols of other cemeteries on Halloween eve during the years that followed. I spoke to many people, then in their thirties and forties, who recalled taking part in JDL patrols at cemeteries on Halloween eve.

[4] Rosh Hashana: Meir Hacohen (pseudonym of Meir Kahane), "Israel Through Laughter and Tears," *Jewish Press*, October 11, 1968, p. 13.

Judea and Samaria: "Amman and Jerusalem," *Jewish Press*, November 22, 1968, p. 9, in RZ Archives, folder 596, reprinted in *Beyond Words*, 1:133-137.

Wives of rabbinical students: "A Small Voice," *Jewish Press*, October 18, 1968, p. 10, in RZ Archives, folder 596.

"Leftist Accuses Slumlord," *Jewish Press*, December 13, 1968, p. 3.

[5] "Delaware Police Find Army of Racist Militant Weapons," *Jewish Press*, September 20, 1968, pp. 3, 22, 27, in RZ Archives, folder 596; "Arab Students Hail Black Militants," *Jewish Press*, October 11, 1968, p. 1, in RZ Archives, folder 595.

Meir drew on his files of clippings, now in RZ Archives, for "Spotlight on Extremism." Folders 310-340 have newspaper clippings on such extremist groups as the Ku Klux Klan, Christian Defense League, Liberty Lobby, Minutemen, National Socialist White People's Party, National States' Rights Party, Progressive Labor Party, Trotskyites, and Black Panthers. Meir clipped items on these subjects from the late 1960s to the mid-1970s.

Meir later collected similar material for the Museum of the Potential Holocaust, which operated in Jerusalem from 1979 to1990.

[6] Photograph of Meir at rostrum, Young Israel of Hillcrest, Queens, New York, October 1968, in RZ Archives, picture folder, no. 354, and in photo section of this book.

Letter from Murray Schneider to Libby, July 1, 2002, in RZ Archives, Appendix.

E-mail from Peter Eisenstadt, April 19, 2005, citing *Inside Rochdale*, February 1969.

[7] The full text of the poem is on the Internet: http://query.nytimes.com.

See also: Henry Raymont, "Teachers Protest Poem to FCC," *New York Times*, January 16, 1969, p. 48; Leonard Buder, "Board Is Asked to Oust Teacher Over Poem Called Anti-Semitic," *New York Times*, January 18, 1969, p. 19.

[8] [*Leslie Campbell*, by Meir Kahane], flyer headed only "Jewish Defense League," in YU Archives, folder 12/4.

Leslie Campbell, "The Devil Can Never Educate Us," *African-American Teachers Forum,* November 1968.

[9] Interview with Sy Polsky, June 13, 1997.

[10] Letter from Ralph Weinstein to Libby, August 11, 1997, in RZ Archives, Appendix.

Meir presents the full case against Campbell in *Story of the Jewish Defense League,* pp. 106-109.

[11] "Members of the Jewish Defense League Picket at P.S. 30, Rochdale Village," [photo caption] *Long Island Press,* January 17, 1969, p. 1. Thanks to Murray Schneider for this clipping, reproduced in the photo section of this book.

[12] Henry Raymont, "Crisis-Level Anti-Semitism Found Here by B'nai B'rith," *New York Times,* January 23, 1969, p. 1; "Decision Reserved in Bias Hearing," *Long Island Press,* January 25, 1969, in YU Archives, folder 12/4; Thomas F. Brady, "Outcry Against Growing Bigotry," *New York Times,* January 25, 1969, p. 15.

[13] "Mayor Asks School Bias Code," *Daily News,* January 24, 1969, pp. 3, 4, in YU Archives, folder 12/4. The *Daily News* had a circulation of 2,080,906. See *Ayer Directory,* 1969, p. 764.

[14] Letter from Meir to JDL members, January 24, 1969, in YU Archives, folder 9/6.

[15] "Rival WBAI Pickets Clash," *Daily News,* January 31, 1969, in YU Archives, folder 12/4; "WBAI-FM Rejects Jewish Group's Demands on Anti-Semitism," *New York Times,* January 28, 1969, p. 27; "Jews Demand Muzzling of Anti-Semitic Radio Show," *Long Island Press,* January 27, 1969, in RZ Archives, folder 63. See also: *Story of the Jewish Defense League,* pp. 109-110.

[16] Letter from Sy Polsky to Libby, January 7, 2000, in RZ Archives, Appendix.

[17] "Freedom of Lampshades," *Jewish Press,* February 7, 1969, pp. 17, 18, in RZ Archives, folder 596.

[18] "The Face of Fascism," *Jewish Press,* April 25, 1969, p. 67, in RZ Archives, folder 596.

Excerpted in: Harold Saltzman, *Race War in High School* (New Rochelle, N.Y.: Arlington House, 1972), pp. 73-74. Saltzman, a teacher at Franklin K. Lane High School in Brooklyn, presents an overview of New York City's 1968 school strike and Lindsay's part in the growth of racial tensions between 1968 and 1969.

Letter from Saltzman to Meir, March 2, 1970, requesting permission to excerpt "Face of Fascism," and Meir's letter to Saltzman, March 11, 1970, in YU Archives, folder 6/2.

[19] The *New York Times Index,* 1969, under "Jews – United States – Anti-Semitism."

[20] Jim Smith and Tom Fox, "Irate Bandits Beat 2 in Synagogue," *Philadelphia Daily News,* February 15, 1969, p. 5, in RZ Archives, folder 50A.

[21] John L. Hess, "Orleans Shops Are Victims of Anti-Semitic Rumor," *New York Times,* June 10, 1969, p. 12, in RZ Archives, folder 50A.

[22] "Acid Bomb Thrown at Boston Rabbi," *Jewish Press,* July 25, 1969, pp. 1, 18, in RZ, folder 50A.

[23] "Gravestones Toppled by Vandals During the Night Lie Row on Row at Ansonia-Derby Hebrew Cemetery," [photo caption] *Hartford Times,* August 25, 1969, in RZ Archives, folder 50A.

[24] American Jewish Committee, *Fact Sheet:* "Not for Publication or Distribution, no. 70-970-2." (New York: February 1970), 8 pp., in RZ Archives, folder 61A. Update, 1971, in RZ Archives, folder 484.

This cites "Growth," *Jewish Defense League Newsletter,* November 14, 1969, p. 2, in RZ Archives, folder 716B.

The founding meeting of JDL's Philadelphia chapter was held September 23, 1969, at the city's Young Men's Hebrew Association (YMHA). See: Letter from Meir to Rabbi Green, YMHA, undated, YU Archives, folder 7/15. See also: FBI file 105-207795, correlation summary, October 20, 1972, p. 4, in RZ Archives, Appendix.

25 "Board of Education Agrees to Meet JDL," *Jewish Press*, March 7, 1969, p. 45; *Story of the Jewish Defense League*, p. 112; FBI file 105-207795, report, December 21, 1970, p. 3, in RZ Archives, Appendix.

26 Don Pride, "Jewish Defense League: 'We'll Riot if Necessary,'" *Manhattan Tribune*, March 15, 1969, p. 5, in RZ Archives, folder 63. Excerpted with the author's permission.

For the JDL's role in Dideon Goldberg's reinstatement, see *Story of the Jewish Defense League*, pp. 113-114.

27 "Blacks Demand Church Money," *World Almanac*, 1970, p. 918.

28 Edward B. Fiske, "Forman Burns a Court Order Barring Disruption in Church," *New York Times*, May 10, 1969, p. 32.

29 Interview with Sy Polsky, June 13, 1997. Polsky recalled that the JDL demonstration began long before sunset on Friday (as did services at Temple Emanu-El) but ended close to Shabbat, so several participants spent Shabbat at his nearby apartment.

See also "Forman Challenged by JDL," *Jewish Press*, May 16, 1969, pp. 1, 2, and *Story of the Jewish Defense League*, pp. 97-105.

Regarding the concept of *chillul Hashem*, desecration of G-d's name, Rabbi Jacob Chinitz of Philadelphia's Temple Beth Ami wrote, "Is the synagogue obliged to tolerate blackmail against itself and its people? ... Crimes tolerated against Jews are a greater *chillul Hashem* than [accusations of vigilantism]." Chinitz, "Letter to the Editor," *Young Israel Viewpoint*, October 31, 1969, in RZ Archives, folder 1203.

30 Cy Egan, "Forman Says He'll Be at Riverside," *New York Post*, May 10, 1969, p. 2, in RZ Archives, folder 435A.

The article, noting Forman's plan to read his manifesto at Temple Emanu-El, is accompanied by a photo, captioned: "Jewish Defense League members with baseball bats and lead pipes wait outside Temple Emanu-El, Fifth Av. and 65th St., for black militant James Forman, who reportedly was to show up to read his demands for church reparations for Negroes. Forman didn't appear."

Phone interview with Joseph Alster, July 8, 2002. Alster, then age 46, is in the photo, holding a baseball bat.

"The City: Jewish Vigilantes," *Time*, July 4, 1969, p. 18, in RZ Archives, folder 63. The picture in *Time* is the same one used in the ad, "Is This Any Way for a Nice Jewish Boy to Behave?" See note 32.

See also: "Temple Emanu-El Agrees to Consider Manifesto," *Jewish Post and Opinion*, June 12, 1970, p. 1.

31 Sol Raffalow, "Letter to the Editor," *New York Times*, October 21, 1969, p. 46, in RZ Archives, folder 683a. This is a response to Theodore Bikel's attack on the JDL in his "Letter to the Editor," *New York Times,* October 15, 1969, p. 46.

32 "Is This Any Way for a Nice Jewish Boy to Behave?" [ad] *New York Times*, June 24, 1969, p. 31, in RZ Archives, folder 63. The ad was three columns wide and ran the entire length of the page.

The catchy heading inspired the title of a 1971 four-page article about the JDL: Martin Flusser, "Any Way for Nice Jewish Boys to Behave?" *Newsday*, January 9, 1971, pp. 8W-12W, in RZ Archives, folder 60A.

33   McCandish Phillips, "Jewish Militants Step Up Activity," *New York Times*, June 25, 1969, p. 25.

34   "Fighting Black Militancy: Jewish 'Vigilantes' Under Fire," *Jewish Chronicle* (London), July 4, 1969, p. 14, in RZ Archives, folder 435A.

35   "Black Militants Make Demands on St. Louis Jews," *Daily News Record*, September 24, 1969, in RZ Archives, folder 315A. This clipping from a menswear trade newspaper was sent to Meir by Ruby Markowitz, who heard him speak at the Young Israel of Queens Valley, Flushing, New York.

See note 24, "Confrontation in Philadelphia," *Newsletter*, p. 1; Lester Kinsolving, "Black Power Stopped by Jewish Power," *Pittsburgh Post-Gazette*, August 15, 1970, in Center for Jewish History (New York), JDL folder.

Kinsolving wrote that JDL chapter chairman Rabbi Harold Novoseller's loud objection to Kenyatta's disrespectful use of four-letter words in a synagogue led many in the audience to leave.

36   See note 33.

37   *Minutes*, Rochdale Village Traditional Synagogue board meeting, June 17, 1969, in RZ Archives, Appendix. The minutes indicate that Meir worked part-time as of June 1. The minutes also show that the Board of Directors first discussed Meir's involvement with the JDL at a meeting on April 29, 1969.

Rabbi Zvi Block, now of Los Angeles, recalled being interviewed by Meir for the position of assistant rabbi. Interview with Rabbi Zvi Block, November 18, 2003, Jerusalem.

See also: Hyman S. Frank, "Inside Meir Kahane," *Jewish Press*, November 15, 1974, p. 8. Details in chapter 10, note 3.

38   The principle of trusting in G-d's protection was discussed by our son Binyamin, expounding on a talk by Meir about *Ezra* 8:21, in: *Hameir La'aretz* [Hebrew] (Jerusalem: Yeshivat Haraayon Hayehudi, 1990), p. 42. Binyamin's words are cited in Lenny Goldberg, *The Wit and Wisdom of Rabbi Meir Kahane* (Ariel: Hameir, 2007), pp. 173-174. Meir's commentary on *Ezra* 8:21 was published posthumously in: Meir Kahane, *Perush Hamacabee: Isaiah, Latter Prophets, Scriptures* [Hebrew] (Jerusalem: Institute for Publication of the Writings of Rabbi Meir Kahane, 1996), p. 419.

39   *Minutes*, Rochdale Village Traditional Synagogue board meeting, June 30, 1969, in RZ Archives, Appendix. June 30 was a Monday; the blacks came to our door on June 29.

Meir's relationship with the synagogue did not end with our move to Brooklyn. The souvenir journal of the dinner of the Jewish Identity Center, March 14, 1976, includes an ad honoring "Our Former Rabbi... from the Traditional Synagogue of Rochdale Village, Philip Lebowitz, President." And former synagogue president Ralph Weinstein wrote: "After I relocated to Florida I would see the Rabbi every year when he came to Florida. He would always embrace me and introduce me as 'my president.'" See note 10.

40   We moved to Flatbush on August 6, 1969. See: FBI file 105-207795, report, December 21, 1970, p. 2, in RZ Archives, Appendix.

Among the JDL members who moved our furniture was schoolteacher Barry Fox, chairman of the Sheepshead Bay chapter in Brooklyn. He wrote: "Rabbi Kahane had more influence on my life than anyone." E-mail from Barry Fox, March 7, 2007.

Even when a phone number was unlisted, the operators would inform callers, "Yes, Mr. X lives at that address, but his number is unlisted." For our address to remain secret, our phone had to be under a different name.

41   FBI file 105-207795, report, February 8, 1971, pp. C, 5, in RZ Archives, Appendix. We lived at 632 East 5 Street, Brooklyn, N.Y.

When asked for his address, Meir usually gave that of the JDL office. For example, on a car rental application dated October 28, 1970, he used the address of the office at 440 West 42nd Street in Manhattan. FBI file 105-207795, report, December 21, 1970, pp. 7, 8, in RZ Archives, Appendix.

Chapter 15

[1] See chapter 14, note 33, McCandish Phillips.

[2] E-mail from Samson Levine, November 22, 1999.

[3] Eli Schwartz, quoted in *Jewish Defense League Newsletter*, Fall 1970, p. [18], in YU Archives, folder 9/8.

[4] Jan Geliebter, "Camp Jedel," *Achdut: The National Voice of the Jewish High School Activist*, June 1971, p. 12, in RZ Archives, Appendix. Excerpted with the author's permission.

[5] E-mail from Martin Lewinter, February 18, 2000.

[6] "This Camp Is Not for Fun and Games!" [ad] *Jewish Press*, February 20, 1970, p. 26, in RZ Archives, folder 61A; reproduced in *Jewish Defense League Newsletter*, February 13, 1970, p. 9, in RZ Archives, folder 1202.

[7] John Peterson, "Camp Builds Cadre of Street Fighters," *National Observer*, July 28, 1969, in RZ Archives, Appendix.

The first to plunge into the Red Sea was Nachshon ben Aminadav (*Talmud, Tractate Sotah* 37a).

[8] Phone interview with Bob Duchanov, January 3, 1998. The Gartenberg family owned the Pioneer Hotel, also called the Pioneer Country Club, in Greenfield Park, N.Y.

Interview with Mal and Yetta Lebowitz, November 3, 1998, Jerusalem.

Fees are noted in ads in *Jewish Press*, June 20, 1969, p. 16, in RZ Archives, folder 596, and in *Jewish Defense League Newsletter*, January 9, 1970, p. 4, in YU Archives, folder 7/1.

Other documents in YU Archives indicate that the camp was subsidized by J.O.Y. (Jewish Operation Youth), a tax-deductible foundation incorporated as the educational arm of the JDL.

[9] E-mail from Dave Sommer, December 21, 1997.

Interview with Sy Polsky, June 13, 1997.

Polsky qualified for a National Rifle Association instructor's certificate after a crash course at the Palmach Rifle and Pistol Club, a legally chartered gun club in Manhattan patronized by many Jewish Defense League members.

[10] Phone interview with Lillian Kaufman, November 3, 1996.

See note 3, *Newsletter*, p. [18].

[11] E-mail from Dave Sommer, June 14, 1999.

Sy Polsky recalled that Lillian Kaufman made the decision to use paper plates. See note 9.

Meir's meeting with the local Board of Health is noted in his 1971 appointment book, in RZ Archives, Appendix.

[12] See chapter 44 for the 1975 season.

[13] Letter from Dave Sommer to Libby, November 17, 1997, in RZ Archives, Appendix.

[14] Interview with Dave and Shoshana Sommer, January 26, 1998, Jerusalem.

The Holocaust survivor who lectured was Joseph Greenblatt of the United Zionist Revisionists. Letter from Meir to Joseph Greenblatt, July 23, 1969, in YU Archives, folder 6/2.

[15] Gil Weisinger, "Sullivan Jewish Camp Stresses Self-Defense," *Times Herald Record*, July 19, 1969, pp. 44, 45; Roger Director, "Camp Is Serious," *Newsday*, August 19, 1970; Gershon

Jacobson, "Yiddishe Zelbst-Shutz... [Jewish Self-Defense Youth Complete Military Training]," *Day-Jewish Journal* (*Der Tog-Morgen Zhurnal*), September 8, 1969, pp. 1, 2. Thanks to Dave Sommer for photocopies of these articles.

Photos of Camp Jedel in: Shlomo Shamir, "Hasisma: 'Lo Od' [The Motto: 'Never Again']," *Ha'aretz*, January 29, 1971, supplement, pp. 20-21, in JNUL Archives, folder ARC 4=1748, clippings album.

See also: "Militants: Armed Summer Camp," *Time*, August 30, 1971, p. 21, in RZ Archives, folder 435A.

[16] See note 13.

[17] Jewish Defense League, Second International Annual Convention, [*Minutes*], June 6, 1971, p. 12, in RZ Archives, Appendix. The convention was held in New York City's Waldorf-Astoria Hotel.

Russ Kelner, age 30, was assistant director of the camp in 1970 and its director in 1971. A high school teacher, he headed the Philadelphia JDL chapter until September 1974, when he left teaching to be JDL's National Director in New York. E-mail from Kelner, July 25, 2000.

[18] See "Militants: Armed Summer Camp," note 15.

[19] E-mail from Sommer, April 21, 1999.

[20] Meir's original Hebrew version of the anthem was titled *Hahimnon*. The Hebrew text began: *Mitokh yoman am dakhui*. This English translation, by Meir, appeared in *The Jewish Defense League: Principles and Philosophies* (New York: Educational Department of the Jewish Defense League, [1973]), p. 2, in JNUL, call no. S74B2962=2.

A different English translation, unsigned, appeared in the *Jewish Defense League Weekly Newsbulletin*, May 3, 1972, in RZ Archives, folder 716B. It may have been written by Stella Gelbard, the *Newsbulletin*'s editor. The music and Hebrew text are in RZ Archives, folder 64B.

Avigdor Herzog, former head of the JNUL's National Sound Archives, recognized the melody as that of a Russian song popular in the 1940s and 1950s.

[21] Jewish Defense League, "Affirmation," *Oz – The Special Group*, p. 3, in RZ Archives, folder 482. See also: "The Pledge of Allegiance to the JDL" in NBC News Archive, media no. 0065054, June 24, 1971.

[22] "Kahane Talk Saturday Sparks Lively Session," *Young Israel Viewpoint*, October 31, 1969, pp. 15, 16, in RZ Archives, Appendix.

Talks at Camp HILI (July 17) and the Gibber Hotel (August 29) are noted in Meir's 1971 appointment book, in RZ Archives, Appendix.

[23] See note 14. Sommer's severe sentence was due to a concerted government crackdown on the JDL at the time his case came to trial. See: Edith Evans Asbury, "8 in JDL Are Indicted for Protests in City," *New York Times,* January 19, 1971, p. 1, in RZ Archives, folder 1203; "2 Are Accused of Hiding Identity to Buy 3 Rifles," *New York Times,* August 29, 1972, p. 18.

[24] Eleanor Blau, "Kahane Enters Guilty Plea on One Charge, in a Deal," *New York Times*, July 10, 1971, p. 1, in RZ Archives, folder 62A. Meir was given a five-year suspended sentence that was activated in 1975. See chapters 24 and 42.

[25] FBI file 105-207795, report, October 14, 1970, p. 11, in RZ Archives, Appendix.

[26] *Confidential: Jewish Defense League, Inc.* ([New York: Anti-Defamation League], September 12, 1969), in RZ Archives, folder 63.

The memo, signed only S.R., stated that the report was based on material supplied by Jerry Bakst, archivist of the Anti-Defamation League. The anonymous sympathizer who sent it to Meir attached a handwritten note, "From ADL."

[27] "Police in Passaic Seize 12 in Looting," *New York Times*, August 4, 1969, p. 11; "Passaic City Hall Hit by Firebomb," *New York Times*, August 5, 1969, p. 55.

See note 5, e-mail from Martin Lewinter.

Sommer recalled this occasion: "A Jewish manufacturer in Passaic phoned Meir at the JDL office, and Meir phoned the camp. We sent four guys." See note 14.

[28] Sylvan Fox, "School Is Firebombed in Fourth Night of Violence in Passaic," *New York Times*, August 7, 1969, p. 25:1. Copyright © 1969 by The New York Times Co. Excerpted with permission.

[29] "JDL Aids NJ Jewish Merchants," *Jewish Press*, August 15, 1969, pp. 1, 13.

[30] "JDL Stops Bungalow Attack," *Jewish Press*, August 22, 1969, pp. 1, 26, in RZ Archives, folder 63.

Chapter 16

[1] Irving Spiegel, "Rabbi Urges U.S. to Guard Worship," *New York Times*, May 19, 1969, p. 33. This article was reprinted in a JDL flyer that featured a photo of Joseph Alster, Irving Calderon and others holding baseball bats and lead pipes. "We Are Talking of Jewish Survival!" flyer, in RZ Archives, folder 63. The photo is from the *New York Post*, May 10, 1969, p. 2.

See also: *Story of the Jewish Defense League*, pp. 101-105, and pp. 175-180.

[2] "Dream or Nightmare?" [editorial] *New York Times*, June 25, 1969, p. 46. This is about the ad, "Is This Any Way for a Nice Jewish Boy to Behave?" (See chapter 14, note 32.) See chapter 14 for text of ad.

Irving Spiegel, "Jewish Extremists Scored by Council for View on Force," *New York Times*, July 1, 1969, p. 20, in RZ Archives, folder 63.

[3] "From a Jewish Father, to My Dear and Beloved Children," *Jewish Press*, July 11, 1969, p. 22. On October 20, after Meir was again condemned by a coalition of Jewish organizations, he placed this article as an ad in the *New York Times*. See note 29.

"Where there are no men, endeavor to be a man," is from *Mishnah*, *Avot*, 2:5.

[4] See: www.mfa.gov.il. Choose Terrorism.

[5] Jewish Defense League, "In response to the concerted world-wide Israel...," press release, August 27, 1969, in YU Archives, folder 10/9.

The rally was held at the center of the garment district, 39th Street and Seventh Avenue.

"U.S. Jet With 113 Hijacked to Syria by 2 Young Arabs," *New York Times*, August 30, 1969, p. 1.

FBI file 105-207795, see chapter 14, note 24. This report cites the interview with Meir on WNEW-TV (Channel Five) and quotes comments on the JDL raid from the Arabic-English newspaper, *Action*, September 15, 1969.

See also: "Mehdi Complains About Jewish Defense League Break-In to P.L.O. Office," *Spotlight on Extremism, Jewish Press*, October 3, 1969, pp. 3, 30.

Alfonso A. Narvaez, "Marchi Lays 'Urban Crisis' to Fear and Distrust," *New York Times*, September 5, 1969, p. 35. The news report noted that mayoral candidates Mario Procaccino and John Marchi had been invited to speak at the JDL rally.

[6] Letter from Rabbi Meir Kahane, National Director, Jewish Defense League, to "Gentlemen," [governments of Syria, Jordan, Lebanon, Iraq, and the United Arab Republic (Egypt)], September 10, 1969, in YU Archives, folder 10/9.

[7] Michael J. Berlin, "Militants Admit Threat to Arabs," *New York Post*, September 12, 1969, p. 14, in YU Archives, folder 10/9.

[8] Letter from Rabbi Meir Kahane, National Director, Jewish Defense League, to "Dear Friends and Brethren," September 10, 1969, in YU Archives, folder 10/9.

See also: Jewish Defense League, "The escalation of Arab terror against American Jews...," press release, undated, in YU Archives, folder 10/9. This details the parade route.

[9] "There Will Be No Arab Terror Here!" [ad] *Jewish Press*, undated clipping, in YU Archives, folder 10/9.

[10] "Arabs at U.N. Guarded After Reported Threats," *New York Times*, September 16, 1969, p. 5. See also note 7.

[11] FBI New York office file 157-5767, report, October 14, 1970, p. 9, in RZ Archives, Appendix. For Meir's comments on the FBI probe, see *Story of the Jewish Defense League*, p. 282.

[12] "Jewish Defense League Protests at U.N. Missions," *New York Times*, September 21, 1969, p. 6. This reports that JDL members traveled to Washington to petition the Justice Department to expel foreign students linked to subversive Arab groups.

[13] Robert I. Friedman in *False Prophet*, p. 104, maintains – among his many other inaccuracies – that Meir was deliberately not invited to the gala. Since I was there with Meir, I wrote to the New York City Hall of Records seeking a list of invitees. On August 29, 1997, Stephen Barto, Public Records Officer, sent me a photocopy from the guest list where Meir's name (misspelled Kehane) appears as "Associate Editor, *Jewish Press*." See: "Record Series: Special Event Files, Office of the Mayor, Lindsay Administration," in New York City Municipal Archives; copy in RZ Archives, Appendix.

"Mrs. Meir Arrives in City on Monday," *New York Times*, September 26, 1969, p. 3. See also: Maurice Carroll, "Lindsay Will Bolster 4th Platoon; Plans for Jewish Holy Days," *New York Times*, September 12, 1969, p. 32.

Jews numbered roughly 25% of New York City's population. See: *American Jewish Year Book*, 1970, p. 351.

[14] Meir was seated in the *sukkah* with other religiously observant men. Since women are not obligated to eat in a *sukkah*, and space there was limited, I was seated with the wives of other men who were in the *sukkah*. Among them were Blu Greenberg of Riverdale, married to a former BTA classmate of Meir's, Rabbi Irving Greenberg, and Malka Schick, whose husband Marvin was an advisor to Lindsay.

Lawrence Van Gelder, "Quest for Peace Keeps Mrs. Meir on Go Here," *New York Times*, October 1, 1969, p. 16.

[15] "On the Nature of Anti-Semitism," *Jewish Press*, June 20, 1969, p. 31, in RZ Archives, folder 596.

"Reverse Bias in Medical Schools Limits Admissions for Whites," *Jewish Press*, August 1, 1969, pp. 2, 27, in RZ Archives, folder 595.

"Color It Lindsay: Lindsay and the Jews," *Jewish Press*, September 26, 1969, pp. 35, 45.

[16] "No Apology Necessary," *Jewish Press*, September 5, 1969, p. 17, in RZ Archives, folder 596.

"U.S. Churches, Refugee Group Supporting Al Fatah Operations," *Jewish Press*, September 19, 1969, pp. 1, 36, in YU Archives, folder 10/9. Al Fatah, see note 6.

[17] "Tisha B'Av, 5729," *Jewish Press*, July 25, 1969, pp. 28, 38, in RZ Archives, folder 596, reprinted in *Beyond Words*, 1:153-156.

See also: Henry Kamm, "Soviet Is Said to Arrest Jew Who Seeks to Emigrate to Israel," *New York Times*, April 10, 1969, p. 8. The article erroneously spells his name Kochubinsky.

[18] "I Spent a Night in Canada Last Week," *Jewish Press*, October 10, 1969, p. 38, in RZ Archives, folder 594, reprinted in *On Jews and Judaism*, pp. 30-31.

The segment was filmed at the beginning of October in Waterloo-Kitchener, near Toronto. My efforts to locate a video copy were unsuccessful. Roy Harris, archivist at the Canadian Broadcasting Company, wrote that *Under Attack* was not a CBC-owned television production and therefore it was not in their archives. (E-mail from Harris, March 2000.) Dan Somers of the National Archives of Canada wrote that programs at that time were shot on relatively expensive two-inch video tape that was recycled rather than archived. It was very unlikely that a copy of the broadcast had survived. (E-mail from Somers, July 31, 2000.)

See also: "Student Activism, New Left and Anti-Semitism," chapter 10, note 22.

Rabbi Philip (Shraga Feivel) Rosensweig was rabbi of the Beth Jacob Synagogue in Waterloo. His name was misspelled as Rosenzweig in the original article.

[19] Meir Kahane, "The Jews of New York City Cannot Afford Four More Years of John Lindsay," [ad] *New York Times*, October 6, 1969, p. 35, in RZ Archives, Appendix.

Anti-Lindsay articles by Meir in the *Jewish Press* were in his *Commentary* column: June 14, 1968, pp. 1, 2, 28; July 5, 1968, pp. 3, 41; October 25, 1968, p. 13; December 13, 1968, pp. 9, 23; August 8, 1969, pp. 23, 28; "Lindsay," October 25, 1968, pp. 19, 34; "Twenty Questions for Lindsay," January 31, 1969, p. 9. See also note 15, "Color It Lindsay."

See also chapter 12.

[20] Jewish Defense League, telegram, October 7, 1969, in YU Archives, folder 7/9. Begins: "Please send the following telegram and charge to our phone bill." It gives the text and a list of recipients and their addresses.

[21] Jewish Defense League, "The Jewish Defense League advertisement in yesterday's (Oct. 6) *New York Times*...," press release, October 7, 1969, in YU Archives, folder 7/9.

E-mail from Dave Sommer, December 21, 1997.

[22] "Lindsay Sets Off a Mixed Reaction," *New York Times*, October 8, 1969, p. 37.

Letter from Meir to Editor, *New York Post*, October 8, 1969, in YU Archives, folder 7/9.

[23] Irving Spiegel, "Mayoral Candidates Bar Bloc Appeal," *New York Times*, October 10, 1969, p. 52. Meir wrote about the "Jewish vote" in *Story of the Jewish Defense League*, pp. 175-176.

[24] Pressure on Klass: Meir named the Joseph Jacobs advertising agency in *Story of the Jewish Defense League*, p. 198.

Meir's last articles in the *Jewish Press* , October 10, 1969: "Israel Through Laughter and Tears," by Meir Hacohen (pseudonym of Meir Kahane), pp. 17, 37; "Spotlight on Extremism," pp. 3, 44; and "I Spent a Night in Canada Last Week," p. 38.

After Meir's dismissal from the *Jewish Press*, *Spotlight on Extremism* appeared under the byline Ben Greenberg. Arnold Fine, explained: "Rabbi Klass asked me to continue it under a nom de plume. (E-mail from Fine, February 15, 2000). Fine narrowed the column's focus to extremist groups in the city school system. By July 1971 the column's title had become *Spotlight on Discrimination*, and in 1975 it became *Spotlight on Education.*

See chapter 20 for a discussion of Meir's newsletter, *Spotlight on Extremism*. The *Spotlight* column was succeeded by *Exposing the Haters*. See chapter 25, note 15.

Meir's Dismissal: *New York Times*, October 11, 1969, p. 75. This was listed in the printed *New York Times Index*, 1969, under "Kahane, Meir," but the article did not appear in the microfilmed edition. Jack Begg of the *New York Times* explained: "It is possible that this article was published in an early edition, and then dropped for the later editions. However, if this were the case, the *New York Times Index* should not have picked it up. (The Index only catalogs the Late City edition [the edition which is microfilmed]) So, we are at a loss to explain its inclusion in the *Index*." E-mail from Jack Begg, Supervisor, News Research, *New York Times*, May 19, 2006.

[25] Jewish Defense League, "In response to the Lindsay-maneuvered denunciation...," press release, October 9, 1969, in YU Archives, folder 7/9.

Jewish Defense League Newsletter, November 1969, p. 2, in RZ Archives, folder 716B. This details the flyers and pamphlets distributed at the press conference.

Jewish Defense League, "Press Conference, Overseas Press Club, Reference Material," October 10, 1969, in YU Archives, folder 7/9.

The press kit included "Twenty Questions for Lindsay." See note 19.

[26] "Answer to WCBS Radio Editorial to Be Aired on October 14 at 12:20, 3:20, 8:20 and 11:20 P.M. and October 15, 8:20 A.M.," in YU Archives, folder 7/9.

[27] "Ballad of Fun City" and "Questions for Mr. Lindsay," audio recording, in JNUL, National Sound Archives and in RZ Archives, Appendix. See: *Story of the Jewish Defense League*, p. 177: "We even put out a really clever record based on the hit song, *Those Were the Days*, sung by one of our members Roz Nesis, and played it over loudspeakers..."

See: Letter from Roz Nesis to "Dear Member," October 14, 1969, in YU Archives, folder 7/9.

The words of the song were printed on a JDL flyer headed "Please Stop and Sing With Us ... Ballad of Fun City," flyer in RZ Archives, Appendix. There were six stanzas plus the chorus. Murray Schneider sent me this flyer and noted at the bottom, "Words composed by Meir."

[28] Jewish Defense League, "News: The Jewish Defense League will unveil...," press release, in YU Archives, folder 7/9. Another news release in this folder announces a press conference at JDL headquarters, 156 Fifth Avenue, [October 19] at 2:30 P.M., prior to the rally.

[29] Meir Kahane, "From a Jewish Father, to My Dear and Beloved Children," [ad] *New York Times,* October 20, 1969, p. 52, in RZ Archives, folder 63. The three-column ad spanned the length of the page's outer edge. For details of the original article, see note 3.

[30] See note 25, *Newsletter*.

[31] E-mail from Mallenbaum, March 29, 1998.

See also: *Jewish Defense League Newsletter*, November 14, 1969, p. 4, in RZ Archives, folder 716B. This notes Mallenbaum's appointment as administrative director and thanks "Jack Schecterson, Industrial Designer, who contributed his time and talents to designing our new logo [and] letterhead." The font is a bold script. Examples of the letterhead: Press release dated October 19, 1969, in YU Archives, folder 9/3; "A Modest Suggestion to Arthur Goldberg," [press release] December 19, 1969, in RZ Archives, folder 63.

[32] Shalom Klass, "Statement From the Publisher: *Jewish Press* Disassociates Itself from the Leaders of the JDL," *Jewish Press*, October 24, 1969, pp. 1, 23, in YU Archives, folder 7/9.

The editorial goes on to praise both Lindsay and Mario Procaccino for approving a program to aid yeshivas but rather than endorse either one it says, "... our readers can decide for themselves."

[33] See note 25, *Newsletter*, pp. 2, 3.

It is uncertain who wrote these words. Allan Mallenbaum, administrator of the JDL then, wrote: "... I did write parts of the newsletter. I can't, however, state honestly whether I'm responsible for that quote or not." E-mail from Allan Mallenbaum, June 8, 2006.

[34] Marvin Schick, "Kahane and Lindsay: A Different Version of Events," *Jewish World*, June 1, 1990, p. 7, in RZ Archives, folder 699. Excerpted with the author's permission.

The allegations about Rabbi Klass in Robert I. Friedman's *False Prophet*, p. 103, are among the book's numerous inaccuracies.

"The Jewish Vote," [editorial] *Jewish Press*, October 17, 1969, p. 4. This editorial says only: "The *Jewish Press* has opened its pages to all the mayoralty candidates to document their views." See: "Letter[s] of Intent," submitted by Mayor John V. Lindsay and Comptroller Mario

Procaccino, *Jewish Press*, October 17, 1969, p. 17; "The Candidates and the Issues," [statements from the three candidates] *Jewish Press*, October 17, 1969, pp. 28-29. Editorials in subsequent issues of the *Jewish Press* did not touch on the elections.

[35] "Intergroup Relations and Tensions in New York City," *American Jewish Year Book*, 1970, pp. 217-219.

[36] See note 31, *Newsletter*, p. 2. Youth headquarters were on the third floor at 440 West 42 Street, between 9th and 10th Avenues.

See note 25, *Newsletter*, p. 4. See chapter 18 for more about youth activities.

[37] David Gumpert, "Militant Jewish Group Sparks a Controversy in New York City Area," *Wall Street Journal*, November 4, 1969, pp. 1, 24. For details on Operation Hagana, see *Story of the Jewish Defense League*, pp. 136-137.

[38] See note 31, *Newsletter*, p. 3. Farber's show aired on radio station WOR.

[39] See note 37.

Meir spoke at the Young Israel of Chomedy, near Montreal, on Sunday evening, November 2, 1969. The fee paid to the JDL was $150 plus expenses. See: Letter from Nathan Yacowar to Meir, October 13, 1969, RZ Archives, folder 714B.

Meir spoke in Philadelphia on Tuesday evening, December 9, 1969. Letter from Edward Smiley, Wolfe Baron-Brith Sholom Lodge, Overbrook Park, to Meir, October 2, 1969, in RZ Archives, folder 714B.

[40] Rabbi Irving J. Rosenbaum, "Why Did the Jewish Defense League Leader Find an Attentive Audience for His Message in Chicago?" *Jewish Sentinel* (Chicago), December 4, 1969, pp. 13, 15, in RZ Archives, folder 63. Excerpted with permission.

Meir's talk was sponsored by the Religious Zionists of Chicago.

The *Jewish Sentinel* of November 6 announced this speaking engagement and reported on plans for "judo and karate classes for youths in the 11-16 and 16-18 age groups."

[41] *Jewish Defense League Newsletter*, December 5, 1969, in RZ Archives, Appendix.

See also: Hillel Levine, *Death of an American Jewish Community* (New York: Free Press, 1992), pp. 252-271; "Never Again... to Us," *Cambridge Phoenix*, February 5, 1970, pp. 6, 7, in RZ Archives, folder 61B; *Story of the Jewish Defense League*, pp. 70, 122-123, 218-219.

[42] E-mail from Alan Mandel, May 18, 1999. Mandel's talk at JDL's First International Convention, Hotel New Yorker, June 28, 1969, is reported in *Jewish Defense League Newsletter*, August 5, 1970, p. 8, in RZ Archives, folder 716B.

[43] "Jewish Defense League Wins Backing in Newton," *Boston Evening Globe*, December 15, 1969; "Large Gathering at JDL Meeting Split on Organization's Activities," *Jewish Advocate*, December 18, 1969, both in RZ Archives, Appendix.

[44] Jewish Defense League, "The JDL Is the Hagana...," press release, undated, in YU Archives, folder 9/8. The quotations are from, respectively, *The Boston Herald Traveler*, June 1, 1970; *The Jewish Advocate*, June 4, 1970; and *The Reconstructionist*, March 27, 1970.

[45] "Orthodox Rabbi Urges Self-Defense Groups but Raps Existing JDL," *Jewish Week*, December 3, 1970, p. 6, in RZ Archives, folder 61B.

[46] *Fiddler* deals with several issues, among them intermarriage, anti-Semitism, and socialism, as a solution to the persecution of Jews in the Diaspora. My granddaughters' Israeli high school class produced *Fiddler* in Hebrew in 2001, and in the process learned about the harsh life endured by Jews in Eastern Europe.

[47] Interview with Tova Ettinger, December 1, 2003, Jerusalem.

Chapter 17

1 "Save Soviet Jewry," *Jewish Press*, May 22, 1964, p. 25.

2 "JDL Clashes With Black Panthers," *Jewish Press*, May 15, 1970, p. 3. See also: *The Story of the Jewish Defense League*, pp. 202-203.

Most JDL members agreed with Meir that they should do all they could for Soviet Jewry, but some believed the JDL should confine itself to protecting Jews in America. Interview with Sy Polsky, June 13, 1997.

3 Meir was dismissed from the *Jewish Press* in October 1969 and reinstated in June 1970.

A test of the phone communications system to call members to demonstrations is noted in *Jewish Defense League Newsletter*, December 5, 1969, p. 3, in RZ Archives, folder 482. See also chapter 19, note 2, Michael T. Kaufman.

Rabbi Naftali Tzvi Halberstam, the Bobover Rebbe, who heard Meir speak in Brooklyn's Borough Park section, remarked that his fiery style was typical of the Sanzer chasidim, from whom he was descended. Related to Baruch Kahane by R. Naftali Wachstein, April 25, 2007.

4 Iver Peterson, "Soviet Jew Who Got Out After 11 Years Tells How Difficult It Was," *New York Times,* December 6, 1969, p. 9.

5 *Story of the Jewish Defense League* (Radnor, PA: Chilton Book Co., 1975), x, 338 p., ISBN 0-80-1962471. An enhanced edition was published in 2000 by the Institute for Publication of the Writings of Rabbi Meir Kahane, ISBN 965-7044 04 9. A Hebrew translation was published by the Institute in 2002, ISBN 965-7044-05-7.

6 "Big Four Talks Go On," *New York Times*, December 24, 1969, p. 3; "Jews Protest Soviet Bias," *New York Times*, December 26, 1969, p. 18.

7 Letter from Allan E. Mallenbaum, Committee Coordinator, and Rabbi Meir Kahane, National Chairman, to "Dear Friends," [December 1970], in YU archives, folder 10/2.

Some public figures who replied to decline the JDL's invitation were Roy Wilkins, director of the NAACP; New York Congressmen Joseph P. Addabbo and William F. Ryan; Ruhama Saphir, executive assistant to Israeli ambassador Yitzhak Rabin; and Michigan Congressman Gerald R. Ford. See their letters in YU Archives, folder 6/1.

Archpriest George Grabbe of the Russian Orthodox Church spoke at the opening ceremony. See: "Spokesman for Russian Orthodox Church Denounces Soviet Religious Persecution," JDL press release, December 18, 1969, in YU Archives, folder 9/6.

8 "Police Restrain Jewish Militants at Soviet Office," *New York Post*, December 29, 1969, p. 83, in RZ Archives, folder 63.

9 E-mail from Samson Levine, November 22, 1999.

10 Irving Spiegel, "14 Jews Arrested in Soviet Protest," *New York Times,* December 30, 1969, p. 46, in YU Archives, folder 7/1, and RZ Archives, folder 683A.

"N.Y. Jewish Youths in Anti-Soviet Move," *Jerusalem Post*, December 31, 1969, reproduced in *Jewish Defense League Newsletter*, January 9, 1970, p. 3, in YU Archives, folder 7/1.

Meir and two youths, Samson Levine and Abraham Muallem, were arrested at the Tass office. Russel Kelner, David Kanensky and Avraham Hershkowitz were arrested at the Intourist office. Paul Stein, Eli Schwartz, Martin Templeman, Steven Lang, Alex Sternberg and Eugene Keller were arrested at Aeroflot.

11 See note 10, *Newsletter*, p. 6.

12 "JDL Declares Soviets Will Have No Peace Until Russian Jewry Goes Free," press release, December 30, 1969, in YU Archives, folder 7/14.

"Picketing Suit Dismissed," *New York Times*, August 9, 1969, p. 12.

[13] NBC News Archive, media no. 0040738, December 30, 1969; Daniel O'Grady, Mel Greene and William McFadden, "Seize Rabbi, 6, as Jews, Cops Clash," *Daily News*, December 31, 1970, pp. 3, 28, in RZ Archives, folder 63; "27 Young Jews Seized After Soviet Union Protest," *New York Times*, December 31, 1969, p. 18.

[14] See note 10, *Newsletter*, p. 5.

[15] FBI New York office file 157-5767, report, October 14, 1970, file NY, p. 2.

The New York City Police Department gave the FBI the names of those arrested that night and details of the charges against them.

The FBI report, p. 6, cites "JDL Rabbi Hits Cops in Row on Picketing," *New York Post*, December 31, 1969.

"Lindsay Is Accused in Protest Clash," *New York Times*, January 1, 1970, p. 14, in YU Archives, folder 7/1.

Meir was usually paroled on his own recognizance. Judges knew that he was not going to flee New York City. For him, a court hearing was another platform from which to campaign for Soviet Jews.

[16] E-mail from Samson Levine, June 14, 1999.

Jay Levin, "Kahane Trial Ends in Deadlock," *New York Post*, March 31, 1971, in RZ Archives, Appendix.

[17] E-mail from Samson Levine, August 5, 1999.

[18] "Summer Is Coming," *Jewish Press*, June 25, 1971, p. 9, in RZ Archives, folder 592, reprinted in *Writings 5731*, p. 106, and in *Beyond Words*, 1:198-201.

The case dragged on until March 6, 1972, when, with their pleas changed to criminal mischief and criminal trespass, the government dropped its charges of conspiracy and the three were fined.

See: Shlomo Mordechai Russ, *The 'Zionist Hooligans:' The Jewish Defense League* (Ph.D. diss., City University of New York, 1981), pp. 1092-1093.

See also: chapter 26, excerpts from letter from Meir to Libby, March 8, 1972.

[19] Meir explained this aim at a talk on February 4, 1970, before 150 people at the auditorium of the High School of the Fashion Industries in Manhattan. See note 15, FBI report, p. 7.

[20] "J.D.L. Interrupts Red Lullaby," *Shore Record* (Brooklyn), February 1, 1970, p. 1, in YU Archives, folder 9/6; "Protest at Concert Laid to 'Hooligans,'" *New York Times*, February 3, 1970, p. 39; Donal Henahan, "Protesters Upset Russians' Recital," *New York Times*, February 2, 1970, p. 30.

The disruption of the Moscow Philharmonic Orchestra concert at Brooklyn College appears in the printed index to the *New York Times* 1970, p. 1940, with a reference to January 25, 1970, p. 70, but there is no article in the microfilmed Late City Edition. See message from John Begg, chapter 16, note 24.

"Don't Go In!" flyer, in RZ Archives, Appendix. Part of this flyer is a reproduction of a 1970 *Chicago Daily News* political cartoon captioned, "Carrier of the Plague," depicting the Soviet Union covered with swastikas.

[21] "Don't Try to Perform Here, Russian Artists Warned," *Cleveland Press*, September 28, 1970, cited in FBI file 105-207795, correlation summary (chapter 14, note 24).

"Moiseyev Performance Disrupted by Tear Gas," *New York Times*, August 27, 1970, p. 27.

[22] *Never Again* (Jewish Defense League of Philadelphia), October 1970, p. 1, in RZ Archives, Appendix.

Rabbi Novoseller: Bernard Gwertzman, "Moscow Cancels Visit by Bolshoi Opera, Ballet," *New York Times*, December 12, 1970, p. 1.

Hurok offer: *Story of the Jewish Defense League*, pp. 6-7.

23 Almost a year later, the Kazakovs received exit permits. "Soviet Said to Let 7 Families Leave," *New York Times*, February 15, 1971, p. 11.

When Kazakov went to America in December 1969 with fellow Soviet émigré Dov Sperling, the Israeli officials leaked stories that they were Soviet spies and most of their sponsors cancelled their speaking dates. See: *Story of the Jewish Defense League*, page 10.

24 "The Shame of American Jewry," [ad] *New York Times*, March 26, 1970, p. 34. The two-column ad was more than half the length of the *Times'* page. Robert I. Friedman referred to this quarter-page ad as a full-page ad (*False Prophet*, p. 112).

25 "Israel Calls on Soviet Émigré to End Hunger Strike at U.N.; Massive Rally Cancelled," *New York Times*, March 30, 1970, p. 14.

26 *Jewish Defense League Newsletter*, March 20, 1970, p. 4, in RZ Archives, folder 716B.

27 *Jewish Defense League Newsletter*, August 5, 1970, p. 1, in RZ Archives, folder 716B.

28 The Seder protest was held on April 19. See: "JDL Member Arrested at Soviet Mission Protest," *Jewish Press*, April 24, 1970, p. 46. This arrest is listed in: FBI file 105-207795, report, December 21, 1970, p. 3, in RZ Archives, Appendix. The report lists the charge as 240.08, the code for incitement to riot.

29 "J.D.L. Announces Operation 'Ten Plagues' Against Soviet Anti-Semitism," press release, April 17, 1970, in YU Archives, folder 11/2. Emphasis added.

30 Balfour Brickner, [Report on the Jewish Defense League] (New York: Union of American Hebrew Congregations [Reform], Commission on Interfaith Activities, January 13, 1971), p. 3, in RZ Archives, folder 482. The report is introduced by a letter from Balfour Brickner and ends with the initials B.B.

31 Edward B. Fiske, "Synagogue Scene of Soviet Protest by Jewish League," *New York Times*, May 21, 1970, p. 14; "Jewish Group Taunts Reds," *Daily News*, May 21, 1970, cited in note 15, FBI report, p. 7.

Photos of the sit-in are in the photo section of this book.

By coincidence, many years earlier my father's uncles were members of the Park East Synagogue, then called Congregation Zichron Ephraim. Uncle Morris Blum, was president of the congregation in the 1930s. (E-mail from Gerald Blum, July 6, 2007.)

32 "Communist Paper Invaded by Jewish Defense League," *New York Times*, June 4, 1970, p. 6; C. Gerald Fraser, "Jews Raid Office of Amtorg Here," *New York Times*, June 24, 1970, p. 14.

33 Meir Kahane, "Letter to the Editor," *New York Times*, July 9, 1970, p. 36, in RZ Archives, folder 63.

34 *The Plight of the Soviet Jew* (New York: Jewish Defense League, Educational Department, [1970]), 20 pp., 35 cm, in JNUL, call no. S2=2003B6892.

This has reproductions of letters of esteem written to Meir up to March 1970. Pages 25-55 of the book co-authored by Meir, *The Jewish Stake in Vietnam*, are reprinted on pp. 1-3, 7-12.

35 "U.N. Ambassador Yost Meets with JDL; Warns of Soviet Retaliation Against U.S.," *Jewish Press*, July 17, 1970, p. 11, in RZ Archives, folder 61A. See also: *The Story of the Jewish Defense League*, p. 14.

36 *Jewish Defense League Chapter Information Bulletin*, October [1970], p. [8], in RZ Archives, Appendix. The contents indicate that this was published at the end of November 1970.

During Rabbi Teitz's frequent trips to Russia in the early 1960's he was an apologist for the Chief Rabbi of Moscow. See: Rivkah Teitz Blau, *Learn Torah, Love Torah, Live Torah: HaRav Mordechai Pinchas Teitz, the Quintessential Rabbi* (Hoboken, N.J.: 2001).

Later, Rabbi Feinstein endorsed a mass prayer meeting for Soviet Jews held at the Manhattan

Center on January 10, 1971. See: "Jewish Militants Plan Harassment," *New York Times,* January 11, 1971, p. 15. In 1976, Rabbi Feinstein sent a message of support to the Solidarity Sunday for Soviet Jewry Rally. See: "The Following Message from Hagaon Harav Moshe Feinstein *Shlita* Will Be Delivered...," [ad] *Jewish Press*, April 30, 1976, p. 13.

Another prominent rabbi, Rabbi Yaakov Kamenetsky, opined that anything that anyone did for Soviet Jewry could not hurt. He came to this conclusion after he visited the Soviet Union in 1963. Phone interview with his son, Rabbi Noson Kamenetsky, June 29, 2000.

[37] Bert Zweibon, "The JDL Answers the *Issur* (Ban) of Harav Moshe Feinstein," *Jewish Press*, January 1, 1971, p. 36.

[38] "The Jewish Defense League to begin photographing Soviet Mission..." press release, August 3, 1970, in YU Archives, folder 9/3.

[39] *Jewish Defense League Newsletter*, Fall 1970, p. [14], in YU Archives, folder 9/8. See also: "JDL to Change Street Signs..." press release, [August 10, 1970], in YU Archives, folder 9/3.

[40] "100-Mile March on Washington to Protest for Soviet Jewry," *Jewish Press*, July 31, 1970, p. 25. A map of the route is given in: "Aug. 16-23: 100-Mile March..." flyer, in RZ Archives, folder 61B.

The costs of the 100-Mile March included over $1,000 for phone calls. See note 36, *Bulletin*, p. [10].

Photo of rally in Independence Park, in RZ archives picture file, no. 331, and in photo section of this book. The Liberty Bell was displayed in Independence Park until 1976, when it was moved to Liberty Bell Pavilion nearby.

[41] William J. Storm and Chas. Montgomery, "Held in Gun Charges: 4 Jewish Militants Seized Here," *Evening Bulletin* (Philadelphia), August 16, 1970, pp. 1, 30; "Militant Jewish League Starts Washington March," *Philadelphia Inquirer*, August 17, 1970, in RZ Archives, Appendix.

NBC News Archive, media no. 0052132, August 16, 1970.

See note 39, *Newsletter*, p. [2].

[42] See note 39, *Newsletter*, p. [3].

[43] See note 15, FBI report, pp. 11, 12.

In Baltimore the marchers were hosted by Rabbi Israel Tabak of the Shaarei Zion synagogue. E-mail from Rabbi Blitz, July 27, 2000.

Congressional candidate Thomas M. Boggs spoke at the Wheaton rally at the request of Rabbi Herzel Kranz. Phone interview with Rabbi Kranz, October 1, 2002.

[44] NBC News Archive, media no. 0052402, August 21, 1970. The JDL march probably garnered media coverage because Congress was not in session and very little was happening in Washington.

[45] The rabbi of Shaare Tefila, Martin Halpern, gave the marchers the use of his synagogue at the request of Rabbi Herzel Kranz. Phone interview with Rabbi Herzel Kranz, October 1, 2002.

[46] See note 15, FBI report, p. 12. See also: "Jewish Defense League Plans to Harass Russians," *New York Times*, January 11, 1971, p. 1.

[47] Israel Broadcasting Authority Radio News Archive, media no. 6594, August 23, 1970.

"Protection Asked Here by Soviet," *New York Times*, August 30, 1970, p. 9.

[48] Yosef Mendelevich, speaking at a memorial meeting for Meir, Binyamin, and Talya Kahane, October 23, 2002, Jerusalem.

The memorial meeting, arranged by Rabbi Eliezer Melamed, was filmed and an edited version was produced on computer disk (in RZ Archives, Appendix). The disk does not include the part of Mendelevich's speech quoted here, but it is confirmed in: Letter from Yosef Mendelevich to Libby, May 20, 2005, in RZ Archives, Appendix.

[49] Patrick Doyle and William McFadden, "Girl Militant's Car Hits 6 Cops," *Daily News,* November 24, 1970, p. 22; Letter from Marilyn Betman to Libby, postmarked December 9, 2002, in JNUL Archives, folder ARC 4=1748; NBC News Archive, media no. 0056425, November 23, 1970.

[50] Alfonso Narvaez, "Bomb Damages Russian Office Here," *New York Times*, November 26, 1970, p. 1; Israel Broadcasting Authority Archives, media nos. 40156-70-5 and 40171-70-4, November 25, 1970.

[51] Bernard Gwertzman, "Moscow Cancels Visit by Bolshoi Opera, Ballet," *New York Times*, December 12, 1970, p. 1; "Drive to 'Liberate' Jews in Soviet Urged by Kahane," *New York Times*, December 14, 1970, p. 53. The tour had been arranged by Sol Hurok under the Soviet-American Exchange Agreement.

[52] "Bye Bye Bolshoi," [editorial] *Daily News*, December 15, 1970, p. 47, in RZ Archives, folder 63. © New York Daily News, L.P.; reprinted with permission.

[53] Bernard Gwertzman, "Soviet Dooms Two Jews in Plane Hijacking," *New York Times*, December 25, 1970, p. 1.

[54] Daniel O'Grady, Mel Greene and William McFadden, "Jews, Cops Clash; Rabbi, 9 Seized," *Daily News*, December 28, 1970, pp. 3, 24, in YU Archives, folder 8/3. © New York Daily News, L.P.; reprinted with permission; "11 in Protest Held by Cops...," *Newsday*, December 28, 1970, pp. 7, 27, in RZ Archives, folder 1202; Lawrence Van Gelder, "Protecting Russians Here a Hard Job," *New York Times*, January 7, 1971, p. 3, in RZ Archives, folder 60A; "Vigil to Protest Soviet Policy," *Jewish Press*, December 25, 1970, p. 18.

JDLers remained on the balcony of the Park East Synagogue for several hours, until synagogue officials decided to call the police to evict them.

Letter from Barbara Ginsberg, January 8, 1998, in RZ Archives, Appendix.

[55] Irving Spiegel, "Lindsay Urges U.S. Stand," *New York Times*, December 29, 1970, p. 5.

[56] Yitta Halberstam, "The 100-Hour Vigil for Soviet Jewry," *Bas-Kol*, January 29, 1971, p. 5, in YU Archives, folder 13/5, and RZ Archives, folder 1203. Excerpted with the author's permission.

[57] Bernard Gwertzman, "Soviet Spares Two Jews," *New York Times*, January 1, 1971, p. 1.

[58] Ernest E. Barabash, "News and Views," *Day-Jewish Journal (Der Tog-Morgen Zhurnal)),* January 14, 1971, pp. 1, 2.

[59] "Reflections on a Vigil," *Jewish Press*, January 8, 1971, p. 23, in RZ Archives, folder 594. Meir resumed writing in the *Jewish Press* in June 1970. See chapter 18.

Chapter 18

[1] Geula Cohen, "Be'arba Einayim Im Haliga Lehagana Yehudit [Face to Face With the Jewish Defense League]," *Ma'ariv*, January 2, 1970, p. 10. Excerpted with permission.

Cohen had been active in Lechi, the pre-state military unit, and was a member of the Herut party. Opposed to Menachem Begin's 1980 retreat from Sinai, she left Herut. As a founder of the Tehiya party, she was a member of Knesset from 1981 to 1992.

[2] Interviews: Mal Lebowitz, November 13, 1997, Jerusalem; Allan Mallenbaum, May 18, 1988, Jerusalem. Phone interview, Avraham Hershkowitz, July 26, 1999. Letter from Renee Brown, December 15, 1997, in RZ Archives, Appendix.

[3] Kenneth Braiterman, "The Jewish Defense League: What Safety in Karate?" *Midstream*, April 1970, p. 8, in RZ Archives, folder 61A. Excerpted with the author's permission.

4 Joel Griffith, "A Talk With Rabbi Meir Kahane," *Manhattan Tribune*, January 17, 1970, pp. 1, 6, 7, in RZ Archives, Appendix.

5 *Story of the Jewish Defense League*, pp. 199-201.

6 See note 5, pp. 157-160, 162-164.

7 See note 5, pp. 201-203.

8 See note 5, pp. 113-114, 116.

9 See note 5, p. 138.

10 See note 5, pp. 193-194.

11 See note 5, pp. 275-277. See also: Letter from Dr. Arnold H. Einhorn to the JDL, September 7, 1972, in RZ Archives, folder 63. See also "Lincoln Hospital," *American Jewish Year Book*, 1971, pp. 153-155.

12 Letter from Samuel Shoshan, Public Relations Director, JDL, to George Sharman, Channel Five, [May 1970], in RZ Archives, Appendix.

13 Irving Spiegel, "Burials Stalled as Gravediggers Strike," *New York Times,* January 13, 1970, p. 36; "Jews Win Ruling on Burials Here," *New York Times*, January 15, 1970, p. 59.

14 "JDL to Aid Orthodox Burials," *Jewish Press*, January 30, 1970, p. 30; reproduced in *Jewish Defense League Newsletter*, February 13, 1970, p. 8, in RZ Archives, folder 1202.

Phone interview with Avraham Hershkowitz, February 24, 1997. Hershkowitz, who was born in a German concentration camp in 1944 (10 Av), suffered from diabetes for many years and died in Israel in 2001 (19 Tevet).

15 "Defense League Protects Burial," *Jewish Post and Opinion*, January 30, 1970, p. 3; "A Burial Delayed," *Daily News*, January 15, 1970, pp. 1, 5. Both noted in *Newsletter*, p. 8, see note 14. The *Jewish Post and Opinion* related that the story had been on TV.

16 Phone interview with Hershkowitz, February 24, 1997.

17 Interview with Janice Stern, June 7, 2000, Jerusalem.

18 Simcha Mallenbaum (son of Allan Mallenbaum, JDL's administrative director), "Pompidou's Tour," *Jewish Defense League Newsletter*, March 20, 1970, pp. 1-2, in RZ Archives, folder 716.

The JDL protest, which Pompidou witnessed, contrasted sharply with one organized by the Jewish Community Council of Greater Washington. That rally took place about three hours before Pompidou arrived in Washington, and he never saw it. "Pompidou Arrives in U.S.; One Thousand Protesters Stream Into Capital," *Jewish Week-American Examiner*, February 26, 1970, pp. 1, 12.

19 Interview with Malcolm Lebowitz, November 3, 1998, Jerusalem.

An FBI report confirms: "… The juveniles arrested were released in care of Kahane for return to Queens, New York." FBI report 105-207795, correlation summary (chapter 14, note 24).

20 "At Pompidou Dinner, Leaders Trade Praise," *New York Times*, February 25, 1970, p. 1.

See note 19, FBI report, p. 4. Recognizance is a written promise to appear in court when required. See: www.utcourts.gov/resources/glossary.htm.

21 See note 18.

22 There were monthly seminars for the members, beginning on Wednesday, December 17, 1969, at Congregation Zichron Moshe, at 342 East 20th Street in Manhattan. See: *Jewish Defense League Newsletter*, December 5, 1969, p. 2, in RZ Archives, Appendix.

JDL seminars in later years were also held at Congregation Zichron Moshe. See chapter 44, note 37. Many people recalled Meir's inspiring seminars there.

23 *Jewish Defense League Newsletter*, Fall 1970, p. [16], in YU Archives, folder 9/8.

24 "Student Activism, New Left and Anti-Semitism," see chapter 10, note 22; "Intergroup Relations in the United States," *American Jewish Yearbook*, 1971, p. 132; "Campuses Called Harmful to Jewry," *New York Times*, May 5, 1971, p. 52.

Abbie Hoffman quoted in: Ram Oren, "Harav Kahana Mul Doktor Mehdi [Rabbi Kahane vs. Dr. Mehdi]," *Yedioth Ahronoth*, February 26, 1971, *Shiv'a Yamim* section, pp. 10-11, in JNUL Archives, folder ARC 4=1748.

[25] *Jewish Defense League Newsletter*, November 14, 1969, p. 2, in RZ Archives, folder 716B. The newsletter credits Yossi Templeman, college coordinator, with the success on college campuses.

[26] See note 23, *Newsletter*, p. [20].

[27] Among the editors of the *Jewish Defense League Newsletter* were Sue Greitinger, Sheldon Davis, Neil Perelstein, and Stuart Cohen.

Youth office: See note 14, *Newsletter*, p. 10.

Rifle range: See note 23, *Newsletter*, p. [20].

Board meetings: Interview with Neil Rothenberg, August 18, 2000, Jerusalem.

[28] Interviews with Sy Polsky, June 13, 1997; Garth Kravat, November 9, 1999; and Neil Rothenberg, August 18, 2000. See also: *Oz – the Jewish Defense League Elite Group*, 3 pp., in RZ Archives, folder 482.

[29] See note 23, *Newsletter*, pp. [1, 19]. Eli Schwartz and Neil Rothenberg made most of the arrangements for the Seminar, held from August 30, 1970, to September 4, 1970.

[30] *Hadar Yisrael, Barzel Yisrael* and *Mishma'at Yisrael* are derived somewhat from the teachings of Zeev Jabotinsky.

[31] *The Jewish Defense League: Principles and Philosophies* (New York: Jewish Defense League, [1970]). [24] pp., 28 cm. JNUL call no. S74B2961=2.

[32] *Jewish Defense League Newsletter*, February 1971, p. [4], in RZ Archives, Appendix. As a formal rabbinical seminary, plans for Yeshiva Torah Ve'Oz never materialized, despite Meir's attempts to establish it in 1973 and 1977. He finally realized his dream with the founding of the Yeshiva of the Jewish Idea (Yeshivat Haraayon Hayehudi) in Jerusalem in 1987.

[33] "JDL to Open Rabbinical Military School," *Jewish Press*, November 20, 1970, pp. 2, 22; the ad, on p. 35, announced a fundraising event for the Jewish Identity Center on December 6.

A *Newsletter* report on the event said: "Rabbi Kahane spoke to a packed hall at a fundraiser in Brooklyn for the Jewish Identity Center. Cantor Larry Fine sang and Alex Sternberg gave a karate exhibition." See note 32, *Newsletter*, p. [14].

[34] Gruner was the brother of my aunt by marriage, Helen Friedman. Family members collected money for her to fly to Palestine to plead for her brother's life. She arrived February 13, 1947, visited Dov and met with British authorities several times. On April 16, she was granted another visit. Without telling her that Dov had been hanged at 2 A.M. that morning, a British police escort led her taxi directly to Safed for his burial. See: Itzhak Gurion, *Triumph on the Gallows* (New York: 1950), pp. 83-131.

[35] See note 32.

[36] "Dov Gruner Month," flyer, in YU Archives, folder 7/4.

Meir spoke at Brooklyn College twice that day: at 12:30 in the Student Union Building and at 8:30 P.M. in the Knickerbocker Lounge, to evening session students. See: *Ken* (Brooklyn College), November 9, 1970, p. 12, in YU Archives, folder 7/4.

The Lechi group, formed by Avraham (Yair) Stern, was also called the Sternist group.

[37] "Rabbi Kahane: The JDL Is Fighting for 'Love' of Jews," *Long Island Press*, February 18, 1970, in RZ Archives, folder 61A.

[38] FBI file 105-207795, memorandum from W. R. Wannall to E. S. Miller, January 7, 1972, 2 pp., in RZ Archives, Appendix. See also: FBI file 105-207795, report, March 24, 1971, pp. 14, 15, in RZ Archives, Appendix.

Direct interviews: FBI New York office file 157-5767, report, October 14, 1970, p. 9, in RZ Archives, Appendix (see chapter 16); *Story of the Jewish Defense League*, pp. 193-194; FBI file 105-207795, teletype message, September 11, 1972, p. 1, in RZ Archives, Appendix (see chapter 30).

[39] See note 19, FBI report, pp. 7-8.

[40] Jewish Defense League, Second International Annual Convention, June 6, 1971, [*Minutes*], p. 1, in RZ Archives, Appendix.

[41] FBI file 105-207795, report, December 21, 1970, p. 5, in RZ Archives, Appendix.

[42] Meir spoke at the University of Missouri at Columbia on October 28, 1970. See note 41, FBI, pp. 7, 8. See also "Request for Speaker" form, signed by Rabbi Abraham Pimontel, Hillel Foundation, in RZ Archives, folder 714B.

[43] Dick Langlois, "Jewish Defense League's Kahane Speaks Here," *The Williams Record*, November 3, 1970, p. 1, in RZ Archives, Appendix.

[44] Agreement signed by Robert Elias, Associated Students, University of California, Los Angeles, for December 3, 1970, lecture by Meir Kahane, stipulating a fee of $150, in RZ Archives, folder 714B. Letter from Rabbi Robert Elias, rabbi of Knesseth Israel synagogue, Los Angeles, to Libby, September 14, 1999, in RZ Archives, Appendix.

Elias referred to this article: "Superjew," *Esquire*, August 1970, in RZ Archives, folder 683B. This in-depth interview gave Meir the opportunity to present his ideas nationwide. Despite its risqué pictures, *Esquire* had a reputation for publishing articles with high literary merit.

[45] "Kahane Relates JDL Actions," *Daily Bruin*, December 4, 1970, p. 7, in RZ Archives, Appendix. Excerpted with permission.

An announcement on page one of the *Daily Bruin,* December 3, 1970, said: "[Rabbi Kahane] will be speaking at noon on 'The Crisis for American Jewry.' A question-answer period will follow the speech."

Haines Hall 39 held about 300 people. E-mail from Richard Macales, July 20, 1999.

[46] Associated Students, University of California, Los Angeles, "Speakers Program: Rabbi Meir Kahane," December 3, 1970, audio tape in RZ Archives, audio folder. Side 1: Speech, Side 2: Questions and Answers.

Thanks to Rabbi Robert Elias, who suggested there might be an audio tape of Meir's speech in the Student Association's archives, and to Richard Macales, who sent it to me.

[47] *Jewish Defense League Newsletter*, February 1971, p. 5, in RZ Archives, Appendix.

[48] FBI file 105-207795, report, April 8, 1971, p. 3, in RZ Archives, Appendix.

[49] "Students Battle at JDL Rally in Grand Ballroom," *Observation Post*, December 11, 1970, pp. 1-3, in YU Archives, folder 10/9.

Chapter 19

[1] American Jewish Committee, *Fact Sheet*. See chapter 14, note 24.

This discusses JDL philosophy, activities, and membership, and names chapter chairmen and their occupations in greater New York, Philadelphia, Boston, Hartford, Cleveland, Miami, Montreal, and Toronto.

[2] Michael T. Kaufman, "Jewish Activists See Ranks Growing," *New York Times*, May 25, 1970,

p. 4, in RZ Archives, folder 683. Copyright © 1970 by The New York Times Co. Excerpted with permission.

3   Correspondence connected with bookings through the Jewish Welfare Board Lecture Bureau and the Spotlight on Extremism office is in RZ Archives, folder 714B. The Jewish Welfare Board Lecture Bureau took 15% of the fee, which ranged from $50 to $150 per lecture.

4   FBI file 105-207795, report, April 8, 1971, p. 3, in RZ Archives, Appendix.
   See note 15.

5   Milton Winston, "Kahane Says Jews Must Strike Back," *Canadian Jewish Chronicle Review*, May 17, 1970, p. 17, in RZ Archives, Appendix. Excerpted with permission.
   Parts of this report were quoted in the *Jewish Post and Opinion*, vol. 37, June 5, 1970, p. 1, which was in turn reproduced in the *Jewish Defense League Newsletter*, August 5, 1970, p. 7, in RZ Archives, folder 716B.

6   E-mail from Seymour Lecker, February 10, 2000.

7   "Leaving Synagogue After Yom Kippur: Old Story: Worshippers Attacked," *Jewish Post and Opinion*, October 16, 1970, p. 4.
   "Temple Cleans Up After Mob Attack," *New York Times*, October 12, 1970, p. 23, in RZ Archives, folder 50A.
   Jewish Telegraphic Agency, *Daily News Bulletin*, October 19, 1970, p. 4, in YU Archives, folder 12/5.
   Story of the Jewish Defense League, p. 39. The walk to Borough Park from our home in Flatbush took about 45 minutes.

8   E-mail from Alan Mandel, May 18, 1999. In the same vein, Meir wrote in 1988: "Half the children who attend the Presbyterian school in Sherman Oaks [California] are Jewish." See: "Kahane Speaks," *Jewish Press,* July 22, 1988, p. 14.

9   Trenton: FBI file 105-207795, report, February 8, 1971, pp. 7, 8. Stamford: FBI file 105-207795, report, December 21, 1970, p. 10. Both in RZ Archives, Appendix.

10   See note 9, FBI report, p. 8. The report only states that the audience reaction was favorable.
   See also: Jewish Welfare Board Lecture Bureau, Lecturer Confirmation of Booking, October 12, 1970: Temple Emanuel, Providence, November 4, 1970, in RZ Archives, folder 714B. The fee to the JDL was $200, less 15% commission to the Jewish Welfare Board.

11   See note 9, FBI report, pp. 9, 10. Meir spoke in Chicago on November 29, 1970.

12   *Jewish Defense League Newsletter*, February 1971, p. 5, in RZ Archives, Appendix.
   Sherri Okin recalled that this December 2, 1970, speaking engagement was arranged by Sy Gaibor. Interview with Sherri Okin, November 19, 1999, Jerusalem.
   Meir's talk to students at UCLA, noted in Chapter 18, took place the following day, December 3.

13   Letter from Norman Duberstein, Harvest Lodge, to Meir, September 21, 1970, in RZ Archives, folder 714B.

14   See note 12, *Newsletter*. The JDL International Leadership Conference was held from December 11 to December 13. Representatives from Canada, London and Paris were invited.
   See chapter 17, note 51, "Drive to 'Liberate' Jews in Soviet Urged by Kahane."

15   Letter from Renee Brown to Libby, October 1, 1997, in RZ Archives, Appendix.
   Meir's speaking engagements in 1970 not mentioned above, but documented in RZ Archives, folder 714B, were as follows:
   In Greater New York: February 5, Temple Israel, Jamaica; March 23, Rockwood Park Jewish Center; April 12, Bayside Oaks Jewish Center; May 3, Midchester Jewish Center, Yonkers; May 7, Valley Stream synagogue; May 17, Bellerose Jewish Center, Floral Park; September 20, Dix

Hills Jewish Center; December 17, Rosedale Jewish Center, Queens; December 20, Flatbush Park Jewish Center, Brooklyn.

Outside New York: October 7, Philadelphia (See note 9, FBI report, p. 6); November 11, Temple Israel Community Center, Cliffside Park, N.J.; November 22, Brith Sholom Community Center, Bethlehem, Pa.; November 29, Mather High School, Chicago.

Meir even spoke at high schools. At Stuyvesant High School in Manhattan there was standing room only when he appeared there. E-mail from Ira Friedman, November 25, 2000.

[16] Balfour Brickner, [Report on the Jewish Defense League]. See chapter 17, note 30.

[17] Jewish Telegraphic Agency, *Weekly Bulletin*, January 15, 1970, pp. 2, 4, in RZ Archives, folder 60A.

[18] See note 2.

[19] Letters in YU Archives, folder 6/1. These letters, all dated December 3, 1969, were in response to the December 2 ad: "Operation Hagana," [ad] *New York Times*, December 2, 1969, p. 35, in RZ Archives, folder 63. The ad was 3 columns wide and half-a-page long.

[20] Michael Pousner, "Never Again," *Daily News*, July 27, 1970, p. 34.

[21] Morris Drucker: *Jewish•Defense League Newsletter*, November 1969, p. 4, in RZ Archives, folder 716B.

JDL had to pay for paper. A December 31, 1971, invoice from the McAliece Paper Company for $894.74 has a handwritten note, "Drucker can't get us any more paper until we pay part of this!" That bill was paid by Samuel Shoshan, chairman of the JDL chapter in Fairfield County, Connecticut, who raised $250 from Harry C. Schnur and paid the rest from his chapter's bank account. Documents on the payment of the McAliece invoice, from the collection of Samuel Shoshan, in RZ Archives, Appendix.

Ari Calderon: *Jewish Defense League Newsletter*, November 14, 1969, p. 2, in RZ Archives, folder 716B.

A stencil was used to produce the master copy for a duplicating machine known as a mimeograph. See: http://en.wikipedia.org/wiki/Mimeograph.

Letter from Stanley Schumsky to Meir, November 10, 1969, in RZ Archives, folder 716B.

[22] "*Jewish Press* Ad Nets $9,000 Bail Money," letter to the editor from Free the Prisoners Committee, *Jewish Press*, October 23, 1970, p. 4. See: "Free the Hershkowitz's," [ad] *Jewish Press*, October 9, 1970, p. 32, in RZ Archives, folder 61B; "Bail Drive for Accused Hijackers," [news item by Meir], *Jewish Press*, October 9, 1970, p. 3. See also: "JDL'er Arraigned on False Passport," *Jewish Press*, November 20, 1970, p. 3, in RZ Archives, folder 683A.

Annual budget: See note 9, FBI report, p. 8.

[23] *Jewish Defense League Newsletter*, February 13, 1970, p. 6, in RZ Archives, folder 1202.

Albuquerque chapter: Raphael Rothstein, "Harav Kahana Me'orer Ahada [Rabbi Kahane Arouses Sympathy]," *Ha'aretz*, June 9, 1971, p. 19, in JNUL Archives, folder ARC 4=1748.

Victor Picciotto, "Jewish Defense League Opens Chapter in Bergen," *Sunday Record*, June 21, 1970, in RZ Archives, Appendix. See also: note 12.

The Chicago chapter was formed at a July 19, 1970, meeting. See: Louis Shoichet, "Chicago Dateline," *Jewish Press*, July 31, 1970, p. 29.

In 1977, American Nazis planned a march through Skokie, a largely Jewish Chicago suburb where many Holocaust survivors lived. JDL threats helped prevent the march.

[24] Letter from Meir to Marilyn Betman, March 11, 1970, in YU Archives, folder 6/3.

Betman later wrote: "... He came to Detroit with Irving Calderon to explore the possibility of a Detroit chapter." Letter from Marilyn Sue Betman to Libby, postmarked December 9, 2002, in JNUL Archives, folder ARC 4=1748.

25 "Never Again," [JDL organizational outline], 4 pp., in RZ Archives, folder 482.

26 *Jewish Defense League Newsletter*, August 5, 1970, p. 8, in RZ Archives, folder 716B; International Jewish Defense League, *Convention '71*, June 6, 1971, "Agenda," in RZ Archives, Appendix.

Chapter 20

1 Letter from Meir to Anglo-Jewish newspaper editors, [November 26, 1969], in RZ Archives, folder 1008.

2 Letters from *California Jewish Record* editor David B. Reznek to Meir, December 1, 1969, and January 10, 1970, in RZ Archives, folder 1007.

"The Jewish Vigilantes," *Newsweek*, January 12, 1970, pp. 34-35, in RZ Archives, folder 683B. The article ends: "We are saying, you hit a Jew, you gonna be hit back."

Meir Kahane, "Spotlight on Extremism: Cheers for the Panthers," *California Jewish Record*, January 30, 1970, p. 6, in the JNUL, call number PB2970=2X.

Tannah Hirsch, "The JDL: Heroes or Hooligans?" *Jerusalem Post*, March 4, 1970, p. 4.

I checked the entire bound volume of the *California Jewish Record* for 1970 in the JNUL. Since Anglo-Jewish newspapers were usually supported by the local Jewish federation, it was probably the opposition of the Establishment that led to the short period of syndication in the *Record* and the lack of response from other newspapers.   •

3 In 1971, Meir's JDL salary was $6,825. See: U.S. income tax form 1099, 1971, in RZ Archives, Appendix.

Employment ads of the period show that this was equivalent to the salary of a secretary, while salaries for jobs commensurate with Meir's education and ability were more than double that. Meir's 1971 salary was close to the average wage for that year: $6,497.

I do not have documentation for his JDL salary in 1970, but it may be assumed that it was close to the average wage for 1970, which was $6,186. Average wage given on Internet at Social Security Online.

Meir's subscriptions to extremist publications were under pseudonyms. For example, he used the name J. Blym, a variation of my father's name, Jacob Blum, and his address. See: Pro-forma invoice from the John Birch Society to J. Blym for *American Opinion*, $10, November 10, 1971, in RZ Archives, folder 326.

The extremist literature is in RZ Archives, folders 310-340. Details in chapter 14, note 5.

4 "If You Miss Reading Meir Kahane," [ad] *Jewish Press*, February 13, 1970, p. 34. The ad was two columns wide and two inches high.

Spotlight on Extremism was also advertised in *Jewish Defense League Newsletter*, November 1969, pp. 3-4, in RZ Archives, folder 716B.

5 Ten of the eleven issues of *Spotlight on Extremism*, January-November 1970, are in RZ Archives, folder 100. Number 7 is lacking.

See note 4, *Newsletter*, pp. 3-4.

The cost of an annual subscription was raised to $4.50, with a single issue still 25 cents, in *Spotlight on Extremism*, November 1970.

6 "Mr. Bernstein and the Panther," *Times of Israel*, February 20, 1970, p. 7. See also: *Story of the Jewish Defense League*, pp. 199-200.

Goldfoot's letters to Meir, January 13, 1970, February 3, 1970, and June 28, 1970, in RZ Archives, folder 1007. On June 28 he wrote, "I enclose herewith our check for $20 and will be glad to pay you on this basis for each article published."

One article which had no byline but was definitely written by Meir was "Profile of a Fallen Soldier: It's All in the Family," *Times of Israel*, July 10, 1970, p. 11. The raw material for this article about David Uzan (Hebrew news items, photocopies of letters from Uzan to his parents) are in RZ Archives, folder 41. Another indication that Meir wrote it is that he took the liberty of reprinting it in the *Spotlight on Extremism* newsletter (see text). It is likely that other articles by Meir appeared anonymously in the *Times of Israel*.

7 See chapter 19, note 2, Michael T. Kaufman.

8 Ben Greenberg (pseudonym of Arnold Fine), "Spotlight on Extremism," *Jewish Press*, July 24, 1970, pp. 3, 30, in RZ Archives, folder 61A.

9 "Israel Through Laughter and Tears" and "Israel News Analysis" both appeared on August 21, 1970, p. 21.

10 "Time to Go Home," *Jewish Press*, June 26, 1970, p. 22, reprinted in *Times of Israel*, July 24, 1970, p. 7, and in *Writings 5731*, pp. 3-4.

11 "The Way of the Mount," *Jewish Press*, July 26, 1968, p. 36, in RZ Archives, folder 596; reprinted in: *Jewish Press*, August 14, 1970, p. 40, in *Writings 5731*, pp. 57-58, and in *Beyond Words*, 1: 119-121. A copy of the article hand-dated only "1962" is in RZ Archives, folder 592.

This homily appears under *Parshat Yitro* in *Chanukat Hatorah Hechadash* by Avraham Yehoshua Heshel ben Yaakov (Ashdod: 1989); in *Tiferet Shmuel* by Shmuel Tzvi Danziger (Jerusalem: 1996, reprint of Lodz: 1920); and in *Amud Haemet* by R' Menachem Mendel of Kotzk (Tel Aviv: 1956 and 1985). It does not appear in the writings of any of the Gerrer Rebbes. Meir probably heard this homily orally from someone who misattributed it to the Gerrer Rebbe.

12 "Beat Me Again," *Jewish Press*, July 24, 1970, p. 27, reprinted in *Times of Israel*, August 21, 1970, p. 6, and in *Writings 5731*, pp. 11-12.

13 "Freedom of Filth," *Jewish Press*, November 27, 1970, p. 16, in RZ Archives, folder 1206, reprinted in *Writings 5731*, pp. 34-35, and in *Beyond Words*, 1:168-171.

"Next Year in Jerusalem – Maybe," *Jewish Press*, November 27, 1970, p. 30, in RZ Archives, folder 1206, reprinted in *Jewish Press*, December 24, 1971, pp. 9, 14, in *Writings 5732*, pp. 30-32, and in *Beyond Words*, 1:236-240.

"Blueprint for Soviet Jewry," *Jewish Press*, three parts, December 4, 1970, p. 27; December 11, 1970, pp. 22, 28; December 18, 1970, pp. 9, 36, in RZ Archives, folder 1206, reprinted in *Writings 5731*, pp. 38-47.

"Confession," *Jewish Press*, December 25, 1970, p. 16, in RZ Archives, folder 1206, reprinted in *Writings 5731*, pp. 52-54.

14 "Jewish Money," *Jewish Press*, September 25, 1970, p. 36, reprinted in *Writings 5731*, pp. 22-24.

15 Irving Spiegel, "Jews Are Urged by Fund Head to Back Religious Day Schools," *New York Times*, November 14, 1971, p. 26.

See also: Rabbi Isaac Trainin, "Letter to the Editor," *Jewish Press*, October 9, 1970, "... Federation has just completed a comprehensive study which is being presented to the Board of Trustees, and which calls for greater support for Jewish education." Rabbi Trainin, Meir's maternal uncle, headed the Federation's Department of Religious Affairs.

Manhattan Supreme Court barred the JDL "from committing disruptive acts" at the Federation headquarters. See: "Jewish Federation Seeks to Bar Disruptive Acts," *New York Times*, November 13, 1970, p. 46.

Meir's activities had a long-term influence on increased funding for Jewish education. See: Memo from Federation of Jewish Philanthropies, June 11, 1975, in RZ Archives, folder 418.

See also: *Story of the Jewish Defense League*, pp. 157-166.

[16] Geula Cohen, "Be'arba Einayim Im Haliga Lehagana Yehudit [Face to Face with the Jewish Defense League]," *Ma'ariv*, January 2, 1970, p. 10; Jewish Defense League, Second International Annual Convention, [*Minutes*], June 6, 1971, p. 6, in RZ Archives, Appendix; "Nelekh Ad Hasof Bemilchamtenu Lema'an Yehudei Rusya [We Will Do Everything Necessary in Our Fight for Russian Jews]," *Yedioth Ahronoth*, January 7, 1971, pp. 3, 12, in RZ Archives, folder 60A.

[17] A letter from Chaim Mageni (d. 2001) praising Meir's work for Soviet Jewry (and mentioning my visit to Hebron) was published that year in the JDL booklet, *The Plight of Soviet Jewry* (New York: 1970), p. 16.

Shortly after arriving in Israel in 1971, Meir visited Rabbi Moshe Levinger at the military compound in Hebron. A snapshot shows the two standing on a bare hill with a Kiryat Arba building in an early stage of construction in the background. Miriam Levinger later spearheaded the resettlement of Hebron in May 1979, when she and a group of women and children occupied the abandoned Hadassah Hospital building there. Meir led a number of demonstrations between 1976 and 1980 in this historic Jewish city, whose population now was mainly Arab, to protest the Israeli government ban on Jews living in Hebron.

Chapter 21

[1] Interview with Geula Cohen, January 10, 1997, Jerusalem.

Cohen's visit to the JDL office is described in chapter 18.

This was Meir's first overseas flight. In those years, people flew infrequently and many wrote a last will and testament before a plane trip. Printed wills were even sold from vending machines at airports. Meir wrote one by hand on a blank sheet of paper: "I hereby leave all my worldly possessions to my wife, Libby." [signed] Meir Kahane, [dated] December 30, 1970. Copy in RZ Archives, Appendix.

[2] Robert I. Friedman, "The Kahane Connection: How Shamir Used J.D.L. Terrorism," *Nation*, October 31, 1988, p. 424. See also Friedman's *False Prophet*, pp. 106-107.

Friedman's claim that Meir acted on instructions from the Israeli right wing has no basis in fact. Herut leaders sought Meir out in order to co-opt him to their party. A 1972 newspaper report said that Meir was "widely spoken of as a Herut candidate for the Israeli Knesset in the next national elections." (See chapter 27, note 6, Menachem Israel.) Yitzhak Heimowitz, a Herut member, confirmed this. (E-mail from Yitzhak Heimowitz, May 5, 2006.) Another indication of the interest of Herut members in co-opting Meir to their party was that during the early 1970's Meir and I were invited to social evenings at the homes of Herut members Geula Cohen, Shmuel Tamir, and Uri Zvi Greenberg.

[3] Herzl Rosenblum, "Meir Kahane," [editorial] *Yedioth Ahronoth*, May 26, 1970, p. 2, in RZ Archives, folder 59.

"Ligat Hahagana Hayehudit Marchiva Et Shuroteha [The JDL is Expanding]," *Hatzofe*, May 27, 1970, in RZ Archives, folder 59. The article cited was: "Jewish Activists See Ranks Growing." See chapter 19, note 2.

Brady, Thomas F., "Three Arabs Beaten Near U.N. After Bus Is Attacked in Israel," *New York Times*, May 23, 1970, p. 1.

[4] Barbara Rosenberg, "Hahagana Nosach America [The Hagana, American-Style]," *Ma'ariv*, September 18, 1970, *Yamim Velelot* section, pp. 28-29.

Israel Broadcasting Authority Radio News Archive, media no. 6775, October 8, 1970.

[5] Israel Broadcasting Authority Television News Archive, media no. 7-17-21764, January 1, 1971.

Israel Broadcasting Authority Radio News Archive, media no. 6971, January 7, 1971.

"JDL Leader to Settle Here," *Jerusalem Post*, January 8, 1971, p. 8.

See chapter 20, note 16, "Nelekh..." The byline is: "Yedioth Ahronoth Correspondent."

6   Uri Dan, "Al Ta'azru... [Don't Help and Don't Interfere]," *Ma'ariv*, January 7, 1971, pp. 9, 14.

7   Benko Adar, "'Hapanterim Hayehudiyim' Shel Harav Kahana [Rabbi Kahane's 'Jewish Panthers']," *Al Hamishmar*, January 22, 1971, *Hotam* section, pp. 3-4.

"Higi'a Hasha'a Lashuv Habayta," the Hebrew translation of "Time to Go Home" was first printed in *Tefutzot Yisrael*, November-December 1970, pp. 31-33. Original: "Time to Go Home," *Jewish Press*, June 26, 1970, p. 22.

"Higi'a Hasha'a Lashuv Habayta" was also printed in *Zot Ha'aretz*, together with a supportive article by Zvi Shiloah, "Ma'avako Shel Harav Kahana [Rabbi Kahane's Struggle]," *Zot Ha'aretz*, January 22, 1971, pp. 3, 8, in RZ Archives, folders 60A and 592.

Shlomo Shamir, "Hasisma – Lo Od [The Motto – Never Again]," *Ha'aretz*, January 29, 1971, *Musaf* section, pp. 20-21, in JNUL Archives, folder Arc 4=1748.

8   Murray Schumach, "Jewish Defense League Plays Grim Game With the Russians," *New York Times*, January 13, 1971, pp. 1, 15, in RZ Archives, folder 1203. Copyright © 1971 by The New York Times Co. Excerpted with permission.

For Meir's first mention of the harassment tactic in August 1970, see chapter 17, note 15.

See also: *Story of the Jewish Defense League*, pp. 28-48.

9   Max Lerner, "The Harassment Mess," *New York Post*, January 13, 1971, p. 45, in RZ Archives, folder 60C. Excerpted with the permission of his son, Dr. Michael Lerner.

Bernard Gwertzman, "U.S. Cars Damaged in Soviet Actions," *New York Times*, January 10, 1971, p. 21, in RZ Archives, folder 60A.

10   "Jewish Militant Arrested for Failing to Appear on Riot Charge," *New York Times*, January 13, 1971, pp. 1, 15, in RZ Archives, folder 60A. See photo section of this book for a photo of Meir waiting to be brought before a judge.

The missed hearing concerned the December 27, 1970, arrest at the 100-Hour Vigil.

In August, the Justice and State Departments asked Congress to pass a law giving them authority to prosecute cases involving attacks on foreign officials. See: Robert M. Smith, "U.S. Asks for Laws to Protect Officials," *New York Times,* August 6, 1971, p. 2.

11   Israel Broadcasting Authority Television News Archive, media nos. 41309-71-7, 41402-71-0, 41407-71-9, January 12, 1971.

Israel Broadcasting Authority Radio News Archive, media no. 6976, January 13, 1971.

Paul Montgomery, "Spearhead of the JDL: Meir David Kahane," *New York Times*, January 13, 1971, p. 15.

12   NBC News Archive, media no. 0058359, January 12, 1971.

13   E-mail from Glenn Richter, July 6, 1999.

Jacob Birnbaum quoted in: Walter Ruby, "The Role of Nonestablishment Groups," *A Second Exodus: The American Movement to Free Soviet Jews*, eds. Albert D. Chernin and Murray Friedman (Hanover, N.H.: Brandeis University Press, 1999), p. 208.

14   Transcript of *Today* show, January 13, 1971. From: FBI file 100-460495-1039, January 15, 1971, p. 6, in RZ Archives, Appendix.

15   See note 10. This article lists Meir's pending court cases.

16   Lawrence Van Gelder, "Grand Jury Will Hear Charges Against Jewish Defense League," *New York Times*, January 14, 1971, p. 1; "U.S.-Soviet Tension Seen Cooling Off," *Newsday*, January

14, 1971, in RZ Archives, folder 60A. *Newsday* has a photo of Meir and Zweibon at the press conference.

[17] Fern Marja Eckman, "Rabbi Kahane & the JDL," *New York Post Magazine*, January 16, 1971, p. 5, in RZ Archives, folder 1082. Excerpted with the author's permission.

[18] Murray Schumach, "A Brick Shatters Aeroflot's Window Here," *New York Times,* January 15, 1971, p. 8. The driver of the car was never apprehended.

NBC News Archive, media no. 0058463, January 14, 1971.

[19] Mark R. Arnold, "Militant Defense League Cries: 'Jewish Is Beautiful,'" *National Observer*, January 18, 1971, in RZ Archives, folder 60A. Excerpted with the author's permission.

See also: Michael Pousner, "Never Again," *Daily News*, July 27, 1970, p. 34.

[20] Arnold H. Lubasch, "3 in J.D.L. Indicted on Gun Charges," *New York Times*, January 16, 1971, p. 11. See also chapter 15 concerning David Sommer.

[21] NBC News Archive, media no. 0058524, January 15, 1971.

"Some Soviet Émigrés in Israel Back Harassment Tactics Here," *New York Times*, January 16, 1971, p. 11, in RZ Archives, folder 60A. Among those who signed the cable were Dov Sperling and Mordecai Lapid. Copyright © 1971 by The New York Times Co. Excerpted with permission.

Tovia Preschel, "A *Jewish Press* Profile: Dov Sperling," *Jewish Press*, January 22, 1971, pp. 14, 31, in RZ Archives, folder 1203.

[22] Edith Evans Asbury, "8 in J.D.L. Indicted for Protests in City," *New York Times*, January 19, 1971, p. 1; Peter Coutros, "Rabbi Kahane and 7 Indicted for JDL Riots," *Daily News*, January 19, 1971, p. 5, in RZ Archives, folder 1203; Israel Broadcasting Authority Radio Archives, January 18, 1971, media no. 6989.

Names of the seven other defendants and their ages and occupations are given in the *New York Times* report.

[23] See Peter Coutros, note 22.

[24] Juan M. Vasquez, "J.D.L. Calls a Halt to Its Harassment of Soviet Diplomats," *New York Times*, January 20, 1971, p. 1.

[25] *Story of the Jewish Defense League*, p. 44.

[26] Will Lissner, "Jewish Defense League to Boycott Products of Concerns Dealing With Soviet," *New York Times*, January 21, 1971, p. 9. See also: NBC News Archive, media no. 0058747, January 20, 1971.

On April 13, Meir led a peaceful sit-in at the Manhattan headquarters of the Satra Corporation, which traded with the Russians. See: "Kahane Sentenced to Pay Fine of $500," *New York Times*, April 14, 1971, p. 50.

[27] See chapter 17, note 18, "Summer Is Coming."

[28] Bob Mastro, "Hansen: Press Helped Torpedo Mack at Kama River," *Metalworking News*, November 15, 1971, p. 22, in JNUL Archives, folder ARC 4=1748. Sam Shoshan, JDL's public relations officer, penciled in at the top of the clipping, "An example of JDL's effectiveness." One demonstration by JDL is described in: "Mack Truck Offices Picketed," *New York Times*, June 22, 1971, p. 22.

Yak-40 aircraft: "Washington Roundup," *Aviation Week and Space Technology*, May 17, 1971, p. 13, in YU Archives, folder 9/9.

[29] Irving Spiegel, "Jewish Defense League Plans to Resume Harassing Russians," *New York Times*, January 30, 1971, p. 34, in RZ Archives, Appendix.

"Russia Cancels U.S. Tour," *Daily News*, February 7, 1971, p. 32, in RZ Archives, folder 60B.

[30] "The Kremlin vs. the Jews," [editorial] *Daily News*, January 3, 1971, p. 44, in RZ Archives, folder 1203. © New York Daily News, L.P.; reprinted with permission.

[31] "How to Lose Friends," [editorial] *Daily News*, January 12, 1971, in RZ Archives, folder 60A; Michael T. Kaufman, "The Complex Past of Meir Kahane," *New York Times*, January 24, 1971, p. 1; "Pressure Groups: Kahane's Commandos," *Newsweek*, January 25, 1971, pp. 31-33, in RZ Archives, folder 60A; "The Private Jewish War on Russia," *Time*, January 25, 1971, pp. 20-21, and "The Harsh Plight of the Soviet Jews," ibid., pp. 25-26.

"League Officials Quit," *New York Times*, January 19, 1971, p. 42.

"Israel Condemns 'Terrorism' in U.S. in Support of Soviet Jews," *New York Times*, January 18, 1971, p. 6. This report notes that during a radio debate aired on January 17, 1971, opposition Knesset member Shmuel Tamir denounced the government statement.

Ariel Ginai, "Moskva Alula Lehakshiach Emdata Nokhach Alimut... [Moscow Liable to Harden Its Stance Because of JDL Violence]," *Yedioth Ahronoth*, January 19, 1971, pp. 3, 30, in RZ Archives, folder 60A.

[32] "Under Heavy Attack, JDL Undaunted," [editorial] *Jewish Post and Opinion*, January 22, 1971, p. 2, in RZ Archives, folder 1203. Excerpted with permission.

Yisrael Eldad, "Mikhtav Galui Larav Meir Kahane [An Open Letter to Rabbi Meir Kahane]," *Yedioth Ahronoth*, January 22, 1971, p. 17, in RZ Archives, folder 60C.

Chapter 22

[1] Juan M. Vasquez, "Kahane Is Guilty in Disorder Case," *New York Times*, February 24, 1971, p. 6, in RZ Archives, folder 60B. This trial began February 19. See: "Kahane, at Trial, Says Police Blocked Access to Synagogue," *New York Times*, February 23, 1971, p. 3.

[2] "Kahane Sentenced to Pay Fine of $500," *New York Times*, April 14, 1971, p. 50; "Sentence Rabbi Meir Kahane to Serve 90 Days in a NY Jail," *Jewish Sentinel* (Chicago), April 22, 1971, in RZ Archives, folder 60C.

[3] Felonious riot: See note 1.

Williamsburg case: FBI file 105-207795, report, April 8, 1971, p. 1, in RZ Archives, Appendix. Meir's 1971 appointment book, in RZ Archives, Appendix.

For more on the Tass case see chapter 17.

[4] "Kahane & 5 Are Seized on Gun Rap," *Daily News*, May 13, 1971, in RZ Archives, Appendix; "Kahane Says Gun Charge Is an Attempt to Gag JDL," *New York Post*, May 13, 1971, reproduced in the *Jewish Defender* (Jewish Defense League of Staten Island), July 1971, p. 2, in RZ Archives, Appendix.

See also chapter 15, note 23.

[5] Letter from Barry Slotnick to Libby, June 29, 2000, in JNUL Archives, folder ARC 4=1748.

Slotnick's uncle, Rabbi Harry (Chaim Yehuda) Hurwitz, was an official of the Kashruth Supervisors Union.

Morris Kaplan, "Kahane and Colombo Join Forces to Fight Reported U.S. Harassment," *New York Times*, May 14, 1971, pp. 1, 60, in RZ Archives, folder 1188B.

TV coverage of Colombo's support for Meir was extensive. NBC News, for example, showed the two speaking to reporters outside the courthouse. See: NBC News Archive, media no. 0063283, May 13 1971. See also: Israel Broadcasting Authority Television News Archive, media no. 44180-71-9, May 13, 1971, and media no. 44182-71-5, May 14, 1971.

[6] *Indictment*, May 27, 1971, 4 pp., in YU Archives, folder 4/7.

[7] "Kahane Defends Alliance With Italian Group," *Jewish Press*, June 11, 1971, p. 21, in RZ Archives, folder 1211; Meir Kahane, "Observations on a Week That Was," *Jewish Press*, May

21, 1971, p. 22, in RZ Archives, folder 594; Bertram Zweibon, "Kahane, Colombo and You," *Jewish Press*, July 30, 1971, p. 9, in RZ Archives, folder 1202; *Story of the Jewish Defense League*, pp. 185-190.

[8] Robert Lipsyte, "Handicaps and Other Small Moments," *New York Times*, June 5, 1971, in RZ Archives, folder 62A.

[9] Interview with Bennett Levine, June 30, 1998, New York.

The court appearance that morning concerned Meir's December 27, 1970, arrest at the Soviet Mission. It is noted in Meir's 1971 appointment book, in RZ Archives, Appendix.

[10] William E. Farrell, "Colombo Shot, Gunman Slain at Columbus Circle Rally Site," *New York Times*, June 29, 1971, p. 1; NBC News Archive, media no. 0065213, June 28, 1971, and media no. 0065209, June 29, 1971.

In the early years, Meir was chronically late for appointments and speaking engagements. In November 1977, when I accompanied him on a trip to the U.S., I noticed that he was making an effort to change this habit. He was usually prompt from then on.

Colombo died almost seven years later, on May 22, 1978.

[11] See note 9, interview with Bennett Levine.

[12] "Defense League Resumes Protests Against Russians," *New York Times*, February 15, 1971, p. 11, in RZ Archives, folder 60B; Linda Charlton, "Police Seize Head of Defense Group," *New York Times*, February 16, 1971, p. 15, in RZ Archives, folder 60B.

After his formal response to Federov's complaint, Meir was released to appear in Manhattan Criminal Court on March 2.

The police restriction on picketing in front of the mission was later endorsed by an injunction issued on July 6, 1971, by Judge Isidore Dollinger permitting no more than twelve people to picket on the actual block of the Soviet Mission.

In November 1978, the injunction was contested in New York State Supreme Court by Glenn Richter and the Student Struggle for Soviet Jewry, joined by a number of other individuals and organizations, including Meir and the Jewish Defense League. They were represented by attorney Steven Shapiro of the American Civil Liberties Union. (See: "On East 67th Street, an Injunction Against 'the World,'" *New York Times,* November 25, 1978, p. 23.)

Richter's affidavit stated: "Even these twelve are restricted to a pen, constructed with police barricades and several hundred feet from the Soviet Mission. In addition, the use of any sound equipment on 67th Street at any time is absolutely forbidden, no matter how small or weak the equipment may be. The effect of these restrictions is to severely inhibit the effectiveness of any demonstration." (Index No. 10560/1971, pp. 1-2, affidavit and brief, in JNUL Archives, folder ARC 4=1748.) The result of the suit was "the small triumph of increasing our demonstrators to a legal 40." (E-mail from Glenn Richter, July 6, 1999.)

[13] Harry Smoler, "Letter to the Editor," *Jewish Post and Opinion*, February 19, 1971, in RZ Archives, folder 60B. For statistics showing the effectiveness of JDL tactics, see chapter 23. The Susskind show was aired on February 14, 1971.

[14] "American Response to Soviet Anti-Jewish Policies," *American Jewish Year Book,* 1965, pp. 312-313; "American Response to Soviet Anti-Semitism," *American Jewish Year Book,* 1969, pp. 111-113.

[15] See note 1, "Kahane, at Trial..."

Meir had been scheduled to leave for Brussels on Sabena flight 542, departing New York at 5:45 P.M. He forgot his passport at home, however, and instead boarded flight 548, departing at 9 P.M. FBI file 105-207795, report, March 24, 1971, p. 12, in RZ Archives, Appendix.

Sam Shoshan sent a telegram to Bert Zweibon at the Plaza Hotel in Brussels about the flight change: "Arriving Sabena flight 548 at 10:20 A.M." Telegram from Shoshan to Bert Zweibon, stamped February 24, 1971, in RZ Archives, Appendix.

[16] Bertram Zweibon, "The Brussels Affair," *Jewish Press*, April 16, 1971, p. 26.

[17] Edwin Eytan, "Harav Kahana Ba, Cholel Se'ara – Vegorash [Rabbi Kahane Came, Caused a Storm – and Was Ousted]," *Yedioth Ahronoth*, February 25, 1971, p. 2. English translation in *Jewish Echo – Bat Kol*, March 1971, p. 2.

Henry Giniger, "World Jews Make a Plea to Moscow," *New York Times*, February 26, 1971, pp. 1, 2. This reports that Begin's allegation was denied by Dr. William Wexler, president of the American Conference of Jewish Organizations.

Carl Hartman, "Kahane Kicked Out," *Daily Argus* (Mount Vernon, N.Y.), February 25, 1971.

[18] "Soviet Jewry: Pressures Mount on a Still Unyielding Kremlin," *Daily News*, February 28, 1971, p. 38, in RZ Archives, folder 60C.

[19] Conference declaration: See note 17, Giniger.

Detained by the Belgian police together with Meir but not deported, Sam Shoshan bought every newspaper on sale in Brussels the next day. He kindly gave me his collection of newspapers to consult for this book.

[20] Henry Giniger, "U.S. Jewish Militant Expelled From Belgium After Detention," *Herald Tribune*, February 25, 1971, pp. 1, 2, in RZ Archives, folder 681.

Mike [pseudonym], "A Strange People," [cartoon caption] *Yedioth Ahronoth*, February 26, 1971, p. 19. The Russian in the cartoon is labeled "General D. A. Dragunsky." Dragunsky, a Jewish member of the Soviet Union's Central Auditing Committee, had expressed opposition to the conference in Brussels. See: Bernard Gwertzman, "Moscow Assails a Conference Set for Belgium on Soviet Jews," *New York Times*, February 17, 1971, pp. 1, 4.

[21] Max Lerner, "Kahane and Brussels," *New York Post*, February 26, 1971, p. 35, in RZ Archives, folder 60B. Excerpted with the permission of his son, Dr. Michael Lerner.

Similar sentiments were expressed in "The Editor's Chair," *National Jewish Post and Opinion*, March 12, 1971, in RZ Archives, folder 60B. ("The Brussels Conference should have permitted the speech and... not have created the martyr that it did and meanwhile earned itself the reputation of being afraid to hear all viewpoints....")

[22] NBC News Archive, media no. 0060189, February 24, 1971; NBC News Archive, media no. 0060196, February 25, 1971; Israel Broadcasting Authority Radio Archives, February 24, 1971, media no. 7067; February 25, 1971, media nos. 7068, 7069; Israel Broadcasting Authority Television Archives, February 24, 1971, media no. 42454-71-0; February 25, 1971, media nos. 42426-71-8, 42452-71-4, 42380-71-7, 35165-71-1, 890-83-0, 881-83-9.

See also: *Story of the Jewish Defense League*, pp. 49-57.

William Sherman, "Jewish Aide Rips Kahane in TV Debate," *Daily News*, February 26, 1971, p. 16, in RZ Archives, folder 60B.

[23] "Picketing at the U.N.," *New York Times*, March 11, 1971, p. 9; Israel Broadcasting Authority Television Archives, March 10, 1971, media no. 42741-71-0; e-mail from Isaac Jaroslawicz, November 16, 2006.

A photo shows Isaac Jaroslawicz reciting the Scroll of Esther, with Meir at his side. Photo in RZ Archives, Appendix.

[24] *JOYS/Jewish Orthodox Youth Speaks*, March 1971, p. 3, in RZ Archives, Appendix; Letter to JDL members, in RZ Archives, folder 482. The JDL stationery had the address 440 West 42 Street, New York City.

On the rally in Providence: *The 'Zionist Hooligans,'* p. 414 (see chapter 17, note 18).

Yosef Schneider, "Yosef Schneider Speaks," *Achdut: The National Voice of the Jewish High School Activist*, June 1971, p. 3, in JNUL Archives, folder ARC 4=1748.

25 [Meir Kahane,] "This Is the Price of Silence," [ad] *New York Times*, March 19, 1971, p. 36, in RZ Archives, folder 60B. The ad was two columns wide and full-page length.

A news story also promoted the rally: "Thousands to Attend Huge Rally for Soviet Jewry at White House," *Jewish Press*, March 19, 1971, pp. 1, 30.

See chapter 23 for details of Meir's speaking dates preceding the rally.

26 Martin Weil, "City Jails 1,000 in Protest," *Washington Post*, March 22, 1971, pp. A1, A11 (with a photo of the demonstrators seated in the street); "Grab 800 in Jewish Protest at D.C. Embassy," *Daily News*, March 22, 1971, p. 5, in RZ Archives, folder 1082; Dick Belsky, "Kahane: Arrests Won't Stop Us," *New York Post*, March 22, 1971, p. 1, in RZ Archives, folder 60B.

Yossi Templeman headed Student Activists for Soviet Jewry (SASJ), co-sponsor of the rally. SASJ, established by JDL college students in 1971, should not be confused with SSSJ (Student Struggle for Soviet Jewry) formed in 1964. For a comprehensive report on the demonstration and SASJ's role in it, see *The 'Zionist Hooligans,'* pp. 410-413 (see chapter 17, note 18).

Templeman recalled: "They let everyone go immediately (i.e within hours) without trial in exchange for the $10 collateral. Keep in mind that this is close $80 in today's money. This caused us tremendous problems since we paid for everybody out of the money collected to pay for the buses..." E-mail from Yossi Templeman, April 17, 2007.

27 Carl Bernstein, "'I Kind of Hate to Do It,' Policeman Making Arrest Says," *Washington Post*, March 22, 1971, pp. 1, 11, in RZ Archives, folder 60B. Excerpted with permission.

28 Letter from Dr. William Perl to Libby, February 26, 1998, in RZ Archives, Appendix.

Dr. Perl died on December 24, 1998. See: Richard Goldstein, "William R. Perl Is Dead at 92; Built Sealift Rescue of Jews," *New York Times*, December 29, 1998, p. 15.

The total number of arrests is given as 1,347 in *Story of the Jewish Defense League*, pp. 144-145.

29 Bobby Rosenberg, "In Cell No. 2," *Achdut: The National Voice of the Jewish High School Activist*, June 1971, pp. 12, 15, in JNUL Archives, folder ARC 4=1748.

Meir took our son Baruch, age 12, to that demonstration. Baruch recalled waiting with friends for Meir to be released. Robert I. Friedman erroneously wrote that Baruch was arrested (*False Prophet*, p. 130).

30 Israel Broadcasting Authority Radio Archive, media no. 7097, March 22, 1971; Israel Broadcasting Authority Television Archive, media no. 42988-71-7, March 23, 1971; NBC News Archive, media no. 61193, March 24, 1971. Photos of the demonstration in Washington are in the photo section of this book.

31 "A Remarkable Event," *Jewish Press*, April 9, 1971, p. 37, in RZ Archives, folder 592, reprinted in *Writings 5731*, pp. 89-91, and in *Beyond Words*, 1:194-197. Similar sentiments were expressed in Shaul Shiff's, "Anachnu Hechezarnu Lador Hatza'ir Ketzat Mehaga'ava Hayehudit [We Gave Youth Some Jewish Pride]," *Hatzofe*, March 26, 1971, p. 5, in RZ Archives, Appendix.

32 E-mail from Charles Levine, January 24, 2000.

33 Philip Hochstein, "The Rabbi Seems to Pick Up All the Marbles!" *American Examiner–Jewish Week*, April 1, 1971, p. 6, in RZ Archives, folder 60C. Excerpted with permission.

34 Bill Kovach "Stolen Files Show F.B.I. Seeks Black Informers," *New York Times*, April 8, 1971, p. 22; Bill Kovach, "Stolen F.B.I. Papers Described as Largely of a Political Nature," *New York Times*, May 13, 1971, p. 18. This report notes that the stolen documents include the start of an FBI file on the JDL.

35 Letter signed "Barry Wingard for Resist" to Samuel Shoshan, May 14, 1971, with enclosure:

FBI memorandum to SAC 105-18173, October 21, 1970, from collection of Samuel Shoshan, in JNUL Archives, folder ARC 4=1748.

[36] "Observations on a Week That Was – Informers," *Jewish Press*, May 21, 1971, p. 22, in RZ Archives, folder 594.

Shulchan Arukh, Choshen Mishpat 388:5, forbids informing on a fellow Jew.

[37] Mel Ziegler, "The Jewish Defense League and Its Invisible Constituency," *New York* [weekly], April 19, 1971, pp. 28-36, in RZ Archives, folder 683B.

Conservative rabbis were also critical of ADL. See: "ADL Under Heavy Fire for 'Informing' on JDL," *Jewish Post and Opinion*, May 28, 1971, p. 1, in RZ Archives, folder 62A. See also: Arnold Forster, "The Anti-Defamation League States Its Position on Release of JDL Names," *Jewish Post and Opinion*, August 27, 1971, p. 11.

[38] See chapter 18, note 24, Ram Oren. The show was hosted by Terry Noble-Efrati.

[39] Jewish Defense League of Boston, "On the Night of July 11, 1971..." flyer in Jewish Defense League collection, Center for Jewish History, New York City.

[40] *Newsletter* (Jewish Defense League of Southshore [Queens, New York]), April 1971, p. 3, in RZ Archives, folder 716B.

[41] "Rabbi Meir Kahane Vows to Start Drive to Smash Heads," *Jewish Sentinel* (Chicago), April 22, 1971, p. 3, in RZ Archives, folder 60C; Dave Sobel, "Young Jewish Activists," *Jewish Press*, April 23, 1971, p. 21; "JDL in Battle on Muggers," *Daily News*, April 13, 1971, p. 26, summarized in FBI file 105-207795, report, May 7, 1971, p. 5, in JNUL Archives, folder ARC 4=1748; NBC News Archive, media no. 62599, April 27, 1971.

[42] Irving Spiegel, "Parade Here Salutes Israel's 23d Year," *New York Times*, April 26, 1971, pp. 1, 21. After the parade, JDL marchers gathered in Central Park. See photo section of this book.

[43] Sy Polsky, "Triumph and Tragedy," *Jewish Defender* (Jewish Defense League of Staten Island), June 1971, pp. 9, 10, in RZ Archives, Appendix.

[44] "Fights, Marches, Demonstrations Mark JDL, Third World Conflict," *Kingsman* (Brooklyn College), May 7, 1971, pp. 1, 6, in RZ Archives, folder 961; Mitch Biderman, "Confrontation at Brooklyn College," *Achdut: The National Voice of the Jewish High School Activist* , June 1971, p. 15, in RZ Archives, Appendix. See also *Story of the Jewish Defense League*, pp. 279-281.

Frank Ross, "Kahane Barred on Campus, After B'klyn College Clash," *Daily News*, May 6, 1971, p. 73, in RZ Archives, folder 62A.

For an overview of the problems of Jewish students in the colleges of the City University of New York, see Howard Adelson, "City University: A Jewish Tragedy," *American Zionist*, September 1971, pp. 17-29, in RZ Archives, folder 1202.

[45] Charlayne Hunter, "Kahane and Black Leader Promise Unity," *New York Times*, May 19, 1971, p. 20, in RZ Archives, folder 62A; "U.S. Group Appeals to Kosygin to Allow Visit to Jewish Area," *New York Times*, August 4, 1971, p. 5.

[46] E-mail from Yossi Templeman, December 20, 1999.

Linda Charlton, "Jewish Youths Here Visit 'Plague' on Soviet Aides," *New York Times*, April 14, 1971, p. 42. Copyright © 1971 by The New York Times Co. Excerpted with permission.

[47] "16 Jews Among 21 in Iraq to Be Tried in Money Case," *New York Times*, April 15, 1971, p. 11. Amnesty International reported that at least thirty-eight Jews had been detained in Iraq, including women and children: "Iraqi Jewish Prisoners Identified," *Jewish Press*, April 23, 1971, p. 2, in RZ Archives, Appendix.

Patrick Doyle, "3 Cops Felled; Seize Kahane & 6 Marchers," *Daily News*, April 21, 1971, p. M-1, in RZ Archives, Appendix; "Kahane Facing Riot Rap," *New York Post*, April 21, 1971, p.

12, in RZ Archives, folder 62A; "Kahane Is Arrested in Protest on Iraq," *New York Times*, April 21, 1971, p. 5.

1969: James Feron, "Eshkol Appeals for World Help," *New York Times*, January 28, 1969, p. 1. The execution took place on January 27, 1969.

See also *Story of the Jewish Defense League*, pp. 281-282. The date given there, April 11, is incorrect.

48 Court hearing on August 10, 1971, noted in Meir's 1971 appointment book, in RZ Archives, Appendix. Shiva date confirmed in interview with Rabbi Solomon Kahane, June 24, 1998, New York City.

49 "Rabbi Kahane Acquitted of Two Criminal Charges," *New York Times*, August 19, 1971, p. 25; "Jury Acquits Rabbi Kahane," *Jewish Post and Opinion*, September 10, 1971, in RZ Archives, folder 62A.

Chapter 23

1 "From the Press Wires: Reds Quietly Letting Soviet Jews Go," *Long Island Press*, April 12, 1971, p. 2, in RZ Archives, folder 62A; Harry Trimborn, "Soviets Letting Jews Out at Record Rate," *New York Post*, March 16, 1971, p. 1, in RZ Archives, folder 60B

Both reports credited the *Los Angeles Times*. The *Long Island Press* said, "The figures were made available to the *Los Angeles Times* yesterday from unimpeachable sources that cannot be identified."

The total number of Jews allowed to leave the Soviet Union in 1971 was an astounding 14,000. See: Bernard Weinraub, "Moscow Is Berated on Eve of Brussels Meeting on Soviet Jews," *New York Times,* February 17, 1976, p. 6.

2 Martin Arnold, "Bomb Explodes in Midtown Soviet Trading Office," *New York Times,* April 23, 1971, p. 41, in RZ Archives, folder 716A; "Blast Rips Red Office," *Daily News*, April 23, 1971, pp. 1, 3, 38, reproduced in the *Jewish Defender* (Jewish Defense League of Staten Island), June 1971, p. 2, in RZ Archives, Appendix.

3 "Soviet Protests Harassment Here," *New York Times,* April 25, 1971, p. 23, in RZ Archives, folder 62A.

4 "Hail to Our Chiefs," *Jewish Press*, March 12, 1971, p. 32, reprinted in *Beyond Words*, 1:184-187.

5 "JDL Invaders Smash Up Board of Rabbis Office," *Jewish Week*, May 6, 1971, p. 2, in RZ Archives, folder 60C; "23 Arraigned Here for Invading Office of Board of Rabbis," *New York Times,* April 30, 1971, p. 79; *Jewish Defense League Newsletter*, August 1, 1971, p. 1, in RZ Archives, folder 1202; "Two JDL Members Get Prison Terms," *Jewish Press*, February 11, 1972, p. 2.

Meir wrote several articles in the *Jewish Press* urging the Board of Rabbis to drop the charges. "The Shepherds," April 30, 1971, pp. 31, 36, in RZ Archives, folder 594; "Ahavat Yisrael – Love of Israel," May 7, 1971, p. 19, in RZ Archives, folder 594. See also unsigned news item, "JDL to Call Board of Rabbis to Din Torah," May 14, 1971, pp. 16, 45.

6 Irving Spiegel, "77 in J.D.L. Seized in Sitdown on 3d Ave. Near Soviet Mission," *New York Times,* May 3, 1971, p. 26, in RZ Archives, folder 62A; "89 Arrested at Protest for Jews in Russia," *Daily News*, May 3, 1971, reproduced in the *Jewish Defender* (Jewish Defense League of Staten Island), June 1971, p. 5, in JNUL Archives, folder ARC 4=1748.

7 Interview with Mal and Yetta Lebowitz, November 11, 1998, Jerusalem.
The Tenth Police Precinct was at 230 West 20 Street.

Mal summed up those years: "Meir was a tremendous leader and a tremendous thinker – an inspiration to the rest of us. My family – we spent the best years of our lives with Meir Kahane. Life was a challenge, life was interesting, life was productive."

8 *Battle Song of the Jewish Defense League,* lyrics by Raphael Perl, music by Michael Garin, 1971, in RZ Archives, folder 985. The lyricist, Raphael Perl, son of William Perl, is named "JDL spokesman and tactician" in: "Publicity a Weapon for Militant Jews," *Washington Post*, November 1, 1971, pp. C1, C7, in RZ Archives, folder 734.

9 E-mail from David Fisch, June 14, 1999.

10 "Arrest Kahane, 130 in Sit-Out," *New York Post*, June 11, 1971, in RZ Archives, folder 62A.

This quotes another speaker, Natale Marcone, president of the Italian American Civil Rights League, who said, "Keep fighting. The Italian American Civil Rights League is behind you every inch of the way." See also: "100 J.D.L. Backers Seized in Protest," *New York Times,* June 11, 1971, p. 32.

11 Meir's attorney for this case was Harvey J. Michelman. See: *The 'Zionist Hooligans,'* p. 446 (chapter 17, note 18).

12 The picture was published later, without a photographer's name, in the *Chicago Sun-Times*, April 29, 1973, Showcase section 3, p. 17. Queries to the *Chicago Sun-Times* were not answered. The photographer was probably Barbara Kanegis, a member of the JDL in Washington.

13 Letter from Charlotte Levin to Libby, December 2, 1999, in RZ Archives, Appendix.

JDLers recalled that at a demonstration in Manhattan Meir once jumped on the hood of a car whose driver stopped to curse the demonstrators. (Interview with Baruch Ben Yosef, October 9, 1997, Jerusalem; e-mail from Yerachmiel Gersh, July 15, 1998.)

Charlotte Levin described the lapel pin: "A yellow Magen David is superimposed on a red star [symbolizing the USSR] and on top of that are prison bars in black. The words 'Free Soviet Jews' are in caps in yellow, with 'Free' at the top, and 'Soviet Jews' at the bottom." E-mail from Charlotte Levin, December 26, 1999.

14 NBC News Archive, media no. 65249, June 27, 1971.

15 "Arrest Kahane at Soviet HQ," *Daily* News, June 28, 1971, p. 8, in RZ Archives, folder 62A; "Kahane and 37 Arrested," *New York Times,* June 28, 1971, p. 18; Dave Sobel, "Young Jewish Activists," *Jewish Press*, June 18, 1971, p. 22.

See: *Story of the Jewish Defense League*, p. 293-295. Meir noted that in the ensuing trial, the ordinance forbidding an individual to bring a foreign state into disrepute was struck down.

16 The drawing is signed "H. Becerra." I was unable to identify the artist.

17 Israel Broadcasting Authority Television Archives, media nos. 45274-71-9, 44503-71-2, June 27, 1971; NBC News Archive, media no. 0065120, June 27, 1971.

See also: Robert E. Tomasson, "Jewish Defense League Gains Adherents in Cities Across the Country," *New York Times,* June 28, 1971, p. 18, in RZ Archives, folder 62. This comprehensive report on JDL's growth noted that 37 marchers were arrested in Washington for "insulting the Soviet Union."

"Guest Editorial," *Daily News*, June 29, 1971, p. 43. Information about this editorial in e-mail from David Fisch, June 16, 1999.

18 "Anti-Anti-Semitism Rules: Media Continues to Bow," *Middle East Perspective*, October, 1971, p. 2, in RZ Archives, folder 316.

The Frost show was taped on June 28, 1971. Noted in Meir's 1971 appointment book, in RZ Archives, Appendix.

July 9 broadcast date confirmed by e-mail from Jewish Telegraphic Agency, Client Services, January 14, 2003.

Letter about Schary from Brenda Berlin to Meir, December 8, 1971 [*sic*], in RZ Archives, folder 713a.

[19] [Larry Ankewicz], "Through the Jewish Looking Glass," *Or* (B'nai B'rith Hillel Foundation, York University and University of Toronto), February 1971, p. 1, 2, in RZ Archives, folder 60B. Excerpted with the author's permission.

[20] Joe Polonsky, "Little Big Jew," *Or*, p. 8. (See note 19.)

[21] Meir Kahane, "Jewish Is Beautiful," *Or*, p. 7. (See note 19.)

[22] January 26, 1971: Dickinson College, sponsored by the Hillel Jewish students' organization. See: FBI file 105-207795, report, March 24, 1971, p. 4, in RZ Archives, Appendix.

January 17: Temple Sinai, Summit, N.J.; January 20: East Northport Jewish Center; January 25: Congregation Sons of Abraham, Albany, N.Y. Booking agreements, correspondence, and memos in RZ Archives, folder 714B.

[23] Phil Donahue telecast: see note 22, FBI, p. 7.

Baltimore telecast, February 21, 1971: Ticket stub, Delta Air Lines.

Philadelphia telecast, May 25, 1971: Meir's 1971 appointment book, in RZ Archives, Appendix.

[24] Jack Luria, "Noise in Place of Numbers," *National Jewish Monthly*, February 1971, p. 33, in RZ Archives, folder 60B.

[25] E-mail from Liz Berney, March 21, 2004.

[26] The march on Washington is discussed in chapter 22.

[27] Speaking dates in February and March: February 11, 1971, Temple Beth Ami, Philadelphia (See note 22, FBI, p. 6.); February 14, 1971, Temple Avodah, Oceanside; February 21, 1971, Hebrew Institute of White Plains; March 7, 1971, Malverne Jewish Center. Booking agreements and correspondence in RZ Archives, folder 714B.

"Protest March on Washington Urged by JDL," *Jewish Week*, February 4, 1971, in RZ Archives, folder 1203. This describes Meir's appearance in New Rochelle.

Meir had been invited to the Young Israel of New Rochelle by its rabbi, Stanley Wexler, despite opposition by some synagogue members. So many people came that the speech had to be wired into another hall in the building. Interview with Rabbi Stanley Wexler, November 17, 1999, Jerusalem.

[28] *Newsletter* (United Zionist Revisionist Organization of America), February-March 1971, in RZ Archives, Appendix.

[29] Hank Burchard, "JDL Founder Gets Ovation: End Nonviolence, Jews Urged," *Washington Post*, March 1, 1971, p. 1, in RZ Archives, folder 681. Excerpted with permission.

Another report on Meir's talks in Washington pointed out: "He spoke in measured tones... stating his case calmly and logically." [Lillian Levy], "Kahane's Ouster Made Him a Hero," *Jewish Post and Opinion*, March 5, 1971, p. 3. Cited in "The Editor's Chair," *Jewish Post and Opinion*, March 12, 1971, in RZ Archives, folder 60B.

[30] Buffalo: "Jewish Leftists, Arabs Harass Rabbi Kahane," *Jewish Post and Opinion*, March 12, 1971, in RZ Archives, folder 60B. See also: *Story of the Jewish Defense League*, p. 152.

Colgate: "Kahane to Lead Capital Protests," *Daily Mirror* (New York), February 18, 1971, in RZ Archives, folder 1203.

February 8, 1971, Syracuse University (see note 22, FBI, p. 9); February 3, 1971, Staten Island Community College (see note 22, FBI, p. 11); February 7, 1971, Brooklyn College ("Jewish Operation Youth Presents Solidarity for Soviet Jewry and Israel..." flyer, in RZ Archives, folder 435B).

31 McGill: "Scuffle Disrupts Kahane Talk," *New York Times,* March 16, 1971, p. 44. In contrast, he was warmly received that evening in Montreal at the Place Bonaventure, Salle Westmount. See note 34.

Brown: FBI file 105-207795, report, April 8, 1971, pp. 6-7, in RZ Archives, Appendix. Brown University speech: March 24, 1971.

32 Chuck Petrowski, "JDL Head Hits Oppression," *Diamondback* (University of Maryland), March 17, 1971, p. 1. Excerpted with permission.

33 Dick Polman, "Kahane Advocates Resistance," *Hatchet* (George Washington University), March 18, 1971, p. 1. Excerpted with the author's permission.

34 Letter from Bryna Weinberger, Montreal, to Libby, March 29, 1997. The talk took place at Place Bonaventure, Salle Westmount.

35 Tamara Goldman, "Rabbi Meir Kahane Hits Home...," *Jewish Standard*, March 26, 1971, in RZ Archives, folder 60B.

More on appearances at New Jersey synagogues in: Simon Bloom, "Extraordinary Phenomenon of America Today: Meir Kahane of Jewish Defense League," *American Jewish Ledger*, April 23, 1971, pp. 1, 3, 5, in RZ Archives, folder 62A.

On March 7, 1971, Meir debated Rabbi Samuel Silver in Fair Lawn. See: Jewish Welfare Board Lecture Bureau, Confirmation of Booking, Fair Lawn Jewish Center, in RZ Archives, folder 714B.

36 *Newsletter* (Jewish Defense League of South Shore [Queens, New York]), April 1971, p. 3, in RZ Archives, folder 716B.

37 *Never Again*, speech by Rabbi Meir Kahane, March 28, 1971, rpm phonograph record.

Hager signed Meir to a contract that stipulated: "We hereby agree to pay you a royalty of $1.00 per record sold to retail outlets, to wholesale distributor: 50 cents per record. You hereby agree not to record for any other record company in the world for one year until April 1972." Contract between Meir and Isaac Hager, Fran Record Company, March 16, 1971, in RZ Archives, folder 1002.

In the late 1980s the rpm was copied to cassette tapes and distributed by the U.S. office of Kach. The speech, on computer disk and on the original rpm record, is in the National Sound Archives, Jerusalem.

Apparently, the record was not a commercial success; it was not followed by others. In July 1971, Hager made a 45-minute video of a speech by Meir. It was taped at Hager's home, without an audience, and was never produced commercially. Phone interview with Isaac Hager, October 1, 2007. A DVD of this video is in RZ Archives, Appendix.

38 FBI Los Angeles office file 105-29135; 105-29629, report, April 29, 1971, pp. 1-3, in RZ Archives, Appendix.

This report names the synagogues where Meir spoke: Stephen S. Wise Temple, Temple Akiba, Beth Jacob Synagogue, and Leo Baeck Temple. The college campuses were UCLA, University of California at San Diego, Valley Junior College at Van Nuys and San Fernando Valley State College. He also spoke at two high schools. The heckler at UCLA noted in FBI report, p. 1.

See also: "Kahane Fined $500, Hailed in California," *Jewish Post and Opinion*, April 23, 1971, in RZ Archives, folder 62A.

39 Interview with Rabbi Zvi Block, November 18, 2003, Jerusalem; Letter from Sherri Okin to Libby, received November 30, 2003, in RZ Archives, Appendix.

40 Interview with Sherri Okin, November 19, 1999, Jerusalem.

See note 38. The May Company demonstration was led by Al Epstein. Sy Gaiber, a mainstay of the JDL chapter in Los Angeles, also helped set up JDL chapters in Chicago, Cincinnati and Detroit. Phone interview with Gaiber, November 2, 1999.

May 12 demonstration: U.S. Secret Service, Los Angeles office file 105-29629-30, intelligence report, April 26, 1971, p. 2, in RZ Archives, Appendix. JDL membership statistics are in this report.

[41] Wayne State University and the University of Michigan, April 14, 1971. See: FBI file 105-207795, report, May 7, 1971, p. 5, in RZ Archives, Appendix.

Northeastern University, Boston, April 21, 1971; Princeton University, April 22, 1971. Noted in Meir's 1971 appointment book, in RZ Archives, Appendix.

Geri Sprung, "Defense League Founder Urges Jewish Nationalism, Brotherhood," *Michigan Daily*, April 15, 1971, p. 7; "Jewish Militants Defended," *Ann Arbor News*, April 15, 1971, p. 7.

[42] "To My Four Children," *Jewish Press*, March 19, 1971, p. 20, reprinted in *Writings 5731*, pp. 87-89, and in *Beyond Words*, 1:188-191.

[43] Patrick Clark, "Bomb Rips Temple Expecting Kahane," *Daily News*, April 19, 1971, in RZ Archives, folder 62A. See also: "Despite Bombing Kahane to Speak," *New York Post*, April 19, 1971.

[44] Les A. Somogyi, "Kahane Would Ship All U.S. Jews to Israel," *Jewish Post and Opinion*, May 7, 1971, p. 1.

Larry S. Pollack, "Letter to the Editor," *Ohio Jewish Chronicle*, February 8, 1990, p. 2, in RZ Archives, folder 127B.

[45] Naphtali J. Rubinger, "The Jewish Defense League," *Jewish Spectator,* May 1971, pp. 8-9, in RZ Archives, folder 62B. Excerpted with permission of Robert Bleiweiss, editor emeritus.

The *Spectator* had published editorials against the JDL in February and March 1971. The author was rabbi of Congregation Habonim in Chicago.

Efforts by the Canadian Jewish Congress to cancel Meir's appearance at the University of Toronto and at York University on January 21, are described in "The Editor's Chair," *Jewish Post and Opinion*, March 12, 1971, in RZ Archives, folder 60B. I found no information about similar efforts in Springfield, Massachusetts, in 1970 or 1971.

[46] "Editor Casts Lone Vote in Defense of the JDL," *Jewish Post and Opinion*, August 6, 1971, in RZ Archives, folder 62A. Excerpted with permission.

[47] "On Violence," *Jewish Press*, January 29, 1971, p. 15, in RZ Archives, folder 64D, reprinted in *Writings* 5731, p. 62. This article was later reprinted as a flyer.

For an analysis of violence in Jewish tradition and how JDL violence helped Soviet Jewry, see: Reuben E. Gross, "In Behalf of the JDL's Militancy," *Young Israel Viewpoint*, October 28, 1971, in RZ Archives, folder 62B.

[48] Mickey Gerelick, editor of the Omaha *Jewish Press*, quoted in: "Editor Casts Lone Vote in Defense of the JDL." See note 46.

[49] "ADL Policy Needs Revising," [editorial] *Jewish Post and Opinion*, August 27, 1971, p. 6, in RZ Archives, folder 62A.

[50] "Kahane & 5 Are Seized on Gun Rap," *Daily News*, May 13, 1971, in RZ Archives, Appendix. See chapter 22.

[51] Speaking engagements in May 1971: May 15 and May 16, synagogues in Atlantic City and Fort Lee; May 22 at the Avenue N Jewish Center, Brooklyn. Noted in Meir's 1971 appointment book, in RZ Archives, Appendix.

Meir spoke at a rabbinical conference in Miami on Wednesday morning May 5 and at the Bellmore Jewish Center in Queens, N.Y. that evening. See: Frank Ross, "Kahane Barred on Campus, After B'klyn College Clash," *Daily News*, May 6, 1971, p. 73, in RZ Archives, folder 62A.

Farewell dinner in Toronto, May 26: "ADL Under Heavy Fire for 'Informing' on JDL," *Jewish*

Post and Opinion, May 28, 1971, p. 1, in RZ Archives, folder 62a; Meir's 1971 appointment book, in RZ Archives, Appendix.

Activities of the Toronto chapter: *Toronto Daily Star*, April 27, 1971, April 28, 1971, and October 26, 1971, in RZ Archives, folder 62A and Appendix.

Toronto chapter chairman, Judy Feld, requested 300 copies of the leaflet *Three Most Asked Questions of the* JDL. Letter from Judy Feld to Samuel Shoshan, November 1971, in RZ Archives, Appendix.

Three Most Asked Questions, leaflet, in RZ Archives, folder 683.

[52] "Rabbi Kahane Explains JDL Activities," *Chicago Illini* (University of Illinois at Chicago), May 10, 1971, p. 3, in RZ Archives, Appendix.

[53] Meir was present at a meeting of chapter chairmen on June 13, 1971, that lasted six hours. *Forest Fire: Newsletter of the Rego Park-Forest Hills Chapter of the* JDL, June 25, 1971, in RZ Archives, folder 716B. The masthead names chapter chairman Raymond Solomon and treasurer Bernard Ratowitz.

[54] *Newsletter* (Jewish Defense League of South Shore [Queens, New York]), March 1971, p. 1, in RZ Archives, in folder 716B; Dave Sobel, "Young Jewish Activists," *Jewish Press*, September 3, 1971, p. 11.

[55] JDL *Bulletin Briefs*, [September 13, 1971], p. 3, in RZ Archives, folder 716B.

Murray Schneider quoted in: Jewish Defense League, Second International Annual Convention, [*Minutes*], June 6, 1971, p. 12, in RZ Archives, Appendix.

Chapter 24

[1] M. Hirsch Goldberg, "Where Does Meir Kahane Go From Here?" *Times of Israel and World Jewish Review*, January 1975, p. 50, 51.

[2] E-mail from Ed Nash, July 12, 2000.

The Nash Publishing Company, 9255 Sunset Boulevard, Los Angeles, was founded in 1969. It was acquired in the mid-1970s by a small New York publisher, Books for Libraries, which used the imprint New York: Nash Publishing.

Arthur J. Horwitz, the attorney who handled the liquidation of Books for Libraries, suggested that Ed Nash might still be living in the Los Angeles area. (Letter from Arthur J. Horwitz to Libby in JNUL Archives, folder ARC 4=1748.) I wrote to several Edward Nashes there and finally received a reply from the founder of Nash Publishing.

[3] Letter from Edward L. Nash to Meir, April 20, 1971, in JNUL Archives, folder ARC 4=1748. "Mr. Avram" was probably Avraham Hershkowitz.

[4] E-mail from Edward L. Nash to Libby, July 17, 2000.

[5] Letter from Edward L. Nash to Meir, April 22, 1971, in JNUL Archives, folder ARC 4=1748.

[6] Letter from Edward L. Nash to Meir, April 29, 1971, in JNUL Archives, folder ARC 4=1748.

[7] Letter from Edward L. Nash to Meir, May 19, 1971, in JNUL Archives, folder ARC 4=1748.

[8] The telegram was phoned in to the JDL office and transcribed by Sue Levine. Telegram from Nash to Meir, June 16, 1971, in JNUL Archives, folder ARC 4=1748.

[9] More about Laurie and three other informers, Richard Rosenthal, Herb Eisner and Mark Gold, in *The 'Zionist Hooligans*,' pp. 191-258, 389-467 (see chapter 17, note 18).

See also: Richard Rosenthal, *Rookie Cop* (Wellfleet, Mass.: Leapfrog Press, 2000).

[10] Eleanor Blau, "Wiretap Hearing Set Here Today," *New York Times,* June 25, 1971, p. 23. This reported that attorney general John N. Mitchell, in a statement accompanying the sealed transcript

of overheard telephone conversations, contended that the electronic surveillance had been authorized by President Nixon on the grounds that national security was involved.

Beginning October 7, 1971, attorney Bert Zweibon took the case of the wiretaps through a
series of lower courts. On June 23, 1975, the U.S. Court of Appeals decided that wiretaps carried
out without a court order are illegal. However, it did not award damages to any JDL members. See:
Lesley Oelsner, "Appeals Court Curbs U.S. on Warrantless Wiretap," *New York Times*, June 24,
1975, pp. 1, 69.

Zweibon continued to litigate for payment of damages, to no avail. In 1983, the U.S. Court of
Appeals declared Attorney General John Mitchell immune from suit. See: "Mitchell Held Free of
Damages," *Washington Post*, October 21, 1983, p. A2; "Nixon Attorney General Wins Appeals
Ruling on Wiretaps," *New York Times*, October 22, 1983, p. 8. See also: U.S. District of Columbia
Circuit Court of Appeals Reports, Zweibon v. Mitchell, 82-1626, 720 F 2d 162 (D.C. Cir. 1983)

In a blatant inaccuracy, Yair Kotler wrote: "Bertram Zweibon brought a lawsuit on behalf of
JDL against the wiretaps and asked for $782,000 in damages. The government pleaded 'national
security' but the court found for Zweibon and awarded the sum." Yair Kotler, *Heil Kahane*, p.
53.

[11] "Our Dissenters Also Have Rights," *Jewish Week*, July 1, 1971, in RZ Archives, folder 683B.

[12] Marcia Kramer and Lester Abelman, "Cop Who Infiltrated JDL to Testify at Kahane Trial,"
Daily News, July 7, 1971, p. 51, in RZ Archives, folder 62A; Eleanor Blau, "Hearings Opened
for Kahane Trial," *New York Times*, July 7, 1971, p. 75.

[13] "Fair Trials for Jews," [ad] *Jewish Press*, July 16, 1971, p. 14a. The ad was 3 columns wide
and 6 inches high.

Jewish Defense League Newsletter: Flash, August 1, 1971, pp. 1, 2, in RZ Archives, folder
1202.

The names of the lawyers appear in "Deposition of Harvey J. Michelman," June 20, 1973, in
YU Archives, folder 3/1.

[14] Interview with Mal and Yetta Lebowitz, November 13, 1997, Jerusalem.

[15] Eleanor Blau, "Kahane Enters Guilty Plea on One Charge, in a Deal," *New York Times*, July
10, 1971, pp. 1, 24, in RZ Archives, folder 62A.

[16] Emanuel Perlmutter, "Kahane, Facing Jail Term, Vows More Attacks on Russians," *New York
Times*, July 13, 1971, p. 11, in RZ Archives, folder 62A.

[17] "Reflections," *Jewish Press*, July 16, 1971, p. 9, in RZ Archives, folder 594.

[18] "Pack the Courtroom," [ad] *Jewish Press*, July 16, 1971, p. 17. The ad was 2 columns wide
and 8 inches high.

Rabbi Yehoshua Neeman took part in the all-night vigil. Telephone interview with Rabbi
Neeman, August 2, 2001.

See *The 'Zionist Hooligans,'* p. 514 (see chapter 17, note 18).

[19] Dov Hikind, in a public address, February 18, 2003, Jerusalem. More on Hikind, a New York
State Assemblyman, in: http://assembly.state.ny.us/mem.

[20] For the complete text, see: "Preface," *Story of the Jewish Defense League*, pp. ix-x. In the second edition (Jerusalem: 2000), see pp. xv-xvi.

[21] NBC News Archive, media no. 66399, July 23, 1971; Israel Broadcasting Authority Television
Archive, media no. 45985-71-0, July 23, 1971.

[22] Jack B. Weinstein, "Conditions of Probation," countersigned by Meir, July 23, 1971, in RZ
Archives, folder 714B.

23 Opinion: [*689] Memorandum and Order by Judge Weinstein, May 7, 1975. See: LEXIS 12468.

The complete text of Judge Weinstein's decision is in *The 'Zionist Hooligans,'* p. 519-525 (see chapter 17, note 18), and in the Jewish Defense League collection, Center for Jewish History, New York City.

Weinstein wrote that Meir was free to immigrate to Israel with his family.

24 Telegram from George H.W. Bush, U.S. ambassador to the U.N. (1971-1973) to American Embassy, Tel Aviv, and to Secretary of State, Washington, D.C., July 23, 1971, in RZ Archives, Appendix.

George H.W. Bush was U.S. President, 1989-1993. His son, George W. Bush, became U.S. President in 2001.

25 "Kahane Draws Suspended Sentence," *Jewish Press*, July 30, 1971, p. 2.

26 "Nazi Camp Survivor Slain Here," *New York Times*, August 21, 1971, p. 1.

"JDL Begins Patrols: Arming Jews in East Flatbush Area of Brooklyn," *Jewish Press*, September 31, 1971, p. 36; Morris Kaplan, "Kahane Gets 5-Year Suspended Sentence in Bomb Plot," *New York Times,* July 24, 1971, p. 26, in RZ Archives, folder 62A; Marcia Kramer, "Hint Kahane's Remarks Could Imperil Probation," *Daily News,* August 26, 1971, p. 67, in RZ Archives, folder 62A; "Gun Drive Opened by Jewish League," *New York Times,* August 6, 1971, p. 38; Emanual Perlmutter, "Kahane Plans Armed Patrols to Cut Crime in East Flatbush," *New York Times,* August 25, 1971, p. 18; Israel Broadcasting Authority Television Archives, August 5, 1971, media nos. 46648, 46708-71-5.

27 See chapter 29, note 11, pp. 3-4.

The address given for Meir in this report is 1814 East 2nd Street, Brooklyn, which was my parents' address then. Meir prudently did not reveal our home address.

28 Bruce Drake and Martin McLaughlin, "Cheer Kahane at B'klyn Rally," *Daily News*, August 31, 1971, p. 16, in RZ Archives, folder 62A. © New York Daily News, L.P.; reprinted with permission.

29 "A Sad Commentary," [editorial] *Jewish Press*, August 13, 1971, p. 5; "Kahane and *Jewish Press* Tiff on Arming of Jews," *Jewish Post and Opinion*, August 20, 1971, in RZ Archives, folder 62A.

30 "The Wisdom of the Nations," *Jewish Press*, August 13, 1971, p. 28, in RZ Archives, folder 592, reprinted in *Writings 5731*, pp. 121-124, and in *Beyond Words*, 1:214-217.

31 U.S. Secret Service, Los Angeles office file 105-29629-30, intelligence report, March 26, 1971, pp. 2, 3, in RZ Archives, Appendix.

32 See note 28.

33 New York City's Human Resources Administration confirmed that Jews were the third largest poverty group in the city. See: Peter Kihss, "Jewish Poor Seen as Under-Served," *New York Times*, September 14, 1971, p. 45.

34 Jewish Defense League, Second International Annual Convention, [*Minutes*], June 6, 1971, p. 15, 16, in RZ Archives, Appendix. This project is reported in: Jean Herschaft, "Wexler Asked to Destroy Records on JDL Members," *Jewish Post and Opinion*, June 11, 1971, in RZ Archives, folder 62A.

35 "The Rape of the Jew," *Jewish Press*, June 4, 1971, p. 18, 22, reprinted in *Writings 5731*, pp. 100-103.

36 *Council of Oppressed Jewish Neighborhoods,* four-sided quarto flyer, in YU Archives, folder 10/2.

Marcia Kramer, "Says City Neglects Poor Jews," *Daily News,* August 18, 1971, p. 55, in RZ Archives, folder 62A.

[37] "Jewish Defense Sits In to Protest Jewish Poverty; HRA Agrees to Talks," *Jewish Press,* August 27, 1971, p. 20, in RZ Archives, folder 62A.

See also: Dave Sobel, "Young Jewish Activists," *Jewish Press,* September 3, 1971, p. 11. Sobel called the group the Jewish Neighborhood Power Council.

This project led to the formation of the Association of Jewish Anti-Poverty Workers. See: *Story of the Jewish Defense League,* p. 217.

[38] "Kahane, 20 Aides Stage Sit-In at Kennedy's Office," *International Herald Tribune,* August 7-8, 1971, in RZ Archives, folder 62A; "JDL Takes Over Kennedy Offices; Demands Action for Soviet Jews," *Jewish Press,* August 13, 1971, p. 2; "Edward M. Kennedy Facing Off With Rabbi Kahane," [photo caption], www.corbis.com.

[39] "Largest Rally Looms," [ad] *Jewish Press,* September 3, 1971, p. 11.

[40] "Cops Grab 34 in JDL Action," *Daily News,* September 10, 1971, in RZ Archives, folder 62A.

The day before this demonstration, seven JDLers were indicted for planting bombs at the Soviet trade agency, Amtorg, on April 22. See: Morris Kaplan, "7 Members of Jewish Defense League Accused in a Plot to Bomb Soviet Offices," *New York Times,* September 9, 1971, in RZ Archives, folder 62A.

[41] JDL *Bulletin Briefs,* [September 13, 1971], p. 1, in RZ Archives, folder 716B; Association of the Bar of the City of New York, Special Committee on Demonstration Observations, *Report,* October 4, 1971, pp. 1, 4, 5, in YU Archives, folder 6/4.

[42] Dave Sobel, "Young Jewish Activists," *Jewish Press,* September 3, 1971, p. 11; "2 in Jewish Defense League Seized at Soviet Embassy," *New York Times,* September 21, 1971, p. 7; "Taiwan Official Vows 'Fight to the Last' at U.N.," *New York Times,* September 20, 1971, p. 13.

[43] "Time to Go Home," *Jewish Press,* June 26, 1970, p. 22, reprinted in *Writings 5731,* pp. 3-4.

[44] "And One More," *Jewish Press,* April 23, 1971, p. 26, in RZ Archives, folder 592 and YU Archives, folder 10/2, reprinted in *Writings 5731,* p. 98-100. Typescript in RZ Archives, folder 28B.

[45] Irving Spiegel, "Kahane Appears at Zionist Parley," *New York Times,* September 6, 1971, p. 17, in RZ Archives, folder 131.

[46] Ernest E. Barbarash, "News and Views," *Day-Jewish Journal (Der Tog-Morgen Zhurnal),* September 14, 1971, pp. 1, 2, in YU Archives, folder 13/4.

[47] "The Courage to Fear," three parts, *Jewish Press,* September 3, 1971, pp. 15, 36; September 10, 1971, pp. 28, 41; September 17, 1971, p. 18.

[48] "Jew Go Home," [ad] *Jewish Press,* August 20, 1971, p. 15.

JDL held another farewell event on August 18 at the Westbury Music Fair. See note 13, *Flash.*

[49] JDL *Bulletin Briefs* [September 13, 1971], p. 1, in RZ Archives, folder 716B.

[50] NBC News Archive, media no. 68705, September 12, 1971.

Snapshots taken at the airport send-off are in RZ Archives, picture folder nos. 329-330. One is in the photo section of this book.

Three youngsters were arrested late that night, after Meir's departure, for causing a disturbance at the Pan American Airlines counter while the airline was receiving passengers off a flight from Russia. See: "Three in JDL Are Arrested," *Daily News,* September 14, 1971, in RZ Archives, folder 62A. See also: *Story of the Jewish Defense League,* pp. 318-319.

[51] "Jewish Leader Arrives," *Daily News,* September 14, 1971, in RZ Archives, folder 62A.

[52] "Holding a Letter Addressed to the Soviet Ambassador in London..." [photo caption], *Jeru-*

salem Post, September 14, 1971, p. 2. See also: Photo of the demonstration, in RZ Archives, picture folder, no. 434.

Zalmanson's plight is described in Meir's article "One Life." See chapter 25, note 38.

"Kahane Visits London Today," *Jerusalem Post*, September 13, 1971, p. 2.

Many years later, a man who had been in the audience at Hyde Park recalled the lasting impression Meir made on him. Phone interview with Barbara Oberman, November 2, 2003.

[53] National Photo Collection, Israel Government Press Office, picture code D-128099. See: www.mof.gov.il/pictures. Pictures of Meir at Lod airport are in the photo section of this book.

[54] Israel Broadcasting Authority Television Archives, September 14, 1971, media 39919-71-7.

[55] Meir's appointment book shows Baruch's eighth-grade graduation ceremony on June 17 and Tova's on June 21. Baruch was a year younger than Tova, but he had skipped a grade.

[56] In 1967, 1,771 Jews made aliya from the U.S.; 2,275 in 1968; 9,601 in 1969; 11,405 in 1970; and 12,885 in 1971. *Statistical Yearbook of Israel*, 2005, section 4.2.

For Meir's speech before the Zionist Organization of America, see note 45.

[57] This custom is noted in *Zemirot Leshabbat* [*Sabbath Songs*] (Bnei Brak: Am Olam, 2004), p. 22.

Grammatical rules require this word to be transliterated as *aleikhem*. However, the spelling of name of the author Sholom Aleichem has made the "ch" more acceptable in transliterating this word.

[58] The song, *Bilvavi*, is based on a verse in *Sefer Chareidim* by R. Eliezer Azkari (Safed, 16th century). The words and music are by Rabbi Yitzchak Hutner (1906-1980), founder of Mesivta Chaim Berlin. Phone interview with Rebbetzin Bruria Hutner David, April 30, 2007. For the words of the song, see: http://www.usy.org/songs/view_song.php?songID=120.

[59] Rabbi Professor Nachum Rakover recalled Rabbi Kook's request in a conversation with Baruch Kahane, February 2, 1999, Jerusalem.

Phone interview with Rabbi Yaakov Filber, May 17, 1999. The photos are in RZ Archives, picture folder, no. 421-423.

Rabbi Yosef Bramson, another student of Rabbi Kook, maintained that this was one of only two occasions that the rabbi initiated a photograph. Interview with Rabbi Bramson, April 29, 2002, Jerusalem.

Two snapshots taken with Rabbi Kook that day are in the photo section of this book.

[60] "If I Forget Thee, O Jerusalem," *Jewish Press*, October 8, 1971, p. 15, reprinted in *Writings 5732*, p. 3 and in *Beyond Words*, 1:218-220.

Chapter 25

[1] "JDL Opening HQ in Israel...," *Jewish Press*, July 9, 1971, p. 35; "Israel HQ planned for Kahane League," *Daily News*, July 6, 1971, p. 5. Photo of Neil Rothenberg and Yosef Schneider at press conference, in RZ Archives, picture folder, no. 347. Schneider sat in a cage near the White House for a week in March, 1970 (see chapter 16).

[2] "Galut in Israel," *Jewish Press*, July 23, 1971, p. 30, in RZ Archives, folder 592, reprinted in *Writings 5731*, p. 115-117, and in *Beyond Words*, 1:210-213. Meir referred to Amos Kollek, son of Teddy Kollek, mayor of Jerusalem.

[3] Menachem Barash, "Meir Sheli Hu Ben Tov Lehorav – Ulekol Am Yisrael [My Meir is a Good Son to his Parents – and to the Entire Jewish People]," *Yedioth Ahronoth*, August 6, 1971, p. 11, in RZ Archives, folder 69A.

[4]   "Israel News Analysis," *Jewish Press*, October 8, 1971, p. 38, reprinted as "Seeds of Strife" in *Writings 5732*, pp. 6-8.

[5]   Rachel Primor, "Lo Nelamed Po Yeladim Lirot Beneshek... [We Won't Teach Children Here How to Shoot...]," *Ma'ariv*, September 15, 1971, p. 4, in RZ Archives, folder 74B.

[6]   "Kahane Declares If Prisoner Dies, Russians Will, Too," *New York Times*, September 28, 1971, p. 11, in RZ Archives, folder 62A; "Rabbi Kahane Warns Russians...," *Jewish Sentinel* (Chicago), September 30, 1971, in RZ Archives, folder 60C; "Harav Kahana: Shnei Diplomatim Sovyetiyim Yutzu Lahoreg Al Kol Yehudi Sheyipaga Bivrit Hamo'atzot [Rabbi Kahane: Two Soviet Diplomats Will Be Executed for Every Jew Harmed in the USSR]," *Davar*, September 28, 1971, p. 3.

See photo section of this book for a picture of Meir and Avraham Zalmanson at the press conference.

[7]   A snapshot of Meir shaking hands with Rabbi Mordechai Peron is in the photo section of this book.

Meir's meetings with Natan Peled were on October 5 and October 12. Noted in Meir's 1971 appointment book, in RZ Archives, Appendix.

Memo (Hebrew) from Meir Kahane to minister of absorption Natan Peled, October 12, 1971, 2 pp., in RZ Archives, folder 94.

[8]   Her"o [Herzl Rosenblum], "Eineni Terorist Velo Ish Machteret [I Am Neither a Terrorist Nor a Member of an Underground]," *Yedioth Ahronoth*, October 22, 1971, p. 4, in RZ Archives, folder 62A. Excerpted with permission.

[9]   Meir's salary from the *Jewish Press* was about $120 a week. The low cost of living in Israel at that time made it an important part of our income. My salary as a librarian at the National Library in Jerusalem was a useful supplement.

[10]   Letter from Arnold Fine, *Jewish Press* editor, to Meir, November 28, 1973, in RZ Archives, folder 70A.

[11]   This changed with the introduction of fax machines in the late 1980s. Meir would fax his article to the Kach office in Brooklyn and secretary Adele Levy would retype it and personally deliver it to the *Jewish Press*.

[12]   The clippings are now located in the Rabbi Meir Kahane Collection, Archives for Religious Zionism, Bar Ilan University, Ramat Gan (RZ archives).

[13]   "Lansky," *Jewish Press*, October 15, 1971, p. 20, reprinted in *Writings 5732*, p. 10.

The charges against Lansky were not covered by the extradition treaty between Israel and the United States, so there was no question of extraditing him. See: "Non-Returnable Lansky," *Time*, September 25, 1972.

The halakha states: "It is forbidden to hand over a Jew to Gentiles, neither his person nor his property, even if he was a wicked person who committed crimes." *Shulchan Arukh, Choshen Mishpat* 388:5.

[14]   Another explanation: Rabbi Aharon David Borac taught at Brooklyn's Ohel Moshe yeshiva and at Yeshiva University. Meir may have thought of the name without consciously recalling him.

[15]   *Exposing the Haters*, by David Borac, appeared in the *Jewish Press* from October 8, 1971, to Aug. 22, 1975; from September 3, 1976, to the end of 1978; and once in 1980, on April 18. The first few columns had the byline Meir Kahane.

[16]   David Borac (pseudonym of Meir Kahane), "Exposing the Haters," *Jewish Press*, December 3, 1971, p. 14, in RZ Archives, folder 331.

[17]   David Borac (pseudonym of Meir Kahane), "Exposing the Haters," *Jewish Press*, December

31, 1971, p. 10, in RZ Archives, folder 1207. *Thunderbolt* was published by the National States Rights Party, a white supremacist group.

See also: *Exposing the Haters* ([New York:] Jewish Defense League, Education Department, [1970]), 16 pp., in RZ Archives, folder 26.

18 "Hafgana Betel Aviv Neged 'Tokhnit Rogers' [Demonstration in Tel Aviv Against the 'Rogers Plan']," [photo caption] *Yedioth Ahronoth*, October 14, 1971, p. 3, in RZ Archives, folder 74B; NBC News Archive, media no. 0070186, October 14, 1971. A photo of the demonstrators is in the photo section of this book.

DOV is the Hebrew acronym for *Diku'i Bogdim*, freely translated as "Down With Traitors." DOV regarded the leftist Jews who align themselves with Arabs as traitors. For more on DOV's participation in the demonstration, see: http://www.hermon.com/dov/dov.htm.

19 "JDL Head Tours Negev," *Jewish Journal*, October 22, 1971, p. 4, in RZ Archives, folder 60C; "Harav Kahana Bedimona: Im Hakushim To'anim... [Rabbi Kahana in Dimona: If the Black Hebrews Claim God is Black – That's Their Problem]," *Yedioth Ahronoth*, October 14, 1971, p. 24, in RZ Archives, folder 74B.

The group had first emigrated from Chicago to Liberia, but Liberia turned them away. They arrived in Israel as tourists, renounced their U.S. citizenship, and refused to leave. By 2003 their number had grown to 3,000. "Black Hebrews Become Citizens," *Jerusalem Post*, August 29, 2003, p. 6A.

20 NBC News Archive, media no. 0070185, October 14, 1971.

21 "Kahane Detained at Montreal," *New York Times*, October 19, 1971, p. 9. See also: *Story of the Jewish Defense League*, p. 243.

The next day, about 7,500 Canadian Jews marched through downtown Ottawa demanding that Kosygin allow Soviet Jews to emigrate. See: "Canadian Jews March to Press Kosygin on Emigration," *New York Times*, October 20, 1971, p. 3.

Jewish Defense League Newsbulletin Weekly, [October 22, 1971], p. 1, in RZ Archives, folder 716B. At this time, JDL executive offices were still at 440 West 42 Street. The Jewish Identity Center at 4002 New Utrecht Avenue in Brooklyn had opened in March (see chapter 23).

22 "Highlights of Meeting of Joint Executive Board Held October 19, 1971," pp. 2, 3, published as part of *Jewish Defense League Newsbulletin Weekly*, [October 29, 1971], in RZ Archives, folder 1202.

The price of apartments is given at the exchange rate set in August 1971, when the dollar was worth 4.2 lirot.

23 Jewish Defense League, Second International Annual Convention, [*Minutes*], June 6, 1971, p. 12, in RZ Archives, Appendix.

A full-page ad in the *New York Times* cost about $10,000 in 1971, according to Samuel Shoshan, interviewed June 1, 1999, Jerusalem.

24 *Jewish Defense League Newsletter / Flash*, August 1, 1971, p. 2, in RZ Archives, folder 1202.

25 See note 22, "Highlights," p. 1.

26 See note 21, *Jewish Defense League Newsbulletin Weekly*.

27 "You Don't Have to Agree...," [ad] *New York Times Book Review*, December 5, 1971, Section 7, p. 62, in RZ Archives, Appendix.

28 Robert J. Milch, "[Review of] *Never Again! A Program for Jewish Survival*," *Saturday Review*, January 8, 1972, p. 32; Letters to the Editor, February 5, 1972, p. 70, in RZ Archives, folder 62B; reprinted in *Iton* (Jewish Defense League), Purim 5732 [March 1972], p. 4, in RZ Archives, folder 73B. Excerpted with the author's permission.

[29] Sidney J. Jacobs, "The New Jewish Militancy," *Chicago Sun-Times, Showcase*, December 12, 1971, in RZ Archives, folder 62B.

[30] "Kahane Speaking," *Sunday Times Advertiser* (Trenton, N.J.), December 5, 1971, in RZ Archives, folder 62B.

[31] H. Borovik, "Meir Kahane Hot Zich Genumen Tzu Der Pen [Meir Kahane Has Taken Up the Pen]," *Sovetish Heymland*, April 1972; Hyman Lumer, "Kahane's 'Mein Kampf,'" *Daily World*, January 15, 1972, p. M10, both in RZ Archives, folder 62B.

Jim Bishop, review of *Never Again!*, King Features Syndicate, for release on January 7, 1972, in RZ Archives, folder 62B.

Other reviews appeared in the *Herald American and Call-Enterprise*, January 13, 1972, and the *San Antonio Light*, June 25, 1972, in RZ Archives, folder 62B.

[32] In 1971, Nash paid Meir $6,666 in royalties. Source: Meir's 1971 U.S. income tax form 1099, in RZ Archives, Appendix.

The royalty statement for the period ending September 30, 1972, indicates that the final payment of $3,334 was made on February 18, 1972. According to this statement, Nash owed Meir $5,625 for the sale of paperback rights to Pyramid Books. However, because the royalties he had received exceeded the percentage due him on sales, Meir now owed Nash $4,700. JNUL Archives, folder ARC 4=1748.

[33] "The Debate," *Jewish Post and Opinion*, November 19, 1971, p. 5, in RZ Archives, folder 62B.

Letter from Rabbi Samuel Silver to Samuel Shoshan, August 9, 1971, in RZ Archives, Appendix. This confirms the October 28, 1971, date at a $500 fee and mentions the Bridgeport radio station. The radio station's call letters, WSTC, are given in Rabbi Silver's letter to Samuel Shoshan, September 13, 1971, in RZ Archives, Appendix.

Earlier debates with Rabbi Samuel Silver were held on March 7, 1971, (see chapter 23, note 35) and on November 15, 1970, at the Wantagh Jewish Center in New York (see chapter 19.)

[34] Letter from Norwalk Jewish Center to Samuel Shoshan, August 30, 1971, in RZ Archives, Appendix.

[35] "Follow Blacks Lead: Kahane," *Hudson Dispatch* (Union City, N.J.), November 8, 1971, in RZ Archives, folder 62B. Meir spoke in Englewood on November 6.

[36] Meir spoke at Yale on November 9. Other speaking dates during this period: October 31, Bayside, N.Y.; November 1, Albany, N.Y.; November 3, Chicago and Milwaukee. Noted in Meir's 1971 appointment book, in RZ Archives, Appendix.

[37] See note 22, "Highlights," p. 1.

[38] "One Life," *Jewish Press*, November 26, 1971, p. 16, reprinted in *Writings 5732*, p. 20-22, in *Beyond Words*, 1:227-230, and in *Hadar* (Lower Manhattan Chapter, Jewish Defense League), December 1973, p. 1, in RZ Archives, 716B.

[39] "Silva Zalmanson's Address to the Court," flyer, edited by Stella Gelbard, illustrated by Allan Glass, in RZ Archives, Appendix.

[40] David Welcher, "Kahane Rallies Students; Deplores Jewish Apathy," *Ken* (Brooklyn College), November 1, 1971, pp. 1, 6, in RZ Archives, Appendix. Excerpted with permission: The Brooklyn College Library Archive & Special Collections and David Welcher.

[41] *Jewish Defense League Newsbulletin Weekly*, [October 29, 1971], p. 1, in RZ Archives, folder 716B. Among the schools were Queens College, Long Island University, Yeshiva University, and the Yeshiva of Flatbush.

42 Feuer, Michael, "Kahane at Queens College," *Jewish Journal*, November 12, 1971, p. 12, in RZ Archives, folder 60C.

This is a reprint from *Newsbeat* (Queens College), November 2, reporting on Meir's talk "before a crowded lecture room in Remsen Hall." The date of Meir's talk was October 28, 1971. E-mail from Stephen C. Barto, Archivist, Queens College Archives, November 19, 2003. Excerpted with permission of Queens College Provost.

The excerpt refers to a plan to build a housing project in Forest Hills that would serve mostly non-whites. See: "Forest Hills Controversy," *American Jewish Year Book*, 1972, p. 117-119.

43 "Youth Seized in Firing at Soviet Mission," *New York Times*, October 22, 1971, p. 45.

44 "Kahane at LIU," *Jewish Journal*, November 12, 1971, p. 12, in RZ Archives, folder 60C. The article noted that Meir spoke to an audience of 200 and that the usual fee for Meir's personal appearances was $500, but he agreed to speak at LIU for $150.

This is a reprint of an article in the Long Island University student newspaper, *Seawanhaka*, November 4, 1971, p. 3. Meir spoke at the LIU downtown Brooklyn campus on October 28. E-mail from Denise Millman, Coordinator of Reference, Long Island University, September 30, 2003.

45 "Cops Uninvited at the JDL's Block Party," *Daily News*, November 8, 1971, centerfold, in RZ Archives, folder 1203; "75 J.D.L. Members Are Arrested Here," *New York Times*, November 8, 1971, p. 25. A picture taken at the demonstration is in the photo section of this book.

46 "Action Memorandum" from George S. Springsteen, Deputy Assistant Secretary of State for European Affairs, to Acting Secretary of State, December 4, 1971, in U.S. National Archives, file PS 11-3 US; copy in RZ Archives, Appendix.

47 "Kahane Speaks at YU on Behalf of Jewess and Senator Jackson," *Commentator* (Yeshiva University), November 10, 1971, in YU Archives. A photo shows him at this speech on November 4 dressed "Israeli style," tieless, with his open shirt collar folded over his jacket collar. For more on Meir's support for Jackson, see "Israel News Analysis," *Jewish Press*, October 29, 1971, p. 19, reprinted as "Jackson" in *Writings 5732*, pp. 13-15.

48 *Jewish Defense League Newsbulletin Weekly*, [October 22, 1971], p. 1, in RZ Archives, folder 716B. Meir spoke at the Rotary Club on October 20.

49 "Israel News Analysis," *Jewish Press*, October 22, 1971, pp. 11, 43, reprinted in *Writings 5731*, p. 124A.

50 "Prison Protest Movements," *American Jewish Year Book*, 1972, p. 126-127.

51 Letter from Herbert X. Blyden to Meir, October 23, 1971, in YU Archives, folder 6/4.

52 FBI Los Angeles office file 105-29629, report, November 26, 1971, p. 1, in RZ Archives, Appendix.

53 Young Israel: See note 52, FBI, p. 2. The admission fee at this talk was $2.00 per person.

Radio interviews: FBI Los Angeles office file 105-29629, report, November 9, 1971, Tentative Schedule, p. [3], in RZ Archives, Appendix.

Temple Akiba: "Kahane to Arrive in Los Angeles; Busy Speaking Agenda," *B'nai B'rith Messenger*, November 5, 1971, p. 44. This is a list of Meir's appearances in Los Angeles submitted to the newspaper by Jan Okin, JDL's West Coast coordinator.

54 Pierce Junior College: See note 52, FBI, p. 2.

Rabbi Zvi Block, a teacher at Emek Hebrew Academy, took his eighth grade class to Pierce Junior College to hear Meir. He saw it as an important part of their education. Interview with Rabbi Zvi Block, November 18, 2003, Jerusalem.

See note 53, FBI, November 9, 1971.

[55] FBI Los Angeles office file 105-29629, report, November 13, 1971, 3 pp., in RZ Archives, Appendix.

[56] Letter from Bob Manning to Libby, October 27, 2003, in RZ Archives, Appendix.

FBI Los Angeles office file 105-29629, report, November 15, 1971, pp. 1, [3] in RZ Archives, Appendix. Epstein's and Manning's names are blacked out, but their file numbers are not. I identified them through other reports in which both their names and file numbers appear.

[57] Letter from Ian Gardenswartz, president, American Students for Israel, University of Colorado at Denver, to Meir, undated, in RZ Archives, folder 714B. This speaking engagement is confirmed by Tentative Schedule, p. [3], see note 53.

[58] Temple Beth Shalom: See note 52, p. 4. Temple Solael and radio interviews: See note 53, Tentative Schedule, p. [3].

[59] Letter from Rabbi Philip Schroit to David Braverman, February 20, 1987, in RZ Archives, Appendix. It refers to Meir's talk on February 2, 1987, and to the many times Meir had spoken at his synagogue.

[60] Letter from Marsha Wernick to Meir, November 14, 1971, in YU Archives, folder 6/4. Sherman Oaks Manor, where she heard Meir speak, was probably the private home where he spoke Sunday morning, November 14.

[61] "The Jewish Federation sent out letters telling people not to let the Rabbi speak." Letter from Bob Manning to Libby, October 27, 2003, in RZ Archives, Appendix.

[62] "On Majorities," *Jewish Press*, December 3, 1971, p. 30, reprinted in *Writings 5732*, pp. 25-27, and in *Beyond Words*, 1:231-235.

Chapter 26

[1] Meir Kahane, "Zionism, Kahanism, and Racism," *Jewish Press*, March 15, 1985, pp. 14, 24.

[2] Walter Goodman, "Rabbi Kahane Says, I'd Love to See the JDL Fold Up. But," *New York Times*, November 21, 1971, section 6, pp. 32-33,115-116, 118-119, 121-122, in RZ Archives, folder 60A. © The New York Times News Service. Excerpted with permission.

Sonny Carson was a leader of the black group, CORE (Congress on Racial Equality).

Three letters to the editor commenting on this article were subsequently published in the *New York Times* magazine section on December 19, 1971, p. 50.

Demonstration for Silva Zalmanson at the U.N. on October 25, 1971, reported in: *Jewish Defense League Newsbulletin Weekly*, [October 29, 1971], p.1, in RZ Archives, folder 716B. See also: "U.N. Isaiah Wall Mass Rally," flyer, in RZ Archives, folder 403.

One week after Goodman's article, the *New York Times* magazine section had an article about singer Bob Dylan in which Meir was named the inspiration for Dylan's return to Judaism. See: Anthony Scaduto, "Won't You Listen to the Lambs, Bob Dylan?" *New York Times*, November 28, 1971, section vi, pp. 48, 50.

[3] The words "Office of the Reb" were sprayed on the wall by Isaac Jaroslawicz. E-mail from Isaac Jaroslawicz, November 15, 2006.

[4] Cable from U.S. Secretary of State William P. Rogers to U.S. Embassy-Tel Aviv, U.S. Embassy-Moscow, U.S. Mission to the United Nations, November 19, 1971, (Department of State cable number 1971STATE210576), in RZ Archives, Appendix.

[5] "Two-Day Visa for Kahane in Britain," *Jerusalem Post*, November 21, 1971, p. 2.

[6] Phone interview with Barbara Oberman, October 30, 2003.

[7] "Clash Over Protests on Soviet Jewry," *Jewish Chronicle* (London), November 19, 1971, p.

8; "Board of Deputies Condemns Kahane," *Jewish Chronicle* (London), November 26, 1971, p. 7; Photo of Meir speaking at Westminster Hall, November 18, 1971, in RZ Archives, picture folder, no. 434.

8 Phone interviews with Barbara Oberman, October 30, 2003 and November 23, 2006.

Gloria Tessler, "Can 'Jewish Power' Infect British Youth?" *Jewish Chronicle* (London), November 26, 1971, p. 22.

9 E-mail from Sonja Cohen Illouz, August 13, 2006. She moved to Israel in 1979. ".. Your husband certainly changed my life, for which I shall be eternally grateful," she wrote.

10 John L. Hess, "3 Arab Lands Said to Oppress Jews," *New York Times*, January 28, 1970, p. 7; "Young Jewish Escapee Charges Syria With Terror," *New York Times*, November 19, 1971, p. 17; "Jews in Arab and Moslem Countries," *American Jewish Year Book*, 1971, p. 446.

11 "And What of Damascus," *Israel News Analysis*, *Jewish Press*, January 21, 1972, reprinted in *Writings 5732*, pp. 42-44.

12 Eldad, a leader of Lechi, the pre-state military unit, had a weekly column in the popular *Yedioth Ahronoth*, was a professor of Jewish history at the Technion, and appeared often on radio and television as a proponent of right-wing policies. He wrote several books. One in English translation is *The Jewish Revolution* (New York: 1971).

See Eldad's laudatory article, "The Jewish Defense League of Shushan Habira: Thoughts for Purim 1970," *Times of Israel*, March 25, 1970, p. 8-9. (I did not find a Hebrew version among Eldad's columns in *Yedioth Ahronoth*.)

13 "Kahane: Would Act With Violence over Arab Lands Jewry," *Jerusalem Post*, December 3, 1971, p. 12, in RZ Archives, folder 62B; phone interview with Shimon Rachamim, January 27, 2001.

14 Memorandum from Abraham S. Karlikow, American Jewish Committee, Paris Office, to David Geller, American Jewish Committee, New York City, December 17, 1971, in RZ Archives, folder 62B.

FBI file 105-207795, cablegram, December 22, 1971, 3 pp., in RZ Archives, Appendix. The cablegram is addressed to the FBI office in Paris, requesting that information from French publications relating to "subject" be sent to the FBI agent in Tel Aviv.

The report includes the reminder that "New York, Baltimore and Washington field offices were instructed December 14, 1971, to target sources in order to establish subject's current location and to be aware of his activities and location on a day-to-day basis. Because of the extreme sensitivity and high level interest surrounding the investigation of the JDL plot to blow up the Soviet Mission to the United Nations, and the new alleged plot of JDL to launch a sniper attack against the Soviet Embassy within the next few days, we should be constantly aware of subject's location and activities."

In fact, although there was a sniper shooting into the Soviet Mission on October 20, 1971, there was none following this December 1971 warning.

15 Edwin Eytan, "Hasovyetim Vehasurim Kan Yimtze'u Shehachayim Einam Ko Nochim [The Soviets and the Syrians Will Find Life Here Uncomfortable]," *Yedioth Ahronoth*, December 16, 1971, p. 2, in RZ Archives, folder 74B.

Edwin Eytan, "Hateror Hayehudi Yashiv Lateror Ha'antishemi Makhriz Irgun 'Massada' Betzarfat [Jewish Terror Will Answer Anti-Semitic Terror Proclaims the 'Massada' Group in France]," *Yedioth Ahronoth*, October 5, 1972, p. 2.

16 Shmuel Halperin, "Hahakala Bematzav Hayehudim Ba'acharona – Be'ikar Todot Lifulot Harav Kahana [The Recent Alleviation in Conditions for Jews Is Due Mainly to Rabbi Kahane's Actions]," *Ma'ariv*, December 15, 1971, p. 14, in RZ Archives, folder 60C.

[17] This figure is confirmed in "Moscow Is Berated..." See chapter 23, note 1.

[18] "Salvation Is Still to Come," *Israel News Analysis, Jewish Press*, January 14, 1972, p. 43, reprinted in *Writings 5732*, p. 40-42.

[19] W. E. Hall: *A Treatise on International Law*, 6th ed. (London: Oxford, 1909). This was a text-book Meir had used in a course for his masters' degree. See chapter 6.

[20] "Israel News Analysis," *Jewish Press*, December 10, 1971, p. 14, reprinted as "Russian Logic" in *Writings 5732*, pp. 53-55.

[21] Meir's 1971 appointment book, in RZ Archives, Appendix.

[22] "Syrian Delegate Accuses J.D.L. of 'Continuing Its Harassment,'" *New York Times*, December 30, 1971, p. 52, in RZ Archives, folder 62B; FBI file 105-207795, memorandum, January 7, 1972, p. 1, in RZ Archives, Appendix.

Subsequent protests for Syrian and Iraqi Jews included these:

1) January 23, 1972: Rally for Syrian Jews in New York. *Daily News*, January 24, 1972, in RZ Archives, folder 73A. A photo shows mounted police riding into the crowd.

2) January 26, 1972: Protest at Iraqi Embassy in Washington. *Jewish Defense League Newsbulletin Weekly* February 16, 1972, p. 3, in RZ Archives, folder 716B.

3) June 8, 1972: Protest for Iraqi Jews at Red Cross offices in Israel. *Yedioth Ahronoth*, June 9, 1972, p. [4], in RZ Archives, folder 74A.

4) June 22, 1972: Demonstration for Syrian Jews at U.N. headquarters in Jerusalem. *Yedioth Ahronoth*, June 23, 1972, p. 9, in RZ Archives, folder 74B.

5) November 30, 1972: JDL hunger strike in Jerusalem for Iraqi and Syrian Jews. "Bemisgeret Ma'amatzenu [As Part of Our Efforts...]," press release in RZ Archives, folder 96.

[23] "J.D.L. Forms Group to Fight Lindsay's Presidential Bid," *New York Times*, January 4, 1972, p. 23; Thomas P. Ronan, "Jackson to Run in Primary Here," *New York Times*, January 12, 1972, p. 19.

[24] Phone interview with Nat Rosenwasser, November 24, 2003. Miami JDL member Sharon Katz helped Rosenwasser arrange Meir's speaking engagements.

Interview with Sharon Katz Mittman, November 19, 1999, Jerusalem. She sent me clippings of photos of the picketing from the *Hollywood Sun-Tattler*, January 24, 1972, p. 1; *Miami Herald*, February 16, 1972, p. 20a; *Newsweek*, February 28, 1972, p. 67.

Neither Lindsay nor Jackson was nominated. George McGovern was the Democratic candidate, and Republican candidate Richard Nixon was reelected.

Bill Kovach, "Lindsay in Bay State Test..." *New York Times*, January 14, 1972, p. 14.

[25] See chapter 18 for more on *Jewish Defense League: Principles and Philosophies* and the five principles.

["Calendar"], *Kol Jedel*, January 14, [1972], p. 3, in RZ Archives, Appendix. Editors of *Kol Jedel* were Izzy Jaros (Isaac Jaroslawicz) and Alan Rocoff.

[26] Attica demonstration, January 11; Carnegie Hall protest, January 22; Syrian Jewry protest, January 23; demonstration for Jewish poor, January 31. See: note 25, ["Calendar,"], p. 3.

The disruption of the performance of the Osipov Balalaika Orchestra was reported in: "7 Held at Concert After Disruption," *New York Times*, January 27, 1972, p. 30.

Another demonstration to promote the exchange of Silva Zalmanson for Attica prisoners: "J.D.L. Stages a Sit-In at 6 Candidates' Offices," *New York Times*, February 17, 1972, p. 23. See chapter 25 for more on this prisoner exchange.

[27] Letter from Ben Weintraub, youth chairman, JDL Washington, to Irving Calderon, December 8, 1971, in RZ Archives, folder 62B. The protest took place on November 18, 1971.

"Synagogue Is Picketed: Class Sees Superstar," *Jewish Post and Opinion*, December 10, 1971, in RZ Archives, folder 62B.

Protest at Symphony Hall in Newark, December 12, 1971. See: *Newsletter* (Northern New Jersey Council, Jewish Defense League), [December 1971], in RZ Archives, folder 62B.

"Jewish Defense League," *American Jewish Year Book*, 1972, p. 115. The demonstration in Philadelphia was held on December 23, 1971.

28 "Machar – Mishpat Harav Meir Kahana [Tomorrow – Trial of Rabbi Meir Kahane]," *Ha'aretz*, January 9, 1972, p. 2; Letter from Meir to Libby, March 8, 1972, in RZ Archives, Appendix.

See chapter 17 for more about the Tass case.

29 "On Greatness," *Jewish Press*, January 7, 1972, p. 9, reprinted in *Writings 5732*, pp. 37-40, and in *Beyond Words*, 1:253-257.

Meir acted according to his conscience even though he was aware that his life might be in danger. A proposal by KGB official Arkadi Guk to assassinate him is noted in: Christopher Andrew and Oleg Gordievsky, *KGB: The Inside Story of Its Foreign Operations from Lenin to Gorbachev* (New York: Harper Collins, 1990), p. 585.

30 Speaking engagements in January: Temple Adath Yeshurun, Syracuse, January 9, 1972, arranged by Harry Walker lecture agency. Invoice dated January 6, 1972, for plane tickets, New York-Syracuse-New York, in RZ Archives, folder 468.

East Nassau Hebrew Congregation, Syosset, N.Y., January 15, 1972, and Long John Nebel show, December 30, 1971, noted in Meir's appointment book for 1971, in RZ Archives, Appendix. (Entries in Meir's 1972 appointment book begin on January 17.)

Printed invitation to fundraiser at the home of Charles Schreiber, January 12, 1972, in RZ Archives, folder 73B.

Chapter 27

1 "Kahane Demands 3 Congress Seats," *Jerusalem Post*, December 24, 1971, p. 10.

Letter from Meir to the World Zionist Organization, December 19, 1971, in RZ Archives, folder 473. The letter is written on stationery headed Jewish Defense League of Israel, 26 Ben Maimon, P.O.B. 7287, Jerusalem, Israel."

The "shameful Brussels incident" is described in chapter 22.

2 "Kahane 'Will Speak' at Congress," *Jerusalem Post*, December 27, 1971, p. 9; "Haliga Lehagana Yehudit Lo Teyutzag Bakongres [The Jewish Defense League Will Not Be Represented at the Congress]," *Ha'aretz*, January 4, 1972, p. 10, in RZ Archives, folder 74B.

3 See for example: Morris B. Abram, "An Answer to Kahane," *New York Times*, June 2, 1972, p. 37, in RZ Archives, folder 131.

4 "Moment of Truth," *Jewish Press*, January 14, 1972, pp. 22, 23, 27, 30, reprinted as a two-sided quarto flyer for distribution to the Congress delegates, in RZ Archives, folder 1202, reprinted in *Writings 5732-33*, pp. 44-48.

5 Charles Chanover: Meir's 1972 appointment book, January 17, 1972, in RZ Archives, folder 713B.

Noah Kliger, "Harav Kahana Bevo'o Leyisrael: Anaseh Shuv Vashuv Lin'om Bacongres... [Rabbi Kahane Upon His Arrival in Israel: I Will Try Over and Over Again to Speak at the Congress, Until They Arrest Me]," *Yedioth Ahronoth*, January 20, 1972, p. 2, in JNUL Archives, folder ARC 4=1748; Israel Broadcasting Authority Television News Archive, media no.

53379-72-3, January 18, 1972; Peter Grose, "Zionists Divided as Parley Opens," *New York Times*, January 19, 1972, p. 2.

In a 14-minute interview on Israel radio's English program, Meir repeated his belief in an imminent holocaust. A transcript of the interview was sent to the FBI by the U.S. Information Service in Israel. The interview, which is mainly biographical, is dated January 17, 1972. Since Meir flew to Israel only on January 18, the January 17 date is either a typographical error or the interview was taped before he left for Israel. See: FBI file 105-207795, memorandum, January 21, 1972, p. 1, in RZ Archives, Appendix.

6   Menachem Israel, "Israeli News Digest: The Same Old Zionists," *Jewish Press*, February 11, 1972, p. 39, in RZ Archives, folder 73B. Meir's meetings with Begin, Paglin and Cohen noted in his 1972 appointment book, in RZ Archives, folder 713B.

See also: "Harav Kahana Ba Lakongress – Velo Na'am [Rabbi Kahane Came to the Congress – And Did Not Speak]," *Hatzofe*, January 21, 1972, p. 1 (with photo); "Congress Votes Against Hearing Meir Kahane," *Jerusalem Post*, January 21, 1972, p. 3; reprinted in "Highlights of the 28th Zionist Congress in Jerusalem," *Iton* (Jewish Defense League), Purim 5732 [March 1972], p. 5, in RZ Archives, folder 73B; "Barred, Rabbi Kahane Wins Moral Victory," *Jewish Post and Opinion*, January 28, 1972, p. 3, in RZ Archives, folder 73B.

7   Cable no. 0537 [1972TELAVIV501] from U.S. Embassy, Tel Aviv, to Secretary of State, Washington, D.C., January 21, 1972, in RZ Archives, Appendix.

A photo of Meir surrounded by reporters is in the photo section of this book.

See also: Cable number 0481 [STATE010672], from Secretary of State, Washington, D.C., to U.S. Embassy-Tel Aviv, U.S. Embassy-Moscow and U.S. Mission to the United Nations, January 20, 1972, in RZ Archives, Appendix. This reports on Meir's departure for Israel on January 19 and adds: "Department requests full reporting on Kahane's activities while in Israel, including those connected with the 28th World Zionist Congress in Jerusalem."

8   Israel Broadcasting Authority Radio News Archive, media no. 7791, January 20, 1972; Israel Broadcasting Authority Radio News Archive, media no. 7792, January 22, 1972.

The appeal was set for January 24. See: Menachem Barash, "Beit Din Hakongres Yadun Hayom Bitlunat Kahana [The Court of the Congress Will Discuss Kahane's Appeal Today]," *Yedioth Ahronoth*, January 24, 1972, p. 35, in RZ Archives, folder 74A.

9   Mati Golan, "Yahadut Shel Ga'ava [Jewish Pride]," *Ha'aretz*, January 28, 1972, *Musaf* section, pp. 8, 9, 42, in JNUL Archives, folder ARC 4=1748. Copyright © *Ha'aretz* Daily Newspaper Ltd. Excerpted with permission.

10   Noah Kliger, "Harav Kahana Yofi'a Machar... [Rabbi Kahane Will Appear Tomorrow Before the Youth of the Congress; Will Celebrate Son's Bar Mitzvah at the Western Wall]," *Yedioth Ahronoth*, January 23, 1972, p. 34, in RZ Archives, folder 74B; "Kahane Finds Platform to Predict Perils for U.S. Jewry," *Jerusalem Post*, January 23, 1972, p. 9.

Photo of Meir and Baruch at the Western Wall in: *Yedioth Ahronoth*, January 25, 1972, p. 33, in RZ Archives, folder 74A. A different pose is in the photo section of this book. Baruch had started putting on *tefillin* one month earlier.

Meir appealed the decision of the court of the World Zionist Organization to a higher court, the Zionist Congress' Court of Appeals. On February 10, 1972, it issued its decision upholding the lower court's rejection of JDL's application for membership in the American Zionist Federation. See: "Kahane to Protest 'Missionaries' in Zichron Yaakov," *Jerusalem Post*, February 11, 1972, p. 12.

11   Gil Sadan, "Haliga Lehagana Irgena Kongres Tziyoni Biyerushalayim [The Liga Organized a Zionist Congress in Jerusalem]," *Yedioth Ahronoth*, January 25, 1972, p. 35, in RZ Archives, folder 74B. Excerpted with permission.

Israel Broadcasting Authority Radio News Archive, media no. 7794, January 24, 1972; Israel Broadcasting Authority Television News Archive, media no. 53506-72-1, January 24, 1972.

Ad: "Ezrach Yakar! [Dear Citizen!]" Clipping without name of newspaper, without date, in RZ Archives, folder 74B. The ad was 2 inches wide and 4 inches high.

[12] Malka Rabinowitz, "Kahane, Supporters, Meet Press in Capital," *Jerusalem Post*, January 30, 1972, p. 10.

[13] "To Baruch on His Bar Mitzvah," *Jewish Press*, January 28, 1972, p. 21, in RZ Archives, folder 594, reprinted in *Writings 5732-33*, pp. 48-50, and in *Beyond Words*, 1:258-262.

[14] Les Ledbetter, "Fire Bomb Kills Woman, Hurts 13 in Hurok Office," *New York Times*, January 27, 1972, p. 1.

[15] "Kahane Calls It 'Insane' Act," *New York Times*, January 27, 1972, p. 30.

See chapter 29 regarding the arrests.

[16] Meir's 1972 appointment book, in RZ Archives, folder 713B.

[17] Phone interview with Oscar Zimmerman of Kibbutz Bror Chayil, September 11, 2003.

[18] "A Declaration of War Against Judaism," *Jewish Press*, July 13, 1984, p. 23; "McCarthy, Witches, Kahane," *Jewish Press*, August 24, 1984, p. 53.

[19] [Kahane, Meir,] *Jewish Defense League Movement Handbook* (Brooklyn, N. Y.: Jewish Defense League, 1972), 62 pp., 21 cm., in RZ Archives, Appendix. (Added pages: 3A, 39A, 49A, 57A, 57B.)

[20] Letter from Meir to Bennett Levine, undated (from the collection of Bennett Levine), in RZ Archives, Appendix. The letter's content places it in this period.

See *The Jewish Idea*, vol. 1, pp. 684-688, for an exposition on "religio-nation."

[21] [Meir Kahane], *The Jewish Identity Center in Jerusalem, Israel* [Brooklyn, N. Y.: 1972] [12] pp., 21 cm., in RZ Archives, folder 930.

The cover shows a helmeted Israeli soldier, still in full battle gear, his forehead resting on the Western Wall, in prayer.

The Jewish Identity Center was incorporated in 1972. Directors were: Charles Schreiber, Irving Bunim, Reuben Mattus, Nat Maidenbaum, Harry Walker, Alex Friedman, Morris Appleman, Murray Wilson, Chaim Stern, Jerry Kay, Joe Baer, A.B. Joffe and Bernard Deutsch. See: Jewish Identity Center, Certificate of Incorporation, in YU Archives, folder 8/1.

[22] "Israel News Analysis," *Jewish Press*, March 31, 1972, p. 18, reprinted as "Do Not Sin Against the Child," in *Writings 5732-33*

[23] "Jews and Israelis," *Jewish Press*, March 24, 1972, p. 8.

Two books on the issue in Meir's personal library were: Simon N. Herman, *Israelis and Jews; the Continuity of an Identity* (Philadelphia: 1971) and Amos Elon, *The Israelis: Founders and Sons* (New York: 1971).

[24] *Story of the Jewish Defense League*, p. 170. The Zionist Organization ran a similar leadership school in Jerusalem, the *Makhon Le'madrikhei Chutz La'aretz*, for members of Zionist youth groups.

[25] Letter (Hebrew) from Moshe Dayan, minister of defense, to Meir, February 1, 1972, in RZ Archives, Appendix. Thanks to Murray Schneider for a photocopy of the letter.

Meeting with Dayan noted in Meir's 1972 appointment book, in RZ Archives, folder 713B.

Ishur Mosad Tzibburi [Permit for a Pubic Institution] no. 4503545, Yeshiva Torah Ve'Oz – Jewish Identity Center, granted on June 17, 1972, effective February 7, 1972, to March 31, 1974, in RZ Archives, folder 700.

[26] "Leadership Training School Open for Applicants," *Jewish Press*, February 11, 1972, p. 43.

"Jewish Defense League Yeshiva for Jewish Leadership in Israel," mimeographed flyer, in RZ Archives, Appendix. This flyer announced the meetings on February 27 and 28 and named Dov Hikind as contact person.

[27] "In the Shadow of the Cross," *Jewish Press*, March 9, 1962, p. 12, reprinted in *On Jews and Judaism* (Jerusalem: Institute for Publication of the Writings of Rabbi Meir Kahane, 1993), pp. 8-10.

In France – and in Israel – the Pe'ilim organization set up free Jewish schools and persuaded parents to take their children out of the Christian schools.

[28] In July 1972, Emma Berger, planning a school for young children in Nazareth Ilit, offered IL75,000 for a building whose value had been estimated at IL50,000. Opponents to her missionary activities tried to stop her, but the Supreme Court upheld her right to buy the building. See: Yaakov Ardon, "Supreme Court Backs Emma Berger's Right to Zichron Property," *Jerusalem Post*, July 20, 1972, p. 9; "Emma Berger Menassah Lifto'ach Mosad Liyeladim Benatzrat Ilit [Emma Berger Is Trying to Open a Children's Institution in Nazareth Ilit]," *Ma'ariv*, August 28, 1972, p. 11. See Supreme Court decision in the case of Emma Berger v. District Planning Committee in *Piske Din* [*Decisions of the Supreme Court*], 1972, vol. 27, part 2, p. 764.

Tamar Hausman, "Germans in Israel Work to Protect Jews Against Poison-Gas Attack," *Wall Street Journal*, February 7, 1998. According to this article, about 160 members of the sect still lived in Zichron Yaakov and were continuing their missionary activities.

[29] "Kahane to Protest 'Missionaries' in Zichron Yaakov," *Jerusalem Post*, February 11, 1972, p. 12; "Harav Kahana Yafgin Neged Hamisyon Bezichron [Rabbi Kahane Will Demonstrate Against the Mission in Zichron]," *Yedioth Ahronoth*, February 11, 1972, p. 4.

"... laws against missionaries." Letter from Meir to Micha Reiser, chairman of the Knesset House Committee, July 23, 1986, in RZ Archives, folder 579.

[30] "JDL to Demonstrate Against Germans in Zichron Today," *Jerusalem Post*, February 13, 1972, p. 9; Avraham Arnon, "Harav Kahana Lo Ba... [Rabbi Kahane Did Not Come...]," *Yedioth Ahronoth*, February 14, 1972, p. 35, in RZ Archives, folder 74B. At the end of the article: "Noah Kliger reports [on Meir's absence]: Rabbi Kahane had to leave for the U.S. for a court appearance connected with a demonstration at the Soviet Mission two years ago. In a round of speaking engagements he will speak to American Jews about the urgency of aliya." There is a photo of the protesters holding placards.

[31] "Haliga Hifgina Neged Hamisyon... [The Liga Demonstrated Against the Missionaries...]," *She'arim*, May 4, 1972, p. 4, in RZ Archives, folder 74B.

Flyer "Haliga Mazmina Et Hatzibur Lehafgana Neged Pe'ulot Hamisyon... 19 Iyar 5732 [The Liga Invites the Public to a Demonstration Against the Christian Missionaries... May 3, 1972]," in JNUL Archives, folder V1797.

On March 15, 1972, JDL executive secretary Yosef Schneider and two others stood outside a missionary book store in Jaffa holding placards reading, "Danger! These Are Missionaries." When they entered the store and began throwing books out onto the street, they were arrested. See: "J.D.L. Protest Against Jaffa Missionaries," *Jerusalem Post*, March 21, 1972, in RZ Archives, folder 96.

Chapter 28

[1] Craig Aronoff, "The Wit and the Wisdom of Meir Kahane," *Hayom* (Philadelphia Union of Jewish Students), March 15, 1972, pp. 1, 7, in RZ Archives, folder 73A. Includes photos. Reprinted with the permission of Craig Aronoff, Ph.D.

See: Contract between Harry Walker, Inc., and University of Pennsylvania, for March 2, 1972, signed October 4, 1971, in RZ Archives, folder 714B.

Breaking international law: Following katyusha missile attacks on northern settlements that killed three and injured seven, Israeli forces attacked terrorist bases in southern Lebanon. The U.N. censured Israel. See: "Israel Reports Pullout From Lebanon," *New York Times*, February 29, 1972, p. 3.

[2] Speaking engagements at colleges in February: Columbia University, February 23; Yeshiva University, February 24 and March 20; Brooklyn College, February 25; City College, February 28; Queens College and the State University at Stonybrook, N.Y., February 29; University of Arizona at Tucson, March 16. Noted in Meir's 1972 appointment book, in RZ Archives, folder 713b.

For a report on Meir's talk at Brooklyn College, see: Ezra Ogarek, "Kahane Wants to Send 50,000 Jews to Israel," *Jewish Journal*, February 25, 1972, p. 4, in RZ Archives, folder 73A. A week later the *Jewish Journal* carried an ad for the leadership school headed "A Jewish Leader Is Made, Not Born," *Jewish Journal*, March 3, 1972, p. 7, in RZ Archives, folder 73A.

[3] Vincent O'Brien, "A Bitter Day of Extremes at Hofstra," *Long Island Press*, February 23, 1972, pp. 1, 3, in RZ Archives, folder 73A.

[4] Charles E. Kinzie, "Swastika at Hofstra," *Midstream*, May 1972, pp. 21-26, in RZ Archives, folder 73B; "Kahane Visits Post and Hofstra," *Pioneer* (Long Island University, C.W.Post Campus), February 24, 1972, p. 1, in RZ Archives, Appendix. See also note 3, *Long Island Press*. A photo in the *Long Island Press* shows students giving Meir a standing ovation.

Earlier that month, when William Pearce, former editor of the neo-Nazi newspaper *White Power*, spoke at George Washington University, he was barraged with eggs and a stink bomb by JDLers. "Nazi Assailed by Eggs, Stink Bomb," *Hatchet*, February 7, 1972, reproduced in *Iton*, Purim 5732, in RZ Archives, folder 73B.

[5] "Israel News Analysis," *Jewish Press*, March 24, 1972, p. 46.

[6] See note 4, *Pioneer*.

[7] Irving Spiegel, "Study Finds Rise in Anti-Semitism," *New York Times*, November 20, 1972, p. 11.

[8] Jim Remsen, "Rabbi Kahane's Aliyah Pitch – 'It Is Happening Here – Now,'" *Jewish Exponent* (Philadelphia), March 10, 1972, pp. 1, 103, in RZ Archives, Appendix. Excerpted with permission.

Quoted verbatim in: Irving J. Rosenbaum, "Rabbi At Random: Rabbi Meir Kahane – Is He Really 'A Jewish Dick Gregory – George Wallace – Billy Graham'?" *Jewish Sentinel* (Chicago), March 30, 1972, in RZ Archives, folder 73B.

[9] Letter from Meir to Libby, February 28, 1972, in RZ Archives, Appendix.

[10] Meir began to work with the Harry Walker lecture agency in August 1971. Walker demanded high fees for Meir's talks, fees which went directly to the JDL. (The University of Pennsylvania, $1,000; Temple B'nai Abraham, $500; Midway Jewish Center, $1,000; Temple Beth El, $1,000.) Walker probably received 30% of the fee, the usual commission on speakers' fees. See: www.writersmarket.com. Meir and Walker parted ways in July 1972 (see chapter 29).

Speaking dates arranged by Harry Walker: March 5, Temple B'nai Abraham, Beverly, Mass.; March 8, Midway Jewish Center, Syosset, N.Y.; March 12, Temple Beth El, Gary, Indiana. See contracts in RZ Archives, folder 714B.

Speaking dates listed in Meir's 1972 appointment book, in RZ Archives, folder 713B: March 1, Norman, Oklahoma; March 5, King David Hotel, Long Beach, N. Y.; March 14, Houston, Texas; March 16, Tucson Jewish Community Center.

[11] See note 8, *Jewish Sentinel*. Rabbi Irving J. Rosenbaum's report on Meir's speech in Philadelphia included a description of his talk in Des Plaines on March 13, 1972.

[12] Leslie Taylor, "Jeers Interrupt Jewish Speaker," *Austin American*, March 16, 1972, p. A-2, in RZ Archives, Appendix. Copyright 1972 *Austin American-Statesman*; excerpted with permission.

A snapshot of Meir arriving via Texas International Airlines to speak at the University of Texas at Austin is in the photo section of this book.

[13] Dotty Jacobus, "Kahane Draws Catcalls, Cheers," *Daily Texan* (University of Texas at Austin), March 16, 1972, p. 1, in RZ Archives, folder 73A. Includes photos of Meir and students arguing.

[14] Avi Reich, "[Rabbi Kahane Comes to the Campus]," *Bit'on Irgun Hastudentim Vehamishtalmim Hayisra'elim Be'arhab Vecanada* [*Newsletter, Organization of Israeli Students Studying in the United States and Canada*], no. 8, June 1972, p. 9, in RZ Archives, folder 73B.

[15] E-mail from Michael Abramowitz, January 27, 2000.

Meir arrived at Houston Airport on March 14. He was met by Michael Abramowitz, Ed Fagan and Dr. David Cotlar and made the three-hour drive to Austin with them. He spent the night in Michael and Ed's dorm room at Hebrew House and spoke at the university the next day. E-mail from Michael Abramowitz, December 10, 2006.

[16] Lynn Ketchum, "Militant Rabbi Warns Against 2nd Germany," *Arizona Daily Wildcat*, March 17, 1972, pp. 1, 3. The talk, which took place on March 15 at Arizona State University, was announced in another university newspaper, the *State Press*, on March 15, 1972. Both clippings in RZ Archives, Appendix.

[17] "Here Is the Week in Review... [datelined] London, March 15, 1972," in *Jewish Defense League Newsbulletin*, March 22, 1972, p. 1, in RZ Archives, folder 716B.

[18] "Raiza Palatnik," *Jewish Press*, March 3, 1972, pp. 15, 22, in RZ Archives, folder 594, reprinted in *Beyond Words*, 1:267-271.

[19] "JDL Leader Is Refused Soviet Visa," *Washington Post*, March 7, 1972, pp. 1, A17, in RZ Archives, folder 73A; "Kahane Trying to Go to Moscow," Jewish Telegraphic Agency report. Clipping from unidentified newspaper (perhaps *Jewish Journal*), hand-dated March 10, 1972, in RZ Archives, folder 73A.

[20] Letter from William Perl to Libby, February 26, 1998, in RZ Archives, Appendix.

Meir's application for a visa to the USSR, with photo, in RZ Archives, folder 73A.

Bert Zweibon, Sam Shoshan, and Irving Calderon were among those who accompanied Meir. See: *Iton* (Jewish Defense League), Passover 5732 [April 1972], p. 8, in RZ Archives, folder 1202.

[21] See note 19.

[22] Letter from Meir to the children, March 8, 1972, in RZ Archives, Appendix.

[23] Julius Gottesman, "In Defense of the J.D.L.," [op-ed] *New York Times*, March 25, 1972, p. 31, in RZ Archives, folder 73A.

[24] Meir's 1972 appointment book, in RZ Archives, folder 713B. Other speaking engagements for this period: March 18, Shabbat, Young Israel of Ocean Parkway; Saturday night, Mount Sinai Jewish Center, Manhattan; March 19, North American Jewish Youth Council, Pittsburgh; March 20, Yeshiva University at 6 P.M. and JDL Brighton chapter 8:30 P.M.; March 21, Belle Harbor Jewish Center.

[25] Irving Spiegel, "Shanker Boycotts Teachers Luncheon Featuring Kahane," *New York Times*, March 20, 1972, p. 48, in RZ Archives, folder 683A; "Award to Golda Meir Nixed by Kahane Talk," *Jewish Post and Opinion*, March 24, 1972, p. 1. Albert Shanker was president of the

United Federation of Teachers (a labor union), the New York City affiliate of the American Federation of Teachers.

[26] Stanley Marlin, "Letter to the Editor," *United Teacher*, April 9, 1972, in RZ Archives, Appendix. Excerpted with permission. Marlin wrote, "Rabbi Kahane was a great inspiration to me." Letter from Stanley Marlin to Libby, June 8, 2006.

[27] Letter from Meir to Libby, February 28, 1972, in RZ Archives, Appendix.

[28] Interview with Rabbi Nachman Kahane, October 16, 1999, Jerusalem. The owner of the property was a religious trust, Ne'emanei Hekdesh Sima Belilius, whose officers had to approve any transfer of key-money rights. Nachman had earlier signed a separate agreement with the officers that did not involve any payment.

Meir purchased the key-money rights from Yitzchak Bivas, in March 1972. The purchase contract is not in Meir's files, but he sold the rights back to Bivas in October 1972 and that contract is on file. The purchase price was probably close to the sale price, which was 100,000 lirot ($23,809). See chapter 31, note 54.

[29] Meir was in Israel from March 23 to April 27, according to dates stamped in his passport.

Meir's 1972 appointment book, in RZ Archives, folder 713B: April 24, Chorev High School, Jerusalem; April 18, Bar Ilan Yeshiva High School, Tel Aviv. See also: Letter of thanks from the head of the Bar Ilan Yeshiva to Meir, April 20, 1972, in RZ Archives, Appendix.

Tel Aviv Bar Association, April 21. See: Yair Amikam, "Hametichut Hagiz'anit Be'artzot Habrit Mesakenet Et Shlom Hayehudim [Racial Tensions in the U.S. Endanger Jews' Welfare]," *Yedioth Ahronoth*, April 23, 1972, p. 15, in JNUL Archives, folder ARC 4=1748.

Meir Kahane, "Yehudei Arhab Al Chavit Avak Serefa [The Jews in the United States Are Sitting on a Powder Keg]," *Yedioth Ahronoth*, April 28, 1972, in RZ Archives, folder 73B.

This is very similar to Meir's op-ed article, "A Call for Mass Emigration to Israel," *New York Times*, May 26, 1972, p. 35, in RZ Archives, folder 607. See abstract in chapter 29.

[30] Letter from Meir to Sam Shoshan, April 2, 1972, in RZ Archives, Appendix.

[31] "Jew Go Home," [ad] *New York Times*, April 24, 1972, p. 44, in RZ Archives, folder 131. The ad, four columns wide and about eight inches high, was placed at the page's outer margin.

At the bottom of the ad were coupons: a membership application, an application to attend the conference (the fee was $5 but "Students need not pay") and a request for a donation to cover the expense of the ad.

The ad was signed "Office of Aliyah Alert," 4002 New Utrecht Avenue, Brooklyn, New York. The name, Aliyah Alert, was used as early as August 27, 1971, when a letter about Meir's farewell aliya party on September 12 was sent to members. See: Letter from Sol Taubenfeld, Chairman of Aliyah Alert, to JDL members [September 1971], in RZ Archives, folder 60C.

[32] Interview with Sam Shoshan, June 1, 1999, Jerusalem.

[33] *Daniel* 5:28 describes the mysterious handwriting on the wall to warn the king of Babylonia, and gives the meaning of each word: Mene: God has numbered your kingdom, and finished it. Tekel: You have been weighed in the balance and found wanting. Pharsin: Your kingdom has been divided and given to the Medes and Persians.

The text of the flyer was slightly different from the text of the ad. Another version of this flyer had the same Hebrew heading and graphic image but the closely-printed text covered four quarto pages. Instead of Aliyah Alert it was signed Habayta-Return, 1133 Broadway, New York City and was inserted as pages 5-8 in *Iton* (Jewish Defense League), Lag Ba'omer 5732 [May 1972], in RZ Archives, folder 1202.

Habayta-Return was founded at the Aliya Conference on May 7, 1972. See: "Aliyah: Yes or No," *Jewish Journal* (Brooklyn), May 11, 1972, p. 1, in RZ Archives, folder 73A.

Application for the incorporation of Habayta, June 6, 1972, in YU Archives, folder 6/4. This gives the address of Habayta as 1133 Broadway and lists the officers: Eli Schwartz, Sheila Lidz, Neil Rothenberg, Fay Lloyd and Meir Kahane. The address of JDL's Brooklyn headquarters, 4002 New Utrecht Avenue, is given as Meir's home address.

Chapter 29

[1]   "Kahane Talk Here Sunday Under Fire," *Washington Post*, April 29, 1972, p. E11. Noted in Meir's 1972 appointment book, in RZ Archives, folder 713B.

The ad calling for aliya, "Jew Go Home," appeared on April 24, 1972. See chapter 28.

E-mail from Rabbi Mitchell Wohlberg, October 25, 2006.

[2]   Sidney Schaffer, "Rabbi Meir Kahane Visits West Hempstead," *Newsletter* (Young Israel of West Hempstead), May 1972, in RZ Archives, Appendix. Meir's visit was May 5-6.

Rabbi Shalom Gold was rabbi of the Young Israel of West Hempstead from 1972 to 1983, when he moved to Israel.

[3]   Jean Crafton, "Kahane Asks U.S. Jews to Go to Israel," *Daily News*, May 8, 1972, p. 40, in RZ Archives, folder 683A. © New York Daily News, L.P.; reprinted with permission.

Moshe Amirav spoke on "Israel Today," James Rapp on "Weimar Germany vs. America 1972," and Eli Schwartz on "Anti-Semitism: Sources and Literature." *Program* [Aliya Conference], May 7, 1972, in RZ Archives, folder 131.

[4]   George Dugan, "Jewish Congress Keeps Kahane Out," *New York Times*, May 12, 1972, p. 9.

An article that sided with Meir against the American Jewish Congress was: Yossi Klein, "The AJCongress or Kahane, Which Should Be Expelled?" *Jewish Post and Opinion*, May 26, 1972, pp. 9, 10, in RZ Archives, folder 73A.

[5]   Meir Kahane, "A Call for Mass Emigration to Israel," [op-ed] *New York Times*, May 26, 1972, p. 35, in RZ Archives, folder 73B.

[6]   "Israel – State of," *New York Times Index*, 1972, p. 1047.

[7]   Morris B. Abram, see chapter 27, note 3. Folder 131 has similar letters which appeared in Anglo-Jewish newspapers.

[8]   Harry Golden, "Letter to the Editor," *New York Times*, June 12, 1972, p. 34.

[9]   Irving Spiegel, "Jewish Leaders Score 'Alarmists,'" *New York Times*, July 1, 1972, p. 24. The council, a coalition of national and local Jewish organizations and federations, issued the statement at its Plenary Session, June 30, 1972.

[10] Robert E. Segal, "New Guides for Perplexed," *American Jewish World*, June 30, 1972, p. 3, in RZ Archives, folder 131. Excerpted with the publisher's permission.

[11] *Report on Violation of Probation*, submitted March 21, 1972, to Honorable Jack B. Weinstein, U.S. District Court Judge, Eastern District, by James F. Haran, Chief U.S. Probation Officer, prepared by Irving Gold, in RZ Archives, folder 714B. See also: "Government Moves to Jail Rabbi Kahane," *Jewish Press*, March 31, 1972, p. 3.

[12] Letter from John N. Irwin, Acting Secretary of State, to John B. Connally, Secretary of the Treasury, December 14, 1971, in U.S. National Archives, file PS 11-3 US; copy in RZ Archives, Appendix. See response from Connally, note 23.

[13] Judge Jack B. Weinstein, Order 71 CR 479, May 15, 1972, in RZ Archives, folder 73A. See also: "Kahane Is Warned on Advocating Guns," *New York Times*, May 3, 1972, p. 18.

"... trying to muzzle me..." quoted in: Cable from Ambassador George H.W. Bush to U.S. Embassy, Tel Aviv, stamped May 4, 1972, in RZ Archives, Appendix.

[14] Documentation on indictment and May 30, 1972, sentence in JNUL Archives, folder ARC 4=1748.

[15] "Rabbi Kahane of JDL to Speak in Brookline," *Jewish Advocate*, May 4, 1972, p. 3. "Rabbi Kahane will speak to students at the Boston University Hillel House..." Meir's appointment book shows him at Boston University on May 10 and again on May 14. The May 14 trip is listed as an expense of the leadership school, indicating that he returned for a follow-up meeting with potential students. List of expenses in RZ Archives, folder 694.

[16] Meir spoke at the University of Rochester on May 8, 1972. See: Rhonda Ores, "Kahane Returns: Highlights of '72," *Connection – Kesher* (University of Rochester Jewish Student Magazine), Fall 1984, p. 5, in RZ Archives, folder 187A; Meir's 1972 appointment book, RZ Archives, folder 713B.

[17] May 12, Young Israel of Kew Gardens; May 13 and June 4, Young Israel of Hillcrest. Noted in Meir's 1972 appointment book, in RZ Archives, folder 713B.

May 9: Young Israel of Brookline, near Boston. This was his fourth talk at the congregation since November 1969. See "Rabbi Kahane of JDL to Speak in Brookline," *Jewish Advocate*, May 4, 1972, p. 3.

Speaking dates at the end of May on the East Coast: May 26-27, Brunswick Hotel, Lakewood, New Jersey. See: FBI Los Angeles office, file 105-29629-79, cable, May 16, 1972, pp. 1-2, in RZ Archives, Appendix.

May 28, Pioneer Hotel, Greenfield Park, N.Y. Noted in Meir's 1972 appointment book, in RZ Archives, folder 713B.

[18] See note 17, FBI.

[19] FBI Los Angeles office file 105-29629-81, memorandum, May 18, 1972, p. 1, in RZ Archives, Appendix. The report notes that Epstein drove a Cadillac.

[20] FBI Los Angeles office file 105-29629-82, memorandum, May 22, 1972, p. 1, in RZ Archives, Appendix. Information on three Los Angeles students at the leadership school in e-mail from David Fisch, September 22, 2000.

Photocopies of a letter from Barbara Javor to Meir, May 26, 1972, and the check stub of an honorarium of $250 from the Associated Students, May 26, 1972, are attached to FBI Los Angeles office file 105-29629-85, report, June 27, 1972, 3 pp., in RZ Archives, Appendix.

[21] FBI Los Angeles office file 105-29629-84, report, June 9, 1972, 2 pp., in RZ Archives, Appendix.

Rambam: FBI Los Angeles office file 105-29629-83, report, June 9, 1972, 3 pp., in RZ Archives, Appendix.

House parties: FBI Los Angeles office file 105-29629-80, teletype report, May 17, 1972, pp. 1-3, in RZ Archives, Appendix.

[22] *Iton* (Jewish Defense League), Passover 5732 [April 1972], p. 7, in RZ Archives, folder 1202.

[23] Letter ("Confidential") from John B. Connally, Secretary of the Treasury, to William P. Rogers, Secretary of State, January 15, 1972, in U.S. National Archives, file PS 11-3 US. Copy in RZ Archives, Appendix. The firearms division was part of the Treasury Department's Alcohol, Tobacco and Firearms Division.

[24] "Bush Cancels Out of TV Appearance With Rabbi Kahane," *Cleveland Jewish News*, June 2, 1972, p. 2, in RZ Archives, folder 73B; John T. McQuiston, "Kahane Protest Delays a Taping," *New York Times*, May 26, 1972, p. 71. Meir was to have appeared on the Cavett Show on May 25.

[25] Jerry D. Barach, "An Editor's Notes," *Cleveland Jewish News*, June 2, 1972, p. 14, in RZ Archives, folder 73B.

[26] Letter from Clarence Mann to Meir, June 12, 1972, in RZ Archives, folder 713A.

[27] Bracha Hollander, "300 Jewish Student Activists Gather at Network Convention," *Jewish Free Press*, October 1972, pp. 1, 7, in RZ Archives, folder 73B. A photo on page one shows Meir surrounded by students. This was the second annual network convention, June 8-12, 1972.

See also: "Israel News Analysis," *Jewish Press*, June 23, 1972, p. 26, in RZ Archives, folder 594. Meir wrote that leftist students had gained control of the World Union of Jewish Students, which received large sums from Jewish sources. He urged his readers to write letters of protest to the Jewish Agency, the World Jewish Congress and their local Jewish Federation demanding that they cease funding the Union and Network. For example, he wrote, a petition was circulated at the Network convention demanding that Israel cease its policy of colonization – civilian settlement – in the Gaza Strip and the West Bank, because it is "extremely prejudicial for peace in the Middle East..."

[28] "3 in J.D.L. Plead Not Guilty in Bombing at Hurok Office," *New York Times*, June 21, 1972, p. 27. Bail of $35,000 each was set by Judge Arnold Bauman.

[29] "Israel News Analysis," *Jewish Press*, July 7, 1972, p. 17, reprinted as "Who Is Not a Jew," in *Writings 5732*, pp. 90-92.

[30] Letter from Sheldon Davis to Libby, July 21, 1997, in RZ Archives, Appendix.

Meir had been in the U.S. since April 28. He remained until June 22 in order to raise bail for the young men.

[31] Arnold H. Lubasch, "Two in JDL Cleared in Hurok Bombing After Witnesses Balk," *New York Times*, June 28, 1973, pp. 1, 80, in RZ Archives, folder 733.

See chapter 43, concerning two of the prosecution's essential witnesses, Richard Huss and Jeffrey Smilow, who refused to testify against the accused for religious reasons.

Sheldon Siegel, who was also called as a prosecution witness, won the right not to testify because the government had used illegal wiretaps to gain information. His attorney was Alan Dershowitz.

Legal briefs dealing with the government's 1975 decision to cease prosecution of the case (*nolle prosequi*) are in YU Archives, folder 2/1. Other briefs on the Hurok case are in YU Archives, folders 2/2 and 2/3.

[32] Interview with Hy Bieber, June 30, 1998, Brooklyn, N.Y.

See also chapter 24 ("He had taught them the basics...") and chapter 26 ("Brooklyn headquarters at 4002 New Utrecht Avenue...") for examples of JDLers' independence.

See: The '*Zionist Hooligans*,' p. 657 (see chapter 17, note 18).

[33] E-mail from Samson Levine, November 22, 1999.

Charged with conspiracy and bomb possession, Levine spent a year in prison. See: David A. Andelman, "Anti-Soviet Bomb Plot Is Laid to 4 on L.I.," *New York Times*, May 25, 1972, pp. 1, 16; "4 Held in Bomb Work at [Lido Beach] Jewish Center," *Newsday*, May 24, 1972. See also Levine's "Jewish and in Prison," *Jewish Press*, March 2, 1973, p. 37.

[34] Interview with Alan Rocoff, June 11, 1999, Jerusalem.

[35] Walter Ruby, "The Role of Nonestablishment Groups," *A Second Exodus: The American Movement To Free Soviet Jews*, edited by Albert D. Chernin and Murray Friedman (Hanover, N.H.: Brandeis University Press, 1999), p. 207-208.

[36] "Israel News Analysis: Eretz Yisrael," *Jewish Press*, June 30, 1972, pp. 26, 30, reprinted in *Writings 5732*, pp. 85-87, and in *Beyond Words*, 1:297-300.

[37] "Israel News Analysis," *Jewish Press*, June 9, 1972, pp. 47, 49; reprinted as "Lessons of Lydda," in *Writings 5732*, pp. 79-80.

"25 Die at Israeli Airport As 3 Gunmen from Plane Fire on 250 in a Terminal," *New York*

Times, May 31, 1972, p. 1; "Lod Death Toll Reaches 26 Dead," *Jewish Post and Opinion*, June 9, 1972, p. 3.

Because the Japanese had been trained at a P.L.O. camp in Lebanon, Meir led a demonstration of JDLers at the Lebanese U.N. Mission in Manhattan. This quick response against the country hosting the terrorists was also broadcast on Israel TV. Israel Broadcasting Authority Radio News Archive, media no. 64650-72-4, May 31, 1972.

[38] Meir Kahane, *Time to Go Home* (Los Angeles: Nash Publishing, 1972), 287 pp. ISBN 0840213069.

[39] Letter from Harry Walker to Meir, July 3, 1972, in JNUL Archives, folder ARC 4=1748.

The letter bore the address that we used before our street was named: It was simply Kiryat Itri, Entrance 4, Jerusalem, Israel.

Meir's June 19, 1972, meeting with Walker is noted in his 1972 appointment book, in RZ Archives, folder 713B.

[40] Letter from Edward L. Nash to Harry Walker, with a copy to Meir, June 27, 1972, in JNUL Archives, folder ARC 4=1748.

[41] "I just received your wire and have already mailed the manuscript to Nash..." Letter from Harry Walker to Meir, July 12, 1972, in JNUL Archives, folder ARC 4=1748.

[42] Letter from Harry Walker to Meir, July 19, 1972, in JNUL Archives, folder ARC 4=1748.

[43] Meir Kahane, "Foreword," in Menachem Begin, *The Revolt* (Los Angeles: Nash Publishing, 1972), pp. [i-iv]. Foreword dated January 1972. Typescript of the foreword and copy of book jacket in RZ Archives, Appendix.

Other editions of *The Revolt* in English were published in 1951, 1964, 1977, and 2002. In 1977, following Begin's election victory, the Nash edition was reprinted – without Meir's introduction.

The Revolt was recommended reading for JDLers. See JDL's "Jewish Liberation Reading List," in RZ Archives, folder 986. It was advertised by JDL as one of "Three Great Books by Three Great Jewish Leaders: *The Revolt* by Menachem Begin, *The Jewish Revolution* by Israel Eldad, *Never Again* by Rabbi Meir Kahane." See: "Three Great Books," [ad] *Jewish Press*, May 9, 1975, p. 31.

[44] Letter from Edward L. Nash to Meir, July 17, 1972. Nash mailed this letter to Meir's parents' former address, 254 Quentin Road, Brooklyn, N.Y.

[45] Letter from Edward Nash to Meir, August 10, 1972, addressed to the Jewish Identity Center Leadership School, 10 Dorot Rishonim Street, Jerusalem, in JNUL Archives, folder ARC 4=1748.

[46] Letter from Edward Nash to Meir, October 24, 1972, in JNUL Archives, folder ARC 4=1748. This was addressed to our home at 13 Sorotzkin Street, Jerusalem. By this date, our street had a name!

[47] Letter from Edward Nash to Meir, November 27, 1972, in JNUL Archives, folder ARC 4=1748.

[48] Letter from Edward Nash to Harry Walker, December 1, 1972, in JNUL Archives, folder ARC 4=1748.

[49] See chapter 31. Meir's passport was confiscated by the Israeli police on October 1, 1972.

[50] Letter from Edward Nash to Meir, December 8, 1972, in JNUL Archives, folder ARC 4=1748.

[51] Letter from Contracts Manager [signature illegible], Nash Publishing, to Meir, February 2, 1973, with Meir's handwritten note at the bottom, dated February 11, 1973, in JNUL Archives, folder ARC 4=1748. Meir sent the original and kept a photocopy.

[52] Check stub, $2,000 for "royalties on account," March 6, 1973, in RZ Archives, folder 478.

[53] Letter from Sherry Gottlieb, Credit Manager, Nash Publishing, to Meir, March 27, 1973, with Meir's handwritten reply at the bottom, in JNUL Archives, folder ARC 4=1748. Meir sent the original and kept a photocopy.

[54] Letter from Meir to Steve Smason, May 2, 1973, in JNUL Archives, folder ARC 4=1748.

[55] Photocopies, front and back, of check no. 4404, $3,623.21, May 8, 1973, in JNUL Archives, folder ARC 4=1748. Meir was in jail from June 3, 1973, to July 6, 1973. See chapter 33.

[56] Letter from Meir to Nash Publishing, July 6, 1973.

Nash offered 3,000 copies at $1.25 each. See: Letter from R.A. Miller, Chief Accountant, Nash Publishing, Freeport, N.Y., to Shifra Hoffman, September 9, 1973. Both letters in JNUL Archives, folder ARC 4=1748.

[57] Phone interview with Rabbi Kenny Cohen, September 24, 1997.

Nash did not find a paperback publisher for *Time to Go Home*. In 1975 Meir raised the money to reprint it in softcover. See chapter 45.

[58] Reuben E. Gross, "It Can Happen Here? [*sic*]" *Jewish Life*, July 1973, pp. 51, 53, in RZ Archives, folder 131, reprinted in *Jewish News* (New Jersey), July 5, 1973, in RZ Archives, folder 985.

[59] Roy Larson, "The Hand Writes on the Wall," *Chicago Sun-Times*, April 29, 1973, section 3, p. 17, in RZ Archives, folder 714B. Book reviews stamped "Luce Press Clippings" were probably sent to Meir by Nash Publishing.

Chapter 30

[1] David Fisch, who was in the program that summer, wrote that there were "approximately 25 students... 20 fellows and five women... three guys from Los Angeles. The rest were mostly from New York." E-mail from David Fisch, September 22, 2000.

[2] Phone interview with Avraham Hershkowitz, July 7, 1997.

[3] Meir met with lecturers Joseph Nedava and Dov Shilansky on July 7, 1972. Noted in Meir's 1972 appointment book, in RZ Archives, folder 713B.

See chapter 26, note 12, for Dr. Israel Eldad's biography.

Dr. Joseph Nedava, a well-known historian, authored over 100 Hebrew books. Two in English translation are: *Trotsky and the Jews* (Philadelphia: Jewish Publication Society, 1972) and *Vladimir Jabotinsky: The Man and His Struggles* (Tel Aviv: Jabotinsky Institute, 1986).

Dov Shilansky, a Holocaust survivor, was active in the Irgun in Europe. He was a member of Knesset (Likud) from 1977 to 1992 and its Speaker from 1988 to 1992. His books are listed in: www.knesset.gov.il.

Shmuel Tamir served as a member of Knesset (various parties) from 1965 to 1980 and as minister of justice, 1977-1980.

Amichai Paglin, see: http://www.us-israel.org/jsource/biography/Paglin.html.

David Niv wrote several books in Hebrew; some were translated into English.

Aharon Pick was an expert on the history and geography of Israel. He was director of the Geographical Biblical Study Center in Tekoa (Judea). See: Aaron Pick, *Geographical Biblical Study Center* [brochure], November 1981, in RZ Archives, folder 385.

[4] This creative JDL activity is described in chapter 41.

[5] Many of the photocopied texts used as course materials are in RZ Archives, folder 48B.

[6] E-mail from Seymour Lecker, February 10, 2000.

[7] Transcript of lecture [mimeographed], July 13, 1972, in RZ Archives, folder 48A.

Doreinu was published by the Baltimore-Washington Union of Jewish Students. The January 1971 issue has a letter to the editor referring to Waskow's letter in the December 1970 issue. I did not see the 1970 issues because the JNUL's holdings of *Doreinu* start with 1971.

[8] Transcript of lecture, "Jewish Basics" [mimeographed], July 13, 1972, pp. 11-13, in RZ Archives, folder 403.

[9] E-mail from David Fisch, July 8, 1997. Another student, Neil Rothenberg, also recalled that Dov Shilansky, Aaron Pick, and Amichai Paglin were among the lecturers. Interview with Neil Rothenberg, August 17, 2000, Jerusalem.

[10] Letter from Marilyn Sue Betman to Libby, received January 10, 2003, in RZ Archives, Appendix.

[11] Hershkowitz was accused of planning to hijack a plane, but he was convicted only of falsifying information on his passport application. (See chapter 18.) Attorney Nathan Lewin arranged for Hershkowitz to be paroled from prison for deportation to Israel on May 15, 1972, after he had served one year and seven months of his five-year sentence. Phone interview with Avraham Hershkowitz, February 24, 1997. See: "Kochubievsky Defends JDL on Arrival Here," *Jewish Post and Opinion*, April 28, 1972, p. 1, in RZ Archives, folder 73A; *Iton* (Jewish Defense League), Lag Ba'omer 5732 [May 1972], p. 12, in RZ Archives, folder 1202.

His administrative duties: See note 2.

[12] The Achdut Yisrael synagogue was founded by veterans of the pre-state military units. The synagogue is in the Baruch Mashi'ach Alley behind 91 Jaffa Street, Jerusalem.

[13] See note 9.

[14] Letter from Meir to Bert Zweibon and Bennett Levine, postmarked August 24, 1972, in RZ Archives, Appendix.

See chapter 31 regarding the confiscation of Meir's passport.

[15] David Fisch recalled that Meir wanted them to hear prime minister Golda Meir's speech at the opening session. Wrote Fisch: "He still liked many things about Golda at the time. He liked the way she told the ZOA people that they need to make aliya. He liked that she did not recognize a separate 'Palestinian' people." E-mail from David Fisch, February 3, 2004.

See: "At ZOA Convention Mrs. Meir Warns of Assimilation Danger," *Jerusalem Post*, July 14, 1972, p. 1.

See chapter 24 for more about the ZOA conference in Pittsburgh on September 5, 1971.

[16] "An Open Letter to the Delegates of the Zionist Organization of America from the Jewish Defense League of Israel and the Aliya Organization *Habayta*," [ad] *Jerusalem Post*, July 13, 1972, in RZ Archives, folder 131.

The ad invited delegates to "stop by at the offices in Jerusalem at the Jewish Identity Center, 10 Rechov Dorot Rishonim, near Zion Square."

[17] Daniel Dagan, "Kol Galut Hi Kelala... [Every Exile Is a Curse and America Is Not Different From Other Exiles]," *Ma'ariv*, July 17, 1972, p. 7, in RZ Archives, folder 131; Noah Kliger, "Krova Hasha'a Ba Yakumu Negdekhem [The Time Nears When They Will Rise Up Against You]," *Yedioth Ahronoth*, July 17, 1972, p. 15, in RZ Archives, folder 131.

Meir's talk at ZOA House, Tel Aviv, was on July 16, 1972.

Dagan's lengthy article includes quotes from Meir's speech.

Parts of Kliger's article appear in English translation in *Story of the Jewish Defense League*, p. 262.

Moshe Barkai, "Kor'im Kotvim: Bein Kalman LeMeir [Readers Write: Between Kalman and Meir]," *Ma'ariv*, July 23, 1972, p. 14.

18 "The Wandering Jew," *Jewish Press*, July 14, 1972, p. 37, reprinted in *Writings 5732*, pp. 92-94.

19 Ohel Shem, August 8, 8:30 P.M.; Bnei Akiva group, July 20, 1972; Moshav Azriel, July 30, 1972, 8 P.M. Noted in Meir's 1972 appointment book, in RZ Archives, folder 713B.

20 E-mail from Charles Levine, January 24, 2000.

21 "Soviet Jew Is Sentenced to 3 Years at Hard Labor," *Washington Post*, August 12, 1972, p. E8.

22 Yair Amikam, "Chavrei 'Haliga Lehagana' Punu... [Members of the Liga Were Forcibly Removed From the Offices of the Finnish Embassy in Tel Aviv]," *Yedioth Ahronoth*, August 10, 1972, p. 13, in RZ Archives, folder 74B; "Police Evict JDL From Embassy," *Jewish Press*, August 18, 1972, pp. 2, 18; "JDL Youths Detained," *Jerusalem Post*, August 10, 1972, p. 3.

"Hifsiku Shevitat Ra'av Leyad Misrad Hatzlav Ha'adom [Hunger Strike Near Red Cross Offices Ended]," *Ha'aretz*, August 31, 1972, p. 3, in RZ Archives, folder 74B.

23 Hedrick Smith, "Soviet Journalist Privately Urges Jews Not to Pay New Exit Tax," *New York Times*, August 28, 1972, p. 4.

"Russian Exit Fees 'Fantastic,'" *Jewish Press*, September 1, 1972, p. 49, in RZ Archives, folder 594; "Soviet Tells Public of Emigration Tax," *New York Times*, September 14, 1972, p. 10; "Will Russia Yield on Exit Ransom?" *Jewish Post and Opinion*, September 29, 1972, p. 1.

See also: "Ransom Tax," *American Jewish Year Book*, 1973, pp. 221-222; "Diploma Tax," *American Jewish Year Book*, 1974/75, p. 202.

24 "Mehana'aseh Batenua Hale'umit [News of the National Movement]," *Yesh Berera*, [September-October 1972], p. 4, in RZ Archives, folder 74B. Meir is pictured at the podium.

The other sponsors were Hatenua Hale'umit, Agudat Ma'oz and Va'adat Hape'ula Shel Olei Brit Hamo'atzot; other speakers were Leah Slovin, Avraham Shifrin, and Yosef Lipski.

The rally also commemorated the twenty years since Stalin's execution of thirteen Jewish poets and intellectuals on trumped-up charges on August 12, 1952.

25 "Jews Ask Nixon to Bar Credits to Soviet Until Exit Taxes End," *New York Times*, September 28, 1972, p. 12.

26 "Israel News Analysis," *Jewish Press*, September 8, 1972, p. 46, in RZ Archives, folder 594.

27 "Warning by Kahane," *New York Times*, August 22, 1972, p. 3; "Kidnapping of Soviets Threatened," *Washington Post*, August 22, 1972, p. A6. These reports quoted only a few lines of the letter.

Letter [carbon copy] from Rabbi Meir Kahane, International Chairman, to Secretary of State William P. Rogers, August 21, 1972, in RZ Archives, folder 73B. The letter is written on stationery headed Jewish Defense League in Israel, 26 Ben Maimon Street, P.O. Box 7287, Jerusalem.

A slightly different version, distributed at the press conference, is given in: FBI Los Angeles office file 105-29629-86, cable from Acting Director to field offices, August 22, 1972, 2 pp., in RZ Archives, Appendix. The cable reported that this letter had not yet been received by Secretary of State William P. Rogers.

28 FBI file 105-207795-240, cable, from Acting Director to Los Angeles and New York offices, August 25, 1972, pp. 1-2, in RZ Archives, Appendix.

29 Meir's 1972 appointment book, in RZ Archives, folder 713B. The wedding [couple not named] was scheduled for 7 P.M.

30 Avraham Rotem, "Irgun Anonymi 'Nakam'... [An Anonymous Organization, 'Nakam,' Plans to Kidnap Russians]," *Yedioth Ahronoth*, August 29, 1972, p. 7; Israel Broadcasting Authority Television News Archive, media no. 59372-72-2, August 28, 1972.

FBI file 105-207795-257, memo, August 29, 1972, 3 pp., in RZ Archives, Appendix;

FBI file 105-207795-242, cable from Acting Director, FBI, to FBI offices in U.S. cities and to Legal Attache, Tel Aviv, August 29, 1972, pp. 2-4, in RZ Archives, Appendix. This mentions the interview on ABC-TV.

FBI file 105-207795-262, cable from Legat [legal attaché, i.e. FBI agent] Tel Aviv to Acting Director, September 12, 1972, p. 1, in RZ Archives, Appendix.

Press conference, August 28, noted in Meir's 1972 appointment book, in RZ Archives, folder 713B.

[31] Letter from Edward S. Walker, Jr., U.S. Embassy, Tel Aviv, to Meir, September 5, 1972, in RZ Archives, folder 96.

[32] Yair Amikam, "Harav Kahana Huzman Lifgisha Beshagrirut... [Rabbi Kahane Was Invited to a Meeting at the American Embassy in Tel Aviv]," *Yedioth Ahronoth*, September 12, 1972, p. 13, in RZ Archives, folder 74A. A photo of Meir speaking into a bullhorn at the demonstration accompanies the article. See also: Israel Broadcasting Authority Radio News Archive, media no. 8281, September 11, 1972.

Meir told reporters afterwards that the American Embassy was taking Nakam's threat very seriously, even though the organization had not yet acted and "may never act."

[33] See note 30, FBI, pp. 1-4.

Meir's information probably came from the *Daily News*, which reported that two FBI men, Harold Rubenstein and Theodore Goble, had arrived in Israel to follow JDL activities. See: "FBI Watching Jews?" *Daily News*, August 28, 1971, in RZ Archives, folder 62A. The *Daily News* cited *Davar* as its source.

[34] See chapter 18, "Under FBI Scrutiny," for details of two earlier FBI interviews.

[35] "Biram and Ikrit," *Jewish Press*, September 1, 1972, pp. 49, 53, in RZ Archives, folder 594.

[36] "Haliga Tafgin Neged Masa Hatzlav Shel Raya [The Liga Will Demonstrate Against Raya's Crusade]," *Yedioth Ahronoth*, August 16, 1972, p. 8, in RZ Archives, folder 74B. Were it not for this brief item about Archbishop Raya, there probably would have been no historical record of the session at Beit Haam.

Henry Kamm, "Arabs and Jews Protest in Israel," *New York Times*, August 24, 1972, p. 2. See the photo section of this book for a picture of the demonstrators.

[37] "Harav Kahana Mul Habishof Raya [Rabbi Kahane Against Bishop Raya]," *Ma'ariv*, May 2, 1973, p. 3, in RZ Archives, folder 71B. The debate took place on April 30, 1973.

[38] See: www.hebron.org.il.

[39] E-mail from David Fisch, May 27, 1997.

[40] Letter to Ja'abari signed Yitzhak Ben Avraham, August 27, 1972, in RZ Archives, folder 94. Written on JDL of Israel stationery (see note 27).

The signature, Yitzhak Ben Avraham (Isaac the son of Abraham) referred to the Patriarch buried in Hebron's Cave of the Patriarchs.

[41] Avishai Amir, "Anshei Ha-liga Tzatzu La-feta... [League Members Suddenly Appeared in Hebron Despite Roadblocks]," *Ma'ariv*, August 28, 1972, p. 3, in RZ Archives, folder 96; Gil Sadan, "Yesh Kan Rova Yehudi She'en Bo Adayin Yehudim [There's a Jewish Quarter Here, But No Jews There Yet]," *Yedioth Ahronoth*, August 28, 1972, pp. 9, 15, in RZ Archives, folder 96; Anan Safadi, "Dayan Assures Against J.D.L. Activity," *Jerusalem Post*, August 28, 1972, p. 1, in RZ Archives, folder 74B; "Nikhbedei Har Hevron... [Arab Leaders of Hebron Area Decided Not to Demonstrate Against Liga People]," *Ha'aretz*, August 27, 1972, p. 8, in RZ Archives, folder 74B; "Dayan Etzel Ja'abari: Ein Yesod Leda'agatekha [Dayan to Ja'abari: There Is No Basis for Your Worry]," *Ma'ariv*, August 28, 1972, p. 3, in RZ Archives, folder 96; Israel Broad-

casting Authority Radio News Archive, media no. 8271, August 27, 1972; "Kahane in Hebron in Refugee Protest," *New York Times*, August 28, 1972, p. 8.

[42] Meir's 1972 appointment book has the notation "Press Conference 2 P.M.," which might indicate that the press conference had been scheduled even before the group was asked to leave Hebron.

[43] "Kahane Says Rights Were 'Denied,'" *Jerusalem Post*, August 29, 1972; "Harav Kahana Mevakesh Bevagatz Tzav Neged Sar Habitachon [Rabbi Kahane Requests an Order from the High Court Against the Minister of Defense]," *Ha'aretz*, August 29, 1972, p. 4.

Schechter appealed Judge Etzioni's decision; the appeal was refused: "Nidcheta Atirat Harav Kahana... [Rabbi Kahane's Appeal to Be Allowed to Visit Hebron Refused]," *Yedioth Ahronoth*, September 14, 1972, p. 13; "Court Rebukes Kahane, Dismisses Order *Nisi*," *Jerusalem Post*, September 14, 1972, p. 3.

[44] Yizhar Arnon, "Hatizkoret Shel Harav Kahana [Rabbi Kahane's Reminder]," *Ma'ariv*, September 3, 1972, p. 15, in RZ Archives, folder 96. Excerpted with permission.

[45] Menachem Chevroni, "Ma Oseh Harav Kahana [What Rabbi Kahane Is Doing]," [letter to the editor] *Ma'ariv*, September 5, 1972, p. 5, in RZ Archives, folder 74B; "Hasheikh Ja'abari Matzhir Shelo Haya Lo Kesher... [Sheikh Ja'abari Declares He Had No Connection with the 1929 Riot]," *Ha'aretz*, September 1, 1972, p. 2, RZ Archives, folder 96.

[46] "Open Letter," flyer and press release, September 5, 1972, in RZ Archives, folder 94; "Mitbakshim: Edim... [Requested: Witnesses...]" poster about public trial of Ja'abari on September 28, 1972, in RZ Archives, poster folder, no. 11.

A Liga flyer stated, "Today a group of Liga members went to Hebron to collect testimony about Ja'abari, accompanied by *Yedioth Ahronoth* reporter Gil Sadan. They acted decorously, but three of them were detained for 'fear of disturbance of the peace.'" See: *Gilayon Hasbara, Mispar 1 [Information Sheet, No. 1]*, September 14, 1972, flyer from the collection of Shimon Rachamim, in RZ Archives, Appendix.

[47] "Ne'esar Al Anshei Haliga Lehikanes Leyehuda Veshomron [Liga People Banned from Entering Judea and Samaria]," *Yedioth Ahronoth*, September 24, 1972, p. 5, in RZ Archives, folder 74A; "Hasar Hillel: Mad'iga Oti Tofa'a Shel Hakamat Machteret [Minister Shlomo Hillel: I Am Worried by the Phenomenon of an Underground]," *Ma'ariv*, September 24, 1972, p. 4, in RZ Archives, folder 74A; [Untitled, brief report], *New York Times*, September 24, 1972, p. 9.

[48] "With All Due Respect," *Jewish Press*, September 15, 1972, pp. 42, 45, reprinted in *Writings 5732*, pp. 245-249.

The "right to Haifa" refers to Ja'abari's statement that Jews could return to Hebron on the condition that all the Arabs could return to Haifa. See: Gil Sadan, "Hafganat 'Haliga Lehagana' [The Liga's Demonstration]," *Yedioth Ahronoth*, August 28, 1972, p. 15, in RZ Archives, folder 96.

Mock trial of Ja'abari postponed. See: "Mesarvim Lehaskir Ulam Lemishpat Haliga Neged Ja'abari [Refuse to Rent the Hall for the League's Trial Against Ja'abari]," *Ha'aretz*, September 12, 1972, p. 4, in RZ Archives 74B. See also: "JDL Will Run for Knesset," *Jerusalem Post*, September 28, 1972, p. 2. This report states that the mock trial of Ja'abari was put off because JDL could not raise the IL 50,000 bank guarantee demanded by the Association of Journalists for renting a hall in Beit Agron.

Chapter 31

[1] "Milchemet Kiyum [A War for Survival]," *Yedioth Ahronoth*, September 14, 1972, p. 15, in RZ Archives, folder 62B. Translation of "No Illusions, Please," *Jewish Press*, August 25, 1972,

pp. 26, 28, 31, reprinted in *Writings 5732*, pp. 103-106, and in *Beyond Words*, 1:310-316. The text is also in *Our Challenge*, pp. 29-34.

[2]   Martin Arnold, "Leaders Around the World Express Horror at the Guerrilla Attack at Olympics," *New York Times*, September 6, 1972, p. 19; Martin Arnold, "New Yorkers Grieve Over Israeli Dead," *New York Times*, September 7, 1972, p. 19.

[3]   "The Honor of the Jewish People," *Jewish Press*, October 27, 1972, pp. 15, 24, 42, in RZ Archives, folder 683A, reprinted in *Beyond Words*, 1:333-334, and in *Letters from Prison* (Jerusalem: 1974), pp. 34-41, in RZ Archives, booklet folder.

[4]   Meir's 1972 appointment book, in RZ Archives, folder 713B, shows an appointment with Amichai Paglin on September 11. That same day, Meir had a meeting at the American Embassy in Tel Aviv concerning threats by "Nakam" to kidnap Soviet diplomats (see chapter 30).

Phone interview with Avraham Hershkowitz, February 24, 1997. Hershkowitz was kept in jail for three weeks. The fact that this specific crate was opened for inspection may point to the existence of a police informer in the Liga.

Apparently, Hershkowitz delivered the crate to the airport on Thursday morning, September 14, and then went to Hebron with two others to collect testimony for the "public trial" against Ja'abari. In Hebron the three were taken into custody. When they arrived at the police station in Jerusalem, only Hershkowitz was jailed. See: "Ne'etzar Ish Haliga Sheba Lechevron [A Liga Member Who Came to Hebron Was Arrested]," *Yedioth Ahronoth*, September 19, 1972, p. 5, in RZ Archives, folder 74B.

Shlomo Nakdimon, "Hashavu'a shel Amichai Paglin," *Yedioth Ahronoth*, September 24, 1972, pp. 9, 20. At first, Paglin was taken to the lockup at Abu Kabir, but was soon transferred to house arrest at the Basle Hotel in Tel Aviv.

[5]   "JDL Reports Arms Sent to U.S., Europe: Jewish Group Reveals Counterterror Plan," *International Herald Tribune*, September 20, 1972, in RZ Archives, folder 83; "An Ex-Terrorist Is Held in Israel: Police Say He's Linked With Anti-Arab Underground," *New York Times*, September 22, 1972, p. 11; "Haliga Lehagana: Sukla Tokhnitenu... [The Liga: Our Plan to Kidnap Arab Hostages Was Thwarted]," *Yedioth Ahronoth*, September 20, 1972, p. 13, in RZ Archives, folder 74A; "Haliga Mevakeshet Lehakim Irgun Olami Leteror Neged Mechablim [The Liga Wants to Set Up a Worldwide Counterterror Organization]," *Ha'aretz*, September 20, 1972, p. 6, in RZ Archives, folder 74B.

The press conference was held on September 19 at 4 P.M. at Victor (Avigdor) Perry's public relations firm, 105 Rothschild Blvd., Tel Aviv. See: Hoda'at Haliga Lehagana Yehudit Be'eretz Yisrael [Announcement by the Liga], undated, begins "Beyom chamishi she'avar... [Last Thursday...]," press release from the collection of Shimon Rachamim, in RZ Archives, Appendix.

[6]   Hoda'at Haliga Lehagana Yehudit [Announcement by the Liga], undated, begins: "Miyad achar hatevach [Immediately after the massacre]," flyer from the collection of Shimon Rachamim, in RZ Archives, Appendix.

[7]   "Harav Kahana: Haderekh Hayechida Lehilachem Beteror Hi Beteror [Rabbi Kahane: The Only Way to Fight Terror Is With Terror]," *Yedioth Ahronoth*, September 22, 1972, p. 2; Yosef Tzuriel, "Harav Kahana: Haliga Tif'al Bechul... [Rabbi Kahane: The Liga Will Act Against Arab Terror Overseas]," *Ma'ariv*, September 22, 1972, p. 4, in JNUL Archives, folder ARC 4=1748; Israel Broadcasting Authority Radio News Archive, media no. 8299, September 21, 1972.

A snapshot taken at the September 21 press conference is in the photo section of this book.

[8]   "The Country That Loses Its Heart," *Jewish Press*, October 20, 1972, p. 47, in RZ Archives, folder 594.

Schneider's arrest: "Ba Lezahot Et Mazkir Haliga... [He Came to Identify the Administrative

Director of the Liga...]," *Yedioth Ahronoth*, September 25, 1972, p. 5, in RZ Archives, folder 74A.

When asked about Paglin, Meir would only say, "He is a national hero." See: Yosef Tzuriel, note 7

On September 28, Paglin was transferred from house arrest in the Basle Hotel (note 4, Nakdimon) to a police lockup. Gideon Alon, "Paglin – Lema'atzar Bekeleh Mishtarti [Paglin – To Jail in a Police Lockup]," *Ha'aretz*, September 29, 1972, p. 3, in RZ Archives, folder 74B.

See also: "An Ex-Terrorist Is Held in Israel..." (note 5); Shlomo Nakdimon and Shabtai Portnoy, "Ne'etzar Ketzin Hamivtza'im... [Former Operations Officer of the Etzel Was Arrested]," *Yedioth Ahronoth*, September 21, 1972, p. 1.

Reports of the arrests of Liga members included: "Hamishtara Mechapeset et Willy Hochhauser [The Police Seek Willy Hochhauser]," *Ha'aretz*, September 27, 1972, p. 3, in RZ Archives, folder 74B. See also note 17.

9 "Tzarikh Latet Hada'at La'efsharut... [We Must Consider Declaring the Liga an Illegal Organization]," *Yedioth Ahronoth*, September 24, 1972, p. 4, in RZ Archives, folder 74A; "Jordan Says Bombs Are Found in Malls," *New York Times*, September 24, 1972, p. 9; Amos Shapira, "Abirei Ha'egrof [Knights of the Fist]," *Ha'aretz*, September 25, 1972, p. 11; Aharon Papo, "Pe'ulot Harav Kahana [Rabbi Kahane's Activities]," [letter to the editor] *Ha'aretz*, October 2, 1972, p. 16, in RZ Archives, folder 74B. This page has additional letters to the editor about Meir.

Another letter to the editor about Shapiro's article expounded on Liga ideology: Yoel Lerner, "Hashkafat Anshei Haliga Lehagana Yehudit," *Ha'aretz*, September 29, 1972, p. 26, in RZ Archives, folder 74B.

10 "Sar Hamishpatim Nifgash Im Harav Kahana [The Minister of Justice Met With Rabbi Kahane]," *Ma'ariv*, September 25, 1972, p. 1, in RZ Archives, folder 74A; Mati Golan, "Harav Kahana Ma'ashim... [Rabbi Kahane Accuses Minister Shapiro of Leaking the Minutes of Their Meeting]," *Ha'aretz*, September 27, 1972, p. 1, in RZ Archives, folder 74B; Shabtai Portnoy and Shlomo Nakdimon, "Hamishtara Tevakesh Hayom Leha'arikh... [Today the Police Will Request Extension of Paglin's Detention]," *Yedioth Ahronoth*, September 26, 1972, p. 8, in RZ Archives, folder 74A. See also note 21.

11 Shabtai Portnoy, "Kahana: Ha'iyumim La'itonim Provokatzya [Kahane: The 'Threats' to Newspapers Are a Provocation]," *Yedioth Ahronoth*, September 26, 1972, p. 8, in RZ Archives, folder 74A.

"Larav Kahana Tzafui Krav Im Tze'irei Tenuat Ha'avoda [A Battle With the Labor Party Young Leadership Is Foreseen for Rabbi Kahane]," *Ma'ariv*, September 27, 1972, p. 9, in RZ Archives, folder 74A.

12 See Mati Golan, chapter 27, note 9.

13 Letter from Meir to Tuvia Friedman, Haifa, August 30, 1972, in RZ Archives, Appendix.

14 "Kahane to Run for Office in Israel," *New York Times*, September 28, 1972, p. 17; "Haliga: Einenu Kevassim... [We Are Not Sheep; We'll Run in the Elections]," *Ha'aretz*, September 28, 1972, p. 3, in RZ Archives, folder 74B; Nahum Barnea, "Le'olam Lo Od, Harav Kahane! [Never Again, Rabbi Kahane!]" *Davar*, September 29, 1972, pp. 11, 16, in JNUL Archives, folder ARC 4=1748; Mati Golan, "Kahana Ratz Laknesset [Kahane Runs for Knesset]," *Ha'aretz*, September 29, 1972, p. 12, in RZ Archives, folder 96; "JDL Will Run for Knesset," *Jerusalem Post*, September 28, 1972, p. 2; "Haliga Lehagana: Narutz Laknesset [The Liga: We Will Run for Knesset]," *Yedioth Ahronoth*, September 28, 1972, p. 5, in RZ Archives, folder 74A.

15 Phone interview with Yoel Lerner, February 27, 2004. Lerner recalled that one of the newsmen handed him a copy of the press release he had just read from and asked him to autograph it, "because one of these days it will be worth a lot of money."

16 Israel Broadcasting Authority Radio News Archive, media no. 70036-72-8, September 27, 1972.

17 "Hamishtara Arkha Halayla Peshita Al Bateihem Shel Chavrei Haliga [Last Night the Police Searched the Homes of Liga Members]," *Yedioth Ahronoth*, September 29, 1972, p. 8.

Statements of Shalom Cohen and Uri Avneri: See note 11, *Ma'ariv*, and note 14, *Jerusalem Post*.

18 Shmuel Shnitzer, "Sakanat Hamachteret [The Danger of an Underground]," *Ma'ariv*, September 29, 1972, p. 13, in RZ Archives, folder 72A; "Ra'ayon Im Orekh Hadin Shmuel Tamir [Interview With Attorney Shmuel Tamir]," *Ma'ariv*, September 29, 1972, pp. 22, 28 in RZ Archives, folder 74A.

19 "Hamishtara: Hachakira Befarashat Havrachat Haneshek Matzrikha Berur Yesodi [Police: The Investigation Into the Arms Smuggling Case Requires a Thorough Investigation]," *Yedioth Ahronoth*, September 26, 1972, p. 13.

See also: Yehoshua Kahana, "Ma'atzaro Shel Paglin Hu'arakh Bashlishit [Paglin's Detention Renewed for the Third Time]," *Ma'ariv*, October 1, 1972, p. 7.

20 Herzl Rosenblum, "Klaf Meshuga [Wild Card]," [editorial] *Yedioth Ahronoth*, September 28, 1972, p. 2, in RZ Archives, folder 596; Herzl Rosenblum, "Milchemet Elem [A Silent War]," [editorial] *Yedioth Ahronoth*, October 1, 1972, p. 2, in RZ Archives, folder 596.

21 Terence Smith, "Rabbi Kahane Is Arrested in Jerusalem," *New York Times*, October 2, 1972, p. 10, in RZ Archives, folder 697. Copyright © 1972 by The New York Times Co. Excerpted with permission.

22 See note 14, Mati Golan. Copyright © *Ha'aretz* Daily Newspaper Ltd. Excerpted with permission.

Among the discussions in the press were: "Mi Yelachem Bateror [Who Will Fight Terror]," [editorial] *Ha'aretz*, September 25, 1972, p. 11 and "Symposion: Mi Veketzad Tzarikh Lehilachem Bateror? [A Symposium: Who and How To Fight Terror?]" *Yedioth Ahronoth*, September 29, 1972, *Musaf* section, p. 1, in RZ Archives, folder 74A.

23 "JDL Chief Seized by Police In Israel," *Los Angeles Times*, October 2, 1972; Yosef Tzuriel, "Ne'etzar Harav Meir Kahana... [Rabbi Meir Kahane Was Arrested; He Was Not Permitted to Fly to the U.S.]," *Ma'ariv*, October 1, 1972, p. 1, in RZ Archives, folder 74A; Gideon Reicher, "Harav Kahana Ne'etzar Haboker Biyerushalayim [Rabbi Kahane Was Arrested This Morning in Jerusalem]," *Ha'aretz*, October 1, 1972, p. 1; "Kahane Arrested in Israel," *New York Post*, October 2, 1972, p. 4; Israel Broadcasting Authority Television News Archive, media no. 70098-72-8, October 1, 1972. See also note 21.

Newspaper reports differed on the location of the lockup. *Ha'aretz* and *Yedioth Ahronoth* said it was in Rishon Letziyon, while *Ma'ariv* said it was in Nes Tziyona. See: Avi Valentin, "Hamishtara Hecherima Reshimat Ketovot... [The Police Confiscated a List of Addresses...]," *Ha'aretz*, October 2, 1972, p. 3, in RZ Archives, folder 74B; "Harav Kahana Nechkar Bema'atzaro Berishon Letziyon [Rabbi Kahane Interrogated in Rishon Letziyon]," *Yedioth Ahronoth*, October 2, 1972, p. 1; Yehoshua Kahana, "Ne'etzar Od Chashud... Kahana Mesarev Leshatef Pe'ula Im Chokrav [Another Suspect Was Arrested, Kahane Refuses to Cooperate With Investigators]," *Ma'ariv*, October 2, 1972, pp. 1, 7, in RZ Archives, folder 74A.

The law has since been amended to reduce the number of hours of administrative detention.

24 "Willy Hochhauser Amad Lekabel Et Argaz Haneshek Bechul [Willy Hochhauser Was to Receive the Crate of Arms in Europe]," *Ha'aretz*, October 3, 1972, p. 10, in RZ Archives, folder 74B.

Confiscation of files: See note 23, Avi Valentin. See also note 7. A similar police act in New York was decried by the American Jewish Congress: "We oppose any police action that violates constitutional guarantees.... [Police] seized files and other documents, including membership lists, to which they were not entitled." See chapter 33, note 16.

25 See Yehoshua Kahana, note 23 and Yehoshua Kahana, "Hayom Hachlata Im Paglin, Kahana Vehershkowitz Yeshuchreru Be'arvut [Decision Today Whether to Release Paglin, Kahane and Hershkowitz on Bail]," Ma'ariv, October 3, 1972, p. 1, in RZ Archives, folder 74A.

26 "Harav Kahana Megaleh: Pa'alti Besherut Ha-FBI; Chakarti et Pe'ulot Ha'irgun Hakitzoni 'Birch' [Rabbi Kahane Reveals: I Worked for the FBI; I Investigated the John Birch Society]," Ma'ariv, October 2, 1972, p. 1, in RZ Archives, folder 74A; "Bera'ayon Liktav Ha'et Playboy, Rabbi Kahana: Pa'alti Shenatayim Vachetzi Besherut Ha-FBI Ha'amerikani [In an Interview in Playboy, Rabbi Kahane: I Worked Two-and-a-Half Years for the FBI]," Ha'aretz, October 3, 1972, p. 2, in RZ Archives, folder 74B; "Harav Kahana Mesaper Hakol – Le-Playboy [Rabbi Kahane Tells All – To Playboy]," Davar, October 3, 1972, p. 3, in JNUL Archives, folder ARC 4=1748.

Walter Goodman, "Meir Kahane: A Candid Conversation with the Militant Leader of the Jewish Defense League," Playboy, October 1972, pp. 69-78, in RZ Archives, folder 484.

The October issue of Playboy was apparently released in mid-September. A brief review of the article appeared in James F. Clarity, "Notes on People," New York Times, September 15, 1972, p. 22.

27 Menachem Shmuel, "Harav Kahana Masbir Matza'o Hamiflagti: Laliga Lehagana Yesh Tafkid Lehagen Al Ofyo Hayehudi Shel Ha'am Hayehudi Beyisrael [Rabbi Kahane Explains His Party's Platform: The Liga's Function Is to Guard the Jewish Character of the Jewish People in Israel]," Ma'ariv, October 15, 1972, p. 9, in RZ Archives, folder 74A.

Later, Meir wrote, "Think of all the Jewish readers of Playboy, and who needs the teachings of JDL more than they." Story of the Jewish Defense League, p. 272.

28 See Playboy, p. 74 (note 26). See also: Psalms 139:21: "... For indeed those who hate You... I hate them..." This concept is discussed in The Jewish Idea, vol. 1, pp. 127-131.

See chapter 26, note 2, for Walter Goodman's article about Meir in the New York Times.

29 "Harav M. Kahana Bikesh Ezrachut [Rabbi M. Kahane Requested Israeli Citizenship]," Ma'ariv, October 3, 1972, p. 9, in RZ Archives, folder 74.

The news item also noted that Meir had applied for Israeli citizenship about five weeks earlier. It quoted a spokesman for the Interior Ministry who said there was no reason to deny Meir's application; it was being processed routinely – a procedure that usually took three to four months. See chapter 32.

30 Avi Valentin, "Paglin, Hershkowitz VeHochhauser Shuchreru Be'arvut [Paglin, Hershkowitz and Hochhauser Freed on Bail]," Ha'aretz, October 4, 1972, p. 3, in RZ Archives, folder 74B; "Harav Kahana Ne'etzar Le-4 Yamim... [Rabbi Kahane Jailed for 4 Days]," Yedioth Ahronoth, October 4, 1972, p. 4.

31 "Lema'an Yahadut Brit Hamo'atzot [For the Sake of Soviet Jewry]," [ad] Ma'ariv, October 3, 1972, p. 32, in RZ Archives, folder 74A. The ad measured 14 cm. by 11 cm.

Flyers were distributed: "Bal Tachzor Hahashtaka [The Shame of Silence Will Not Be Repeated]," flyer for demonstration on October 3, 1972, in RZ Archives, Appendix, from the collection of Shimon Rachamim.

Photo of demonstrators holding placards, Tel Aviv, October 3, 1972, in RZ Archives, picture file, no. 332-333. A large sign behind them "Air France," was over the Air France ticket office, across the street from the American Embassy.

[32] Meir's bail was IL40,000 (about $9,500), as was that of Paglin and Hershkowitz. Yosef Schneider's bail was IL20,000 (about $4,750). See notes 30 and 35.

[33] FBI New York office file 157-5767, cable, October 6, 1972, 2 pp., in RZ Archives, Appendix.

[34] "Kahane Says He Got Votes in Israeli Jail," *New York Times*, October 7, 1972, p. 3, in RZ Archives, folder 96.

[35] "Harav Kahana Shuchrar Be'arvut, Yevakesh Hayom Heter Latzet Le'arhab [Rabbi Kahane Freed on Bail; Will Ask for Permission to Travel to the U.S.]," *Ha'aretz*, October 8, 1972, p. 8, in RZ Archives, folder 74B; "JDL Suspects Freed but Cannot Travel Abroad," *Jerusalem Post*, October 8, 1972, p. 3.

[36] "Yugshu Kanir'eh Kitvei Ishum Neged Paglin, Kahana, Schneider, Vehershkowitz [Indictments Will Probably Be Presented Against Paglin, Kahane, Schneider, and Hershkowitz]," *Ha'aretz*, October 10, 1972, p. 3, in RZ Archives, folder 74B.

"Kahane Gets His Passport – For One Month," *Jerusalem Post*, October 12, 1972, p. 2; "Kahana Hursha Latzet Lechul Lechodesh Akh Lo Le'arhab [Kahane Permitted to Leave the Country for One Month, but Not to the U.S.]," *Ha'aretz*, October 12, 1972, p. 3, in RZ Archives, folder 74A; Israel Broadcasting Authority Radio News Archive, media no. 8376, October 11, 1972.

"Ne'esra Yetzi'at Harav Kahana [Rabbi Kahane's Departure Forbidden]," *Ha'aretz*, October 16, 1972, p. 10, in RZ Archives, folder 74B.

Details on Meir's speaking date in San Francisco: FBI file 105-207795, Teletype from San Francisco (105-26688), October 18, 1972, in RZ Archives, Appendix.

On November 15, 1972, Meir again petitioned the court for a permit to leave the country. "Harav Kahana Yevakesh Heter Latzet Le'arhab [Rabbi Kahane Will Request a Permit to Go to the U.S.]," *Ha'aretz*, November 16, 1972, p. 2, in RZ Archives, folder 74A.

On November 22, 1972, his appeal was denied: "Nidcha Ir'ur Harav Kahana [Rabbi Kahane's Appeal Refused]," *Ha'aretz*, November 23, 1972, p. 6, both in RZ Archives, folder 74A.

[37] Letter (Hebrew) from Nat Rosenwasser to Meir, November 12, 1972, in RZ Archives, folder 713A.

[38] Interview with Dan Gottlieb, November 2, 1999, Jerusalem.

[39] Letters from members in England, South Africa and Australia in RZ Archives, folder 94. France: See chapter 26, note 15.

[40] Letter from Barbara Ginsberg to Libby, January 8, 1998, in RZ Archives, Appendix.

[41] "School Board's Minority Tells of East Side 'Threats,'" *New York Post*, February 3, 1972, p. 14; "JDL Raids District 1M," *Teachers Action Caucus Newsletter*, February 1972, in RZ Archives, folder 73B.

[42] "J.D.L. Member Pours Blood Over Soviet Aide's Head," *New York Times*, March 16, 1972, p. 5.

[43] "Six Protesters Arrested as Soviet Research Ship Docks," *Miami Herald*, March 26, 1972, pp. 1, 2A, in RZ Archives, folder 73B; Interview with Sharon Katz Mittman, November 19, 1999, Jerusalem.

[44] "JDL Sets Crush American Nazism Day," *Jewish News*, March 17, 1972; "Jewish League to Ask Nixon Support," *Detroit News*, March 22, 1972; both in RZ Archives, folder 73A.

[45] Letters from Russel D. Kelner, JDL chapter coordinator, to the American Friends Service Committee [Quakers], dated May 26, 1972, and June 11, 1972. Newspaper articles: "Quakers Rebuff JDL's Plan to Aid Arab Jews," *Jewish Exponent* [no date], in YU Archives, folder 7/2. "A Jewish Protest at Quaker HQ" [no journal title], April 20, 1973, in RZ Archives, folder 70.

Anti-Nazi protest: "A Confrontation of Extremists," *Philadelphia Daily News*, May 25, 1972, p. 4, in RZ Archives, folder 734.

[46] "JDL Men to Patrol Inlet," *Press* (Atlantic City), June 2, 1972, pp. 1, 10, in Jewish Defense League collection, Center for Jewish History, New York City.

[47] Letter from Rabbi Herschel Shifrin, Congregation Chovevei Torah, to Jewish Defense League, July 18, 1972, in RZ Archives, folder 73B; YU Archives, folder 6/4.

Flyers distributed in Crown Heights, calling on blacks not to allow "blood sucking Jews" to take over the community council, in RZ Archives, folder 438A.

Dave Sobel, "Young Jewish Activists: A 'Yasher Koach' to Crown Heights, et al," *Jewish Press*, reproduced in *Iton*, Cheshvan 5733 [November 1972], p. 13, in RZ Archives, folder 683B. Elections took place on July 25, 1972.

[48] Yossi Klein, "Yossi Tells Why Dancers Bloodied," *Jewish Post and Opinion*, August 18, 1972, p. 2, in RZ Archives, folder 683B; "Ukrainian Dance Company Target of Protesters Here," *New York Times*, August 3, 1972, p. 67.

Ron Stepneski, "Soviet Dance Troup Picketed," *Record* (Bergen, N.J.), November 28, 1972, in RZ Archives, folder 73B.

Chicago chapter's disruption in: "Over the past year," [mimeographed page listing JDL achievements, September 1972-May 1973], in RZ Archives, folder 986.

[49] "Metropolitan Briefs," *New York Times*, October 19, 1972, p. 51.

[50] "Soviet Embassy Melee," *Washington Post*, December 22, 1972, pp. B1, B3, in RZ Archives, folder 73B.

[51] "JDL Starts Course for Overseas Leaders," *Jerusalem Post*, August 9, 1972, p. 2. This reports on a press conference Meir held on August 8, 1972.

"Hamerkaz Letoda'a Yehudit [The Jewish Identity Center]," [ad] *Ma'ariv*, August 25, 1972, p. 14. List of courses.

Documents about the courses are found in RZ Archives, folders 96 and 404.

[52] Phone interview with Shimon Rachamim, August 9, 1999.

[53] "Jewish Identity Center Course Outline," flyer, in RZ Archives, folder 692B.

[54] Contract between Meir and Yitzchak Bivas, the previous holder of key-money rights, October 19, 1972, in RZ Archives, folder 692B. The contract gave the price as 100,000 lirot ($23,809) and stipulated that Meir would pay 1,250 lirot rent per month from November 1, 1972, to January 31, 1973, so that he could continue to use the building for Jewish Identity Center classes until January 31.

[55] Letter from Meir to the JDL International Board, November 28, 1972, from the collection of Samuel Shoshan, in RZ Archives, Appendix.

[56] E-mail from David Fisch, June 1, 2004.

Chapter 32

[1] "Kahana Masbir Madu'a Hechlit Lehakim Miflaga [Kahane Explains Why He Decided to Form a Political Party]," *Ha'aretz*, October 16, 1972, p. 4, in RZ Archives, folder 74B. See also: Menachem Shmuel, chapter 31, note 27.

[2] "Israel News Analysis," *Jewish Press*, November 17, 1972, pp. 17, 37, reprinted as "A Mezuza," in *Writings 5732*, pp. 133-135, and in *On Jews and Judaism*, pp. 35-38.

In this article, Meir notes the possibility that halakha may not require the Old City's gates to have a *mezuza,* due to its Arab majority, but emphasizes that the aim was to show Jewish sovereignty.

3   "Atzuma Shel Toshavei Yisrael [Petition of Israeli Residents]," petition for *mezuza,* with signatures, in RZ Archives, folder 96.

4   "Nikba Mezuza Besha'ar Shechem Bashavu'a Haba [We Will Affix a *Mezuza* to Damascus Gate Next Week]," *Yedioth Ahronoth,* October 24, 1972, p. 2.

5   "Tzav Al Tnai Bekesher Limezuza Besha'ar Shechem [Conditional Order Requested Regarding a *Mezuza* on Damascus Gate]," *Yedioth Ahronoth,* October 27, 1972, p. 3.

Petition presented by attorney Meir Schechter: "Atira Lematan Tzav Al Tnai Ulematan Tzav Beinayim [Petition for a Conditional Order and an Interim Injunction]," High Court for Justice, October 26, 1972, 2 pp., in RZ Archives, folder 94.

6   Menachem Barash, "Ne'etzar Harav Kahana Benasoto Likbo'a Mezuza Besha'ar Shechem [Rabbi Kahane Was Arrested As He Tried to Affix a *Mezuza* to Damascus Gate]," *Yedioth Ahronoth,* October 31, 1972, p. 5; "Kahana Ve'anashav Shuchreru Be'arvut [Kahane and His Men Were Released on Bail]," *Ha'aretz,* November 1, 1972, p. 10, in RZ Archives, folder 74A; "Kahane Freed on Bail," *New York Times,* November 1, 1972, p. 29.

Meir and his supporters were released on bail pending trial. Meir's bail was the highest: IL30,000 ($7,150). There were pre-trial conditions for Meir only: He was forbidden to be in the Old City, except for prayer at the Western Wall, and he was forbidden to be in a public place with more than four people, except for his family.

Phone interview with Yoel Lerner, April 17, 2004.

Crowd at Damascus Gate, October 30, 1972, photo in RZ Archives, Appendix.

7   "Mevukash! Ha'im Kakha Mitnaheg Rav Beyisrael? [Wanted! Is This How a Rabbi Should Act?]" flyer, in RZ Archives, folder 94. See note 6, Menachem Barash. Another picture of Meir flanked by two policemen is in the photo section of this book.

8   "Kahane Fined for Breach of Peace," *Jewish Press,* December 22, 1972, p. 2; "Harav Kahana Niknas Al Nisayon Likbo'a Mezuza Besha'ar Shechem [Rabbi Kahane Was Fined for Trying to Affix a *Mezuza* to Damascus Gate]," *Yedioth Ahronoth,* December 13, 1972, p. 12; *Psak Din* [Verdict] by Judge Moshe Shalgi, undated, in RZ Archives, folder 96.

9   FBI file 105-207795, cablegram, December 13, 1972, 2 pp., in RZ Archives, Appendix. This cites the article, "Jerusalem Court Fines Kahane," *Star-Times* (Washington, D.C.), December 12, 1972.

See also: "JDL Head Jailed on New Count," *Herald Examiner* (Los Angeles), October 31, 1972. Cited in: FBI Los Angeles office file 105-29629-106, memo to U.S. Embassy, Tel Aviv, November 4, 1972, in RZ Archives, Appendix.

10   "Israel Issues Protest," *New York Times,* October 31, 1972, p. 10.

11   "Enough Lamentations," [op-ed] *New York Times,* November 29, 1972, p. 45, reprinted in *Beyond Words,* 1:347-349.

12   "Hartza'ato Shel Harav Meir Kahane Biyerushalayim [Address by Rabbi Meir Kahane in Jerusalem]," [ad] *Ma'ariv,* October 25, 1972, p. 12, in RZ Archives, folder 74A; mimeographed flyers advertising the event, in RZ Archives, folder 715B.

The public address was to take place at 8.30 P.M., admission free.

13   "Eretz Yisrael Hashelema Hi Shel Ha'am Hayehudi [The Entire Land of Israel Belongs to the Jewish People]," [ad] *Ma'ariv,* October 23, 1972, p. 12, in RZ Archives, folder 74A.

"Haliga Lehagana Yehudit Vehahitnachluyot Be'eretz Yisrael [The Liga and Settlements in the Land of Israel]," mimeographed flyer, in RZ Archives, folder 96.

The meeting was held at the Jewish Identity Center, 10 Dorot Rishonim Street, Jerusalem, on November 5, 1972.

[14] Speaking engagements: November 8, Bnei Akiva yeshiva, Raanana; November 8, evening parlor meeting, Ramat Eshkol (See: Letoshavei Ramat Eshkol: [To Ramat Eshkol Residents:], flyer, in RZ Archives, folder 96); November 9, Lodge of Freemasons, Tel Aviv; November 14, Hebrew University, Givat Ram; November 15, Hebrew University, Mount Scopus; November 22, Jewish Identity Center (See: Mimeographed flyer, in RZ Archives, folder 96. The agenda included an ideological lecture and elections to the board of the Jerusalem chapter); November 30, *Ironi Aleph* high school, 128 Rothschild, Tel Aviv; December 2, Parlor meeting, Herziliya; December 6, Jewish Identity Center (See: Mimeographed pages to accompany the ideological lectures on November 22 and December 6 in RZ Archives, folder 96); December 11, Technikum School, Tel Aviv; December 15, *Ironi Heh* high school, 227 Ben Yehuda Street, Tel Aviv; December 17, Junior Chamber of Commerce, Tel Aviv (See: Letter from *Lishka Hatze'ira, Tel Aviv-Yafo* to its members, undated, in RZ Archives, folder 714B); December 31, Lifshitz Teachers Seminary, Jerusalem (See: Letter from Uri Dassberg, Educational Director, Lifshitz Teachers College, to Meir, January 1, 1973, in RZ Archives, Appendix. Dassberg thanked Meir for his "edifying lecture last night... What you said is very important, especially to future teachers.")

The speaking engagements for which a specific source is not indicated are noted in Meir's 1972 appointment book, in RZ Archives, folder 713B.

[15] "Harav Kahana Matzi'a Hagirat Aravim Miyisrael [Rabbi Kahane Suggests Arab Emigration from Israel]," *Ha'aretz*, November 30, 1972, p. 5, in RZ Archives, folder 74A.

Press release announcing Meir's lecture at the Technion on November 29, 1972, in RZ Archives, folder 94; Letter from the Technion Students Association to Meir, December 4, 1972, in RZ Archives, folder 713A. The letter thanked Meir for taking part in the Wednesday afternoon lecture series.

[16] "Israel News Analysis," *Jewish Press*, November 3, 1972, pp. 25, 34, in RZ Archives, folder 594, reprinted as "Facing Up to the Arab Presence," in *Writings 5732*, pp. 131-133.

[17] "Israel News Analysis," *Jewish Press*, December 15, 1972, pp. 11, 43, reprinted as "What Palestinians?" in *Writings 5732*, pp. 147-150 and in *Beyond Words*, 1:350-355.

[18] This figure included the Arabs in East Jerusalem. In 2006, Israeli Arabs, including Arabs in East Jerusalem, were 19.5% of Israel's population. See: http://en.wikipedia.org/wiki/Israeli_Arab.

[19] "Defusing the Time Bomb," *Jewish Press*, January 19, 1973, pp. 22, 27, 44, reprinted in *Writings 5732*, pp. 158-161, and in *Kahane: The Magazine of the Authentic Jewish Idea*, May 1976.

[20] Meir's 1972 appointment book, in RZ Archives, folder 713B. This was on Friday evening, December 1, 1972. The program conformed to the halakhot of Shabbat: There was no entrance fee and there were no microphones.

See chapter 31, note 11, for Yehiel Leket's opposition to Meir's ideas.

[21] Letter (Hebrew) from Yehiel Leket to Meir, September 26, 1975, in RZ Archives, folder 65C.

[22] Ziva Yariv, "Ma'aseh Humani [A Humanitarian Deed]," *Yedioth Ahronoth*, December 21, 1972, p. 15, in RZ Archives, folder 96.

Press release with text of letters to Arabs in English and Hebrew, in RZ Archives, Appendix. There is no evidence that these letters were written in Arabic. Yoel Lerner typed the Hebrew letters. (Phone interview with Lerner, July 28, 1999.) Similar letters sent in 1985 were in Arabic.

[23] "Misrad Hapnim Isher Ha'anakat Te'udat Oleh Larav Meir Kahana [The Interior Ministry Granted New Immigrant Status to Rabbi Meir Kahane]," *Ma'ariv*, December 21, 1972, p. 7, in

RZ Archives, folder 73B; "Israel to Accept Kahane as Citizen," *New York Times*, December 21, 1972, p. 4; "Kahane Appeals to Court in Israel Citizenship Bid," *New York Times*, December 15, 1972, p. 12; "Israel Terms Citizenship '99% Certain' for Kahane," *New York Times*, December 14, 1972, p. 5.

Meir's Israeli identity number was 1268340.

[24] Gabi Baron, "Le'achar Hase'ara She'orer Kruz Mita'am 'Haliga Lehagana Yehudit' Shenishlach Le'arviyei Yisrael Mitbarer: Chazon Hahagira Shel Haliga Lehagana Mivtza Ta'amula Im Kupa Reka [After the Storm Raised by the Liga's Letter to the Arabs: The Emigration Idea Is a Propaganda Stunt Without Money]," *Yedioth Ahronoth*, January 3, 1973, p. 17, in RZ Archives, folder 71B.

[25] "Defusing the Time Bomb," see note 19.

[26] "Sulcha Ne'erkha Bein Harav Meir Kahana La'eida Hadruzit [Reconciliation Meeting Between Rabbi Kahane and the Druze Community]," *Yedioth Ahronoth*, January 8, 1973, p. 12, in RZ Archives, folder 71B; "Kahane Apologizes for Bid to Druzes to Leave Israel," *New York Times*, January 8, 1973, p. 12; David Landau and Yoel Dar, "Apologizes to Druze: Kahane May Be Prosecuted for Anti-Arab Circular," *Jerusalem Post*, January 8, 1973, in RZ Archives, folder 71B.

Phone interview with Shimon Rachamim, June 11, 2004.

[27] Phone interview with Yoel Lerner, May 27, 2004.

[28] "Kahane to Be Charged Under Law of Sedition," *Jerusalem Post*, January 9, 1973, p. 3; "Kahane to Be Prosecuted on Criminal Charges," *Jewish Press*, January 12, 1973, p. 5.

The Law of Sedition was enacted by the British Mandatory government in 1936 and was carried over to Israel's legal system.

[29] "Mikhtav Galui Lerosh Hamemshala [An Open Letter to the Prime Minister]," [ad] *Ma'ariv*, January 11, 1973, p. 32, in RZ Archives, folder 71B.

Another inciteful statement of Golda Meir's was quoted in the *Jerusalem Post:* "Golda Meir once quipped that she does not wish to wake up every morning asking herself how many Arab babies were born during the night." In: Arieh O'Sullivan, "Does the IDF Oppose a Gaza Evacuation?" *Jerusalem Post*, February 10, 2004.

The ad gives the addresses of the Liga as 83 Rechov Dizengoff, Tel Aviv, and 10 Rechov Dorot Rishonim, Jerusalem.

[30] Israel Broadcasting Authority Television News Archive, media no. 00439-73-7, January 11, 1973.

[31] Noah Kliger, "Harav Kahana Mosif Leshager... [Rabbi Kahane Continues Sending Letters to Arabs Encouraging Emigration]," *Yedioth Ahronoth*, January 12, 1973, p. 2, in RZ Archives, folder 71B. Excerpted with permission.

In fact, it was Israeli government policy to purchase the property of Israeli Arabs who wished to emigrate. This is confirmed by U.S. Department of State report, note 33.

[32] Yosef Tzuriel, "Shelosha Mukhtarim Mehagalil Yipagshu Im Harav Kahana [Three Village Heads From the Galilee Will Meet With Rabbi Kahane]," *Ma'ariv*, January 21, 1973, p. 11, in RZ Archives, folder 71B. Excerpted with permission.

[33] Noah Kliger, "'Kan Lo Medinati' Amar Ha'aravi Vehitgayes Laliga Lehagana Yehudit ['This Is Not My State' Said the Arab, and Joined the Liga]," *Yedioth Ahronoth*, January 31, 1973, p. 5, in RZ Archives, folder 71B.

U.S. Department of State report 137 TELAVIV 3378, from U.S. Embassy, Tel Aviv, to Secretary of State, May 16, 1973, p. 3, in RZ Archives, Appendix.

Several payments to Emmanuel Khoury are listed by Meir in RZ Archives, folder 694.

34 "Kahane on Bail for Sending Letters to Arabs," *Jerusalem Post*, February 5, 1973; "Kahane Charged in Israel With Inciting Arabs to Go," *New York Times*, February 5, 1973, p. 12; Phone interview with Yoel Lerner, July 28, 1999. See also note 33, U.S. Department of State.

Summons to report to the police station, February 4, 1973, in RZ Archives, folder 714B.

35 "Six Suspects Held for Arson at Mission Centre," *Jerusalem Post*, February 8, 1973, in RZ Archives, folder 71B; "4 JDL Members Arrested, *Jewish Press*, February 16, 1973, p. 3; "Hutzat Merkaz Misyoneri Behar Hazetim [A Missionary Center on the Mount of Olives Was Set Afire]," *Ha'aretz*, February 7, 1973, p. 12, in RZ Archives, folder 71B; Israel Broadcasting Authority Radio News Archive, media no. 8610, February 7, 1973. See also: "Israel News Analysis: Jerusalem of Golda," note 41.

Source for halakha: *Shulchan Arukh, Orach Chaim* 306:14. One may violate the Sabbath to prevent a Jew from converting to another religion. It is similar to saving a life.

36 "Israel May Banish Christian Missionaries," *International Herald Tribune*, February 17-18, 1973, p. 1, in RZ Archives, folder 71B. Excerpted with permission of United Press International.

37 "Why Are All These People Smiling?" *Jewish Press*, May 26, 1972, p. 13, in RZ Archives, folder 594.

An indication of widespread efforts to convert Jews: "*New York Post* Rejects Ad Seeking Jewish Converts," *Jewish Post and Opinion*, April 21, 1972, p. 11.

38 "Israelis Alarmed by Jews for Jesus," *New York Times*, March 31, 1973, p. 11; "Rabbi Goren Asks Law to Curb Missionary Activities," *Jewish Press*, March 16, 1973, p. 3.

See also note 36.

39 "Higi'a La'aretz Yoshev Rosh Hava'ad Lema'an Hagira Bamizrach Hatikhon Be'artzot Habrit; Haliga Makhriza Al Irgun Chadash: Notzrim Be'ad Moshe [Head of the United States Committee on Middle East Emigration Arrives in Israel; The Liga Announces the Formation of a New Organization: Christians for Moses]," press release, February 20, 1973, in RZ Archives, Appendix. In Hebrew and English.

See chapter 22, note 28, for a biography of William Perl.

40 Israel Broadcasting Authority Radio News Archive, media no. 8657, March 1, 1973; Noah Kliger, "Biteshuva Liyehudim Lema'an Yeshu Hitzig Harav Kahana Et Hanotzrim Lema'an Moshe [In response to Jews for Jesus Rabbi Kahane Presented Christians for Moses]," *Yedioth Ahronoth*, March 2, 1973, p. 2, in RZ Archives, folder 71B. Excerpted with permission.

It is likely that Cummings, Simpson and Thompson were American Jews who acted the roles of Christians for Moses for the news media.

41 "Israel News Analysis: Jerusalem of Golda," *Jewish Press*, April 20, 1973, p. 19, in RZ Archives, folder 594.

The article also told of the plight of Yosef Schneider and Yoel Lerner, family men with children, accused of anti-missionary acts, who were being held without bail pending trial. They were released after four and a half months, in June 1973.

42 "Christians for Moses Begins Its Campaign to Save Christian Tourists," flyer, hand-dated April 2, 1973, in RZ Archives, folder 71B.

43 Sarah Honig, "Christians for Moses to Combat Jews for Jesus," *Jerusalem Post*, March 2, 1973, in RZ Archives, folder 71B.

44 Menachem Rahat, "Harav Kahana Matza Befassuta Tomkhim Betokhnito... [Rabbi Kahane Found Supporters in Fassuta for His Emigration Plan]," *Ma'ariv*, March 4, 1973, p. 4, in RZ Archives, folder 71B. Excerpted with permission.

See also: Meir Hacohen (pseudonym of Meir Kahane), "Israel Through Laughter and Tears: The Emigration Fund," *Jewish Press*, February 23, 1973, p. 56.

A survey taken in the Palestinian Authority in 2004 showed that 37% of the population would agree to leave their "homeland" in exchange for material benefits. See: www.IsraelNationalNews.com (Arutz Sheva News Service, February 5, 2004).

45 Letter from Meir to William Perl, undated [probably mid-March 1973]. Original in the William Perl collection, Gelman Library, George Washington University, Washington, D.C.

"Haliga Lehagana Yehudit Mevakeshet Lehasig Visa Le'arhab [The Liga Wants to Obtain a Visa to the U.S.]," *Ha'aretz*, April 5, 1973, p. 2; "Arab Villager Quits JDL," *Jerusalem Post*, May 16, 1973, p. 2; U.S. Department of State report 137 TELAVIV 3378, from U.S. Embassy, Tel Aviv, to Secretary of State, May 16, 1973, p. 3, in RZ Archives, Appendix.

46 Several letters from Jews wishing to buy Arab property in Israel are in RZ Archives, folder 67. A plan to set up a business syndicate to purchase Arab properties is detailed in a letter from Sheila Lidz to Paul Flacks, December 4, 1974, in RZ Archives, folder 92A.

47 "Kahane Charged With Incitement," *Jerusalem Post*, April 30, 1973, p. 2.

Meir's statements in: Meir Hacohen (pseudonym of Meir Kahane), "Israel Through Laughter and Tears," *Jewish Press*, January 26, 1973, p. 41; June 22, 1973, p. 15.

48 Phone interview with Yoel Lerner, July 7, 1997; e-mails from Yoel Lerner, July 29, 2005 and March 18, 2007.

Letters from attorney Aharon Papo regarding this case (criminal case no. 92/73), May 11, 1973, January 23, 1975, and May 11, 1975, in RZ Archives, folder 714B.

49 "Israel News Analysis," *Jewish Press*, July 21, 1972, p. 22, reprinted as "Jewish Babies," in *Writings 5732*, p. 96-98, and in *Beyond Words*, 1:306-309.

Chapter 33

1 The rental contract between Meir and owners Israel and Ilana Perl was signed on February 18, 1973, for one year, through February 21, 1974. The monthly rent was 900 lirot (about $125). Contract in RZ Archives, folder 700.

The building at 38 Jaffa Road, like others near it, has high arched windows overlooking Jaffa Road. The floor-to-ceiling windows open onto balconies with railings of ornately designed wrought iron. The children and I watched the Independence Day Parade that year from the excellent vantage point of the office balcony.

The phone number of the Jerusalem office was 02-228594. Its mailing address was P.O. Box 7287. The 26 Ben Maimon Street address does not appear in any documents after September 1972. Until January 31, 1973, all Liga press releases and flyers bore the address of the Jewish Identity Center, 10 Dorot Rishonim Street, Jerusalem.

2 Phone interview with Shimon Rachamim, July 19, 2006.

The phone number of the Tel Aviv office was 03-286543. Its mailing address was P.O. Box 36431. Meir gave an interview shortly after the Tel Aviv office was opened. See: Moshe Yahalom, "Ma Ata, Harav Kahana? [What Are You, Rabbi Kahane?]," *Yatush* (Tel Aviv University), April 29, 1973, p. 2, in RZ Archives, folder 71B.

3 *Kol Haliga*, March 25, 1973, from the collection of Shimon Rachamim, in RZ Archives, Appendix.

Protokol Shel Asefa Klalit Shenitkayma Beyom 2.4.73 [Minutes of Meeting Held on April 2, 1973.] From the collection of Shimon Rachamim, in RZ Archives, Appendix.

Letter sent to Liga members, signed Shimon Rachamim, *Mazkir* [Administrative Director], April 1, 1973, from the collection of Shimon Rachamim, in RZ Archives, Appendix.

4 Meir's Ministry of Interior certificate of name change is dated April 3, 1973, in RZ Archives,

Appendix. On his U.S. passport application dated April 9, 1979, he used the name Martin Meir David Kahane. See passports in RZ Archives, folder 582.

5   Letter from Mr. E. Netzer, Principal, ORT High School, Ramat Gan, to Meir, February 19, 1973, in RZ Archives, Appendix.

Letter from Cultural Committee, Kfar Hittim, to Meir, February 11, 1973, in RZ Archives, folder 473.

Letter from Meir to Major Horowitz, Judea and Samaria Regional Headquarters, March 26, 1973, in RZ Archives, Appendix. Meir wrote: "I was asked by members of Rosh Tzurim to lecture to them. Since I am prohibited to enter the liberated territories, I request a one time permit for April 15, 1973 – April 16, 1973."

Letter of thanks from the Segula Bnei Akiva high school for girls to Meir, April 25, 1973.

Letter of thanks from Histadrut Poalei Agudat Yisrael, Tel Aviv, to Meir, June 19, 1973 (for lecture on June 1, 1973).

Letter of thanks from Rabbi Shmuel Heller, Yeshivat Pirchei Aharon, Kiryat Shmuel, May 29, 1973, in RZ Archives, folder 713A.

6   Uri Avneri, "Ledavid Frost Megama Brura [David Frost Has a Clear Objective]," [letter to the editor] *Ma'ariv*, March 15, 1973, p. 5, in RZ Archives, folder 71B; Moshe Shamir, "Eichut Hasicha [The Quality of Talk]," *Ma'ariv*, March 13, 1973, p. 5.

"On the Air," *Jerusalem Post*, March 11, 1973, p. 8. The Frost show aired at 9:40 P.M.

7   "Harav Meir Kahana Hitchapes Le'itona'i Vetakaf Komunistim [Rabbi Meir Kahane Disguised Himself as a Reporter and Attacked Communists]," *Yedioth Ahronoth*, April 16, 1973, p. 4, in RZ Archives, folder 71B; "Harav Kahana: Takafti et Harusi Biglal Ha'elbon Shebevikuro [I Attacked the Russian Because His Visit Is an Insult]," *Hatzofe*, April 16, 1973, p. 1.

See also: FBI Los Angeles office file 105-29629-118, report, June 1, 1973, p. 3, in RZ Archives, Appendix.

8   "Geveret Meir: Shetikatekh Alula Lehamit Sho'a Chadasha! [Mrs. Meir: Your Silence May Bring Another Holocaust!]," [ad] *Ma'ariv*, May 3, 1973, p. 27, in RZ Archives, folder 71B.

The ad was signed with the post office box and phone number of the Tel Aviv branch. See note 2.

9   "A Time To Pluck," *Jewish Press*, May 11, 1973, pp. 53-57, reprinted in *Writings 5732*, pp. 217-220.

10   William Korey, "The Struggle Over Jackson – Mills – Vanick," *American Jewish Year Book*, 1974/75, pp. 199-224. Korey is a leading American and international authority on East European anti-Semitism and human rights.

11   William Orbach, *The American Movement to Aid Soviet Jewry* (Amherst: University of Massachusetts Press, 1979), p. 142.

12   Letter from Meir to Rabbi Shalom Klass, undated, [photocopy] from collection of Bennett Levine, in RZ Archives, Appendix. Although Meir tried to avoid its interception by mailing it to a JDL member who would hand-deliver it to Klass, it was stopped by the postal censor in Israel.

13   "... Lehalan Keta Mehane'um... May 17, 1973 [... The Following Is an Excerpt from the Speech... May 17, 1973...]," press release with text of part of Meir's speech, in RZ Archives, folder 715B.

Hoda'a La'itonut... Tekes Hakhnasat Sefer Torah [Press release... Torah Dedication Ceremony], May 17, 1973, at Soviet immigrants' synagogue in Sanhedria Murchevet, Jerusalem, in RZ Archives, folder 71A.

The Torah scroll, a gift from a New York synagogue that had closed, was brought to Israel by Gene Singer. He recalled that the ceremony included singing, dancing and refreshments. Interview with Gene Singer, Jerusalem, August 23, 1999.

14 *Report on Probation Violation*, see chapter 41, note 36.

15 "Israel News Analysis: Day of the Holocaust and the Bravery," *Jewish Press*, May 25, 1973, pp. 16, 21, reprinted in *Writings 5732*, pp. 206-209.

The Jackson amendment failed to garner support during that period because Nixon had succeeded in convincing the major Jewish organizations not to back it.

16 "F.B.I. Says Threat Led to J.D.L Raid: Contends Action Was Based on Peril to U.N. Missions," *New York Times*, May 25, 1973, p. 70; Joseph Feurey and Joseph P. Cotter, "FBI, Cops Ransack JDL Headquarters," *New York Post*, May 23, 1973, p. 18, in YU Archives, folder 13/2; "Raid May Delay JDL Trial," *Daily News*, [May 25], 1973, reproduced in: *Iton* (Jewish Defense League), Rosh Hashana 5734 [September / October, 1974], p. 8, in RZ Archives, Appendix.

JDL headquarters were at 144 West 27 Street in Manhattan.

The American Jewish Congress protested the raid on JDL offices: "We oppose any police action that violates constitutional guarantees.... the raiding forces destroyed property and seized files and other documents, including membership lists, to which they were not entitled." American Jewish Congress, "For Immediate Release," May 25, 1973, in RZ Archives, folder 70B.

Lawrence Dickter, "B'nai B'rith Protests on Bugging, but Silent About Same for JDL," [letter to the editor] *Jewish Post And Opinion*, July 6, 1973, p. 12. Dickter was co-chairman, South Brooklyn chapter, JDL.

17 E-mail from Glenn Richter, June 13, 2004.

18 "Police Arrest 29 During Protests," *Washington Post*, June 19, 1973, p. A13; "U.S.-Russian Pact Seen on A-Power," *Newsday*, June 18, 1973.

"800 Demonstrate for Hour at Soviet Mission's Estate," *New York Times*, June 21, 1973, p. 16; John Sibley, "Soviet Diplomat's Car Is Fire-Bombed in Queens," *New York Times*, June 21, 1973, p. 17; "Nixon, Brezhnev Agree on Arms," *Newsday*, June 21, 1973, p. 7.

19 E-mails from Si Frumkin via Glenn Richter, July 10, 2004 and July 12, 2004. Frumkin recalled: "We were met in San Clemente by some very polite, mysterious people in suits who followed our trucks, filmed us as we released the balloons and told us that they were from a news agency with a fictitious name and phone number."

Brezhnev arrived in California on Friday, June 22, met with Nixon in San Clemente (about 70 miles from Los Angeles) on June 23 and flew back to Washington on June 24. See: Hedrick Smith, "Nixon and Brezhnev, on Coast, Hold Final Round of Talks," *New York Times*, June 24, 1973, pp. 1, 7.

20 See note 7, FBI report. The appeal was probably heard on June 1, the date of this report.

21 "Israel Court Forbids Visit to U.S. by Rabbi Kahane," *New York Times*, June 5, 1973, p. 38; "State Attorney Refuses to Return Kahane's Passport," *Jewish Press*, June 8, 1973, p. 3; "Kahane Detained Again for Letters to Arabs," *Jerusalem Post*, June 7, 1973, p. 3.

See also: Letter from attorney Meir Schechter to State Attorney Gabriel Bach, May 27, 1973, in RZ Archives, folder 71A. This was an informal request prior to filing an appeal.

Hoda'a La'itonut: Praklitut Hamedina Hefera Havtacha Be'al Peh... [Press release: The State Attorney Violated a Verbal Agreement...], undated [probably June 2, 1973], in RZ Archives, folder 71A.

A demonstration at the Israeli Consulate in New York was planned for August 7, too: See: "JDL Vigil at Israeli Mission," *Jewish Press*, August 3, 1973, p. 41.

22 Letter from Meir to an unnamed JDL member, undated, [photocopy] from collection of Bennett Levine, in RZ Archives, Appendix. Cited in *Report on Probation Violation*, p. 7. See note 14.

Iraq broke off relations with the United States after the 1967 Six Day War.

23 Meir alluded to government tampering with his mail in a magazine interview. "The fact is the democratic way of life in Israel is not everything it should be.... The concept that the government can tamper with your mail..." See: Avi Oren, "The Jewish Defense League in Israel," *Israel Magazine*, July-August, 1972, p. 18.

In the *Jewish Press* he wrote that there were "rumors that Rabbi Kahane's mail is tampered with." He advised readers, "Send all mail to P. O. Box 439, Bronx, N.Y. [i.e. to Shifra Hoffman]..." See: Meir Hacohen (pseudonym of Meir Kahane), "Israel Through Laughter and Tears," *Jewish Press*, May 24, 1974, p. 11.

Earlier, he had written to Hoffman (see chapter 38, note 30) to address all mail to our neighbor Al Storch, because he suspected that the government was tampering with his mail.

Shabak is the acronym of *Sherut Bitachon Klali*, the General Security Service.

An example of *Shabak* infiltration: In DOV, an organization that participated in Liga demonstrations in 1971 and 1972, a leading member was an undercover policeman. See: Memoir by Haim Hermon, http://www.hermon.com/dov/dov.htm.

24 "JDL Leader Still Sending Emigration Letters to Arabs," *Jerusalem Post*, June 4, 1973, p. 3; Avishai Amir, "Manhig Haliga Le-15 Yemei Ma'atzar: Bevaksho Le'esor Pirsum Chomer Hara'ayot, He'eshim Praklit Hamedina: Harav Kahana Laliga Bechul: Lechabel Bevikur Ishiyut Mesuyemet Bemedina Mesuyemet [Liga Leader to Jail for 15 Days: In a Request to Bar Publication of Evidence, the Attorney General Accused: Rabbi Kahane Instructed JDL in America: Sabotage the Visit of a Certain Personage in a Certain Country]," *Ma'ariv*, June 8, 1973, p. 4, in RZ Archives, folder 71A; "Notes on People," *New York Times*, June 9, 1973, p. 39; "Kahane Jailed for Urging Demonstrations," [editorial] *Jewish Press*, June 15, 1973, p. 5; "Meir Kahane Jailed," *Jewish Press*, June 15, 1973, p. 45. See also: "Kahane Detained Again...," note 21.

25 E-mail from Yoel Lerner, June 25, 2004.

26 Letter from Meir to Libby, [June 1973], in RZ Archives, Appendix.

27 Letter from Tzippy to Meir, June 25, 1973, in RZ Archives, folder 714B. While Meir was in jail, the Schwartz family invited us to spend Shabbat, June 23, at their home in Moshav Chemed. It was a welcome change of scene.

Interview with Tzippy Kaplan, December 10, 2006.

28 Letter from Meir to the children, [June 1973], in RZ Archives, Appendix. This was probably written June 13 or 14, 1973, because in his letter to Binyamin, he referred to them studying together "last week." The letter begins: First a few words to all of you and then a few to each of you."

When Meir would bless the children on Friday nights, he always added the words in this letter, "Remember what is important and what is not important." This principle guided him always.

29 Letter from Meir to Libby and children, June 12, 1973, in RZ Archives, Appendix.

30 Letter from Meir to Libby, June 18, 1973, in RZ Archives, Appendix.

31 "How Sweet It Is," *Letters from Prison* (Jerusalem: Jewish Identity Center, 1974), pp. 14-15, in RZ Archives, booklets folder. Reprinted in *Writings 5734-5-6*, p. 18-19, in *Beyond Words*, 1:453-455, and in *Kahane: The Magazine of the Authentic Jewish Idea*, March-April 1988, p. 14.

Two Hebrew translations were published: 1) "Talmud Torah Keneged Kulam," *Hara'ayon Hayehudi: Bit'on Tenuat Kach*, no. 7, August 13, 1982, pp. 2-3, in RZ Archives, Appendix. 2) "Kama Shezeh Matok," translated by Binyamin Kahane, in *Kohen Venavi* [Selected Articles by Rabbi Meir Kahane] (Jerusalem: Institute for Publication of Writings of Rabbi Meir Kahane, 2001), vol. 1, p. 31-32.

32 This commandment in *Leviticus* 19:16 was translated by Meir's father as: "Do not stand idle when your fellow man is in danger." See: Yechezkel Shraga Kahane, *Torah Yesharah*, chapter 1, note 12.

33 *Igeret Hagra* [The Vilna Gaon's Letter] written by Eliyahu ben Shlomo Zalman, 18th century Lithuanian rabbi known as the Vilna Gaon, the Sage of Vilna. Meir wrote this paragraph in the original Hebrew. The English translation is from the website: www.pirchei.co.il.

34 Letter (Hebrew) from Meir to the children, June 24, 1973, in RZ Archives, Appendix.

35 "Harav Meir Kahana – Korban Lekesher Hashetika [Rabbi Meir Kahane – Victim of a Conspiracy of Silence]," [ad] *Ma'ariv*, June 12, 1973, p. 13, in RZ Archives, folder 71A.

Posters announcing the First National Convention of the Liga at the Jerusalem International Convention Center on Tuesday, June 12, 1973, 7:30 P.M., in RZ Archives, poster folder, no. 195.

36 Noah Kliger wrote for *Yedioth Ahronoth*. Shimon Rachamim recalled that Shmulik was the correspondent for *Itim*, the Israeli news agency. Phone interview with Shimon Rachamim, October 28, 2004.

37 *Matza Haliga Lehagana Yehudit Likrat Habechirot Laknesset Hashminit.* [*The Platform of the Liga for the Eighth Knesset.*] 16 pp., 18 cm., in JNUL Archives, folder V1797; "Haliga Lehagana Ishra Matza'a [The Liga Approved Its Platform]," *Ha'aretz*, June 13, 1973, p. 2.

38 Yosef Tzuriel, "Harav Kahana Lo Shuchrar Leve'idat Haliga [Rabbi Kahane Was Not Released for the Liga Convention]," *Ma'ariv*, June 13, 1973, p. 2. This describes Emmanuel Khoury's speech.

39 Letter (Hebrew) from Meir to Dr. Israel Eldad, dated June 14, 1973, in RZ Archives, folder 714B.

40 Typescript of Hebrew speech by Rabbi Yechezkel Kahane, June 12, 1973, 3 pp., in RZ Archives, folder 71A.

41 Four letters from Meir to Shimon Rachamim, undated, but probably written between June 8 and June 12, 1973, from the collection of Shimon Rachamim, in RZ Archives, Appendix.

See chapter 31, note 54, for details on the contract with Bivas.

42 Letter from Meir to an unnamed JDL member, June 12, 1973, [photocopy] from the collection of Bennett Levine, in RZ Archives, Appendix. Cited in *Report on Probation Violation*, pp. 7-8. See note 14.

43 Israel Police, "Doch Chipus [Search Report]," June 18, 1973. Witnesses: Aryeh Julius, Avinoam Biton.

44 "Kahane Held 10 More Days," *Jerusalem Post*, June 21, 1973, p. 3; "Rabbi Kahane Held 10 More Days; Letter Smuggled Out of Meir Kahane's Jail," *Jewish Press*, June 29, 1973, pp. 2, 50.

45 Dosh [Kariel Gardosh], "Al Titragesh! Zeh Rak Harav Kahana! [Don't Get Excited! It's Only Rabbi Kahane]," [cartoon] *Ma'ariv*, June 22, 1973, p. 13, in RZ Archives, folder 71A. This cartoon was later reproduced on Liga election flyers.

46 Letter from Meir to Libby, [June 1973], in RZ Archives, Appendix.

47 "Eretz Yisrael and the Burning Fire: Letter Smuggled Out From Meir Kahane's Jail," *Jewish Press*, July 20, 1973, pp. 9, 20, reprinted in *Letters from Prison* (Jerusalem: Jewish Identity Center, 1974), pp. 42-45, in RZ Archives, booklets folder. The article bore the dateline, "Jerusalem Central Prison, 25 Sivan, [June 25]," i.e. it was written after his detention was extended on June 20 for another 10 days.

As Meir foresaw in this article, the Brezhnev letters trial was indeed held behind closed doors. See chapter 37.

48 Letter from Meir to Libby and children, undated [probably June 20, 1973] from Jerusalem Central Prison, in RZ Archives, Appendix.

After Meir was released, one of our family outings was to the recently opened Wax Museum in the Shalom Meir Tower, Tel Aviv, then Israel's tallest building. Later that summer, we went to the Galei Sanz hotel in Netanya for a few days.

49 "The Fire in My Bones," *Jewish Press*, February 23, 1990, p. 22, in RZ Archives, folder 1188A.

The verse quoted is from *Jeremiah* 20:9.

Letter from V. L. Terdiman to Meir, March 13, 1990, in RZ Archives, folder 127D.

Meir also compared himself to Jeremiah and other prophets in these articles: "Meir Kahane's Speech Before the Military Court in Ramallah," *Jewish Press*, August 29, 1980, pp. 8, 25; "Arabs and Jews: The Ultimate Contradiction," *Jewish Press*, March 27, 1981, p. 24, 26 (reprinted in the introduction to *They Must Go*); and "Reflections on an Election," *Jewish Press*, July 17, 1981, pp. 12, 18.

50 See note 44, *Jewish Press*.

51 Michal Tzur, *The (Emergency) Defense Regulations, 1945. Position Paper No. 16.* (Jerusalem: Israel Democracy Institute, 1999).

Over the years, the Knesset changed or repealed many of the old mandatory laws, but the emergency measures remained basically the same.

52 "Notes on People," *New York Times*, June 29, 1973, p. 19; "JDL Raps Rabbi Kahane's Detention," *Jewish Telegraphic Agency Bulletin*, [dateline:] June 28, 1973, in RZ Archives, folder 71A; "B'ni Bakele Ve'af Echad Lo Zo'ek... [My Son Is in Jail and Nobody Cries Out...]," *Yedioth Ahronoth*, June 28, 1973, p. 4.

53 "Israel Indicts Kahane in Abduction Plot," *New York Times*, June 30, 1973, p. 5; "Kahane Admits Plan to Abduct Soviet in U.S.," *Jerusalem Post*, July 1, 1973, p. 3; "Kahane Indicted in Israel," *Jewish Press*, July 6, 1973, pp. 1, 2.

The telegram had no specific directives. See note 14, *Report on Probation Violation*, p. 8.

54 Letter from Meir to Libby, [July 1973], in RZ Archives, Appendix.

55 "Protest the Harassment and Imprisonment of Rabbi Meir Kahane," [ad] *Jewish Press*, July 6, 1973, p. 23. The ad was almost a quarter-page.

Protest letters also appeared in the *Jewish Press*. For example: George Torodash, "Protests Jailing of Kahane," [letter to the editor] *Jewish Press*, June 29, 1973, p. 5. JDL member Torodash, a probation officer, gave his credentials: President, Local 1114, American Federation of Police.

Printed form letter replying to protests, signed David Zohar, First Secretary, Israeli Embassy, Washington, D.C., July 11, 1973, in RZ Archives, folder 683B.

56 Letter from Samuel Shoshan to Shaul Ramati, Israel Consul General, Chicago, July 11, 1973, in RZ Archives, Appendix.

57 "Gilui Da'at [Open Letter]," [ad] *Ma'ariv*, July 9, 1973, p. 4, in RZ Archives, folder 71A.

58 "Adishut Mul Ma'atzar Harav [Indifference to the Rabbi's Imprisonment]," [letters to the editor] *Yedioth Ahronoth*, July 10, 1973, p. 14, in RZ Archives, folder 71A.

59 "Ar'ar... [Appeal...]" to the Supreme Court presented by attorneys David Rotlevy and Meir Schechter, July 7, 1973, in RZ Archives, folder 714B. David Rotlevy was a prominent Tel Aviv attorney. See: www.intjewishlawyers.org/docenter/viewDocument.asp?id=9268.

"Kahane Wins Appeal, Released on Bond," *Jerusalem Post*, July 8, 1973, p. 3; "Harav Kahana Shuchrar Be'arvut [Rabbi Kahane Freed on Bail]," *Davar*, July 8, 1973, p. 8, in RZ Archives, folder 71A; "Notes on People," *New York Times*, July 7, 1973, p. 17. The *New York Times* gives the amount of bail as $12,000, i.e. 50,000 lirot, but this is an error.

Meir's parents' presence in the judge's chambers during the appeal is noted in the printed reply to those who wrote to protest Meir's imprisonment. See note 55, Zohar.

Check stub no. 020814 for 83.05 lirot from Israel Prison Service, dated July 17, 1973 [*sic*], in RZ Archives, folder 714B.

60 "Charges in Israel Denied by Kahane," *New York Times*, July 21, 1973, p. 7, in RZ Archives, folder 71A. This was criminal case number 167/73.

Time frame considered reasonable: Letter (Hebrew) from attorney Meir Schechter to Libby, June 27, 2004, in RZ Archives, Appendix. Legal proceedings ended on June 28, 1974, when Meir received a two-year suspended sentence. See: "Israel Convicts Kahane in Plot on Embassies," *New York Times*, June 29, 1974, p. 48.

Chapter 34

1 "Harav Kahana Mavti'ach Masa Bechirot Benosach America [Rabbi Kahane Promises an American-Style Election Campaign]," *Yedioth Ahronoth*, July 17, 1973, p. 4, in RZ Archives, folder 71A; "Kahane 'Running For Knesset With List of 40,'" *Jerusalem Post*, July 17, 1973, p. 3; "Kahane Says He Proposed Bombing Iraqi Office in the U.S.," *New York Times*, July 17, 1973, p. 11.

The website of the National Photo Collection, Israel Government Press Office, has three pictures of Meir at this press conference. See: www.mof.gov.il/pictures, picture codes D128-100, D128-101, D128-102. Number D128-102 is in the photo section of this book.

See also: "Harav Meir Kahana... Bechevrato Shel Grisha Feigin... [Rabbi Meir Kahane... with Grisha Feigin...]," [photo caption] *Yedioth Ahronoth*, July 24, 1973, p. 13, in RZ Archives, folder 71A.

The large number of copies printed is verified by Hebron Press shipping slips in RZ Archives, folder 692B.

2 Phone interview with Yoel Lerner, May 2, 2000.

Meir Kahane, *Ha'etgar: Eretz Segula* [*Our Challenge: The Chosen Land*] (Jerusalem: Jewish Identity Center, 1973), 183 pp., 16 cm.

In 1992, a hardcover memorial edition was published by the Yeshiva of the Jewish Idea (Yeshivat Haraayon Hayehudi) in Jerusalem with a different layout: 107 pp., 24 cm.

Meir Kahane, *Our Challenge: The Chosen Land* (Radnor, Pa.: Chilton Book Company, 1974), 181 pp.

Meir was writing directly in Hebrew by the 1980s. One example is his booklet *Al Ha'emuna Ve'al Hage'ula* [*On Faith and Redemption*].

3 *Our Challenge*, pp. 14-15.

4 "Zeh Ata Yatza La'or! [Just Published!]" [ad] *Daf Hasbara* [*Information Page*], four-sided tabloid-size flyer, p. [4], in RZ Archives, folder 68A.

See also: "Hofi'a! [Published!]," [ad] *Ma'ariv*, September 16, 1973, p. 16, in RZ Archives, folder 71A and RZ Archives, poster folder, no. 193. This announced an election rally on September 20, 1973, where Meir would autograph copies of *Ha'etgar*.

5 Interview with Moshe Lebowitz of Betar Ilit, February 18, 2003.

Steimatzky received 1,000 copies of *Ha'etgar*, sold 325, and returned 675. They paid 487.50 lirot for 325 copies sold at IL3 each, less 50% discount. See: Steimatzky, [*payment report*], November 10, 1974, in RZ Archives, folder 692A.

The price, 3 lirot, less than a dollar, was the average price of books during that period. See: *Katalog Hasefarim Haklali, 1973* [*General Book Catalog, 1973*]. (Tel Aviv: Book Publishers Association of Israel, 1973).

The total cost for 10,000 copies, including editing, proofreading and graphic design, was 15,200 lirot ($3,600). Invoice from Hebron Press, August 5, 1973, in RZ Archives, folder 703.

Phone interview with Yehoshua Ben Zion, July 20, 2004.

[6] Letter from Shoshana Mageni to Meir, February 7, 1974, in RZ Archives, folder 715B.

[7] Letter from Benton M. Arnovitz to Libby, October 19, 1997 in RZ Archives, Appendix.

[8] Telegram from Benton M. Arnovitz to Meir, stamped June 7, 1973, in JNUL Archives, folder ARC 4=1748.

[9] Telegram from Benton M. Arnovitz to Libby, July 10, 1973, in JNUL Archives, folder ARC 4=1748.

Letter from Benton M. Arnovitz to Meir, July 25, 1973, in JNUL Archives, folder ARC 4=1748. This refers to Arnovitz' letter of June 11 urging Meir to change the title to one that would "capture the potential buyer's imagination." Since the working title on the contract was *Our Challenge*, it is clear that Meir did not change it.

[10] Letter from Benton M. Arnovitz to Libby, August 20, 1973, in JNUL Archives, folder ARC 4=1748.

Letter from Benton M. Arnovitz to Libby, September 21, 1973, in JNUL Archives, folder ARC 4=1748.

Letter from Meir to Benton M. Arnovitz, November 4, 1973, in JNUL Archives, folder ARC 4=1748.

Meir later wrote in the *Jewish Press* of "rumors that Rabbi Kahane's mail is tampered with." See chapter 33, note 23.

[11] Letter from Benton M. Arnovitz to Meir, September 21, 1973, in JNUL Archives, folder ARC 4=1748.

[12] Letter from Meir to Benton M. Arnovitz, November 4, 1973, in JNUL Archives, folder ARC 4=1748.

[13] Letter from Stan Stephenson, Manager, Marketing Services, Chilton Book Company, to Meir, December 6, 1973, in JNUL Archives, folder ARC 4=1748.

[14] Meir went to the United States only in August 1974.

[15] Contract with Chilton Book Company for publication of *Our Challenge: The Chosen Land*, signed July 25, 1973; Advance Tip Sheet, July 30, 1973. Both in JNUL Archives, folder ARC 4=1748.

[16] Letter from Benton M. Arnovitz to Meir, February 26, 1974, in JNUL Archives, folder ARC 4=1748.

Regarding the sentence in the fourth paragraph of the jacket copy, Arnovitz attached a sheet showing the original text and the revision headed, "This is the revised copy," in JNUL Archives, folder ARC 4=1748.

[17] *Publisher's Weekly*, February 25, 1974, p. 108, in RZ Archives, folder 72A.

[18] Arthur I. Waskow, "Slouching Toward Israel," *New York Times Book Review*, July 21, 1974, section 7, pp. 15-16, in RZ Archives, folder 715A.

See Meir's comments on Waskow in chapter 30.

[19] Isaac L. Swift, "Two Books by Rabbi Kahane Tell JDL History, Controversy, Aims," *Jewish Bookland*, March 1976, p. 2. This was a review of both *Our Challenge* and *Story of the Jewish Defense League*.

[20] Arnold Ages, "Kahane Plays Right Into Hands of Israel's Enemies," *Jewish Western Bulletin*, January 3, 1975, p. 10, in RZ Archives, folder 64C. Reprinted as: "In the World of Books," *Jew-*

ish Post (Toronto), October 30, 1975, in RZ Archives, folder 713B. Excerpted with the author's permission.

Udi Adiv: "Five Israelis Are Convicted of Treason," *New York Times*, March 26, 1973, p. 3.

[21] "[Review]," *Kirkus Reviews*, April 15, 1974, in RZ Archives, folder 72A. Excerpted with permission.

[22] "[Review]," *Choice*, September 1974, p. 1024, in RZ Archives, folder 72A. Excerpted with permission from *Choice*, copyright by the American Library Association.

Other reviews, mostly brief and negative, appeared in: *America*, October 12, 1974, and *Brief: Quarterly Newsletter of the American Council for Judaism,* Autumn, 1974, pp. 3-4, both in RZ Archives, folder 64C; *Philadelphia Inquirer*, June 16, 1974, and *Reconstructionist*, June 1974, both in RZ Archives, folder 72A.

[23] "Jewish Defense League's leader..." press release from Chilton Book Company for *Our Challenge*, April 24, 1974, in RZ Archives, folder 91.

[24] Letter from Chilton Book Company to Meir, March 2, 1978, in JNUL Archives, folder ARC 4=1748. The letter does not say how many books remained. Arnovitz estimated the original printing run at 5,000 – 6,000 copies. Letter from Benton M. Arnovitz to Libby, October 19, 1997, in JNUL Archives, folder ARC 4=1748.

Letter from Benton M. Arnovitz to Meir, July 29, 1974, in JNUL Archives, folder ARC 4=1748.

E-mail from Benton M. Arnovitz to Libby, June 13, 2000. Arnovitz added, in this message, "A great many books, maybe even most, never earn beyond their advance."

[25] Letter from Meir to Shifra Hoffman, November 6, 1973, in RZ Archives, folder 704.

[26] Notices about the planned book of articles appeared in: "Israel News Analysis," *Jewish Press*, April 20, 1973, p. 19, in RZ Archives, folder 594; "Israel News Analysis," *Jewish Press*, May 11, 1973, p. 14, in RZ Archives, folder 1207.

There are about 50 advance orders in RZ Archives, folder 704.

[27] Printer's proofs of *Writings 5731* headed Michlol Ltd., 35 Rachel Imenu Street, Jerusalem, in RZ Archives, folder 596. "Typesetting by Michlol Ltd.," appears on the verso of the title pages of the volumes for 5731 and 5732. The proofs are in RZ Archives, folders 593, 594 and 1207.

[28] Letter from Meir to Libby, June 18, 1973, in RZ Archives, Appendix.

[29] Handwritten "Publisher's Introduction," in RZ Archives, Appendix. A comparison of the manuscript with the printed pages reveals many typographical errors. See: "Publisher's Introduction," *Writings 5731*), pp. 1-2.

[30] Letter from Meir to Libby, undated [probably June 20, 1973], in RZ Archives, Appendix.

[31] Invoices from Hebron Press in RZ Archives, folders 692A, 692B and 694; invoice for 3,150 lirot ($750) from Hebron Press, November 6, 1973, in RZ Archives, folder 478.

"The plates of my *Jewish Press* articles went out to [Morris] Drucker today." Letter from Meir to Shifra Hoffman, October 28, 1973, in RZ Archives, folder 92B.

Ordering information in: Meir Hacohen (pseudonym of Meir Kahane), "Israel Through Laughter and Tears," *Jewish Press*, November 9, 1973, pp. 18, 31; "Finis," *Jewish Press*, September 21, 1973, pp. S8, 39, in RZ Archives, folder 1207.

[32] Letter from Meir to Benton M. Arnovitz, Chilton Book Company, November 4, 1973, in JNUL Archives, folder ARC 4=1748.

The circulation of the *Jewish Press* is given as 154,310 in the *Ayer Directory*, 1971, p. 691, and as 172,000 in the *Ayer Directory*, 1972, p. 556.

[33] E-mail from Benton M. Arnovitz, June 12, 2000.

[34] *Writings 5732* had 268 pages and the imprint Jerusalem: Jewish Identity Center, 1973.

Hebron Press invoice for 8,576 lirot (about $2,000) for "English book, 268 pages, typesetting," July 31, 1974, in RZ Archives, folder 692B.

[35] Torodash wrote: "I put Shifra Hoffman in touch with Zvi Kraushar. Bookazine will order 1,000 copies." Letter from George Torodash to Meir, December 8, 1973, in JNUL Archives, folder ARC 4=1748.

Zvi Kraushar's brother, Shmuel, introduced 14-year-old Meir to Betar (see chapter 4).

Letters from Shifra Hoffman to Meir, February 5, 1974, and April 28, 1974, in RZ Archives, folder 713A.

Letter from Abe Levine, Managing Editor of *Kahane: The Magazine of the Authentic Jewish Idea*, to subscribers, September 19, 1977, in RZ Archives, folder 735.

In 1976 a *Jewish Press* ad offered *Writings 5731* as part of a special package deal: Six books for $18, including, in hardcover: *Never Again, Story of the Jewish Defense League,* and *Our Challenge*, and in softcover: *Writings 5731, Time to Go Home,* and *Numbers 23:9.* "Does Your Library Have the Writings of Rabbi Meir Kahane?" [ad] *Jewish Press*, May 14, 1976, p. 29, in RZ Archives, folder 90B.

[36] Mimeographed letter signed Rabbi A. Julius, to publishing firms, October 1973, in RZ Archives, folder 1010.

[37] Letter from Viking Press to Rabbi A. Julius, November 9, 1973; Postcard with printed message from Atheneum, November 5, 1973; Letter from Alfred A. Knopf to Meir, November 5, 1973; Letter from Prentice-Hall to Meir, November 28, 1973; Letter from Delacorte Press to Meir, November 8, 1973; Letter from Little, Brown and Co. to Meir, November 8, 1973; Letter from McGraw-Hill to Meir, December 27, 1973; all in JNUL Archives, folder ARC 4=1748.

[38] Letter from Norman Kotker, editor, Charles Scribner's Sons, to Meir, November 13, 1973, in RZ Archives, folder 713A. Norman Kotker has written several books on Jewish topics.

[39] "Going to the Knesset," *Jewish Press*, June 1, 1973, pp. 26, 39, reprinted in *Writings 5732*, pp. 226-228. Reprinted as a flyer, in RZ Archives, folders 1202 and 714A.

[40] "Kahane to the Knesset," [ad] *Jewish Press*, June 22, 1973, p. 25. An earlier ad was: "The JDL IS Going to The Knesset," *Jewish Press*, May 18, 1973, p. 35.

[41] "Attention Organizations," [ad] *Jewish Press*, July 6, 1973, p. 37. The ad gave Rabbi Julius' qualifications: "Formerly director of the Religious Education Department of the Jewish Agency in the U.S., now a broadcaster on Israel radio." Rabbi Julius presented the news on the Yiddish language program. To ease the adjustment of new immigrants, Israel radio had programs in various languages.

[42] Letter from Hilton Goldman to Meir, July 15, 1973, in RZ Archives, folder 71A. "The mountains" refers to the Catskill Mountain area in upstate New York, where many Jews spent their summer vacations.

At first, fundraising was handled by Renee Brown, using Post Office Box 64 in Manhattan's Old Chelsea station. By June 1973, Post Office Box 1836 in Newark, closer to Hilton Goldman's home, was used. See: Letters from Hilton Goldman to Meir, in RZ Archives, folders 713A and 714A.

Goldman was chief fundraiser for Meir's later Knesset campaigns as well.

[43] "Be Sure to Listen," [ad] *Jewish Press*, July 6, 1973, p. 23. The Barry Farber Show was broadcast on July 5 on station WOR at 9 P.M. On July 7, Rabbi Julius spoke at Congregation Poalei Agudah, 4922 14 Avenue, Brooklyn, at 9 A.M.

Letter from Liz Greenbaum to Meir, June [i.e. July] 12, 1973, in RZ Archives, folder 713A. Greenbaum's report on the meeting included this tribute: "I am only writing a brief note to thank you from the bottom of my heart for giving me back the greatest gift of all, the gift of my heritage.... The awareness and the final progress is all due to you and your influence. I cannot find the words to thank you, all I can say is that whenever and wherever you need my help, please be assured that I will give it unhesitatingly."

Charlotte Levin, secretary of the Washington, D.C., chapter, reported, "Rabbi Kranz will host Rabbi Aryeh Julius. He estimates he can raise $2,000." Letter from Charlotte Levin to Meir, June 19, 1973, in RZ Archives, folder 713A.

Minutes of JDL Board meeting, July 2, 1973, in RZ Archives, Appendix.

44 Printed letter headed "Kahane for Knesset Committee." Note at the bottom from Hilton Goldman to Libby, undated but probably November 1997, in RZ Archives, Appendix.

45 Invitation to "An Evening for Kahane to the Knesset" at Café Yaffo, 460 West 42 Street, New York City, August 8, 1973, 7.30 P.M., in RZ Archives, folder 714A.

Dr. Morris Mandel's speech in: JDL *Admin Bulletin*, August 14, 1973, p. 2, in RZ Archives, folder 70B. Shifra Hoffman, Lorraine Schumsky and Gene Singer were on the Dinner Committee.

"We're Sorry!" [ad] *Jewish Press*, August 17, 1973, p. 32, in RZ Archives, folder 70B. The room at Café Yaffo seated between 200 and 225 people.

46 JDL *Admin Bulletin*, October 30, 1973, p. 1, in RZ Archives, folder 70B; Letter from Meir to Dr. William Perl, undated, but after Perl's election on August 30, 1973, to JDL National Chairman, in the William Perl collection, Gelman Library, George Washington University, Washington, D.C.

47 JDL *Admin Bulletin*, August 14, 1973, p. 2, in RZ Archives, folder 70B.

48 "Rabbi Meir Kahane Speaks from Israel," [ad] *Jewish Press,* August 10, 1973, p. 41, in RZ Archives, folder 70B.

"Message from Jerusalem," audio tape, in RZ Archives, audio folder.

49 Meir Hacohen (pseudonym of Meir Kahane), "Israel Through Laughter and Tears," *Jewish Press,* August 24, 1973, p. 32.

50 Letter from Meir to Gene Singer, June 12, 1973, in RZ Archives, Appendix.

Letter from Hilton Goldman to Meir, July 15, 1973, in RZ Archives, folder 71A.

Letter from Shmuel Knopfler to Meir, September 29, 1973, in RZ Archives, folder 713A.

51 Interview with Gene Singer, August 23, 1999, Jerusalem.

Chapter 35

1 "Am Segula [A Chosen People]," flyer, in RZ Archives, folder 473. Abridged translation.

"Oxford educated" refers to Abba Eban, Israel's foreign minister, 1966-1974.

2 Flyers gave contact information for Liga offices: 38 Jaffa Road, 3rd floor, Jerusalem, Tel. 02-228594 and 83 Dizengoff Road, 3rd floor, Tel Aviv, Tel. 03-286543.

Meir wrote, "Every flyer should have a coupon at the bottom." See: Letter (Hebrew) from Meir to Shimon Rachamim, June 1973, from the collection of Shimon Rachamim, in RZ Archives, Appendix.

Completed coupons are in RZ Archives, folder 473.

3 "Eikh Mitgabrim Al Hapa'ar? [How Do We Overcome the Gap?]" flyer, in RZ Archives, folder 94. Abridged translation.

4 Uzi Benziman, "Hachevra Hayisra'elit Le'achar Sheshet Hayamim [Israeli Society After the

Six Day War]," *Ha'aretz*, June 5, 1973, p. 14, reproduced in *Daf Hasbara* [*Information Page*], four-sided tabloid-size flyer, undated, p. [3], in RZ Archives, folder 68A.

Sprinzak, a professor of political science at the Hebrew University of Jerusalem, held views that were generally leftist.

5   "Mevukash! [Wanted!]" flyer, in RZ Archives, folder 94. Meir's arrest at Damascus Gate: see chapter 32, note 7.

6   "Kenes Tze'irim Datiyim... Likrat Ma'arekhet Habechirot [Conference of Religious Youth... for the Approaching Elections]," Tel Talpiot hall, Jerusalem, July 28, 1973, 9 P.M., poster in RZ Archives, poster folder, no. 198. This is a large poster with sky blue letters on a white background.

During this time there was talk of forming a right-wing bloc for the elections. Meir's comments on this were reported in: "She'on Habechirot [Elections Countdown]," *Yedioth Ahronoth*, August 7, 1973, p. 5.

7   "Va'ad Bet Haknesset Neged Harav Kahana [Synagogue Committee Against Rabbi Kahane]," *Ha'aretz*, August 23, 1973, p. 9, in RZ Archives, folder 71A.

8   "Kiddush Hashem," *Jewish Press*, September 7, 1973, pp. 12, 13, in RZ Archives, folder 1207, reprinted in *Writings 5732*, pp. 265-268, and in *Beyond Words*, 1:493-498. "From a speech given by Meir Kahane in Tel Aviv, August 1973."

9   "Anu Hachatumim Mata, Yehudim Ge'im... [We, the Undersigned, Proud Jews...]," mimeographed petition, in RZ Archives, folder 71A.

Meir announced the petition at a press conference held at Beit Sokolov. See: "Haliga Lehagana Yehudit Koret Lehitnagdut Hamonit Likhni'a [The Liga Calls for Mass Resistance to Surrender]," *Ha'aretz*, August 15, 1973, in RZ Archives, folder 71A.

10   "Ma Era Bechug Habayit Shel Harav Kahana? [What Happened at the Parlor Meeting of Rabbi Kahane?]" *Yedioth Ahronoth*, September 6, 1973, p. 5, in RZ Archives, folder 71A. The meeting took place on September 4.

Postcard (Hebrew) from Pinchas Hershler, Ponevezh Yeshiva, to Meir, September 6, 1973, in RZ Archives, folder 71A.

Letter (Hebrew) from Meir Gross of the Ezra religious youth group, to Meir, September 29, 1973, in RZ Archives, folder 713A. Meir spoke at an Ezra seminar at the Givat Michael campus in Nes Tziyona.

11   "Finis," *Jewish Press*, September 21, 1973, pp. S8, 39, in RZ Archives, folder 1207, reprinted in *Writings 5732*, pp. 255-258. "From a speech delivered by Meir Kahane in Jerusalem, September 1973." This was probably at the Jerusalem International Convention Center. See: Letter from Morris (Moshe) Saperstein, dean of the American College in Jerusalem, to Meir, September 16, 1973, in RZ Archives, folder 473. "We enjoyed your talk at Binyanei Ha'uma [the Jerusalem International Convention Center]."

12   "Assimilation," *Jewish Press*, September 7, 1973, pp. 12, 24 in RZ Archives, folder 1207, reprinted in *Writings 5732*, pp. 258-260, and in *Beyond Words*, 1:489-492. "From a speech given in Rehovot, September 1973."

13   "Pras 'Kekhol Hagoyim...' ['Like All the Nations' Award...]," [ad] *Yedioth Ahronoth*, September 2, 1973, [sports section] p. 12, in RZ Archives, folder 71A.

"JDL Protests Arab-Jewish Summer Camps," *Jerusalem Post*, September 4, 1973, p. 4.

"Hakol Kol Moshe [The Voice Is the Voice of Moshe]," [ad] *Yedioth Ahronoth*, September 30, 1973, p. 28; "Haliga Metakhnenet 'Mishpat' Neged Hasar Kol [The Liga is Planning a 'Trial' Against Minister Kol]," *Yedioth Ahronoth*, September 10, 1973, in RZ Archives, folder 71A.

14   The Elections Committee cited Elections Law 1969, paragraph 61(a). See: Avishai Amir,

"Atirat Haliga Neged Yoshev Rosh Va'adat Habechirot – Hayom [The Liga's Petition Against the Election Committee Chairman – Today]," *Ma'ariv*, October 4, 1973, p. 4, in RZ Archives, folder 71A.

Tentative approval of *kaf-kaf*: Letter (Hebrew) from Judge Haim Cohn, Chairman, Central Elections Committee, to Shimon Rachamim, Secretary, Jewish Defense League of Israel, July 24, 1973, from the collection of Shimon Rachamim, in RZ Archives, Appendix.

Interview with Shimon Rachamim, February 9, 1998, Jerusalem.

The first ten candidates on the Liga list were: Meir Kahane, Shimon Rachamim, Yosef Schneider, Yoel Lerner, Moshe Reich, Tzippora Levine, Avraham Hershkowitz, Avraham Haraf, Yitzchak Ben Hevron, and Michael Horowitz. See: *Matza'ei Reshimot Laknesset Hashminit* [*Platforms of the Lists to the Eighth Knesset*], in JNUL Archives, folder V2182.

15 "JDL Loses Court Fight for Its Letters," *Jerusalem Post*, October 5, 1973, p. 3; "Nidcheta Atirat Haliga [Liga's Petition Denied]," *Ma'ariv*, October 5, 1973, p. 4.

High Court of Justice, case no. 402/73, decision by Justices Yitzhak Kahan, Moshe Landau and Shimon Agranat, October 4, 1973, in *Piskei Din* [*Decisions of the Supreme Court*], 1973, vol. 27, part 2, p. 532.

16 See note 14, interview.

The new letters *kaf-kaf sofit* were approved on October 21. See: Letter (Hebrew) from Judge Haim Cohn, chairman, Central Elections Committee, to Shimon Rachamim, October 21, 1973, from the collection of Shimon Rachamim, in RZ Archives, Appendix.

The letters *kaf-kaf sofit* spelled the Hebrew word *kach* (thus), the name Meir gave to the movement formed in July 1974.

Because of the change of letters, a rumor circulated in America that "by some legalist measure, the Liga list was stricken off." Letter from William Perl to Meir, October 21, 1973, in the William Perl collection, Gelman Library, George Washington University, Washington, D.C.

17 Yom Kippur War, see: www.jewishvirtuallibrary.org/jsource/History/73_War.html.

18 "Hamo'ed Hechadash Shel Habechirot... [The New Date of Elections...]," *Yedioth Ahronoth*, October 25, 1973, p. 4; "Delay Held Likely in Israeli Vote," *New York Times*, October 13, 1973, p. 15.

19 Letter from Meir to Samuel Shoshan, October 27, 1973, in RZ Archives, Appendix.

20 Letter from Meir to Hilton Goldman, November 6, 1973, carbon copy in RZ Archives, folder 713A.

21 See chapter 34 for efforts to find a publisher for *Story of the* JDL.

22 Letter from William Perl to Meir, November 25, 1973, in RZ Archives, folder 70A.

Morris "Mike" Fox of Miami was a leader of the JDL group in Miami in the early 1970s, together with his wife, Fremette Fox.

23 E-mail from David Fisch, November 18, 1999. Meir's note about Fisch in RZ Archives, folder 694. Meir's repayments of personal loans in RZ Archives, folders 692 and 693.

24 See RZ Archives, poster folder, nos. 190, 192, 194, 196, 197, 198, 216.

25 "What Will Be?" *Jewish Press*, November 2, 1973, pp. 23, 27, in RZ Archives, folder 1207, reprinted in *Writings 5734-5-6*, pp. 33-35, and in *Beyond Words*, 1:499-502. "From a speech by Meir Kahane in Jerusalem, October 20, 1973, the 14th day of the war."

26 "Nitzachon La'aravim [Victory to the Arabs]," [ad] *Ha'aretz*, October 25, 1973, p. 4, in RZ Archives, folder 68A. Abridged translation. See also note 17.

27 "A Statement to United States Ambassador Kenneth Keating," flyer, in RZ Archives, folder 71A.

Maccabee Dean, "Citizens' Group Calls on U.S. to Act in Prisoner Exchange," *Jerusalem Post*, November 6, 1973, p. 2. Clipping of AP photo of Meir captioned "Rabbi Meir Kahane and nine members of the Jewish Defense League who held a sit-in at the U.S. Embassy in Tel Aviv are carried away in a police car," in RZ Archives, folder 71A.

"Asefat Am [Election rally]," November 4, 1973, Jerusalem International Convention Center, in RZ Archives, poster folder, no. 197.

"Lo Yakum Velo Yih'yeh Shum Heskem Kni'a [There Will Be No Surrender Agreement]," flyer announcing Knesset demonstration, November 13, 1973, in RZ Archives, folder 71A.

28 "The Nuisance," *Jewish Press*, August 29, 1975, pp. 4, 34, reprinted in *Writings 5734-5-6*, pp. 35-40, and in *Beyond Words*, 1:511-518.

Before this article appeared in the *Jewish Press*, the text was mimeographed and circulated as a flyer. The typescript, in RZ Archives, folder 1001, has a note: "From a speech delivered by Rabbi Meir Kahane in Tel Aviv, November 7, 1973."

The speech was advertised: "Haliga... Mazmina Et Hatzibur Lishmo'a... [The Liga... Invites the Public to Hear...]," [ad] *Ha'aretz*, November 7, 1973, p. 14. Meir's lecture was held at the Bnei Brith Hall, Kaplan Street, Tel Aviv.

That same day, David Fisch led a JDL rally at the U.S. mission to the U.N. in New York on the same theme. See: "JDL Rally to Call for Unity Against Communism...," flyer, in RZ Archives, folder 70B.

29 Letter from Arnold Fine, editor, *Jewish Press*, to Meir, November 28, 1973, in RZ Archives, folder 70A.

30 "We Can Do Without Jews. We Can't Do Without Oil," *Jewish Standard*, November, 30, 1973, reprinted in Northern New Jersey Council News Letter, Adar 5734 [March 1974], p. 1, in RZ Archives, folder 734.

See also: http://en.wikipedia.org/wiki/1973_oil_crisis.

Meir later wrote: "As the energy crisis unfolded, the extreme right hastened to take full advantage of it.... The National Youth Alliance said, 'The International Gang of Zionists is responsible for the whole mess.'" David Borac (pseudonym of Meir Kahane), "Exposing the Haters," *Jewish Press*, March 1, 1974, p. 21. See also: "Exposing the Haters," *Jewish Press*, September 1, 1974, p. 47.

31 "Jewish Eternity and Triumph," *Jewish Press*, November 23, 1973, pp. 16, 23, in RZ Archives, folder 594, reprinted in *Beyond Words*, 1:508-510.

Booklet: Meir Kahane, *Netzach Yisrael Venitzchono* [*Jewish Eternity and Triumph*] (Tel Aviv: Haliga Lehagana Yehudit, 5734=1973), 12 pp., 17 cm., in JNUL, call no. S74A2605.

Poster: "Netzach Yisrael Venitzchono [Jewish Eternity and Triumph]," wall poster in RZ Archives, folder 714A.

Additional flyers and posters relating to the 1973 Knesset campaign in folder 714A.

32 Letter (Hebrew) from Yehoshua Ben Zion to Meir, December 2, 1973, in RZ Archives, Appendix. Ben Zion was referring to an ad with pictures of Meir and Menachem Begin, "Hu Tzarikh Oto Baknesset [He Needs Him in the Knesset]," [ad] *Yedioth Ahronoth*, November 30, 1973, p. 5 and *Yedioth Ahronoth*, December 19, 1973, p. 4.

"Netzach Yisrael Venitzchono [Jewish Eternity and Triumph]," [ad] *Ma'ariv*, December 2, 1973, p. 12 and *Yedioth Ahronoth*, December 2, 1973, p. 12, in RZ Archives, folder 68B.

Netzach Yisrael Venitzchono, flyer on newspaper stock, reproduction of the ad, in RZ Archives, folder 384B.

33 "Tzav Hasha'a: Pe'ula Uma'as [Today's Imperative: Deeds and Actions]," [ad] *Ma'ariv*, December 13, 1973, p. 9, in RZ Archives, folder 68A. The same ad appeared in *Yedioth*

Ahronoth, December 13, 1973, p. 12. It announced that chartered buses would take people to the airport from Jerusalem and from Tel Aviv.

The Middle East Peace Conference, promoted by Kissinger, was to open in Geneva on December 21, 1973.

34 Rachel Primor, "Hamafginim Chiku Lekissinger – Akh Hu Chamak Bemasok [The Demonstrators Waited for Kissinger – But He Evaded Them in a Helicopter]," *Ma'ariv*, December 17, 1973, in RZ Archives, folder 71A; "Me'ot Nosei Kerazot Umitriot Ba'u Etmol... [Hundreds Carrying Placards and Umbrellas Came Yesterday...]," *Yedioth Ahronoth*, December 17, 1973, p. 5, in RZ Archives, folder 71A; Marilyn Berger, "Israel Balks at Talks," *Washington Post*, December 17, 1973, p. A1, in RZ Archives, folder 71A; "Israel Cops Nab Kahane at Protest," AP report [December 17, 1973], reproduced in *Iton* (Jewish Defense League), Pesach 5734 [April 1974], p. 8, in RZ Archives, folder 987.

Meir faced criminal charges for the demonstration at Lod. Criminal case no. 797/73 was heard in Ramle Magistrate's Court on March 19, 1974, and Meir was fined 50 lirot. Legal documents in RZ Archives, folders 714B and 715B.

35 "She'on Habechirot [Elections Countdown]," *Yedioth Ahronoth*, December 18, 1973, p. 4; "Kahana Ye'argen Hafganot Be'arhab Kesheyekabel Darkono [Kahane Will Organize Demonstrations in the United States When He Receives His Passport]," *Yedioth Ahronoth*, December 19, 1973, p. 4.

36 Form letter (Hebrew) from Liga, Tel Aviv, to Ashkelon Municipality, undated, in RZ Archives, Appendix.

Invoice for 150 lirot, Mitzpor Hotel, Safed, October 1, 1973, in RZ Archives, folder 692A. The note: "From a speech delivered in Safed, September 1973," appears over Meir's article, "Golden Opportunity," *Jewish Press*, September 28, 1973, p. 44, reprinted in *Writings 5732*, pp. 253-255.

"Erev She'elot Uteshuvot [Question-and-Answer Evening]," [ad] *Ma'ariv*, November 30, 1973, p. 4, in RZ Archives, folder 68A. This announces a rally at the Mishkenot Israel synagogue hall, Ramat Gan, Saturday night, December 1, 1973, and requests that people invite Meir to their homes for parlor meetings.

37 "Asefot Am [List of Rallies]," [ads] *Ma'ariv*, December 10, 1973, p. 8; *Yedioth Ahronoth*, December 9, 1973, p. 18; *Ma'ariv*, December 11, 1973, p. 26; *Ma'ariv*, December 16, 1973, p. 13; *Yedioth Ahronoth*, December 16, 1973, p. 19; *Ma'ariv*, December 23, 1973, p. 30; *Yedioth Ahronoth*, December 23, 1973, p. 39, in RZ Archives, folder 68A.

Invoices and check stubs in RZ Archives, folder 692A. Receipts from Beit Sokolov and the Jerusalem International Convention Center in RZ Archives, folders 692A, 692B.

38 Payments to Igra Press were: 3,500 lirot on November 29, 1973; 1,500 lirot on December 15, 1973; 2,045 lirot on January 1, 1974; and 3,500 lirot on December 1, 1974. Invoices in RZ Archives, folders 692A and 694.

Invoice from *Yedioth Ahronoth*, lists ads and cost of each, December 2, 1973-December 31, 1973, total: 68,607 lirot (about $16,335), in RZ Archives, folder 692A.

Most ads placed by Meir cost about 300 lirot ($70). The charge for slightly larger ads, measuring 2 columns by 5 or 6 inches was about 600 lirot ($140).

39 Agudat Yisrael: "Tenu 'Kavod' [Give 'Honor']," [ad] *Ma'ariv*, December 27, 1973, p. 35; [ad] *Yedioth Ahronoth*, December 27, 1973, p. 7. Another ad aimed at Agudat Yisrael voters was "Mikhtav Galui Letzibur Bnei Torah [An Open Letter to the Torah Community]," [ad] *Yedioth Ahronoth*, December 16, 1973, p. 11, in RZ Archives, folder 71A.

Likud: "*Chaval Al D'avdin* [Alas For Those That Have Gone]," [ad] *Yedioth Ahronoth*, December 21, 1973, p. 19; *Ma'ariv*, December 20, 1973, p. 12.

Mafdal: "Kahana, Mi Ata? [Kahane, Who Are You?]" *Ma'ariv*, December 30, 1973, p. 50. Details about picture with Rabbi Tzvi Yehuda Kook in chapter 24.

Anti-Kissinger protest: "Ma Nishtana [What's the Difference]," [ad] *Ma'ariv*, December 24, 1973, p. 27; *Yedioth Ahronoth*, December 24, 1973, p. 16.

40 "Ha'azinu [Listen]," [ad] *Yedioth Ahronoth*, December 12, 1973, p. 19 and December 27, 1973, p. 18; *Ma'ariv*, December 12, 1973, p. 12 and December 27, 1973, p. 34, in RZ Archives, folder 68A.

The TV broadcasts took place on December 13 at 8 P.M., December 22 at 8:06 P.M., and December 27, at 8 P.M. The radio broadcasts were on December 13, at 6.05 P.M, December 18 at 1:55 P.M., December 25 at 1:55 P.M., December 27 at 7:45 A.M., and December 28 at 7:45 A.M. The final TV broadcast, on December 27, was originally scheduled for 9:13 P.M., but according to the December 27 ad, it was moved to 8 P.M.

41 Phone interview with Dov Lederberg, August 16, 2004. Lederberg was paid 2,000 lirot for his work on the TV presentation and the use of a studio cost another 2,000 lirot. (Total cost: about $950.) Check stubs in RZ Archives, folder 692A.

42 Meir Kahane, "Bemerchak Shnot Dor Mikav Hayahadut [A Great Distance from Judaism]," [letter to the editor] *Yedioth Ahronoth*, November 28, 1973, p. 10, in RZ Archives, folder 71A.

43 "Letalmidei Tikhon... [To High School Pupils...]," [ad] *Yedioth Ahronoth*, December 5, 1973, p. 5, in RZ Archives, folder 68A.

The demonstration had originally been called for December 2, 1973, but was postponed "because of mourning for David Ben Gurion, first prime minister." Original ad: "Mimisrad Hachinukh Vehatarbut – Ra'ayon 'Mavrik' Venivzeh! [From the Ministry of Education and Culture – a 'Brilliant,' Contemptible Idea!]," [ad] *Yedioth Ahronoth*, November 27, 1973, p. 7.

The ad gave a reference for the Ministry of Education's plan: "Kenes Mechankhim Dan Behasbara Letalmidim Bemikreh Nesiga [A Conference of Educators Discussed How to Explain Possible Retreat to Pupils]," *Yedioth Ahronoth*, November 25, 1973, p. 8.

44 "Haknesset Hi Lo Ha'ikar [The Knesset Is Not the Main Thing]," [ad] *Yedioth Ahronoth*, December 28, 1973, p. 8; *Ma'ariv*, December 27, 1973, p. 24, in RZ Archives, folder 68A. The closely written text of this quarter page ad refers to Meir's talk at a secular high school in Kiryat Motzkin on December 14, 1973.

45 "Mechdal Ushmo Chinukh [A Failure Named Education]," [op-ed] *Yedioth Ahronoth*, December 27, 1973, p. 10. Abridged translation.

Two other candidates wrote op-eds on the same page: Yosef Tamir (Likud) and Moshe Carmel (Labor).

In the newspaper, the second paragraph begins: "When I sat in Ramle prison..." However, as of December 1973, Meir had never been held in Ramle prison. He had been in the lockup in Rishon Letziyon / Nes Tziyona (see chapter 31, note 23), in Jerusalem Central Prison (see chapter 33) and in the prison at Kfar Yona, near Netanya (see chapter 33). A possible explanation might be that he underwent "processing" in Ramle before being moved to Kfar Yona. Or this may simply be a typographical error.

46 "Sinai Settlers Complain of Eviction," *Jerusalem Post*, December 24, 1973, p. 3. The press conference was held at Beit Sokolov.

Document signed by Meir, undated, authorizing Aryeh Baruch and Mario Kogan to open a branch of the Liga in Shalhevet, in RZ Archives, Appendix.

47 "The JDL Has From Its Inception...," typescript of English press release about Shalhevet, December 23, 1973, from collection of Samuel Shoshan, in RZ Archives, Appendix.

Shoshan, then visiting in Israel, wrote on the typescript: *Ma'ariv, Yedioth Ahronoth*, and JTA [Jewish Telegraphic Agency]. Apparently, Meir gave it to Shoshan to forward to them.

48 "Kahane Calls for American Jewry to Organize Political Action to Force Change in Israel Government Policy," press release about Meir's talk at Bar Ilan University datelined Tel Aviv, December 23, 1973, distributed by the Jewish Defense League, New York, December 26, 1973, in RZ Archives, folder 72B.

"Asefot Am [List of Rallies]," [ad] *Yedioth Ahronoth*, December 24, 1973, p. 12.

"Asefot Am [List of Rallies]," [ad] *Ma'ariv*, December 25, 1973, p. 31, in RZ Archives, folder 68A.

"Asefot Am [List of Rallies]," [ad] *Yedioth Ahronoth*, December 27, 1973, p. 33.

"Asefat Am... [Rally, Saturday night, December 29, at 10 P.M., at Tel Talpiot, Jerusalem]," poster in RZ Archives, poster folder, no. 216. The rent for Tel Talpiot was 1,000 lirot (about $240). See receipt in RZ Archives, folder 692B.

49 Letter from Samuel Shoshan to his wife Renah, December 25, 1973, in RZ Archives, Appendix. He and Meir stayed at the Florida Hotel in Tiberias, owned by a Kahane relative. Check stub for 90 lirot paid to the Florida Hotel, December 23, 1973, in RZ Archives, folder 692A. A snapshot of Meir and Shoshan on Election Day is in the photo section of this book. It was taken outside our neighborhood polling station, a school on Rechov Zikhron Yaakov.

See also: Photo of Meir, Shoshan and young supporters, in RZ Archives, picture folder, no. 10.

50 Letter from Hilton Goldman to Libby, undated, but probably February 1998 (my reply is dated March 9, 1998).

In the same letter, Goldman wrote: "On balance, he was a tremendous, positive influence on my life.... It was destiny that you and the kids had to share him with the Jewish nation. For that we are deeply indebted to you."

51 Interview with Alan Rocoff, June 11, 1999, Jerusalem.

52 Gil Sadan, "Kahana: Ulai Eshev Ketzat – Lo Baknesset [Kahane: Perhaps I'll Sit a Little – Not in the Knesset]," *Yedioth Ahronoth*, January 2, 1974, p. 5, in RZ Archives, folder 68B.

53 "15,000 Ezrachim Hodi'u Al Temikhatam Barav Kahana [15,000 Citizens Declared Their Support for Rabbi Kahane]," [ad] *Yedioth Ahronoth*, December 26, 1973, p. 40, in RZ Archives, folder 68A. The same ad was published in *Ma'ariv*, December 25, 1973, p. 13.

"Tenu Lanu Et Hamandat Hashelishi [Give Us the Third Seat]," [ad] *Yedioth Ahronoth*, December 24, 1973, p. 13.

An ad introducing Shimon Rachamim, number two on the Liga list, had his picture and C.V. "Haker Na [Please Meet]," *Yedioth Ahronoth*, December 27, 1973, p. 19.

The Liga also put up candidates for the Jerusalem Municipal Council: Shimon Rachamim and Yoel Lerner. (Municipal elections were held the same day as national elections.) Newspaper ads included: "Besorot Tovot Teddy [Good News, Teddy]," [ad] *Yedioth Ahronoth*, October 4, 1973, p. 20, in RZ Archives, folder 71A and *Ma'ariv*, October 4, 1973, p. 32; "Terumat Haliga Leteddy Kollek [The Liga's Gift to Teddy Kollek]," [ad] *Ma'ariv*, December 25, 1973, p. 22 and *Yedioth Ahronoth*, December 23, 1973, p. 30, in RZ Archives, folder 714A. The Liga received many votes, but not enough for a seat on the council. Interview with Shimon Rachamim, February 9, 1998, Jerusalem.

54 Interview with Rabbi Aryeh Julius, August 1, 1999, Jerusalem.

55 Interview with Shimon Rachamim, November 11, 1997, Jerusalem.

The lack of sufficient poll watchers can be deduced from the fact that our children Tova, age 16, and Baruch, age 15, were appointed poll watchers for the Liga in Jerusalem. See: Forms headed "Mashkif Leva'adat Kalpi [Poll Watchers]," naming the polls each was to watch, in RZ Archives, folder 714A.

[56] Hyman S. Frank, "Inside Meir Kahane," *Jewish Press*, January 31, 1975, pp. 18, 19. Details in chapter 10, note 3.

[57] "JDL Threatens to Hold 'Angry Demonstrations,'" *Jerusalem Post*, January 8, 1974, p. 3; Israel Broadcasting Authority Radio News Archive, media no. 9220, January 7, 1974.

[58] "Berigshei Toda [With Thanks]," [ad] *Ma'ariv*, January 13, 1974, p. 14, in RZ Archives, folder 473; [ad] *Yedioth Ahronoth*, January 13, 1974, p. 5, in RZ Archives, folder 714B. For those who wanted to join, a coupon was printed at the bottom of the ad.

Chapter 36

[1] Handwritten letter (Hebrew) from Meir to Hillel Seidman, November 3, 1973, in RZ Archives, folder 713A. Carbon copy.

[2] Handwritten letter from Meir to Judge Jack Weinstein, November 3, 1973, in RZ Archives, folder 713A. Carbon copy.

[3] Letter from Reuben E. Gross to Hon. Jack Weinstein, November 12, 1973, in RZ Archives, folder 70A.

Letter from Reuben E. Gross to Meir, November 21, 1973, in RZ Archives, folder 713A.

Letter from Reuben E. Gross to Meir, November 22, 1973, in RZ Archives, folder 714B.

"Court Move Starts for Kahane Return," *Daily News*, November 22, 1973, in RZ Archives, folder 714B.

[4] *Memorandum* to the Honorable Jack B. Weinstein, United States District Judge, Docket No. 71-CR-479, for hearing January 2, 1974, submitted by James F. Haran, Chief U.S. Probation Officer for the Eastern District of New York, in RZ Archives, folder 72A.

[5] This petition was heard on January 27. See note 18.

[6] Letter from Meir to Dr. William Perl, January 5, 1974, in the William Perl collection, Gelman Library, George Washington University, Washington, D.C.

[7] Letter from Dr. William Perl, to Meir, January 8, 1974, in RZ Archives, folder 72A.

Meir held a brief hunger strike at the Jerusalem office of Ministry of the Interior, which was in charge of issuing passports. "Meir Kahane Begins Fast," *Jewish Press*, January 11, 1974, p. 1.

[8] Letter from Meir to Dr. William Perl, January 18, 1974, in the William Perl collection, Gelman Library, George Washington University, Washington, D.C.

[9] Letter from Dr. William Perl to Meir, February 4, 1974, in the William Perl collection, Gelman Library, George Washington University, Washington, D.C.

[10] Letter from Samuel Sternfeld to Meir, January 28, 1974, in RZ Archives, folder 72A. Other members of the committee for the return of Meir's passport: Hesh Morgan, Asher Moskowitz, and Richie Aroll.

[11] Letter from Nat Rosenwasser to Meir, November 12, 1972, in RZ Archives, folder 713A.

[12] Hillel Seidman, "Harav Kahana's Hundert Felern Un Eyn Zkhus [Rabbi Meir Kahane's Hundred Mistakes and One Great Deed]," *Algemeiner Journal*, August 10, 1973, p. 4, in RZ Archives, folder 92B.

The article was translated into English and distributed by the Committee for the Return of Rabbi Meir Kahane, which used Hilton Goldman's "Kahane for Knesset" post office box in Newark, New Jersey.

[13] See note 9.

Biaggi sent Meir a copy of his letter to the Israeli ambassador. See: Letter from Meir to Dr.

William Perl, February 10, 1974, in the William Perl collection, Gelman Library, George Washington University, Washington, D.C.

14 Letter from Dr. William Perl to Meir, January 15, 1974, in the William Perl collection, Gelman Library, George Washington University, Washington, D.C. See also: "JDL National Chairman Resigns," *Jewish Press*, January 25, 1974, p. 3.

15 Letter from James F. Haran, Chief U.S. Probation Officer, United States District Court, Eastern District of New York, to Meir, February 14, 1974, in RZ Archives, folder 72A. Haran "was informed" that the statement by Meir was dated October 23, 1973, but it was dated November 3, 1973.

16 Letter from Rabbi Shalom Klass to Meir, January 4, 1974, in RZ Archives, folder 72A.

17 Letter from Meir to Libby, undated but between August 14 and October 28, 1974 (during his trip to the United States), in RZ Archives, Appendix. Meir was very fond of Rabbi Klass, but he liked to pun.

18 "Hoda'a La'itonut... Beyom Rishon, 4 Shvat... [Press Release... On Sunday, January 27, 1974...]" January [25], 1974, in RZ Archives, folder 92B. Abridged translation.

See: Telegram from Benton M. Arnovitz, Senior Editor, Chilton Book Company, to the Minister of Justice, Jerusalem, February 19, 1974, in RZ Archives, folder 92B. It said, "Promotion of Rabbi Meir Kahane's forthcoming book is being hampered by his inability to travel to America. Will appreciate your cooperation."

19 "JDL Begins a 'No Russia, No Sakharov-Solzhenitsyn Here' Campaign," press release, January [30], 1974, and similar Hebrew press release, "Berusya Hakomunistit Medak'im... [In Soviet Russia They Oppress...]," both in RZ Archives, folder 92B. The press release announced that the hunger strike would begin on Sunday, February 3, but it actually began two days later, on Tuesday, February 5.

20 Telegram from U.S. Embassy, Tel Aviv, to U.S. Department of State, Washington, D.C., February 1, 1974, in RZ Archives, folder 582.

21 Letter from Larry W. Roeder, U.S. Consul General, Tel Aviv, to Meir Shamgar, Attorney General, Jerusalem, February 5, 1974, in RZ Archives, folder 92B.

22 Telegram from U.S. Embassy, Tel Aviv, to U. S. Department of State, Washington, D.C., February 6, 1974, in RZ Archives, Appendix. Meir began the hunger strike on February 5, immediately after Supreme Court Justice Joel Sussman denied his petition. He arrived in Tel Aviv on February 6.

23 "Notes on People," *New York Times*, February 7, 1974, p. 46. A photo of Meir in the van during his hunger strike is in the photo section of this book.

24 "You Are Invited to Demonstrate Your Solidarity," flyer, in English, distributed February 6, 1974, at U.S. Embassy, Tel Aviv, in RZ Archives, folder 92B.

25 Herzl Rosenblum, "Bilti Musari," [editorial] *Yedioth Ahronoth*, February 10, 1974, p. 2, in RZ Archives, folder 92B.

26 "Harav Kahana Patach Etmol Bishevitat Ra'av... [Rabbi Kahane Began a Hunger Strike Yesterday...]," [photo caption] *Ma'ariv*, February 7, 1974, p. 15, in RZ Archives, folder 92B.

"Kahane: A Fast," [photo caption] *B'nai B'rith Messenger*, August 15, 1975, p. 31, in RZ Archives, folder 65D.

27 "Emergency Aliya Conference," press release, February 10, 1974, in RZ Archives, folder 92B.

28 "Message to Western Jewry," [ad] *Jerusalem Post*, March 18, 1974, p. 6, announces cocktail party to introduce Habayta, March 24, at 6 P.M., Sheraton Hotel, Tel Aviv. Enlargement of the ad, in RZ Archives, posters folder, no. 100.

World Zionist Organization, Press Release no. 74/3/9/904, about Habayta conference on March 17; letters from Moshe Dayan and Shimon Peres, in RZ Archives, folder 131. The name Habayta was used by the JDL in 1972. See chapter 30, note 16.

Ratner's support for the Liga: Interview with Rabbi Aryeh Julius, August 1, 1999, Jerusalem.

[29] "Shagrirut Arhab Ta'anik Darkon Chadash Larav Kahana Im Yesarev Hayo'etz Hamishpati Lehachzir Et Hayashan [The U.S. Embassy Will Give Rabbi Kahane a New Passport if the State Attorney Refuses to Return His Old One]," Ha'aretz, February 14, 1974, p. 5.

Telegram from Ambassador Kenneth Keating, U.S. Embassy, Tel Aviv, to Department of State, Washington, D.C., February 15, 1974, in RZ Archives, folder 582. Keating noted in this telegram that the report in Ha'aretz was "apparently based on inquiry February 13 by Rabbi Julius, Kahane's associate..."

In August 1974 the U.S. Embassy requested the return of the passport in possession of the police, stating: "Regulations prohibit holding two valid passports." Letter from U.S. Embassy, Tel Aviv, to Meir, August 6, 1974, in RZ Archives, folder 715B.

Passport no. Z1595113, issued July 14, 1972, was returned to the U.S. Embassy by the Israel Police on September 12, 1974. See: Memo from U.S. Embassy, note 32.

[30] Letter from Israel State Attorney Gabriel Bach to Larry W. Roeder, Consul General, U.S. Embassy, Tel Aviv, February 15 1974, in RZ Archives, Appendix.

Meir Shamgar was Attorney General of Israel, 1968-1975; Gabriel Bach was State Attorney and then Attorney General, 1969-1982.

[31] Letter from John H. Adams, Consul, U.S. Embassy, Tel Aviv, to Meir, February 20, 1974, in RZ Archives, folder 92B.

[32] Memo from U.S. Embassy, Tel Aviv, to Department of State, Washington, D.C., September 13, 1974, in RZ Archives, folder 582.

On the passport application, dated February 14, 1974, Meir gave his occupation as "writer."

Telegram from Ambassador Kenneth Keating, U.S. Embassy, Tel Aviv, to U.S. Department of State, Washington, D.C., February 21, 1974, in RZ Archives, folder 582.

[33] Protokol [Minutes], meeting of the Liga, January 6, 1974, in RZ Archives, folder 92B. Attending were: Meir, Shimon Rachamim, Yoel Lerner, Yossi Schneider, Moshe Reich, Rabbi Aryeh Julius, Tzippy Levine, Moshe Potolski, Moshe Simon, Menachem Levi, and two members whose personal names are not noted: Schlesinger and Galili. Abridged translation.

[34] Protokol [Minutes], meeting of the national board of the Liga, Jerusalem, January 27, 1974, in RZ Archives, folder 92B. Attending were Meir, Rabbi Aryeh Julius, attorney Rachamim Cohen, attorney Moshe Simon, Tzippy Levine, Yoel Lerner, Moshe Potolski, Amos Kliger, Shimon Rachamim, and Yossi Schneider. Abridged translation.

[35] Interview with Avery and Chana Gross, February 27, 1997, Jerusalem.

[36] Letter from Reuben Gross to Meir, March 21, 1974, in RZ Archives, folder 92A.

Sub-lease between the Shmuel Ezra and Rivka Gross Foundation and the Jewish Identity Center – Yeshiva Torah Ve'oz, March 15, 1974, in RZ Archives, folder 700. The contract stipulated: "This sub-lease remains in force and is conditional upon the continuance of Rabbi Meir Kahane as head of the Yeshiva."

The Gross Foundation signed a key-money agreement with the owner of the property, Zalman Zeidel Heisler.

[37] "Ma Metzapeh Ha'am Mehaknesset Hashminit [What Do the People Expect from the Eighth Knesset?]" [ad] Ma'ariv, January 20, 1974, p. 11, in RZ Archives, folder 473.

See also: "Haketz Lediburim – Et La'asot [Enough Talk – It's Time for Action]," flyer, in RZ Archives, folder 92B. The meeting was held at ZOA House on January 22, 1974.

Letter from Adina Drechsler, Gesher, to Meir, February 7, 1974, in RZ Archives, folder 92B.

"Im Ata Choshev... [If You Think...]," flyer, in JNUL, folder V1797. This announced a meeting at Canada Building, Givat Ram campus, Hebrew University, January 31, 1974, 3 P.M.

38 "Jerusalem Police Seize 12 in Blasts," *New York Times*, February 14, 1974, p. 5; Abraham Rabinovich, "Arson at Jerusalem Church Institutions," *Jerusalem Post*, February 12, 1974, p. 2.

"Nab 6 More for Arson in Israel," [reproduction of article from unnamed, undated newspaper] in: *Iton* (Jewish Defense League), Pesach 5734 [April 1974], p. 8, in RZ Archives, folder 987.

The halakha on preventing conversion to another religion: chapter 32, note 35.

39 Interview with Rabbi Aryeh Julius, August 1, 1999, Jerusalem.

The "scoundrel" was barred from the Liga after that. However, he continued to claim that he was a JDL/Kach member and defrauded many people out of their savings. In 1988, Meir heard many accounts of his chicanery and issued a warning about him in the *Jewish Press*. He wrote: "Beware of Shimon Lerner... preying on innocent people... defrauding teenagers." (See: "News We Doubt," *Jewish Press*, November 18, 1988, p. 27.) See also open letter: Lekhol Man D'vai [To Whom It May Concern] from Meir Kahane, June 20, 1988, in RZ Archives, Appendix. It stated: "To Whom It May Concern: Shimon Lerner was expelled from the JDL in 1973 and has had no connection with Kach since then."

40 Interview with [name withheld], March 13, 1997, Jerusalem.

41 Letter from Meir to Nat Rosenwasser, postmarked April 4, 1974, in RZ Archives, Appendix. Meir's handwritten lists of personal loans and repayments are in RZ Archives, folders 692-694.

42 "Ha'irgun Hame'uchad Neged Hamisyon [Union of Anti-Mission Organizations]," flyer and press release, in RZ Archives, folder 92B.

43 *Protokol* [*Minutes*], meeting of the expanded board of the Liga, Tel Aviv, February 24, 1974, in RZ Archives, folder 92B. Attending were Meir, Rabbi Aryeh Julius, Tzippy Levine, attorney Moshe Simon, Moshe Potolsky, and Shimon Rachamim. Abridged translation.

44 Letter from Meir to Dr. William Perl, February 15, 1974, in the William Perl collection, Gelman Library, George Washington University, Washington, D.C.

Chapter 37

1 "Major Kahane Trial Opens March 10 in Jerusalem District Court," *Jewish Press*, March 8, 1974, p. 23; "Kahane Goes On Trial," *Jewish Press*, March 15, 1974, p. 1; "Israel Begins Kahane Trial; Bomb Conspiracy Charged," *New York Times*, March 11, 1974, p. 10.

Summons to Meir to appear in Jerusalem District Court on March 10, 12 and 17, 1974, for Criminal Case No. 167/73, dated February 18, 1974, in RZ Archives, folder 92B.

See excerpts of letters in chapter 33.

2 "Weigh Decline in Emigration," *Jewish News* (Newark, N. J.), March 14, 1974, in RZ Archives, folder 734; Hedrick Smith, "Soviet Emigrants Said to Decrease," *New York Times*, March 3, 1974, p. 5.

3 Letter [from Meir] to "Dear Editor," [English mimeographed letter sent to newspapers, undated] in RZ Archives, folder 92B.

See: http://en.wikipedia.org/wiki/Rudolf_Kastner for more about Rudolf (Israel) Kastner and about Joel Brand, who planned the evacuation of Hungarian Jews to the land of Israel but was betrayed to the British by Jewish Agency officials.

4 "Kahana: Ahafokh Mishpati Lemishpat 'Kastner 1974' [Kahane: I Will Turn My Case Into a '1974 Kastner Case']," *Yedioth Ahronoth*, March 6, 1974, p. 2. See also note 1, "Major Kahane Trial..."

The press conference, whose theme was "Am I Brezhnev's Keeper?" was held at Beit Sokolov, Tel Aviv, on March 5.

Nativ: See: http://en.wikipedia.org/wiki/Lishkat_Hakesher.

Kastner was killed one night by a lone assassin near his home in Tel Aviv. See: "Israeli 'Quisling' Dead of Wounds; Dr. Kastner, Branded a Nazi Collaborator, Succumbs to an Assassin's Bullets," *New York Times*, March 16, 1957, p. 3.

5 "Mishpat Kastner 1974 [The 1974 Kastner Case]," [ad] *Ma'ariv*, March 8, 1974, p. 8, in RZ Archives, folder 92A.

6 Affidavit of Golda Meir, prime minister and acting foreign minister, March 8, 1973, in RZ Archives, folder 92A.

7 "Kahana Diber Bidlatayim Segurot... [Kahane Spoke Behind Closed Doors]," *Ma'ariv*, March 11, 1974, p. 6, in RZ Archives, folder 92A; "Kahana He'id Bidlatayim Segurot [Kahane Testified Behind Closed Doors]," *Yedioth Ahronoth*, March 11, 1974, p. 4; "Israel Begins Kahane Trial; Bomb Conspiracy Charged," *New York Times,* March 11, 1974, p. 10; "Kahane Goes on Trial," *Jewish Press*, March 15, 1974, p. 1.

8 Letter from Meir to Shimon Rachamim, June 1973, from the collection of Shimon Rachamim, in RZ Archives, Appendix; "Eretz Yisrael and the Burning Fire:" see chapter 33, note 47.

9 Interview with Julie Thornberg, June 21, 2001, Jerusalem. In 1974 she lived in Tel Aviv and was an active member of the Liga. She passed away on September 20, 2002, at age 84.

"Madu'a Mefachedet Golda Mikahana? [Why is Golda Afraid of Kahana?]," flyer [March 10, 1974], from the collection of Shimon Rachamim, in RZ Archives, Appendix.

"Harav Kahana Yu'asham Benisayon Lehafitz Kruzim Bevet Hamishpat [Rabbi Kahane Will Be Charged With Distributing Flyers at the Courthouse]," *Ma'ariv*, March 13, 1974, p. 7, in RZ Archives, folder 92A.

10 "Pidyon Shevuim [Redemption of Prisoners]," [ad] *Jewish Press*, March 15, 1974, p. 18, in RZ Archives, folder 92A.

The JDL newspaper, *Hadar*, has the text of a letter to Judge Yaakov Bazak asking for a fair trial for Meir and the dismissal of all charges. Readers were asked to clip the letter and mail it to Judge Bazak with a 26 cent airmail stamp. See: *Hadar* (Lower Manhattan Chapter, JDL) 1:4, Special Issue, [March 1974], p. 3, in RZ Archives, folder 91.

The argument about halakha was also aimed at Judge Bazak, who was an observant Jew.

One letter to Judge Bazak was sent by Meir's long-time supporter, Barry Dov Schwartz, rabbi of Temple B'nai Sholom, Rockville Centre, New York. See: "U.S. Rabbi Appeals in Behalf of Kahane," *Jewish Post and Opinion*, April 12, 1974, p. 12, in RZ Archives, folder 715A.

11 Irene Klass, "I Remember Meir Kahane," [editorial] *Jewish Press*, March 15, 1974, p. 3.

12 "Rabbi Meir Kahane's Statement to the Court Explaining His Refusal to Participate Further in the Proceedings of His Trial, March 12, 1974," *Jewish Press*, April 5, 1974, pp. 44, 45. (The *Jewish Press* printed "Statement" with a disclaimer: "We have no way of knowing whether the allegations made are exactly as presented...")

Reprinted in *Iton* (Jewish Defense League), Pesach 5734 [April 1974], insert, p. S3, in RZ Archives, folder 987 and in *Hadar* (see note 10), p. 2.

Reprinted as "Boycott" in *Letters from Prison* (Jerusalem: Jewish Identity Center, 1974), pp. 17-19, in RZ Archives, booklets folder.

Hebrew version: "Hatzharato Shel Harav Meir Kahana Leveit Hamishpat Hamasbira Et

Seruvo Lehamshikh Uleshatef Pe'ula Im Halikhei Hamishpat," 2 mimeographed pp., in RZ Archives, folder 92A.

References in excerpt: Judge Haim Dvorin's decision: Shaul Hon, "Shuv Nidcheta Bakashat Harav Kahana Lehatir Lo Linso'a Lechul [Again Rabbi Kahane's Request to Travel Overseas Refused]," *Ma'ariv*, November 30, 1973, p. 5, in RZ Archives, Appendix.

Judge Joel Sussman's decision: Telegram from U.S. Embassy, Tel Aviv, to U. S. Department of State, Washington, D.C., February 6, 1974, in RZ Archives, Appendix.

[13] "Kahane to Supreme Court, Says 'Muzzled' in Trial," *Jerusalem Post*, March 13, 1974, p. 3; "Bet Hamishpat Ha'elyon Yikba Im Medini'ut Hamemshala Chasuya [The Supreme Court Will Determine Whether Government Policy Is Classified Information]," *Ma'ariv*, March 13, 1974, p. 17, both in RZ Archives, folder 92A; "Sanegoro Shel Kahana Yifneh Levet Hamishpat Ha'elyon [Kahane's Attorney Will Petition the High Court]," *Yedioth Ahronoth*, March 13, 1974, p. 7.

[14] "Will Those Who Bled for Selma Keep Quiet About Golda?" flyer, in RZ Archives, folder 92A. The 85th Annual Convention of the Central Conference of American Rabbis was held in Jerusalem, March 13-18, 1974.

"Kahane Asks to Address Reform Rabbis," press release in Hebrew and English, March 13, 1974, in RZ Archives, folder 92A.

[15] "Urgent Press Conference..." press release, March 14, 1974, in RZ Archives, folder 92A.

[16] "Declaration to the Court," 3 folio leaves, mimeographed, in RZ Archives, folder 92B. Reprinted in *Writings 5734-5-6*, pp. 20-25, in *Letters from Prison*, pp. 24-29, and in *Hadar* (see note 10), pp. 2-3.

Hebrew version, "Hatzhara Levet Hamishpat," 3 folio leaves, mimeographed, in RZ Archives, folder 92B. Reprinted as "Emunati Hadatit Veha'emunatit [My Religious Tenets and Beliefs]," *Yesh Breira; Bit'on Tziyoni*, no. 25, Iyar [May] 1974, pp. 1, 4.

Original "Declaration to the Court," handwritten in pen on lined paper, [June 1973], 11 pp., in RZ Archives, folder 1193.

[17] [Announcement of press conference on March 17, 1974], press release, March 12, 1974, in RZ Archives, folder 92A. This invited the press to our home, 13 Sorotzkin Street, Jerusalem, on Sunday, March 17, 1974, 8 P.M.

[18] "A Statement to the Press," [begins: "Rabbi Aryeh Julius"] [March 13, 1974], in RZ Archives, folder 92A. Hebrew version, "Hoda'a La'itonut," in RZ Archives, Appendix.

[19] *The Chosen State* [mimeographed], 14 folio leaves; *Medinat Segula* [mimeographed], 11 folio leaves, mimeographed; both in RZ Archives, folder 92A.

The Chosen State was reprinted in *Letters from Prison*, pp. 1-13, *Writings 5734-5-6*, pp. 7-18, and *Story of the Jewish Defense League*, pp. 301-316.

The cover page of the packet distributed to the press on March 17, 1974, headed Supplementary Declaration to the Court, noted: "I wrote this in June 1973, when I was jailed for a month to appease Nixon."

Meir wrote *The Chosen State* in the Kfar Yona prison. In a letter to me from Kfar Yona he wrote: "Re: the 20-page [handwritten] article. Please title it 'Supplementary Declaration to Court' and mail one photocopy to Shifra [Hoffman]. Tell her to type it on stencil and run off copies to mail to all the newspapers and groups she has [on list]. But not to MAIL it until she gets further word from me.... Have them ready to give to press the last day of the trial." See: Letter from Meir to Libby, [July 1973] (excerpts in chapter 33), in RZ Archives, Appendix.

[20] Letter from Shifra Hoffman to Meir, March 26, 1974, in RZ Archives, folder 92A.

[21] Ruth Alexandrovich *et al*, "Petichat Hadelatot – Upetichat She'arim [Opening Doors – And Opening Gates]," [letter to the editor] *Yedioth Ahronoth*, March 20, 1974, p. 10, in RZ Archives, folder 92A.

Herzl Rosenblum, "Stimat Peh [Suppressing Speech]," [editorial] *Yedioth Ahronoth*, March 25, 1973, p. 2.

Golda Yellin *et al*, "Kol Koreh [Open Letter]," petition to High Court of Justice, March 26, 1974, in RZ Archives, folder 92A.

"Immigrants Wary of *In Camera* Trial," *Jerusalem Post*, April 12, 1974, p. 3.

[22] Letter from Golda Yellin to Judge Yaakov Bazak, May 20, 1974, in RZ Archives, folder 91. "Since the High Court refused Rabbi Kahane's request to lift the secrecy order and allow an open trial, I ask that you call on me to testify."

Yellin enclosed a twelve page petition (see note 21, Golda Yellin). There were no witnesses for the defense at the trial.

[23] "El Talmidei Bet Hasefer... [To the students of Denmark High School]," March 28, 1974, flyer and press release, in RZ Archives, folder 92A.

Cited: *Min Hameitzar*, p. 25. See chapter 11, note 21.

Cited: Yehuda ben Shmuel Halevi (ca. 1075-1141), *The Kuzari* (Northvale, N.J.: J. Aronson, 1998). This classic on Jewish thought was published in several English translations.

[24] "J.D.L. Ends Sit-In After Promise by Churches to Study Demands," *New York Times*, February 23, 1973, p. 9; "JDL Quits Church Offices After a Long 24-Hour Sit-In," *Jewish Post and Opinion*, March 2, 1973, p. 1.

[25] "Pickets Protest Bolshoi Ballet," *Miami Herald*, July 25, 1973, p. 4-B; "Bolshoi Protest," *Daily Sun Reporter*, July 25, 1973.

[26] "Paint Hurled at Standard Oil Buildings," *San Francisco Chronicle*, August 7, 1973, in RZ Archives, folder 70B.

[27] "To the Publisher and Editors of the Philadelphia *Jewish Exponent*," petition from Philadelphia chapter, JDL, dated July 1973, stamped August 21, 1973, in RZ Archives, folder 1202.

[28] "Sit-in at Austrian Consul's," *San Francisco Examiner*, October 4, 1973, in RZ Archives, folder 70B; "Protest Over Camp," *Los Angeles Times*, October 3, 1973, p. 1, in RZ Archives, folder 70B.

"Austria Rejects Mrs. Meir's Plea on Transit Routes," *New York Times*, October 3, 1973, pp. 1, 13.

"Austria's Former U.N. Mission Attacked by 75 Militants," *New York Times*, October 5, 1973, p. 3.

[29] "Helmeted Members of the JDL Confront Police Near the Israeli UN Mission," *New York Post*, October 8, 1973, p. 19, in RZ Archives, folder 70A; NBC News Archive, media no. 301555, October 8, 1973.

Los Angeles: "Shouting Match Disrupts Teach-In on Middle East," *Daily Bruin*, October 17, 1973.

"Jewish League Burns Arab Flag Here," *Evening Bulletin* (Philadelphia), October 8, 1973.

[30] "300 Jews, Protesting 2 Fires, Seek Added Police Protection," *New York Times*, November 23, 1973, p. 39, in RZ Archives, folder 734; "Yeshiva Fire Brings a March," *Daily News*, November 23, 1973.

[31] Letter from David Fisch to Meir, December 31, 1973, in RZ Archives, folder 91.

Letter from Dr. William Perl to Meir, January 15, 1974, in the William Perl collection, Gelman Library, George Washington University, Washington, D.C. See chapter 36.

[32] "Kahane Says He Is Quitting as J.D.L.'s Militant Chief," *New York Times*, April 17, 1974, p. 92; "Kahane Quits as JDL Chief," *New York Post*, April 17, 1974, p. 17, in RZ Archives, folder 91; David Rosenthal, "Kahane's Successor: A Columbia Junior," *New York Post*, April 19, 1974, p. 51, in RZ Archives, folder 434A; "Harav Meir Kahane Poresh Min Haliga Lehagana Yehudit

[Rabbi Meir Kahane Resigns from JDL]," [mimeographed press release], April 17, 1974, 1 folio page, in RZ Archives, Appendix.

[33] "Kahane Resigns from JDL," [Jewish Telegraphic Agency] *Jewish Press*, April 26, 1974, p. 2, in RZ Archives, folder 435A.

[34] Letter from Dr. William Perl to Meir, April 26, 1974, in the William Perl collection, Gelman Library, George Washington University, Washington, D.C.

When Meir wanted to resign in November 1972, members of the executive board persuaded him to remain. See chapter 31, note 56.

The *Jerusalem Post* was the only newspaper that noted a possible connection between the trial and Meir's resignation from the JDL: "[Attorney Meir] Schechter emphasized, Rabbi Kahane had reached the conclusion that his methods were 'hopeless' in view of the government's position, and this prompted him to resign as head of the JDL." It is doubtful that Meir's words were quoted precisely. See: "Kahane Convicted of Attempted Conspiracy; Sentencing Today," *Jerusalem Post*, June 28, 1974, p. 3, in RZ Archives, folder 91.

[35] Dov Genachowski, "Al Mi Natashta Hatzon, Rabbi Meir [To Whom Did You Abandon the Sheep, Rabbi Meir?]," *Yedioth Ahronoth*, April 19, 1974, p. 17, in RZ Archives, folder 91.

[36] Marvin Schick, "In The City," *Jewish Press*, April 26, 1974, pp. 2, 16, in RZ Archives, folder 435A. Excerpted with the author's permission.

In September 1974, Meir was interviewed by reporter M. Hirsh Goldberg, who wrote: "Kahane himself admits that he now sees he did not prepare adequately for a leadership to take over with his move to Israel." See: M. Hirsh Goldberg, "Where Does Meir Kahane Go From Here?" *Times of Israel and World Jewish Review*, January 1975, pp. 50-51, in RZ Archives, folder 72B.

Chapter 38

[1] "Harav Meir Kahane Poresh Min Haliga Lehagana Yehudit [Rabbi Meir Kahane Resigns from JDL]," press release, April 17, 1974, 1 mimeographed folio page, in RZ Archives, Appendix. Abridged translation.

All press releases at this time gave our home phone number. There was a phone in the office but only a part-time secretary to answer it.

[2] Gil Sadan, "Im Lo Yefachadu Ha'aravim, Tihye Lanu Od Kiryat Shmonah [If the Arabs Won't Fear Us, There Will Be Another Kiryat Shmonah]," *Yedioth Ahronoth*, April 18, 1974, p. 4, in RZ Archives, folder 91.

Yosef Wachsman, "Harav Kahana Parash Mehaliga Hayehudit Lehagana [Rabbi Kahane Resigned from the JDL]," *Ma'ariv*, April 18, 1974, p. 11.

[3] Jewish Identity Center, "Courses and Lecture Series," 1 mimeographed page, in RZ Archives, folder 91. In Hebrew and English.

[4] "This Saturday Night and Every Saturday Night – Rabbi Meir Kahane Speaks," flyer, in RZ Archives, folder 91.

Interview with Baruch Ben Yosef, October 9, 1997, Jerusalem.

[5] "Jew Get Out," flyer, prior to April 2, 1974, in RZ Archives, folder 131.

"A Message of Solidarity to the Jews of the Exile," *Meir Kahane News Letter* 2, May 10, 1974, pp. 4-6, in RZ Archives, folder 1010.

[6] "Arab Guerrillas Kill 18 in Israeli Town," *New York Times*, April 12, 1974, p. 65. See also: http://www.eretzyisroel.org/~samuel/plohistory.html.

[7] See note 2, Sadan.

Sadan noted that Meir had a thin beard that day because the period of *sefirat ha'omer*, between Passover and Shavuot, when shaving is prohibited, had just begun. Once again newspaper photos showed him looking unkempt!

8 Meir Kahane, *"Chillul Hashem* [Desecration of G-d's Name]," 3 folio pp., in RZ Archives, folder 91. An English translation appeared in *Meir Kahane News Letter* 1, April 26, 1974, pp. [5-8], in RZ Archives, folder 1010.

A similar theme is found in the following *Jewish Press* articles: "Only Thus [first version]," *Jewish Press*, June 8, 1973, p. 22; "Only Thus [second version]," *Jewish Press*, February 21, 1975, pp. 36, 37. See also note 9.

The desecration of G-d's name is discussed at length in *The Jewish Idea*, vol. 1, pp. 355-362, 384-396.

9 See chapter 35, note 8, "Kiddush Hashem." Excerpts in chapter 35.

10 Meir Kahane, "Rak Kach: Tokhnit Pe'ula Letipul Biva'ayat Hateror Ha'aravi [Only Thus: Operational Program for Dealing With the Problem of Arab Terror]," 1 folio p., in RZ Archives, folder 91.

"Kahane to Present Anti-Terror Program, Monday, April 22, 1974, 11 A.M., at Dir Yassin," press release (in Hebrew and English), mimeographed, poorly typed, in RZ Archives, folder 91.

UPI cable, datelined April 22, 1974, in RZ Archives, folder 91. This notes that Dir Yassin was "the site of an alleged Jewish massacre of Arabs in 1948." See: Klein, Morton A., *Deir Yassin: History of a Lie* (Jerusalem: Israel Resource News Agency, 1997), 33 pp.; Uri Milstein, *Alilat Hadam Bedir Yassin: Hasefer Hashachor* [The Blood Libel of Dir Yassin: The Black Book] (Tel Aviv: Hamidrasha Haleumit, 2007), 239 pp.

11 Gil Sadan, "Harav Kahana Matzi'a Hakamat Irgun Yehudi Leteror-Negdi [Rabbi Kahane Proposes the Creation of a Jewish Counterterror Organization]," *Yedioth Ahronoth*, April 23, 1974, p. 5, in RZ Archives, folder 91. Excerpted with permission.

See also: Yosef Wachsman, "Yukam Irgun Olami Lemilchama Be'irgunei Hachabala Ha'arviyim [A Worldwide Organization to Fight Arab Terror Groups Will Be Formed]," *Ma'ariv*, April 23, 1974, p. 15, in RZ Archives, folder 91.

12 Charles Mohr, "Israeli Toll Is 24 As 4 Students Die; 4 or 5 More of the Original 70 Wounded at Maalot Are on Serious List," *New York Times*, May 17, 1974, p. 16; "24 Korbanot Hatevach Bema'alot... [24 Victims of the Massacre at Maalot...]," *Yedioth Ahronoth*, May 16, 1974, p. 1; Tova Kamins, "15,000 Rally at U.N.," *Jewish Press*, May 24, 1974, pp. 1, 2.

Lawrence Van Gelder, "10,000 Here Protest Terrorist Incident at Maalot; Religious Leaders Express Outrage and Grief," *New York Times*, May 17, 1974, p. 16, in RZ Archives, folder 697. This notes: "Brooklyn District Attorney Eugene Gold and seven others, including Rabbis Haskel Lookstein, Steven Riskin, Avraham Weiss, Shaul Berman, and Reuven Grodner, chained themselves to a U.N. fence..."

Dick Belsky, "Arab Spokesman Mehdi Is Beaten Near the U.N.," *New York Post*, May 17, 1974, in RZ Archives, folder 697.

On counterterror: *Meir Kahane News Letter* 3, May 24, 1974, p. 1, in RZ Archives, folder 1010.

13 Meir was conscripted according to Israeli law on April 16, 1974, and did basic training until May 14, 1974. Source: His application for a U.S. passport, April 9, 1979, in RZ Archives, folder 582. His profile was 89, and his army I.D. number was 273854. Source: Application for gun permit, May 7, 1987, in RZ Archives, folder 1147.

The Civil Defense unit is now known as the IDF Homefront Command.

14 Ad for the newsletter in *Numbers 23:9* (Jerusalem: [July] 1974), p. 34.

Excerpts from *Our Challenge* (Radnor, Pa.: Chilton Book Company, 1974), pp. 29-34. Details on other reprints of this text in chapter 31, note 1.

"A Secret Trial in Israel" is reproduced from *Hadar* (Lower Manhattan Chapter, JDL) 1:4, Special Issue, [March 1974], p. 1, in RZ Archives, folder 91.

"The Chosen State," 14 pp. [pp. 10-24] was double-spaced on folio sheets. Reprinted in *Letters from Prison*. See note 17.

15 "Happy Intermarriage," flyer and press release about demonstration at U.S. Consulate on Agron Street, Jerusalem, April 24, 1974, 10 A.M., in RZ Archives, folder 91.

16 "With Deep Regret," *Meir Kahane News Letter* 6, July 5, 1974, p. 1, in RZ Archives, folder 1010.

The six issues, in RZ Archives, folder 1010, are: 1, April 26, 1974; 2, May 10, 1974; 3, May 24, 1974; 4, June 7, 1974; 5, June 21, 1974; 6, July 5, 1974.

17 Meir Kahane, *Letters from Prison* (Jerusalem: Jewish Identity Center, 1974), 46 pp., 24 cm., softcover, in RZ Archives, booklets folder. *Letters from Prison* is in the JNUL and in the University of California at Berkeley library.

Contents: The Chosen State, pp. 1-13 (reprinted in *Story of the Jewish Defense League*, pp. 301-316, and in *Writings 5734-5-6*, pp. 7-18; mimeographed text distributed in March 1974 as "Supplementary Declaration to the Court" in RZ Archives, folder 92A); How Sweet It Is, pp. 14-16 (see chapter 33, note 31); Boycott, pp. 17-19 (printed as "Statement to the Court," *Jewish Press*, April 5, 1974, pp. 44, 45); Letter to a Jewish Prisoner, pp. 20-23 (see note 18); Declaration to the Court, pp. 24-29 (reprinted in *Writings 5734-5-6*, pp. 20-25); A Letter to My Children, pp. 30-32 (*Jewish Press*, July 6, 1973, p. 45, reprinted in *Beyond Words*, 1:464-467); The Honor of the Jewish People, pp. 33-41 (see chapter 31, note 3.); Eretz Yisrael and the Burning Fire, pp. 42-45 (see chapter 33, note 47).

Five of these articles are excerpted in this book: "How Sweet It Is" and "Eretz Yisrael and the Burning Fire," in chapter 33; "Boycott" (originally "Statement to the Court") and "Declaration to the Court," in chapter 37; "Letter to a Jewish Prisoner" in this chapter.

18 "Letter to a Jewish Prisoner," *Jewish Press*, November 10, 1972, p. 22; reprinted in *Beyond Words*, 1:335-340.

19 Meir Kahane, *The Jewish Idea: A Jewish Program for Jewish Survival* (Jerusalem: Jewish Identity Center, [June] 1974), [20] pp., 28 cm., softcover. (The excerpt in the text is from page 7.) In JNUL, call number S74B2962=2.

The first mimeographed edition of this booklet had an introduction which did not appear in the printed booklet. Cover and introduction of mimeographed edition sent to me by Lore Perl, widow of Dr. William Perl; copies in RZ Archives Appendix.

Another imprint: New York: Jewish Defense League, 1975, in RZ Archives, folder 69B.

These concepts are discussed by Meir in *The Jewish Idea*, vol. 1, pp. 115, 509, 519-522, and in *Perush Hamaccabee: Devarim* [Hebrew] (Jerusalem: Institute for Publication of Writings of Rabbi Meir Kahane, 1995), pp. 250, 320, 406.

Jewish Defense League: Principles and Philosophies, see chapter 18.

The Jewish Defense League Movement Handbook, see chapter 27.

20 Meir Kahane, *Numbers 23:9* (Jerusalem: Jewish Identity Center, [July] 1974), 34 pp., 28 cm., softcover. In JNUL, call number S74B1962=2; in RZ Archives, booklets folder. See also chapter 45, note 23, item 18.

My personal copy has the dedication, "To Libby, With Everlasting Love, Meir."

Excerpts from *Numbers 23:9* appeared in *Meir Kahane News Letter* 5, June 21, 1974, pp. [3-9], in RZ Archives, folder 1010.

Numbers 23:9 later reprinted in smaller format: Miami Beach: I. Block, 1975, 58 pp., 19 cm. In JNUL, call number S75B3155.

Hebrew edition: *Bamidbar Khaf-Gimel:Tet* (Jerusalem: Tenuat Kach, [1974]), 30 pp., 24 cm., softcover. In JNUL, call number S75A7312. Hebrew translation by Rabbi Aryeh Julius. (Interview with Rabbi Julius, August 1, 1999, Jerusalem.) This was published shortly after the founding of Tenuat Kach in July 1974.

[21] Meir Kahane, *Madmen and Murderers* (Jerusalem: Jewish Identity Center, 1974), 8 pp., 20 cm., softcover, in RZ Archives, folder 589A and booklet folder. Another imprint: New York: Jewish Identity Center, 1975.

Reprinted in *Meir Kahane News Letter* 3, pp. [3-6] (see note 12); in *Writings 5734-5-6*, p. 40-44, dated March 1974; and in the *Jewish Press*, July 18, 1975, pp. 31, 32.

Noted in the excerpt: *Min Hameitzar*. See chapter 11, note 21.

Noted in the excerpt: Yitzhak Rabin said, "I am ready to obtain a visa for going to Gush Etzion." Quoted in Uri Avnery, "Yom Hazikaron Ha'amiti [Rabin's Real Memorial Day]," *Ma'ariv*, October 31, 1999, p. 6.

[22] Letter from Meir to Gene Singer, Shifra Hoffman, Sam Shoshan, Hilton Goldman, and Reuben Gross, July 3, 1974, in RZ Archives, folder 91.

The letter began, "Once again forgive me for the form of this joint letter to you but I want all of you to read everything here and it is simply too long to write separately."

[23] "Meir Kahane's Writings," [ad] *Jewish Press*, May 31, 1974, p. 27.

Ads for Meir's writings appeared on the last pages of *Meir Kahane News Letter*, nos. 2-6, in RZ Archives, folder 1010.

[24] Letter from Meir to book publishers, February 26, 1974, in JNUL Archives, folder ARC 4=1748.

[25] Letter from McGraw-Hill to Meir, March 20, 1974, in JNUL Archives, folder ARC 4=1748.

[26] Letter from Little, Brown and Company to Meir, March 19, 1974, in JNUL Archives, folder ARC 4=1748.

[27] See note 22.

[28] Ads in *Letters from Prison*, p. 46, and *Numbers 23:9*, p. 33. Meir used my father's address in an effort to prevent the government from tampering with his mail.

By May 1974, the Jewish Identity Center of Jerusalem had been granted tax deductible status by the U.S. Internal Revenue Service. Letter from attorney Arthur H. Miller to attorney Hilton Goldman, May 6, 1974, in RZ Archives, folder 692B.

[29] Letter to Meir from Gabriel Cohen, publisher, *Jewish Post and Opinion*, March 8, 1974, in RZ Archives, folder 1007.

[30] David Borac (pseudonym of Meir Kahane), "Exposing the Haters," *Jewish Press*, March 1, 1974, p. 21, in RZ Archives, folder 1212; "Exposing the Haters," *Jewish Press*, April 12, 1974, pp. 8, 9.

Letter from Meir to Shifra Hoffman, April 25, 1974, in RZ Archives, folder 713A.

[31] Meir Hacohen (pseudonym of Meir Kahane), "Fear on the Heights," *Jewish Press*, May 24, 1974, pp. 4, 8; Meir Hacohen (pseudonym of Meir Kahane), "The Last Long Day," *Jewish Press*, April 26, 1974, pp. 14, 33. Meir relied largely on the *Knesset Minutes* for "The Last Long Day."

[32] See note 8, *Meir Kahane News Letter* 1.

[33] Irving Spiegel, "Hans Morgenthau Attacks Kissinger on Mideast Policy," *New York Times*, May 6, 1974, p. 7.

[34] "Citizens Group Formed to Back Jackson for President and to Fight Kissinger's Policy and

Kennedy's Plans," press release, April 24, 1974, in RZ Archives, folder 91; "Citizens for Jackson and Against Kissinger," [ad] *Jerusalem Post*, April 29, 1974, in RZ Archives, folder 91.

The Democratic party's presidential candidate in 1976 was Jimmy Carter.

35 Inge Deutschkron, "Harav Kahana Koreh: Jackson Lanesi'ut [Rabbi Kahane Declares: Jackson for President], *Ma'ariv*, May 2, 1974, p. 14, in RZ Archives, folder 91.

36 "Lo – Lenixon Vekissinger [No to Nixon and Kissinger]," *Yedioth Ahronoth*, May 7, 1974, p. 4, in RZ Archives, folder 91. This has a photo of Meir speaking to crowd, while a newsman holds a microphone up to him. The caption says, "Rabbi Meir Kahane, who resigned as head of the Liga, appeared again yesterday as the 'fighting rabbi.'"

Kissinger arrived in Tel Aviv on May 4, 1974. See: Bernard Gwertzman, "Kissinger Urges Israelis to Map a New Truce Line," *New York Times*, May 6, 1974, pp. 1, 73.

"Join Us," English flyer, in RZ Archives, folder 91. The flyer gave addresses for further details and for contributions: Attorney Bob Persky in Jersey City, N.J. and Mrs. Julie Thornberg in Tel Aviv.

37 "Tza'ir Yehudi... [Young Jew...]," mimeographed quarto flyer dated Sivan 5734 [June 1974] in RZ Archives, folder 72B. Abridged translation.

The flyer included a coupon for potential members.

38 "Kol Hakavod Lehafganot [Demonstrations Are Great]," flyer announcing meetings on civil disobedience, Rechov Ussishkin 31, Jerusalem, May 14, 8 P.M.; ZOA House, Tel Aviv, May 20, 8 P.M., in RZ Archives, folder 91. Abridged translation.

39 See note 5, *Meir Kahane News Letter* 2, pp. 1, 2.

40 See note 39.

41 "Mitnachalei Shechem Servu La'azov Ufunu Bekho'ach Al Yedei Chayalei Tzahal [Shechem Settlers Refused to Leave and Were Forcibly Evicted by IDF Soldiers]," *Yedioth Ahronoth*, June 6, 1974, p. 3; "Group of 120 Ready to Settle at Shechem," *Jerusalem Post*, January 7, 1974, p. 3.

Raphael Bashan, "Kol Hanesigot Hen Totza'a Shel Chulsha Ruchanit... Harav Tzvi Yehuda Hacohen Kook [All Withdrawals Are the Result of Spiritual Weakness... Interview With Rabbi Tzvi Yehuda Hacohen Kook]," *Yedioth Ahronoth*, June 28, 1974, *Musaf Leshabbat* section, p. 7.

Hamdi Kan'an was mayor of Shechem until 1969. Ma'zoz Masri was elected in 1971 and Bassam Shak'a was elected in 1976. See: www.nablus.org

42 "Shchem," *Meir Kahane News Letter* 4, June 7, 1974, p. 2, in RZ Archives, folder 1010.

43 "On Law and Order in Israel," *Jewish Press*, August 23, 1974, pp. 18, 43, reprinted in *Beyond Words*, 2:33-44. A two-part article with the same title, with only slight changes in the text, appeared in the *Jewish Press*, March 11, 1977, p. 58; March 18, 1977, pp. 53, 54.

A Hebrew translation, an abridgement of the 1974 *Jewish Press* article, was *Chok Vaseder O Hefker Beyisrael*, 2 mimeographed pages, dated August 1, 1974, in RZ Archives, folder 92A.

The Hebrew translation of the 1977 *Jewish Press* article was a booklet, *Chok Vaseder Beyisrael* (Jerusalem: Tenuat Kach, [1977]), [10] pp., 18 cm. The booklet was reprinted in 1980, 1982, and 1986. In JNUL, call numbers S77A1614, S88A1616, S2000A5450.

In 1986, after an objection was raised to Meir's modification of the standard pledge to the Knesset, one columnist quoted from "Law and Order in Israel," to show that Meir's first allegiance was to Torah law. Allan E. Shapiro, "Unseat Kahane," *Jerusalem Post*, December 25, 1986, in RZ Archives, folder 521.

44 See note 42.

45 Letter (Hebrew) from Meir to mayors of Shechem, Ramallah, Tulkarem and Ramallah, June 9, 1974, in RZ Archives, folder 91.

[46] "Oness Bishechem [Rape in Shechem]," flyer announcing speech at Beit Agron, June, 12, 1974, in RZ Archives, Appendix and folder 91.

The *Altalena* was shelled on June 22, 1948. See: www.jewishvirtuallibrary.org. Search Altalena.

Chapter 39

[1]   "Finally, A Verdict," *Meir Kahane News Letter* 5, June 21, 1974, p. 1, in RZ Archives, folder 1010.

[2]   "Kahane Convicted of Attempted Conspiracy: Sentencing Today," *Jerusalem Post*, June 28, 1974, p. 3, in RZ Archives, folder 91; "Kahane Gets Suspended Term for Conspiracy Bid," *Jerusalem Post*, June 30, 1974, p. 3, in RZ Archives, folder 91; "Harav Kahana – Lema'asar Shenatayim Al Tenai [Rabbi Kahane – Two Year Suspended Sentence]," *Ma'ariv*, June 30, 1974, p. 11, in RZ Archives, folder 91; "Harav Kahana Hursha Benisayon Lechabel Beyachasei Yisrael-Artzot Habrit [Rabbi Kahane Found Guilty of Attempt to Harm Israel-U.S. Relations]," *Yedioth Ahronoth*, June 28, 1974, p. 2; "Shenatayim Al Tenai [Two Year Suspended Sentence]," *Yedioth Ahronoth*, June 30, 1974, p. 4; "Israel Convicts Kahane in Plots on Embassies," *New York Times*, June 28, 1974, p. 7; "Kahane Sentenced in Israel," *New York Times*, June 29, 1974, p. 58.

[3]   "Not Happy," *Meir Kahane News Letter* 6, July 5, 1974, p. 1, in RZ Archives, folder 1010.

Beginning in the mid-1960s, Beate Klarsfeld and her husband Serge, French citizens, tracked down and brought to justice Nazis and Nazi collaborators. The most famous of them was Klaus Barbie, the "Butcher of Lyons."

[4]   Arye Avneri, "Ani Me'ukhzav Mehano'ar Hayisraeli [I Am Disappointed by Israeli Youth]," *Yedioth Ahronoth*, May 23, 1974, p. 20, in RZ Archives, folder 91.

[5]   Meir lectured at Ramot Shapira on June 3 and August 4, 1974, and was paid 30 lirot an hour for each lecture plus 22 lirot for taxi fare (55.98 for the first lecture and 33.12 for the second). Check stubs in RZ Archives, folder 479.

Letter from "Students and Teachers," Mitrani Comprehensive High School, Holon, to Meir, June 17, 1974, in RZ Archives, folder 715B.

Letter from Esther Goldblatt, Association of Americans and Canadians in Israel, Netanya, to Meir, June 4, 1974, in RZ Archives, folder 91. Confirms lecture on June 17, 1974.

Letter from Rabbi Shmuel Heller, Yeshivat Pirchei Aharon, Kiryat Shmuel, to Meir, June 24, 1974, in RZ Archives, folder 713A. This was Meir's second invitation to the school. See chapter 33, note 5.

Mimeographed letter (Hebrew) to members of Hachug Lezugot Nesu'im Leyad Hamishmeret Hatze'ira-Chazon [the Chazon group in the Mafdal party]: "Rabbi Meir Kahane will speak at the home of Sara and Dudu Taubman in Rishon Letziyon," on August 3, 1974, 9 P.M., in RZ Archives, folder 715B.

Letter from Lanny and Evelyn Yellin to Meir, August 6, 1974, in RZ Archives, folder 713A. Meir spoke at their home "last Thursday," i.e. August 1.

See also: Check stub for 145 lirot from the Tel Aviv municipality for an unspecified lecture, August 1974, in RZ Archives, folder 479.

[6]   "Jericho," *Meir Kahane News Letter* 6, July 5, 1974, p. 1, in RZ Archives, folder 1010; Yosef Dan, "Tokhnit Yericho Palestina'it [Plans for a Palestinian Jericho]," *Yedioth Ahronoth*, July 15, 1974, *24 Hours* section, p. 3.

In light of the 1994 Gaza and Jericho agreement, in which Jericho was transferred to the Palestinian Authority, Meir showed foresight in his concern that Jericho remain under Israeli sovereignty.

The campaign for a settlement near Jericho led to the establishment of Mitzpeh Yericho in 1977. See: www.geocities.com/m_yericho/index.html.

7 Menachem Barash, "Talmidei Yeshiva Mevakshim Lehitnachel Biyericho [Yeshiva Students Ask to Settle in Jericho]," *Yedioth Ahronoth*, June 21, 1974, p. 1; Yosef Wachsman, "B'nai Yeshivot Panu Lerabin Bevakasha Lehitnachel Biyericho [Yeshiva Students Approached Rabin with a Request to Settle in Jericho]," *Ma'ariv*, June 21, 1974, p. 4; "Yeshiva Mitnachelet [Settlers Yeshiva]," press release, [June 19, 1974], all in RZ Archives, folder 91.

8 "Yeshivat Aderet Eliyahu," [ad] *Jerusalem Post*, July 1, 1974, p. 4, in RZ Archives, folder 91. A coupon printed at the bottom of the ad gave Tel Aviv P.O. box 36431 and phone number 03-268894, and Jerusalem P.O. box 15027 and our home phone number, 02-526127.

"Anu Ge'im Lehakhriz Al Hakamata... [We Are Proud to Announce the Establishment...]," [ad] *Yedioth Ahronoth*, July 2, 1974, p. 30, in RZ Archives, folder 91.

9 See chapter 38, note 22, letter from Meir to Gene Singer, et al.

10 "Kahane's New Centre to Open in Jericho," *Jerusalem Post*, July 17, 1974, p. 3; "Harav Kahana Hekim Tenua Chadasha [Rabbi Kahane Formed a New Movement]," *Davar*, July 17, 1974, p. 3.

"Rabbi Meir Kahane to Announce Formation of New Movement... July 16, 11 A.M., Beit Sokolov," press release in English and Hebrew, July 14, 1974. This includes an announcement about the Institute on Human Relations. Receipts for telegrams to the King family, July 12, 1974, all in RZ Archives, folder 91.

11 "Kahana Mekim Tenua Chadasha Beshem 'Kach' [Kahane is Forming a New Movement Named 'Kach']," *Yedioth Ahronoth*, July 14, 1974, p. 8; "Harav Kahana Hekim 'Tenua Amamit' Beshem 'Kach' [Rabbi Kahane Formed a 'Popular Movement' Named 'Kach']," *Ma'ariv*, July 17, 1974, p. 6, in RZ Archives, folder 82; "Kahane Forms New Movement," *Jerusalem Post*, July 12, 1974, p. 3.

Press release about the new movement, together with its platform, dated July 10, 1974, in RZ Archives, folder 82. News reports about the formation of Kach that appeared before the July 16 press conference were based on the press release.

Dr. William Perl commented: "The name Kach is in my opinion entirely unsuited for America. a) It does not say anything to the 99.9% Americans who do not speak Hebrew. b) It can too easily serve for jokes." Letter from Dr. William R. Perl to Meir, July 14, 1974, in RZ Archives, folder 713A.

12 See chapter 38, note 22, letter from Meir to Gene Singer, et al.

13 See press release, note 10.

"Kahana Mitkaven 'Larutz' Pa'am Nosefet Laknesset [Kahane Intends to Run for the Knesset Again]," *Yedioth Ahronoth*, July 17, 1974, p. 6.

Principles and program: "Kach" [Hebrew] (Jerusalem: Tenuat Kach, [1974]), 8 mimeographed folio leaves, in RZ Archives, folder 82. Meir hand-dated this July 16, 1974. English version: "Kach – Thus!" 7 mimeographed folio leaves, in RZ Archives, folder 82.

A reprint with the font reduced was: *Tenuat "Kach," Berashut Harav Meir Kahane, Ekronot Vekavei Pe'ula* (Jerusalem: no date), 6 pp., 28 cm., in RZ Archives, folder 714A.

The Hebrew version was probably translated by Rabbi Julius; the 6-page Hebrew version was used for the 1977 elections. (Phone interview with Shimon Rachamim, January 27, 2001).

14 National Photo Collection, Israel Government Press Office: www.mof.gov.il/pictures. This shows four photos by Yaakov Saar, July 16, 1974, nos: 017374, 17375, 017381, and 17382.

See the photo section of this book for no. 17375.

[15] Transcript of a radio report by Jay Bushinsky, WINS radio, July 12, 1974, in RZ Archives, folder 82. Dave Sobel sent the transcript to Meir. Letter from Dave Sobel to Meir, July 13, 1974, in RZ Archives, folder 713A.

See also: Israel Broadcasting Authority Television News Archive, media no. 09377-74-8, July 16, 1974.

[16] See chapter 38, note 22, letter from Meir to Gene Singer, et al.

Meir scheduled his return to Israel for November 1 because his trial for the weapons shipment was scheduled for November 17 in Tel Aviv District Court.

[17] Letter from Meir to "Dear Friend," undated, but after July 16, 1974, in RZ Archives, folder 715B. The enclosure is *Kach – Thus* (see note 13).

[18] Letter from Meir to Samuel Shoshan, undated but probably March 13, 1974, in RZ Archives, Appendix.

[19] Letter from Shelley Blum to "Dear Community Leader," [July 1974], in RZ Archives, folder 546.

[20] Letter from Hilton Goldman to Meir, July 28, 1974, in RZ Archives, folder 715B. Goldman wrote that he was lining up media events. He signed this letter with his Hebrew name, Hillel.

[21] Albin Krebs, "Notes on People," *New York Times*, August 15, 1974, p. 34.

Letter from Meir to Gene Singer and Samuel Shoshan, July 29, 1974, in RZ Archives, Appendix.

[22] Letter from Meir to Libby and children, August 19, 1974, in RZ Archives, Appendix.

"Beshel Ee-havana Nimne'a Yetzi'at Kahana Min Ha'aretz [A Misunderstanding Prevented Kahane from Leaving Israel]," *Yedioth Ahronoth*, August 13, 1974, p. 7; "Israeli Police Take Kahane Off a Plane Bound for U.S.," *New York Times*, August 13, 1974, p. 11.

William T. Slattery. "We'll Picket Kissinger – Kahane," *New York Post*, August 15, 1974, p. 16, and photo, captioned "Kahane Returns," p. 3, in RZ Archives, folder 72B.

A snapshot showing Meir standing before a microphone at the airport press conference is labeled, "Return to U.S., August 14, 1974," in RZ Archives, picture folder, no. 12. The snapshot is in the photo section of this book.

See also: "Kahane Ready for Action," *Jewish Press*, August 23, 1974, p. 2, in RZ Archives, folder 72B.

[23] Letter from Meir to Libby and children, undated but probably August 29, 1974, in RZ Archives, Appendix.

[24] Letter from Dr. William Perl to Meir, July 14, 1974, in RZ Archives, folder 713A.

[25] Letter from Samuel Shoshan to Meir, January 21, 1974, in RZ Archives, Appendix.

[26] Letter from Norman Karr to Samuel Hirschman, July 7, 1974, in RZ Archives, Appendix.

[27] Press release from David Fisch to "Jewish News Media," July 3, 1974, in RZ Archives, folder 91.

[28] Interview with Barbara and Chaim Ginsberg, January 14, 1998, Jerusalem.

[29] Letter from Bertram Zweibon to "Dear Member," undated, but before Rosh Hashana (September 17, 1974), in RZ Archives, folder 483B.

"The JDL Is NOT Holding a Convention," [ad] *Jewish Press*, September 6, 1974, p. 41. The 3 column x 3.5 inch ad was signed Bertram Zweibon, Chairman of the Board, JDL, 315 Seventh Avenue, New York.

Decision to expel adult members: *Minutes*, Executive Board Meeting, September 4, 1974, in YU Archives, folder 6/4.

[30] Letter from Meir to Bertram Zweibon, November 17, 1972; letter from Meir to Nat Rosenwasser, postmarked November 21, 1972, both in RZ Archives, Appendix.

Letter from Dr. William Perl to Meir, January 22, 1974, in the William Perl collection, Gelman Library, George Washington University, Washington, D.C.

[31] "Pursuant to the By-Laws...," [ad] *Jewish Press*, September 6, 1974, p. 44, in RZ Archives, folder 72B.

[32] International Jewish Defense League, *Program of Convention 1974*, Belmont Plaza Hotel, New York, September 8, 1974, in RZ Archives, folder 72A and folder 435B.

[33] Letter from Meir to Dear Fellow Jew, September 1974, in RZ Archives, folder 72B.

Quoted in: Barry Cunningham, "Power Struggle in the JDL," *New York Post*, October 21, 1974, pp. 4, 40, in RZ Archives, folder 683A.

[34] "A Message to the Jewish Community from the JDL led by Rabbi Meir Kahane," [ad] *Jewish Press*, September 27, 1974, p. 17.

Chapter 40

[1] Letter from Meir to Libby and children, August 19, 1974, in RZ Archives, Appendix.

Meir appeared on the Long John Nebel radio show, WMCA, on August 19, 1974, at midnight. See: "Today's Radio," *New York Post*, August 19, 1974, p. 50, in RZ Archives, folder 72B.

False bomb threats had become an everyday event in general and for Meir in particular. Crank callers hoped for the cancellation of an event. Meir always refused to take the threats seriously, and there was never a real bomb.

When I worked as a secretary at a public high school in Brooklyn in 1971, I was told matter-of-factly how to deal with phoned-in bomb threats (usually from students who were not prepared for exams): "Simply record the date and hour and how the caller's voice sounded in our 'bomb threat' notebook."

My brother and his wife rented a two-room bungalow in the Catskill mountain area during the summer to give their children the benefits of country air. Later on, Meir stayed at their home in Brooklyn.

My brother wrote: "I met Meir at the airport Wednesday night... [Meir spent Shabbat with them and spoke at their synagogue.] He spoke for two hours and hasn't lost his charisma.... Saturday night, he cancelled some appointments and baby-sat for us. He was asleep when we came home. I guess that jet lag really gets to you!" Letter from Phil Blum to Libby, August 18, 1974, in RZ Archives, Appendix.

[2] Contract for *Story of the Jewish Defense League*, between Meir Kahane and the Chilton Book Company, August 9, 1974, in JNUL Archives, folder ARC 4=1748.

In a telegram at the end of March 1974, Arnovitz wrote: "Ability to contract for new book depends on orders for *Challenge*. Am monitoring." (Telegram from Benton M. Arnovitz to Meir, March 28, 1974, in JNUL Archives, folder ARC 4=1748.)

In July, a telegram from Arnovitz said, "*Challenge* sales remain modest. No interest from paperbackers. Management will authorize twenty five hundred dollars only." Meir agreed to those terms, which were the same as those for *Our Challenge*. (Telegram from Benton M. Arnovitz to Meir, July 25, 1974, and telegram from Meir to Arnovitz, July 28, 1974; both in JNUL Archives, folder ARC 4=1748.)

Letter from Benton M. Arnovitz's secretary to Meir, October 31, 1974, in JNUL Archives, folder ARC 4=1748. "Enclosed is our check in the amount of $1,250 representing the second half of the advance for the *Story of the Jewish Defense League*."

"... but WHY." Letter from Meir to Libby and children, [August 25, 1974], in RZ Archives, Appendix. The book came off the press in May 1975 rather than March 1975. See chapter 45, note 37.

3   Letter from Meir to Libby, see note 2.

On Saturday morning, August 24, Meir spoke at Congregation B'nai Yosef in Brooklyn, the synagogue attended by supporter Charles Cohen. See: "Meir Kahane will speak on Kissinger and Israel...," [ad] *Jewish Press*, August 23, 1974, p. 32.

At first, the Jewish Identity Center had an office at 5 Beekman Street, Room 425. By mid-September it had moved to 1133 Broadway, Room 426. Letter from Meir to Libby and children, [September 20, 1974,] in RZ Archives, Appendix.

4   Letter from Meir to Libby and children, September 4, 1974, in RZ Archives, Appendix.

5   David Friedman, "[Report]," *Jewish Telegraphic Agency News Dispatches*, August 30, 1974, p. 20, in RZ Archives, folder 72B. The rally took place on August 28.

A photo of Meir at the Garment Center rally shows him speaking into a hand-held mike, with an attentive audience. See: "Kahane on Tour," [photo caption] *Baltimore Jewish Times*, September 6, 1974, p. 3, in RZ Archives, folder 72B. The picture is in the photo section of this book, reproduced with the permission of the *Baltimore Jewish Times*.

See also: "Kahane Is Back and the Fight Against Kissinger Has Begun... Wednesday, August 28, 12:30, at 7th Avenue and 37th Street," flyer, in RZ Archives, folder 1205.

6   Letter from Meir to Libby and children, [August 29, 1974], in RZ Archives, Appendix.

7   "Rabbi Meir Kahane Is Back!" [ad] *Jewish Press*, September 6, 1974, p. 41. The ad gave the phone numbers of Sheila Lidz and Shelley Blum. The number 516 374 6057 was confirmed by e-mail from Lidz, April 19, 2005.

8   Letter from Rabbi Morris J. Rothman to Rabbi Sholom Rivkin, Young Israel of Wavecrest and Bayswater, August 25, 1974, in RZ Archives, folder 72A. Meir spoke at the Young Israel of Wavecrest and Bayswater on Saturday, August 31.

9   Letter from Meir to Libby and children, September 4, 1974, in RZ Archives, Appendix.

An ad announced Meir's talk on Saturday afternoon, September 7, 4 P.M., at the Young Israel of Long Beach and at 11 P.M. (prior to *Selichot*) at the Young Israel of Hillcrest. "The Public Is Invited to Hear..." [ad] *Jewish Press*, September 6, 1974, p. 41.

"... Most provocative, challenging aspect of our convention." Letter from Howard Sherizen, Committee for 15th National Convention of Yavneh, National Religious Jewish Students Association, to Meir, October 14, 1974, in RZ Archives, folder 72B.

Aaron I. Reichel recalled Meir's "rousing" speech at the Yavneh convention. Letter from Reichel to Libby, January 26, 1998, in RZ Archives, Appendix.

10   "Myths to Be Shaken at Pickwick by Controversial Rabbi Kahane," *Baltimore Jewish Times*, September 6, 1974, p. 18, in RZ Archives, folder 72B.

11   SOIL was set up in August 1974 with the same addresses as the Jewish Identity Center. See note 3.

At the initiative of Sam Shoshan, Norbert Rosenthal backed the project. Letter from Samuel Shoshan to Dov Hikind, November 18, 1974, in RZ Archives, Appendix.

Membership forms set annual dues at $5.00 in the U.S. and 20 lirot in Israel.

Hikind later became a New York State assemblyman. See chapter 24, note 19.

Flyer for SOIL, with coupon for membership registration, in RZ Archives, folder 91.

When Meir was in Israel in November and December, Hikind led SOIL demonstrations. See: Dov Hasdai, "JDL Analysis," *Jewish Press*, November 15, 1974, p. 15, and November 22, 1974, p. 45, both in RZ Archives, folder 697; "S.O.I.L Sits In at A.D.L. Offices," *Jewish Press*, December 13, 1974, p. 52, in RZ Archives, folder 683A.

[12] "Why Do Jews Always Wait...," [ad] *Jewish Press*, September 6, 1974, p. 41.

[13] J. William Joynes, "Jewish Leader Calls Kissinger Threat," *Baltimore News American*, September 15, 1974, p. 2B, in RZ Archives, folder 72B. Excerpted with the author's permission.

"Kahane blasts *Jewish Times*, Kissinger in Pickwick Center Speech," *Northwest Star* (Pikesville, Maryland), September 19, 1974, in RZ Archives, folder 72B; M. Hirsh Goldberg, "Where Does Meir Kahane Go from Here?" *Times of Israel and World Jewish Review*, January 1975, pp. 50-51, in RZ Archives, folder 72B. See the photo section of this book for photos by Eric Feinberg that accompany Goldberg's interview. Reproduced with the photographer's permission.

"Kissinger's Israel Policy Assailed," *Baltimore Sun*, September 15, 1974, p. A18, in RZ Archives, folder 72B. This report on Meir's talk at the Pickwick Jewish Center said that police received phone calls that a bomb had been placed there. The building was not evacuated and the meeting was not disrupted.

University of Maryland: FBI file 105-207795, teletype, September 12, 1974, 2 pp., in RZ Archives, Appendix.

Gerald Ford was appointed Vice President in 1973, when Spiro Agnew resigned because of income tax evasion. In August 1974, when Richard Nixon was forced to resign because of the Watergate scandal, Ford became President.

[14] See note 6.

Greek Cypriots accused Kissinger of responsibility for the Turkish invasion and domination of Cyprus in 1974. See: www.hellenicnews.com/readnews.html?newsid=1575&lang=US.

[15] "Kissinger's Home Picketed," *Jewish Press*, September 20, 1974, p. 3, in RZ Archives, folder 72B.

Names of co-sponsors: FBI file 105-207795-408, report, September 24, 1974, 5 pp., in RZ Archives, Appendix.

Probation violation: See note 13, FBI teletype.

[16] "An Open Letter to the President," *Jewish Press*, August 30, 1974, pp. 3, 44.

Details on the conduct of the rally and handouts distributed: See note 15, FBI file 105-207795-408.

[17] Isaac Rehert, "'Bagels and Lox Judaism' Berated by Rabbi Kahane," *Baltimore Sun*, September 24, 1974, p. B1, in RZ Archives, folder 72B. Excerpted with permission.

Israel Broadcasting Authority Television News Archive, media no. 12224-74-7, September 15, 1974.

"Anti-Kissinger March," [photo caption] in *Newsday* (Long Island [Melville], New York), September 16, 1974, "The Nation" section, in RZ Archives, Appendix.

The entire caption read: "Representatives of the Jewish Defense League and Greek, Ukrainian and other ethnic groups demonstrate at Henry Kissinger's home in Washington yesterday for his removal as Secretary of State for what they feel are the shortcomings of U.S. foreign policy."

[18] "Rabbi Meir Kahane speaks at Silver Spring Jewish Center, September 15, 1974, 8 P.M.," flyer in RZ Archives, folder 72B.

[19] See note 23, letter.

[20] See note 13, J. William Joynes.

[21] Mark Toor, "Rabbi Kahane Urges U.S. Jews to Emigrate to Israel," *Hatchet* (George Washington University), September 23, 1974, p. 2, in RZ Archives, Appendix.

[22] Letter from Meir to Tova, September 20, 1974, in RZ Archives, Appendix. Meir wrote a similar letter about the salamander to Tzippy that day.

[23] Letter from Meir to Libby and children, [September 19, 1974], in RZ Archives, Appendix.

This notes that he spent Rosh Hashana at the home of Rabbi Moshe (Marcel) Blitz. Meir spoke at George Washington University on September 19, 1974.

Clippings: The newspaper clippings that Meir periodically sent home, together with many clippings and other documents that he kept on file, make up the Rabbi Meir Kahane Collection at the Archives for the Research of Religious Zionism, Bar Ilan University.

"Why Is Kahane Here?" [editorial] *Baltimore Jewish Times*, September 13, 1974, p. 12, in RZ Archives, folder 72B.

The following week, a report on Meir's talk at the Pickwick Jewish Center appeared in the *BJT*. It had many photos of Meir and the audience. See: Gary Rosenblatt, "A Fiery Kahane Berates the Establishment," *Baltimore Jewish Times*, September 20, 1974, pp. 6-7.

Responses to the hostile editorial were also printed. For example: Paul L. Brodsky, "You Hide," [letter to the editor] *Baltimore Jewish Times*, September 20, 1974, p. 12, in RZ Archives, folder 72B.

[24] Ian Newmark, "Kahane Accuses Kissinger of Selling Out to Arabs; Calls for All Jewish 'Exiles' to Return to Israel," *Kingsman* (Brooklyn College), September 25, 1974, p. 1, in RZ Archives, folder 961.

The Washington Heights Congregation was at Pinehurst Avenue and 179th Street. Meir spent Shabbat with Martin and Elsa Gruenspecht, members of the congregation.

"Not One Inch... " flyer announcing march on Arab missions to the U.N. on Saturday night, September 21, 1974, (sponsored by SOIL), in RZ Archives, folder 72B; "Not One Inch," [ad] *Jewish Press*, September 20, 1974, p. A2.

Bayside: "The Public Is Invited to Hear..." [ad] *Jewish Press*, September 20, 1974, p. 25, in RZ Archives, folder 72B.

[25] Letter from Meir to Tzippy, September 25, 1974, in RZ Archives, Appendix. Letters written that day to the other children were similarly worded.

[26] Letter from Meir to Libby, October 2, 1974, in RZ Archives, Appendix.

Meir's speaking engagement, Colony Hotel, Atlantic City, October 1, 1974, 4 P.M., noted in *Colony News*, September 30, 1974, in RZ Archives, folder 72B.

Binyamin's birthday was on 19 Tishrei, during the intermediate days of *Sukkot*. Tithing all cash gifts was an integral part of the children's upbringing.

Speaking dates: "The Public Is Invited to Hear..." [ad] *Jewish Press*, September 27, 1974, p. 31. Saturday, September 28, on Manhattan's Lower East Side: East Side Torah Center, 9 A.M.; Bialystoker synagogue, 4 P.M.; Young Israel of New Hyde Park, 8 P.M.; Sunday, September 29, Bellmore Jewish Center.

[27] Letter from Jacob Blum, my father, to Meir, October 6, 1974, in RZ Archives, folder 714B. Meir quoted the letter (especially the last paragraph) in many talks. One was at the Dix Hills Jewish Center, February 2, 1976. See chapter 48 for the transcription of part of an audio recording of that talk.

Construction in Ramot, a new neighborhood directly north of us, began in 1974.

[28] Letter (Hebrew) from Meir to Julie Thornberg, October 3, 1974. Julie gave me the letter when I interviewed her on June 21, 2001.

Letter (Hebrew) from Meir to Shimon Rachamim, October [3], 1974, from the collection of Shimon Rachamim, in RZ Archives, Appendix.

In 1976, Meir reversed his decision to keep out of politics in Israel. He ran in the 1977 Knesset elections in the hope that a Knesset seat would further his ideological goals.

[29] Terence Smith, "Israel Turns Back 5,000 Trying to Settle West Bank," *New York Times*, October 10, 1974, pp. 1, 97; Ehud Sprinzak, "Gush Emunim: The Tip of the Iceberg," *Jerusalem Quarterly*, 21 (Fall 1981) p. 30; "Kama Kevutzot Mitnachalim Partzu Machsomei Tzahal

Bedarkhei Hagada [Several Groups of Settlers Broke Through Army Roadblocks on the West Bank]," *Yedioth Ahronoth*, October 9, 1974, pp. 1, 8.

30 Letter from Meir to Baruch, October 21, 1974, in RZ Archives, Appendix.

Meir had ample experience with police spies, beginning with JDL in New York (see chapter 24, note 9). He used to say they were his group's most efficient workers.

31 "Strength With Sanity...," [ad] *Jewish Press*, September 27, 1974, p. 17.

"... Monday, September 30, at noon: Presentation of Auschwitz booklet for Kissinger to U.S. ambassador to U.N., John Scali." I asked many JDLers about the "Auschwitz booklet." No one recalled anything about it, nor could I find any reference to it in library catalogues or other sources.

The ad gave the location of the JDL office: Room 1026, 1133 Broadway (near 24 Street) in Manhattan.

Rabbi Azriel Miller, protesting the recognition of the P.L.O. by the United Nations in November, complained to Ambassador Scali that when Rabbi Meir Kahane wanted to meet with him a few months earlier, he sent a minor official to speak with him in the lobby. But he met with Mohammad T. Mehdi, who was not even an American citizen, and thus gave encouragement to terror. See: Philip Ben, "Mishlachat Artzot Habrit Ba'um Ben Hapatish Hayehudi Vehasadan Shel Ashaf [The U.S. Delegation to the U.N. Is Between the Jewish Hammer and the P.L.O. Anvil]," *Ma'ariv*, November 11, 1974, p. 14.

March on Syrian Mission: "Jewish Defense League Open House," flyer, in RZ Archives, folder 72B; "Jewish Defense League Open House," [ad] *Jewish Press*, September 27, 1974, p. 17; October 4, 1974, p. 19.

Audio tape, interview on the Barry Farber show, [October 10, 1974], in RZ Archives, Appendix. I dated this October 10 because during the interview Meir said he was returning to Israel in "two and a half weeks," and his return date was October 29. Taped by Abe Levine.

David Borac (pseudonym of Meir Kahane), "Exposing the Haters," *Jewish Press*, October 11, 1974, p. 35, in RZ Archives, folder 1212. This article briefly mentions the debate with Brickner.

32 Cara Selinger, "Kahane Wants Change," *Phoenix* (Queens College), October 15, 1974, p. 2, in RZ Archives, folder 72B. Excerpted with permission of Queens College.

See also: Howard Steifel, "Kahane Speaks at the College," and Jerry Simonowits, Shirley Agronin and Howard Steifel, "Exclusive Interview with Rabbi Meir Kahane," *Ha'or* (Queens College), October 16, 1974, pp. 1, 3, 5, 8; Susan Scharf, "Rabbi Meir Kahane: 'Jewish Is Beautiful,'" *Newsbeat* (Queens College), October 15, 1974, p. 5, in RZ Archives, folder 72B.

33 Lee Crane Schwartz, "Students Crowd to Hear Kahane Cite Danger in U.S.," *Jewish Post and Opinion*, October 25, 1974, p. 2, in RZ Archives, folder 72B. Excerpted with permission.

One flyer distributed by the Jewish Socialist Alliance was headed, "You Don't Have to Be Jewish to Hate Meir Kahane (But It Helps)," in RZ Archives, folder 72B.

See also: Robert Irwin, "Rabbi: Holocaust Is Coming," *Sun-Bulletin* (Binghamton, N.Y.), October 11, 1974, p. 3, in RZ Archives, folder 72B.

Since Meir's trip to Binghamton would have taken almost five hours by car, he probably flew there.

34 E-mail from Jonathan Libber, February 22, 2005. Libber, a student at the University of Maryland, arranged a speaking engagement there for Meir during this period.

35 Michael Pollack, "Kahane: Militants Accepted," *The Record* (Bergen County, N.J.), October 14, 1974, p. B-4, in RZ Archives, folder 72B. Excerpted with permission.

"Autographed Copy," [photo headline] *Jewish Standard*, October 25, 1974, p. 23, in RZ Archives, folder 72B.

[36] "Rabbi Kahane Raps Kissinger," *Evening Bulletin* (Philadelphia), October 14, 1974, p. 10, in RZ Archives, folder 72B.

[37] Kahane Ad Is Rejected," *Jewish Post and Opinion*, October 25, 1974, p. 2, in RZ Archives, folder 72B; "Kahane to Speak Here," *Philadelphia Jewish Times*, October 10, 1974, p. 1, in RZ Archives, folder 72B.

[38] Letter from Meir to Libby, [October 15, 1974], in RZ Archives, Appendix.

"Rabbi Meir Kahane is currently in the U.S. to promote *Our Challenge*. He is scheduled to appear on 'Tomorrow,' NBC TV (October 15)." Report in: *Publishers Weekly*, October 7, 1974, in RZ Archives, folder 64C.

[39] Carol Pogash, "Rabbi Kahane Warns City's Jews of Doom," *San Francisco Examiner*, October 15, 1974, p. 2, in RZ Archives, folder 72B.

FBI Los Angeles office file 105-29629-130, report, November 22, 1974, 5 pp., in RZ Archives, Appendix; "Tough Talk Here From Kahane," *San Francisco Chronicle*, October 16, 1974, in RZ Archives, folder 72B; JDL of San Francisco, flyer for talks October 15 and October 16, in RZ Archives, folder 72B.

Berkeley students' flyers in RZ Archives, folder 72B.

[40] Allan Rabinowitz, "Jewish Militant Preaches Self-Interest, Survival," *Daily Californian* (University of California at Berkeley), October 23, 1974, p. 6, in RZ Archives, folder 72B. Excerpted with the author's permission.

[41] "Rabbi Kahane to Speak at Religious Zionists Meeting," *Jewish Sentinel* (Chicago), October 10, 1974, p. 19, in RZ Archives, folder 72B.

"First City-Wide Cultural: Rabbi Meir Kahane," *The Sabbath Voice – Kol Hashabbat* (Religious Zionist of Chicago), October 4, 1974, p. 1, in RZ Archives, folder 714B.

Shoshan also invited local congressman Sidney R. Yates to the gathering after the speech. Letter from Samuel Shoshan to Congressman Sidney R. Yates, October 7, 1974, in RZ Archives, Appendix.

Invitation to midnight champagne cocktail party at the home of Mr. and Mrs. Seymour H. Persky, October 19, 11 P.M., in RZ Archives, folder 72B.

"Rabbi Meir Kahane: Exclusive Chicago Appearance..." poster, in RZ Archives, poster folder, no. 200.

"Rabbi Meir Kahane Will Speak," [ad] *North Town News*, October 16, 1974, in RZ Archives, folder 72B.

[42] "Our Rabbis & Lay Leaders Bankrupt Pygmies – Kahane," *Jewish Post and Opinion* (Chicago edition), October 25, 1974, pp. 1, 15, in RZ Archives, folder 72. Page 15: Larry Gittleson, "Unseen in the Audience, They Stand at the Ready," part one of a two-part article about the JDL in Chicago.

Jay Branegan, "Use Violence If Need Be, Says Militant Israeli," *Chicago Tribune*, October 20, 1974, p. 34, in RZ Archives, folder 72B.

[43] Letter from Norbert Rosenthal to Meir, October 23, 1974, in RZ Archives, folder 82.

[44] "Echad: We Are All Jews – We Are All One," flyer, in RZ Archives, folder 715A. Ads about Echad: *Jewish Press*, October 11, 1974, p. 30; October 18, 1974, p. 20.

Echad was termed "the moderate nationalist group" in: Dov Hasdai, "JDL Analysis," *Jewish Press*, November 22, 1974, p. 45, in RZ Archives, folder 697.

Planning for Echad began months before. See: "U.S. Religious Zionist Nationalist Groups Urged to Form a Coalition," *Jewish Telegraphic Agency* [*Daily News Bulletin*], dateline April 29, 1974, in RZ Archives, folder 64A.

See note 38, letter from Meir to Libby.

[45] Meir Kahane, "For Shame," *Jewish Press*, October 18, 1974, p. 44, in RZ Archives, folders 72B and 1208.

[46] David Friedman, "Kahane Would Dump on Israeli Consulate," *Jewish Week*, October 31, 1974; Barry Cunningham, "Power Struggle in the JDL," *New York Post*, October 21, 1974, pp. 4, 40, in RZ Archives, folder 683A.

Letter from Meir to Tova, October 21, 1974, in RZ Archives, Appendix. Referring to her participation in Operation *Hakafot*, he wrote that he told the crowd, "May G-d give you the *nachat* [joy] that I have from my daughter."

[47] "Rabbi Meir Kahane speaks... October 21, 1974," [ad] *Achshav: The Jewish Voice of Lehman College*, October 1974, in RZ Archives, folder 72B. The talk was sponsored by Yavneh.

Report on the speech: Sheila Leonard, "Go Home Before You Can't Go Home," *Achshav*, December 1974, in RZ Archives, folder 65A.

Letter from Dr. William Berkowitz to Meir, July 30, 1974, in RZ Archives, folder 715B. The letter thanks Meir for agreeing to speak on October 21, 1974.

In October 1975, Meir gave a series of four lectures at B'nai Jeshurun on "The History and Ideology of Jewish Activism." See chapter 46.

[48] Cassandra Thornton, "Militant Rabbi to Speak on Campus," *Falcon Times* (Dade Junior College, North), October 23, 1974, p. 3, in RZ Archives, folder 72B.

"Kahane Is Coming," flyer, in RZ Archives, folder 72B. Morton Maisel is named as the contact person for Meir's visit in Miami.

"Kahane Is Coming," [ad] *Miami Herald*, October 18, 1974, p. 5-D, in RZ Archives, folder 72B. The ad said, "Exclusive South Florida appearance.... Students Free." On the same page, with other social announcements: "Rabbi Meir Kahane to Speak in Area."

See also: Leo Mindlin, "The Rabbi Was a Pussy Cat," *Jewish Floridian*, November 1, 1974, pp. 4A, 12A, in RZ Archives, folder 72B.

[49] "Crowd Cheers Kahane," *The Journal* (Long Beach, N. Y.), October 31, 1974, pp. 1, 3, in RZ Archives, Appendix; "An Evening Honoring Rabbi Meir Kahane," [ad] *Jewish Press*, September 27, 1974, p. 32; October 18, 1974, p. 29. The dinner was held at the Hebrew Academy of Long Beach, catered by Bob Duchanov, with music by "The Messengers."

"Walking and Talking," [photo caption] *Daily News*, October 28, 1974, in RZ Archives, folder 72A. See also: "Rally Planned on Funds for Ethnic Minority Groups," *New York Times*, October 25, 1974, p. 25; "Jewish Poverty Sunday," [ad] *Jewish Press*, October 25, 1974, p. 13. The ad was signed by the Association of Jewish Anti-Poverty Workers. The purpose of the walk, from City Hall to Gracie Mansion, was to protest the uncertain future of city antipoverty programs.

[50] "Save Our Israel: Rally to Support the Settlers... at Israeli Consulate, October 27, 1974, 2 P.M...." [ad] *Jewish Press*, October 25, 1974, p. 13.

Later that afternoon, Meir spoke at a synagogue in Brooklyn. See: "Rabbi Meir Kahane Will Be Speaking in Borough Park, October 27, 1974, at 4.30 P.M.," [ad] *Jewish Press*, October 25, 1974, p. A3.

Chapter 41

[1] "Kahane, Paglin Get Suspended Sentences," *Jerusalem Post*, November 18, 1974, p. 3; "Paglin Verashei Haliga – Lema'asar Al Tnai [Paglin and the Liga Leaders – Suspended Prison Sentences]," *Yedioth Ahronoth*, November 18, 1974, p. 4.

Meir and Hershkowitz were given two-year suspended sentences; Paglin and Schneider one-year suspended sentences.

2   Summons to court for December 18, 19 and 23, 1974, in RZ Archives, folder 713A.

Letters from attorney Aharon Papo, May 11, 1973, January 23, 1975, and May 11, 1975, regarding this case (criminal case no. 92/73), in RZ Archives, folder 714B.

Phone interview with Yoel Lerner, July 7, 1997.

Another reason the case was dropped may have been that attorney Aharon Papo planned to present evidence that Mapai [Labor] party leaders were on record in favor of encouraging Arab emigration. In the early 1950s, a government agency even devised a plan (later shelved) to implement their emigration. Phone interview with Shimon Rachamim, November 1, 2007.

3   The fact that Meir was working on the manuscript of *Story of the Jewish Defense League* during this period can be seen in his reference to General George S. Brown's anti-Semitic statements of November 1974 in *Story*, chapter 7, p. 268, and a reference to the events of January 1975 in the Epilogue.

His statement in chapter 9, p. 300, that he is writing in August 1974, does not contradict the later dates. He was probably rewriting until close to the publication date.

Circulation statistics: *Ayer Directory,* 1975, p. 591.

4   "A Letter to Soviet Jewry," *Jewish Press*, January 31, 1975, pp. 37, 41, reprinted in *Writings 5734-5-6*, pp. 103-105, and in *Beyond Words*, 2:111-114.

5   "The Fahmy Aliyah," *Jewish Press*, February 7, 1975, p. 20, in RZ Archives, folder 589A, reprinted in *Writings 5734-5-6*, p. 105-107.

6   "Rabbi Meir Kahane Points to General Brown Statement...," press release, November 13, 1974, in RZ Archives, folder 72B.

John W. Finney, "Chairman of Joint Chiefs Regrets Remarks on Jews," *New York Times*, November 14, 1974, pp. 1, 97. Brown's statement had been made at Duke University on October 21, but it became public knowledge only in mid-November.

Two years later, General Brown stated that Israel was a "burden" to the United States. For Joseph Churba's comments, see chapter 10, note 1.

7   "Bashan," *Jewish Press*, February 14, 1975, pp. 15, 17, reprinted in *Writings 5734-5-6*, pp. 107-110, and in *Beyond Words*, 2:115-119.

8   "One Little Word," *Jewish Press*, January 17, 1975, pp. 39, 42, reprinted in *Kahane: The Magazine of the Authentic Jewish Idea*, May 1976, in RZ Archives, folder 589A.

9   "It Has Only Begun," *Jewish Press*, January 3, 1975, p. 34, reprinted in *Writings 5734-5-6*, pp. 83-85.

10   Letter from Paul Liptz, Institute for Youth Leaders from Abroad, Jerusalem, to Meir, December 23, 1974, in RZ Archives, folder 72B. Liptz wrote, "Your talk the other day was much appreciated... Thank you for the collection of pamphlets... I have placed them in the library... If you have any other material, we'd be pleased to receive it."

"Jewish Pride and Responses to Anti-Semitism," mimeographed booklet prepared in connection with his lecture, dated December 10, 1974, in RZ Archives, folder 715B. The Institute for Youth Leaders from Abroad was sponsored by the Jewish Agency.

"Kahane Ignores Fahmy Demands," press release announcing Meir's speech at ZOA House, Tel Aviv, December 18, 1974, in RZ Archives, folder 72B.

11   "Hyde Park at Bar Ilan, noon, December 19, 1974," poster, in RZ Archives, poster folder, no. 201; "Kahane – Change the Israeli Policy?" *Jewish Journal*, January 3, 1975, p. 15, in RZ Archives, folder 733.

12 Call-up papers for reserve duty at the Nes Tziyona *Haga* training center, December 22-26, 1974, in RZ Archives, folder 714B.

13 "Christians for Zion," [ad] *Jerusalem Post*, December 26, 1974, p. 6, in RZ Archives, folder 72B; "Kahane Calls Upon Americans... January 2, 1975," press release announcing meeting, in RZ Archives, folder 65A.

The "Christians for Zion" ad cost 190 lirot (about $32). See: [Income and Expenses], April 26, 1974, to January 8, 1975, handwritten list in RZ Archives, folder 694.

14 "Christians for Zion," *Jewish Press*, January 24, 1975, p. 34, reprinted in *Writings 5734-5-6*, pp. 100-103, and in *Beyond Words*, 2:106-110.

15 Paul Hofmann, "Arafat to Speak at the U.N. Today," *New York Times*, November 13, 1974, pp. 1, 89.

Peter Kihss, "100,000 Rally at the U.N. Against Palestinian Voice," *New York Times*, November 5, 1974, pp. 1, 74; "60,000 Rally Here Against P.L.O.," *New York Post*, November 4, 1974, p. 1, in RZ Archives, folder 435B.

16 E-mail from David Fisch, January 14, 2005.

"U.N. Guard Tight as Palestinians Fly In for Debate," *New York Times*, November 12, 1974, pp. 1, 15; Peter Kihss, "J.D.L. Aide Held in Threat to Kill Palestinian Leader," *New York Times*, November 13, 1974, pp. 1, 89; Tom Goldstein, "J.D.L. Aide Held on Catch-All U.S. Law for Threat; Threat Was Broadcast," *New York Times*, November 13, 1974, p. 16; Irving Spiegel, "Court Cuts Bail of J.D.L. Official [from $100,000 to $10,000]," *New York Times*, November 16, 1974, p. 13; "Threat Prompts Arrest," [caption of photo showing Kelner seated at table displaying .38 revolver] *Los Angeles Times*, November 13, 1974, p. 2.

17 Interview with Gene Singer, August 23, 1999, Jerusalem.

Kelner recalled this differently: "The late Congressman Mario Biaggi brought cash to the federal courthouse in Manhattan to get me released on bail. I don't recall who from the JDL had communicated with Biaggi." E-mail from Russel Kelner, January 30, 2005.

The JDL raised funds for Kelner's legal defense. See: "Killers of Jews Must Be Stopped... Russel Kelner Defense Fund," [ad] *Jewish Press*, June 27, 1975, p. 25. Meir wrote a *Jewish Press* editorial that said, in part: "If a Jew can be jailed (and he faces 5 years!) for exploding in frustration and anger at the appearance of a killer of women and children, we are undone.... Your letters to the judge are more than a plea to help a Jew. They are your self-respect." See: "The Incredible Case of Kelner," [editorial] *Jewish Press*, June 20, 1975, p. 5.

Judge Richard Owen, noting Kelner's "absence of intent" to carry out the threat, fined him $1,000, gave him a one-year suspended sentence, and placed him on probation for four years. See: "Metropolitan Briefs," *New York Times*, July 10, 1975, p. 33.

In December 1976, Kelner was given a prison sentence for transporting weapons across state lines. See: "A Former Leader of J.D.L. Is Sentenced to 3 Years in Violent-Harassing Plot," *New York Times*, December 16, 1976, p. 40.

18 Henry Kamm, "Israelis Bury Four Victims amid Grief, Anger, Shame," *New York Times*, November 21, 1974, pp. 1, 97.

19 "A Different Jewish View: There Is No Palestinian People" was printed as a flyer handed out at the demonstration on January 19, 1975. (See below in text.) It did not appear in the *Jewish Press* or in *Writings*.

The theme of this flyer was promoted earlier by Meir in speeches, press releases and ads. See chapter 40, note 50, "Save Our Israel," and chapter 41, note 10, "Kahane Ignores Fahmy Demands."

United Nations Resolution 3236, November 22, 1974, recognized the "inalienable national rights of the Palestinian people."

It was only in the 1978 Camp David Accords, in the "Framework for Peace in the Middle East" agreement, that Israel explicitly recognized a Palestinian people. In 1974, it is not clear that this was the case, except by implication, as Israel still looked to Jordan as representing the Palestinians. E-mail from Dr. Mordechai Nisan, January 13, 2005.

20 "Palestine, My Palestine," [editorial] *B'nai B'rith Messenger*, January 3, 1975, in RZ Archives, folder 65A. Excerpted with the permission of Joe Bobker, publisher.

Regarding editorials about Meir in the *B'nai B'rith Messenger*, Los Angeles journalist Tom Tugend wrote: "I have just been able to get in touch with Ted Sandler, the paper's long-time managing editor. Ted tells me that he himself wrote the editorials and that he was instrumental in introducing your husband to the West Coast." E-mail from Tom Tugend, June 9, 2007.

21 See chapter 10, note 3, October 18, 1974, p. 17.

22 "The Jewish Identity Center Announces the Chug (The Circle)," [ad] *Jewish Press*, January 17, 1975, p. 14, in RZ Archives, folder 65B. The Chug became the framework for teaching Meir's ideas until the end of 1978.

23 "Vandalism at U.N. Information Office," *Washington Star News*, January 20, 1975, p. B4, in RZ Archives, folder 65A. Plans were made for simultaneous demonstrations in Boston, Washington, Philadelphia, Chicago, Los Angeles and San Francisco. See: "JDL Calls Rally for 'No Palestine' Day," *Jewish Press*, December 20, 1974, p. 31, in RZ Archives, folder 72B.

24 "Israel Go Under?" [ad] *New York Times*, January 15, 1975, p. 16, in RZ Archives, folder 732. This was a quarter-page ad for the rally on January 19.

"Proposed Program of Organization for January 19," dated December 18, 1974, in RZ Archives, folder 482; "JDL Calls Rally for 'No Palestine' Day," *Jewish Press*, December 20, 1974, p. 31, in RZ Archives, folder 72B; "Join a Mass Nationwide Rally: 'There Is No Palestine Day,'" [ad] *Jewish Press*, January 17, 1975, p. 29.

Interview with Baruch Ben Yosef, October 9, 1997, Jerusalem.

25 David Friedman, "Kahane Launches National 'No Palestine' Campaign," *Jewish Telegraphic Agency Daily News Bulletin*, January 20, 1975, p. 3, in RZ Archives, folder 65A; Martin Gottlieb and William McFadden, "Kahane and 46 Seized in Protest," *Daily News*, January 20, 1975, in RZ Archives, folder 734; Robert D. McFadden, "48 Seized in Clash at Soviet Mission," *New York Times*, January 20, 1975, p. 25.

Photo of Meir speaking at the Diplomat Hotel, hand clenched, wearing a black high-necked sweater, dated January 19, 1975, in RZ Archives, poster folder, no. 463.

Route of the march: From the Diplomat Hotel, 43 Street near Sixth Avenue, to the American Mission to the U.N., Second Avenue near 42 Street, to the Soviet Mission, Third Avenue and 67 Street.

FBI New York office file 157-5767, report, January 30, 1975, 2 pp., in RZ Archives, Appendix.

26 Letter from Meir to Libby and children, [January 30, 1975], in RZ Archives, Appendix.

"Police Increase Kahane Charges," *Jewish Press*, February 7, 1975, pp. 2, 22, in RZ Archives, folder 733. Attorney Hy Dechter represented Meir in this case.

27 "JDL Will Begin a 24-Hour Fast... Wednesday, January 22, 1975..." and "JDL to Confront Israeli Consulate and Temple Emanu-El... Wednesday, January 22," press releases, January 21, 1975, both in RZ Archives, folder 65A; "JDL Demonstrates in Front of Temple," *New York Times*, January 23, 1975, p. 22.

"Jewish Defense League Going to B'nai B'rith, AJC Offices," flyer and press release in RZ

Archives, folder 65A. The text of the flyer gives the details: "... The picketing will take place on Thursday, January 23 at 10 A.M.... On Monday, January 27 at 12.30 P.M., a major Garment Center rally... against American pressure and Israeli government willingness to concede.... Rabbi Meir Kahane will speak."

Long John Nebel: "Radio," *New York Times*, January 27, 1975, p. 51.

"Demonstration at the home of Arnold Forster... February 2..." flyer, in RZ Archives, folder 65A. The flyer was signed by Russel Kelner, Operations Officer and Malcolm Lebowitz, JDL Executive Director.

28 Letters from Meir to Libby and children, January 22, 1975, and [January 30], 1975, in RZ Archives, Appendix.

"JDL Pitches Tents on Rabbi's Lawn," press release, in RZ Archives, folder 65B. Joachim Prinz, 1902-1988, president of the American Jewish Congress, said Israel should give up land for peace. Search Prinz in www.commentarymagazine.com.

29 "Israel Go Under?" flyer, January 1975, in RZ Archives, folder 1204. The flyer is a reprint of an ad for "There Is No Palestine" Day. See note 24.

SOIL, set up in August 1974 with the same aim as CAIR (see chapter 40), was now an independent group under Dov Hikind. Many ads about SOIL demonstrations against retreat from the liberated lands appeared in the *Jewish Press* in 1975: Feb. 28, p. 34; Mar. 21, p. 44; Apr. 18, p. 20; May 4, p. 25; May 26, p. 25; Jul. 25, p. 8; Aug. 22, p. 23; Oct. 17, p. 25; and more.

30 "Wanted: A New Firm Israeli Government," flyer, February 1975. The flyer was printed as an ad in Anglo-Jewish newspapers: *B'nai B'rith Messenger*, February 21, 1975, p. 16; *Connecticut Jewish Ledger*, February 20, 1975, p. 5; *Detroit Jewish News*, February 21, 1975, p. 19; *Jewish Standard*, February 21, 1975, p. 22, all in RZ Archives, folder 65A.

Ads in the *Jewish Press* publicized CAIR. One was "While Israel Chokes..." [ad] *Jewish Press*, February 14, 1975, p. 23.

31 Yirmiyahu Yovel, "An Israeli's Open Letter to Kissinger," *New York Times*, February 13, 1975, p. 25.

Preceded by a note: "Excerpts from an open letter to Secretary of State Kissinger written by Professor Yirmiyahu Yovel, head of the Hebrew University Institute of Philosophy and an outspoken dove. It first appeared in the daily *Ha'aretz* just before Kissinger began his last round of Middle Eastern diplomacy [before February 10]."

Hans Morgenthau: Irving Spiegel, "Hans Morgenthau Attacks Kissinger on Mideast Policy," *New York Times*, May 6, 1974, p. 7.

Another report quoted Ariel Sharon, special security advisor to prime minister Yitzhak Rabin: "Kissinger is the most dangerous man for Israel to come out of the U.S. Administration in the 27 years of our existence.... Every time Kissinger comes to the Middle East, 50,000 Jews should demonstrate at the White House." See: "Henry a Peril, Israeli Says," *Daily News*, May 27, 1975, in RZ Archives, folder 732.

32 Brooklyn, New York: "Noar Mizrachi" group, Borough Park, Friday night, January 24; Yeshiva Etz Chaim and Mishkan Yosef, Saturday, January 26; Young Israel of Canarsie, Friday night, January 31; NCSY Shabbaton at Congregation Beth Tikvah, Saturday, February 1. See: Flyers in RZ Archives, folder 65A, and telegram from Yehoshua Livnat, Noar Mizrachi, New York, to Meir, December 30, 1974, in RZ Archives, folder 715B; "Rabbi Meir Kahane Speaks in Canarsie," flyer, in RZ Archives, folder 67D.

Queens, New York: Young Israel of Forest Hills, Friday night, February 7; Queens Jewish Center, Forest Hills, Saturday, February 8. See: Letter from Meir to Libby, [February 4, 1975], in RZ Archives, Appendix.

"Rabbi Meir Kahane," *The Sage* (B'nai B'rith Hillel Foundation, Syracuse University), January 1975, pp. 1, 4; Laurie Lucas, "Rabbi Meir Kahane Urges Aliya," *Syracuse Post Standard*, January 27, 1975, both in RZ Archives, folder 65A.

[33] "'Never Again!' Rabbi Meir Kahane... February 3, 1975, 8 P.M.," [ad] *Jewish Civic Leader*, January 23, 1975, p. 1, in RZ Archives, folder 65D. The ad specified, "No admission charge, no solicitation."

Sheila Lidz arranged this speaking engagement: Letter from Ira Brody, Executive Director of ZOA, New England Region, to Sheila Lidz, October 25, 1974, in RZ Archives, folder 72B. A press conference and a cocktail reception preceded the speech.

Worcester is about 45 miles west of Boston.

[34] Letter from Meir to Libby, [February 4, 1975], in RZ Archives, Appendix.

Meir also wrote about the offer to buy $150,000 worth of Israel Bonds in "Israel Through Laughter and Tears," *Jewish Press*, February 21, 1975, p. 27.

[35] Yosef Gotlieb, "Rabbi Kahane in Worcester," *Homeward Bound* (Clark University Zionist Alliance), February 25, 1975, p. 4, in RZ Archives, folder 64B.

[36] *Report on Probation Violation*, Docket No. 71-CR-479, submitted to the Honorable Jack B. Weinstein, United States District Judge, by James F. Haran, Chief U.S. Probation Officer for the Eastern District of New York, prepared by Philip J. Bigger, February 6, 1975, in RZ Archives, folder 64A.

Max H. Seigel, "Kahane Faces Loss of Probation on Kidnap and Arms Charges," *New York Times*, February 8, 1975, p. 41, in RZ Archives, folder 65B; Irving Lieberman, "U.S. Asks Court to Jail Kahane," *New York Post*, February 8, 1975, in RZ Archives, folder 733.

[37] "Why I Came Back," *Jewish Press*, February 21, 1975, pp. 8, 49, reprinted in *Writings 5734-5-6*, pp. 110-112.

Slotnick was not a scheduled speaker at the convention. See: International Jewish Defense League, Convention 1975, February 9, 1975, *Agenda*, in RZ Archives, Appendix.

The convention was held at the New York Hilton Hotel. The officers elected were: Meir, International Chairman; Mal Lebowitz, Executive Director; David Fisch, CAIR coordinator; Garth Kravat, Chief of Security; and Alan Rocoff, College Coordinator. Stanley Schumsky, Russ Kelner and Howie (Chaim) Ginsberg worked on organizing the convention. See: *Jewish Defense League Bulletin*, [March 1975], p. 1, in RZ Archives, folder 65B.

[38] "Jewish Defense League Takes Over AJC, Temple Emanu-El," *Jewish Press*, February 14, 1975, p. 41, in RZ Archives, folder 1212. See also: "Kahane, 6 Followers Arrested," *New York Post*, February 11, 1975, in RZ Archives, folder 65A; "News Flashes: Kahane, Six Other JDL Members Arrested," *B'nai B'rith Messenger*, February 21, 1975, p. 6, in RZ Archives, folder 64A.

Kissinger's arrival in Israel: Bernard Gwertzman, "Kissinger Opens Talks in Israel on Sinai Accords," *New York Times*, February 11, 1975, pp. 1, 81.

[39] Photos of demonstrators in the snow, February 12, 1975, in RZ Archives, picture folder, nos. 2-6.

Frank Lynn, "Ford Says He Named Rockefeller to Oversee Work of Domestic Council," *New York Times*, February 14, 1975, p. 12. See also note 38, "Jewish Defense League Takes Over..."

"Announcement... a series of demonstrations...," flyer, in RZ Archives, folder 65D. February 11: JDL pickets a gathering honoring Treasury Secretary William Simon; February 13, JDL demonstrates against President Ford.

[40] Letter from Meir to his parents, [February 12, 1975], in RZ Archives, Appendix.

[41] "Noon JDL Rally at Syrian Mission, February 17, 1975," press release, in RZ Archives, folder 65B; "While Israel Chokes and Syrian Jewry Slowly Dies, You Do Nothing," [ad] *Jewish Press*,

February 14, 1975, p. 23. The same ad urged readers to demonstrate against President Ford on Thursday, February 13 (the *Jewish Press* bore Friday's date but was on the newsstands by Wednesday night).

42 Letter from Meir to Libby, undated but between February 9 and February 20, in RZ Archives, Appendix. There is no testimony by Elie Wiesel in the stenographic transcript of the trial; Leah Slovin came from Israel to testify. See: *Transcript of Hearing*, note 50.

43 "Save Meir Kahane," [editorial] *Jewish Press*, February 14, 1975, p. 5.

44 Letter from George Torodash, president of local 1114, New York State Parole Officers Association, to Judge Jack B. Weinstein, February 11, 1975, in RZ Archives, folder 65B.

45 Letter from Benton M. Arnovitz to Judge Jack B. Weinstein, February 11, 1975, in RZ Archives, folder 64A.

46 Letter from Saly Zloczower to Judge Jack B. Weinstein, February 17, 1975, in RZ Archives, Appendix.

47 Letter from Judge Jack B. Weinstein to Saly Zloczower, February 20, 1975, in RZ Archives, Appendix.

48 "Kahane Faces 5 Yr. Jail Sentence," *Jewish Press*, February 14, 1975, p. 3.

49 Telegram from Ambassador John Scali, U.S. Mission to the U.N., to American Embassy, Tel Aviv, February 10, 1975, 4 pp., in RZ Archives, Appendix. Texts of the letters in *Report on Probation Violation* (see note 36). See also chapter 33.

50 *Transcript of Hearing before Judge Jack B. Weinstein*, Brooklyn Federal Court, February 21, 1975, in JNUL Archives, folder ARC 4=1748.
    Tuvia Preschel, "*Jewish Press* Profile: Leah Slovin," *Jewish Press*, March 14, 1975, p. 32, in RZ Archives, folder 65B.

51 Letter from Meir to Libby, February 24, 1975, in RZ Archives, Appendix; *Transcript of Hearing* (see note 50).

52 *Transcript of Hearing* (see note 50).

53 *Transcript of Hearing* (see note 50).

54 *Transcript of Hearing* (see note 50).
    Meir was indeed aware that the government was tampering with his mail. See chapter 33 and chapter 34.

55 "From the Official Transcript of the Kahane Trial," *Jewish Press*, February 28, 1975, pp. 4, 49, in RZ Archives, folder 435; *Transcript of Hearing* (see note 50).

56 Judge Weinstein referred to the leniency he showed on July 23, 1971, when he gave Meir a suspended sentence, and again at a hearing on May 15, 1972, when he issued an order amending the terms, instead of revoking probation. Details of the order in chapter 29, "Severe Probation Conditions."

57 *Transcript of Hearing* (see note 50); Marcia Kramer, "Rabbi Kahane Is Sentenced to Jail Term," *Daily News*, February 22, 1975, in RZ Archives, folder 697; "Kahane Gets Year in '71 Conviction," *New York Times*, February 22, 1975, p. 18; "Rabbi Kahane Sentenced to Year," *Jewish Press*, February 28, 1975, pp. 2, 50.

58 "Kahane to Begin Serving Year Sentence March 18," *New York Times*, February 27, 1975, p. 39; "Kahane Ordered to Prison," *Jewish Press*, March 7, 1973, p. 3; Telegrams from John Scali, U.S. Mission to the U.N., to Department of State, Washington, D.C., February 21, 1975, and February 27, 1975, in RZ Archives, Appendix.

59 "Rabbi Sentenced," [photo caption] *San Francisco Chronicle*, February 22, 1975, p. 8, in RZ Archives, folder 64A. This AP wirephoto appeared the same day in many papers, including the

Detroit News, and the *Chicago Daily News*. See note about the photo from David Fisch, in RZ Archives, folder 64A.

[60] Letter from Meir to the children, February 21, 1975, in RZ Archives, Appendix.

[61] Letter from Meir to Libby, February 24, 1975, in RZ Archives, Appendix.

[62] Letter from Meir to Libby, undated but prior to March 5, 1975, in RZ Archives, Appendix. (In a letter to the children dated March 5, he referred to the contents of this letter to me.)

[63] Letter from Meir to Libby, February 28, 1975, in RZ Archives, Appendix.

[64] "The Sentencing of Meir Kahane," [editorial] *Jewish Press*, February 28, 1975, p. 5.

[65] Letter from Moshe Brodetzky to Judge Jack B. Weinstein, March 5, 1975, in RZ Archives, folder 65B. Brodetzky had been a member of Betar.

[66] Reuven Leib, "Yitbe'u Pidyon Hashavui Kahana [They Will Demand Freedom for Captive Kahana]," *Yedioth Ahronoth*, March 6, 1975, p. 12; Nachman Kahana, ["Letter to the Editor"], *Hatzofe*, March 7, 1975, both in RZ Archives, folder 65B. The letter gave Judge Weinstein's address in English.

[67] Letter from Rabbi Tzvi Yehuda Kook to Judge Jack B. Weinstein, March 3, 1975, in RZ Archives, folder 65B. The letter was sent with a typed English translation.

[68] Letter from David Rotlevy, chairman of the Tel Aviv Bar Association, and Max Seligman, vice president of the Tel Aviv Commercial and Industrial Club, to Judge Jack B. Weinstein, March 19, 1975, in RZ Archives, folder 65C.

[69] Letter from Meir to Libby, March 26, 1975, in RZ Archives, Appendix.

[70] Letter from Judge Jack B. Weinstein to Libby, June 12, 1975, in RZ Archives, folder 64D.

[71] Letter from Meir to Libby, March 11, 1975, in RZ Archives, Appendix.

Chapter 42

[1] "Jewish Power Day... February 24, 10 A.M., Statler Hilton, 18th Floor..." flyer and press release in RZ Archives, folder 65D; Volunteer Forces for Israel membership card in RZ Archives, folder 714B; "Jewish Power Day," [ad] *Jewish Press*, February 21, 1975, p. 37. See also: Martin G. Berck, "Cookies, Ginger Ale and Saber-Rattling," *New York Post*, February 6, 1975, p. 13.

[2] John Mullane, "Kahane Seeks Army for Israel," *New York Post*, February 24, 1975, p. 6, in RZ Archives, folder 64A; *Jewish Defense League Bulletin*, March 1975, p. 2, in RZ Archives, folder 985.

Flyer: "Projects and Events... March 17, 1975... 7 P.M.... JDL Training Center..." flyer, in RZ Archives, folder 65B.

Meir wrote about the need for a volunteer army for Israel made up of Jews from abroad in: "One People," *Jewish Press*, January 10, 1975, p. 27, reprinted in *Our Town: Manhattan's Community Newspaper*, May 16, 1975, p. 6, in RZ Archives, folder 64D, in *Writings 5734-5-6*, pp. 98-100, and in *Beyond Words*, 2:103-105.

[3] Shifra Hoffman, "An Open Letter to Mrs. Meir Kahane," *Jewish Press*, March 14, 1975, p. 57, in RZ Archives, folder 435A.

[4] Long John Nebel: "Radio," *New York Times*, March 6, 1975, p. 75. An audio tape of the interview, recorded by Abe Levine, is in RZ Archives, audio folder.

Henry Kamm, "Israelis Report Capturing Ship Used by Guerrillas," *New York Times*, March 7, 1975, pp. 1, 73; "Tel Aviv Raider Says He Trained in Syria," *New York Times*, March 9, 1975, p. 2. The attack took place on March 5.

"Kahane Urges Counter-Terror," *Jewish Week*, March 13, 1975, p. 8, in RZ Archives, folder 732. This is a report on Meir's March 6 press conference.

In an unsigned feature article, Meir wrote about Menachem Begin living incognito at the Savoy Hotel while he directed the Irgun: "The Remarkable Past of the Savoy Hotel," *Jewish Press*, March 14, 1975, p. 66.

5 Letter from Sholom Inbar, Associate Director, Aliyah Center, Brooklyn, New York, to Meir, January 15, 1975, in RZ Archives, folder 65D.

Meir wrote about the Aliyah Center's sponsorship in "Israel Through Laughter and Tears," *Jewish Press*, February 21, 1975, p. 27.

The Israeli government's aliya efforts can be seen in the contemporary Anglo-Jewish press. Examples: "News Highlights: Sapir Calls for New Aliyah From North America," *Jewish Times* (Boston), January 30, 1975, p. 6; "Have You Ever Considered a Meaningful Life in Israel?" [ad placed by Israel Aliyah Center] *Jewish Press*, February 14, 1975, p. 16.

6 Letter from Meir to Libby, [January 30, 1975]; Letter from Meir to Libby, undated but prior to March 5, 1975, in RZ Archives, Appendix. (In a letter to the children dated March 5, he wrote that he had sent me the Aliyah Department clippings.)

7 "Kahane Sees Jewish Crisis," *Asbury Park Press*, February 17, 1975, in RZ Archives, folder 64A. A photo of Meir on page 1 is captioned, "Rabbi Meir Kahane emphasizes a point..."

Letter from Dr. Leon Hellerman, Hewlett High School, to Meir, February 20, 1975, dated February 20, 1975, in RZ Archives, folder 64A. Hellerman wrote, "Throughout the day I heard the youngsters commenting on what you said... Your talk had [the students] thinking, questioning." This speaking engagement is listed in: FBI New York office file 157-5767, report, January 30, 1975, 2 pp., in RZ Archives, Appendix.

Letter from Ralph Pelcovitz, rabbi of Congregation Knesseth Israel (the "White *Shul*"), to Meir, February 27, 1975, in RZ Archives, folder 64A. This letter indicates that the JDL fee agreed upon with Sheila Lidz was $150.

8 Roslyn Middleman, "JDL Chief Condemns American Jewish Leadership," *Bay News*, March 10, 1975, pp. 5, 10, in RZ Archives, folder 65B. See also: Mike Meaney, "Kahane Speaks of Need for Force, Lack of Jewish Leadership," *Bay News*, March 10, 1975, p. 4, in RZ Archives, folder 65B.

On February 27, Meir spoke at City College in Manhattan, where students applauded him enthusiastically. See: Barry Smuckler, "JDL's Kahane Blasts Jewish Leaders," *The Source: The Jewish Voice of City College*, March 13, 1975, pp. 1, 6, in RZ Archives, folder 64D.

9 "Kahane in Silver Spring," *Jewish Week*, March 6, 1975, p. 5, in RZ Archives, folder 65B.

Antero Pietila, "Rabbi Asks Fundamentalists to Support Israeli Position," *Baltimore Evening Sun*, March 3, 1975, p. C1; Larry Singer, "Kahane on World Jewry: 'We Must Be for Ourselves...,'" *Northwest Star* (Pikesville, Md.), March 6, 1975, pp. 1, 2; both in RZ Archives, folder 65B. The Pickwick Jewish Center sponsored Meir's talk Saturday night at Northwestern High School in Hyattsville and Rabbi Moshe (Marcel) Blitz introduced the speakers.

10 "Aliyah Expo," flyer, in RZ Archives, folder 64A. The flyer announced that Meir would speak on Sunday, March 2, 1975... sponsored by the Jewish Students Coalition, SUNY-Albany, and by the Israel Aliyah Center, New York.

"Israel JDL Chief to Speak," *Knickerbocker News-Union Star*, March 1, 1975, p. 7A, in RZ Archives, folder 64A. The meeting was held at the Beth Abraham-Jacob Synagogue iñ Albany on Sunday evening, March 2.

11 Larry Gordon, "The Importance of Being Meir Kahane," *Jewish Look*, [April 1975], pp. 6, 7, in RZ Archives, folder 65B. Excerpted with the author's permission.

"Brooklyn College Chapter of JDL presents Rabbi Meir Kahane, March 3, 1975, 12 noon, in cooperation with the Israel Aliyah Center," flyer, in RZ Archives, folder 64A.

Richard Harary, "Kahane Speaks on Jewish Youth," *Calling Card* (Brooklyn College), March 12, 1975, p. 1, in RZ Archives, folder 64B.

Brooklyn College's Walt Whitman Auditorium easily held 800 people.

Arrest of sixty: "Jewish Youths Ousted From West Bank Site," *New York Times*, March 3, 1975, p. 5.

[12] Su Katz, "Jail-Bound Kahane Condones Violent Action: 'Not So Bad When Nothing Else Helps,'" *Kingsman* (Brooklyn College), March 7, 1975, p. 1, in RZ Archives, folder 65D. Excerpted with permission, The Brooklyn College Library Archive & Special Collections.

[13] John Kiffney, "War Seen Likely in Mideast," *Providence Journal*, March 4, 1975, pp. B1, B4, in RZ Archives, folder 64A. Meir urged the audience to join CAIR.

[14] Laura Lopatin, "Meir Kahane: Portrait of an Angry Man," *Brown Daily Herald / Fresh Fruit*, March 12, 1975, pp. 4, 5, in RZ Archives, folder 65B.

[15] "Kahane Says Israel Should Keep Lands," *Buffalo Courier Express*, March 5, 1975, in RZ Archives, folder 65D.

Meir spoke at Kingsborough Community College the same afternoon. See: "Rabbi Meir Kahane Is Speaking," [ad] *Jewish Press*, February 28, 1975, p. 26. This ad listed Meir's speaking dates from February 26 through March 5. Entrance Pass to admit a car to the Kingsborough campus, stamped March 4, 1975, in RZ Archives, folder 64D.

[16] Letter from Meir to the children, March 5, 1975, in RZ Archives, Appendix.

[17] Mike Livingston and Jeff Bialos, "Kahane Blasts Jewish Leaders, Calls for Emigration to Israel," *Cornell Daily Sun*, March 6, 1975, p. 7, in RZ Archives, folder 64A. Flyers, signed by Revolutionary Student Brigade, Young Socialist Alliance, Cornell Arab Club, in RZ Archives, folder 64A. The distance from Buffalo to Ithaca is about 150 miles, a three-hour drive. It is likely that Meir flew.

[18] "A New Life...," [ad] *Jewish Press*, February 28, 1975, p. 30.

[19] E-mail from Lorraine and Stanley Schumsky, January 30, 2005.

"JDL weekend at Grossinger's, March 7-9," *Jewish Defense League Bulletin*, February 1975, p. 2, in RZ Archives, folder 683B.

Photo of Meir at Grossinger's Hotel in RZ Archives, picture folder, no. 8.

David Fisch recalled that he accompanied Meir on the Saturday night drive to Grossinger's from Monsey, where Meir had spoken at Rabbi Tendler's synagogue on Shabbat. E-mails from David Fisch, February 1, 2005 and February 2, 2005.

[20] Tova L. Kamins, "Kahane Blasts Jewish Leadership," *Hunter Envoy*, March 14, 1975, p. 1, in RZ Archives, folder 65B. Excerpted with permission, Archives & Special Collections of the Hunter College Libraries.

A short news item in the *New York Times* noted that there were no pickets and very little heckling when Meir spoke at Hunter College, sponsored by the school's Jewish Coalition. "Notes on People," *New York Times*, March 11, 1975, p. 41.

[21] "Rabbi Cheered for Tough Stance on Nazis," *Milwaukee Sentinel*, March 11, 1975, in RZ Archives, folder 64B; "Kahane Urges Jews to 'Break Nazis' Heads,'" *Milwaukee Journal*, March 11, 1975, section 2, in RZ Archives, folder 64B.

Meir's flight to Milwaukee left Laguardia airport at 5:55 in the afternoon, March 10. Ticket stub in RZ Archives, folder 712. He spoke at the Jewish Community Center there.

[22] F.K. Plous, Jr. "Jewish Leadership Is Timid: Kahane," *Chicago Sun-Times*, March 12, 1975, p. 42, in RZ Archives, folder 65B. Excerpted with permission.

[23] Typescript of letter from Jacob Blum to the *Reader's Digest*, [March 1975], in RZ Archives, Appendix. The letter refers to: William E. Griffith, "It's Our Move in the Middle East," *Reader's Digest*, February 1975. Professor Griffith was an advisor to the State Department.

Reader's Digest circulation given as 18,487,284 copies, in *Ayer Directory*, 1976, p. 658. An estimated 60 million people read it.

[24] Audio tape, Meir's talk at M.I.T., March 12, 1975, in RZ Archives, audio folder.

"Rabbi Meir Kahane Speaking on Time to Go Home," *Jewish Advocate*, March 6, 1975, p. 3, in RZ Archives, folder 69A. This named the sponsors: the Israel Aliyah Center, the Zionist Organization of America and the M.I.T. Hillel club.

Letter from Meir to Libby, March 11, 1975, in RZ Archives, Appendix. This notes Meir's visit to the Shoshan family.

Stub of plane ticket from Chicago to Boston, March 12, in RZ Archives, folder 712.

[25] Letter from Meir to the children, March 11, 1975, in RZ Archives, Appendix.

Letter from Meir to Libby, see note 24.

Yehoshua Yadlin was Director of the Israel Aliyah Center in the United States and Canada.

[26] "JDL Coming Events," [ad] *Jewish Press*, March 7, 1975, p. 35. It noted that JDL would begin recruiting volunteers for the Israeli army on March 17.

"JDL Projects and Events," flyer, in RZ Archives, folder 65B.

[27] Letter from Meir to Libby and children, March 26, 1975, in RZ Archives, Appendix.

Flyer announcing lecture, "Is Kissinger Doing Us All In?" March 15, 10 A.M., Hebrew Institute of Riverdale, in RZ Archives, folder 65B.

The text of this talk is given in "The Broken Reed," *Jewish Press*, two parts, May 16, 1975, pp. 23-24; May 23, 1975, p. 13, reprinted in *Writings, 5734-5-6*, pp. 174-178. At the end of the article, Meir noted, "This is what I said to the Jews of Riverdale on March 15.

[28] "Jewish Is a Complete Identity," [ad] *Jewish Press*, February 14, 1975, p. 29, in RZ Archives, folder 1205.

"Come Say Farewell to Rabbi Meir Kahane... March 15, 1975... coffee and cake... musical entertainment," [ad] *Jewish Press*, March 7, 1975, p. 28, in RZ Archives, folder 65A.

Letter from Hilton Goldman to Libby, November 1997, in RZ Archives, Appendix.

"Meir Kahane Iz Unter Arrest [Meir Kahane Is Under Arrest]," *Algemeiner Journal*, March 21, 1975, in RZ Archives, folder 697. Photo caption: "Meir Kahane Zitst Fartrakht in Kafe 'Yafo' Beym der Gezegenung Erev Zayn Geyn In Tfise [Meir Kahane Sits Deep in Thought in Café Yaffo During the Farewell Party Before Going to Jail]." The photo, by Yossi Melamed, appears in the photo section of this book. Reproduced with the photographer's permission.

[29] "Announcement," press release, in RZ Archives, folder 65D; "Youth Farewell to Meir Kahane," [ad] *Jewish Press*, March 14, 1975, p. 45.

"Jews arrested for inhabiting Jewish land?! NO WAY!... March 16... 2 P.M.," flyer, in RZ Archives, folder 65B.

[30] "JDL Sit-In at Israeli Consulate Goes On," *Jewish Press*, March 21, 1975, p. 57.

Photo of Meir and supporters at Israeli Consulate sit-in, March 17, 1975, in RZ Archives, picture folder, no. 7.

[31] Telegram from Ambassador William Schaufele, U.S. Mission to the United Nations, to Department of State, Washington, D.C., March 20, 1975, 2 pp., in RZ Archives, Appendix.

[32] [Meir Kahane], "A Tale of Two Parents," *Jewish Press*, March 21, 1975, p. 63.

This feature article concludes: "The letter of Yitzhak Gazit was read inside the Israeli Consulate in New York by Meir Kahane as JDL and CAIR sat-in this week to demand, 'Not one inch of retreat.'"

See also note 30.

[33] See notes 30 and 31.

[34] "Kahane Starts Sentence," [photo caption] *New York Post*, March 18, 1975, p. 2, in RZ Archives, folder 733.

See also note 31 and "Kahane Begins Jail Term," *Jewish Press*, March 28, 1975, p. 2.

Bob Lipson, "Kahane Appears at Baruch," *Ticker*, March 11, 1975, pp. 1, 7, in RZ Archives, folder 65B. Meir spoke at Baruch College, City University of New York, Monday, March 17, 6:30 P.M.

[35] Irving Lieberman, "Kahane Starts His Prison Term," *New York Post*, March 18, 1975, p. 6, in RZ Archives, folder 733. See also: Marcia Kramer, "One-Year Jail Term Begun by Kahane," *Daily News*, March 19, 1975, p. 27; "Rabbi Kahane Asks J.D.L. to 'Redouble' Its Efforts," *New York Times*, March 21, 1975, both in RZ Archives, folder 65B; Telegram from Ambassador William Schaufele, see note 31.

Letter from Meir to Libby, see note 6. Excerpts in chapter 41.

[36] Letter from Meir to Libby, March 18, 1975, in RZ Archives, Appendix.

Newspapers gave the address of the halfway house as 38 West 31 Street in Manhattan. Meir probably did not have the exact address when he wrote this letter. See: Emanuel Perlmutter, "Jailed Kahane Is Allowed Out 7 Hours a Day to Pray and Eat," *New York Times*, April 17, 1975, p. 22, in RZ Archives, folder 64B.

Slotnick's application to the court for a furlough for Passover, granted March 25, 1975, in RZ Archives, folder 706.

Meir needed an electric shaver because shaving with a razor is forbidden by halakha.

[37] Typed list, headed in Meir's handwriting "Weinstein's Order," [February 21, 1975], in RZ Archives, folder 64D.

[38] "Forget Meir Kahane," [ad] *New York Times*, March 4, 1975, p. 14, in RZ Archives, folder 64A. The ad filled about one sixth of the page. Its cost was probably about $4,000. The JDL address was 1133 Broadway, room 1026.

The same ad, headed "To Hell With Meir Kahane" was published in *Newsday*, April 4, 1975, p. 9A, in RZ Archives, folder 65B. It covered more than a quarter of the tabloid-size page. See also: "To Hell With Meir Kahane," [ad] *Jewish Press*, February 28, 1975, p. 18, in RZ Archives, folder 65B, and "To Hell With Meir Kahane," flyer, in RZ Archives, folder 65B.

[39] Letter from Barry Slotnick to Meir, March 21, 1975, in RZ Archives, folder 65B.

[40] Letter from Meir to Libby, March 20, 1975, in RZ Archives, Appendix.

The consulate did not press charges, and the protesters remained at the consulate for several days. When they commandeered an elevator, the owner of the building called the police, so they left. Interview with Baruch Ben Yosef, October 9, 1997, Jerusalem.

Arrest of Settlers: See: "12 Mafginim Neged Kissinger Ne'etzru Etmol Biyerushalayim, [12 Demonstrators Against Kissinger Arrested Yesterday in Jerusalem]," *Yedioth Ahronoth*, March 21, 1975, p. 4; Bernard Gwertzman, "Kissinger in Aswan Again, Relays New Israeli Views," *New York Times*, March 21, 1975, p. 3.

[41] "Of Prisoners and Free Men," *Jewish Press*, April 25, 1975, pp. 20, 22, reprinted in *Writings 5734-5-6*, pp. 121-123, and in *Beyond Words*, 2:136-139. Datelined Federal Prison, New York, March 25, 1975.

[42] Letter from Meir to Libby and children, March 26, 1975, in RZ Archives, Appendix. Meir's departure was postponed from April 4, the day after Passover, to April 7 because April 4 fell on a Friday, too close to Shabbat to travel and get settled in prison in Allenwood.

[43] The charge stemming from Meir's arrest on January 19, 1975, docket N506314, was abated

by death on December 13, 2002. Letter from Claire Amster, New York City Criminal Court, to Libby, January 6, 2003, in RZ Archives, Appendix.

The charge on trespass at Temple Emanu-El on February 10, 1975, docket no. N510421, was adjourned on April 4, 1975, ("now in federal custody") and abated by death, December 13, 2002. See: Letter from Claire Amster, above.

On May 30, 1972, after Meir pleaded guilty to a December 1970 charge of inciting to riot and unlawful assembly, he was sentenced by Judge Harold Baer to a period of probation (see chapter 29). On March 14, 1975, he pleaded guilty to violation of probation, and was sentenced to 60 days in prison, with execution of sentence stayed to May 20, 1975. On May 20, with Meir already in prison, Judge Baer amended his decision to Unsatisfactory Discharge (docket no. B10809-71). Summons to appear before Judge Harold Baer for hearing on probation status, March 12, 1975, Manhattan Supreme Court, Room 1029. Letter from Charles J. Christian, Probation Officer, to Meir, February 27, 1975, in RZ Archives, folder 64A; Certificate of Disposition no. 27222, signed by Claire Amster, New York City Criminal Court, January 6, 2003, in RZ Archives, Appendix.

[44] "Ten JDLers Arrested at Israeli Consulate," *Daily News*, April 1, 1975, in RZ Archives, Appendix; Terence Smith, "Israeli Marchers Ask Settling of the West Bank," *New York Times*, April 1, 1975, p. 3; "25,000 Attempt to Settle Judea-Samaria," *Jewish Press*, March 28, 1975, pp. 3, 43. See also: "Listen Jew!... Here is where YOU Should Be: Israeli Consulate... March 31 (Fifth Day of Passover)," [ad] *Jewish Press*, March 28, 1975, p. 12, in RZ Archives, folder 65B.

[45] Letter from Meir to Tzippy, April 17, 1975, in RZ Archives, Appendix. Meir wrote the Talmudic saying "Three things..." (*Berachot* 5A) in Hebrew.

Chapter 43

[1] Order by Judge Jack B. Weinstein, 18 U.S.C. § 3653, cited in *United States of America v. Meir Kahane*, May 7, 1975. See: 75-C-624, 396 F. Supp. 687; 1975 U.S. Dist. (LEXIS 12468). Order given at sentencing, February 21, 1975.

[2] "Kahane: Mass Arrests," *Long Island Press*, April 8, 1975, p. 5, in RZ Archives, folder 65B; "Kahane Refused Kosher Food; Kahane Demanding Minyans for Jewish Prisoners," *Jewish Press*, April 11, 1975, p. 1, in RZ Archives, folder 65B; Emanuel Perlmutter, "Jailed Kahane Is Allowed Out 7 Hours a Day to Pray and Eat," *New York Times*, April 17, 1975, p. 22, in RZ Archives, folder 64B.

A provision for Meir to attend prayer services is on a typed sheet, headed in Meir's handwriting "Weinstein's Order," [February 21, 1975], in RZ Archives, folder 64D.

[3] "Give Me a Present," *Jewish Press*, April 11, 1975, pp. 38, 29, reprinted in *Writings, 5734-5-6*, pp. 92-98. Datelined Federal Prison, March 1975. A week later, Meir placed an ad thanking the participants: "Thank you! To all who gave me a present in prison by sitting down on the streets of New York. You were seen and heard in the Soviet Union and Israel. G-d bless you. [signed] Meir Kahane." See: "Thank You!" [ad] *Jewish Press*, April 18, 1975, p. 28, in RZ Archives, folder 64B.

[4] "It Is a Time of Distress for Jacob...," [ad] in RZ Archives, *Jewish Press*, April 4, 1975, p. 22, in RZ Archives, folder 65B.

JDL members were to take part in the official parade. "... The JDL position in the parade is Section F, 69th Street and Park Avenue, at 11:45 A.M.... JDL dress is blue shirts and black pants." See: *Jewish Defense League Bulletin*, March 1975, in RZ Archives, folder 985.

[5] "This Is No Time for a Picnic," flyer, in RZ Archives, folder 64B.

[6] Irving Spiegel, "100,000 March Here in Support of Soviet Jewry," *New York Times*, April 14, 1975, p. 49, in RZ Archives, folder 65B.

[7] See note 10.

[8] "Kosher Food," *Jewish Press*, April 18, 1975, p. 22, in RZ Archives, folder 589A. Datelined Federal Prison, April 9, 1975. This spoke of a new group, the Committee for Jewish Prisoners. See also Union of Jewish Prisoners, chapter 47, note 44.

Huss and Smilow were two of the prosecution's essential witnesses in the Hurok case (see chapter 29). Their refusal to testify against the accused followed *Shulchan Arukh, Choshen Mishpat* 388:5: "It is forbidden to hand over a Jew to Gentiles, neither his person nor his property, even if he was a wicked person who committed crimes."

For various reasons their contempt case started only on July 16, 1974. They received a harsh sentence for contempt of court: one year in prison. "Two in J.D.L. Sentenced in Hurok Bomb Case," *New York Times*, August 1, 1974, pp. 31, 63.

[9] See Emanuel Perlmutter, note 2.

It is not extraordinary for federal judges in different districts to rule differently on the same issue. The conflict is normally resolved by appealing to a higher court. E-mail from David Fisch, September 22, 1999.

[10] Letter from Meir to Libby, undated but after April 7, 1975, in RZ Archives, Appendix.

[11] William Sherman, "Kahane Kosher Bid: Why Not West St.?" *Daily News*, April 17, 1975, p. 5, in YU Archives, folder 13/3. © New York Daily News, L.P.; reprinted with permission.

The *Daily News* had a circulation of 1,941,917 and the *Sunday News* had 2,790,760. This surpassed the *New York Times*, with a daily circulation of 806,495 and a Sunday circulation of 1,415,515. See: *Ayer Directory*, 1976, pp. 640, 651.

[12] "The Law and Rabbi Kahane," [editorial] *Daily News*, April 17, 1975, p. 71, in YU Archives, folder 13/3. © New York Daily News, L.P.; reprinted with permission.

[13] See Emanuel Perlmutter, note 2.

[14] "Kahane Accuses Government of Planting News Story," *Jewish Press*, April 25, 1975, pp. 1, 36. This is an unsigned news item, but it is clear that Meir wrote it.

See also: "Press Release," [undated] with a similar text, signed by Meir, in RZ Archives, folder 64B.

[15] Letter from Meir to Libby, undated, but probably April 17 or 18, 1975, in RZ Archives, Appendix.

[16] "Kosher Food Offer Made for Prisons," *New York Times*, April 23, 1975, p. 46, in RZ Archives, folder 733; Donald Singleton, "5 Orthodox Rabbis Back Kahane's Fight for Diet," *Daily News*, April 23, 1975, p. 22.

[17] "Clark, Koch, RCA, Join Kosher Food Fight," *Jewish Press*, May 2, 1975, p. 2, in RZ Archives, folder 64B.

Edward Koch, later mayor of New York City, was one of New York state's representatives in Congress.

Ramsey Clark later became actively pro-Palestinian and anti-Israel. It is likely that he supported Meir's cause because of his sincere belief in freedom of religion.

[18] Peter Kiernan, "Kosher Food & Jail Rights," *New York Post*, April 28, 1975, in RZ Archives, folder 64B.

[19] Brief presented to Judge Jack B. Weinstein by attorney Barry Slotnick, April 23, 1975, in RZ Archives, folder 112A. The National Jewish Commission on Law and Public Affairs, COLPA, under the direction of attorney Howard Rhine, submitted a supporting brief.

"Federal Courts Hear Kosher Food Case," *Jewish Press*, May 2, 1975, p. 3, in RZ Archives, folder 64B.

Rabbi Siegman testified that the Synagogue Council of America, which assisted the Federal Bureau of Prisons in providing Jewish chaplains, regularly requested that the Bureau provide kosher food to Jewish prisoners, but had been unsuccessful. See note 20.

Rabbi Shapiro: See note 16.

[20] See note 1. Rabbi Tendler's testimony had been given on February 21, 1975.

Jerry Capeci and Leo Standora, "Rabbis Testify on Kosher Diet," *New York Post*, April 24, 1975, p. 42, in RZ Archives, folder 733.

[21] "Petition," April 25, 1975, prepared by attorney Barry Slotnick, in RZ Archives, folder 706.

Marcia Kramer, "Judge Reserves Decision in Kahane's Kosher Case," *Daily News*, April 25, 1975, p. 31, in RZ Archives, folder 733.

[22] Letter from Meir to Libby, postmarked May 1, 1975, in RZ Archives, Appendix. Meir wrote that he spent every Shabbat at the home of his cousins Solomon and Betty Kahane who lived nearby, on West 34 Street.

[23] Letter from Meir to Libby, May 6, 1975, in RZ Archives, Appendix.

Stipend of $4.00 daily noted in "Kahane Enjoys Freedom as Inmate," chapter 46, note 54.

[24] Letter from Meir to Libby, July 31, 1975, in RZ Archives, Appendix.

[25] Letter from Meir to Libby, October 30, 1975, in RZ Archives, Appendix.

[26] Yitta Halberstam, "A Day in the Life of an 'Imprisoned' Rabbi: Sets a Furious Pace Making Rounds of His Multi-Front Crusade," *Jewish Week*, October 26, 1975, p. 27, in RZ Archives, folder 66B. Excerpted with the author's permission.

[27] *United States of America v. Meir Kahane*, May 7, 1975. See: 75-C-624, 396 F. Supp. 687; 1975 U.S. Dist. (LEXIS 12468).

[28] Letter from Meir to Libby, May 8, 1975, in RZ Archives, Appendix.

[29] "Rabbi Meir Kahane During Press Conference at Federal Community Training Center," [photo caption] *Daily News*, May 7, 1975. Photo by Richard Corkery. To view the image, see http://www2.dailynewspix.com and search by photo caption.

[30] Mark Liff, "Kahane Gets a Kosher Ruling," *Daily News*, May 8, 1975, in RZ Archives, folder 65C; "Metropolitan Briefs," *New York Times*, May 8, 1975, p. 43; Marcia Kramer, "Feds to Appeal Kosher Case," *Daily News*, June 11, 1975, in RZ Archives, folder 716A.

On June 17 Judge Jack B. Weinstein informed Slotnick that the matter was before the Second Circuit Court of Appeals. See chapter 44.

[31] "J.D.L. Inmates Lose Kosher-Food Plea," *New York Times*, May 7, 1975, p. 87, in RZ Archives, folder 754A; Eric Fettman, "JDL Youths Lose Kosher Food Case," *Jewish Press*, May 9, 1975, pp. 3, 43.

The decision was handed down late on Monday, May 5. An appeal by attorney Nathan Lewin was dismissed on narrow technical grounds. See: "Court Dismisses Kosher Food Case," *Jewish Press*, August 1, 1975, pp. 2, 26, in RZ Archives, folder 733.

For a legal analysis of the decisions of Judge Weinstein and Judge Griesa, see: Marvin Schick, "In the City," *Jewish Press*, May 16, 1975, pp. 2, 51, in RZ Archives, folder 733.

Yossi Klein, "Jewish Political Prisoners in Jail," *Jewish Post and Opinion*, May 9, 1975, in RZ Archives, folder 64D.

[32] See note 9, Fisch.

[33] Letter from Jeffrey Smilow to Meir, May 8, 1975, in RZ Archives, folder 715B. This was reprinted as a letter to the editor, "A Letter from Jeffrey Smilow to Meir Kahane," *Jewish Press*, July 4, 1975, p. 39.

Meir never abandoned JDLers who were in prison. A report that said he did not communicate with them does not contradict this. (Leonard Levitt, "A New Style for Jewish Militants," *Newsday*, June 3, 1975, in YU Archives, folder 13/3.) One JDLer explained: "Meir would never have written to me in jail. He was too smart and I was too well indoctrinated into what the system wants to see and what the system doesn't want to see.... Can you imagine a parole board reviewing a half-way house request with the notation in my file that Meir was corresponding with me?" E-mail message, from [name withheld], June 22, 1999.

[34] Letter from Meir to Libby, May 6, 1975, in RZ Archives, Appendix.

[35] Letter from Ari Calderon to Libby, July 15, 1997, in RZ Archives, Appendix. Calderon's moving tribute came in response to my query about Shuva's Galilee project.

[36] Letter from Meir to Libby, May 17, 1975, in RZ Archives, Appendix.

Shuva's office was at 1130 Broadway, room 914. See: Letter from Meir to JDL members, May 1975, in RZ Archives, folder 1205.

[37] "Begin a New Life in Israel," [ad] *Jewish Press*, May 2, 1975, p. 20, in RZ Archives, folder 1205.

[38] "East Brooklyn JDL Meeting," [ad] *Jewish Press*, May 16, 1975, p. 10. The meeting was to be held on May 19 at the Midwood Public Library, 8 P.M. to 10 P.M.

"Mass Meeting for Israel," [ad] *Jewish Press*, May 30, 1975, p. 29. This was to be held at Congregation Derech Emuna, 53 Charles Street, at 3:30 P.M. on June 1.

[39] "A Limited Number of People...," [ad] *Jewish Press*, May 30, 1975, p. 31; June 20, 1975, p. 31.

[40] "Kahane Sets Aliya Seminars in Prison," *Jewish Press*, June 6, 1975, p. 41. Prison sanctions detailed in: "Kahane Enjoys Freedom as Inmate," chapter 46, note 54.

[41] Meir Hacohen (pseudonym of Meir Kahane), "Israel Through Laughter and Tears," *Jewish Press*, June 20, 1975, p. 31.

Publicity for Shuva: "Israel Through Laughter and Tears," *Jewish Press*, May 23, 1975, p. 21; May 30, 1975, p. 33; June 13, 1975, p. 16; and July 4, 1975, p. 29.

Cheri Feldman was featured in: "Shuva Aliya Group Sets Date for First Aliya," *Jewish Press*, June 20, 1975, p. 29 and Tuvia Preschel, "*Jewish Press* Profile: Shuva," *Jewish Press*, July 18, 1975, p. 21.

In July, a Shuva press conference resulted in an AP report that the JDL was calling for the evacuation of six million American Jews to save them from a new holocaust, and had organized 2,000 Jews in four aliya groups. Israeli papers published the report: "Masa'iyot Im Ramkolim Yikre'u Lefinui Yehudei Artzot Habrit Leyisrael [Vans With Loudspeakers Will Call for American Jews to Evacuate to Israel]," *Yedioth Ahronoth*, July 31, 1975, p. 8, in RZ Archives, folder 65D; "Anshei Kahana: Al Kol Yehudei Arhab La'alot [Kahane's People: All American Jews Must Go to Israel]," *Davar*, August 3, 1975, p. 4.

[42] "The Week That Was," *Jewish Press*, May 30, 1975, p. 41.

Meir blamed the failure of Israel's Aliyah department on the patronage system. When Yehiel Leket became director of the Aliyah Center, he wrote, "It is not talent or experience or knowledge of the subject that are the criteria for Aliyah directors.... [It] is political patronage.... The main thing [for them] is not successful aliya, but guaranteed control of aliya by the perpetual Labor party." See: "The Week That Was," *Jewish Press*, August 15, 1975, pp. 13, 14.

[43] "Galut Realities and Galut Mentalities" *Kahane: The Magazine of the Authentic Jewish Idea*, September 1976, pp. 22-23; flyer, in RZ Archives, folder 431.

"A Jew Dies in Brooklyn," *Jewish Press*, October 17, 1975, pp. 9, 10, in RZ Archives, folder 65C, reprinted in *Writings 5734-5-6*, p. 238-241, and in *Beyond Words*, 2:178-183. This article argues that the murder of a Jew by hoodlums should convince Jews that the best place for them is Israel.

See also Shuva ad: "Jew, Get Out. It Is Time to Go Home," [ad] *Jewish Press*, May 18, 1975, p. 29; May 23, 1975, p. 30.

44 Letter from Meir to Libby, June 2, 1975, in RZ Archives, Appendix.

45 Letter from A. Frank to B. Gorodish, with copy to Yehiel Leket, Director, Israel Aliyah Center, October 8, 1975, in RZ Archives, folder 69B.

Letter from Meir to Libby, December 7, 1975, in RZ Archives, Appendix.

Shifra Hoffman led a Shuva pilot tour to Israel in February 1976. See: Shifra Hoffman, "Shuva's Pilot Tour to Israel," *Jewish Press*, April 9, 1976, p. 16, in RZ Archives, folder 1205.

46 Meir's note, "All the aliya letters...." undated, in RZ Archives, folder 69B. His "phony letter" was: Melvin Gresham, "Attacks JDL on Aliya," [letter to the editor], *Jewish Press*, May 30, 1975, p. 5. Five letters arguing against Gresham and in favor of promoting American aliya, in: "Letters to the Editor," *Jewish Press*, June 20, 1975, p. 33.

47 "President Ford Must Go," [ad] *New York Times*, May 19, 1975, p. 20, in RZ Archives, folder 64D. The ad is 2 columns wide by 9 inches.

See also: "Ford Must Go," *Jewish Press*, May 9, 1975, pp. 34, 35, in RZ Archives, folder 1208; "The Week That Was," *Jewish Press*, June 20, 1975, pp. 41, 42, reprinted as "Just Once" in *Writings 5734-5-6*.

Letter from Meir to Libby, May 17, 1975, in RZ Archives, Appendix.

The price of the ad is noted in: "Jews Against Ford Sponsor Large Ad," *Jewish Post and Opinion*, June 6, 1975, p. 7, in RZ Archives, folder 69A. This also notes that the National Chairman of AJAF was Ed Linn [a writer] and that Alan Cornet, the associate director, was a regular panelist on the Long John Nebel radio show.

48 Letter from Meir to Libby, May 11, 1975, in RZ Archives, Appendix. The AJAF office was in Room 916, 1133 Broadway, one floor below the JDL office.

49 "The Week That Was," *Jewish Press*, May 30, 1975, p. 41, in RZ Archives, folder 1208.

There was also criticism from non-Jews. Meir received an unsigned letter that said, "Shame on you for your propaganda campaign to discredit President Ford... You kikes are creating an anti-Jew backlash that eventually may destroy you. You didn't learn a thing from Hitler. Your collective stupidity amazes me..." Unsigned letter to Meir, June 7, 1975, in RZ Archives, folder 64D.

50 *Ford Must Go* (New York: American Jews Against Ford, 1975), 8 pp., 21 cm., in RZ Archives, folder 1204. AJAF flyers are in RZ Archives, folders 64B and 64D. AJAF demonstrations:

May 28: Picketing the Republican State Committee offices in New York City, demanding the dismissal of Henry Kissinger. See: "American Jews Against Ford to Hold Initial Protest," press release, May 1975, in RZ Archives, folder 69A.

June 15: A march "in support of the territorial integrity of the Land of Israel" from U.N. Plaza to the Jewish Agency at 515 Park Avenue, where prime minister Yitzhak Rabin would be speaking. See: "Premier Yitzhak Rabin Will Be in New York..." [ad] *Jewish Press*, June 13, 1975, p. 18, in RZ Archives, folder 64D.

June 12: Picketing a Republican party dinner at the Waldorf Astoria Hotel. See: "Members of AJAF will peacefully picket... tonight," press release, June 12, 1975, in RZ Archives, folder 64D.

"A Petition... " [ad] *Jewish Press*, April 18, 1975, p. 8; "Petition" in RZ Archives, folder 64B.

51 "The Christian American Interest in the Middle East," *Jewish Press*, July 4, 1975, p. 8, in RZ Archives, folder 1208. Typescript with handwritten corrections in RZ Archives, folder 1235.

[52] Meir Kahane, "Only Choice: Support of Israel," [op-ed] *Newsday*, July 1, 1975, p. 41, in RZ Archives, folder 589A.

Meir was paid $150 for this article. See: Memo from *Newsday* to Meir, July 1, 1975, in RZ Archives, folder 64D.

[53] Meir Kahane, "The Sinai Covenant for Israeli Retreat," [op-ed] *Newsday*, September 16, 1975, p. 45, in RZ Archives, folder 715A. See also: "Congress Has Questions on Sinai Personnel," *Jewish Press*, August 22, 1975, p. 3.

Bernard Gwertzman, "Israel and Egypt Agree on Text of Sinai Accord," *New York Times*, September 1, 1975, pp. 1, 31.

[54] "Jewish Activists to Spend Two Weeks Lobbying in D.C. Against U.S. Personnel to Sinai," press release, announcing press conference, September 2, 1975, 10:30 A.M. at offices of American Jews Against Ford, 1133 Broadway, Suite 916, in RZ Archives, folder 65D.

[55] When reporters discovered Meir's connection with AJAF in May, he admitted that the JDL had helped the AJAF financially, but said it was "not a branch of the League." See: "Jewish Organization to Oppose President Is Established Here," *New York Times*, May 25, 1975, p. 55; Martin G. Berck, "JDL Cash Backing Anti-Ford Group," *Newsday*, May 21, 1975, in RZ Archives, folder 69A.

[56] "The Jewish Defense League Statement on the Sinai Capitulation," press release, September 2, 1975; "The Activist's Column: A Retreat From More Than Sinai," *Jewish Press*, September 12, 1975, p. 42, reprinted in *Writings 5734-5-6*, p. 214-216. The text of this article was distributed at the press conference.

Chapter 44

[1] Standing committees listed in: *Jewish Defense League Bulletin*, July 25, 1975, in RZ Archives, folder 69B.

Phone numbers for the various organizations (Jewish Identity Center, CAIR, AJAF, Shuva, JDL Training Center, JDL headquarters, JDL answering machine) were listed in *Jewish Defense League Bulletin*, June 1975, in RZ Archives, folder 64D.

Invitation: Letter from Meir to [members and supporters], June 5, 1975, in RZ Archives, folder 754A. The meeting was held at the Summit Hotel in Manhattan.

Pledge card, headed "Israel Will Live!" in RZ Archives, folder 69B. The pledge card said, "For tax deductible purposes, checks may be made out to J.I.C. (Jewish Identity Center), and funneled to the area that you indicate above."

[2] Hilton Goldman and others confirmed the accuracy of this description. See: Letter from Hilton Goldman to Libby, November 1997, in RZ Archives, Appendix.

The description is from a novel by Ira Levin, *The Boys from Brazil* (New York: Random House, 1976), pp. 232-234. The novel works JDLers into the plot as Nazi-hunters. Its depiction of the character who is supposed to be Meir is inaccurate. Goldman and others I interviewed confirmed that Meir never used swear words as the book's character "Gorin" does.

[3] E-mail from Russel Kelner, August 22, 2000. The flyer coded N-PS-275-1 is in RZ Archives, folder 65A.

[4] "Telephone Squad Schematic: Jewish Defense League Phone Chain," October 1975, in RZ Archives, folder 65C. Code: N-P19-1075.

See: "JDL Announces Telephone Chain for Demonstrations," *Jewish Press*, June 13, 1975, p. 51. An ad on the same page said, "Want to Be Informed of JDL Demonstrations? Phone 255- 0211 and Let Us Know."

5 *Jewish Defense League Bulletin*, July 25, 1975, p. 1, in RZ Archives, folder 69B.

6 Letter from Russel Kelner to "Speakers Listed on Agenda... 9 February Convention...," February 4, 1975, in RZ Archives, folder 65B. "Please make note of your allotted time for speaking."

Form letter from Russel Kelner to members, April 9, 1975, in RZ Archives, folder 483B. The Solidarity Sunday parade took place on April 13, 1975.

7 *Jewish Defense League Bulletin*, March 1975, p. [3], in RZ Archives, folder 985. The JDL Training Center was at 227 West 29 Street (between Seventh and Eighth Avenues), Manhattan.

8 "J.D.L. Burns Rocket Model Here in Protesting Détente," *New York Times*, July 16, 1975, p. 19; "Dump Détente... Rally at Soviet Mission, July 15, 1975, noon," flyer, in RZ Archives, folder 1204.

"JDL Takes Over Finnish Consulate to Protest Détente," *Jewish Press*, August 1, 1975, p. 26, in RZ Archives, folder 733.

See also: Bernard Gwertzman, "Solzhenitsyn Says Ford Joins in Eastern Europe's 'Betrayal,'" *New York Times*, July 22, 1975, pp. 1, 63; "Excerpts From the Declaration to Be Issued by the European Security Parley," *New York Times*, July 30, 1975, p. 8.

9 Interview with Abe Levine, November 11, 1998, Jerusalem. On March 30, 1975, JDLers protested the Soviet government's disruption of Passover services in Moscow. Twenty-two members were arrested on charges of throwing containers of red paint at the Soviet Mission. See: "Metropolitan Briefs," *New York Times*, March 31, 1975, p. 35.

See also: Christopher Wren, "Jews Dispersed by Moscow Police," *New York Times*, March 30, 1975, p. 5.

10 Letter from Rabbi Meir Kahane, International Chairman, Jewish Defense League, to "Dear Friend," August 1975, in RZ Archives, folder 732.

11 Letter from Isadore Rabinowitz, Brooklyn, N.Y., to Meir, September 26, 1975, in RZ Archives, folder 65D.

12 The purses were made in Lebanon. See: Joy Allen, "JDL Pickets Over Purses," *Newsday*, August 3, 1972, p. 26, in RZ Archives, Appendix. The article quoted the leader of the protest: "Lebanon supports the Palestinian underground."

13 Interview with Yetta Lebowitz, November 3, 1998, Jerusalem.

Letter from Bazaar Committee to [manufacturers and store owners], November 5, 1975, in RZ Archives, folder 732. Annette Cohen, Rosalie Goldstein, Lillian Greenblum, Yetta Lebowitz, Lorraine Schumsky and Norma Singer were on the committee.

"JDL flea market...," *Jewish Defense League Bulletin*, May 1975, in RZ Archives, folder 985.

14 The Camp Da-Ro site was in Linlithgo, a small town in New York's Hudson Valley, near Germantown. It was a two-and-a-half hour drive from New York City. E-mail from David Fisch, February 19, 1998. Preparations for the 1975 camp began shortly after Meir was permitted to travel to the United States in August 1974.

The last JDL summer camp had been held in 1971. There was an unsuccessful effort to open one in 1974. See: "Learn Jewish Pride and Leadership: Camp Jedel," [ad] *Jewish Press*, February 15, 1974, p. 42.

15 Letter from Rabbi Meir Kahane, JDL International Chairman, to "Dear Member, Former Member, Supporter," May 1975, in RZ Archives, folder 69A.

16 "Learn Jewish Pride and Leadership," [ad] *Jewish Press*, April 25, 1975, p. 24, in RZ Archives, folder 64B.

"The Proudest and Most Unique Camp in America: Camp Jedel... Now Accepting Applications for 1975 Summer Season... Ages 13-21," [ad] *Jewish Press*, January 17, 1975. Reprinted in *Hadar* (Lower Manhattan Chapter, Jewish Defense League), [January 1975], p. 8, in RZ Archives, folder 754A.

"We Are Accepting Applications to Camp Jedel," *Jewish Defense League Bulletin*, March 1975, p. 2, in RZ Archives, folder 985.

See also: "They used to send us to camps... but 'Never Again.' Now we have our own camps to make sure 'Never Again.'" Camp Jedel brochure and application form, December 1974, in RZ Archives, folder 734.

"Applications Being Accepted for Camp Jedel, 1975 Summer Season," flyer, in RZ Archives, folder 89A.

[17] Interview with Baruch Ben Yosef, October 9, 1997, Jerusalem.

E-mail from Garth Kravat, May 26, 2005.

E-mail from Menachem Gottlieb, May 26, 2005. "All camp participants had to learn the *himnon* [anthem] in Hebrew by heart. For those who could not read Hebrew, it was written in transliteration." See chapter 15 for the words of the anthem.

[18] Letter from David Fisch to [selected JDL members], April 1975, in RZ Archives, folder 64B.

[19] "Young Revolutionaries Wanted on Campus," flyer, in RZ Archives, folder 64B.

[20] "Campers came from..." *Jewish Defense League Bulletin*, July 25, 1975, p. 2, in RZ Archives, folder 985.

Interview with Dan Gottlieb, November 2, 1999, Jerusalem.

E-mail from Menachem Gottlieb, April 6, 2005.

[21] E-mail from David Fisch, May 27, 1997.

A *Bet Sefer* (seminar) at the end of the summer was advertised but never took place. "*Bet Sefer* on Jewish Militancy," [ad], *Jewish Press*, August 8, 1975, p. 18; August 15, 1975, p. 24; "*Bet Sefer* on Jewish Militancy," poster, in RZ Archives, poster folder, no. 9.

[22] *Jewish Defense League Bulletin*, July 25, 1975, p. 1-4, in RZ Archives, folder 985.

[23] E-mail from David Fisch, February 19, 1975.

[24] See note 13.

[25] *Camp Jedel Songbook: Songs from the Underground, Camp Jedel and Other Fun Songs*, compiled by Menachem Gottlieb and Dan Gottlieb (Jerusalem: Segev Press, 1979), 50 pp. Photocopy (partial) in RZ Archives, Appendix.

The songs were those sung at Camp Jedel in 1975, but the songbook was not printed until 1979. Songs were printed in Hebrew, Hebrew transliteration and English.

The words of the three songs named in the text are on the internet. See: www.saveisrael.com (Choose Jabotinsky; Anonymous) and www.internationalwallofprayer.org

[26] See note 23.

[27] E-mail from Baruch Ben Yosef, May 28, 2005.

[28] See note 23.

[29] Many of the campers went to live in Israel: Baruch Ben Yosef, Menachem Gottlieb, Dan Gottlieb, Garth Kravat, Ellen Greenblum, and Glenn Perlman.

[30] "JDL Camp Makes Reality of Slogan, 'Never Again,'" *Poughkeepsie Journal*, July 27, 1975, pp. 1, 18, in RZ Archives, folder 69B. Excerpted with permission.

See also: "Experimental Jewish Camp Starts," *Register-Star* (Hudson, N.Y.), July 4, 1975, in RZ Archives, folder 64C. Reprinted as a flyer, code number N-C-775-1A.

[31] Miguel Perez, "Jericho Battle Reenacted by Pickets for Education," *The Miami Herald*, September 18, 1975, in RZ Archives, folder 65C. Excerpted with permission.

[32] "A Protest in Chains," *Miami News*, September 17, 1975, in RZ Archives, folder 65C.

33 Rudy Johnson, "Gas Hoses Slashed at 10 Gulf Stations," *New York Times*, September 17, 1975, p. 95; "10 Gulf Stations Struck by Anti-Arab Vandals," *Star Ledger* (Newark), September 17, 1975, p. 12, in RZ Archives, folder 733.

34 "JDL Sit-In Yields Meeting Monday, Sept. 8, with Senator Javits," press release, September 4, 1975, in RZ Archives, folder 65D.

35 "Egyptian and Indian Missions Defaced..." press release, December 11, 1975, in RZ Archives, folder 731. JDLers followed diplomatic personnel shouting "Free Syrian Jewry."

36 "Moscow Circus Target Here of Demonstrators in Hall," *New York Times*, December 17, 1975, p. 49, in RZ Archives, folder 66A.

"Eggs Interrupt Hockey," *New York Times*, December 29, 1975, p. 29.

37 "Invite Rabbi Meir Kahane," [ad] *Jewish Press*, July 11, 1975, p. 21; July 25, 1975, p. 21; August 1, 1975, p. 20. The ad gave the telephone numbers of the Shuva and JDL offices.

The weekly seminars were usually held at Congregation Zichron Moshe, 342 East 20 Street in Manhattan. See: "Jewish Identity Center 'Chug' Seminars," *Jewish Press*, October 17, 1975, p. 25; November 7, 1975, p. 33. See also chapter 46, note 44. For earlier seminars at Cong. Zichron Moshe, see chapter 18, note 22.

38 Letter from Berryl Septimus, Metropolitan Coordinator, to members, June 1975, in RZ Archives, folder 69A.

"Religious Services," *New York Times*, June 13, 1975, p. 42, in RZ Archives, folder 69B. Meir's lecture at the Lincoln Square Synagogue on Saturday at 7 P.M. is noted.

The halfway house was located at West 54 Street near Broadway.

39 Letter from Meir to Libby, June 29, 1975, in RZ Archives, Appendix. Claire Dienstag was a librarian at the New York Public Library's Jewish Division and Jacob Dienstag was a bibliographer. We became acquainted at meetings of Judaica librarians.

40 Letter from Meir to Libby, June 2, 1975, in RZ Archives, Appendix.

Motion for Reduction of Sentence, June 11, 1975, in RZ Archives, folder 706A.

Federal Rules of Criminal Procedure, rule 35, modification of sentence. E-mail from Avery Gross, Esq., February 10, 2005.

41 Marcia Kramer, "A Reduced Sentence Denied Kahane," *Daily News*, June 18, 1975; "Kahane Loses Plea for Holiday Time," *Jewish Week*, July 5, 1975, p. 11, both in RZ Archives, folder 754A.

Judge Weinstein's statement indicates that the Bureau of Prisons had already filed a notice of appeal in the Court of Appeals.

Another motion for reduction of sentence was heard by the Second Circuit Court of Appeals on October 9, 1975. The court's decision, given on November 26, 1975, was that since 120 days had elapsed since the original sentence, the court had lost the power to reduce sentence under Rule 35 of the Federal Rules of Criminal Procedure. See: *Meir Kahane v. Norman Carlson, Director of the Federal Bureau of Prisons, et al.*, 527 F.2d 491, 1975 U.S. App. LEXIS 11747.

42 Letter from Meir to Libby, July 1, 1975, in RZ Archives, Appendix.

43 Letter from Meir to the children, July 18, 1975, in RZ Archives, Appendix.

44 "Government Cracks Down on Kahane: JDL Leader Defiant," *Jewish Press*, July 25, 1975, p. 18, in RZ Archives, folder 69B. Letters to the Parole Board asking for clemency are in folders 64B, 65B and 69B.

45 "Kahane Files Motion to Hold Government in Contempt," *Jewish Press*, August 1, 1975, p. 24, in RZ Archives, folder 69B; "Kahane: Parole Board Decides: Not to Decide," *Jewish Press*, September 5, 1975, p. 2, in RZ Archives, folder 733. The Regional Parole Board, which was to hand down a decision within two weeks, did not grant parole.

46 Letter from Meir to the children, July 7, 1975, in RZ Archives, Appendix.

Meir's words, "... for which I am in prison – counterterror and Arab emigration," probably refer to the revocation of his probation on the basis of Israeli court decisions. He received suspended sentences for the Brezhnev letters and the arms shipment (counterterror). Regarding the charge of incitement for sending letters to Arabs recommending that they emigrate, the case was discontinued shortly after Meir wrote this letter (see chapter 32).

See also: Terence Smith, "13 Die, Scores Hurt in Jerusalem Blast," *New York Times*, July 5, 1975, pp. 1, 39; "Bombing Claims 15th Victim," *Jewish Press*, July 18, 1975, p. 1.

47 "JDL Calls Israeli Government Responsible for Terrorist Successes," press release, July 7, 1975, in RZ Archives, folder 64C.

48 *Revised Sign-In/Sign-Out Schedule*, July 9, 1975, in RZ Archives, folder 64D. This gave the new hours of Meir's furloughs: 7 A.M.-9:30 A.M., 12:30 A.M.-1:30 P.M., 6 P.M.-7:30 P.M.

See also: William Sherman, "On 7-Hour Furlough, Kahane Leads Protest," *Daily News*, July 9, 1975, in RZ Archives, folder 64C. The news item said, "Rabbi Meir Kahane... used one of his daily seven-hour furloughs yesterday to lead JDL members through mid-Manhattan in a march of protest against Arab terrorist attacks in Israel."

As a result of the protest march, many reporters came to his press conference and his ideas about fighting Arab terror appeared in the media. See: "Kahane Insists Counterterror Is the Answer," *Jewish Week*, July 19, 1975, p. 6, in RZ Archives, folder 683B.

49 Letter from Meir to Matthew Walsh, Community Treatment Center, July 10, 1975, in RZ Archives, folder 754A. The letter was typed on the stationery of the Committee Against Israeli Retreat (CAIR).

50 Memo from Matthew Walsh to Meir, undated but between July 10 and July 14, 1975] in RZ Archives, folder 754A. Walsh's reply was handwritten on Meir's typed letter.

51 Letter from Meir to Matthew Walsh, June [i.e. July] 14, 1975, in RZ Archives, folder 754A.

52 "Resident Check Out/In Sheet," in RZ Archives, folder 64A. It had columns for time out, destination, expected time of return, and staff initial.

53 See note 44, *Jewish Press*, July 25, 1975.

54 See note 45, *Jewish Press*, August 1, 1975.

Judge Weinstein's order, [February 21, 1975], in RZ Archives, folder 64D.

55 Memoranda of calls for Meir received at halfway house, in RZ Archives, folder 1234.

56 Letters from Meir to Libby, August 4, 1975, and August 7, 1975, in RZ Archives, Appendix.

57 "U.S. Fed Up With 'Imprisoned' Kahane," *Jerusalem Post*, August 6, 1975, p. 5, in RZ Archives, folder 754A; "Notes on People," *New York Times*, August 5, 1975, p. 23; "Kahane Claims Time Is Cut as Ford Reprisal," *Jewish Week*, August 23, 1975, in RZ Archives, folder 733.

58 "Kahane – Government in Battle over Prison Rights," *Jewish Press*, August 15, 1975, p. 34.

"Rabbi Meir Kahane Speaks During Press Conference at Gefen's Dairy Restaurant," [photo caption] *Daily News*, August 7, 1975. Photo by Frank Giorandino. To view the image, see http://www2.dailynewspix.com and search by photo caption.

Gefen's Dairy Restaurant was at 297 Seventh Avenue, near West 26 Street.

59 "Government Seeks Full Imprisonment for Rabbi Meir Kahane," [ad] *Jewish Press*, August 8, 1975, p. 16, in RZ Archives, folder 733.

60 "Weinstein Upholds Kosher Food Right in Prison," *Jewish Press*, August 22, 1975, p. 3.

61 U.S. Department of Justice, Bureau of Prisons, *Incident Report*, Register no. 72712-158, August 13, 1975, and *Incident Report*, Register no. 72712-158, August 27, 1975, in RZ Archives, folder 754A.

After the Court of Appeals refused Trager's August 12 petition to send Meir to Allenwood prison, Meir wrote of the Incident Reports: "Having won the decision last week, the prison officials seem to have given up, and they do not even bother to give me 'reports.' Just as well, since I was running out of walls [to paste them on]." See: Letter from Meir to Libby, August 18, 1975, in RZ Archives, Appendix.

[62] Letter from Congressman Mario Biaggi to U.S. Attorney General Edward Levi, August 14, 1975, in RZ Archives, folder 754A.

[63] "Furlough Application," September 4, 1975, approved by Matthew Walsh, in RZ Archives, folder 65A. "Purpose: To participate in religious services during the High Holidays. Person to be visited: Mr. Philip Blum."

Sukkot holiday: Letter from Meir to Libby, September 25, 1975, in RZ Archives, Appendix.

[64] U.S. Department of Justice, Bureau of Prisons, *Incident Report*, Register [I.D.] no. 72712-158, September 20, 1975, in RZ Archives, folder 754A.

[65] Letter from Meir to Libby, August 12, 1975, in RZ Archives, Appendix.

[66] Letter from Meir to Baruch, August 12, 1975, in RZ Archives, Appendix. The principle that Jews suffer the natural consequences of their actions is discussed in *Perush Hamaccabee: Devarim* [Hebrew] (Jerusalem: Institute for Publication of Writings of Rabbi Meir Kahane, 1995), pp. 152, 273, 280-282, 295.

Chapter 45

[1] Letter (Hebrew) from Meir to Binyamin, February 13, 1975, in RZ Archives, Appendix.

[2] Letter (Hebrew) from Meir to Binyamin, March 5, 1975, in RZ Archives, Appendix. The story of the rabbi and the miser is related by Meir in *Time to Go Home*, pp. 13-14.

[3] Letter (Hebrew) from Meir to Binyamin, July 27, 1975, in RZ Archives, Appendix. The source of the principle that all Jews are responsible for one another is *Talmud, Shvu'ot*, 39a.

[4] Letter (Hebrew) from Meir to Binyamin, September 25, 1975, in RZ Archives, Appendix.

[5] Letter (Hebrew) from Meir to Binyamin, November 23, 1975, in RZ Archives, Appendix.

Report card noted in: Letter (Hebrew) from Meir to Binyamin, August 27, 1975, in RZ Archives, Appendix.

[6] Letter from Meir to Baruch, February 2, 1975, in RZ Archives, Appendix.

[7] Letter from Meir to Baruch, June 25, 1975, in RZ Archives, Appendix.

[8] Letter from Meir to Baruch, September 25, 1975, in RZ Archives, Appendix.

[9] Letter from Meir to Baruch, undated, but probably mid-September 1975 (includes wishes for the New Year), in RZ Archives, Appendix.

[10] Letter from Meir to Baruch, December 5, 1975, in RZ Archives, Appendix.

Gush Emunim attempted to settle in Samaria in December, but the army again removed them. "Arabs on West Bank in Clash with Israelis," *New York Times*, December 5, 1975, p. 2; David Landau, "Gush Emunim Settlers Removed from Sebastia," *Jewish Press*, December 5, 1975, p. 2.

[11] Letter from Meir to Baruch, August 11, 1975, in RZ Archives, Appendix.

[12] Letter from Meir to Baruch, August 7, 1975, in RZ Archives, Appendix.

[13] Letter from Meir to the children, July 1, 1975, in RZ Archives, Appendix. Since halakha forbids military service for girls, Tova did national service as a school aide in a development town.

[14] Letter (Hebrew) from Meir to the children, June 1, 1975, in RZ Archives, Appendix.

[15] Letter from Meir to Libby, August 10, 1975, in RZ Archives, Appendix.

[16] Letter from Meir to Libby, October 20, 1975, in RZ Archives, Appendix.

[17] Letter from Meir to Tzippy, June 11, 1975, in RZ Archives, Appendix. "Make the words of Your Torah pleasant..." is from the daily prayer book.

[18] Letter from Meir to Tzippy, July 21,1975, in RZ Archives, Appendix.

[19] Letter from Meir to the children, July 18, 1975, in RZ Archives, Appendix.

[20] Letter [signed] Sheila Lidz, Jewish Identity Center, to [editors and publishers of Anglo-Jewish newspapers], March 1975, in RZ Archives, folder 64A.

The letter was written on the stationery of the Jewish Identity Center. The Officers' names were listed at the side: Hilton Goldman, President; Arthur Miller, Treasurer; Sanford Goldstein, Assistant Treasurer; Norma Singer, Secretary. Directors included Rabbi Max Schreier, Rabbi Gedalia Schwartz, Dr. Morris Mandel, Dr. Hillel Seidman, Charles Cohen, Alan Cornet, Edith Goldman, Reuben Gross, Shifra Hoffman, Ben Karpen, Shmuel Knopfler, Abe Levine, Linda Levine, Max Lidz, Sheila Lidz, Reuben Mattus, Rose Mattus, Fran Prager, and Nat Rosenwasser.

[21] *What Makes Bernie Run* (New York: Jewish Identity Center of Jerusalem), 8 pp.

The booklet was widely distributed: "Over 10,000 have been distributed to colleges and synagogues." Letter from Sheila Lidz to "Dear Friend," March 22, 1976, in RZ Archives, folder 1205.

What Makes Bernie Run, datelined Federal Prison, April 29, 1975, reprinted: *Jewish Press*, July 16, 1976, pp. M7, M8; *Writings 5734-5-6*, p. 154-160; *Kahane: The Magazine of the Authentic Jewish Idea*, December 1976, pp. 28-31; *Beyond Words*; 2:278-289; *Israel Today* (Los Angeles), November 26, 1976, p. 6, in RZ Archives, folder 90F.

Typescript, with handwritten corrections, in RZ Archives, folder 1234.

Meir's choice of the name Bernie is explained in chapter 42, p. 468.

[22] *Letters from Prison*, 1974, is discussed in chapter 38. In 1992, Bertha Klausner informed me that she had tried unsuccessfully to find a publisher for the 1975 manuscript.

[23] The collection had 20 new articles in typescript, in this order: (This list indicates where they were published.)

Introduction, "Ignorance About Jews and Judaism Is an Ancient Malady," dated May 23, 1975.

1. "Excerpts from the Hearing before Judge Jack B. Weinstein, February 21, 1975." The entire transcript of the hearing appeared in the *Jewish Press*, February 28, 1975, pp. 4, 49.

2. "Why I Regret Going to Prison," *Jewish Press*, March 14, 1975, pp. 28, 36, reprinted in *Writings, 5734-5-6*, pp. 112-115.

3. "The Jewish Way," *Jewish Press*, September 19, 1975, p. 37, reprinted in *Writings, 5734-5-6*, pp. 222-224, and in *Beyond Words*, 2:168-172. Datelined May 1975.

4. "The Gathering Storm," *Jewish Press*, April 4, 1975, pp. 28-30, reprinted in *Writings, 5734-5-6*, pp. 134-137. Datelined March 21, 1975.

5. "Ford Must Go." See chapter 43, note 47. The manuscript has the original booklet, with a note attached: "Written March 25, 1975, at Federal Prison in Manhattan."

6. "In the Name of the L-rd of Hosts," *Jewish Press*, April 18, 1975, pp. 31-34, reprinted in *Writings, 5734-5-6*, pp. 128-131, and in *Beyond Words*, 2:130-135. Datelined Federal Training Center, March 24, 1975.

7. "What Makes Bernie Run?" See note 21.

8. "On the Beach." Datelined Federal Prison, April 8, 1975. See text.

9. "There Is No Other Way," *Jewish Press*, two parts, May 30, 1975, p. 30; June 6, 1975, pp. 18, 21, in RZ Archives, folder 101, reprinted in *Writings, 5734-5-6*, pp. 160-165, and in *Beyond Words*, 2:140-146. Datelined April 1975.

10. "1947," *Jewish Press*, November 28, 1975, p. 20, reprinted in *Kahane: The Magazine of the Authentic Jewish Idea*, May 1976 and September-October 1988. Datelined Federal Prison, April 28, 1975.

11. "The Land of Israel – The Real Issue," a mimeographed flyer, in RZ Archives, folder 589, reprinted in *Writings, 5734-5-6*, pp. 170-174, in *Kahane: The Magazine of the Authentic Jewish Idea*, May 1976, and in *Beyond Words*, 2:256-263. Datelined Federal Prison, Manhattan, May 2, 1975.

12. "My Son Was Arrested Last Week," *Jewish Press*, March 28, 1975, pp. 16, 18, reprinted in *Writings, 5734-5-6*, pp. 119-121. Datelined Federal Prison, New York, March 23, 1975.

13. "The Thunderous Silence of Détente," *Jewish Press*, three parts, February 27, 1976, p. 33; March 19, 1976, p. 38; March 26, 1976, p. 57. Datelined Federal Prison, Manhattan, May 4, 1975.

14. "The Broken Reed." See chapter 42, note 27.

15. "Détente," *Writings, 5734-5-6*, pp. 85-92. Dated January 8, 1975.

16. "What Will Be?" *Jewish Press*, June 27, 1975, pp. 33, 37, reprinted in *Writings, 5734-5-6*, pp. 123-126, and in *Beyond Words*, 2:150-155. Datelined Federal Prison, New York, Passover eve, March 26, 1975.

17. "Of Prisoners and Free Men." See chapter 42, note 41.

18. "Numbers 23:9," *Jewish Press*, six parts, December 19, 1975, p. 43; December 26, 1975, p. 14; January 2, 1976, p. 8; January 9, 1976, p. 36; January 16, 1976, pp. 14, 15; January 23, 1976, p. 14, reprinted in *Kahane: The Magazine of the Authentic Jewish Idea*, three parts, January, April and May 1977. Originally printed as a booklet in 1974, see chapter 38, note 20; reprinted 1975, see note 29.

19. "What Is It All About?" *Jewish Press*, two parts, April 23, 1976, p. 32; April 30, 1976, p. 22, reprinted in *Writings, 5734-5-6*, pp. 165-170. Datelined Federal Prison Manhattan, May 7, 1975.

20. "Give Me a Present." See chapter 43, note 3.

The collection included six articles written in Jerusalem Central Prison in 1973 that had appeared in *Letters from Prison*, 1974: The Chosen State, Letter to a Jewish Prisoner, Declaration to the Court, A Letter to My Children: Tova, Baruch, Cippora, Binyamin, The Honor of the Jewish People, Eretz Israel and the Burning Fire. Details in chapter 38, note 17.

[24] Meir Kahane, *On the Beach*, unpublished typescript, in RZ Archives, Appendix.

[25] "Israel Through Laughter and Tears" ceased after August 22, 1975, and resumed from June 11, 1976, to November 3, 1978. "Exposing the Haters" ceased after August 22, 1975, and resumed from September 3, 1976, to December 15, 1978. It then appeared once more, on April 18, 1980. Meir wrote under pseudonyms because Rabbi Klass did not want the same byline to appear more than once in each issue.

Letter from John H. Kliever, Americans for Middle East Neutrality, to Abe Levine, January 16, 1975, in RZ Archives, Appendix.

[26] Letter from Meir to Libby, May 17, 1975, in RZ Archives, Appendix.

[27] "The Week That Was" was published from May 30, 1975, through August 15, 1975. Its name may have been derived from an NBC-TV satirical series, 1964-1965, *That Was The Week That Was*.

"The Activist's Column" appeared from August 29, 1975, through November 4, 1977. It is likely that Meir chose the name as a tie with the new group, Conference of Presidents of Major American Jewish Activist Organizations, discussed in chapter 46.

28 "The Activist's Column," *Jewish Press*, August 29, 1975, pp. 12, 35, in RZ Archives, folder 594, reprinted as "Sense and Nonsense," in *Writings 5734-5-6*, pp. 209-213.

29 *Numbers 23:9* (Miami Beach: I. Block, 1975), 58 pp., 19 cm.

The size of the 1974 edition was 34 pp., 28 cm. Both editions are in the JNUL, call numbers S74B1962=2 and S75B3155. Reprints are listed in note 23.

Madmen and Murderers (New York: Jewish Identity Center of Jerusalem, 1975), [8] pp., 20 cm., in RZ Archives, booklets folder. Details of the 1974 edition in chapter 38.

The Jewish Idea: *A Jewish Program for Jewish Survival* (New York: Jewish Defense League, 1975), 20 pp., 28 cm., in RZ Archives, folder 69B. The cover has the Hebrew words *Am Yisrael Chai* (The people of Israel lives). Details of the 1974 edition in chapter 38. Both editions in JNUL, call numbers S2005B1311=2 and S74B2962=2.

30 *Time to Go Home* was published in hardcover in 1972. See chapter 29.

Price estimate submitted by Hebron Printing Press Ltd., January 1, 1975, in JNUL Archives, folder ARC 4=1748. It specified 60 gram paper, 2 color softcover, size 17x12.5 cm., 296 pages. The price included shipping to port and was "based on the rate for the premium for exporting books."

Letter from Meir to Shifra Hoffman, February 24, 1974: "How much would it cost to photo offset in pocket book size *Time to Go Home*. Please ask Drucker." Letter from Shifra Hoffman to Meir, April 28, 1974, both in RZ Archives, folder 713A.

See also: chapter 38, note 22, Letter from Meir to Gene Singer, et al.

31 Letter from Meir to Libby, see chapter 42, note 6.

32 Letter from Meir to Libby, March 18, 1975, in RZ Archives, Appendix.

33 Epilogue to *Time to Go Home,* from *Numbers 23:9* (Jerusalem: Jewish Identity Center, 1974), pp. 6-13.

34 Letter from Meir to Libby, May 1, 1975, in RZ Archives, Appendix.

35 Letters from Meir to Libby, May 11, 1975, mid-May 1975, and June 8, 1975, in RZ Archives, Appendix.

36 Letter from Meir to Libby, June 29, 1975, in RZ Archives, Appendix. In this letter, Meir lists typos he found in the copy he received from Hebron Press. Sadly, the same typos were in the original hardcover edition.

Letter from Meir to Libby, July 11, 1975, in RZ Archives, Appendix.

The paperback edition of *Time to Go Home* bore the same imprint as the hardcover, with the date given as 1975 (Los Angeles: Nash Publishing, 1975) but Meir's subsequent letters indicate that the book was actually printed in New York from plates prepared by the Hebron Press. In October, he asked me get the plates from Hebron Press and give them to a tourist, Mordechai Pollan, who would bring them to New York. (Letter from Meir to Libby, October 26, 1975, in RZ Archives, Appendix.) Hebron Press apparently refused to give me the plates because they had not yet been fully paid, so he wrote: "Leave the Hebron Press debt alone and forget the plates for the time being." (Letter from Meir to Libby, December 7, 1975, in RZ Archives, Appendix.) Then, in a letter to my parents: "Please tell Libby to have Hebron Press ship the plates for my book immediately." (Letter from Meir to Jacob and Leah Blum, December 29, 1975, in RZ Archives, Appendix.) In January, he wrote, "Send plates by SHIP to Gene Singer." (Letter from Meir to Libby, January 10, 1976, in RZ Archives, Appendix.)

The paperback was printed early in 1976, but the title page, prepared by Hebron Press, had the date 1975. Its size is 287, 11 pp., 16 cm.

[37] Letter from Benton M. Arnovitz to Meir, May 19, 1975, in RZ Archives, folder 64C. Details of contract with Chilton, August 1974, in chapter 40.

[38] Letter from Meir to Libby, May 20, 1975, in RZ Archives, Appendix.
Letter from Meir to Libby, undated, but after May 20, 1975, in RZ Archives, Appendix.
Letter from Meir to Libby, June 18, 1975, in RZ Archives, Appendix.

[39] Meir Kahane, "So Easy to Forget," [op-ed] *New York Times*, June 16, 1975, p. 27, in RZ Archives, folder 65C, reprinted in *Beyond Words*, 2:147-149. The drawing was three columns wide. See chapter 31 for an article with a similar text: "No Illusions Please," *Jewish Press*, August 25, 1972, pp. 26, 28, 31.

Most of the text of "So Easy to Forget" was reprinted in: "N.Y. Times Publishes Kahane 'J'Accuse,'" *B'nai B'rith Messenger*, August 15, 1975, p. 31, in RZ Archives, folder 65D.

When Meir submitted this article to the *Times* a month earlier, he received this reply: "We would be happy to consider your article on the Middle East situation at 600 words. As is, it's too long for us." Letter from Charlotte Curtis, Associate Editor, *New York Times,* to Meir, May 23, 1975, in RZ Archives, folder 69A.

New York Times payment slip, $150 for "So Easy to Forget," in RZ Archives, folder 64B.

Previous op-ed articles by Meir in the *Times* were: "A Call for Mass Emigration to Israel," *New York Times*, May 26, 1972, p. 35; "Enough Lamentations," *New York Times*, November 29, 1972, p. 45, both in RZ Archives, folder 607.

[40] Herbert Gold, "The Story of the Jewish Defense League," *New York Times Book Review*, June 8, 1975, Section 7, pp. 4-5, in RZ Archives, folder 64D. Copyright © 1975 by The New York Times News Service. Excerpted with permission.

The review is accompanied by a photo of Meir on an outdoor platform, an American flag behind him, shouting through a bullhorn, wearing a suit jacket over a light-colored sweater. The caption says only, "At a J.D.L. rally in New York, January 1975." His light-colored clothing indicates that this photo was taken at a rally against Israeli retreat held at the Garment Center on January 27. At the "There Is No Palestine" rally on January 19, 1975, Meir wore a black high-necked sweater. See photo in RZ Archives, picture folder, no. 463. Both rallies are described in chapter 41.

[41] Meir Hacohen (pseudonym of Meir Kahane), "Israel Through Laughter and Tears," *Jewish Press*, June 27, 1975, p. 28. See also "*Story of the Jewish Defense League*," [unsigned review] *Jewish Press*, June 27, 1975, p. 39.

Ads for the book appeared in the *Jewish Press*, May 16, 1975, p. 16; May 30, 1975, p. 41; July 4, 1975, p. 20.

[42] Lenora Berson, "Some People Are More Chosen Than Others," *Philadelphia Inquirer*, August 10, 1975, in RZ Archives, folder 713B. Excerpted with permission.

[43] Donald L. Wolberg, "Reviews of Books," *Minnesota Daily*, August 11, 1975, p. 9, in RZ Archives, folder 713B. Excerpted with the author's permission.

[44] Ron Mehler, "The Bookshelf," *Wisconsin Jewish Chronicle*, August 20, 1975, in RZ Archives, folder 713B.

[45] A.H. [sic], "New JDL Book Tells Same Story," *Detroit Jewish News*, July 25, 1975, in RZ Archives, folder 713B.

[46] Letter from Meir to Libby, October 13, 1975, in RZ Archives, Appendix.
"Chronology of a Miracle" is discussed in chapter 11.

[47] Letter from Meir to Libby, October 20, 1975, in RZ Archives, Appendix.

[48] "The Six Day War," [ad] *Jewish Press*, November 21, 1975, p. 47.

Chapter 46

[1]   Letter from Meir to Libby, May 17, 1975, in RZ Archives, Appendix. Echad, the group Meir formed in October 1974, had similar aims. See chapter 40.

The "organization that came in out of the cold" is a play on words referring to *The Spy Who Came in from the Cold*, a 1963 espionage novel by John le Carré.

[2]   Letter from the American Zionist Federation to Eugene Singer, Jewish Defense League, July 14, 1975, in RZ Archives, folder 483B.

At a meeting on June 29, 1975, the National Jewish Community Relations Advisory Council decided to reject JDL membership. See: "JDL Denied Affiliation by Umbrella Group..." *Jewish Week*, July 19, 1975, p. 6, in RZ Archives, folder 64D; Irving Spiegel, "J.D.L. Rejected by Advisory Council on Membership Bid," *New York Times*, July 6, 1975, p. 29.

"JDL Sues to Compel Major Jewish Umbrella Groups to Accept JDL Membership," press release, May 12, 1975, in RZ Archives, folder 64D. The press release named the Conference of Presidents of Major American Jewish Organizations and the American Zionist Federation.

An ad in the *Jewish Press* said, "The JDL has applied for membership in the Conference of Presidents of Major American Jewish Organizations. Not only have they not replied, they have chosen to totally disregard the three *hazmonos* (summons) of the *Beth Din* (rabbinical court) of the Rabbinical Alliance of America.... The JDL, in accordance with Jewish law (*Choshen Mishpat*, 11) will pursue this matter in civil court. [signed] Nat Rosenwasser, Executive Director, JDL." See: "The JDL Has Applied...," [ad] *Jewish Press*, May 30, 1975, p. 44, in RZ Archives, folder 985.

Dr. Irving Moskowitz, who represented the Zionist Organization of America at the convention of the Presidents Conference, wrote: "... The Presidents Conference... is attempting to stifle opposing ideas in the Jewish community. It is ridiculous to call the Presidents Conference a Conference of Presidents of Major American Jewish Organizations while excluding the Jewish Defense League." Letter from Irving Moskowitz to Rabbi Joseph Sternstein, president, Zionist Organization of America, June 19, 1975, in RZ Archives, folder 69B. See also: Irving Moskowitz, "Presidents Conference Should Admit JDL," [letter to the editor] *Jewish Post and Opinion*, June 27, 1975, p. 12.

[3]   Letter from Meir to Libby, May 20, 1975, in RZ Archives, Appendix.

[4]   Conference of Presidents of Major American Jewish Activist Organizations, *Minutes*, June 11, 1975, in RZ Archives, folder 754A.

[5]   "Why Can There Be No Unity Among the Jewish Activist Organizations?" [ad] *Jewish Press*, June 27, 1975, p. 10. Ads were also placed in the general press: "Founding Convention of Conference of Presidents..." [ad] *New York Post*, June 27, 1975, in RZ Archives, folder 64B.

The *Jewish Press* ad named additional charter members of the new umbrella group: Jewish Alliance of Businessmen, Shuva Aliya Movement, International League for the Repatriation of Russian Jewish Identity Center, and Masada. The organizations were also listed in "Activists Calendar and Contacts," *Jewish Press*, August 29, 1975, p. 25.

See also: "New Major Jewish Umbrella Group Being Formed," [unsigned news report] *Jewish Press*, June 27, 1975, p. 10. Meir wrote enthusiastically about the unity of Jewish groups and the coming convention in his column "The Week That Was," *Jewish Press*, June 27, 1975, p. 12.

[6]   "The Week That Was," *Jewish Press*, July 4, 1975, p. 18, in RZ Archives, folder 594.

[7]   Large Crowd at Founding Convention of New Activist Conference," *Jewish Press*, July 4, 1975, p. 31, in RZ Archives, folder 64B.

Meir Hacohen (pseudonym of Meir Kahane), "Israel Through Laughter and Tears," *Jewish Press*, August 1, 1975, p. 14.

"Agenda, Activist Conference," [memo], July 9, 1975, in RZ Archives, folder 64C. This type-script is typical of Meir's typing, with the heading in his handwriting. It also discusses by-laws, dues, fundraising, hiring an executive director, and suggested activities.

8 Letter from Meir to Libby, July 7, 1975, in RZ Archives, Appendix.

9 "Sanctification Day," flyer, in RZ Archives, folder 64C.

Ads about Sanctification Day appeared in the *Jewish Press*: July 4, 1975, p. 26, and July 11, 1975, p. 17. Ads were placed in other Anglo-Jewish newspapers as well. For example: "Sanctifi-cation Day," [ad] *Jewish Week*, in RZ Archives, folder 1204.

10 Printed letter signed Stanley Schumsky to "Dear Rabbi," undated, but prior to July 17, 1975, in RZ Archives, folder 64C. The letter was clearly composed by Meir, and Schumsky's signature is in Meir's handwriting. The stationery had the logo of the Conference, a stylized Star of David made up of six partially joined triangles.

11 "The Week That Was," *Jewish Press*, July 11, 1975, p. 17, in RZ Archives, folder 1208.

"Tisha B'Av Reading at U.N.," *Jewish Press*, July 4, 1975, pp. 3, 42. See also: "Tisha B'Av Torah Reading at U.N.," press release, stamped July 8, 1975, in RZ Archives, folder 64C.

12 "Sanctification Day Program, Tisha B'Av 5735," July 17, 1975, 2 pp., in RZ Archives, folder 1234. The program is in typescript, with Meir's handwritten corrections in the text of his message.

A photo of Meir in *tallit* and *tefillin* at the Sanctification Day ceremonies appeared in a Yiddish newspaper over a month later. "Harav Kahana Ruft Americaner Iden Tzu Shtitzen Yisroel Op [Rabbi Kahane Calls on American Jews to Support Israel]," *Algemeiner Journal*, August 29, 1975, back page, p. 14. Photographer: Yossi Melamed.

13 "Moynihan Asked to Meet With Activist Conference," *Jewish Press*, July 25, 1975, p. 25. This includes a report on the Tisha B'Av demonstration.

Letter from Shlomo Thaler, Vice President, Conference of Presidents of Major American Jew-ish Activist Organizations, to Hon. Daniel P. Moynihan, U.S. Ambassador to the U.N., July 17, 1975, in RZ Archives, folder 65D. The letter requested a meeting with Moynihan on August 17, before the demonstration, but Moynihan did not meet with him.

14 Letter from Meir to Libby, July 11, 1975, in RZ Archives, Appendix.

15 Yossi Klein, "Young Jewish Activist," *Jewish Post and Opinion*, September 5, 1975, in RZ Archives, folder 754A; "Anti-Kissinger Demonstrations Continue," *Jewish Press*, August 29, 1975, p. 1.

Interview with Baruch Kahane, July 30, 2007, Jerusalem.

16 "The Week That Was," *Jewish Press*, August 15, 1975, pp. 13, 14; "Mass Rally Asks Moynihan to Meet Jewish Activists," *Jewish Press*, August 1, 1975, p. 26; "Huge Washington Israel Rally Called...," *Jewish Press*, August 22, 1975, p. 22, in RZ Archives, folder 1208.

See also: "Israel Now Forever!" [ad] *Jewish Press*, August 8, 1975, p. 29.

17 Letter from Meir to Libby, August 18, 1975, in RZ Archives, Appendix.

18 Letter from Rabbi Israel Miller, president, Conference of Presidents of Major American Jewish Organizations, to Shlomo Thaler, Conference of Presidents of Major American Jewish Activist Organizations, August 25, 1975, in RZ Archives, folder 65D.

"What Confusion?" *Jewish Press*, September 12, 1975, p. 42, reprinted in *Writings 5734-5-6*, p. 216-218.

19 "American Pressure Is Destroying Israel's Security," poster, 74 cm. by 114 cm., in RZ Archives, poster folder, no. 202. The poster gave the Conference of Activists' phone number for bus reservations.

Phone interview with Shlomo Thaler, July 28, 1999.

20 "Rally to Launch Nationwide Drive," [ad] *New York Post*, August 26, 1975, in RZ Archives, folder 64D. The ad outlined the objectives of the rally: Defeat Ford and oust Kissinger in 1976 – Demand that the present Rabin government cease its collapse before Ford and Kissinger – Create a coalition with Christian fundamentalists – Call for immediate and unrestricted Jewish settlement in every part of the Land of Israel.

21 Letter from Meir to Matthew Walsh, Director, Community Treatment Center, September 9, 1975, in RZ Archives, folder 754A.

22 Letter from Matthew Walsh to Meir, September 10, 1975, in RZ Archives, folder 754A.

23 Telegram to Meir from John Sparkman, Chairman, Committee on Foreign Relations, U.S. Senate, September 31, 1975, in RZ Archives, folder 754A.

24 See note 19, Shlomo Thaler. See also: Bernard Gwertzman, "Senators Hear Opposition to Sinai Pact," *New York Times*, October 7, 1975, p. 3, in RZ Archives, folder 754. This reports that Dr. William Perl, of the JDL, and Rabbi Herzel Kranz, of the United Zionists-Revisionists of America, and Shlomo Thaler were among fifteen Jews who testified against the Sinai agreement.

25 Cara Selinger, "Kahane – 'Rally for Israel Now,'" *Phoenix*, September 30, 1975, in RZ Archives, folder 754A. Excerpted with permission of Queens College.

26 Sharon Yellin, "Stern Girls Arrested in DC," *Observer* (Stern College for Women), October 30, 1975, p. 1; Aviva Brojges, "Kahane Questions Jewish Silence," *Observer*, October 30, 1975, p. 3, in RZ Archives, folder 65C. Six Stern College students were among those arrested for sitting down in the street.

Meir spoke at Yeshiva University at lunch hour on October 1. See: "Rabbi Meir Kahane Will Be Speaking..." poster, in RZ Archives, folder 754A. The poster features the cover of *Our Challenge*.

Jewish Press ads for the March for Israel were: "Silence Kills!" August 22, 1975, p. 24; "March for Israel," September 12, 1975, p. 12; "Save Israel From the Jaws of Kissinger's Pressure," September 19, 1975, p. 10, in RZ Archives, folder 754A.

27 "Silence Kills!" flyer, August 1975, in RZ Archives, folder 65D. Similar flyers in RZ Archives, folder 1204.

"March for Israel," stickers, signed Conference of Presidents of Major American Jewish Activist Organizations, in RZ Archives, folder 65D. The stickers say: "For reservations call 212 255 8517."

"REASSESS" alludes to Ford's anti-Israel "reassessment" of America's Mideast policy in the spring of 1975.

28 "Daddy, Where Were You When They Tried to Destroy Israel?" [ad] *Jewish Press*, August 29, 1975, p. 40, in RZ Archives, folder 64D.

The ad was signed: Conference of Presidents of Major American Jewish Activist Organizations, 156 Fifth Avenue, Room 1214, New York City, Tel. 212-255-8517. See also: "March on Washington for Israel," [ad] *Jewish Press*, September 26, 1975, p. 18, in RZ Archives, folder 65D. Details of buses leaving from seven locations in Greater New York at 7:30 A.M. were given in: "March for Israel," [ad] *Jewish Press*, October 3, 1975, p. 16.

29 Letter from Meir to Libby, September 11, 1975, in RZ Archives, Appendix.

Lobbyists: See note 24.

30 Letter from Meir to Libby, September 15, 1975, in RZ Archives, Appendix.

31 Bernard Gwertzman, "Ford Seeks Help of Jewish Leaders," *New York Times*, September 9, 1975, p. 7. This reported that Ford had invited Rabbi Israel Miller, head of the Conference of Presidents of Major American Jewish Organizations, and thirty-three other Jewish leaders to the White House. After a 40-minute meeting, a spokesman said that they had assured Ford of the support of the organized Jewish community for... the stationing of American technicians... in Sinai. This report also noted that mail to the White House was running against support for the agreement 511 to 54.

[32] "The Activist's Column: A Retreat From More Than Sinai," *Jewish Press*, September 12, 1975, p. 42, reprinted in *Writings 5734-5-6*, p. 214-216.

An editorial against "A Retreat From More Than Sinai" was published in the same issue: "In Support of Peace," [editorial] *Jewish Press*, September 12, 1975, pp. 5, 16.

The following week, Meir responded to the editorial. Because the editorial had referred to his supporters as "misguided militants," he titled his rebuttal "A Vigorous Jewish Dissent on Sinai, or Confessions of a Misguided Militant," *Jewish Press*, September 19, 1975, p. 38, reprinted in *Writings 5734-5-6*, p. 219-222; typescript with handwritten corrections in RZ Archives, folder 65D.

[33] Letter from Dr. Irving Moskowitz to Meir, September 8, 1975, in RZ Archives, folder 754A. Moskowitz, an important figure in Zionist affairs, became a significant supporter of Jewish settlement efforts, especially in East Jerusalem.

[34] Letter from Meir to Libby, October 3, 1975, in RZ Archives, Appendix.

[35] "The Following Is the Text of Rabbi Meir Kahane's Remarks at the Activist Demonstration... October 5, 1975," mimeographed on stationery of the Conference of Presidents of Major American Jewish Activist Organizations, 2 pp., in RZ Archives, folder 1204. Meir's typescript with handwritten corrections in RZ Archives, folder 1234.

[36] "85 Jewish Demonstrators Arrested at White House," *Washington Star*, October 6, 1975, p. B-10, in RZ Archives, folder 733. Excerpted with permission.

[37] "Police Arrest 108 in Sit-Down Protest Against Sinai Pact," *Jewish Week*, October 9, 1975, pp. 1, 8, in RZ Archives, folder 734.

"100 in Jewish Protest Seized at White House," *New York Times*, October 6, 1975, p. 6; "Protest at White House," *New York Post*, October 6, 1975, p. 41; "95 Forfeit Bonds In Protest Arrests," *Springfield Leader-Press* (Missouri), October 6, 1975, p. 1; all in RZ Archives, folder 65C; "Lo Tih'yeh Vietnam Besinai [There Will Be No Vietnam in Sinai]," *Ma'ariv*, October 7, 1975, p. 3, in RZ Archives, folder 754A; "Yehudim Hifginu... [Jews Demonstrated...]," [photo caption], *Yedioth Ahronoth*, October 7, 1975, p. 1, in RZ Archives, folder 65C.

[38] Letter from Meir to Baruch, August 28, 1975, in RZ Archives, Appendix.

[39] "The Jewish Speaker's Bureau," [ad] *Jewish Press*, October 10, 1975, p. 21, in RZ Archives, folder 754. The same ad appeared on October 31, 1975, p. 29. It gave the home address and phone number of Renee Brown, who scheduled Meir's speaking dates. It featured the familiar drawing by Becerra of Meir in handcuffs.

[40] Letter from Abe Levine, chairman, Jewish Speaker's Bureau, to "All Speakers and All Chapter Chairmen," October 21, 1975, in RZ Archives, folder 684.

Schedule of speaking dates, in Abe Levine's handwriting, in RZ Archives, folder 684 and 696. These lists cover October 20, 1975, through December 13, 1975.

[41] Speaking dates:

September 25, Queens College: C.S. Selinger, "Kahane – 'Rally For Israel Now,'" *Phoenix*, September 30, 1975, in RZ Archives, folder 754A.

October 1, Borough Park Public Library: "West Brooklyn JDL Meeting," [ad] *Jewish Press*, September 26, 1975, p. 26.

October 20, East Nassau Hebrew Congregation: "Kahane Steps Out in Syosset," see note 46.

October 22, Stern College: "Kahane Discusses 'One Jew, One Vote,'" *Observer*, November 13,

1975, p. 1, in RZ Archives, folder 65C.

October 24, Kingsborough Community College: "Kahane Blasts Apathy," *Scepter*, October 31, 1975, p. 3, in RZ Archives, folder 484.

October 29, Queensborough College: Gail Cohen, "Kahane Urges Jews to Go Home," *The Burro*, November 5, 1975, p. 1, in RZ Archives, folder 66B.

October 29, evening, Young Israel of Manhattan: "Rabbi Meir Kahane Will Speak..." [ad] *Jewish Press*, October 24, 1975, p. 16.

November 3, Young Israel of Ocean Parkway: "An Open Meeting... All Welcome," [ad] *Jewish Press*, October 31, 1975, p. 31.

November 9, Young Israel of Borough Park: See note 40, schedule.

November 10, Akiva Club of Canarsie High School: "Rabbi Meir Kahane will be speaking... Akiva Club ... November 10, 1975, Room 307, Periods 8 and 9," flyer, in RZ Archives, folder 66A.

November 12, Stern College: "Kahane Discusses 'One Jew, One Vote,'" *Observer*, November 13, 1975, p. 1, in RZ Archives, folder 65C.

November 12, evening, Rosedale Jewish Center: See note 40, schedule.

November 14, noon, Young Israel's Women's League: "Meir Kahane to Speak at Kosher Kitchen Luncheon," [ad] *Jewish Press*, October 31, 1975, p. 30, in RZ Archives, folder 754A.

November 14, evening, Sutton Place Synagogue: Letter from Meir to Libby, November 17, 1975, in RZ Archives, Appendix.

November 19, Queens Jewish Center: See note 40, schedule.

November 20, 1 P.M., City College: See note 40, schedule.

November 20, evening, Forest Park Jewish Center: See note 40, schedule.

November 22, Grand Central Synagogue: See note 40, schedule.

November 25, Hebrew Institute of Long Island: See note 40, schedule.

See also: "Rabbi Meir Kahane Will Be Speaking at..." [ad] *Jewish Press*, November 14, 1975, p. 35, in RZ Archives, folder 66B. This lists speaking dates from November 12 to December 1. Clearly, the ad was submitted before Meir's transfer to Allenwood Prison on November 27.

Snapshots of Meir at two speaking engagements during this period are in the photo section of this book. One was not dated but it was probably taken in October because an October newspaper photo shows him wearing the same suit. See "Kahane Steps Out in Syosset," note 46.

On September 30, 1975, Meir was interviewed for the student newspaper of the State University of New York in New Paltz. See: Letter from Bruce Tannenbaum to Meir, October 2, 1975, in RZ Archives, folder 754A. An interview with Meir was also published in the journal of the Orthodox college students: "Kahane Decries American Jewish Scene," *Kol Yavneh*, November-December 1975, p. 10, in RZ Archives, folder 484.

[42] Joyce White, "Kahane Set to Teach on Free Time," *Daily News*, October 9, 1975, in RZ Archives, folder 754A.

Perhaps the reporter saw the ad mentioning Meir's lecture series in the *Jewish Press* (which reached newsstands on Wednesday): "We're Celebrating Our Birthday – Join Us," [ad] *Jewish Press*, October 10, 1975, p. 15, in RZ Archives, folder 713A. See also: Letter from Dr. William Berkowitz to Meir, September 23, 1975, in RZ Archives, folder 65C.

Meir's lectures were scheduled for October 21, 22, 23 and 26. Other lecturers at the Institute of Adult Jewish Studies were Zalman Schachter, Eli Carlebach, Shlomo Carlebach, David Feldman, and Abraham Carmel.

For Meir's lecture at B'nai Jeshurun on October 21, 1974, see chapter 40.

[43] Letter from Matthew Walsh to Meir, October 15, 1975, in RZ Archives, folder 66B.

[44] "Jewish Identity Center 'Chug' seminar," [ad] *Jewish Press*, September 26, 1975, p. A5, in

RZ Archives, folder 65D. The ad explicitly stated, "Rabbi Meir Kahane Speaks." The topic of his October 2 lecture was given as *"Ma Yih'yeh* – What Will Be?"

"Jewish Defense Corps," [ad] *Jewish Press*, November 7, 1975, p. 33. "We believe that the coming economic crisis may lead to attacks on Jews and property. Therefore, we are organizing a Jewish Defense Corps. Men will be trained in the legal use of firearms and placed into neighborhood reserve units to be ready if needed. Vital meeting, November 13, 7:30 P.M., Congregation Zichron Moshe. Rabbi Meir Kahane will speak."

45 "Call Mr. E. Kelly, New York Police Department, Southern Community Affairs," phone message memo, October 16, 1975, in RZ Archives, folder 1193.

The rally was scheduled for Sunday, October 19, 1975, 1 P.M., at the corner of Kingston Avenue and Eastern Parkway. See: "Street Corner Rally," press release in RZ Archives, folder 65C.

There was also a request from the Lubavitcher Rebbe, via Dr. Hillel Seidman, to cancel the rally. See: Letter from Hillel Seidman to Meir, October 19, 1975, 10:45 A.M., in RZ Archives, folder 65D. A letter from Meir indicates that the rally was held. See: Letter from Meir to Baruch, October 26, 1975, in RZ Archives, Appendix. Shlomo Thaler also recalled that the rally took place. Interview with Shlomo Thaler, November 3, 1997.

46 U.S. Department of Justice, Bureau of Prisons, *Incident Report*, Register no. 72712-158, October 20, 1975, in RZ Archives, folder 66B.

Aileen Jacobson, "Kahane Steps Out in Syosset," *Newsday*, October 21, 1975, in RZ Archives, folder 65C; "Kahane Urges Jews to Lobby for Own Needs," *Long Island Press*, October 21, 1975, in Jabotinsky Archives, Meir Kahane collection.

Meir wrote to me afterwards, "I spoke last night in Syosset, and Jack Blum [my father's cousin – Libby] and his wife were there." Letter from Meir to Libby, October 20, 1975.

47 "Herzog Asserts Jews Didn't Aid Israelis in U.N. Zionism Debate," *New York Times*, October 25, 1975, p. 3. The resolution was first adopted by the General Assembly's Third Committee on October 17. For text of Herzog's speech defending Zionism at the U.N. on November 10, 1975, see: www.jewishvirtuallibrary.org/jsource/UN/herzogsp.html. Excerpts from the speech in: "Excerpts From Israeli Talk," *New York Times*, November 12, 1975, p. 16.

"Raise Your Glass and Shout: L'Chaim / To Chaim! To Chaim Herzog, You Were Right!" [ad] *New York Times*, November 10, 1975, p. 10. The ad, signed "Rabbi Meir Kahane," urged attendance at the JDL rally Saturday night, November 15.

Arafat spoke at the United Nations on November 13, 1974. See chapter 41.

48 Paul Hofmann, "U.N. Votes, 72-35, to Term Zionism Form of Racism," *New York Times*, November 11, 1975, pp. 1, 65.

John F. Burns, "Huge Rally Here Condemns U.N. Anti-Zionism Move," *New York Times*, November 12, 1975, pp. 1, 89.

49 "Zionism Is Judaism," [editorial] *B'nai B'rith Messenger,* December 5, 1975, p. 28, in RZ Archives, folder 66A. Excerpted with the permission of Joe Bobker, publisher. Ted Sandler wrote the editorial (see chapter 41, note 20).

The article excerpted in the above editorial was printed as: "Militant Activist Decries Forsaking G-d," *Jewish Post and Opinion* [New York edition], December 19, 1975, p. 5, in RZ Archives, folder 66A. A letter from the editor of the *Jewish Post* thanked Meir for his submission, noting: "We have a token remuneration... enclosing $5." Letter from Charles Roth, editor, *Jewish Post* of New York, to Meir, December 19, 1975, in RZ Archives, folder 66A.

Similar ideas were expressed by Meir in "Ma Nishtana" (*Jewish Press*, November 14, 1975, p. 10), but the wording was different.

[50] Meir has the I AM A ZIONIST button pinned to the lapel of his jacket in a photo taken at the Carnegie Endowment Center, January 31, 1976. See chapter 48, note 8.

"Many, many JDLers wore that button." E-mail from Barbara Ginsberg, February 12, 2007.

[51] "Great Rally for Zionism..." *Jewish Press*, November 7, 1975, p. 31; November 14, 1975, p. 20.

"A Rally For Zionism," [ad] *Jewish Press*, October 31, 1975, p. 30. This quarter-page ad for the rally also advertised the Open Jewish Youth Conference on November 16, 1975, at the West Side Jewish Center, where Meir's cousin, Solomon Kahane, was rabbi.

The slogan of the demonstration, "Listen U.N., We Are All Zionists," is echoed in the title of Meir's important book on the history of Zionism, *Listen Vanessa, I Am a Zionist*, published in 1978. Later editions of this book were titled *Listen World, Listen Jew*. See bibliography.

Meir cancelled a speaking engagement originally scheduled for that night in order to address the protesters. Poster announcing Meir's speaking engagement on Saturday night, November 15, at Temple Beth Shalom, Babylon, N.Y., in RZ Archives, poster folder, no. 12.

[52] Speaking dates detailed in note 41.

[53] Eric Fettman, "Boro Park Synagogues Are Firebombed," *Jewish Press*, November 14, 1975, p. 52, in RZ Archives, folder 733; Deirdre Carmody, "Jews in Borough Park Asking Police for Increased Protection," *New York Times*, November 14, 1975, p. 41, in RZ Archives, folder 733; Alfonso A. Narvaez, "2 Synagogues and Homes Fire-Bombed in Boro Park," *New York Times*, November 12, 1975, p. 47; Jerry Adler, "Puerto Ricans, JDL Clash in Boro Park," *Daily News*, November 11, 1975, p. 29, in RZ Archives, folder 732; "Yehudim Hutkefu, Beit Knesset Hutzat... Harav Kahana Nisa La'arokh Mitz'ad Za'am [Jews Attacked, Synagogue Set Afire... Rabbi Kahane Tried to Hold Angry March]," *Yedioth Ahronoth*, November 19, 1975, p. 14, in RZ Archives, folder 66B.

JDL patrols for self-defense were set up in Borough Park. See: "Metropolitan Briefs," *New York Times*, November 21, 1975, p. 47.

David Friedman, "Kahane Denies Charges That He and JDL's Presence in Boro Park Are Heating Up Jewish-Hispanic Tensions," *Jewish Telegraphic Agency Bulletin*, November 18, 1975, in RZ Archives, folder 66A; "Kahane to Reply to Attacks by News Media, Minority Groups," press release, November 16, 1975, in RZ Archives, folder 66A. The press conference was called for November 18, 12:45 P.M., Summit Hotel.

JDL in Borough Park: "The Activist's Column," *Jewish Press*, November 21, 1975, pp. 22, 23, in RZ Archives, folder 1206.

[54] Deirdre Carmody, "Kahane Enjoys Freedom as Inmate," *New York Times*, November 15, 1975, pp. 56, 60, in RZ Archives, folder 65C. Copyright © 1975 by The New York Times Co. Excerpted with permission.

One day before this report appeared, Meir received an Incident Report because he returned late on Friday night, November 14. Meir explained that he had to walk both ways on Friday night [because Orthodox Jews may not travel on Shabbat] and one and a half hours is not sufficient. "He stated that he will be late until we give him more time," said the report. See: U.S. Department of Justice, Bureau of Prisons, *Incident Report*, Register no. 72712-158, November 14, 1975, in RZ Archives, folder 66B.

[55] See note 54. Carmody's article on Meir included the fact that Commissioner Norton had written a letter of complaint to Judge Weinstein. Carmody apparently informed Commissioner Norton of her findings in the course of writing her article.

[56] "Metropolitan Briefs," *New York Times*, November 17, 1975, p. 35; Stewart Ain, "Kahane's

Rally Role Gets Him 2 Guards," *Daily News*, November 17, 1975, in RZ Archives, folders 66A and 733. Ain notes that the marshals began to accompany him on November 15.

57 Letter from Meir to Libby, November 17, 1975, in RZ Archives, Appendix.

58 Letter from Meir to Libby, November 25, 1975, in RZ Archives, Appendix.

59 Letter from Meir to Matthew Walsh, Director, Community Treatment Center, November 17, 1975, in RZ Archives, folder 706.

Letter from Community Treatment Center case managers, Kenneth I. Kaufman and Elle B. Kelly, to Meir, November 18, 1975, in RZ Archives, folder 706.

60 Meir defined his aims in April. See chapter 43, note 14.

61 "Kahane Gets Year in Jail," *Jewish Post and Opinion*, February 28, 1975, p. 8, in RZ Archives, folder 65B.

Joseph Egelhof, "Rabbi Kahane Still Fighting for Has-Been Cause," *Chicago Tribune*, March 16, 1975, p. A9, in RZ Archives, folder 65B.

Chapter 47

1 "The Week That Was," *Jewish Press*, July 25, 1975, pp. 16, 17, reprinted as "Democracy" in *Writings 5734-5-6*, pp. 190-193.

Other articles written by Meir about DIJL were: "The Week That Was: Who Elected Them? Part 2," *Jewish Press*, August 15, 1975, pp. 13, 14; "Democracy," *Jewish Press*, October 10, 1975, p. 16, reprinted as "But What Choice Did Israel Have?" in *Writings 5734-5-6*, pp. 235-238, and in *Beyond Words*, 2:173-177; and "Ma Nishtana," *Jewish Press*, November 14, 1975, p. 10, reprinted in *Writings 5734-5-6*, pp. 252-254.

On May 27, 1975, the Reform movement, wanting a greater voice in Jewish community affairs, called for more democratization in the decision making process in the American Jewish community. See: "Presidents Shelve Plea for Democracy," *Jewish Post and Opinion*, June 27, 1975, p. 1, in RZ Archives, folder 762. An editorial said, "We suggest... a long range program which would see the final emergence of a democratic body in the Jewish community." See: "Democracy in Jewish Life," [editorial], *Jewish Post and Opinion*, June 27, 1975, p. 6, in RZ Archives, folder 762.

This may have led Meir to believe that the time was ripe to act on the DIJL idea.

2 "The Week That Was: Who Elected Them? Part 1," *Jewish Press*, August 1, 1975, p. 8, reprinted in *Beyond Words*, 2:156-158.

3 Letter from Meir to Libby, July 28, 1975, in RZ Archives, Appendix.

4 *Democracy in Jewish Life* (New York, 1975), 15, [5] pp., 21 cm., in RZ Archives, folder 81, and in YU Archives, SSSJ Collection, JDL folder.

The text was later reprinted in installments in *Kahane: The Magazine of the Authentic Jewish Idea*, May, June, November, December 1976, and February 1977.

Typescript of text with handwritten corrections in RZ Archives, folder 65D.

Mailing of 3,000 copies noted in: "First DIJL Executive Meeting, December 10, 1975," audio tape, in RZ Archives, Appendix. Abe Levine, committee chairman, taped the meeting.

5 "The Uneasy American Jew," *Newsweek*, February 3, 1975, pp. 48, 49, in RZ Archives, folder 733; "Jewish Power Structure Related to Wealth," *Jewish Post and Opinion*, February 28, 1975, p. 1.

6 "In This Bicentennial Year," [ad] *Jewish Press*, August 22, 1975, p. 28. A coupon had blanks to complete: I want to help form a Committee for Democracy in Jewish Life. Enclosed is $ __to help.

[7] Letter from Meir to Libby, September 11, 1975, in RZ Archives, Appendix.

[8] Letter from Meir to Libby, September 25, 1975, in RZ Archives, Appendix.

[9] "Jewishness Without Representation Is Tyranny," [ad] *New York Times*, October 14, 1975, p. 24, in RZ Archives, folder 65C.

The ad was signed Rabbi Meir Kahane, Chairman; Eugene Singer, Vice Chairman; and Shifra Hoffman, Coordinating Secretary. It gave the address P.O.B. 1847, GPO, New York City, and phone number, 255-8518.

A coupon at the end of the ad had a box to check: "I pledge to vote in the election for Democracy." It had blanks for contributions, for inviting a speaker, and for volunteering to form a local committee.

The ad had two logos. One showed the American flag over a candelabrum. The second had an American bald eagle over the slogan, "One Jew, One Vote!"

The ad was reprinted as a flyer. Some flyers had a petition sheet on the back, headed: "I support the idea of an open, direct election of a truly representative Jewish leadership body that can speak for me, having been chosen democratically. I pledge myself to vote in any such election." Flyer in RZ Archives, folder 65A.

[10] "Kahane: One Jew, One Vote," *Wisconsin Jewish Chronicle*, October 23, 1975, pp. 3, 14, in RZ Archives, folder 65C. This Jewish Telegraphic Agency article was also published as: Yitzhak Rabi, "Kahane Launches Campaign for Democracy in Jewish Life," *Jewish Press*, October 24, 1975, p. 44.

The Summit Hotel press conference took place on October 14. See: Yitzhak Rabi, "Democracy in Jewish Life," *Jewish Advocate*, October 16, 1975, p. 1, in RZ Archives, folder 66B. Yitzhak Rabi's article in the Jewish Telegraphic Agency's *Bulletin* was datelined October 14.

[11] Letter from Meir to Libby, October 3, 1975, in RZ Archives, Appendix.

[12] Emanuel Rackman, "Naive Hope, Unfair Judgment," *Jewish Week*, October 19, 1975, in RZ Archives, folder 66B.

[13] "Kahane Argues Polling of U.S. Jews Is Not a Practical Impossibility," *Jewish Week*, October 26, 1975, p. 10, in RZ Archives, folder 65C.

Meir also rebutted Rabbi Rackman in "The Assault on Democracy in Jewish Life," *Jewish Press*, October 31, 1975, pp. 14, 16, in RZ Archives, folder 66B.

[14] Meir Kahane, "A Plan for Elections," [letter to the editor] *Jewish Week*, November 2, 1975, in RZ Archives, folder 66A.

A computer program that was capable of handling 13 million registrations was written for the elections. Description, design and specifications of the program are in RZ Archives, folders 79 and 81; worksheets are in RZ Archives, folders 761-765.

[15] Marvin Schick, "In the City," *Jewish Press*, October 31, 1975, pp. 2, 39, in RZ Archives, folder 733.

[16] "Klutznick, Sternstein Say Conference Failed to Rally American Jews," *Jewish Week*, October 12, 1975, p. 2, in RZ Archives, folder 762; Eric Fettman, "ZOA Urges End of Presidents Conference," *Jewish Press*, October 10, 1975, p. 3. Philip N. Klutznick was chairman of the Governing Council of the World Jewish Congress and a founder of the Presidents Conference in 1954.

[17] "Kahane Opens Daily Round of Street Corner Rallies to Demand Democracy in Jewish Life," press release announcing rallies during the week of November 2, in RZ Archives, folder 66A.

"Democracy in Jewish Life," [ad] *Philadelphia Jewish Times*, October 30, 1975, p. 10, in RZ Archives, folder 65C; "An Historic Event... The Great Preparatory Conference on Democracy in Jewish Life," [ad] *Jewish Press*, November 21, 1975, p. 35.

"... Kahane Calls Press Conference..." press release for November 10 press conference, in RZ Archives, folder 66B.

18 Interview with Charlie Cohen, November 11, 1998, Jerusalem.

19 Letter from Meir to Tzippy, November 24, 1975, in RZ Archives, Appendix. Meir alluded to the children's pet hamsters.

20 "Kahane Asks JDL Take Back Seat in Move for Democratic Community," *Jewish Week*, November 29, 1975, in RZ Archives, folder 81.

Several of the speakers at the conference were taped by Abe Levine: Rabbi Abraham Gross, Rabbi Avi Weiss, Shifra Hoffman and Howard Barbanel. "DIJL Convention, General Proceedings, New York Hilton, November 24, 1975," audio tape, in RZ Archives, Appendix.

21 See note 4, audio tape of committee meeting, "First DIJL Executive Meeting...."

Ira Silverman, "How Much Democracy – And For Whom?" *Present Tense*, Winter 1977, pp. 59-63, in RZ Archives, folder 81; Melvin I. Urofsky, "Do American Jews Want Democracy in Jewish Life," *Interchange: A Monthly Review of Issues Facing Israel and the Diaspora*, March 1976, pp. 1, 5-7, in RZ Archives, folder 97C.

22 Letter from Barry Slotnick to Meir, September 30, 1975, in RZ Archives, folder 65D.

23 See chapter 44.

24 *United States of America v. Meir Kahane*, No. 274, Docket 75-2088, U.S. Court of Appeals, Second Circuit, argued October 9, 1975, decided November 26, 1975. 527 F.2d 492 (1975) / Federal Reporter, 2nd series (527), p. 492-500, LEXIS 11746, in RZ Archives, folder 482.

The Second Circuit Court had jurisdiction in New York, Connecticut and Vermont.

25 "Kahane Ordered to a U.S. Prison," *New York Times* [Late City Edition], November 27, 1975, p. 66, in RZ Archives, folder 733.

According to an early edition of the *Times* (in RZ Archives, folder 66A), Meir spent Wednesday night at the Metropolitan Correction Center (known as "The Tombs") at Foley Square. But according to *The 'Zionist Hooligans*,' p. 915 (see chapter 17, note 18), Meir was taken directly from the courthouse to Allenwood on Wednesday.

See also: Marcia Kramer, "Court Assures Kahane Kosher Diet in Prison," *Daily News*, November 27, 1975, p. 44, in RZ Archives, folder 66B.

U.S. Department of Justice, Bureau of Prisons, *Inmate Personal Property Record*, November 28, 1975, in RZ Archives, folder 66A.

26 "Rabbi Kahane in Allenwood," *Daily News*, November 29, 1975, p. 28, in RZ Archives, folder 66B.

27 "Kahane Is Reported on Hunger Strike," *New York Times*, November 28, 1975, p. 34; "Rabbi at Allenwood on Hunger Strike," *The Daily Item* (Northumberland, Union, Snyder and Montour Counties [Pennsylvania]), November 28, 1975, p. 1, in RZ Archives, folder 66A.

28 *The 'Zionist Hooligans*,' p. 916-919 (see chapter 17, note 18). The information given here is from author Shlomo Russ' interview with Barry Slotnick. (E-mail from Shlomo Raziel, formerly Russ, May 26, 2005.)

29 "Kahane Ends Prison Fast," *New York Times*, November 29, 1975, p. 20.

30 Letter from Meir to Libby, December 25, 1975, in RZ Archives, Appendix. Meir typed this with carbon copies, and sent the copies to his parents and mine.

31 *Inmate Informational Handbook: Guidelines and Procedures* (Montgomery, Pa.: Allenwood Federal Prison Camp, May 1975), 42 pp.

32 "The Fight for Jewishness in Allenwood Federal Prison," *Jewish Press*, two parts, December 26, 1975, pp. 17, 18; January 2, 1976, p. 41, reprinted in *Writings 5734-5-6*, p. 280-283.

[33] Letter from Meir to Libby, November 30, 1975, in RZ Archives, Appendix. Meir typed this letter with carbon copies and sent the copies to his parents and mine.

[34] "Kahane Blasts Warden, Prison System for Bureaucratic Hardness, Anti-Semitism: Struggle for Rights at Allenwood Prison Continues on Court, Administrative Levels," press release, December 16, 1975, in RZ Archives, folder 66A.

[35] "Kahane Granted Kosher Meat in Prison," *Jewish Press*, December 19, 1975, pp. 3, 27, in RZ Archives, folder 66B.

[36] See note 34.

[37] See note 33, letter.

[38] See note 30, letter.

[39] Letter from Meir to Libby, December 21, 1975, in RZ Archives, Appendix.

[40] See note 30, letter.

[41] "The Activist's Column," *Jewish Press*, December 19, 1975, pp. 10, 12, reprinted in *Writings 5734-5-6*, pp. 262-266.

Rabbi Louis Bernstein of the Rabbinical Council of America sent a pair of *tefillin*. (See note 32.) A proper set of *tefillin* can cost a few hundred dollars, but one set can be used by several people if necessary.

[42] Letter from Louis Goldberg to Meir, December 21, 1975, in RZ Archives, folder 66A. A prayer book and Bible were also donated by Nathan Safren of Brooklyn. (Letter from Nathan Safren to Chaplain Harold Washburn, in RZ Archives, folder 97A.)

[43] Letter from Julius Briller, National Director of Information, Synagogue Council of America, to Meir, December 30, 1975, in RZ Archives, folder 66A.

[44] "Historic Torah Scrolls Ceremony at Allenwood Federal Prison," press release, January 4, 1976, on stationery of Union of Jewish Prisoners, in RZ Archives, folder 97A. The address of the Union of Jewish Prisoners was same as the JDL's address. See also Committee of Jewish Prisoners, chapter 43, note 8.

[45] "Friday Evening Service; Sabbath Morning Service," [prayer sheet], in RZ Archives, folder 93. The prayer sheet was clearly typed by Meir. The repeated X's over typos were typical of the way he typed.

[46] See note 30, letter.

[47] Letter from Robert V. Owens to Judge K.K. Hall, U.S. District Court, Charleston, West Virginia, December 24, 1975, in RZ Archives, folder 1234. At the top, in Meir's handwriting, is the note, "I wrote this as a favor to one of the prisoners."

[48] The Black Muslims followed Islamic dietary law forbidding pork.

Meir's aid to Black Muslim prisoners was reported in the media. See: "Muslims Turn to Kahane," *Jewish Standard*, December 19, 1975, in RZ Archives, folder 66A.

Special offenders were denied many privileges, including furloughs. See note 33.

[49] Letter from Meir to Libby, December 7, 1975, in RZ Archives, Appendix.

[50] Letter from Meir, see note 30. See chapter 46, note 49, for the articles referred to in the letter.

[51] Joseph Alsop, "Open Letter to an Israeli Friend," *New York Times*, December 14, 1975, Sunday Magazine section, pp. 5-6.

Meir Kahane, "Open Letter to Joseph Alsop, an American Friend," *American Zionist*, February 1976, pp. 12-19. Reprinted in *Kahane: The Magazine of the Authentic Jewish Idea*, April 1976, pp. 1, 3-9, in RZ Archives, folder 97B.

The article is summarized in "Kahane Article in *American Zionist* Warns of American Abandonment of Israel," press release, April 12, 1976, in RZ Archives, folder 731.

[52] Letter from Meir to Libby, January 26, 1976, in RZ Archives, Appendix.

Alsop's letter was addressed to Amos Eiran, director general, Office of the Prime Minister of Israel. See: Amos Eiran, "Open Answer From an Israeli Friend," *New York Times*, February 8, 1976, Sunday Magazine, pp. 55-57, 63.

[53] Letter (Hebrew) from Meir to Shimon Rachamim, January 4, 1976, in RZ Archives, Appendix.

[54] See note 33, letter.

[55] Letter from Meir to Libby, January 16, 1976, in RZ Archives, Appendix.

See: *Sentence Computation Record, Meir Kahane*, in RZ Archives, folder 66A. This form has the notation "1/30/76/ 8 EGT W/2 PL" indicating that Meir received eight days of "extra good time" (8 EGT). Since this advanced his release date to February 1, a Sunday, they gave him two Public Law days (W/2 PL) in order to process him out on Friday, January 30.

"Public Law days were created to prevent inmates from being released on weekends and holidays when most of the staff is off." E-mail from Mark E. Race, Operations Manager, Federal Bureau of Prisons, Designations and Sentence Computation Center (DSCC), Grand Prairie, Texas, October 4, 2006.

The abbreviated notation is also explained in: Letter from Andrew Bobbe, U.S. Probation Officer, Eastern District of New York, to Libby, July 28, 2005, in RZ Archives, Appendix.

[56] Interview with Shifra Hoffman, June 3, 1998, Jerusalem.

Letter from Meir to Libby, December 7, 1975, in RZ Archives, Appendix.

[57] Note from Sheila Lidz to Libby, undated, in RZ Archives, folder 66A.

[58] Letter from Meir to Baruch, December 28, 1975, in RZ Archives, Appendix. He sent similar letters to Tzippy and Tova that day.

[59] Letter from Meir to Congressman Mario Biaggi, December 18, 1975, in RZ Archives, folder 66A.

Biaggi was unable to attend the Torah Dedication. See: Letter from Congressman Mario Biaggi to Meir, undated, in RZ Archives, folder 97A.

Meir also wrote to Biaggi: "Two Jewish prisoners here, Erwin Weiss and James Glass, have been refused kosher food and have begun a hunger strike. I am joining them tomorrow in sympathy." See: "Inmate Request to Staff Member," from Erwin Weiss, December 23, 1975, in RZ Archives, folder 93.

Weiss' request was refused on the grounds that he had not kept kosher previously. Meir wrote: "May a prisoner who entered non-observant get kosher food? Two inmates are now demanding kosher food. They are regular participants in Jewish studies courses given by Rabbi Meir Kahane and now appreciate what Judaism really is and are capable of changing their ways. Robert Persky has filed a class action writ in Washington Federal Court." See: "Kashruth Prison Dispute Centers on Philosophical Dispute: Can a Jew Change?" *Jewish Press*, January 23, 1976, p. 15.

[60] E-mail from Stanley Schumsky, June 15, 2005; see also note 44.

[61] See note 30, letter from Meir.

[62] Meir had written to Congressman Biaggi: "Despite great difficulties that have been placed in our way by a hostile prison administration..." See note 59.

[63] Memo from Superintendent Eldon Jensen, January 8, 1975, in RZ Archives, folder 97A. Allenwood prison did not have a full-time Jewish chaplain. Rabbi Abraham Yeret, who served a synagogue in nearby Shamokin, went to Allenwood once a week on a regular basis as well as for special occasions. (E-mail from Sarah Yeret Rosenblum, June 22, 2005.)

Rabbi Yeret recalled that when Jews who had not been previously observant requested kosher food, he approved their requests. He told the warden, "If there are born-again Christians, there can be born-again Jews." (Phone interview with Rabbi Abraham Yeret, June 24, 2005.)

Several people visiting Jewish prisoners were present at the dedication. Their comments are in: Charlotte Levin, "Allenwood Prisoners Rejoice at Torah Dedication; Discuss Ford, Conditions," *Intermountain Jewish News*, January 23, 1976, p. 42, in RZ Archives, folder 93.

[64] Among those who attended were Rabbi Moshe (Marcel) Blitz, Renee Brown, Larry Dickter, Barbara and Chaim Ginsberg, Sandy Goldstein, Shmuel Knopfler, Rabbi Herzel Kranz, Joshua Lepman, Morty Lloyd, Dr. William Perl, Mordechai Pollan, Richard Rolnick, Lorraine and Stanley Schumsky, Stanley W. Schlessel (representing the National Council of Young Israel), Gloria Schlessel (see note 72), Dr. Hillel Seidman, Gene Singer, Shlomo Thaler and Fran Trager. Some were identified by Rabbi Blitz and Gene Singer from photos in the commemorative journal *Allenwood Prison Torah Dedication* (see note 68). E-mail from Rabbi Moshe (Marcel) Blitz, June 29, 1999; interview with Gene Singer, August 23, 1999, Jerusalem.

Letter from Barbara Ginsberg to Libby, January 8, 1998.

Interview with Fay Lloyd, July 23, 2000, Jerusalem.

[65] "Torah Dedication Ceremony," program, January 11, 1976, Allenwood Federal Prison Camp, Montgomery, Pennsylvania, in RZ Archives, folder 97A.

[66] Untitled song sheet, with Meir's handwritten notation, "Song sheet we printed for the Torah dedication," in RZ Archives, folder 97A. The transliteration was according to Ashkenazi pronunciation.

Photos of the Torah dedication in RZ Archives, picture folder, nos. 348, 349, 433.

[67] Meir's closing speech is quoted in "Torah Dedicated at Allenwood Prison," *Jewish Press*, January 16, 1976, p. 1. His place on the program is noted in the printed program, note 65.

[68] *Allenwood Prison Torah Dedication* [commemorative journal] ([New York:] Jewish Defense League, 1976), 24 pp., in YU Archives, JDL Collection, Addition. Compiled and edited by Gene Singer. Cover by Shmuel Knofler. Photos by Nachum Bar-Berel [Stern].

"We published it as a fundraiser, at $4.00 per copy," said Singer. (Interview with Gene Singer, August 23, 1999, Jerusalem.) See: "Now Available: 24 Page Souvenir Journal...," [ad] *Kahane: The Magazine of the Authentic Jewish Idea*, November 1976, p. 25.

The journal includes photos of the event and reproductions of printed material: Meir's *Jewish Press* article, "The Fight for Jewishness in Allenwood Federal Prison" (see note 32); a news release about the ceremony dated January 8, 1976; the program; a news item with photo: "Torah Dedicated at Allenwood," *Jewish Press*, January 16, 1976, pp. 1, 2, in RZ Archives, folder 97A; and the article by Charlotte Levin, note 63.

Nachum Stern recalled that his photos were also used in newspaper reports. He no longer had the negatives. E-mail from Nachum Stern, June 21, 2005.

Lore Perl, widow of Dr. William Perl, sent me the snapshots of the ceremony that are in the photo section of this book.

[69] E-mail from Stanley Schumsky, 15 June 2005.

The *Sefer Torah* probably remains in Allenwood Prison to this day. It was certainly there up to 1980, while Rabbi Yeret was still there. (Phone interview with Rabbi Abraham Yeret, June 24, 2005.)

[70] Phone interview with Rabbi Herzel Kranz, rabbi of the Silver Spring Jewish Center, January 24, 1999.

[71] E-mail from Richard Rolnick, July 28, 1999.

[72] See note 55, letter from Meir.

See also: Hillel Seidman, "Simchas Torah... [Rejoicing With the Torah...]," *Algemeiner Journal*, January 16, 1976, pp. 1, 15, in RZ Archives, folder 97A.

"Rabbi Meir Kahane Participates in Torah Reading," [photo caption] *Cleveland Jewish News*, January 23, 1976. p. 4, in RZ Archives, folder 93. The photo, accompanied by a brief report on the dedication ceremony, shows Meir with Rabbis Kranz and Yeret around the open Torah. The same photo illustrates "Torah Scroll, Ark Are Dedicated at Allenwood Federal Prison," *San Francisco Jewish Bulletin*, February 13, 1976, p. 8, in RZ Archives, folder 733, and Levin's article in the *Intermountain Jewish News* (see note 63).

Gloria Schlessel, "Jews Should Support Religious Programs in Penitentiaries," [letter to the editor] *Jewish Press*, March 5, 1976, p. 44.

73 Letter to Meir from Allenwood Jewish Congregation, January 29, 1976, in RZ Archives, folder 1234. Approximately forty prisoners signed the letter.

Chapter 48

1 Letter from Meir to Libby, January 9, 1976, in RZ Archives, Appendix.

2 *Mordecai Manuel Noah... An Exhibit Marking 150 Years Since His Program "Ararat,"* arranged by Libby Kahane (Jerusalem: Jewish National and University Library, 1975), 10 pp. English and Hebrew. (JNUL call number S76A84). The exhibit opened on December 21, 1975. See also: Libby Kahane, "Mordecai Manuel Noah in Hebrew Periodical Literature and in Israel," *American Jewish Historical Quarterly*, March 1978, pp. 260-263.

3 Letter from Meir to Libby, September 19, 1975, in RZ Archives, Appendix.

4 Letter from Meir to Libby, January 10, 1976, in RZ Archives, Appendix.

5 Letter from Meir to Libby, January 16, 1976, in RZ Archives, Appendix; E-mail from Rabbi Meir Fund, son-in-law of Dr. Hillel Seidman, conveying Mrs. Seidman's recollections.

6 "A Statement by Rabbi Meir Kahane on the Eve of Release from Allenwood Prison," press release, [January 25, 1976], in RZ Archives, folder 93. See also: "Kahane to Campaign Against Israeli Policy Shift," *Jewish Press*, January 23, 1976, p. 34; *Jewish Telegraphic Agency Daily News Bulletin*, January, 29, 1976, p. 3, in RZ Archives, folder 93.

7 Letter from Meir to Libby, January 26, 1976, in RZ Archives, Appendix.

8 "Rabbi Meir Kahane Goes Free on January 30. Come Hear Him Speak on: 'Treachery in Washington, Confusion in Jerusalem,' January 31," [ad] *Jewish Press*, January 23, 1976, p. 30, in RZ Archives, folder 93. See also: "Rabin, Here, Assails U.N.'s Lebanon Role," *New York Times*, February 1, 1976, p. 30. The Carnegie Endowment Center was at 46 Street and First Avenue, near United Nations Plaza.

Photo of Meir at the Carnegie Endowment Center, January 31, 1976, in RZ Archives, picture folder, no. 441, and in the photo section of this book. It shows the button "I Am A Zionist" pinned to the lapel of Meir's jacket.

"Rabbi Meir Kahane Goes Free! Listen to Him Speak," [ad] *Jewish Press*, January 30, 1976, p. 30, in RZ Archives, folder 696.

The speaking dates listed in this ad are: Grand Central Synagogue, February 1, 3 P.M.; Young Israel of Pelham Parkway, February 1, 7:30 P.M.; Dix Hills Jewish Center, February 2; Columbia University, February 3; Cong. Sons of Israel, Lakewood, N. J., February 4; Yeshiva University, February 5, 2:30 P.M.; Temple Beth-El, Bellmore, N.Y., February 5, 8:30 P.M.; Talmud Torah of Flatbush, February 6, 8 P.M.; Lido Beach Hotel, February 7, 8 P.M.; Young Israel of Staten Island, February 8, 9 A.M.; Temple in Highland Park, N.J., February 8, 8 P.M.; Brooklyn College, February 9, noon; home of Mr. and Mrs. Martin Gruenspecht, February 9, 8 P.M.; Queens College, February 10, 1 P.M.; Manetto Hill Jewish Center, February 10, 8 P.M.; Fleetwood Synagogue, Mt. Vernon, N.Y., February 11; Forest Park Jewish Center, February 12; Educational Alliance, Manhattan, February 13, 10 P.M.; Young Israel of Spring Valley, February 14, 8 P.M.; Cong. Shaarei Zion, Baltimore, Md., February 15.

Meir's speaking dates were coordinated by the Jewish Speakers Bureau under the direction of Renee Brown. See also flyers and announcements in RZ Archives, folder 93.

Meir's speaking engagement in Baltimore was arranged by Rabbi Joshua Shapiro and Cantor Jacob Rozencweig of Congregation Shaarei Zion. E-mail from Rabbi Blitz, July 7, 2005.

[9] Letter from George Topas to Meir, February 12, 1976, in RZ Archives, folder 715B. Meir spoke in Lakewood, N.J., on February 4.

For more on Topas' reference to the story of Elijah, see chapter 8 concerning the title of Meir's *Jewish Press* column "A Small Voice."

[10] Rabbi Meir Kahane Speaking at Dix Hills Jewish Center, February 2, 1976, in RZ Archives, audio tape 2, in RZ Archives, audio folder.

The letter from my father, Jacob Blum, is cited in chapter 40. The letter's wording is slightly different: "... after I went through the cholera and hunger in Vilna in 1919, I was racing my grand-children up the Judean mountains."

Blizzard conditions, with winds up to 59 miles per hour, were reported in "Weather Reports and Forecast," *New York Times*, February 3, 1976, p. 61.

[11] "Rabbi Meir Kahane and the J.D.L.," *Herald of Freedom*, March 26, 1976, pp. 1-2. This anti-Semitic newspaper was published by the Christian Defense League, Box 493, Baton Rouge, La.

[12] Phone interview with Yaakov Zev, February 29, 2000. Meir spoke Saturday night, February 7, at the annual convention of the Association of Americans and Canadians for Aliyah (AACA), in Lido Beach, N.Y. See: "AACA Seventh Annual National Convention," *Aliyon*, February-March 1976, p. 10, in RZ Archives, booklets folder. "Convention Photo Album," *Aliyon*, pp. 14-15, shows Meir at the podium.

[13] "Successful Aliya Requires Commitment: Kahane," *Jewish Telegraphic Agency Daily News Bulletin*, February 10, 1976, p. 3, in RZ Archives, folder 93. Excerpted with permission.

[14] "To Go Up Or To Go Down," *Jewish Press*, January 30, 1976, p. 17, in RZ Archives, folder 844, reprinted in *Writings 5734-5-6*, pp. 287-291, and in *Beyond Words*, 2:234-240. Typescript with handwritten corrections in RZ Archives, folder 28C.

[15] Dave Kahn, "Rabbi Kahane Released From Federal Prison Strongly Attacks American Jewish Leaders," *Commentator* (Yeshiva University), February 11, 1976, p. 1. Excerpted with the author's permission.

[16] See chapter 23, note 1, "Moscow Is Berated..." Similar statistics in: Bernard Postal, "Brussels II and Who Is Attending," *Jewish Week*, February 8, 1976, p. 2, in RZ Archives, Appendix.

[17] "Mrs. Meir Pleads for Soviet Jews," *New York Times*, February 19, 1976, p. 7. The Second World Conference of Jewish Communities on Soviet Jewry was held in Brussels, February 16-19, 1976.

[18] "The Activist's Column: Brussels," *Jewish Press*, January 23, 1976, p. 43, reprinted in *Writings 5734-5-6*, p. 291-292.

[19] "JDL Raps National Conference on Soviet Jewry," *Jewish Press*, January 30, 1976, p. 3; "JDL Demonstrators Arrested After Full-Day Occupation of NCSJ Offices," press release, January 23, 1976, in RZ Archives, folder 731; Marcus Rosenberg, "National Conference on Soviet Jewry Prosecutes Jewish Youths," [letter to the editor] *Jewish Press*, March 26, 1976, p. 5; "JDL Seizes Soviet Jewry Office, Face Charges," Jewish Week, February 1, 1976, p. 10, in RZ Archives, folder 1209.

20 For more on the *Jewish Week*'s dependence on UJA-Federation subsidies, see note 22.

21 Meir Kahane, "Kahane Wants Hearing," [letter to the editor] *Jewish Week*, February 1, 1976, hand-dated clipping in RZ Archives, folder 93.

Mimeographed letter sent out by Meir: Letter from Meir to "Dear Editor," January 18, 1976, in RZ Archives, folder 93.

22 "Kahane Blasts 'Federation Controlled Newspapers,'" *Jewish Press*, January 16, 1976, p. 19, in RZ Archives, folder 93.

This topic remains relevant. In December 2004, Rob Eshman, editor of the *Jewish Journal* (Los Angeles) wrote: "... even when there is little question of outside editorial influence, as at the superb New York *Jewish Week* or at this paper, the arrangement is less than ideal. It diverts Federation dollars from urgent philanthropy, it involves a charitable organization in a business where it has little expertise and it creates a temptation for either censorship or self-censorship." See: http:// www.jewishjournal.com/home/preview.php?id=13457.

23 "Will It Be Kahane II?" [editorial] *B'nai B'rith Messenger*, February 6, 1976, p. 26, in RZ Archives, folder 93. Excerpted with the permission of Joe Bobker, publisher. Ted Sandler wrote the editorial (see chapter 41, note 20).

24 "Why the Defense League Should Go to Brussels," *Jewish Post and Opinion*, January 30, 1976, p. 6, in RZ Archives, folder 97A. Excerpted with permission.

25 "Conference on Soviet Jewry Rejects Kahane Compromise," press release, undated, but probably shortly before February 12, 1976, in RZ Archives, folder 93.

26 Telegrams to National Conference on Soviet Jewry, 11 West 42 Street, New York City, from Mr. and Mrs. Sol Wolkoff, February 11, 1976; Dr. and Mrs. Sol Seltzer, February 10, 1976; and George Topas, February 8, 1976, in RZ Archives, folder 76A. See also: Letter from Rabbi Avraham Weiss to National Conference, February 11, 1976, and Letter from Rabbi Benjamin Blech to National Conference, January 26, 1976, both in RZ Archives, folder 97B.

Petition to the National Conference on Soviet Jewry, [February 1976], in RZ Archives, Appendix. Several of those who signed this petition became Meir's supporters only after the first Brussels conference. Dr. Alexander Temkin (sometimes spelled Tiemkin), former Prisoner of Zion, did not leave the Soviet Union until 1973. The names are listed in the order that they appear on the petition.

27 "An Important Release from the Jewish Defense League," undated but before February 17, 1976, press release, in RZ Archives, folder 093.

Under the heading "A Concrete Program," the press release presented the speech that Meir planned to give at the Brussels conference. It was reprinted as "Final Opportunity," dated February 9, 1976, in *Writings 5734-5-6*, pp. 306-312.

Meir's request to Shoshan to travel with him: Letter from Meir to Sam Shoshan, January 20, 1976, in RZ Archives, Appendix.

28 "The Brussels Conference Has Barred Kahane," [ad] *Jewish Press*, February 13, 1976, p. 31.

29 "Rabbi Kahane Stirs Controversy at Brussels II," *Jewish Press* (Omaha), March 12, 1976, p. 3, in RZ Archives, folder 1209. This notes the noisy chants of Meir's supporters.

See the photo section of this book for a picture of Meir speaking into a portable loudspeaker at the KLM rally. Abe Levine sent me snapshots showing supporters at the rally: Annette Cohen, Martin Gruenspecht, Mal Lebowitz, Abe and Rita Levine, Mickey Lidz, and Dr. Hillel Seidman.

30 Interview with Samuel Shoshan, June 1, 1999, Jerusalem; e-mails from Samuel Shoshan, October 6, 1999 and June 4, 2003.

Shoshan wrote of his personal experiences: "Like Meir, I was arrested and expelled. At the airport in Amsterdam, I went to Avis, gave them the key and the parking ticket so they could pick up the car. They were very understanding of the circumstances. Although I was barred from entering Belgium after that, I went back on business three or four times, but I went by train from Amsterdam. I just didn't land at Brussels because the lists were there."

[31] Among the newspapers that ran the photo and reported the incident were: *New York Post*, February 18, 1976, pp. 1, 15, in RZ Archives, folder 75A; *Het Volk*, February 19, 1976; *Daily Telegraph*, February 19, 1976, both in RZ Archives, folder 97A; *Le Soir*, February 19, 1976, p. 3; *Chicago Sun-Times*, February 19, 1976, pp. 1, 13; *International Herald Tribune*, February 19, 1976, pp. 1, 2; Yuenger, James, "Radical Rabbi Bounced from Brussels Parley," *Chicago Tribune* (Final Edition), February 19, 1976, pp. 1, 17. Thanks to Sam Shoshan for these newspapers.

Other reports were: Bernard Weinraub, "Meeting Appeals to Soviet on Jews," *New York Times*, February 20, 1976, p. 5; CBS Television News Archive, media no. 0-316566 and 0-316557, February 19, 1976. See also: "Mrs. Meir Pleads...," note 17.

See also: David Nussbaum, "Reflecting on Brussels II," *Exodus* (Soviet Jewry Action Group, San Francisco), May-June 1976, in RZ Archives, folder 90B.

[32] Letter from Samuel Shoshan to Meir, February 23, 1976, in RZ Archives, folder 715B.

[33] Madeline P. Becker, "For Kahane," [letter to the editor] *Jewish Exponent*, March 5, 1976, p. 32, in RZ Archives, folder 97B.

[34] Judith Ratner, "Resents Ban on Kahane," [letter to the editor] *Jewish Week*, March 14, 1976, hand-dated clipping in RZ Archives, folder 1209.

[35] Glenn Richter, "Brussels II – An Opportunity Missed," *Soviet Jewry Action Newsletter*, March 1976, pp. 1-2, in YU Archives, SSSJ collection, box 219, folder 15. Excerpted with the author's permission.

Richter pointed out positive results of this conference: "International publicity (more in Europe than in the U.S.) for Soviet Jews was generated. A number of key activists who otherwise might not have been released were set free..."

A reprint of this article, sent to JDL members by Dave Solomon, chairman of JDL's Committee on Oppressed Jewry, in RZ Archives, folder 986.

[36] "The Kahane Bounce," [editorial] *B'nai B'rith Messenger*, February 27, 1976, p. 26, in RZ Archives, folder 97B. Excerpted with the permission of Joe Bobker, publisher. Ted Sandler wrote the editorial (see chapter 41, note 20).

[37] "On to Brussels," *Jewish Press*, February 20, 1976, p. 10, reprinted in *Writings 5734-5-6*, pp. 317-318.

[38] Deuxieme Conference Mondiale des Communautes Juives. Comite D'Organization, 17-19 fevrier 1975 [Second World Conference of Jewish Communities, February 17-19, 1975], "About Meir Kahane," in YU Archives, SSSJ collection, JDL folder.

[39] Meir Kahane, "Jewish Defense League's Meir Kahane Sees 'Murderers' at Brussels II," *American Jewish World* (Minneapolis), April 9, 1976, p. 8, in RZ Archives, folder 97C, reprinted as "Brussels" in *Writings 5734-5-6*, pp. 322-324.

This did not appear in the *Jewish Press*. It was probably one of the articles that Meir used to send to Anglo-Jewish newspapers to be printed as op-eds.

[40] A photo in *Yedioth Ahronoth* showed Tzippy welcoming Meir at the door of our apartment, which was decorated with a poster saying *Baruch Haba – Baruch Ata Hashem Matir Asurim* [Welcome Home – Blessed Are You Who Frees Prisoners]. See: "Baruch Matir Asurim [Blessed Is He Who Frees Prisoners," [photo caption] *Yedioth Ahronoth*, February 22, 1976, p. 13, in RZ Archives, folder 97A. The photograph, by Batsheva and Meir Indor, is reproduced in the photo section of this book with the photographers' permission.

Glossary of Hebrew Terms*

Ahavat Yisrael: Love of fellow Jews, involving a special feeling of responsibility for them.

Aliya (plural, aliyot; alternate spelling: aliyah): Jewish immigration to the Land of Israel.

Bar mitzvah, bat mitzvah: A ceremony to mark the day a child is obligated to fulfill the commandments – age 13 for boys (bar mitzvah) and age 12 for girls (bat mitzvah).

Challah (plural, challot): A traditional Jewish yeast bread eaten on the Sabbath.

Chasid (plural, chasidim; adjective, chasidic): An Orthodox Jew of the chasidic movement. Chasidism stresses emotional involvement in prayer, the power of joy and of music. A chasid usually has a spiritual attachment to a saintly leader, a Rebbe.

Chillul Hashem: Desecration of G-d's name.

Etzel: Acronym of Irgun Tzva'i Leumi. See **Irgun**.

Galut: The Exile; any place outside of Israel where Jews live since their exile from the Land of Israel in the year 70 C.E. Euphemistically called the Diaspora.

Halakha (plural, halakhot; adjective, halakhic): The corpus of Jewish religious law, including biblical law and later Talmudic and rabbinic law.

High Holidays: **Rosh Hashana** and **Yom Kippur**.

Irgun: Short for Irgun Tzva'i Leumi, a pre-state military unit that fought British rule in (then) Palestine during the 1930s and 1940s.

Kashrut (also kashrus, noun): See adjective, **Kosher**.

Kiddush Hashem: The sanctification of G-d's name.

Kippa (plural, kippot; alternate spellings: kipah, kipa; Yiddish: yarmulke, yarmulka, yarmelke): A skullcap worn by observant Jews.

---

* This glossary includes only terms that are not defined in the text.

Kohen (also cohen; plural, kohanim): A direct male descendant of the Biblical Aaron, brother of Moses. Kohanim have a distinct personal status within Judaism and are bound by special laws.

Kosher food: Food that conforms to **halakhic** dietary rules.

Lechi: Acronym of Lochamei Herut Yisrael, a pre-state military unit that fought British rule in (then) Palestine during the 1940s.

Maccabee (plural, Maccabim; adjective, Maccabean): Jews who fought Greek rule in the Land of Israel and established an independent state from 165 BCE to 63 BCE. Their victory is commemorated by the Chanuka holiday.

Mitzvah (plural, mitzvot): A commandment or rule of conduct mandated by the Torah or later Jewish law.

Purim: The holiday that commemorates the deliverance of the Jews from Haman's plot to exterminate them, as recorded in the biblical Book of Esther.

Rabbi (abbreviation: **R.**): A Jewish religious leader who serves as the legal and spiritual guide of a congregation or community. The title is conferred after considerable study of traditional Jewish sources. A person who is learned but holds no communal position may also be called Rabbi.

Refusenik: Soviet Jews who were *refused* permission to emigrate.

Rosh Hashana: The Jewish New Year. It usually falls in September.

Selichot: Penitential prayers, recited prior to the **High Holidays**.

Shabbat: The Jewish Sabbath, a period of rest and sanctification, observed from sunset Friday until approximately one hour after sunset Saturday.

Shofar: A ram's horn trumpet, sounded on **Rosh Hashana** and **Yom Kippur**.

Shul: Synagogue.

Sukkah: see Sukkot.

Sukkot: A week-long festival during which Jews live in booths (sukkot; singular sukkah), temporary huts with thatched roofs, to commemorate the forty years that the Children of Israel wandered in the desert, living in temporary shelters.

Tefillin (phylacteries): Small boxes containing biblical verses, with black leather straps attached to them, which are worn during the morning prayer services.

Torah: Primarily, the first five books of the Bible, the Pentateuch. The term also refers to all of Judaism's written and oral law and encompasses the entire spectrum of religious teachings, including the Talmud, the Midrash, and more.

Yom Kippur: The Day of Atonement. It falls ten days after **Rosh Hashana**.

Books in English by Rabbi Meir Kahane

Beyond Words: *Selected Writings of Rabbi Meir Kahane, 1960-1990*. Jerusalem: Institute for Publication of the Writings of Rabbi Meir Kahane, [To be published 2008].* 7 vols.

Forty Years. Miami Beach: Institute of the Jewish Idea, 1983. 82 pp.

___. 2nd edition: Jerusalem and New York: Institute of the Jewish Idea, [1989], c1983. 112 pp.

Israel: *Referendum or Revolution*. Secaucus, N.J.: Barricade Books, 1990. 185 pp.

The Jewish Idea (Translation of *Or Haraayon*). Jerusalem: Institute for Publication of the Writings of Rabbi Meir Kahane, 1996-1998.* 2 vols.

The Jewish Stake in Vietnam, by Meir Kahane, Joseph Churba and Michael King. New York: Crossroads Pub. Co., 1967. 224 pp.

Listen Vanessa, I am a Zionist. Tucson, Ariz.: The Desert Ulpan for the Institute of the Jewish Idea, 1978. 163 pp.

Listen World, Listen Jew. Jerusalem: Institute of the Jewish Idea, 1983, c1978. xiv, 145 pp.

___. Corrected edition. Jerusalem: Institute for Publication of the Writings of Rabbi Meir Kahane, 1995.* 236 pp.

Never Again: A Program for Survival. Los Angeles: Nash Publishing, 1971. 287 pp.

___. Softcover edition. New York: Pyramid Books, 1972 c1971. 256 pp.

On Jews and Judaism: *Selected Articles, 1961-1990*. Jerusalem: Institute for Publication of the Writings of Rabbi Meir Kahane, 1993.* 168 pp.

---

* Posthumous publications by the Institute for Publication of the Writings of Rabbi Meir Kahane, P.O.B. 39020, Jerusalem, Israel. The Institute is a non-profit foundation; Israel registration no. 58-120-521-9.

Our Challenge: the Chosen Land. Radnor, Penna.: Chilton Book Co., 1974. 181 pp.

The Story of the Jewish Defense League. Radnor, Pa.: Chilton Book Co.,1975. 338 pp.

___. Enhanced edition. Jerusalem: Institute for Publication of the Writings of Rabbi Meir Kahane, 2000.* 344 pp.

___. Hebrew translation. Jerusalem: The Institute, 2002.* 288 pp.

They Must Go. New York: Grosset & Dunlap, 1981. 282 pp.

___. Softcover edition. Jerusalem and New York: The Jewish Idea, 1985. 282 pp. Reprinted: 1987.

Time to Go Home. Los Angeles: Nash Publishing, 1972. 287 pp.

Uncomfortable Questions for Comfortable Jews. Secaucus, N.J.: Lyle Stuart, 1987. 324 pp.

Why Be Jewish? Intermarriage, Assimilation, and Alienation. New York: Stein and Day, 1977. 251 pp.

___. Softcover edition. New York: Stein and Day, 1983. 251 pp.

___. Softcover edition. Miami: Copy Service Inc., [1987]. 252 pp.

Writings (5731): Selected Writings by Meir Kahane from the Year 5731 (1971-72). Jerusalem: Jewish Identity Center, 1973. 126 pp.

Writings (5732-33): Selected Writings by Meir Kahane from the Year 5732-33 (1971-73). Jerusalem: Jewish Identity Center, 1973. 264 pp.

Writings (5734-5-6): Selected Writings by Meir Kahane from the Year 5734-5-6 (1974-6). New York: Jewish Identity Center, 1977. 379 pp.

Booklets in English by
Rabbi Meir Kahane

Democracy in Jewish Life. New York: DIJL, [1975]. 15, [5] pp., 21 cm.

Détente. New York: American Jews Against Ford, [1975]. 7 pp., 21 cm.

Ford Must Go! New York: American Jews Against Ford, [1975]. 8 pp., 21 cm.

The Ideology of Kach: The Authentic Jewish Idea. New York: [The Jewish Idea], 1987. 25, [2] pp., 27 cm. Reprinted: 1990.

The Jewish Defense League: Aims and Purposes. New York: Jewish Defense League, 1969. 14 pp., 30 cm.

The Jewish Defense League: Principles and Philosophies. New York: Educational Department of the Jewish Defense League, [1969]. 24 pp., 28 cm. Reprinted: 1973. 32 pp., 21 cm.

The Jewish Defense League Movement Handbook. New York: Jewish Defense League, 1972. 62 pp., 21 cm.

The Jewish Idea: a Jewish Program for Jewish Survival. Jerusalem: Jewish Identity Center, 1974. 20 pp., 27 cm. Reprinted: New York: [1975].

The Jewish Identity Center in Jerusalem, Israel; Statement of Purposes. New York: Jewish Identity Center, Yeshiva Torah V'oz, [1976]. [12] pp., 21 cm.

Letters from Prison. Jerusalem: Jewish Identity Center, 1974. 45 pp., 24 cm.

Madmen and Murderers. [New York, Jewish Identity Center of Jerusalem, 1974]. [7] pp., 21 cm. Reprinted: New York: 1975.

Numbers 23:9. Jerusalem: Jewish Identity Center, 1974. 34 pp., 27 cm. Reprinted: Miami Beach: I. Block, [1974]. 57 pp., 18 cm.

The Plight of the Soviet Jew. New York: Jewish Defense League Educational Program, [1970]. [2], 20, [2] pp., 35 cm.

What Makes Bernie Run? New York: Jewish Identity Center of Jerusalem, 1975. [2], 8, [2] pp., 22 cm.

Index of Selected Names and Subjects

ב"ה

Dear Friend,

Work on a Hebrew translation of this book has begun, to enable the Israeli public to learn about Rabbi Meir Kahane's ideas. It will be published, please G-d, by the Institute for Publication of the Writings of Rabbi Meir Kahane, Israeli foundation no. 58-020-521-9.

We would greatly appreciate your assistance in making this a reality.*

For information about a dedication page or any other clarification, please contact me, at:
- Institute for Publication of the Writings of Rabbi Meir Kahane
  1412 Avenue M #2387, Brooklyn, NY 11230
  P. O. Box 39020, Jerusalem, Israel
- E-mail: mrslkahan@yahoo.com
- Phone: Libby Kahane, 972-2-654-0217.

Sincerely,
Libby Kahane

* Contributions are tax-deductible if sent to:
  PEF Israel Endowment Funds, Inc.
  317 Madison Avenue, Suite 607, New York, NY 10017.

(Write your check to the order of the PEF (IRS no. 13-6104086) and specify: "Enclosed is my contribution of __ with a recommendation to your trustees that it be used for: **Institute for Publication of the Writings of Rabbi Meir Kahane**.")